Literature Criticism from 1400 to 1800

Guide to Gale Literary Criticism Series

For criticism on	Consult these Gale series
Authors now living or who died after December 31, 1999	*CONTEMPORARY LITERARY CRITICISM (CLC)*
Authors who died between 1900 and 1999	*TWENTIETH-CENTURY LITERARY CRITICISM (TCLC)*
Authors who died between 1800 and 1899	*NINETEENTH-CENTURY LITERATURE CRITICISM (NCLC)*
Authors who died between 1400 and 1799	*LITERATURE CRITICISM FROM 1400 TO 1800 (LC)* *SHAKESPEAREAN CRITICISM (SC)*
Authors who died before 1400	*CLASSICAL AND MEDIEVAL LITERATURE CRITICISM (CMLC)*
Authors of books for children and young adults	*CHILDREN'S LITERATURE REVIEW (CLR)*
Dramatists	*DRAMA CRITICISM (DC)*
Poets	*POETRY CRITICISM (PC)*
Short story writers	*SHORT STORY CRITICISM (SSC)*
Literary topics and movements	*HARLEM RENAISSANCE: A GALE CRITICAL COMPANION (HR)* *THE BEAT GENERATION: A GALE CRITICAL COMPANION (BG)*
Asian American writers of the last two hundred years	*ASIAN AMERICAN LITERATURE (AAL)*
Black writers of the past two hundred years	*BLACK LITERATURE CRITICISM (BLC)* *BLACK LITERATURE CRITICISM SUPPLEMENT (BLCS)*
Hispanic writers of the late nineteenth and twentieth centuries	*HISPANIC LITERATURE CRITICISM (HLC)* *HISPANIC LITERATURE CRITICISM SUPPLEMENT (HLCS)*
Native North American writers and orators of the eighteenth, nineteenth, and twentieth centuries	*NATIVE NORTH AMERICAN LITERATURE (NNAL)*
Major authors from the Renaissance to the present	*WORLD LITERATURE CRITICISM, 1500 TO THE PRESENT (WLC)* *WORLD LITERATURE CRITICISM SUPPLEMENT (WLCS)*

ISSN 0740-2880

Volume 109

Literature Criticism from 1400 to 1800

Critical Discussion of the Works of Fifteenth-, Sixteenth-, Seventeenth-, and Eighteenth-Century Novelists, Poets, Playwrights, Philosophers, and Other Creative Writers

Linda Pavlovski
Project Editor

THOMSON

GALE

Detroit • New York • San Francisco • San Diego • New Haven, Conn. • Waterville, Maine • London • Munich

THOMSON

GALE

Literature Criticism from 1400 to 1800, Vol. 109

Project Editor
Linda Pavlovski

Editorial
Jessica Bomarito, Kathy D. Darrow, Jeffrey W. Hunter, Jelena O. Krstović, Julie Landelius, Michelle Lee, Ellen McGeagh, Thomas J. Schoenberg, Lawrence J. Trudeau, Russel Whitaker

Data Capture
Francis Monroe, Gwen Tucker

Indexing Services
Synapse, the Knowledge Link Corporation

Rights and Acquisitions
Margie Abendroth, Jacqueline Key, Mari Masalin-Cooper

Imaging and Multimedia
Dean Dauphinais, Leitha Etheridge-Sims, Lezlie Light, Mike Logusz, Dan Newell, Christine O'Bryan, Kelly A. Quin, Denay Wilding, Robyn Young

Composition and Electronic Capture
Kathy Sauer

Manufacturing
Rhonda Williams

Product Manager
Janet Witalec

LIBRARY OF CONGRESS CATALOG CARD NUMBER 94-29718

ISBN 0-7876-8726-X
ISSN 0740-2880

Printed in the United States of America
10 9 8 7 6 5 4 3 2 1

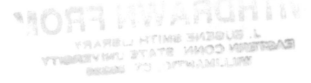

Contents

Preface vii

Acknowledgments xi

Literary Criticism Series Advisory Board xiii

Preface

*L*iterature Criticism from 1400 to 1800 (*LC*) presents critical discussion of world literature from the fifteenth through the eighteenth centuries. The literature of this period is especially vital: the years 1400 to 1800 saw the rise of modern European drama, the birth of the novel and personal essay forms, the emergence of newspapers and periodicals, and major achievements in poetry and philosophy. *LC* provides valuable insight into the art, life, thought, and cultural transformations that took place during these centuries.

Scope of the Series

LC provides an introduction to the great poets, dramatists, novelists, essayists, and philosophers of the fifteenth through eighteenth centuries, and to the most significant interpretations of these authors' works. Because criticism of this literature spans nearly six hundred years, an overwhelming amount of scholarship confronts the student. *LC* organizes this material concisely and logically. Every attempt is made to reprint the most noteworthy, relevant, and educationally valuable essays available.

A separate Thomson Gale reference series, *Shakespearean Criticism,* is devoted exclusively to Shakespearean studies. Although properly belonging to the period covered in *LC,* William Shakespeare has inspired such a tremendous and ever-growing body of secondary material that a separate series was deemed essential.

Each entry in *LC* presents a representative selection of critical response to an author, a literary topic, or to a single important work of literature. Early commentary is offered to indicate initial responses, later selections document changes in literary reputations, and retrospective analyses provide the reader with modern views. The size of each author entry is a relative reflection of the scope of the criticism available in English. Every attempt has been made to identify and include the seminal essays on each author's work and to include recent commentary providing modern perspectives.

Volumes 1 through 12 of the series feature author entries arranged alphabetically by author. Volumes 13-47 of the series feature a thematic arrangement. Each volume includes an entry devoted to the general study of a specific literary or philosophical movement, writings surrounding important political and historical events, the philosophy and art associated with eras of cultural transformation, or the literature of specific social or ethnic groups. Each of these volumes also includes several author entries devoted to major representatives of the featured period, genre, or national literature. With volume 48, the series returns to a standard author approach, with some entries devoted to a single important work of world literature and others devoted to literary topics.

Organization of the Book

An *LC* entry consists of the following elements:

■ The **Author Heading** cites the name under which the author most commonly wrote, followed by birth and death dates. Also located here are any name variations under which an author wrote, including transliterated forms for authors whose native languages use nonroman alphabets. If the author wrote consistently under a pseudonym, the pseudonym will be listed in the author heading and the author's actual name given in parenthesis on the first line of the biographical and critical information. Uncertain birth or death dates are indicated by question marks. Topic entries are preceded by a **Thematic Heading,** which simply states the subject of the entry. Single-work entries are preceded by the title of the work and its date of publication.

■ The **Introduction** contains background information that introduces the reader to the author, work, or topic that is the subject of the entry.

- A **Portrait of the Author** is included, when available.

- The list of **Principal Works** is ordered chronologically by date of first publication and lists the most important works by the author. The genre and publication date of each work is given. In the case of foreign authors whose works have been translated into English, the title and date (if available) of the first English-language edition is given in brackets following the original title. Unless otherwise indicated, dramas are dated by first performance, not first publication. Lists of **Representative Works** by different authors appear with topic entries.

- Reprinted **Criticism** is arranged chronologically in each entry to provide a useful perspective on changes in critical evaluation over time. The critic's name and the date of composition or publication of the critical work are given at the beginning of each piece of criticism. Unsigned criticism is preceded by the title of the source in which it appeared. All titles by the author featured in the text are printed in boldface type. Footnotes are reprinted at the end of each essay or excerpt. In the case of excerpted criticism, only those footnotes that pertain to the excerpted texts are included. Criticism in topic entries is arranged chronologically under a variety of subheadings to facilitate the study of different aspects of the topic.

- Critical essays are prefaced by brief **Annotations** explicating each piece.

- A complete **Bibliographical Citation** of the original essay or book precedes each piece of criticism. Source citations in the Literary Criticism Series follow University of Chicago Press style, as outlined in *The Chicago Manual of Style,* 14th ed. (Chicago: The University of Chicago Press, 1993).

- An annotated bibliography of **Further Reading** appears at the end of each entry and suggests resources for additional study. In some cases, significant essays for which the editors could not obtain reprint rights are included here. Boxed material following the further reading list provides references to other biographical and critical sources on the author in series published by Thomson Gale.

Indexes

A **Cumulative Author Index** lists all of the authors that appear in a wide variety of reference sources published by Thomson Gale, including *LC*. A complete list of these sources is found facing the first page of the Author Index. The index also includes birth and death dates and cross references between pseudonyms and actual names.

A **Cumulative Nationality Index** lists all authors featured in *LC* by nationality, followed by the number of the *LC* volume in which their entry appears.

A **Cumulative Topic Index** lists the literary themes and topics treated in the series as well as in *Nineteenth-Century Literature Criticism, Twentieth-Century Literary Criticism,* and the *Contemporary Literature Criticism* Yearbook, which was discontinued in 1998.

An alphabetical **Title Index** accompanies each volume of *LC*. Listings of titles by authors covered in the given volume are followed by the author's name and the corresponding page numbers on which the titles are discussed. English translations of foreign titles and variations of titles are cross-referenced to the title under which a work was originally published. Titles of novels, dramas, nonfiction books, and poetry, short story, or essay collections are printed in italics, while individual poems, short stories, and essays are printed in roman type within quotation marks.

In response to numerous suggestions from librarians, Thomson Gale also produces an annual paperbound edition of the LC cumulative title index. This annual cumulation, which alphabetically lists all titles reviewed in the series, is available to all customers. Additional copies of this index are available upon request. Librarians and patrons will welcome this separate index; it saves shelf space, is easy to use, and is recyclable upon receipt of the next edition.

Citing *Literature Criticism from 1400 to 1800*

When citing criticism reprinted in the Literary Criticism Series, students should provide complete bibliographic information so that the cited essay can be located in the original print or electronic source. Students who quote directly from reprinted criticism may use any accepted bibliographic format, such as University of Chicago Press style or Modern Language Association (MLA) style. Both the MLA and the University of Chicago formats are acceptable and recognized as being the current standards for citations. It is important, however, to choose one format for all citations; do not mix the two formats within a list of citations.

The examples below follow recommendations for preparing a bibliography set forth in *The Chicago Manual of Style,* 14th ed. (Chicago: The University of Chicago Press, 1993); the first example pertains to material drawn from periodicals, the second to material reprinted from books:

Morrison, Jago. "Narration and Unease in Ian McEwan's Later Fiction." *Critique* 42, no. 3 (spring 2001): 253-68. Reprinted in *Literary Criticism from 1400-1800.* Vol. 76, edited by Michael L. LaBlanc, 212-20. Detroit: Gale, 2003.

Brossard, Nicole. "Poetic Politics." In *The Politics of Poetic Form: Poetry and Public Policy,* edited by Charles Bernstein, 73-82. New York: Roof Books, 1990. Reprinted in *Literary Criticism from 1400-1800.* Vol. 82, edited by Michael L. LaBlanc, 3-8. Detroit: Gale, 2003.

The examples below follow recommendations for preparing a works cited list set forth in the *MLA Handbook for Writers of Research Papers,* 5th ed. (New York: The Modern Language Association of America, 1999); the first example pertains to material drawn from periodicals, the second to material reprinted from books:

Morrison, Jago. "Narration and Unease in Ian McEwan's Later Fiction." *Critique* 42. 3 (spring 2001): 253-68. Reprinted in *Literary Criticism from 1400-1800.* Ed. Michael L. LaBlanc. Vol. 76. Detroit: Gale, 2003. 212-20.

Brossard, Nicole. "Poetic Politics." *The Politics of Poetic Form: Poetry and Public Policy.* Ed. Charles Bernstein. New York: Roof Books, 1990. 73-82. Reprinted in *Contemporary Literary Criticism.* Ed. Michael L. LaBlanc. Vol. 82. Detroit: Gale, 2003. 3-8.

Suggestions are Welcome

Readers who wish to suggest new features, topics, or authors to appear in future volumes, or who have other suggestions or comments are cordially invited to call, write, or fax the Product Manager:

Product Manager, Literary Criticism Series
Thomson Gale
27500 Drake Road
Farmington Hills, MI 48331-3535
1-800-347-4253 (GALE)
Fax: 248-699-8054

Acknowledgments

The editors wish to thank the copyright holders of the excerpted criticism included in this volume and the permissions managers of many book and magazine publishing companies for assisting us in securing reproduction rights. We are also grateful to the staffs of the Detroit Public Library, the Library of Congress, the University of Detroit Mercy Library, Wayne State University Purdy/Kresge Library Complex, and the University of Michigan Libraries for making their resources available to us. Following is a list of the copyright holders who have granted us permission to reproduce material in this volume of *LC*. Every effort has been made to trace copyright, but if omissions have been made, please let us know.

COPYRIGHTED MATERIAL IN *LC*, VOLUME 109, WAS REPRODUCED FROM THE FOLLOWING PERIODICALS:

College Literature, v. XII, 1985. Copyright © 1985 by West Chester University. Reproduced by permission.—*Comitatus,* v. 29, 1998. Copyright © 1998 by the Regents of the University of California. Reproduced by permission.—*Criticism,* v. 40, summer, 1998. Copyright © 1998, Wayne State University Press. Reproduced with permission of the Wayne State University Press.—*Early Modern Literary Studies,* v. 1, April, 1995. Copyright © 1995 by David Carlson. Reproduced by permission.—*Eighteenth-Century Life,* v. 26, spring, 2002. Copyright © 2002 by The Johns Hopkins University Press. Reproduced by permission.—*English,* v. XVI, autumn, 1967. Copyright © 1967 by The English Association. Reproduced by permission.—*History of Religions,* v. 3, 1964. Copyright © 1964 by The University of Chicago. Reproduced by permission.—*Indian Literature,* v. 29, 1986. Copyright © 1986 by *Indian Literature*. Reproduced by permission.—*Modern Language Review,* v. 95, October, 2000. Copyright © Modern Humanities Research Association 2000. Reproduced by permission of the publisher.—*Modern Philology,* v. 97, February, 2000. Copyright © 2000 by The University of Chicago. Reproduced by permission.—*Philological Quarterly,* v. 54, 1975 for "King James and Some Witches: The Date and Text of the *Daemonologie*" by Rhodes Dunlap. Copyright © 1975 by The University of Iowa. Reproduced by permission of the author.—*Quarterly Journal of Speech,* v. 54, December, 1968 for "Performing Nahum Tate's *King Lear*: Coming Hither by Going Hence" by Peter L. Sharkey. Copyright © 1968 by the Speech Communication Association. Reproduced by permission of Speech Communication Association and the author.—*Renaissance Quarterly,* v. LIV, winter, 2001. Copyright © 2001 by the Renaissance Society of America. Reproduced by permission.—*Review of English Studies,* v. 23, February 1972 for "Tradition and Innovation in Alexander Barclay's *Towre of Vertue and Honoure*" by R. J. Lyall. Copyright © 1972 by Oxford University Press. Reproduced by permission of the publisher and the author.—*Romance Notes,* v. 26, spring, 1986. Reproduced by permission.—*Selected Papers from the West Virginia Shakespeare and Renaissance Association,* v. 6, spring, 1981. Reproduced by permission.—*Studies in English Literature, 1500-1900,* v. 3, winter, 1963; v. 7, summer, 1967; v. 12, spring, 1972; v. 38, 1998; v. 40, summer, 2000. Copyright © 1963, 1967, 1972, 1998, 2000 by The Johns Hopkins University Press. All reproduced by permission.—*Theatre Notebook,* v. 42, 1988. Reproduced by permission.—*University of Toronto Quarterly,* v. XLIV, winter, 1975. Copyright © 1975 by University of Toronto Press. Reproduced by permission of University of Toronto Press Incorporated.

COPYRIGHTED MATERIAL IN *LC*, VOLUME 109, WAS REPRODUCED FROM THE FOLLOWING BOOKS:

Bell, Sandra. From "Writing the Monarch: King James I and Lepanto," in *Other Voices, Other Views: Expanding the Canon in English Renaissance Studies.* Edited by Helen Ostovich, Mary V. Silcox, and Graham Roebuck. University of Delaware Press, 1999. Copyright © 1999 by Associated University Presses, Inc. Reproduced by permission.—Bly, Robert. From *The Kabir Book: Forty-Four of the Ecstatic Poems of Kabir.* Seventies Press-Beacon Press, 1971. Copyright © 1971, 1977 by Robert Bly.—Chaudhuri, Sukanta, From *Renaissance Pastoral and Its English Developments.* Clarendon Press, 1989. Copyright © 1989 by Sukanta Chaudhuri. Reproduced by permission of Oxford University Press.—Dickens, A. G. From *The Counter Reformation.* W. W. Norton & Company, Inc., 1979. Copyright © 1968 by A. G. Dickens. All rights reserved. Reproduced by permission of W. W. Norton & Company, Inc.—Evennett, H. Outram. From "St. Ignatius and the Spiritual Exercises," in *The Spirit of the Counter-Reformation: The Birkbeck Lectures in Ecclesiastical History given in the University of Cambridge in May 1951.* Edited by John Bossy. Cambridge University Press, 1968. Copyright © Cambridge University Press 1968. Reprinted with the permission of Cambridge University Press.—Ezekiel, Isaac. From *Kabir the Great Mystic.* Radha Soami Satsang Beas, 2003. Copyright © 1966 and 2003 by Sewa Singh, Secretary, Radha Soami Satsang Beas. All rights reserved. Reproduced by permission.—Fox, Alistair, From *Politics and Literature in the*

Thomson Gale Literature Product Advisory Board

Alexander Barclay
c. 1475-c. 1552

Scottish poet, translator, and nonfiction writer.

INTRODUCTION

Barclay is credited with being the first poet to write English pastorals. He enjoyed a brief literary career spanning about fifteen years, during which he produced poems, translations, and a French textbook. While many of his writings are translations, Barclay's writing style allowed him to keep the spirit of the original work while successfully adapting each piece to incorporate his own ideas concerning English society. Barclay was among the first writers to enjoy a wider circulation of his works as a result of the invention of the printing press, which allowed large quantities of his works to be distributed relatively inexpensively. Consequently, Barclay had an important role in introducing Continental literature to the English public.

BIOGRAPHICAL INFORMATION

Little is known with certainty regarding Barclay's life, and many scholars turn to his writings to obtain information on his life and experiences. Most critics believe he was born in Scotland around 1475. He is thought to have moved to England very early in his life and was raised in Croydon or Lincoln. In *The Ship of Fools* (1509), Barclay claims that he was comprehensively educated in a variety of disciplines, but no records of his formal education have been found. Most scholars agree that Barclay most likely earned a degree at an English university and traveled abroad to study. Over a period of five weeks beginning in March 1508, Barclay was ordained as subdeacon, deacon, and priest. This sequence of events most likely took place in order for Barclay to secure a position at the collegiate church of Ottery Saint Mary in the Exeter diocese. The following year Barclay published *The Ship of Fools,* and it is believed that he left Ottery Saint Mary sometime before 1514. Around this time Barclay joined the Benedictine monks at the Ely Cathedral and enjoyed an association with several important religious figures, including Bishop James Stanley. Barclay completed the remainder of his literary works while a member of the Benedictine order, including *The gardyner's passetaunce* (c. 1512), *The Towre of Vertue and Honoure* (c. 1514), and *The Mirror of Good Manners* (c. 1518). Lacking evidence to the contrary, scholars believe that Barclay's literary

career ended after his publication of *The Introductory to Write and to Pronounce Frenche* in 1520. Details of Barclay's life after this point are unknown. In June, 1552, a priest named Alexander Barclay died and was buried at Croydon, but scholars are not sure this was the poet.

MAJOR WORKS

Barclay is most widely known for *Ship of Fools,* a rendering of Sebastian Brant's poem *Das Narrenschiff.* Barclay's version, which significantly lengthens the work and adapts the story to his own view of English society, established him as a satirist of the social evils of the time. *The gardyner's passetaunce* is an allegory of English-French hostility, in which a gardener prefers the English rose to the French lily. Along the same lines, *The Towre of Vertue and Honoure* is an allegory glorifying English military campaigns against the French. Barclay's eclogues, pastoral poems modeled after Italian humanists, are the first of their kind to have been written in English. Written sometime between 1509 and 1514, the five eclogues were not published together until 1570. The first three form a unit that depicts the miseries of court life. Barclay's *Life of St. George* (1515), a translation, was intended to have a patriotic appeal and a tone of pious respectability. *The Mirror of Good Manners* is a moral work analyzing the four cardinal virtues of prudence, justice, fortitude, and temperance. *The Introductory to Write and to Pronounce Frenche* is a type of textbook that provides a comprehensive guide to the language; it was published shortly after peace was concluded between England and France.

CRITICAL RECEPTION

Many critics have attempted to assemble what is known of Barclay's life and career in an effort to assess his particular achievement and influence. John Richie Schultz has sought to gauge Barclay's contemporary reputation and fame, despite the paucity of surviving information on the poet. Nicholas Orme has explored *The Ship of Fools* within the contexts of Barclay's own life and the larger social and political events of his time. R. J. Lyall has analyzed *The Towre of Vertue and Honoure,* arguing that it was influential in the development of the English elegy, written in a style that presents a freshness and originality not seen before.

Sukanta Chaudhuri has examined Barclay's eclogues, judging them "the most important English ones before [Edmund] Spenser's." Critics agree that Barclay was significant for introducing European works and literary forms to a wide audience in England. His translations typically reworked the foreign material to present patriotic messages that found favor with English readers.

PRINCIPAL WORKS

This present boke named the shyp of folys of the worlde was tr. out of Laten, Frenche, and Doche in the college of saynt mary Otery by A. Barclay [translator; from Sebastian Brant's poem *Das Narrenschiff*] (poetry) 1509

The gardyners passetaunce touching the outrage of fraunce (poetry) 1512?

The Towre of Vertue and Honoure (poetry) 1514

Here begynnyth the lyfe of the gloryous martyr saynt George [translator; from a work by Giovanni Battista Spagnolo of Mantua] (poetry) 1515?

The fyfte eglog of Alexander Barclay of the cytezen and Uplondyshman (poetry) 1518?

Here begynneth a ryght frutefull treatyse, intituled the myrrour of good maners, conteynyng the .iiii. vertues [translator; from Domenico Mancini's treatise *De quattuor virtutibus*] (treatise) 1518?

The boke of Codrus and Mynalcas. The fourthe eglog of A. Barcley (poetry) 1521?

Here begynneth the introductory to wryte, and to pronounce Frenche (prose) 1521

Here begynneth the Egloges of Alexander Barclay prest wherof the fyrst thre conteyneth the myseryes of courters & courtes (prose) 1530?

The Ship of Fooles . . . with diuers other workes [edited by John Cawood] (poetry) 1874

The Ship of Fools. 2 vols. [edited by T. H. Jamieson] (poetry) 1874

The Mirrour of Good Manners by Alexander Barclay (poetry) 1885

The Eclogues of Alexander Barclay [edited by Beatrice White] (poetry) 1928

The Life of St. George [edited by William Nelson] (poetry) 1955

The Gardyners Passetaunce [edited by Franklin B. Williams, Jr., and Howard M. Nixon] (poetry) 1985

CRITICISM

John Richie Schultz (essay date July 1919)

SOURCE: Schultz, John Richie. "The Life of Alexander Barclay." *The Journal of English and Germanic Philology* 18, no. 3 (July 1919): 360-68.

[In the essay below, Schultz suggests that too many critics have focused on Ship of Fools *in order to define Barclay's impact on English literature and proposes that literary critics examine the bulk of Barclay's writing as well as his biographical information in order to study his importance in literary history.]*

To students of literature the name of Alexander Barclay is linked with his **Ship of Fools**—a translation, or rather a derivation, from the *Narrenschiff* of Sebastian Brant. Brant's poem had such universal appeal that it was translated into several languages, and was popular throughout Europe in the sixteenth century. Barclay was fortunate in his original, and his rendition came at an opportune time. But the reputation of Barclay does not rest upon the **Ship of Fools** alone. He was industrious in literary work and the list of his writings includes many books. Among them are the **Introductory to Write and Pronounce Frenche,** a translation of Sallust, the **Myrrour of Good Manners,** and the five **Eclogues.** Besides the foregoing, he is the author of many works that have not survived. Such a writer must have had considerable fame in his own day. That he was known at court is shown by the fact that he was considered a suitable poet to devise "Histoires and Convenient Raisons" for the Field of the Cloth of Gold. John Bale, a contemporary, in spite of a bitter personal prejudice, speaks of him as "poeta ac rhetor insignis." If he were so well known as all this would imply, it seems curious that the facts of his life should be so uncertain. The date and place of his birth are unknown, his nationality is a matter of dispute, and the surviving details of his career are few. His biographers have collected the scattered facts of his life, drawn conclusions from them, and deduced others on the theory that in his works Barclay reproduces his own experience. Such to a certain extent, is the character of the most elaborate discussion that has yet appeared—the sketch prefixed by Jamieson to his edition of the **Ship of Fools.**[1] Koelbing in the latest criticism of Barclay, the section devoted to him in the *Cambridge History of English Literature,*[2] follows rather closely the work of his predecessor. But further light is thrown upon Barclay's career by the *Letters and Papers of the Reign of Henry VIII*[3] which was published subsequent to Jamieson's work, and was apparently unknown to Koelbing. It is barely mentioned by Jusserand[4] in his history of English Literature. Gardiner, in his introduction to the *Letters and Papers,* calls attention to the letters concerning Barclay as a source of biographical material, but apparently no attempt has been made to reconstruct the details of Barclay's life in the light of this new information.

An examination of the majority of the accounts of Barclay's life discloses the fact that stripped of all speculation and doubtful statements they draw their information very largely from John Bale's short sketch printed in his *Scriptorum Illustrium Maioris Brytannie,*[5] published seven years after Barclay's death. When this account is carefully analysed at least one point that has puzzled Barclay's biographers, the question of whether he was a Franciscan or a Benedictine, can be cleared up; and by the aid of the *Letters and Papers* Barclay's later career may be traced.

The following is Bale's account of Barclay in full:

> "Alexander Barkeley, quem alii Scotum, alii Anglum fuisse contendunt, poeta ac rhetor insignis, ab eruditis artibus magnam sibi, dum viveret, existimationem peperit. Plures sectas ille probavit, quandoque sacrificulum, quandoque Benedictum aut Franciscanum indunes, nulli certus; sed in illis omnibus veritatis osor, & sub coelibatus fuco foedus adulter perpetue mansit. Multa tamen in Anglicum sermonem eleganter ille transtulit ac scripsit, praesertim

De miseriis aulicorum,	Illustres poetae novem Musis.
Contra Skeltonum,	
Vitam Georgii, ex Mantuano,	
Quinque Eglogas eiusdem,	
Vitam D. Catharinae,	
Vitam D. Margaretae,	
De pronounciatione Gallica,	Multii ac varii homines literati.
Salustium de Bello Iurguthino,	Memini me superioribus annis
Navim Stultiferam,	
Vitam D. Etheldredae,	
Bucolicam Codri,	
Eglogam quartam,	
Castellum laboris,	
Mancinum de virtutibus,	
Aliique plura fecit. Obiit anno Domini 1552, in mense Iunio, Croydone prope	
Londinum sepultus."	

The work quoted above is a valuable and interesting source of information. In recent years Bale's veracity has been questioned, but through the publication of his autograph notebook in 1902[6] we are able to see his *modus operandi.*[7] What Bale did was to gather information from various sources and combine this material into one publication. In his lists of books he distinguishes those he had seen by reproducing the first line of each, as shown by the list presented, and in the case of works so noted there is no duplication. This is not true of the notebook, however, where there is repetition both in title and first line. In other words, he makes corrections by striking out the duplicates; otherwise they remain, as a reference to the lists will show.

From the notebook we learn that there are four sources for his account of Barclay. These are the lists received from "Nicolaus Brigan et alii," "ex officina Roberti Toye,"[8] "ex museo Joannis Alen," and "ex hospitis domo Dubline." In the first of these we have this statement prefixed to the list: "Alexander Barkeley, Scotus, Benedicti Monachus in Anglia primum, postea Franciscanus, scripsit," etc. Heading another list is, "Alexander Barclay, Anglus, doctor et poeta, scripsit," etc. Since these statements are given on the authority of

different sources it is easy to see how contradictions may appear. Thus in the lists cited he is claimed by one to be a Scot and by another an Englishman. It is evident, then, that any inference drawn from one source in the notebook may be incorrect; and that Bale's final summary itself may not be entirely reliable.[9]

With these facts in mind, Bale's account may be discussed together with the work of later writers. There is no need to review the discussion concerning Barclay's nationality. The dispute goes back to Bale's time, and Jamieson has given fully the arguments of both sides.[10] His decision is that Barclay was a Scot, an opinion that seems to have the weight of evidence. The main testimony is that of Wm. Bullein,[11] a contemporary of Barclay and a native of the Isle of Ely where for a time Barclay lived and wrote. Bullein says of Barclay that he was "borne beyonde the cold river of Twede." Another argument is that in the *Ship of Fools* there is an acrostic passage in eulogy of James IV of Scotland. Moreover, throughout the works of Barclay there is a large number of Scottish words. Jamieson lists several examples from the *Ship of Fools,* while in other works many dialectic peculiarities occur that are undoubtedly of northern origin. It seems safe, therefore, to assume that Barclay was a Scot.

Jamieson's conjecture that Barclay in his early days lived at Croyden seems plausible because of his frequent mention of that town throughout the *Eclogues,* and the fact that he was buried in the church there. At what university he studied it is impossible to say. He is claimed for Cambridge because of a single mention of the place in the *Eclogues*; and for Oxford on the ground that he received his first preferment from Thomas Cornish, the Suffragan Bishop of Tyne, in the diocese of Bath and Wells, who was earlier a Provost of Oriel College. It is also impossible to say whether he traveled and studied abroad. Certain passages in his works would indicate such travels, if we are to believe that Barclay puts his own experience into the mouths of his characters, and his apparent knowledge of foreign languages might lead to the same inference. But there is no direct evidence. At any rate he entered the church and became chaplain at the College of Saint Mary Ottery in Devonshire. Here he wrote his first work, *The Ship of Fools,* as is stated in the preface, in the year 1508.[12]

After leaving Devonshire, Barclay is next heard of, says Jamieson, "in monastic orders, a monk of the order of St. Benedict, in the famous monastery of Ely." This brings up the question whether Barclay was a Benedictine or a Franciscan, or as Jamieson says, following the statements of preceding writers, at different times both. The statement of Mackenzie,[13] for which no authority is given, that "he entered into the Order of St. Benedict, and the Rules of that Society not pleasing him, he changed his Habit, and entered into the Order of St. Francis," and other statements equally unsupported, may be disregarded. The only indication that Barclay was at any time of the order of St. Benedict is that he speaks of himself in the title of his version of the *Myrrour of Good Manners*[14] as "Monke of Ely"; that in the letter of Sir Nicholas Vaux to Wolsey[15] concerning the arrangements for the Field of the Cloth of Gold he is called "the Blacke Monke and Poete"; and Barclay's own reference in the prologue to the *Eclogues* to his "habite blacke." In one of Bale's lists, quoted earlier,[16] Barclay is spoken of as first a Benedictine and later a Franciscan. But that Bale himself did not consider this statement of value is shown by his remark that the matter is "nulli certus."

In the last analysis, then, the question of Barclay's having been a member of the order of St. Benedict depends upon the fact that he is called by himself and others a monk, that he speaks of his black habit, and that he was at one time located at Ely where there was a Benedictine monastery. The term monk, however, was, and still is, so loosely used that it may have been applied to a friar, and in that capacity he may have been at Ely without being a member of the monastery there. Moreover, he may well have been one of the so-called "Black Franciscans."[17] There is no question of his having been a Franciscan since his contemporary Bullein[18] speaks specifically of "the five knots upon his girdle after Francis tricks." This testimony of Bullein is significant in another way. Perhaps the best argument that Barclay was a Benedictine is his connection with Ely Monastery. But it is at this place that he was known by Bullein, who tells us that he was a Franciscan. Although it was possible for a monk to become a friar, and no one can say for certain that Barclay did not, the probability is against what would be considered going from a higher to a lower spiritual state. In view of these facts, and of Bale's doubt upon this point, it seems reasonable to assume that Barclay was never a Benedictine, but that some time after he left the chaplaincy of St. Mary Ottery he entered the order of St. Francis.

Barclay's biographers are silent upon the interval between 1520, the year of the letter from Vaux to Wolsey, and 1546, when he became Vicar of Much Badew in Essex. During this period, which covers Wolsey's height of power and later fall, the dissolution of the monasteries, and the separation of the Church of England and the Church of Rome, Barclay's own career must have undergone many changes in his transition from a Franciscan Friar to a position in the English Church.

Light is thrown upon this period of Barclay's life by the *Letters and Papers of the Reign of Henry VIII,* already mentioned. In a letter from Herman Rinck to Wolsey, dated at Cologne, Oct. 4, 1528,[19] the writer acknowledges the receipt of letters delivered to him by John West, an Observant, concerning the arrest of certain heretics. Among other things he offers to go to the

Emperor to obtain the renewal of privileges for English merchantmen, "as there was a clause for the prevention of English rebels or heretics taking refuge in the empire," etc. He adds that "William Roy, William Tyntaell, Jerome Barlo, Alexander Barckley, and their adherents, and George Constans and others ought to be delivered up." This would indicate that Barclay's criticism of certain abuses of the Church and Clergy, which had appeared in his earlier works, had ripened into something stronger until he was compelled to flee to the continent.

That Barclay returned, or was brought back, to England is shown by a letter from John West to Wolsey, dated 1529.[20] The letter "asks that he may speak with him secretly before he sees Brother Alysander Barkley, who has called Wolsey a tyrant and other opprobrious and blasphemous words."[21] Barclay had already made a veiled attack on Wolsey in the *Eclogues*[22] written many years before, where in his tribute to Bishop Alcock he tells of the harm done by "butchers dogges wood," a term that must refer to Wolsey.

The next reference to Barclay appears in a letter of Robert Ward to Cromwell, Oct. 9, 1538.[23] "In Barking Parish Suffolk," says Ward, "where Mr. Richard Redman is parson the word of God is not preached unless a stranger comes by chance, and those that have come have not set forth the king's title nor defaced the usurped power of the Bp. of Rome; no, not Alex. Barkley who preached in Wytson Holidays. Spoke to him of his negligence after the sermon before the Parson and Mr. Walter Watlond, one of the Justices."

Three days later in a letter to Cromwell[24] William Dynham tells of a visit to the Priory of St. Germayne in Cornwall where he "sat at supper with the prior, accompanied by Alex. Barclay, who the day before preached in honor of the Blessed Virgin." Here Barclay is spoken of as "a frere in a somewhat honester weed." Dynham describes the conversation in which Barclay is quoted as saying "I would to God that at the least the laws of God might have as much authority as the Laws of the Realm," and that he thought men were "too busy pulling down images without special commandment of the Prince." Dynham takes exception to these remarks, and in the heat of the argument finally tells Barclay that his "cankered heart is disclosed," and calls him a "false knave and a dissembling frere." Some one, perhaps one of the writers quoted above, has also written to Latimer about the same matter. Latimer sends word to Cromwell[25] that he has been informed "that Frere Bartlow does much hurt in Cornwale and in Daynshire, both with open preaching and private communication."

The final reference in this connection is given by Foxe.[26] "Hereunto also pertaineth the example of Friar Bartley, who wearing still his Friar's cowl after the suppression of the religious houses, Cromwell, coming through

Paul's Churchyard and espying him in Rheines's shop, 'Yea,' said he, 'Will not that cowl of yours be left off yet? And, if I hear by one o'clock that this apparel be not changed, thou shalt be hanged immediately for example of all others.' And so, putting his cowl away, he durst never wear it after." This incident probably took place shortly before the writing of the letters quoted above since Dynham speaks of him as "a Frere in a somewhat honester weed."

From the foregoing documents we are able to gain a general idea of Barclay's activities during the period left blank by his biographers. In the Roman Church he had been a reactionary. He wished the Church to be remodeled and reformed, but from within. This led him to attack Wolsey with the result that he was compelled to flee to the continent. The next year he is brought back and charged with these attacks. But it must not be inferred from this that Barclay had become a Protestant. As he attacked Wolsey, so he apparently attacks Cromwell. It must be remembered that the Reformation in England was political as well as religious. Barclay accepted the political, but not the religious reformation. The result is that we find him a few years later preaching in Cornwall and Devonshire. He had put off his cowl, had outwardly conformed, but is attacked by the extreme party as too conservative. He has not "defaced the usurped power of the Bp. of Rome," and thinks that men are "too busy pulling down images." Latimer himself takes up the matter and writes about it to Cromwell. These things account for the animosity of Bale, and his attacks upon Barclay's character. Bale belonged to the party of Latimer and Cromwell, and to him Barclay was a wolf in sheep's clothing. But Barclay was not within the reach of his enemies, and received preferment in the English Church. He became Vicar of Much Badew in Essex on Feb. 7, 1546, and of St. Mathew at Wokey in Somerset on March 30, of the same year. On April 30, 1552 he was presented with the rectory of All Hallows, Lombard Street,[27] but a few weeks later he died, as Newcourt's record shows, and was buried at Croyden.[28] The Croyden Parish Register reads, "June 10, 1552. Alexander Barkley sepult," thus corroborating the statement of Bale.

These, then, are the scanty facts in the life of Alexander Barclay. It is possible that the speculations and deductions from Barclay's works made by Jamieson and other writers referred to previously may be true in part at least. But this outline, bare as it is, may clear up some matters hitherto unsettled; and it shows Barclay more clearly than ever as a typical representative of the transition period between Humanism and Scholasticism.

Notes

1. T. H. Jamieson, Ed. *The Ship of Fools. Translated by Alexander Barclay.* 1, 1-85.

2. Arthur Koelbing, *Cambridge History of English Literature,* 3.4.63.

3. *Letters and Papers of the Reign of Henry VIII.* Ed. Brewer and Gardiner, London, 1862-1910.

4. J. J. Jusserand, *Histoire Littéraire du Peuple Anglais,* Paris, 1904, p. 103 N.

5. No. 723.

6. *Index Britanniae Scriptorum,* 19.

7. Cf. Berdan, *Alexander Barclay, Poet and Preacher,* Modern Language Review, 8. 296.

8. A London Printer and Bookseller, 1542-60.

9. An instance of this in the question of the authorship of *The Castell of Labor* is given by Berdan, *op. cit.,* 296.

10. *Op. Cit.,* XXV-XXXI.

11. *A Dialogue Both Pleasaunt and Pietiful . . . against the Fever Pestilence.* Cf. Jamieson, *op. cit.,* XXII.

12. Cf. Jamieson, *op. cit.,* CXVI.

13. *Lives and Characters of Eminent Scots Writers,* 287.

14. Cf. Jamieson, *op. cit.,* CV.

15. *Letters and Papers,* 3.1., 737.

16. *Op. cit.,* p. 117.

17. For much of this information I am indebted to Father Aldrich, of the Dominican Fathers of New Haven, Conn.

18. Jamieson, *op. cit.,* XXIII.

19. *Letters and Papers,* 4. 4810.

20. *Ibid.,* 4. 3. 5462.

21. Father Aldrich (mentioned previously) suggests that there is here additional evidence that Barclay was a Franciscan in the fact that John West, an Observant, speaks of him as "Brother."

22. *Eclogue 1.* 349.

23. *Letters and Papers,* 13. 2. 571.

24. *Ibid.,* 13. 2. 596.

25. *Ibid.,* 13. 2. 709, dated 28 Oct. 1538.

26. *Acts and Monuments* (Townsend's Ed.), 5. 396.

27. Newcourt, *Reportorium Ecclesiasticum Parochiale Londinense* (under respective parishes named).

28. Lysons, *The Environs of London* (under Croyden).

R. J. Lyall (essay date February 1972)

SOURCE: Lyall, R. J. "Tradition and Innovation in Alexander Barclay's *Towre of Vertue and Honoure.*" *Review of English Studies* 23, no. 89 (February 1972): 1-18.

[*In this essay, Lyall asserts that little critical attention has been given to the poem* The Towre of Vertue and Honoure *and contends that the poem is a representation of Barclay's originality and was influential in the development of the English elegy.*]

Set in the fourth of his **Eclogues, The Towre of Vertue and Honoure** (1513-14) is unique among the works of Alexander Barclay. It represents his only sustained attempt at formal, courtly allegory, if we agree with the consensus of modern critical opinion and reject the ascription to him of 'The Castell of Laboure'.[1] The **Towre** is an occasional poem, concerned with the death in battle of Sir Edward Howard, the son of Thomas Howard, duke of Norfolk, who was soon to become Barclay's patron. Such formal poems are not unusual in the later Middle Ages, and the **Towre** has received little critical comment. Dr. Beatrice White, editing Barclay's **Eclogues** in 1928, suggested that the inspiration for this poem may have been Jean Lemaire's *Temple d'Honneur et de Vertus* (1503), but acknowledged that 'Barclay has taken but little detail from Lemaire's "Temple"'.[2] Beyond indicating the likely influence of Lemaire, Dr. White gave little attention to the **Towre,** and did not suggest in what way the poem made its avowed 'claim to originality'. It is the intention in this article to explore Barclay's purpose in writing **The Towre of Vertue and Honoure,** stressing the poet's independence of all the probable sources, and then to examine the place of Barclay's poem in the development of English elegy.

II

Lemaire, like Barclay, sets his allegorical poem within the framework of a pastoral. *Le Temple d'Honneur et de Vertus* falls into two principal parts: the first a eulogy of Pierre II de Bourbon and his wife, Anne of France, and an account of Pierre's illness and death; the second the description of a dream experienced by Anne after her husband's death, in which the Temple of Honour and Virtue has an important role. These two sections have a clear thematic relationship: the emphasis in the first half of the poem is upon the prosperity and natural harmony which prevailed in Pierre's dominions, against which the tragedy of his death is set for dramatic effect:

> Trop estions nous joyeuses
> Ma seur, m'amye, et trop nous dégoisions;
> Trop avions voix de chanter envieuses,
>   Riens que desbat nous ne nous devisions.
> Mais apres joye il s'ensuyt tousjours dueil;

A quoy bien peu certainement visions.

(490-5)[3]

The problem thus stated, the temporary nature of human happiness and prosperity, is partially resolved in the latter part of the poem, where it is made clear that Pierre's virtue during his lifetime has led to his elevation to a special position in the Temple of Honour and Virtue. The comfort which this solution offers is directed partly towards Anne, to whom the poem is dedicated, and partly towards seven shepherds and shepherdesses, who act as spokesmen in the first part, and who are Anne's companions in her dream. The role of these pastoral figures appears to be primarily to emphasize the natural prosperity of Pierre's domains, which is generally the theme of the seven songs which make up the first four hundred lines.

The pastoral machinery in Barclay's poem, by contrast, does not directly relate to the theme of the allegory. Freely adapted from Mantuan's fifth eclogue, **'Eclogue IV'** takes the form of a discussion between Codrus, a wealthy shepherd, and Minalcas, who remains poor despite his ability as a poet. The principal theme of the poem is the misery of the contemporary poet; unable to survive by his art alone, Minalcas is confronted with a dilemma, since to return to the shepherds' life will not leave him sufficient time to write, and the great patrons of the past have no equivalents in the present. Besides, how can a poet write of the deeds of great men such as the 'sonnes of noble lorde Hawarde' (l. 621), when he himself lives in abject poverty? Minalcas' appeals to Codrus for assistance receive little attention, and a little further on, another problem of the artist becomes apparent. In response to Codrus' requests, Minalcas begins to recite a poem, extolling the virtuous life, which is not however to Codrus' liking:

> Ho there Minalcas, of this haue we ynough,
> What should a Ploughman go farther then his plough,
> What should a shepherde in wisedome wade so farre,
> Talke he of tankarde, or of his boxe of tarre.
> Tell somewhat els, wherein is more conforte,
> So shall the season and time seeme light and short.

(791-6)

Minalcas now takes up Codrus' point concerning the praise of great men, and says that since he has already referred to the death of Sir Edward Howard, he will recite a poem which he knows on that subject. The link between the formal allegory and its pastoral setting is thus structurally much less important in Barclay's eclogue than in Lemaire's 'Temple'.

A further significant difference may be noted at the outset. The allegorical temple is portrayed, as I have noted, as part of a dream-vision experienced by Pierre's widow, of which she is the chief protagonist. Such a device is familiar in later medieval allegory,[4] and here it is closely related to the purpose of the poem. Lemaire is offering consolation to his patron, and to do so, he shows her receiving consolation through her dream, both from the counsel of Entendement (817-982) and from her vision of the enthronement of Pierre in the Temple of Honour and Virtue (983-1192). ***The Towre of Vertue and Honoure,*** by contrast, has no such dramatic pattern, and is, formally at least, a rhetorical lament in the tradition of Geoffrey de Vinsauf's elegy on the death of Richard I.[5] Barclay makes use, much more directly than does Lemaire, of apostrophe, eulogy, and of rhetorical argument, and his technique is that of description and formal statement, rather than of a narrative situation.

Enough has been said to suggest that Barclay's work is more than a mere englishing of a French original. An examination of the details of the two poems indicates that Barclay has taken little from Lemaire's poem except, probably, his title. The tower, like the temple of Anne's dream, is set on a high mountain, but the first stanza of the English poem indicates the great difference between the two approaches:

> High on a mountayne of highnes maruelous,
>   With pendant cliffes of stones harde as flent,
> Is made a castell or toure moste curious,
>   Dreadfull vnto sight, but inwarde excellent.
> Such as would enter finde paynes and torment,
>   So harde is the way vnto the same mountayne,
> Streyght, hye and thorny, turning and different,
>   That many labour for to ascende in vayne.
>
> (823-30)

Dr. White tentatively suggests a parallel with the opening description of Lemaire's 'Temple', but the mountain in the French poem is quite different in character. It is, certainly, 'haute et spectable', but it is also

> tant floury, tant verdoyant et tant revestu d'arbrisseaux aromaticques et d'autres jolivetez de grant redolence, comme se ce feust ung second paradis terrestre,
>
> (673-6)

and the temple is set upon a 'plaine spacieuse et herbue'. A crucial distinction between the two buildings is thus to be made: while both are richly decorated, Lemaire's temple is set in surroundings which are equally splendid, while the tower in Barclay's poem can only be reached by hard physical effort. Allegorical buildings of this general kind abound in English poetry after Chaucer, and can also be related to the castles, frequently with magical qualities, which are found in French and English romances.[6] It may therefore be argued that both poets are in reality making use of a common poetic tradition, a further reason for playing down the significance for Barclay of Lemaire's poem.

Not only in its surroundings, but also in its occupants, Barclay's tower differs from Lemaire's temple. For his

enthronement, Pierre is part of a great company of princes and nobles of former times, including his ancestors and extending from King Daniel to Charles VIII of France, who had died only five years before the writing of the poem Anne's vision is of the welcoming of her dead husband into this illustrious band, and the ceremony gives dramatic point to the counsel of Entendement:

> Il fault plourer ceulx desquelz les corps & les noms ensemble par leur coulpe & ignavite sont enseveliz en oblivion perpetuelle. Mais ceulx ne sont point plourables, ne lamentables qui, par la memoire de leurs gestes vertueux, revivent et reflourissent de jour en jour et volent en la bouche des meilleurs.
>
> (853-9)

But while famous men are the inhabitants of Barclay's tower also, they are living, not dead, heroes, and this fact is the key to an understanding of the poem.

In his third stanza Barclay makes clear the basis for entry to the tower:

> This towre is gotten by labour diligent,
>   In it remayne such as haue won honoure
> By holy liuing, by strength or tournament,
>   And moste by wisedome attayne vnto this towre:
> Briefely, all people of godly behauour,
>   By rightwise battayle, Iustice and equitie,
> Or that in mercy hath had a chiefe pleasour:
>   In it haue rowmes eche after his degree.
>
> (839-46)

Its occupants, the poet adds, include Henry VIII, the duke of Norfolk, Sir Gilbert Talbot, and Robert Curzon (847-62).[7] What Barclay means by honour is not at once perfectly obvious, but it is clear that, since all the representatives of the quality are alive at the time of writing, 'honour' must be attainable within one's own lifetime. In this respect also, therefore, Barclay has moved away from his supposed source, and this last distinction will prove to be particularly important in the interpretation of his poem.

III

Having established several typical ways in which Barclay's poem differs from that of Lemaire, we can now approach the ***Towre*** as an independent work, and attempt a full analysis of it.[8] As I have already suggested, the first part of the poem (823-950) is primarily concerned with the image of the Tower itself, and the monster which guards its gate. The castle is outwardly forbidding and difficult of access, but inside it is beautifully and elaborately decorated. Quite early in the poem, Barclay offers a preliminary definition of honour, using the allegorical figures of the castle and its occupants:

> Of this stronge castell is porter at the gate
>   Stronge sturdy labour, much like a champion,

But goodly vertue a lady moste ornate
  Within gouerneth with great prouision:
But of this castell in the moste hyest trone
  Is honour shining in rowme imperiall,
Which vnrewarded of them leaueth not one
  That come by labour and vertue principall.

(863-70)

This stanza presents a simple moral equation: labour +
virtue = honour. The close association of virtue and
honour originates with Aristotle, but the prevailing religious and philosophical view during the Middle Ages
grouped the pursuit of honour with other worldly concerns as a vain and foolish distraction from the serious
business of devotion to God.[9] Yet Barclay devotes much
of the first part of his poem to a consideration of Honour
in precisely these terms, returning to the point at l. 919
to argue that labour cannot by itself sustain a man, 'To
lady vertue if he not well intende.'

Between these two statements of Barclay's view of
honour, there is an account of the ordeals which a man
must undergo before entering the Tower: Labour, the
monster at the gate, is a fearsome figure, capable of
changing his shape like Proteus when bound by
Aristeus. Dr. White points to an echo of Virgil's
Georgics in the description of the transformed Labour
(886-910). But the other classical allusions in this passage are equally interesting:

Here must man vanquishe the dragon of Cadmus,
  Against the Chimer here stoutly must he fight,
Here must he vanquish the fearefull Pegasus,
  For the golden flece here must he shewe his might:
If labour gaynsay, he can nothing be right,
  This monster labour oft chaungeth his figure,
Sometime an oxe, a bore, or lion wight
  Playnely he seemeth, thus chaungeth his nature.

(879-86)

. . . . .

I trowe olde fathers (whom men nowe magnify),
  Called this monster Minerua stoute and soure,
For strength and senewes of man moste commonly
  Are tame and febled by cures and laboure.
Great Hercules the mighty conquerour
  Was by this monster ouercome and superate,
All if he before vnto his great honour
  The sonne of Uenus had strongly subiugate.

(911-18)

The reference to Minerva is, at first sight, rather surprising: she is, after all, primarily the goddess of Wisdom and of War, rather than a representative of Labour.
Of course, Barclay may in part be taking up Minerva's
military associations as an extension of the theme of
challenge and conflict which runs through the passage.
But another aspect of the goddess's complex personality, a result of her identification with Pallas Athene, is

that of patroness of handicrafts, as Barclay would have
known if he had read, for example, Ovid's *Fasti*. Ovid
mentions Minerva's role in learning and in war, but he
devotes most of his section on the feast of Minerva on
March 19 to her patronage of handicrafts:

  Pallade placata lanam mollire puellae
    discant et plenas exonerare colos.
  illa etiam stantis radio percurrere telas
    erudit et rarum pectine denset opus.
  hanc cole, qui maculas laesis de vestibus aufers,
    hanc cole, velleribus quisquis aëna paras . . .[10]

Even more significantly, he says of her in conclusion:
'mille dea est operum'—sufficient justification for
Barclay's remark. It may be because of classical sources
such as Ovid that at least one medieval artist appears to
have seen Minerva as the representative of the Active
Life in the familiar allegorization of Venus, Minerva,
and Juno.[11]

The linking of Minerva with the 'monster' Labour also
recalls her appearance in the *Lyfe of saynt George,*
which Barclay translated two years later from Mantuan's
Georgius (first published in Milan in 1507). Despite his
use here and elsewhere of classical mythology, Barclay
sometimes follows his sources in condemning pagan
deities; and one notable example is in the *Lyfe of saynt
George* where Minerva is a leader of the 'damnyd
spirites', inciting them to the persecution of the Christian martyr. Mantuan describes her as 'truculenta
Minerva', which Barclay translates as 'This cruell pallas
| the goddes infernall.'[12] That he may have been in a
similar frame of mind when writing *The Towre of
Vertue and Honoure* is suggested by the slighting reference to classical authors 'whom men nowe magnify',
a clear indication that Barclay was out of sympathy
with the contemporary humanist vogue. At any event,
his sketch of Minerva is scarcely one that would have
been recognized by classical writers.

There is the further interesting possibility that Barclay
based his list of classical references here upon a passage in Lydgate's *Fall of Princes,* drawn directly from
Boccaccio's *De casibus virorum illustrium.* Lydgate,
explaining God's judgement, emphasizes that He does
not expect men to undertake great tasks, such as defeat-
ing the 'Chimere off Licie', going 'into Colchos to
conquere with Iason | The Flees off Gold', killing the
Minotaur 'halff man, halff bole', or, like Hercules, undertaking 'pereilous deedis that been marciall'.[13] Barclay
has exactly reversed the argument, stating that such
deeds *are* necessary before one can reach the Tower,
but notwithstanding this reversal and the commonplace
nature of the examples, the coincidence does seem sufficiently remarkable to make one wonder whether
Barclay was recalling Lydgate's poem. This being the
case, it is at least possible that there was in Barclay's
mind some confusion of Minerva and the monstrous
Minotaur.

But whatever the intention behind this reference, the general purpose of the first section is to emphasize, by a blend of classical allusion and chivalric allegory, the difficulty which the aspiring hero will have in reaching his goal. His claim to honour, it is clear from the allusions to Henry VIII and others, is to be made during his lifetime. But towards the end of the first phase of the poem, Barclay's conception of honour begins to become more equivocal. Having reaffirmed the interdependence of Virtue and Labour, the poet gives a brief hint of the course the elegy is going to take:

> But noble heartes to win immortall name,
>   Fight at these gates till they ouercome labour,
> Then lady vertue with good report and fame
>   Suche knightes gideth to laude and hye honour.
>
> (947-50)

The preceding lines have contained no suggestion that the immortal aspects of honour are under discussion, and indeed Barclay immediately reverts to his narrower sense of the word. In doing so, he puts forward one of the two ethical problems around which the poem is built, both of which are developed in the central section (951-1078).

There is no doubt in Barclay's mind that Sir Edward Howard deserved the reward of honour; he was noble and courageous, 'of auncient stocke and noble progenie':

> Longe he contended in battayle stronge and harde,
>   With payne and labour, with might repelling wrong,
> No backe he turned as doth some faint cowarde,
>   But with this monster boldly contended long,
> When he had broken the locke and doores stronge,
>   Ouercome the porter, and should ascende the toure,
> To liue in honour hye conquerours amonge,
>   Then cruell fortune and death did him deuoure.
>
> (959-66)

It is this ethical problem which is at the centre of the poem: Howard deserves fame and honour for his exploits, for his nobility and his virtue, and yet fortune has intervened to prevent him from enjoying them. In terms of the original definition, death and honour are now seen to be mutually exclusive. The assertion of Howard's virtues is perhaps the most superficial aspect of the poem, the one most closely linked with Barclay's role as a court poet, but it is given a more philosophical dimension by the careful contrast of the fate Howard deserves with the fate he has actually met. Thus far the poem is quite orthodox: we are told how the noble prince has been deprived of worldly honour, and after reading a number of fifteenth-century works in this vein we expect Barclay to move directly into the usual attack on worldly aspiration and a moralistic injunction to humility and virtue, and to an acceptance of God's will.

But now Barclay changes direction. Having asked how it is possible for so virtuous a man to have been robbed of the honour which is his due, he does not answer the question immediately, but turns instead (at l. 975) to the other moral question with which he is confronted. He apostrophizes in turn Fortune, Death, and God, asking in each case why it was necessary for Howard to die. This passage in particular derives from the rhetorician Geoffrey de Vinsauf: the popularity of the tradition is satirized by Chaucer, and Barclay's contemporaries provide several examples of the mode. But Barclay uses the device for his own purposes; after a further eulogy of Howard, showing how he overcame each of the Seven Deadly Sins (1015-38), he returns to the dilemma which lies behind his apostrophes:

> Whom may I accuse, whom may I put in blame,
>   God, or death, or fortune, or impotent nature,[14]
> God doth his pleasour, and death will haue the same,
>   Nature was mightie longe able to endure.
>
> (1043-6)

This passage brings to a crisis the philosophical questions underlying the poem's central section: Barclay, in the face of such an apparent travesty of natural justice, is trying to assess its significance and assign the responsibility. His conclusions will not be unorthodox, but at this point we are shown the 'confusion' in the poet's mind, and the issue at least *seems* to be open.

For Barclay's predecessors in formal lament, the apostrophe was simply a rhetorical device to express the magnitude of the tragedy. Geoffrey de Vinsauf, standing at the head of this rhetorical tradition, laments the death of Richard I as follows:

> O Veneris lacrimosa dies! O sidus amarum!
> Illa dies tua nox fuit et Venus ille venenum.
> Illa dedit vulnus; sed pessimus ille dierum,
> Primus ab undecimo, qui, vitae vitricus, ipsam
> Clausit. Uterque dies homicida tyrannide mira . . .
>
> Ausus es hoc in eum? Scelus hoc, scelus istud es ausus?
> O dolor! O plus quam dolor! O mors! O truculenta
> Mors! Esses utinam, mors, mortua! Quid meministi
> Ausa nefas tantum? Placuit tibi tollere solem
> Et tenebris damnare diem: scis quem rapuisti?[15]

These lines raise no serious questions about the nature of mortality; they simply assert the injustice of such a death, and emphasize the poet's sense of outrage. The same remarks apply to later elegies within the same tradition. Two elegies on the death of Henry Percy, earl of Northumberland, who was murdered by his tenants in 1488, illustrate the currency of the device at the beginning of the Tudor period:

> Nunquid es ludo satur, O Quirine?
> Tam gravi quanto, furibunde, pulsu
> Cogis humanos animos furenti
>   Currere motu! . . .

Quid feros, O Mars truculente! agrestes
Dexteris movit, duce te, cruentis
(Proh scelus!) tantum comitem nefanda
        Perdere morte.[16]

O cruell Mars, thou dedly god of war!
    O dolorous tewisday, dedicate to thy name,
When thou shoke thy sworde so noble a man to mar!
    O ground vngracious, vnhappy be thy fame,
    Which wert endyed with dede bloud of the same
Most noble erle! O foule mysuryd ground,
Whereon he gat his finall dedely wounde!

O Atropos, of the fatall systers iii
    Goddes most cruel vnto the lyfe of man,
All merciles, in the is no pite!
    O homicide, which sleest all that thou can,
    So forcibly vpon this erle thou ran,
That with thy sword, enharpit of mortall drede,
Thou kit asonder his perfight vitall threde![17]

We do not have any sense of development within the poem in these examples; the function of the apostrophe, as in Geoffrey's case, is to emphasize the poet's attitude which we have already been shown in other ways.

But Barclay, it is fairly clear, is doing something rather different. Technically, he is using the *color* of apostrophe, *dubitatio,* defined by Geoffrey as

> color quando dubitamus de duobus vel de pluribus quod eorum velimus dicere.[18]

His use of the device, however, represents a considerable advance on the rhetorical techniques of Geoffrey, André, and Skelton which we have just noted: through his statement of the alternatives, Barclay communicates a genuine impression of confusion arising from the death of Howard. Thus, although the conclusions which he reaches are at this point quite conventional, and particularly characteristic of the fifteenth-century allegorists,[19] his actual handling of the subject is rather more original, and the innovation is significant in an overall reading of the poem.

Having, by l. 1046, achieved this effect of confusion, Barclay advances the poem by immediately resolving one of his questions:

> In fortune is the fault nowe am I sure,
>   I would if I durst his tiranny accuse:
>
> (1047-8)

In fact, he does dare, and he accuses the tyranny of Fortune in four highly conventional stanzas of complaint. This passage is surely the least original in the whole poem, and it is very close in tone and terminology to the mood, for instance, of the *Fall of Princes:*[20]

> When man is worthy a rowme imperiall,
>   On him thou glowmest with frowarde countenaunce,
> Weake is thy promis reuoluing as a ball,

Thou hast no fauour to godly gouernaunce,
No man by merite thou vsest to aduaunce,
    O blinded fortune ofte time infortunate,
When man thee trusteth then falleth some mischaunce,
    Unwarely chaunging his fortune and estate.

(1063-70)

The assertions of the earlier part of the poem thus seem to have been refuted: virtue and labour are not a true index to honour, since Fortune may intervene arbitrarily at any time.[21] By reaching such a conclusion, Barclay appears to have answered the two ethical questions with which he has been concerned, although he can hardly be said up to this point to have moved very far towards the poem's supposedly consolatory goal. That the solution he has so far offered is not adequate is made clear in the final section (1079-1134).

Turning first to address Howard's father, the duke of Norfolk, Barclay still does not appear to have much comfort to offer. Many other princes, he says, have suffered similarly, and he proceeds to cite a number of classical *exempla.* As has been the case throughout the poem, Barclay is on the surface simply reaffirming medieval ideas, quoting Pompey, Caesar, Alexander, and other classical heroes to support the great medieval generalization:

> What is all honour and power but a blast,
>   When fortune threatneth the life to breuiate.
>
> (1101-2)

Even now, and in the following stanza, there does not seem to be any answer to this proposition, or any way of reconciling this view with the praise of Honour as a worthy ideal which permeates the opening of the poem. Only in the last three stanzas, by two deft advances in his argument, does Barclay produce his ultimate solution. It has always been the case, he says, possibly echoing Ecclesiastes,[22] that 'boldest heartes be nearest ieopardie', and it is appropriate that Sir Edward, like the noble captain that he was, should have died in battle. And it is at this point, in the last stanza, that he at last takes up the notion of Honour as an immortal quality, after nearly two hundred lines of ambiguity and doubt:

> But death it to call me thinke it vnright,
>   Sith his worthy name shall laste perpetuall,
> To all his nation example and clere light,
>   But to his progeny moste specially of all,
> His soule is in pleasour of glory eternall,
>   So duke most doughty ioy may that noble tree,
> Whose braunches honour shall neuer fade ne fall,
>   While beast is on earth or fishes in the sea.
>
> (1127-34)

This reading of Barclay's *Towre* brings out a number of significant points. As I have already argued, the rhetorical structure of the poem, which is founded upon the middle section, marks a considerable advance on the tradition of formal lament. By a skilful combination of rhetorical devices and a more informal, discursive technique, Barclay produces an effect of contemplation, of the actual thinking-through of a complex moral problem.[23] The outcome may be inevitable, and Barclay may be open to a charge of legerdemain for the way in which he switches definitions of Honour to produce his solution in the final stanza, but we are much more conscious here than we are in other formal medieval elegies of the author, as a personality and in relation to the moral issues which are raised by the inevitability of death. It follows that the poem is also significant for the manner in which Barclay approaches its consolatory function. The *Towre* is, after all, addressed to Howard's father, and it is tactically necessary that the omnipotence of death should not be over-stressed. And yet, Barclay has designed his poem to follow the typical patterns of grief: rather than attempt to deny outright the natural nihilism of bereavement, he is careful to give such feelings due weight, indeed for a time appears to share them, and then reverses them at the last moment to assert Howard's triumph over physical death.

In his portrayal of this triumph, Barclay reflects a change in attitudes. By limiting the power of Fortune, and by affirming the validity of Honour, he has clearly marked himself off from traditional medieval opinion. The difference is more obvious because of his association of Honour with Virtue, a link for which there was, as noted above, ample classical precedent, but which was not generally acknowledged by medieval authors.[24] The medieval attitude is well illustrated by a short verse of John Lydgate's:

> Þer beoþe foure thinges þat makeþ man a fool.
>   Honnour first puteþe him in oultrage
> And aldernexst solytarye and sool.
>   Þe secound is vnweldly crooked aage,
>   Wymmen also bring men in dotage,
> And mighty wyne in many dyuers wyse
> Distempren folk wheche beon holden wyse.[25]

Barclay, on this point at least, is obviously closer to the views of Sir Thomas Elyot:

> And like as an excellent physician cureth most dangerous diseases and deadly wounds, so doth a man that is valiant advance himself as invincible in things that do seem most terrible, not unadvisedly, and as it were in a beastly rage, but of a gentle courage, and with premeditation, either by victory or by death, winning honour and perpetual memory, the just reward of their virtue.[26]

Nor is it going too far to assert that such a change in attitudes was a prerequisite for the development of the funeral elegy in its later form.

IV

Very little has been written on the early history of the funeral elegy in England. The greatness of *Lycidas,* and the ready availability of classical sources for that poem, have tended to distract critics from the earlier development of an English elegiac form. A line is usually traced for the pastoral elegy from Theocritus through Virgil and Petrarch to the later Italian humanists, and thence to Milton. If any earlier English poet is mentioned, there is a brief notice of Spenser's November eclogue and *Astrophel.*[27] The problem is compounded by the variety of meanings of 'elegy': F. W. Weitzman manages to discern eight more or less distinct senses of the term.[28] In its classical sense, the word referred to a metrical form rather than to any category of content, the form defined by Puttenham as a 'limping Pentameter after a lustie Exhameter'. An examination of Elizabethan and Jacobean poetry makes it clear that no particular thematic concerns were universally associated with the term, although Spenser's *Astrophel* (1587), a series of laments, includes one 'Pastoral Elegie', and while Drayton's *Elegies upon Sundry Occasions* (1627) suggest a more general meaning, nearly half the poems are in fact funeral elegies.[29] Thus, we can identify, well before Milton, an English tradition (though clearly based in part on classical models) of formal obituary verse, already associated with this adapted sense of the term 'elegy'.

Even before the word came into general use in this sense, however, and before it was employed in English at all, poems of this kind certainly existed, along with many other works in closely related modes. I would suggest a four-part classification of those medieval English poems which are relevant to the development of an English elegaic tradition. First, there are those poems which I would call *dramatic elegies*. It happens that the two most important and most-read medieval English elegies, *Pearl* and Chaucer's *Book of the Duchess,* fall into this category. They share, with each other and with a number of European poems, the familiar patterns of dream-allegory: the poet, suffering from profound grief, falls asleep, and in a dream encounters a figure who offers him consolation (in the case of *Pearl*) or who makes his own complaint (in Chaucer's poem). The threnody, the lament itself, is here presented as a secondary part of the poem, through a narrative framework which is itself designed to elucidate the point: consolation for the fictional narrator and hence, in a formal poem like Chaucer's, for the person to whom the poem is addressed.

Other poems, more directly concerned with the moral aspects of the mutability of human affairs, but not themselves elegies, are those on the fall of princes, such as Lydgate's early poem 'Of the sodeine fal of princes in oure days.'[30] The message, reinforced in greater bulk in *The Fall of Princes* itself and then throughout the next century and a half, is made fully explicit in the first stanza of a similar poem found in MS. Rawlinson C 813:

Musyng vppon the mutabilite
   off worldlye changes & grett vnstablenes,
& me remembering howe grett aduersite
I haue seen falle to men off highe noblenes—
   furst welthe, and then ageyn distres,
   nowe vppe, nowe downe, as fortune turnethe hur
   whele,
Best is, me thinke, for mannys sikernes
   to trust in god & labour to doo well.[31]

The emphasis in such poetic lists of *exempla* as this piece is clearly upon the moral point, in which the individual question of a man's death, or rather the poet's reaction to a single death, is subordinated to a series of illustrations of a general ethical commonplace.

For similar reasons, certain political poems, which are closely related in some ways to the development of elegy, cannot really be included under that general heading. Such poems are concerned not with the death of the subject and its moral and religious significance, but with the political issues involved, on one side or the other. Two poems on the arrest and death of the duke of Suffolk (1450), and the earlier carol on the death of Archbishop Scrope (1405), show in different ways the possibilities of this approach.[32] Within these three poems one can discern several recurrent devices: the use of popular sayings and of heraldic badges for the identification of the protagonists in 'Now is the fox drevin to hole!'; dramatic presentation through dialogue and ironic use of the Office for the Dead in 'In the moneth of May'; and the casual, thrown-away quality of the sung carol in the Scrope poem:

The bysshop Scrope that was so wyse,
now is he dede, and lowe he lyse;
To hevyns blys yhit may he ryse,
   Thurghe helpe of Marie, that mylde may.

At their best, poems such as these have a brevity and directness very different from the rather ponderous moralization of many more 'serious' mutability poems.

It is, however, in the final group that the real roots of later elegy may be seen, whatever these other categories may contribute to the developing tradition. This consists of those formal threnodies on the deaths of kings which we have already encountered, and of which the model was Geoffrey de Vinsauf's poem on the death of Richard I. The currency of the tradition in the later Middle Ages is attested by the number of imitators, by the large number of manuscripts of the *Poetria Nova* which have survived, and by Chaucer's use of the elegy as the butt of a parody of exaggerated rhetorical techniques in the *Nun's Priest's Tale*.[33] The purpose of Geoffrey's elegy, and of others in the tradition, is twofold: to assert the benignity and virtue of the dead monarch, and to remind the reader of the transience of human life and glory:

Se in hac re suire dedisti
Quam brevis est risus, quam longa est lacrima mundi.[34]

Two English poems on the death of Edward IV (1483) illustrate two of the more common methods of dealing with such subjects.[35] 'Wher is this Prynce', found in Rylands Engl. MS. 113, is demonstrably in the tradition of Geoffrey's lament for Richard I. In addition to the apostrophic technique, which here avoids the rhetorical excesses of Geoffrey's poem, the author employs the *ubi sunt?* motif to emphasize the mutability theme, and to point up the contrast between England under Edward and England after his death. The pattern of the poem is hardly original: after lamenting in a general way the king's death, and appealing to Edward himself, the poet ends with a prayer for the welfare of the dead man's soul and a pious reminder to the reader that we must all share Edward's fate.

The other poem, attributed to Skelton, adopts the strategy of speaking through Edward himself. This is a fairly common practice, which may in part be influenced by the *planctus Mariae* and 'the appeal of Christ from the cross', both of which were recurrent types of religious lyric in the fifteenth century. There is, as a further example, a lament of the duchess of Gloucester (1441), in which the poet combines a supposed political confession with a strong moral lesson.[36] The political element is not so strong in the lament of Edward IV, although it includes a recognition of some of his sins:

I se wyll, they leve that doble my yeris:
   This dealid this world with me as it lyst,
And hathe me made, to yow that be my perys,
   Example to thynke on Had I wyst:
   I storyd my cofers and allso my chest
With taskys takynge of the comenalte;
   I toke ther tresure, but of ther prayyeris mist;
Whom I beseche with pure humylyte
For to forgeve and have on me pety;
   I was your kynge, and kept yow from yowr foo:
I wold now amend, but that wull not be,
   Quia, ecce, nunc in pulvere dormio![37]

Again, the *ubi sunt?* motif is used to make clear the vanity of human glory, and it is this tone of conventional moralization which limits the success of these poems as elegies. Even here, where the poet's attention is undeniably on the death of an individual, there is no sense that he is endeavouring to come to terms with what Dylan Thomas calls 'a grave truth', with a fundamental ethical or spiritual problem which is raised by the fact of death. And it is such questions, which tend to be assumed as solved in these medieval poems, which are at issue in, and which substantially contribute to the greatness of, *Lycidas*.

Enough has been said to show that there were in medieval English poetry a number of traditions which are relevant to the development of elegy in its later form.

By 1500, however, it is necessary to take account of a further element: the *déploration* or *élégie déplorative* which was much in vogue among the *rhétoriqueurs.*[38] It is within this group that we must place Jean Lemaire's *Temple d'Honneur et de Vertus,* and hence it is clear that the French tradition had some influence at least upon Barclay. The elegies of the *rhétoriqueurs* contained at least two new elements. First, they made considerable use of the conventions of dream allegory: a notable example is Jean Molinet's *Le Trosne d'Honneur* (1467), commemorating the death of Philippe, duke of Burgundy.[39] This work, to which Lemaire may have been indebted, presents a dream vision of the poet's, in which Noblesse laments the death of Philippe and is promised remedy by Virtue, and in which we finally see Philippe welcomed to eternal life before the throne of Honour. The other significant characteristic of this group of poems is the association of pastoral with elegy, a link which is well established by the beginning of the sixteenth century. The pastoral machinery seems, in a poem like Cretin's *Déploration sur le trespas du feu Okergan* (1496-8), to grow naturally out of the wealth of classical allusion,[40] but there is a tendency for the pastoral elements to assume a greater role, as Lemaire's *Temple* testifies. The influence of a revived interest in Latin pastoral, dating back to Petrarch, is suggested by the existence of Simon Nanquier's eclogue on the death of Charles VIII of France (1498).[41]

This evidence suggests that Barclay's **Towre of Vertue and Honoure** is of some historical importance, since it represents the first English attempt at pastoral elegy, and reveals better than most of Barclay's work both a certain interest in innovation and a considerable awareness of the literary trends of his time. As I have already argued, the **Towre** breaks new ground for English poetry both in a formal, rhetorical sense and in a thematic sense. But in taking his poem in these directions, Barclay was clearly reflecting the current preoccupations of the *rhétoriqueurs.* The significance of the **Towre** is more striking because Barclay twice describes his poem as an 'elegy'. Weitzman argues that the word here means a general complaint, but there are reasonable grounds for believing that it carries, at least at its second appearance, a narrower meaning:

> Lo Codrus I here haue tolde thee by and by
>   Of shepheard Cornix the wofull elegy,
> Wherin he mourned the greeuous payne and harde,
>   And laste departing of the noble lorde Hawarde
> . . .

(1135-8)

Alexander Barclay's continuing (and rather surprising) popularity in the sixteenth century is borne out by the new edition of several of his works, including the **Eclogues,** which was published by John Cawood in 1570. There is a need for a much more detailed study of the funeral elegies written in English in the sixteenth and earlier seventeenth centuries, and an evaluation of their influence on Milton. It seems very likely that Barclay's role in the development of this tradition has been underestimated.

Notes

1. See, for example, Beatrice White, *The Eclogues of Alexander Barclay* (Early English Text Society, London, 1928), p. x. All line references to Eclogue IV are based on this edition.

2. Ibid., pp. 260 ff.

3. Jean Lemaire de Belges, *Le Temple d'Honneur et de Vertus* ed. H. Hornik (Geneva, 1957). All line references to the *Temple* are based on this edition.

4. A useful list of such allegorical buildings can be found in W. A. Neilson, *The Origins and Sources of the 'Court of Love'* (Boston, 1899).

5. Geoffrey de Vinsauf, *Poetria Nova,* printed in E. Faral, *Les Arts Poétiques du XIIᵉ et du XIIIᵉ Siècle* (Paris, 1924). See Lyall, R. J. "Tradition and Inovation in Alexander Barclay's *Towre of Vertue and Honoure.*" *Review of English Studies* 23, no. 89 (February 1972): 1-18, pp. 9-10, 15-16.

6. Glynne Wickham's *Early English Stages,* vol. i (London, 1959), contains much evidence of the popularity of the castle as an allegorical device, in practice as well as in literature. There may also be in Barclay's description an echo of the opening of Dante's *Purgatorio.*

7. Thomas Howard, earl of Surrey, was created duke of Norfolk after Flodden (1513). He died in 1524. Talbot and Curzon both took part in the 1513 French campaign. See White, op. cit., p. 262.

8. To speak of the 'Towre' as an 'independent' work does not, of course, imply that Barclay was not indebted to convention for most of his images, rhetorical techniques, and so on. It is simply necessary to establish that the poem is not based on any single work for its form and argument.

9. C. B. Watson, *Shakespeare and the Renaissance Concept of Honor* (Princeton, 1960), pp. 19-75. Watson acknowledges the existence of an alternative view, that of the chivalric ideal, which held honour to be a legitimate pursuit. But poems such as Barclay's clearly fall outside that tradition.

10. Ovid, *Fasti,* iii. 817-22.

11. See Jean Seznec, *The Survival of the Pagan Gods,* trans. B. F. Sessions (New York, 1952), pp. 89, 107-9. Seznec traces this *allegoria* back to the *Mythologiae* of Fulgentius Planciades, but it is important to note that in Fulgentius' account of the

Judgment of Paris, the Active Life is represented by Juno, and Minerva is the representative of the Contemplative Life (*Auctores Mythographi Latini* ed. A. van Staveren (1742), pp. 663-6). This version is of course in greater harmony with the Roman view of Minerva.

12. *The Life of St. George,* ed. W. Nelson (E.E.T.S., London, 1955), pp. 61-5.

13. *The Fall of Princes,* ed. H. Bergen (E.E.T.S., London, 1918), i. 22-5.

14. Dr. White follows Cawood (1570) in printing 'God for death', but the balance of the following line suggests that this is a printer's error. Death and God are clearly distinguished in l. 1045.

15. Vinsauf, op. cit., ll. 375-9, 385-9.

16. Bernard André, *Vita Henrici Septimi,* printed in *Memorials of King Henry VII,* ed. James Gairdner (Rolls Series, London, 1858), pp. 48-9.

17. John Skelton, *Poetical Works,* ed. A. Dyce (London, 1843), i. 6-14 (ll. 112-26).

18. See Vinsauf, *De arte versificandi,* in Faral, ed. cit., p. 271.

19. This preoccupation with the power of Fortune is particularly clear in *The Kingis Quair,* where a resolution of the powers of God and Fortune is attempted. See the edition by W. Mackay Mackenzie (London, 1934), pp. 90-4.

20. Cf. for instance Lydgate's envoy to Duke Humphrey, ed. cit., iii. 1013-19.

21. On the powers of Fortune, see H. R. Patch, *The Goddess Fortuna in Medieval Literature* (New York, 1923), pp. 57-80 and (on her power over Death) pp. 117-20.

22. 'This shall be, this is, and this hath euer bene' (l. 1115). Cf. Eccles. 1: 9.

23. It is tempting here to take up Jon S. Lawry's suggestion (in his article 'Eager Thought: Dialectic in *Lycidas*', *P.M.L.A.* lxxvii (1962), 27-32) that 'we . . . may take an additional step toward reconciling the supposedly antagonistic modes of statement in *Lycidas* by considering the poem as in part a dialectical process, in the Hegelian sense: the initial dogmatic proposition (thesis) is opposed by a skeptical second (antithesis); from their encounter there arises a third statement, one of mystic certainty (synthesis)'. A similar structure, primitively executed but unmistakable, can be discerned in Barclay's 'Towre'. But it is unnecessary to resort to Hegel for a logical or rhetorical model: the pattern of assertion-denial-resolution is clearly apparent in the scholastic *quaestio* from Abelard to Aquinas and beyond, a possible influence on both Barclay and Milton.

24. Watson, op. cit., pp. 21-32.

25. *Minor Poems,* ed. H. N. MacCracken (E.E.T.S., London, 1934), ii. 708.

26. *The Book named the Governor,* ed. S. E. Lehmberg (London, 1907), pp. 183-4.

27. For an extreme statement of this view, see J. H. Hanford, 'The Pastoral Elegy and Milton's *Lycidas*' in *Milton's Lycidas,* ed. C. A. Patrides (New York, 1961), pp. 27-55, esp. pp. 42 ff.

28. F. W. Weitzman, 'Notes on the Elizabethan *Elegie*', *P.M.L.A.* (1935), 435-43.

29. Drayton, *Works,* ed. J. W. Hebel (2nd edn., Oxford, 1962), iii. 203-41.

30. *Minor Poems,* ed. cit., ii. 660-2.

31. R. H. Robbins, *Historical Poems of the XIV and XV Centuries* (New York, 1959), pp. 184-6.

32. Ibid., pp. 186-9, 90.

33. Chaucer, *Works,* ed. F. N. Robinson (2nd edn., Cambridge, Mass., 1957), p. 204.

34. *Poetria Nova,* Faral, ed. cit., p. 210.

35. Robbins, op. cit., pp. 111-13; Skelton, ed. cit., i. 1-5.

36. Robbins, op. cit., pp. 176-80.

37. Skelton, ed. cit., p. 3.

38. For an outline history of these developments, see E. Dubruck, *The Theme of Death in French Poetry of the Middle Ages and the Renaissance* (The Hague, 1964) and C. M. Scollen, *The Birth of the Elegy in France 1500-1550* (Geneva, 1967).

39. Molinet, *Les faictz et dictz,* ed. N. Dupire (S.A.T.F., Paris, 1936-7), i. 36-58.

40. Cretin, *Œuvres poétiques,* ed. K. Chesney (S.A.T.F., Paris, 1932), pp. 60-73.

41. W. L. Grant, *Neo-Latin Literature and the Pastoral* (Chapel Hill, 1965), pp. 314-20.

Nicholas Orme (essay date 1989)

SOURCE: Orme, Nicholas. "Alexander Barclay, Tudor Educationist." In *Education and Society In Medieval and Renaissance England,* pp. 259-70. London: The Hambledon Press, 1989.

[*In the following essay, Orme provides a brief synopsis of Barclay's biographical information as well as an analysis of Barclay's translation of* The Ship of Fools, *focusing on how the work reflects his background and writing style.*]

Few sixteenth-century Englishmen had such a varied career as Alexander Barclay. By origin a Scot, he spent most of his life in England but also travelled widely on the continent. By career, he was in turn a secular priest in a collegiate church, a monk, a friar, and finally (after the dissolution of the friaries), a secular priest again, this time a parish clergyman. He is best known today as a poet and translator, but he was also an educationist. He held at least two teaching posts, one in a song and one in a grammar school, and he wrote educational works. Yet much of his life remains obscure.[1] Even some of his contemporaries were doubtful whether he was born a Scot or an Englishman (the former is more likely), and the date of his birth is uncertain. It is usually given as 1475-6 on the grounds that he speaks in his *Eclogues* of being 38, parts of which were written as early as 1513-14. But we do not know when the statement of his age was written, and it may be better to postpone his birth nearer to 1484. This is the latest possible date, since Barclay had to be aged 24 in order to be ordained priest in 1508. He does not appear in records before his ordination, and all that we can gather of his previous life is that he journeyed in France and Italy. If he studied, he did not gain a university degree higher than that of BA. Only one reference before the 1530s calls him 'Master Barclay', and the rest describe him as if he were below the rank of MA.[2] The span of his life from 18 to 24 is enough to accommodate what we can infer of his early career, and to extend it by another eight years seems too long. On being ordained, as we shall see, Barclay took up a comparatively junior post, which also points towards a younger man.

The register of Hugh Oldham, bishop of Exeter, shows that Barclay was ordained subdeacon by Oldham at Exeter on 18 March 1508, deacon on 8 April and priest on 22 April.[3] He had not been previously living in Exeter diocese but in that of Lincoln, and had 'letters dimissory' from the bishop of Lincoln enabling him to be ordained elsewhere. His 'title'—the means of support which ordinands had to show—was provided by the collegiate church of Ottery St Mary, twelve miles east of Exeter, evidently because the college was going to give him a job. Barclay probably came to Ottery, therefore, in about March 1508. His stay at the collegiate church is important because it was there that he translated his first major work, *The Ship of Fools* by Sebastian Brant, but he did not stay long. A note in the first printed edition of *The Ship of Fools* states that he made the translation at Ottery in '1508' (which in terms of the early-Tudor calendar means March 1508 to March 1509), being 'at that time chaplain in the said college'.[4] The phrase 'at the time' indicates that Barclay had left Ottery when the printing of the book was completed on 14 December 1509. His stay in Devon was therefore less than a year and three quarters, and possibly only about a year. The most likely person to have brought him to Ottery is Thomas Cornish, the warden or chief officer of the collegiate church and a figure of some importance in the south west of England. A graduate of Oxford, Cornish combined being warden of Ottery, precentor of Wells Cathedral, titular bishop of Tine and suffragan bishop in the dioceses of Exeter and Bath and Wells.[5] More than anyone else at Ottery he had the wide connections capable of bringing a young man from elsewhere to take up a job there. The likelihood is strengthened when we find that Barclay dedicated *The Ship of Fools* to Cornish, with an acknowledgement that Cornish had 'promoted' (presumably sponsored) him to holy orders and given him many other benefits.[6] No other member of the college is mentioned in the book with such respect.

On the basis of the word 'chaplain' applied to Barclay in the printed book, he is usually thought to have held the post of chaplain (or clerk) of the Lady chapel while he was at Ottery. The duties of this office were twofold. He had to teach the choristers and adolescent clerks or 'secondaries' of the college to sing, and to organise the daily series of services, accompanied by polyphonic music, which took place in the Lady chapel in honour of the Virgin Mary.[7] These services were sung by the choristers and secondaries, along with the adult vicars choral of the college. Barclay mentions the secondaries in *The Ship of Fools,* but he does not actually say that he was their teacher. We know, however, that he was not one of the dignitaries or canons of Ottery (whose names are recorded), nor (in view of his age) a secondary or chorister. It is unlikely that he would have come to the college to be a vicar choral, since many similar posts could be had elsewhere at more important places such as the cathedrals, and those at Ottery were probably filled by local men. There was only one office in the college apart from that of chaplain of the Lady chapel to which a man would be likely to have come from elsewhere: that of master of the grammar school. Barclay was well up in Latin grammar when he translated *The Ship of Fools*[8] and taught for a time in a grammar school, as we shall see, in the 1540s. But it was not necessary to be ordained to be schoolmaster of Ottery collegiate church, and if Barclay had held that office we would expect him to have been described in print as a schoolmaster, rather than as a chaplain. On the whole, the likelihood seems to favour Barclay having been chaplain of the Lady chapel, though the fact itself is never overtly stated.

The Ship of Fools by Sebastian Brant, published in Germany in 1494, is a long, rather diffuse poem, further extended by Barclay with his own additions. It satirises various groups in society: gentlemen, clergy and scholars, parents, women and children, and complains of their follies and faults. In the course of the work, opinions are stated about some aspects of education, notably parents and children, academic study, and the ignorance of gentlemen and clergy. On the first of these topics,

Barclay is traditional and unexceptional. Parents should set a good example to their offspring, and correct them when they do wrong. In return, children should be obedient and care for their parents when they are old. To fathers who say that children are too tender to be chastised, Barclay replies like Langland,

> What hurtyth punysshement with moderacion
> Unto yonge children? Certaynely, no thynge;
> It voydeth vyce, gettynge vertue and cunnynge.

Like an Oxford writer of his own period, he asks is it not better for your son to be beaten than to grow up wicked and be hanged?[9] In the section on study, Barclay is more original because he takes sides with the humanists against the medieval grammarians. Many scholars who study logic and law, he says, do so without having mastered grammar properly, which is the basis of all the liberal arts. They read the old *Doctrinale* of Alexander of Ville-Dieu (a work then still in print in England), and disdain Priscian and Sulpizio, the classical and Renaissance authorities on grammar:

> If he have onys red the olde Dotrinall
> With his diffuse and unparfyte brevyte,
> He thynketh to have sene the poyntis of grammer all,
> And yet of one errour he maketh two or thre;
> Precyan or Sulpice disdayneth he to se.
> Thus many whiche say that they theyre grammer can,
> Ar als great folys as whan they firste began.[10]

When it comes to promotion to ranks and offices in the world, however, the studious do not get their just deserts:

> Eche is nat lettred that nowe is made a lorde,
> Nor eche a clerke that hath a benefyce.[11]

Criticism of clerical education was a well-worn theme among satirists, but Barclay shows the typical humanist tendency to extend it to the nobility and gentry. He was to repeat the charge a few years later in the preface to his translation of Sallust's *Jugurthine War* (published c. 1520). 'The understandyng of Latyn . . . at this tyme is almost contemned of gentylmen.'[12]

Some literary works tell us nothing about the places in which they were written. *The Ship of Fools* is not of that kind, since Barclay greatly enlarged the German text in his translation and took the opportunity to include several references, both complimentary and disparaging, to people whom he had met in Devon. Two of these people were dignitaries whose favour Barclay had or wished to have. The whole work, as has been said, was dedicated to Cornish, and in a section on foolish and wicked sheriffs and knights, Barclay explains that there is an exception to them: 'Kyrkham', who is not to be put into the ship along with the rest, because he is 'manly, righteous, wise, discreet and sad', a man of 'perfect meekness' and a supporter of men in poverty.

Barclay asserts that he himself is Kyrkham's 'servitor, chaplain and bede-man'; he promises to remain so during his life, and prays to God to raise Kyrkham to honour and give him the favour of the king.[13] 'Kyrkham' was evidently Sir John Kirkham of Paignton, who had been sheriff of Devon two years previously, from December 1505 to December 1506, and was to hold the office a second time in 1523-4.[14] Barclay appears to have done some travelling while he was in Devon; he later mentions Exeter and Totnes as if he had visited them,[15] and it is possible that he met Kirkham either at Paignton or at Ottery. Sir John's third wife, Lucy, was the daughter of Sir Thomas Tremayle of Sand in Sidbury parish near Ottery, and the knight may well have passed by the collegiate church on visits there from time to time.[16]

As well as applauding his patrons, Barclay inserted six stanzas into *The Ship of Fools* in praise of 'his well-beloved friend Sir John Bysshop of Exeter' who, he said, was the first person to see his translation and encouraged him not to keep it in the dark but to publish it.[17] 'Bysshop', as Barclay makes clear, was a cleric, and there is no reason to dissent from the late Professor Nelson's suggestion that he was the John Bishop who was ordained deacon at Ottery on 4 December 1500 to the title of Ottery collegiate church.[18] The title implies that Bishop came from Ottery or nearby, and Barclay could easily have met him there on in Exeter. In 1508 Bishop may already have been rector of St Paul's church, Exeter,[19] the benefice he definitely held in 1522.[20] He seems to have been ambitious to rise in the Church and Barclay calls him 'covetous', though he also expresses a hope that Bishop's fortunes will grow and that he will one day be a bishop in fact as well as in name. This hope was not fulfilled. In 1522 the rectory of St Paul's was worth £10 a year and Bishop's own possessions were valued at £26.13s.4d., but he never got a better benefice, and his resignation of the parish in 1537 to become priest of the Grandisson chantry in Exeter Cathedral, worth a little over £6 a year, looks like a retirement by a man of failing powers.[21] It is the last that we hear of him, and he probably died in the 1540s. Barclay, as the incumbent of two or three parishes in his last years, ended up better off than his former friend.

The rest of the local allusions in *The Ship of Fools* are unfavourable ones, suggesting that Barclay held a poor opinion of most Devonians, as did his fellow-poet Herrick a hundred and forty years later. It may be Ottery that he had in mind in his sketch of the disorders of contemporary church choirs: the musical director running hither and thither holding his staff of office, while the clergy gossip about the latest battle in France.[22] Barclay certainly mentions the eight secondaries of Ottery who, he says, are worthy to receive first place in the ship of fools because they know nothing and will learn nothing, even though they receive their tuition free of charge and live in a building next to the school itself.[23] He is scathing too about the local clergy, asserting as elsewhere that the least learned are promoted to the best benefices,

> For if one can flater, and bere a hawke on his fyst,
> He shalbe made person of Honyngton or of Clyst.[24]

Once in possession of these benefices, such people employ a hired chaplain to do their work—a 'Sir John of Garnesey'—and think themselves absolved of all responsibility.[25] No chaplain of this name can be discovered in early-Tudor Devon, so Barclay was either bestowing a nickname on some local priest who came from Guernsey, or using a stock name current at the time.[26] We should be careful, however, not to assume that the pre-Reformation clergy were as uniformly bad as he and other literary writers asserted. The secondaries of Ottery were probably a mixture of studious and ignorant, idle and conscientious youths, like their counterparts at Exeter Cathedral in the early sixteenth century.[27] And while we cannot now be sure which rector Barclay had in mind in the five parishes called Clyst, it is clear that his picture of the rector of Honiton was an inadequate one. Barclay may not indeed have had any personal knowledge of Henry Ferman, who held the parish from 1505 to 1527, since Ferman was studying at Oxford at about the time that Barclay was in Devon. But Ferman's ability to take a university degree in canon law, his promotion by the bishop to be precentor of Ottery in 1523 and his bequests to the fabric of Ottery and Honiton churches in 1526, shows that there was more to him than Barclay's canard suggests.[28]

Barclay reserved his rudest remarks for a group of people who seem to have been mainly lay inhabitants of Ottery. Foremost among them was a certain Mansell, whom he portrays as a man with a huge belly who went about seeking for prey and despoiling the poor, presumably as a steward, rent collector, or summoner of the Church courts.[29] Barclay suggested that if Mansell arrived too late to get into the fools' ship, he should be made the captain of a separate barge of 'bawds' or scoundrels. Later, the poet changed his mind and allocated Mansell a place in the filthiest part of the ship—the stinking bilges—along with Jack Chard, Robin Hill, millers and bakers who cheated with weights and measures, and 'all stealing tailors' such as Soper.[30] The court rolls of Ottery manor mention a Chard family in 1515-17,[31] but it is unfortunately impossible to identify any of Barclay's enemies as such, due to a lack of contemporary local records. Nevertheless, his criticisms of these people, along with the absence of any compliments to the staff of the collegiate church excepting Cornish, show plainly that Barclay was not very happy during his stay in Ottery. In one respect *The Ship of Fools* was his revenge: a squib to startle his enemies when he had left. It is amusing to picture their indignation when Barclay's book exploded in Ottery, some time in 1510, when he himself was safely far away.

On leaving Devon, Barclay moved both geographically and vocationally. By 1513 he had become a Benedictine monk of Ely cathedral priory, and since in 1516 he is listed as sixteenth among the thirty brethren, it is likely that he went there straight from Ottery. Was the change due to economic or spiritual motives? He may have despaired of getting patronage with which to leave Ottery and get a more comfortable benefice, such as a parish church. Ely offered a better standard of living, being a large and well endowed foundation, where a monk would have his personal servant, a private room, and a good library at hand. But Barclay had hardly been in Devon long enough to feel a sense of failure in the search for patronage, and his later career suggests a strong vocation to live in a religious order. His life at Ely must have been relatively comfortable, and he was able to go on writing. Six of his works were published wholly or partly during this period, up to the mid 1520s, falling into two groups: literary and educational.[32] The first were all translations of texts by classical or Renaissance authors: *The Life of St George* by Battista Mantovano (published c. 1515), five *Eclogues,* nos 4-5 by Mantovano (published 1518-21) and nos. 1-3 by Aeneas Sylvius Piccolomini (published 1523-30), and Sallust's *Jugurthine War* (published c. 1520). The educational group began with a translation of *The Mirror of Good Manners* by the humanist scholar Domenico Mancini, a Renaissance work in the medieval genre of treatises on behaviour and etiquette aimed at young people. Next came a revision of John Stanbridge's popular *Vocabula* (published 1519), an early humanist vocabulary in Latin and English for use in schools, and successful enough in Barclay's edition to be reprinted in 1524 and 1526. Finally, an *Introductory to Wryte and to Pronounce Frenche* was published in 1522, the latest of a long line of such treatises in England, stretching back to the thirteenth century.[33] Barclay drew on these, admitting in his work that he had 'seen the draughtes of others' made before his time, and sometimes he perpetuated out-of-date spellings of French words. The book was treated scornfully by John Palsgrave, the author of a much longer work on French, *L'Esclarcissement de la langue francoyse,* published in 1530, who stated

> I have seen an old book written in parchment in manner in all things like to his said *Introductory* which by conjecture was not written this 100 years. I wot not if he happened to fortune upon such another.

But Palsgrave was self-consciously trying to write a new kind of treatise, in which French grammar was thoroughly reduced to rules. Barclay belonged to an older tradition which gave the learner practical advice, rather than aiming at grammatical completeness.[34]

The best known of Barclay's Ely works are the *Eclogues,* which were the first formal poems of their kind to be written in English. They belong to humanist literature since they are translations from two fifteenth-century Italian authors, but Barclay sympathised enough with pre-humanist Latin poetry to pay a compliment in his prologue to the *Eclogue of Theodulus,* the ninth-century poem which was widely read in English grammar schools up to the early sixteenth century:[35]

> What shall I speake of the father auncient,
> Which in briefe language both playne and eloquent,
> Between Alathea, Sewstis stoute and bolde,
> Hath made rehearsall of all thy storyes olde,
> By true historyes us teaching to object
> Against vayne fables of olde Gentiles sect.[36]

Barclay himself may have read Theodulus at school, and it is interesting that despite his acquaintance with humanist writing, he still valued its 'playne and eloquent' style and content (the debate of Pseustis and Alathea as to whether Greek mythology or Hebrew history was better). His opinion did not prevail, however, and Theodulus ceased to be printed in England after 1515.[37] Elsewhere in Barclay's *Eclogues* there are some brief but vivid references to childhood. The mother sits on the doorstep with her children on her lap, kissing and hugging them, delousing and combing them, and rubbing their necks with butter—perhaps to soothe sunburn. The street boys busy themselves with their tops in Lent, and sing and hop for joy in the fruit season. In winter, torn and ragged, they watch men killing pigs, in hope of a good dinner, and claim the bladder into which they put beans and peas to make it rattle, blow it up well, and play handball and football with it to drive away the cold.[38] There is also a more formal discussion about whether the royal court is a place of education for good or ill. Coridon, one of the shepherd characters, asserts that at court you find wise men, good music and the reading of chronicles which stir young princes to imitate the worthy deeds of their predecessors. But Cornix, who tends to represent Barclay, disagrees; most of the talk at court is of war, novelties and abominable deeds. The wise cloak their sayings with flattery to gain promotion. Some great men indeed send their sons to court to learn virtue and manners, but all that the youths absorb is malice, bad manners and vice. Courtiers boast of their sexual exploits, the murders they have done, the frauds they have committed, and you must not think to find any chaste or sober young men among them; instead 'all sueth vices, all sue enormitie'.[39] Once more the vein is the familiar humanist one of telling the aristocracy to reform their manners.

In the middle of the 1520s, somewhere between 1521 and 1528, Barclay's career experienced another change with his departure from Ely to become a Franciscan friar.[40] A move of this kind was most unusual—monks and friars had different traditions, objectives and ways

of life—and it undoubtedly signified a major shift of outlook in the man himself. He ceased to write, either poetry or practical works, and his only important publication afterwards, the first three *Eclogues* of 1530, was probably written before he joined the friars. Instead, he acquired a reputation as a religious activist, even a non-conformist. In about 1528 the German informer Hermann Rinck wrote to Cardinal Wolsey that various dissidents, including 'William Roy, William Tyndale, Jerome Barlow, Alexander Barclay and their adherents, etc., formerly Observants of the Order of St Francis but now apostates, . . . ought to be arrested, punished and delivered up on account of Lutheran heresy'. As the others mentioned were all living in Germany, it looks as though Barclay was also settled there. The Observants were the reformed branch of the Franciscan Order, with six houses in England, and this is the chief evidence that Barclay joined them rather than the larger 'Conventual' section of the order. It seems to be supported by a letter to Wolsey of April 1529 by another Observant friar, John West, who was about to meet Barclay whom he accused of calling the cardinal a 'tyrant' and other 'opprobrious and blasphemous words'. The Observants were noted for their fervour, by contemporary religious standards, and if Barclay joined them, he did so as a religious challenge not merely for personal convenience. It is unlikely that he was a Lutheran. He may have been interested in some of Luther's writings (like other eventually conservative men of his day), but Rinck's letter is not wholly accurate (Tyndale was not a friar), and his linking of Barclay with the admittedly Lutheran Roy and Barlow may be a mistake. In the event Barclay remained a friar, returned to England and became known not for his Lutheranism but for his religious conservatism.[41]

We know little of Barclay's life as a friar, but friars were great students and it is likely that part of his time was spent studying theology at a university and taking a doctor's degree—a process of several years. He is described as 'Doctor Barclay' in 1538,[42] and if this is correct (as it certainly was by 1546), he must have taken his degree in the late 1520s or 1530s in a foreign university, since he does not appear in the degree registers of Oxford or Cambridge. Study in Germany would account for his mention there in 1528. In 1534 the Observant houses in England were closed because of their hostility to the king's supremacy over the Church, and the surviving members were transferred to the Conventual houses, themselves suppressed in 1538. Barclay thus experienced further changes of life, this time changes forced on him and unwelcome. The London chronicler Charles Wriothesley singled him out by name, under the year 1538, as one who was reluctant to give up wearing his friar's habit in public until he was compelled to do so, and John Foxe the martyrologist later recounted a story in which Thomas Cromwell personally threatened Barclay with a hanging unless he changed his clothes. In the summer and autumn of 1538 Barclay carried out a number of preaching engagements: at Barking (Suffolk) at Whitsuntide and in the diocese of Exeter in October. It is not recorded whether he revisited Ottery, but three reports of his demeanour subsequently reached Cromwell. At Barking he had not preached in favour of the king's supremacy or against the pope; at St Germans in Cornwall he had made his conservatism known, albeit in a circumspect way; and in Cornwall and Devonshire generally he was doing 'much hurt' with 'open preaching and private communication'.

What action Cromwell took, if any, is not clear, because Barclay drops out of records for the next eight years. When he reappears it is in the role of a beneficed clergyman, indeed a clerical pluralist—a different role by far from that of an Observant friar. This suggests that Barclay accepted that the friars were done for and decided to come to terms with the situation. In 1546 the subdean of Wells Cathedral presented him to be vicar of Wookey (Somerset), close to Wells and with an income of £12.15s.8d.; he probably lived in one or other of those places for the next couple of years.[43] Then, in the summer of 1547, the headmaster of Wells Cathedral School, Richard Edon, fell ill and Barclay was persuaded to take his place, probably on a temporary basis, with a further salary of £13.6s.8d.[44] He did the task until Michaelmas or Christmas 1548, when he moved abruptly from Somerset to the other side of England to become resident vicar of Great Baddow in Essex. It has always been said that Barclay was admitted as vicar of Great Baddow on 7 February 1547 (new style), but this is a mistake of the eighteenth-century historian Richard Newcourt. The true date is 1549, and we know from other evidence that Barclay went to live in Great Baddow in January of that year.[45] It was a more valuable benefice than Wookey, with an income of £18.6s.8d., and as Barclay obtained permission to go on holding Wookey as well,[46] his net income rose to a respectable £25 even if he paid a curate to serve his Somerset parish. In 1552 he was given a third, even wealthier benefice: the rectory of All Hallows Lombard Street, London, with an income of £22.6s.8d., which involved him giving up one of his other two parishes. In the event, before he could do so, he died at Croydon (Surrey), early in June 1552, and was buried there on the tenth of the month.

If we had to write his epitaph, it would be difficult to sum him up concisely. As a Latinist, he was a humanist, dismissive of Alexander of Ville-Dieu and steeped in classical and Renaissance literature. Yet he could write appreciatively of Theodulus, compile a treatise in French of a very traditional kind, and make customary observations about parents and children. He also became a monk and a friar, both of which we associate with the middle ages. Yet the humanist monk-poet of

Ely is parallelled by Robert Joseph, the humanist monk-letter writer of Evesham,[47] and the old religious orders were perfectly capable of absorbing new ideas, not to mention heretical ones as we see with Roy and Barlow. Once upon a time, Barclay would have been called 'a transitional figure', with a foot in the medieval and the Renaissance worlds. The truth is that every generation is transitional, and that all innovators are conservative in some respects. We shall witness the same when we pass on to Shakespeare.

Notes

1. On Barclay's life, see principally his translation of *The Ship of Fools,* ed. T. Jamieson, 2 vols (Edinburgh and London, 1874), i, pp ix-xcii; *Dictionary of National Biography,* article by A. W. Ward; *The Eclogues of Alexander Barclay,* ed. Beatrice White, Early English Text Society, original series, clxxv (1926), pp i-liv, and Barclay, *The Life of St George,* ed. W. Nelson, EETS, original series, ccxxx (1955), pp ix-xxv.

2. *Eclogues,* ed. White, p xli.

3. Devon Record Office, Chanter XIII, ff 92^v, 95^v. The evidence was first brought to light by W. Nelson, 'New Light on Alexander Barclay', *Review of English Studies,* xix (1943), pp. 59-61. The mentions of Barclay's 'admission by the schoolmaster' in the bishop's register refer to John Calwoodleigh, master of Exeter high school, who acted as one of the examiners of the ordinands (Orme, [Nicholas, *Education in the] West of England, [1066-1548,* Exeter: University of Exeter, 1976,] pp 50, 56).

4. *The Ship of Fools,* ed. Jamieson, i, p cxvi.

5. For Cornish's career, see Emden, *BRUO,* i, 491-2.

6. *The Ship of Fools,* ed. Jamieson, i, pp cxvi-vii.

7. J. N. Dalton, *The Collegiate Church of Ottery St Mary* (Cambridge, 1917), pp 93, 98, 100, 145, 262.

8. *The Ship of Fools,* ed. Jamieson, i, 144.

9. Ibid., pp 45-52, 234-8; ii, 147-52. On hanging, compare *A Fifteenth Century School Book,* ed. W. Nelson (Oxford, 1956), p 14.

10. *The Ship of Fools,* ed. Jamieson, i, 142-7; compare *A Fifteenth Century School Book,* ed. Nelson, p 19.

11. *The Ship of Fools,* ed. Jamieson, i, 21-2, 158.

12. Sallust, *The Jugurthine War,* trans. Barclay (London, R. Pynson, c. 1520), f A5^v. For similar contemporary references, see Richard Pace, *De Fructu* (Basel, 1517), p 15; John Skelton, *Poetical*

Works, ed. A. Dyce, 2 vols (London, 1843), i, 334-5; Sir Thomas Elyot, *The Governor* (London, 1531), book i, chapter 12.

13. *The Ship of Fools,* ed. Jamieson, ii, 81.

14. *Lists of Sheriffs for England & Wales,* PRO, Lists and Indexes, ix (1898), p 36.

15. *Eclogues,* ed. White, pp 19-20.

16. On Kirkham, see John Prince, *Danmonii Orientales Illustres: or, The Worthies of Devon* (London, 1810), pp 554-6.

17. *The Ship of Fools,* ed. Jamieson, ii, pp vii, 278-80.

18. *Review of English Studies,* xix (1943), p 60; Devon Record Office, Chanter XII part ii, f 42.

19. Devon Record Office, Deeds (Exeter, St Paul's), ED/BC/6-8. For another reference to Bishop, see PRO, C 1/287/78 (and possibly C 1/303/53 and C 1/317/53).

20. *Tudor Exeter: Tax Assessments, 1489-1595,* ed. Margery M. Rowe, Devon and Cornwall Record Society, new series, xxii (1977), p 14.

21. Devon Record Office, Chanter XIV, ff 88, 90; Nicholas Orme, *The Minor Clergy of Exeter Cathedral* (Exeter, 1980), p 83. The stipend of the Grandisson chantry was £5.6s.8d., but the priest could earn about another 19s.0d. by attending obit masses for the dead in the cathedral.

22. *The Ship of Fools,* ed. Jamieson, ii, 155.

23. Ibid., i, 179. For the locations of the secondaries' house and the school, see Dalton, op. cit., p 75 and plan between pp 80-1.

24. *The Ship of Fools,* ed. Jamieson, i, 22.

25. Ibid., p 160.

26. The term 'Sir John' for an ordinary priest was, of course, very common.

27. Orme, Nicholas. *Education and Security in Midieval and Renaissance England.* London: Hambledon Press, 1989, pp 194-5.

28. For Ferman's career, see Emden, *BRUO,* iv, 202.

29. *The Ship of Fools,* ed. Jamieson, ii, 82.

30. Ibid., ii, 307. In this reference Mansell is spelt 'Manshyll' in order to rhyme, and perhaps in parallel with Prince Hal's gibe at Falstaff: 'a huge hill of flesh' (*1 Henry IV,* II.iv.239).

31. Devon Record Office, CR 1288, mm 105, 107ᵛ, etc.

32. On these works, see A. W. Pollard and G. R. Redgrave, *A Short Title Catalogue of Books Printed in England, 1475-1640,* 2nd ed., 2 vols (London, 1976-86), nos 1383.5-1386, 3545, 10752, 12379, 17242, 21626, 22992.1 and 23181.

33. Orme, *Education,* p 11.

34. Kathleen Lambley, *The Teaching and Cultivation of the French Language in England during Tudor and Stuart Times* (London and Manchester, 1920), pp 3-4, 77-80.

35. Orme, [Nicholas,] *English Schools* [*in the Middle Ages,* London: Methuen, 1973,] p 103.

36. *Eclogues,* ed. White, p 2.

37. Pollard and Redgrave, *Short Title Catalogue,* nos 23939.5-23943.

38. *Eclogues,* ed. White, pp 184, 191-2.

39. Ibid., pp 60-3, 128-9.

40. For references to the rest of Barclay's career, unless otherwise given, see ibid., pp xli-liv.

41. On Roy and Barlow, see E. G. Rupp, *Studies in the Making of the English Protestant Tradition* (Cambridge, 1949); this contains no evidence of Barclay's involvement with them.

42. Charles Wriothesley, *A Chronicle of England, 1485-1559,* ed. W. D. Hamilton, vol i, Camden Society, new series, xl (1875), p 82, assuming that the entry was written at the time.

43. *The Registers of Thomas Wolsey, etc., Bishops of Bath and Wells, 1518-1559,* ed. Sir H. C. Maxwell-Lyte, Somerset Record Society, lv (1940), pp 113-14.

44. Orme, *West of England,* pp 87-8, 90.

45. Barclay was admitted as vicar of Great Baddow on 7 February 1549 (new style) (London, Guildhall Library, MS 9531/12 part i (The Register of Edmund Bonner), f 164ᵛ). For the other evidence, see *Eclogues,* ed. White, pp xlviii-li.

46. Barclay was licensed to hold an additional benefice with Wookey on 28 January 1549 (D.S. Chambers, *Faculty Office Registers, 1534-1549* (Oxford, 1966), p 316).

47. Orme, *Education,* pp 39-40.

Alistair Fox (essay date 1989)

SOURCE: Fox, Alistair. "*Beatus ille*: The *Eclogues* of Alexander Barclay." In *Politics and Literature in the Reigns of Henry VII and Henry VIII,* pp 37-55. Oxford: Basil Blackwell Ltd., 1989.

[*In the essay below, Fox examines Barclay's motivations for writing the* Eclogues *as well as for translating Brandt's* Ship of Fools.]

The patronage system affected different people in different ways, and these differences conditioned the kind of literature they contrived. Skelton wrote from within the court, having enjoyed the benefits that the system could impart. His problems were not ones of frustration at being excluded from court, but of insecurity and anxiety arising from the need to maintain his position and moral integrity once there. Consequently, he used the fiction of *The Bowge of Courte* to analyse and objectify the sources of that anxiety as a preparation for taking steps to resolve it. The case of Alexander Barclay is quite different, since at the time when he confronted the issue in his *Eclogues,* he had conspicuously failed to gain court patronage, and this is reflected in the nature and function of the work. Whereas *The Bowge of Courte* is an instrument of analysis preparatory to future action, the *Eclogues* are a retrospective justification of Barclay's failure, designed to make a virtue out of necessity; while Skelton narrows the distance between the action in his poem and his personal situation, Barclay seeks to distance it by placing it clearly in the past; and whereas Skelton seeks to involve the reader in deciding what he might do, Barclay instructs him or her on the merit of what he pretends he has already done. The rhetorical strategies of the two works are thus quite different.

There are, nevertheless, striking similarities that show *The Bowge of Courte* and the *Eclogues* to be characteristic of their age. Both seek to confirm their author's viewpoint by exploiting conventional anti-court themes, yet handle them in ways that are innovative in form. Both seek to 'establish the will' of the author,[1] by dramatizing the process through which he evolves towards his final attitude; and both end up being ambivalent in that attitude because of divided impulses in each author that belie his fictional stance. Though a much maligned writer, therefore, Barclay takes his place as a genuine contributor to the early Tudor literature of complexity.

* * *

Barclay's early career explains the frustration and disappointed expectations that eventually moved him to write the *Eclogues.* Like so many others who sought a literary career, Barclay went to either Oxford or Cambridge, and certainly gained a degree from one of them.[2] From his various references to foreign universities and foreign scholars (particularly French ones), it can be inferred that he travelled to the continent where he may have undertaken further study. Up to this point, Barclay's career is remarkably similar to that of Skelton or Stephen Hawes, and Barclay might well have expected that it would lead to advancement similar to theirs.

On his return to England, Barclay entered holy orders, being ordained by Thomas Cornish, titular bishop of Tyne, and suffragan bishop of Bath and Wells. Cornish was also provost of Oriel College, Oxford (1493-1507), and warden of the College of Saint Mary, Ottery, in Devonshire, between 1490 and 1511,[3] and it was probably through his offices that Barclay gained his first preferment as chaplain at Saint Mary, Ottery, where he combined the duties of librarian and instructor to the choirboys.[4] Saint Mary's was a college of secular priests, and would therefore have given Barclay plenty of scope for further advancement, had he sought it.

There are, indeed, plenty of signs that Barclay wanted to secure promotion to higher positions at this time. The main evidence is provided by the ***Ship of Fooles,*** the translation of Sebastian Brandt's satire which Barclay completed in 1508, while at Saint Mary's, Ottery. Barclay's verse translation vastly expands on the original, and his periphrastic additions often reveal a great deal of self-projection on his part.

Two specific themes emerge in these additions: resentment at the numbers of unsuitable people gaining promotion, and an implicit assertion of Barclay's own suitability for advancement. Barclay seems particularly resentful of the advantages that those with wealth, noble birth, or powerful connections have over other more worthy aspirants in the competition for promotion. For instance, in the section 'of unprofitable study' he asserts that he dare not let on board 'all the fooles promoted to honours . . . of hye progenitours' because, together with the servants of Cupid and Venus, these would cause the ship to sink.[5] These are the scholars that make good not because of mind or talent, but because of noble lineage. The problem, however, is general in England:

> Eche is not lettred that nowe is made a lorde,
> Nor eche a Clerke that hath a benefice:
> They are not all lawyers that plees do recorde,
> All that are promoted are not fully wise.[6]

> This is the speciall cause of this inconuenience,
> That greatest fooles, and fullest of lewdnes,
> Hauing least wit, and simplest science
> Are first promoted, and have greatest reuerence.
> For if one can flatter, and beare a Hauke on his fist,
> He shalbe made Parson of Honington of Clist.[7]

> The company of men that lacketh witte,
> Is best exalted (as nowe) in every place,
> And in the chayre or hyest rowme shall sit,
> Promoting none but suche as sue their trace.[8]

In the expanded phrasing of passages like these one can detect Barclay's envy at the promotion of others less worthy than he is to positions he feels he is better equipped to occupy. The phrasing with which he proposed the remedy for England's ills (in a section marked '*Anglie defectus*' in the margin) also implies Barclay's belief that he should be among those who are advanced to an honourable office:

If the noble realme of Englande would aduance
In our days men of vertue and prudence,
Eche man rewarding after his gouernaunce,
As the wise with honour and rowme of excellence,
And the ill with greeuous payne for their offence,
Then should our famous laude of olde obtayned,
Not bene decayed, oppressed and thus distayned.

If men of wisdom were brought out of the scoles,
And after their vertue set in moste hye degree,
My ship should not haue led so many fooles.[9]

The phrasing with which he translated the Latin here creates an unnecessary repetition, betraying Barclay's conviction that he would benefit from such a reform. *He* is the wise man from the schools that might very profitably be advanced to a 'room of excellence'.

Even though Barclay professes that he translated the book 'neyther for hope of rewarde nor laude of man',[10] there are indications that his motives were rather more practical than he pretends. The work contains a number of strategically placed panegyrics praising the English king, which were manifestly composed with Henry VII in mind. Henry is praised as 'the red Rose redolent' who has quelled insurrection, expelled war and shown exemplary qualities of meekness, chastity, justice and pity, to whom Englishmen are to do obedience 'with faythfull heart'.[11] These encomiastic passages offer exactly the same kind of flattery through which other writers, such as Skelton, Hawes, or More, sought to attract the attention, and hence the patronage, of the current monarch. Having embedded these encomia in the work, Barclay may have hoped that his mentor, Bishop Cornish, to whom *The Ship of Fooles* is dedicated, might bring it to the king's notice to procure him advancement. Henry VII, however, died in 1509 before the work appeared in print. Hasty emendations to the text confirm the idea that Barclay had patronage from the king in mind. In the case of one encomium, a marginal note simply substitutes Henry VIII for Henry VII as the subject of praise:

But ye proude galants that thus your selfe disguise,
Be ye ashamed, beholde vnto your prince:
Consider his sadness, his honestie deuise,
His clothing expresseth his inwarde prudence
Ye see no example of such inconuenience.
In his highnes, but godly wit and grauitie,
Ensue him, and sorowe for your enormitie.

The marginal comment reads: 'Laus summa de grauitate eximia Henrici Anglorum regis, viij' ('a high commendation of the extraordinary seriousness of Henry VIII, King of England').[12] Whatever else Henry VIII may have been in the early years of his reign, he was not the epitome of *gravitas* and sober dress—but his father was. Another sign of hasty reworking occurs later in the work when Barclay, forgetting that he has already praised Henry VII as the 'red rose redolent' who has

been leading England into a state of millenial peace, inserts a long panegyric of the new king who is just beginning a reign of unprecedented glory:

One hope we have our enemies to quell,
Which hope is stedfast if we our selfe do well,
For Henry the eyght replete with hye wisedome,
By iust title gideth our scepter of kingdome.
This noble prince beginneth vertuously,
By iustice and pitie his realme to maynteyne,
So that he and his without mo company,
May succour our sores by his manhode souerayne,
And get with his owne hande Jerusalem agayne,
He passeth Hercules in manhode and courage,
Hauing a respect vnto his tender age.[13]

Much of this is simply drawn from Brandt's original praise of the Emperor Maximilian as the leader who will defeat the Turks, liberate Jerusalem, and recover the holy cross, as the marginal note makes clear: 'Mutatur laus Maximiliani Romanorum regis, in laudem Henrici octaui anglorum regis' ('the praise of Maximilian, King of the Romans, is changed into a praise of Henry VIII, King of the English).' However, Barclay praised the young Henry for a virtue that is not mentioned in the source—liberality:

He passeth Achilles in strength and valiaunce,
His fame here as great, but as for his larges
And liberalitie, he showeth in countenaunce
That no auarice can blinde his righteousnes,
Couetice hath left behinde him his riches,
Unto the high possession of liberalitie,
Which with the same shall kepe our libertie.[14]

These lines show Barclay hastening to ingratiate himself with the new regime by (like so many others) attacking the old. He implicitly personifies Henry VII as Covetousness, whose wealth his liberal son, Henry VIII, has inherited, to the happiness of potential beneficiaries—like himself. It is all rather cynical, as Barclay had earlier praised the old king as 'one who spared no expence upon the poore', when it looked as if the father and not the son would be the source of liberality for him.[15] At any rate, these inconsistencies and emendations prove that Barclay was not as disinterested in putting forth his work as he pretended. He hoped to gain preferment and, if he had observed the careers of scholars such as André, Skelton, and Hawes, he might justifiably have expected that it would come his way.

In this hope, however, he was to prove disappointed. Just at the point when Barclay could look to see his literary efforts rewarded, his intended patron, Henry VII, died, and his successor, Henry VIII, favoured a style of man and writing which was far removed from anything Barclay had to offer. The new king was interested in disguisings and joustings, not in didactic treatises—he had enough of those inflicted on him by his tutors—and in poets who would entertain, not instruct him. To add

to this misfortune, Bishop Cornish, Barclay's old patron, retired from the wardenship of Saint Mary, Ottery,
in 1511 and died shortly after, thus depriving Barclay
of any intercessor with the new regime. And to cap
Barclay's bad luck, just at this time John Skelton decided that he had had enough of country life as a parish
priest, and energetically sought to return to court.[16]
Skelton had the advantage over Barclay in every respect. He was already personally acquainted with the
king, having been his tutor, and in spite of a deeply serious vein of morality, had the wit and racy style to
provide Henry with what he wanted, as his bawdy lyrics and colourful invectives show.

For a number of reasons Skelton became a particular
bête noire for Barclay, even before he added insult to
injury by gaining the court patronage Barclay would
have liked. Barclay's first attack on his rival came at
the end of ***The Ship of Fooles***:

> Holde me excused, for why my will is good,
> Men to induce vnto vertue and goodnes,
> I write no iest ne tale of Robin Hood,
> Nor sowe no sparkles ne sede of viciousnes,
> Wise men loue vertue, wilde people wantonnes,
> It longeth not to my science nor cunning,
> For Philip the Sparowe the *Dirige* to singe.[17]

This reference to Skelton's *Phyllyp Sparowe* reveals not
only Barclay's disapproval of the frivolity and sexual
lubricity displayed by his rival in that poem, but also
the difference between them as poets. Barclay is unwilling, and unable, to write jests of fiction for entertainment's sake, preferring instead to write didactically;
Skelton, on the other hand, is both willing and able, and
Barclay despises him for it.

Such an attitude was bound to disqualify Barclay in the
eyes of the boisterous and pleasure-loving young king,
and so it eventually proved. Yet Barclay nevertheless
appears to have been given a chance to prove his worth
at court. One of Skelton's first tasks as newly appointed
court poet was to stage a 'flytyng' or ritual exchange of
verbal abuse, with Sir Christopher Garnesche, one of
Henry VIII's gentleman ushers, for the entertainment of
the court in late 1513 or early 1514.[18] Although
Garnesche's side of the flytyng does not survive, we
can infer from Skelton's, which does, that Garnesche
called upon the services of another poet, whom Skelton
alludes to sarcastically as 'gorbellyd Godfrey' with 'that
grysly gargons face'.[19] There is every reason to suspect
that this other poet is not Stephen Hawes, as has been
claimed,[20] but Alexander Barclay himself. Gordon adduced that 'gorbellyd Godfrey' was Hawes because of
the similarity between that name and the name of a
misshapen dwarf, 'Godfrey gobylyue' who occurs in
Hawe's *Passetyme of Pleasure*.[21] 'Godfrey', however, is
an ironic name that is frequently applied, in various alliterative combinations with adjectives beginning with

'g', to other nefarious types in the early Tudor period.
Barclay himself uses it in his ***Eclogues*** to refer, I believe, to none other than Skelton. Replying to Cornix's
assertion that 'a ribaudes blame is commendation',
Coridon says:

> Nowe truely my heart is eased with the same,
> For *Godfrey Gormand* lately did me blame.
> And as for him selfe, though he be gay and stoute,
> He hath nought but foly within and eke without.
> To blowe in a bowle, and for to pill a platter,
> To girne, to braule, to counterfayte, to flatter,
> He hath no felowe betwene this and Croydon,
> Saue the proude plowman (Gnato) of Chorlington.
> Because he alway maligneth against me,
> It playne appereth our life doth not agree.
> For if we liued both after one rate,
> Then should I haue him to me a frendly mate.[22]

In late 1513-early 1514, when the ***Eclogues*** were
worked up, the most likely recent occasion for vituperation would have been the Garnesche-Skelton flytyng,
and in this passage Barclay seems to be reliving the encounter. Godfrey Gourmand, he says, is unmatched in
his dubious ability

> To blowe in a bowle, and for to pill a platter,
> To girne, to braule, to counterfayte, to flatter.

This picks up the level of Skelton's own vituperative
manner when, for example, he abuses Garnesche:

> Ye bere yow bolde as Barabas, or Syr Terry of Trace.
> Ye gyrne grymly with your gomys and with yor grysly
>   face.[23]

Barclay is thus purloining Skelton's style and adapting
the sobriquet Skelton had given him in order to throw
both back in his face. He even alludes to the idea that
must have formed the main line of his attack on Skelton,
when he declares that his opponent's life-style and his
own do 'not agree'. Skelton's own verses confirm that
this was one of the main tactics used by his opponent to
slander him. Warning Garnesche that he, Skelton, has
detected the hand of his 'skrybe' behind his letter,
Skelton adds:

> I caste me nat to be od
> With neythyr of yow tw[ey]ne:
>   . . . . .
> Lewedely your tyme ye spende,
> *My lyvyng to reprehende.*[24]

This implies that Garnesche and his poet have singled
out improprieties in Skelton's personal life (he kept a
concubine) as ammunition for an *ad hominem* attack,
which is entirely consistent with the attitude Barclay
displays towards Skelton elsewhere. In the ***Eclogues*** he
refers to him in thinly veiled terms as having been
'decked as Poete laureate, / When stinking Thais made
him her graduate',[25] and in ***The Life of Saint George*** he

asserts that 'he which is lawreat / Ought nat his name with vyce to vyolate', implying that at least one notable laureate (that is, Skelton) had done so.[26]

One final piece of evidence exists to clinch the identification of Barclay as the poet Garnesche hired to counter Skelton. John Bale attributes to Barclay a work to which he gives the Latin title **Contra Skeltonum.**[27] In the light of the other evidence, it would seem probable that this work, no longer extant, is the missing side of the flytyng, the counterblast to Skelton's *Agenst Garnesche*.

Time has obliterated any further traces of the quarrel between Barclay and Skelton, but we do know that it left him with an abiding detestation of his rival, and resentment at his success. He had good reason to be perturbed. Skelton, the charismatic court wit, was in tune with the times, and Barclay, the sage and serious moralist, was not. If he were indeed the rival poet in the Garnesche flytyng, the whole experience must have shown him that he could not expect to find advancement at court, far less fit comfortably into it. He was left with no option but to seek a living elsewhere, and he found one by becoming a Benedictine monk at the cathedral house of Ely. It was here that he drew breath, and chose the moment to reflect on the meaning of his experience in his next major literary work, his five pastoral *Eclogues.*

* * *

The first three of Barclay's five *Eclogues* were printed separately by Wynkyn de Worde at an unknown date, and form a discrete group on their own. They may have been written earlier in Barclay's career, for he says in the 'Prologe' that he had first compiled the *Eclogues* in youth; then, having rediscovered them accidentally, has worked them up, 'adding and bating where I perceyved neede.'[28] This protestation closely imitates the Dedicatory Epistle of Mantuan's *Eclogues,*[29] and as such may be largely convention, but references to Henry VII as recently dead and Dudley and Empson as traitors suggest that there may have been some truth in it.[30] Also, whereas Mantuan refers to himself as 'quinquagenarius', Barclay declares that he is 'fortie yere saue twayne'.[31] The more specific age of 38 suggests a particular occasion for the work and, given other internal references dating the *Eclogues* to 1514, it seems likely that the occasion was Barclay's entry into the Benedictine monastery at Ely after his encounter with Skelton in the Garnesche flytyng. Such circumstances would explain the bitterness Barclay still shows towards Skelton, as when he sardonically contrasts his own black monk's robes with the green robe Skelton had been given as *orator regius*:

> No name I chalenge of Poete laureate.
> That name vnto them is mete and doth agree

> Which writeth matters with curiositee.
> Mine habite blacke accordeth not with grene,
> Blacke betokeneth death as it is dayly sene,
> The grene is pleasour, freshe lust and iolite,
> These two in nature hath great diuersitie.
> Then who would ascribe, except he were a foole,
> The pleasaunt laurer vnto the mourning cowle.[32]

While Barclay disavows any ambition to gain the reputation and position that Skelton has, the ironic tone and his insistence on the blackness of his cowl, with its symbolism of mourning, nevertheless betrays more than a hint of sadness and self-pity.

Eclogues I-III translate the *De Curialium Miseriis* by Aeneas Sylvius Piccolomini, later Pope Pius II, but in the course of doing so transforms the original.

Piccolomini's satire on life at the imperial court is written in the form of a Latin prose letter to John Aich. Barclay recasts it as three pastoral dialogues spoken between two shepherds—Cornix, who is old and experienced, and Coridon, who is young, inexperienced, and eager to escape his life of poverty in the country by finding a place at court. Cornix gradually talks him out of this plan by describing to him all the miseries of courtiers.[33]

Barclay's decision to present this anti-court satire in the form of the pastoral dialogue has been denounced as 'ideally unfortunate'.[34] It is no such thing, for the associations inherent in the pastoral conventions meant that Barclay could exploit them as a metaphor for his own situation as a self-imposed exile in Ely. The device of 'shepherds' perfectly suggested the religious vocation of Barclay and his fellow monks, and the traditional setting of the countryside accurately signified his location. Moreover, the countryside had conventionally been attributed with greater innocence, happiness, and virtue than the city, and so the pastoral genre helped Barclay justify his failure to gain preferment at court, on the grounds that his current situation was in any case superior.

The pastoral genre, therefore, helped Barclay to turn Piccolomini's satire into a vehicle for self-projection and self-assertion. The original attack is an extended literary paradox in which Piccolomini proves that all who dwell at court are fools because, in seeking honour, praise, power, wealth, and pleasure, they end up with the opposites of these things. Barclay dutifully reproduces the substance of Piccolomini's proof, while suppressing the element of facetiousness in the original, so that it becomes a serious statement of his own fictionalized reaction to court. **'Eclogue 1'** proves that the honour to be found there is false honour because it arises neither from virtue nor merit—and itemizes the disadvantages of power and riches.[35] **'Eclogue II'** describes how any pleasures offered to the five senses are outnumbered by unpleasant experiences, such as drinking out of cups 'in which some states or dames late did pis', or eating fish that is 'corrupt, ill smelling, and fiue dayes olde'.[36] **'Eclogue III'** expands the catalogue of miseries: having to put up with the farting, snorting, and stinking breath of unwelcome bedfellows; the difficulty of getting stipends paid; and the horrors of a troubled conscience.[37] Barclay deliberately obscures the careful structure of the original by introducing Coridon as an interlocutor, who breaks in to voice doubts and queries. His interruptions add a verisimilitude that helps to disguise the rhetorical character of the original, so that its points may be taken more seriously.

The dialogue form of the *Eclogues* was just as useful to Barclay as the generic conventions of the pastoral, for he needed not only to justify a life away from court, but also to reconcile himself to his rural existence. By changing Piccolomini's epistle into a series of dialogues, Barclay turned the *Eclogues* into an instrument for 'establishing his will', through confronting doubts in order to overcome them. By personifying his own divided impulses as two separate characters, Barclay was able to dramatize as an external action, an internal process of self-persuasion.

Cornix and Coridon both reveal traces of their creator. In a passage that has no source in Piccolomini, Cornix who is old and experienced, says that in youth he dwelt in Croydon, and often brought coals to sell at court, where 'none regarded me'.[38] Barclay mentions Croydon so often that his biographers have supposed that he resided there as a boy. The fact that he was buried in Croydon in 1552 lends some credence to this supposition.[39] In some respects, therefore, Cornix is likely to embody aspects of Barclay's older, disillusioned self. Coridon, on the other hand, the young man who is tired of country life and does not want to live in poverty any longer, shows the same belief in his own worthiness and capacity that Barclay had projected in *The Ship of Fooles.* 'I were a man mete to serue a prince or king', he declares, and later adds:

If I had frendes I haue all thing beside,
Which might in court a rowme for me prouide.[40]

Coridon may therefore represent some of Barclay's own earlier expectations. By setting the two together in a debate, during which Cornix talks Coridon out of seeking a place at court, Barclay attempted to allay doubts about his chosen course that still troubled his mind.

The youthful Coridon acts as the devil's advocate. When Cornix asserts that a life at court is merely vile and full of shame, Coridon asks why, if that is really so, have there been so many 'worthy shepheardes' such as 'the riche shepheard which woned in Mortlake' (John

Morton, Archibishop of Canterbury and Lord Chancellor), or John Alcock (the 'cock in the fens'), Bishop of Ely, Master of the Rolls, and also Lord Chancellor.[41] All that Cornix is able to reply, is that things have got a lot worse since they died, and that any good shepherds who resorted to court went there against their will.[42] Here we see Barclay struggling against his fear that virtue and a life at court may not, indeed, be incompatible, as the worthiest churchmen have always enjoyed high rank there. To admit this would be to deprive himself of the comforting thought that it was his virtue that had prevented him from getting court patronage. However lame Cornix's reply, it does show Barclay using the dialogue to confront the sources of lingering perturbation in his mind.

Another instance occurs when he makes Coridon catch Cornix out on an inconsistency over his attitude to wealth:

Cornix, thy promise was not to preache,
But me of the courtiers misery to teache.
Against thine owne selfe thou speakest nowe perdie,
For first thou grutched against pouertie.
Agayne, thou blamest plentie of riches nowe,
But fewe men liuing thy saying will alowe.
For without riches, thou sayest openly
Uertue nor cunning nowe be nothing set by.[43]

The terms in which this paradox is put are not in the source, and reflect Barclay's awareness that he is making Cornix protest too much. In reply, Cornix havers: it is not wrong for a man to possess riches, but for riches to possess the man. The idea is commonplace, but its inclusion at this point dangerously threatens the premise of the case Cornix has been trying to maintain—that a life of poverty in the country is preferable to a wealthy one at court. For the rest of his life Barclay tried energetically to touch money, which exposes a degree of disingenuousness in the attitude propounded in the *Eclogues.*

Indeed, many traces of regret and resentment remain in the *Eclogues,* as when Cornix claims that the kind of power gained at court is worthless:

There none hath honour by vertue and cunning,
By maners, wisedome, sadnes nor good liuing.
But who hath power, hye rowmes or riches,
He hath moste honour and laude of more and lesse.
For what poore man, a playne and simple soule,
Though he were holy as euer was Saint Powle,
Haste thou euer seene exalted of a king
For all his maners and vertuous liuing.
These be the wordes of Shepherde Siluius,
Which after was pope, and called was Pius.[44]

Even though the words italicized in this passage are a fairly close translation from Piccolomini's Latin,[45] Barclay's need to remind the reader that the words are

Piccolomini's and not his own suggests that he felt their relevance to his own personal situation was in danger of becoming rather too apparent. Passages in other works too enhance the probability that Barclay was investing these lines with more than a little self-interest. In *The Mirrour of Good Maners,* for example, he wrote:

> When from this wretched life at last thou must depart,
> And come to heauen gates to see the eternall king,
> It shall not be asked what countrey man thou art,
> Frenche, English, Scot, Lombard, Picard or Fleming,
> But onely shalbe asked thy merite and liuing,
> *A poore Scot of good life shall find him better then,*
> *Then some riche Lumbarde, or noble English man.*[46]

Barclay, who was a Scot,[47] seems to have thought that his nationality, as well as his poverty, had acted as a barrier to preferment. In spite of the homiletic platitudes Barclay utters in the *Eclogues,* therefore, he was sufficiently honest to allow his grievances and regret to show through.

As a result of Barclay's fictive strategy, a final, perhaps unintended paradox emerges: whereas Barclay wrote the work to warn those seeking court patronage that they were better off without it, his fiction betrays his own ambivalence on that score. Predictably, Cornix ends up voicing the conventional exhortation:

> Flee from the court, flee from the court I crye,
> Flee proude beggery and solemne miserye.[48]

Coridon accepts this as wise advice, but in a passage of Barclay's own invention, he asks about the alternative:

> But tell me Cornix one thing or we departe,
> On what maner life is best to set my harte?
> In court is combraunce, care, payne, and misery,
> *And here is enuy, ill will and penury.*[49]

In this passage Coridon is altering the terms on which the attack was predicated: that a life in the country is preferable to one at court. Coridon's words let slip a realization that rural life has its own miseries. All that Cornix can offer, ultimately, is the necessity for stoical endurance:

CORNIX.

> Sufferaunce ouercommeth all malice at the last,
> Weake is that tree which can not bide a blast,
> But heare nowe my counsell I bid thee finally,
> Liue still a shepheard for playnly so will I.

CORIDON.

> That shall I Cornix thy good counsell fulfill,
> To dye a shepheard established is my will.[50]

Coridon concurs, but it takes an effort of will, suggesting that he, like Barclay, is making the best of a bad deal.

The ambivalence generated in *Eclogues* I-III, shows why fiction was so useful to those who had to confront the realities of early Tudor politics. Because of its capability for representing or figuring forth experience, it could be used as a device for dramatizing and objectifying tensions that arose from personal predicaments such as Barclay's, or Skelton's (as was shown in the previous chapter). The distinctive complexity of early Tudor literature arises from its need to confront such predicaments.

* * *

The other one of Barclay's *Eclogues* to have a political bearing, the fourth, serves a completely different function. It is a skilfully contrived bid for patronage which makes the protestations of the first three eclogues seem all the more disingenuous.

Based on Mantuan's fifth eclogue, Barclay's **'Eclogue IV'** treats of 'the behauour of Rich men agaynst Poetes', in the form of a dialogue between Codrus, who has riches but lacks wisdom, and Minalcas, a poet 'with empty belly and simple poore aray'.[51] In the course of their talk Minalcas laments the difficulty of attaining the kind of financial support that would enable him to write, and then, when he agrees to sing a song for Codrus in exchange for a fee, discovers that even he finds a pretext for putting off the promised payment. The effectiveness of the work depends upon its function as an indirect means of negotiation between Barclay as suppliant and the second Duke of Norfolk as prospective patron.

As in *Eclogues* I-III, Barclay makes sure that the details of the pastoral context reflect his personal situation. In a long autobiographical insertion of 140 lines he projects his discontent with monastic life at Ely, through the unhappiness of Minalcas with his pastoral lot. Minalcas is 'wery of shepheardes company', hates the isolation, mud, and stink of the fens, and resents being poor when other shepherds are rich:

> Seest thou not Codrus the fieldes rounde about
> Compassed with floudes that none may in nor out,
> The muddy waters nere choke me with the stinke,
> At euery tempest they be as blacke as inke:
> Pouertie to me should be no discomforte
> If other shepheardes were all of the same sorte.
> But Codrus I clawe oft where it doth not itche,
> To see ten beggers and halfe a dosen riche,
> Truely me thinketh this wrong pertition,
> And namely sith all ought to be after one.[52]

Minalcas, in fact, has suffered a rude shattering of his expectations:

> When I first behelde these fieldes from a farre
> Me thought them pleasant and voyde of strife or warre,
> But with my poore flocke approching nere and nere

Alway my pleasour did lesse and lesse appeare,
And truely Codrus since I came on this grounde
Oft vnder floures vile snakes haue I founde.[53]

However unpleasant the physical environment may be, 'yet the dwellers be badder then the place.' Minalcas has encountered brawling and envy amongst the shepherds, who have shown hatred and malice towards him because he is a newcomer whose learning they resent. As a result Minalcas is determined 'to seke a newe pasture', so long as he can be assured that it will improve his conditions.[54] If these details are translated into the autobiographical facts they signify, one can infer that Barclay was highly disillusioned with life in the monastery at Ely, and was seeking to change it for something better. In particular, he wanted leisure and material support. When Codrus asks him why he no longer 'endites', Minalcas replies that being a shepherd absorbs all his energy in tending his flock, whereas 'a stile of excellence / Must haue all laboure and all the diligence'; Minalcas cannot do both. Also, a poet needs material comfort to produce good work, for

. . . without repast who can indite or sing:
It me repenteth, if I haue any wit,
As for my science, I wery am of it.
And of my poore life I weary am, Codrus,
Sith my harde fortune for me disposeth thus.[55]

Barclay's piety, however genuine, was evidently not strong enough to expunge the wordly ambition that he had earlier shown.

When Codrus advises several remedies, the terms in which Minalcas rejects them imply the particular frustrations Barclay had felt. Codrus suggests, first, that he seek to join the service of a rich prelate:

Thou well perceyuest they be magnificent.
With them be clerkes and pleasaunt Oratours,
And many Poetes promoted to honours,
There is aboundaunce of all that men desire.[56]

Minalcas laments, however, that all the former bounteous ecclesiastical patrons such as Morton, are dead and 'They, nor their like shall neuer returne agayne.' Minalcas, therefore, has given up any idea of finding that kind of patronage, and has now trimmed his sights so that he is prepared to accept a more modest kind of advancement:

Graunt me a liuing sufficient and small,
And voyde of troubles, I aske no more at all.
But with that litle I holde my selfe content,
If sauce of sorowe my mindes not torment.[57]

The fact that these passages are more particular than anything in Mantuan's original makes it probable that they describe Barclay's actual experience.

Barclay also seems to have given up hope of gaining any preferment at court. When Codrus proposes that he seek a place in a prince's court, Minalcas observes bitterly that 'the coyne auaunceth' so that only the rich get promotion, and apart from that, all the 'iugglers and Pipers, bourders and flatterers / Baudes and Ianglers, and cursed aduoutrers' who infest the court 'do good Poetes forth of all courtes chase.'[58] Barclay/Minalcas's special resentment is reserved for the 'rascolde poets' who pander to the vices of princes and get decked as Poet Laureate in return. As usual, he has Skelton in mind, and seems to feel that Skelton's success has hindered his chances:

Thus bide good Poetes oft time rebuke and blame,
Because of other which haue despised name.
And thus for the bad the good be cleane abiect,
Their art and poeme counted of none effect.[59]

As if to illustrate his point, Barclay has Codrus offer Minalcas a payment if he will recite 'some mery fit / Of mayde Marion, or els of Robin hood, / Or Bentleyes ale which chaseth well the bloud.' Minalcas refuses to speak about vice or wantonness, but launches instead into a ballad on the moral maxims of Solomon. Eventually Codrus intervenes to shut him up.[60] The whole episode serves as a dramatic exemplum of the claims Barclay has just made. Princes and courtiers want 'vicious' entertainment—the kind of thing Skelton could produce with gusto—while Barclay was only prepared to offer them poetry 'sownynge in vertu', as Chaucer might have said. In Barclay's own mind, and he was probably right, this essential difference between the two poets had barred him unjustly from court promotion.

Up until his ballad on Solomon's wise saws, Barclay had followed Mantuan's fifth eclogue quite closely, because it served admirably as a disguised representation of his own dilemma. Nevertheless, the fourth *Eclogue* was calculated to remedy the dilemma, not just depict it, and to that end Barclay boldly inserts into his source an elegy on the death of Edward Howard, second son of the Duke of Norfolk, who, as Lord High Admiral, was killed in a naval engagement with the French off Brest in 1513. The elegy itself, 'The Towre of Vertue and Honour', is a chivalric allegory of the Franco-Flemish kind, in which Howard contends with the monster Minerva in order to ascend the Tower of Vertue. By writing the poem, Barclay is offering to immortalize the fame and honour that Howard should have attained, had Fortune not maliciously cut him off at the very moment of his success.

The elegy is an elegant compliment in its own right, but it is even more important for its function within the whole *Eclogue.* Being set into a work complaining of the niggardly behaviour of rich men towards poets, it implicitly invites the Duke of Norfolk, to whom it is explicitly and flatteringly addressed, not to imitate them.[61] The ending is designed to make it even more difficult for Norfolk to withhold his bounty, for Codrus, having promised to reward Minalcas for the poem he has just recited, reneges on the agreement and earns Minalcas's parting curse. In the course of his fiction, Barclay has thus managed to depict his need, offer a sample of the flattering panegyrics he can provide for his intended patron, and give a cautionary exemplum of the obloquy which that patron could suffer should he withhold patronage. In this way, **'Eclogue IV'** is not merely a plea for patronage, but also a kind of fictional blackmail by proxy.

* * *

It worked. Several decades later William Forrest declares, in dedicating his *History of Joseph the Chaiste* to the fourth Duke of Norfolk, that Barclay had commended **The Mirrour of Good Maners** to his great-grandfather, the second Duke, 'withe other workes mo'. These books, continues Forrest, were received 'in acceptation' for their worthiness and noble fame.[62] We know what some of the other works were. Barclay dedicated both his translation of Sallust's *Jugurthine War,* published by Pynson in the early 1520s, and his **Introductory to Wryte and to Pronounce Frenche,** published in 1521 by Copland, to the second Duke of Norfolk, at whose command he says they were compiled. In the prologue to his French primer, Barclay drops hints that it was the Duke's munificence that had stimulated him to write. He explains that whereas he had once used to write diligently to alleviate the dullness of mind of his native countrymen, some time before he had ceased his literary activity; now, however, he has picked up his pen once more:

> lyke as the naked trees depryued of fruyt and leaf stoppeth
> the byrdes tune: & al that wynter depryueth ye somer restoreth agayne / ryght so though dyuers causes have withdrawen my pen from my olde dylygence / the mocyon of
> certayne noble gentylmen hath renued and excyted me agayne
> to attempt my accustumed besynesse.[63]

Although Barclay does not say explicitly what the diverse causes of his silence had been, they can be inferred from the symbolism he uses. The images of naked trees deprived of fruit and leaf because of the deprivations of winter suggest the poverty and lack of patronage of which he had complained in the **Eclogues.** Likewise, the idea of summer restoring the dearth of winter suggests that the poet has received new bounty, and that that is why his song has resumed.

Other evidence strengthens the likelihood that Norfolk secured for Barclay some of the advancement he desired. It was probably Norfolk who promoted Barclay's interests at court. In April 1520 Sir Nicholas Vaux wrote to Wolsey from Guisnes begging him to send over

'Maistre Barkleye, the Blacke monke and poete, to devise histoires and convenient raisons to florisshe the buildings and banquet house withal' for the meeting of Henry VIII and Francis I at the Field of Cloth of Gold.[64] For Barclay to have been given this important assignment proves two things: first, that he was not as averse to supplying the offices of a court poet as he had pretended in the *Eclogues,* and, second, that his reputation at court had risen considerably.[65] For that to have happened, he would have needed a mediator, and his patron, Norfolk, was undoubtedly the man. Barclay, in fact, ultimately arrived where he had wished to go all along—at court—if only in a rather minor way. As a final piece of corroborating evidence, we have William Forrest's statements in *The Life of the Blessed Virgin Mary* that 'Alexander Barkeleye . . . to the Cowrte dyd eke beelonge', and that 'hee in Courte had manye freynde.'[66] So much for Barclay's disingenuous assertion of the miseries of courtiers.

Barclay's literary output ceased when the second Duke of Norfolk died. He fell out of favour with the administrations of both Wolsey and Cromwell by managing both to flirt with the new religion and also to oppose the royal supremacy.[67] These attitudes, plus his uncompromising moralism, probably cost him his chance of any further advancement. In any case, it had been the problem of gaining patronage that had excited his literary imagination; once he had tasted it, he abandoned both political aspiration and the literary impulse together.

Notes

1. I use Barclay's phrase. See *The Eclogues of Alexander Barclay from the Original Edition by John Cawood,* ed. Beatrice White, Early English Text Society, Original Series, 175 (London, 1928), *Eclogue* III, p. 139, l. 820. All references are to this edition.

2. He has been claimed for Oriel College, Oxford, by Wood, and for Cambridge by Watson; see Beatrice White, ed. cit., p. viii.

3. *DNB,* I, p. 1077.

4. Ibid., I, p. xiv.

5. *Stultifera nauis, qua omnium mortalium narratur stultitia . . . The Ship of Fooles, Wherein is shewed the Folly of all States. . . . Translated out of Latin into Englishe by Alexander Barclay Priest* (London 1570), fo. 54ᵛ. All references are to this edition.

6. Ibid., fo. 2ʳ, paraphrasing 'Seu studiam, seu non, dominus tamen esse vocabor' (fo. 1ᵛ).

7. Ibid., fo. 2ᵛ. There is nothing in the Latin to suggest this passage, which may refer to an actual incident (See White, p. xix).

8. Ibid., fo. 235ᵛ, paraphrasing 'Ascendit celebres stultorum turba cathedras, / Stultitia mentes quae violare solet' (fo. 234ʳ).

9. Ibid., fo. 235ᵛ, based on: 'Si modo prudentes aleret Germania pugnax, / Et daret ingenuis praemia digna viris: / non sic deserta fluerent praeconia fama, / Parta quidem, quae nunc Theutona terra premit. / Si gradus insignis sophiae cultoribus esset, / Non veheret fatuos tot modo nostra ratis' (fo. 234ʳ). My italics.

10. Ibid., sig. ¶¶ 1ᵛ.

11. Ibid., fo. 127ʳ.

12. Ibid., fo. 9ᵛ.

13. Ibid., fo. 205ʳ.

14. Ibid., paraphrasing 'Viribus Alcidem superat, praecellit Achillem, / Caesaris hoc vno est principe, fama minor' (fo. 200, misnumbered 100).

15. Ibid., fo. 127ʳ.

16. See Edwards, [H. L. R.], *Skelton,* [Lodon: Cape, 1949,] pp. 129-32.

17. *Ship of Fooles,* fo. 259ʳ.

18. See Helen Stearns Sale, 'John Skelton and Christopher Garnesche', *Modern Language Notes,* 43 (1928), pp. 518-23.

19. *Agenst Garnesche* (ii), Skelton, [John. *John Skelton: The complete English*] *Poems,* ed. [John] Scattergood, [New Haven, Conn.: Yale University Press, 1983,] p. 123, ll. 29-36.

20. By Ian Gordon, 'A Skelton Query', *Times Literary Supplement,* 15 November 1934, p. 795.

21. *The Passetyme of Pleasure,* ed. William Edward Mead, Early English Text Society, Original Series, no. 173 (London, 1928), p. 141/3746.

22. *Eclogues,* I, ll. 837-48. My italics.

23. *Agenst Garnesche,* (ii), ll. 11-12.

24. Ibid., (iii), ll. 1-16. My italics. Scattergood prints 'tewyne'.

25. *Eclogues,* IV, ll. 685-6.

26. *The Life of Saint George,* ed. William Nelson, Early English Text Society, Original Series, no. 230 (London 1955), p. 14/113-19.

27. John Bale, *Index Britanniae scriptorum,* ed. Reginald Lane Poole, Anecdota Oxoniensia (Oxford, 1902), p. 19.

28. *Eclogues,* I, ll. 65-79.

29. Quoted by White, *Eclogues,* p. 220, n. 7.

30. Ibid., p. lvii.

31. *Eclogues,* I, l. 69.

32. Ibid., I, ll. 104-12.

33. *Aeneae Sylvii Piccolominei . . . opera quae extant omnia* (Basel, 1557), pp. 720-36.

34. Berdan, [John Milton,] *Early Tudor Poetry,* [Hamden, Conn.: Shoe String Press, 1961,] p. 242; cf. C. S. Lewis, *English Literature in the Sixteenth Century,* [London: Oxford University Press, 1973,] p. 131.

35. *Eclogues,* I, ll. 719-910, 911-1072, 1073-308.

36. Ibid., II, ll. 642, 783.

37. Ibid., III, ll. 82-112, 265-74, 620-42.

38. Ibid., I, ll. 389-93.

39. See T. H. Jamieson (ed.), *The Ship of Fools* (Edinburgh, 1874), I, p. xxxi; White, p. viii.

40. *Eclogues* I, ll. 328, 353-4.

41. Ibid., I, ll. 494-550.

42. Ibid., I, ll. 545-6, 557-9.

43. Ibid., I, ll. 1123-30.

44. Ibid., I, ll. 729-38. My italics.

45. 'Nam quem vnquam pauperem, tametsi praestanti virtute praeditum, Regum aliquis sublimauit?' (White, p. 25).

46. *Stultifera nauis . . . The Ship of Fooles . . . Translated out of Latin into Englishe by Alexander Barclay Priest* (1570), ed. Cawood, sig. F6ᵛ. My italics.

47. For the evidence of Barclay's Scottish origins, see Jamieson, pp. xxv-xxx. It seems not to have been noticed that Skelton corroborates this disputed point. In *Collyn Clout* he criticizes the monks for being slack in refuting heresy, and lists those who could effectively do so. Having scanned the other three orders, when he comes to the black friars he makes the following observation, unquestionably with reference to Barclay:

>   Or elles the poore Scot,
>   It must come to his lot
>   To shote forthe his shot.

(Skelton, *Poems,* ed. Scattergood, p. 265, ll. 749-51.) Either this is an allusion to the passage quoted from *The Mirrour of Good Maners,* or else Barclay's complaint at the discrimination he suffered because he was a Scotsman had become sufficient of a mannerism for Skelton to be able to mock it thus.

48. *Eclogues,* III, ll. 779-80.

49. Ibid., III, ll. 811-14. My italics.

50. Ibid., III, ll. 815-20.

51. Ibid., IV, l. 26.

52. Ibid., IV, ll. 52, 93-102.

53. Ibid., IV, ll. 103-8.

54. Ibid., IV, ll. 123, 124-33, 134-5.

55. Ibid., IV, ll. 179-80, 226-30.

56. Ibid., IV, ll. 498-501.

57. Ibid., IV, ll. 515-18.

58. Ibid., IV, ll. 545-52, 665-9.

59. Ibid., IV, ll. 711-14.

60. Ibid., IV, ll. 720-2, 791.

61. Ibid., ll. 1079, 1120, 1132.

62. Quoted by White, pp. xxxi-xxxii.

63. *The Introductory to Wryte and to Pronounce Frenche,* (London, 1521?), sig. A2ʳ.

64. *Letters and Papers, Foreign and Domestic, of the Reign of Henry VIII,* ed. J. S. Brewer and others (London, 1862-1932), III, i, no. 737. Hereafter cited as *LP.*

65. Significantly, Skelton had fallen into disfavour at this time (see Chapter Fox, Alistar. *Politics and Literature in the Reigns of Henry VII and Henry VIII,* Oxford: Basil Blackwell, 1989.).

66. Quoted by White, pp. xxxiii-xxxv.

67. See White, pp. xlii; xlviii.

Sukanta Chaudhuri (essay date 1989)

SOURCE: Chaudhuri, Sukanta. "English Pastoral before Spenser." In *Renaissance Pastoral and Its English Developments,* pp. 113-31. Oxford: Clarendon Press, 1989.

[*In this excerpt, Chaudhuri suggests that Barclay's* Eclogues *represent significant pastoral works before Spenser's because of their emphasis on the hardship of a shepherd's life.*]

BARCLAY'S ECLOGUES: SATIRE AND THE
SUFFERING RUSTIC

Roughly between 1500 and 1513,[1] Alexander Barclay wrote five *Eclogues* which must be accounted the most important English ones before Spenser's. They are the reverse of Arcadian. Rather, they emphasize the poverty and hardship of the shepherd's life, and are full of satirical and didactic passages. In fact, the first three eclogues are based upon *De curialium miseriis,* a prose satire of court life by Aeneas Silvius Piccolomini, later Pope Pius II. The two other pieces are modelled on Mantuan V and VI.

The Argument to **'Eclogue I'** describes the old shepherd Cornix's poverty in spite of a life of toil. The eclogue itself opens with an account of the shepherds' miseries after a storm. Here Barclay borrows from Mantuan III to commence on a note of suffering and questioning that Aeneas Silvius does not provide:

> If God (as men say) doth heauen and earth sustayne,
> Then why doth not he regarde our dayly payne?[2]

As a rule, however, the anger and resentment seek a different object. Cornix has already noted the contrast between their state and that of the rich. At first his speech echoes Mantuan; but Barclay introduces more and more touches of his own, building up to a completely original climax:

> They do nought els but reuell, slepe and drinke,
> But on his foldes the poore shepheard muste thinke.
> They rest, we labour, they gayly decked be
> While we go ragged in nede and pouertie
> . . . . .
> But what bringeth them to this prosperitie,
> Strength, courage, frendes, crafte and audacitie.

> (ll. 343-6, 351-2)

There are many such passages in Barclay, mostly original to the poet. In **'Eclogue IV',** the poor shepherd Minalcas complains:

> Pouertie to me should be no discomforte
> If other shepheardes were all of the same sorte.
> But Codrus I clawe oft where it doth not itche,
> To see ten beggers and halfe a dosen riche . . .[3]

In **'Eclogue V'** the protest and satire reach a climax:

> In lust, in pleasour, and good in aboundaunce
> Passe they their liues, we haue not suffisaunce.

> (ll. 143-4)

As in the source-poem, Mantuan VI, the town-country debate is turned into a more basic contrast between rich and poor—and further, between duty and pleasure, moral sense and irresponsibility. Barclay adapts his original towards this end. The interlocutors in Mantuan VI, Fulica and Cornix, had differed in nothing except their views on town and country. But Barclay reallocates their speeches up to line 236 so that Amintas becomes a vain upstart, flaunting his smattering of city ways, while Faustus is the traditional, dour, moralizing shepherd.

Barclay introduces much new matter on the shepherd's toil and poverty. The following six lines from **'Eclogue IV'** expand as many words in Mantuan:

> Bye strawe and litter, and hay for winter colde,
> Oft grease the scabbes aswell of yonge as olde.
> For dreade of thieues oft watche vp all the night,
> Beside this labour with all his minde and might,
> For his poore housholde for to prouide vitayle,
> If by aduenture his wooll or lambes fayle.

> (ll. 173-8)

The idyllic world of classical pastoral is far away. This is shown in **'Eclogue II'** by an interesting reference to Virgil III. 70 (again this is Barclay's own addition to Aeneas Silvius):

> Thy princes apples be swete and orient,
> Suche as Minalcas vnto Amintas sent,
>
> In sauour of whom thou onely haste delite,
> But if thou shouldst dye no morsell shalt thou bite.

> (ll. 879-80, 883-4)

Virgil's shepherd-world (though that was not all Arcadia) becomes a remote Never Never Land associated with the city and the court!

Along with this goes much satire. Of course, Barclay's sources are basically satirical, but he adds to the plenty. **'Eclogue II'** contains a long piece of satire against women (ll. 399ff.), and another on eating and drinking at court (ll. 538ff.). The latter sticks to Aeneas Silvius, but the former far exceeds the original. The account of cheating traders in **'Eclogue V'**. 686ff. is largely Barclay's own invention. In the same poem (ll. 803-30) he inserts a passage from Mantuan (II. 67-78) on the abuse of the Sabbath in the country. But he prefaces this with an original passage (ll. 779-802) on similar irreverence among city-dwellers. He cannot let the criticism of rural life stand by itself.

In a word, Barclay's **Eclogues** mark an extreme development of the 'suffering shepherd' vein. They show a pronounced satirical and moral bent, vivid accounts of a shepherd's hardships, and a keen awareness of injustice and exploitation, the contrast between rich and poor. We may relate this to Barclay's concern with the concept of the three estates, as pointed out by Ruth Mohl.[4]

All this strongly suggests an independent influence in addition to Mantuanesque pastoral. The obvious model would be *Piers Plowman,* commonly thought to be the first English satire.[5] It circulated widely in manuscript in the Renaissance,[6] ran into four printed editions in mid-century, and was mentioned by many authors.[7]

Even more influential, perhaps, was an extensive body of 'Plowman literature', inspired by the more satirical and demotic aspects of Langland's work. *Pierce the Ploughman's Crede* was twice printed in addition to manuscript copies. *The Plowman's Tale* was ascribed to Chaucer, included in his manuscripts, and (from 1542) printed in his works. *The Praier and Complaynte of the Ploweman vnto Christe* was printed in 1531 and 1532 and—crowning proof of popularity—included from 1610 in Foxe's Book of Martyrs. Yet another tract was printed c.1550 and reprinted some forty years later during the Martin Marprelate controversy.[8]

In his primary identity, Piers was the figure of the common man, and frequently of the oppressed peasant. As is well known, 'Piers Plowman' was a code-name in a letter written by John Ball during the Peasants' Revolt. Langland's own work provides a strong basis for such use,[9] and later Plowman-literature is dominated by protest and criticism. *The Plowman's Tale* makes a sustained attack upon the wealth and power of the clergy. In *Pierce the Ploughman's Crede,* the humble ploughman knows the Creed while friars sunk in sloth and luxury do not. *The Praier and Complaynte of the Ploweman* is most vehement of all:

> For the pore man mote gone to hys laboure in colde & in hete, in wete & drye, & spende his flesch & hys bloude in the rych mennes workes apon gods grounde to fynde the rych man in ese, & in lykynge, & in good fare of mete & of drinke & of clothinge. Here ys a gret ʒifte of the pore man. For he ʒeueth his own body. But what ʒeueth the rych man hym aʒeynwarde? Sertes febele mete, & febele drinke, & feble clothinge.[10]

The opposition of clergy and laity has become a simple contrast of rich and poor, proud and meek.

Even in a work of humanist affinities like the early Tudor play of *Gentleness and Nobility,* the ploughman tells the knight and the merchant that private possession stems from tyranny and extortion (ll. 608-16).[11] The sober political tract *Pyers Plowmans Exhortation, vnto . . . Parlyamenthouse* (c.1550) exposes contrasts of wealth and poverty, ending with a stern warning of 'the plage and vengeaunce of Good, ready to be powred doune upon the whole realme, for this cruell oppression of the pore' (sig. B4ʳ). Earlier, at a more popular level, *God Spede the Plough* had listed the ploughman's burden of taxes and other exactions.

This is precisely the complaint made in the Wakefield Second Shepherds' Play:

> we ar so hamyd,
> ffor-taxed and ramyd,
> We ar mayde hand tamyd,
>   with thyse gentlery men.[12]

The hard labour of the Wakefield shepherds is very like the ploughman's, as described in *God Spede the Plough* and the *Crede.* In the Wakefield First Shepherds' Play too, the First Shepherd's reflections on earthly transience soon focus upon his own poverty and loss. The Second Shepherd complains how the townsmen exploit them:

> If he hask me oght I that he wold to his pay,
> ffull dere bese it boght I if I say nay;
>
> (ll. 73-4)

Shepherd and ploughman become kindred figures in this demotic literature, part of a whole gallery of rustic types. Langland himself associates 'Plowmen and pastours and pouere commune laborers, I Souteres and shepherdes' (Passus X. 466-7). In John Ball's 'Piers Plowman' letter, Ball himself is 'Iohan schep' (shepherd),[13] perhaps because he is a priest. Skelton's Colin Clout, a spokesman for the common rustic, bears a name that may already have been applied to shepherds.[14] In the Catholic *Banckett of Iohan the Reve* (BL MS Harley 207), the members of the proletarian symposium are exactly (and perhaps consciously) the same as in the lines quoted from Langland: 'peirs ploughman, Laurens laborer. Thomlyn Tailyer. And hobb of the hill. with other' (fo. 1ʳ). Hob is a shepherd, the best read among the rustics, and to him falls the honour of the conclusive defence of the doctrine of transubstantiation. In *I playne Piers* . . . the Ploughman preaches his subversive message to all fellow-labourers, including 'hoggeherdes sheperhedes and all youre sorte dyspysed'.[15]

From the other direction, in Mantuan VI, God in his curse upon the younger sons of Eve equates the shepherd with all poor labourers in both town and country:

> vester erit stimulus, vester ligo, pastina vestra;
> vester erit vomer, iuga vestra, agrestia vestra
>   omnia; . . .
>   . . . . .
> sed tamen ex vobis quosdam donabimus urbe
> qui sint fartores, lanii, lixae artocopique
> et genus hoc alii soliti sordescere . . .
>
> (ll. 95-101)

[Yours shall be the goad, yours the mattock, yours the dibbles; yours the ploughshare, yours the yokes, yours all things rustic . . . Some of you, however, we shall give to the city. They shall be poulterers, butchers, sutlers, bakers, and the tribe of all others accustomed to demean themselves with work . . .]

The old *Kalender of Shepardes* has some lines to the ploughman beginning 'Peers go thou to plowe.'[16] In line with such precedents, Barclay in his fourth eclogue equates shepherd and ploughman as similar rustic types:

> What should a Ploughman go farther than his plough,
> What should a shepherde in wisedome wade so farre
>   . . .
>
> (ll. 792-3)

And again, in **'Eclogue V'**:

> It were a maruell if Cornix matter tolde
> To laude of shepheardes, or plowmen to vpholde . . .
>
> (ll. 399-400)

These brief touches underscore my earlier point about the 'suffering shepherd': he is not a distinct type or symbol, but a figure of the rustic poor generally. His higher symbolic functions are forgotten. In Barclay's *Eclogues,* this is particularly in evidence owing to conflation with the 'Piers Plowman' tradition.

Plowman-literature preserves one function of the pastoral metaphor: the ecclesiastical. The clergy are habitually presented as neglectful hireling shepherds or wolves in sheep's clothing.

> Lorde of all schepherdes blessed mote thou be. For thou louedest more the scheep then her wole. For thou fedest thy sheep both in body & in soule. [But the prelates] distroyen thy schepe, . . . that for drede they ben disparpled a brode in mownteynes, & there the wilde beestes of the felde distroyeth hem, & deuoureth hem for defaute of a good schepherde.[17]

For all its forensic detail, this is a single-noted metaphor, an overworked pastoral image rather than genuine pastoralism. Moral approbation, philosophic appeal, such suggestive detail as there might be—all these have passed to the ploughman-figure. Moreover, the ploughman is basically 'real', an actual rustic; the shepherd is a metaphoric or allegorical one, with the ploughman and his fellows as his 'sheep'.

Such division is unfortunate; but union, as we have earlier seen, is nearly impossible. The literal and metaphorical shepherds come to clash. In Barclay I. 485, Christ is 'the shephearde of Nazareth'; in Aeneas Silvius's non-pastoral context, he had been merely 'Salvator noster Iesu' [Jesus our saviour].[18] Morton, Archbishop of Canterbury, becomes 'the riche shepheard which woned in Mortlake' (**'Eclogue I'**. 499). But this is spoken by an actual shepherd who would be one of the shepherd-priest's 'flock'. Morton visits Coridon's family cottage as 'the patron of thinges pastorall' (**'Eclogue I'**. 511), an aristocrat or overlord rather than a true herdsman. With Alcock, Bishop of Ely, Barclay can avoid this metaphoric maze by exploiting a common pun on Alcock's name: 'He all was a cocke, he wakened vs from slepe' (**'Eclogue I'**. 521). But incongruously, the cock is also 'a father of thinges pastorall' (l. 531); and in **'Eclogue III'**. 470-1 Barclay sadly mixes the two metaphors: 'the gentle Cocke whiche sange so mirily, I He and his flocke were like an vnion'. Exactly the same clash between ruler-shepherd and commoner-shepherd occurs in **'Eclogue IV'** in a secular context. In the city,

> The riche and sturdie doth threaten and manace
> The poore and simple and suche as came but late
>   . . . . .

And suche be assigned sometime the flocke to kepe
Which scant haue so muche of reason as the shepe,
And euery shepheard a other hath enuy,
Scant be a couple which loueth perfitely . . .

(ll. 124-5, 129-32)

In fact, in line 131, 'euery shepheard' seems to be neither ruler nor subject but mankind generally. The significance of sheep and shepherd differs from line to
line. One sees the need to define the pastoral mode
clearly once again.

When Spenser set about doing so in *The Shepheardes
Calender,* he would have found in Barclay—and in
Plowman literature generally—a model for his moral,
didactic, and satiric vein.[19] But this is a subsidiary element in Spenser's design. In a general way, he emphatically moves *away* from Barclay's model.

J. R. Schultz failed to find any correspondence, beyond
the most accidental, between Barclay's **Eclogues** and
The Shepheardes Calender.[20] Yet, as Mustard, Schultz,
and White have all noted,[21] it is unlikely that Spenser
would not have known of Barclay's work—which was
not only appended to John Cawood's edition of **The
Ship of Fools** in 1570 but published separately several
times before.[22] The probability is increased by the fact
that, as Mustard points out, E. K.'s Epistle to Harvey
clearly echoes Barclay's **'Prologe'.**

In any case, there is one fundamental matter in which
Spenser draws upon the poetic tradition of which
Barclay's **Eclogues** form a part. This consists in an important element of the language of the *Calender,* E. K.'s
'rusticall rudenesse of shepheards, eyther for that theyr
rough sounde would make his rymes more ragged and
rustical, or els because such olde and obsolete wordes
are most vsed of country folke'.[23] Philologists, most notably B. R. McElderry,[24] have tried to minimize the importance of this element. Others have tried to show that
the archaic and dialectal diction is most pronounced in
the moral and satiric eclogues, where satiric roughness
merges with that demanded by 'pastoral decorum'.[25] But
the other eclogues make the same demand, and it seems
idle to deny that the language has an archaic and dialectal element all through.[26] Alexander Lyle admits (p.
164) that 'Januarye' has the same substantial presence
of archaic and rustic words as 'Februarie', though with
a very different effect. I shall cite two other local instances, both at the openings of poems and thus condi-
tioning our response to what follows. The first eighteen
lines of 'March' yield *alegge, sicker, thilke, studde,
bragly, vpryst.* 'Aprill' begins

Tell me good Hobbinoll, what *garres* thee *greete*?
What? hath some Wolfe thy tender Lambes *ytorne*?[27]

The words italicized (by me) were all archaic at that
date, on the testimony of the *OED.*[28] The stress-based
rhythm that Lyle and Ingham consider characteristic of

the moral eclogues, as of earlier rustic and satiric literature, is found equally in the framework of 'August'—a
fact they do not recognize.

I shall make no attempt at a philological or metrical
study of the *Calender.* I have cited sample passages
only to confirm the presence of this element in
Spenser's language all through the work. He is recreating with his own resources an equivalent for the
diction, idiom, and register of utterance that he and his
age found in Chaucer and late Middle English literature, especially Plowman literature—whose affinities
with Barclay's **Eclogues** I have tried to show. Spenser's
debt to Chaucer is well authenticated. He has also been
shown to echo *The Plowman's Tale* in 'Maye'.[29] In his
concluding verses to the *Calender,* 'the Pilgrim that the
Ploughman playde a whyle' may refer to the *Tale* or to
Piers Plowman. In either case, Spenser is professing
formal allegiance to a conservative poetic ideal to which
Barclay's **Eclogues** form an adjunct—with the vital difference that Spenser applies the mode to subject-matter
that Barclay and the Plowman-poets know nothing of:
love, poetry, simple sport, and the appreciation of nature.

These themes are in line with continental art-pastoral;
but the distinctive, purportedly rustic element in
Spenser's language invests them with a special simplicity and spontaneity, checks their sophistication with a
constant hint at rustic directness and sincerity. This
leads us beyond the *Calender* to the considerable body
of pastoral lyrics written after it and, I shall argue, in
line with it. Such lyrics (epitomized by the collection in
England's Helicon) have practically nothing in common
with Barclay's **Eclogues**; but from Barclay, via Spenser,
they preserve a special strain of the 'honest shepherd'
in their treatment of idealized pastoral life.

Notes

1. As estimated by Beatrice White in her edn. of the
   Eclogues (EETS os 175; Oxford, 1928).

2. *Eclogue I.* 213-14; all refs. to White's edn. (cit. n.
   8).

3. *Eclogue IV.* 97-100. Cf. *Eclogue II.* 789ff. (based
   on Aeneas Silvius); *Eclogue IV.* 305ff. (4 ll. in
   Mantuan expanded to 30); *Eclogue V.* 663-4
   (original to Barclay).

4. [Mohl, Ruth,] *The Three Estates in Medieval and
   Renaissance Literature* (New York, 1933), 143-9.

5. See Puttenham, *The Arte of English Poesie*
   (Gregory Smith (ed.), *Elizabethan Critical Essays,*
   ii. 62. l. 25, p. 64, l. 34-p. 65, l. 6); Francis Meres,
   Palladis Tamia (ibid. ii. 320, l. 19); Henry
   Peacham, *The Compleat Gentleman,* ch. 10 (J. E.
   Spingarn (ed.), *Critical Essays of the Seventeenth*

Century (Oxford, 1908), i. 132-3); Milton, *Apology for Smectymnuus* (Milton's *Works,* Columbia edn., iii/1 (New York, 1931), 329, ll. 9-10).

6. At least 5 new MSS were made: Bodl. MS Digby 145 (see A-Text, ed. G. Kane (London, 1960), 9-10); BL Royal Lib. MS 18 B. xvii (see C-Text, ed. W. W. Skeat (EETS os 54, 1873), p. xlviii); Caius College, Cambridge MS 201, made from the printed 1561 text (see B-Text, ed. W. W. Skeat (EETS os 38; 1869), p. xxx); Cambridge Univ. Lib. MS Gg. 4. 31 (see B-Text, ed. G. Kane and E. T. Donaldson (London, 1975), 8); Sion Coll. MS Arc. L. 40. 2/E(S) (ibid. 15).

7. For a list see W. W. Skeat (ed.), *Piers Plowman,* iv/2 (EETS os 81, 1885), 863-70. However, many of Skeat's instances actually concern the 'Plowman literature' I shall describe in the next few pages.

8. STC 19903a, 19903a.5. The 1550 title-page reads 'I playne Piers which can not flatter . . .'.

9. See e.g. B-Text Passus X. 67-8, Passus XIV. 174-8. (All refs. to the B-Text, ed. Kane and Donaldson.)

10. 1531 edn., sig. E5^v.

11. Refs. to the Malone Society repr., 1950.

12. ll. 15-18; refs. to *The Towneley Plays,* ed. G. England (EETS ES 71, Oxford, 1897; repr. 1952).

13. R. H. Robbins (ed.), *Historical Poems of the XIVth and XVth Centuries* (New York, 1959), 55.

14. See Cooper, [Helen,] *Pastoral, [: Medieval into Renaissance. Ipswich: Brewer, 1977,]* p. 153.

15. 1550 edn., sig. A8^r.

16. *The Kalender of Shepardes,* printed by Thomas Este for John Wally (1570?), sig. A5^r.

17. *The Praier and Complaynte of the Ploweman vnto Christe* (n.p., 1531?), sig. E8^{r-v}.

18. *De curialium miseriis,* ed. W. P. Mustard (Baltimore, 1928), 26.

19. The matter has been treated, and through exclusive attention over-emphasized, in Alexander Lyle, 'The Shepheardes Calender and Its English Antecedents' (B.Litt. Oxford, 1969). See also the brief account in David R. Shore, *Spenser and the Poetics of Pastoral* (Kingston, Ont., 1985), 29-30.

20. 'Alexander Barclay and the Later Eclogue Writers', *Modern Language Notes* 35 (1920), 52-4.

21. W. P. Mustard, 'Notes on the *Eclogues* of Alexander Barclay', *MLN* 24 (1909), 10; Schultz, *MLN* 35; White (ed.), *Barclay's Eclogues,* p. lxi.

22. *Eclogues I-III* (*c.*1530, *c.*1548, *c.*1560), IV (*c.*1521), V (*c.*1518): dates as in STC.

23. Epistle to Gabriel Harvey preceding *The Shepheardes Calender.*

24. 'Archaism and Innovation in Spenser's Poetic Diction', *PMLA* 47 (1932), 144-70.

25. See Lyle (cit. n. 26), ch. vi; P. Ingham, 'Spenser's Use of Dialect', *ELN* 8 (1971), 166-7.

26. It seems both futile and unnecessary to attempt to separate the archaic from the strictly dialectal, as both are being used to give the language a simultaneously primitive and rustic flavour. Because of the belief in the 'purity' of early Chaucerian English, archaisms would in any case be placed in the same register as unsophisticated and dialectal forms.

27. All Spenser refs. to [*Poetical Works,* ed. J. C. Smith and E. de Seliincourt (Oxford, 1912, repr. 1970)]. . . .

28. For *ytorne* see McElderry, [Bruce Robert. *Spenser's Poetic Diction,* State University od Iowa, 1925,] pp. 156-7. My sample suggests that McElderry is grossly over-cautious in estimating the number of archaisms in the *Calender.* Except for *alegge,* he does not note any of the words listed above.

29. See Variorum notes on ll. 1-8, 39: *The Works of Edmund Spenser: A Variorum Edition,* ed. E. Greenlaw *et al.* (Baltimore, 1932-57), *Minor Poems,* i. 297-8.

David R. Carlson (essay date April 1995)

SOURCE: Carlson, David R. "Skelton and Barclay, Medieval and Modern." *Early Modern Literary Studies* 1, no. 1 (April 1995): 2.1-17.

[*In the essay below, Carlson explores the literary conflict between Barclay and John Skelton and how this antagonistic relationship signals a shift in English literary history.*]

Early Tudor literature was done in distinct circles, the centres of which were not coincident, and which overlapped little: the humanist circle, around More and Erasmus; in the later decades of the reign of Henry VIII, the "new company" of courtier-poets, in Puttenham's phrase, around Wyatt; and earlier, the less well-defined group of vernacular makers, professional or nearly professional English writers, comprising John Skelton, Alexander Barclay, and Stephen Hawes.[1] Within these circles, relations varied. Generally, they were amicable and supportive amongst the courtier-poets and the humanists, though intergenerational and other quarrels occurred. Amongst the vernacular makers, however, things were otherwise. Evidence of friendship or shared respect is wanting. The courtier Hawes stood apart, as far as can be confirmed, and Skelton and Barclay fought.[2] There is something to be said for finding in their quarrel symptoms of the epochal clash, between modern and medieval, difficult as these terms can be to define agreeably, and even though the terms would have meant little to the antagonists. Neither Skelton nor Barclay fits easily in either category, however, and in the end it appears their quarrel would have come less of their differences than of their likeness: they were similarly situated in the Tudor literary system.

In December 1509, Barclay saw printed a stanza at the conclusion of his **Ship of Fools** ([ed. Jamieson] II: 331), characterizing his own work as inducing "unto vertue and goodnes," while charging Skelton, somewhat obliquely, with "vyciousnes" and "wantones." "Holde me excusyd," Barclay wrote,

> for why my wyll is gode
> Men to induce unto vertue and goodnes.
> I wryte no Jest ne tale of Robyn hode,
> Nor sawe no sparcles ne sede of vyciousnes;
> Wyse men love vertue, wylde people wantones.
> It longeth nat to my science nor cunnynge
> For Phylyp the Sparowe the Dirige to synge.

This would not have been withering vituperation, perhaps, when addressed to Skelton, a man who made his name out of rude remarks uttered in public about other people. From one end of his career to the other, from the "Manerly Margery Mylk and Ale" to *A Replycacion agaynst Certayne Yong Scolers Abjured of Late,* the list of persons whom Skelton attacked and insulted, not exempting even the dead, is a lengthy one, and the terms Skelton chose show a Bach-like inventiveness when it came to invective. For Skelton, in other words, on a scale from one to ten, Barclay rated a two, maybe: small beer.

Nevertheless, Skelton replied to Barclay. As Barclay's stanza castigating Skelton and the poem *Phyllyp Sparowe* had concluded his "Brefe addicion of the syngularyte of some newe Folys," so Skelton cast his reply in the form of "An Addicyon" to the *Phyllyp Sparowe.* This Skeltonic addition—with its exaggeratedly long conjuration of all the impotent demons and heroes of the pagan underworld on Skelton's behalf—is such as to suggest that Skelton did not take Barclay altogether seriously. He neither names him nor singles him out for characterization. The substance of Skelton's reply is summed up in the final (Latin) line of the addition, where Skelton imputes *invidia* to his detractors ("Est tamen invidia mors tibi continua": "Your ceaseless envy will be the death of you"): envy of Skelton's poem, of Skelton's talents, and of Skelton's success,

> The gyse now a dayes
> Of some janglynge jayes
> Is to discommende
> That they cannot amend,
> Though they wold spend
> All the wyttes they have.

(*Phyllyp Sparowe* 1268-1273)

John Bale, in his list of Barclay's writings, attributes to him a work entitled "Contra Skeltonum," which is not known to survive and about which nothing more can be said (Bale 19). Bale's claim suggests, though, that squabbling between Barclay and Skelton may have extended beyond the 1509 exchange. Skelton republished his addition to the *Phyllyp Sparowe* as part of the 1523 *Garland of Laurel* (1261-1375), with a further remark about "sum" who "grudge" at the *Phyllyp Sparowe* "with frownyng countenaunce" (1254- 1260)—possibly with reference to Barclay, though not pointedly so, and not with exclusive reference to Barclay:

> Of Phillip Sparow the lamentable fate,
> The dolefull desteny, and the carefull chaunce,
> Dyvysed by Skelton after the funerall rate;
> Yet sum there be therewith that take grevaunce
> And grudge therat with frownyng countenaunce;
> But what of that? Hard it is to please all men;
> Who list amende it, let hym set to his penne.

For his part, in his **Eclogues** and in his **Life of St. George,** Barclay offered up a few (characteristically bland, generalized) castigations of "laureates," which may have been jabs at Skelton:

> No name I chalenge of Poete laureate.
> That name unto them is mete and doth agree
> Which writeth matters with curiositee.
> Mine habite blacke accordeth not with grene.
> Blacke betokeneth death, as it is dayly sene;
> The grene is pleasour, freshe lust and jolite.
> These two in nature hath great diversite.
> Then who would ascribe, except he were a foole,
> The pleasant laurer unto the mourning cowle?

("**Eclogue I**": 104-112 [ed. White 4])

> Another thing yet is greatly more damnable:
> Of rascolde poetes yet is a shameful rable,
> Which voyde of wisedome presumeth to indite
> Though they have scantly the cunning of a snite;
> And to what vices that princes moste intende,
> Those dare these fooles solemnize annd commende.
> Then is he decked as poete laureate,
> When stinking Thais made him her graduate.
> When muses rested, she did her season note,
> And she with Bacchus her camous did promote.
> Such rascolde drames promoted by Thais,
> Bacchus, Licoris, or yet by Testalis,
> Or by suche other newe forged muses nine
> Thinke in their mindes for to have wit divine.
> They laude their verses, they boast, they vaunt and jet,
> Though all their cunning be scantly worth a pet.

("**Eclogue IV**": 679-694 [ed. White 165])

Let raylynge poetes for help on Venus call,
Which hath in Venus theyr pleasour and delyte,
Whose wrytynge uttreth theyr lyvynge bestyall.
With barayne termys, suche thynges they indyte
Which may the reders to vicious lyfe excyte
And nat to vertue. He which is lawreat
Ought nat his name with vyce to vyolate.

(***Life of St. George*** 113-119 [ed. Nelson 14])

While Skelton was among the writers attached to the early Tudor court who styled themselves "laureate"—others included Bernard André, Pietro Carmeliano, and Andrea Ammonio—they were a pretty bad lot, all of them probably guilty of the faults (frivolity and vanity, chiefly) that Barclay charges to laureates in general. Here too, Barclay by no means singles Skelton out or unequivocally refers to him; Barclay's scattered remarks about laureates are different from the passage in his ***Ship of Fools*** in this regard.

It has been suggested that Barclay became "Wolsey's poet" at some point and would therefore have attracted Skelton's ire (Kinney 132-3, 194; cf. Webb 300-305); and it has been maintained that Barclay was the amanuensis employed by Christopher Garnesche for his lost half of the c. 1514 "flyting" with Skelton, whose half survives as the five-part serial *Agenst Garnesche,* in which Skelton answers Garnesche's provocations and imputes employment of a *scriba* to him (Fox 42-5). As attractive as these suggestions may be in their own ways, the evidence supporting both is equivocal or slight and so they remain speculative. Given the present state of the primary evidence, the 1509 exchange between Barclay and Skelton, with the addition to the ***Ship of Fools*** in which Barclay accuses Skelton of "wantones" and Skelton's answering addition to the *Phyllyp Sparowe* in which he charges envy, remains the sole definite evidence for their quarrel.

The evidence of this 1509 unpleasantness between Skelton and Barclay can be enlisted as support for constructing an image of a deeper, more substantive antipathy between them. They were bound to clash because they were fundamentally different as writers, and in their quarrel can be discerned the lineaments of the major shift taking place in English literary history in the early Tudor period, from medieval to modern. Defined empirically, this can be seen in terms of the writers' affiliations with traditions and institutions, literary and social, that had flourished in the Middle Ages but would cease to matter early in the modern period (monasticism, for example, or Chaucerian dream-vision) and with other characteristically modern practices and institutions that were substantively new at the time (publication in print, most saliently, or humanism).

In this perspective, Barclay's attack on Skelton can be used to corroborate other evidence indicating that Barclay was medieval: pious, clerical, conservative, fundamentally backward. The tendency of the critical heritage to depreciate Barclay as medieval, in order to praise Skelton as modern, is most pronounced perhaps in Ian Gordon's book, where Barclay is characterized as "deeply immersed in didactic and mediaeval morality": "the cast of his mind is essentially mediaeval" (Gordon 8-9). To some degree, for Gordon as for others, "medieval" is code for "bad," only "a vague pejorative term meaning 'outmoded,' or 'hopelessly antiquated,'" as Fred Robinson showed (Robinson 745). On the other hand, Barclay's affiliations with characteristically medieval institutions and literary traditions that would not long outlive him lends substance to the image of an "essentially mediaeval" Barclay, the sort of person who would attack "modern" Skelton.

Barclay was a priest and later became a monk of the Benedictine Order—he was of the last generation of English Benedictines, for it was during his life that the order was dissolved in England. Moreover, he wrote saints' lives at a time when the genre, having enjoyed a brief revival in the sometimes odd, always oxymoronic form of humanist hagiography, was finally moribund: lost lives of Etheldrede (who founded the monastic community at Ely in which Barclay lived), Catherine, and Margaret (Bale 19), and a surviving ***Life of George.*** Barclay also wrote moralities—a disquisition on the cardinal virtues (his ***Mirror of Good Manners***), for example, and a hortatory ballad "Of Sapience," made up of sage precepts: "Spende not on women," "All wealth is transitory," and so on ([ed. White] 167-168). As his castigation of Skelton as wanton and vice-prone would suggest, Barclay's writings tend be explicitly, unremittingly righteous. For example, his best-known work, the ***Ship of Fools,*** with the attack on Skelton, is a translation, to which Barclay's chief original addition is the series of translator's envoys put at the end of each chapter of the work, in which he spells out the already clear moral of each chapter still more clearly.

By contrast with this old-fashioned, medieval Barclay—myopically, pedantically monkish and moral—John Skelton looks wantonly, amblingly modern: sceptical, irreverent, and idiosyncratic. To quote Gordon again, whereas "the verse of his contemporaries is dead, Skelton's has a restless, bustling energy that can vitalize even the formulae of allegory" (Gordon 9). Here too, there is much to be said in favour of such a characterization. Important recent work on Skelton as a "transitional" figure, by Halpern, Walker, and Blanchard, has emphasized that Skelton is intractably difficult to classify as a literary-historical specimen. Unlike Barclay, Skelton evidently defied the various contemporary categories that might have applied to him. At court, he was a figure of learning and piety, by turns a royal tutor of humanist proclivities and a local Jeremiah, inveighing against sin and corruption. The story that he kept women is not going to go away, however (Fox 44), with its implication that Skelton was also roguish for a priest if not dissolute. More to the point, Skelton's best writings have also evaded categorization. In metrical, stylistic, generic, and topical terms, Skelton's most characteristic work is wholly unlike anything else being done at the time, before or since, and such idiosyncrasy is unmedieval all by itself.

Much can be said for the opposition of a medieval Barclay and a modern Skelton. It can also be a false, misleading opposition, however. In Skelton's work, for all its idiosyncracy, there is also a persistence of medieval traditions, as A. R. Heiserman and A. C. Spearing have established. For example, Skelton had frequent recourse to personification allegory—at the beginning and end of his career, in the *Garland of Laurel* that he seems to have published and later republished (Brownlow, *Book of the Laurel* 17-36), and in such important works as the *Bowge of Court* and *Magnificence*—a tradition with roots in antiquity, of course, though it flourished most widely in the Middle Ages, beginning with Prudentius. Skelton was likewise deeply traditional in his use of liturgical schemes to frame and orient his writings—the salient example being the *Phyllyp Sparowe* (Brownlow, "*Phyllyp Sparowe* and the Liturgy"; Kinney)—and, as also proper for the priestly poet that Skelton was, he wrote effective, affecting devotional lyrics, drawing knowingly on his Middle English antecedents (Scattergood, "John Skelton's Lyrics"). Finally, as John Scattergood has recently shown, Skelton's rhyme-royal dream-visions—the *Garland of Laurel* and the *Bowge of Court* again—are self-consciously in a medieval, Chaucerian tradition (Scattergood "Skelton's *Garlande*"; cf. Spearing 234-247).

In the light of these aspects of Skelton's work, Barclay's writings appear modern. Barclay responded more quickly and knowingly to recent developments of continental literature, especially those taking place in Italy. Barclay's ***Tower of Virtue and Honour*** ([ed. White] 170-179) is the one clear, successful effort to render in English the conventions Franco-Burgundian allegory—a peculiar amalgam of classicism and neo-feudalism that Stephen Hawes also tried but Skelton never did (Lyall "Tradition and Innovation"). However, Barclay is best known for having written eclogues in English. While there had been medieval eclogues—Theodulus and other poets of the Carolingian classical revival supplying the chief examples—the eclogue was an ancient genre revived only recently, along with much else, amongst the Italians. In bringing the genre into English, Barclay was bringing the Renaissance (Cooper, esp. 100-123). The same impulse evidently informed his choice of sources to translate: Dominico Mancini for the ***Mirror of Good Manners,*** Eneo Silvio Piccolomini for ***Eclogues*** I-III, and Mantuan—the chief neo-Latin poet of the Renaissance—for the ***Life of St. George*** and for ***Eclogues***

"**IV**" and "**V.**" For translating and adapting in his characteristic way, Barclay chose the work of recent, even modish exponents of the Italianate New Learning.

For his living, Barclay evidently was dependent on patronage, including peculiar ecclesiastic forms of patronage that ceased to be available with the reformation: Barclay's priestly and monastic vocations left him time to write. Skelton too was a priest, enjoying ecclesiastic incomes, and he too had royal and aristocratic patrons. The difference here is that, while Skelton seems to have avoided printers, Barclay had important ties with one and may have derived income from the relationship. Barclay's writing circulated in the new medium with a consistency unparalleled among living writers at the time, including Hawes.[3]

A small portion of Skelton's work was printed during his life. These publications in print appear to have been of two kinds. First, there are a few items of propaganda—the *Ballade of the Scottyshe Kynge* written and printed, as a broadside, by Fakes, in 1513, and the *Replycacion* written and printed, by Pynson, in 1528—which rushed into print, probably at the behest of the printers or possibly officers of the court at Westminster, the chief printer of such propaganda being an officer of the court, the royal printer Richard Pynson. Barclay too saw print on such occasions, as did others. The second sort of publication in print that Skelton's work saw while he lived was the piratical, printerly speculation: writings leaked into print, belatedly, after Skelton's name was made, evidently without his authorization or involvement. The best examples are the two collections of poems known as *Agaynste a Comely Coystrowne* and *Dyvers Balettys,* both printed by John Rastell c. 1527, within a year or two of Skelton's death, at a time when he had all but stopped writing, although the poems date from Skelton's first period at court, in the late fifteenth century (Kinsman "The Printer and Date of Publication").[4] Probably similar in origin are the editions of the *Bowge of Court,* printed by de Worde, c. 1499 and c. 1510, though the poem itself is as early as the early fourteen-eighties (Brownlow "The Date of *The Bowge*"), and the edition of the *Elynour Rummynge,* printed c. 1521 by de Worde again, though possibly written a few years earlier, c. 1517 (Kinsman "Eleanora Rediviva"; Schulte). About the dates and circumstances of these last two publications much is uncertain; in none of these cases, however, is there evidence to suggest that Skelton co-operated with the printers. These appear to be instances, instead, in which the printers, having come by a literary property, indirectly, from the pen of a writer with a marketable reputation, sought to make money by exploiting it, without the writer's participation.

The 1523 *Garland of Laurel,* printed by Fakes, is an exception. Neither simple propaganda nor a printer's belated speculation, this work appears to have been printed at least with Skelton's co-operation, if not at his behest. The printed book contains materials that Skelton can be believed to have passed recently, directly into the printer's hands (Erler 19-23, 28). However, this kind of co-operation between printer and living writer that occurred in the exceptional case of the 1523 *Garland of Laurel* was the rule in relations between Pynson and Barclay. For a period of fifteen years or so, from 1508 or 1509 to the early fifteen-twenties, Barclay seems to have worked for or with Pynson, as Hawes may have worked for Wynkyn de Worde, albeit on a reduced scale (Edwards "Poet and Printer"). The relationship between Pynson and Barclay began with the ***Ship of Fools,*** what Barclay called "meorum primicias laborum qui in lucem eruperunt," which Pynson printed and signed 14 December 1509 ([ed. Jamieson] I: cxv). Barclay's letter dedicating his work to Thomas Cornish, Bishop of Tyne and Suffragan of Bath and Wells, is signed at its conclusion "Ex Impressoria officina Richardi Pynson. iij. Idus Decembris" ([ed. Jamieson] I: cxv), and in the final stanza of the ***Ship*** ([ed. Jamieson] II: 337), Barclay takes his leave of his audience by directing those wanting to buy copies of the work to Pynson's shop:

> Our Shyp here levyth the sees brode
> By helpe of God almyght, and quyetly
> At Anker we lye within the rode.
> But who that lysteth of them to bye
> In Flete strete shall them fynde truly,
> At the George, in Richarde Pynsonnes place,
> Prynter unto the Kynges noble grace.
> Deo gratias.

Finally, most tellingly, at one point in the middle of the ***Ship,*** Barclay claims to admit another group of fools even though Pynson had directed him to keep the work brief, as if Pynson were exercising some editorial control over Barclay's writing: "To you [sc., ironically, 'Ye blaberynge folys'] of Barklay it shall nat be denayde, / How be it the charge Pynson hathe on me layde / With many folys our Navy not to charge" ([ed. Jamieson] I: 108).

Beginning with this 1509 publication, Pynson was always the first to print new writing by Barclay, with a characteristic woodcut author portrait of Barclay that he used over and over, and a characteristic, peculiar bilingual layout for Barclay's translations from Latin that must have been worked out between printer and writer (Smith 333-338). Because of the disappearance of all the earliest editions of Barclay's most popular, commercially successful work, the five ***Eclogues***—the earliest surviving is a c. 1520 edition of the fifth ***Eclogue,*** printed at least five years after the work's initial appearance—it is not possible to say much about the circumstances of the ***Eclogues'*** first appearances in print. With this exception, Pynson evidently printed first editions of

all of Barclay's later writings, doing so without delay, always shortly after the writings' completion. One of the last signs of literary activity on Barclay's part, before he ceased to write, about 1523, twenty-five years before his death, was signed editorial work on a grammar book issued by Pynson.

By comparison with Skelton, Barclay was the better informed about recent continental literature, and he did more to put the products of Italianate literary fashions before English audiences; likewise, Barclay worked regularly with a printer, seeing to the circulation of his writing by the newly invented means of printing, whereas Skelton remained aloof, sticking to manuscript circulation, except in limited, unusual circumstances. In these respects, Barclay was the more forward-looking, the more modern, of the two. By this light, Barclay's attack on Skelton in the ***Ship of Fools,*** albeit couched in monkish, moralistic terms, appears to have been the attack of a newcomer, publishing his first work, against an old, established figure, well-known, with a substantial body of writing already behind him. Evidently, these are the terms in which Skelton understood the attack, as his counter-charge of envy indicates. "Medieval" Barclay was a young upstart; "modern" Skelton was the old guard.

Finally, however, aside from this generational difference—apparently, Skelton was ten to fifteen or twenty years older—the similarities between Skelton and Barclay probably outweigh the differences. Each was medieval in characteristic ways, Barclay in his monkish moralism and generic pieties, Skelton in his allegorism and Chaucerian affiliations; at the same time, each was also modern, Skelton in ways still unique to him, Barclay in his affiliations with humanism and printing. However, by contrast with the professional humanists active and influential in England at the time—André, Carmeliano, Polydore Vergil, Erasmus, and the rest—and by contrast with the amateur, aristocratic courtier poetry soon to emerge, Skelton and Barclay look much alike. For both, ordination to the priesthood seems to have been initially a rung on a careerist ladder; both began their careers as pedagogues, Barclay in a collegiate church, and Skelton in an aristocratic or the royal household; both enjoyed (or sought) the patronage of the Howards and of the royal family; both wrote works of pedagogy and translations of ancient historians; both worked with the allegorical "ship of fools" topic; and both wrote pro-English propaganda, and political and social satire, in English. Skelton and Barclay occupied—or sought to occupy (Skelton, in addition to being the older, was also the more successful)—the same niche in the transitional literary economy of the late fifteenth and early sixteenth centuries, between medieval and modern. They competed with one another, and, not surprisingly, they clashed. The clash was the result of professional, generational competition, however, not a fundamental, inevitable difference of outlook or allegiance.

Notes

1. This paper was originally presented at a session of the 1993 *Kalamazoo International Congress on Medieval Studies,* on "John Skelton: The Medieval and Classical Heritage," to the organizer and other participants of which I am grateful: Ann Deno, M. J. Tucker, and Frank Brownlow.

2. On Skelton, the best single treatment of his life and works remains Nelson's *John Skelton, Laureate;* and for Skelton's writings the basic source of information, as well as the quotations herein, is Scattergood's edition. On Barclay, still the best source of biographical information, incorporating also basic bibliography and information about Barclay's sources, is White (i-liv). Since White's work was published, a number of significant biographical studies of Barclay have appeared, including Colchester, Nelson (ed. *The Life of St. George by Alexander Barclay* xi-xiii; Lyall ("Alexander Barclay"); and Orme. On Hawes, the basic work is Edwards (*Stephen Hawes*). Except as indicated otherwise, biographical and bibliographical information in this paper comes from these sources. In quoting writings of Skelton and Barclay from the editions of others, I have felt free to make minor adjustments to punctuation without comment.

3. The discussion of Skelton's and Barclay's relations with printers that follows is abbreviated from a paper with the title "Alexander Barclay and Richard Pynson: A Tudor Printer and his Writer," forthcoming in *Anglia,* where the evidence is discussed in somewhat greater detail.

4. Rastell evidently printed more of Skelton than has survived, as is confirmed by the inventory published by Rogers (34-42) and Boffey (24) suggests that Skelton and Rastell may have been working together.

Works Cited

Bale, John. *Index Britanniae Scriptorum.* Ed. R. L. Poole and Mary Bateson, intr. Caroline Brett and James P. Carley. Cambridge: Brewer, 1990.

Blanchard, W. Scott. "Skelton: The Voice of the Mob in Sanctuary." *Rethinking the Henrician Era.* Ed. Peter C. Herman. Urbana: U Illinois P, 1994. 122-144.

Boffey, Julia. "Early Printers and English Lyrics: Sources, Selection, and Presentation of Texts." *Papers of the Bibliographical Society of America* 85 (1991): 11-26.

Brownlow, F.W. "*The Book of Phyllyp Sparowe* and the Liturgy." *English Literary Renaissance* 9 (1979): 5-20.

———. "The Date of *The Bowge of Courte* and Skelton's Authorship of 'A Lamentable of Kyng Edward the IIII.'" *English Language Notes* 22 (1984): 12-20.

———, ed. *The Book of the Laurel: John Skelton.* Newark: U Delaware P, 1990.

Colchester, L. S. "Alexander Barclay." *Modern Language Review* 37 (1942): 198.

Cooper, Helen. *Pastoral: Medieval into Renaissance.* Ipswich: Brewer, 1977.

Edwards, A. S. G. "Poet and Printer in Sixteenth Century England: Stephen Hawes and Wynkyn de Worde." *Gutenberg Jahrbuch* (1980): 82-8.

———. *Stephen Hawes.* Boston: Twayne, 1983.

Erler, Mary C. "Early Woodcuts of Skelton: The Uses of Convention." *Bulletin of Research in the Humanities* 87 (1986-1987): 17-28.

Fox, Alistair. *Politics and Literature in the Reigns of Henry VII and Henry VIII.* Oxford: Blackwell, 1989.

Gordon, Ian A. *John Skelton Poet Laureate.* 1943. New York: Octagon, 1970.

Halpern, Richard. "John Skelton and the Poetics of Primitive Accumulation." *Literary Theory / Renaissance Texts.* Ed. Patricia Parker and David Quint. Baltimore: Johns Hopkins UP, 1986. 225-256.

Heiserman, A. R. *Skelton and Satire.* Chicago: U of Chicago P, 1961.

Jamieson, T. H., ed. *The Ship of Fools Translated by Alexander Barclay.* 2 vols. 1874. New York: AMS, 1966.

Kinney, Arthur F. *John Skelton, Priest as Poet: Seasons of Discovery.* Chapel Hill: U of North Carolina P, 1987.

Kinsman, Robert S. "The Printer and Date of Publication of Skelton's *Agaynste a Comely Coystrowne* and *Dyvers Balettys.*" *Huntington Library Quarterly* 16 (1953): 203-10.

———. "Eleanora Rediviva: Fragments of an Edition of Skelton's *Elynour Rummyng,* ca. 1521." *Huntington Library Quarterly* 18 (1955): 315-27.

Lyall, R. J. "Alexander Barclay and the Edwardian Reformation 1548-1552." *Review of English Studies* ns 20 (1969): 455-461.

———. "Tradition and Innovation in Alexander Barclay's 'Towre of Vertue and Honoure.'" *Review of English Studies* ns 23 (1972): 1-18.

Nelson, William. *John Skelton, Laureate.* New York: Columbia UP, 1939.

———, ed. *The Life of St. George by Alexander Barclay.* EETS OS 230. London: Early English Text Society, 1955.

Orme, Nicholas. "Alexander Barclay, Tudor Educationalist." *Education and Society in Medieval and Renaissance England.* London: Hambledon, 1989. 259-270.

Roberts, R. J. "John Rastell's Inventory of 1538." *The Library* 6th ser. 1 (1979): 34-42.

Robinson, Fred C. "Medieval, the Middle Ages." *Speculum* 59 (1984): 745-756.

Scattergood, John, ed. *John Skelton: The Complete English Poems.* New Haven: Yale UP, 1983.

———. "John Skelton's Lyrics: Tradition and Innovation." *Acta* 12 (1988): 19-39.

———. "Skelton's *Garlande of Laurell* and the Chaucerian Tradition." *Chaucer Traditions.* Ed. Ruth Morse and Barry Windeatt. Cambridge: Cambridge UP, 1990. 122-138.

Schulte, Edvige. "John Skelton nella tradizione poetica inglese." *Annali Istituto Universitario Orientale Napoli—Sezione germanica* 4 (1961): 166-171.

Smith, Julie A. "Woodcut Presentation Scenes in Books Printed by Caxton, de Worde, Pynson." *Gutenberg Jahrbuch* (1986): 322-43.

Spearing, A. C. *Medieval to Renaissance in English Poetry.* Cambridge: Cambridge UP, 1985.

Walker, Greg. "'Ordered Confusion'?: The Crisis of Authority in Skelton's *Speke, Parott.*" *Spenser Studies* 10 (1989): 213-228.

Webb, Geoffrey. "The Office of Devisor." *Fritz Saxl 1890-1948: A Volume of Memorial Essays.* Ed. D. J. Gordon. London: Nelson, 1957. 297-308.

White, Beatrice, ed. *The Eclogues of Alexander Barclay.* EETS OS 175. London: Early English Text Society, 1928.

FURTHER READING

Biography

Lyall, R. J. "Alexander Barclay and the Edwardian Reformation 1548-52." *Review of English Studies* 20, no. 80 (November 1969): 455-61.

Explores various sources to develop a concrete portrayal of Barclay's life and its importance in literary history.

White, Beatrice. "Introduction: The Life of Alexander Barclay." In *The Eclogues of Alexander Barclay,* edited by Beatrice White, pp. i-liv. London: Oxford University Press, 1961.

Explores the controversy surrounding Barclay's life by examining how Barclay's work provides biographical details.

Criticism

Berdan, John M. "Alexander Barclay, Poet and Preacher." *Modern Language Review* 8, no. 3 (July 1913): 290-300.

Illustrates Barclay's method of translation for *Ship of Fools* and how this text signals a specific timeline and influences.

Nelson, William. Introduction to *The Life of St. George,* Edited by William Nelson, pp. ix-xxv.: Oxford University Press, 1955.

Identifies the historical background of Barclay's *The Life of St. George* and events in Barclay's life which influenced the poems publication.

Schultz, John Richie. "The Method of Barclay's *Eclogues.*" *The Journal of English and Germanic Philology* 32, no. 4 (October 1933): 549-71.

Examines Barclay's method of writing in the *Eclogues* and how this method demonstrates Barclay's importance as a writer.

Additional coverage of Barclay's life and career is contained in the following sources published by Thomson Gale: *Dictionary of Literary Biography,* Vol. 132; and *Literature Resource Center.*

James VI of Scotland, I of England
1566-1625

Scottish poet, essayist, critic, translator, and nonfiction writer.

INTRODUCTION

At a time when monarchs were expected to be highly literate and cultured, King James VI of Scotland and I of England was one of the most accomplished and prolific. During his reign, he wrote poetry, political theory, theological meditations, tracts against smoking and witchcraft, and literary criticism. He also authorized the creation of the King James Bible, which is regarded as his most enduring literary achievement.

BIOGRAPHICAL INFORMATION

Born in Edinburgh on June 19, 1566, James was the only son of Mary, Queen of Scots and her second husband, Lord Darnley. Mary was an incompetent ruler, and James's birth was clouded by rumors of illegitimacy and his mother's adultery. Darnley was murdered a few months after James's birth; historians assert that he was killed to avenge the slaying of Mary's secretary and possible lover, David Rizzio. After her husband's murder, Mary married her lover, the Earl of Bothwell. Deposed by rebellious Scottish lords in June 1567, she fled to England to procure the protection of Queen Elizabeth I. She was immediately incarcerated and James became King James VI of Scotland on July 29, 1567. The young monarch was educated by a series of notable tutors, the best known being the poet, dramatist, and humanist George Buchanan and the scholar Peter Young. Buchanan instilled in James an insatiable interest in political theory; from Young he learned to appreciate poetry and theological debates. Under the tutelage of these great teachers, James became a skillful debater, a voracious reader, and an aspiring poet. He also showed a burgeoning fascination with the theater—particularly the plays of William Shakespeare and Ben Jonson—and was very fond of the masque, which would become the leading form of court entertainment when he became king. In 1579 the first of a series of male favorites, Esmé Stuart (or Stewart), Seigneur d'Aubigny, arrived in Scotland and quickly charmed the young king. Esmé's meteoric rise from courtier to Duke of Lennox and his intimate relationship with James caused much consternation among the Scottish nobles and English ar-

istocracy, including Elizabeth. Some historians claim that the two men were lovers and that the relationship inspired James to fulfill his literary ambitions and patronize a group of prominent poets as well as to undertake other artistic pursuits. In 1582 a group of Scottish nobles convinced James to separate from Esmé for the good of the monarchy, and Esmé was ordered to leave the country. From an English prison, Mary wrote to James with a plan to share power; James rejected her offer and she was executed on February 8, 1587. In 1589 James married Anne of Denmark in Oslo.

After Elizabeth's death on March 24, 1603, James was crowned King James I of England at Westminster. As king, he aimed to unite England and Scotland, strengthen England's power, and end the war with Spain. The power structure in England was wary of a Scottish king and often perceived him as foreign and a barbarian. Moreover, he continued to raise suspicion with his system of favorites in which his close male friends gained power, titles, and prestige through their intimacy with the monarch. In 1611 James authorized a translation of the Bible; this Authorized Version, or King James Bible, as it came to be known, was technically not a new translation of the bible but a synthesis of several earlier versions of the scriptures. He survived several assassination attempts during his reign, most notable among them the Gunpowder Plot of 1605. Tension between the English Parliament and the Scottish-born king did not abate during his reign; in fact, issues such as the official policy toward Spain and the generation of income exacerbated conflict. In 1613 a new scandal erupted, as James's favorite, Robert Carr, was implicated in the murder of Sir Thomas Overbury, who had a sexually intimate relationship with Carr. James was also derided for his next involvement, an intense relationship with George Villiers, Duke of Buckingham; James eventually made Villiers an earl in 1617 and a marquess in 1618. The last few years of James's life were preoccupied with England's relationship with Spain and the growing dissension with his foreign policies. James died on March 2, 1625.

MAJOR WORKS

James's best-known written works focus on theological issues and the principle of divine right of kings, which is the doctrine that sovereigns derive their right to rule solely from God. *The True Lawe of Free Monarchies* (1598) is a clear explanation of the theory of divine right for the general public. Another well-regarded work, *Basilikon Doron* (1599), contains practical advice for his son, Prince Henry, on the responsibilities and logistics of power. It is comprised of three sections: "Of a King's Christian Duty Towards God," "Of a King's Duty in His Office," and "Of a King's Behavior in Indifferent Things." Several thousand copies were put into circulation and the book was translated into several different languages. His *Counter-Blaste to Tobacco* (1604) is regarded as one of the best attacks on smoking ever written. In a religious vein, James published *Triplici Nodo, Triplex Cuneus. Or, An Apologie for the Oath of Allegiance* (1607), a defense of the oath of allegiance that all Catholics were required to take to the Protestant king; *A Meditation upon the Lord's Prayer* (1619); and several other biblical studies and reflections. His fierce interest and personal encounters with witchcraft inspired his *Daemonologie* (1597), which recounts his collected knowledge and experience with the subject. James also published works of poetry and literary criticism. His first published poetic work, *The Essayes of a Prentise, in the Divine Art of Poesie* appeared in 1584 and was followed by another collection *His Maiesties Poeticall Exercises at Vacant Houres* in 1591. This work contains his epic poem, *Lepanto*, which chronicles the decisive victory of Christian forces over the Turkish fleet in 1571. Critics note that James employed poetry for the dissemination of his religious and

political beliefs and assumed that his position as monarch allowed him a privileged viewpoint from which to write religious poetry. His *Some Reulis and Cautelis to Be Observit and Eschewit in Scottish Poesie,* included in *The Essayes of a Prentise,* was the first treatise ever written on Scottish poetry and underscores the value he placed on Scottish culture.

CRITICAL RECEPTION

Commentators argue that the mixed reaction to James's reign throughout the years shaped his reputation as a literary figure. His work—especially his tracts on political and theological concerns—was quite influential in his time, and critics point to his support for Scottish poetry and English masques as particularly significant. After his death, his literary reputation declined because scholars asserted that it was only James's privileged position that allowed him any critical attention as a literary figure. In fact, such prestigious critics as Sir Walter Scott and David Harris Willson eviscerated James's literary reputation, but in the early twentieth century commentators rediscovered James's political work, and a reevaluation of James's reign and literary achievements occurred. Through the efforts of the scholar James Craigie, reissues of James's poems, psalms, and essays appeared and brought increased critical attention to his literary achievements. James is now recognized as a critic and poet as well as a political and religious theorist. Although some of his political positions, such as his stand on the divine right of kings, are now viewed as obsolete, critics commend his lively, clear prose and deft use of imagery. It is the King James Bible, however, that constitutes his most lasting and influential literary achievement.

PRINCIPAL WORKS

The Essayes of a Prentise, in the Divine Art of Poesie (essays, poetry, and translations) 1584

Ane Frutfull Meditation Contening ane Plane and Facill Expositioun of ye 7.8.9 and 10 Versis of the 20 Chap. of the Revelatioun in Forme of ane Sermon (essays) 1588

Ane Meditatioun upon the xxv., xxvi., xxvii., xxviii., and xxix. Verses of the xv. Chapt. of the First Buke of the Chronicles of the Kingis (essays) 1589

His Maiesties Poeticall Exercises at Vacant Houres (poetry) 1591

Daemonologie, in Forme of a Dialogue, Divided into Three Bookes (nonfiction) 1597

The True Lawe of Free Monarchies: or The Reciprock and Mutuall Dutie Betwixt a Free King, and His Naturall Subjectes (nonfiction) 1598

Basilikon Doron: Devided into Three Books (nonfiction) 1599; revised 1603

A Counter-Blaste to Tobacco (essay) 1604

Triplici Nodo, Triplex Cuneus. Or, An Apologie for the Oath of Allegiance, against the Two Breves of Pope Paulus Quintus, and the Late Letter of Cardinal Bellarmine to G. Blackwel, the Arch-priest (nonfiction) 1607

Declaration du Serenissimie Roy Jacques I. Roy de la Grand' Bretagne France et Irlande, Defenseur de la Foy. Pour le droit des rois & independance de leurs Couronnes, contre la Harangue de L'Illustrissime Cardinal du Perron pronouncée en la chambre du tiers Estat le XV. de Janvier 1615 [A Remonstrance of the Most Gratious King James I. King of Great Brittaine, France, and Ireland, Defender of the Faith, &c. for the Right of Kings, and the Independence of Their Crownes. Against an Oration of the Most Illustrious Card. of Perron, Pronounced in the Chamber of the Third Estate. Jan. 15. 1615. Translated out of His Majesties French Copie] (nonfiction) 1615

The Workes of the Most High and Mightie Prince, James, by the Grace of God, King of Great Britaine, France and Ireland, Defender of the Faith, &c. Published by James, Bishop of Winton, and Deane of His Maiesties Chappel Royall (essays, poetry, and nonfiction) 1616; enlarged edition 1620

A Meditation upon the Lords Prayer, Written by the Kings Majestie, for the Benefit of All His Subjects, Especially of Such as Follow the Court. Joh. 16.23 (essay) 1619

A Meditation Upon the 27, 28, 29, Verses of the XXVII. Chapter of S^t. Matthew. Or a paterne for a Kings inauguration (essays) 1620

The Psalmes of King David, Translated by King James [translator] (poetry) 1631

Letters of Queen Elizabeth and King James VI of Scotland [edited by John Bruce] (letters) 1849

Correspondence of King James VI of Scotland with Sir Robert Cecil and Others [edited by Bruce] (letters) 1861

New Poems of James I of England, from a Hitherto Unpublished Manuscript (Add. 24195) in the British Museum [edited by Allan F. Westcott] (poetry) 1911

The Political Works of James I, Reprinted from the Edition of 1616 [edited by Charles Howard McIlwain] (essays) 1918

The Basilicon Doron of King James VI. 2 vols. [edited by James Craigie] (nonfiction) 1944, 1950

The Poems of James VI of Scotland. 2 vols. [edited by Craigie] (poetry) 1955, 1958

Minor Prose Works of King James VI and I [edited by Craigie and Alexander Law] (essays) 1982

Letters of King James VI & I [edited by G. P. V. Akrigg] (letters) 1984

King James VI and I: Political Writings [edited by Johann P. Sommerville] (essays) 1994

CRITICISM

Robert S. Rait (essay date 1900)

SOURCE: Rait, Robert S. Introduction to *A Royal Rhetorician: A Treatise on Scottis Poesie, A Counterblaste to Tobacco, etc. etc. by King James VI and I,* edited by Robert S. Rait, pp. ix-xlvii. Westminster: A. Constable and Co., 1900.

[*In the following essay, Rait offers an overview of King James's literary, political, and theological works.*]

'Your Inheritance consists as much in the workes of your Father's Royall Vertues, as in the wealth of his mighty Kingdomes.' So wrote the courtier Bishop of Winchester in his 'Epistle Dedicatorie to the Thrice Illustrious and most Excellent Prince, Charles, the Onely Sonne of Our Soveraigne Lord the King'—an epistle prefixed to the Bishop's edition of King James's Works, published in 1616. The goodly folio[1] volume of some six hundred pages may have seemed to the prelate and his master to justify the compliment, or the sentence may have served for taking up the wager of battle against those who held that writing became not the majesty of a king, and to whose confutation the editor devoted a 'Preface,' wherein he appealed to 'the King of Kings, God Himselfe, who, as he doth all things for our good; so doeth he many things for our Imitation. It pleased his Divine wisdome to bee the first in this Rancke, that we read of, that did ever write. Hee wrote, and the writing was the writing, saith Moses, of God.'

We have fallen heirs to this portion of Prince Charles's inheritance; but it can scarcely be said that any generation, later than King James's own, has received its heritage with the Bishop's triumphant cry: 'God hath given us a Solomon.' Yet it would be matter of regret if King James, as an author, were to pass into complete oblivion. We are, of course, not dealing with literature in any true sense. But, in the King's writings, we have, in the first place, the work of one of the best educated men of his time. Brought up under the care of the greatest living humanist, he was, if a pedant, none the less a scholar. 'Thay wald haif me learn Latin before I can speik Scots,' he had scrawled on the margin of his copybook in his strange, dreary, motherless boyhood in Stirling Castle, and George Buchanan had allowed no whipping-boy to bear vicarious suffering for the shortcomings of the Lord's Anointed. By nature, too, he was shrewd and capable, seeing clearly if not far. His mind was precisely fitted to appreciate the intricacies of Formal Logic, and his thought naturally ran in syllogisms. He revelled in the hard, logical, and crude discussions on Divinity, which could bear no mystery, and found superstition congenial and mysticism impossible. The opinions of such a man are better fitted than writings which bear even faint traces of unusual intellectual force, to picture for us the attitude of the men of his time. The political theses which the King impugns and supports, throw an interesting sidelight upon English history and go far to explain the tragedy of his House. But, above all, these interminable treatises are interesting as bringing into relief the personality of perhaps the oddest figure in our national history. James was not a great king; in some respects he was a fool. But, as Henry IV. remarked about him, he was the wisest fool in Christendom. The cautious shrewdness which was ever waging war against the pride of Kingship and the arrogance of intellectual self-confidence; the simpleness and *naïveté* which strove in vain to hide themselves under an affectation of cunning statecraft and an assertion of fierce wrestlings with the evil spirits of ignorance and heresy; the quaint humour, now unconscious, and now scoring an obvious or verbal point, but rarely affording salvation from the worst errors that lack of humour can bring; the worldly-wisdom which only at times rose above the level of garrulous advice; the piety which honestly strove to be unaffected, and which succeeded in clothing the royal prejudices in language of unctuous and suspicious sanctity; the rashness of a mind filled with but one idea and of an ambition which sought vainglory in good and evil alike, mingled with a keen moral sense and with that cowardice which 'would not play false and yet would wrongly win'; the humility, genuine enough in its way, which boasted that even kings must acknowledge God—all these and a thousand other incongruities make this king real to us in his own pages.

The present selection[2] from the works of King James comprises his *Treatise on Scottish Poesie,* and his more widely-known *Counterblaste to Tobacco.* The former was written as a preface to a volume of *Essayes of a Prentise in the Divine Art of Poesie,* printed at Edinburgh in 1585, when the royal author was eighteen years of age. These *Essayes,* with *His Majesty's Poetical Exercises at Vacant Houres* (published in 1591), some sonnets, and 'The Psalms of KING DAVID translated by KING JAMES,' constitute the whole of the king's production of verse. They possess little interest of any sort.[3] It is otherwise with the *Schort Treatise,* which, if it proves the king's words that 'if Nature be not the chief worker in this art, Rules will be but a bond to Nature,' remains valuable, not only as showing the æsthetic and intellectual fibre of the writer, but also as the only work of its kind in existence. It is a schoolboy's essay, and it represents the fruit of George Buchanan's teaching. James himself thus apologised for his early work: 'I composed these things in my verie young and tender yeares: wherein Nature (except shee were a monster) can admit of no perfection'; and, fortunately for our enjoyment of the *Treatise,* he never revised it. 'Being of riper yeares, my burden is so great

and continuall, without anie intermission, that when my ingyne and age could, my affaires and fasherie would not permit mee to remark the wrong orthography committed by the copiars of my unlegible and ragged hand, far less to amend my proper errours.' The present editor has added a glossary and a few notes to the *Treatise* and to the *Counterblaste.* The latter will explain itself. It was published, anonymously, shortly after King James's accession to the English throne, and the authorship was first openly avowed in 1616. It shows King James in a lighter vein. He calls it 'but a toy,' and 'the fume of an idle braine'; and in Bishop Montagu's Latin translation of his works, which appeared in 1619, it is described as 'Misocapnus, sive De Abusu Tobacci Lusus Regius.' But it is a case of Pegasus on stilts, and the humour is, for the most part, unconscious, although the pamphlet might have warranted the Bishop in applying to the royal rhetorician the title of 'Doctor Subtilis.'

Of King James's remaining writings, the most interesting is his *Basilikon Doron,* or book of advice to his eldest son, Henry, afterwards Prince of Wales. It deals with a king's duty towards God, his duty in his office, and his behaviour in things indifferent. A fierce attack upon Presbytery and 'the proud Puritanes' explains why it was necessary, in 1599, to limit the first edition to a secret issue of seven copies. 'Paritie is the mother of confusion, and enemie to Unitie, which is the mother of order. . . . Take heede therefore (my sonne) to such Puritanes, verie pestes in the Church and Commonweale, whom no deserts can oblige, neither oathes nor promises binde, breathing nothing but sedition and calumnies, aspiring without measure, railing without reason, and making their owne imaginations (without any warrant of the word) the square of their conscience.' The English succession had removed all need of hiding such sentiments from the Church of Scotland, but the sentence throws a light upon James's religious policy in England and the consequent separation of the Puritans from the Church. James never failed more egregiously to understand men's minds than when he confused English Puritanism with Scottish Presbytery. We find, too, an anticipation of James's Irish policy in his advice regarding the Scottish Highlands:—'As for the Hie-lands, I shortly comprehend them all in two sorts of people: the one, that dwelleth in our maine land, that are barbarous for the most sorte, and yet mixed with some shewe of civilitie; the other that dwelleth in the Iles, and are all uterly barbares, without any sort or shew of civilitie. For the first sort, put straitly to execution the Lawes made alreadie by me against their Over-lords, and the chiefes of their Clannes, and it will be no difficultie to danton them. As for the other sort, follow forth the course that I have intended, in planting Colonies among them of answerable In-land subjects, that within short time may reforme and civilize the best inclined among them; rooting out or transporting the barbarous and stubborne sort, and planting civilitie in their roomes.'

The transference of King James's energies to England reserved the suppression of the clan-system for the government of George II. And, again, we are reminded of the **Book of Sports,** when James urges, as a means of preventing people from speaking 'rashly of their Prince,' the appointment of 'certaine dayes in the yeere, for delighting the people with publicke spectacles of all honest games, and exercise of armes; as also for conveening of neighbours, for entertaining friendship and heartlinesse, by honest feasting and merrinesse: For I cannot see what greater superstition can be in making plays and lawfull games in Maie, and good cheere at Christmas, than in eating fish in Lent, and upon Fridayes, the Papists as well using the one as the other.'[4]

The king's personal advice is not less interesting than his political maxims. Prince Henry should 'not marry for money, but marry where money is.' For 'beautie increaseth your love to your wife, and riches and great alliance doe both make her the abler to be a helper unto you.' In things indifferent, he was to be wise and discreet:—

> In the forme of your meate-eating, bee neither uncivill like a grosse cynicke, nor affectatlie mignarde, like a daintie dame; but eate in a manlie, round, and honest fashion. . . . Be also moderate in your raiment, neither over superfluous, like a deboshed waster, nor yet over base, like a miserable wretch . . . but in your garments be proper, cleanely, comely and honest, wearing your clothes in a careless yet comely forme.[5] . . . Especially eschew to be effeminate in your cloathes, in perfuming, preening [pinning] and such like, and make not a foole of yourselfe in disguising or wearing long haire or nailes. . . . In your language be plaine, honest, naturall, comely, cleane, eschewing both the extremities, as well in not using any rusticall corrupt leide [language], as booke language, and pen and inkehorne termes, and least of all mignard and effeminate termes . . . not taunting in Theologie, nor alleadging and prophaning the Scripture in drinking purposes [conversations], as over many doe. . . . If yee would write worthily, choose subjects worthie of you, that bee not full of vanitie, but of vertue, eschewing obscuritie, and delighting ever to be plaine and sensible. And if yee write in Verse, remember that it is not the principall part of a Poeme to rime right, and flow well with many pretie wordes: but the chief commendation of a Poeme is, that when the verse shall be shaken sundrie in prose, it shall bee found so rich in quicke inventions, and poetick flowers, and in faire and pertinent comparisons, as it shall retaine the lustre of a Poeme, although in Prose. And I would also advise you to write in your owne language: for there is nothing left to be saide in Greeke and Latine alreadie, and ynew [enough] of poore schollers would match you in these languages; and beside that, it best becommeth a king to purifie and make famous his owne tongue; wherein he may goe before all his subjects, as it setteth him well to doe in all honest and lawfull things. And amongst all unnecessarie things that are lawfull and expedient, I think exercises of the bodie most commendable to be used by a young Prince, in such honest games or pas-

times, as may further abilitie and maintaine health . . . but from this count I debarre all rough and violent exercises, as the foote-ball, meeter for laming then making able the users thereof. . . . But the exercises that I would have you to use are running, leaping, wrastling, fencing, dancing, and playing at the caitch or tennise, archerie, palle maille, and such like other faire and pleasant field-games. And the honourablest and most commendable games that yee can use, are on horseback, for it becommeth a Prince best of any man, to be a faire and good horseman. . . . I cannot omit heere the hunting, namely with running hounds, which is the most honourable and noblest sorte thereof: for it is a theevish forme of hunting to shoote with gunnes and bowes, and greyhound hunting is not so martiall a game. . . . When ye are wearie of reading, or evill disposed in your person, and when it is foule and stormie weather; then, I say, may ye lawfully play at the cardes or tables. For as to dicing, I thinke it becommeth best deboshed souldiers to play at, on the head of their drums, being onely ruled by hazard, and subject to knavish cogging. And as for the chesse, I think it over fond, because it is over-wise and Philosophicke a toy. For where all such light playes are ordained to free men's heades for a time, from the fashious thoughts on their affaires; it by the contrarie filleth and troubleth men's heades, with as many fashious toyes of the play, as before it was filled with thoughts on his affaires.

So he rambles garrulously on, playing with keen zest the part of Polonius (which his future subject must about the same time have been creating). It is all wise and shrewd, and the language redeems the commonplace of the thought. He refers now and again to the circumstances of his youth and the troubles of his mother's reign, describing his uncle, the Regent Murray, as 'that bastard, who unnaturally rebelled, and procured the ruine of his owne Soverane and sister,' and urging the destruction of 'such infamous invectives as Buchanan's or Knoxes Chronicles.' In command of Scriptural quotation the king cannot have been surpassed by any of the hated Presbyterians who 'claiming to their Paritie, and crying, "Wee are all but vile wormes," yet will judge and give Law to their king, but will be judged nor controlled by none.' It is with them in mind that he advises the prince to study well the Psalms of David 'for teaching you the forme of your prayers. . . . So much the fitter are they for you then for the common sort, in respect the composer thereof was a king: and therefore best behoved to know a king's wants, and what things were meetest to be required by a king at God's hand for remedie thereof.' The sentence seems to resound with the echoes of ecclesiastical controversies, and it reveals the storehouse from which King James borrowed his armour when he went forth to face Andrew Melville himself.

Next in interest to the **Basilikon Doron** is a treatise on **Daemonologie, in Forme of a Dialogue,** which also saw the light in 1599. James is well known as a persecutor of witches, and here we have his *Apologia.* It was written 'not in any wise to serve for a shew of my learning and ingine,' but as a protest 'against the damnable opinions of two principally in our age, whereof the one called Scot,[6] an Englishman, is not ashamed in publike Print to deny, that there can be such a thing as witchcraft: and so maintaines the old errour of the Sadduces in denying of spirits; the other called Wierus, a German Physitian, sets out a publike Apologie for all these craftsfolkes, whereby, procuring for their impunitie, he plainely bewrayes himselfe to have bene one of that profession.' The interlocutors are Philomathes, the willing disciple, and Epistemon, the wise instructor. Epistemon begins by proving (largely by means of the Witch of Endor) the possibility of magic, and then proceeds to divide it into Necromancie and Sorcerie or Witchcraft.

PHI.:

> What difference is there between Necromancie and Witchcraft?

EPI.:

> Surely, the difference vulgare put betwix them is very merry, and in a manner true; for they say, that the Witches are servants onely, and slaves to the divel; but the Necromanciers are his masters and commanders.

PHI.:

> How can that be true, that any men being specially addicted to his service can be his commanders?

EPI.:

> Yea, they may be: but it is onely *secundum quid*; for it is not by any power that they can have over him, but *ex pacto* allanerlie; whereby he obliges himselfe in some trifles to them, that he may on the other part obteine the fruition of their body and soule, which is the onely thing he huntes for.

After a discussion of the use of charms, we come to the 'difference between God's miracles and the Divel's':—

> God is a creatour, what he makes appeare in myracle, it is so in effect. As Moyses Rod being casten downe, was no doubt turned into a naturall serpent; whereas the divel (as God's ape) countersetting that by his magicians, made their wandes to appeare so, onely to men's outward senses: as kythed [was shown] in effect by their being devoured by the other; for it is no wonder that the divel may delude our senses, since we see by common proofe, that simple jugglars will make an hundredth things seeme both to our eyes and eares otherwayes then they are.' Passing now to witchcraft, Epistemon declines to believe that witches can travel to their diabolical conferences in the shape of a little beast or fowl, but thinks it credible that they can be 'caried by the force of the spirit which is their conducter, either above the earth, or above the Sea swiftly, to the place where they are to meete: which I am persuaded to be possible in respect that as Habakkuk was carried by the Angel[7] in that forme, to the den where Daniel

lay; so thinke I, the divell will be readie to imitate God as well in that as in other things: which is much more possible to him to doe, being a Spirit, then to a mighty wind, being but a naturall meteore.

The idea of witchcraft naturally suggests a question which gives King James an opportunity for one of his most characteristic sentences:—

PHI.:

> What can be the cause that there are twentie women given to that craft, where there is one man?

EPI.:

> The reason is easie, for as that sexe is frailer then man is, so is it easier to be intrapped in these grosse snares of the divell, as was overwell prooved to be trew by the serpent's deceiving of Eva at the beginning, which makes him the homelier with that sex sensine.

The discussion on witchcraft ends with a reminiscence of 'the Logicks':—

EPI.:

> Doubtlesse who denieth the power of the Divell would likewise denie the power of God, if they could for shame. For since the Divel is the very contrarie opposite to God, there can bee no better way to know God, then by the contrarie; as by the one's power (though a creature) to admire the power of the great Creatour: by the falshood of the one to consider the trewth of the other: by the injustice of the one to consider the justice of the other: and by the cruelty of the one, to consider the mercifulnesse of the other, and so foorth in all the rest of the essence of God, and qualities of the Divell. But I feare indeed, there bee over many Sadduces in this world, that denie all kinds of Spirits: for convicting of whose errour, there is cause enough if there were no more, that God should permit at sometimes Spirits visibly to kyith.

The third book deals with Ghosts, which are explained as being evil spirits which 'have assumed a dead bodie, whereinto they lodge themselves.' The bodies of the righteous may be used for this purpose for 'the rest of them that the Scripture speakes of, is not meaned by a locall remaining continually in one place, but by their resting from their travailes,' and 'there is nothing in the bodies of the faithfull, more worthie of honour, or freer from corruption by nature, nor in these of the unfaithfull, while time they be purged and glorified in the *latter Day,* as is daily seene by the wilde diseases and corruptions, that the bodies of the faithfull are subject unto.' The story of the wer-wolf he rejects in a characteristically matter-of-fact way: 'If any such thing hath beene, I take it to have proceeded but of a naturall superabundance of melancholy, which as we reade, that it hath made some thinke themselves pitchers, and some horses, and some one kinde of beast or other, so suppose I that it hath so viciat the imagination and memory of some, as *per lucida intervalla,* it hath so highly oc-cupied them, that they have thought themselves very woolfes indeed at these times . . . but as to their hav-ing and hiding of their hard and schelly fluiches, I take that to be but eiked [added], by uncertaine report, the author of all lies.' The Brownies, on the contrary, are genuine, being evil spirits sent to haunt houses 'without doing any evill, but doing as it were necessarie turnes up and downe the house,' the more readily to deceive ignorant Christians in times of Papistrie and blindness, and make them account God's enemy their own par-ticular friend. The 'Phairie,' again, are merely illusions, 'objected' by the devil to men's fantasie and not pos-sessing any real existence, apart from the common herd of evil spirits. And so we reach the conclusion of the whole matter—the duty of suppressing, at any cost, the sin of witchcraft. Epistemon will not admit that there is any real difficulty in detecting guilt. If witchcraft cannot be absolutely proved in all cases, yet the accused are al-ways sure to be 'of a very evill life and reputation,' and so no real injustice is done. 'And besides that, there are two other good helps that may be used for their triall: The one is, the finding of their marke, and the trying the insensiblenes thereof: the other is their fleeting on the water . . . for it appears that God hath appointed . . . that the water shall refuse to receive them in her bosome that have shaken off them the sacred water of baptisme, and wilfully refused the benefite thereof: No, not so much as their eyes are able to shed teares (threaten and torture them as ye please) while [till] first they repent . . . albeit the womenkind especially be able otherwayes to shed teares at every light occasion when they will, yea although it were dissemblingly like the crocodiles.' We are thus brought from comedy to tragedy, for the darkest stain on the wonderful history of seventeenth-century Scotland is the record of the cruel tortures and executions of many innocent old women whom an unfortunate combination of circum-stances or the malice of personal enemies had accused of witchcraft.

King James's purely theological work[8] consists of *A Paraphrase upon the Revelation of S. John,* dedicated to 'the whole Church Militant,' *A Meditation upon* 1 *Chron. xv. 25-29,* and a *Declaration* against the Dutch heretic, Vorstius,[9] which bears the extraordinary inscrip-tion:—'To the Honour of our Lord and Saviour Jesus Christ . . . in signe of Thankfulnes, His Most Humble and Most Obliged Servant, James, by the Grace of God, King of Great Britaine, France, and Irelande, Defender of the Faith, Doeth Dedicate and Consecrate this his Declaration.' The *Paraphrase* was written before the king was twenty years of age, and the *Meditation* a little later, and they are just what might be expected from a clever boy who had received James's training and possessed his self-confidence. The *Declaration* is addressed to the States-General of the United Prov-inces, and its aim was to persuade them to deprive

Vorstius, a follower of Arminius, of his office in the University of Leyden, and, if possible, to bring him to the stake. His main offence consisted in his *Tractatus Theologicus de Deo,* and his *Exegesis Apologetica,* in which he had argued that 'nothing forbids us to say that God hath a Body, so as we take a Body in the largest signification,' and had expressed similar and consequent tenets. James described him as 'a wretched Heretique or rather Athiest,' and used his whole diplomatic power to secure his ruin. He professed his readiness to have controverted Arminius in person; but 'it was our hard hap not to heare of this Arminius before he was dead,' and he had to content himself with warnings regarding the dangers of heresy in general, and the pernicious ef-fect of the teaching of Vorstius in particular. The books in question were solemnly burned in London, Oxford, and Cambridge; and James, who was invited to act as umpire between Vorstius and his opponents in Leyden, succeeded in obtaining his expulsion from Leyden, and afterwards his banishment from the States. The *Decla-ration* shows considerable debating power, and a knowledge of orthodox Theology, and it proves that the Calvinistic teaching in which James was educated had not lost its hold upon his mind.

Two further treatises deal with the relation of Church to State, and they may be next described. *A Defence of the Right of Kings against an oration of the Most Il-lustrious Cardinal of Perron*[10] arose out of a speech made by the Cardinal in the Chamber of the Third Es-tate in France, at the meeting of the States-General in 1614 (the last instance of their being convened till the Assembly of 1789). The assassination of Henry III. in 1589, when under a Papal sentence of excommunica-tion, and the murder of Henry IV. in 1610 (of which the Jesuits were, probably unjustly, suspected to have been the instigators), had drawn attention to the ever-recurring question of the relation of a monarch to the Papacy. A motion was under discussion which was in-tended, as King James puts it, to disavow the sentiment that 'the Pope may tosse the French King his Throne like a tennis ball,' and the Cardinal's speech, which turned the current of opinion in a Papal direction, was printed with the Pope's recommendation, and a copy was sent to King James 'by the Author and Orator himselfe; who presupposed the reading thereof would forsooth drive me to say, "Lord Cardinall, in this high subject your Honour hath satisfied me to the full."' The main portion of the argument is occupied with a discus-sion of historical instances adduced by the Cardinal to show the powers which had been exercised by Popes over Kings in the past, and James disputes the ground inch by inch. As regards wider considerations, he ob-serves that, while the Cardinal had asserted the Pope's power of deposing a king only in cases of Apostasy, Heresy, and persecution of the Church, these powers had, in fact, been claimed on a very much wider scale, and 'Heresy' may include anything whatsoever. 'Among the crimes which the Councel of Constance charged Pope John XXII. withall, one was this, that hee denied the immortalitie of the soule . . . Now if the Pope shall be caried by the streame of these or the like errours, and in his Hereticall pravitie shall depose a king of the contrary opinion, I shall hardly bee persuaded, the said king is lawfully deposed.' He points out also the evil effects likely to follow from the authorisation of such teaching by the Roman Church, and makes a profession of tolerance, which was probably justified as far as Roman Catholicism was concerned:—

> As for myselfe, and my Popish Subjects, to whom I am no lesse then an heretike forsooth; am I not by this doctrine of the Cardinall, pricked and whetted against my naturall inclination, to turne clemencie into rigour; seeing that by his doctrine my subjects are made to believe, they owe me subjection onely by way of *proviso*, and with waiting the occasion to worke my utter destruction and finall ruine. . . . Who seeth not here how great indignitie is offered to me a Christian King, paralleld with Infidels, reputed worse then a Turke, taken for an usurper of my kingdomes, reckoned a Prince, to whom subjects owe a forced obedience by way of provision, untill they shall have meanes to shake off the yoke, and to bare my temples of the Crowne, which never can be pulled from the sacred Head, but with losse of the head itselfe? . . . The plotters and practisers against my life are honoured and rewarded with a glorious name of Martyrs: their constancie (what els?) is admired, when they suffer death for treason. Wheras hitherto during the time of my whole raigne to this day (I speake it in the word of a king, and trewth itselfe shall make good the king's worde) no man hath lost his life, no man hath indured the Racke, no man hath suffered corporall punishment in other kinds, meerely or simply, or in any degree of respect, for his conscience in matter of religion; but for wicked conspiring against my life, or estate, or Royall Dignitie; or els for some notorious crime, or some obstinate and wilfull disobedience.

James was acute enough to see the weakness of the Cardinal's admission that 'the Church abhorreth sudden and unprepensed murders [of kings] above the rest . . . because in sudden murders oftentimes the soule and the body perish both together,' and he compares it to the well-known quibble of the Jesuit Mariana:—

> For Mariana liketh not at any hand the poisoning of a Tyrant by his meat or drinke: for feare lest he taking the poison with his owne hand, and swallowing or gulping it downe in his meate or drinke so taken, should be found *felo de se* (as the common Lawyer speaketh), or culpable of his owne death. But Mariana likes better, to have a Tyrant poysoned by his chaire, or by his apparell and robes . . . that being so poysoned onely by sent, or by contact, he may not be found guiltie of selfe-fellonie, and the soule of the poore Tyrant in her flight out of the body may be innocent. O hel-houndes, O diabolical wretches, O infernall monsters! Did they onely suspect and imagine, that either in kings there is any remainder of kingly courage, or in their subjects any sparke left of ancient libertie; they durst as soone

eat their nailes, or teare their owne flesh from the bones, as once broach the vessell of this diabolicall device. How long then, how long shall kings whom the Lord hath called his Anointed, kings the breathing images of God upon earth; kings that with a wry or frowning looke, are able to crush these earthwormes in pieces; how long shall they suffer this viperous brood, scot-free and without punishment, to spit in their faces? how long the Majestie of God in their person and Royall Majestie, to be so notoriously vilified, so dishonourably trampled under foot?

Apart from its rhetoric, the *Defence* shows James at his best as a controversialist. It was a subject on which he felt strongly and with regard to which he had a good case; and he knew his position to be so strong that he could speak of his adversary with courtesy and respect, except when he was carried away by his own denunciations. It was a subject, too, which afforded an opportunity for a display of his very considerable learning, and he was not insensible of the importance, for this purpose, of marginal references, if judiciously employed.

The other politico-theological treatise is *An Apologie for the Oath of Allegiance,* imposed upon Roman Catholics after the Gunpowder Plot. Pope Paul v. had issued two Briefs forbidding English Romanists to take the oath, and Cardinal Bellarmin, the ex-Jesuit, had enforced the Papal briefs in a strongly worded letter. James now published, under a veil of anonymity, a remarkably temperate defence of the position of the Government, pointing out that the oath did not involve any acknowledgment of the Royal Headship of the Church, and was a promise of political obedience. Two answers made to this *Apologie* led to the king's publishing a second edition, in his own name, with a vigorous preamble, entitled, 'A Premonition to all Most Mightie Monarchs, Kings, Free Princes, and States of Christendom.' One of these answers was in English, and was the work of an English Roman Catholic resident abroad.[11] Him James dismissed in a few words, considering 'a rope the fittest answer' for him:—

> As for the English Answerer, my unnaturall and fugitive Subject; I will neither defile my pen, nor your sacred eyes or eares with the describing of him, who ashames, nay, abhorres not to raile, nay, to rage and spew foorth blasphemies against the late Queene of famous memory. A subject to raile against his naturall Soveraigne by birth; a man to raile against a Lady by sexe; a holy man (in outward profession) to insult upon the dead; nay, to take Radamanthus office over his head, and to sit downe and play the judge in hell.

The other antagonist had written in Latin, and his name led the king into a play upon words—'Hee calleth himselfe Mattheus Tortus, Cardinall Bellarmins Chaplaine. A throwne[12] Evangelist indeed, full of throward Divinitie.' Tortus brought three main accusations against James, that he was an Apostate, having been baptized into the Roman Faith; that he had been a

Puritan in Scotland, and now persecuted the Puritans; and that he was a Heretic. Against each of these James defended himself in his characteristic manner, making incidentally a number of interesting statements, and concluding with an assertion of the Anglo-Catholic position which is strangely reminiscent of modern controversies:—

> I am no Apostate . . . not onely having ever bene brought up in that Religion which I presently professe, but even my Father and Grandfather on that side professing the same. . . . And as for the Queene my Mother of worthy memorie; although she continued in that Religion wherein she was nourished, yet was she so farre from being superstitious or *Jesuited* therein, that at my Baptisme (although I was baptized by a Popish Archbishop) she sent him word to forbeare to use the spettle in my Baptisme; which was obeyed, being indeed a filthy and an apish tricke, rather in scorne then in imitation of Christ. . . . As also the Font wherein I was Christened, was sent from the late Queene here of famous memory, who was my Godmother; and what her Religion was, Pius V. was not ignorant. And for further proofe, that that renowned Queene my Mother was not superstitious; as in all her Letters (whereof I received many) she never made mention of Religion, nor laboured to persuade me in it; so at her last words, she commanded her Master-houshold, a Scottish Gentleman, my servant and yet alive, she commanded him (I say) to tell me; that although she was of another Religion then that wherein I was brought up; yet she would not presse me to change, except my owne Conscience forced mee to do it. . . . Neither can my Baptisme in the rites of their Religion make me an Apostate, or Heretike in respect of my present profession, since we all agree in the substance thereof, being all Baptized *In the Name of the Father, the Sonne, and the holy Ghost*: upon which head there is no variance amongst us. . . . I cannot enough wonder with what brasen face this Answerer could say *that I was a Puritane in Scotland, and an enemie to Protestants*: I that was persecuted by Puritanes there, not from my birth onely, but even since foure moneths before my birth?[13] I that in the yeere of God 84 erected Bishops, and depressed all their popular Paritie, I being then not 18 yeeres of aage? I that in my Booke to my Sonne doe speake tenne times more bitterly of them nor of the Papists; having in my second Edition thereof, affixed a long Apologetike Preface, onely *in odium Puritanorum*? . . . And now for the point of Heretike, I will never bee ashamed to render an accompt of my profession, and of that hope that is in me, as the Apostle prescribeth. I am such a CATHOLIKE CHRISTIAN, as beleeveth the three Creeds . . . and I beleeve them in that sense, as the ancient Fathers and Councels that made them did understand them. . . . I reverence and admit the foure first generall Councels as Catholique and Orthodoxe. . . . As for the Fathers, I reverence them as much and more then the Jesuites doe. . . . As for the Scriptures, no man doubteth I will beleeve them. . . . As for the Saints departed, I honour their memory, and in honour of them doe we in our Church observe the dayes of so many of them, as the Scripture doeth canonize for Saints. . . . For the blessed Virgin Marie, I yeeld her that which the Angel Gabriel pronounced of her . . . that all generations shall call her blessed. . . . And I freely confesse that shee is in glory both above angels and men, her owne Sonne (that is both God and man) onely excepted. But I dare not mocke her and blaspheme against God, calling her not onely *Diva* but *Dea,* and praying her to command and controule her Sonne, who is her God and her Saviour: Nor yet not I thinke, that shee hath no other thing to doe in heaven than to heare every idle man's suite, and busie herselfe in their errands; whiles requesting, whiles commanding her Sonne, whiles comming downe to kisse and make love with Priestes, and whiles disputing and brawling with Devils. . . . That Bishops ought to be in the Church. I ever maintained it, as an Apostolique institution. . . . If the Romish Church hath coined new Articles of Faith, never heard of the first 500 yeeres after Christ, I hope I shall never bee condemned for an Heretike, for not being a Novelist. . . . Since I beleeve as much as the Scriptures doe warrant, the Creeds doe perswade, and the ancient Councels decreed; I may well be a Schismatike from Rome, but I am sure I am no Heretike. . . . And I will sincerely promise, that whenever any point of the Religion I professe, shalbe proved to be new, and not Ancient, Catholike, and Apostolike (I meane for matter of Faith) I will as soone renounce it.

But the Anglican Catholic, before he concludes, appears as a sixteenth-century Protestant, and devotes many pages, and much wealth of Scriptural and historical allusion, to proving that the Pope is Antichrist.[14] From this we pass naturally to an Appendix consisting of 'A Catalogue of the Lyes of Tortus, together with a Briefe Confutation of them,' and there we leave this part of our subject.

It remains to mention King James's more purely political writings. These have reference, mainly, to three topics—the proposed Union of the Kingdoms, the Gunpowder Plot, and the general relations between king and subject. In his first speech to his English Parliament, on 19th March 1603-4, the king brought forward his proposal for a complete union of the two kingdoms. The words in which he commended it to his new people are very characteristic:—

> What God hath conjoyned, let no man separate. I am the Husband and all the whole Isle is my lawfull wife; I am the Head, and it is my Body; I am the Shepherd, and it is my flocke; I hope therefore no man will be so unreasonable as to thinke that I that am a Christian King under the Gospel, should be a Polygamist and husband to two wives; that I being the Head, should have a divided and monstrous Body; or that being the Shepheard to so faire a Flocke (whose fold hath no wall to hedge it but the foure seas) should have my Flocke parted in two. . . . And as God hath made Scotland the one halfe of this Isle to enjoy my Birth, and the first and most unperfect halfe of my life, and you heere to enjoy the perfect and the last halfe thereof: so can I not thinke that any would be so injurious to me . . . as to cut asunder the one halfe of me from the other.

The incorporating Union proposed by King James was more thorough than that which afterwards was carried in 1707. It involved the abolition of Scots Law, and the Scottish Church would have become part of the Church of England. The Parliament did not welcome the proposal, and, in 1607-8, James had again to devote his oratorical power to persuade his English subjects to consent:—

> You here have all the great advantage by the Union. Is not here the personall residence of the King, his whole Court and family? Is not here the seate of Justice, and the fountaine of Government? must they [the Scots] not be subjected to the Lawes of England, and so with time become but as Cumberland and Northumberland, and those other remote and Northern Shires? you are to be the husband, they the wife: you conquerours, they as conquered, though not by the sword, but by the sweet and sure bond of love. . . . Some thinke that I will draw the Scottish nation hither, talking idlely of transporting of trees out of a barren ground into a better . . . doe you not thinke I know England hath more people, Scotland more wast ground? so that there is roumth in Scotland rather to plant your idle people that swarme in London streets, and other Townes, and disburden you of them? . . . The Kings my successours, being borne and bred heere, can never have more occasion of acquaintance with the Scottish nation in generall, then any other English King that was before my time. . . . Since my comming from them I doe not alreadie know the one halfe of them by face, most of the youth being now risen up to bee men, who were but children when I was there, and more are borne since my comming thence.

James failed to convince the English Parliament. The question became connected with the difficult constitutional problems of the time, and the project was definitely abandoned. Like James's foreign policy, the scheme possessed a distinct note of statesmanship, but it resembled it also in its impracticability. It was premature, and could not but have ended in disaster: the ecclesiastical conditions alone would have been sufficient to work its ruin.

In connection with the Gunpowder Plot, the king published *A Discourse of the maner of the Discoverie of the Powder Treason, joyned with the examination of some of the prisoners,* and he also devoted to the subject his speech to Parliament after the discovery. In neither does he add anything that is not otherwise known; but his personal allusions are, as usual, interesting, and he gives us incidentally such a piece of information as the fact that Salisbury was accustomed to end an audience with the king 'with some merry jeast.' In his Speech to Parliament, James laid great stress on the 'two great and fearefull Domesdayes, wherwith God threatned to destroy mee.' The first was the mysterious Ruthven Raid: the second, the Gunpowder Plot:—

> By three different sorts in generall may mankinde be put to death. The first, by other men and reasonable creatures, which is least cruell . . . and the second way

more cruell then that, is by Animal and unreasonable creatures, for as they have less pitie then men, so is it a greater horror and more unnaturall for men to deale with them. . . . But the third, which is most cruell and unmercifull of all, is the destruction by insensible and inanimate things, and amongst them all, the most cruell are the two elements of Water and Fire: and of those two, the fire most raging and mercilesse. . . . The discovery hereof is not a little wonderfull, which would bee thought the more miraculous by you all, if you were as well acquainted with my naturall disposition, as those are who be neere about me: For as I ever did hold suspition to be the sicknes of a Tyrant, so was I so farre upon the other extremity, as I rather contemned all advertisements, or apprehensions of practises. And yet now at this time was I so farre contrary to myselfe, as when the Letter was shewed to me by my Secretary, wherein a generall obscure advertisement was given of some dangerous blow at this time, I did upon the instant interpret and apprehend some darke phrases therein, contrary to the ordinary Grammar construction of them,[15] (and in another sort then I am sure any Divine, or Lawyer in any Universitie, would have taken them) to be meant by this horrible forme of blowing us up all by Powder.

Finally, we have King James's political philosophy stated in a discussion of *The Trew Law of Free Monarchies,* written before he left Scotland, and in three speeches to his English Parliament. His view was that which is known as the Divine Right of Kings. 'Kings are justly called Gods.' for

> God gives not kings the style of Gods in vaine.

The king is the father of his people, and they may in no case oppose his will. If he is a bad king, he 'is sent by God for a curse to his people, and a plague for their sinnes: but that it is lawfull for them to shake off that curse at their owne hand, which God hath laid on them, that I deny, and may do so justly.' To God alone is any king responsible. The king is above the law. 'A good king will frame all his actions to be according to the Law, yet is hee not bound thereto but of his good will, and for good example-giving to his subjects.' This theory he grounded upon the law of nature which makes the king stand to the people as the father to the children or the head to the members; upon the statements of chroniclers regarding early history; upon deductions from the laws (*e.g.* the law of treasure-trove); and upon the teachings of Scripture. In his *Trew Law,* he makes a clever use of Samuel's description of the office of a king, when the Israelites demanded a king to rule over them, and the old prophet attempted to dissuade them, by drawing a picture of the powers of an absolute monarch.[16] This speech of Samuel being part of Holy Scripture, 'it must necessarily follow that these speeches proceeded not from any ambition in Samuel, as one loath to quite the reines that he so long had ruled, and therefore desirous, by making odious the government of a king, to disswade the people from their farther importunate craving of one. For, as the text proveth it plainly, he then conveened them to give them a resolute grant of their demand, as God by his owne mouth commanded him, saying, "*Hearken to the voice of the people.*" And to presse to disswade them from that, which he then came to grant unto them, were a thing very impertinent in a wise man; much more in the Prophet of the most high God.'

In his speeches to his English Parliaments, James stated his position with regard to the rights and privileges of Parliament. 'It is no place for particular men to utter their private conceipts, nor for satisfaction of their curiosities, and least of all to make shew of their eloquence by tyning [losing] the time with long studied and eloquent Orations: No, the reverence of God, their King, and their Countrey being well setled in their hearts, will make them ashamed of such toyes. . . . Men should bee ashamed to make shew of the quicknesse of their wits here, either in taunting, scoffing, or detracting the Prince or State in any point, or yet in breaking jests upon their fellowes.' The duty of a Parliament is to 'give advice in such things as shall by the king be proposed,' to propose anything that, after mature judgment it shall consider to be needfull, to supply the king with money, and to inform him of grievances. But, under the pretext of grievances, Parliament must not presume to 'meddle with the maine points of Government,' or with ancient Rights received by the king from his predecessors, or to attempt to disturb 'any thing that is established by a setled Law,' which they know the king is unwilling to alter. Both in his speeches to Parliament and in **'A Speach in the Starre Chamber,'** James stated his belief in the doctrine that the king is the fountain of law. And he warned the judges of the Star Chamber not to decide anything affecting the royal prerogative or mysteries of State, without first consulting the king. 'The absolute Prerogative of the Crowne is no subject for the tongue of a Lawyer, nor is lawfull to be disputed. It is Athiesme and blasphemie to dispute what God can doe . . . so, it is presumption and high contempt in a subject to dispute what a king can doe or say that a king cannot doe this.' These speeches abound in valuable illustrations of the domestic history of the reign, though the topics are too varied to find mention here.

Only once does James refer to the great political theory which was being debated in his time—the theory of the Social Contract, afterwards associated with the name of Locke. 'There is, say they, a mutuall paction, and contract bound up, and sworne betwixt the king and the people: Whereupon it followeth, that if the one part of the contract or the Indent bee broken upon the king's side, the people are no longer bound to keepe their part of it, but are thereby freed of their oath.' James denies the existence of any such contract, 'especially containing such a clause irritant as they alledge,' but admits

that, at his coronation, a king 'willingly promiseth to his people' to discharge his office honourably. But God alone can judge whether or not the promise has been broken: 'the cognition and revenge must only appertaine to him,' and he must first 'give sentence upon the king that breaketh.'

'Our play is played out.' It is easy to speak severely of the puppets; but the feeling of the reader will probably be directed rather towards a sympathetic judgement. The faults of King James lay largely on the surface. If he has not deserved the prophecy of his flatterers:—

> The Monarks all to thee shall quit their place:
> Thy endless fame shall all the world fulfill.
> And after thee, none worthier shal be seene,
> To sway the Sword, and gaine the Laurell greene,

yet we may apply to him the often-quoted words that were written of his grandson: 'He had as good a claim to a kind interpretation as most men. It there might be matter for objections, there is not less reason for excuses; the defects laid to his charge, are such as may claim indulgence from mankind. Should nobody throw a stone at his faults but those who are free from them, there would be but a slender shower.'

Notes

1. The works contained in the folio edition had been frequently printed; some of them under various titles. (Cf. The British Museum Catalogue.) Several speeches, delivered after the publication of the folio of 1616, were separately published. They have reference to incidents in the political history of the reign, and scarcely come within our province.

2. For a selection on a somewhat larger scale, see Arber's English Reprints, *James VI. of Scotland and I. of England.* Westminster: A. Constable & Co.

3. The reader will find a few specimens on pp. 61-79.

4. The Scottish Parliament had, after the Reformation, made stringent rules for maintaining the old customs regarding the eating of fish in Lent. These Acts were passed in the interests of the fishing trade, which, as in England, had, since the fifteenth century, contributed largely to the prosperity of the towns on the East Coast.

5. Cf. Sir Walter Scott's description of James's person in *The Fortunes of Nigel*, chap. v.

6. Reginald Scot (1538?-1599) was the author of *The Discoverie of Witchcraft* (1584), in which he advanced views far beyond his age with regard to witchcraft and sorcery. He had adopted, in part,

the enlightened opinions of John Wier (1515-1588), who published, in 1566, a work entitled *De Praestiqiis Demonum.* Cf. Mr. Sidney Lee's article on Scot in the *Dictionary of National Biography.*

7. Bel and the Dragon.

8. Subsequently to the folio edition, King James published two purely theological writings, *A Meditation upon the Lord's Prayer* (1619), and *A Meditation upon St. Matthew* xxvii. 27-29 (1620). After his death, there appeared *Cygnea Cantio or Learned Decisions, and most Prudent and Pious Directions for Students in Divinitie, delivered by our late Soveraigne of Happie Memorie, King James, at Whitehall, a few weekes before his death* (1629). It was edited by Daniel Featly, the well-known controversialist, chaplain to Archbishop Abbot, and is a report of a 'scholastick duel' between the king and Featly.

9. Conrad Vorstius (1569-1622) succeeded Arminius in his Chair in the University of Leyden in 1610.

10. Jacques Davy du Perron, Cardinal (successively Bishop of Evreux, and Archbishop of Sens). The Cardinal's oration was translated into English in 1616. He wrote a reply to King James's *Defence,* but it did not appear in English till 1630, when it was translated by the Viscountess Falkland.

11. Parsons the Jesuit.

12. Being a proper word to express the trew meaning of *Tortus* [original note].

13. A reference to the circumstances of the murder of Rizzio.

14. The Gunpowder Plot and the Perron controversy had driven James to this extreme attitude. At the time of his arrival in England he held quite different language:—'I acknowledge the Romane Church to be our Mother Church, although defiled with some infirmities and corruptions.'—*Speech in Parliament,* March 1603.

15. The words (which occurred in a letter to Lord Mounteagle, warning him not to go to the meeting of Parliament) were:—'For though there be no appearance of any stirre, yet I say, they shall receive a terrible Blow this Parliament, and yet they shall not see who hurts them. This counsell is not to be contemned, because it may doe you good, and can doe you no harme; for the danger is past so soone as you have burnt the Letter.' The last clause was construed by the king to indicate 'the suddaintie and quickenesse of the danger, which should be as quickly performed and at an end as that paper should be of bleasing up in the fire; turning that word of *as soone* to the sense of *as quickly,*' and

this suggested gunpowder.—*Discourse of the Powder Treason.*

16. Samuel viii, 11-18.

Ronald D. S. Jack (essay date autumn 1967)

SOURCE: Jack, Ronald D. S. "James VI and Renaissance Poetic Theory." *English* 16, no. 96 (autumn 1967): 208-11.

[*In the following essay, Jack perceives* Some Reulis and Cautelis to Be Observit and Eschewit in Scottish Poesie *to be a valuable contribution to Renaissance poetic theory.*]

During the Renaissance many critical treatises appeared in Europe. Scholars turned to a more minute study of classical authors and discovered that many of the metrical and theoretical principles underlying classical verse could not be applied to works in the vernacular. As a result it became clear that the critical manuals of Cicero and Quintilian were inadequate for evaluating art written in the vulgar tongue. In Italy, Trissino had suggested that Italian verse worked on a different idea of rhythm than Latin or Greek. For Trissino the Italian innovation was intimately connected with dancing:

> Rithmo e anchora quello, che risulta dal danzare con ragione, e dal sonare, e cantare; il che volgarmente si kiama misura e tempo.[1]

The Pléiade too were concerned with comparisons between classical and vernacular verse. Most of all they were conscious that French could not rival the older tongues in wealth of vocabulary. Thus when Du Bellay argued for the use of the vernacular in composition, it was only after adding the reservation, that 'nostre Langue n'est si copieuse que la Greque ou Latine'.[2] In England Puttenham spoke out for the superiority of modern poetry in having introduced rhyme, while Ascham adduced rules to bring English into close alignment with Latin.[3]

As this idea of vernacular composition lay behind the treatises, it is not surprising that they betray a spirit of nationalism, ranging from the open chauvinism of Vida's *Ars Poetica* to the more muted patriotism of Puttenham's *Arte of English Poesie.* Nearly all the critics are agreed that art has degenerated since antiquity and that the Renaissance will herald the first reversal of this process. But the location of the revival depends on the poet's birthplace. Vida believes the leaders of the vernacular revolution to be the Tuscan poets under Medici patronage:

> Iampridem tamen Ausonios invisere rursus
> Coeperunt Medycum revocatae munere Musae

Thuscorum Medycum, quos tandem protulit aetas
Europae in tantis solamen dulce ruinis.[4]

Ronsard puts his faith in the Pléiade, and Puttenham advances a less vitriolic case for English supremacy.

Renaissance criticism thus had a strongly vernacular and patriotic bias. It is perhaps fitting that the quieter Scottish movement should produce but one contribution to this wealth of critical material, and that a work of less than twenty quarto pages, composed by a teenage king. Yet James VI's *Ane Schort Treatise Conteining some Reulis and Cautelis to be obseruit and eschewit in Scottis Poesie,*[5] shows its author to have been aware of the larger European tradition. Apart from differences in terminology, James approaches poetry in the same way as Vida, Du Bellay, and Puttenham. He too opens by justifying his work in terms of the new problems besetting a writer:

> As for them that wrait of auld, lyke as the tyme is changeit sensyne, sa is the ordour of Poesie changeit. For then they observit not Flowing, nor eschewit not ryming in termes, besydes sindrie uther thingis, quhilk now we observe, and eschew, and dois weil in sa doing.[6]

It was this sense of particular and present need which motivated the major European treatises. Like Vida and Du Bellay, James sees the Renaissance poet as being in a unique and fortuitous position. He can take advantage of all the errors or advances made by earlier poets, and so speak of poetry 'as being come to mannis age and perfectioun'. It was in a similar light that Vida had seen the Tuscan movement, Ronsard and Du Bellay the Pléiade.

The nationalistic bias is reflected in the title of James's essay and expanded upon in the prologue. One of the king's justifications for writing is that among the many critical writers of the period, 'there hes neuer ane of them written in our language'. Nor is Scots to be confounded with English, for 'we differ from thame in sindrie reulis of Poesie'. He is intent on pleading for a Scottish poetic and linguistic autonomy. No language, however similar in structure to another, can be equated with it. This type of argument was already familiar to readers from the first chapter of Du Bellay's *Deffence,* where he advanced his famous account of language evolution. All tongues originate like the plant from a single root, and their diverse developments depend on national character and idiosyncrasy.

The *Reulis* is primarily a technical account of poetry. Like most European critics James is mainly concerned with devising rules for rhyme, rhythm, and stanza formation. This prevalent attitude to poetry resulted from its still being considered a secondary branch of rhetoric. The idea of the close relationship of the seven liberal arts had survived the Medieval period, while rhetoric had gained primary importance for literary men since Il Trapezunzio's *Rhetoricum Libri* of 1435.[7] As a result four of the six books in Trissino's *Poetica* deal with technical problems and only the second of Gascoigne's sixteen rules touches on general poetic theory.[8] In the same way, seven of the eight chapters in the *Reulis* teach the poet his craft by means of arbitrary laws.

From this brief comparison of the *Reulis* with other examples of Renaissance critical theory, it becomes clear that it belongs to the same tradition. It originates from an interest in the vernacular. It shares with many other European manuals the patriotic tone and the view of the sixteenth century as a golden age. It sees poetry as the metrical branch of rhetoric and devotes a large section to metrical problems. With this general similarity established, a more detailed study of the work is necessary. This is especially so as James set up a poetic school at court and encouraged writers like Stewart of Baldynneis, William Fowler, and William Alexander to follow his critical views.

In the discussion on rhyming James puts forward three ideas, continuing the almost mathematically logical approach of the prologue. He forbids identical rhymes, like those used by Chaucer, yet goes even further by not permitting a 'proue'/'reproue' or 'houe'/'behoue' rhyme. At first sight this stricture seems to be only an echo of Du Bellay's rule in the *Deffence*:

> Ces equivoques donq' et ces simples rymez avecques leurs composez, comme un baisser et abaisser, s'ilz ne changent ou augmentent grandement la signification de leurs simples, me soint chassez bien loing.[9]

But Du Bellay, unlike James, lays the stress on a meaning criterion. 'Baisser' and 'abaisser' were synonyms in sixteenth-century French. The Scottish critic is widening the scope of the rule to cover cases in which there is a wide divergence of sense. It would seem that James is no servile imitator.

The tendency of his changes is to a stricter poetics than any hitherto advanced. For example, he insists that, without exception, the rhyme should be carried by the last long syllable in the line, even if this involves rhyming on the antepenultimate. No other critic seems to agree with this viewpoint, and indeed only Puttenham considers the problem at any length. Similarly he argues that only the iamb should be used in Scottish verse. This decision he justifies by ear, and it seems strange to ignore all the other possible types on the strength of so flimsy an argument, especially when Puttenham had advocated the use of all the ancient feet.

Despite strange rules like these, James is often enlightening. In no case is this more so than when he treats decorum, one of the main topics in Elizabethan criticism.[10] It had been fully sketched out by Puttenham in book 3, chapter 6, of the *Arte of English Poesie*. He defined the three styles as high, mean, and base, as well as introducing a series of topics to fit each level. The high style was to be used in hymning the gods or princes; the mean style for matters concerning lawyers, gentlemen, and merchants, and the base for the 'doings of the common artificer'. This social division James at first ignores. Instead he confines himself to those aspects omitted by Puttenham or falsely treated in his account. On the subject of tragedy he openly disagrees with the English critic, who had assigned it to the high style. James advocates the use of 'lamentable wordis with some heich', thus extending the principle to mood and introducing a more complex system of graded levels of diction. The effect of this is to allow a freer, less rigid application of the device, enabling it to enrich rather than restrict the free flowing of verse.

Secondly, he extends the principle from the level of style to that of argument. If the lover is to use passionate but unaffected words, his reasoning must also proceed from passion. If country people are to speak colloquially, their argument must fit this style. In short, decorum is not only a linguistic but a social phenomenon. James takes up Puttenham's social division from a different angle, expanding the implications of his ideas, to show that the merchant will not only use the mean style but also arguments fitted to his mental capacity and social position. The king breaks down the artificial and harmful rigidity of the three stylistic levels set out by Puttenham. He also extends their relevance from the linguistic to the rhetorical; from style to argument.

James has thus successfully dealt with the principle of decorum, yet not been content merely to accept the ideas laid down by his predecessors. His views on imitation are equally interesting. He ignores the first interpretation of this topic—art as an imitation of Nature, and instead concentrates on imitation of classical authors. In this context most early critics had based their theory on some modification of Petrarch's statement in the *Familiares*. He had argued for imitation alongside ingenuity, by seizing on Seneca's image of the bee. The modern poet steals from classical models as the bee steals from flowers:

> Apes in inventionibus imitandas, quae flores, non quales acceperint, referunt, sed ceras ac mella, mirifica quadam permixtione, conficiunt.[11]

Just as both bee and flower profited from their interrelationship, so imitation of the classics benefited the vernacular. Just as the bee did not retain the pollen in its original form but converted it into honey, so the good imitator transformed his model into something new.

James is not of this opinion. Beginning with invention as one of the chief poetic virtues, he says that this qual-

ity is best exercised 'if ye inuent your awin subiect, yourself', and don't 'compose of sene subiectis'. Imitation, it is implied, hinders the free action of this prime poetic virtue. This is especially so in translation, where 'ye are bound as to a staik, to follow that buikis phrasis, quhilk ye translate'. In his discussion of both imitation and translation James's approach is valuable, for he is thinking of lesser writers. Other critics tended to deal with first-rank poets, in whose hands imitation might have the beneficial effects suggested by Petrarch's image. But minor writers, following in their footsteps, adopted a more literal approach, which produced poetry sounding like the first awkward steps in French or Latin translation.

A salient feature of the king's poetic theory has by now come to light. He simplifies previous accounts by concentrating on technical rather than metaphysical aspects. By refusing to discuss imitation in Neo-Platonic or Aristotelian terms he is forced into a further simplification, this time with regard to invention. This concept was very important for the sixteenth-century critic, who saw it as closely connected with the theory of art as imitative of nature. By assigning art's terms of reference to the realm of the 'probable' rather than the 'actual', it was an easy matter to reconcile imitation with invention. The poet was not restricted to a reproduction of the real world as sensuously perceived but could imitate the potential values by means of his invention. But James had ignored imitation in this sense. In the same way he views invention narrowly, equating it with originality, the antithesis of literary imitation:

> Bot sen Inuention, is ane of the cheif vertewis in a Poete, it is best that ye inuent your awin subiect, your self, and not to compose of sene subiectis.[12]

This closely resembles Gascoigne's approach. He also saw invention as 'the first and most necessarie poynt' in poetic craftsmanship and asserted that it was opposed to imitation.

In fact Gascoigne and James are fulfilling a different function from Puttenham and Du Bellay. In modern terms, they are producing a textbook on elementary versifying rather than a full poetic theory. That is why they put a heavier emphasis on technical elements than usual. That is why they ignore the far-reaching metaphysical speculations on art's function in order to confine themselves to more practical problems of the poet's craft. They are not writing for the master poets but for the apprentices. As a result no discussion of the imagination is necessary, for it is a quality which is inherited, not imparted by 'reulis'. Imitation and invention are accepted as tools and their value assessed, but wider questions of the relationship of finished artefact to the world at large are outside the scope of the discussion.

Only once does James move outside the limits of a purely technical treatise. This is when he discusses the

Horatian theory of a 'divine fury' animating great artists. Vida, Du Bellay, Ronsard, and Puttenham all stressed the poet's divinity, but the clearest statement is in Thomas Lodge's *Defence of Poetry,* where he uses it as a means of distinguishing the poet from the orator:

> It is a pretye sentence, yet not so pretty as pithy, Poeta nascitur, Orator fit: as who should say, Poetrye commeth from above, from a heavenly seate of a glorious God, unto an excellent creature man; an Orator is but made by exercise.[13]

Such a theory is clearly out of place in a technical treatise and Gascoigne ignores it. But James not only mentions it, he opposes the mainstream of critical thought resolutely. For him, the poet must avoid 'materis of commoun weill' as 'they are to graue materis for a Poet to mell in'. Uncharacteristically he is departing from purely literary criteria and considering the poet's function in general terms. Such a departure must be accounted for.

The solution probably lies in his unique social position and his belief in divine right. In the **Basilicon Doron** he stressed that only the king is inspired by God. Yet he was aware that Ronsard had mocked Henri II's claim to near-deity, while Vida in the *Poetica* had placed the poet above earthly kings:

> Ultores sperate Deos, sub numine quorum
> Semper vita fuit vatum defensa piorum.
> Illi omnes sibi fortunas posuere volentes
> Sub pedibus, regumque et opes, et sceptra superba
> Ingenti vincunt animo, ac mortalia rident.[14]

James therefore ignores the technical nature of his treatise on this isolated occasion to warn Scottish poets that interference in court matters will be frowned upon.

A more detailed study of the **Reulis** thus reveals that its broad similarity to other critical treatises goes along with a number of hidden differences. The most important of these is its stature as a technical handbook of poetry on the model of Gascoigne's *Notes of Instruction.* As a consequence, the emphasis on rhetoric, versification, and metre is even more pronounced than in the *Deffence* or the *Arte of English Poesie.* Most of the major theoretical ideas are mentioned but their scope of reference is severely limited, as questions of poetic imitation of Nature or the relationship between invention and imagination would be irrelevant in the given context. On the other hand, the young king shows good sense in realizing that his youth and lack of poetic experience render him a poor rival to Du Bellay and Ascham on their own ground. If the **Reulis** are seen as a guide to versification written by a young man and not as a national poetic manifesto, they do constitute a valuable contribution to Renaissance learning.

Notes

1. Giovan Trissino, *La Poetica* (Vicenza, 1529), p. xii r.

2. J. du Bellay, *La Deffence et Illustration de la Langue Francoyse,* ed. Henri Chamard (Paris, 1948), p. 22.

3. George Puttenham, *The Arte of English Poesie,* ed. Arber, English Reprints, vii (London, 1869), p. 22. Roger Ascham, *The Scholemaster,* ed. W. A. Wright (Cambridge, 1904), p. 260.

4. *Ars Poetica Marci Hieronymi Vidae Cremonensis* (Lugduni apud Gryphium, 1536), p. 10.

5. James VI, 'Essayes of a Prentise in the Divine Arte of Poesie', in *The Poems of King James VI of Scotland,* ed. J. Craigie, Scottish Text Society, 2 vols. (Edinburgh and London, 1948), i. 66-83.

6. Ibid., p. 67.

7. See E. R. Curtius, *European Literature and the Latin Middle Ages,* tr. W. R. Trask (London, 1953), pp. 36-79.

8. George Gascoigne, 'Certayne Notes of Instruction', in *Elizabethan Critical Essays,* ed. G. Gregory Smith, 2nd ed., 2 vols. (London, 1950), vol. 1.

9. Du Bellay, *La Deffence,* p. 146.

10. See Rosemund Tuve, *Elizabethan and Metaphysical Imagery,* for a modern discussion of decorum.

11. The comparison between the author and the bee is a commonplace in classical literature. See Seneca, *Epist.* 84; Pindar, *Pyth.* X; Plato, *Ion.*

12. James VI, *Essayes,* p. 79.

13. Thomas Lodge, 'Defence of Poetry', in *Elizabethan Critical Essays,* ed. G. Gregory Smith (Oxford, 1950), i. 71.

14. Vida, *Ars Poetica,* p. 21.

Emrys Jones (essay date 1968)

SOURCE: Jones, Emrys. "*Othello, Lepanto,* and the Cyprus Wars." *Shakespeare Survey* 21 (1968): 47-52.

[In the following essay, Jones explores the link between Lepanto *and Shakespeare's* Othello.]

In 1604 the theatrical company for which Shakespeare wrote and acted was taken under the patronage of the new king; and it is becoming increasingly clear that at least two of the plays written by Shakespeare during the early years of the new reign were probably intended to reflect James I's opinions and tastes.[1] *Othello,* acted at court on 1 November 1604, seems never to have been considered in relation to Shakespeare's new patron. I want to suggest that, like *Measure for Measure,*

Macbeth, and possibly other plays written during these years, *Othello* was also designed as a work appropriate to the chief dramatist of the King's Men.

James's various interests as a man, theological, political and scholarly, as well as his multiple roles as king—in particular his peculiar historical position as the first *British* king of modern times—provided panegyrists with a number of possible themes. He could be celebrated for his wisdom and learning, his piety, and his love of peace, as well as for the British unity which his accession to the English throne had achieved. Allusions could be made to his views on the theory of kingship and on witchcraft, and his own published works, **Basilikon Doron** and **Daemonologie,** could be searched for usable material. In poems, masques and processions he could be figured as David, Solomon, Augustus or Brute. There was also one other aspect of James's public personality which was eagerly taken up at the time of his accession: he could be acclaimed by poets as one of themselves. For while still a young man in Scotland James had not only written but published poems, so that along with his other roles he could be celebrated as a poet-king—and poets in particular were naturally anxious that no one should forget the fact. A sonnet by Drayton addressed to James opens, 'Of Kings a Poet, and the Poets King', and an epigram of Jonson's calls him 'best of Poets'. Of course other English monarchs of recent date had also written poetry: Henry VIII and Elizabeth I had done so. But their poems had been no more than brief lyrics, while James's poetical works were more ambitious. Among the poems and translations which he had published the best known was his original heroic poem **Lepanto.** It is this poem, I suggest, which provides the link between *Othello* and the king.

Lepanto was first published in James's second volume of verse, **His Maiesties Poeticall Exercises at Vacant Houres**; the earliest known edition is dated 1591. It was written several years before, probably in 1585, when James was nineteen.[2] The poem is hardly of much interest in its own right; yet whatever its poetic deficiencies it had at least the merit of a striking subject: an heroic action taken from recent history and of large political importance.[3] James's poem celebrates the great naval victory over the Turks won by the confederate Catholic states. The battle of Lepanto was the culmination of a military episode which had begun in 1570 with the Turkish attack on Cyprus, at that time one of Venice's richest territorial possessions. Spain and Rome, who were in a confederation with Venice, came to her assistance, and in the autumn of 1571 the combined Christian fleet of Spain, Venice and the Papacy set sail from Messina under the command of Don John of Austria, the illegitimate half-brother of Philip II. Battle was joined with the Turkish fleet at the gulf of Lepanto (near Corinth) on Sunday 7 October 1571. There were

heavy losses on both sides, but the greater part of the entire Turkish fleet was destroyed or captured. Lepanto was not only an overwhelming victory for the Christians: it was also the only great Christian victory over the Turks in the sixteenth century. It was usually interpreted as a victory for Christendom as a whole, Protestant as well as Catholic, and so, although the king of a fiercely Protestant nation, James could take it as a suitable theme for his Christian muse.

James's **Lepanto** quickly became famous. Poets and scholars in England paid it tribute; Du Bartas translated it into French. In his edition of James's poems James Craigie collects a number (27 in all; the collection is not exhaustive) of contemporary references to James as a poet; among the writers are Sidney, Gabriel Harvey, Francis Meres, Sir William Alexander, and Ben Jonson.[4] Some of them refer explicitly to **Lepanto**: e.g. Gabriel Harvey, who in *Pierces Supererogation* (1593) declares of James that he

> hath not only translated the two diuine Poems of Salustius du Bartas, his heavenly Vrany, and his hellish Furies, but hath readd a most valorous Martial Lecture unto himselfe in his own victorious Lepanto, a short, but heroicall, worke, in meeter, but royal meeter, fitt for a Dauids harpe—Lepanto, first the glory of Christendome against the Turke, and now the garland of a soueraine crowne.

As might have been expected, there was a sharp revival of interest in James's poem—as there was in all his published works—at the time of his accession to the English throne. A separate edition of **Lepanto** was printed in London in 1603; the poem was called on the title-page **His Maiesties Lepanto, or, Heroicall Song. Naupactiados,** a Latin version of **Lepanto** by Thomas Moray, appeared in 1604. In *Sorrows Joy* (1603), a collection of elegies for Elizabeth I and panegyrics to James, a poem by 'T. B.' asks what poet is worthy to praise the King and answers, predictably enough:

> Lo then the man which the *Lepanto* writ;
> Or he, or els on earth is no man fitt.[5]

And in the same year, 1603, Richard Knolles dedicated his *Generall Historie of the Turkes* to James, and in his dedicatory epistle argued the aptness of the dedication: 'and the rather, for that your Maiestie hath not disdained in your **Lepanto,** or *Heroicall Song,* with your learned Muse to adorne and set forth the greatest and most glorious victorie that ever was by anie the Christian confederate princes obtained against these the *Othoman* Kings or Emperors.'

There is further evidence that James was especially famed as a poet for **Lepanto,** and also that the poem was made to contribute to the coronation celebrations of 1604—possibly the year in which *Othello* was composed. In March 1604 the King made a coronation progress through the City of London. (The ceremony was described by Dekker in his tract, *The Magnificent Entertainment given to King James.*) The *Italians Pageant,* one of several before which the King and his party were required to pause, consisted of a great triumphal arch inset with illustrative panels.[6] The main panel on the front side of the arch depicted James's main claim to the English throne by showing James receiving the sceptre from Henry VII. On the reverse side of the arch James's *poetic* achievements were the subject:

> The middle great Square, that was aduanc'd over the *Freeze* of the Gate, held *Apollo,* with all his Ensignes and properties belonging vnto him, as a *Sphere, Bookes,* a *Caducaeus,* an *Octoedron,* with other *Geometricall* Bodies, and a Harpe in his left hand: his right hand with a golden Wand in it, poynting to the battel of *Lepanto* fought by the Turks, (of which his Maiestie hath written a Poem) and to doe him Honour, *Apollo* himselfe doth here seeme to take vpon himself to describe . . .

Othello was probably the first of Shakespeare's tragedies to be written for the King's Men, but it has apparently never been related to this setting of allusive compliment. That this is so may be largely due to the peculiarly private or even domestic nature of its action. Among Shakespeare's mature tragedies *Othello* is exceptional in taking its main plot not from history but fiction; and its apparent confinement to the private and domestic sphere sets it apart from *Hamlet, King Lear, Macbeth* and the Roman tragedies. Indeed its difference from them has seemed so marked that it has often been described as Shakespeare's closest approach to domestic tragedy, a *genre* concerned not with the crimes and misfortunes of heads of state but with the essentially private, and so unhistorical, lives of citizens. However, the opening scenes of the play present a world which could not be at all adequately described in private and domestic terms. These scenes evoke a world of public events: affairs of state, war, and military heroism. This is the world in which history is made; and it is accordingly in this part of the play—the Venetian part—that *Othello* comes closest to the public and historical concerns of the other tragedies.

The early Venetian scenes are usually regarded as a prelude to the main Cyprus action. The conflict of Othello and Brabantio can be seen as foreshadowing the much more difficult, because concealed and oblique, conflict of Othello and Iago, just as the trial scene in I, iii can be seen as anticipating the passing of judgement that takes place in the last scene of all. But otherwise the political events of which we hear in Act I are usually regarded as no more than dramatic machinery for effecting the move of the main characters from Venice to Cyprus (which from one point of view they are) and are seldom scrutinized for their own sakes. The modern

playgoer probably never spares a thought for the 'Cyprus wars' mentioned early on by Iago or for the manoeuvres of the Turkish naval forces which so much exercise the Duke and Senators of Venice. The question arises whether Shakespeare had any further intentions in including this political material.

Shakespeare has so arranged it that the night of Othello's elopement with Desdemona is also the night when the news arrives in Venice of the movements of the warlike Turkish fleet. The Venetian Senate is alarmed for the safety of Cyprus, and accordingly Othello is sent to Cyprus to supervise its defences. Now although these events are in themselves fictitious (since Othello is a fictitious character), they could hardly have failed to arouse the memory of anyone in Shakespeare's audience who was at all aware of recent European history. For if we were to seek to give an approximate date to the action of *Othello,* we should be driven to the crucial years round about 1570, the year of the Turkish attack on Cyprus. The Turks had landed in Cyprus in 1570; one of the two chief Cypriot towns, Nicosia, soon fell; the other, Famagusta, underwent a long siege. It was these events which led to the Lepanto engagement. But the victory of Lepanto did not in fact restore Cyprus to Venice. Famagusta fell to the Turks on 1 August 1571, which left them in possession of the island. At the time of *Othello*'s composition therefore (*c.* 1602-4), Cyprus had been in Turkish hands for over thirty years.

The connexion of the action of *Othello* with these events, at least in approximate date, is allowed by the *Variorum* editor. He quotes Isaac Reed's note on the play:

> Selymus the Second formed his design against Cyprus in 1569, and took it in 1571. This was the only attempt the Turks ever made upon that island after it came into the hands of the Venetians (which was in the year 1473), wherefore the time of the play must fall in with some part of that interval.[7]

In the story by Cinthio, which is Shakespeare's only known source of *Othello,* there is no mention of a Turkish threat to Cyprus. Cinthio's story was after all written before the Turkish attack; the *novelle* were first published in 1565. So the story of Cinthio's Moor takes place in time of peace. If Cinthio was in fact his only narrative source, then Shakespeare has deliberately brought the action closer to the events of 1570-1. In Act I everything seems—or perhaps would have seemed to Shakespeare's first audience—to be moving towards the naval action which culminated in Lepanto and which was fought over the same issue as that presented in the play: the possession of Cyprus. Thus Iago says of Othello in the opening scene:

> . . . he's embark'd,

> With such loud reason to the Cyprus wars,
> Which even now stand in act . . .

—a remark which seems, among other things, to be a direct pointer ('Which even now stand in act') to the approximate date of the action. And in the senate scene the Duke tells Othello:

> The Turk with a most mighty preparation makes for Cyprus.

Given the fame of the battle of Lepanto, Shakespeare's audience could not have been blamed if they had expected the play to run along lines much more true to history than the play they were actually given. But what happens is that as soon as the main characters are arrived in Cyprus, the action moves into an entirely fictive realm, and the military background involving Venice and Cyprus, Christian and Turk, is allowed to recede from the attention. The military and naval clash which we seem led to expect never takes place. For instead of a battle between Christians and Turks Shakespeare substitutes a storm which disperses the Turkish fleet. An anonymous Gentleman announces:

> News, lads! Our wars are done.
> The desperate tempest hath so bang'd the Turk
> That their designment halts . . .

A little later, on his entry, Othello dismisses all thought of the Turks in a single line:

> News, friends: our wars are done; the Turks are drown'd.

And finally the war theme is allowed to die with the Herald's proclamation:

> It is Othello's pleasure, our noble and valiant general, that, upon certain tidings now arriv'd, importing the mere perdition of the Turkish fleet, every man put himself into triumph . . .

The fate of the Turks is left purposely vague, and apart from one or two phrases which help sustain the atmosphere of an exposed garrison town ('this warlike isle', 'what! in a town of war, / Yet wild, the people's hearts brimful of fear'), the Turkish threat to Cyprus is allowed to be forgotten.

The connexion of *Othello* with the 'Cyprus wars' is not only of a general kind; there are one or two precise details which suggest that Shakespeare had the events of 1570-1 in mind. At the beginning of I, iii the Duke and Senators are comparing the different reports of the numbers of the Turkish galleys and their movements:

1 SENATOR:

> My letters say a hundred and seven galleys.

DUKE:

> And mine a hundred and forty.

2 SENATOR:

>   And mine two hundred . . .

In his *Generall Historie of the Turkes* Knolles says of the Turks at the time of their first landing in Cyprus: 'The whole fleet at that time consisted of two hundred gallies.' And later, after Lepanto, he notes: 'Of the enemies gallies were taken an hundred threescore and one, fortie sunk or burnt.'[8] The Turks had two hundred galleys; and this is the number which Shakespeare keeps last, in a position of emphasis or climax, for his Second Senator. This may be a coincidence, but at any rate the size of the Turkish fleet in *Othello* and at Lepanto was roughly the same. A little later in the same scene a messenger reports news of the Turkish movements:

> The Ottomites, reverend and gracious,
> Steering with due course toward the isle of Rhodes,
> Have there injointed them with an after fleet.

1 SENATOR:

> Ay, so I thought. How many, as you guess?

MESSENGER:

> Of thirty sail; and now do they restem
> Their backward course, bearing with frank appearance
> Their purposes toward Cyprus.

These movements correspond exactly to Knolles's account of the Turkish invasion plans:[9] 'For *Mustapha*, author of that expedition . . . had before appointed *Piall Bassa* at a time prefixed, to meet him at the RHODES, and that he that came first should tarrie for the other, that so they might together sayle into CYPRUS.' Knolles goes on to say that Mustapha Bassa 'together with *Haly Bassa* and the rest of the fleet, departed from CONSTANTINOPLE the six and twentieth of May, and at the RHODES met with Piall as he had before appointed. The whole fleet at that time consisted of two hundred gallies . . .'[10]

Shakespeare could of course have taken for granted a general interest in the Ottoman empire which is very remote from what a modern audience brings to *Othello*. The Turkish menace to Christendom was a fact of Shakespeare's entire lifetime; it remained of pressing concern to the West until late in the seventeenth century. This fact may of itself have given *Othello*'s Cypriot setting an ominous character which is lost on us. As Knolles put it: 'The Venetians had ever had great care of the island of CYPRUS, as lying far from them, in the middest of the sworne enemies of the Christian religion, and had therefore oftentimes determined to have fortified the same.'¹¹ So Cyprus could be seen as an out-post of Christendom, rich, vulnerable, and perilously situated: a highly suitable setting for a play showing Christian behaviour under stress. After Cassio's drunken brawl has been put down, Othello is to say:

> Are we turn'd Turks, and to ourselves do that
> Which Heaven hath forbid the Ottomites?
> For Christian shame, put by this barbarous brawl.

His words, skilfully placed in the scene, are emphatic and ironic. For if Shakespeare's fictitious action can be said to belong to the years 1570-1, those were histori-cally the very years when Cyprus underwent a violent conversion from Christian to Turkish rule—the years when it literally 'turned Turk'.

However, over thirty years had elapsed between Lepanto and the writing of *Othello*. The battle in itself was no longer a matter of topical interest as it had been (for example) to Gascoigne when, in his Mountacute Masque of 1572, he had incorporated a dramatic eye-witness account of the sea-fight. But in the interval be-tween 1571 and 1604 an event had taken place which had had the effect of reviving interest in the battle, at least indirectly. The event was, as I have argued, the ac-cession of James, whose heroic poem was promptly re-printed in 1603.

It has to be admitted that Shakespeare seems to have no direct indebtedness to James. What is relevant here is Lepanto as an historical event rather than any specific reminiscences of the poem.¹² Even so the general affini-ties between *Othello* and **Lepanto** are sufficiently strik-ing. Both are concerned, **Lepanto** centrally, *Othello* pe-ripherally, with the 'Cyprus wars', which for Shakespeare's contemporaries could only have pointed to the events of 1570-1. And a major topic of the poem—the conflict of Christian and Turk—is present in *Othello* as it is in no other of Shakespeare's plays. Knolles's dedication of his *Generall Historie of the Turkes* has already been quoted; it can surely be as-sumed that Shakespeare and his fellow actors would have been quite as adroit in publicly saluting their new patron.

Notes

1. See Henry N. Paul, *The Royal Play of 'Macbeth'* (New York, 1950); David L. Stevenson, 'The Role of James I in Shakespeare's *Measure for Measure*', *E.L.H.* XXVI (1959), 188-208; Josephine Waters Bennett, '*Measure for Measure' as Royal Enter-tainment* (New York and London, 1966); I have argued the case for *Cymbeline* in *E.C.* XI (1961), 84-99.

2. *The Poems of James VI of Scotland* (vol. 1), ed. James Craigie (Edinburgh and London, 1955), p. xlviii.

3. The subject inspired several Venetian painters. Paolo Veronese's *Battle of Lepanto* is reproduced in Samuel C. Chew's *The Crescent and the Rose. Islam and England during the Renaissance* (New York, 1937). Chew quotes (p. 126) Jonson's *Cynthia's Revels,* IV, i, 48 ('He looks like a Vene-tian trumpeter in the battle of Lepanto in the gal-lery yonder') as evidence for the existence of paintings on the subject in England.

4. Craigie, *op. cit.* Appendix A.

5. Quoted by Craigie, *op. cit.* p. 276.

6. *The Dramatic Works of Thomas Dekker,* ed. Fredson Bowers (Cambridge, 1955), II, 262-5.

7. *Othello,* ed. H. H. Furness (Philadelphia, 1886), 357. The editor wrongly attributes the comment to Henry Reed, author of *Lectures on English His-tory and Tragic Poetry* (1856). It should be attrib-uted to Isaac Reed; it occurs in his prefatory note to *Othello* in his edition of Shakespeare (1799-1802).

8. Knolles (2nd edn. 1610), pp. 846, 863.

9. This was noted by Isaac Reed.

10. Knolles, *op. cit.* p. 846.

11. Knolles, *op. cit.* p. 847.

12. In '*Othello' as the Tragedy of Italy* (1924), an at-tempt at a cryptic reading of the play, Lilian Winstanley wrongly states (p. 21) that the battle of Lepanto is directly referred to. In this context of the Christian and Turkish conflict in *Othello,* see F. N. Lees's article, 'Othello's Name' (*N.Q.,* n.s., VIII (1961), 139-41), for the suggestion that Shakespeare adapted Othello's name from that of Othoman, the founder of the Ottoman (or Othoman) empire. Shakespeare could have found an account of Othoman in Knolles.

G. P. V. Akrigg (essay date winter 1975)

SOURCE: Akrigg, G. P. V. "The Literary Achievement of King James I." *University of Toronto Quarterly* 44, no. 2 (winter 1975): 115-29.

[*In the following essay, Akrigg assesses King James's achievement as an author, translator, critic, and patron of the arts.*]

Speaking at the University of Cambridge a good many years ago, Professor W. P. Ker assured his audience that King James I had 'abilities which would have entitled him to be a Professor of Literature.'¹ Of James's peda-gogical bent there has never been any doubt—he has been described as a Scottish dominie at heart. Characteristically, King James, daily visiting his young favourite, Robert Ker, while the young man was recovering from a leg injury, used the opportunity to teach him Latin. But a desire to teach is not enough to create a professor. There is a further consideration: the man must be a publishing scholar. With this in mind, let us consider the bibliography of King James.

His *Essayes of a Prentise* in 1584 and *Poetical Exercises* in 1591, being mere verse, would be excluded by some austere academics from any professorial bibliography. But His Majesty had more substantial publications. When not yet twenty he wrote his formidable *Paraphrase on Revelations,* an admirably documented piece of scholarship. In 1597 he published his *Daemonologie,* and in 1598 his *True Law of Free Monarchies.* In 1599 he wrote his *Basilikon Doron.* In 1604 he published his *Counterblast to Tobacco,* and in 1606 his *Apologie for the Oath of Allegiance.* In 1609 King James published, both in English and in his own Latin translation, his *Praemonition to all Christian Monarches.* In 1612 he composed in French his weighty *Declaration against Vorstius* and in 1615, also in French, his *Defence of the Rights of Kings.* He also wrote a number of lesser pieces. On the whole, this must be accepted as quite an impressive record, especially since, throughout this period, King James was carrying a very considerable administrative load. Moreover, we may note that King James was not only a publishing scholar himself but a cause of publication in other men. He deserves credit for setting the bishops and professors of theology to work on the King James Bible, and he actively encouraged such younger writers as John Donne and Ben Jonson.

The purpose of this present essay is to assess the literary achievement of King James himself as a practising man of letters. It may, however, be germane first to take a glance at the family from which he sprang. It is a commonplace of British history that, though the Stuarts were on the whole unsatisfactory politically, where the arts are concerned they were the most gifted royal family ever to possess the throne. Certainly if literary taste and talent are heritable (and a fair bit of evidence suggests that they may be), James might reasonably have been expected to show a flair for literature. In his realm of Scotland, our King was James VI and his Stuart ancestor there, James I, author of *The Kingis Quair,* was one of the really major Scottish poets. But there is no need to reach that far back for family literary antecedents. James's own mother, Mary Queen of Scots, according to Brantôme, delighted in poets and poetry. She wrote poems, in French, herself; and Ronsard, a particular friend of hers, paid tribute to her lines. We are told that King James had in his possession, and 'esteemed as a most precious jewell,' a manuscript of his mother's verses on 'The Institution of a Prince,' written in her own hand and bound in a cover decorated with her own meticulous needlework. On his father's side also James came of a literary line. Contemptible as the weak and vicious Lord Darnley may have been as a person, he was the author of poems which Lady Antonia Fraser has recently characterized as 'pleasant.' Darnley's mother, the Countess of Lennox, was, like her daughter-in-law, Queen Mary, a poetess. All in all we may say that if genes have anything to do with the matter, James was made for some sort of a career in literature.

James Stuart became King of Scotland at the age of one year. When he advanced into his teens, he gathered about him a court circle of poets, 'The Castalians.'[2] Chief among them was Alexander Montgomery, saluted by James as 'master of our art.' Montgomery almost certainly helped the young king with the revision of his own verses. Others in the group were Alexander Hume, John Stewart, William Fowler (to whom James assigned the translating of Petrarch's *Trionfi*), and Robert Hudson, whom he set translating the *Judith* of Du Bartas. Du Bartas was held in very high regard by James, and in 1587 he visited Scotland at the royal invitation. The creation of this literary circle was the more remarkable because at this time there was hardly one of the rough Scots lords who could be regarded as a patron of literature. The subjects assigned for translation by members of the King's circle are significant. As Professor Craigie has noted, James was for a while bringing Scottish poetry 'back into the main stream of European Literature.'[3] King James's own library, by the way, contained three books in French for every one in English. At times, however, a homely Scots flavour marks 'The Castalians.' One of James's own poems bears the thoroughly Burnsian title 'An admonition to the Master poet to be warr of great bragging hereafter, lest he not onlie slander himselfe; bot also the whole professours of the art.' In consequence of his interest in poetry and his poets, James wrote *Ane Schort Treatise, Conteining Some Reulis and Cautelis to be Observit and Eschewit in Scottis Poesie.* Banal and obvious though most of its declarations are, this little work is in fact the first critical treatise to be written on Scottish poetry. The *Short Treatise* was printed in 1584 as part of the King's first volume of verse, which he published under the modest title of *The Essayes of a Prentise, in the Divine Art of Poesie.*

With mention of the *Essayes* we come directly to appraisal of James as an author. In this matter a notorious split verdict has been delivered over the centuries. During the King's own lifetime nobody, either in Britain or on the Continent, seems to have regarded James's writings with anything less than respect—if we except Henri IV, who felt that it was beneath the dignity of a king to be an author. James's troubles began later, in the eighteenth century, when his political views became reprehensible. The real damage was done by Alexander Pope in a speech which he provided for the Goddess Dullness in *The Dunciad*:

> 'Oh' (cry'd the Goddess) 'for some pedant Reign!
> Some gentle JAMES to bless the land again;
> To stick the Doctor's Chair into the Throne,
> Give law to Words, or war with Words alone,
> Senates and Courts with Greek and Latin rule,
> And turn the Council to a Grammar School!'

[IV:175-80]

Although Pope made not the slightest reference to James's abundant works in English, he had effectively set the note for subsequent literary criticism: as an author King James was a dull pedant. This view has persisted right into our own day. *The Concise Cambridge History of English Literature* speaks contemptuously of 'the jejuneness and insipidity which characterize the literary efforts of the royal pedant.'[4]

A contrary view had been expressed, however, as early as 1816 by Isaac Disraeli who, in his 'Inquiry into the Literary and Political Characters of James the First' quietly observed:

> . . . James the First was a literary monarch at one of the great eras of English literature, and his contemporaries were far from suspecting that his talents were inconsiderable, even among those who had their reasons not to like him. The degradation which his literary character has suffered has been inflicted by more recent hands; and it may startle the last echoer of Pope's "Pedant-reign" to hear that more wit and wisdom have been recorded of James the First than of any one of our sovereigns.[5]

In our own century James has found defenders, not only in Dr Craigie, the editor of his collected poetry, but in Caroline Bingham, who has found James's works 'pungently readable'[6] and, more notably, in C. J. Sisson, who after observing that 'the writings of James the Sixth and First are of the highest importance and of great variety' sardonically added 'unfortunately they are very seldom read.' Speaking subsequently of James's works, Sisson remarks on 'the invincible freshness and vividness that is his most notable characteristic.'[7]

Caught between such wildly varying opinions, we are left to reach our own conclusions about King James as an author. Since he began as a poet, and wrote most of his poetry during his early years, though he intermittently returned to poetic authorship in later life, we may well begin with some consideration of James as a poet. Right at the outset we encounter a significant fact: the two volumes of poetry which James published in early life do not contain much of the best of his poetry. For that we had to wait for Professor A. F. Westcott's *New Poems by James I* in 1911, and Dr Craigie's second volume of his definitive edition of James's poetry, published in 1958. These works seem to have been largely ignored by literary historians, who keep passing on verdicts based on the poems published in 1584 and 1591. Clearly any just appraisal must take into account the entire corpus of the King's poetry.

Making survey of that entire corpus, one finds that, as a poet, King James was quite remarkably uneven. Despite his own warning against making translation provide the substance for one's poems, in his early years he spent far too much time in mechanical uninspired translations of the Psalms and of his admired Du Bartas. Only very occasionally do we have a vivid phrase. One remembers his description of Hunger from Du Bartas's *Furies*:

> Lo, Hunger comes at ones,
> Her blackened skin is pierced with
> The sharpe points of her bones.[8]

Still, by and large, the King's translations are poor stuff, and it would be folly to claim any real merit for them.

King James did considerably better when being original. Surely a kind word is merited by the earliest surviving piece of original verse by our royal author, written when he was fifteen:

> Since thought is free, think what thou will
> O troubled heart to ease thy pain.
> Thought unrevealed can do no ill.
> But words passed out comes not again,
>   Be careful aye for to invent
>   The way to get thy own intent.[9]

So runs the first stanza of the poem by the boy king in which he reveals already the political shrewdness which would permit him to master his turbulent Scottish lords. At about the time of the writing of this poem, Queen Elizabeth, shocked at finding herself out-manoeuvred by young James exclaimed, 'That false Scotch urchin! What can be expected from the double dealing of such an urchin as this!'[10]

In another early poem, **'Phoenix,'** James laments the forced banishment of his dazzling French kinsman and favourite, Esme, Duke of Lennox. He sees Lennox as the resplendent Phoenix who has made her home in Scotland:

> . . . this country cold,
> Which naught but hills and darkness aye does bear.

Now, attacked by Envy and Malice, the Phoenix has flown back to France:

> Where she was bred, where storms doth never blow,
> Nor bitter blasts, nor winter snows, nor rain,
> But summer still.[11]

A special place among these early poems must be reserved for James's poem on the Battle of Lepanto. Translated by Du Bartas, it established for the King his poetic reputation upon the Continent.

James could always turn out a competent, adroit sonnet. Typical is one which he addressed to his bride, Anne of Denmark, which begins with mention of his dangerous voyage from Scotland to wed her:

> As on the wings of your enchanting fame
> I was transported o'er the stormy seas,
> Which could not quench that restless burning flame
> Which only ye by sympathy did mease [assuage];
> So can I troubled be with no disease
> But ye my only mediciner remains,
> And easily whenever that ye please
> May salve my sores and mitigate my pains.
> Your smiling is an antidote againes [against]
> The melancholy that oppresseth me,
> And when a raging wrath into me reigns
> Your loving looks may make me calm to be.
>   How oft you see me have an heavy heart
>   Remember then, sweet doctor, on your art.[12]

Many years later, after Anne's death in 1619, he wrote verses which one finds preserved in many of the commonplace books of the period:

> Thee to invite, the great God sent a star,
> Whose friends and nearest kin good princes are,
> For though they run the race of men and die,
> Death seems but to refine their majesty.
> So did the Queen her court to Heaven remove
> And left of earth to be enthroned above.
> Then she is gone not dead, no good prince dies
> But only with the day-star shuts their eyes.[13]

Poetically competent, though politically distasteful by the eighteenth century, is the sonnet in which James instructed his heir in the duties of kingship:

> God gives not kings the style of gods in vain,
> For on his throne his sceptre do they sway:
> For as their subjects ought them to obey,
> So kings should fear and serve their God again.
> If, then, ye would enjoy a happy reign,
> Observe the statutes of your heavenly King
> And from his Law make all your laws to spring,
> Since his lieutenant here ye should remain.
> Reward the just. Be steadfast, true, and plain.
> Repress the proud, maintaining aye the right.
> Walk always so as ever in His sight,
> Who guards the godly, plaguing the profane:
>   And so ye shall in princely virtues shine,
>   Resembling right your mighty King Divine.[14]

If anything is needed to refute *The Cambridge History*'s absurd description of James's poetry as jejune and insipid, it is the wonderful pungent poem which the King wrote around 1623 when he had been goaded beyond endurance by the ever-increasing demands of Parliament. The immediate occasion for the writing of the poem was the discovery within the precincts of the court of a pro-Parliament and pro-Puritan lampoon entitled *The Commons' Tears*. His Majesty retorted to it with his own **'Verses Made Upon a Libel Let Fall at Court.'** The poem is much too long to be quoted in full here, but a few excerpts may serve:

> O stay your tears, you who complain,
> Cry not as babes do all in vain,
> Purblind people, why do you prate,
> Too shallow for the deep of state?
> You cannot judge what's truly mine,
> Who see no farther than the rin[d].
> Kings walk the heavenly milky way.
> But you by by-paths gad astray.
>   . . . . .
> Religion is the right of kings
> And they know best what good it brings,
> Whereto you must submit your deeds
> Or be pulled up like stubborn weeds.
>   . . . . .
> Oh, what a calling were a king
> If he might give or take no thing
> But such as you should to him bring!
> Such were a king but in a play
> If he might bear no better sway.[15]

The political sentiments may have been completely reprehensible for several centuries; but literary criticism should not be concerned with politics but with literature, with the skill, the adroitness, the effectiveness with which language is used, regardless of the sentiments expressed. Judged properly on literary grounds, this poem deserves a good rating. Seldom have racy octosyllabic couplets been better employed for political satire.

Almost as pungent is a poem written by the King in 1622 when he learned that, despite a royal proclamation commanding the gentry to return to their country mansions and tend their estates, many were lingering in London. King James had no doubt that the womenfolk were to blame:

> Ye women that do London love so well
> Whom scarce a proclamation can expell,
> And to be kept in fashion, fine and gay,
> Care not what fines your honest husbands pay . . .

Sardonically he advises these women who dote on the pleasures of the city and the court that a good life awaits them back in the shires:

> Your husbands will as kindly you embrace
> Without your jewels or your painted face.
> And there your children you may educate
> As well as they of French and Spanish prate.
> Visit your sick and needy, and for plays
> Play the good housewives, waste not golden days.[16]

The whole poem is both amusing and pithy.

The prose works of King James are not the easiest of reading, but then neither are those of Milton nor Sir Thomas Browne. The reasons are the same: a Latinate sense of style which calls for elaborate cumulative sentences, freighted with complexities of antithesis, parenthesis, and alliteration. Even so, once we begin to get attuned to the prose of an earlier age, King James offers good reading for he is vivid and energetic in his phrases, clear and systematic in the marshalling of his ideas. A good sample of his prose can be found in Book II of his ***Daemonologie,*** in a passage wherein he tells how the Devil recruits witches:

> At which time, either upon walking solitary in the fields, or else lying pansing [thinking] in their bed, but always without the company of any other, he either by a voice, or in the likeness of a man, inquires of them what troubles them, and promiseth them a sudden and certain way of remedy, upon condition on the other part that they follow his advice, and do such things as he will require of them. Their minds being prepared beforehand, as I have already spoken, they easily agree unto that demand of his, and syne [afterwards] sets another tryst, where they may meet again. At which time, before he proceed any further with them, he first persuades them to addict themselves to his service, which being easily obtained he then discovers what he is unto them, makes them to renounce their God and baptism directly, and gives them his mark upon some secret place of their body, which remains sore unhealed, while [until] his next meeting with them, and thereafter ever insensible, howsoever it be nipped or pricked by any, as is daily proved, to give them a proof thereby, that as in that doing he could hurt and heal them; so all their ill and well doing thereafter must depend upon him. And besides that, the intolerable dolour that they feel, in that place where he hath marked them, serves to waken them and not to let them rest, while [till] their next meeting again: fearing lest otherwise they might either forget him, being as new prentises, and not well founded yet in that fiendly folly; or else remembering of that horrible promise they made him at their last meeting they might skunner at the same, and press to call it back.[17]

By the standards and practice of most seventeenth-century writers this is certainly good, clear, straightforward prose. And in fact King James was a great believer in plain direct utterance. 'I study clearness not eloquence' he declared to Parliament in a speech in 1607. In the preface to his ***Basilikon Doron*** he can refer to 'the concised shortness of my style.' He tells us that his reason for casting ***The Daemonologie*** in the form of a dialogue was to make it 'more pleasant and facile' for his readers.

In fact, once we become acclimatised to seventeenth-century idioms, punctuation, spelling, and word meanings James does emerge as a writer who combines originality of thought with clarity of expression. Far from being 'insipid,' to return to that unhappy epithet of the *Cambridge History,* James's prose is pungent, strenuous, and alive. Good phrases abound. To James, the Devil is 'God's hangman,' and he tells us that, 'being so learned a knave as he is,' the Devil has little trouble getting the 'tinsel' of the souls of those who lack spiritual strength. His Majesty's famous ***Counterblast to Tobacco*** is full of fine vituperative phrases for those who are addicted to 'this precious stink.' When the King discusses how deep a matter 'The Book of Revelation' is for him as a theological commentator, he speaks of 'these high and profound Mysteries in the Revelation, wherein an Elephant may swim' (***A Meditation upon the Lord's Prayer***).

But at this point a caveat must be given. Today proverbs are little used, though clichés abound. In King James's day proverbs were used abundantly and James, with his feeling for a telling phrase, is a great user of proverbs. His works are of course sprinkled with Latin tags, but they contain a large number of English proverbs also, and others in good homely Scots. Sometimes a proverb is signalled by italics, or by specific identification as when (speaking of the Puritans) James remarks:

> I cannot wonder enough at the inconstancy of too many among us in our days that *like fools fain of flitting,* as the Scottish proverb is, are so greedy of novelties.[18]

Often, however, James will use proverbs without a hint that he is borrowing. One may, at first glance, credit James with still another good phrase when he tells us that the Devil is 'God's ape.' Then, with a start, one discovers that he has just given us a proverb popular in his age.

Not surprisingly, James was a master of the well-turned phrase, epigram, or apothegm. To quote the most famous, we have his declaration at the Hampton Court conference:

> I approve the calling and use of bishops in the church and it is my aphorism 'No bishop, no king.'

One can easily draw up a little florilegium to illustrate His Majesty's way with a phrase:

> [Leave] the envious to the food of their own venom.
>
> . . . the preposterous humility of one of the proud Puritans, claiming to be of their party and crying 'We are all but vile worms,' and yet will judge and give law to their King, but will be judged nor controlled by none.
>
> Let your countenance smell of courage.
>
> Beauty without bounty, wealth without wisdom, and great friendship without grace and honesty are but fair shows and the deceitful masques of infinite miseries.
>
> Jesuits are nothing but Puritan papists.
>
> Knowledge and learning is a light burden, the weight whereof will never press your shoulders.

Indicative of James's reputation as a coiner of pithy and telling phrases is the fact that two years after his death, when flattery could no longer be a motive, a little book of *The Apothegms of King James* was published in London.

One cannot read far into the works of James without being impressed by how habitually the King employs vivid and original images. A few examples will show how effectively imagery gives emphasis to his writing. In the preface to *The True Law of Free Monarchies,* James, wanting to indicate that too extended a preface will leave him little to say in the work proper, puts the matter thus:

> But lest the whole pamphlet run out at the gaping mouth of this preface, if it were any more enlarged, I end . . .

Counselling Prince Henry in his *Basilikon Doron,* James tells him:

> In your prayers be neither over strange with God, like the ignorant common sort, that prayeth nothing but out of books, nor yet over homely with him, like some of the vain Pharisaical Puritans that think they rule him upon their fingers.

Clear as he was in the principles which he was convinced should govern good writing, James was a shrewd critic of other men's literary style. We may pass over his somewhat profane comment upon Bacon's *Novum Organum,* that 'like the peace of God it passeth all understanding,' and go on to His Majesty's comment upon the labyrinthine sentences of the Earl of Northampton, who at one time had lectured at the University of Cambridge. His lordship's prose, said James, was too 'Asiatic.' The term was a technical one, used with perfect exactness, taken from the treatises of the ancient Roman rhetoricians. By 'Asiatic' they referred to a conspicuously ornate and elaborate style. One of the reasons for the excellence of the King James Bible may be that the translators were well aware that their royal master put a very high value on literary simplicity, directness, and vigour.

The best place to see James functioning as a literary critic is in his *Basilikon Doron,* the treatise which he wrote to instruct his heir in what he liked to term the 'craft' of kingship. It is indicative of the whole literary bent of James that he considered instruction in the use of language a necessary part of such a manual. Here is some of James's literary advice to Prince Henry:

> In your language be plain, honest, natural, comely, clean, short and sententious [ie, really having something to say], eschewing both the extremities, as well in not using any rustical corrupt leide [speech], as book-language and pen and inkhorn terms; and least of all mignard and effeminate terms. But let the greatest part of your eloquence consist in a natural, clear and sensible form of delivery of your mind, builded ever upon certain and good grounds; tempering it with gravity, quickness or merriment according to the subject and occasion of the time . . .
>
> Now as to your writing, which is nothing else but a form of en-registrate speech; use a plain, short, but stately style, both in your proclamations and missives, especially to foreign princes.[19]

In an interesting passage James has some counsel for the young Prince if, following in his father's path, he should turn to writing poetry:

> And if ye write in verse, remember that it is not the principal part of a poem to rime right and flow well with many pretty words. But the chief commendation of a poem is, that when the verse shall be shaken sundry in prose, it shall be found so rich in quick inventions, and poetic flowers, and in fair and pertinent comparisons as it shall retain the lustre of a poem, although in prose. And I would also advise you to write in your own language: for there is nothing left to be said in Greek and Latin already; and enough of poor scholars would match you in these languages. And besides that, it best becometh a king to purify and make famous his own tongue, wherein he may go before all his subjects as it setteth him well to do in all honest and lawful things.[20]

If, in the above passage on the requirements of poetry, we recall that by 'quick inventions' the King meant lively and stimulating concepts, by 'poetic flowers' turns of phrase of a particular richness, and by 'fair and pertinent comparisons' imagery of a particularly fit and interconnecting kind, we will realize that James's requirements are not far from those of a present day professor of English taking a class in practical criticism.

So far, in making survey of the canon of James's writing, we have left out of account two special categories: his speeches and his letters. The former pose particular problems for, though a surprising number of them survive, they have generally reached us in varying degrees of inexactness, depending upon the competency of the stenographer who took down the royal utterance. Even so, it is quite surprising how often the same arresting phrases reappear in variant accounts of a particular speech. Five of King James's speeches were published in 1616 by James Montague, Bishop of Winchester, in his thick folio edition of *The Workes of the Most High and Mightie Prince, James.* One of these speeches has the somewhat apologetic heading **'A Speach in the Parliament House, As Neere the Very Words As Could be Gathered at the Instant.'** The other four speeches carry no such caveat and would appear to have been printed from the King's own script. For a sample of James as an orator we may look at his speech of 19 March 1604, the first he ever delivered before an English Parliament. In it he spoke feelingly of the union of England and Scotland under his reign:

> Hath not God first united these two kingdoms both in language, religion, and similitude of manners? Yea, hath he not made us all in one island, compassed with one sea, and of itself by nature so indivisible as almost those that were borderers themselves, on the late Borders, cannot distinguish, nor know, or discern their own limits? These two countries being separated neither by sea, nor great river, mountain, nor other strength of nature, but only by little small brooks, or demolished

little walls, so as rather they were divided in apprehension than in effect. And now in the end and fullness of time united, the right and title of both in my person, alike lineally descended of both the crowns, whereby it is now become like a little world within itself, being entrenched and fortified round about with a natural, and yet admirable strong pond or ditch, whereby all the former fears of this nation are now quite cut off: the other part of the island being ever before now not only the place of landing to all strangers that was to make invasion here, but likewise moved by the enemies of this state by untimely incursions to make enforced diversion from their conquests, for defending themselves at home, and keeping sure their back door, as then it was called, which was the greatest hinderance and let that ever my predecessors of this nation got in disturbing them from their many famous and glorious conquests abroad. What God hath conjoined, then, let no man separate, I am the husband, and all the whole isle is my lawful wife. I am the head and it is my body. I am the shepherd and it is my flock.[21]

As far as the letters of King James are concerned, we are in a rather different area, and one which has too long been overlooked. Renaissance rulers did little of their own letter writing. Normally a secretary was given the gist of what the king wanted said, drafted a letter, and submitted it for his master's signature. A letter entirely in a monarch's own hand was something exceptional, usually a special act of courtesy and compliment when corresponding with another monarch. It is symptomatic of the whole literary bent of James I that again and again he grabbed a pen and wrote his own letter. The present writer has found and transcribed some 250 letters surviving entirely in James's holograph. They range a great deal in literary merit. Many are offhand jottings—one unfriendly critic has characterized James as 'an inveterate scribbler.' Others of the letters are so full of private jokes and allusions as to make their editing something of a nightmare; but some have just those virtues of clarity, energy, and personality which we commented upon earlier.

For examples we may turn to letters addressed to his wife, Anne of Denmark, and his heir, Prince Henry, at the time of his accession to the English throne. Anne was full of dire apprehensions that courtiers who were her enemies were turning King James against her. After various reassurances, James continued:

> . . . I say over again, leave these forward womanly apprehensions, for I thank God I carry that love and respect unto you which, by the law of God and nature, I ought to do to my wife and mother of my children, but not for that ye are a King's daughter, for whether ye were a King's or a cook's daughter, ye must be all alike to me, being once my wife. For the respect of your honourable birth and descent I married you; but the love and respect I now bear you is, because that ye are my married wife, and so partaker of my honour as of my other fortunes. I beseech you excuse my rude plainness in this; for casting up of your birth is a need-

less impertinent argument to me. God is my witness I ever preferred you to all my bairns, much more than to any subjects; but if you will ever give place to the reports of every flattering sycophant that will persuade you that when I account well of an honest and wise servant for his faithful service to me, that is to compare, or prefer him to you, then will neither ye or I be ever at rest at peace.[22]

In a second undated letter, plainly of the same period, James warns Prince Henry not to let the good news of the Stuarts' acquisition of the English throne inspire in him any foolish vainglory:

> . . . let not this news make you proud or insolent, for a king's son and heir was you before, and no more are ye yet, the augmentation that is hereby like to fall unto you, is but in cares and heavy burdens, be therefore merry but not insolent, keep a greatness but *sine fastu,* be resolute but not wilful, keep your kindness, but in an honourable sort . . .[23]

Among the best of James's letters is one which he wrote on 12 November 1617. At the time the King was revisiting his native Scotland and he had charged his Privy Council in England to use his absence to make a drastic retrenchment of the royal finances. (As usual James was deeply in debt, and he hoped that the Council could get things sorted out and made manageable during his absence.) The letter reads:

> My Lords:
>
> No worldly thing is so precious as time. You know what task I gave you to work upon during my absence, and what time was limited unto you for performance thereof. This same Chancellor of Scotland was wont to tell me 24 years ago that my house could not be kept upon epigrams. Long discourses and fair tales will never repair my estate. *Omnis virtus in actione consistit.* Remember that I told you that the shoe must be made for the foot, and let that be the square of all your proceedings in this business. Abate superfluities in all things, and multitudes of unnecessary officers wherever they be placed. But for my household, wardrobe and pensions, cut and carve as many as may agree with the possibility of my means. Exceed not your own rule of £50,000 for the household. If ye can make it less, I will account it for good service. And that you may see I will not spare mine own person, I have sent with this bearer a note of the superfluous charges concerning my mouth, having had the happy opportunities of this messenger in an errand so nearly concerning his place. In this I expect no answer in word or writing, but only the real performance for a beginning to relieve me out of my miseries. For now the ball is at your feet, and the world shall bear me witness that I have put you fairly to it.
>
> And so, praying God to bless your labours, I bid you heartily farewell.
>
> Yours own, James R.[24]

No letters bring us closer to James as a man than those he wrote, in 1623, to Prince Charles and Buckingham, far off in Spain, seeking the Infanta as a bride for the

Prince. The first of these letters opens bravely as he addresses 'My sweet boys and dear venturous knights, worthy to be put in a new romance,' but even in this first letter one senses the loneliness of James in their absence. As the months passed, with both his son and his favourite still in Madrid, involved in ever more complicated negotiations, the old King's cries for their return become increasingly urgent. The anguish is real and insistent in his letter of 14 June:

> My sweet boys your letter by Cottington hath struck me dead, I fear it shall very much shorten my days. . . . Come speedily away, if you can get leave, and give over all treaty, & this I speak without respect of any security they can offer you, except ye never look to see your old dad again, whom I fear ye shall never see, if ye see him not before winter. Alas I now repent me sore that ever I suffered you to go away. I care for match nor nothing so I may once have you in my arms again. God grant it. God grant it. God grant it. Amen, amen, amen. I protest ye shall be as heartily welcome as if ye had done all thing[s] ye went for, so that I may once have you in my arms again. And so God bless you my only sweet son & my only best sweet servant, & let me hear from you quickly with all speed, as ye love my life. And so God send you a happy and joyful meeting in the armes of your dear dad.
>
> James R.[25]

A few things may be said by way of conclusion. One cannot work at all closely with King James without feeling that one is dealing with a man who is profoundly a man of letters. One of the most significant things here is the King's habitual use of images. Like a poet he thinks in terms of images. The trait is inherent and basic. Words were tremendously important to James. He had a literary man's sensitivity to words and, like so many literary men, instinctively fell back on them as weapons. Responding as he did to the power of language, he counted too much upon language. He expected his words to prevail with Parliament. He expected his publications and letters to modify the policies of other sovereigns. For James was a king who would send abroad a treatise of his inditing where a more practical monarch would have dispatched a fleet. But such is the price of having a literary man as the ruler of a realm. And James was a literary man, and one of no mean competence or achievement.

In 1938 C. J. Sisson, in his essay 'King James the First of England as Poet and Political Writer' observed of King James: 'The time will come, and may well come soon, when popular views concerning his character, his policy and its results, will sway strongly in his favour.' Without going into King James's policies, this writer would like to express a hope that, at least in matters of literature, opinion will soon sway strongly in his favour.

Notes

1. See C. J. Sisson, 'King James the First of England as Poet and Political Writer,' *Seventeenth Century Studies Presented to Sir Herbert Grierson* (Oxford 1938) 50

2. On 'The Castalians' see Ian Ross, 'Sonneteering in Sixteenth-Century Scotland,' *University of Texas Studies in Literature and Language* IV (Summer 1964) 255-68.

3. *The Poems of James VI of Scotland,* ed. James Craigie (Edinburgh 1955-8) I: xxv. This edition will hereafter be referred to simply as 'Craigie.'

4. George Sampson, *The Concise Cambridge History of English Literature,* 2nd edition (Cambridge 1961) 398

5. Isaac Disraeli, *Literary Character of Men of Genius,* ed. the Earl of Beaconsfield (London, nd) 385

6. *The Making of a King: The Early Years of James VI and I* (London 1968) 98

7. Sisson, 48, 60

8. Craigie, I.140. Throughout this article the quotations from King James's works have uniformly been given in modern anglicized form. After all major quotations a footnote is made to the standard edition, where one exists. These old-spelling editions sometimes are able to supply the text in the original Scots of the King, but more often reproduce the anglicized text of some sixteenth- or seventeenth-century printer or transcriber.

9. Craigie, II:132-3

10. *Calendar of State Papers relating to Scotland,* III:35

11. Craigie, I:49, 53

12. Ibid., II:69

13. Ibid., II:174-5

14. Ibid., II:170

15. Ibid., II:182-5

16. Ibid., II:178-81

17. *Daemonologie, in Forme of a Dialogue* (Edinburgh 1597) sig. G4v, H1r

18. *A Meditation upon the Lords Prayer* (London 1619) sig. K5v, K6r

19. *Basilikon Doron* in C. H. McIlwain, ed., *The Political Works of James I* (Cambridge, MA 1918) 46-7

20. Ibid., 48

21. McIlwain, ed., *The Political Works of James I*, 271-2

22. John Nichols, *The Progresses, Processions, and Magnificent Festivities of King James the First* (London 1828) I:153-4

23. *Harl.* MS 6986, f 67

24. BM Add. MS 5503, ff 96-7

25. *Harl.* MS 6987, f 100

Rhodes Dunlap (essay date 1975)

SOURCE: Dunlap, Rhodes. "King James and Some Witches: The Date and Text of the *Daemonologie*." *Philological Quarterly* 54 (1975): 40-6.

[*In the following essay, Dunlap investigates the publication date of* Daemonologie *through an analysis of the manuscript and dates of events included in the volume.*]

MS 1125.1 in the Folger Shakespeare Library at Washington is described as follows in Seymour de Ricci's *Census of Medieval and Renaissance Manuscripts in the United States and Canada*:[1] "James VI, Daemonologie in forme of ane dialogue. Pap. (ca. 1597), 64 ff. (20 × 16 cm.). Written by a professional scribe, but with numerous additions and corrections in the King's autograph. . . . There is every reason to believe that this is the actual ms. used by the Edinburgh printer Robert Waldegrave for the first edition (1597)." This description needs to be modified in several respects. The manuscript contains in fact three hands—that of the copyist, in a regular print-like italic; another italic hand which has supplied a few revisions and some marginal notes; and the clear though somewhat untidy script of the King himself. The copyist need not have been a professional scribe; he could have been a calligraphically adept member of the court circle such as Sir James Semple, a friend and companion of the King since boyhood, who in 1599 copied out in elegant italics another of the King's works before it was published.[2] De Ricci's suggestion that the present manuscript served as printer's copy for the 1597 edition of the *Daemonologie* is not supported by a detailed comparison of the two texts, though the manuscript helps to correct and explain some glaring defects of the printed version.

The interest of the manuscript is not exclusively textual. Most of its marginal notes are also to be found in the printed *Daemonologie,* but this is not true of three sets of initials which stand in the margin of p. 39 in the manuscript. The discussion at this point (corresponding to p. 30 as printed) has to do with the skeptical notion that so-called witches are really self-deluded melancholics, a notion which James undertakes to refute by describing obviously unmelancholic witches as he has actually known them: "sume of thame riche, and worldlie wyse, sum of thame fat or corpulent in thair bodies and maist pairt of thame altogether geuin ouer to the pleasours of the flesche, contenuall haunting of companie, and all kynde of mirrines baith laufull and unlawfull." In the margin by "riche, and worldlie wyse" are written the initials EM; by "fat or corpulent," RG; and by "geuin ouer to the pleasours of the flesche," BN. These initials, which invite identification with particular persons, may well point to the immediate background of the *Daemonologie* and help determine the date of its composition.

James had indulged some special curiosity about witchcraft as early as 1589, when at Aberdeen he insisted on seeing the "notorious and rank" witch Marioune McIngaruch; she showed him three "stanis" or drinking-vessels used in her art, and seems to have gone unpunished for what might have been considered a violation of the severe statute "Anentis Witchcraftes" passed by the Ninth Parliament of Queen Mary in 1563. In 1590 her client Hector Munro was charged with murder by witchcraft but acquitted.[3] But in 1590-91 James found his own life threatened by witches in league with his rebel cousin the Earl of Bothwell. Abundant evidence seemed to show that they had used demonic aid to raise a tempest while he was sailing home from Denmark after his marriage, and that they had also tried to work his destruction by a toad, a wax image, and other devices. James followed the examinations with understandably close attention, especially since the criminal complicity of Bothwell could be established only on the witches' testimony; and in May 1591 he intervened in one of the trials, that of Barbara Napier, who was charged with treasonable practice against the King's life as well as previous murder by witchcraft. She was the wife of Archibald Douglas, a burgess of Edinburgh. Her identification with BN as "geuin ouer to the pleasours of the flesche" may perhaps be supported by testimony at the trial of another witch earlier in the year, in which Barbara Napier was said to have obtained a bonny small "pictour" or image of yellow wax to be used against "a man callit Archie" that "had done hir grit wrang."[4] On May 9, 1591 the assize convicted her of consulting with witches, but found her innocent of attending witch meetings or of using witchcraft to commit murder and treason. Her punishment they referred to the King's pleasure.[5] Two days later James pronounced in favor of death, and had the fourteen members of the assize charged with wilful error. These threw themselves on the royal mercy, pleading that their error was ignorant rather than wilful,[6] and James forgave them after lecturing them (June 7, 1591) in the Tolbooth at Edinburgh in a long discourse which is his first detailed discussion of witchcraft.[7] Surely no more prominent witch with the initials BN could be found than Barbara Napier.

Equally plausible is the identification of the "riche, and worldlie wise" EM as Ewfame Makcalzane, who was the only daughter and heiress of Mr. Thomas Makcalzane Lord Liftounhall, one of the Senators of the College of Justice; her husband, Patrick Moscrop, was himself the son of a respected advocate. In reporting her trial, Robert Pitcairn expresses wonder that "a person, moving in the rank of society which Ewfame Makcalzean occupied, should have leagued with the obscure and profligate wretches who figure in the Trials for Witchcraft at this period, for the destruction of her sovereign."[8] The twenty-eight crimes of which she was charged included treasonable conspiracies enterprised by witchcraft "to haif destroyit oure souerane lordis persoune." On June 24, 1591 she was burnt on Castle Hill in Edinburgh. Her property, which was forfeited to the crown, was in part restored to her three daughters in 1592, the King being "tuichit in honour and conscience" that they should suffer.[9]

Finally, who was RG? Here the identification must be much more doubtful because there are two possibilities. Robert Grierson, a ship's captain of Prestonpans, figures prominently in accounts of the witch-meetings along with Barbara Napier and Ewfame Makcalzane. He was concerned in particular with raising the tempest which was intended to prevent the return from Denmark of the King and his new Queen. At a meeting of witches, more than a hundred in all, in the Kirk of North Berwick, Grierson was one of the six men present, all the rest being women, and was involved in a vividly recorded incident: the Devil, calling the roll, should have used nicknames for his followers but mistakenly called Grierson's true name instead of Robert the Comptroller or Rob the Rover, whereat the participants "ran all hirdie-girdie and wer angrie." Nothing awed, Grierson complained to the Devil that the King's image was not given to them, as promised, to be roasted.[10] That he was "fat or corpulent" there seems to be no evidence, but the supplier of the initials RG in the Folger manuscript might well have had Robert Grierson in mind. An even better-known bearer of the initials, however, and far worthier of specification in the royal margins, was Richard Graham, who had been notorious for some years as a sorcerer. Barbara Napier was said to have consulted with him "in Johnne Ramsayis hous, outwith the West-poirt of Edinburgh" and rewarded him with three ells of bombesie cloth and five quarters of brawn. He told her, according to the testimony, that she, along with Effie Makcalzane and another witch, were destined to destroy the King.[11] Sir James Melville, who was present when Graham was examined before the King, says that he was "a West-land man," who had a familiar spirit but denied being a witch. The Earl of Bothwell "had knowledge of him by Effe Machalloun, and Barbary Naper, Edinburgh Women. Whereupon he was sent for by the Earl Bothwel," first for aid in obtaining restoration to the King's favor by a drug or herb, then (this proving ineffectual) for aid in destroying the King. Graham told Bothwell he could not raise tempests, but referred him to a witch who could.[12] The prominence of Graham in the witchcraft proceedings is emphasized by the fact that he is the only prisoner named in a warrant to pay £200 to the jailer of the Tolbooth, "be his majesties precept, for furnesing of Richart Grahame and utheris witcheis."[13] He was burnt at the Mercat Cross in Edinburgh on February 28, 1592.

There was renewed excitement over witchcraft in 1597, more than sufficient to explain James's sending his *Daemonologie* to the press in that year. But it does not appear possible to fit the initials with which we have been concerned with any appropriately prominent persons who are named in the proceedings of 1597. The identifications suggested here would indicate that James composed his work, in the substantially complete form which we find in the Folger manuscript, at a time early enough for Ewfame Makcalzane, Barbara Napier, and Richard Graham (or, quite conceivably, Robert Grierson) to be still the most vivid examples of the sorts of witches described in the text. The hand in which the three sets of initials are written may be that of James Carmichael, Minister of Haddington, who according to Melville[14] wrote a "History" of the 1591 cases "with their whole Depositions"; at least it resembles the hand in which Carmichael subscribed a letter which he wrote to King James from Haddington on March 27, 1615 recalling that he had formerly been employed by the King to "penne ane pairt of ye Comoun grammar" (printed in 1587) and "to attend sestein monethes vpoun ye examinationes of divers Witches."[15] In 1590 he also wrote an account of the coronation of Anne of Denmark, James's Queen.[16] His work on the witch trials has not survived under his name, but seems almost certain to be the basis of a pamphlet called *Newes from Scotland* which appeared in London in 1591, "Published according to the Scottish Coppie"; this pamphlet summarizes the examinations of some of the main witches "as they uttered them in the presence of the Scottish King," and concludes with special praise of King James for his magnanimous and undaunted mind, "not feared with their inchantmentes, but resolute in this, that so long as God is with him, hee feareth not who is against him." It is apparently to Carmichael's work that James refers in the manuscript version of his Preface, where he cites "thair confessions that haue beine at this tyme apprehendit: quilkis all are to be set furthe in prent"; the last nine words are crossed through—apparently by James, to judge from the color of the ink—and do not appear in the printed version of 1597, when they would have been no longer timely.

In the light of these considerations we may plausibly reconstruct the inception of the *Daemonologie* as follows. It was one of two works which the King planned in 1591—one an account of the testimony at the witch trials, to be written by James Carmichael, the other his own treatise on the main theoretical and judicial aspects, developing more systematically some of the ideas expressed in his speech to the members of the assize for Barbara Napier. After completing his first draft he had a fair copy made but kept it for some further revisions instead of sending it at once to the printer.

But if the *Daemonologie* was substantially completed in 1591-92, why would James have been so tardy about publication? He himself provides a possible answer in the preface to *His Maiesties Poeticall Exercises at Vacant Houres,* 1591: "my burden is so great and continuall, without anie intermission, that . . . my affaires and fasherie will not permit mee, to re-mark the wrong orthography committed by the copiars of my unlegible and ragged hand, far les to amend my proper errours: Yea scarslie but at stollen moments, haue I the leasure to blenk vpon any paper, and yet not that, with free and vnuexed spirit." The contents of the *Poeticall Exercises* were themselves several years late in appearing; manuscripts had been circulating in England at least two years previously, as is proved by an entry in the Stationers' Register on 7 August 1589, and according to the King's own account one of the pieces, the *Lepanto,* was composed even earlier, in 1585. In 1591 James also had on his desk other unpublished work: his paraphrase of the Book of Revelation, which did not reach print till the collected *Workes of the Most High and Mightie Prince, James* of 1616, and a number of versified Psalms which remained in manuscript until the present century.

The published *Daemonologie, in Forme of a Dialogue* which came from the press in 1597 contains surprising faults for an authorized edition issued by the King's printer. There are three clear errors in the speech-divisions (on pp. 34, 35, and 40), and a number of words seem to have been dropped or misread. The Folger manuscript not only offers what seem to be correct readings, but it also helps to explain how the speech-divisions went wrong. Apparently when he composed his work in the form of a dialogue the King did not decide at first what to name his two speakers. In a brief fragment of manuscript at the Bodleian Library (MS Bodley 165), entirely in James's hand, the speeches are marked simply Q and A. In the Folger manuscript the copyist left spaces where the names of the speakers might be supplied, and they were subsequently written in for the heading and the first four speeches only. But some of the spaces left between speeches are only a little larger than the ordinary spaces between sentences. It is thus not surprising that a few errors in the assignment of speeches should have occurred when copy was prepared for the printer. On p. 34 of the printed text the inquiry of Philomathes ending "I would faine heare what is possible to them to performe in verie deede" is run together with what should be the answer of

Epistemon beginning "Although they serue a common Master"; on p. 35, conversely, there is a mistaken change of speakers at "In two partes their actiones may be diuided," though this properly continues Epistemon's long speech which should have begun with "Although they serue a common Master" on the previous page; on p. 40 a change of speakers is again missed: "The reason that moues me to thinke" should begin a new speech by Epistemon, as is indicated by a blank for the speaker's name in the manuscript. There are also many verbal differences between manuscript and printed text, some of them by no means insignificant, though they cannot be catalogued here.

Not only are a number of additions and revisions written into the Folger manuscript, but others might readily have been introduced in preparing the printer's copy, which seems clearly to have been based on this manuscript, whether directly or indirectly. Some changes were made even after the printing had begun: in sheet I, for which the inner forme exists in two states,[17] the uncorrected readings correspond with those of the manuscript. But the mistakes in the printed *Daemonologie* are numerous enough to warrant surprise that James should have allowed them to stand. Ordinarily he was by no means indifferent to such matters. Errors less gross in *His Maiesties Poeticall Exercises* were corrected in ink apparently at the printing house; and in 1609 he called in by proclamation a defective issue of his *Apology and Monitory Preface.* But though the *Daemonologie* was several times reprinted in his lifetime, James did nothing to correct the text—which, for that matter, has been reproduced in its original imperfect state in all subsequent reprints. The Latin translator in the *Opera* of 1619 did indeed correct one of the three wrong speech-divisions, but this was apparently by the light of nature only. No doubt by 1597, troublesome though the problem of witchcraft still remained in that year, the *Daemonologie* itself no longer claimed James's principal attention as an author. He must already have been meditating other problems of importance for *The True Lawe of Free Monarchies,* which he was to publish in the following year as his next serious work.

Notes

1. (New York: H. W. Wilson, 1935), I, 371.

2. *The Basilicon Doron of King James VI,* ed. James Craigie, Scottish Text Society, Third Series, No. 18 (Edinburgh: Blackwood, 1950), II, 314.

3. Robert Pitcairn, *Ancient Criminal Trials in Scotland* (Edinburgh: H.M.S.O., 1833), I, iii, 201-04.

4. Pitcairn, I, iii, 240.

5. Pitcairn, I, iii, 242-43.

6. Pitcairn, I, iii, 244-47.

7. *Calendar of Scottish Papers* (Edinburgh: H.M.S.O., 1936), X, 522-25. An abstract of King James's speech, sent by the English agent Robert Bowes to Lord Burghley, is in the Public Record Office, S.P. 52.67 (61 I).

8. Pitcairn, I, iii, 247-57.

9. *The Acts of the Parliaments of Scotland* (Edinburgh, 1814), III, 608-09.

10. Pitcairn, I, iii, 211-12, 236-39, 245-46.

11. Pitcairn, I, iii, 243-45.

12. *Memoires of Sir James Melvil of Hal-hill* (London, 1683), pp. 194-95.

13. *Rotuli Scaccarii Regum Scotorum. The Exchequer Rolls of Scotland* (Edinburgh: H.M.S.O., 1903), XXII, 160.

14. Melville, *Memoires,* p. 195.

15. British Museum, Add. MS 19402, fol. 120.

16. *Calendar of Scottish Papers,* X, 307.

17. *The Carl H. Pforzheimer Library: English Literature 1475-1700* (New York: Morrill, 1940), p. 536.

Jacqueline E. M. Latham (essay date 1975)

SOURCE: Latham, Jacqueline E. M. "*The Tempest* and King James's *Daemonologie.*" *Shakespeare Survey* 28 (1975): 117-23.

[*In the following essay, Latham identifies James's* Daemonologie *as a possible source for the character of Caliban in Shakespeare's* The Tempest.]

The Tempest offers a twentieth-century audience more problems for a full understanding than most of Shakespeare's plays, and these problems are the more insidious because action, language and characters seem transparently clear. Yet the play is highly intellectual and despite the work of scholars who have explored many of the ideas raised by the varied but scant sources there remain elements that still seem to fit uneasily, and one character, Caliban, who eludes even the simplest definition. This essay seeks to develop two aspects of contemporary thought by means of which Caliban can be seen not more clearly but in even greater complexity, and it proposes King James's *Daemonologie* as a possible source for these ideas. Contemporary beliefs about devils could, of course, be found elsewhere, but James's relationship to Shakespeare as patron of the King's Men, the clarity and dialectical skill of his *Daemonologie* as well as its content make the King's famous work a likely source for some of the ideas of Shakespeare's strange play.

The problem of Caliban's birth, while receiving little attention on its own account, crops up from time to time in more general discussions of *The Tempest*. Unfortunately, though many critics agree that Caliban is the touchstone by which the civilised world is judged, his actual status—human, sub-human or demi-devil—is rarely subjected to close examination, and critics tend to take the view which suits their particular interpretation of the play. To cite an obvious example, Professor Kermode, in his brilliant Arden Introduction, places the 'salvage and deformed slave' within the tradition of the European savage man, and in a note added when this edition was in proof, draws attention to *Wild Men in the Middle Ages* by R. Bernheimer, whose views, incidentally, are far more complex than Kermode's brief summary allows.[1] In the same way, Caliban can be seen in the context of the exploration of the New World, corrupted by a supposed civilisation or corrupting the civilised. These are two important dimensions within which Caliban can fruitfully be viewed, but there are others, like the problem of his birth.

For Kermode, 'Caliban's birth, as Prospero insists, was inhuman; he was "a born devil", "got by the devil himself upon thy wicked dam". He was the product of sexual union between a witch and an incubus, and this would account for his deformity, whether the devil-lover was Setebos (all pagan gods were classified as devils) or, as W. C. Curry infers, some aquatic demon.'[2] Yet, even in this simple account of Caliban's origin there lurk ambiguities, as I intend to show.

In what would appear to be a key study, 'The Magic of Prospero', C. J. Sisson merely remarks in passing that 'the powers of Sycorax derived from evil communion with the devil, the father of her son Caliban',[3] thus distinguishing the source of her powers from those of Prospero. More recently, Robert Egan in his interesting article 'This Rough Magic: Perspectives of Art and Morality in *The Tempest*' comments, 'Caliban is not a devil—thoroughly evil and unredeemable—but a type of humanity' and in a footnote on the same page adds that Caliban, who makes frequent references to his mother and her god, never mentions an infernal father,[4] apparently missing the point that Setebos is probably his father, in the tradition that false gods are to be identified with devils. Yet Egan is surely correct in his insistence that Caliban's 'qualities as a character are clearly not satanic but human'. There is, then, an apparent contradiction: the text proclaims (and critics sometimes accept) the demonic origin of Caliban: 'A devil, a born devil', cries Prospero (IV, i, 188); yet if we wish to see Caliban as the touchstone of the civilised (or semi-civilised) world, we need to see him in relation to the world of nature or in some definable sense outside it—not, of course, in the world of art but, perhaps, as a symbolic figure, as Bernheimer's book would suggest, representing social, psychological and sexual aspects of man. Alternatively he can be seen as an intermediate link in the chain of being, below man but higher than the animals.

An examination of sixteenth-century views about the incubus may enable certain aspects of *The Tempest* to be seen more clearly. Although it is important to bear in mind R. H. West's wise warning in the first chapter of his study, *The Invisible World,* that 'the literature of pneumatology was rarely so cool and judicial as the ideal required', we can, I think, agree with him that there can be little doubt 'that, within degrees proper to works of art, and each in its own way, these plays [*Doctor Faustus, Macbeth* and *The Tempest*] and others accommodate it'.[5]

Traditions of witchcraft in England and on the Continent were very different. This is stressed by Barbara Rosen in her perceptive introduction to the collection of English texts entitled *Witchcraft* and by Keith Thomas in his widely acclaimed *Religion and the Decline of Magic.* In England trials were chiefly concerned with *maleficium,* harm to others, either their person or possessions; the familiar in the form of a domestic creature like cat, toad or fly was also a typically English manifestation. On the other hand, continental witchcraft was frequently concerned with the diabolic nature of the witches' compact and the sexual orgy of the witches' sabbath. As Barbara Rosen says, 'The English witch was frequently unchaste, but in the usual prosaic fashion.'[6] The incubus is, therefore, late in appearing in native accounts of witch trials and Keith Thomas claims that 'the more blatantly sexual aspects of witchcraft were a very uncommon feature of the trials, save perhaps in the Hopkins period', the mid-seventeenth century.[7] We have, then, an odd situation when we look at *The Tempest.* Shakespeare's island world, for all its concern with magic, is far from the witch hunts and trials of his own country. And yet, untypical as Sycorax and Caliban are of the English tradition of witchcraft, there were notorious continental studies of witchcraft (some translated into English) and other ways in which the idea of diabolic intercourse could have become familiar to an educated Elizabethan.

If we accept the likelihood that Shakespeare kept one eye on his royal master while writing *Macbeth* and *The Tempest,* then King James's **Daemonologie,** first published in Edinburgh in 1597 but reprinted in London on James's accession to the English throne, provides a helpful gloss on this aspect of *The Tempest;* it has, moreover, further aspects which suggest that Shakespeare may well have read it closely.[8]

King James was writing in a particular and personal context. *Newes from Scotland declaring the damnable life and death of Doctor Fian, a notable Sorcerer* had been published anonymously in Scotland and London

in 1591. The story of the tempest, supposedly raised by witchcraft, which sank one boat-load of jewels and provided a contrary wind for King James, though not for his accompanying vessels, is well known. But more significant is that the account of the trial of Dr Fian and the witches included torture, the devil's mark, a witches' sabbath, and obscene kiss,[9] a christened cat bound to the 'cheefest partes' (p. 16) of a dead man, and intercourse with the devil. James followed the trial closely, and when he came to write his **Daemonologie** he explicitly directed it against two sceptics: John Weyer, the German physician, whose *De Praestigiis Daemonum* (1563) remains untranslated, and Reginald Scot, the Kentish author of *The Discoverie of Witchcraft* (1584) which it is thought Shakespeare read. Scot's immensely long and overtly sceptical work serves as an advertisement of the continental views that he is refuting. His sources include Jean Bodin's untranslated *De la Démonomanie des Sorciers* (1580), Cornelius Agrippa and the notorious *Malleus Maleficarum* (1486?), and though his refutation of the continental writers is based on common sense and a skilful use of *reductio ad absurdum,* he betrays an almost prurient enjoyment of some of the more scabrous tales, including a detailed account, which takes up most of Book IV, of the problems of sexual relations with an incubus, whetting his readers' appetite at the end of Book III by urging those whose 'chaste eares cannot well endure to heare of such abhominable lecheries' to skip the next pages with their 'bawdie stuffe'. His major discussion in Book IV leans heavily upon J. Sprenger and H. Institor's *Malleus Maleficarum.*[10] It seems then likely that the Elizabethan and Jacobean public could derive a fairly full account of continental witchcraft practices from *Newes from Scotland* and from *The Discoverie of Witchcraft,* but even, for example, Samuel Harsnett's *A Declaration of egregious Popish Impostures,* which Shakespeare knew well, ascribes to Bodin the belief that devils may 'transforme themselves into any shape of beasts, or similitude of men, and may [. . .] have the act of generation with women, as they please'.[11]

King James's **Daemonologie** has a remarkably balanced tone. This derives in part from its dialogue form, in which the good tunes are distributed fairly equally between the credulous Epistemon and the more sceptical Philomathes. The argument is close, clear and free from the tedious capping of scriptural quotations which makes Henry Holland's *A Treatise against Witchcraft* (Cambridge, 1590) such unrewarding reading for us. In chapter 3 of the Third Book Epistemon explains that the devil has two means of effecting the union between himself and a woman—the male authors of works on demonology are strangely reluctant to discuss the mechanics of the succubus. He can steal sperm from a man, dead or alive, and inseminate the witch, or by inhabiting a dead body he can have visible intercourse with her. In both cases the sperm is cold; hence the fact that witches so often report the coldness of union with the devil. Spirits, having no sex, can have no seed of their own; in this James is following the traditional Christian view. A child born of the union of witch and incubus is therefore human. But even the credulous Epistemon is doubtful whether this union can actually take place; this kind of devil, he says, 'was called of old' (p. 67) an incubus or succubus, and his account of the intercourse is hedged with the proviso 'might possibly be performed' (p. 67). So when the inquirer Philomathes asks 'How is it then that they say sundrie monsters have bene gotten by that way' (p. 68), Epistemon can dismiss the notion with 'These tales are nothing but *Aniles fabulae*' and go on to explain that if it were possible '(which were all utterly against all the rules of nature) it would bread no monster but onely such a naturall of-spring, as would have cummed betuixt that man or woman and that other abused person'. The devil's part is merely carrying 'And so it coulde not participate with no qualitie of the same' (p. 68).

James is surprisingly cavalier in dismissing monstrous births as old wives' tales; Shakespeare was obviously more interested in them. There had, after all, been a very long tradition of extraordinary offspring of unusual parentage: Romulus and Remus and Augustus Caesar were, presumably, a tribute to their unusual fathers. In *Mandeville's Travels* the 'fendes of Helle camen many tymes and leyen with the wommen of his generacoun and engendred on hem dyverse folk, as monstres and folk disfigured, summe withouten hedes, summe with grete eres, summe with on eye . . .'.[12] Here we are nearer to the 'mooncalf' of *The Tempest*. But Britain, too, had its monstrous births. Geoffrey of Monmouth's *Historia Regum Britanniae,* incorporating Merlin's prophecies, was popular Tudor propaganda, and gives an account of Merlin's mother being visited in a convent by an incubus in the form of a handsome young man. Nearer home for James is Hector Boece's *Scotorum Historiae* translated by John Bellenden in 1531. In Book VIII chapter 14 he follows an account of Merlin's birth with recent examples of intercourse with the devil, in the last of which the woman is delivered of 'ane monstir of mair terribill visage' than had ever been seen before. From this digression Boece returns quietly to his 'dedis of nobill men'.[13] Shakespeare possibly read Holinshed's close paraphrase of Boece's narrative, which inserted, as Boece had done, the fifteenth-century events immediately after reference to Merlin: 'It is foolishlie supposed that this Merline was got by a spirit of that kind which are called *Incubi*.'[14] Holinshed's scepticism contrasts with Boece's credulity.

Shakespeare emphasises not merely Caliban's demonic paternity but his monstrous birth; he is described as a 'deformed slave' in the list of characters, and in II, ii Stephano calls him a mooncalf and is followed by Trinculo with 'monster', repeated thirteen times in that scene and becoming the name by which Stephano and Trinculo usually address Caliban. Shakespeare is prepared to accept—or exploit—the tradition having before him many of the same examples as James, as well as *The Mirror for Magistrates,* the 1578 edition of which added the tragedies of Eleanor, Duchess of Gloucester, and her ill-fated husband Humphrey Plantagenet, whose story Shakespeare had told in *2 Henry VI.* In *The Mirror* the Duke says that King Henry II reported:

> that his Auncient Grandame
> Though seeminge in Shape, a Woman naturall,
> Was a Feende of the Kinde that (*Succubae*) some call.[15]

Caliban is not, however, Shakespeare's only 'salvage and deformed slave'. As early as *3 Henry VI* the birth of Richard, Duke of Gloucester, is described in unmistakable terms. After the owl had shrieked, his mother brought forth:

> To wit an indigest deformed lump,
> Not like the fruit of such a goodly tree.

> (V, vi, 51-2)

The most interesting of the references to Richard as monster, however, comes in *Richard III* when Queen Margaret cries:

> Thou elvish-mark'd, abortive, rooting hog!
> Thou that was seal'd in thy nativity
> The slave of nature and the son of hell!

> (I, iii, 228-30)

Here Richard, like Caliban, is a monster whose outer form indicates a moral depravity which itself has explicit demonic overtones. As Barbara Rosen points out, 'Imperfection was one of the traditional marks of anything created by the Devil in imitation of God'.[16] (Hence the search for the devil's mark in Continental and Scottish witch-hunts.)

Moreover, the Broadside ballads of the sixteenth century reflect a grossly morbid interest in deformed births where the crudity of description is made more offensive by the moralising tone.[17] Such births were accounted for not by intercourse with Satan but by the more homely sins of vanity, pride or fornication. The Reverend Stephen Batman, too, in *The Doome Warning all men to Judgement* (1581) gives a hideous collection of monsters illustrated by woodcuts as a warning to blasphemers and adulterous women. Although continental writers are concerned with demonic intercourse, they give similar horrific descriptions of monstrous births, while some take a more naturalistic—though still moralistic—view. N. Remy in Book I chapter 6 of *Daemonolatreiae Libri Tres* (1595) describes the birth of a shapeless mass like a palpitating sponge, arguing that it is the impression of the demon on the mother's imagination that has produced the monstrosity; physically the child is wholly human. Bodin has an account of a hideous monster without head or feet, with a liver-coloured mouth in the left shoulder, and Boguet in *Discours des Sorciers* (1590) believes, like the English writers, that monstrous births may be God's punishment for men's sins. A much more scientific view is given in *Des Monstres et Prodiges* (1573) by the surgeon Ambroise Paré, though his illustrations are quite as extreme as those of Stephen Batman. Anyone who has seen Peter Hall's 1974 production of *The Tempest* for the National Theatre has only to recall the 'living drollery' (III, iii, 21) of 'monstrous shape' (III, iii, 31) bringing in the banquet to have an unforgettable image of these sixteenth-century monsters. Even Stephano's discovery of Caliban and Trinculo under the gaberdine with four legs, two at either end, can be paralleled from contemporary illustrations of headless monsters. Therefore, if King James's reference to monsters is tersely dismissive, it appears to assume both mythical and, more important, popular information; on the other hand, Shakespeare makes his interest manifest, and his monster's relevance to the concerns and images of the age is very close indeed.

King James was clearly more aware of the continental tradition of witchcraft than were most Englishmen, and the chief value for our understanding of *The Tempest* in James's discussion of the incubus is that biologically even Epistemon, the credulous expositor of demonology, would consider Caliban human, as indeed would Reginald Scot and most continental writers. If, then, Shakespeare and his audience like their King were sceptical of the possibility of demonic paternity, then Caliban's essential humanity must be emphasised and his character qualified only by those human factors of nature and nurture so persuasively discussed by Professor Kermode in his Introduction.

At this point the evidence seems decisive, the interpretation of Caliban simply as natural man acceptable and we can return with confidence to accounts of natives in the New World or wild men in the old, forgetting demonology—as most critics have—but perhaps with the image of the monster more clearly fixed in our minds. Yet *The Tempest* is more elusive and interpretation more difficult than is allowed by the argument so far put forward. If Shakespeare had read King James's *Daemonologie,* why did he make Prospero so insistent upon Caliban's demonic nature? After all, though the incubus was not a protagonist in English witch trials, the audience would be likely to accept Prospero's repeated statements with the same kind of willing suspension of disbelief with which in a romance it accepted Ariel and the spirits presenting the Masque.

It seems probable that, as so often, Shakespeare seized upon ambiguities in order to exploit them; Caliban perhaps has more facets than have previously been recognised: as a native of the New World, wild man, demi-devil and monster. As a new-found primitive man he serves as touchstone of the civilisation which has, in one sense, usurped his island as Prospero's throne has been usurped; he seems in this context superior to Trinculo and Stephano though inferior to Ferdinand. As a wild man, he may symbolise the untamed within us, but like Spenser's Sir Satyrane offer hope of ultimate self-discipline. As a man—whether primitive or wild—despite the attempted rape of Miranda and his glorying in the physical details of the proposed murder of Prospero, he may be capable of redemption. However, if we see him as a 'demi-devil' his state is lost; his last intention, to 'seek for grace' (V, i, 295) is, then, a tactical move born of cunning. Moreover, the associations of 'monster' in neo-Platonic, demonic and popular thought emphasise the distortion of human nature by evil; for the twentieth century 'monster' has become trivialised, so that we need to recall its power in the sixteenth century. The reiteration of the word in *King Lear* indicates that Shakespeare felt its force adequate for the most terrible of the tragedies; and the word surely retains some of its strength even in the new context of *The Tempest*. Caliban is literally a malformed creature, a mooncalf; he may, too, take on something of the word's further sense as a creature part brute part human ('a man or a fish?' II, ii, 25); finally, there is the new sixteenth-century sense, exploited in *Lear,* of moral depravity. The connotations, therefore, of 'monster' serve to emphasise Caliban's evil. Moreover, the moralising interpretation of monsters in contemporary popular writing may also give some support to the view of Caliban as externalising Prospero's own propensity to evil, since for Prospero, as for the audience, Caliban's monstrous form must, as I have shown, have had a religious and moral message lost to us. Prospero's concession, 'this thing of darkness I / Acknowledge mine' (V, i, 275-6), now takes on a new resonance.

King James's ***Daemonologie,*** however, has further relevance to *The Tempest*. His Preface includes a reference to the power of magicians who can 'suddenly cause be brought unto them, all kindes of daintie disshes, by their familiar spirit'. This point is developed more fully in Book I chapter 6. Here Epistemon repeats the traditional view (only to reject it) that at the fall of Lucifer some spirits fell into the elements of air, fire, water and land, the spirits of air and fire being 'truer' (p. 20) than those of water and land. However, he grants a spirit the ability to carry news 'from anie parte of the worlde' (p. 21) and refers to the 'faire banquets and daintie dishes, carryed in short space fra the farthest part of the worlde' (p. 22). In this the devil deceives through his agility, as he does when he produces 'impressiones in the aire' of 'castles and fortes' (p. 22). The similarity of this to *The Tempest* is obvious; even the 'insubstantial pageant' (IV, i, 155) of Prospero's great speech is prefigured.

There remains some slight additional evidence that Shakespeare had read the **Daemonologie.**[18] James, as one would expect, refers to magicians making circles, as Prospero does to charm the court party in Act V. More interesting, however, in chapter 2 of Book I James gives the three ways the devil 'allures' (p. 7) persons by the 'three passiones that are within our selves' (p. 8). These are curiosity, thirst of revenge and 'greedie appetite of geare' (p. 8). Although James goes on to relate the allurement of curiosity to magicians or necromancers, and the last two to sorcerers and witches, they remain oddly relevant to three important temptations in *The Tempest* as a whole. First, it is the curiosity of Prospero that has led to his secret studies and to his downfall as Duke of Milan. Second, though Antonio was dry for sway Prospero overcomes his thirst for revenge saying 'the rarer action is / In virtue than in vengeance' (V, i, 27-8). Finally the greedy appetites of the three men of sin could be tempted by the illusory banquet, and Trinculo and Stephano, too, are far from controlling their unrestrained passions when confronted by the 'geare' that Prospero displays to distract them.

Notes

1. *The Tempest,* ed. F. Kermode (1958), Introduction, pp. xxxix, lxii-lxiii. All quotations from *The Tempest* are from this, the sixth, edition. References to passages in other Shakespeare plays are from the single-volume Oxford edition of W. J. Craig.

2. *The Tempest,* Introduction, p. xl.

3. *Shakespeare Survey 11* (Cambridge, 1958), 75.

4. *Shakespeare Quarterly,* 23 (1972), 179.

5. *The Invisible World* (Athens, Georgia, 1939), p. 4.

6. *Witchcraft* (1969), p. 338 footnote.

7. *Religion and the Decline of Magic* (1971), p. 568.

8. I have used the Bodley Head Quarto of the *Daemonologie* edited by G. B. Harrison (1924). All quotations from the work are followed by parenthetical page references which are identical with the 1597 edition. *Newes from Scotland* is usefully included in the same volume, but since the original is unpaginated the page reference refers only to the reprint.

9. English innocence is demonstrated by Peele's *The Old Wives' Tale* where Madge telling the burlesque romance to her sleepy listeners threatens them, 'Hear my tale, or kiss my tail.'

10. This remained unavailable in English until Montague Summers edited and translated it in 1928.

11. *A Declaration of egregious Popish Impostures* (1603), p. 133. It should be noted that Shakespeare echoes Harsnett in *The Tempest.* See II, ii, 10-11 and Kermode's note.

12. *Mandeville's Travels,* ed. M. C. Seymour (Oxford, 1967), p. 160. I owe this example to R. R. Cawley's pioneering study, 'Shakspere's use of the Voyagers', *PMLA,* XLI (1926), 722.

13. *The Chronicles of Scotland,* trans. J. Bellenden, ed. R. W. Chambers and E. C. Batho, The Scottish Text Society, 3rd ser. (Edinburgh and London, 1938), I, 348.

14. *Holinshed's Chronicles of England, Scotland and Ireland, Scotland* (London, 1808), V, 146. In the same volume Holinshed refers to Alphonse, King of Naples, and his son, Ferdinand, p. 454.

15. *The Mirror for Magistrates,* ed. L. B. Campbell (New York, 1960), p. 447.

16. *Witchcraft,* p. 18.

17. See J. H. Pafford's Arden edition of *The Winter's Tale* (1963) for his footnote list of references on p. 105.

18. H. N. Paul, *The Royal Play of Macbeth* (1950), pp. 255ff. and K. Muir, *Shakespeare's Sources,* 1 (1957), p. 178, provide some of the evidence.

Sheldon Hanft (essay date spring 1981)

SOURCE: Hanft, Sheldon. "The True King James Version: His Bible or His *Daemonologie*?" *Selected Papers from the West Virginia Shakespeare and Renaissance Association* 6 (spring 1981): 50-7.

[*In the following essay, Hanft asserts that James's intense interest in spirituality and religious practice led not only to his call for a new translation of the Bible but also to his study of witchcraft,* Daemonologie.]

The effort to mark the emergence of modern society in Great Britain is an endeavour which has stirred substantial controversy among scholars over the last three decades. While different interpretations have suggested a variety of dates, events, and institutions prominent from the close of the War of the Roses to the entrenchment of the Reformation, all agree that modernity was firmly settling on Britain by the early seventeenth century.[1] King James, whose peaceful ascent to Elizabeth's throne in 1603, appears as the embodiment of this development because he unified the English and Scottish crowns, secured the Reformation, and became embroiled in conflicts which led Britain into the "age of democratic revolutions."[2]

Despite these and other contributions to the process of modernization, the first Stuart king of England remains an enigmatic figure. Although he was a champion of the Protestant Cause, he is rarely portrayed as a leader in the Whig chronicles of Britain's march to greatness. While he authorized the most influential translation of the Bible, he defended the Anglican Church from attack by Catholics, Puritans and Separatists, and he married his daughter to Elector Frederick of the Palatinate—the great martyr of the 30-Years War—the mantle of the great Defender of the Protestant Faith is not one which seems comfortable on his shoulders. It fits poorly because it cannot cloak James' active interest in witchcraft, his repugnant behavior, or cover his proposals to the Pope discussing the conversion of his heir to Catholicism. Instead of gaining renown for his theological debates with Cardinal Bellarmine and for his other religious projects, these activities earned him notoriety as the "Wisest Fool in Christiandom."[3]

James' accession to the throne did not bring toleration, instead it resulted in the passage of the most severe statutes for the persecution of Catholics and witches in British history.[4] For the first time in England communing with the devil became a sin punishable by death.[5] While this legislation was enacted with the King's approval, James took great pleasure in discovering witches, and as Goodman noted, vigorously endeavoured "to sound the depths of brutish impostures and he discovered many." Sometimes James went to great lengths in his investigations. In one case he arranged the seduction of a maid to show how "Cupid's arrows drove out the pretended darts of the devil."[6]

While scholars have not been unanimous in their assessment of the duration or the degree of commitment James invested in these activities, most scholars treat these seemingly contradictory aspects of the royal character as unique and separate developments.[7] While some recent biographers like David Mathews go so far as to try to "explain away" *Daemonologie,* most like D. H. Willson, consider each as an individual episode or phase related only to those events and policies with which they are in close chronological proximity.[8] I would like to suggest in this paper that most of these diverse activities and antithetical proposals can be reconciled by examining James' cosmology as he developed in his *Daemonologie.*[9]

King James, who prided himself on his learning and his piety, was shocked and stimulated by his experiences in Scotland during the last decade of the sixteenth century. He endeavoured to develop a synthesis which would, through an examination of Biblical Scripture and an account of his encounters with witches, explain the existence and actions of divine and supernatural forces in the world. He sought not only to understand the principles which guided the operation of these forces but also to show the various forms evil assumed and to provide a practical guide for his subordinates in the proper ways of dealing with devilish practitioners. The principles James perceived in the operations of divine and

supernatural forces in Scotland influenced his actions and policies in England. His proposals to the Pope for an ecumenical council, his desire for a new translation of the Bible, and his antics during the examinations of witches are all expression of James' view of the role and responsibilities of a "lawful magistrate." These were structured by his encounters with the Scottish witches.

In *Daemonologie,* James was determined to refute the arguments of Reginald Scott not only because he knew them to be false in theory and by virtue of his personal experiences, but also because he desired to fulfill his obligations as God's "lawful magistrate." In the preface he tells his readers that he intends to correct two "damnable opinions" of contemporaries in England and on the continent who are "not ashamed in public print to deny that there can be such a thing as witchcraft."[10]

As he asserted in the Introduction, his purpose was to demonstrate clearly that "Magic in general and necromacie in special . . . have been and are." Not only was the reality of these practices incontestable, but he felt strongly that those who practiced these evil arts must be severely punished. To support his philosophical and scriptural evidence and provide further illumination for his subjects he appended to *Daemonologie* a section entitled *Newes from Scotland.* This was an account of his encounter with the coven of Dr. Fian and his coven of Scottish witches who unsuccessfully attempted to murder their King.[11]

James provided a detailed account of how toads were roasted and venom extracted to be used in the ceremonies through which the coven hoped to invoke the power of the devil to murder James. He learned that the witches had cast a cat into the sea and chanted incantations which they hoped would raise a storm and drown him and his wife as they returned from Denmark. Since his ship did in fact encounter a fierce storm, James became frightened as these confessions were revealed. Soon, however, his initial reaction turned to curiosity as he sought to account for the irregular pattern of effectiveness which was apparent in the practice of witchcraft. The King alone seemed immune to the most extreme acts of black magic. James felt triumphant in the knowledge that even though a coven of witches was employed by one of the great peers of the realm, he was unaffected when they burned his waxen effigy slowly to cause his consumption in the pains of agony. These practices and the exercise of magic impressed him and stimulated his curiosity. Thus James wrote *Daemonologie,* not because he surrendered to his fears, as Professor MacElwee has suggested,[12] but because he felt there was a rational theological explanation for both the existence and the exercise of evil in the real world. He also believed that his experience had taught him that God had reserved within this supernatural cosmology a distinctive role for magistrates. In all countries where the Church was established by law, as it was in England and Scotland, the godly magistrate must be made aware of his responsibilities of combating the conspiracies of the damned.

It is important to remember that James published *Daemonologie* not for his Scottish subjects, most of whom shared his viewpoint, but to impress the godly of England with his learning, his piety, and his understanding of his responsibilities as God's chief magistrate. This was a concern expressed not only in *Daemonologie* but also in the first book of his *Basilikon Doron.* His concern with the spiritual and supernatural responsibilities of Kings was shown in the opening lines of the poem he chose to begin this primer on Kingship, dedicated to his son:

> God gives not Kings the style of God in vain
> For on his throne, his Septer do they sway
> And as their subjects ought them to Obey
> So Kings should fear and serve their God, again.[13]

This view of the demonic was also reflected in his first interview with Elizabeth's godson who was considered to be very learned. James told the Queen's godson that he knew of Elizabeth's death long before a messenger arrived with the news. A sorcerer, who saw a floating head, recognized it as that of the English Queen. James also sought to impress his listener by citing foreign works on witchcraft and by indicating those views he wished to discuss. Like many scholars since the event, Sir John Harrington was confused by his new sovereign and could draw few conclusions from this strange interview.[14]

While he was dazzled and confused by the terminology, and by James' accent, the fact remains that James' views were not distant from his own. The King was a staunch Calvinist who believed in predestination and salvation through God's Grace. The world was corrupt because man had fallen from God's favor, James wrote, and "is but restored again in part by Grace only to the elect."[15] The omnipotence of God was certain, and as he asserted toward the end of the second book of *Daemonologie,* "God hath before all beginnings preordained as the particular sorts of Plagues as of benefits for every man."[16] But the lesson of Job—as James' experiences had confirmed—was relevant to every man. Salvation must not be taken for granted but confirmed daily. The increased evil and errors of the Papists were constant reminders that those of the Elect who were not diligent would lose the Lord's blessing.

Those of this second group, whom he described as "falling away from God to be given over to the Devil," he divided into two categories—necromancers and witches. "Witches," King James wrote, "are servants only and slaves to the devil; Necromancers are his familiars and commanders."[17] While he believed that most witches were women because they were frail and more susceptible than men to Satan's snares, he believed that the devil's supporters came from three groups: sinners, impostors and the frail.

While Satan's delusions are most appealing to those wicked people who commit horrible sins, the devil is not without power among "the Godly who are sleeping in any great sins or informities." The remaining group of susceptible souls are those who may practice their religion but at heart are weak in their faith. All of these, regardless of how they were induced to abandon their profession, were doomed for eternity. Those who convened with the devil were condemned to "wander through the world, as God's hang-men, to execute such turns as he employs them in." Thus the devil is "God's Ape" and "God's hang-man" and his agents are merely carrying out the directions of an omnipotent and omniscient God.[18]

But as James knew from his own experiences, just as God operates through evil agents so too does he have his "lawful lieutenants" and magistrates to assist him. These magistrates were to fight the Lord's fight and keep their subjects both diligent and fervent in their profession and practice of the lawful religion. To this end, magistrates were to use every power at their disposal to expose and punish both real and pretended witches. If a magistrate were negligent in persecuting familiars, magicians, witches or impostors, he would incur the wrath of God for "his sloth." But a vigilant magistrate was indomitable and indestructible for "God will not permit their master to trouble or hinder so good a work."[19] James devoted much of his energies to these pursuits.

Daemonologie warned the magistrate to exercise care so that he succeeds in protecting the innocent as well as punishing the guilty. As James later wrote in a letter to his son, "Ye have oft heard me say that most miracles now a days prove illusions . . . judges should be wary in trusting accusations without an exact trial." Despite this warning James did not abandon his belief in true magic. In the next decade James informed one of his peers who was examining a woman given to prolonged trances, "It becomes us to lose no opportunity of seeking after the real truth of pretended wonders, that if true we may bless the creator who has shown such marvels to men." But he warned, if the occurrences prove false, then James reminded his kinsman that he was bound to punish severely the impostor.[20] The execution of the dual functions of the magistrate make many of his actions seem inconsistent and hypocritical. Yet, as James' behavior illustrates, an effective magistrate had to play the devil's advocate, on occasion, to do the work of the Lord.

Thus James offered pardons to induce impostors to confess their errors. When Archbishop Abbot, in 1613, questioned the King's views in a divorce proceeding by noting there had been no recorded case of impotence caused by witchcraft since the coming of the Reformation to England, James had a ready reply. He drew himself up and told the good archbishop, "Look you my *Daemonologie.*"[21]

James did not ignore the problems created by the occurrence of the Reformation. He argued that the time before the revelation of true religion was a period when the devil could visibly converse and ensnare his victim. But the light of Scriptures revealed during the Reformation made these practices, "commonest in the time of Papistry," ineffective and so Satan has been forced to operate through the agency of witches, impostors and heretics. Thus the Pope and his disciples, like the devil and his agents, operated to entice and beguile those who were weak in their faith and lead them from the path of salvation. Therefore, the legal monarch was responsible to denounce and expose these false prophets and treat them just like agents of the devil, because both groups of evil creatures seek "to obtain the perpetual hurt of their souls of so many that by these false miracles may be induced . . . in the profession of that eroneous Religon."[22] The similarities of these two kinds of witches were obvious to James. He notes the comparison between a witch's sabbath and the actions of "papist priests, dispatching a haunting mass."[23]

James believed that the lawful magistrate must frustrate and expose the plots and activities of Papists. Thus he saw nothing inconsistent in his negotiations with the Pope in the last years of Elizabeth's reign. Since they were conducted to prevent a Catholic from securing the English throne, James was merely discharging his duties as a lawful lieutenant by making sure that God's will was enacted. In this age of divine enlightenment, James was still acutely aware that despite the best efforts of the lawful magistrate, witchcraft and heresy still flourished. "We now being of sound religion," James observed, "and in our life rebelling to our profession, God justly, by that sin of rebellion as Samuel called it, accuseth our life so willfully fighting against our profession."[24]

This concern with fulfilling the role of the godly magistrate motivated his interest in a new translation of the Bible. James was dissatisfied with the editions available in England at his accession. When the Puritans at the Hampton Court conference, in 1604, requested a new translation of the Bible, James agreed. In expressing his dislike of the Geneva edition, he used the same formulation he expressed in *Daemonologie* to note his objections to the marginal notes of the Geneva translation. He felt that some of the comments were "partial, untrue, seditious and savouring of traiterous conceits." It

was the source of error and must be corrected. Of particular interest to James was the commentary on Second Chronicles, XV, 16. James wanted the account of King Asa expanded to note that he not only deposed his mother for her idolatrous practices but also had her executed. James wanted the role of the lawful monarch clearly marked in his new translation of the Bible for his new subjects in England.[25]

Thus, as King James concluded at the end of his narrative on the events in Scotland, "The King is the child and servant of God and they but servants to the devil . . . He is the Lord's annointed . . . they but the vessels of God's wrath: He is a true Christian . . . they worse than Infidels."[26] Throughout his life he sought to implement this message and demonstrate to his subjects how to treat those he considered worse than infidels. He used every device at his command to fulfill the obligation of a lawful magistrate and to protect his flock from the temptations and spells of witches, false prophets, heretics and impostors. These activities were motivated by the same concerns which caused him to authorize a new translation of the Bible. While the two sets of interests seem contradictory to modern scholars and make a monarch, who was contemporary with Bacon, Kepler and Galileo seem medieval, for King James these forces were part of the same cosmology. To deny the devil was to deny God and his omnipotence. Thus the true version of King James was a combination of the two with each being the reference for the other. As King James said at the conclusion of Book II of *Daemonologie*:[27]

> For since the Devil is the very contrary opposite of God, there can be no better way to know God than by the contrary; as by ones power (though a creature) to admire the power of the great Creator; by the falsehood of the one to consider the truth of the other, by the injustice of the one, to consider the Justice of the other; and by the cruelty of the one, to consider the mercifulness of the other and so forth in all the rest of the essence of God and qualities of the Devil.

Notes

1. For a useful summary of the major elements in this continuing controversy see Norman Cantor, *The English* (New York, 1967), pp. 278-310 or Lawrence Stone, *The Causes of the English Revolution, 1529-1642* (New York, 1972), pp. 58-117. For the most recent reassertion by a principal in the debate see Geoffrey R. Elton's review of Penry William's *The Tudor Regime* in the *Times Literary Supplement,* (February 15, 1980) p. 183.

2. While this concept was developed by R. R. Palmer to expand Michael Kraus' view of a transatlantic eighteenth-century revolution it is now used to unify a broad spectrum of revolutionary activity which occurred between 1770 and the Congress of

Vienna. Students of the "English Revolution" were quick to adopt this paradigm and to characterize the events in England between 1640 and 1689 as the first in a series of major, modern, "democratic revolutions." For examples of this view see Christopher Hill, *The Century of Revolution* (London, 1961) and Stuart Prall, *The Bloodless Revolution* (New York, 1972) especially pp. VII-XV, passim.

3. Two historians of Scotland—Gordon Donaldson *Scotland James V-James VII* (Edinburgh, 1965), pp. 212-240 and Maurice Lee, Jr., "James VI's Government of Scotland After 1603," *Scottish Historical Review,* LV (1976), 41-53————and one student of English history—Marc L. Schwarz, "James I and the Historians: Toward a Reconsideration," *Journal of British Studies,* XIII (1974), 114-134————are the only modern scholars to suggest that some aspects of King James' reputation might be rehabilitated. Most scholars accept the judgements of David H. Willson, *King James VI and I,* (New York, 1956) whose biography is scholarly, judicious, and presents a depiction of the Stuart monarch which is highly unflattering.

4. I James I, cap. 12.

5. Alan D. J. Macfarlane, *Witchcraft in Tudor and Stuart England* (New York, 1970) pp. 14-16. The text and table compares the provisions of this act with the 1563 Elizabethan "Act against Conjurgations, Enchantments, and Witchcraft." For the full text of the Elizabethan law see V Elizabeth I, cap. 16.

6. D. H. Willson, *King James VI and I,* pp. 309-310.

7. R. Trevor Davies, *Four Centuries of Witch-Beliefs,* (London, 1947) pp. 58-60. He quotes Nicholas Fuller *Church History of Britain,* X, p. 54, to assert that James had abandoned his belief in witchcraft by 1621. Macfarlane notes that the general pardon issued by James in 1624 excluded the practitioners of witchcraft from its benefits, p. 16. While James may have wearied of exposing impostors, it is my contention that it was philosophically impossible for James to repudiate the devil and his agents. They were an essential part of his religious world view. Without them, James' justification for the claims of the divine "rights" of the monarchs would be undermined. Since the system James developed expended much effort to explain the role and functions of false witches, it is unlikely that James would abandon it at the very end of his reign. Witchcraft was an integral part of James' religious and philosophical writings and his official actions, to the very end of his reign, affirmed his belief in the reality of Satan and his agents.

8. David Mathews, *James I* (London, 1967) pp. 75-80. David H. Willson, *King James VI and I.* pp. 103-6, 308-312.

9. King James I; *Daemonologie* (1597) and *Newes From Scotland* (1591) in George B. Harrison, ed., *Elizabethan and Jacobean Quartos* (New York, 1966). This standard version is a reproduction of the 1922-26 Bodley Head Quartos based on Bodlean MSS—Douce I, 230 and Wood B21. All citations in this paper refer to this edition. All spelling has been modernized.

10. *Ibid.,* pp. xi-xii.

11. *Ibid.,* pp. xii. *Newes From Scotland,* pp. 1-29. John Harrington, ed., *Nugae Antiquae,* I, 367.

12. William L. McElwee, *The Wisest Fool in Christiandom* (London, 1958), pp. 70-71.

13. King James, *Basilikon Doron,* (London, 1601), p. 1, and in Charles H. McIlwain, ed., *The Political Works of James I* (Cambridge, Mass., 1918).

14. John Harrington, ed., *Nugae Antiquae,* I, 367.

15. *Daemonologie,* p. 6.

16. *Ibid.,* p. 48.

17. *Ibid.,* p. 9

18. *Ibid.,* pp. 20, 23, XIV, "God by the contrary draws ever out of that evil, glory to himself."

19. *Ibid.,* p. 50.

20. Willson, *James VI and I,* p. 309.

21. W. Cobbett, T. B. Howell, et. al., *A Complete Collection of State Trials,* II (London, 1809-1829), 799.

22. *Daemonologie,* p. 77.

23. *Ibid.,* p. 72.

24. *Ibid.,* p. 54.

25. William Barlow (Bishop), *Sum and Substance of the Conference . . .* (London, 1604), pp. 44-48. Most of this is reprinted in J. R. Tanner, *Constitutional Documents of the Reign of James I, 1603-1625* (Cambridge, 1961), pp. 63-64.

26. *Newes From Scotland,* p. 29.

27. *Daemonologie,* p. 55.

Terrell L. Tebbetts (essay date spring 1985)

SOURCE: Tebbetts, Terrell L. "Talking Back to the King: *Measure for Measure* and the *Basilicon Doron.*" *College Literature* 12, no. 2 (spring 1985): 122-34.

[In the following essay, Tebbetts asserts that individuals fare better in "a society based on what is organic to human life," such as that portrayed in Shakespeare's Measure for Measure, *than in the paternalistic society of* Basilikon Doron.*]*

The relationship of *Measure for Measure* to James I's **Basilicon Doron** has interested critics for some time. The King's little book advising his son on statecraft was London's best-seller in 1603. Critics early in this century disputed its relationship with Shakespeare's play; W. W. Lawrence, for example, claimed that any resemblance between the works was likely to be "accidental" (108).[1] But more recently those resemblances have seemed too strong for most readers to doubt that Shakespeare deliberately drew on the **Basilicon Doron** in writing *Measure for Measure,* perhaps even taking his title from James's concluding allusion to Scripture: "And above all, let the measure of your love to everyone be according to the measure of his virtue . . ." (156-57).[2] Ernest Schanzer, for instance, finds "a great deal of plausibility" in the thesis that *Measure for Measure* "was deliberately made to turn upon themes which were of special interest to James" (122).[3] J. W. Lever agrees that Shakespeare "could hardly have been impervious to the political atmosphere of the time or quite uninfluenced by the most widely discussed book of 1603" (22).[4]

In light of this kind of agreement, critical debate has begun to focus on the nature of the relationship between the works, and of course various writers have expressed varying opinions. Josephine Bennett holds that Shakespeare used James's book primarily to make his play more topical, mining it for "allusions easily caught by the majority of the audience" in order to build the play's "comic effect" (82).[5] David Stevenson, on the other hand, sees an effort by Shakespeare to please the King, "to dramatize the intellectual interests of his new patron" (147).[6] Whatever the differences between these opinions and others, many critics in recent years have shared two assumptions. First, they agree that the Duke speaks for and embodies the King's ideas. Second, they agree that the play's presentation of the Duke is almost entirely positive.

This near unanimity of opinion among critics dealing with the relationship of the two works is most puzzling. The second assumption is especially so, since critics approaching the play along other lines have frequently found the Duke's character to be problematic; they have questioned both his motivation and his accomplishments, not only in fulfilling his large responsibilities but also in dealing with the specific personalities and problems within the framework of the play. When a full account of these views is taken, it appears that though the Duke may indeed echo the King and may indeed use his advice in bringing events to apparently successful conclusion, in subtler ways the characterization of the Duke brings some of James's assumptions into real question. Only a few critics investigating the relationship of *Measure for Measure* to the **Basilicon Doron** have seen the play as a critical response to the book. Among the best of these few, Roy Battenhouse finds

the play "altering and deftly bettering James's precepts, in order to propose obliquely . . . a more satisfying version of government than James had so far formulated" (193).[7] But even this stops short, for Battenhouse sees in the play only a plea that James add a fuller, more Christian mercy to his otherwise acceptable views on statecraft. This stops short because there is a real possibility that the play finds the King's views anything but acceptable. The King's statecraft, as embodied in the Duke, may in fact be the object of Shakespeare's subtlest satire in *Measure for Measure*. The play may well be the playwright's way of talking back to a very opinionated king.

A close look at the **Basilicon Doron** reveals a good deal for Shakespeare to pause over. Certainly the book is full of good advice. James writes as a two-fold father—the father of Prince Henry who will become King, and the father of the nations of England and Scotland. And certainly that role was one the Renaissance expected its kings to play. In fact, as Elizabeth Pope explains it, Renaissance expectations of the King went beyond mere fallible fatherhood: "According to Renaissance theory, the authority of all civil rulers is derived from God. Hence, they may be called 'gods' . . . because they act as God's substitutes" (57).[8]

James's stance in his little book clearly fulfills these high expectations. Repeatedly he assumes for himself a kind of perfection not ordinarily available to human kind. He admits to a former flaw or two (the kind of early laxness that Shakespeare's Duke admits), but these flaws have, he assumes, been overcome, so that the best his son and his nation can do is to submit totally to his habits, his judgment, his will. He goes so far as to counsel Henry that any "unreverent writing or speaking of your parents" ought to be held "unpardonable" (38), and that Henry's choice of servants and advisers ought to be limited to those his father had chosen, with Henry keeping "constant love toward them that I loved" and "constant hatred to them I hated" (79). He advises his son to "foster true humility" toward his parents (115) and to avoid "judging your superiors" and incurring the "curse of the Parents" (116).

The father is suggesting, through these and other demands, that the son deny the validity of his own experience and judgment, and become a puppet for the father, an empty shell in which the father can live and extend his life another generation. He makes the demand based on the assumption of his own perfection. He is a king who has become able to subject "his own private affections and appetites to the weal and standing of his subjects, ever thinking the common interest his chiefest particular" (29). He is a king who can administer justice "only for the love of justice and not for satisfying any particular passions" of his own (35). Naturally such perfection has a right to dominate the kingdom and the son, space and time. Apotheosis is the only just reward for the perfect patriarch.

Can a critic really believe that Shakespeare could read such naive assumptions of patriarchal perfection and respond to the King who wrote it only with echoes, compliments, and gentle additions? Evidence suggests otherwise. Unkingly fathers filled with such stuff appear elsewhere in such guises as Polonius, full of high sentence yet almost indeed a fool. Kingly fathers fare no better, for serving as God's substitute does little to make Claudius, Macbeth, and Lear any less guided by their own "particular passions" than any other mortal. Shakespeare was too clear a seer to take Renaissance political theory or King James I's use of it at face value. He saw too clearly the fallibility of kings to accept the perfection of their judgments and the right of their wills to control both their own world and their children's. *Measure for Measure* takes on this disparity between royal assumptions and royal realities. It beguiled its first royal audience and its most recent critics alike, for its words echo those royal assumptions rather comfortably. Its actions, on the other hand, are another matter. For a sensitive reader, the play's actions dramatically question those patriarchal assumptions and the political theory supporting them.

Textual and historical evidence supports this position. The material Shakespeare added to his dramatic sources in creating *Measure for Measure* shows the Duke to be Shakespeare's major addition. He took a bit character whose role in Whetstone had been nothing but that of a convenient *deus ex machina* and turned him into the chief character and key to the whole action of the play. Introducing such a figure surely suggests that the playwright had something more than topicality and flattery on his mind. The disparity between the actual behavior of James and the grand assumptions of his little book suggests what Shakespeare may in fact have had in mind. The King's extravagance as James VI of Scotland and his excessive devotion to personal pursuits and pleasures had already established a pattern which E. K. Chambers describes as "loose-fibred self-indulgence" and which would quickly lead to "a marked degeneration in the standard court life" in England (1:107).[9] Such evidence compels us to a close look at how the Duke behaves in the play and how that behavior might offer subtle but firm correction to the man whose words he frequently echoes.

It might be best to begin such a close look by acknowledging that the Duke's words, his announced intentions, are indeed noble. No doubt they inspire not only those who see flattery in the play but also those who see the Duke as representing Divine Justice and Divine Mercy. He speaks to Escalus of his respect for Angelo, and claims to have "dressed him in our love" (1.1.20).[10] He speaks to Angelo of the deputy's virtues and puts aside

Angelo's request for more testing of those virtues before they're given full scope. He speaks to Friar Thomas of his own fault in letting liberty get out of hand and of his desire to remedy that fault. He speaks to Claudio of the small worth of dull, sublunary existence and soliloquizes on the importance of "grace" and "virtue" in a ruler (3.2.278). He soliloquizes on his desire to bring Isabella "heavenly comforts" out of her "despair" (4.3.114).

But even in acknowledging how admirable these words sound, we must also acknowledge their problematic nature and the sometimes equal importance of words which the Duke does not bother to speak. Robin Grove questions a number of the Duke's speeches, seeing in them reflections of a man "sensitive to his own dignity above all," adding that the play gives "not the slightest sign" that the Duke is ever touched by others' sufferings (10,22).[11] Rosalind Miles agrees, noting that the Duke "registers no distress or passion" for those he finds in pain (177).[12] These critics miss only the potential application of their observations to James I as the probable source for the Duke's character and the King before whom the play was to be performed. We can only imagine how much that performance may have been like the one Hamlet arranges for Claudius, but Battenhouse must be right when he calls the play a "trap for meditation" (212). Perhaps, "Mousetrap" would be better, for the problem here is greater than Battenhouse sees it when he accepts James's premises in the **Basilicon Doron** as sound but only a bit short of being "integrally Christian" (195). The point seems to be that a system of government cannot function when built on Stuart assumptions, particularly on what Stevenson calls the "bland assumption of [a monarch's] personal right to interfere in the lives of all subordinate persons" (159). The play's response to King James and his bland assumption seems to be that noble views and apparently noble objectives can very easily mask one's self-seeking even from oneself. Such a position would certainly have been daring, especially if the King were subtle enough to catch it, but if the King was as self-deceived as the Duke is, Shakespeare had little to fear. R. A. Foakes sees this feature of the play, characterizing the Duke as both "deceiving others" and "deceived himself" (25).[13] To Foakes, though, the negative characteristics of the Duke are so strong as to rule out the possibility that he is a dramatization of James's kingship. To others it is tantalizing to see Shakespeare warning his monarch that noble words and even noble objectives, when masking one's own self-magnification, can lead to results anything but noble, results that offer destruction masked as reformation and totalitarianism masked as community.

Masked destruction and tyranny do indeed seem to be the result of the Duke's activity. His masking is one of the most obvious devices of the play, one that has drawn varying misinterpretations. Miles is a recent spokesman for the positive school, seeing "the disguise of the kindly father" as preparing us to see the Duke as "an ultimately benevolent authority" (190). She thus lines up with Lawrence's earlier claim that the duke-disguised-as-friar was a mere theatrical convention aimed at giving the figure the "binding force or constituted and final authority" but at the same time leaving the figure "of minor importance" as a study in character (103, 110). The problem with this positive interpretation of the Duke's friar mask is that it too greatly contradicts the historical conclusion that Miles herself draws: "the ironic possibilities of the friar disguise must have been so obvious to an audience of 1604 that they needed only allusion rather than explanation . . . playwrights were using it with a specific intention, in order to provoke a specific response, usually ironic" (167). Miles is more nearly right when she uses this finding to contradict Lawrence, holding that historical evidence gives "no indication that a friar would automatically command respect from an audience of 1604, or necessarily represent venerated authority" (170).

Irony is, in fact, the key to the mask. The friar's robe wraps the Duke in holy garb not his own just as his pious words enwrap his actions. From a Freudian perspective, for example, the disguise as a celibate friar could suggest the father's asexual discourse, his assurances that the taboos he enforces in the family have nothing to do with his own sexual/political interests but are sanctioned by a higher, impersonal authority. Such an application of the irony in the Duke's disguise is strengthened when we realize that the Duke drops the disguise—his convenient manipulative mask—in the same scene in which he claims sexual possession of Isabella, his virginal "daughter." The irony becomes doubly important when it applies not just to the father of one family (James and Henry) but to a sometime political theorist positioning himself as father of the nation. The mask of personal perfection and social disinterest, Shakespeare hints, disguises serious threats to individuals and the community.

Individual characters clearly do feel the destructive hand of Shakespeare's Duke, especially Angelo and Isabella. The Duke destroys the personalities and plans his "son" and "daughter" have constructed for themselves and substitutes his own will for their lives, even though Isabella's and Angelo's own intentions are harmless enough and potentially productive. Miles has described the repeated "disintegration of the carefully erected self-image" of characters in the play (125); we would correct Miles by noting that the self-images collapse not because they fail to be whole (what "image" is an adequate substitute for reality?) but because the Duke violently rips them apart rather than nurturing them or allowing them to mature naturally.

Isabella has chosen a life of "strict restraint" in the convent. In so doing she has chosen to put aside a sexual life and to live apart from any sexual claims of men. Though an asexual life of prayer and devotion certainly is not to everyone's taste, it is an honorable calling—especially honorable in the Vienna of the play—and one that holds much promise for a young woman to develop her potential even unto sainthood. Certainly Angelo makes the first assault on Isabella in acts one and two; he is the first to assert a sexual claim on her that denies her self-defined status. Yet in the latter half of the play, the Duke misleads her, lies to her, shocks her doubly with her brother's supposed death and sudden resurrection, and then when she is as incapable of making a sound decision or of asserting her own wishes as any human can be, he makes his own sexual claim on her and cancels her right to self-definition. Her silence at the end of the play is not so hard to understand: it is the natural result of such shock as the Duke has put her through, and also the appropriate symbol for the Duke's effective cancellation of what was authentically "Isabella" in her. She is now his and will henceforth continue to speak the scripts he feeds her.

Criticism's rush to the Duke's defense in all of this is more than a bit puzzling, especially in light of Shakespeare's repeated depictions of admirable young women in pursuit of their own, independent goals. His Violas, his Rosalinds, his Beatrices pursue men rather than sainthood, to be sure, but they pursue them independently, because the men they choose suit them. Yet from critics we hear sanguine remarks on the Duke's having "cleansed the prospective bride (Isabella) of her lack of charity" (211),[14] and having made her more human, more compassionate (65-69),[15] and we get psychological assurances that Isabella reaches a final "acceptance of herself as a woman" through the Duke's ministry (181).[16] What leads critics to take the Duke's brutal treatment of Isabella for spiritual and psychological nurture? The misreading itself suggests that they operate from two mistaken assumptions: that the play accepts the right of a dominant patriarch to claim available females despite their wishes (i.e., though Isabella rejects Angelo's claim, she should accept the Duke's), and that the play accepts the Duke at his own valuation (i.e., if he *says* he is bringing her heavenly comforts, then that must be what he *does* bring her).

Angelo's character suffers a similar destruction at the Duke's hand. Certainly Angelo participates more fully in his destruction than Isabella does in hers, specifically through his persecution of Isabella and Claudio. When he is publicly disgraced, he has done much to "deserve" that disgrace. But acknowledging this much does not cleanse the Duke of his responsibility in Angelo's fall. Critics have long noted the importance of the idea of mercy in *Measure for Measure*; in so doing they have examined the need of Angelo and Isabella to learn the ways of mercy, while seeing the Duke most often as the teacher of those ways. Bennett, for instance, holds that "the Duke embodies Divine mercy which watches over man, giving him power to do both good and evil, yet guiding, teaching . . ." (126). With such insight into the play, critics have still missed commenting on how the theme of mercy becomes problematic when applied to the Duke's treatment of Angelo. Certainly keeping Angelo from raping Isabella and killing Claudio prevents his worst intentions from becoming reality, and granting him his life would be widely viewed as an act of mercy. The problem arises, however, in looking at the Duke's earlier actions and inactions, and in comparing them with what we might expect from a truly merciful individual, especially from a disinterested and perfect patriarch.

What the earlier actions show us is that the Duke recognizes Angelo's probity, his "stricture and firm abstinence" (1.3.12) but that he mistrusts that probity partly because of Angelo's putting aside his engagement and partly for the very strength of that probity itself, since Angelo "scarce confesses / That his blood flows or that his appetite / Is more to bread than stone" (1.3.51-53). He suspects, therefore, that Angelo may fail in his difficult assignment. Perhaps we should ask what anyone in Angelo's position would want of his superior in such a case—what, for instance, a Shakespearean scholar would want of his dean if that dean were making him acting department chair. Surely normal professional responsibility, let alone Christian mercy, would call for some counsel on areas of weakness, some advice on how to avoid the traps the new responsibility brings with it, especially when the "patriarch" sees that the initiate may fail. Yet the Duke offers Angelo only flattery:

> There is a kind of character in thy life,
> That to th'observer doth thy history
> Fully unfold. Thyself and thy belongings
> Are not thine own so proper as to waste
> Thyself upon thy virtues, they on thee.
>
> (1.1.28-32)

And just as surely that same professional responsibility and Christian mercy would call for a trial run, a testing of the new person's ability in small areas before entrusting that person with the largest job. Angelo even asks for such a trial:

> Let there be some more test made of my metal
> Before so noble and so great a figure
> Be stamped upon it.
>
> (1.1.49-51)

But the Duke responds by calling such requests "evasions." It seems fair to conclude that the Duke himself is like Angelo, a "seemer" whose real "being" lies hidden. Angelo's later actions certainly reveal him to be a hypocrite; the Duke's early actions suggest that he is one too. He takes a rising young statesman and sets him up for a fall, without a single word or action to prevent it, hiding his expectation of that fall from everyone in Vienna, even old Escalus. When the expected fall comes, it destroys Angelo's future in statecraft, and Vienna's rising star, perhaps a potential rival for the Duke in statesmanship, is sunk. The Duke spares Angelo his life after assuring that it will be lived in obscurity and shame with no one to blame but himself. The Duke remains Vienna's unrivaled and only statesman and its most successful masked avenger.

The Duke's destruction of Isabella and his participation in Angelo's are subtle but firm responses to King James and his Stuart concept of kingship. The Duke's participation in the collapse of these individuals' lives perhaps most closely responds to King James's view of his position as Prince Henry's father in the *Basilicon Doron,* the view that the son's best hope lies in following all of his father's policies and employing all of his father's ministers. But of course the idea extends beyond this one possible application, reaching finally to the real problematic nature of patriarchy. It suggests to the monarch-father that his position is far more complex than is suggested by his easy assumption of his own present perfection and of the "right" granted by that perfection to dominate the lives of the subjects-children. The coin of his realm may bear the image a perfect king on its obverse, but only if it bears the image of ruin on its reverse. Look on both sides, the play seems to say.

And it says more. The Duke's destructiveness moves beyond what he does to the individuals Isabella and Angelo. He does a pretty good job on political and social institutions, too. Both law (and thus the state) and marriage (and thus the family) suffer at his hands. Stuart statecraft, the play seems to say, not only can damage individual lives but can also undermine the very bases of social life.

The Duke masks his destructive effect on law and the state with the same noble sentiments that masked his destruction of individuals. He tells Escalus that he admires his knowledge of the properties of government, his experience in the "city's institutions, and the terms / For common justice" (1.1.11-12), and he tells Friar Thomas that he regrets having neglected enforcing the city's laws to the point that "our decrees / Dead to infliction, to themselves are dead" (1.3.27-28). This regret, of course, echoes King James's admission in the *Basilicon Doron* that he had been too lenient in the past: if, he warns Prince Henry, you are too merciful early in your reign, "the offenses would soon come to such heaps, and the contempt of you grow so great, that when you would fall to punish, the number of them to be punished would exceed the punishers" (36-37). The King says he learned this lesson from his own experience: "I confess, where I thought (by being gracious at the beginning) to win all men's hearts to a loving and willing obedience, I by the contrary found the disorder of the country and the tinsel of my thanks to be all my reward" (37). But the play quickly moves beyond the Duke's humble confession, polite admiration, his seemingly responsible intentions—that is, beyond the mask of his words—and shows as what his actions actually accomplish.

They do not do much to strengthen the law and the state. By the end of the play the law has been shown to be overharsh, and its most visible enforcer has been exposed as a hypocrite. Yet there is no promise, no hint even, that the law will be changed, that it will be brought into accord with what the people of Vienna need in order to live together with civility. Instead the Duke has inserted himself between the people and the law, making himself superior to it—becoming, in effect, the savior of the people from the law. Thus he turns Mariana, Isabella, and the friars over to Escalus for trial but then returns to make a mockery of the due process of law and to usurp the role of justice he just handed over to Escalus. And when he then hands out justice, naturally, he substitutes his own idiosyncratic sentences for what the law demands. What are the people of Vienna likely to learn in this spectacle? Probably not that law is the binding force that makes their city what it is. Probably not that judges and courts are capable of administering the law. But they probably do learn that the Duke knows better than the law and is the only reliable source of justice. He has become the law.

Shakespeare would not have had to rely only on the **Basilicon Doron** to see that the statecraft of that little book could have such consequences. Certainly such consequences would be suggested by its simplistic patriarchal stance, its intolerance of opposition, and many of its specific recommendations (e.g., that the King should spy on the proceedings of his courts). But Shakespeare also had the evidence of the King's own behavior on the throne. The King's emptying of England's jails as he journeyed from Scotland to London but then choosing to have the Newark pickpocket summarily hanged is as idiosyncratic as the Duke's justice. His treatment of the Raleigh conspirators—his arrangement to have his last-minute clemency delivered only when the men were on the scaffold and at the point of execution—was as disruptive a substitution of his own will for due process of law as the actions of the Duke are. Statecraft that assumes the patriarch's omniscience, statecraft that places the patriarch's will between the law and the people, finally destroys the law. It forces society to organize itself around the person of the patriarch. To the degree that that person is erratic, so will social structures be.

Perhaps the Duke's destructiveness is most fully revealed in what he does to the family. In all of Shakespeare's dramatizations of successful marriages, the indispensible feature is mutuality. In the romantic comedies, characters preparing for successful marriages first develop strong, independent lives; their marriages result from their mutual choice of each other and their willingness to give up some of that independence in establishing their family. Maturer marriages—where they are portrayed in Shakespeare—continue to be successful to the degree that couples continue their mutual respect for each other as individuals, still largely independent within their new bonds. Perhaps *The Merry Wives of Windsor* provides the best illustration since its plots present a full range of marriages in the romantic and mature stages. The principal difference between the successful marriage of the Pages and the rockier one of Fords is the degree to which the husband trusts his wife to live chastely on her own—independently, without the husband's oversight. And the principal quality that recommends Fenton as young Anne Page's best suitor is that their attraction to each other is mutual. *Othello* offers similar illustrations: the romantic stage of the marriage of Othello and Desdemona is successfully based on mutual attraction and voluntary surrender, notably on the part of Desdemona, who has established her independence in rejecting suitors offered by her father and then selecting Othello as her husband. Their marriage fails tragically for the same reason the Fords' almost failed comically—because the husband fails to trust the wife to live up to her responsibility to him while maintaining her independent will.

Now in *Measure for Measure* marriage is central. Profligacy that makes independence the only good runs rampant; prostitution, fornication, and adultery threaten the kind of mutual surrender that Shakespeare's successful marriages seem to be based on. The Duke uses language drawn from the family when describing the sorrowful state of disorder in Vienna: "The baby beats the nurse, and quite athwart / Goes all decorum" (1.3.30-31). Even the comic scenes suggest problems in the family—in that of Elbow and his respected wife, the only married couple mentioned in the play apart from the semi-married Claudio and Juliet. By the end of the play, all this seems to be solved: the Duke's major visible accomplishment is the claiming of Isabella as his wife, the forced marriages of Angelo and Mariana and of Lucio and his punk, and the completion of the marriage of Claudio and Juliet. With marriage instituted as the new rule in Vienna, the family would seem to be returning to its proper form and proper place as the basis of the larger social structures. The problems would seem to be solved.

Certainly most criticism has taken this somewhat sanguine line. Battenhouse sees the marriages as properly ending the near worship of self that has marked the behavior of the "independence" party: ". . . the Duke is mercifully providing for their welfare, while justly ending their evasions of duty to themselves and to the public" (200). Arthur Kirsh goes even further, rhapsodizing that "marriage always in Shakespeare has sacramental value, and never more than in *Measure for Measure,* where it is seen as a sanctification of impulses that could otherwise damn us, as the means through procreation by which we can make true coin of the currency of our lives, by which we can—literally—remake ourselves in the image of our Creator" (100).[17] The problem with this approach, of course, is its naivete. It is based on the notion that marriage is good in every case, that all marriages are equal. Note, for instance, Kirsch's "always." The plays, on the other hand, present repeated evidence that Shakespeare knew much better than this. For Shakespeare, marriage is as problematic as fatherhood. The question remains, then, whether the marriages made by the Duke are like Shakespeare's successful ones or his unsuccessful ones, whether they strengthen the family or hide its weakness under a mask of strength.

The evidence in Shakespeare and in everyday life is that the Duke's marriages do the latter. Angelo has been tricked and then forced into a disadvantageous marriage with Mariana, one that Renaissance law held he had every right to repudiate. What kind of relationship is he likely to have with the woman who connived in the trick and consented to his public disgrace? Lucio's marriage is likely to be worse. Will being forced into a marriage with a "whore" make him suddenly "responsible" to her or *their child*? And Isabella's ability to participate mutually in her marriage to the Duke is already indicated by her silence; unless modern productions interpreting the silence as defiance are accurate, she participates not out of mutual surrender but out of vanquishment, and a marriage forced upon a defiant individual, of course, would fare no better. The utter lack of mutuality in all of these marriages suggests that they are little more than whited sepulchres. They are monuments to the Duke's power to form society along the lines of his own will. They have not arisen organically out of real needs of the people involved—as law ought to have but didn't—but they have been imposed from the top. In taking this right to form families at his will, the Duke in effect becomes not only "law" but "society" as well. Why not, when all that is whole lies in himself, all that is corrupt, without?

What a far-reaching, firm response Shakespeare makes to his monarch's little book on statecraft. The playwright offers the King a vision of his egoistic, paternalistic assumptions played out with apparent success, with their spokesman the great and only victor in Vienna and its Savior. But Shakespeare challenges King James and his readers to look beneath the friar's robe, the pious words, the masks of success. He challenges us to understand the complex role of the father—in a family and in a state—and the fragile nature of both marriage and law—the basis of society on the one hand, and its framework on the other. He implies the need for a society based not on the ***Basilicon Doron****'s* paternalism but on what is organic to human life and is mutually agreed on. Such a society, *Measure for Measure* implies, might give each individual a chance to be a victor, and might leave no individual in need of a human savior.

Notes

1. William W. Lawrence. *Shakespeare's Problem Comedies.* New York: Ungar, 1960.

2. James I. *Basilicon Doron.* 1599. Menston, England: Scholar Press, 1969.

3. Ernest Schanzer. *The Problem Plays of Shakespeare: A Study of Julius Caesar, Measure for Measure, and Antony and Cleopatra.* London: Paul, 1963.

4. J. W. Lever. "The Disguised Ruler." *Twentieth Century Interpretations of Measure for Measure.* Ed. George Greckle. Englewood: Prentice, 1970.

5. Josephine W. Bennett. *Measure for Measure as Royal Entertainment.* New York: Columbia UP, 1966.

6. David L. Stevenson. *The Achievement of Shakespeare's Measure for Measure.* Ithaca: Cornell UP, 1966.

7. Roy Battenhouse. "*Measure for Measure* and King James." *CLIO*7 (1978).

8. Elizabeth M. Pope. "The Renaissance Background of *Measure for Measure.*" *Twentieth Century Interpretations of Measure for Measure.* Ed. George Greckle. Englewood: Prentice, 1970.

9. E. K. Chambers, *et al. Shakespeare's England: An Account of the Life and Manners of His Age.* 2 vols. 1916. Oxford: Clarendon, 1950.

10. William Shakespeare. *The Complete Works.* Ed. G. B. Harrison. New York: Harcourt, 1968. All subsequent references are to this edition.

11. Robin Grove. "A Measure for Magistrates." *The Critical Review* 19 (1977): 10, 22.

12. Rosalind Miles. *The Problem of Measure for Measure: A Historical Approach.* New York: Barnes, 1976.

13. R. A. Foakes. *Shakespeare: The Dark Comedies to the Last Plays: From Satire to Celebration.* Charlottesville: UP of Virginia, 1971.

14. Battenhouse.

15. Bennett.

16. Marilyn Williamson. "Oedipal Fantasies in *Measure for Measure.*" *The Michigan Academician* 9 (1976).

17. Arthur Kirsh. "The Integrity of *Measure for Measure.*" *Shakespeare Survey* 28 (1975).

J. Derrick McClure (essay date 1990)

SOURCE: McClure, J. Derrick. "'O Phoenix Escossois': James VI as Poet." In *A Day Estivall: Essays on the Music, Poetry and History of Scotland and England & Poems Previously Unpublished: In Honour of Helena Mennie Shire,* edited by Alisoun Gardner-Medwin and Janet Hadley Williams, pp. 96-111. Aberdeen, Scotland: Aberdeen University Press, 1990.

[*In the following essay, McClure surveys James's verse and assesses his contribution to Scottish poetry.*]

In the great pageant of European royalty, King James the Sixth of Scots occupies a place all of his own. Not even the features of Henry VIII or Louis XIV can be more familiar than the oft-portrayed, very Scottish face of James, with its ungracious yet disconcertingly penetrating glower. By the mere fact of dying peacefully in his bed he attained to a distinction rare enough among Scottish kings; and by doing so after a long and on the whole successful reign lasting from his childhood he achieved a status unique in the annals of the House of Stewart. His political achievements, as King of Scots, King of England and an active player on the European scene, are by any standards remarkable; and his success in maintaining order in both his kingdoms, and exercising a powerful influence for peace in Europe, is all the more extraordinary through being achieved in defiance of almost unending criticism directed at—from different quarters and at different times of his life—his religion, his political theories, his nationality, his physique, his recreations, his drinking, his scholarship, his choice of companions, his artistic tastes, his personal hygiene, his sense of humour and much else. An idiosyncratic blend of political acumen and personal eccentricity, such as James displayed, is not so unusual among European monarchs; but James adds to this a truly amazing capacity for provoking diametrically opposite reactions, from his own time to the present, in each of his two kingdoms: Scottish accounts of James VI and English accounts of James I can scarcely be understood as referring to the same man.[1] All these factors make of James perhaps the most fascinating and (with the obvious exception of his mother) certainly the most controversial figure ever to occupy the Scottish throne: for the scholarly attempts at undercutting the heroic stature of Robert Bruce, in the first half of the present century, represent a passing aberration, now happily resolved, rather than part of an enduring debate.

Beyond controversy is the guid conceit which James had of himself; and no doubt his lasting fame would have pleased him greatly. Yet in one respect he has not had the attention which he would certainly have considered his due. As self-appointed head of the Castalian Band he exerted considerable influence on Scottish literature during a short-lived but interesting and distinctive phase, and his leadership has been acknowledged and discussed. But James, besides being an enthusiastic patron of poets, was—or at least tried to be—a poet in his own right. On poetic theory he wrote with sense and shrewdness: his **Schort Treatise,** derivative though much of it is, is the work of a man who had not only studied but clearly understood the precepts and the practice of earlier poets and scholars. His prescriptions on 'the wordis, sentences, and phrasis necessair for a Poete to vse in his verse' are sound practical advice. More interesting are his observations on metre: his technical terminology is sometimes idiosyncratic and sometimes erroneous (though he can hardly be censured for a mistake as widespread, in the sixteenth century and much later, as the misleading use of *long* and *short* to mean *stressed* and *unstressed*; but a modern reader familiar with metrical theory can see beyond this to the fact that he had come much nearer to grasping the principle of stress-timing and the prosodic structure of English (and Scots) words than many of his contemporaries. His own poetic effusions, too, were widely remarked on in his time, often in terms of high praise.[2] The complimentary sonnets prefaced to his **Essayes of a Prentise** need not, of course, be taken as the writers' true estimate of James's work: Montgomerie's fulsome eulogy in particular:

> Can goldin *Titan* schyning bright at morne
> For light of Torchis, cast ane greater shaw?
> Can *Thunder* reard the heicher for a horne?
> Craks *Cannons* louder, thoght ane *Cok* sould craw?

admirable though it is as rhetoric, must provoke some scepticism. (One should remember, however, that those poets were not only judiciously flattering their king but kindly encouraging a very young man of unmistakable promise.) Much more significant is the tribute paid by Du Bartas in the dedicatory introduction to his translation of James's **Lepanto**:

> Hé! fusse-je vrayment, ô Phoenix escossois,
> Ou l'ombre de ton corps, ou l'echo de ta voix,
> Si je n'avoy l'azur, l'or, et l'argent encore
> Dont ton plumage astré brilliantement s'honnore,
> Au moins j'auroy ta forme; et si mon rude vers
> N'exprimoit la douceur de tant d'accords divers,
> Il retiendroit quelque air de tes voix plus qu'humaines,
> Mais, pies, taisez-vous pour ouyr les Camœnes.[3]

Du Bartas, perhaps, had appreciated James's enthusiasm for his own work (the young king, in inviting the French poet to visit his court, had expressed himself as eager to meet Du Bartas as Alexander to meet

Diogenes)[4] and been pleased with the royal entertainment he received at Falkland: nonetheless, he was in no way dependent on James's patronage as the Scottish court poets were; and this dignified compliment is surely a genuine expression of regard.

Yet James's personal contribution to Scottish poetry, as distinct from his indirect influence on the development of it at his court, has rarely received the attention of critics: even by the standards of Scottish poets apart from the very greatest, he is a neglected figure.[5] Assuredly he is no Montgomerie or Drummond, and—unlike his great ancestor James I—nothing can make his achievements in the poetic field seem comparable in magnitude to those in the political; but his poetry is at least of sufficient interest to warrant a serious assessment.

A difficulty in judging the work of a poet who is also a major historical figure with an exceptionally well-documented life story is that of considering his poems as poems and not as outcomes of events in his personal history or evidence regarding his thought or character. The song 'Sen thocht is frie', for example, is discussed by some historians as a revelation of the cunning and secretive cast of mind which James perforce acquired in early adolescence.[6] No doubt it is this; but it is also a very good lyric. The simplicity and clarity of the language (in several cases defying, but to no ill effect, James's later precept against filling a line with monosyllables), the regular but not inflexible metre, and the skilful matching of the clause and sentence structure with the lineation and rhyme scheme—a feature conspicuously lacking in much of James's later work—shows technical aptitude of a respectable order. One is tempted to wonder whether the boy who wrote this song, which not only unites thought and expression in a less contrived manner but has the ring of spontaneity to a far greater extent than many of James's more mature writings, might have developed into a really considerable lyric poet if he had not become so fascinated with reulis and cautelis.

In sharp contrast to this early effort, the *Essayes of a Prentise* are clearly the work of a practitioner who, in his own belief at least, had learned exactly what poetry was and how he was expected to proceed in writing it. The graceful apologia in sonnet form which James appended to the collection makes the entirely just point: these are the works of a mere beginner in the craft, and:

> Then, rather loaue my meaning and my panis,
> Then lak my dull ingyne and blunted branis.
>
> (13-14)

James's ambitions as a poet were lofty indeed, at any rate in his youth, but throughout his poetic career his meaning and his pains were very often in excess of his ingyne. The twelve sonnets which open his *Essayes* show this, at times all too clearly. The theme of these poems—a series of prayers to the various gods in turn, for the gift of poetry so inspired that readers will think they see and hear the gods' own works—could only have suggested itself to a man whose imagination was capable of being profoundly stirred by poetry; and his youthful eagerness cannot fail to arouse the sympathy, at the very least, of any reader. And in the last sonnet of the series if nowhere else, his ambitions are stated with real dignity:

> I shall your names eternall euer sing,
> I shall tread downe the grasse on *Parnass* hill
> By making with your names the world to ring. . . .
>
> (7-9)

The couplets in these sonnets are in some cases so weak as to suggest that James did not even realise the necessity to the sonnet form of a decisive conclusion; but this poem ends with firmness:

> Essay me once, and if ye find me swerue,
> Then thinke, I do not graces such deserue.
>
> (13-14)

James knew well what poetry can do: his sonnet sequence is in effect a catalogue of traditional poetic themes (the stories of the gods, the changing seasons, the sea and voyages, heroic tragedy, warfare); and his technical competence is unfailing in the sense that he never writes a grossly unmetrical or cacophonous line. Nor is the writing without some felicitous touches. He can use alliteration judiciously, produce onomatopoeic lines such as:

> . . . the whiddering *Boreas* bolde,
> With hiddeous hurling, rolling Rocks from hie,
>
> (Sonnet 6, 5-6)

add colour to an address to Neptune by the use of technical terms from seafaring: 'That readars think on leeboard, and on dworce', (Sonnet 7, 3) and make a metrical list of sea creatures whose names (*seahorse, mersvynis, pertrikis,* that is, soles) or another feature ('*Selchs* with oxin ee') suggest the conceit:

> In short, no fowle doth flie, nor beast doth go,
> But thow hast fishes lyke to them and mo.
>
> (Sonnet 8, 13-14)

The classical references, too, are sometimes turned to good effect: the cleverest instance, perhaps, being (from the same sonnet):

> As *Triton* monster with a manly port,
> Who drownd the *Troyan* trumpetour most raire. . . .
>
> (3-4)

Bathos and vacuity intrude with distressing frequency, no doubt; and even the least practised of poets should not have been reduced to filling up a line with 'seasons dowble twyse' (2:8) (as likewise in the first two lines of a later **"Sonnet to Chanceller Maitlane"** he made twelve years into '. . . the space / That Titan six tymes twise his course does end'); making the phrase 'that be / Myle longs' cross a line break (8:9-10); comparing a smooth sea to *alme* for the sake of a rhyme with *calme* (7:14), or ending a sonnet with 'visited by him' (9:14). Yet as juvenilia, these sonnets show promise, and occasionally more than this.

The sonnet form continued to entice James, and some of his later exercises show considerable improvement in technique and inspiration over this early sequence. Certain easily-recognisable faults he never outgrew: blatant padding of lines, feeble rhyming tags, lines ending bathetically on semantically unimportant words, failure to counterpoint grammar with metre resulting in distortions of word order or ineptly run-on lines, and a general tendency to peg entire poems on ideas or conceits of insufficient weight to sustain them. A sonnet with an arresting opening may lapse into disappointing banality: examples are the third of the **"Amatoria"** sequence:

> As on the wings of your enchanting fame
> I was transported ou'r the stormie seas
>
> (1-2)

and the **'Sonnet painting out the perfect Poet'**, where after the promising opening line, 'A ripe ingine, a quicke and walkened witt', the task of rendering as poetry a list of poets' qualities defeated James entirely. Sonnets which show a tolerable degree of competence throughout may be marred by a weak conclusion: the **'Sonnet against the could that was in January 1616'**, after a strongly alliterative lament on the baleful effects of the weather ends:

> Curst bee that loue and may't continue short
> That kills all creaturs *and doth spoile our sport.*
>
> (13-14)

The witty **'Sonnet on Sir William Alexanders harshe vearses after the Inglishe fasone'** opens effectively with the parody-rhetoric of:

> Hould hould your hand, hould, mercy, mercy, spare
> Those sacred nine that nurst you many a yeare,
>
> (1-2)

proceeds to the deliberately jarring prosody of 'Bewray there harsh hard trotting tumbling wayne' (12), and then concludes with the solecism of making the Muses use a mixed metaphor: 'Our songs are fil'd with smoothly flowing fire' (14); and the fine line, 'Although that crooked crawling Vulcan lie' (**"Amatoria"** 5, 57), leads

through a notably lifelike account of the fire spreading through 'the greene and fizzing faggots made of tree', only to fall flat in the hopelessly prosaic last line: 'I houpe Madame it shall not be for noght' (70). His poetic taste failed him much less often than his technique: the crass over-literalism of the second sonnet in the **"Amatoria"** sequence: 'I frie in flammes'—'my smoaking smarte'—'And all my bloode as in a pann doeth playe'—is a breach of decorum of which he is rarely guilty.

On the occasions when he is able to sustain his verbal technique throughout and match it with a thought or idea of sufficient content, however, James can produce sonnets fully worthy of preservation. The two associated with the **Basilikon Doron,** particularly the verse summary of the argument of the book, can hardly be faulted on any count. The second of the three sonnets **'When the King was surprised by the Earle Bothwell'** effectively employs an unusually forceful vocabulary, a skilful weaving of alliteration within and across lines, and a striking anaphora in the last quatrain:

> How long shall Furies on our fortunes feede
> How long shall vice her raigne possesse in rest
> How long shall Harpies our displeasure breede
> And monstrous foules sitt sicker in our nest.
>
> (9-12)

The rhetorical catalogue, a frequent device, is turned to expert use in the sonnet which concludes the **Poeticall Exercises,** where the things of the created universe are listed in due order from 'The azur'd vaulte, the crystall circles bright' to 'the bounded roares and fishes of the seas'; and the same theme and method are applied in the second of his poetic tributes to Tycho Brahe, which summarises in imposing language the Christian model of the universe. The names of classical deities appear with monotonous frequency in James's verse and rarely suggest anything but the routine application of a stock poetic device; but the conceit of Minerva, Diana and Venus competing to bestow their favours on his queen results in an inspired and delightful sample of poetic wit (**"Amatoria"** 3). The attractive sonnet **'On the moneth of May'** likewise turns classical allusions to good effect, including the memorable line 'Of sadd Saturnus tirrar of the trees'. Jack has pointed out the indebtedness of this poem to one of Desportes's,[7] but James's adaptation is very free: a much closer translation, resulting in another distinguished sonnet, is his rendering of Saint-Gelais's 'Voyant ces monts de veue assez lointaine' (**"Amatoria"** 5). His rather touching naturalisation of the poem by the change of 'ces monts' to 'the Cheuiott hills' is far from the most important of his modifications to the original. The French poem opens non-committally with 'Je les compare à mon long desplaisir'; James anticipates the result of the comparison in:

The Cheuiott hills doe with my state agree
In euerie point excepting onelie one.

(1-2)

He elaborates on 'Haute est leur chef, et haut est mon desir' by introducing a contrast between the height of *cloudes* and that of *skies,* embellishes Saint-Gelais's 'grands vents' with a characteristic onomatopoeia by making them 'hurle with hiddeous beir', and relates the points of comparison in 'Ils sont sans fruict, mon bien n'est qu'aparence' at least somewhat more closely by his use of 'no fruicts . . . no grace'. And for once the use of a personal pronoun as a rhyme-word in the final couplet does not sound bathetic: in 'That snowe on them, and flames remaines in me', if anything the word-order renders the antithesis more strikingly than in the original 'Qu'en eux la neige, en moy la flamme dure'.

That James should have embarked on a project as ambitious as a translation from Du Bartas, even 'the easiest and shortest of all his difficile, and prolixed Poems', is a further measure of his youthful poetic ambition. Though the French poet has no longer the reputation, in his own country or elsewhere, which he had among his contemporaries, it is easy to recognise the qualities in his work that appealed to James: the devoutly Protestant orientation of his thought, his erudition and firmly intellectual approach, his grandiose choice of subjects. As a fluent speaker and reader of French, too, James would no doubt have been intrigued by Du Bartas's neologisms and linguistic experimentation. But little can be said in praise of James's **"Uranie."** The movement of his pentameters is inflexible and plodding compared to the alexandrines of his original, and his use of couplets instead of Du Bartas's *abba* quatrains has a dismally confining effect on the expression of his thought. The translation is close, at times almost literal:

Exerce incessament et la langue, et ta plume
Exerce but cease thy toung and eke thy pen

(108)

Chacun reuereroit comme oracles vos vers
Echone your verse for oracles wolde take

(183)

Qui, sage, le profit auec le plaisir mesle
Who wysely can with proffit, pleasure ming. . . .

(280)

The only instances in which he shows any degree of linguistic enterprise are the very rare cases where he simply adopts a word, until then not naturalised into Scots, from the original (such as *macquerel* or *mignarde*), or alters the meaning of *oweryere* (normally in Scots 'left over from last year') to make a calque on

surannée, rendering *ces fables surannées* as 'those oweryere lyes'. Flashes of inspiration such as the rendering:

Car il vaut beaucoup mieux n'estre point renommé
Que se voir renommé pour raison de son vice

as:

For better it is without renowme to be
Then be renowmde for vyle iniquitie

(231-2)

—where the terser and blunter Scots considerably increases the force of the statement—are outnumbered by infelicities such as the rhyme of 'Parnass' with 'lyke as', or rhyme-enforced syntactic distortions like 'It that the hevinly court contempling bene' (56).

The fourteeners which James used for his second translation from Du Bartas, *The Furies,* at least move with greater fluency than his pentameters; but to counter this advantage they intensify the tendency to line-padding which constantly bedevils his poetry. 'Puisses-tu quelque jour reprendre ta couronne' becomes 'Mot thou win home thy crowne againe, *The which was reft away*' (Exordium, 43-4); and the exigencies of metre and rhyme compel him to eke out 'From Edens both chas'd ADAMS selfe And seed . . .' (11-12), rendering 'Bannit des deux Edens Adam et sa semence', with '. . . for his pretence' (in both versions the line rhymes with 'offence'). More creditable additions to the original are James's augmentations of Du Bartas's lists of mutually attractive and mutually antipathetic beings with examples of his own: this piece of esoteric learning clearly aroused his interest.

An examination of James's translations of Du Bartas suggests, rather oddly, a great opportunity lost through the accidents of spatio-temporal contiguity. Du Bartas is a fascinating and highly individual representative of the exuberant literary and linguistic efflorescence which French, like English but unlike Scots, was enjoying in this period; and his verbal inventiveness—his use of technical terms, onomatopes, new compounds and derivations, Gasconisms—is in principle characteristic of a gifted poet consciously participating in a new and lively movement in his national literature. The finest Scottish poets of the reigns of James III and IV, and of the present century, made enthusiastic and effective use of all these devices. And Du Bartas's fondness for lists and catalogues, the precision and detail of his visual and other sensual images, his combination of factual and scientific knowledge ostentatiously displayed with a pervasive sense of numinous awe and delight, all are features which have a habit of recurring in Scottish poetry. If this French poet had been translated by Douglas, or MacDiarmid, what masterpieces of Scots verse might the sympathy of tastes and talents have produced! But alas, he only got James, who could render his meaning with unimpeachable competence, but whose language is barren compared to that of his model.

Of greater interest are the two original long poems in James's early collections, **Phoenix** and **Lepanto.** The former, if once again the poet's execution does not fully measure up to his intention, certainly is among his most competent works. The difficulty, already mentioned, of assessing James's poems apart from their known origins in events of his life is particularly pressing here, since much of the merit of the poem inheres in the careful allegorical presentation of Esmé Stewart's career in Scotland as the story of James's Phoenix; and the description of the bird's beauty, the emphasis on the cruelty and malice of her attackers, and the pathetic picture of her fleeing vainly for protection to the speaker of the poem, are undoubtedly made more poignant by the historical fact of the boy king's helpless grief and fury at the dismissal of his adored cousin. However, the poem has other commendable features. The carefully-balanced preliminary meditation, with its parallel listing of Fortune's blows and the consolatory reflections for each of them, is well-conceived as an introduction, though not all readers would find particularly admirable the sentiment of:

> For death of frends, although the same (I grant it)
> Can noght returne, yet men are not so rair,
> Bot ye may get the lyke.
>
> (17-19)

The narrative flows steadily in unfailingly regular verse—lack of clarity is never one of James's faults—enlivened by such touches as the account of the Phoenix's glorious colours and the hyperbole:

> . . . whill she did shame
> The Sunne himself, her coulour was so bright,
> Till he abashit beholding such a light.
>
> (61-3)

A moral point is effectively underscored by anaphora in:

> Lo, here the fruicts, whilks of *Inuy* dois breid,
> To harme them all, who vertue dois imbrace.
> Lo, here the fruicts, from her whilks dois proceid,
> To harme them all, that be in better cace
> Then others be.
>
> (127-31)

And James attains to real eloquence in the four apostrophising stanzas beginning:

> O deuills of darknes, contraire unto light,
> In *Phœbus* fowle, how could ye get such place,
> Since ye are hated ay be *Phœbus* bright?
>
> (225-7)

The cumulative effect of the rhetorical questions and exclamations here is to produce a passage of unusual power.

A more impressive poem, and one of the few in either of James's early collections for which a reader does not have to make continuous allowance for the poet's youth, is **Lepanto.** Prolix it is, and prone as always with James to unsubtle and bathetic passages; but as a Protestant scholar-poet's narrative account of one of the great battles of the sixteenth century it is a fine achievement. The racy fourteeners bear the reader along at an exciting pace; the story is competently told, incidents being selected, balanced and commented on with considerable skill; the alternation of narrative passages with other material (for example, the description of Venice (97-112), the classical 'autumn' passage (345-56), or the list of artisans and their activities (431-40)) makes for an interesting variety of tone. James's gift for onomatopoeia is again in evidence:

> Like thunder rearding rumling raue
> With roares the highest Heauen:
>
> (621-2)

his insistence on the *noise* of the battle is indeed one of the most noteworthy features of his description of it. The simple language at times acquires an almost ballad-like quality, as these two examples show:

> With willing mindes they hailde the Tyes,
> And hoist the flaffing Sayles. . . .
>
> (297-8)

> The foming Seas did bullor vp,
> The risking Oares did rashe,
> The Soldats peeces for to clenge
> Did shoures of shotts delashe.
>
> (305-8)

There is also evidence of careful structural arrangement. The poem opens with an authorial apostrophe, a scene in Heaven, and a scene in Venice; and concludes with a similar sequence in reverse order, mourning in Venice now giving place to rejoicing and hostile confrontation between Christ and Satan to an angelic chorus of praise. A further Heavenly episode occurs at a pivotal point in the story, before the joining of battle; shortly before it a speech by a Christian commander is quoted, shortly after it a speech by a Turk. Authorial interventions are placed to mark new phases in the narrative: the short passage concluding the account of the sorrowing city of Venice, the introduction to the lengthy battle sequence with its engagingly honest disclaimer:

> No, no, no man that witnes was
> Can set it out aright,
> Then how could I by heare-say do,
> Which none can do by sight:

But since I rashlie tooke in hand,
   I must assay it now,
With hope that this my good intent
   Ye Readers will allow:

(589-96)

and the dramatic interruption of the vigorous passage describing the wholesale slaughter:

O now I spie a blessed Heauen,
   Our landing is not farre:
Lo good victorious tidings comes
   To end this cruell warre.

(769-72)

The fervour of religious partisanship in Scotland and all Europe at this period makes it natural that *Lepanto* should have provoked violent political and religious controversy, but the fact is that James's theological standpoint is stated as clearly as it could possibly be, and is admirably moderate and enlightened. The final *chorus angelorum* contains an extended series of variations on the theme expressed in the lines:

For since he shewes such grace to them
   That thinks themselues are just,
What will he more to them that in
   His mercies onelie trust?

(969-72)

and the line put into the mouth of God:

All christians serues my Sonne though not
   Aright in everie thing

(79-80)

could hardly be bettered as a concise encapsulation of a wholly respectable moral and religious position. In the present age, when the context of the poem is less likely to arouse strong feelings, the work itself can more easily be appreciated on its own merits; and the verdict must be that James has written a thoroughly good and enjoyable poem.

Another attractive poem in a different vein is **"A Complaint of his mistressis absence from Court."** James's ability, on occasion, to write genuinely musical verse is in evidence here: the opening lines with their unusually intricate sound-patternings show a degree of technical expertise to which he rarely attained, and at other points in the poem, too, alliteration and vowel harmony are again skilfully applied:

Inflam'd with following fortunes fickle baite . . .

(9)

The Sunne his beames aboundantlie bestowes . . .

(16)

When the image of the sea voyage through sunshine and storm is dropped the quality of the writing flags somewhat; but interest is added to the latter part of the poem by the characteristic Castalian mannerisms: the quasi-correction in 'The like, ô not the like bot like and more' (43), the anaphora with its pointedly contrasting third element in 'Whose comelie beautie . . . Whose modest mirth . . . Whose absence . . .' (47-9), the sequence of similes in:

The Court as garland lackes the cheefest floure
The Court a chatton toome that lackes her stone
The Court is like a volier at this houre
Whereout of is her sweetest Sirene gone . . .

(50-3)

complemented in the last line of the stanza by the ordered sequence 'Our light, our rose, our gemme, our bird' (56).

"A dreame on his Mistris my Ladie Glammis" is less felicitous as poetry: the relentless fourteeners, admirably suited for fast-moving narrative, are much less so for a meditative poem of this kind. Yet it is of interest in demonstrating James's propensity for expressing his knowledge in poetic form: the discussion of dreams, the extended account of the properties of the amethyst, and the interpretation of the tablet show at any rate considerable ingenuity in arranging the products of his learning and imagination into verse, and the poem can be read with pleasure as an interesting discourse. Perhaps the most extreme instance in all James's work of a poem written purely to display his knowledge in witty form is **"A Satire against Woemen,"** where, the title notwithstanding, the anti-feminist matter is restricted to two stanzas, preceded by no fewer than six in which every single line enumerates a characteristic of some living thing. This stichomythic bestiary is a minor literary tour de force.

The possibility has been raised that James might have been a better poet if his gifts had been less circumscribed by his own conception of how poetry should be written. To some extent this is supported by two of the few poems written in the latter part of his reign, the **"Elegie written by the King concerning his counsell for Ladies & gentlemen to departe the City of London according to his Majesties Proclamation,"** and the **"Answere to the Libell called the Comons teares."** These are not 'poetic' in the conscious and prescriptive sense of most of his earlier work: they contain neither classical allusions (except a cleverly-applied reference to Caesar's wife) nor decorative language, and make no parade of learning. They are, however, pointed, forceful and at times witty compositions, expressing the king's argument in forthright fashion.

In the first, James gives free reign to his satirical propensities, employing such weapons as word-play, as in these two examples:

& to be kept in fashion fine & gay
care not what ffines your honest husbands pay

(3-4)

Visite the sicke & needy & for playes
play the good huswifes. . . .

(41-2)

He uses sarcastic overstatement: 'the world hath not a more deboshed place' (20), and understatement:

your husbands will as kindly you embrace
without your jewels or your painted face. . . .

(37-8)

And the conclusion is menacingly epigrammatic:

and ye good men 'tis best ye gette these hence
least honest Adam pay for Eves offence.

(49-50)

James in the second poem falls into his old habit of verbosity; but though the sentiments of the poem can hardly have been gratifying for those at whom it was directed, surely few kings have ever delivered so scathing a dismissal—through the medium of verse—to their critics:

Kings walke the milkye heavenly way
but you by bye paths gad astray.
God and Kings doe pace together,
but vulgars wander light as feather.

(7-10)

There is no sign in this poem of the sad, senile figure that James had, by some accounts, become in the last years of his reign. The king who aimed such shafts as:

Whereto you must submitt your deeds
or be puld vp like stinkinge weeds

(27-8)

And to no vse were Counsell Tables
if State affaires were publique bables

(78-9)

was still the man who, in one mood, had written the **Basilikon Doron** with its unique blend of exalted pride in his God-given calling and shrewd common sense in the methods of putting it into practice, and in another had modestly but devastatingly demolished the vaunting even of 'Belouit sandirs maister of oure airt'.

A reading of James's poems and his observations on poetry in Scotland prompts the disconcerting question: to what extent was he aware of the great achievements of his compatriot makars of the earlier Stewart period? That some at least of the poetry and song of pre-Reformation Scotland had survived to contribute its influence to a poet such as Montgomerie has been clearly demonstrated, notably by the recipient of the present volume;[8] but the fact that the works of, say, Henryson or Dunbar were there for James to read does not prove that he had read them. His poetic models, as has always been recognised, were French and Italian rather than Scottish; and the one contribution which he by his actual example made to the subsequent course of poetry in Scotland was the introduction of the Petrarchan sonnet form. The only Scottish poet, other than his contemporaries, whom he mentions by name is David Lyndsay; and in more than one respect his writing suggests a curious ignorance, rather than mere ignoring, of Lyndsay's predecessors. Would the language of his seasonal descriptions have been so tame if he had modelled it on Dunbar or Douglas; would his **"Schort Poem of Tyme"** have been so banal if he had read Henryson's *The Preiching of the Swallow* or *The Testament of Cresseid*? (The line 'The mous did help the lyon one a day' is hardly evidence that the version of the fable he had in mind was Henryson's.) These questions can evoke nothing but guesses; but a much more definite one also arises: would he have argued with Hudson that Virgil was 'inimitable to vs, whose toung is barbarous and corrupted',[9] or proclaimed 'I lofty *Virgill* shall to life restoir' (Sonnet 12.10, in **Essayes**), if he had been acquainted with the *Eneados*? His reference in a letter to Du Bartas to his 'douleur que ce pais n'a esté si heureusement fertil que d'avoir produict un tel colosse ou arc triomphal'[10] is of course primarily an expression of his enthusiasm for the recipient's work; but would even this have taken the form of a direct denial of the existence of half a dozen Scottish poets of the late fourteenth, fifteenth and earlier sixteenth centuries whose merits are comparable at least to those of Du Bartas if he had been familiar with their works? The sentence in his **Reulis and Cautelis** 'Thairfore, quhat I speik of Poesie now, I speik of it, as being come to mannis age and perfectioun, quhair as then [the meaning of 'then' is not specified] it was bot in the infancie and chyldheid' is taken by Craigie[11] to be a contemptuous dismissal of his Scottish predecessors; but the present writer finds it inconceivable that a man possessing any degree of poetic sensitivity or patriotic pride—and James incontrovertibly had both—would have rejected the superb national poetic achievement from Barbour to—with reservations—Lyndsay *en bloc* if he had been to any serious extent acquainted with it. That this argument is not purely intuitive is shown by his manifest admiration for Montgomerie, who is in his poetic assumptions and techniques the direct heir of the Makars.

James in his youthful zeal may indeed have seen himself as a poetic revolutionary in Scotland; but that he consciously rejected, on literary grounds, the work of his Scottish predecessors seems to me less likely than another possibility: that he was an early and illustrious victim of the Protestant syndrome memorably exposed and excoriated by Fionn MacColla: the unthinking and uninformed attribution of 'darkness and ignorance' to all periods between classical antiquity and the triumph of Protestantism.[12] Barbour, James I as poet, Holland, Blind Harry, Henryson, Dunbar, Douglas: all these were representatives of the Christendom which, to James and his government—and, more importantly, to Buchanan and the king's other early mentors—was founded on superstition and idolatry; and therefore their works had probably never been allowed to form any part of James's education. Lyndsay, because of his vigorous campaigning for reform at least from within the Church, would be the only one of the pre-Reformation poets who was not beyond the pale; but even in his case, James's use of the phrase 'of old' in reference to his work (**Phoenix,** 24)—if it has any importance other than as a rhyme tag—is rather oddly applied to a poet whose death preceded James's birth by less than a dozen years, and suggests that James perceived a gulf between himself and Lyndsay which the chronological gap is hardly sufficient to explain. It is surely not without significance, too, that James's favourite among his contemporary French poets was a Huguenot.

If the argument of the preceding paragraph is correct, it is a striking instance in support of the theory that the Reformation has had a long-term effect of steadily and cumulatively weakening the Scots' awareness of their national culture and sense of national identity.

James's poetry is of considerable importance to students of his life and reign. No serious reader could regard it simply as evidence for his supposed vanity and pedantry: if those qualities are visible so too are humaneness, piety and, regarding his own poetic skill, an unmistakeably genuine modesty; and it is of course true that displays of learning are commonplace in mediaeval and Renaissance poetry, and that James's being one of the few monarchs to proclaim his Divine Right in print does not mean that the belief itself was his own idiosyncrasy. But his work deserves to be considered as literature too: in a period when the Scottish poetic scene gives, on the whole, the impression of a fair number of good or very good practitioners rather than a few great ones, he is fit to be mentioned in company with the Aytons, Fowlers and Alexanders of his court. James was clever and witty, he had ideas worthy of expression in verse, he had an ear for rhythm and sound-patterning, and his concept of poetry was high and serious. These qualities were not sufficient to make him a great poet or even a consistently good one; but the best work that can be salvaged from his poetic oeuvre show him to have been not only an effective patron, but a not unworthy practising member, of the Castalian Band.

Notes

1. See Jenny Wormald, 'James VI and I: two kings or one?', *History,* LXVIII (1983), 187-209.

2. The edition of King James's poems used is that prepared for the Scottish Text Society by James Craigie, published as Numbers 22 (1955) and 26 (1958) of the Third Series, hereafter 'Craigie, 1955'. This edition presents different early texts of several of James's poems on facing pages. Since textual questions are not the concern of the present paper, quotations in such cases have been taken from the more standardised version: normally a printed as contrasted with a manuscript text. On the contemporary response to James's own poetry, see Craigie, 1955, 274-80.

3. See *The Works of Guillaume De Salluste Sieur du Bartas,* ed. U. T. Holmes, J. C. Lyons and R. W. Linker, 3 vols (Chapel Hill, 1935-40), III, 506.

4. Ibid., I, 203.

5. But see R. D. S. Jack's discussion and bibliography, 'Poetry under King James VI', in *The History of Scottish Literature. Volume I: Origins to 1660,* ed. R. D. S. Jack (Aberdeen, 1988), 125-40.

6. For example, see Caroline Bingham, *The Making of a King: The Early Years of James VI and I* (London, 1968), p. 153, and Antonia Fraser, *King James VI of Scotland, I of England* (London, 1974), p. 397.

7. *A Choice of Scottish Verse 1560-1660* (London, Sydney, Auckland and Toronto, 1978), p. 173.

8. See Helena Mennie Shire, *Song, Dance and Poetry of the Court of Scotland under King James VI* (Cambridge, 1969).

9. *Thomas Hudson's Historie of Judith,* ed. W. A. Craigie, STS Third Ser. 14 (Edinburgh and London, 1941), 3.

10. Holmes et al., *The Works of du Bartas,* I, 203.

11. Craigie, 1955, xiii.

12. See his *At the Sign of the Clenched Fist* (Edinburgh, 1967), pp. 130-2.

Jenny Wormald (essay date 1991)

SOURCE: Wormald, Jenny. "James VI and I, *Basilikon Doron* and *The Trew Law of Free Monarchies*: The Scottish Context and the English Translation." In *The Mental World of the Jacobean Court,* edited by Linda Levy Peck, pp. 36-54. Cambridge: Cambridge University Press, 1991.

[*In the following essay, Wormald elucidates James's political theory and places* Basilikon Doron *and* The True Lawe of Free Monarchies *into their historical and political contexts.*]

The Trew Law of Free Monarchies was published in 1598. It is significant that the only writings in English of the period of the reign of Elizabeth that definitely formulate a doctrine of absolute monarchy were written by a Scot in Scotland, and by a man who suffered from the drawback of being himself a King.[1]

Thus in 1928 did J. W. Allen debar James VI from serious consideration, because of the twin disabilities of Scottishness and royalty. Much more recently, and much more surprisingly, this political theorist received even more dismissive treatment from Quentin Skinner, whose *Foundations of Modern Political Thought,* published in 1978, omitted the king's works entirely from his list of primary sources, mentioned him only four times in the course of the book, and coped with the 'Scottish problem' in the index by referring to him simply as 'James I, King of England'. Yet, even if we were not now far removed from the perception of James VI and I as the pedantic buffoon, beloved of Sir Anthony Weldon and Sir Walter Scott,[2] it would still remain true that the writings of a king have a peculiar, indeed a unique importance. Not since Alfred had a ruler combined the practice and the theory of kingship in his own person; and if all political theory, to a greater or lesser degree, is a response to immediate political reality, the view from the throne has its own peculiar fascination and relevance to the debate about that fundamental question which underlies all theory, the nature and source of power. It would be an unwise historian, in this age of revisionism, who attempted to resurrect 1603 as a crucial milestone on the road to civil war. Yet it was the date chosen by Dr Sommerville as the starting-point for his compelling analysis of *Politics and Ideology in England, 1603-1640,* that thought-provoking work which, as Dr Christianson has pointed out in his recent review, offers both 'a perspective not entirely dissimilar to the old whig interpretation' and 'the best formal analysis of English political theory in early Stuart England that has ever appeared in print'.[3] So if 1603 is not the essential prelude to the battlefield, it still has its place in the history of ideological conflict.

This is surely because the mental world of the English court—and the world beyond the court—were jolted on to a new level of theoretic debate simply because of a foreign king whose leisure pursuits included not only the normal royal enthusiasm for hunting (if, as they saw it, to an obsessional degree) but the very abnormal one of writing books. It was an aberration made all the worse because, as Nicholas Fuller said in the parliament of 1610, he was 'in truth very wise yet is he a straunger to this government', so that the Commons had to take to themselves the awesome responsibility to be 'true to the King and true to ourselves, and let him know what by the laws of England he may do'. This was not, of course, just an 'ideological' comment. It related to that potential flashpoint, impositions; and it was made on 22 May, in response to the deeply worrying

speech by the king on 21 May. The crunch comes in Fuller's insistence that the reason why the Commons had to remind the King of England about the laws of England was that 'the king speaks of France and Spain what they may do'; and the same point was made by Thomas Wentworth, citing Fortescue on the difference between France and England, 'in that . . . by the law of England no imposition can be made without assent of parliament as in France etc. etc'.[4]

It was of course quite clever of Fuller and Wentworth to single out these frightening creatures, the Catholic and arbitrary kings of France and Spain. But they were only partially quoting. For what James had said the previous day was that 'all kings Christian as well elective as successive have power to lay impositions, I myself in Scotland before I came hither, Denmark, Sweden that is but newly successive, France, Spain, all have this power. And as Bellarmine abuses me in another sense *solus rex Angliae timet,* so shall *solus rex Angliae* be confined? Besides to call in question that power which all your kings have ever had, which two women have had and exercised, I leave it to yourselves to think what dutiful subjects ought to do in it'.[5] And there is the huge distinction between king and English MPs. The MPs argued their case on the basis of Fortescue and English law. The king, in asserting his, moved in a huge sweep from Scotland round the other major continental monarchies, Catholic and Protestant, and even threw in a reference to Bellarmine before arriving at English government—and petticoat government at that.

What could better illustrate the problem: the deep, and probably unbridgeable ideological gulf between a traditional attitude memorably satyrized in Flanders and Swann's song, 'The English are best' and the approach now translated into the English political world, which was grounded in continental, and Scottish, theories of kingship, as well as Scottish practice. Because of that approach, of course, tactlessness was writ large virtually every time James opened his mouth in England; and tactlessness hardly made for mutual trust. This was sad, because at the political level, there was actually much less to frighten the English in their king's understanding of his role than his language suggested. It was indeed unfortunate that James picked up English constitutional rhetoric with such enthusiasm and then turned it into a constant reminder of his passionate interest in an ideological debate which was very definitely not English. It masked all too effectively the king's ability to separate when necessary his love of theorizing from his firm grasp of the real world of politics. The Commons leapt like hungry trouts at the gaudy fly of continental theory. They paid no attention to the much less colourful little fly also cast by the king in his speech: his unwelcome complaint that 'fourteen weeks have now been spent in the parliament, yet you cannot allege nor say that for the principal errand you have bestowed so many days, nay scarce half so many days as weeks have been spent in the parliament'.[6] The theorist had a very practical point to make to the castigators of his theory.

Therein surely lies the supreme irony. For not only was James naturally unaware that his unusual leisure pursuit would provide wonderful evidence for the whig historians of later centuries. He was also unaware that it would deeply disturb his English subjects, for two reasons. First, it is highly doubtful if the two great works on kingship written in Scotland were primarily designed to inform his future English subjects of their king's extreme views of his kingship. Second, it is arguable that his major misreading of his kingdom of England lay not so much in his assumption that it was the land flowing with milk and honey, as in his expectation that there he could indulge the pleasure of talking political 'shop' as well as the theological 'shop' which he had enjoyed in Scotland. For the English took themselves all too seriously. They made the mistake of taking their new king too seriously also.

To illustrate this, let me begin with the mental world of Scotland. For what has never been given sufficient emphasis is that not only was it highly unusual for a king to write books. It was remarkable in the extreme for a Scottish king to do so, not because of a lack of an intensive and up-to-date education—James was, after all, taught by one of Europe's leading scholars, George Buchanan—but because before the sixteenth century there had been, in sharp distinction to England, virtually no tradition of political theorizing: no Magna Carta, no Provisions of Oxford, no theoretic justification such as accompanied the depositions of Edward II and Richard II, no Fortescue or Thomas Smith, and certainly no history of demands by those Scottish lairds, whose English equivalents sat in the lower house of parliament, for rights and privileges. And whereas only Richard III and Henry VII are missing from the line of seven English kings from Edward III to Henry VIII (and to the list can be added Henry VI's son Edward Prince of Wales) who were the recipients of at least one letter of advice to princes,[7] Scottish kings were not. There were, in the fifteenth century, Scottish contributions to the *speculum principis* genre, such as the anonymous poem known as *The Harp* which contained the singular advice that the king should choose his councillors because of ability rather than birth; Gilbert Hay translated the pseudo-Aristotelian *Secreta Secretorum,* but this was a work commissioned not for a king but by the Earl of Orkney; and only John Ireland's *Merroure of Wisdome,* which drew heavily on five sermons preached by Gerson to Charles VI, was actually intended for a king, James IV.[8] But for the clearest example of a specific connection we have to wait until a king himself turned writer, when James VI produced his manual of Scottish kingship for his son Henry.

This does not mean that Scotland was wholly without political theory. A country which produced a document as moving and dramatic as the Declaration of Arbroath of 1320 can hardly be dismissed as lacking ideological awareness. But the Declaration is itself an excellent guide to the nature of Scottish political theory. It was an appeal to the pope, John XXII, by the barons of Scotland that the ban of excommunication on their king, Robert Bruce, should be lifted, and Robert recognized as ruler of an independent kingdom, in no way subservient to England. To illustrate their utter resistance to English claims of overlordship, they asserted that if Robert—the king who had led them to freedom—were to depart from this cause, they would depose him and choose another in his place.[9] This was indeed resistance theory. But it was hypothetical resistance not to a tyrant but to a deserter, in one particular circumstance. Even more important, it was a theory drawn up in order to persuade a foreign power. It admirably demonstrates how different was the Scottish approach from the much more internalized attitude of the English; for the English explained things to themselves. And the Scottish approach had not substantially changed when the next great burst of theorizing took place in the 1560s, provoked by the crisis created by Mary Queen of Scots. Once again, the Scots were explaining themselves to a foreign power, this time Elizabeth.

By then, however, there were two new elements. First, the theorizing of King James was not Scotland's earliest experience of continental ideas being brought to bear on Scottish kingship. For sound political reasons—the fright the Scots had had when the succession to the Crown collapsed in 1290, and the sustained and aggressive English attempts at colonialism which followed—succession by primogeniture had been emphatically established. The Crown was entailed twice in the fourteenth century, in 1318 and 1371, according to rules of primogeniture, and never again was there a dynastic threat to the Scottish royal house. One might, indeed, ruminate in passing on the curious fact that the much more sophisticated kingdom of England so signally failed to sort out that most fundamental issue of how men became kings that it plunged itself into political mayhem in the fifteenth century. Meanwhile, and more to my purpose, there was another kind of crisis going on in Europe: papal mayhem, and the Conciliar Movement. And it was conciliarist theory which belatedly threw its shadow across accepted norms of Scottish kingship in the early sixteenth century. For one of the great latter-day conciliarists was the Scot John Mair, theologian and historian, teacher at Paris and subsequently principal of the universities of Glasgow and then St Andrews.

Mair wrestled with the problem of the source and nature of authority, not always consistently, but in the end clearly enough assigning to the ruler—ecclesiastical or secular—a role subordinate to and contained by the state. He recognized the need for, or at least advantages of, a prince of sorts; for, as he said, republics tended to be short-lived. And on occasion he did seem to veer towards assigning very considerable power to the ruler; as J. H. Burns has pointed out, his argument that it was best to have a monarch who would not only guide but, having taken counsel of wise men, decide, whether they agreed or not, might have been stated by Bossuet. But when he faced the question of whether the supreme power which is absolute and belongs only to Christ could ever be brought down to earth, his answer was that there was indeed a power which was not just superior but supreme—*potestas fontalis*—and that power was vested in the community. And the state, and the monarchy, which he used to illustrate this most fully was Scotland; in his *History of Greater Britain,* this concept was applied with ruthless logic to argue for the power of the state over the king, the right of deposition, and the elective nature of kingship.[10] As a political theorist Mair was more influential in the academic circles of Europe than in his native country. But if his impact was relatively limited, there was another's which was not. Mair's greatest European pupil was John Calvin. His greatest Scottish one was George Buchanan, future tutor of James VI. Both turned against the teachings of their master. Yet by a different route, Buchanan did arrive at conclusions about power in the state very similar to Mair's.

Buchanan's theory, particularly as applied to Scotland, derived more directly from a contemporary of Mair, Hector Boece, another luminary of Paris, principal of the new university of Aberdeen, and friend of Erasmus. Boece produced the same answer, by way not of logic but of an invented source, Veremundus, and an equally invented line of forty kings, each deposed because of their vicious lives, by the people of Scotland. And while the cool and logical Mair had little influence, the much more riotous Boece—far more popular in his own day, when he was given the royal patronage denied to Mair—was a wonderful source. None of it particularly mattered in the first half of the sixteenth century. But Boece's writings came to matter very much indeed in the late sixteenth century. He provided the witches for *Macbeth*; and he provided, for Buchanan, the necessary basis for the 'Ancient Constitution' of Scotland, by which 'the people' elected and deposed kings. The fact that the ancient Scots apparently got the choice wrong forty times over seems to have worried no one. Much more to the point, Buchanan could use ideas of Mair (without, as it were, adequate footnotes), and reinforce them with the supposed facts of Boece, to demonstrate to Elizabeth that the people of Scotland were justified in deposing Mary in 1567; and he could then go on to add his weight to the contractual theories advanced by

the Huguenot writers of the 1570s.[11] He could also, of course, teach—indeed, hammer—such theories into his own great pupil, King James.

The second, and, for the Scots, crucial new element was religion. For Mary's unique—and uniquely irresponsible—stance as a ruler who insisted on one religion for herself while allowing, and even paying for, another for her subjects, created a uniquely radical strand in Scottish reforming thought from the beginning, in the assertion of the superiority of the spiritual over the temporal power, and the extension beyond the natural leaders of secular society of the right and duty of resistance. The leading figure here was, of course, John Knox, with his appeal in 1558 to the nobility to 'hear the voice of the Eternal your God' and fulfil their divinely ordained role to act against an ungodly magistracy; and if they failed, Knox appealed beyond them to the commons, so that 'vox populi', invoked in England in 1327 to justify the deposition of Edward II, was now introduced to Scotland as the defender of the true religion against idolatry—except that when that defence turned into iconoclasm in Perth in May 1559, Knox's commons promptly became 'the rascal multitude'.[12] Yet despite the fright which the reforming leaders had when seeing 'vox populi' in action, they, like Buchanan, continued to appeal in the most general terms to the people; in practice, both were looking to the nobility, but they never limited the responsibility for action against ungodly rule to the lesser magistracy, as continental theorists like Beza and Philippe Du Plessis-Mornay did. Thus Knox could reduce Mary to stunned silence by insisting on his right to dictate her choice of husband as a subject born within the realm. And in the General Assembly of 1564, the former Dominican and minister of Edinburgh, John Craig, followed up a lengthy debate between Knox and Mary's secretary Maitland of Lethington about the right of the ministers to remove Mary, by citing the debate he had been present at in the university of Bologna in 1553, when it had been successfully held that all rulers could be deposed by their subjects if they broke their oaths to them; in answer to a 'claw-backe of the corrupt court' who objected that Bologna, being a commonwealth, was irrelevant to the kingdom of Scotland, he argued that 'everie kingdome is a commoun wealth . . . albeit everie commoun wealth is not a kingdome', and came close to Ponet by asserting that in each, the negligence of the people as well as the tyranny of princes might mean that laws contrary to God could be made, and yet that people or their posterity 'could justlie crave all things to be reformed, according to the originall institutioun of kingdoms and commoun wealths; and suche as will not doe so deserve to eate the fruict of their owne foolishnesse'.[13]

The Scottish context of *Basilikon Doron* and the *Trew Law* was therefore, from the point of view of their author, confusing and potentially very dangerous. In the long term, he inherited a kingdom in which, in theory and in practice, politics had been very low-key. Mainly because of their personal strength and ruthlessness, his Stewart predecessors between 1424 and 1542 had ruled with great authority, but the repeated minorities which beset the Stewart dynasty had militated against the move towards absolutist rule, with its ideological underpinning, already detectable in the French and Spanish kingdoms by the fifteenth century. This did not mean that the other end of the ideological spectrum, the elective and contractual theories of Mair and Buchanan, in any way disturbed the theoretic basis of a monarchy so firmly grounded, since the early fourteenth century, in the principle of primogeniture. But there was another aspect of Scottish political life which did more closely correspond with their ideas. One important consequence of the intermittent exercise of royal rule was that the localities remained unusually autonomous, by the standards of the major kingdoms of the sixteenth century; and they were presided over by men whose local power and influence were, from the mid-fifteenth to the early seventeenth century, given formal written recognition in the numerous bonds and contracts made between lords and their followers.[14] Mair and Buchanan did not significantly change, let alone dictate, the realities of Scottish politics (even in the sensational events of January 1649, it was the English, not the Scots, who were to agree with Buchanan that a people could bring a tyrannous king before the courts, try him, condemn him and kill him). Rather, they were subsuming the Scottish contract, as it had existed in practice at least since the fifteenth century, into their political theory. But the very existence of these contracts, as the fundamental means of social control, created a context in which contractual theories of kingship, when pushed hard for immediate political motives, could evoke vibrant echoes. More than that, they enabled the Scots of the late sixteenth century to move naturally towards a convenanting theology. It was the heirs of both theorists and politicians of the sixteenth century who were to draw up that supreme example of the Scottish bond, the National Covenant of 1638. More immediately, however, James also suffered from his short-term inheritance.

He can hardly be said to have been fortunate. He succeeded a ruler who was politically discredited and personally scandalous, but who was still alive, and wanted her throne back. In particular, he was vulnerable to aspersions on his legitimacy because of Mary's supposed affair with David Rizzio. Hence Henry IV's famous sneer at the Scottish Solomon, son of David, and the insults hurled at him in Perth on 5 August 1600, the day of the Gowrie conspiracy, as the 'son of seigneur Davie'; these things may give us a clue to his curious choice of phrase in the *Trew Law*, when describing the effect on the law of the conquest of England by the 'bastarde of Normandie'.[15] He was educated— savagely—by the man who was Mary's most outspoken

and vicious critic, and whose personal attack on her had been subsumed into a political theory which made James's power ultimately dependent on the will of the community; as the first coinage of his reign succinctly put it, 'pro me si mereor in me' (for me; against me if I deserve it), the phrase referring to the sword on the coins. At his coronation, when he was aged thirteen months, it was promised on his behalf that he would uphold the Protestant faith, and this, to the Protestant reformers, undoubtedly meant acting as the godly magistrate under their direction. Between them, his mother, his tutor, and the leading Protestants had reduced his position, at least in theory, to one of a subservience which would have been unacceptable to any of his predecessors, and was certainly unacceptable to him.

Basilikon Doron and the ***Trew Law*** have been castigated as unoriginal, even dismissed as stating no meaningful theory.[16] In one sense, they were unoriginal, as they were bound to be. For there was nothing new about the question whether power could be absolute and, if so, whether it was vested in the monarch or the community, even if in the late sixteenth century the focusing of the ruler's sacerdotal power as something precise and potentially immense had brought a new intensity to the debate. James had learned the contractual theory from Buchanan. But he was also aware of something very different; for by 1577 the royal library contained a copy of Guillaume Budé's *Institut du Prince,* and it also contained Bodin's *République,* and both offered him an answer utterly opposed to Buchanan's. How soothing it must have been to turn from the thunderings of Buchanan, with his terrifying stories of what had happened to wicked kings—which gave James nightmares years later—to assertions such as 'Maiestie or Soveraigntie is the most high, absolute, and perpetuall power over the citizens and subiects in a Commonweale . . .'.[17] But when, twenty years later, James adopted in his own writings the theories of the 'absolutists' rather than the 'contractualists', he was, in the Scottish context, doing something very original indeed. For he gave to Scottish monarchy an ideological base wholly different from anything in the past; and he gave it not just as a theorist, but as the man who had to translate theory into practice. And it is this which explains the difference between ***Basilikon Doron*** and the ***Trew Law.***

Space does not allow discussion of the practice, the subtlety and skill with which James restored royal authority in the state, and gained ascendancy over the extremists in the church, the hard-line group of Presbyterians known, from their leader Andrew Melville, as the Melvillians.[18] But the chronology of the gradual imposition of the new ideological base can be briefly sketched in. As Ian Stewart has shown, the 'Buchanan' propaganda of the first coinage gave way to royal propaganda, and the dates are instructive. In 1578, the year when the last of James's regents, the harsh and Anglophile Earl of Morton, fell from power, with the eleven-year-old king cheerfully asserting his ability to rule, and showing the first signs of saying no to Elizabeth, the coins for the first time used the famous Scottish motto 'Nemo me impune lacessit' (no one may meddle with me with impunity); ten years later, his coins announced 'florent sceptra piis regna his Iova dat numeratque' (sceptres flourish with the pious; God gives them kingdoms and numbers them); and in 1591, the new gold piece gave the name of Jehovah in Hebrew, with the inscription 'te solum vereor' (Thee alone do I fear), while the silver had a pair of scales over a sword, declaring 'his differt rege tyrannus' (in these a tyrant differs from a king).[19] Meanwhile, other propaganda methods had been brought into use. In 1583, when James, unlike in 1578, was genuinely emerging from his minority, he asserted his intention to be a 'universal king', above faction.[20] It was an intention which was to be fulfilled—to the fury, *inter alia,* of Cecil in the first decade of his English rule. In 1610, he burst out furiously to Sir Henry Yelverton that 'it fareth not with me now as it did in the Queen's time . . . for then . . . she heard but few, and of them I may say myself the chief, the king heareth many, yea of all kinds. Now as in hearing too few, there may be danger, so in hearing so many cannot be but confusion';[21] but confusion to Cecil was, and had long been, for James, the intelligent assertion of the over-riding authority of the king.

Moreover, the ruler who was to upset his English Commons by high-handed statements about his power, deliberately invoked the authority of his Scottish parliament in order to establish the authority of the king as he understood it. In 1584, parliament gave its support to enhancing royal prestige, when it passed two acts dealing with the king's estate. The first 'perpetuallie confirmis the royall power and auctoritie over all statis alsweill spirituall as temporall within this realme in the persoun of the kingis maiestie our soverane lord his airis and successouris', who will be 'Juges competent to all persounis . . . of quhatsumevir estate degrie functioun or conditioun . . . spirituall or temporall'. The second promised the full rigour of the law against any who uttered calumnies 'to the dishonour hurt or preiudice of his hienes his parentis and progenitouris', and specifically called in for suppression Buchanan's *De Iure Regno apud Scotos* and his *History of Scotland*; it was James's view of kingship, not Buchanan's, to which his subjects must now subscribe. But along with this went an attempt to repair the damage done by Mary not just to the prestige of monarchy but to Scottish government as a whole; her misuse of parliament was now to be rectified by the king's assertion of the 'honour and the auctoritie of his supreme court of parliament continewit past all memorie of man unto thir dayis as constitute upoun the frie votis of the thrie estaits of this ancient kingdome'.[22]

In practice, the authority of the supreme court of parliament was both built up and contained with immense skill. In the great parliament of 1587 the dignity of parliament was given considerable emphasis; this included its visual dignity, for James, following a precedent set by James II, took it upon himself to design clothes fitting for MPs, and the opening and closing public ceremony of the Riding of Parliament through Edinburgh undoubtedly became in his reign a splendid affair. At last an effective system of shire elections was introduced, which both met the rising aspirations of the lairds to turn up and give their voices, and at the same time imposed limits on the numbers who could actually do so.[23] And meanwhile in a series of acts in 1587 and the parliaments of the early 1590s, control of composition, notably of that crucial committee the Lords of the Articles, and control of business were relentlessly extended. It was effective; and yet it did not produce the kind of tension which marked James's dealings with his English parliaments. Perhaps there was a considerable safety-valve in the fact that James had not yet adopted English rhetoric; only after 1603 did his Scottish parliaments discover that their 'soverane lord' had greatly elevated his style, and now expected them to regard him as 'his sacred majestie'; more generally, only after 1603 were there signs of unease about what his sacred majesty, remote in England and raising the level of the actions of royalty as well as its language, was up to.[24]

Before 1603, his achievements did not of course solve all problems. But they marked a significant move towards the creation of a new Scottish context, after the troubles and confusions of the previous two decades. During the twelve years after the 1584 parliament, the king gradually translated the claims made there into practice. After 1596, apart from the extraordinary and quixotic Gowrie affair, his control of church and state was becoming irresistible. And after 1596, he settled down to write about it.

The texts of both his political tracts are well known. Neither is a long work; the *Trew Law* in particular is very short, so much so that it has recently been reprinted under the surprising title of *The Minor Prose Works of James VI and I.* Both are highly readable. And both are firmly set within the context of Scottish kingship. There the similarities end. **The *Trew Law*** deliberately—perhaps even defiantly—takes up the familiar Scottish theme of contract, and gives it a twist; the subtitle **The Reciprock and Mutuall Dutie betwixt a free King and his naturall Subiectes** has nothing whatsoever to do with a contract which may be broken by the inferior party if the superior does not fulfil his part. It was a new interpretation of 'reciprock'. It also rewrites Scottish history. Boece's forty kings, so crucial to Buchanan's theory, no longer exist. But the arguably historical figure of Fergus, fifth-century King of the Scots of Dalriada, is invoked to prove that 'as our

Chronicles beare witnesse', this king from Ireland and his successors settled in a country 'skantly inhabited' and 'skant of civilitie', and therefore kings in Scotland 'were before any estates or rankes of men within the same, before any Parliaments were holden or lawes made; and by them was the land distributed (which at the first was whole theirs) states erected and decerned & formes of government devised & established. And so it follows of necessitie, that the Kinges were the authors & makers of the lawes, and not the lawes of the Kings'. It was an appeal to history and logic of which Mair would surely have approved, even if his own logical approach—that despite rules of primogeniture, the first king must have been elected—resulted in a very different conclusion. Indeed, James himself allowed for Mair's idea, when he insisted that his Scottish 'model' was not universal. In other societies 'in the time of the first age', men were chosen to rule and protect their fellows. But not in Scotland, which stands somewhere between such societies and others, which were 'reft by conquest from one to another, as in our neighbour countrie in England, (which was never in ours)'. The parenthetical clause looks somewhat specious, for James had already acknowledged that Fergus arrived with his followers from Ireland and 'maid himself maister'. But the inconsistency could be resolved by the fact that he clearly saw Fergus and his followers, unlike the Saxons or the Normans, as coming in peaceably, to be welcomed by the few existing barbarous inhabitants; it was a particular and very muted kind of 'conquest', in which Fergus introduced law and government where previously there had been none, whereas the Conqueror 'changed the lawes (and) inverted the order of governement'.[25] His argument against Buchanan's theory therefore remained valid. But if this theory was to be answered on historical and logical grounds, that of Knox and Melville meant scripture; and Samuel's terrible warning to the Israelites about what their insistence on having a king would bring down on them was duly rehearsed.

This may appear a less than happy method of asserting divine right—as unhappy, indeed, as the forty mythical kings as props for the authority of the people—but it certainly established the case that what the Lord gave, the people must accept. There is no doubt whatsoever that the _Trew Law of Free Monarchies_ was an unequivocal defence of the theory of the divine right of kings. And inasmuch as it was written by a king, it raised the possibility, and indeed, especially among his English subjects, the spectre, that this was the thinking of a man who was in a position such as Mair and Buchanan could never be, of translating theory into practice. But one does not need to turn only to James's political actions to find that fears about his understanding of his office were often exaggerated. We only have

to read the end of his book. His most terrible warning was not to subjects who must accept the will of God. It was to the monarch. The tyrant would not escape punishment:

> but by the contrary, by remitting them to God (who is their only ordinary judge) I remit them to the sorest and sharpest Schoolemaister that can be devised for them. For the further a king is preferred by God above all other ranks and degrees of men, and the higher that his seate is above theirs: the greater is his obligation to his maker . . . The highest benche is sliddriest to sit upon.

Indeed, the absolute insistence on the providence of God led him to acknowledge the loophole in his own theory. The evocative homeliness of the 'sliddriest benche', so typical of much of James's writing, gave way to the compelling need, equally typical, to explore the full implications of his argument; and in one of the most deliberately powerful passages in the book, he went on:

> neither thinke I by the force & argument of this my discourse so to perswade the people, that none wil herafter be raised up, and rebel against wicked Princes. But remitting to the justice and providence of God to stirre up such scourges as pleaseth him, for punishment of wicked kings (who made the verie vermine & filthy dust of the earth to bridle the insolency of proud Pharaoh).

It may then 'please God to cast such scourges of princes and Instruments of his furie in the fire'. But the hand of God could reach out to punish the tyrant even in this life, and would surely punish him in the next. There were to be men in England who felt that this king was slipping out of human control. The _Trew Law_ tells us about the awesome control imposed on the king who was controlled only by God.[26]

Basilikon Doron is very different. It is a manual of kingship, firmly set in the _speculum principis_ genre. Indeed, the immediate model may have been the work believed to be Charles V's _Political Testament_ to his son Philip; certainly an Italian version of it was sent to James in 1592 by an Italian scholar and fugitive from the Inquisition, Giacomo Castelvetro, who had turned up in Scotland in 1591, hoping for the job of the king's Italian teacher.[27] In any event, it is a practical handbook and emphatically not a statement of highly developed political theory. Only in the first section, called 'A Kings Christian Duetie towards God', is there an overt nod towards divine right: 'for that he made you a little God to sitte on his throne, and rule over other men'.[28] But it is a very little nod; most of the section is about the king and his God. In the second part, 'A Kings Duetie in his Office', it becomes very clear that James's major concern, in developing the theory of the _Trew Law_ and in setting out his advice here, was the Melvillians, those 'vaine Pharasaicall puritanes', who will cry 'Wee are all but vile worms, & yet wil judge and give law to their king, but will be judged nor controlled by none: Surely there is more pride under such a ones black-bonnet nor under great Alexander's Diademe.' He had reason to know. He also had reason to know of both the dangers and the advantages of aristocratic power, and advised his son to harness the one and use the other, as indeed he had done with considerable success. His lack of understanding of economic matters comes out in his moan—the eternal moan of the 'layman'—about high prices and poor quality as the fundamental problem. His passionate desire for peace is equally apparent, although he admits and advises on unavoidable war. His discussion of marriage would of course send any modern self-respecting feminist into paroxysmic fury, but is in fact, by contemporary standards, a moderate and reasonable account, leavened with humour and a certain affection.[29] And the third part, on 'Indifferent Things', deals with the ideal lifestyle of a king: moderation—the same keynote—in all things, in food, language, recreation, even armour which provokes the unashamedly unheroic, if eminently practical comment that it should be light for easier 'away-running'. Hunting is highly praised; silly pedantry condemned.[30] What above all informs this remarkable book is not its theory of kingship. It is its low-key and admirable commonsense and wit.

Both works, however, posed considerable problems. Naturally James while King of Scotland was of considerable interest to the English; and the accounts of English diplomats give us a clear picture of a very effective ruler, controlling factions, controlling parliaments, asserting his will. So far, so good. But he was also the author of books which laid down a view of kingship, from the controlling of property to the making of law; and that was anything but good. Elizabeth believed, as much as James did, in kingship by divine right, and had no hesitation in warning her subjects off areas which were reserved to the monarch; but she was 'mere English', and she never offended English susceptibilities by making the claims, and showing an indifference to the rules, which the king from Scotland was to do.[31] It is inconceivable that she would ever have insisted, as James did in his famous exchange with Sir Edward Coke, that in effect he could be 'judge competent', as the 1584 act had said, because 'the law was founded on reason, and that he and the others had reason as well as the (English) judges'; and he then went on to make matters worse by retorting, when Coke pointed out that for all his great endowments, English law demanded long study and experience, that this put him under the law 'which is treason to affirm'.[32] It did not help very much that *Basilikon Doron* could on occasion be pressed into service by those whom James made profoundly uneasy; in 1610 Nicholas Fuller cited its advice to Prince Henry to be careful not to impoverish his sub-

jects—something which in practice James appeared all too guilty of doing. It is a nice illustration of Maurice Lee's reminder that '*Basilikon Doron,* like scripture, can be used for many purposes'.[33] But on the whole, the translation of James's Scottish writings into the English context, reinforced by some of James's own assertions after 1603, contributed to, if they did not wholly create, an atmosphere of unease. Yet it can be argued that this was not so much, as the English thought, because the king did not understand them. It was because they did not understand the king.

Few authors write only for themselves; and it may appear inconceivable that James, who was not a modest man, could have done so. Yet, as I shall suggest, it does appear that, at least at the time of their conception, neither of James's tracts was designed for an open readership, and neither was written with an English readership particularly in mind. In later years, James did write for his public; the *Apologie for the Oath of Allegiance* and the *Premonition to all Christian Monarchies* are obvious cases in point. But these were very different works, deliberately designed to refute papal claims and therefore naturally composed for a European market. This was not the case with the Scottish writings. Indeed, there are various clues about James's approach to writing—and to controversy—which suggest that the political tracts of 1598-9 should be viewed, initially at least, as the product of a mind at work rather than a closed and fixed one having already determined on the theme he had decided to lay before the world. Not the least of these clues is the manuscript of *Basilikon Doron* itself, a delightful piece of evidence of an author searching for words and ideal expression of arguments, scribbling, scoring out, scribbling again—and the whole lovely mess, which would call down the wrath of any tutor were a student to present it as an essay, bound up in purple velvet, and stamped in gold leaf with thistles, the Scottish emblem, and the royal initials, as befitted a king. There is also James's justification for a piece of early writing, his *Paraphrase on Revelations* (1588), which is 'asvell to teach my self as others'.[34] And it is arguable that the *Reulis and Cautellis of Poesie* (1585) and the *Daemonologie* (1597) were written in a state of anything but certainty, the first because of the dawning awareness that he could not match the great circle of poets in the Scottish court, the second because of the dawning fear that even if witchcraft existed, many of those who had died for it in Scotland had not been witches.

We have, then, a picture of a man who turned to writing to clarify his thought, who found writing a release; as Bishop Goodman later said of him, 'he did love solitariness, and was given to his study'.[35] *Basilikon Doron* and the *Trew Law* do not absolutely parallel the *Reulis* and the *Daemonologie,* but they should surely be seen in similar terms: that is, they were written for refreshment and for pleasure, for the sheer delight in temporarily shutting the door on a world which, in his early years, had posed so many problems, but which were now being overcome, and could now be analysed by the pen. *Basilikon Doron* was certainly written for Prince Henry. But both were surely written primarily for King James. It may even be that he was following in the footsteps of two great rulers of the past who had turned to writing; for the *Meditations* of Marcus Aurelius, and Alfred's *Boethius* and *Augustine* were composed because of the awareness of these men that the vanity and pride that might too easily accompany great power must be controlled by internal contemplation. Much more prosaically, there was also the consideration that *Basilikon Doron* would greatly upset the Melvillians; as indeed, when they became aware of it, it did.[36]

It is not only the appearance of the manuscript of *Basilikon Doron* which is suggestive of an author not principally motivated by the desire to rush into publication. The *Trew Law* was anonymous when first published in 1598; the author called himself 'C. Philopatris' (a hybrid which is, incidentally, hardly a tribute to Buchanan's teaching of the classics!). Moreover, the passage describing the effect of the Norman Conquest on English law and government was, as James can hardly have failed to be aware, one which touched on a somewhat raw English nerve. James was not averse to the occasional assumption of Scottish superiority, such as his change of New Year's Day to 1 January in 1600, to bring Scotland into line with 'all utheris weill governit commoun welthis and cuntreyis', though he must have realized when he said this that his hoped for succession to the country which, unlike well-governed ones, retained 25 March, could not be much longer delayed.[37] But that was very different from the pointed contrast between Scotland and the conquered, subservient England; and this surely indicates that this book was not intended as a means of trumpeting to his future subjects his political theory of divine right. The fact is that we make too much of the *Trew Law* because it sounds very familiar. But it was not the final and comprehensive statement of the deeply convinced and unshakeable divine right theorist, bound by the confines of his own theory. We only think that because after 1603, James expressed his ideas, and refined them, a great deal more than he had done in Scotland, in response to the English common lawyers. Before 1603, it was not even typical of his utterances. It was brought into being as a direct reaction to the secular theory of Buchanan and the much more dangerous religious theories and claims of the Melvillians.

Basilikon Doron was written in thorough-going Middle Scots, a fact which, as the editor of the Scottish Text Society edition, Dr James Craigie, rightly points out, is itself worthy of note; for already some thirty years ear-

lier John Knox's *History of the Reformation* had been written in a version of Scots which showed distinctly anglicizing tendencies, the late sixteenth century witnessed a continuation of the process in both literary and non-literary writings, and James himself in his great plea for Union in 1607 used linguistic similarity as one of his arguments for the common ground between his kingdoms of England and Scotland. All this does suggest a very private approach when James wrote *Basilikon Doron* in 1598; indeed, the immense secrecy which surrounded it and the fact that James wrote what he called his 'testament & latter will' because he was in fear of death—as Charles V had been when he wrote his testament—were described to Cecil by his agent George Nicolson, who begged him to keep quiet about it.[38] When the ideas began to emerge from the study for the first printing in 1599, the text was indeed anglicized; even so, James himself swore the printer, Robert Waldegrave, to secrecy, and only seven copies were produced, for designated people: his wife, his son, his son's tutor, the reasonably reliable Marquis of Hamilton, and the three northern Catholic earls who had caused him such trouble in the early 1590s but who were now cooperative subjects, Huntly, Erroll and Angus.[39] And then in March 1603 the situation changed entirely. The book appeared on the London market.

I have previously described this—impressionistically—as 'becoming a bestseller'; his new subjects wanted a sight of 'the king's book'. But I had no idea of the scale of it until Peter W. M. Blayney, who has made a very detailed study of the printing of *Basilikon Doron,* told me of his findings and very kindly allowed me to make use of them. They are dramatic in the extreme. The *Trew Law* was also published in that year, after *Basilikon Doron,* and in two of the three printings the king's name did appear. But it was very small-scale compared to the huge success of *Basilikon Doron.* One copy of Waldegrave's Edinburgh edition was sent to London before Elizabeth's death on 24 March. Only four days later, on 28 March, the publisher John Norton and five partners 'entered' the work in the Stationers' Hall, thus registering their claim to copyright. By 13 April, eight 1603 editions were almost certainly out; at that point plague hit London—and the booktrade—and very little was produced from then until 30 May. Dr Blayney estimates that there were between 13,000 and 16,000 copies printed: up to 10,500 of the Norton editions, two pirate editions by one Edward Allde, who printed 3,000 and was fined on 13 April for doing so and for undercutting the price of the official editions, and in addition copies of the Waldegrave edition made available on the London market. The printer of all the official editions was Felix Kingston, who began by roping in other printers in order to get the sheets ready but then took over the enterprise almost exclusively. Norton himself, publisher of all eight editions, was a friend of Cecil; and, as Dr Blayney suggests, Cecil—no doubt anxious to please his new master—may have been in-volved in bringing the initial Waldegrave copy to London before Elizabeth's death and its registration with the Stationers' Company immediately afterwards. This friend in high places, however, did not save Norton from being up before the court of the Stationers' Company on the same day as Allde, 13 April, not for under-cutting, but for overcharging. The king's book was undoubtedly a best-seller.

Whether it was a popular read is a quite different matter. Normally very few copies survive from the editions of books which capture the market: one or two from the first edition, a few more from the second, and so on. In the case of **Basilikon Doron,** a lot survives from each edition, and this suggests that it was bought, perhaps read once, and put on the bookshelf.[40] This seems to me to raise a very interesting possibility. By March 1603, James does seem to have decided that his book should be made generally available to his future subjects; in the 1603 Edinburgh edition he referred to Elizabeth as being still alive, and apologised to his English readers for anything which might offend them in a text written originally for private purposes, commenting on Scottish affairs, and not intended for general publication.[41] The highly significant fact is that the work he chose to make available was not the theoretic and potentially controversial *Trew Law*; that simply trailed in behind *Basilikon Doron* later in 1603. Although like the *Trew Law, Basilikon Doron,* as he now acknowledged, did contain things which might appear critical of the English, it was nevertheless the book brought into circulation because it was his account of the practical exercise of royal authority, realistic, moderate rather than arbitrary, compromising. That was the style of kingship which he wanted to demonstrate to his new subjects. If they did not read it, then it explains an error which has been remarkably persistent: the belief that an English king called James I wrote a book about absolute kingship called **Basilikon Doron.** The idea gains support from the fact that after the frenzied printings of the first two and a half weeks of the reign, there was virtually no interest in England for further editions. It was taken up on the Continent; some thirty translations into Latin, French, Italian, Spanish, Dutch, German and Swed-ish—as well as one in Welsh—were produced in James's lifetime. But it did not appear in England again until the publication of the *Workes* in 1616. So the English seem, on the whole, to have treated it as the equivalent of a coronation mug.[42] But it was not a coronation mug. It was a guide to their new king. It was, in other words, not just a missed opportunity. It was an opportunity which James, the stranger, the incoming foreign king was keen to offer, as reassurance; and it went very badly awry.

The sad thing was that once this had happened, the problem could only be compounded. For James was certainly more than a solitary author. He was a delighter in controversy. In Scotland, it had been theological controversy—sometimes impassioned, even bad-tempered controversy, but always with the spice of enjoyment. There is a revealing little thumbnail sketch of a row between the king and one of the Melvillian ministers, John Davidson, in 1598—a row in which, incidentally, Davidson, like Andrew Melville himself on a much more famous occasion, clutched at the king's sleeve. It could hardly be said that they parted in agreement. But as they parted, 'the king turned backe, and taking him by the shoulder, said, "Mr Johne, yee sall be welcomer with me becaus yee are plaine."'[43] Not the least of James's difficulties in the new world of England was that the English were not so plain.

Moreover, they took him too literally, at every turn. They failed to make allowance for bursts of irritation and visible exaggeration in the heat of argument, of which the exchange with Coke, and the famous out-burst at Hampton Court are obvious examples. And, perhaps precisely because he was a notable political theorist as well as a leading political figure, they failed to make sufficient allowance for flexibility of mind—that flexibility which produced works as different in character as *Basilikon Doron* and the *Trew Law* within a year, and twelve years later, in the parliament of 1610, the very well-received speech of 21 March on the nature of monarchy which was far more acceptable than either, commanding 'the great Contentment of all Parties'. This reaction, among MPs all too ready to show their touchiness, and the text of the speech itself, suggest that Dr Sommerville's view of it as 'little more than pleasantries' may be an understatement.[44] It was surely more than that, a genuine assertion of James's belief that kingship did indeed involve vast powers, but that wise kings did not invoke them without concern for the law and for the bond between monarch and subjects. But I have already referred to a speech of 1610, made exactly two months later, which did not create contentment; flexibility included irritability and, with it, the tendency to emphasize theory when practice caused frustration. Inevitably that made it difficult for his English subjects—especially the English common law-yers—to distinguish between theory and practice.

There were even occasions when it was hard for them to see the theory for what it was. In the genial and hopeful atmosphere surrounding the opening of parliament in 1621, James took up the delicate question of the nature of monarchy and parliament. He told his parliament that 'Things proper to yourselves are the making of laws in that nature as he [the king] shall call for them. The king, he is the maker of them and ye are the advisers, councillors, and confirmers of them . . .'. The very idea of the king as the maker of laws no doubt struck horror into his listeners. One wonders whether they had listened attentively to an earlier passage: 'for kings and kingdoms were before parliaments . . . but when people began to be willing to be guided by laws, then came the first institutions of parliaments'.[45] It was the appeal to logic expressed in very similar terms two decades earlier in the *Trew Law.* Indeed, if anything, it was a modified version of that earlier claim. But the modification was not enough. James was not claiming that he alone could 'make' law. But it was possible to interpret him as believing that he could; and that, to his English subjects, was profoundly disturbing.

Yet in reacting as they did, they missed not one but two crucial points about King James. It was not only that he never translated his most extreme theoretic claims into practice. It was also the fact that the political issue which concerned him most when he succeeded to the English throne was not divine right monarchy at all, but union. And this brings me finally to a much neglected figure, James's major ally in the union project, the great Scottish lawyer Sir Thomas Craig of Riccarton. Craig was an enthusiastic unionist, influenced not only by the king, but by the vision of union expressed by Protector Somerset in his influential *Epistle* of 1547.[46] It was to be a union of equal partners. That meant asserting Scotland's antiquity and independence as a kingdom, as against the dismissive views of the vassal status of the Scottish kingdom most recently expressed by Holinshed. Craig gives us a wonderful little description of the eternal reaction of the Scot when faced with assertions of English superiority: having read Holinshed, 'I found my Choler begin to rise, and that it happened to me exactly as Holinshed had foretold; for there is nothing, says he, which will vex a Scotsman more, or that he takes worse, than to tell him, that Scotland is a Fee-Liege of England.' But he was concerned with far more than the defence of Scottish independence. This friend and legal adviser of the king was the one notable exception to the general rule that debate in Scotland was religious debate. His political theory was very moderate. An admirer of Bodin, he nevertheless stopped far short of Bodin's view of kingship; indeed, he managed to maintain good relations with James despite the fact that he could describe George Buchanan as 'my very intimate friend'. For Craig, the law was of two kinds, mutable and immutable. The Prince could alter the first, for the good of the state; for it related to particular times and circumstances, and must change as they changed. But the immutable law is that which always binds the Prince, because he has sworn to observe it, by sacred oath; and 'as God himself is invoked witness of the Oath given, so he will avenge the violation of it. The Prince has not made his promise to men, but to the Omnipotent God, who can and uses to require a strict account of it.' And what did Craig mean by the Prince? 'When I speak of a Prince, I mean a Prince in the Parliament or Great Court of the kingdom. For then he has the Rights of Majesty more eminently, because otherwise he cannot make a law, that obliges the subjects,

nor impose Taxes upon them.'[47] Despite the very different emphasis of the *Trew Law* and, indeed, many of the assertions James made to his English subjects after 1603, this view, advanced by a man close to the king, trusted and respected by him, was not one from which the king would have dissented. But neither was it a view which made its mark on his English subjects. The English translation of James's Scottish views was not a happy one. But that was not simply because the Scottish views were unacceptably extreme.

King James adored theological debate. In Scotland and England he got plenty of it. In Scotland, when he turned to political theory, he was, apart from Craig, a more isolated figure. When he entered the English world, he found a preoccupation with political issues which to him was both stimulating and entertaining. James's Scottish subjects were well aware that their king was a man of wit and humour. Even the hostile Anthony Weldon paid grudging tribute to that. But it is not something which James's English subjects—or later historians of King James I—have particularly appreciated. The difficulty was that royal enjoyment, even occasional tail-twisting, could only add to English worry.

Notes

1. J. W. Allen, *Political Thought in the Sixteenth Century* (London, 1928), p. 252. For the writings discussed here: *Basilikon Doron of King James VI,* ed. J. Craigie (Scottish Text Society, Edinburgh, 1944-50), 2 vols.; *The Trew Law of Free Monarchies* is in *Minor Prose Works of King James VI and I,* ed. J. Craigie and A. Law (Scottish Text Society, Edinburgh, 1982), pp. 57-82. Both are also printed, in English, in *The Political Works of James I,* ed. C. H. McIlwain (Cambridge, Mass., 1918; reprint, 1965), pp. 3-70; the introduction, pp. xv-cxi, is a masterly analysis of James's thought.

2. Sir Anthony Weldon, *The Court and Character of King James,* in *The Secret History of the Court of James I,* ed. Sir Walter Scott (Edinburgh, 1811), II, pp. 1-20. Scott's own views are made all too clear in his novel *The Fortunes of Nigel* (Edinburgh, 1822).

3. J. P. Sommerville, *Politics and Ideology in England, 1603-1640* (London, 1986). P. Christianson, 'Political Thought in Early Stuart England', *Historical Journal,* 30 (1987), 960.

4. *Proceedings in Parliament, 1610,* ed. Elizabeth Read Foster (New Haven, 1966), II, pp. 109, 108.

5. *Ibid.,* II, p. 102.

6. *Ibid.,* II, p. 101.

7. Jean-Philippe Genet, 'Ecclesiastics and Political Theory in Late Medieval England: The End of a

Monopoly', in *The Church, Politics and Patronage in the Fifteenth Century,* ed. R. B. Dobson (Gloucester, 1984), pp. 31-2.

8. 'The Harp' is printed in *Liber Pluscardensis,* ed. F. J. H. Skene (Edinburgh, 1877-80), I, pp. 392-400. *Gilbert of the Haye's Prose MS* (1456), II, *The Buke of the Ordre of Knychthede and The Buke of the Governance of Princis* (Scottish Text Society, Edinburgh, 1909). J. H. Burns, 'John Ireland and *The Merroure of Wyssdome*', *Innes Review,* 6 (1955), 77-98. R. J. Lyall, 'Politics and Poetry in Fifteenth and Sixteenth Century Scotland', *Scottish Literary Journal,* 3 (1976), 5-29. R. A. Mason, 'Kingship, Tyranny and the Right to Resist in Fifteenth Century Scotland', *Scottish Historical Review,* 66 (1987), pp. 125-51. Sally L. Mapstone, 'The Advice to Princes Tradition in Scottish Literature, 1450-1500' (DPhil., Oxford, 1986); I have much benefited from reading this thesis, and from discussions with Dr Mapstone.

9. Sir James Fergusson, *The Declaration of Arbroath* (Edinburgh, 1970); A. A. M. Duncan, *The Nation of Scots and the Declaration of Arbroath* (Historical Association Pamphlet, 1970); G. W. S. Barrow, 'The Idea of Freedom in Late Medieval Scotland', *Innes Review,* 30 (1970), pp. 16-34.

10. John Major, *History of Greater Britain* (Scottish History Society, 1892). My debt in this section to the work of Professor J. H. Burns is very clear: see Burns, 'The Conciliarist Tradition in Scotland', *Scottish Historical Review,* 42 (1963), pp. 89-104, and '*Politia Regalis et Optima*: The Political Thought of John Mair', *History of Political Thought,* II (1981-2), 31-61; I also learned a great deal from his Carlyle Lectures on 'Lordship, Kingship and Empire, 1400-1525', given in the University of Oxford, 1988.

11. Hector Boece, *The History and Chronicles of Scotland . . . translated by John Bellenden,* ed. T. Maitland (Edinburgh, 1821). George Buchanan, *De Iure Regni apud Scotos* (Edinburgh, 1579: facsimile reprint, Da Capo Press, Amsterdam and New York, 1969). Among the wealth of writing on these authors, see in particular A. A. M. Duncan, 'Hector Boece and the Medieval Tradition', *Scots Antiquaries and Historians* (Abertay Historical Society, Dundee, 1972), pp. 1-11; J. H. Burns, 'The Political Ideas of George Buchanan', *Scottish Historical Review,* 30 (1951), 60-8; H. R. Trevor-Roper, 'George Buchanan and the Ancient Scottish Constitution', *English Historical Review,* Supplement 3, 1966; R. A. Mason, '*Rex Stoicus*: George Buchanan, James VI and the Scottish Polity', in *New Perspectives on the Politics and Culture of Early Modern Scotland,* ed. J. Dwyer,

R. A. Mason and A. Murdoch (Edinburgh, 1982), pp. 9-33; and, most recently, the excellent new approach by D. Norbrook, '*Macbeth* and the Politics of Historiography' in *Politics of Discourse: The Literature and History of Seventeenth-Century England,* ed. Kevin Sharpe and Steven N. Zwicker (Berkeley, 1987), pp. 78-116. For the development of theories of resistance, Q. Skinner, *The Foundations of Modern Political Thought* (Cambridge, 1978), II, part 3.

12. John Knox, *Appellation to the nobility and estates of Scotland* and *Letter addressed to the Commonalty of Scotland* (both 1558) in *The Works of John Knox,* ed. D. Laing (Edinburgh, 1864), IV, pp. 469-520 and 521-38; the quotation is on p. 495. The reference to 'the rascal multitude' is in John Knox, *History of the Reformation in Scotland,* ed. W. C. Dickinson (Edinburgh, 1949), I, p. 162.

13. *Ibid.,* II, pp. 82-3; David Calderwood, *The History of the Kirk of Scotland* (Wodrow Society, Edinburgh, 1842-9), II, pp. 277-9. John Ponet, *A Short Treatise of Politic Power* (Scolar Press facsimile, London, 1970).

14. Jenny Wormald, *Lords and Men in Scotland: Bonds of Manrent, 1442-1603* (Edinburgh, 1985). As king, James recognized and made use of the idea of contract for political purposes; he entered into bonds himself, and in 1587 he revived the idea of the General Band, which formally bound highland and border lords to take responsibility for their followers and tenants: *Lords and Men,* pp. 130, 153, 165. But unlike Mair and Buchanan, he did not subsume practice into his political theory; he was no 'contractualist'. Not surprisingly, he shared his predecessors' belief in hereditary succession as the basis for his position as King of Scotland—and potential King of England: *Trew Law,* ed. Craigie, pp. 73, 80-1.

15. Maurice Lee Jr, *James I and Henry IV: An Essay in English Foreign Policy, 1603-1610* (Illinois, 1970), p. 10. *Trew Law,* ed. Craigie, p. 71.

16. Allen, *Political Thought,* pp. 252-3.

17. 'The Library of James VI, 1573-1583' is listed in *Scottish History Society, Miscellany* 1 (Edinburgh, 1893), pp. xi-lxxv; references to Budé and Bodin are on pp. xli-ii and lvi—there were two copies of Budé. An appealing aspect of this list is that it includes bows, arrows, a shooting glove and golf clubs (p. lxx): 'mens sana in corpore sano'! Jean Bodin, *The Six Bookes of a Commonweale,* ed. K. D. McRae (Harvard, 1962), p. 84.

18. M. Lee Jr, *John Maitland of Thirlestane and the Foundation of the Stewart Despotism in Scotland* (Princeton, 1959); *Government by Pen: Scotland

under James VI and I (Illinois, 1980); 'James VI and the Revival of Episcopacy in Scotland, 1596-1600', *Church History,* 43 (1974), pp. 55-7.

19. I. H. Stewart, *The Scottish Coinage* (London, 1967), pp. 92-6.

20. *Calendar of State Papers Scottish,* VI, p. 523.

21. 'Mr Henry Yelverton, his Narrative of what passed on his being restored to the King's favour in 1609 . . .', *Archaeologia,* 15 (1806), p. 51.

22. *Acts of the Parliaments of Scotland,* ed. T. Thompson and C. Innes (12 vols., Edinburgh, 1814-75), III, pp. 292-3, 296, cc. 2, 8; p. 293, c. 3.

23. *Ibid.,* III, p. 443, c. 16; pp. 509-10, c. 120, an act which revived legislation first passed in 1428 but never put into effect.

24. For greater control before 1603, see, for example, *ibid.,* III, p. 443, c. 16, and p. 530; IV, pp. 8, 56, 69, c. 28. In the second parliament held after his departure to England, the king tried to nominate the Lords of the Articles, probably unsuccessfully: *ibid.,* IV, p. 280 (the record is mutilated here, and the king's list does not survive). James's visit to Scotland in 1617, when he spent twelve days sitting with the Lords of the Articles, produced something of a show-down. He was forced to concede that no more than eight from each estate, and from among the officers of state—the real point of the demand—would be elected to the Articles: *ibid.,* IV, p. 527. Despite this, royal control of the Articles seems to have reached a new level in the parliament of 1621, when James was straining every nerve to push through his ecclesiastical policy and a new form of taxation; for the extent of royal manipulation in this parliament, Calderwood, *History,* VII, pp. 488-507.

25. *Trew Law,* ed. Craigie, pp. 70-1. This description of the effect of the Norman Conquest on English law and government—reinforced by the point that the laws in England were written in a foreign language—was certainly touching on a somewhat raw English nerve: see Christopher Hill, 'The Norman Yoke' in *Puritanism and Revolution* (Penguin Books reprint, 1986), pp. 58-125; J. P. Sommerville, 'History and Theory: The Norman Conquest in Early Stuart Political Thought', *Political Studies,* 34 (1986), pp. 249-61. That being so, the passage may support the argument suggested on p. 50, that the *Trew Law,* when written, was not primarily directed towards an English readership.

26. *Trew Law,* ed. Craigie, pp. 70, 71, 64-6, 81.

27. According to Castelvetro, in his dedication to James, the king had asked to see this work. Whether it was genuine or not remains uncertain. There are, as Craigie has pointed out, certain similarities between *Basilikon Doron* and Charles V's 'Instrucciones' to Philip in 1543 and 1548; and James may well have known about these. But the Castelvetro manuscript was his holograph of the dubious 'political testament' of 1555. An English translation of this work by Lord Henry Howard was presented to Queen Elizabeth in the 1590s; and Castelvetro had ties with the English court. The literary link between two royal fathers, Charles V and James VI, writing for their sons, is therefore tenuous; more probably the manuscript given to James had only the spurious authority of Charles's name rather than the genuine one of his authorship. This does not, however, affect the idea that James saw himself as following Charles's example. *Basilikon Doron,* ed. Craigie, II, pp. 63-7; *The Works of William Fowler,* ed. H. W. Meikle, J. Craigie and J. Purves (Scottish History Society, Edinburgh, 1940), III, pp. cxxvi-xxxi; R. B. Merriman, *The Rise of the Spanish Empire* (New York, 1962), III, pp. 407-9; Karl Brandi, *The Emperor Charles V* (London, 1949), pp. 484-95, 582-6.

28. *Basilikon Doron,* ed. Craigie, I, pp. 24-5.

29. *Ibid.,* I, pp. 39, 140-3, 82-93, 120-35.

30. *Ibid.,* I, pp. 174-5, 180-1, 188-91.

31. This became immediately apparent at the beginning of the reign, even before James had left Scotland, in an exchange of letters between the king and the English councillors, in which James talked of the blessings of God, while the councillors, instructed to keep things going until his arrival, had to send messengers post-haste to Scotland to tell him the right form of words to authorise them to do so. Apparently English government ceased to function for a few days! Bodleian MS Ashmole 1729, ff. 41r-42r, 56r-v.

32. S. R. Gardiner, *History of England, 1603-1642* (London, 1884-9), II, pp. 38-9.

33. *Parliamentary Debates in 1610,* ed. S. R. Gardiner, Camden Society o.s. 81 (London, 1861), p. 10. M. Lee Jr, 'James VI and the Aristocracy', *Scotia,* 1 (1977), p. 19.

34. British Library, Royal MS 18 B xv (Basilikon Doron); 18 B xiv, f. 1 (Revelations).

35. Godfrey Goodman, *The Court of King James the First,* ed. J. S. Brewer (London, 1839), I, p. 173.

36. *Basilikon Doron,* ed. Craigie, II, pp. 8-15.

37. *Register of the Privy Council of Scotland,* ed. J. H. Burton and others (Edinburgh, 1877-), VI, p. 63.

38. *Basilikon Doron,* ed. Craigie, II, pp. 117, 6.

39. *Ibid.,* I, p. 13; II, pp. 7-8.

40. I am deeply indebted to Dr Blayney for the information contained here, and for his permission to use it; and I should like to record the pleasure and fascination which his discussion of his discovery gave me.

41. *Basilikon Doron,* ed. Craigie, I, pp. 21, 13, 14, 18.

42. One manifestation of this is, however, a good deal more remarkable than the average mug. As a pleasing compliment to the king and his son Henry, the classical scholar and artist Henry Peacham produced two delightful books containing emblems illustrating quotes from *Basilikon Doron,* accompanied by appropriate classical tags; one, with pen-and-ink drawings, was dedicated to the king, the other, using water-colour, to Henry Prince of Wales: British Library, Royal MS 12 A lxvi and Harleian MS 6855, art. 13.

43. Calderwood, *History,* V, p. 680.

44. *Political Works of James I,* ed. McIlwain, pp. 306-25; Sommerville, *Politics and Ideology,* p. 134.

45. *Commons Debates, 1621,* ed. W. Notestein, F. H. Relf and H. Simpson (New Haven, 1935), II, pp. 3-4. A similar note had been struck in the first speech James ever made to the English parliament, on 29 March 1604. In the opening sentences, he stated his view of parliament: 'you who are here presently assembled to represent the Body of this whole Kingdome'. Later in the speech he was even more specific, when he talked of the 'making of Lawes at certain times, which is onely at such times as this in Parliament'. There is no doubt that this is how he saw it. But he immediately followed it up by promising 'that I will ever preferre the weale of the body and of the whole Commonwealth, in making of good Lawes and constitutions, to any particular or private ends of mine, thinking ever the wealth and weale of the Common-wealth to bee my greatest weale and worldly felicitie: A point wherein a lawful King doeth directly differ from a Tyrant.' It might have been more tactful to resist the temptation to talk about his 'special subject' on this occasion; it was an intrusion of his personal role in the making of law which could too easily give rise to confusion and misinterpretation. *Political Works of James I,* ed. McIlwain, pp. 269 and 277.

46. Edward Seymour, Protector Somerset, 'Epistle or exhortacion to uniti & peace to the inhabitauntes of Scotland', appendix to *The Complaynt of Scotlande,* ed. J. A. H. Murray (Early English Text Society, Extra Series 17, 18, London, 1872).

47. Thomas Craig of Riccarton, *Scotland's Sovereignty Asserted* (London, 1695), p. 3. He wrote his rebuttal of Holinshed because 'none of our Country-men had answered that Calumny, as if they seem'd to own the Truth of it by their Silence': he himself would not have bothered, 'except that learned men, such as Bodin, fell into this error' (pp. 3-4). Bodin's opinion clearly mattered. In *The Right of Succession to the Kingdom of England, in Two Books: against the Sophisms of Parsons the Jesuite, who assumed the counterfeit Name of Doleman* (London, 1703), Craig took up the theme of royal power and the law, and cited with approval Bodin's distinction between mutable and immutable laws, which 'pleases me much better than other distinctions' (p. 129), while making clear the grounds for his disagreement. So far, indeed, did he emphasize the supremacy of law that, in the passage referred to here, he invoked the testimony of Jeremiah, 'that God himself is bound, as it were, by Laws to observe his Covenant with Mankind' (pp. 128-9). These works set out the position held by a man very much in James's confidence; the king undoubtedly knew about Craig's ideas. They were not published in his day, however, because the ease with which James succeeded to the throne of England made them unnecessary. But the battle went on. A century after Craig wrote *Scotland's Sovereignty,* an edition and translation by George Ridpath was produced in 1695 because, as Ridpath complained, English historians were still attacking the honour of Scotland, including 'now by Mr Rymer Historiographer to his Majesty king William, who hath publish'd a Form of Homage said to be performed by Malcolm the Third King of Scots to Edward the Confessor for the Kingdom of Scotland' (pp. x-xi); and this in turn provoked William Atwood's *The Superiority and direct dominion of the Imperial Crown of England over the Crown and Kingdom of Scotland asserted. In answer to Scotland's Sovereignty asserted, tr. by G. Ridpath, 1695* (London, 1704). But this was, of course, all very topical because of a very different union.

Kevin Sharpe (essay date 1993)

SOURCE: Sharpe, Kevin. "Private Conscience and Public Duty in the Writings of James VI and I." In *Public Duty and Private Conscience in Seventeenth-Century England: Essays Presented to G. E. Aylmer,* edited by John Morrill, Paul Slack, and Daniel Woolf, pp. 77-100. Oxford: Clarendon Press, 1993.

[*In the following essay, Sharpe argues that an understanding of James's perceptions of conscience and duty is central to any study of his work.*]

Conscience: 'a man cannot steal, but it acuseth him; a man cannot swear but it checks him; a man cannot lie with his neighbour's wife but it detects him. 'Tis a blushing shame fac'd spirit that mutinies in a man's bosom . . .'

—2nd Murderer, *Richard III,* I. iv. 133-9

Let not our babbling dreams afright our souls;
Conscience is but a word that cowards use,
Devis'd at first to keep the strong in awe.
Our strong arms be our conscience, swords our law.

—*Richard III,* V. iii. 308-11.

'Private conscience' and 'public duty' are in our usage terms that usually imply opposites. Though numerous events and controversies—politicians' sexual indiscretions, the publication of offensive books, the responsibility for riot and disorder—belie a simple distinction between them, we adhere to a belief in the separateness of private and public spaces. Indeed, commitment to that separateness and the idea of the ownership of the self are fundamental to both modern psychology and the modern state. Almost from the time that the word became respectable, the business of politics has been that of a negotiation between the individual and the State, private interests and public interests. Indeed, the acceptance and validation of a world of politics—of contest and party, lobby and propaganda—marked a recognition of the artificiality of the social state, and of a public morality that might differ from the ethical values that governed personal behaviour. Brave would be the historian who endeavoured confidently to assign an exact date to, or list of causes for, what were truly revolutionary developments. But we know that by the end of the seventeenth century, despite lingering pejorative associations, parties had become enshrined in the social and political life of the nation; that the Toleration Act signalled a degree of separation of Church and State; and that the language of 'interest' had gained respectability.[1] Such developments, it has been suggested, were inextricably linked with a new attitude to the autonomous individual and a sphere of self-determination.[2] By the end of the seventeenth century the conscience was defined as part of that sphere: as, in Locke's words, 'nothing else but our own opinion or judgement of the moral rectitude or pravity of our own Actions'.[3]

Before the Civil War, however, such distinctions were not so readily made and ideas of conscience were correspondingly different and less individualistic. The normative texts of politics were the works of Aristotle and the Bible. Following Aristotle, it was held that the State was an ethical community and there was no contradiction between the good person, the good citizen, and the good ruler. The concept of the commonweal precluded clear delineation of the public and the private. The human body and 'self' were as much a part of the public as the 'body politic' was anthropomorphized. Because it was natural, the commonweal united all in one interest. Because all were members of a Christian commonweal that shaped its laws and codes according to God's decrees, there should no more have been contention over the 'right course' in public action than in private.[4] There was one God, one Scripture, and therefore—in theory—one conscience for the commonwealth. Conscience was the inner law-giver, the 'deity within us', that element of knowledge of God that remained even in fallen man. Those who claimed God or Scripture spoke to them differently from the prescriptions of the commonweal were, it was held, betrayed by a false conscience or pretended to conscience, *as they themselves knew,* out of evil intent. Nor, in this model, was conscience at odds with duty. Both implied a moral obligation, that is an obligation to a shared morality. The Geneva Bible's translation of Eccles. 12: 13 enjoined: 'Feare God and keep his commandments: for this is the duty of man.'[5] Among God's commandments was obedience to divinely instituted authority. As the conscience was God's lieutenant in the soul, so the king was God's lieutenant in the commonweal, responsible for guiding the *respublica Christiana* according to the divine decrees. Loyalty to the king was an act of conscience as well as a duty and an interest. Resistance to the ruler was rebellion not only against God but against the self, the rise of ignorance and passion against the knowledge and reason which distinguished men from beasts.

Such ideal prescriptions had perhaps always been compromised by observed human experience: theological controversy, popular and baronial revolt, conflicting loyalty to family and ruler. But the rent of Christendom massively exacerbated the tensions and bequeathed to the era between the Reformation and the age of toleration fundamental practical and theoretical problems which could not be resolved nor even fully conceptualized within the prevailing paradigms. Many of those problems and questions—the nature of 'true religion', the extent of obedience to the prince, the relation of man to God and his fellows, the ends and organization of society and the State—were intimately bound up with and revolved around issues of 'conscience'. As old vocabularies and value systems lived on in radically new circumstances, the very word conscience, once a symbol of unity, was deployed to defend violence, rebellion, and division. As a consequence a few thinkers, most notably Niccolò Machiavelli, advocated the radical course of freeing public life and government from religion and morality. But, to an age which still hoped for an ecumenical solution to the division of Christendom, Machiavelli's secular politics were anathema.[6] Faced, then, with the enduring ideals of Christian humanism and the experience of religious division and contest, rulers and citizens had to define—and redefine—their own conscience. It is hardly surprising that in doing so they faced contradiction—not only from others, but also within themselves.

Often in early modern England the theatre staged (and attempted to contain) those contradictions. As our opening quotations remind us, Shakespeare glaringly presents a world in which conscience both preserves some of its unifying moral authority and yet lies at the mercy of 'Machiavels'—illegitimate princes—who would subject it to personal ambition and force. It is no coincidence that, in the works of Shakespeare and other Elizabethan and Jacobean dramatists, we encounter debates about conscience in plays self announcedly about kings.[7] For many of the tensions and contradictions in early modern English society were examined through a notion which had an 'important heuristic function in the period of transition from medieval to modern political thought': the concept of the king's two bodies.[8] On the one hand, in his mystical body, the king was the head, the reason, the conscience of the commonweal, exemplifying the oneness of private and public, duty and interest. On the other, in his natural body, the king was 'but a man as I am', as Henry V puts it, having but 'human conditions' and being subject to human frailties.[9] The virtuous king was he who harmonized his natural to his mystical body, who subjected his passions to his reason, and so through his own example of wholeness applied holistic medicine to the body politic. Yet, even in the case of Shakespeare's good king, questions and tensions remained. The virtuous quality of sincerity required that the king display his 'crystal heart' to his subjects, but diplomacy and discretion, in Henry V's case even intercourse with his subjects, necessitated disguise and deceit. Though the king was responsible for his subjects, yet 'he is not bound to answer the particular endings'.[10] Similarly the king might keep the conscience and command the duty of the realm, 'but every subject's soul is his own' and it was for every subject to 'wash every mote out of his conscience'.[11] As Professor Goldberg reminds us, even this most heroic monarch and mirror for princes appears to different observers—within and outside the play—differently; 'whether he is most Machiavellian or most pious has divided critical response to him'.[12]

Historians have similarly been as divided over their characterization of Tudor and Stuart monarchs. Was Henry VIII a ruthless manipulator of circumstance, or a man who sincerely governed himself as well as the polity according to his conscience? Was Charles I genuine in his claim to rule only for the weal of his people, or did he act—in *both* senses—only to establish his power as absolute? The historiographical differences of interpretation of 'actual rulers', like the critical disagreements about Henry V and other kings represented on the stage, owe much to the self-contradictions of the age and so especially of its rulers, particularly over questions of conscience and duty.[13] In one case, we are fortunate to have a monarch who not only reigned during the period of the richest dramatic representations of these tensions, but also, in (what we would delineate

as) both public and more private genres of writing, contributed to the debate of these issues. Indeed it was in 1599, the year of the first performance of *Henry V,* that James VI penned his own reflections on kingship, the **Basilikon Doron** or **'His Majesty's Instructions to his dearest son, Prince Henry'.**

James VI and I's most public pronouncements on kingship, as well as the **Basilikon Doron, The Trew Law of Free Monarchies,** the **Apology for the Oath of Allegiance,** the **Remonstrance for the Right of Kings,** and the speeches to Parliament, have been easily available in C. H. McIlwain's **The Political Works of James I** since 1918. It is surprising that they have attracted little critical study as political theory or discourse.[14] Perhaps even more regrettably, no study has been made of James's letters, devotional tracts, commentaries on Scripture, and, especially, his poetry as self-examinations and as self-explications of the king's person and concept of office. Central to any such investigation must be an understanding of James's perceptions of conscience and duty—his own, and his subjects' in a Christian commonweal—and of the contradictions within them.

In his most public and avowedly political works, James outlined what conscience and duty meant to him. No more for his subjects than for himself could they be divided. It was the duty of the people to obey their sovereign 'in all things except directly against God', and subjects were 'bound to obey their princes for conscience sake'.[15] 'The bond of conscience', James once wrote to James Hamilton in Scotland, was 'the only sure bond for tying of men's affections to them whom to they owe a natural duty'.[16] Herein, of course, lay the central problem of the early modern state: if conscience were the foundation of the duty of obedience to princes, yet conscience informed some subjects that the ruler acted 'directly against God', how could monarchy and the commonweal survive? James himself conceded that it was the duty of the clergy to encourage disobedience of commands contrary to God's—'it is always better to obey God than man'—yet continued to maintain that there was no conflict, rather a harmony, between faith and allegiance.[17] In part this seeming contradiction was resolved in theory by another: the notion of civil obedience. In the case of his Catholic subjects, the King separated their civil obedience from their conscience. Never believing that 'the blood of any man shall be shed for diversity of opinions in religion', James left them to their 'opinion', requiring only subscription to an oath of allegiance.[18] That oath he regarded as the solution to the pull between conscience and the duty of obedience: 'I never conceived the difference between real obedience and promise by subscription to obey.'[19] However, the promise involved in an oath itself rested on one's obligation and accountability to God—in other words on conscience.[20] In order to reconcile the conscience and duty of his Catholic subjects, James was forced to separate what he intrinsically believed should be inviolable—the civic and the religious.

For, whilst his defence of the Oath of Allegiance seemed to imply it, elsewhere James denied that the sphere of conscience could be separated as a personal realm outside the public. In *A Premonition to All Most Mighty Monarchs* he went so far as to refute the sacred secrecy of the confessional when the public interest was at stake.[21] Most of all he was at pains to deny the Puritan claim to personal conscience, that is to a personal interpretation of what God ordained. Parity of conscience, he realized, would soon lead to equality (and hence anarchy) in the commonwealth.[22] Conscience was not identical with mere opinion: sinners confused the dictates of conscience with those of appetite, and many did 'prattle of' a conscience they did not feel.[23] True conscience was not opinion but knowledge, 'the light of knowledge that God hath planted in man'.[24] 'Conscience not grounded on knowledge', James once put it, 'is either an ignorant fantasy or an arrogant vanity.'[25] Knowledge of God came to man through Scripture, the principal tutor to the conscience. Therefore, 'in making the Scripture to be ruled by their conscience and not their conscience by the Scripture', the Puritans subverted conscience no less than they did authority.[26]

In matters of dispute, of course, the interpretation of Scripture rested with the Church. So, though on occasions he appears to regard conscience as an individual's personal negotiation with God, for the most part James believed in a 'common quality conscience' in which all (himself included) shared, rather than 'distinct individual consciences'.[27] Perhaps, he saw that acceptance of the idea of individual conscience ultimately threatened not only diversity of religious sects but moral and religious relativism. What most upset James about the teachings of Conrad Vorstius was his contention that God had 'some kind of diversity or multiplicity in himself yea even a beginning of a certain mutability'.[28] Against Vorstius no less than Montaigne, James reasserted a theoretical axiom of the early modern polity: 'God is unity itself and verity is one.'[29] But, though necessary, the belief in a common conscience of the commonweal was fraught with difficulties and inconsistencies. For in certain passages the King discerns the light of conscience in all men. God, he concludes in the second book of the *Basilikon Doron,* has 'imprinted in men's minds by the very light of Nature the love of all moral virtues' and an awareness of wrongdoing.[30] Even malefactors retained, like Richard III's murderer, a sense of their own evil, a residual conscience which, as James described it in his *Daemonologie,* 'haunted' them, until 'the purging of themselves by amendment of life from such sins as have procured that extraordinary plague'.[31] But, if such were the case, why could not a man's conscience be autonomous? How was it

that Puritans professed a conscience that was false or pretended, if God planted the light of his knowledge in all? Or, to put the question simply and fundamentally, why did all not agree about the right course for a Christian commonweal?

At times James wants to claim that they did. 'You know in your conscience', he told Members of the House of Commons in 1624, 'that of all the kings that ever were . . . never was king better beloved of his people than I am.'[32] But there is a silent *ought to* implicit before that 'know', a silent phrase that alone can bridge the gap between the theory of common conscience and James's experience, not least with his Parliaments, of fundamental disagreement. Whatever should be, conscience was not common to all. Their conscience led the Puritans to become a 'sect', as James described them, whose members 'refuse to obey the law and will not cease to stir up a rebellion'.[33] Theirs led the Powder Plotters into 'denying the king to be [their] lawful sovereign or the anointed of God'.[34] God had his own ways of expressing the dictates of true conscience. When Catesby and others were wounded when the powder for their plot exploded on them, James thought they were 'wonderfully stroken with amazement in their guilty consciences, calling to memory how God had justly punished them with that same instrument which they should have used for the effectuating of so great a sin'.[35] Yet it was the role of the State to lend some assistance even to 'the wonderful power of God's justice upon guilty consciences'. Accordingly, Guy Fawkes was imprisoned (and, not mentioned, tortured) to help him to 'advise upon his conscience'.[36] Conscience may have been to James the foundation of his authority, but, paradoxically, his authority was an essential prop of a true conscience. To answer the cynic, then, who would dismiss the whole notion as a disingenuous disguise for power, we must look at how James interpreted conscience and duty when he turned to examine his own.

Too much that has been written about the King's theory of divine right has failed to grasp that James saw his position as God's lieutenant not as a power but as a duty—and an awesome duty, in the sense of religious observance as well as feudal obligation, at that. 'Being born to be a king,' he instructed Prince Henry, 'ye are rather born to Onus than Honos: not excelling all your people so far in rank and honour as in daily care and hazardous pains in the dutiful administration of that great office that God hath laid upon your shoulders.'[37] A king owned himself even less than private men. For the commonweal, James wrote in 1593, 'I am born more than for myself'.[38] Even as a parent, a king did not own his son. Henry was 'not ours only as the child of a natural father, but as an heir apparent to our body public in whom our state and kingdom are essentially interested'.[39] If the king's body and flesh were not his own, no more was his conscience. As in his mystical form he was head of the body politic, so the king's conscience was not only personal but the conscience of the realm. James was explicit about how his conscience was bound to the codes of the polity that it was his duty to rule—to law, justice, and equity. 'Certainly,' as he put it in *The Trew Law of Free Monarchies,* 'a king that governs not by his law can neither be countable to God for his administration.'[40] 'A King that will rule and govern justly', he told his parliamentary audience in March 1610, 'must have regard to conscience . . .'[41]

Now, our cynic (or Dr Sommerville) might point out that justice was the king's justice and that the laws too were—James himself used the possessive—'his'. The conscience of the king's mystical self was then one and the same with his personal conscience and so autonomous and untrammelled. James, however, had sworn a coronation oath to see law, justice, mercy, and truth maintained, and felt himself as bound to execute that promise as were the Catholics by the Oath of Allegiance.[42] It had been, he recalled in a speech of 1616, his principal care to keep his conscience clear in all points of his coronation oath.[43] For an oath was to God as well as to the other party and so, as Bishop Sanderson was to put it, 'not to be taken with a relucting and unsatisfied conscience'.[44] That conscience was inextricably part of the honour of the king, 'without which', James proclaimed in 1607, 'I have no being'.[45] Indeed, so much was the king's conscience the realm's as much as the king's own that at times, it would appear, he came close to subordinating his 'private conscience' for the sake of the commonweal. Where his policy towards the papists was concerned, for example, 'I must', James acknowledged in a speech in the Lords, 'put a difference betwixt mine own private profession of mine own salvation and my politic government of the realm for the weal and quietness thereof.'[46] He did so because, 'as I would be loather to dispence in the least point mine own conscience for any worldly respect than the foolishest precisian of them all; so would I be as sorry to straight the politique government of the bodies and minds of all my subjects to my private opinions . . .'[47] In theory, of course, in the ideal commonweal there should have been no such disjuncture. The king's personal and public consciences should have accorded with each other and those of his subjects. The reality was otherwise. The reality of politics threatened the separation of the king's two bodies at a time when their conjunction was essential for—indeed was a device for—the cohesion of the body politic.[48] It was not least because he fully grasped that necessity that James struggled to reconcile and to harmonize all those consciences: to be (as we shall argue) the crystal mirror in and through which his subjects could come to a shared knowledge of God.

In the first place, James went to some lengths to remove and deny any barrier between his private and public selves. Kings, he advised Prince Henry, should have no secret thoughts that they were afraid publicly to avouch. A prince ought to keep 'agreeance and conformity . . . betwixt his outward behaviour and the virtuous qualities of his mind'.[49] 'By the outward using of your office . . . testify the inward uprightness of your heart.'[50] 'I never with God's grace', he once wrote to Cecil, taking his own counsel, 'shall do anything in private which I may not without shame proclaim upon the tops of houses.'[51] Because discourse was 'the true image' of the king's mind (a 'testament' as he called the *Basilikon Doron*), it was important that monarchs spoke and wrote what they meant.[52] Accordingly James vowed to his Parliament that he would promise nothing which he intended not to deliver.[53] His 'tongue should ever be the true messenger of his heart'.[54] Today we would be inclined to interpret this as a *claim* to sincerity—something we tend to doubt in public figures, dismissing such talk as itself political rhetoric or strategy. And this is the point. James was intending more than to secure belief in his word. He was specifically opposing those Machiavels who sought to justify deceit and disguise as stratagems of power in an amoral political universe.[55] And his counter-argument not only opposed Machiavellian premises; it deployed to opposite purpose Machiavelli's own language. As a king James spoke 'without artifice'; 'as a prince', he wrote to Elizabeth, perhaps choosing his self-description carefully, 'it becomes me not to feign'.[56] In 1621, subverting the metaphors of to follow that 'alike Christian as politic rule to measure as I would be measured unto'.[57] 'Peace be with you', James took as the fit 'motto of a king' because 'the blessing of a God'.[58]

James's tracts, speeches, and letters contain constant applications of Scripture to issues and problems of State. Scripture was for him a text of State because the Christian and political realms were one and shared a discourse. 'Let our souls be bound for our bodies,' he urged in 1618, 'our bodies for our souls, and let each come in at the General Sessions to save his bail, where he shall find a merciful judge.'[59] No less than his actions, the King's words, his *Works,* were mediations of God's will', as revealed in Scripture. Their function, as Bishop Montagu saw it when he introduced them to their readers in 1616, was to operate on men's consciences so that they might be 'converted by them'.[60] James described his own *Basilikon Doron* as a 'discharge of our conscience'.[61] *Basilikon Doron* means the royal gift. James so described others of his works, dedicated to Prince Charles or the Duke of Buckingham. In a larger sense, they were, when published, gifts to all his subjects. For, by bringing readers closer to God, leading them to know him, James might indeed convert men by bringing them to the knowledge of God, which, when shared, united all in a Christian commonweal. The author (writer/authorizer) of the tag to the frontispiece to James's works was the earthly no less than the heavenly king: 'Ecce do tibi animum sapientem et intelligentem.'[62]

A king who saw it as his duty to be an apostle as well as a prince, to mediate God's word and will, faced an awesome responsibility to ensure the uprightness of his own conscience. And, in the main, he faced it alone. It may be the duty of MPs 'upon *your* consciences plainly to determine' for 'the weal both of your king and your country'.[63] And the king had his counsellors, bishops, and chaplains close to his bosom. But these were men chosen 'out of my own judgment and conscience' who owed loyalty and service to their master.[64] The acclaim of others could not be relied upon as a mark of the king's virtuous courses. Reputation, James once wrote, was but other men's 'opinion'—and for that a prince should not risk his soul.[65] Ultimately the keeper of the nation's conscience was alone—with his own, before God. In his epistle to the Reader of 'His Majesty's Instructions to his . . . son', James explained his resolution 'ever to walk as in the eyes of the Almighty, examining ever so the secretest of my drifts, before I gave them course, as how they might some day bide the touchstone of a public trial'.[66] Kings had, he put it in the *Trew Law,* 'the count of their administration' to give to God.[67] Not only was that an account more strict than that any other servant owed his master; it was a count of each and every word and deed. Justice demanded of kings that, 'as we reign by [God's] grace . . . we should turn all our energies and thoughts to His glory'.[68] This was not rhetoric. Every day, James commanded his son, he should take the reckoning with himself, his conscience, and his God:

> remember ever once in the four and twenty hours, either in the night or when ye are at greatest quiet, to call yourself to account of all your last days actions, either wherein ye have committed things ye should not, or omitted the things ye should do, either in your Christian or kingly calling: in that account let not yourself be smoothed over with that flattering Φιλαμτία . . . but censure yourself as sharply as if ye were your own enemy.[69]

Never, he concluded 'ever wilfully or willingly . . . contrare your conscience'. The king more than any must fear as well as serve God.[70] 'Let hell afright thee', he advised his fellow rulers, 'and let thy conscience describe it to thee'.[71] When alone taking the count of his obedience and service to God, the king needed only to turn to Scripture—'the statutes of your heavenly king'—to determine whether he had acted (as good kings should) as a true subject of *his* sovereign.[72] 'Would ye then know your sin by the law? read the books of Moses . . . Would ye know . . . Christ? looke the Evangelists.'[73] With Scripture, especially the books of Kings and Chronicles, James told his son, he should be familiarly acquainted: 'for there will ye see yourself (as in a mirror) either among the Catalogues of the good or

evil kings.'[74] Self-knowledge, conscience, the same as the knowledge of God, came from meditation upon *His* word, as in turn the King's **Works** written and enacted were the mirror in which subjects saw their God and themselves.

It is in this context that we must glance specifically (if briefly) at the more neglected of James I's writings: the king's own exegeses of and commentaries on scriptural texts. James called them 'paraphrases' and 'meditations'. And they stand, indeed, as evidence of his personalizing the Scriptures, meditating upon their message to himself and communicating their meaning to his subjects. The King's **Paraphrase upon the Revelation** is an exegesis, a decoding of that most complex of biblical books and a specific application of its symbolic figurations to his own and his contemporaries' world. James deconstructs, as we would now say, the visions of Chapter 10, explaining how Christ was the Angel foretold and how the rainbow signified His covenant with his elect. Similarly the woman of Chapter 12 represents the Church, he explains, and the twelve stars stand for the prophets and the patriarchs.[75] Throughout, James puts his own words as if they were spoken by St John and so joins, as if in a dialogue, the text of Revelation and his reflections upon it. As a consequence it is no less the King's than the apostle's words we read when he writes 'and [God] said unto me, Write and leave in record what thou hast seen'.[76] James saw much that was for the edification of himself. He read again, as Scripture in many places showed him, that 'the hearts of the greatest kings as well as of the smallest subjects are in the hands of the Lord'. The book of the last things forcefully urged him: 'Be watchful then and sleep no longer in negligence and careless security . . . revive your zeal and fervency.'[77] His discursive dialogue with Scripture sharpened his conscience. As he turned to meditate on some verses of the fifteenth chapter of the first book of Chronicles (which he had, we recall, recommended to Prince Henry), he was reminded clearly of the first duty of kings.[78] David after his victory over his enemies immediately translated the ark of the Covenant to his house, 'whereof *we* [sic] may learn first that the chief virtue which should be in a Christian prince . . . is a fervency and constant zeal to promote the glory of God'.[79] James applied his text closely to his place, comparing the elders of the Chronicles to the barons and burgesses of his kingdom and underlining his own responsibility for 'choosing good under-rulers'.[80] At all points the 'opening up of the text' was the basis for examining 'how pertinently the place doth appertain to us and our present estate', guiding the king, for example, on the lawfulness of Sunday sports.[81]

James's meditations on Scripture were a form of self-counsel, a didactic engagement with the commands in Scripture as a means of tutoring conscience. And not only his own. The meditation on the twentieth chapter of Revelations reads also like a sermon. Introducing his meditation upon the first book of the Chronicles, James expressed his desire that 'these meditations of mine may after my death remain to the posterity and a certain testimony of my upright and honest meaning . . .'.[82] Like the overtly *Political Works* (as McIlwain defined them) from which they have been artificially separated, James's paraphrases and explications of Scripture were a discharge of his conscience, an image of the king, at once a crystal and a mirror for all men as well as for magistrates.

Perhaps we see their public and, as well as personal, heuristic function most clearly in two little-studied works, the *Meditation upon The Lords Prayer* of 1619 and the *Meditation upon the . . . XXVII Chapter of St Matthew* of 1620. The first, though dedicated as a New Year's gift to the Duke of Buckingham, was 'written by the King's Majesty for the benefit of *all* his subjects, especially of such as follow the court'.[83] The meditation was a plea for Christian unity at a time of mounting tension and division; as in *The Peace-Maker* of 1618 James had called on the 'monarchical bodies of many kingdoms' to 'be one mutual Christendom',[84] so he now urged all his subjects to join in the fellowship of the sacraments and prayer. The Arminians, he wrote, sought to rob God of his secret will; at the 'other extremity', 'some puritans . . . make God author of sin'.[85] Exposition of the prayer taught by Christ warned all to 'trust not to that private spirit which our Puritans glory in' but to remember, through the words 'Our Father', that 'every one of us is a member of a body of a church that is compacted of many members'.[86] James commends confession to churchmen for the clearing of the conscience and, through reflection on the Lord's Prayer, finds the 'true visible church . . . now in this kingdom' the best hope for salvation.[87]

The Meditation upon St Matthew began, James informed his son Charles, as a private reading 'to myself the passion of Christ'.[88] But, as he thought on the crown of thorns, James contemplated 'the thorny cares which a king . . . must be subject unto as (God knowes) I daily and nightly feel in mine own person'.[89] As he meditated further, 'I apprehended that it would be a good pattern to put inheritors to kingdoms in mind of their calling by the form of their inauguration' and 'whom can a pattern for a king's inauguration so well fit as a king's son and heir being written by the king his father and the pattern taken from the king of all kings'. And so the work became for Charles what the *Basilikon Doron* had been for Henry, James's gift of knowledge of God to his son. Indeed, James informed the reader of his meditation that, if God gave him days and leisure, he intended to expand it to cover 'the whole principal points belonging to the office of a king'.[90] Meantime, the *Meditation upon . . . St Matthew* was a forewarning of the heavy burden of kingship: 'make it therefore',

he instructed the prince, 'your vade mecum'. As he laid out for his son the verses describing Christ's crowning with plaited thorns and mock coronation with sceptre of reed and the soldiers' laughing 'obeisance', James detailed the cares and duties of the prince who was to take his 'pattern' from Christ. The thorns, he explained, made a king remember 'that he wears not that crown for himself but for others'; the reed sceptre instructed a ruler to correct gently and govern 'boldly yet temperately'. In general, Christ's crowning passion reminded kings that they were 'mixtae personae . . . bound to make a reckoning to God for their subjects' souls as well as their bodies'.[91] 'In a word,' James concludes, 'a Christian king should never be without that continual and ever wake-riffe care of the account he is one day to give to God of the good government of his people and their prosperous estate both in souls and bodies, which is a part of the health of his own soul.'[92] As often with James, it was counsel to himself as well as to his son. Just as Pilate proclaimed Christ King of the Jews in Hebrew, Greek, and Latin, so 'upon St George's day and other high festival times the chief Herald Garter . . . proclaims my titles in . . . Latin, French and English'.[93] We can almost hear James meditating with himself as he tells Prince Charles that the purple robe of office was to remind him 'to take great heed of his conscience, that his judgements may be without blemish or stain'.[94]

Our final texts of the king's conscience have all but rested unexamined by historians—doubtless, not least, because they are poetry. James, however, was a major influence on the Renaissance poetry of Scotland, and both his poems and treatise on poetry are rich in evidence of his values and ideals. Like his paraphrase of Revelations, James's verse translations of the Psalms of David were a form of meditation on Scripture, by means of absorbing its meaning into his own words—a placing 'before thy holy throne this speech of mine'.[95] Translation, James decreed, did not license reinterpretation of Scripture; those who adulterated Holy Writ with their own opinions were accursed.[96] The translator was a glass through which Scripture could be read, and poetry might be the instrument by which it was read most clearly.[97] So the King of Scotland, through David, the King of Israel, addressed, as in prayer, his heavenly King, a 'king that last for ever shall quaire all the nationis perish & decayes'.[98] Through David, James learnt (as he taught) that the Lord was a lord of justice, that he abominated the 'creuell and bloodthristie tyran' and those false princes who 'speake with pleasant lippes and dowble myndis'.[99] He read that the Lord preserved his anointed king and bestowed his grace on the virtuous, 'thaim of conscience iust & pure'.[100] James therefore prayed for protection from his enemies without and from temptations of wickedness within; he asked 'lett all my judgement ay proceid from thy most holy face'.[101] Urging, as he was to do in the *Basilikon Doron,* 'all princes sonnes yield to the lorde', he vowed to place his trust 'in Iehova's might'.[102] Trust here meant not only his confidence but his responsibility, his kingdom. In the exercise of his office James, with David, knew the Lord would guide and 'cousaile me', as in turn he would give account to God how he had heeded His counsel:

> the lorde doth iustice give unto the nationis sure
> then judge me lorde according to my iustice great & pure[103]

James's Psalms, *The Psalmes of His Maiestie* as they were titled, were not his only poetical exercises that we should consider as meditations on God and self-examination of the royal conscience. Only when we recall James's admonition to his son to reflect upon God and take his reckoning with himself at quiet moments free from worldly business may we understand the significant epithet in *His Maiesties Poeticall Exercises at Vacant Houres.* In his translation of 'divine' Du Bartas's *The Furies,* a poem about the Fall, James advised that the reader (and reader/writer) might 'see clearly, as in a glass, the miseries of this wavering world: to wit, the cursed nature of mankinde and the heavie plagues of God. And especiallie | heere maye thou learne not to flatter thyselfe, in cloaking thy odious vices with the delectable coulour of vertue . . .'.[104] In *The Furies,* we read how authority had once been natural and kings could rule, like Adam over beasts, not by force but with a wink or a nod. But disobedience to God had as its consequence the collapse of all natural hegemony, as well as the disintegration of order and harmony into chaos. The animals now formed 'rebellious bands' against Man:

> Man in rebelling thus against
> The soveraigne great, I say,
> Doth feele his subjects all enarm'd
> Against him everie way . . .[105]

Wolves, leopards, and bears now challenged the lion, king of beasts:

> Most jealous of the right divine
> Against their head conspire.[106]

Even kings themselves were stained by the Fall:

> The King of beasts . . . of himselfe
> Is not the maister now.[107]

Yet poetry, Sir Philip Sidney, had claimed, could bring fallen man closer again to God. As James himself summarized him: 'a breath divine in Poets breasts doth blow.'[108] Through *The Furies,* therefore, James learnt and taught the emptiness of man's 'outward show', the illegitimacy of princes who advanced themselves 'by false contracts and by unlawfull measures', and the wisdom of those who had 'the feare of God | Imprinted

deeply . . .' and who obeyed his will.[109] Similarly, from his verse account of the battle of Lepanto we know James learnt and taught the duty of kings: to be God's generals against the devil, to prefer the 'honour of the Lord' before all else, and to be 'volunteers of conscience' in the Lord's ranks.[110]

In and through his poetry, which awaits a critical/political reading, James, as the poet Gabriel Harvey put it, 'read a . . . lecture to himself'.[111] He did more than tutor his own conscience, however. The 'heavenly furious fire' of poetry, he believed, might reignite the embers of conscience and knowledge of God in all men.[112] Poets are 'Dame Natures trunchmen, heavens interprets trewe'.[113] So James offered instruction in the art of poetry as he penned advice on the art of kingship. And, in his *Essayes of a Prentise in the Divine Art of Poesie,* he prayed that he, as poet and king, might have the power to represent the wind, the seas, and the seasons, nature—the created works of a living God whom men through verse may come to know and follow:

> For as into the wax the seals imprent
> Is lyke a seale, right so the Poet gent
> Doeth grave so vive in us his passions strange,
> As makes the reader, halfe in author change
> For verses force is sic that softly slydes
> Throw secret poris and in our sences bydes
> As makes them have both good and eville imprented
> Which by the learned works is represented.[114]

David, Job, and Solomon had been poets as well as kings. The poet like the good king prayed to his God 'That I thy instrument may be', so that, as *The Furies* concludes, 'this worke which man did write' also 'by the Lord is pend'.[115] Poetry for James VI and I, like his devotional works, was a meditation with himself and God and a representation to his subjects of himself and God—his purest crystal. In purifying his own conscience, he equipped himself to teach; by teaching, he learnt. So the wise poet of *Uranie* was told:

> In singing kepe this order shown you heir,
> Then ye your self, in feeding men shall leir
> The rule of living well . . .[116]

And, thus, the King published rules for poetry as well as for government, that 'reading thir rules ye may find in yourself such a beginning of Nature . . .'. In the words of the sonnet to the reader, 'Sic docens discans'.[117]

In early modern Europe, as circumstances challenged traditional beliefs, all rulers faced difficult choices. Either they accepted the realities and were forced to compromise long-held beliefs and codes, or they fought to reassert the paradigms and to reconstruct a shattered world. Even though faced with the obvious fact of religious wars in Europe and theological wrangles at home, James VI and I pursued hopes of, and policies towards, an ecumenical resolution to the divisions of Christendom. He endeavoured to make the Church of England a platform for the reunification of a truly Catholic church, a *unum corpus* of which all Christians could be members. In his own countries he sought to minimize dispute over theology and ceremony. And we now see that, as an essential part of his ambitious designs, he sought to lead his subjects to a knowledge of God's dictates, so that all might partake of a common conscience, as well as be members of one church and commonweal. He faced, inevitably, inconsistencies in his own exposition of his ideal, because the means to obtain his goal (a coincidence of private and public belief) were the goal itself. His only answer to the new challenges was the reassertion of the old ideals. James, however, went beyond reassertion; his **Works** were a strategy of reenactment. By his own example, he attempted to demonstrate that conscience was neither mere opinion, nor, as the 'politics' would have it, a disguise, nor yet the inevitable victim of force. And he tried to heal the divisions in the commonwealth, by resolving the disjunctures in himself—between his natural and mystical body, his person and office—ruling his own conscience and his kingdom, as he claimed, according to Scripture.

In the public sphere it is clear that he failed: religious differences and even moral positions continued to polarize. The King perforce took political decisions which accorded uneasily with his conscience. Furthermore, even in his own person James exemplified not only the ideals but also the failings he discussed, to the point that he became a microcosm of the human frailties that always threatened a Christian society. In his quest for the English Crown after Elizabeth's death, the young James acquiesced in his mother's execution, for all his formal protest, and so failed in the filial devotion he believed was owed to parents.[118] Similarly, for all his injunctions to honesty, it would appear that he was prepared to mislead about his willingness to convert to Rome.[119] More tragically still, the king who thundered against the vices of intemperance, drunkenness, and especially sodomy (a crime he exempted from pardon and which, he told Henry, 'ye are bound in conscience never to forgive') was a drunkard and homosexual.[120] How, then, could James counsel his son not to commend what he did not practise or boast—as, in 1616, that 'both our theorique and practique agree well together'?[121] The simple answer would be that James was a straightforward hypocrite, but it would be too simple an answer. For James's denunciations of what were also his own sins were part of his meditations, and may have been a form of the confession that he recommended to others, for 'amendment of life'. We cannot know how, in his private moments, James faced his God and himself. But knowing, as he told his son, that Christ did not come for the perfect, he found 'in the religion we profess . . . so much comfort and peace of conscience'.[122]

Notes

1. See S. Zwicker, 'Lines of Authority: Politics and Literary Culture in the Restoration', in K. Sharpe and S. Zwicker (eds.), *Politics of Discourse: The History and Literature of Seventeenth-Century England* (1987), 230-70; also pp. 5-7.

2. M. McKeon, *The Origins of the English Novel, 1600-1740* (1987).

3. J. Locke, *An Essay Concerning Human Understanding* (1824 edn.), 25.

4. Cf. K. Sharpe, *Politics and Ideas in Early Stuart England: Essays and Studies* (1989), 11-14.

5. *Oxford English Dictionary,* s.v. 'Conscience'.

6. Sharpe, *Politics and Ideas,* 25-8; F. Raab, *The English Face of Machiavelli* (1964).

7. As well as *Richard III, Richard II, Henry V, Lear, Hamlet,* and *The Winter's Tale* are obvious texts in which the king's conscience both faces dilemmas and is yet central to the integrity of the realm.

8. See E. H. Kantorovicz, *The Kings's Two Bodies: A Study in Mediaeval Political Theology* (Princeton, NJ, 1957), *passim* and p. 447.

9. E. Forset, *A Comparative Discourse of the Bodies Natural and Politique* (1606); D. G. Hale, *The Body Politic* (The Hague, 1971); Shakespeare, *Henry V,* Act IV, sc. i.

10. *Henry V,* Act IV, sc. i.

11. Ibid.

12. J. Goldberg, *James I and the Politics of Literature* (Baltimore, Md., and London, 1983), 161. I am grateful to Jonathan Goldberg for his brilliant insights both in this work and in discussion.

13. The historiographical disagreements are especially heated for early modern British history, not least because the period set itself contrary criteria of judgement.

14. They find no place in Quentin Skinner's survey, *The Foundations of Modern Political Thought* (2 vols.; Cambridge, 1978). See, however, L. Avack, *La ragione dei re: Il pensiero politico di Giacomo I* (Milan, 1974).

15. *The Trew Law of Free Monarchies,* in *The Political Works of James I,* ed. C. H. McIlwain (Cambridge, Mass., 1918), 61; *Apology for The Oath of Allegiance,* ibid. 72; HMC, *Salisbury,* XV. 300, James I to Thomas Parry, Nov. 1603.

16. *The Letters of King James VI and I,* ed. G. P. V. Akrigg, (1984), 166-7.

Title page from The Works of James I.

17. *A Remonstrance for the Right of Kings,* in *Political Works,* 213.

18. *Letters,* 204; *Apology for Oath of Allegiance,* in *Political Works,* 72 and *passim.*

19. *Letters,* 223.

20. See R. Sanderson, *De juramento: Seven Lectures Concerning the Obligation of Promisory Oaths* (1655), a work revised by Charles I.

21. *Political Works,* 167.

22. James I, *A Meditation upon The Lords Prayer* (1619), 18: 'trust not to that private spirit or Holy Ghost which our Puritans glory in, for then a little fiery zeal will make thee turn separatist.'

23. *The Basilikon Doron of King James VI,* ed. J. Craigie (2 vols.; Scottish Text Soc.; Edinburgh, 1944-50) i. 40, 124.

24. Ibid. i. 40.

25. James I, *Flores regii, or Proverbes and Aphorismes . . . Spoken By His Majesty* (1627), 104-5.

26. *Basilikon Doron,* i. 16.

27. *OED,* s.v. 'Conscience', history of usage.

28. *A Declaration Concerning the Proceedings with the States General of the United Provinces . . . in the Cause of D. Conradus Vorstius,* in *The Workes of The Most High and Mighty Prince James* (1616), 365.

29. Ibid. 372.

30. *Basilikon Doron,* i. 160.

31. James I, *Daemonologie,* in *Workes of Prince James,* 125.

32. *Cobbett's Parliamentary History of England,* i (1806), 1376.

33. *Basilikon Doron,* i. 16.

34. *A Discourse of the . . . Discoverie of the Powder Treason,* in *Workes of Prince James,* 231.

35. Ibid. 245.

36. Ibid. 241.

37. *Basilikon Doron,* i. 6-7.

38. *Letters,* 25.

39. HMC Salisbury, xv. 302.

40. *Political Works,* 63.

41. Ibid. 318.

42. See *The Ceremonies, Form of Prayer and Services Used in Westminster Abbey at the Coronation of King James 1st* (1685).

43. *Political Works,* 329.

44. Sanderson, *De juramento,* 144, 197-8, 236, 269.

45. *Political Works,* 298.

46. Ibid. 274.

47. Ibid.

48. Cf. Sharpe, *Politics and Ideas,* 61-3, 68-9.

49. *Basilikon Doron,* i. 15.

50. Ibid. i. 200.

51. *Letters,* 192.

52. *Basilikon Doron,* i. 21-2.

53. *Political Works,* 305.

54. Ibid. 280.

55. Though Machiavelli was not available in English until 1640, *The Prince* was translated into Scotch by W. Fowler, a Court poet, who contributed a celebratory verse to James's own collections of poems. See *His Maiesties Poetical Exercises at Vacant Houres* (Edinburgh, 1591), sig. 4; *The Essayes of a Prentise in the Divine Art of Poesie* (Edinburgh, 1585), sig. 3v; *The Poems of James VI of Scotland,* ed. T. Craigie (2 vols.; Scottish Text Soc.; Edinburgh, 1955-8), i. xxii.

56. *Commons Debates 1621,* eds W. Notestein, F. H. Relf, and H. Simpson (7 vols.; New Haven, Conn., 1935), v. 85; *Letters,* 162.

57. *Letters,* 181.

58. *The Peace-Maker,* sig. A4.

59. Ibid. sig. E4^v.

60. *Works . . . of Prince James,* epistle to the Reader.

61. *Basilikon Doron,* i. 22.

62. *Serenissimi Potentissimi Principis Jacobi . . . Opera* (1619), motto at foot of frontispiece depicting the figures of Religion and Peace.

63. *Political Works,* 288.

64. *Letters,* 261.

65. *The Peace-Maker,* sig. D4.

66. *Basilikon Doron,* i. 12.

67. *Political Works,* 54.

68. *Letters of the Kings of England,* ed. J. O. Halliwell (2 vols.; 1848), ii. 68.

69. *Basilikon Doron,* i. 44.

70. Ibid. 5, 'The Argument'.

71. *The Peace-Maker,* sig. C2.

72. *Basilikon Doron,* i. 5.

73. Ibid. i. 34.

74. Ibid.

75. *Paraphrase upon The Revelation,* in *Workes of Prince James,* esp. pp. 13-14, 19-21, 36-9, 63-4, 78.

76. Ibid. 65.

77. Ibid. 11, 56.

78. *A Meditation upon the XXV, XXVI, XXVII, XXVIII, XXIX Verses of the XVth Chapter of The First Book of The Chronicles of The Kings,* in *Workes of Prince James,* 81-90; see p. 92.

79. Ibid. 82.

80. Ibid. 83.

81. Ibid. 86-7.

82. Ibid. 81.

83. *Meditation upon The Lords Prayer.* The full title includes this address.

84. *The Peace-Maker,* sig. B1.

85. *Meditation upon The Lords Prayer,* 42, 116-17.

86. Ibid. 18, 22.

87. Ibid. 62, 66, 15.

88. *Two Meditations of the King's Maiestie* (1620), Epistle dedicatory.

89. *A Meditation upon the . . . XXVII Chapter of St Matthew or A Pattern for a King's Inauguration* (1620), Epistle dedicatory.

90. Ibid. Advertisement to the Reader.

91. Ibid. 25, 50, 124, and *passim.*

92. Ibid. 125-6.

93. Ibid. 78-80.

94. Ibid. 120.

95. BL Royal MS 18 B xvi, fo. 9; *Poems of James VI,* ii. 11. James's father-in-law, the King of Denmark, had written too a manual of selected psalms which 'was his continual vade mecum' (*Meditation upon The Lords Prayer,* 96).

96. *Paraphrase upon The Revelation,* 72.

97. Bodl. MS 165 fo. 20.

98. *Psalmes of His Maiestie,* in *Poems of James VI,* ii. 20.

99. Ibid. ii. 11, 23.

100. Ibid. ii. 42.

101. Ibid. ii. 21, 26, 27.

102. Ibid. ii. 9, 36.

103. Ibid. ii. 14, 26.

104. *Poems of James VI,* i. 98; James I, *Workes of Prince James,* 328.

105. *The Furies,* ll. 224-7, in *Poems of James VI,* i. 126.

106. Ibid. ll. 381-2, (i. 134).

107. Ibid., ll. 1359-60 (i. 184).

108. *Poems of James VI,* ii. 68.

109. *The Furies,* u. 1167-8, 1451-2, 1461-2 (i. 175, 190).

110. 'The Lepanto of James The Sixth', ll. 283, 317-18, in *Poems of James VI,* i. 216-18, and *passim.*

111. *Poems of James VI,* i. 274. Cf. Goldberg, *James I,* 17-28. I am preparing an essay on 'The Politics of James VI and I's Poetry'.

112. *Poems of James VI,* ii. 70.

113. James VI, *The Essayes of a Prentise in the Divine Art of Poesie,* ed. E. Arber (1869), 29.

114. Ibid. 29.

115. *The Furies,* ll. 29, 1515-16 (i. 114, 192).

116. *Essays of a Prentise,* 37.

117. James VI, *An Schort Treatise Conterning Some Reulis . . . to be Observed . . . in Scottis Poesie,* ed. E. Arber (1869), Preface to the reader, p. 55, Sonnet of the author, p. 56.

118. See *Letters,* 81-2; *Letters of Queen Elizabeth and King James VI of Scotland,* ed. J. Bruce (Camden Soc.; 1849), 46; Goldberg, *James I,* 14-17.

119. *Letters,* 308.

120. Ibid. 315; *Basilikon Doron,* i. 64, 102, 122, 136, 168.

121. James I, *Workes of Prince James,* 379.

122. HMC, *Salisbury,* xv. 302.

Susan Campbell Anderson (essay date 1998)

SOURCE: Anderson, Susan Campbell. "A Matter of Authority: James I and the Tobacco War." *Comitatus* 29 (1998): 136-63.

[*In the following essay, Anderson examines James's attitude toward tobacco and its use through a survey of his writing on the subject.*]

In the summer of 1604, only a year after acceding to the English throne, King James I implemented a daring, and some might say foolhardy, measure: complaining that, "at this day, through evil custom and the toleration thereof . . . a number of riotous and disordered persons of mean and base condition . . . do spend most of their time in that idle vanity,"[1] he raised the duty on tobacco from 2d. to 6s.8d. per pound, a staggering increase of 4000 percent. Given the enormous popularity of smoking at the time, his decree was bound to be unpopular. At roughly the same time, an anonymous pamphlet, *A Counterblaste to Tobacco,* appeared in the bookstalls, and was quickly, and correctly, presumed to be James's handiwork.[2] The shared focus of James's earliest fiscal policies and his first published work as king of England reflects a coherent political strategy. Just what that strategy was meant to accomplish, however, is less than obvious. Some have suggested that James hated tobacco in particular because it was the only vice to which he did not subscribe, and others that the plant became a means of focusing his hatred for its supposed "father," Sir Walter Ralegh.[3] But none of these admittedly worthwhile explanations seems sufficient in itself to account for his adoption of this particular cause. The vice argument is almost tautological; after all, it amounts to saying that James hated tobacco because he did not like it. Moreover, participating anonymously in a pamphlet exchange would have been a hopelessly oblique method of discrediting Ralegh.

In fact, despite the vehemence of the *Counterblaste* and traditional opinion to the contrary, it is not clear that James hated tobacco at all. On several occasions, roughly concomitant with the *Counterblaste,* for example, he closed letters to his "little beagle," Lord Cecil, with affectionate salutations involving tobacco. "I bid you heartily farewell," one such letter reads, "having enjoined the bearer to drink good pipes of tobacco to all your company."[4] Another missive, referring to his trusted servant Roger Aston, reads:

> Now that the Master Falconer doth return, I cannot but accompany him with these few lines, although indeed I might very evil have spared him at this time, as well for running of the hawks as for being so fit a man for trying our hounds. Yet, since he will needs be gone, I pray you let him be saluted with a good pipe of tobacco. And I pray you put him out of his new custom, which is to drink nothing but ale after supper.[5]

Intriguingly, James posits tobacco as a remedy for a vice of which he himself was often accused, overindulgence in alcohol. He playfully opposes the two substances, alcohol and tobacco, as vice and redeeming virtue, respectively. The jocular tone is a far cry from that of the *Counterblaste,* which appears to reveal a hatred of both the plant and the most notorious of smokers, Ralegh:

> It is not so long since the first entry of this abuse amongst us here, as this present age cannot yet very

well remember the first Author, and the forme of the first introduction of it amongst us. It was neither brought in by King, great Conqueror, nor learned doctor of Physick.

> With the report of a great discovery for a Conquest, some two or three Savage men, were brought in, together with this Savage custom. But the pity is, the poor wild barbarous men died, but that vile barbarous custom is yet alive, yea in fresh vigor: so as it seems a miracle to me, how a custom springing from so vile a ground, and brought in by a father so generally hated, should be welcomed on so slender a warrant.[6]

The James of the *Counterblaste* is outraged that tobacco appears to exist outside the realm of accepted authority. It is the discovery, not of a king or a doctor, but rather a mere explorer who, significantly, relies on *report* rather than real conquest, allowing threatening icons—strange plants and savage men—to speak for him. Tobacco and Ralegh are undoubtedly linked, but in a far more intricate way than hitherto acknowledged.

This seeming disjunction between James's public and private treatment of the subject of tobacco, however, can be resolved in part by recognizing James's faith in the written document as a means of both forming and articulating his own power and identity. Of his absentee rule over the country of his birth, James once said, "Thus must I say of Scotland . . . here I sit and govern it with my pen: I write and it is done."[7] Perhaps it is not surprising, then, that so many of his letters exist in holograph; for James, the process of active rule could be as simple as setting pen to paper. Indeed, James continued to write many of his own letters long after arthritis forced him to use a stamp to sign less important documents. His letters initiate or continue a process of exchange that both describes and determines the nature of James's relationship to his subjects, hence shaping his own public identity. Telling in this light is his preference for the singular pronoun "I," as opposed to the royal "We,"[8] for it indicates an understanding of the written document as the extension of the individual.[9] Thus, if "James did not write his letters as additions to his literary corpus,"[10] his personal letters nevertheless illustrate the very technique used in the *Counterblaste.* That James continually resorts to devices like proverbs and sustained metaphor indicates the strong literary bent of his correspondence. If his letters are not public discourse in the way his pamphlets are, they are not entirely private, either. Composed with a self-consciously perceived audience, they thus serve as a means of self-presentation. James's work, then, reflects an understanding that the world is constructed through language, or rather through the dialogic exchange of both utterances and material objects.

Consider James's letters to Robert Cecil, the earl of Salisbury. Despite the intermittent tensions that reportedly plagued their relationship, James's opening salutations invariably read, "My little beagle": hardly, as many have noted, the expected or appropriate address for one's Secretary of State. The letters sometimes simply continue a hunting motif, in keeping with their composer's abiding interest in hunting, the reason for his absence and occasion for the letters in the first place.

Yet James often allows this hunting language to slip into a metaphor for his relationship with the State, and Cecil in particular. The term "beagle" establishes a sense of intimacy and affection, at the same time reminding Cecil of his inferior position with respect to the king: Cecil is a harmless, faithful servant who acts without autonomy in James's interest. Indeed, Cecil is not even one of the better sorts of hounds, and his endeavors are less noble than the ones James pursues while hunting bigger quarry at Royston and Newmarket. "I bid you heartily farewell," one letter ends, "having so much mind for good large hounds in this rainy deep weather as I have forgotten all beagles till I come back to the chimney corner again to hunt a mouse."[11] Similarly, one letter, addressed on the outside "To the little beagle that lies home by the fire quhen all the good hounds are daily running on the fields,"[12] apparently chides Cecil for neglecting his duties in the king's absence. Yet another links hunting with political action: "I thank my patient Beagle for stopping the suit at Gray's Inn. . . ."[13] James frequently reminds Cecil that the bearer of the letters is Sir Roger Aston, referring to the latter not in his role as courtier and courier, but as Master Falconer, blurring further the distinction between governing and hunting. Thus, with a slip of the tongue—or rather, pen—James effectively transforms the hunt into a better sort of statecraft.

This trick of the pen, of course, answers complaints, sometimes explicitly acknowledged, that some people do not approve of his diversions and resulting absenteeism.[14] James once praises Cecil's answers to the Bishop of York's reprimands:

> I am thoroughly pleased with your answer; and specially concerning my hunting ye have answered it according to my heart's desire, for a scornful answerless answer became best such a senseless proposition.[15]

James seems to be aware of a dialogic protocol that insists that empty propositions be answered with empty words. Further references to Roger Aston both establish and belie the intimate tone of the letters:

> Surely you have made a brave choice of him for presenting your ciphered letters unto me, for he himself can write nothing but ciphers. But in good faith he had almost put me in a fray at the receipt of them, for he came very grandie unto me while I was sitting at supper and whispered in my ear very quietly that he had letters from you unto me but he durst not give me them till I were all alone in my chamber, and left me to guess what kind of matter it could be.[16]

The king recounts a public display of his own need for privacy, aggrandizing himself and playfully deriding Cecil's "brave" choice of messenger. Aston essentially becomes a cipher for the letters themselves—after all, he is suited to the task because he can "write nothing but ciphers himself"—and so calls attention to both the medium and the means of exchange. Letter, letter writer, and letter bearer all become indispensable to this writer's self-presentation.

Clearly, then, the letters are an intricate process of negotiation. Simultaneously heaping praise and insult on his addressee, James asserts his authority through demeaning apostrophe, equivocal threats, patronizing jibes, and mock humility. He even manages to recognize his dependence on his subordinates, while at the same time turning his overspending into a courtly virtue and his hunting escapades into a type of penance. Of his financial problems, he writes,

> It is true my heart is greater than my rent, and my care to preserve my honor and credit by payment of my debts far greater than my possibility. This cannot but trouble me at home and torture me abroad, for I confess though I have more exercise of body here, I have less contentment of spirit than at home, for there by conference I get some relief and here I do only dream upon it with myself. . . .[17]

Giving up his hunting would be the easy way out; instead, he would rather do exactly as he pleases and be admired for refusing to share the burden of responsibility with his ministers. His customary address to Cecil is in itself an effort to shape through language the identity of the other, through dialogue, and so reflexively on himself. Implicitly, James recognizes, as he does in his published writing, that his image as king is as much constituted in others as in himself. After all, what he finds most gratifying about Cecil's answer to the archbishop is that it is the same answer that he himself would like to have given. The difficulty is one of decorum: if he were to offer the rebuke himself, it would lose effect. Only the speech of the other can effectively articulate the kind of sovereignty James desires. To be what he would be, he must have others to speak for him, and this desire is the same impulse that leads him to attempt to control the *vox populi* with his populist pamphlet.

Another reason other scholars have neglected the complexity of James's relationship to the tobacco industry is simply that they have underestimated the importance of that industry in contemporary consciousness. As Jerome Brooks, the pre-eminent tobacco historian states,

> Four and a half centuries now contain the record of tobacco—a complex and vivid chronicle of which some parts, being unexpected, are all the more dramatic. It is a global history of so composite a character that the subject of tobacco will be found in almost every field

of intellectual and scientific inquiry. Indeed, no other product of the vegetable world has inspired such an abundant body of writing.[18]

His statement might seem hyperbolic, but today we live in a world in which tobacco is so much a part of the mundane that many of us no longer even notice its presence. Yet if one reads the literature inspired by tobacco when it was a marvelous new discovery, it quickly becomes clear that the commodity was a powerful part of the cultural moment. Nearly every major dramatist of the late Elizabethan and Jacobean periods mentions the tobacco user at some point,[19] and representations of the plant abound in texts as varied as elite medical and botanical treatises, popular ballads, and paintings. If we are to understand why James would dedicate these two of the most significant public actions of his early tenure as king to tobacco, we must first recover the cultural moment when tobacco was as alien as a new world and as valuable as gold.

There is little disagreement among historians[20] that the vast and extremely rapid spread of the plant itself received impetus primarily from two quarters: initially, from the scientific curiosity of botanists and physicians and later, from the increasing popularity of the habit of tobacco use itself. Natural philosophers began to cultivate the herb in their own physic gardens before 1560, and by 1570, tobacco appeared in English gardens.[21] The curiosity about tobacco's scientific value was widespread; learned treatises touted the plant's curative value. Francisco Hernández, the Spanish court physician, had brought Philip II specimens from Mexico and there was a growing Portuguese interest in the weed's medicinal value.[22] The French were especially aggressive in promoting its pharmaceutical use. Jean Nicot, ambassador to Portugal, was given credit for sending tobacco seeds to Catherine de Medici—then Queen Mother of France—in 1560 and was lauded for his use of tobacco poultices. This praise annoyed natural philosopher and explorer André Thevet, who had nurtured the plant in his own garden since his return from Brazil in 1556, and had hoped to turn his experience with the plant to his advantage.[23] Significantly, then, tobacco literature found its roots, so to speak, in the houses of European royalty; it is fitting in that sense that James would offer his contribution many years later as a means of solidifying his sometimes tenuous position in the community of monarchs. While the plant quietly made its way around the world, and sailors carried their pipes, cigars, and leaf along marine trade routes to Africa and Asia, conventional wisdom about the topic grew out of elite discourse. For better or worse, the tobacco issue became inextricably tied to issues of class, power, and authority.

Sometime during this period, tobacco use reached England. Although the exact date of its arrival is not known, its spread was obviously hindered by poor relations with Spain, by then the primary producer of the commodity.[24] The English were undoubtedly familiar with tobacco by the 1580's. In 1583, Edward Cotton asked the captain of his eponymous ship to bring some home from America,[25] and Sir Richard Grenville purchased some for Ralegh in 1585.[26] According to Hakluyt's *Principall Navigations,* Native Americans on the west coast of North America had presented tobacco to Sir Francis Drake's men, on the assumption that they were gods.[27] Ralph Lane comments that when he and his fellow Roanoke settlers were rescued by Drake, the latter had just come from Santo Domingo, St. Augustine, and Cartagena. Lane also notes that planting was going well before Drake's arrival.[28] Lane's account supports Joseph Robert's assumption that the ship was heavily laden with tobacco when it finally arrived in England, marking the first major shipment of tobacco and the beginning of widespread tobacco use in the country.[29] Returned settler Thomas Harriot's words attest that both the habit and its fantastic reputation would be thoroughly appropriated by the English:

> We ourselves during the time we were there, used to suck it after their manner, as also since our return, and have many rare and wonderful experiments of the virtues thereof: of which the relation would require a volume by itself: the use of it by so many of late, men and women of great calling as else, and some learned Physicians also, is sufficient witness.[30]

In the fifteen years or so following Drake's return from Roanoke, tobacco became a fairly common commodity. Travelers' references to the herb during these years began to give fewer descriptions of its properties and methods of use. The novelty of smoking may have begun to wear off, but its use had increased dramatically. According to one report, "before the end of the century, the demand for tobacco had grown to such an extent that English sailors were beginning to regard West Indian islands as valuable or otherwise according to the amount of tobacco they produced."[31] Demand continued to grow despite the fact that unadulterated commercial tobacco often drew its weight in silver, and could even draw its weight in gold.[32] Tobacco clearly had become the precious commodity the Spanish had looked for in South America.

Obviously, Sir Walter Ralegh, commonly regarded as the father of English smoking, introduced neither the plant nor its use to England. Ralegh, however, was one of the first courtiers to take to smoking a pipe, and is seen as a major force in popularizing pipe smoking among the aristocracy.[33] Regardless of the accuracy of this perception, even Ralegh's contemporaries distinguished him with a special link to tobacco. A marginal gloss in Hakluyt reads, "Sir Walter Ralegh was the first that brought Tobacco into use, when all men wondered what it meant."[34]

Many historians sensibly point out that no one person could possibly be held responsible for this popularization. The novelty of both the act of smoking and the plant itself, the sometimes exhilarating effects of smoking, and the feeling of social fellowship[35] produced by the sharing of tobacco made its popularity inevitable. Most obvious, and most overlooked by the historians of tobacco, is the simple fact—which we are only beginning acknowledge now—that tobacco is an extremely addictive drug, and thus a self-perpetuating commodity.

As recreational smoking became increasingly popular, fashion called for expensive, elaborate equipment, and although tobacco use spanned all classes, these apparatuses helped to signify those who belonged to a better class, much as certain types of dress did. Like the many upstarts who hoped to better themselves by breaking dress codes, many of those who adopted the practice of "cultured" smoking invited ridicule from those who felt they smoked by right of class. A properly equipped gallant would carry several "clays" (pipes) in a case, along with a special box containing tobacco, silver ember tongs, a pick, metal stopper, knife, scoop, and mirror.[36] Ralegh himself had a gold case set with candles for lighting up.[37]

The better tobacco shops, often apothecaries, had separate sections for smokers, who could go sit behind a curtain and smoke a rented pipe for 3d. Because of tobacco's Native American origins, the telltale figure of the midget blackamoor with a huge cigar tucked under his arm became the sign for tobacco. Whether American or African—the two apparently indistinguishable in a contemporary English mind—the representation of non-Europeans carried similar connotations; both evoked images of transgression, savagery, and sexual liberty. Simultaneously, because the pipe's shape invited both phallic and vaginal associations, tobacco itself became a sign for something else: promiscuity. Tobacco use and sexual licentiousness were thought to be intimately linked; contemporary drama and pamphlets are riddled with tobacco users who smoke while wenching. This was one case where a cigar was not just a cigar; eventually, brothels even began to display the sign of the tobacco pipe.[38]

As smokers' habits became ridiculously extravagant, tobacco dealers fell into disrepute. At the same time, medical claims about tobacco's efficacy as a drug became more and more outrageous. In response, a concerted voice of dissent with respect to tobacco use arose for the first time in England. Sensible thinkers decided that no substance could possibly cure all ailments, and medical men who felt their control of the tobacco industry slipping away sought to keep tobacco use strictly in the therapeutic realm. Whereas for Ralegh, as Jeffrey Knapp and Stephen Greenblatt both discuss, tobacco had been a source of authority and a means of authoring

himself,[39] its rampant use now made it a means of undermining authority. The debate moved into popular discourse, and learned physicians found themselves either championed by common pamphleteers or forced to undertake their own defense in the bookstalls of Paul's yard. Tracts suddenly threatened that tobacco, if used without the appropriate supervision of a physician, could produce sterility, melancholy, vomits, and intestinal decay. They publicized the frightening results of autopsies of excessive smokers with oily, sooty lungs and blackened brains.[40]

The growing protests against tobacco were further fueled by the English public's awareness that Spain controlled virtually all tobacco trade. Since trade with Spain was tightly circumscribed, almost all the tobacco imported into England came through illicit channels.[41] Not surprisingly, English, French, and Dutch piracy aimed specifically at the precious substance abounded;[42] Drake's seagoing exploits, however, only served to whet English appetites for tobacco. In the minds of many, tobacco posed a threat to social, political, economic, and even religious stability; James could not have picked a more apt focus for his own experiment in self-fashioning.

The establishment of the colony at Jamestown stoked the controversy yet again. At first, this settlement, like Roanoke before it, seemed doomed to failure. Initially the colonists found no suitable staple crop,[43] but John Rolfe managed to save the colony by importing seeds from the Spanish West Indies. Some intrigue must have been involved for Rolfe to have acquired the seeds. Spanish planters considered it treasonous to give away even a tiny number of the precious seeds to an Englishman; Spanish law by this time required that all Spanish tobacco be cleared through the port of Seville, and selling harvested leaf directly to foreigners was punishable by death.[44]

Fortunately for Rolfe and his companions, the seed, when planted in the new soil, produced a distinctive and highly satisfactory leaf, but Virginian leaders continued to be wary of the new staple. Governor Thomas Dale, fearing famine, decreed that tobacco could be raised only if two acres of corn accompanied it. The fear of famine influenced Virginia's governmental policy well into the 1640's.[45] Rolfe's marriage to Pocahontas ensured the English the time and technology to perfect the crop; and when Rolfe returned to England, he too participated in the pamphlet war, apologetically addressing a treatise to the king extolling the virtues of Virginia, including "the principal commodity the colony for the present yieldeth."[46]

Upon returning to Virginia, he found tobacco grown in every available nook and cranny.[47] Captain Smith commented with embarrassment upon Governor Samuel Argall's arrival in 1617:

In Jamestown [Argall] found but five or six houses, the Church down, the Palizado's broken, the Bridge in pieces, the Well of fresh water spoiled; the store house they used for the Church, the market-place, and streets, and all other spare places planted with Tobacco, the Savages a frequent in their houses as themselves, whereby they were become expert in our arms, and had a great many in their custody and possession, the colony dispersed all about, planting Tobacco. Captain Argall not liking these proceedings, altered them agreeable to his own mind. . . .[48]

The threat of starvation was not the only aspect of tobacco that the governors of Virginia feared, then. Smith's account reveals a suspicion of commerce, a fastidious fear of the violation of boundaries: the threshold, the well, the altar, the border all undermined by tobacco, an American grotesque. Apparently, tobacco was a menacing tool by which the "frequent" Indians could corrupt an entire Christian community.

In Virginia, tobacco came to dominate every aspect of colonial life. In keeping with the interchangeability of tobacco and gold in London, tobacco became an alternative currency, and was even accepted in payment of taxes. Tobacco bought the first slaves and similarly paid the captain who brought a shipment of wives for the colonists who remained. Even clergymen demanded tobacco in lieu of a proper salary, giving Sunday sermons on the moral importance of raising and curing the herb correctly.[49] The significance of tobacco's widespread acceptance as a form of currency cannot be overemphasized. Tobacco was not, as Knapp argues, simply a morally viable substitute for riches; it *was* money. That it was not just valuable, but actually a form of currency, meant that those who coveted it, craved it, and burned it indiscriminately could be perceived as committing the same sin of avarice as those—like the stereotypical Spaniard—who single-mindedly pursued gold. That tobacco was a corruptive object of obsession, or on the other hand, something that could benefit many, stems directly from its monetary significance, and is apparent in much of the literature discussed below.

Since the controversy surrounding tobacco use obviously continues today, it is hardly surprising that no clear consensus of opinion regarding the propriety of its use was reached in the short time from tobacco's discovery in the Americas until the end of the reign of James I. Nevertheless, the abundance of contemporary published material on the subject reveals that the debate was not simply a stalemate; instead, tobacco polemic continually hovered around a number of recurrent themes, constantly reworking those themes and recreating them anew as each polemicist sought to answer those who came before him. Thus, each pamphlet is both a product of its own agenda and a single utterance in a decades-long dialogue shaped by and shaping the discourse surrounding it.

Before tobacco was commonly in use in England—*i.e.,* before the 1587 return of the first Virginians—Englishmen relied primarily on the translated reports of continental authorities for their information on the subject. John Frampton's *Joyfull Newes ovt of the newe founde worlde,* a heavily revised translation of the Spanish doctor Monardes's work, was available in London by 1577. As the English title of Thevet's 1568 treatise, *The New founde Worlde, or Antarctike, wherein is contained wonderful and strange things,* suggests, these reports portray tobacco as a miraculous and divine gift whose esoteric properties were virtually unbounded. Thevet calls it a "secrete herb," which is "marvelous profitable for many things," and which the Indians use for "secrete talk or counsel among them selves."[50] These works capitalize on the very sense of "wonder" and "marvel" that Stephen Greenblatt suggests was cultivated to justify the exploration and eventual appropriation of the New World.[51] The early accounts describe tobacco almost exclusively in positive terms; dissent on its use in these early works is conspicuously absent.[52]

The minor poet Anthony Chute's treatise, *Tabacco,* published posthumously in 1595, is primarily a summarization of these earlier authorities; he relies mainly on the works of Monardes and Nicot to reveal tobacco's mysteries to an uninformed public. As with his sources, the mystical efficacy of the herb is a paramount theme. Adam Islip, the original publisher of the work, writes in his preface that Chute knew of tobacco both firsthand and "by private conference with men of learning, as by the strange and wonderful operations thereof. . . ." Yet by this time, tobacco use had become common enough in England for Chute to write of the virtues of Indian tobacco:

> Indeed it would seem somewhat much for any man to say, that if the drying of [tobacco] were according to the care of them, who here with vs make it their trade to gain by, that we might attribute so much power to it, being dried after such a manner; but surely I cannot thine, but that coming from those poor people, where covetousness hath not taught the child to cut his fathers throat for gain, or to dissemble with any for profit, we may esteem it either as good as the green, or at least as that green which grows here in our clime, which reason persuades us is unapt to bring forth the herb in her natural heat and virtue being so hot and our soil so cold.[53]

To decipher Chute's garbled prose is no easy task. In short, Chute says that the unspoilt Indians can cure tobacco better than greedy European traders, imparting some sort of implicit virtue to the commodity; and that this tobacco, although cured, is just as good as any fresh tobacco found in England. To these comments he adds that the older authorities do not often discuss pipe use either because it is a fairly new practice or perhaps because it has been used to such extremes, since "every extreme virtue is a vice."[54]

Of this implied abuse and the dissent it had already aroused, he complains,

> I doubt not but some hath both done themselves wrong, wronged vs, and done other injury, who (if They had not heard of some whom unrespective drinking had harmed) would happily have been soon drawn to use it for their health, who now remaining reared with examples shun it as an inconvenience, which else they had entertained as a public good.[55]

The basic premises of the conflict over the tobacco trade had been established by this time, then; for although he praises tobacco strongly, Chute cannot ignore the avarice of the European tobacco trader, the corruption of the New World's innocence, or the growing problem of tobacco abuse.

By 1602, the offenses of tobacco users had become serious enough to prompt a full-fledged attack on tobacco use. *A Work for Chimny-sweepers: or A warning for Tabacconists,* published anonymously, describes itself as a "vain discourse of the pernicious and vulgar use, or rather abuse of Tabacco."[56] The work outlines eight reasons for the author's "dislike . . . of the use and practice of Tabacco,"[57] and then gives a chapter supporting each with personal anecdotes and classical examples. *Chimny-sweepers* portrays vividly the stereotypical tobacco abuser, commonly known as a "tobacconist," for the author accepts that he will "draw . . . no small hatred among our smoky gallants, who having long time glutted themselves with the fond fopperies and fashion of our neighbor Countries: yet still desirous of novelties, have not stuck to travel as far as India to fetch [them]. . . ."[58]

Almost immediately, *A Defence of Tabacco: With a friendly Answer to the late printed Booke called Work for Chimny-sweepers, etc.* responded to the previous pamphlet by refuting its eight contentions one by one. At one point the author states in mock exasperation, "I must needs think, that you were very near driven to the hedge for a stake, when you picked out this argument." This particular tract is thought to have been written by Dr. Roger Marbecke,[59] the queen's chief physician and a former provost at Oriel College, Oxford; naturally, the text is written in the disputatious style of a university wit and so is not without humor. Its author recognizes that, for all the vivacity of the interchange, the debate was, thus far, rather conventional. A poem dedicates the *Defence* in this way, playfully creating its author's name in an acrostic:

> Much here is said Tabacco to defend,
> And much was said, Tabacco to disgrace:
> Read, mark, and scan: then censure in the end:
> Both you are men, most fit to judge the case.
> Esteem of me, as you in me shall find:
> Crave pardon, first I do: and that obtained,
> Know this, that no man shall with better mind,

> Each where declare to you his love unfeigned.

> Come what shall come, to this poor Indian toy:
> Unto you both, I with immortal joy.

Marbecke, then, is not proposing a case as the champion of the irrefutable right to tobacco use. The plan is only a "toy" with which he performs an argumentative exercise; he then expects his readers to "read, mark, and scan," to determine a winner. He calls his opponent "a man, well read, and of sufficient learning, and understanding,"[60] and his later remarks confirm the detached mood of the treatise:

> Loath I am, I confess, to intermeddle in any such matters: nevertheless, for so much, as modest, and scholarly disputations, and conference between such, as have been civilly brought up in schools, are not to be disliked: for that oftentimes they do much good, and give great contentment to the Reader if they be done with due regard, of time, place and person . . . everything is, as it is taken: and my hope is, that nothing shall be ill taken there, where all is well meant.[61]

Marbecke is willing to inject his voice into the debate, but the stakes in the contest do not seem to warrant raising his voice. At this point, the disputation reflected intellectual curiosity rather than social crisis.

But the intervention of the monarch in 1604 made playful detachment far more difficult, for James's *A Counterblaste to Tobacco*—his first, although anonymously, published treatise as king of England[62]—posed the abuse of tobacco as a political issue, and one which jeopardized the State itself. The *Counterblaste* depicts tobacco use as the predictable but undesirable result of the recent arrival of peace and wealth:

> Our peace hath bred wealth: And Peace and wealth hath brought forth a general sluggishness, which makes vs wallow in all sorts of idle delights, and soft delicacies, the first seeds of the subversion of all great Monarchies.[63]

Many readers guessed the author's identity, for the pamphlet stressed the importance of the king as the physician to the body politic; and between the pamphlet and the king's controversial official policy towards tobacco, not to mention the establishment of tobacco plantations in England and Virginia, the immediacy of the issue became apparent in contemporary pamphlets. Pamphleteers could no longer afford to use their opinions on tobacco for mere entertainment. They had been warned implicitly that a public statement about the issue carried potential political consequences.

With the revival of the colonial endeavor in 1607, reports from Virginia described the Indian use of the plant with an invigorated sense of wonder, perhaps with a renewed need to justify the appropriation of new land. But given James's public position on the issue, these writers were forced to tread softly. John Rolfe's *A True Relation of the State of Virginia* (1615), deceptive in its hesitation to mention the crop, mentions first a store of other commodities from Virginia but later calls tobacco the "principal" one. His argument is constructed carefully, to counteract the familiar stereotype of the tobacco-crazed Virginian described by men like John Smith. He subtly seeks favor for tobacco by first combatting fears that Virginians might starve themselves in their greed for profit. He cites the many products of a fruitful land: maize, wheat, peas, beans, hemp, flax, silkworms, carrots, parsnips, and pumpkins, slyly adding, almost as an afterthought,

> Likewise Tobacco (though an esteemed weed) very commodious, which there thriveth so well that (no doubt) after a little more trial and experience thereof, it will compare with the best in the West Indies.[64]

In a similar vein, he later points out the Virginian law that required settlers to plant food as well as tobacco. Rolfe clearly emphasizes the fact that for the Virginians, tobacco is necessary for the very survival of the colony. Of the two-fold system of food and tobacco production, he says:

> . . . the Magazine shall be sure yearly to receive their Rent of Corn, to maintain those who are fed thereof, being but a few, and many others if need be, they themselves will be well stored to keep their families with an overplus and reap Tobacco enough to buy clothes, and such necessaries as are needful for themselves and household.[65]

Rolfe further states that, a short distance away from Jamestown, a group of twenty-five men ". . . are employed only in planting and curing Tobacco, with the profit thereof to clothe themselves, and all those who labor about the general Business."[66] By including these observations in his treatise on the state of Virginia as a whole, he makes a quiet case for tobacco to those at home, showing them that the herb can be transformed into the necessities of life.

But in the eyes of tobacco's opponents, the disease was growing uncontrollably. In *The Honestie of this Age* (1615), Barnabe Rich laments:

> But amongst the trades that are newly taken up, this trade of Tobacco doth exceed: and the money that is spent in smoke is unknown, and (I thine) unthought on. . . . I have heard it told, that now very lately, there hath bin a Catalogue taken of all those newly erected houses that have set up the trade in selling of Tobacco, in London and near about London . . . upward of 7000 houses, that doth live by that trade.[67]

Rich claims that tobacco is sold and consumed everywhere, in apothecaries, groceries, chandleries, and private homes. I have been unable to trace the accuracy of this catalogue; the report may well be exaggerated, in which case it simply affirms even more strongly the alarm that this new tobacco culture excited among some.

In light of the ascendancy of Spanish tobacco and the encouragement given Virginians for their alternative product, it is no surprise that the second decade of the sixteenth century saw a rekindled interest in the tobacco debate. *An Advice how to plant Tobacco in England* (1615)[68] proposes to keep English money out of Spanish pockets by encouraging Englishmen to grow tobacco themselves. Thus, most of the text is purely technical, specifying when to plant and how to care for the crop. But the treatise also identifies many contemporary misgivings surrounding the trade, most notably that of tobacco adulteration:

> Now besides these harmful mixtures [added to imported leaf], if out English which delight in Indian Tobacco, had seen how the Spanish slaves make it up, how they dress their sores and pocky ulcers, with the some unwashed hands with which they slubber and anoint the Tobacco, and call it sauce *per los perros Lutheranos*, for Lutheran dogs; they would not so often draw it into their heads and through their noses as they doe: yea many a filthy savor they find therein, did not the smell of honey master it. . . .[69]

Like many of the pamphlets before it, *An Advice* cites the "masters" of the use of the weed, Thevet and Monardes, and gives countless medicinal applications for it.

John Deacon's *Tobacco Tortured, or the Filthie Fume of Tobacco Refined* (1616) attests that the English fervor for smoking was as avid as ever, for Deacon is vehement in his protest against it. He is not satisfied with castigating tobacco as an unclean and unhealthy habit; he insists, like James, that it represents a palpable threat to the State itself. The work is dedicated to the king, and directly echoes James dedication to the **Counterblaste,** asking the king, in his great knowledge of medicine, to prescribe remedies for the illnesses of the body politic. His tedious and dogmatic prose is arranged in the form of a classical dialogue and "proves" his thesis by a series of syllogisms. At the end, he sums up his argument in this way:

> Now then . . . sith those the disordered courses of our graceless Tobacconists are every way exceedingly hurtful to their own proper persons, first by poisoning their bodies and souls, and then by procuring a prodigal dispending of their ancient patrimonies and other preferments; sith they are so unnaturally injurious to their own wives and children, by causing their needless poverty, and woeful complaints; sith they are so barbarously cruel towards their poor Tenants, for the chargeable supply of their unnecessary wants; sith they are so outrageously resolute upon the present spoil of other mens substance; with they are so fearfully opposite to

the well settled peace of our country, with they are so stately repugnant to the good established laws of our land; with they are so dangerously occurring to the public peace of our sovereign Lord the King; sith they are so proudly rebellious to his Majesties sovereign power, sith they are such inevitable provocations to the untimely spilling of their own and other mens blood, of spoiling the present good blessing of God, of opening a fearful gap to foreign invasions of cruel massacres, of an extreme hazard to our happy Estate and most flourishing kingdom.[70]

To the adversaries of tobacco, its use had become treasonous, for the most part because the king despised it. To them it became a contagious disease to the human body, the body politic, and the body of Christ. Deacon appeals to Christian sensibilities in addressing his audience as "good Christian Readers"[71] and in expressing concern for those who carouse too often to devote themselves to the church.

In the midst of this flurry of tobacco pamphlets, the pamphlet form itself did not go unnoticed. In 1617, Richard Brathwait published his *Solemne Ioviall Disputation, Theoreticke and Practicke: Briefly Shadowing The Law of Drinking.* Brathwait, a poet and onetime lawyer educated at both universities, capitalized on the polemic quality of the pamphlets to satirize publications objecting to drinking and smoking. It is divided into two sections; the second, entitled "The Age of Smoking," is devoted entirely to tobacco. Like the preceding pamphlets, it contains an epistle dedicatory, several introductory poems, Biblical and classical marginalia, and a number of anecdotes. The preface of the tobacco section is addressed "To Whomever, whensoever, or wheresoever."[72] One passage reads:

> That the Light of the Law admonisheth us, that some things are to bee daily and duly learned of us. Seeing then, that there is nothing, (so far as I know) more familiarly practiced, nothing more solemnly observed, than the Ceremonies of Bacchus. . . .[73]

Brathwait thus mocks the pamphleteers' dependence on classical and, even more notably, Christian learning to support their arguments. In a similar manner, he satirizes the pithy aphorisms which pervade the pamphlets, saying, "He that has lived to his time, is either a Fool or a Physician; he knows what is best for himself, which he observes as religiously as any Pagan in Christendom."[74] In an oblique and not entirely flattering reference to James, the narrator tells his fictional companions—tobacco merchants trying to enlist him to speak in their favor—"Alexander Severus would have smoked . . . and Xerxes would have pulled their skin over their ears; if these smoky Merchants . . . had vended, or vented those commodities in their time."[75] A Trinidadan tells him that tobacco seeds were thrown in a bed of gourds,

> and in a months space the whole bed of gourds were into leaves of Tobacco changed. Whereat smiling, I

have read [answered the narrator] all Ovid's Metamorphosis, and I find no such transmutation. No marvel (answered he) those were fictions, there true and native relations: besides, you are to know that Travellers in their surveys, assume a privilege above the authority of Authors.[76]

Both statements humorously reveal the faulty logic implicit in using classical authors as evidence for or against tobacco use, since the issue was so startlingly new.

Although neither side seems to have surpassed the other in the success of its argument, both share several recurrent themes. First, it is clear to both the proponents and opponents of tobacco use that the decision to plant, cure, trade in, or use the plant carries a real moral weight. As was shown above, John Rolfe went to great lengths to justify his choice to promote tobacco growth, while the authors of *Tobacco Tortured* and the *Counterblaste* make tobacco use tantamount to treason. Unlike James, and perhaps in direct response to his indictment, Rolfe proposes tobacco as an aid to the Commonwealth instead of a subversion of it. In aligning the crop with family values, hard work, and honest profit, he answers the fears of those who saw tobacco as an unnecessary luxury item.

In *An Advice,* even the simple act of pruning one's plants becomes a significant moral act:

> . . . if you shall neglect [to prune], *coveting* to have many stalks, because many leaves, your Tobacco will be weak and worth nothing. . . .

> And yet *you must not so love your own* as to take it green . . . otherwise, it may prove equally harmful with that which is sophisticate. I must also advise you not to slubber your English with Melrosarum, and other *trumpery,* as many of our own Artificers do, thereby to bring it to the Indian color; it is an *impious practice* to play with the health of men, and make profit by their destruction.[77]

The author's language goes far beyond the technical to project the ethical implications of such an act. He clearly illustrates the self-defeating nature of covetousness, an understandable admonishment given tobacco's value, and warns against vanity and self-love.[78]

Moreover, almost all of the pamphlets were intensely chauvinistic. Tobacco remained primarily a Spanish product, and therefore one to be derided. The pamphleteers distrusted not just Spaniards, but all foreigners. *Tobacco Tortured* warns of trafficking with corrupt nations, but even the English do not remain unscathed. As with Captain Smith's description of a tobacco-obsessed Jamestown, this chauvinism results from a fear of the grotesque violation of boundaries. True to the contemporary obsession with taxonomy, Deacon argues,

. . . from whence it cometh now to passe, that so many of our Englishmen's minds are thus terribly Turkished with Mahometan trumperies; thus treacherously Italianized with sundry antichristian toys; thus spitefully Spanished with superfluous pride; thus fearfully Frenchized with flaring net-works to catch English fools; thus huffingly Hollandized with ruffian like loom-works, and other like ladified fooleries. . . . According to the Italian proverb which portrayeth forth an Englishman thus. . . . An Englishman Italienate, is a very devil incarnate.[79]

Coupled with this chauvinistic tendency is a desire for insularity, and the need to insure that the world remain in certain categories, and thus remain in the realm of understanding. To overexpose oneself to the culture of another nation is to risk becoming something strange and unknowable. Marbecke insults the author of *Chimny-sweepers* by accusing him, "What needed you to have fetched your proofs out of France, to persuade that ill smells do offend? Every dunghill in England, and something else too, can testify that well enough."[80]

It is when the pamphlets extend their chauvinism to include this fear that they become positively xenophobic. The commonly held suspicion towards tobacco's Indian origins ties in with this particular brand of xenophobia. *Chimny-sweepers* reads, ". . . at all times, at all hours, and of all persons, this Indian stranger most familiarly is received . . ."[81]; and James complains in the *Counterblaste,*

. . . shall we I say, without blushing, abase our selves so far, as to imitate these beastly Indians, slaves to the Spaniards, refuse to the world, and as yet aliens from the holy Covenant of God? Why doe we not as well imitate them in walking naked as they doe? in preferring glasses, feathers, and such toys, to gold and precious stones, as they do? yea why do we not deny God and adore the Devil, as they doe?[82]

The chauvinism and xenophobia of the pamphlets, then, are distinct, but often inseparable impulses.

Those two impulses do diverge, however, in *An Advice.* Its anti-Spanish sentiment is readily apparent in what has been shown so far of the pamphlet, but the author combines this sentiment with the belief in the noble Indian origins of the plant. *Natural* tobacco, he writes,

. . . is a deep yellow, or a light tawny: and when the Indians themselves sold it us for Knives, Hatchets, Bells and the like merchandise, it had no other complexion, as all the Tobacco at this day hath, which is bought from the coast of Guiana, from Saint Vincents, from Saint Lucia, from Dominica, and other places, where we buy it but of the natural people; and all these sorts are clean, and so is that of St. Domingo; where the Spaniards have not yet learned the Art of Sophistication.[83]

In contrast, the Spaniards "sophisticate," or render impure and artificial, this natural, "wholesome" tobacco. The adulterated tobacco takes on a blackened color,

which Englishmen in their ignorance see as a sign of quality; the connection between the older meaning of the adjective "sophisticated" and the more modern "culturally complex, fashionable," is perhaps evident here. If they cannot obtain English tobacco, the pamphleteer advises his countrymen to use Indian leaf, "which colors are natural, and forbear the black which is foul, the dyed tobacco which is red, and the leaf brought in by the Portugals, and the like slubbered stuff," for "he that wears the cloth to the end it was intended for, to wit, to defend himself from the cold, and wet, cares more for the goodness than the color."[84] Thus the two types of tobacco, and more particularly their colors, yellow and black, become emblematic of the bright, innocent, unspoilt New World in contrast with the dark, artificial, and rotten practices of the Old World, and of covetous Iberians in particular.

The Spanish exchange the leaf, not for necessities, as do the Indians; rather, ". . . nothing (some Silks, and Cloth of Silver and Gold excepted) but ready Money, and Silver plate could content them."[85] In saying so, the author, like Rolfe, aligns the Indians and the product with an ideology that values a Protestant work ethic above all else. In contrast, James, in asking of the "beastly" Indians, "Why doe we not imitate them . . . in preferring glasses, feathers, and such toys, to gold and precious stones," considers them evil precisely because their ignorance of "civilized" ways leads them to pursue vanities. Contradicting his own policy regarding tobacco, he implies that the pursuit of treasure that has what he considers intrinsic value is in no way covetous.

Thus, a major contrast between the two camps becomes apparent. Both are well aware of the Indian origins of the plant; moreover, both seem to agree that those origins impart some quality, or lack thereof, to it.[86] Supporters, like Chute and the author of *An Advice,* then, identify that quality as a virtue inherent in the "noble savage," while opponents see it as a vice untamed by civilization and a result of the Indians' "devilish" religious practices. Marbecke answers the accusation made to this effect in *Chimny-sweepers* by implying that Englishmen, whose native drug is alcohol, are the real barbarians:

. . . me thinks it were a more charitable notion, to think [tobacco] came from God, who is the author of all good gifts, than from the devil. . . . Touching the taking of it by [Indian] priests, and by and by falling asleep thereupon & c. mark me but that whole discourse well: and ye shall see, it is taken & reported quite amiss; for indeed it maketh all for Tabacco. For take but Monardes his own tale: and by him it should seem; that in the taking of Tabacco: they were drawn up: and separated from all grosse and earthly cogitations, and as it were carried up to a more pure and clear region, of fine conceits & actions of the mind. . . . Marry, if in their trances, & sudden fallings, they had become nasty, & beastly fellows: or had in a most loathsome manner, falling spewing, and vomiting, as drunkards are wont to do: then indeed it might well have been counted a devilish matter, and been worthy of reprehension.[87]

Marbecke's sympathetic narrative anticipates the Rousseavian celebration of the noble savage, but his understanding of Native Americans is by no means anthropological. He does not offer an accurate assessment or representation of a alien culture. Instead, he merely considers tobacco against a background of theological, eschatological, and aesthetic concerns that are decidedly European. The entire conceit of the noble savage is an attempt less to understand a foreign culture in itself than to advance a favorable prejudice based on the cultural norms of the reader.

The pamphlets' shared reluctance to discuss the subject of tobacco without the citation of European authorities who befit the humanist tradition from which their writing springs, illustrates the same point. Knapp, for example, notices *Chimny-sweeper*'s author's preoccupation with authority,[88] and adds, "Beaumont involves tobacco in a rebellion . . . not only against religious or temporal authority but also . . . the authority of the classics."[89] Participants in the pamphlet war can only establish the meaning of tobacco by calibrating it against familiar texts and discourses. Neither those who attack tobacco nor those who defend it wish to acknowledge the possibility of alternative forms of discourse, which might threaten established cultural paradigms. To step outside the classical canon, to allow discourse without authority, was to acknowledge an uncontrollable, unknowable aspect of the universe—a prospect largely incompatible with Renaissance thought.

Yet, perhaps for the first time, an even obliquely reliable authority for a subject was impossible, for these men found themselves contemplating experiences without precedent. Although this aspect of their encounter with the New World thrilled those like Monardes, who found the experience "joyful news," it also, as an unknown, inspired anxiety and prompted much of the retrenchment and xenophobia in the anti-tobacco pamphlets. Contemporary views of tobacco were, in many ways, a microcosm of the reaction to the New World as a whole; the tension between the impulses to embrace the discovery with joy and to run from it in terror continually played into the tobacco controversy. The very newness, the untouched quality that lent the plant and the world that fostered it their implicit virtue in the eyes of some, paradoxically denied the existence of both in classically oriented discourse.

The preface of the 1616 edition of James's **Works,** in which James's authorship of the **Counterblaste** was finally officially acknowledged, cogently illustrates the definition of authority that attaches itself to James. The bishop of Winchester, dedicating the volume to Prince Charles, invoked

. . . the King of Kings, God Himself, who, as he doth all things for our good; so doeth he many things for our imitation. It pleased his Divine wisdom to bee the first in this Rank, that we read of, that did ever write. He wrote, and the writing was the writing, saith Moses, of God.

R. S. Rait claims that this may have been written "to confute the belief that writing became not the majesty of a king."[90] But it is unlikely that, educated in the strongest humanist tradition, and thus practiced in composition, James felt the need to justify his already copious writings. Instead, the bishop's preface aligns the king, as God's anointed leader, in yet another way—he not only retains the power to govern his people, but also the God-like ability to create a new truth from chaos. The writing becomes the writing, or the word becomes Truth, simply from the power of the Utterer. Moreover, in writing as an example for imitation, God, and James, calls for a submission to these truths, allowing for no dissent among the faithful or loyal.

Both Jonathan Goldberg and David Norbrook note that James's anger at the publication of Spenser's *Faerie Queene,* which allegorizes Mary Stuart's execution in the story of Duessa, stemmed from his mistaken idea that it represented official Tudor propaganda. In short, James saw that any publication permitted by a monarch, as *author* of all things in that country, was, in effect, his or her personal opinion.[91] Conversely, then, it was to James's advantage to publish the **Counterblaste** anonymously. Perhaps, in his eyes, a duplication of his opinion sent from elsewhere furthered the impression of his own authority over his kingdom. James probably would not have said that he needed those voices to support his cause, but rather that by illustrating proper submission to his authority, he could strengthen his own created version of the truth. This outside voice allowed James to create his own Other, obliterating all voices but his own.

James's attack on tobacco is among his most well-known and forcefully presented political causes precisely because of this understanding of the construction of power through dialogue. Although James's hatred of the habit may well have been genuine on a personal level, the tobacco trade also presented a dilemma that forced him to consider his own place as an authority figure. Goldberg certainly approaches this question in his study of authority and its representations in the Jacobean literary scene, yet he neglects to acknowledge explicitly and in all its richness the fundamental premise behind all of James's discursive practices—that James presented himself as an authority or author in *every* sense of the word. He presented himself not simply as one with a power to enforce obedience or influence the opinions of others, and not even simply as one entitled to power or entitled by God to acceptance by his subjects, but, in short, as one who is all of those things *and* a creative communicative force.

The tobacco trade, then, posed a number of threats to James's own sense of power. Here were an economic endeavor and a popular habit that, although widely known to displease the new king, threatened to continue indefinitely. As would be later pointed out in the 1616 preface to James's *Works,* one of the purposes of God's, and thus the king's, actions was to provide an example for imitation. In a country that had gone so long without a male sovereign, this ability would be a doubly conspicuous mode of establishing and maintaining power. Yet the culture that had grown up around tobacco use encouraged James's subjects to emulate others than himself, by definition conducting themselves in an ungodly fashion. A popular tradition that credited Sir Walter Ralegh with the establishment of this culture provided a personified, and thus more direct threat to the king's will; and Ralegh certainly did not escape unscathed from the **Counterblaste.**

Conversely, as smoking was happily (for James) a habit which he did not practice, it was certainly a safe subject for discourse.[92] Goldberg sees the tract as a chance for James to "make the great out of small, to use the vice as a way of presenting himself as exemplary, the nation's savior, pure in his life, acute in his wit," by showing up the logic of those who supported tobacco use.[93] True as this point may be, James could prove himself exemplary only if he completely discredited tobacco use and users; to maintain complete authority, he could not allow for dual truths; he had to counter himself with himself. The tract is not, then, one of self promotion, but of negation and recreation of the other. In the end, in James's textual universe, only he remains.

Notes

1. Quoted in Jerome E. Brooks, *The Mighty Leaf: Tobacco through the Centuries* (Boston, 1952), 56.

2. See Brooks, 70, and James Halliday, "Blast and Counterblast," *Blackwood's Magazine* 317 (1975): 327-338.

3. Cf. Andrew Sinclair, *Sir Walter Raleigh and the Age of Discovery* (Hammersmith, England, 1984), who states the point most succinctly, "the king might hardly ever wash or change his clothes. He may drink too much whiskey, but he abhorred tobacco and the man who had brought it to England," 98. More sophisticated discussions appear in Jonathan Goldberg, *James I and the Politics of Literature,* (Baltimore, 1983), 26, and Jeffrey Knapp's fascinating examination of the Elizabethan tobacco issue, *An Empire Nowhere: England, America, and Literature from* Utopia *to* The Tempest (Berkeley, 1988), chap. 4.

4. James I, *Letters,* ed. G. P. V. Akrigg (Berkeley, 1984), 256. Spelling has been modernized in quo-

tations from primary documents when possible, but, following Akrigg's lead, Scottish dialect has been left intact.

5. Ibid., 252.

6. James I, *A Counterblaste to Tobacco,* ed. Edward Arber (London, 1869), 100-101.

7. Quoted, in G. P. V. Akrigg, introduction and notes to *Letters* by James I, 11. Evidently, this absentee rule was quite successful; with the aid of adept advisors, James was able to maintain relative peace and stability without visiting the country from his accession as King of England until 1617, a period of about fourteen years. Ibid., pp. 10-11, credits this success in large part to James's establishment of an efficient mail system; a letter could travel from London to Edinburgh in approximately one week.

8. Ibid., 29.

9. I am careful not to say that the written document *is* a totalizing substitute for the individual; rather, a written document is often *perceived* as such—hence, the fallacy of intent. The more accurate paradigm is far more complicated. A written document is a representation of the individual only inasmuch as the self exists in language, created (per Bakhtin) by dialogic utterance with an other.

10. Akrigg, 30.

11. James I, *Letters,* 252.

12. Ibid., 260.

13. Ibid., 255.

14. Cf. Akrigg: "Some historians have exaggerated the effects of James's absenteeism at his sport; actually he was more in touch than they seem to realize. He had a Clerk of the Signet in attendance upon him, and papers despatched from Whitehall at the end of a day's work normally reached the King at Royston early the next morning," 13.

15. James I, *Letters,* 255.

16. Ibid., 252.

17. Ibid., 261.

18. Brooks, 5.

19. Ibid., 72. Jonson, Chapman, Marston, Nashe, Beaumont and Fletcher, Decker, Middleton, and Field to name a few—F. W. Fairholt, *Tobacco: Its History and Associations* (London, 1859), catalogues these references exhaustively. The conspicuous exception is Shakespeare, who seems to limit himself to less explicit social satire.

20. The most impressive study of European tobacco use is by historian Jerome Brooks, *The Mighty Leaf.* See also C. M. MacInnes, *The Early English*

Tobacco Trade (London, 1926), and Joseph C. Robert, *The Story of Tobacco in America* (Chapel Hill, NC, 1964). Sarah Augusta Dickson, *Panacea or Precious Bane: Tobacco in Sixteenth Century Literature* (New York, 1954) examines numerous references to tobacco in literature, but performs very little literary analysis. The only recent literary study to engage the subject seriously is Knapp, *An Empire Nowhere,* which devotes a chapter to Elizabethan literary representations of tobacco. Knapp reviews the medical benefits tobacco supposedly offered, and attempts to account for the popularity of tobacco in the 1590's, when England had no real New World foothold. England, he says, tried to compensate for its belatedness in the New World by using a strategy of anti-materialism; the "paradoxical combination of inconsequentiality and power," (p. 135) enabled it to serve as a suitable synecdoche for Virginia, and allowed England to make claims to spiritual superiority in the New World. His argument is fascinating but problematic; he does not sufficiently account for tobacco's extremely high monetary value at the time. Furthermore, he rests a large part of his argument on a single passage in *The Faerie Queene* (3.5.32), without accounting for the ambiguity in the passage. When Belphoebe cures Timias with a magical plant, Spenser refuses to commit to the name of that plant, suggesting tobacco as only one of several possibilities. Although Knapp concentrates on Elizabethan literature and I discuss mostly the Jacobean tobacco phenomenon, I think in both cases it would be more accurate to say that rather than using anti-materialist strategies, the English simply substitute one kind of materialism for another.

21. Brooks, 35-36.

22. Robert, 4.

23. Cf. C. T.'s *Advice,* C3r., which says Nicot brought the queen tobacco, but "Thevet vaunts that he sent it into France 10 years before Nicot's Embassage." Brooks, 47, makes a convincing argument that the two men brought different species, Thevet bringing *Nicotiana tabacum,* used as commercial tobacco then and now, and Nicot, *Nicotiana rustica,* the more hardy plant used then medicinally but rarely grown today. Unfortunately for Thevet, history remembers his rival, for both the genus and its most toxic ingredient bear Nicot's name.

24. Brooks, 51-52.

25. Richard Hakluyt, *The Principall Navigations, Voiages and Discoveries of the English Nation,* facs. ed. (1859; Cambridge, 1965), 188.

26. Ibid., 735.

27. Ibid., 643.

28. Ibid., 746-747.

29. Robert, 5.

30. Hakluyt, 74-75.

31. MacInnes, 29.

32. See Robert, 5, and Sinclair, 98.

33. Sinclair, 31. See also MacInnes, 31.

34. Hakluyt, 541.

35. Brooks, 29.

36. Ibid., 66.

37. Sinclair, 41.

38. Brooks, 83-84. For a fascinating discussion of the pipe as an erotic icon in seventeenth-century Dutch painting, see also Simon Schama, *The Embarrassment of Riches: An Interpretation of Dutch Culture in the Golden Age* (London, 1987).

39. See Knapp, chap. 4, and Stephen Greenblatt, *Renaissance Self-Fashioning* (Chicago, 1980), chap. 4.

40. Brooks, 42.

41. MacInnes, 54.

42. Brooks, 59.

43. Robert, 7.

44. Brooks, 58.

45. Robert, 10.

46. Ibid., 9.

47. By 1618, London yearly imports of Virginian tobacco had grown to 20,000 pounds. The colony now could truly compete with Spain, and over the next ten years, Virginian leaf finally would take pre-eminence over Spanish; see Robert, 9, and Brooks, 55.

48. John Smith, *Complete Works, (1580-1631),* ed. Philip L. Barbour (Chapel Hill, NC, 1986), 262.

49. Brooks, 92.

50. André Thevet, *The New found worlde, or Antarcticke, wherein is contained many wonderful and strange things . . .* contemporary trans. from the French (London, 1568), 49.

51. See Stephen Greenblatt, *Marvelous Possessions: The Wonder of the New World* (Chicago, 1991), for a full treatment of this argument. I credit his Clarendon Lectures, delivered in March 1988 at Oxford University, for starting me out on this subject.

52. Most notably, Phillip Stubbes's *Anatomy of Abuses* (1583) contains no mention of tobacco abuse.

53. Anthony Chute, *Tabaco* (London, 1595), 2. Chute's patron, Gabriel Harvey, was a longtime enemy of Thomas Nashe's. Thus it is no surprise that Nashe denounces Chute, in his "Have with you to Saffron Walden," (1596) for his "ignorance, his poverty, and his indulgence in 'posset curd' and tobacco" (*The Concise Dictionary of National Biography: from the Earliest Times to 1985,* 6 vols. [Oxford, 1992], 347-348). Chute's tortuous prose style makes him a deserving target for Nashe's derision.

54. Chute, 4.

55. Ibid.

56. [Philartes], *A Work for Chimny-Sweepers: or, A Warning for Tabacconists* (London, 1602), A3r.

57. Ibid., B1v.

58. Ibid., A3r.

59. [Roger Marbecke], *A Defence of Tabaco: With a friendly Answer to the late printed Booke called work for chimny-sweepers, etc.* (London, 1602), 57. See also the *Concise Dictionary of National Biography,* 1006-1007.

60. *Defence,* 5.

61. Ibid.

62. Brooks, 70.

63. James I, *Counterblaste,* 96.

64. John Rolfe, *A True Relation of the State of Virginia,* ed. Henry C. Taylor, facs. ed. (1616; New Haven, 1951), 35.

65. Ibid., 47.

66. Ibid., 39.

67. Barnaby Rich, *The Honestie of this Age* (London, 1615), 20-21.

68. The author is identified only as "C. T.," but the Epistle to Brathwait's later "Solemne Jovial Disputation" identifies him as a "doctor of Physick."

69. [C. T.], *An Advice How to Plant Tobacco in England: and How to Bring it to Colour and perfection, to whom it may be profitable, and to whom harmful. the vertues of the Hearbe in generall, as well in the outward application as taken in Fume. with The Danger of Spanish Tobacco* (London, 1615), B1r.

70. John Deacon, *Tobacco Tortured: or, the Filthie Fume of Tobacco Refined* (London, 1616), 176.

71. Ibid., A1v.

72. Richard Brathwait, *A Solemne Iovial disputation, Theoreticke and Practicke: briefly Shadowing the Law of Drinking* (London: 1617), 87.

73. Ibid., 1.

74. Ibid., 67.

75. Ibid., 87.

76. Ibid., 90.

77. *An Advice,* B3r. (emphasis added).

78. The author is, of course, working within a long tradition, often represented in contemporary emblem books, that equates good husbandry with positive moral action.

79. Deacon, 10.

80. *Defence,* 25.

81. *Chimny-sweepers,* B2r.

82. James I, *Counterblaste,* 100.

83. *An Advice,* B1r.

84. Ibid., B4r.

85. Ibid., A3v.

86. As Knapp says, "the tobacco critic considers the imported weed pagan and earthly, qualities that infect England and lower its sights profoundly. A tobacco advocate like Beaumont counters that, with less persuasive claims to inherent value than gold, tobacco bespeaks the mind's power to create value, and so continues to alert the English mind . . . to its own abilities," 137.

87. Marbecke, 57-58.

88. Knapp, 140.

89. Ibid., 166.

90. R. S. Rait, introduction to *A Royal Rhetorician: A Treatise on Scottis poesie, A counterblaste to tobacco, etc.,* by James I (London, 1900), ix-x.

91. See Goldberg, 2, and Norbrook, 137.

92. Cf. Sinclair, Brooks, and Robert.

93. Goldberg, 26.

Sandra Bell (essay date 1999)

SOURCE: Bell, Sandra. "Writing the Monarch: King James VI and *Lepanto*." In *Other Voices, Other Views: Expanding the Canon in English Renaissance Studies,* edited by Helen Ostovich, Mary V. Silcox, and Graham Roebuck, pp. 193-208. Newark: University of Delaware Press, 1999.

[*In the following essay, Bell argues that James's heroic poem* Lepanto *formed part of the king's statecraft.*]

A POLITICAL CONTROVERSY

James VI of Scotland entered the print market in an at tempt to shape the role of the monarchy in a rapidly changing Scottish nation. James's writings include the well-known prose treatises *The Trew Law of Free Monarchies* (1598) and *Basilikon Doron* (1599), both of which responded to the volatile political situation in Scotland by outlining the absolute and divine nature of the monarchy.[1] James's lesser known poetical collections—*The Essayes of A Prentise, in the Divine Art of Poesie* (1584), and *His Maiesties Poeticall Exercises at vacant houres* (1591)[2]—are counterparts to the prose treatises in their attempt to legitimate the authority of the monarchy in a country where that authority was in doubt. The *Essayes* include the first treatise ever written on Scottish poetry: *Ane Schort Treatise, conteining some revlis and cautelis [regulations] to be obseruit and eschewit [avoided] in Scottish Poesie.* Vernacular poetry was a means by which James VI would affirm the monarch's place in Scotland's national cultural consciousness. Poetry became part of statecraft, reaching and convincing an audience in a manner not open to other forms of official discourse. An examination of James's long heroic poem *Lepanto* will gauge the success of the king's cultural policy.

Lepanto was written in 1585, entered in the Stationers' Register in London in 1589 (non-extant), and published in 1591 as one of the two poems of James's second collection of verse, the *Exercises.* It was republished in London in 1603.[3] The subject of James's poem is the recent battle of Lepanto, fought in 1571 between a Catholic navy and the Turkish navy under Selim II. By 1570, the Turkish navy had captured all but the capital of the Venetian-occupied island of Cyprus (the capital fell just weeks before the battle of Lepanto). The Catholic league, under the leadership of Don John of Austria (illegitimate half-brother to the Spanish king), challenged and triumphed over the Turks in the Gulf of Lepanto on 7 October 1571; the battle itself lasted a few short hours.[4]

The Catholic success at Lepanto was seen by many to be more generally a Christian victory[5]; the government of Venice had appealed to all Christian princes for support, but only Venice, Spain, and the Papacy joined to form the league. James appears to have envisaged the victory as a Christian rather than specifically Catholic one, and therefore as safe subject matter.[6] James chose the subject of Lepanto to rouse confidence in the newly created league of European Protestant princes. In the years just before the publication of *Lepanto,* the Catholics were an increasing threat, in Europe generally and within England and Scotland specifically; the Spanish Armada in 1588, and the intrigues of a number of Catholic Scottish nobles with the Spanish king, prompted James to arrange a league of European Prot-

estant princes for mutual defense against the Catholic forces. He notes in the poem's preface that he was "to the writing hereof mooued, by the stirring uppe of the league and cruell persecution of the Protestants in all countries" (Craigie, *Poems* 1:198). Rather paradoxically, therefore, the king's praise of a Catholic victory in *Lepanto* is part of James's attempt to bind together the Protestant nations in the face of a Catholic threat.

In the poem, James attempts to circumscribe the Catholic victory in the recent historical battle of Lepanto by what he terms a "poetical comparison" (198): through the success of the Catholic Holy League, the king explores the possibilities open to the "right religion" of Protestantism. James ends his poem with passages explaining the comparison:

> But praise him [God] more if more can be,
>   That so he loues his name,
> As he doth mercie shew to all
>   That doe professe the same:
> And not alanerlie [only] to them
>   Professing it aright,
> But euen to them that mixe therewith
>   Their owne inuentions slight:
>   . . . . .
> For since he shewes such grace to them
>   That thinks themselues are just,
> What will he more to them that in
>   His mercies onelie [only] trust?
> And sith that so he vses them
>   That doubt for to be sau'd,
> How much more them that in their hearts
>   His promise haue engrau'd?

> (ll. 957-64; 969-76)

In a battle of Catholics against Turks, God shows his mercy to the Christian navy; in a battle of Protestants against Catholics, God will surely side with the believers of the true faith, Protestantism.

James explains in his **"Preface"** that the "nature then of this Poeme, is an argument, *a minore ad majus* [from minor to major], largely intreated by a Poetike comparison" (Craigie, *Poems* 1:198). The majority of the poem is spent developing the *minore*; 940 lines describe the preparations for war, the sea battle itself, and the Christian victory over the Turks. James paints a compassionate portrait of the Christian civilians readying themselves for war, compassionate enough to move James himself to tears:

> As Seas did compasse them about,
>   As Seas the Streets did rin [run],
> So Seas of teares did ever flowe,
>   The houses all within.
> As Seas within were joyned with howles,
>   So Seas without did raire [roar],
> Thair carefull cries to Heauen did mount
>   Resounding in the aire.
> O stay my Muse, thou goes too farre,

Shewe where we left before,
Lest trikling teares so fill my penne
That it will write no more.

(ll. 173-84)

Even Ali-Basha, leader of the Turkish navy, is given a "bolde and manly face," though his "tongue did vtter courage more / Then had alluring grace" (ll. 518, 519-20). The bloody battle is outlined in detail, the Turkish navy losing only after Ali-Basha's head is fixed on the Christian galley mast. Don Juan, named the "Spanish Prince" (ll. 774, 797) or "General" (814), is victorious. Only the final ninety lines of the poem outline the poetic comparison which promises Protestant superiority. Despite James's claims that this is a Protestant poem, the imbalance between the purposed and apparent subject matter did not agree well with all of his readership.

James had chosen a battle whose hero was Don Juan of Austria, a contemporary Roman Catholic general and, as it happens, a one-time suitor of Mary, Queen of Scots. The king's Protestant readers feared—with some justification—that James was a closet papist. Considering the threat of Catholicism at the time and the continual suspicions of Scotland's Protestant lords, James's choice of hero could hardly appear acceptable to his Protestant readership. James over-estimated his readers' ability to remain dispassionate about religious differences, an ability he took for granted because of his extraordinarily mixed upbringing. Offering assurances to both his Protestant and Catholic subjects was one means—however unstable—James used to retain control in both Scotland and England; recognizing Catholic heroism in a Protestant poem is analogous to this method of ruling.[7]

In *Lepanto,* James's tolerance for Catholics is seen when God decides, in His mercy, to give victory to the Catholics over the "Infidels" (l. 82), for "All christians serues my Sonne though not / Aright in everie thing" (ll. 79-80). This echoes the sentiments of the *Basilikon Doron,* where James advises his son Henry to "learne wisely to discerne betwixt points of saluation and indifferent things, betwixt substance and ceremonies" (17). Although James clearly states the superiority of Protestantism in *Lepanto,* his tolerance for Catholics—his glorification of Catholics—was treated as suspect. If *Lepanto* were merely a poem written by a private man to praise God's mercy, the victory of Christians—albeit Catholics—over the heathen Turks might not have aroused such suspicion. However, a poem penned by a Protestant king in a Protestant cause which so conscientiously praises the valor and courage of a Catholic navy, could not but anger a Protestant readership.[8]

Meant to inspire readers with a desire for Protestant imperialism, *Lepanto* instead inspired controversy.[9] Some of the negative reactions to James's poem can be dis-cerned from "The Avthors Preface to the Reader" (1591), which James was forced to include to clarify the meaning of his "Poeticke comparison" (Craigie, *Poems* 1:198) and to rid his name of the suspicion of Catholic sympathies. As James states in the preface: "the special thing misliked in it, is, that I should seeme, far contrary to my degree and Religion, like a Mercenary Poet, to penne a worke, ex professo [in public], in praise of a forraine Papist bastard" (Craigie, *Poems* 1:198). The language of the "Preface" makes it clear that James is insulted that his intent could be so misread. The king annoyedly clarifies what he believes is already abundantly clear, and the references to the "beloued Reader," so ready to find fault with the king, take on ironic undertones:

> It falles out often, that the effects of mens actions comes cleane contrarie to the intent of the Authour. The same finde I by experience (beloued Reader) in my Poeme of LEPANTO: For although till now, it haue not bene imprinted, yet being set out to the publick view of many . . . it hath for lack of a Praeface, bene in some things misconstrued by sundry, which I of verie purpose think to haue omitted, for that the writing therof, might haue tended in my opinion, to some reproach of the skilfull learnednes of the Reader. . . .

(Craigie, *Poems* 1:198)

James explains how careful he was in the poem to avoid any implications of Catholic sympathies. He claims he names Don Juan "neither literally nor any waies by description" in the **"Poetique Praeface"** (1:198), and that the final **"Chorus Angelorum"** and the Epilogue should have made it clear that the poem was a "Historicke comparison" (1:200), meant to comment on the strength of the Protestant religion; if God allowed this victory to the Catholics, what might He not do for the Protestants?[10] This *is* repeatedly stated in the angels' chorus and the epilogue:

> since by this defeat ye see,
> That God doth loue his name
> So well, that so he did them aid
> That seru'd [served] not right the same.
> Then though the Antichristian sect
> Against you do conjure,
> He doth the bodie better loue
> Then shadow be ye sure. . . .

(ll. 1021-28)

In his "Preface," James shapes an understanding and learned audience to shift the blame of misinterpretation; any failing rests neither with his ability as poet or king, nor with his choice of subject, but with the reader, who is either too stupid to understand the poem, or who wilfully, maliciously misunderstands it. The equivocal nature of interpretation is not, James implies, the result of the uncertainty of poetic allegory, but of the insubordination of a malevolent readership, determined to misread and to question his authority.

Despite James's protestations that he intends *Lepanto* as an expression of Protestant superiority, the choice of a Roman Catholic victory as the subject is an excellent example of how James tries to play both sides of the religio-political division. While claiming to champion Protestantism, he still manages to describe in detail the humanity and courage of those who declared themselves Catholics. This did not, however, endear him to the Protestant subjects of a recently professed Protestant country. Rather than connecting monarch and nation—the purpose of James's cultural policy—*Lepanto* threatened to separate them. James's attempt to increase his authority by mythologizing the king and by assimilating himself into the country's national consciousness through poetry encounters opposition because of his subject matter, but also because of the medium of print. The next section will examine how the medium of poetry compounds the difficulties raised by the subject matter of *Lepanto,* and examine James's attempt to limit those problems.

A POETICAL CONTROVERSY

Both of the king's collections of poetry are of political importance. James's first collection of poetry, the *Essayes,* were partly instigated by the political situation in Scotland. Poetry was one of the few media through which the young king could express his political opinions, unimpeded by his powerful regents. His regents saw poetry as a means to keep James diverted from political intervention; in 1584, the Earl of Arran urged the king to continue to spend his time "principally in amusement and recreation," part of which was poetry.[11] Perhaps because other forms of political expression were denied to the young James, poetry became the means through which the king entered politics. The publication of James's first collection, the *Essayes* in 1584, gloriously printed and bound, corresponds to James's acquisition of full political control, and is an example of his belief that poetry is an expression of political and national loyalties.

Despite the ostensible separation of poetry from politics in the preface to the *Exercises* in 1591, this second collection is equally involved in the politics of James's reign. In the preface, James complains that the burdens of politics had left him little time for poetry: "my burden is so great and continuall, without anie intermission. . . . Yea scarslie but at stollen moments, haue I the leasure to blenk upon any paper" (Craigie, *Poems* 1:98). While James here appears to separate poetry from his political duties, this collection, and *Lepanto* specifically, are not removed from James's political actions. *Lepanto*—like his other poems—derives from political will, expresses political intention, and results in both political difficulties and—as will be shown—successes.

James's collections are also written in a politically charged medium, poetry. In Scotland, poetical satire had long questioned the role of the monarch, and the flood of Reformation satires from 1560 to 1584—verse which directly questioned the monarchy—further politicized poetry.[12] In order to regain political control, James needed to regain poetical control, and to create a monarch-centered court poetry to counter the criticism of the satires.[13] Early in his reign, James established a court poetry in an attempt to define and limit both the use of poetry and the readers' responses. The "Castalian Band" first gathered in 1579 and comprised a number of musicians and poets, both Protestants and Catholics. James's patronage of the band members, and his kin relationship to a number of them—distant cousins—allowed James some measure of control over the direction of Scottish poetry. Despite his youth when the Band reached its height—James was eighteen—the king was the group's poetic leader, the "poetic lawgiver."[14] In the hope of advancement, and to guarantee the continuing need for court poets, the Castalians were willing to show the usefulness of poetry in promoting James's authority. Many of their poems uphold the king's absolute authority and divine right, and advance James's desires for the English crown and a peaceable Protestant imperialism.

While the Castalian Band did serve to create a body of Scottish poetry which upheld the monarchy, and which mythologizes James in the Scottish cultural consciousness, it was not without its own political difficulties. The Protestant lords feared the Catholic elements of the Band and took James into house arrest in 1583. Ten months later, James escaped and reinstituted the Band, with Alexander Montgomerie as his poetic tutor, whom the king named "belou'd Sanders, master of our art."[15] Montgomerie, arguably the most skilled member of the Band, was distant kin to James and Lennox (James's favorite); he was named an official member of the Royal Household in 1583 and granted a pension of five hundred marks a year.[16] Montgomerie was also a Catholic, and—according to one's interpretations of his poems "I wald see mare" and "A Ladyis Lamentatione"—a supporter of the imprisoned Mary, Queen of Scots.[17] One of James's main political weapons in Scotland was his ability to find a balance by opposing factions, and—as seen in *Lepanto* and in the constitution of the Band—the incorporation of both Protestant and Catholics allowed James to remain completely reliant on neither.

Montgomerie's Catholicism made him politically useful; it had recommended him to King Philip's court and James made use of that affiliation to keep the favor of Spain, should he need their help. Montgomerie was therefore permitted—or required—to travel overseas on the king's business in 1586.[18] It was at this time, however, that Montgomerie's Catholicism ceased to be a benefit and became a threat. Mary was beheaded in England in 1586, and James separated himself from dangerous Catholic connections. Montgomerie was imprisoned by the English, who stopped his boat en route;

he did not return to Scotland until 1589/90, and had meanwhile lost his pension and position at court.[19] Montgomerie responded with a legal suit and an abundance of verse criticizing James and his court, but failed to recover his lost annuity.[20] If James failed to recognize the dangers of the Catholic elements in his poem *Lepanto,* he did recognize them in his "beloved Sanders."

The difficulties surrounding *Lepanto* are the result not simply of the Catholic content of either the poem or James's Castalian Band, but they also arise from the stigma associated with publication. To repeat a passage quoted above, James's readers were angered "that [he] should seem, far contrary to [his] degree and Religion, like a Mercenary Poet, to penne a worke, ex professo, in praise of a forraine Papist bastard." The king might argue that his religion is not compromised by writing of (or with) Catholics, but his "degree" *is* in danger once he collects and publishes his poetry. As Richard Helgerson points out, book writing and making had become a trade, one that was not necessarily equal in degree to the role of the monarch. Helgerson cites James Montague, Bishop of Winchester and the king's chaplain and editor: "'Since that book writing is grown into a trade . . . it is as dishonorable for a king to write books as it is for him to be a practitioner in a profession'."[21] Despite his involvement in poetry and publishing, James appears to agree: "it becomes not the honour of my estate, like an hireling, to pen the praise of any man" (Craigie, *Poems* 1:200). Regardless of his protestations of innocence and his attempt to separate himself from controversy, James fixes himself in print, and once fixed, he is open to interpretation by anyone who can read. The mystery of monarchy, the unknowable and unquestionable nature of the king that James outlines in *Basilikon Doron,* is compromised by the king's attempt to express himself to his subjects in verse.[22]

Despite poetry's potential as a means of political control, James's cultural policy is subject to the equivocal nature of the medium in which it is expressed, and dependent on the acceptance of his audience, his subjects. The meaning of *Lepanto* cannot be contained by writing even more by way of a preface, and, try as he might, James cannot shape his audience to limit their interpretations of his work. The vagaries of author, reader, and medium ensure the need for the king's continual involvement, the continual rewriting of himself.

However, James's hopes for his poetic Renaissance face difficulties on at least two counts. First, James wishes to limit the nature of political poetry. Chapter 7 of his treatise on Scottish poetry ostensibly deals with "invention," but James includes a warning to those poets who might, like their Reformation counterparts, wish to write about politics:

> Ze man also be war [You must also be wary] of wryting any thing of materis of commoun weill, or vther sic graue sene subiectis [such grave subjects] (except Metaphorically, of manifest treuth opinly knawin, zit [yet] nochtwithstanding vsing it very seindill [seldom]) because nocht onely ze essay nocht zour awin [you try not your own] Inuentioun, as I spak before, bot lykewayis they are to graue materis for a Poet to mell in.

(Craigie, *Poems* 1:79)

James here objects to historical or political topics because they are not imaginative or fictional enough, and his insistence on the gravity of matters of the commonwealth implies that poetry and politics are two very separate realms. Jonathan Goldberg notes that while this section limits the poet, the parenthetical addition "reinvest[s] him with power anew. James returns to the poet the power of language that allows him to go beyond mere representation."[23] James recommends metaphorical poetry, an oblique approach to political expression, but on the condition that these "metaphors" are of subjects "of manifest treuth opinly knawin"; the key to the metaphors must be clear, obvious, not leaving the poem liable to dangerous misinterpretations. James's *Lepanto* is an example of such metaphorical poetry—in this case a poetic comparison or allegory—within which the key to the metaphor is made clear; James's **"Chorus Angelorum"** and epilogue explain that the poem which appears to praise Catholics actually praises Protestants. However, while a move to a metaphorical approach to political subject matter does remove the direct critical threat that the Reformation satires present, it opens poems and poets to misunderstanding. As James himself discovered with his *Lepanto,* the author's intent, hidden in allegory and analogy, can easily be misread; one's choice of metaphor—one's "poetic comparison"—is as telling as one's ostensible subject matter.

The second problem is posed by the stigma inherent in the medium of print, which compounds the difficulties of interpretation presented by allegorical poetry. As Helgerson states, one's image in print is "liable to hostile interpretation and even rejection," and while it gives the writer-king authority, it also empowers the reader-subject.[24] Print opens James and his poetry to a larger interpretative community, one to whom the king's allegorical keys are not necessarily clear.

Despite James's recognitions of the limitations of poetry, and of his attempt to curb the political applications of poetry by others, he appears to believe his own poetry is exempt from such stigmas; he is "above the law," even the poetic laws of his own making. The relationship of monarch-subject is meant to inform the relationship of poet-reader, and the duty required of the subject should create an obedient and respectful reader. The publication of James's poetry is meant as an expression of the king's majesty, civility, and power. As

Helgerson notes, James recognizes the medium of print as "a potent source of authority": there is a "particularly intimate relationship between James's absolutist conception of royal power and the medium through which it was expressed."[25] Print allows the king to avoid public and theatrical shows, for which he had a great distaste, and at the same time gives him a medium through which to present himself to his subjects; it is, simultaneously, private and public. Print is one of the most economical, available, and powerful methods of stating one's authority, and James VI, like James IV before him, intended to make it a tool of government.[26]

Despite the ambiguous reception of *Lepanto*, it was James's most popular poem, and certainly connected monarch and nation in the eyes of his English and European readership. The fairly pedestrian level of James's verse, and the almost doggerel sound of the poem's broken fourteeners, were of no concern to other poets, who were far more interested in the king's having written at all.[27] Gabriel Harvey's praise of *Lepanto* is a representative example of how poets praised James's success. Harvey writes:

> I cannot forget the woorthy Prince that is a Homer to himselfe, a Golden spurre to Nobility, a Scepter to Vertue, a Verdure to the Spring, a Sunne to the day, and hath not onely translated the two diuine Poems of Salustius du Bartas . . . but hath readd a most valorous Martial Lecture vnto hiimselfe [sic] in his owne victorious Lepanto, a short, but heroicall, worke, in meeter, but royal meeter, fitt for a Dauids harpe—Lepanto, first of the glory of Christendome against the Turke, and now the garland of a soueraine crowne.[28]

Like James himself, Harvey legitimized poetry as an enterprise fit for a monarch: *Lepanto* is a heroical poem and one in which James reproduces the victories of Christendom peaceably, without human or economic cost. Also, while the king may write in meter, he uses "royal meeter, fitt for a Dauids harpe."[29]

Sir Philip Sidney, in a letter of May 1586 to the Master of Gray, asks to be "in the gracious remembrance of your King, whom indeed I love" (qtd. in Craigie, *Poems* 2:234), and in his *Apologie for Poetrie* claims James as a patron of the arts:

> Sweet poesy, that hath anciently had kings, emperors, senators, great captains . . . not only to favor poets, but to be poets. And of our nearer times can present for her patrons a Robert, king of Sicily, the great King Francis of France, King James of Scotland.[30]

Though Sidney and James never met, they are frequently mentioned together in poetic criticism, James appearing almost as a successor to Sidney, and his connection with Sidney only profited his own reputation:

> Chaucer is dead; and Gower lyes in grave;
> The Earle of Surrey, long agoe is gone;

> Sir Philip Sidneis soule, the Heauens haue;
> George Gascoigne him beforne, was tomb'd in stone
>
> . . . . .
>
> The King of Scots (now liuing) is a Poet,
> As his Lepanto, and his Furies shoe it.
>
> (Richard Barnefield; qtd. in Craigie, *Poems* 1:274)[31]

Again, in 1600, William Vaughan made a connection between the two: "Sir Philip Sidney excelled all our English Poets in rareness of stile and matter. King James the sixt of Scotland, that now raigneth, is a notable Poet, and daily setteth out most learned poems, to the admiration of all his subjects" (qtd. in Craigie, *Poems* 1:276). Foreign response to *Lepanto* was extensive and laudatory. In addition to the French translation by the Protestant poet Salust Du Bartas, there were translations into Latin, Dutch and German.[32] If *Lepanto* caused the Protestant readership some concern within Scotland, it was accepted as a sign of James's civilized authority without Scotland.

The phrase "imagined community" describes the necessary relationship of developing nations and fictional representations.[33] In the Renaissance, such representations are most often produced by the subjects of communities, not by their leaders. James, however, believes in the monarch's direct involvement with the affairs of his country; as he declares to his son Henry in *Basilikon Doron*, the king must "know all crafts: For except ye know euery one, how can yee controll euery one, which is your proper office?"[34] In James's reign, one of these "crafts" is poetry. James's foray into the print market is an attempt to control the changing cultural consciousness of Scotland and to maintain the authority of the monarchy in his subjects' imaginations. This attempt met with limited success. James's Renaissance did create a circle of poets which supported the king's authority and policies, and James's own verse helped to establish him—within and without Scotland—as a powerful Scottish king ruling a civilized nation. However, not even a king's writing can overcome the politics of poetry or the stigmas of print, or can shape an accepting, docile readership. As the reception of *Lepanto* demonstrates, the imagined community is rarely of one mind.

Notes

1. These treatises were reprinted in 1603 in England and read as an introduction to the new king. For English reactions to the treatises, see Jenny Wormald, "James VI and I, *Basilikon Doron* and *The Trew Law of Free Monarchies*: the Scottish context and the English translation" in *The Mental World of the Jacobean Court,* ed. Linda Levy Peck (Cambridge: Cambridge University Press, 1991), 36-54; and James Doelman's "'A King of thine own heart': The English Reception of King James VI and I's *Basilikon Doron,*" *The Seventeenth Century* 9, no. 1 (spring 1994): 1-9. For English

reactions to James's religious writings, see Doelman's "The Accession of King James I and English Religious Poetry," *Studies in English Literature* 34, no. 1 (1994): 19-40.

2. A third collection, *All the kings short poesis that ar not printed,* was edited and arranged, as if for publication, by Prince Charles, the Groom of the Chamber Thomas Carey, and James himself. Craigie notes that this collection may have been intended for publication along with the 1616 *Works,* but it was not published until 1911. All three collections, and some uncollected verse, are found in *Poems of King James VI of Scotland,* ed. James Craigie, 2 vols. (Edinburgh and London: Blackwood, 1955, 1958). *Lepanto* is found in 1:197-259.

3. Publishing information available in Craigie, *Poems* 1:xlv-l.

4. Historical information can be found in Craigie, *Poems* 1:liv-lx. As Craigie states, James had access to possibly three written sources for historical background.

5. Emery Jones, "'Othello', 'Lepanto' and the Cyprus Wars," *Scottish Literary Studies* 21 (1968): 48. Jones also notes that Shakespeare may have used the opportunity of *Lepanto*'s 1603 publication in London to write *Othello,* also concerned with Venetians of this period, at about this time. There are no specific echoes of the king's poem in the play.

6. James's poem emphasizes the generic nature of the "Christian" army: "Christian Princes" (190) lead a "Christian Nauie" (292), a "Christian Host" (358) of "Christian soules" (491). See Kevin Sharpe, "The King's Writ: Royal Authors and Royal Authority in Early Modern England," in *Culture and Politics in Early Stuart England,* eds. Kevin Sharpe and Peter Lake (Stanford, CA: Stanford University Press, 1993): "the poem gestures to an economic hope for a reunified *republica Christiana* which James cherished throughout his life" (129).

7. James's balancing or juggling act with his Protestant and Catholic subjects in both Scotland and England is discussed in Jenny Wormald's "James VI and I: Two Kings or One?" *History* 68 (1983): 187-209. Wormald also outlines how James was increasingly cut off from Scottish methods of control once in England.

8. It is odd that there are no complaints about James's respectful description of the Turks.

9. R. D. S. Jack, "Poetry under King James," in *Origins to 1660,* ed. R. D. S. Jack, vol. 1 of *The History of Scottish Literature,* ed. Craig Cairns (Aberdeen: Aberdeen University Press, 1988), 1:133. Jack does not give specific examples of the "political furore" raised by the poem; however, that there was a controversy is clearly stated in James's own preface and in the need for a preface at all.

10. J. Derrick McClure agrees that "James's theological standpoint is stated as clearly as it could possibly be" in "'O Phoenix Escossois': James VI as Poet" in *A Day Estivall,* eds. Alisoun Gardner-Medwin and Janet Hadley Williams (Aberdeen: Aberdeen University Press, 1990), 105-6.

11. Qtd. in Maurice Lee Jr., *Great Britain's Solomon: James VI and I in His Three Kingdoms* (Chicago: University of Illinois Press, 1980), 127. Lee also states that Esme Stuart—who should become the Duke of Lennox, James's favorite from 1579-1582, and who would effectively rule Scotland in the last two years of that period—initiated, or at least furthered, James's interest in poetry. See also *Calendar of State Papers Relating to Mary, Queen of Scots,* eds. William K. Boyd and Henry W. Meikle, vol. 8, 338: in 1586, Thomas Randolf stated that James "still follows his hunting, riding, and writing 'in miter'."

12. The main collection of Scottish Reformation satires is *Satirical Poems of the Time of the Reformation,* ed. James Cranstoun (Edinburgh: Blackwood, 1891/93; reprint, New York: AMS, 1974). While many of the satires are directed specifically at Mary, Queen of Scots, a number question Scotland's need for a monarchy at all and are thus a threat to James's reign also. The satires spring from a long tradition of satirical verse, verse which flourished under the pens of William Dunbar and Sir David Lyndsay earlier in the sixteenth century.

13. See Sharpe, "The King's Writ," 118: "monarchs endeavoured in the new circumstances they confronted to re-establish their authority by a reassertion of their interpretative [sic] power over rival voices." While Sharpe is more concerned with prose works, religious verse, and the new King James Version of the Bible, this also applies to James's secular poetry.

14. Shire, *Song, Dance and Poetry of the Court of Scotland under James VI* (Cambridge: Cambridge University Press, 1969), 99.

15. In the King's poem "An admonition to the Master poet," James named Montgomerie his "belou'd Sanders, maistre of our art" as well as "friend" (Craigie, *Poems* 2:122, ll. 2, 9). In his epitaph for Montgomerie, James called him "the prince of Poets in our land" (Craigie, *Poems* 2:107, l. 3).

16. A brief outline of Montgomerie's history and connection to James is provided by Alan Westcott, ed., *New Poems by James I* (New York: AMS, 1911), xxvi-xxxiii (erroneously titled, as nearly all the poems were written before James went to England). An outline of Montgomerie's history and an analysis of his works can be found in R. D. S. Jack, *Alexander Montgomerie* (Edinburgh: Scottish Academic Press, 1985). Helena Mennie Shire supplies an overview of the Band, and also provides a history of Montgomerie and an interpretation of his greatest poem, *The Cherrie and the Slae* in *Song,* 80-99.

17. Shire interprets the title of the first poem as "I would see Ma[ria] Re[gina]" (*Song,* 77-78); the poem was sent to James Lauder, servant to the imprisoned Mary. Jack connects "A Ladyis Lamentatione" to Mary in "The Theme of Fortune in the Verse of Alexander Montgomerie," *Scottish Literary Journal* 10 (1983): 25-44. Montgomerie—a generation older than the king—was a poet in Mary's reign.

18. George Stevenson includes an appendix outlining documents granting Montgomerie permission to travel in *Poems of Alexander Montgomerie* (Edinburgh: Scottish Text Society, 1887), Appendix D: 6. Two other Catholic poets, James Lauder and Hugh Barclay of Ladyland, were also sent overseas at this time. Shire notes that the "King could be ridding the court of dangerous elements, entrusting to ambiguous agents a subtly planned and double handed policy or setting his envoys a task that of its very nature was impossible to fill" (*Song,* 107), the task of appealing to Spain and England at the same time.

19. David Daiches notes that the release of Montgomerie after the execution of Mary made him less of a threat, and that he "remained out of favour, all the more so since he was now associated with elements opposed to the King and his policy." *Literature and Gentility in Scotland* (Edinburgh: Edinburgh University Press, 1982), 15.

20. Litigations for the pension ended, unsuccessfully, in 1593. It appeared that the pension had been an illegal gift to begin with (see Jack, *Alexander Montgomerie,* 11).

21. Richard Helgerson, "Milton Reads the King's Book: Print, Performance, and the Making of a Bourgeois Idol," *Criticism* 29, no. 1 (winter 1987): 1.

22. While it is arguable that prose is equally subject to the stigmas of publication, political tracts and speeches do not appear to have received the same criticisms as the more easily misunderstood figurative language of poetry.

23. *James I and the Politics of Literature* (Baltimore, MD: Johns Hopkins, 1983), 19-20.

24. Helgerson, "Milton," 6.

25. Ibid., 3.

26. On the political use James IV made of the printing press, see Michael Lynch: "The royal licence for the setting up of the first Scottish printing press by Chepman and Myllar in 1507, which specified 'bukis of our lawis, actis of parliament, chroniclis, [and] mess buiks' made it clear it was a means of promoting both the King's government and the image of kingship." *Scotland, A New History* (London: Century, 1991), 258. Lynch also claims that "Like no government before it, that of James VI developed an elaborate propaganda machine that used a variety of channels of communication" (238). For information on the introduction and growth of the press in Scotland, see: Robert Dickson and John Philip Edmond, *Annals of Scottish Printing* (Cambridge: MacMillan & Bowes, 1890); Harry Aldis, *A List of Books Printed in Scotland Before 1700* (Edinburgh: Edinburgh Bibliographical Society, 1904); and R. A. Houston, *Scottish Literacy and the Scottish Identity: Illiteracy and Society in Scotland and Northern England 1600-1800* (Cambridge: Cambridge University Press, 1985).

27. Of course, one cannot measure the sincerity of the praise, whether it was inspired by James's attempt or by the poets' hopes of later preferment.

28. Craigie, *Poems* 1:274. Craigie's Appendix A provides twenty-seven examples of the praise inspired by James's poetry: see *Poems,* 1:274-80.

29. This is not to be confused with the "Ballat Royal" meter, which James advocates for "heich & graue subiectis" in the Treatise. *Lepanto* is written in fourteeners, though each line is divided into two in the printing.

30. Sir Philip Sidney, *An Apology for Poetry,* ed. Forrest B. Robinson (Indiana: Bobbs-Merrill, 1970), 68-69.

31. While the feminine ending might suggest that Barnefield did not intend this as a serious comment on James's skill, at least one contemporary took it seriously: in his *Palladis Tamia, Wits Treasury* (1598), Francis Mere cites the above two lines and claims that "'Iames the 6, nowe King of Scotland, is not only a fauorer of Poets but a Poet, as my friend Master Richard Barnefielde hath in this disticke passing well recorded'" (qtd. in Craigie, *Poems* 1:275).

32. The German translation includes the French text on the verso, the German on the recto. This indicates that in some circles James's reputation relied on Du Bartas's translation rather than on the king's original.

33. See Benedict Anderson's *Imagined Communities: Reflections on the Origin and Spread of Nationalism,* rev. ed. (London: Verso, 1991). What Sharpe says of Tudor England is equally applicable to Stuart Scotland: "the power of crown and state depended largely upon its representation of authority" (117).

34. *The Political Works of James I,* ed. Charles Howard McIlwain (New York: Russell & Russell, 1965), 38.

Bibliography

Aldis, Harry. *A List of Books Printed in Scotland Before 1700.* Edinburgh: Edinburgh, Bibliographical Society, 1904.

Anderson, Benedict. *Imagined Communities: Reflections on the Origin and Spread of Nationalism.* Rev. ed. London: Verso, 1991.

Calender of State Papers Relating to Mary, Queen of Scots, eds. William K. Boyd and Henry W. Meikle. 8:338.

Cranstoun, James, ed. *Satirical Poems of the Time of the Reformation.* 2 vols. Edinburgh: Blackwood, 1891/93. Rev. ed. New York: AMS, 1974.

Daiches, David. *Literature and Gentility in Scotland.* Edinburgh: Edinburgh University Press, 1982.

Dickson, Robert and John Philip Edmond. *Annals of Scottish Printing.* Cambridge: MacMillan & Bowes, 1890.

Doelman, James. "The Accession of King James I and English Religious Poetry." *Studies in English Literature* 34, no. 1 (1994): 19-40.

———. "'A King of thine own heart': The English Reception of King James VI and I's *Basilikon Doron.*" *The Seventeenth Century* 9, no. 1 (spring 1994): 1-9.

Goldberg, Jonathan. *James I and the Politics of Literature.* Baltimore, MD: Johns Hopkins, 1983.

Helgerson, Richard. "Milton Reads the King's Book: Print, Performance, and the Making of a Bourgeois Idol." *Criticism* 29, no. 1 (winter 1987): 1-26.

Houston, R. A. *Scottish Literacy and The Scottish Identity: Illiteracy and Society in Scotland and Northern England 1600-1800.* Cambridge: Cambridge University Press, 1985.

Jack, R. D. S. *Alexander Montgomerie.* Edinburgh: Scottish Academic Press, 1985.

———. "Poetry under King James VI." In *Origins to 1660.* Edited by R. D. S. Jack, 125-40. Vol. 1 of *The History of Scottish Literature.* Aberdeen: Aberdeen University Press, 1988.

———. "The Theme of Fortune in the Verse of Alexander Montgomerie." *Scottish Literary Journal* 10 (1983): 25-44.

Jones, Emery. "'Othello', 'Lepanto' and the Cyprus Wars." *Scottish Literary Studies* 21 (1968): 47-52.

Lee, Maurice, Jr. *Great Britain's Solomon: James VI and I in His Three Kingdoms.* Chicago: University of Chicago Press, 1980.

Lynch, Michael. *Scotland, A New History.* London: Century, 1991.

McClure, J. Derrick. "'O Phoenix Escossois': James VI as Poet." In *A Day Estivall.* Edited by Alisoun Gardner-Medwin and Janet Hadley Williams, 96-111. Aberdeen: Aberdeen University Press, 1990.

Montgomerie, Alexander. *Poems of Alexander Montgomerie.* Edited by George Stevenson. Edinburgh: Scottish Text Society, 1887.

Sharpe, Kevin. "The King's Writ: Royal Authors and Royal Authority in Early Modern England." In *Culture and Politics in Early Stuart England.* Edited by Kevin Sharpe and Peter Lake. Stanford, CA: Stanford University Press, 1993.

Shire, Helena Mennie. *Song, Dance and Poetry of the Court of Scotland under King James VI.* Cambridge: Cambridge University Press, 1969.

Sidney, Sir Philip. *An Apology for Poetry.* Edited by Forrest B. Robinson. Indiana: Bobbs-Merrill, 1970.

Stuart, James. *New Poems by James I.* Edited by Alan Westcott. New York: AMS, 1911.

———. *The Poems of King James VI of Scotland.* Edited by James Craigie. 2 vols. Edinburgh and London: Blackwood, 1955, 1958.

———. *The Political Works of James I.* 1616. Edited by Charles Howard McIlwain. New York: Russell & Russell, 1965.

Wormald, Jenny. "James VI and I, *Basilikon Doron* and *The Trew Law of Free Monarchies*: the Scottish context and the English translation." In *The Mental World of the Jacobean Court.* Edited by Linda Levy Peck, 36-54. Cambridge: Cambridge University Press, 1991.

———. "James VI and I: Two Kings or One?" *History* 68 (1983): 187-209.

Robert Appelbaum (essay date February 2000)

SOURCE: Appelbaum, Robert. "War and Peace in *The Lepanto* of James VI and I." *Modern Philology* 97, no. 3 (February 2000): 333-63.

[*In the following essay, Appelbaum explores the meaning of war and peace in* Lepanto, *contending that James's epic poem "tells its tale of peace in a complicated way."*]

War and Peace. The topos antedates Leo Tolstoy's novel by two thousand years, and its utility is obvious. War is one thing. Peace is another. And so a discourse of differences, of contrasts, may begin. But as terms of rhetoric and representation, war and peace can also be held to resemble, to interpenetrate, or even to become one another. "Much remains / To conquer still," Milton writes in his sonnet "To Lord General Cromwell"; "Peace hath her victories / No less renownd than warr."[1] Peace, under the pressure of rhetoric like this, can be a lot like war since it can be said to require militant vigilance; it may even have its own "victories," as fully heroic and glorious as any that war may entail. War may be more often the subject of narrative literature than peace because war gives the teller more to tell. But many tales of war, going back to the first epics, may really be tales of peace: tales about where peace comes from, how it operates, and what it ultimately means. Such, in any case, is the state of affairs in King James VI and I's *The Lepanto,* a heroic poem over a thousand lines long first published in 1591 and probably written in 1585—James's most significant and widely circulated accomplishment as a poet.[2] But *The Lepanto* tells its tale of peace in a complicated way, including not only the representation of what appeared to be a glorious military victory but also an implicit argument about the justice of just wars. It even participates in a European-wide effort to depict the Battle of Lepanto as a glorious victory, despite evidence that the battle was neither unambiguously heroic nor unambiguously triumphant. (In fact, although the allied Christian forces certainly won a battle over the Ottoman armada in 1571, virtually wiping out the enemy fleet, they were very possibly on their way that day toward losing a century-long war.) Moreover, the great hero of the battle and of James's poem, Don Juan of Austria, continued after Lepanto to make a name for himself in military expeditions where not the hated Turk but thousands of Christians were defeated and killed. So James's situation as a memorializing poet was highly complicated. My intention here, however, is not so much to resolve the complexities entailed in James's poem as to underscore them and to raise questions about what it might mean for someone like James—who was among other things, a man of peace—to write a heroic poem about someone else's victory (real or apparent) in someone else's war.

Along the way I intend to raise questions about what it meant for a monarch to be writing heroic verse in the first place, doing so after the fashion not of great kings but of great poets writing in the service of great kings. I also want to consider the problem of what it may have meant in general for any poet of the Renaissance to have turned a single day's fighting—for the Battle of Lepanto lasted no more than a day—into an exemplary story of quasi-epic proportions. But I am mainly concerned with the meaning of war and peace in *The Lepanto,* and how (and why) James uses one to serve as an example of (or for) the other.

A large part of the issue here is what may be called James's self-professions. There were many such self-professions over the course of James's career, and they were not always free of controversy. Styling himself "King of Great Britain," for example, at a time when the ruling elite in England had no desire to see England absorbed into a larger political entity was a self-profession that caused great unrest among the politically powerful segment of the population and provoked some of James's most long-abiding opposition in Parliament.[3] But at least two self-professions held up over time, thanks in large part to the machinery of state mythology that James obdurately supported. One presented James as a Solomon among kings, a ruler of superlative learning, wisdom, and justice; the other presented him as a peacemaker. "The first . . . of the blessings, which God hath joyntly with my Person sent unto you," James told Parliament in his inaugural address of 1604, "is outward Peace: that is, peace abroad with all forreine neighbours: for I thank God I may justly say, that never since I was a king, I either received wrong of any other Christian Prince of State, or did wrong to any: I have ever, I praise God, yet kept Peace and amitie with all." The "second great blessing," he went on to say, was "peace within," peace that is between Scotland and England, now united in his person and rule after centuries of division, and even between the English houses of Lancaster and York, now united in his own blood as they had been in the Tudor monarchs before him.[4]

Beati pacifici, blessed are the peacemakers, had been adopted by James as his motto—another self-profession—soon upon arriving in England; James frequently saw to it that the iconography of peace should be associated with his reign, whether in ceremonies like court masques or in printed matter such as the frontispieces to the books published under his name. This particular self-profession was not adopted without some ambivalence, to be sure. "I know not," James wrote, "by what fortune the diction of *Pacificus* was added to my title at my coming to England, that of the lion, expressing true fortitude, having been my diction before."[5] There was something suspiciously unmanly about being called a peacemaker. It was better to be known as a lion, signifying courage. Still powerful in the seventeenth century, as James himself well knew, were the traditional timocratic, masculinist values of aristocratic warrior culture, as well as the metaphorical belligerence of Christian militancy. Both of these, whether alone or in combination, would often enough explode into genuine belligerence between individuals, factions, and nations.[6] And as he let the public know by the publication of his **Basilicon Doron** (1599), James did not intend his taste for nonaggression to mean that he would never be aggressive in the interest of his nation: "a honourable and just warre," he wrote, "is more tollerable, then a dishonourable and disadvantageous peace."[7] Yet, James could also own up to his reputation as a peacemaker and claim his new motto as his just dessert. "I am not ashamed of this addition," he added concerning his new "diction." "For King Solomon was a figure of Christ in that he was a king of peace. The greatest gift that our Saviour gave his apostles immediately before his ascension was that he left His peace with them."[8]

The principle of "peacemaking" or, as we say today, "pacifism," lay at the heart of James's foreign and domestic policies and increasingly became the byword of his personal mythology.[9] James had not only established a pacific government; peace was also to be, he was proud to say, his particular legacy—that profession of the self that should survive beyond the self, that "apparance of perpetuity or long continuance" that James understood to be attached to his person.[10] Peacemaking was to be a legacy through which James's progeny would govern and bestow "blessings" on the Christian world at home and abroad. In domestic affairs, he was sustaining a kind of sublime order, and passing it on peacefully through the body of his son.[11] In international affairs he was following a policy which on at least one occasion he referred to as the *via regia*, a démarche among the competing states and factions of Europe, moderating their hostilities with the calculated sagacity of an independent negotiator.[12] "O happy moderator, blessed Father," Thomas Middleton wrote in a paean to the king called *The Peace-maker* (1618), which some have believed to have been written by James himself, so closely does it follow James's own program of self-professed pacifism—"not Father of thy country alone, but Father of all thy neighbors countries about thee."[13] In point of fact the Thirty Years' War was about to break out, but James still had hopes of resolving the conflicts through fatherly diplomacy. "Peace is the passage from life to life," Middleton wrote, summoning his readers to an admiration of his king; "come then to the factory of Peace, thou that desirest to have life: behold the substitute of Peace on earth, displaying the flag of Peace, *Beati pacifici*."[14]

The business of professing oneself a man of peace could be complicated, however. Peace for whom? For everyone? And by what means? Any means necessary? How

do honor, the existence of evil, national sovereignty, and religion fit into the picture? And what does peace look like when one has it, anyway? How does one express or represent peace?

Consider for a moment a pair of famous paintings meant to represent the making of peace by James VI and I, the two major end panels to Peter Paul Rubens's ceiling at the Banqueting House at Whitehall. They are part of a group of works that comprises the single greatest monument to the aspirations of James's reign—in politics, in culture, in religion. The paintings are solemnly, even sublimely eulogistic. But they are also puzzling.[15]

In one of the main panels, *The Union of Scotland and England,* James is shown active in life, seated on his throne, uniting his two kingdoms; in another, *The Benefits of Government,* he is shown bestowing blessings that come from a realm being at peace with itself. In the latter picture James presides over a scene where the Goddess of Peace is "hastening, reassuringly, into the arms of Plenty," and Minerva is beating back an assault by War.[16] But the particular power of Rubens's images is their sense not of beatitude or harmony but of exertion and energy. There is nothing peaceful about Rubens's allegories of peace. In *The Benefits of Government,* though Plenty is reaching to the arms of Peace, and Minerva is beating back War, the gestures are incomplete. Peace and Plenty have not yet embraced. War has not yet been cast off from the vicinity of the King and his seat of government. And James is shown to be directing the affairs of state with a somewhat frantic and ambiguous, if biblically majestic, gesture. The benefits of government are not yet realized in this picture; James is shown belligerently commanding the pacification of the realm.

The Union of Scotland and England portrays a still more disturbing scene. A seated but forward-leaning and gesturing James faces the spectacle of two women, Scotland and England, fighting over an infant, the naked Charles. The Goddess Britannia is attempting to crown the infant, but the two women seem to be contending over which of them will get to keep the child, each pulling on one of the infant's arms and one even trying to grab the crown out of Britannia's hands. Like Solomon passing judgment between the two women claiming the same child, King James is adjudicating the conflict, pointing a dagger toward the child. So far as James's legacy is the theme of the picture, the picture implies that James is wisely giving his son Charles to both kingdoms. But it is unclear what decision is actually being rendered in this particular scene; perhaps James is threatening, like Solomon, to cut the child in half. In the biblical story the threat to cut the child in half reveals which woman is really the child's mother and will get to keep him. While James is supposed to be unifying Scotland and England, the biblical allegory nevertheless suggests that the kingdoms cannot be united, that one mother country and not the other is going to have possession of the next king unless James succeeds in imposing his son on both of them regardless.

The complexities of Rubens's allegory can be construed with regard to the moral and political purposes of Rubens, James, Charles, or any number of advisers, including Inigo Jones, all of whom played a role in the design of the ceiling; it is difficult to settle on a single intention. Even the one sure instance of pacification in James's reign, the de facto union of England and Scotland, is mysteriously represented. For if James had ever promised an infant son to the realms of England and Scotland alike, it was not Charles but his elder brother Henry, the more popular and the more martial of the two brothers, whose place in the English imagination, after his death in 1613, Charles was never able to fill.[17] As it has often been remarked about Stuart court masques, which in a certain sense the Rubens paintings supplanted, such productions were intended to be both representational and representative, both mimetic and exemplary. But it is difficult to say what these paintings were to serve as an example of, or what policies and modes of behavior these paintings were to serve as examples for. The pull of competing impulses and the moving drama of these allegories about a legacy of peace all but overpower the architectonic unity of their execution. And those impulses derive not only from Rubens's own complex reading or expert execution of the artistic and ideological project set before him but of complexities inherent to the project itself—to the various masters it was designed to serve, to the political tensions it was compelled to respond to, and in general to the perplexities of war and peace and of leadership and government which the paintings were supposed to solve.

* * *

Now the production and interpretation of *The Lepanto* would seem to present a much simpler situation. *The Lepanto* tells the straightforward story of Don Juan of Austria's leadership in the naval battle of 1571, when in a single day of fighting a Christian fleet of 208 galleys, sailing under the flag of a "Holy League" organized by Pope Pius V, the Spanish monarchy and the Venetian republic won a total victory over a rival Turkish fleet, capturing 180 out of 274 Turkish ships, freeing more than twelve thousand Christian galley slaves, killing over twenty-five thousand Turkish fighters, and taking approximately fifteen thousand Turkish fighters into captivity as slaves.[18] The battle was already famous when James put his hand to it—the subject of chronicles in Spanish, Italian, and Latin and two or three briefer works in Italian and Latin that were James's primary sources.[19] Thus the exercise that James undertook might

seem to have been commonplace: turning a story of action, adventure, and heroic victory into suitable verse. Nor was the exercise without ample precedent. Heroic verse, the stepchild of epic, was among the more popular and esteemed forms of verse in the sixteenth century, and James does not fail to acknowledge Virgil and Homer as his chief models. A young man with artistic aspirations, who had already tried his hand at translations and lyrical poems, could scarcely select a more suitable subject matter or genre—especially, again, a young poet who was also a king.

There was only one problem, or pair of related problems. The hero of this poem was "a forraine Papist bastard," as James confesses in his preface, written after some of his readers had already seen a manuscript version of the poem.[20] Don Juan of Austria's Roman Catholicism and illegitimacy alike exposed James's work to reproach; moreover, Juan's next (and last) great military adventure had been a devastatingly successful Spanish expedition against Protestant forces in the Netherlands. Yet James had a ready if somewhat unusual response for his detractors. The poem, he wrote, was actually "an argument, *a minore ad majus,* largely intreated by a Poeticke comparison, beeing to the writing hereof mooved, by the stirring uppe of the league and cruell persecution of the Protestants in all countries" (p. 198). In other words, the story of the Pope Pius's Holy League of 1571 fending off a Turkish military operation under the leadership of Don Juan was an allegory for the Protestants' conflicts with the French Catholic League which had been "stirring up cruell persecution" since 1576 and especially in 1585, when James found himself "mooved" to write his epic. (This Catholic League in France—whose leaders had been affiliated with Mary Queen of Scots, James's own mother!—was bent on keeping the Protestant Henry of Navarre from the French throne in the likely event that the Catholic Henry III should die without leaving any male heirs. The league may also have had the more ambitious goal of eradicating Protestantism in France altogether, but the claim that it was persecuting Protestants "in all countries," or even really in France, was an exaggeration.[21]) What James represented, then, in a victory of Catholics over Turks, was a dark conceit intended to be representative of the cause of Protestants against its persecution by Catholics. An example of holy war was meant to be exemplary of resistance to holy war. As for the second part of the objection, that his poem makes a hero out of a foreign bastard, James argues that his poem is neither obsequious nor biographically oriented; unlike Virgil or Homer, he has not "penned the whole Poeme" in the praise of a single hero but only brought the hero in when the narrative situation warranted.

Moreover, although the poem has some good things to say about "Don-Joan," as James calls him, "what ever

praise I have given to *Don-Joan* it is neither in accounting him as first or second cause of that victory, but only
as a particular man, when he falls in my way, to speak
the truth of him. For as it becomes not the honour of
my estate, like an hireling, to pen the praise of any
man: So it becomes it far lesse the highness of my
rancke and calling, to spare for the feare of favour of
whomsoever living, to speake or write the truth of anie"
(p. 200). On the one hand, the poem is an allegory and
means something very different from what it may seem
to mean; on the other hand, it is a historically truthful
representation and a truly praiseworthy historical figure
will be represented accurately. A king should be magnanimous in praise; in fact, it is his prerogative, since,
unlike a "hireling" poet, a king owes praise to no one.

James's responses are both logical and plausible. A Renaissance king of the type that James frequently claimed
to be was indeed free to praise any man.[22] And there
was poetical justice in using the Turkish enemy in one
story to stand for the Catholic enemy in another: the
implied association, that Catholics were to Protestants
as Turks were to Christians, bolstered James's assertion
that the Catholic League in France was abhorrent. But
the relationship of the historical to the allegorical in
James's poem is still curious, even puzzling. In order to
condemn Catholic persecution James chooses to tell the
story of Catholicism's own greatest recent campaign
against persecution. In order to respond to a case of
mass victimization, James chooses to tell the story of a
heroic individual leading an army of heroes. And in order to respond to religious persecution, James tells the
story of a glorious military victory as if war were in
fact a solution to the problem of persecution. But then
James is in effect glorifying war, in spite of his commitment in other circumstances to peacemaking and pacifism.

It may be objected that James's pacifism in 1604 or
1619 need not have any bearing on the young king's attitudes toward war in the 1580s. However, most of what
we know about the king suggests that he experienced a
lifelong aversion to violence, and the poem itself, as I
will show, expresses distaste for violence, too, even as
it celebrates a violent victory.[23] We also know that the
French writers Pierre Ronsard and especially Guillaume
Du Bartas, whom James was most fond of studying and
imitating during the 1580s, were themselves noted for
their pacifistic leanings.[24] Ronsard had written a famous
"Ode au Roy Henry II sur la paix faitte entre luy et le
roy d'angleterre, l'an 1550," and an even more famous
"Exhortation pour la paix" in 1558, which inspired a
whole generation of peace poems in France. This exhortation begins:

> Non, ne combatez pas, vivez en amitié,
> Chrestiens, changez vostre ire avecques la pitié,
> Chàngez à la douceur les rancunes ameres,
> Et ne trempez vos dars dans le sang de vos freres.[25]

Du Bartas, James's favorite poet, had similarly written
a "Hymn to Peace" in 1580, and his popular collections, the first and second *Sepmaines* (1578 and 1584,
respectively), parts of which James translated for publication, contained a great deal of pacifist sentiment, too.[26]

Just as important, James was also familiar at an early
age with Erasmian humanism, which propounded an
unmistakably pacifist message. "Peace, praised by the
voices of the gods and men, . . . [is] the fountain, parent, nourisher, augmenter, and defender of all things,
that [either] the air hath or the earth," Desiderius
Erasmus wrote in his *Complaint of Peace* (1521). "All
Christian men's letters and books, whether thou read
the Old or the New Testament, do sound nothing but
peace and amity."[27] In his *Education of a Christian
Prince* (1503), one of the models for James's **Basilicon
Doron,** Erasmus had insisted that the "arts of peace"
were considerably more important to any Christian
prince than the "arts of war," and he asserted that
"Christ himself and Peter and Paul everywhere teach
the opposite" of war.[28]

So the production and publication of **The Lepanto** recalls many of the kinds of interpretive complexities presented more overtly (and perhaps deliberately) in
Rubens's Whitehall paintings. A man of peace is writing a poem about war. In writing about war he is writing about his desire for a certain kind of peace, although hinting (perhaps!) that a military solution is
called for. In writing about war, moreover, he is deliberately co-opting the mythology, or at least the history, of
those he may be claiming to be his enemies. The effect
of the poem on its literal level is unambiguous: an epochal victory at sea through the wise and valorous leadership of Don Juan, the Papist bastard, is commemo-
rated and celebrated in the language of a Christian epic:
"At last the joyfull tidings" of the victory came to the
Venetians; "Sing praise to God both young and olde"
(lines 873, 881). But the allegorical implications of the
victory of Lepanto are difficult to decipher and, even
when deciphered, difficult to accept. James is adopting
a Spanish and Italian story for a diverse audience in
Scotland and abroad; the poem was soon published in
several European languages, including Latin, and Du
Bartas himself translated the poem into French. James
is writing, moreover, as the ruling monarch of a Protestant nation with close diplomatic ties to both Protestant
and non-Protestant nations (especially France, his mother's birthplace, where James was in close contact with
both Protestant and Catholic partisans, as well as the
still-Catholic court) and as a man already ambitious (in
the years contemporary with the imprisonment and execution of his Catholic mother) to succeed to the throne
of an even greater Protestant nation. But James was already partial to pacifism rather than militarism, and as
soon as he acceded to that Protestant throne he would
sign a peace treaty with Spain, which had been En-

gland's bitterest enemy for several decades. This treaty brought new opportunities for economic expansion to England but alienated its allies in France and Venice and, according to many observers then and now, gave away England's military and political advantages over Spain. Whether in life or in art, the *via regia* seems to have been strewn with perils. It seems to have required the distribution of good will and ill, of signs favorable and unfavorable, of political capital credited and debited, where one's intentions belied one's actions, and one might resolve conflict without ever experiencing the condition of resolution itself.

The end result is an always interesting miniature epic where various narrative impulses collide for sometimes clear and sometimes obscure purposes. Catholicism, Protestantism, war, peace, God's grace, and even Turkish infidels are all by terms celebrated within the context of a sea battle of unprecedented violence, about which James and many of his contemporary readers had to have been ambivalent. Still, the poem adheres quite well to the Aristotelian principle of the unity of action; if it raises unresolvable complexities regarding authorial intention, genre, allegory, and the ideologies of war and peace, it creates a sustained poetic effect and a sustained (if somewhat paradoxical) version of the ethic of humanist pacifism.

The Ambiguity of Authorial Intention

The ambiguity of authorial voicing in the poem follows from James's understanding of the nature of poetic inspiration, although it raises political difficulties for the king. James is not speaking in the poem simply "as himself," whatever that might mean. Here, as in other early writings, including his *Paraphrase of the Revelation* (ca. 1584), James notes the dualities coincident with the writing of scholarly and poetic texts. In his official writings—in royal proclamations and speeches to the Parliament, for example—James would be less concerned about this particular complexity. Speaking as king, in his capacity as "speaking law," James assumes a kind of monological unity between the meaning and the force of his words.[29] But in his poetic and scholarly writings James is not writing in his official capacity as king, or not only in that capacity, and the meaning and force of his words are for that reason not necessarily the same. On the contrary, as soon as any of James's literary texts (in which he writes as either a poet or a man of letters) is released to the public, a rift develops between the author and his text, between the author's intended meaning and the public's actual interpretation.

The writer's competence as a poetic craftsman can bridge or widen this rift. Whatever he may assume about the rhetorical force of his official pronouncements, James the poet or scholar was humble about his ability to express himself as well as he would like. Writing

about Du Bartas's poems, for example, James complains that although "I was moved by the oft reading & perusing of them, with a restles and lofty desire, to preas and attaine to the like vertue, . . . God, by nature hathe refused me the like lofty and quick ingyne, and . . . my dull *Muse,* age and Fortune, had refused me the lyke skill and learning."[30] There is no reason to think that James is not being sincere.[31] He was well aware of his limits as a poet and scholar and aware that poetry and scholarship answered to standards which were independent of the social status of the writer and of the force that social status might contribute to one's language. In a very early poem, for example, he noted a difference between a "thought" kept to himself and a "word" pronounced in public, and advised himself to find ways of invention that would best preserve his intentions:

> Since thought is free, thinke what thou will
> O troubled hart, to ease thy paine.
> Thought, unrevealed, can doe no euill;
> Bot words past out, cummes not againe.
> 　　Be cairfull aye for to invent
> 　　The waye to gett thy owen intent.[32]

To the extent that he hoped to excel as a poet he expected to compete on an equal footing with other poets, according to the relatively autonomous standards of poetic discourse. If a king was a "speaking law," a poet-king was, at bottom, only a poet. In fact, the relative autonomy of poetic writing was what attracted the king to it, since this autonomy allowed him to try on other identities and speak in other capacities.

James recognized that rifts could open between literary discourse and authorial intention precisely because literary discourse had its own rules. He was very much attracted to Du Bartas's and others' idea of divine inspiration, and deduced from it the principle that literary production often involved a form of split subjectivity, where the poet, so long as he was inspired, was no longer quite himself when he wrote but, rather, "parted" from himself, removed to a different plane of existence. In his translation of *The Uranie* (1584-85), for example, James writes that "All art is learned by art, this art alone / It is a heavenly gift," strongly suggesting that poetry is an autonomous practice, divine in origin though human in application:

> For man from man must wholly parted be
> If with his age, his verse do well agree.
> Amongst our hands, he must his witts resing,
> A holy trance to highest heaven him bring
> For even as humane fury maks the man
> Les than the man: So heavenly fury can
> Make man pas man, and wander in a holy mist.[33]

For his translation of Du Bartas's *The Furies,* James wrote a "Translator's Invocation" in which he alludes to the split subjectivity that he will have to exemplify if he is going to express the violent and inherently repellent material that a poem on "the furies"—the divine punishments of man—necessarily involves.[34] Sometimes in parting from himself the poet finds himself capable of writing about violence and cruelty. *The Lepanto,* too, opens by invoking the Holy Spirit to "inflame" the author's pen "above [his] skill" (lines 17-24). At one point, while the woes of Venice on the eve of the formation of the Holy League are being recounted, the poet even invokes the muse to stop and move on to something else: "O stay my Muse, thou goes too farre." The poet claims that the mourning he has been caused to write about will with "trikling teares so fill my penne / That it will write no more" (lines 181-84).

So if James writes and eventually publishes a poem about the Battle of Lepanto while sitting as the King of Scotland, he understands that its rhetorical force, such as it is, stems primarily from the language itself and from whatever expressivity divine inspiration and poetic alterity may have contributed to it. The royal poet is to be attended to as any other poet, speaking by way of divine inspiration and aspiring to the skills appropriate to poetic invention. The poem itself, by the same token, is to be attended to as any other poem, according to the conventions, ambitions, and limits of verse. Only, even if a poet is a poet and the poem a poem, the original problem of intention and invention is never entirely resolved. For as James is well aware, insofar as James the king takes responsibility for the authorship of a poem, he is not simply a poet; he is a poet in whom readers are interested because he is both a poet and a king. And the poem then is not simply a poem, since the construal or misconstrual of the poem reflects back on the king who wrote it and the foreign and domestic policies he represents. "It falls out often," he begins in his preface to *Lepanto,* "that the effects of mens action comes cleane contrairie to the intent of the Author. The same finde I by experience (beloved Reader) in my Poëme of *Lepanto*" (p. 198). The danger, moreover, is as much political as it is literary. If the poem is misunderstood as a poem, it is also misunderstood as an act of meaning for which a king in his political capacity has taken responsibility. The poem itself, of course, is already political, since it is a parable about war and peace and religious persecution, and misconstrual may have a variety of unwanted political effects.

The problem is not readily soluble. For his part, James prefers that his poems speak for themselves, saying that adding "Commentarie" is a kind of "reproach of the skillfull learnedness of the Reader," and a thing he would rather avoid lest he make the work "more displeasant" to that reader (p. 198). But how, then, is the allegory of the poem to be construed? In the end we find the poem related to its royal author in much the same way as the Whitehall ceilings are related to the king. The poems, like the ceilings, both refer to the royal author and stem from him: he wrote the poems (albeit in consultation with various sources and with long- and short-term, domestic and foreign, political goals in mind) just as he promoted the allegories of the ceilings (albeit, again, in consultation with a number of others, and, again, with a varied political program in mind). Yet the poems, like the ceilings, are meant to speak for themselves. It is the artistic image that we see, and that allows us to look backward (but only so far) to read the royal intention behind it. On the one hand, the artistic image speaks for and on behalf of the king. On the other hand, the artistic image obeys its own laws and speaks in its own voice. And it is this image with its own laws and its own voice that James wants his "skillfull" readers to construe.

The Choice of Epic

Insofar as *The Lepanto* operates as an epic, it functions as an unambiguous (if not unambivalent) statement, so that the kinds of misconstruals James said his poem has suffered from ought not to have been expected, at least from diligent and competent readers. The epic's dark conceit may work against its literal tenor, but the epic tenor is palpable all the same. Epic form determines the shape and tone of the poem; it establishes the logic of its plot and the affective force of its message. In choosing the epic form, James has made a number of decisions about the significance of the battle. On a literal level, James has decided, the battle betokens a heroic, epic episode in recent history, and betokens it in a conventionally heroic and epic way.

Epic, as David Quint has recently redefined it, and especially an "epic of winners" like *The Lepanto,* tells a story of warfare and of "a power able to end the indeterminacy of war and to emerge victorious, showing that the struggle had all along been leading up to its victory"; the epic thus imposes on its material a "narrative teleology" within which a certain kind of justice is shown to prevail.[35] Thus the Christian navy in James's poem is shown to have been destined to win the battle by divine decree; to have fought the battle for a divine cause, as argued by Christ himself in heaven as well as by a heavenly messenger on earth who stirs the Venetians and other Christians into action; and to have fought the battle valiantly and fairly, thanks in part to the heroism and leadership of an individual rising to the occasion of greatness. This conventional, epic end result is unmistakable; God's purpose has prevailed, and God's purpose has operated in the battle from beginning to end, ultimately revealing itself in full with the phenomenal victory of the Christians over the Turks. Following epic tradition, James even shows the Turks as worthy opponents of the Christian soldiers, although he also shows that their predations on Christian civilization were the aggravating cause of the battle. When the battle is about to begin, the Turkish leader Ali Basha visits all his host "with bold and manly face" and exhorts his men to action in the language worthy of a classic epic hero (line 518). But in the end the Turks finally manifest that "confusion and disorder" that characterize the losers of epic battles, "so that victory over them may be ascribed as a triumph of reason and meaning."[36] Courageous to the end, the Turks finally lose their battle sense and turn back in confusion when their general Ali Basha is beheaded, and Don Juan displays his head on a mast for all to see. "At sight whereof, the faithlesse Host / Were all so sore agast, / That all amas'd gave back at once" (lines 839-41). And thus the poet, having noted the swift victory over a suddenly distracted army, can end his poem by "exhorting all you Christians true / Your courage up to bend" (lines 1020-21). This example of epic victory serves the usual ends of such victory: the teleological legitimacy of a political regime and its place in history has been elucidated and confirmed, and the subjects of that regime have been accordingly consoled.

And yet (as James's own preface cautions us to reconsider the matter), in spite of the poem's epic treatment of it's subject, nothing in the chain of events that preceded, included, or followed the battle was in itself of epic or heroic significance. Relations between Muslims and Christians had been a complicated affair for centuries, involving cooperation, antagonism, and a good deal of mutual indifference. But in the sixteenth century, the major Christian states competed for international hegemony and so did the Ottoman state, which was the single strongest power in the Mediterranean basin.[37] Clashes (as well as alliances) were all but inevitable. But when, in violation of treaties, though not entirely without provocation, the Ottomans wrested Cyprus from Venetian control at a great cost of Christian and Muslim lives, men like Pius V and Philip II reasonably inferred that the very survival of the Christian states in the Mediterranean was at risk. (At risk over the long term, it should be added: there was no immediate danger that Christianity as a religion was going to be exterminated.) The result was the forming of the Holy League, organized by Pius V to defend the common interests of the Roman Catholic states against the Ottoman Empire. Its first order of business was to retaliate for the Turkish reconquest of Cyprus. The immediate result of the Holy League's first offensive naval expedition was their total victory over the Turkish fleet, but it was not entirely clear what that total victory meant. One standard modern reading of the event, which was not unknown even in the sixteenth century, was that it did not mean much at all.[38] Lepanto, it has often been said, was more a moral or symbolic victory than a real one.[39] By 1572—within a year after losing the great battle—the Ottomans had already rebuilt their navy and were making new incursions on the Spanish protectorate of Tunis, overtaking the town for good in 1574. In 1573 the Venetians, working independently of the

League, negotiated a separate peace with the Ottomans, ceding Cyprus and a large indemnity in return for the reestablishment of trade. Far from being a decisive victory in the campaign of Christianity against the infidel, the battle was but a temporary triumph in a sequence of events which ended in a loss of territory, wealth, and prestige for Spain, Venice, and the Christian confederacy alike, and an early dissolution of the confederacy itself. "This victory seemed to open the door to the wildest hopes," Fernand Braudel writes. "But in the immediate aftermath of the battle, it had no strategic consequences." Indeed, "historians have joined in an impressively unanimous chorus to say that Lepanto was a great spectacle, a glorious one even, but in the end leading nowhere."[40]

Nevertheless, from the outset there was a drive to see in the Battle of Lepanto a historical moment of larger, even monumental significance. And it was to this drive that the young King of Scotland contributed his *Lepanto.* His was one of the first attempts not only to transform the battle into a subject of heroic poetry but also to use the model of the classic epic as the key for reconstructing the story. On the Iberian peninsula, apart from the relatively obscure (and unknown to James) epics by Juan Latino (1573), Hieronymo Corte Real (1578), and Juan Rufo (1582), and a canto in the second part of Alonso de Ercilla's well-known *La Araucana* (1578), Lepanto became the subject of popular ballads, written in the key of conventional romance.[41] In this balladry, Don Juan takes the place of many another chivalrous knight fighting against infidels who are also understood in terms of the chivalric code. For all its journalistic realism and dramatic intensity, *La Araucana,* too, has a strong admixture of chivalric ideology, as the Turks momentarily take the place of South Americans, standing for the savagely noble enemy against which the Christian knight may put his honor to the test.

Fernando de Herrera, an educated court poet and cleric in Spain, by contrast, wrote a heroic poem on Lepanto which recalled neither chivalric romances nor classical epic but Judges, Chronicles, and Kings. In his *Canción en albanza de la Divin Majestad por la victoria del señor Don Juan* (1571), Herrara reconstructs the story as a "hymn" celebrating the power of a jealous God, a "God of Battles," who overcame His enemies in the field, His "wrath" having "swallowed them up, as fire does the dry chaff."[42] In this account, the Turk is neither the worthy opponent of Renaissance epic nor the hated but chivalrous enemy of vernacular balladry. On the contrary, he is a "proud Tyrant" driven by "impious madness" to oppress the people of God and defy God himself. "Where is these men's God?" the Grand Sultan demands, noting his power over people throughout the Mediterranean, "Who is he hiding from?"[43] The Sultan calls a council where he and his Levantine allies decide to "make a great lake of [Christian] blood," "destroy them as a nation, together with the name of their Christ," and "feast our eyes upon their death."[44] The victory against these satanic Asiatics, explained with little concern for narrative details, is wholly God's. "Today the eyes and grandeur of the proud man were humiliated, and You alone, Lord, were exalted; for your day is come."[45] In fact, in this hymn on "Don Juan's victory" Don Juan is never mentioned by name; he is only the "Christian prince" through whom God demonstrates his power.

Later on, in the seventeenth century, the heroic model would become a standard form for representing the event.[46] But at a time nearer to the battle itself there was no particular reason for viewing it that way, and only a few attempted to do so. In book 1 of *Don Quixote* (1605), Cervantes, who had himself participated in the battle, is more tragicomically Machiavellian than heroic in his assessment of Lepanto. His character the Captive explains the event as a trial of military valor, where a number of men were able to prove their worthiness as soldiers, and "the world and all the nations learnt how wrong they were in supposing that the Turks were invincible on the sea." In a single day, "the insolent pride of the Ottoman was broken for ever."[47] Long-term strategy with regard to the Ottoman Empire was thus revised, and real long-term success against it made more certain, because Christian soldiers had learned that they were pretty tough and could beat the Turks if they resolved to do so. But this vision of the battle as a definitive test of manliness, leading toward a greater resolve to fight in the future, is not quite heroic. Unlike the spokesmen of conventional heroic verse, Cervantes' Captive dissociates military valor from other manly virtues, and his story has nothing to say about the inevitable triumph of virtue over vice, whether in this life or the next. On the contrary, the Captive carries his story of Lepanto over to the defeat of the apparently virtuous Christians at Tunis and holds up as an example of valor the fact that during the Turkish siege of their fortress the Christian knights were slaughtered to the man.

The vision of Lepanto among the Venetians, although in a much different key, was not heroic in a conventional sense, either. In the immediate aftermath of the battle, Venetians inclined toward construing the event eschatologically. Adapting traditional millenarian and Joachimite doctrine, they saw the victory as a day, earlier forecast by Italian prophets, when the tide of history would turn, and the Byzantine Empire—Venice's ancestral kingdom—would soon be restored.[48] The Venetian stake in this battle was evidently very different from what the Spanish, the Papal, or for that matter the Scottish court might imagine it to be: the Venetian account of Lepanto looked eastward to their future in a way that had become incomprehensible to the Western European powers since the end of the Crusades.

James's *Lepanto,* then, offered a distinctive reading of events against all the counterevidence that history could provide or counterexamples that other literary works could present; it contributed to the mythos of Lepanto by refashioning the events into a parable of epic heroism. Epic heroism is what the poem shows the battle to be an example of; the head of the enemy is displayed, and the story is over. And clearly, then, heroism is what poem is trying to be an example for. On this level of meaning *The Lepanto* is unambiguous. But that still leaves unresolved both James's claim that the poem is actually an allegory about the persecution of Protestants and the conflict between James's apparent pacifism and the poem's apparent glorification of war.

ALLEGORICAL ATTENUATIONS

James hints at his dark conceit throughout the poem— sometimes heavy-handedly, sometimes subtly, and often with considerable ambiguity. At the conclusion of the poem, for example, he differentiates between "all Christians true" and those Christians who "serv'd not right" their God but received God's help anyway, since he "doth love his name / So well" (lines 1022-24). We find out that God "doth the bodie better love" that is the "bodie" of "Christians true," than those Christians who are only the "shadow" of true Christians (lines 1027-28). Yet those Christians whose fortunes the poem has been documenting, the members of the Pope's Holy League fighting against the Turk—those Christians are the "shadow" Christians whom God loves less than others. Christians in name only, their story is but a shadow of the story of "true Christians," that is, the Protestants, members of the church of true believers. This idea is suggested from the beginning. In the opening council in heaven between God, Satan, and Christ (with obvious allusions to the opening scene of Job), Christ complains that Satan has "inflamde" the "maddest mindes" of the "faithles Turkes" "Against them all that doe professe / My name with fervent fayth" (lines 51-56). To profess the "name" of Christianity is important in itself, we learn, when God the Father proclaims, "All christians serves [*sic*] my Sonne though not / Aright in everie thing" (lines 79-80). And he will now put an end to the Turks' oppression of "these Christians" so that it will be seen that "of my holie hallowed name / The force is great and blest" (lines 81, 83-84).

In this epic, evidently, the young poet is already trying to walk the *via regia*: he is at once condemning Catholics and acknowledging their ties to Protestants, allowing them a merited heroism while stipulating that theirs is but a shadow of Protestant heroism and, indeed, their faith but a shadow of Christian faith. "I could wish from my heart," James said in 1604, "that it would please God to make me one of the members of such a generall Christian union in Religion, as laying wilfulnesse on both hands, we might meete in the middest"—although, of course, he cannot because of "the newe and grosse Corruptions of theirs," which they refuse to renounce.[49] "I protest to God," he wrote in a letter to Robert Cecil in 1603, "I reverence their church as our mother church, although clogged with many infirmities and corruptions. . . . I only wish that such order might be taken as the land might be purged of such great flocks of them that daily diverts the soul of many from the sincerity of the gospel."[50] On the one hand the Catholics of Venice, Spain, and the Papal states are members of a "mother church" and "serve" the Christian God and His purposes on earth.[51] On the other hand, they serve God poorly. They are but shadows of what James thought of as the "Trew, Ancient, Catholike and Apostolike faith, grounded upon the Scriptures and expresse word of God."[52] Furthermore, they can be dangerous. James never had any illusions but that the catholic ambitions of members of the Roman Church represented a danger to the equally catholic ambitions of Protestants, as well as to the independent national hegemonies of Protestant rulers. So the Catholics "shadow" the Protestants in various ways, for good and ill.

Finally, however, by way of what seems to be a stunningly unconvincing piece of choplogic, the Battle of Lepanto communicates in this poem an ostensibly unambiguous moral lesson: if God will do so much for his "shadow" Christians, concerned as He is merely to preserve "the name" of Christianity, think what he will do for the real Christians! Think what he will do for Protestants threatened by Catholic persecution! "Then though the Antichristian sect / Against you do conjure," the poem concludes, addressing its Protestant audience (as Catholics can be "Antichristians" as well as worthy "shadows" in James's political theology),

> He doth the bodie better love
>   Then shadow be ye sure:
> Do ye resist with confidence,
>   That God shall be your stay
> And turne it to your comfort, and
>   His glory now and ay.
>
>   (Lines 1027-32)

This choplogic, along with the dark conceit supporting it, is what the poem's early detractors overlooked. It is what James had to use his authorial and kingly authority in a preface to impose on the reading of the text, even though he preferred and indeed insisted that readers discover the meaning on their own. The situation is not perhaps all that different from that more famous and nearly contemporary epic, *The Fairie Queene* (1590-96). The latter too is a story drawn from epic convention, ostensibly glorifying violence and aggression which nevertheless communicates a post-epic, Protestant allegory and ultimately extols Christian rather than timocratic militancy.[53] But leaving aside the problems of

tenor and vehicle suggested by the parallels between *The Faerie Queene* and **The Lepanto,** the practical questions remain: In what way does James suppose that his reader is now to "resist" the incursions of Catholicism? And how does he suppose that learning about the Battle of Lepanto according to heroic models teach the reader to resist them?

Even if James glorifies the battle, he nevertheless disdains its violence. In the beginning of the poem he characterizes his subject matter as "a cruell Martiall warre, / A bloodie battel bolde, / Long doubtsome fight, with slaughter huge / And wounded manifolde" (lines 5-9). There is neither delight in nor awe of violence in this language, although there is a strain of a conventional teaser here too: get ready, the storyteller tells his readers, for a gory tale. In any case, as he begins to describe the actual battle the poet pauses, longer than seems entirely necessary, to excuse himself for presuming to write about an event he did not see and, meanwhile, registering some hesitancy at the task of imagining the violence and suffering of war. The poet does not stint from grisly details, to be sure, but he emphasizes three interesting things, which attenuate the militarism of the poem: first, the horror of warfare, especially so far as this was a battle where gunfire and cannonade played major roles in the combat, and even the "Fishes were astonisht all, / To heare such hideous sound" (lines 617-18); second, the almost mechanical valor of the soldiers on both sides, all of whom were willing to fight to the end; and third, the closeness the battle, the tide not turning until Don Juan finally captured the galley of Ali Basha. James is uninterested in military strategy or in the finer points of combat which led to the Christian victory. He is mainly concerned with the tableau of combat as a whole, the vast spectacle of warfare, of blood and smoke and unrelenting fury. Many things are "cruell," "hideous," "horrible," and "bloodie" in this battle:

> The Azure Skie was dim'd with Smoke
>   The dinne that did abound,
> Like Thunder rearing rumling rave
>   With roares the highest Heaven,
> And pearst with pith the glistering valuts
>   Of all the Planets seaven:
> The piteous plaints, the hideous howles,
>   The greevous cries and mones,
> Of millions wounded sundrie waies,
>   But dying all at ones,
> Conjoynd with former horrible sound,
>   Distemperd all the aire,
> And made the Seas for terrour shake
>   With braying every where.
>
>   (Lines 619-32)

As James claimed, although the victory belongs to Don Juan, the action does not revolve around him. When he finally appears in the decisive encounter with Ali Basha, it is against the backdrop of other Christians fighting similar fights and other Christians similarly poised now at the brink of success, now at the brink of failure, and not able to tell how the combat is going for either side.

It would be overreading the text to see in James's depiction of combat a kind of antiwar propaganda. Observations of the horror of war are also part of the epic tradition and can be used not to diminish but to highlight genuine acts of heroism. But when the "Spanish Prince" finally "did hazard" battle with Ali Basha, in James's account, there was nothing particularly noteworthy about his comportment, and, indeed, "Ali-Basha proov'd so well, / With his assisters brave" that initially Don Juan was beaten back. Only when he was "boldned with spite, / And vernisht red with shame" did Don Juan lead his men back into the fray, this time successfully. He fought to save his honor; so did everyone else. And as it happened, an anonymous "Macedonian soldier . . . / Great honor for to win" actually severed Ali's head from his body (lines 820-30).[54] So, skipping over a great many details which to a military historian would tell the real story of how the battle turned out the way it did, from the complex characters of the participants (note how mechanically Don Juan's motives are characterized: he is "red with shame" and "boldned with spite") to the convergence of tactics, firepower, manpower, and luck—skipping over all this, the poem shows that victory, simply, is won. Honor is won. The head of Ali Basha is displayed. There is no celebration of heroism per se. In fact, the battle is no sooner won than the scene immediately shifts to reports of the victory among the citizens of Venice, who sing a hymn in praise not of any particular heroes or of human heroism but of the grace of God.

Perhaps the "shadowing" of the Christians in this story attenuates their individuality and moral vigor. But to the extent that their heroism is compromised they provide poor models for the kind of vigorous faith James is evoking for Protestants. Indeed, when James exhorts his true Christians to "resist with confidence," he is supposing that passive resistance may be a serious option. And if he is supposing that a more active resistance might be necessary, perhaps Protestants should wait with patience for their opportunity to resist; they should wait until the Antichrist presents Protestants with an opportunity for alliance and victory the way the Turk presented the members of the Holy League with such an opportunity. In other words, they should wait until the occasion arises for undertaking a just war.

The Just War

"Let first the justnesses of your cause be your greatest strength" in the conduct of war, James advises his son.[55] What was meant by "justnesse" in war was by then fairly clear.[56] Apart from the *jus in bello*, rules for the

just conduct of war, there was also a *jus ad bellum*, rules for the just instigation of war. The *jus ad bellum* can be distilled into four conditions: a government is justified in going to war (1) when the sovereignty of the government is certain, (2) when the government or its people has suffered a wrong at the hands of another sovereign government, (3) when warfare is the only means left to redress the grievance and assert the rights of the injured party, and (4) when the war is conducted with the "right intent: the restoration of peace."[57] The application of this doctrine was, of course, open to debate. If, for example, Spanish ships are attacked by Turkish or English pirates, does the government of Spain have the right to wage war against the government of Turkey or England or only to defend itself against pirates? Or if Spanish colonists in the New World are attacked by Native Americans, exactly what is the status, by turn, of the injured party, of the injuring party, and of the injury? Which party, in fact, is which?[58] The doctrine seemed specifically to prohibit aggressive war—war waged for the sake of territory, wealth, or private motives like vengeance and fame. But even this prohibition was subject to several interpretations. In the context of his disputes with the Spanish over the Thirty Years' War and the stalled negotiations for settlement by marriage, Francis Bacon reminded James that a just, defensive war sometimes had to be waged preemptively and, therefore, offensively. "Neither is the opinion of some of the schoolmen to be received," he wrote in a 1612 essay, referring specifically to Aquinas, "that 'a war cannot justly be made but upon a precedent injury or provocation.' For there is no question but a just fear of an imminent danger, though there be no blow given, is a lawful cause of war."[59] Moreover, the very ethic of personal and national honor to which James subscribed (even if he preferred to subscribe to it nonaggressively) demanded the exercise of a kind of Machiavellian *virtù*, not a militant defense of one's integrity but a militant expression of integrity. "No nation which doth not directly profess arms," Bacon continued, "may look to have greatness fall into their mouths. And on the other side, it is a most certain oracle of time, that those states that continue long in that profession (as the Romans and the Turks principally have done) do wonders."[60] Much depended, ultimately, on what it was that one reckoned "peace" to be.

In this context, pacifism cannot be equated with passivity.[61] James himself understood peacemaking to be an aggressive act, even in forming bonds of "firm and unchangeable friendship" and strict mutual "obligations."[62] Even Erasmus had recognized this.[63] The right of a nation to make war was intimately connected to the right of the nation to exist as a sovereign state and the right of its legitimate rulers to enforce the law within its borders.[64] And so in *The Lepanto* James is careful to show that the battle was fought fairly, in keeping with rules of *jus in bello,* and, more important, in keeping with the strictest rules of the *jus ad bellum.* Respecting the rules *jus in bello* and the conventions of epic conflict, James has his combatants fight with equal valor. In James's version, the Battle of Lepanto was an honorable battle fought in keeping with codes of honor.[65] (In Herrera's version, by contrast, there is nothing honorable about the Turkish opponents to the Christians, and the victory itself expresses God's justice to the almost total exclusion of human effort and the honor that might be attached to it.) But again, the rules of *jus ad bellum* require a war to be fought not only honorably but strictly with the "right intent." And James makes it clear that the Christian forces had the "right intent" from the beginning: the battle was fought and won because it was God's intention that it be fought and won.

"Ils faudrait des dieux," Rousseau once said about the need for a supramundane principle if one wanted to warrant human law absolutely.[66] In a similar vein, following both epic convention and biblical precedent, James opens **The Lepanto** with a council of the gods— God the Father, the Son, and Satan—in order to move the cause for war out of the realm of strictly human motives. "Even if there are some [wars] which might be called 'just,'" Erasmus had remarked in *The Education of a Christian Prince,* "yet as human affairs are now, I know not whether there could be found any of this sort—that is, the motive for which was not ambition, wrath, ferocity, lust, or greed."[67] But by putting the cause of the war in the hands of the gods (and ultimately God) James removes this objection. Christ accuses the Turks with unjustly persecuting Christians, having been motivated to it by Satan, and Satan admits to this meddling in human affairs through Turkish imperialism, saying that the Christians deserve the grief that Turks are causing them. God settles the matter. "No more shall now these Christians be / With Infidels opprest" (lines 81-82). God then incites the Christians "to revenge of wrongs the Turks / Have done" (lines 91-92) but to respond to their difficult impasse reasonably. He has the Archangel Gabriel descend to Venice and spread the word among the people (James here defers to Venice's republican government) that the Venetians have tolerated oppression at the hands of the Turks too long, and it is God's will for them finally to take up arms. "They kill our Knights, they brash our forts, / They let us never rest" (lines 123-24). The Duke and the Senate, urged on by the people, meet and agree:

> The Towne was driven into this time,
> In such a piteous strait
> By Mahometists, that they had els
> Given over all debait;
> The turke had conquest Cyprus Ile,
> And all their lands that lay
> Without the bounds of Italie,
> Almost whole I say.
>
> (Lines 141-48)

Although one may disagree with James's assessment of the Venetians' situation, it conforms entirely to the conditions of a just war. The sovereignty of the Venetian government is certain, its people have suffered a series of wrongs at the hands of another sovereign government, warfare is the only means left to redress the grievance, and the war is conducted with the intent of restoring peace. The Venetians fight with divine authority in response to an unambiguous provocation only to recover what is already theirs. What is already theirs, in short, is peace.

As Aquinas put it, peace is not just "concord" (*concordium*) but "ordered concord" (*ordinatum*). It is a "tranquility of order" (*tranquillitas ordinis*), a coordination of parts into a unified whole knit together by the "amity" and "obligations" that James often discussed. But in that case, being a positive value, an active rather than a passive condition, peace is inherently, albeit paradoxically, aggressive. Peace is not the mere absence of conflict but rather a condition of harmony actively enforced and actively expressed. And peace, therefore, can readily become a cause and justification of war.[68] In fact, according to the idea of "right intent," peace is the only justification of war.

If James's poem dwells on the details of "a bloodie battle bolde," it also dwells on a vision of Venetian society—republican, communitarian, sovereign, God-loving, urbane, "a wondrous sight" to see (line 102). This vision of the Venetian peace is only a "shadow" peace with respect to its observance of the principles of "true Christianity" and perhaps something of a shadow, too, in its embrace of republican rather than regal government. Nevertheless, it provides the cause for the Battle of Lepanto. When the war is over, the Venetians draw together to thank God for the *tranquillitas ordinis* of their peace.

James's sensitivity to the idea that war must only be fought for the sake of restoring peace may have allowed him to celebrate a war whose long-term effects were negligible. He probably knew that the Christians gained no land by waging their war against the Turks. What they gained—in reality as in the poem—was only peace with honor, since the Christians had proven themselves by beating the Turkish fleet and asserting the right of Venetian Christians to be left alone and prosper. When it came time for the Venetians to enjoy the benefits of peace, which is to say when it came time for them to hasten into the arms of plenty, they simply signed a treaty (neither ignominiously nor disadvantageously from a point of view like James's) swearing off aggression in return for trade. But of course, it is before this enjoyment of peace's benefits, as in the scene dramatized by Rubens about the benefits of government, that James has his heroic poem come to an end. The rewards are deferred. If some narrative threads are brought to completion, others are left open, as if to leave the reader in a condition of unsatisfied desire, a condition of hopefulness and resolve, perhaps, but first of all, a condition of want.

In a sense, a nonmilitant restoration of peace was all James ever really wanted for the Protestant cause. Militant though he may have been in his conviction that Protestantism was the true church and destined to overcome the predations of the Antichrist, he mainly wanted Protestants to be left alone: "I only wish that such order might be taken as the land might be purged of such great flocks of them that daily diverts the souls of many from the sincerity of the gospel."[69] Protestantism would spread of its own accord, so long as individuals were allowed—and also not "diverted from"—a pursuit of the "sincerity of the gospel."[70] No ecumenist or internationalist (as Kevin Sharpe implies him to be), James believed in the peace of nations as the condition for evangelical militancy. But of course, believers in the Protestant faith (and for James this was one faith, admitting of no schisms while allowing some theological dispute) were not necessarily in conflict with Roman Catholics. Only when Catholics behaved with sufficient belligerence to disturb the peace of Protestantism, preventing their pursuit of the gospel, only then did Protestants have just cause to resist, so long as they resisted fairly. And in any case, in James's politics the integrity of the state as a secular entity, over and above any evangelical or catholicizing purposes that might be attached to it, is an end in itself. It too demands peace and is, in fact, a condition of peace and needs to be left alone, even if its rulers are wicked and its people heretical.[71] The peace of a sovereign state, though it may conflict with the peace of the church of true believers, is a rival value, a rival peace, and hence a rival cause for aggression.

It was convenient for the young poet-king that the story of Lepanto involved a struggle with the one enemy that no one in his audience would have trouble reviling. Even Erasmus recognized that a war against the Ottoman Empire might on some occasion be necessary; when Ronsard called on Christians to embrace one another as brothers, he added without irony that those who needed an outlet for aggression could go fight against the Turks.[72] So if James does not turn the Ottoman Empire into an evil and impious empire, he does deploy it as a symbol of that opposition to peace that a lover of peace may be forced to resist. Peace was always local for James, even if its locality, the true church, was sometimes mobile and in principle powerfully expansive. So love for the victories of peace might naturally engage the paradoxical languages of war with its cruel and bloody victories and its unambiguous celebrations of meaning. And it might do so even though, or, rather, because poems about war rarely mean what they really mean. James leaves us staring up at the ceiling of a painted room, wondering at its richly puzzling ambiguities, waiting for a final decision, a final coming of meaning, to be imposed. And that, too, a great waiting for meaning, in the interests of both war and peace, may be one of the things the poem is trying to mean.

Notes

1. Roy Flannagan, ed., *The Riverside Milton* (Boston, 1998), p. 291.

2. James Craigie, "Introduction," in *The Poems of James VI of Scotland,* ed. James Craigie, 2 vols. (Edinburgh, 1955-58), 1:xlviii and passim. For an assessment of King James's accomplishments as a poet, see both Craigie's introductory remarks and G. P. V. Akrigg, "The Literary Achievement of King James I," *University of Toronto Quarterly* 44 (1975): 115-29.

3. See Bruce Galloway, *The Union of England and Scotland, 1603-1608* (Edinburgh, 1986).

4. James VI and I, *Political Writings,* ed. Johann P. Sommerville (Cambridge, 1984), pp. 133 and 136.

5. Quoted in Harris D. Willson, *King James VI and I* (New York, 1956), p. 272.

6. See Steven Marx, "Shakespeare's Pacifism," *Renaissance Quarterly* 45 (1992): 49-95. "Militancy" as both metaphor and reality, with worldly as well as spiritual implications, is emphasized as a cause of aggression and revolution in Michael Walzer, *The Revolution of the Saints: A Study in the Origin of Radical Politics* (Cambridge, Mass., 1965), esp. pp. 268-99.

7. James VI and I, *Political Writings,* p. 33.

8. Quoted in Willson, p. 272.

9. In his remarkable essay, "Just Wars and Evil Empires: Erasmus and the Turks," Ronald G. Musto distinguishes between a "peacemaker" and a "pacifist" and warns against the anachronism implied in the latter term. "The labels 'pacifism' and 'pacifist,'" he writes, "are meaningless in any context other than that of the internationalists of the early twentieth century by and for whom they were first coined" (in *Renaissance Society and Culture: Essays in Honor of Eugene F. Rice, Jr.,* ed. John Monfasani and Ronald G. Musto [New York, 1991], pp. 197-216; this quotation, p. 198). "Peacemaker," by contrast, is a word as old as the Bible and better describes the activism in pursuit of peace that has often been exemplified in both premodern and modern Christian societies. However, in his comprehensive study, *The Catholic Peace Tradition* (Maryknoll, N.Y., 1986), Musto frequently finds it difficult to describe even ancient movements without occasional recourse to the words "pacifism" and "pacifist." And so I find it here.

10. James VI and I, *Political Writings,* p. 137.

11. The "sublimity" of James's state mythology is discussed in Robert Appelbaum, "The Look of Power: Ideal Politics and Utopian Mastery in Seventeenth-Century England" (Ph.D. diss., University of California, Berkeley, 1997), chap. 2.

12. See G. P. V. Akrigg, ed., *Letters of King James VI and I* (Berkeley and Los Angeles, 1984), p. 284.

13. Thomas Middleton, *The Peace-maker,* in *Works,* ed. A. H. Bullen, 8 vols. (London, 1886), 8:327. For a defense of Middleton's authorship, see Rhodes Dunlap, "James I, Bacon, Middleton, and the Making of *The Peace-Maker,*" in *Studies in the Renaissance Drama,* ed. Josephine W. Bennett et al. (New York, 1959), pp. 82-93.

14. Middleton, 8:326.

15. In my account of the paintings I am drawing upon the findings of a number of scholars: Per Palme, *The Triumph of Peace: A Study of the Whitehall Banqueting House* (Stockholm, 1956); C. V. Wedgewood, *The World of Rubens, 1557-1640* (New York, 1967), and *The Political Career of Peter Paul Rubens* (London, 1975); Roy Strong, *Britannia Inumphans: Inigo Jones, Rubens, and Whitehall Palace* (London, 1980); Christopher White, *Peter Paul Rubens: Man and Artist* (New Haven, Conn., 1987); J. Newman, "Inigo Jones and the Politics of Architecture," in *Culture and Politics in Early Stuart England,* ed. Kevin Sharpe and Peter Lake (Stanford, Calif., 1993), pp. 229-56; Lisa Rosenthal, "The Banqueting House Ceiling: Two Newly Discovered Projects," *Apollo* 139 (1994): 29-34, and "Manhood and Statehood: Rubens's Construction of Heroic Virtue," *Oxford Art Journal* 16 (1993): 92-111. For the political complexities of James's, Charles's, and Rubens's involvements in diplomatic efforts to end the Thirty Years' War, see Willson (n. 5 above), chap. 15; Maurice Lee, *Great Britain's Solomon* (Urbana, Ill., 1990), pp. 261-98; and Simon Schama, "Peter Paul Rubens's Europe." *New Yorker* (May 5, 1997), pp. 206 ff.

16. Palme, p. 241.

17. Strong's suggestion—that the child James is pointing to is neither Henry nor Charles but Great Britain itself—is ingenious but perhaps too ingenious. To the extent that the painting shows James bestowing the union of Scotland and England on a child who is about to be crowned, the painting cannot help suggesting the alternative idea that this child must also represent a real son, Charles or Henry or both.

18. Jack Beeching, *The Galleys at Lepanto* (London, 1982), pp. 220-21. The variety of figures given for battle losses by different historians is discussed in

Michael G. Paulson and Tamara Alvarez-Detrell, *Lepanto: Fact, Fiction, and Fantasy: With a Critical Edition of Luis Vélez de Guevara's "El águila del agua," a Play in Three Acts* (Lanham, Md., 1986), pp. 27-28.

19. See Craigie, "Introduction" (n. 2 above), 1:lix-lx.

20. *The Battle of Lepanto,* in Craigie, ed., 1:198. Future citations will be included in the text, the preface by page number and the verse by line number. I will be following the "English" version of the text that Craigie reproduces, which is the actual work as printed by the Englishman Robert Waldegrave, who altered the Scots' spelling of James's manuscript and rearranged the verse from fourteeners to a ballad form, with alternating lines of eight and six syllables. I have silently changed "u" to "v" and "i" to "j" where appropriate and disregarded the printer's practice of capitalizing as well as italicizing proper names.

21. R. B. Wernham, ed., *The Counter-Reformation and Price Revolution, 1559-1610,* vol. 3 of *The New Cambridge Modern History,* ed. G. N. Clark et al. (Cambridge, 1979), pp. 292-306; and Robert J. Knecht, *The French Wars of Religion, 1559-1598* (London, 1989).

22. See Kevin Sharpe, "The King's Writ: Royal Authors and Royal Authority in Early Modern England," in Sharpe and Lake, eds., pp. 117-38, and "Private Conscience and Public Duty in the Writings of James VI and I," in *Public Duty and Private Conscience in Seventeenth-Century England,* ed. J. Morrill, P. Slack, and D. Woolf (Oxford, 1993), pp. 77-100.

23. For James's lifelong aversion to violence, see Willson (n. 5 above), pp. 273-74; and Akrigg, "Introduction" (n. 12 above), pp. 3-5.

24. See James Hutton, *Themes of Peace in Renaissance Poetry,* ed. Ita Guerlac (Ithaca, N.Y., 1984), esp. pp. 80-168.

25. Pierre Ronsard, *Oeuvres complètes,* ed. Jean Céard, Daniel Mènager, and Michel Simonin, 2 vols. (Paris, 1993), 2:807.

26. "Ventuese ambition," the section titled "La decadence" begins, e.g., "Chaud fuzil de la guerre, / Helas! combien de sang tu verses sur la terre. / O sceptres, ô bandeaux, ô throsnes haut montz, / Combien de trahisons, cruels, vous enfantez!" (*The Works of Guillaume De Salluste Sieur Du Bartas,* ed. Urban Tigner Holmes, Jr., et al., 3 vols. [Chapel Hill, N.C., 1940], 3:442).

27. Desiderius Erasmus, *Complaint of Peace,* ed. William James Hirten (New York, 1946), p. 25.

28. Desiderius Erasmus, *The Education of a Christian Prince,* trans. Lester K. Born (New York, 1936), p. 251.

29. See Jonathan Goldberg, *James I and the Politics of Literature* (Stanford, Calif., 1989), for an extended discussion of this issue, along with Sharpe, "Private Conscience," esp. p. 89. I differ from both Goldberg and Sharpe by arguing that James's poetry operated under rules separate from James's other discourses and by finding a kind of dialogical principle, in Mikhail Bahktin's sense, struggling to operate in the former.

30. James VI, *Poems* (see n. 2 above), 1:16.

31. Sharpe discusses the sincerity of James's sincerity at some length in "Private Conscience."

32. James VI, *Poems,* 2:132.

33. James VI, *Poems,* 2:23-25, lines 85-86 and 113-20.

34. Ibid., 2:112, lines 6-12.

35. David Quint, *Epic and Empire: Politics and Generic Form from Virgil to Milton* (Princeton, N.J., 1993), p. 45.

36. Ibid., p. 46.

37. See Paul Coles, *The Ottoman Impact on Europe* (London, 1968); Fernand Braudel, *The Mediterranean and the Mediterranean World in the Age of Philip II,* trans. Sian Reynolds, 2 vols. (New York, 1972); Bernard Lewis, *Islam and the West* (Oxford, 1993), and *Cultures in Conflict: Christians, Muslims, and Jews in the Age of Discovery* (New York, 1995).

38. For a contemporary expression of this reading, see Michel de Montaigne, "We Should Meddle Soberly with Judging Divine Ordinances," in *The Complete Essays of Montaigne,* trans. Donald Frame (Stanford, Calif., 1958), p. 158.

39. For a modern evaluation, see Wernham, ed. (n. 21 above), 3:252-53, 353-54. Also see Lewis, *Islam and the West,* p. 18.

40. Braudel, 2:1103.

41. Juan Latino, *Austriadis libri duo* (Granada, 1573); Hieronymo Corte Real, *Felicissima concedida del cielo al señor don Juan d'Austria, en el golfo de Lepánto de la pederasa armada Othomana* (Lisbon, 1578); Juan Rufo, *La Austriada,* in *Poemas épicos,* 2 vols., ed. D. Cayetano Rosell (Madrid, 1925), 2:1-136; Alonso de Ercilla Y. Zúñiga, *La Araucana,* trans. Charles Maxwell Lancaster and Paul Thomas Manchester (Nashville, 1945); Manuel da Costa Fontes, "Dona Maria and Batalha de Lepanto: Two Rare Luso-American Ballads," in *Portuguese and Brazilian Oral Traditions in Verse Form,* ed. Joanne B. Armistead et al. (Los Angeles, 1976), pp. 148-57;

Juan de Mendano, *Silva de varios romances recopliados por Juan de Mendano* (Madrid, 1966). For discussion of the heroic poems in Spanish and Latin, see Michael Murrin, *History and Warfare in Renaissance Epic* (Chicago, 1994), esp. pp. 182-96.

42. Fernando de Herrera, *Canción en albanza de la divin majestad,* in *Renaissance and Baroque Poetry of Spain,* ed. and trans. Elias L. River (New York, 1966), pp. 113-14.

43. Ibid., p. 116.

44. Ibid., pp. 116-17.

45. Ibid., pp. 118-19.

46. See Paulson and Alvarez-Detrell (n. 18 above).

47. Miguel de Cervantes Saavedra, *The Adventures of Don Quixote,* trans. J. M. Cohen (Harmondsworth, 1950), p. 348. Thus Braudel also argues that the "moral" or "symbolic" victory at Lepanto had real long-term effects, marking "the end of a period of profound depression, the end of a genuine inferiority complex on the part of Christendom and a no less real Turkish supremacy"; see Braudel (n. 37 above), 2:1103. On Cervantes' tragicomic approach to Lepanto, see Stanislav Zimic, "Un eco de Lepanto en la ironia cervantina," *Romance Notes* 12 (1970): 174-76.

48. See Letizia Pierozzi, "La vittoria di Lepanto nell'escatologia e nella profezia," *Rinascimento: Rivista dell'Istituto Nazionale di Studi sul Rinascimento* 34 (1994): 317-63.

49. James VI and I, *Political Writings* (n. 4 above), p. 140.

50. James VI and I, *Letters* (n. 12 above), p. 205.

51. Venice, of course, was admired by Protestants for its independence from Rome and its own nascent proto-Protestant practices on an ecclesiastical and theological level. But it was Roman Catholic all the same.

52. James VI and I, *Political Writings,* p. 140.

53. On ideology and representation of warfare in Edmund Spenser, see Murrin (n. 41 above), pp. 136-37; and Richard Mallette, *Spenser and the Discourse of Reformation England* (Lincoln, Nebr., 1997), pp. 143-68.

54. As Beeching and others tell it, however, the man who beheaded Ali Basha was a galley slave.

55. James VI and I. *Political Writings,* p. 32.

56. On the just war tradition as James would have known it, see James Turner Johnson, *Ideology, Reason, and the Limitation of War: Secular and*

Religious Concepts, 1200-1740 (Princeton, N.J., 1975); Frederick H. Russell, *The Just War in the Middle Ages* (Cambridge, 1975); and Musto, *Catholic Peace Tradition* (n. 9 above).

57. Musto, *Catholic Peace Tradition,* p. 104.

58. This last question was a topic of particular concern to Francisco Victoria and Francisco Suarez. See James B. Scott, *Spanish Origins of International Law* (Oxford, 1934), which includes translations of some of Victoria's most important works on just war theory, including *De jure belli* (1557) and *De Indis* (1557).

59. Francis Bacon, "Of Empire," in *Francis Bacon,* ed. Brian Vickers (Oxford, 1996), p. 377; Bacon is referring to the *Summa theologica* 2-2.9.40.1.

60. Bacon, "Of True Greatness of Kingdoms and Estates," in Vickers, ed., p. 401. See also Bacon, *Advertisement Touching a Holy War* (1622), in *Works,* ed. James Spedding, Robert Leslie Ellis, and Douglas Denn Heath, 14 vols. (London, 1858-74), 13:171-228; and *Considerations Touching a War with Spain* (1624) in *Certain Miscellany* (London, 1629).

61. See Musto, *Catholic Peace Tradition,* p. 9.

62. James VI and I, *Letters* (n. 12 above), p. 384.

63. See Desiderius Erasmus, *On the War against the Turks,* in *The Erasmus Reader,* ed. Erika Rummel (Toronto, 1990), pp. 318-33.

64. Ibid., pp. 319, 322.

65. This may also be a reason why James neglects to mention the fact that the Christian forces may have had a technological and strategic advantage in the battle.

66. Quoted in Hannah Arendt, *On Revolution* (Harmondsworth, 1963), p. 183.

67. Erasmus, *The Education of a Christian Prince* (n. 28 above), p. 252.

68. For this doctrine, see Saint Thomas Aquinas, *Summa theologica* 2-1.29.1.1; quoted and translated with valuable commentary in John K. Ryan, *Modern War and Basic Ethics* (Washington, D.C., 1933), p. 13. James discussed Aquinas's doctrine with his advisers and friends.

69. James VI and I, *Letters,* p. 384.

70. Ibid., p. 205.

71. See Jenny Wormald, "'Basilikon Doron' and 'The Trew Law of Free Monarchies,'" in *The Mental World of the Jacobean Court,* ed. Linda Levy Peck (Cambridge, 1991), pp. 36-54.

72. Erasmus, *On the War against the Turks,* p. 333.

Peter C. Herman (essay date winter 2001)

SOURCE: Herman, Peter C. "Authorship and the Royal 'I': King James VI/I and the Politics of Monarchic Verse." *Renaissance Quarterly* 54, no. 4 (winter 2001): 1495-1530.

[*In the following essay, Herman contends that James's position as a monarch influenced both his poetry and its reception, and he discusses the diplomatic value of his verse.*]

Despite the reinvigoration of historicism in literary studies over the last twenty years or so, the poetry of King James VI/I has remained practically unexamined despite the copious attention given to his prose works.[1] The lack of attention, however, is part of the general neglect of monarchic verse. While one finds any number of studies on how Wyatt's or the Earl of Surrey's or Sidney's poetry somehow reflects and intervenes in contemporary politics, the fact that monarchs also regularly produced has seemingly gone unnoticed. This lacuna is particularly odd in James's case, for he not only published two books of poetry while king of Scotland, reprinted his **Lepanto** upon his accession to the English throne, and sponsored its translation into French and Latin, but his poetic accomplishments were widely recognized and celebrated (perhaps over-celebrated) during his life.

I

The sonnet James penned for Elizabeth sometime in 1586 especially demonstrates how a monarch could try to use verse as an instrument of diplomacy. Throughout much of that year James and Elizabeth haggled over the terms of the Anglo-Scots treaty, the primary sticking points being the size of James's pension and whether or not Elizabeth would sign an "instrument" guaranteeing that he would be Elizabeth's heir. In March, Elizabeth rejected James's request to sign this document with firm but gentle irony:

> Tochinge an "instrument," as your secretarye terme it, that you desiar to haue me signe, I assure you, thogh I can play of some, and haue bine broght up to know musike, yet this disscord wold be so grose as wer not fit for so wel-tuned musike. Must so great dout be made of fre good wyl, and gift be so mistrusted, that our signe Emanuel must assure? No, my deere brother. Teache your new rawe counselars bettar manner than to aduis you such a paringe of ample meninge. Who shuld doute performance of kinges offer? What dishonor may that be demed? Folowe next your owne nature, for this neuer came out of your shoppe. But, for your ful satisfaction, and to plucke from the wicked the weapon the

wold use to brede your doubt of meanings, thes the be. First, I wil, as longe as you with iuel desart alter not your course, take care for your safety, help your nide, and shun al actes that may damnifie you in any sort, ether in present or future time; and for the portion of relife, I minde neuer to lessen, though, as I see cause, I wil rather augment. And this I hope may stand you in as muche assuranse as my name in parchement, and no les for bothe our honors.[2]

James, however, was not assured. The Scots King wanted something in writing, not a verbal promise of future "performance," and James tactfully responded that he did not want a signed document for himself, but for others:

And as for the instrument, quhairunto I desyre youre seale to be affixit, think not, I pray you, that I desire it for any mistrust, for I protest before God that youre simple promeis uolde be more then sufficient to me, if it uaire not that uoulde haue the quole worlde to understand hou it pleacith you to honoure me aboue my demeritis, quhich fauore and innumerable otheris, if my euill happ will not permitt [me] by action to acquye, yett shall I contend by goode meaning to conteruayle the same at her handis, quhome, committing to the Almichties protection, I pray euer to esteeme me.[3]

James had a fit when he read Elizabeth's reply (now lost), reportedly turning various shades of red and swearing "By God" that had he known "what little account the queen would make of him, she should have waited long enough before he had signed any league, or disobliged his nobles, to reap nothing but disappointment and contempt."[4] Apparently James told Elizabeth so in a letter (sadly, also lost), but the queen replied in a more temperate fashion, wondering "how possiblie my wel-ment letter, prociding from so fauteles a hart, could be ether misliked or misconstred" and reassuring James of her esteem and constant care for him. Yet despite the sweet words, she refused to raise the offered pension, and she refused to sign the instrument, because such a document "fitted not our two frindeships."[5] James realized that he had gotten as much as Elizabeth would give him, and so he "digested all," signing the treaty in July.

Now, according to G. P. V Akrigg, sometime during 1586 James wrote a letter to Elizabeth which included a sonnet, and because both are very important and as yet have passed without notice, I quote them in full:[6]

Madame and dearest sister,

Notwithstanding of my instant writing one letter unto you yet could I not satisfy my unrestful and longing spirit except by writing of these few lines, which, albeit they do not satisfy it, yet they do stay the unrest thereof while the answer is returning of this present.

Madame, I did send you before some verse. Since then Dame Cynthia has oft renewed her horns and innumerable times supped with her sister Thetis. And the bearer

thereof returned, and yet void of answer. I doubt not ye have read how Cupid's dart is fiery called because of the sudden ensnaring and restless burning; thereafter what I can else judge but that either ye had not received it, except the bearer returned with the contrary to report; or else that ye judge it not to be of me because it is *incerto authore*. For which cause I have insert[ed] my name to the end of this sonnet here enclosed. Yet one way I am glad of the answer's keeping up, because I hope now for one more full after the reading also of these presents and hearing this bearer dilate this purpose more at large according to my secret thoughts. For ye know dead letters cannot answer no questions; therefore I must pray you, how unapparent soever the purpose be, to trust him in it as well as if I myself spake it unto you face by face (which I would wish I might) since it is specially and in a manner only for that purpose that I have sent him. Thus, not doubting of your courtesy in this far, I commit you, madame, and dearest sister, to God's holy protection, the day and dates as in the other letter.

Your more loving and affectionate
brother and cousin than (I fear)
yet ye believe.
James R.

[Sonnet enclosed with letter][7]
Full many a time the archer slacks his bow
That afterhend* it may the stronger be.   *afterward
Full many a time in Vulcan'[s] burning stow*   *stove
    or furnace
The smith does water cast with careful ee.*   *eye
Full oft contentions great arise, we see,
Betwixt the husband and his loving wife
That sine* they may the firmlyer agree   *since
When ended is that sudden choler strife.
Yea, brethren, loving others as their life,
Will have debates at certain times and hours.
The winged boy dissentions hot and rife
Twixt his lets fall like sudden summer showers.
Even so this coldness did betwixt us fall
To kindle our love as sure I hope it shall.
Finis J. R.

Given the correspondence at the time between Elizabeth and James, it seems probable that this poem originated in James's desire to get beyond his anger at Elizabeth for refusing to sign the "instrument" and to ameliorate Elizabeth's annoyance at his persistence, the reference to "dissentions" and "contentions" echoing Elizabeth's reference to musical "disscord" in her letter of March, 1586. As such, James's sonnet represents more than an interesting diversion (when he first arrived in Scotland, Randolph reported that "the King still follows his hunting, riding and writing in metre"[8]). The poem argues that occasional strife only strengthens a relationship, and therefore he and Elizabeth are better allies for having had this argument. The sonnet thus demonstrates James using the medium of poetry to achieve a diplomatic goal, in this case, helping to smooth the relationship between Elizabeth and himself after their quarrels over money and the "instrument."

Yet the poem fascinates for a number of additional reasons. First, the imagery in this sonnet and the rhetoric of the accompanying letter together demonstrate James's awareness of and desire to appropriate for his own benefit the politicization of erotic discourse permeating Elizabeth's court. The letter also demonstrates James's sensitivity to the importance of authorship, since he makes absolutely sure that Elizabeth knows that the sonnet comes from *his* pen, not "*incerto authore*," and James ensures that Elizabeth *knows* that he has signed this copy with his initials. Finally, while I recognize the danger of basing an argument on a lack of response, Elizabeth's refusal to acknowledge James's effort, let alone write a verse reply even though she engages in a mock debate in verse with Sir Walter Ralegh at precisely this time, remains among the most intriguing aspects of this poem.

The fact that James writes Elizabeth a love sonnet using Petrarchan imagery is in itself important, for, as many, many critics have shown, from the 1570s onward the rhetoric of love in the Elizabethan court became deeply entwined with the rhetoric of politics. Not only love lyrics, but the language of love itself, as Marotti writes, "could express figuratively the realities of suit, service, and recompense with which ambitious men were insistently concerned as well as the frustrations and disappointments experienced in socially competitive environments."[9] Thus, for example, Sir Christopher Hatton could write to his queen "Madame, I find the greatest lack that ever poor wretch sustained. No death, no hell no fear of death shall ever win of me my consent so far to wrong myself again as to be absent from you one day . . . I can write no more. Love me; for I love you. . . ."[10] Similarly, the erotic frustration of Sir Philip Sidney's *Astrophil and Stella* probably expresses the author's political frustrations, just as *The Lady of May* and *The Triumph of the Fortress of Perfect Beauty* refigure "the queen's relationship to her courtiers as well as with her relationship to Alençon."[11]

James clearly knows about these developments, and in order to ingratiate himself further with Elizabeth, whose political and financial favor he depends on as much any of Elizabeth's courtiers, he evidently decided to try to write using the tropes of political Petrarchism in both his poetry and his prose, with unique results. In no other letter, either before or after, does James use allegory ("Dame Cynthia has oft renewed her horns and innumerable times supped with her sister Thetis," meaning "it has been a long time since I sent the poem to you"[12]) or invoke "Cupid's dart" (which we will return to below). Additionally, this letter nuances Foucault's deconstruction of the author. The speaker's identity matters intensely to James since Elizabeth's silence might be explained by her not knowing the poem's source (unlikely, to be sure). As James writes, she might "judge it not to be of me because it is *incerto authore*

[meaning James had not signed the original manuscript]. For which cause I have insert[ed] my name to the end of this sonnet. . . ." Yet remarkably, James's attempt to speak the erotic language of the Elizabethan court *fails.* Elizabeth ignored the poem the first time James sent it, and so far as we can tell she ignored it the second time as well. I want to offer two possible explanations for Elizabeth's declining to play along.

First, as both Marotti and Montrose point out, courtiers assimilated Petrarchan language so easily because the relationship between the lover and the beloved closely mirrors the relationship between the courtier seeking favor and a distant, withholding sovereign. The gender relationship between the lover and his beloved also mirrored (at least rhetorically) the relationship between the courtier and the queen, the male being in the subservient position of *asking* for favor, which the woman (i.e., Elizabeth) can give or withhold. In his sonnet to Elizabeth, however, James's monarchic status conflicts with his attempts write a conventional piece of Petrarchan verse that would entertain Elizabeth (hence making her more pliable to his political desires) for several reasons.[13] Foremost, Petrarchan verse depends upon an unequal power relationship, be it between lover and rejecting beloved or courtier and withholding monarch. To be the speaker in a Petrarchan drama entails making oneself a "sub-ject," meaning that which is *thrown under.* The problem is that the monarch by definition is *never* a subject. As a clever courtier of Louis XV put it when his monarch commanded him to think of a joke at the king's expense, "le roi n'est pas sujet" ("The king is not a subject"), and this witticism applies equally well to both James and Elizabeth, who—in theory at least—occupied the same exalted plane. That is to say, both James and Elizabeth considered themselves God's anointed on earth, subject to no-one other than God.[14] Yet nearly all the examples James uses in his sonnet are not only explicitly hierarchical, but gendered as well. There is no mutuality between the "archer" or the "smith" (conventionally male) and their instruments, the early modern division of power between "the husband and his loving wife" needs no rehearsing, and the same gender relations obtain between lovers under the influence of "The winged boy." To use mathematical symbols, archer:bow = husband:wife, and smith:furnace = male lover:female beloved. When, therefore, James writes, "Even so this coldness did betwixt us fall," he does more than compare their political disagreements to a lovers' spat; rather, he implicitly compares his relationship with Elizabeth to a series of *un*equal relationships, with himself as the dominant partner. Given the poverty of James and his court as well as his status as a petitioner for the English throne, let alone English gold, Elizabeth might very well have decided not to respond because the poem implicitly figures her as an *inferior,* the bow to James's archer, the water to James's smith, the subservient wife to James as husband. The poem thus inverts the actual power relations between the two as well as serving to remind Elizabeth of the cognitive dissonance surrounding a powerful female monarch ruling "a stratified society in which authority is everywhere invested in men—everywhere, that is, except at the top."[15]

Furthermore, Elizabeth's inferior position in James's poem contradicted Elizabeth's own deployment of her monarchic status in her verse.[16] Whereas courtier verse enacts its politics from a subservient position—as Montrose puts it, "The otiose love-talk of the shepherd masks the busy negotiation of the courtier; the shepherd is a courtly poet prosecuting his courtship in pastoral forms"[17]—Elizabeth used verse as a vehicle to effect and transmit *royal* policy. For example, one aspect of Elizabeth's response to the problem of Mary Stuart and her plea to enter England was the covert circulation of "The Doubt of Future Foes" (1570), which, as Jennifer Summit argues, constituted a brilliant strategy for reassuring her court that she was ready and able to counter the threat posed by James's mother. Elizabeth, as George Puttenham writes, used the poem "to declare that she was nothing ignorant of those secret practices, though she had long with great wisdom and pacience dissembled it."[18] Even further, Elizabeth used the medium of verse and coterie transmission to assert her primacy in foreign policy:[19]

> The daughter of debate, that eke discord doth sowe
> Shal reap no gaine where formor rule hath taught stil
>   peace to growe.
> No forreine bannisht wigh shal ancre in this port,
> Our realme it brookes no strangers force, let them
>   elswhere resort.
> Our rusty sword with rest, shall first his edge employ,
> To polle their toppes that seeke, such change and gape
>   for ioy.

The same paradigm obtains in her more recreational verse. In her response to Sir Walter Ralegh's no doubt playful lament at his losing his queen's favor (written in 1587), Elizabeth makes very clear that she, not Fortune, let alone any man, is in charge:[20]

>   Ah, silly Pug, wert thou so afraid?
> Mourn not, my Wat, nor be thou so dismayed.
> It passeth fickle Fortune's power and skill
> To force my heart to think thee any ill.
> No Fortune base, thou sayest shall alter thee?
> And may so blind a witch so conquer me?
> No, no, my Pug, though Fortune were not blind,
> Assure thyself she could not rule my mind.
> Fortune, I know, sometimes doth conquer kings,
> And rules and reigns on earth and earthly things,
> But never think Fortune can bear the sway
> If Virtue watch and will her not obey.
> Ne chose I thee by fickle Fortune's rede,
> Ne she shall force me alter with such speed
> But if to try this mistress' jest with thee.
> Pull up thy heart, suppress thy brackish tears,

> Torment thee not, but put away thy fears.
> Dead to all joys and living unto woe,
> Slain quite by her that ne'er gave wise men blow,
> Revive again, and live without all dread,
> The less afraid, the better thou shalt speed.

The poem is a remarkable performance, and not the least reason is the contrast between Ralegh's position as a supplicant (e.g., "In vain, my eyes, in vain ye waste your tears; / In vain, my sights, the smoke of my despairs, / In vain you search the earth and heaven above, / In vain you search, for Fortune keeps my love") and Elizabeth's superior position throughout her text. The poem begins with a command ("Mourn not, my Wat, nor be thou so dismayed") and it concludes with Elizabeth instructing her courtier on how to prosecute his courtship ("Revive again, and live without all dread, / *The less afraid, the better thou shalt speed*"; my emphasis). In between, Elizabeth answers Ralegh's reminder that "Fortune conquers kings" by assuring him that she, the queen, is in fact more powerful than even fortune. Indeed, Elizabeth uses the bulk of the poem to assert her independence and power: "It passeth fickle Fortune's power and skill / *To force my heart* to think thee any ill"; "No, no, my Pug, though Fortune were not blind, / *Assure thyself she could not rule my mind*"; "*Ne chose I thee* by fickle Fortune's rede / *Ne she shall force me alter* with such speed" (all the emphases mine). While Elizabeth grants that Fortune "doth conquer kings, / And rules and reigns on earth and earthly things," the admission is only partial: "Fortune, I know, *sometimes* doth conquer kings," the implication being that this is clearly not going to be one of these instances. In sum, throughout this text Elizabeth writes from the position of a ruler, from the position of one who is appealed *to*, not the appellant. She is the one making decisions, never at the mercy of anyone or anything else. Consequently, by writing as if he were addressing an inferior rather than an equal, James thus made a tactless diplomatic blunder.

In addition, whatever James's intentions, the erotic rhetoric in the letter and the sonnet invokes connotations that probably resonated very badly for Elizabeth. In both texts, James adopts the persona of the amorous lover. In the letter, he compares his apprehension at the lack of response to not hearing from one's lover: "I doubt not ye have read how Cupid's dart is fiery called because of the sudden ensnaring and restless burning"; the poem culminates in a similar image: "The winged boy [Cupid] dissentions hot and rife / Twixt his lets fall like sudden summer showers. / Even so this coldness did betwixt us fall / To kindle our love as sure I hope it shall."[21] In virtually all their previous (and following) correspondence, however, James and Elizabeth consistently invoke close family relationships to describe each other. In no. XVI, for example, James begins by calling Elizabeth "madame and deirest sister" and concludes by calling himself "Your trewest and assured brother and cousin."[22] Elizabeth in turn replies by addressing him as "right deare brother" and "my deerest brother and cousin the king of Scots."[23] In an earlier letter, James even calls Elizabeth "Madame and mother," signing himself as "your most loving and devoted brother and son, James R."[24]

The letter with the sonnet begins as most of the others do—"Madame and dearest sister"—but then James does something very unusual by veering into erotic allegory and concluding with a more passionate ending than usual: "your more lovinge and affectionate brother and cousin than (I fear) yet ye believe" (as opposed to "your most louing and deuoted brother and sonn [no. XIV] or "Youre most louing and affectionat brother and cousin" [no. XXXII]) along with (re)enclosing a sonnet comparing himself and Elizabeth as lovers. While James doubtless intended Elizabeth to read this unprecedented use of erotic language as a witty invocation of common tropes and as a demonstration of his ability to "talk the talk" of the Elizabethan court, the concatenation of amorous and familial terms may well have sounded suspiciously like something that haunted Elizabeth from her earliest days: incest.

Elizabeth owed her existence to the putatively incestuous relationship between her father, Henry VIII, and Catherine of Aragon. Without that "scruple," Henry VIII would not have married Elizabeth's mother, Anne Boleyn. But then, Anne herself fell, and Henry charged her with incest with her own brother, Lord Rochford (some even said that Anne was Henry's illegitimate daughter, making Elizabeth's mother guilty of double incest). And Thomas Cranmer, the Archbishop of Canterbury, argued for Elizabeth's illegitimacy on the grounds of Henry's affair with Anne's sister, Mary Carey, since the definition of incest also included marriage to a former mistress's sister.[25] While Elizabeth regularly "portrayed herself in multiple kinships roles" when dealing with other monarchs,[26] James actually *was* related to Elizabeth by blood.[27] The references to "brother," "sister," and "cousin," in other words, are not purely rhetorical. Consequently, when James shifts gears and suddenly starts comparing himself and Elizabeth to lovers, he raises an issue that Elizabeth would have found most unwelcome, since it constituted one of the prime grounds for the challenges to her legitimacy.

Furthermore, Marc Shell argues that "it is at the level of incest both spiritualized and secularized that Elizabeth as monarch later established herself as the national virgin queen who was at once the mother and the wife of the English people."[28] Therefore, when he writes "The winged boy dissentions hot and rife / Twixt his lets fall like sudden summer showers" or describes his agony at waiting for a response to "the sudden ensnaring and restless burning" of Cupid's fiery dart, James

implicitly (and probably unwittingly) *de*spiritualizes incest. It is one thing for a courtier, like Hatton, to use such terms when writing to Elizabeth. He was not actually related to her. But when James uses them, he sets in motion an entirely different set of connotations. Elizabeth evidently believed that the best response was to pretend nothing happened and James got the message. He never used such language with Elizabeth again.

II

Sir Philip Sidney died on 21 September, 1586, and about five months after that, in February, 1587, Alexander Neville edited a volume of Latin verse commemorating Sidney, *Academiae Cantabrigiensis Lachrymae Tumulo Noblilissimi Equitis, D. Philippi Sidneii Sacratae.*[29] The publication of Neville's volume gave James another opportunity to use verse as an instrument of royal diplomacy (although more successfully, and certainly more appropriately). Neville's volume includes English and Latin versions of James's epitaph for Sidney as well as contributions from Lord Patrick Gray, Sir John Maitland, Colonel James Halkerston, Lord Alexander Seton and the Earl of Angus, none of whom are known today as poets, but all of whom were deeply involved with James's highly slippery diplomacy towards England. Significantly, James's mother, Mary, lost her head on February 8th, about two or three weeks before Neville's volume appeared, and I propose that her death constituted the precipitating factor in James's decision to deliver contributions from himself and his courtiers. The printer, John Windet, clearly added the Scots contributions after the compositor set the volume in type: unlike the rest of the volume, the pages with the Scots elegies are not numbered, the signatures for their poems start at "K" even though the final pages of Neville's preceding letter are signatures H3r-v, and the first poem after the Scots elegies, by G. H. (Gabriel Harvey?), is on—using the actual pagination—page 1, sig. A1v. Also, Windet or the compositor put the volume's title and an ornamental design on top of G. H.'s poem,[30] and the page before, signature A1r, repeats the title page. Taken together, these details of book production suggest that the Scottish elegies arrived *after* Windet had completed the volume, which in turn suggests that the Scots wrote and published their poems less out of concern for the late Sir Philip and much more in reaction to Mary's recent execution.[31]

James's contribution, it must be admitted, is neither particularly distinguished nor deep:

> Thou mighty Mars the Lord of souldiers brave,
> And thou Minerve, that dois in wit excell,
> And thou Apollo, that dois knowledge have,
> Of every art that from Parnassus fell
> With all you Sisters that thaireon do dwell,
> Lament for him, who duelie serv'd you all
> Whome in you widely all your arts did mell,

Bewaile (I say) his inexpected fall,
I neede not in remembrance for to call
His race, his youth, the hope had of him ay
Since that in him doth cruell death appall
Both manhood, wit and learning every way,
    But yet he doth in bed of honor rest,
    And evermore of him shall live the best.

But like the sonnet to Elizabeth, the fact of its royal author eclipses all aesthetic considerations. We have already seen James's concern for rendering explicit his authorship, and the typography suggests that James (or one of his ambassadors) and the printer collaborated on making sure that the reader knew that this sonnet constituted a monarchic performance. The poem comes first (thus indicating the social and political preeminence of its creator), and it appears in English (all the other elegies are in Latin or Greek). Windet further distinguishes James's elegy from the others by using italic type and slightly larger font than that used for the rest of the volume. Furthermore, Windet gives the following title:

> IN *PHILIPPI SIDNAEI*
> interitum, Illustrisimi Scotorum
>   Regis carmen

Whereas Windet ascribes all the other poems to a person (either through initials or full names), this one originates from an institution, less by "James Stuart" and more by the "Illustrisimi Scotorum / Regis," the most illustrious King of the Scots. As such, the poem seems nothing more than a royal tribute to Sir Philip Sidney. The political and diplomatic resonances are, however, more complex.

Dominic Baker-Smith suggests that James's elegy for Sidney can be explained partly by their common interest in a "specifically Christian poetics."[32] Yet I know of no extant evidence suggesting that Sidney and James ever discussed poetry (despite their common interest in Du Bartas), nor do I know of any evidence proving that they ever met in person. Furthermore, Baker-Smith does not take into account the ideological gulf separating James and Sir Philip, in particular their different views concerning the role of the monarch. By at least 1580, James thought that a king should be absolute, ruling by divine right, and he expressed these views to Walsingham at their first meeting in 1583 (for which Walsingham roundly rebuked him),[33] while Sidney sided more with Buchanan and the French resistance theorists. Nor was James, as we shall see, as hot a Protestant as Sidney might have liked. The mystery of why James would go to such trouble to write an elegy and to commission elegies for someone with whom he had deep ideological differences lightens when we remember the dictum that nations do not have friends, but interests.[34]

Baker-Smith, however, rightly notes that however much James actually mourned Sidney, the poem also serves the Scots king's desire to "commend his own name to those, in England and abroad, who looked for a fit successor to Elizabeth, one equipped to serve the Protestant interest."[35] In other words, James uses the occasion of Sidney's death to strengthen his claim to the English throne. Yet the matter is murkier than Baker-Smith allows, for if this poem shows James trying to ingratiate himself with Sidney's father-in-law, or more importantly, Elizabeth's trusted Privy Councilor, Walsingham, while implicitly advertising himself as Elizabeth's heir, he was also exploring his options with England's Catholic enemies. In sum, this poem should not be taken as a simple declaration of principle or ambition, as Baker-Smith suggests, but as one more example of the slipperiness of James's diplomatic maneuvering and his penchant for using verse to further his political goals.

While Sidney and James might very well have liked each other, the fact remains that their relations were more diplomatic than personal. Sidney's involvement with James dates back to 1585, when, as Roger Howell puts it, his name starts to "figure prominently in Scots affairs."[36] Specifically, Sidney was deeply involved with Walsingham's negotiations over the amount of Elizabeth's pension for James. For Sidney, his activities on James's behalf formed part of his Protestant activism, as a large grant "would not only strengthen the Protestant cause north of the border but it would also help to thwart the machinations of the continental powers."[37] And although neither Howell nor Baker-Smith mention it, Sidney knew enough about James's interests to send him a gift of bloodhounds (not poems), for which James instructed his English ambassador to be sure to thank him.[38] While the negotiations for an Anglo-Scots alliance were ultimately successful (still, James did not get as large a pension as he would have liked, nor, more importantly, an unequivocal statement about the succession), we need to remember that Elizabeth consistently resisted those who were unqualifiedly in favor of James.

The reason why is not hard to find, for if James appeared to Sidney as pro-English and (no doubt) pro-Protestant, the king was also treating with the Catholic powers. In 1585 (the same year that Sidney sent James the dogs), the king not only refused to keep the Catholic Earl of Arran in prison and out of favor, but—as Walsingham writes with considerable disgust—the Jesuits and the Guise were in Scotland with their own offers for James's "loyalty":

> For myself I give over all hope of Scotland otherwise than by force. I see no reason to think that Bellenden and Maitland's credit (now that Arran and Gray are reconciled) shall be able to prevail to keep the King in good terms with her Majesty. There are lately arrived in that realm one Hay, general of the Jesuits of the Scottish nation and one Durye that hath written against the ministers in Scotland . . . They are sent from the

Duke of Guise with very large offers unto the King. . . . I see so great treachery in that nation as I have no desire at all to have any extraordinary dealing with them.[39]

In another letter, Walsingham concluded that "The best is to deal warily with them all, for they are all born under one climate." Elizabeth evidently agreed with her counselor, for, Walsingham reports, "I can by no means persuade her Majesty to write to Gray, neither will she, in respect of the jealousy had of the King's cunning and unsound dealing, yield unto him the pension promised."[40] We therefore cannot regard James's elegy as unequivocal evidence of James's devotion to Protestant humanism or of his undying devotion to the Leicester-Walsingham-Sidney faction's hostility towards Spain, as Baker-Smith argues,[41] since James clearly adhered to one principle alone: his self-interest (we will return to James's dealings with Catholic powers below).

Of course, the "letting slip" of the Protestant pro-English Ruthven Lords (who had initially fled to England for protection in the wake of James's attack on the Kirk's power) completely changed matters, and he finally signed the Anglo-Scots alliance that Sidney and Walsingham, among others, labored to bring about on 5 July 1586. But when Walsingham brought to light the Babington plot which would lead to the execution of Mary, Queen of Scots, James once more consistently played a double game.

While reports famously vary as to James's reaction to his mother's death,[42] James clearly tried to keep all his options open, not knowing "whether Protestant or Roman Catholic" would eventually win.[43] James may very well have intended, as Baker-Smith argues, his elegy for Sidney as an implicit endorsement of the Anglo-Scots treaty, a reassurance that both he and his chief advisors remained committed to England, and this interpretation accords with James's secret understanding with Leicester that he would not break the alliance if his mother were executed, since that would mean losing the throne of England.[44] Furthermore, James continued his friendship with Henry of Navarre and delighted in the company of his favorite poet, the very Protestant Du Bartas. Yet, at virtually the same time, James refused to receive Elizabeth's ambassador for several months, and he sent letters to Henry III, Catherine de' Medici, and the Guises asking for support.[45] James's chancellor, Maitland, who also wrote in memory of Sidney, several months later made a speech in parliament vowing "vengeance for Mary's blood."[46] In consequence, while the Sidney elegy contributes to the making of the Sidney legend, it figures as much as another front in James's duplicitous diplomacy, an attempt to reassure—through the medium of verse—his English allies while he secretly negotiated with the enemies of his English allies.

III

The fact that James did not include either the epitaph on Sir Philip Sidney or the sonnet to Elizabeth in his books suggests that he considered these works topical ephemera rather than serious bids for poetic immortality. The *Lepanto,* however, is an entirely different story. James wrote this poem in 1585 and he not only included it in his 1591 volume, *His Majesties Poetical Exercises,* but appended a translation into French by Du Bartas. James then republished the *Lepanto* in 1603 and sponsored a Latin translation that appeared in 1604. Clearly, James considered this poem his masterpiece, yet the high estimation he accorded this work only partly accounts for its frequent reprinting. While the latter two appearances are both aspects of his monarchic self-presentation to his new kingdom, since they (obviously) coincided with his accession to the English throne, there is even more. The *Lepanto* partakes of three distinct (if overlapping) sets of contexts, and as we will see, this text performs very different political work in 1585, 1591 and 1603. Furthermore, James alters his authorial self-presentation in accord with these different contexts.[47]

According to the hierarchy of genres popular in the early modern period, the epic—or "Heroicall song," as James terms it—ranks the highest. As Sir Philip Sidney puts it in the *Apology,* "all concurreth to the maintaining the heroical, which is not only a kind, but the best and most accomplished kind of poetry."[48] Consequently, writing an epic is a perfectly appropriate task for a poet-king (indeed, it might be the only genre worthy of a king). Yet in 1585, when James turned to this subject, there was nothing obvious about why James would find attractive either the subject matter or the prospect of writing martial, heroic poetry.

To be sure, the story of the Battle of Lepanto (1571) seems ideally suited for epic treatment: Don Juan, leading a fleet of 208 galleys sailing under the flag of a "Holy League" organized by Pope Pius V, the Spanish monarchy and the Venetian republic, destroyed the Turkish fleet in one day of fighting, and the victory of the Christian forces over the Islamic "Other" was very quickly transformed into the subject of chronicles in Spanish, Italian and Latin.[49] Yet the victory did not mean very much strategically, as within one year the Turks had rebuilt their navy and were making "new incursions on the Spanish protectorate of Tunis, overtaking the town for good in 1574."[50] While, as Ferdinand Braudel writes, "This victory seemed to open the door to the wildest hopes,"[51] and while in the seventeenth-century writers would depict this battle as a heroic event, people closer to the battle itself recognized that the hopes led nowhere[52]. Furthermore, given James's lifelong aversion to both figurative and literal military exploits (his son, Prince Henry, distinguished himself from his father by adopting an explicitly chivalric and bellicose persona[53]), the king's decision to write the poem in the first place and then republish it requires more explanation than ascribing it to a desire for writing an exciting story or demonstrating expertise in a variety of genres.

The ideological work behind James's composition of the *Lepanto* becomes clearer when one takes into consideration his very tenuous grasp on political power in 1585. The year before, James had parliament pass bills asserting "the royal authority in the state, both in theory and in practice," no mean feat given the resistance, both in theory and in practice, of both the aristocracy and the clergy.[54] The clergy were furious at James for ending the Presbyterian system in Scotland and a number had fled to England. The return of the banished Ruthven lords along with an army of 10,000 men added to James's troubles, and we have already noted the tense relations between the young king, Elizabeth, and Walsingham. "Estranged from Elizabeth, menaced by the exiled lords and ministers, and aware of discontent in Scotland,"[55] James chose this moment to write an epic, and as Fischlin argues, the *Lepanto* could be construed as "an empowering literary response to the contingencies of sovereign rule by a monarch struggling to achieve a modicum of internal political stability. . . ."[56] In other words, James composed and distributed the *Lepanto* as part of his (at times desperate) project of asserting monarchic authority within and without Scotland by representing himself through the highest, most "noble" genre. While it would be absurd to assert that James actually thought that he would become Elizabeth's heir and subdue his recalcitrant clergy and aristocracy by writing epic poetry, James likely intended his poem to strengthen his prestige by interjecting himself "into the literary pantheon that contributes to [monarchic and poetic] authority."[57]

In addition to demonstrating James's attempt to add some luster to his crown by appropriating the cultural authority of the epic poet, the *Lepanto* also exemplifies James's sometimes clumsy, sometimes adept strategy throughout his Scottish reign of balancing Catholic interests against the Protestants. First, James calls Don John (in the poem, "Don Joan") a "Generall great" (207), and depicts him as an ideal leader, who knows "the names of speciall men" and, somewhat like a nautical Henry V, rows about his troops, urging them on. James also highlights Don John's nationality, consistently referring to him as "the Spanish Prince" (481, 798), and once uses orthography to emphasize the point: "The SPANIOL Prince" (497). Given the presence of Spain in Scots affairs at this point, it would be hard not to read these references as a deliberate compliment, just as the Sidney elegy could be construed as a declaration of loyalty to the Protestant side. Complimenting the Spanish, however, potentially alienates the Protestants, but James takes them into consideration as well.

The poem itself splits neatly down the middle in its valuation of anti-Turkish forces' religion. On the one hand, in the main body of the epic, James pointedly refuses to condemn either Don John's religion or his nationality. In the Job-like scene at the start of the poem, Christ says to Satan:[58]

> I know thou from that City comes,
>   CONSTANINOPLE great,
> Where thou hast by the malice made
>   The faithless Turkes to freat [fret].
> Thou hast inflamde their maddest mindes
>   With raging fire of wraith [wrath],
> *Against them all* that doe professe
>   My name with fervent fayth.

(49-56; my emphasis)

Christ seems to care only about the profession of his name; none of the doctrinal quarrels dividing Christianity matter very much to him. Similarly, James consistently calls the anti-Turkish forces and the inhabitants of Venice Christians rather than Catholics, thus once more submerging or erasing doctrinal and theological differences in favor of a larger unity. Even God, while not endorsing all forms of observance, nonetheless declines to dwell on these distinctions in his answer to Christ:

> *All christians* serves [sic] my Sonne though not
>   Aright in everie thing.
> No more shall now these *Christians* be
>   With Infidels opprest

(79-82; my emphasis)

The Turkish conquest of Cyprus "moo'ved each Christian King / To make their Churches pray for their / Relief in everie thing" (150-52); urged on by Gabriel's rumor campaign, the town's population and the Venetian senate implore aid from "The Christian Princes" (190) in the conflict "twixt the Turkes / and Christians" (195-96); and the entire fleet, made up of Spanish and Italian ships, are a "Christian Navy" (292).

Yet the angelic chorus at the poem's end displays no such ecumenism. Their odd argument (rather, James's odd argument) is that if God gives victory to such *deficient* Christians, indeed, to people who barely deserve the title at all, imagine what he could do for Protestants:

> But praise him more if more can be,
>   That so he loves his name,
> As he doth mercie shew to all
>   That doe professe the same:
> And not alanerlie [only] to them
>   Professing it aright,

But even to them that mixe therewith
   Their own inventions slight:
As specially this samin time
   Most plainly may appeare,
In giving them such victory
   That not aright him feare:
For since he shewes such grace to them
   That thinks [sic] themselves are just,
What will he more to them that in
   His mercies onelie trust?

(957-72)

One could dismiss these shifts in emphasis as another example of James's lack of rhetorical skill, but they are entirely consistent with his refusal to choose unequivocally between Catholicism and Protestantism, or—perhaps more to the point—between the Catholic powers of Spain and France and the Protestant power of England.

In 1580-81, Esmé Stuart, the Earl of Lennox, dominated James's thinking and affections, and while he might have remained ignorant of the details concerning Lennox's intrigues with the Catholic powers, he nonetheless absorbed their lessons well. As Willson puts it, "he stood on the periphery of them, understanding their general drift, and was introduced to the subtle courses of a double diplomacy."[59] And James soon acquired a nasty reputation for two-facedness. Elizabeth, for instance, exclaimed with no end of annoyance: "That false Scotch urchin! What can be expected from the double dealing of such an urchin as this?"[60] James's strategy of playing Catholics off Protestants and vice versa intensified starting in 1584 and continued through 1585, exactly the period during which he composed the *Lepanto.* We have already noted James's highly tenuous grasp on power due to various domestic problems, and opportunely in 1584 James received a letter from the Catholic Duke of Guise offering friendship and protection. James regarded this letter as a means of shoring up his crumbling authority, and he responded so positively that the Spanish King, Philip, noted "He is quite ready to confess them himself"; Philip thought, in other words, that James would convert to Catholicism, a concept that James encouraged by writing to the pope: "I trust to be able to satisfy your Holiness on all other points, especially if I am aided in my great need by your Holiness."[61] At the same time, James was negotiating with Elizabeth over the fate of his mother, and in May 1585, just before he started the *Lepanto,* Elizabeth opened up negotiations for a league with Scotland.

Ultimately, James realized that his interests lay with England and Protestantism, not with Spain, but James also realized that he could gain even more by keeping both in play. Consequently, as Willson writes, "Even while he sought aid from Catholic powers he strove tenaciously to improve his relations with England."[62] Or one can reframe this strategy from the opposite perspective, i.e., that he strove tenaciously to improve his relations with the Catholic powers while seeking a treaty with England. The matter is more evenly balanced than Willson's rhetoric allows, for, as Willson himself points out, James's negotiations with foreign Catholic powers along with his refusal to curb his domestic Catholic lords served to enhance "his bargaining power with Elizabeth, formed a counterpoise to the Kirk, and offered hope of survival in case of Spanish victory."[63] At the time of its composition, therefore, the *Lepanto* intervenes in James's domestic and foreign diplomacy by exemplifying his attempts to keep all his cards in play. The main body of the text serves to assure the Catholic powers of his esteem for both their military heroes and their religion, and the Angelic Chorus serves to assure the Kirk and the English Protestants who happen to read this poem that James is really on *their* side. James, in other words, does not so much create a poetic attempt at forging a *via media* between the two opposing poles of Christianity as invent a strategy for maintaining maximum diplomatic advantage while avoiding a firm commitment to either side.

By 1591, however, when James published the *Lepanto* as part of his *Poeticall Exercises,* both the domestic and foreign contexts had shifted considerably. James had signed the treaty with England, the crisis over his mother's execution had passed, and James now clearly favored England and Protestantism. The formation of a moderate party within the Kirk made accommodating them easier,[64] and James continued to advertise his preference for Protestantism through his disputation with the Jesuit, James Gordon, his marriage to the Protestant Anne of Denmark and his eventual containment of the Catholic northern earls with Huntly's defeat in 1589. While James continued to infuriate the Protestant powers with his refusal to repress completely the Catholic lords or to sever unequivocally his ties with Spain,[65] he recognized that his interests lay with Protestantism and England, not Spain and Catholicism, and acted accordingly.

But the shift in contexts created a problem. As we have seen, the *Lepanto* carefully endorses both sides because this strategy made diplomatic sense at the time of the poem's composition. James asserts, as so many authors in this period do, that the poem has circulated in manuscript without his knowledge: "For although till now, it have not bene imprinted, yet being set out the publick view of many, by a great sort of stoln Copies, purchast (in truth) without my knowledge or consent . . ." (198).[66] Even so, James concerns himself less with unauthorized transmission and more with unauthorized *interpretation*: "It falles out often, that the effects of mens actions comes [sic] cleane contrarie to the intent of the Author . . . it hath for lack of a Praeface, bene in somethings misconstrued by sundry" (198). In all likelihood, sundry *have* read the poem correctly, but now—in

1591—the original, evenly balanced meaning no longer serves James's interest, and so the "Author" adds a preface in an attempt to "guide" the reader to a more politically correct interpretation. Don John, whom the text unambiguously declares a Christian hero, James now calls "a forraine Papist bastard," and he announces that "I name not DON-JOAN neither literally nor any waies by description" (198), even though James most certainly does name Don John both literally and by way of description. Furthermore, James explicitly denigrates Don John's military accomplishments and Catholicism—"Next followes my invocation to the true God only, and not to all the He and She Saints, for whose vaine honors, DON-JOAN fought in all his wars" (200). The preface, in other words, accommodates the change in political and diplomatic circumstances by trying to tip the poem's careful balance toward Protestantism, even if this means contradicting what the poem actually says.

We have already seen, in his 1586 letter to Elizabeth, James's sensitivity to the question of ascription, and James adopts a similar strategy in this text by highlighting his position as monarch. The (putative) misconstruction of the poem bothers James, but the offence against his royal dignity really annoys him:

> And for that I knowe, the special thing misliked in it, is, that I should seeme, *far contrary to my degree* and Religion, like a Mercenary Poët, to penne a worke, *ex professo,* in praise of a forraine Papist bastard. . . . *For as it becomes not the honour of my estate,* like an hireling, to pen the praise of any man: *becomes it far lesse the highnesse of my rancke and calling,* to spare for the feare of favor of whomseover living, to speake or write the trueth of anie.
>
> (198-200; my emphasis).

James invokes his degree, his estate, the highness, as he says, of his rank and calling to impose his interpretation on his poem. The references to the author's degree, estate, the "highness" of his rank and calling unmistakably mark the speaking "I" of the preface as a *royal* "I," and James offers his interpretation/corrections not just as evidence of authorial intention (i.e., I—the king!—wrote the poem, so I know what it means better than you), but of the absolute monarch's will. As Goldberg suggests, in the preface "the powers of poet and king are parallel . . . They exercise the discourse of power and the power of discourse."[67] The position James adopts, in other words, is that of king, not simply author, speaking to the reader, with the implication that the reader better pay attention.

Yet, ironically, in doing so, James draws not just on royal authority, but on the growing authority of poetic authorship itself, and we can trace this development through an examination of the title pages, organization and page layout of his books. During this period, as Saunders noted, gentlemen simply did not publish poetry.[68] Manuscript transmission was perfectly acceptable, even a mark of aristocratic identity. But because of the associations of print publication with the marketplace,[69] and because of the omnipresence of what I call antipoetic sentiment and what Steven W. May terms "the stigma of verse," publishing a book of one's poems "could damage rather than enhance social status."[70] As John Selden marvelously puts it:

> 'Tis ridiculous for a Lord to print Verses; 'tis well enough to make them to please himself, but to make them public, is foolish. If a Man in a private Chamber twirls his Band-strings, or plays with a Rush to please himself, 'tis well enough; but if he should go into *Fleet-street,* and sit upon a Stall, and twirl a Band-string, or play with a Rush, then all the Boys in the Street would laugh at him.[71]

The issue is not the supposed "stigma of print." As May has shown, many Tudor and Stuart aristocrats had no problem with publishing volumes on topics as various as religious commentaries and the importance of mothers breastfeeding their own children.[72] Moreover, while monarchs had published books before (Henry VIII in particular),[73] and while they even wrote poetry from time to time, the fact remains that no monarch before James had their verses printed in a book for circulation as a commodity in the market-place, and the anonymity of the title page demonstrates the tentativeness with which James approached this precedent-breaking move. Even though the book of poems has a royal author, the printer presents it as an anonymous publication; the first page gives us the title—*The Essayes of A Prentise, In the Divine Art of Poesie* (1584; not insignificantly, the type gets progressively smaller and smaller, "Poesie" being nearly unnoticeable, and certainly subordinated to the more respectable term, "Essayes"[74]), as if the genre were an embarrassing admission. We are told that Vaultrollier printed the book "cum privilegio Regali," but nowhere does the title page reveal that the regal one had also made ("fecit") the book.[75] The introductory sonnets reveal that key fact slowly and enigmatically, and even then the book's authorship is apparent only by the third sonnet (by "M. W."), which concludes with this couplet: "O Phoebus then rejoyce with glauncing glore, / Since that a King doth all thy court decore" (sig. *iii).

With the publication, however, of *His Majesties Poeticall Exercises,* in 1591, James more readily announces his responsibility for his poetic text. The title page boldly declares that "His Majesty" wrote this book, with "Majesties" published in larger type than anything else and in boldface. Even so, the title page of the *Lepanto* marks something of a retreat, since it privileges (like so many of the title pages of playbooks do)[76] the work over the author. Reversing the layout of the initial title page, now the first two syllables of Lepanto are printed in large, boldface letters. The reader now knows the name and rank of the text's author ("James the sixt, King of Scotland"), but the work takes precedence over the royal author. What accounts for this change from James's first book?

On the one hand, it could be argued that the shift in the layout of these title pages proves Goldberg's thesis, i.e., that we have an absolute monarch asserting his authority in the domain of authorship, thereby legitimizing authorship and removing, through the fact of his august presence, the "stigma of verse." But by 1591, the category of "poet-author" had already started to accrue considerable authority on its own as a middle-class, commercial entity. Marotti suggests that the publication of Sir Philip Sidney's literary works in the early 1590s "fundamentally changed the culture's attitudes toward the printing of the secular lyrics of individual writers, lessening the social disapproval of such texts and helping to incorporate what had essentially been regarded as literary ephemera into the body of durable canonical texts."[77] Yet Marotti also provides evidence of this shift starting earlier. In the first edition of George Gascoigne's *A Hundred Sundrie Flowers* in 1573, like James's **The Essayes of a Prentise,** the title page omits Gascoigne's name. But in the second edition (1575), the printer gives this work an architectural frontispiece and retitles the work as *The Posies of George Gascoigne.* Given that Gascoigne himself likely had no say in this, evidently the *printer* considered it commercially advantageous to make the work's authorship explicit and give it a privileged position. The buying public, in other words, had started to become as interested in who wrote the work as in the work itself. This development, however, emanates from the market-place, not the aristocracy, where the notion that it is "ridiculous for a Lord to print Verses" would continue for some time yet. When, therefore, James allows his Scots printer, Robert Waldegrave, to advertise the book's royal authorship, he is not so much legitimizing authorship with his royal presence as seeking to appropriate poetic authorship's growing non-aristocratic prestige for himself. In other words, the king does not confer authority on authorship; rather, authorship confers authority on the king.

Edmund Spenser's construction of himself in the 1590 and 1596 editions of *The Faerie Queene* especially highlights this shift. In the first edition's dedication page, as Louis A. Montrose points out, "the relations between ruler and subject are graphically manifested," the Queen's name in bold, capital letters while Spenser's appears "in the lower right-hand corner of the page, in much smaller and italicized type, with only the initial letters capitalized and his given name abbreviated to 'Ed.'"[78] In the 1596 edition, the printer no longer distinguishes between the ruling subject and the ruled author, as he uses the same size and type of font for both, thus signaling the rise in poetic authorship's cultural capital.

"For Spenser," Montrose writes, "the material process of reproducing and distributing his poetry in printed books was culturally empowering."[79]

James clearly agreed, and I suggest that he wanted to arrogate for himself some of poetic authorship's cultural empowerment upon his ascension to the English throne in 1603. Consequently, in addition to the other festivities, he also reprints the **Lepanto,** this time using the London printers Simon Stafford and Henry Hooke (a Latin edition appeared one year later). Several small changes in book layout from the poem's original publication demonstrate how the printers wanted the reader to interpret the 1603 **Lepanto** as a monarchic performance.[80] First, as the title page shows, Stafford and Hook print "Majesties" in larger type than anything else, and unlike the title page of the 1591 edition, not even a syllable break draws attention away from the poem's royal authorship. Second, whereas "The Lepanto" appears as the running header on the verso pages of the 1591 edition, in 1603 the printer changed this phrase to "The *Kings* Lepanto" (my emphasis, the running header of the recto pages, "Or, Heroicall Song" remained unchanged). In sum, James reprinted this poem in 1603 in order to appropriate for himself once more the cultural capital of poetic authorship, epic poetic authorship in particular, and so to further legitimate himself to a country not known for its high estimation of Scotland's cultural heritage.[81]

. . . . .

Like Elizabeth and like many courtiers during this period, King James VI/I wrote poetry for both pleasure and political advantage. Yet the difference is that James, like his royal predecessors, always writes *as a monarch,* never as a mere poet, and never from the subservient position of a courtier. Thus he reminds Elizabeth of his sonnet's royal authorship, knowing that the poem's meaning derives from the speaker's status, and thus he turns both his elegy for Sidney and the various manuscript and print versions of the **Lepanto** into vehicles for monarchic diplomacy and display. For James, no discourse exists separate from sovereignty. Ironically though, once James established himself on the English throne, his interest in book publication seems to vanish (he continues occasionally to write and distribute politically charged poems), and so, while the title page of his 1616 collected works constitutes the most elaborate construction to date of James as royal author (the full title is **The Workes of the Most High and Mighty Prince, James,** and on both the frontispiece and the title page, "The Works" and "James" are printed in the same size font—larger than the rest—and in boldface),[82] he conspicuously omits poetry from this text.[83] But while James published no verse after 1603, his sovereign discourse nonetheless initially depended upon his manipulation of verse, and as Antonio reminds both the good Gonzalo and his courtly audience in *The Tempest,*[84] a play James may have seen twice, the end should not forget its beginning.[85]

Notes

1. On James's prose, see, for example Wormald and Sommerville. While there are several recent editions of James's political writings, the only complete edition of James's poetry remains Craigie's. As for James's verse, as Sharpe notes, it "has received no historical and little critical evaluation" (1993, 127). Other studies include Goldberg, Sharpe, 1994, and Perry, 15-24. This critical neglect, however, is swiftly changing. See Appelbaum and the forthcoming articles by Bell and Fischlin.

2. Elizabeth I and James VI/I, no. XIX, 30-31.

3. Ibid., no. XX, 32.

4. Ibid., 33.

5. Ibid., no. X1, 34. Even so, Elizabeth adds that she "haue sent you a lettar that I am sure containes all you desired in spetiall wordes, I trust it shal content you" (34). To my knowledge, this letter has been lost, although Willson assumes that it contained "a revised statement concerning the succession" (72).

6. James VI/I, 71-72.

7. The annotations of obscure words are my own.

8. Quoted in Willson, 72.

9. Marotti, 398. See also May, 224-7 and *passim* as well as Montrose, 1980, 153-82.

10. Quoted in Marotti, 1982, 399.

11. Montrose, 1977, 26.

12. I am grateful to Anne Lake Prescott for her help with this reference.

13. See Perry's analysis of the tensions between James's status as monarch and Petrarchan poetics in James's early love poems (21-23).

14. In no. XVII, Elizabeth explicitly endorses James's theory of absolute kingship: "Since God hathe made kinges, let them not unmake ther authorite, and let brokes and smal rivers acknowledge ther springes, and flowe no furdar than ther bankes. I praise God that you uphold euer a regal rule." Elizabeth I and James VI/I, 27.

15. Montrose, 1988, 31.

16. On Elizabeth's verse, see Summit and Jordan.

17. Montrose, 1980, 154.

18. Cited in Summit, 413.

19. Elizabeth I, 307-09. Starting in 1570, Elizabeth's "The Doubt of Future Foes" circulated in several manuscript variants, and the poem was published in two printed versions, George Puttenham's *The Arte of English Poesie* (1589, although probably written twenty years earlier) and Henry Harington's *Nugae Antiquae* (1769). The latter also included a prefatory letter, probably by James Harington, outlining the curious circumstances by which the poem started to circulate: "Herewith I commit a precious jewel, not for your ear, but your eye; and doubt not but you will rejoyce to wear it even in your heart: It is of her Highness own editing, and doth witnhess, how much her wisdom and great learning doth outweigh even the perils of state, and how little all wordly dangers do work no change in her mynde. My Lady Wiloughby did covertly get it on her Majesties tablet, and had much hazard in so doing; for the Queen did find out the thief, and chid for spreading evil bruit of her writing such toyes, when other matters did so occupy her employment at this time; and was fearful of being though too lightly of for so doing. But marvel not, good Madam, her Highness doth frame herself to all occasions, to all times, and all things, both in business, and pastime, as may witness this her sonnet. . . ." (Henry Harington, *Nugae Antiquae,* (London, 1769), vol. 1: 58-59). While presumably all versions result from the manuscript copied by Lady Willoughby, the different copies offer numerous significant variations in diction, grammar, and line length (e.g., in the Digby manuscript, we have "force" for "foes"). I reprint eight versions in Herman, forthcoming.

20. I am indebted to Ilona Bell for providing the original impetus for this reading of the Raleigh-Elizabeth exchange.

21. Akrigg avers that lines 11 and 12 "are unintelligible as they stand. Apparently the King, when copying his poem, carelessly left out some word such as 'joys' after 'his'" (72). Craigie, however, using a later copy of the poem (he dates it from 1604) from a different source (Hatfield Mss., *Historical MSS. Commission, Part XVI* [1933], 393), gives exactly the same reading (James VI/I, 1955, 2:171), suggesting that "his" means "the lovers belong to Cupid" rather than referring Cupid's "joys" or whatever.

22. *Letters,* 24-25.

23. Ibid., no. XVII, 27-28.

24. Akrigg, Letter 15 (3 August? 1585), 64.

25. Shell, 1988, 109-10.

26. Shell, 1993, 69.

27. Henry VII's daughter, Margaret, was James's grandmother.

28. Shell, 1988, 113. Shell expands this argument in the introduction to *Elizabeth's Glass*, 3-73.

29. All citations will be to the facsimile reproduction of this text in *Elegies for Sir Philip Sidney (1587)*.

30. There are in fact two sets of "K" signatures, a fact which caused me no end of confusion when I tried to find James's poem.

31. Baker-Smith, 94.

32. See also Campbell, 45-49.

33. Read, 2: 212-13. According to Willson, Walsingham "told James that his power was insignificant, that he was too young to judge affairs of State, that he should rejoice in such as friend as Elizabeth, and [most interestingly] that young kings who sought to be absolute were apt to lose their thrones" (51).

34. Significantly, James's opinion of Sidney's poetic accomplishments shifted considerably after his accession. In 1618-19, well after James had any need to praise Sidney for diplomatic advantage, he told Ben Jonson that "Sir P. Sidney was no poet" (quoted in Craigie, 2: 234).

35. Baker-Smith, 93-94.

36. Howell, 106.

37. Ibid., 106.

38. Letter to Lewis Bellenden, dated 12 April 1585, in Akrigg, 62.

39. Quoted in Read, 246.

40. Ibid., 248.

41. Cf. Baker-Smith, 95.

42. See the summary of the various reports of James's reactions, which range from being entirely unmoved to implicitly swearing revenge for his mother's death in Stafford, 17.

43. Ibid., 17.

44. Ibid., 13, who relies on Cameron and Rait.

45. Ibid., 18.

46. Ibid., 21.

47. My approach to the thematic significances of book production is deeply indebted to Kastan and Marcus.

48. Sidney, 49.

49. Craigie, "Introduction," 1: lix-lx; Appelbaum, 9.

50. Appelbaum, 22; Wernham, ed., 252-53; 353-4.

51. Braudel, 1103; Appelbaum, 23.

52. Michel de Montaigne, for instance, uses this battle as an example of why we should not use earthly events as indicators of divine will: "It was a notable Sea-battle, which was lately gained against the Turkes, under the conduct of Don John of Austria. But it hath pleased God to make us at other times both see and feele other such, to our no small losse and detriment" (172). Donald Frame translates these lines as: "It was a fine naval battle that was won these past months against the Turks, under the leadership of Don John of Austria; but it has certainly pleased God at other times to let us see others like it, at our expense" (160).

53. See Strong, 115, and Herman, 1997, 2.

54. Lee, 64.

55. Willson, 51.

56. Fischlin, 5.

57. Fischlin, 8.

58. All references to the *Lepanto* are to Craigie's edition, 1: 198-258, and I have silently adopted the modern usage of u/v and i/j.

59. Willson, 39.

60. Ibid., 39, who also cites these other examples of English exasperation to James's "diplomacy": "'The King's fair speeches and promises,' wrote an English noble, 'will fall out to be plain dissimulation, wherein he is in his tender years better practised than others forty years older than he is.' He 'is holden among the Scots for the greatest dissembler that ever was heard of for his years'" (39). Indeed, reading over their correspondence and Walsingham's various reports of his negotiations with James, it is hard not to have the sense that during the early years of James's reign Elizabeth considered him an intensely annoying little twerp who exasperated her beyond measure. Even so, James did get what he wanted, perhaps using apparent weakness to his advantage.

61. Ibid., 51.

62. Ibid., 52.

63. Ibid., 81.

64. Ibid., 71.

65. Even though James threw the Spanish agent, Colonel Semple, in prison after the defeat of the Armada ("with great Protestant zeal," as Willson says), he nonetheless allowed him to escape (Willson, 84).

66. Even though some of James's poetry made its way into two English miscellanies, *Englands Parnassus* and John Bodenham's *Bel-Vedére, Or the Garden of the Muses* (1600), (Perry, 24; May, 1980, 16-17), there is no evidence that the *Lepanto* underwent unauthorized manuscript transmission, which suggests that James is making up this scenario of uncontrolled transmission. Furthermore, James's poetry rarely appears in contemporary miscellanies, and an entry in Stephen Powle's commonplace book suggests that James rather tightly controlled the copying of his lyric verses. Concerning "In Sunny beames the skye doth shewe her sweete," Powle writes that the poem was "Geaven me by Master Britton who had been (as he sayed) in Scotland with the Kinges Majesty: But I rather thinke they weare made by him in the person of the Kinge" (quoted in Marotti, 1995, 14).

67. Goldberg, 18.

68. Saunders, 139-64. May, 1980, 17. See also Helgerson, *passim.*

69. On book publishing's movement from an elite to a mass market, resulting in the industry's loosing "its glamour" and becoming "an almost humdrum affair," see Jardine, 135-80. While Jardine's point is to examine how "the staggering escalation in book production in the course of the sixteenth century was consistently driven by commercial pressures" (179-80), she also implicitly helps explain why aristocrats, who define themselves by their lack of involvement in commercial affairs, would shy away from publishing much themselves.

70. On the Protestant roots of antipoetic sentiment and how attacks on poetry constitute a shaping presence in early modern poetic production, see Herman, 1996, *passim*; Wall, 26. Wall does not dispute the existence of Saunders' "stigma," but she brilliantly elucidates the gender issues involved with "being a man in print."

71. Quoted in Marotti, 1995, 228.

72. May, 1980, 15, 17.

73. However, the title page of Henry's book attacking Luther hardly privileges its royal authorship. The first two words of the title, *Libello Huic,* are printed in bold letters, and are twice as big as the rest, *Regio Haec Insunt.* Underneath we have a table of contents, but Henry is not mentioned until the fifth item, "Libellus regius adversis Martinum" (the title page is reproduced in Williams, 86. In this case, the matter supersedes authorship in importance).

74. One wonders if James intended a reference to Montaigne's *Essais,* first published in 1580-81.

75. Cf. May, 1980, 16.

76. See Kastan, 216-18.

77. Marotti, 1995, 229-30.

78. Montrose, 1996, 87.

79. Ibid., 87.

80. Even so, the reception of the 1603 *Lepanto* pales in comparison to the huge success of the 1603 *Basilikon Doron,* which went through eight editions in 1603 alone (Wormald, 51).

81. In England, according to the Earl of Northumberland, "the name of Scots is harsh in the ears of the vulgar," and the more sophisticated "feared 'swarms of tawny Scots' who, locust-like, would devour office and wealth." The degree of contempt was so great that "the decapitated skull of a Scottish king was used as a flowerpot in the English royal conservatory" (Kishlansky, 78).

82. As part of James's pacifism, he brackets the title with the figures "Religio" and "Pax," Mars being a highly notable absence.

83. Craigie notes, however, that a manuscript in the British Museum (MS.Add.24195), entitled *All the kings short poesis that ar not printed,* may represent "the intention, never carried out," to publish a companion volume to the 1616 collected prose of James's poetry ("Introduction," 2: xxiii). On the other hand, given that the manuscript was revised by Prince Charles and James's Groom of the Chamber, Thomas Carey and corrected by the king himself, it is equally plausible that they wanted this collection to remain private.

84. According to Hallett Smith, Shakespeare's company performed the play at court in 1611 and in 1612-13 (1606).

85. I am very grateful to San Diego State University's College of Arts and Letters for awarding me a Faculty Development Program, half-time leave grant which allowed me to research this essay as well as a CAL Micro-Grant which paid for the illustrations.

Bibliography

Appelbaum, Robert. 2000. "War and Peace in James VI/I's *Lepanto*." *Modern Philology* 97.3: 333-63. Also in Herman, forthcoming.

Baker-Smith, Dominic. 1996. "'Great Expectations: Sidney's Death and the Poets." In *Sir Philip Sidney: 1586 and the Creation of a Legend,* ed. Jan Van Dorsten, et al., 83-103. Leiden.

Bell, Sandra. "Kingcraft and Poetry: James VI's cultural Policy." In Herman, forthcoming.

Braudel, Ferdinand. 1972. *The Mediterranean and the Mediterranean World in the Age of Philip II,* trans. Sian Reynolds. 2 vols. New York.

Cameron, Annie I., and Sir Robert S. Rait. 1927. *King James's Secret.* London.

Campbell, Lily B. 1939. "The Christian Muse." *Huntington Library Quarterly* 8: 29-70.

Elizabeth I. 2000. *Collected Works.* Ed. Leah S. Marcus, Janel Mueller, and Mary Beth Rose. Chicago.

Elizabeth I and James VI/I. 1968. *Letters of Queen Elizabeth and King James VI. of Scotland.* Ed. John Bruce (Camden Society; old series, 46). [London.]

Elegies for Sir Philip Sidney (1587). 1980. Ed. A. J. Colaianne and W. L. Godshalk. Delmar, NY.

Fischlin, Daniel. Forthcoming. "'Like a Mercenary Poët': The Politics and Poetics of James VI's *Lepanto,*" In *Essays on Older Scots Literature,* vol. 3, ed. Sally Mapstone. East Linton.

Goldberg, Jonathan. 1989. *James I and the Politics of Literature: Jonson, Shakespeare, Donne and Their Contemporaries.* Stanford, CA.

Harington, Henry. 1769. *Nugae Antiquae.* 2 vols. London.

Helgerson, Richard. 1983. *Self-Crowned Laureates: Spenser, Jonson, Milton and the Literary System.* Berkeley, CA.

Herman, Peter C. 1997. "'Is this Winning?': Prince Henry's Death and the Problem of Chivalry in *The Two Noble Kinsmen.*" *South Atlantic Review,* 62: 1-31.

————. 1996. *Squitter-wits and Muse-haters: Sidney, Spenser, Milton and Renaissance Antipoetic Sentiment.* Detroit, MI.

————, ed. Forthcoming. *Reading Monarchs, Writing: The Poetry of Henry VIII, Mary Stuart, Elizabeth I, and James VI/I.* Tempe, AZ.

Howell, Roger. 1968. *Sir Philip Sidney: The Shepheard Knight.* Boston.

James VI/I. 1984. *Letters of King James VI & I.* Ed. G. P. V. Akrigg. Berkeley, CA.

————. 1955. *The Poems of James VI. of Scotland.* Ed. James Craigie. 2 vols. Edinburgh.

Jardine, Lisa. 1996. *Worldly Goods: A New History of the Book.* New York.

Jordan, Constance. "States of Blindness: Doubt, Justice and Constancy in Elizabeth I's Avec l'aveualer si estrange." In Herman, forthcoming.

Kastan, David Scott. 1999. "Shakespeare After Theory." *Opening the Borders: Inclusivity and Early Modern Studies, Essays in Honor of James V. Mirollo,* ed. Peter C. Herman, 206-224. Newark, DE.

Kishlansky, Mark. 1996. *A Monarchy Transformed: Britain 1603-1714.* London.

Lee, Maurice. 1990. *Great Britain's Solomon: James VI and I in His Three Kingdoms.* Urbana, IL.

Marcus, Leah S. 1996. *Uneditng the Renaissance: Shakespeare, Marlowe, Milton.* New York.

Marotti, Arthur F. 1982. "Love is not Love: Elizabethan Sonnet Sequences and the Social Order." *ELH* 49: 396-428.

————. 1995. *Manuscript, Print, and The English Renaissance Lyric.* Ithaca.

May, Steven W. 1980. "Tudor Aristocrats and the Mythical 'Stigma of Print,'" *Renaissance Papers*: 1-18.

————. 1991. *The Elizabethan Courtier Poets.* Columbus, MO.

Montaigne, Michel de. 1965. *The Complete Essays of Montaigne.* Trans. Donald Frame. Stanford, CA.

————. n.d. *The Essayes of Montaigne: John Florio's Translation.* New York.

Montrose, Louis A. 1977. "Celebration and Insinuation: Sir Philip Sidney and the Motives of Elizabethan Courtship," *Renaissance Drama* n.s. 8: 3-36.

————. 1980. "'Eliza, Queene of Shepherds,' and the Pastoral of Power." *English Literary Renaissance* 10: 153-82.

————. 1988. "'Shaping Fantasies': Figurations of Gender and Power in Elizabethan Culture." *Representing the English Renaissance,* ed. Stephen J. Greenblatt, 31-64. Berkeley, CA.

————. 1996. "Spenser's Domestic Domain: Poetry, Property, and the Early Modern Subject." In *Subject and Object in Renaissance Culture,* ed. Margreta de Grazia, Maureen Quilligan, and Peter Stallybrass, 83-132. Cambridge.

Peck, Linda Levy, ed. 1991. *The Mental World of the Jacobean Court.* Cambridge.

Perry, Curtis. 1997. *The Making of Jacobean Culture: James I and the Renegotiation of Elizabethan Literary Practice.* Cambridge.

Puttenham, George. 1589. *The Arte of English Poesie.* London.

Read, Conyers. 1925. *Mr. Secretary Walsingham and the Policy of Queen Elizabeth.* 2 vols. Oxford.

Saunders, J. W. 1951. "The Stigma of Print: A Note on the Social Bases of Tudor Poetry." *Essays in Criticism* 1: 139-64.

Sharpe, Kevin. 1993. "The King's Writ: Royal Authors and Royal Authority in Early Modern England." In *Culture and Politics in Early Stuart England,* ed. Kevin Sharpe and Peter Lake. 117-38. Stanford, CA.

————. 1994. "Private Conscience and Public Duty in the Writings of King James VI and I." In *Public Duty and Private Conscience in Seventeenth Century England.* Ed. J. Morrill, Peter Slack, and Daniel Woolf, 77-100. London.

Shell, Marc. 1993. *Elizabeth's Glass.* Lincoln, NB.

————. 1988. *The End of Kinship*: Measure for Measure, *Incest, and the Ideal of Universal Siblinghood.* Stanford, CA.

Sidney, Sir Philip. 1970. *An Apology for Poetry,* ed. Forrest G. Robinson. Indianapolis.

Smith, Hallett. 1974. Introduction to *The Tempest* by William Shakespeare. In *The Riverside Shakespeare,* ed. G. Blakemore Evans, 1606-10. Boston.

Sommerville, J. P. 1991. "James I and the Divine Right of Kings: English Politics and Continental Theory." In Peck, 55-70.

Stafford, Helen G. 1940. *James VI of Scotland and the Throne of England.* New York.

Strong, Roy. 1986. *Henry, Prince of Wales and England's Lost Renaissance.* London.

Summit, Jennifer. 1996. "'The Arte of a Ladies Penn': Elizabeth I and the Poetics of Queenship. "*English Literary Renaissance* 26: 395-422. Also in Herman, forthcoming.

Wall, Wendy. 1993. *The Imprint of Gender: Authorship and Publication in the English Renaissance.* Ithaca.

Wernham, R. B., ed. 1968. *New Cambridge Modern History.* Vol. 3: *The Counter-Reformation and Price Revolution.* Cambridge.

Williams, Neville. 1971. *Henry VIII and His Court.* London.

Willson, David Harris. 1956. *King James VI and I.* London.

Wormald, Jenny. 1991. "James VI and I, *Basilikon Doron* and *The Trew Law of Free Monarchies*: The Scottish Context and the English Translation." In Peck, 36-54.

FURTHER READING

Bibliography

Collier, Susanne. "Recent Studies in James VI and I." *English Literary Renaissance* 23, no. 3 (autumn 1993): 509-19.

Bibliographic article on recent studies of James.

Biographies

Bevan, Bryan. *King James VI of Scotland & I of England.* London: Rubicon Press, 1996, 216 p.

Biographical portrait of James.

Fraser, Antonia. *King James VI of Scotland, I of England.* London: Weidenfeld and Nicolson, 1974, 224 p.

Biography of King James.

Lockyer, Roger. *James VI and I.* London: Longman, 1998, 234 p.

Biography of James, including a bibliographic essay.

Criticism

Barroll, Leeds. "Assessing 'Cultural Influence': James I as Patron of the Arts." *Shakespeare Studies* 29 (2001): 132-62.

Investigates the implications of James's dual image as generous patron of the arts and debauched king.

Bergeron, David M. *King James & Letters of Homoerotic Desire.* Iowa City: University of Iowa Press, 1999, 251 p.

Analyzes the homoerotic element of James's correspondence with his male favorites.

Clark, Stuart. "King James's *Daemonologie*: Witchcraft and Kingship." In *The Damned Art: Essays in the Literature of Witchcraft,* edited by Sydney Anglo, pp. 156-81. London: Routledge & Kegan Paul, 1977.

Assesses the significance of *Daemonologie* to James's political career and mental outlook.

Craigie, James, ed. *Minor Prose Works of King James VI and I.* Edinburgh: Scottish Text Society, 1982, 264 p.

Presents several of James's essays along with a critical introduction to each.

Doelman, James. "The Accession of King James I and English Religious Poetry." *SEL* 34, no. 1 (winter 1994): 19-40.

Considers the growth of religious verse during James's reign and contends that his accession was viewed as "the beginning of a new poetic era."

————. *King James I and the Religious Culture of England.* Cambridge: D. S. Brewer, 2000, 184 p.

Underscores James's role in the rise of religious poetry during his reign.

Fischlin, Daniel. "'Counterfeiting God': James VI (I) and the Politics of *Daemonologie* (1597)." *Journal of Narrative Technique* 26, no. 1 (winter 1996): 1-29.

Explicates the relationship between the monarch and the witch through an examination of *Daemonologie*.

Fortier, Mark. "Equity and Ideas: Coke, Ellesmere, and James I." *Renaissance Quarterly* 51, no. 4 (winter 1998): 1255-1281.

> Traces James's political theory and its impact on the relationship between common law and equity.

Goldberg, Jonathan. "James I and the Theater of Conscience." *ELH* 46, no. 3 (fall 1979): 379-98.

> Elucidates the literary implications of James's metaphor of the "player king."

———. *James I and the Politics of Literature: Jonson, Shakespeare, Donne, and Their Contemporaries.* Baltimore: Johns Hopkins University Press, 1983, 292 p.

> Considers "the relationships between authority and its representations in the Jacobean period" and focuses on how James's writings articulated his power and authority.

Herman, Peter C., ed. *Reading Monarch's Writing: The Poetry of Henry VIII, Mary Stuart, Elizabeth I, and James VI/I.* Tempe: Arizona Center for Medieval and Renaissance Studies, 2002, 330 p.

> Includes critical essays that focus on James's verse.

Rypins, Stanley. "The Printing of *Basilikon Doron*." *Papers of the Bibliographical Society of America* 64 (1970): 393-14.

> Details the printing history of *Basilikon Doron*.

Skrine, Peter. "James VI & I and German Literature." *Daphnis* 18, no. 1 (1989): 1-57.

> Explores the links between James's writings and German literature in the seventeenth century.

Sommerville, Johann P., ed. Introduction to *King James VI and I: Political Writings,* Cambridge: Cambridge University Press, 1994, 329 p.

> Surveys James's political writings.

Kabīr
1398?-1448?

Indian poet, mystic, and religious reformer.

INTRODUCTION

Although he was an illiterate weaver who did not write down any of his more than seven hundred poems and songs, Kabīr is regarded as one of the foremost classical Indian poets and probably the most quoted author in Hindi. His poetry, in the form of couplets, love poems, and mystic songs, satirized the pretensions of orthodox Hinduism and Islam. His work gave new direction to Indian philosophy and the Bhakti movement, which emphasized faith and devotion to God over ritualism and scriptural learning. Kabīr's poems and sayings were written down by his disciples and appeared in various collections after his death, among them the Sikh holy book the *Gurū Granth* which includes over five hundred of his verses. The most authoritative collection of his works is the *Bījak,* which circulated in manuscript form for centuries before being printed for the first time in 1868. Kabīr has an intense and loyal following among many Muslims, who see him as a Sufi mystic; Hindus, who regard him as a saint; and Sikhs, whose religious leader was an admirer of the rebel poet's unorthodox approach. His poetry is characterized by its energy and use of simple language, homespun imagery, and biting satire directed at religious orthodoxy. He was also one of the earliest and most vehement critics of the Hindu caste system. In his poetry Kabīr denounces the hypocrisy of religious leaders and their articles of faith, pointing the way for simple people to forge their own understanding of God and rely on their own, individual experiences to show them true spiritual fulfillment.

BIOGRAPHICAL INFORMATION

Very little is known for certain about Kabīr's life, although there are a number of legends surrounding his birth and religious career. The most popular story holds that he was born to a widow after she was blessed by the Brahmin teacher and ascetic Ramananda. The woman, a Hindu, left her child floating on a lotus leaf on the lake Lahar Talao, where he was found by poor Muslim weavers. This legend was most likely designed by Hindus to claim for Kabīr "pure" Brahmanical roots and play down his Muslim background. Muslim accounts of his life correspondingly emphasize his Islamic birth.

Kabīr was most likely born around 1398 in the city of Benares, also called Kashi, although some accounts put his birth as late as 1440. His father was probably a Muslim weaver named Niru, who lived with his wife, Nima, in dire poverty, as was typical for his caste. Some modern scholars speculate that Kabīr belonged to a family of non-celibate yogis who had recently converted to Islam, partly because his knowledge of Islam is quite superficial. In any event, because Benares was a Hindu city of pilgrimage, Kabīr grew up influenced by Hinduism, and from a young age showed an interest in Hindu teachings and practice. Early on he became a disciple of Ramananda, causing much protest by orthodox Hindus and Brahmins alike. Kabīr was never formally educated and was almost completely illiterate; according to one legend, the only word that he ever learned how to write was "Rama," the name of one of the incarnations of God. He earned his living as a weaver, although he also was part of the circle of thinkers associated with his teacher who were engaged in theological and philosophical arguments. Unlike other religiously minded men of his day, Kabīr had a wife and children, with whom he lived in a hut outside of Benares.

Benares, in Kabīr's day, was the center of Brahminic learning, and Brahmins controlled the religious and social life of the city. Kabīr rejected their teachings and made it his work to satirize and criticize their approach to religion. He attracted followers, who would meditate with him and listen to his preaching, which often took the form of poetic couplets or songs. Like Jesus before him, Kabīr was criticized and ridiculed by the priestly class for preaching to prostitutes and other low castes, but he continued to denounce organized religion in general and Brahminism in particular. He repeatedly condemned the Brahmins' ritualism, religious hypocrisy, and teachings on caste. He roamed about the country singing his songs and gaining a large following among commoners, who for the first time began to question Brahmin orthodoxy. Kabīr also attacked the hypocrisy he perceived among Islamic teachers, and thus he became an object of the wrath of both orthodox Hindus and Muslims. He did not merely attack the beliefs of religious teachers, however, but also the ideas set forth in the *Vedas* and *Quaran,* their sacred texts. He rejected the idea that books, teachers, or any other authority could tell people about God, since God is inexpressible, beyond understanding, and, yet, to be found in the ordinary objects and circumstances of life.

Another legend has it that the emperor Sikander Lodi learned that Kabīr was leading the people astray by preaching false doctrines. When he was brought before the emperor, Kabīr refused to bow to him, asserting that the only emperor he knew and before whom he would prostrate himself was God. The emperor banished Kabīr from the city. This is said to have taken place when Kabīr was almost sixty years old. Another story says that when Kabīr realized his time of death was near, when he was over a hundred, he moved from Banares to the "cursed" city of Magahar. He did this to show his disapproval of the the Brahminical superstition that any one who died in the city of Banares would go to heaven while anyone who died in Magahar would go to hell. Modern scholars think Kabīr probably died around 1448, when he was fifty years old, but again there is disagreement, and some assert that he died as late as 1518. When he died, Kabīr's body was claimed by both Muslim and Hindu religious leaders, a testament to the following he had and the reputation he had garnered. Each group claimed him to be of its faith and wanted to dispose of his body according to its particular religious rites. Legend says that as the two sides were quarreling, Kabīr's voice came from heaven and said that in life he was neither Hindu nor Muslim, and that to those who see clearly, both religions are the same. Kabīr's corpse then miraculously vanished, and in its place were left flowers. Half were taken by the Hindus, who cremated them and built a temple on the ashes, and the other half by Muslims, who buried them and built a mosque over the grave. After his death Kabīr's supporters formed a religious order. The "Kabīrpanthis," as his followers are known, exist to this day. They view Kabīr as a saint, preach simplicity and morality, and sing praises of God.

MAJOR WORKS

Since he was illiterate, Kabīr did not write down any of the poems or songs he composed and recited, nor did he create any systematic treatise of his religious beliefs. Although he himself denounced the authority of the written word, after he died, Kabīr's disciples began to transcribe his verse. The *Bījak,* the most authoritative collection of Kabīr's work and the sacred text of the Kabīrpanthis, has been in circulation in various forms since shortly after his death. His work has also been preserved by different sects of his followers. The founder of the Sikh religion, Nanak, was greatly influenced by Kabīr, and a number of his poems are recorded in the Sikh religious text, the *Gurū Granth.* No printed edition of Kabīr's poetry existed until the nineteenth century, when Western scholars, mostly missionaries, began to take an interest in his work. The Italian monk Padre Marco della Tomaba translated some of his verses into Italian in the late 1700s, but this work was not published. The first printed English version of Kabīr's poems appeared in 1877 in *The Adi Granth,* a

translation of the *Gurū Granth.* The first printed edition of the *Bījak,* in the original Hindi, appeared in 1868. Translations into other Indian languages followed, notably K. M. Sen's Bengali rendering in 1911. Sen's work was translated into English by the poet Rabindranath Tagore in 1914, and Tagore's versions of Kabīr's works are those most familiar to Western readers. In 1928 another important Hindi collection of Kabīr's work, based on manuscripts dating as early as 1504, was published. The *Kabīr-granthāvalī* (complete works) is today considered one the authoritative collections of the poet's writings.

There is some dispute among scholars about the authenticity of some of the poems attributed to Kabīr, but for the most part the verses in the *Bījak* are considered to be canonical. Scholars familiar with the poet's work note that his poems, usually couplets, or *dohas,* are always written using simple but spirited language with images and metaphors drawn from everyday life. In his poems Kabīr criticizes organized religion and its rituals, rejects notions of caste, and offers moral lessons about true righteousness and oneness with God that do not depend on laws and codes devised by humans. He preaches nonconformity and satirizes the superstitions and traditions of Islam and Hinduism as he saw them practiced by the religious leaders of his day. Because he was not writing to the elite but speaking to other illiterate persons, his images are vivid and taken from contexts that would be familiar to them; he does not use literary allusions but refers to ordinary events and objects of daily living. The many weaving metaphors he uses reflect his humble background as well. The most striking feature of Kabīr's poetry, however, is its biting tone and stinging criticism of religious orthodoxy. Over and over he deflates the superiority of those who divide humans by caste, pretend to be holy, and think they have privileged access to God.

CRITICAL RECEPTION

Although it is difficult to separate mythology from fact in the stories that have been handed down about Kabīr, it seems clear that during his lifetime he gained a loyal following and was known as a rebel poet and preacher. Ironically, Kabīr today has achieved the status of a saint among both Hindus and Muslims, and thus is revered as one whose words and ideas can lead people to the truth about God—an idea he probably would have rejected. He is revered as a Sufi mystic, a Hindu saint, and a religious reformer, although during his life he was more interested in dismantling orthodox belief structures than reforming them.

Kabīr's poetry and songs are part of the consciousness of many ordinary Indians, especially in the north of the country, but it was only in the nineteenth century, after they were collected and printed, that they began to be studied systematically by scholars. Critics writing in English have tended to concentrate their analyses on the biographical details or legends of Kabīr's life, his criticism of orthodoxy, and his nature as a Bhakti poet. Evelyn Underhill's introduction to Tagore's translation was one of the earliest critical introductions of the poet's life to the English-speaking world. Underhill stressed the poet's mysticism and his use of images from everyday life. One of the foremost English-language critics of Kabīr's verse, Charlotte Vaudeville, has attempted a textual history of Kabīr's poetry, tracing the written records of his writing from the years shortly after his death. Other critics have examined Kabīr's energetic style, his emphasis on the interior experience of religion, his standing as a poet and not merely a mystic, and Tagore's translation of his work. Some have noted the irony of his status today as a Hindu or Muslim saint among orthodox believers, when so much of his writing denounces the pretensions and narrow-mindedness and formalism of organized religion and the fiction that some humans have greater access to God than others.

PRINCIPAL WORKS

Bījak (poetry) 1868

The Adi-Granth [contributor; translated by E. Trumpp] (religious text) 1877

Bījak [translated by Prem Chand] (poetry) 1911

One Hundred Poems of Kabīr [translated by Rabindranath Tagore with Evelyn Underhill] 1914

The Sayings of Kabīr [translated by Lala Kannoo Mal] (prose) 1923

Kabīr-granthāvalī. 3 vols. [edited by S. S. Das] (poetry and prose) 1928

Kabīr the Great Mystic [translated by Isaac A. Ezekiel] (poetry) 1966

Love Songs of Kabīr [translated by G. N. Das] (poetry) 1992

A Weaver Named Kabīr: Selected Verses With a Detailed Biographical and Historical Introduction [edited and translated by Charlotte Vaudeville] 1993

Maxims of Kabīr [translated by G. N. Das] (prose) 1999

CRITICISM

Evelyn Underhill (essay date 1914)

SOURCE: Underhill, Evelyn. Introduction to *One Hundred Poems of Kabīr,* translated by Rabindranath Tagore with Evelyn Underhill, pp. v–xlii. London: Macmillan & Co. Ltd., 1961.

[*In the following excerpt, from a work originally published in 1914, Underhill recounts the legends surrounding Kabīr's life and discusses his reputation from his own time to the twentieth century, before examining his mystical poetry, which the critic says never loses its touch with common life.*]

The poet Kabīr . . . is one of the most interesting personalities in the history of Indian mysticism. Born in or near Benares, of Mohammedan parents, and probably about the year 1440, he became in early life a disciple of the celebrated Hindu ascetic Rāmānanda. Rāmānanda had brought to Northern India the religious revival which Rāmānuja, the great twelfth-century reformer of Brāhmanism, had initiated in the South. This revival was in part a reaction against the increasing formalism of the orthodox cult, in part an assertion of the demands of the heart as against the intense intellectualism of the Vedānta philosophy, the exaggerated monism which that philosophy proclaimed. It took in Rāmānuja's preaching the form of an ardent personal devotion to the God Vishnu, as representing the personal aspect of the Divine Nature: that mystical 'religion of love' which everywhere makes its appearance at a certain level of spiritual culture, and which creeds and philosophies are powerless to kill.

Though such a devotion is indigenous in Hinduism, and finds expression in many passages of the Bhagavad Gītā, there was in its mediæval revival a large element of syncretism. Rāmānanda, through whom its spirit is said to have reached Kabīr, appears to have been a man of wide religious culture, and full of missionary enthusiasm. Living at the moment in which the impassioned poetry and deep philosophy of the great Persian mystics, Attār, Sādī, Jalālu'ddīn Rūmī, and Hāfiz, were exercising a powerful influence on the religious thought of India, he dreamed of reconciling this intense and personal Mohammedan mysticism with the traditional theology of Brāhmanism. Some have regarded both these great religious leaders as influenced also by Christian thought and life: but as this is a point upon which competent authorities hold widely divergent views, its discussion is not attempted here. We may safely assert, however, that in their teachings, two—perhaps three—apparently antagonistic streams of intense spiritual culture met, as Jewish and Hellenistic thought met in the early Christian Church: and it is one of the outstanding characteristics of Kabīr's genius that he was able in his poems to fuse them into one.

A great religious reformer, the founder of a sect to which nearly a million northern Hindus still belong, it is yet supremely as a mystical poet that Kabīr lives for us. His fate has been that of many revealers of Reality.

A hater of religious exclusivism, and seeking above all things to initiate men into the liberty of the children of God, his followers have honoured his memory by re-erecting in a new place the barriers which he laboured to cast down. But his wonderful songs survive, the spontaneous expressions of his vision and his love; and it is by these, not by the didactic teachings associated with his name, that he makes his immortal appeal to the heart. In these poems a wide range of mystical emotion is brought into play: from the loftiest abstractions, the most other-worldly passion for the Infinite, to the most intimate and personal realization of God, expressed in homely metaphors and religious symbols drawn indifferently from Hindu and Mohammedan belief. It is impossible to say of their author that he was Brāhman or Sūfī, Vedāntist or Vaishnavite. He is, as he says himself, 'at once the child of Allah and of Rām.' That Supreme Spirit Whom he knew and adored, and to Whose joyous friendship he sought to induct the souls of other men, transcended whilst He included all metaphysical categories, all credal definitions; yet each contributed something to the description of that Infinite and Simple Totality Who revealed Himself, according to their measure, to the faithful lovers of all creeds.

Kabīr's story is surrounded by contradictory legends, on none of which reliance can be placed. Some of these emanate from a Hindu, some from a Mohammedan source, and claim him by turns as a Sūfī and a Brāhman saint. His name, however, is practically a conclusive proof of Moslem ancestry: and the most probable tale is that which represents him as the actual or adopted child of a Mohammedan weaver of Benares, the city in which the chief events of his life took place.

In fifteenth-century Benares the syncretistic tendencies of Bhakti religion had reached full development. Sūfīs and Brāhmans appear to have met in disputation: the most spiritual members of both creeds frequenting the teachings of Rāmānanda, whose reputation was then at its height. The boy Kabīr, in whom the religious passion was innate, saw in Rāmānanda his destined teacher; but knew how slight were the chances that a Hindu guru would accept a Mohammedan as disciple. He therefore hid upon the steps of the river Ganges, where Rāmānanda was accustomed to bathe; with the result that the master, coming down to the water, trod upon his body unexpectedly, and exclaimed in his astonishment, 'Rām! Rām!'—the name of the incarnation under which he worshipped God. Kabīr then declared that he had received the mantra of initiation from Rāmānanda's lips, and was by it admitted to discipleship. In spite of the protests of orthodox Brāhmans and Mohammedans, both equally annoyed by this contempt of theological landmarks, he persisted in his claim; thus exhibiting in action that very principle of religious synthesis which Rāmānanda had sought to establish in thought. Rāmānanda appears to have accepted him, and though

Mohammedan legends speak of the famous Sūfī Pīr, Takkī of Jhansi, as Kabīr's master in later life, the Hindu saint is the only human teacher to whom in his songs he acknowledges indebtedness.

The little that we know of Kabīr's life contradicts many current ideas concerning the Oriental mystic. Of the stages of discipline through which he passed, the manner in which his spiritual genius developed, we are completely ignorant. He seems to have remained for years the disciple of Rāmānanda, joining in the theological and philosophical arguments which his master held with all the great Mullahs and Brāhmans of his day; and to this source we may perhaps trace his acquaintance with the terms of Hindu and Sūfī philosophy. He may or may not have submitted to the traditional education of the Hindu or the Sūfī contemplative: it is clear, at any rate, that he never adopted the life of the professional ascetic, or retired from the world in order to devote himself to bodily mortifications and the exclusive pursuit of the contemplative life. Side by side with his interior life of adoration, its artistic expression in music and words—for he was a skilled musician as well as a poet—he lived the sane and diligent life of the Oriental craftsman. All the legends agree on this point: that Kabīr was a weaver, a simple and unlettered man, who earned his living at the loom. Like Paul the tentmaker, Boehme the cobbler, Bunyan the tinker, Tersteegen the ribbon-maker, he knew how to combine vision and industry; the work of his hands helped rather than hindered the impassioned meditation of his heart. Hating mere bodily austerities, he was no ascetic, but a married man, the father of a family—a circumstance which Hindu legends of the monastic type vainly attempt to conceal or explain—and it was from out of the heart of the common life that he sang his rapturous lyrics of divine love. Here his works corroborate the traditional story of his life. Again and again he extols the life of home, the value and reality of diurnal existence, with its opportunities for love and renunciation; pouring contempt upon the professional sanctity of the Yogi, who 'has a great beard and matted locks, and looks like a goat,' and on all who think it necessary to flee a world pervaded by love, joy, and beauty—the proper theatre of man's quest—in order to find that One Reality Who has 'spread His form of love throughout *all* the world.'[1]

It does not need much experience of ascetic literature to recognize the boldness and originality of this attitude in such a time and place. From the point of view of orthodox sanctity, whether Hindu or Mohammedan, Kabīr was plainly a heretic; and his frank dislike of all institutional religion, all external observance—which was as thorough and as intense as that of the Quakers themselves—completed, so far as ecclesiastical opinion was concerned, his reputation as a dangerous man. The 'simple union' with Divine Reality which he perpetually extolled, as alike the duty and the joy of every soul, was independent both of ritual and of bodily austerities; the God whom he proclaimed was 'neither in Kaaba nor in Kailāsh.' Those who sought Him needed not to go far; for He awaited discovery everywhere, more accessible to 'the washerwoman and the carpenter' than to the self-righteous holy man.[2] Therefore the whole apparatus of piety, Hindu and Moslem alike—the temple and mosque, idol and holy water, scriptures and priests—were denounced by this inconveniently clear-sighted poet as mere substitutes for reality; dead things intervening between the soul and its love—

> The images are all lifeless, they cannot speak:
>   I know, for I have cried aloud to them.
> The Purāna and the Korān are mere words:
>   lifting up the curtain, I have seen.[3]

This sort of thing cannot be tolerated by any organized Church; and it is not surprising that Kabīr, having his head-quarters in Benares, the very centre of priestly influence, was subjected to considerable persecution. The well-known legend of the beautiful courtesan sent by the Brāhmans to tempt his virtue, and converted, like the Magdalen, by her sudden encounter with the initiate of a higher love, preserves the memory of the fear and dislike with which he was regarded by the ecclesiastical powers. Once at least, after the performance of a supposed miracle of healing, he was brought before the Emperor Sikandar Lodī, and charged with claiming the possession of divine powers. But Sikandar Lodī, a ruler of considerable culture, was tolerant of the eccentricities of saintly persons belonging to his own faith. Kabīr, being of Mohammedan birth, was outside the authority of the Brāhmans, and technically classed with the Sūfīs, to whom great theological latitude was allowed. Therefore, though he was banished in the interests of peace from Benares, his life was spared. This seems to have happened in 1495, when he was nearly sixty years of age; it is the last event in his career of which we have definite knowledge. Thenceforth he appears to have moved about amongst various cities of northern India, the centre of a group of disciples; continuing in exile that life of apostle and poet of love to which, as he declares in one of his songs, he was destined 'from the beginning of time.' In 1518, an old man, broken in health, and with hands so feeble that he could no longer make the music which he loved, he died at Maghar near Gorakhpur.

A beautiful legend tells us that after his death his Mohammedan and Hindu disciples disputed the possession of his body; which the Mohammedans wished to bury, the Hindus to burn. As they argued together, Kabīr appeared before them, and told them to lift the shroud and look at that which lay beneath. They did so, and found in the place of the corpse a heap of flowers; half of which were buried by the Mohammedans at Maghar, and half carried by the Hindus to the holy city of

Benares to be burned—fitting conclusion to a life which had made fragrant the most beautiful doctrines of two great creeds.

II

The poetry of mysticism might be defined on the one hand as a temperamental reaction to the vision of Reality: on the other, as a form of prophecy. As it is the special vocation of the mystical consciousness to mediate between two orders, going out in loving adoration towards God and coming home to tell the secrets of Eternity to other men; so the artistic self-expression of this consciousness has also a double character. It is love-poetry, but love-poetry which is often written with a missionary intention.

Kabīr's songs are of this kind: outbursts at once of rapture and of charity. Written in the popular Hindī, not in the literary tongue, they were deliberately addressed—like the vernacular poetry of Jacopone da Todi and Richard Rolle—to the people rather than to the professionally religious class; and all must be struck by the constant employment in them of imagery drawn from the common life, the universal experience. It is by the simplest metaphors, by constant appeals to needs, passions, relations which all men understand—the bridegroom and bride, the guru and disciple, the pilgrim, the farmer, the migrant bird—that he drives home his intense conviction of the reality of the soul's intercourse with the Transcendent. There are in his universe no fences between the 'natural' and 'supernatural' worlds; everything is a part of the creative Play of God, and therefore—even in its humblest details—capable of revealing the Player's mind.

This willing acceptance of the here-and-now as a means of representing supernal realities is a trait common to the greatest mystics. For them, when they have achieved at last the true theopathetic state, all aspects of the universe possess equal authority as sacramental declarations of the Presence of God; and their fearless employment of homely and physical symbols—often startling and even revolting to the unaccustomed taste—is in direct proportion to the exaltation of their spiritual life. The works of the great Sūfīs, and amongst the Christians of Jacopone da Todi, Ruysbroeck, Boehme, abound in illustrations of this law. Therefore we must not be surprised to find in Kabīr's songs—his desperate attempts to communicate his ecstasy and persuade other men to share it—a constant juxtaposition of concrete and metaphysical language; swift alternations between the most intensely anthropomorphic, the most subtly philosophical, ways of apprehending man's communion with the Divine. The need for this alternation, and its entire naturalness for the mind which employs it, is rooted in his concept, or vision, of the Nature of God; and unless we make some attempt to grasp this, we shall not go far in our understanding of his poems.

Kabīr belongs to that small group of supreme mystics—amongst whom St. Augustine, Ruysbroeck, and the Sūfī poet Jalālu'ddīn Rūmī are perhaps the chief—who have achieved that which we might call the synthetic vision of God. These have resolved the perpetual opposition between the personal and impersonal, the transcendent and immanent, static and dynamic aspects of the Divine Nature; between the Absolute of philosophy and the 'sure true Friend' of devotional religion. They have done this, not by taking these apparently incompatible concepts one after the other; but by ascending to a height of spiritual intuition at which they are, as Ruysbroeck said, 'melted and merged in the Unity,' and perceived as the completing opposites of a perfect Whole. This proceeding entails for them—and both Kabīr and Ruysbroeck expressly acknowledge it—a universe of three orders: Becoming, Being, and that which is 'More than Being,' *i.e.* God.[4] God is here felt to be not the final abstraction, but the one actuality. He inspires, supports, indeed inhabits, both the durational, conditioned, finite world of Becoming and the unconditioned, non-successional, infinite world of Being; yet utterly transcends them both. He is the omnipresent Reality, the 'All-pervading' within Whom 'the worlds are being told like beads.' In His personal aspect He is the 'beloved Fakīr,' teaching and companioning each soul. Considered as Immanent Spirit, He is 'the Mind within the mind.' But all these are at best partial aspects of His nature, mutually corrective: as the Persons in the Christian doctrine of the Trinity—to which this theological diagram bears a striking resemblance—represent different and compensating experiences of the Divine Unity within which they are resumed. As Ruysbroeck discerned a plane of reality upon which 'we can speak no more of Father, Son, and Holy Spirit, but only of One Being, the very substance of the Divine Persons'; so Kabīr says that 'beyond both the limited *and* the limitless is He, the Pure Being.'[5]

Brahma, then, is the Ineffable Fact compared with which 'the distinction of the Conditioned from the Unconditioned is but a word': at once the utterly transcendent One of Absolutist philosophy, and the personal Lover of the individual soul—'common to all and special to each,' as one Christian mystic has it. The need felt by Kabīr for both these ways of describing Reality is a proof of the richness and balance of his spiritual experience; which neither cosmic nor anthropomorphic symbols, taken alone, could express. More absolute than the Absolute, more personal than the human mind, Brahma therefore exceeds whilst He includes all the concepts of philosophy, all the passionate intuitions of the heart. He is the Great Affirmation, the fount of energy, the source of life and love, the unique satisfaction of desire. His creative word is the *Om* or 'Everlasting Yea.' The negative philosophy, which strips from the Divine Nature all Its attributes and—defining Him only by that which He is not—reduces Him to an 'Emptiness,' is abhorrent to

this most vital of poets. Brahma, he says, 'may never be found in abstractions.' He is the One Love who pervades the world, discerned in His fullness only by the eyes of love; and those who know Him thus share, though they may never tell, the joyous and ineffable secret of the universe.[6]

Now Kabīr, achieving this synthesis between the personal and cosmic aspects of the Divine Nature, eludes the three great dangers which threaten mystical religion.

First, he escapes the excessive emotionalism, the tendency to an exclusively anthropomorphic devotion, which results from an unrestricted cult of Divine Personality, especially under an incarnational form; seen in India in the exaggerations of Krishna worship, in Europe in the sentimental extravagances of certain Christian saints.

Next, he is protected from the soul-destroying conclusions of pure monism, inevitable if its logical implications are pressed home: that is, the identity of substance between God and the soul, with its corollary of the total absorption of that soul in the Being of God as the goal of the spiritual life. For the thorough-going monist the soul, in so far as it is real, is substantially identical with God; and the true object of existence is the making patent of this latent identity, the realization which finds expression in the Vedāntist formula 'That art thou.' But Kabīr says that Brahma and the creature are 'ever distinct, yet ever united'; that the wise man knows the spiritual as well as the material world to 'be no more than His footstool.'[7] The soul's union with Him is a love union, a mutual inhabitation; that essentially dualistic relation which all mystical religion expresses, not a self-mergence which leaves no place for personality. This eternal distinction, the mysterious union-inseparateness of God and the soul, is a necessary doctrine of all sane mysticism; for no scheme which fails to find a place for it can represent more than a fragment of that soul's intercourse with the spiritual world. Its affirmation was one of the distinguishing features of the Vaishnavite reformation preached by Rāmānuja; the principle of which had descended through Rāmānanda to Kabīr.

Last, the warmly human and direct apprehension of God as the supreme Object of love, the soul's comrade, teacher, and bridegroom, which is so passionately and frequently expressed in Kabīr's poems, balances and controls those abstract tendencies which are inherent in the metaphysical side of his vision of Reality: and prevents it from degenerating into that sterile worship of intellectual formulae which became the curse of the Vedāntist school. For the mere intellectualist, as for the mere pietist, he has little approbation.[8] Love is throughout his 'absolute sole Lord': the unique source of the more abundant life which he enjoys, and the common factor which unites the finite and infinite worlds. All is soaked in love: that love which he described in almost Johannine language as the 'Form of God.' The whole of creation is the Play of the Eternal Lover; the living, changing, growing expression of Brahma's love and joy. As these twin passions preside over the generation of human life, so 'beyond the mists of pleasure and pain,' Kabīr finds them governing the creative acts of God. His manifestation is love; His activity is joy. Creation springs from one glad act of affirmation: the Everlasting Yea, perpetually uttered within the depths of the Divine Nature.[9] In accordance with this concept of the universe as a Love-Game which eternally goes forward, a progressive manifestation of Brahma—one of the many notions which he adopted from the common stock of Hindu religious ideas, and illuminated by his poetic genius—movement, rhythm, perpetual change, forms an integral part of Kabīr's vision of Reality. Though the Eternal and Absolute is ever present to his consciousness, yet his concept of the Divine Nature is essentially dynamic. It is by the symbols of motion that he most often tries to convey it to us: as in his constant reference to dancing, or the strangely modern picture of that Eternal Swing of the Universe which is 'held by the cords of love.'[10]

It is a marked characteristic of mystical literature that the great contemplatives, in their effort to convey to us the nature of their communion with the supersensuous, are inevitably driven to employ some form of sensuous imagery: coarse and inaccurate as they know such imagery to be, even at the best. Our normal human consciousness is so completely committed to dependence on the senses, that the fruits of intuition itself are instinctively referred to them. In that intuition it seems to the mystics that all the dim cravings and partial apprehensions of sense find perfect fulfilment. Hence their constant declaration that they *see* the uncreated light, they *hear* the celestial melody, they *taste* the sweetness of the Lord, they know an ineffable fragrance, they feel the very contact of love. 'Him verily seeing and fully feeling, Him spiritually hearing and Him delectably smelling and sweetly swallowing,' as Julian of Norwich has it. In those amongst them who develop psychosensorial automatisms these parallels between sense and spirit may present themselves to consciousness in the form of hallucinations: as the light seen by Suso, the music heard by Rolle, the celestial perfumes which filled St. Catherine of Siena's cell, the physical wounds felt by St. Francis and St. Teresa. These are excessive dramatizations of the symbolism under which the mystic tends instinctively to represent his spiritual intuition to the surface consciousness. Here, in the special sense-perception which he feels to be most expressive of Reality, his peculiar idiosyncrasies come out.

Now Kabīr, as we might expect in one whose reactions to the spiritual order were so wide and various, uses by turn all the symbols of sense. He tells us that he has 'seen without sight' the effulgence of Brahma, tasted the divine nectar, felt the ecstatic contact of Reality, smelt the fragrance of the heavenly flowers. But he was essentially a poet and musician: rhythm and harmony were to him the garments of beauty and truth. Hence in his lyrics he shows himself to be, like Richard Rolle, above all things a musical mystic. Creation, he says again and again, is full of music: it *is* music. At the heart of the Universe 'white music is blossoming': love weaves the melody, whilst renunciation beats the time. It can be heard in the home as well as in the heavens; discerned by the ears of common men as well as by the trained senses of the ascetic. Moreover, the body of every man is a lyre on which Brahma, 'the source of all music,' plays. Everywhere Kabīr discerns the 'Unstruck Music of the Infinite'—that celestial melody which the angel played to St. Francis, that ghostly symphony which filled the soul of Rolle with ecstatic joy.[11] The one figure which he adopts from the Hindu Pantheon and constantly uses, is that of Krishna the Divine Flute Player.[12] He sees the supernal music, too, in its visual embodiment, as rhythmical movement: that mysterious dance of the universe before the face of Brahma, which is at once an act of worship and an expression of the infinite rapture of the Immanent God.[13]

Yet in this wide and rapturous vision of the universe Kabīr never loses touch with diurnal existence, never forgets the common life. His feet are firmly planted upon earth; his lofty and passionate apprehensions are perpetually controlled by the activity of a sane and vigorous intellect, by the alert common sense so often found in persons of real mystical genius. The constant insistence on simplicity and directness, the hatred of all abstractions and philosophizings,[14] the ruthless criticism of external religion: these are amongst his most marked characteristics. God is the Root whence all manifestations, 'material' and 'spiritual,' alike proceed; and God is the only need of man—'happiness shall be yours when you come to the Root.'[15] Hence to those who keep their eye on the 'one thing needful,' denominations, creeds, ceremonies, the conclusions of philosophy, the disciplines of asceticism, are matters of comparative indifference. They represent merely the different angles from which the soul may approach that simple union with Brahma which is its goal; and are useful only in so far as they contribute to this consummation. So thorough-going is Kabīr's eclecticism, that he seems by turns Vedāntist and Vaishnavite, Pantheist and Transcendentalist, Brāhman and Sūfī. In the effort to tell the truth about that ineffable apprehension, so vast and yet so near, which controls his life, he seizes and twines together—as he might have woven together contrasting threads upon his loom—symbols and ideas drawn from the most violent and conflicting philosophies and faiths. All are needed, if he is ever to suggest the character of that One whom the Upanishad called 'the Sun-coloured Being who is beyond this Darkness': as all the colours of the spectrum are needed if we would demonstrate the simple richness of white light. In thus adapting traditional materials to his own use he follows a method common amongst the mystics; who seldom exhibit any special love for originality of form. They will pour their wine into almost any vessel that comes to hand: generally using by preference—and lifting to new levels of beauty and significance—the religious or philosophic formulae current in their own day. Thus we find that some of Kabīr's finest poems have as their subjects the commonplaces of Hindu philosophy and religion: the Līlā, or Sport, of God, the Ocean of Bliss, the Bird of the Soul, Māyā, the Hundred-petalled Lotus, and the 'Formless Form.' Many, again, are soaked in Sūfī imagery and feeling. Others use as their material the ordinary surroundings and incidents of Indian life: the temple bells, the ceremony of the lamps, marriage, suttee, pilgrimage, the characters of the seasons; all felt by him in their mystical aspect, as sacraments of the soul's relation with Brahma. In many of these a particularly beautiful and intimate feeling for Nature is shown.[16]

In [Kabīr's songs are] . . . found examples which illustrate . . . all the fluctuations of the mystic's emotion: the ecstasy, the despair, the still beatitude, the eager self-devotion, the flashes of wide illumination, the moments of intimate love. His wide and deep vision of the universe, the 'Eternal Sport' of creation (LXXXII), the worlds being 'told like beads' within the Being of God (XIV, XVI, XVII, LXXVI), is here seen balanced by his lovely and delicate sense of intimate communion with the Divine Friend, Lover, Teacher of the soul (X, XI, XXIII, XXXV, LI, LXXXV, LXXXVI, LXXXVIII, XCII, XCIII; above all, the beautiful poem XXXIV). As these apparently paradoxical views of Reality are resolved in Brahma, so all other opposites are reconciled in Him: bondage and liberty, love and renunciation, pleasure and pain (XVII, XXV, XL, LXXXIX). Union with Him is the one thing that matters to the soul, its destiny and its need (LI, LII, LIV, LXX, LXXIV, XCIII, XCVI); and this union, this discovery of God, is the simplest and most natural of all things, if we would but grasp it (XLI, XLVI, LVI, LXXII, LXXVI, LXXVIII, XCVII). The union, however, is brought about by love, not by knowledge or ceremonial observances (XXXVIII, LIV, LV, LIX, XCI); and the apprehension which that union confers is ineffable—'neither This nor That,' as Ruysbroeck has it (IX, XLVI, LXXVI). Real worship and communion is in Spirit and in Truth (XL, XLI, LVI, LXIII, LXV, LXX), therefore idolatry is an insult to the Divine Lover (XLII, LXIX) and the devices of professional sanctity are useless apart from charity and purity of soul (LIV, LXV, LXVI). Since all things, and especially the heart of man, are God-inhabited, God-possessed (XXVI, LVI, LXXVI, LXXXIX, XCVII), He may best be found in the here-and-now: in the normal,

human, bodily existence, the 'mud' of material life (III, IV, VI, XXI, XXXIX, XL, XLIII, XLVIII, LXXII). 'We can reach the goal without crossing the road' (LXXVI)—not the cloister but the home is the proper theatre of man's efforts: and if he cannot find God there, he need not hope for success by going farther afield. 'In the home is reality.' There love and detachment, bondage and freedom, joy and pain play by turns upon the soul; and it is from their conflict that the Unstruck Music of the Infinite proceeds. 'Kabīr says: None but Brahma can evoke its melodies.'

Notes

1. Cf. Poems Nos. XXI, XL, XLIII, LXVI, LXXVI. All references are to the poems in Tagore and Underhill's edition.

2. Poems I, II, XLI.

3. Poems XLII, LXV, LXVII.

4. Nos. VII and XLIX.

5. No. VII.

6. Nos. VII, XXVI, LXXVI, XC.

7. Nos. VII and IX.

8. Cf. especially Nos. LIX, LXVII, LXXV, XC, XCI.

9. Nos. XVII, XXVI, LXXVI, LXXXII.

10. No. XVI.

11. Nos. XVII, XVIII, XXXIX, XLI, LIV, LXXVI, LXXXIII, LXXXIX, XCVII.

12. Nos. L, LIII, LXVIII.

13. Nos. XXVI, XXXII, LXXVI.

14. Nos. LXXV, LXXVIII, LXXX, XC.

15. No. LXXX.

16. Nos. XV, XXIII, LXVII, LXXXVII, XCVIII.

Charlotte Vaudeville (essay date 1964)

SOURCE: Vaudeville, Charlotte. "Kabīr and Interior Religion." *History of Religions* 3 (1964): 191-201.

[*In the following essay, Vaudeville emphasizes that Kabīr's religious beliefs were nonconformist and stressed the interiority and mystical nature of the spiritual experience, as he satirized religious orthodoxy and showed contempt for pious sages and prophets.*]

Kabīr (1440-1518)—from his true name Kabīr-Dās, "the servant of the Great (God)"—is one of the great names of the literature and religious history of North India. He belongs to that first generation of poets of the

"Hindi" language who composed couplets and songs for the people in a language which they understood: a mixed Hindī dialect, a kind of dialectal potpourri which is not amenable to the classifications of the linguists. This jargon was first used by the innumerable itinerant preachers who at the time, as from all antiquity, traversed the country in all directions: Yogis covered with ashes, Muslim Sufis draped with picturesque patchwork robes, Jain ascetics dressed in white or only in "cardinal points," *sants* and *bhagats,* as one called the Vishnuite "saints" or "devotees"—all intoxicated with the Absolute or with divine love, all free and bold, exploiting without mercy the inexhaustible liberality of the poor Indian peasant. Kabīr, who knew them well, often evoked them, and not without irony:

> Sweet is the food of the beggar! He collects all kinds
>   of grains,
> He does not depend on anyone and, without distant
>   expeditions, he is a great king!

If Kabīr himself did not disdain to mingle with this motley crowd sometimes, he was, however, never an ascetic, nor a Yogī, nor even a professional "devotee." Born of a caste of weavers recently converted to Islām, a poor artisan lacking in culture, perhaps even illiterate as he boasted, he practiced the ancestral craft in a narrow alley in Kāshi, the modern Banaras. Banaras, the holy city of the "great god" Śiva was then, even more than today, the fortress of Brahmanic orthodoxy where the Pandits and the Pāndés, the Scribes and Pharisees of Hinduism, held sway as masters. For the Pandits and their holy Scriptures, for the Pāndés and their idols, for the immense mystification and exploitation of the ignorance and credulity of the masses, Kabīr felt only a profound contempt joined with the most resounding indignation. He did not cease to pursue them with his sarcasm, in violent, often vulgar, language, in which bursts forth the rebellion of a proud soul against the venality, the baseness, and the hypocrisy of these so-called scholars, these sorry shepherds who with tranquillity lead a great multitude of defenseless sheep to their ruin:

> I am the beast and you are the Shepherd who leads
>   me from birth to birth,
> But you have never been able to make me cross the
>   Ocean of Existence: how then are you my master?
> You are a Brahman, and I am only a weaver from
>   Banaras:
>   Understand my own wisdom:
> You go begging among kings and princes, and I think
>   only of God!

The work of Kabīr contains a resounding satire on Brahmanical orthodoxy and the superstitions of popular Hinduism. Not only does he condemn with finality worship of idols, these "lifeless stones," but he he also rejects with contempt all the proceedings and ceremonies by which popular Hindu devotion manifests itself: purificatory bathings, ritual fasts, pilgrimages, and all sorts of practices:

> What is the good of scrubbing the body on the out-
>   side,
>   If the inside is full of filth?
> Without the name of Rām, one will not escape hell,
>   Even with a hundred washings!

This contempt is not inspired by his Muslim faith and there is no iconoclastic rage in it. If the Brahman and the Pāndé are his favorite targets, he feels scarcely more respect for the official representatives of the Islāmic religion, the Mullah and the Qazi, who are less venial but no less proud and pedantic, and who are still more intolerant:

> The one reads the Veda, the other does the *qutba,*
>   This one is a Maulana, that one is a Pāndé:
> They bear different names,
>   But they are pots from the same clay!
> Says Kabīr, both have gone astray
>   And neither has found God. . . .
> The one kills a goat, the other slays a cow:
>   In quibbles they have wasted their life!

This satire is brought to bear not simply on the vices and weaknesses of men but reaches in them and behind them to the systems themselves which they defend or pretend to represent. It is the authority of the Veda and the Qur'ān, as much and even more than the Pandit or the Qazi, that Kabīr attacks, or, more precisely, he rebels against the pretension of resolving by means of "books" or by way of authority the mystery of the human condition and the problem of salvation:

> Well! Pandit, by virtue of reading and reading, you
>   have become clever:
> Explain to me, then, your Deliverance!
>   . . . . .
> Well, Qazi! What then is this Book that you discourse
>   on?
> Night and Day you are jangling and wrangling,
>   And you do not understand that all systems are the
>   same.

The Paradise to which men aspire and the thought of which makes them forget their own mystery is but a snare:

> Everyone speaks of going there,
> But I do not know where that Paradise is!
> They do not understand the mystery of their own self
> And they give a description of Paradise!

It is therefore rather inaccurate to represent Kabīr as a reformer of Hinduism, or even as an apostle of religious tolerance and of Hindu-Muslim reconciliation. Undoubtedly, he loves to repeat that "the Hindu and the Turk are brothers," since God is present in all. But this reform is a final condemnation, and this tolerance is supported by a kind of rationalism which rejects absolutely every revelation based on an authority extrinsic to the human soul. In this, Kabīr follows the long nonconformist tradition which has its source in the Buddhist "heresy," if it is not still more ancient. In fact, a form of late Buddhism, mingled with practices and concepts of tantric magic, had profoundly impregnated the lower layers of Hindu society in North India several centuries before Kabīr. Some recent researches have made it possible to establish the dependence of Kabīr on the tradition of tantric Yoga. The family of Kabīr belonged to a caste of married "Jogis" or "Jugis" recently converted to Islām. Many of these Jogis were, in fact, weavers. This family origin would explain Kabīr's irreducible opposition to Brahmanical orthodoxy as well as his ignorance of the Islāmic religion, which he seems to have known only from the outside.[1]

The schools and sects of tantric Yoga differ according to their "method" or "practice" (*sādhana*). The metaphysical basis always remains very nearly identical: it is characterized by a pure idealism and by a kind of dualistic monism. Whether Buddhists or Śivaites, the Yogis do not recognize any existence other than that of spirit, "the mental," and no field of experience other than that of the human body, which is itself considered a microcosm. All truth is experimental; it ought not to be discovered but "realized" within the body with the aid of psychological practices: concentration, control of breathing, sexual practices. For the Yogis the Absolute manifests itself under two aspects: negative and positive, static and dynamic, male and female. The supreme goal of their *sādhana* is a state of "non-duality" or of unity transcending the opposites, which ought to be "realized" by the Yogi at the end of a kind of process of regression: reabsorption of the states of consciousness in the consciousness and of the latter in the Undifferentiated. By thus overcoming the "mental" the Yogi attains the liberating trance, *samādhi,* which is conceived as "the great bliss," *mahāsukha,* of which nothing can be expressed. Through this *sādhana* the Yogi's body becomes incorruptible and the Yogi himself obtains immortality. The perfect Yogi claims to overcome death.

These conceptions form the background and, as it were, the terrain for the development of Kabīr's religious thought. However, in his time, two other currents had already penetrated the old substratum of popular Hinduism: that of Vishnuite devotion (*bhakti*), which had come from the South, and that of Islāmic mysticism, which had been spread by the Sufīs in Northwest India since the thirteenth century.

Contrary to Yoga, which is essentially technique, Bhakti is essentially faith, the adoration of a personal God, who is generally "manifested" in an anthropomorphic form, that of an *avatāra* or "descent." It is this visible form of a "qualified" (*saguṇa*) God which is the object of Vishnuite devotion. This God asks of his devotee ("bhakta") or of his servant (*dāsa*) nothing but faith, love, and trust. The attitude of the perfect bhakta, then, is one of humility and of totally giving himself into the hands of his chosen divinity, that is to say, of the divine Form that he has chosen as the object of his worship. The bhakta expects his salvation only by grace, whatever may be his own moral faults. The invocation of the name of the divinity is enough to purify the devotee. In its purest and highest form Bhakti is *prapatti,* "abandon," the total self-surrender of the devotee to his Lord. The religion of Bhakti is one of a deeply felt love for a visible god, a love which suffices for everything and is its own recompense; Bhakti is constantly represented as the "easy path," a kind of *moyen court* which makes all asceticism unnecessary and which manifests itself by a kind of continual exaltation and an abundance of tears. As a religion essentially emotive, based on rather uncertain metaphysical foundations, but strongly monotheistic in its fundamental orientation, Bhakti appears remarkably in harmony with the religious needs of the Indian masses; one can say that it remains, to this day, the truly popular religion. The polytheistic forms which it continues to gather around itself have much less significance than one generally believes. It is remarkable that the entire Hindu tradition recognizes in Kabīr himself a "great bhatka," in spite of his fierce negations and his irreducible opposition to all kinds of idolatry and to all the divine "manifestations" adored by the Vishnuite bhaktas.

The mysticism of the Muslim Sufīs is based on a complete abandonment to the will of an all-powerful and merciful God—but this God is a completely spiritual Being, infinitely removed from all sensible manifestation. The man who discerns in creation a reflection of His Beauty is seized with a love for Him, a love which is above all the intense desire to meet Him, and he rushes toward Him by the path of detachment. Far from being strewn with flowers, this "path" (*tariqa*) is bristling with sorrows; the soul of the lover is tortured by desire for the inaccessible Beauty and by separation from his Beloved. Permanent union with his God is unattainable in this life and will be achieved only after death when the purified soul will be freed from the bonds of the body. But it sometimes happens that God makes himself in some way perceptible for some moments to that mysterious internal organ which is the "heart" (*sirr*) of man. The Sufī, like the Yogi, is turned inward in the quest for a superior Reality which manifests itself in the most profound depths of his soul. It may be pointed out, however, that the forms of Sufism which were widespread in North India at the time of Kabīr had already been influenced by Vedanta monism and had also assimilated some yogic methods, so much so that the Sufīs appeared to the people as a variety of Yogis. And one knows that Kabīr himself, although he was opposed to the Islamic practices and was rather suspicious of all pious mendicity, often associated with the Sufīs, numerous at the time in the west of the country.

The three currents of thought that we have attempted to define summarily agree on one point: the pre-eminence of the interior experience over any other source of religious and metaphysical knowledge. For the Yogi there is only experimental truth; he does not search for the truth and the Truth does not come to him: he "realizes" it, that is, he "makes" it, in proportion as he progresses in his *sādhana* (the word signifying both "method" and "realization"). The bhakta accepts in principle the postulates of Brahmanical orthodoxy, and recognizes at least theoretically the eternal truth of the Veda—but he cares very little about it, for he has no need of it in order to be saved. He needs a visible form or of a manifestation of the divinity in order to "pin" his devotion there, but in the choice of it he remains free to follow the desire of his heart and the inclination of his imagination: it is his own religious experience which largely determines the conception and the image that he makes of his God. The Sufī is apparently less free, since he acknowledges the Qur'ānic revelation and the principles of Islāmic orthodoxy—but he gets around this in his own way, by gnosis: without denying the validity of the traditional path, based on the Qur'ānic prescriptions, he willingly leaves it to the mass of believers, in quest of the joys of "Paradise." He chooses another way for himself, the way of love and of intimate experience of God, a way reserved for the initiates only; in this way he will come to a progressive illumination, symbolized by the rending of the veils which separate him from the perfect Beauty.

The blessedness to which the Sufī aspires is not the Islāmic paradise, but a kind of mysterious life in God, sometimes expressed as a veritable immersion or absorption in Him.

These various currents explain the genesis of the *sādhana* of Kabīr: it does not appear to have precise metaphysical bases, but seems rather to be an original synthesis of Bhakti and of medieval Yoga, with some elements borrowed from the Sufī tradition. Throughout Kabīr's work the accent is on interiorization: man ought to turn his attention away from the exterior world, from all sensible forms, in order to withdraw into the innermost depths of his conscience (undoubtedly analogous to the *sirr* of the Sufīs) where God dwells:

> They say that Hari dwells in the east and that Allah resides in the west:
> Search in your heart, search in your heart—there is his dwelling and his residence!
> I believed that Hari was far off, though he is present in plenitude in all beings,
> I believed Him outside of me—and, near, He became to me far!

The new Yogi has left there all his practices. Love (*prem*) henceforth is his only technique and his goal is the mysterious "meeting" with God:

> Says Kabīr, in love, I have found Him,
> Simple hearts have met Raghouraï. . . .

This meeting between the Lord and the soul in its depths is a mysterious experience which Kabīr calls *paricaya*, from a word which signifies "acquaintance by sight or by contact." Kabīr liked to underline the ineffable and transcendent character of this "experience":

> In the body, the Inaccessible is obtained, in the Inaccessible, an access,
> Says Kabīr, I obtained the Experience, when the Guru showed me the Path.

> Love has lighted the cage, an eternal Yoga has awakened,
> Doubt has vanished, happiness has appeared, the beloved Bridegroom has been found!

Kabīr seems most often to interpret this union as an ultimate absorption of the lover in the Beloved:

> When I was, Hari was not—now Hari is, and I am no more,
> Every shadow is dispersed when the Lamp has been found within the soul. . . .

> The One for whom I went out to search, I found Him in my house,
> And this One has become myself, whom I called Other!

Kabīr willingly borrows the language and metaphors of Yoga in order to describe the conditions of the meeting; this is possible only by the destruction of the "mental," and a final victory over "duality":

> The lamp is dry, the oil is used up,
> The guitar is silent, the dancer has lain down,
> The fire is extinguished and no smoke rises,
> The soul is absorbed in the One and there is no more duality. . . .

Kabīr has lost himself; he has disappeared like salt in meal, like a drop in the ocean:

> You search, you search, O Friend—but Kabīr has disappeared:
> The drop is absorbed in the Ocean: how find it again?
> . . . . .
> By the touch of the magic stone, the copper is changed,
> But this copper, having become gold, is saved!
> By the company of the saints, Kabīr is changed,
> But this Kabīr, having become Rām, is saved!

The frequent allusions to the absorption of the soul in God explain how Kabīr could be considered a monist *nirguṇī,* that is, a partisan of the "non-qualified" (*nirguṇa*) Absolute in opposition to the partisans of Bhakti, worshipers of a personal and "qualified" (*saguṇa*) God. But this monistic interpretation of the thought of Kabīr is contradicted by the essential role that love plays in his *sādhana* and by the nature of the relation which he maintains with his God, Rām. The principal difficulty of interpretation comes undoubtedly from the fact that India, in its totality, conceives the person as a limitation of Being, and cannot accept the idea of a personal God who would not be anthropomorphic at the same time or in some way tainted with "illusion." Now Kabīr formally rejected all the illusory manifestations of the divine which are the object of Vishnuite devotion, and he claimed to direct his love to God, the unfathomable Being, "as He is in Himself." For those who understand only sentimental devotion, this love is a mystery: "Inexpressible is the story of Love: if one told it, who would believe it?"

The attitude of *nirguṇī* Kabīr toward his God, to whom he usually gives the Vishnuite names (Hari, Rām, Govinda), is not that of the philosopher before a metaphysical entity, but rather that of the devotee before the God "who has bound his heart to His own with gentle bonds." The weaver Kabīr entertains relations of the most touching familiarity with this unfathomable and ineffable Being. He retains an acute consciousness of his own misery and looks only to the grace of his Lord for his salvation, that is, the joy of meeting:

> How shall I be saved, O Master, how shall I be saved?
>   Here I am, full of iniquities!
> Weary, I stand at your royal threshold:
> Who then, if not You, will care for me?
>   Let me see your face, open the door!

His confidence is complete; he belongs body and soul to his Master:

> I am your slave, you may sell me, O Lord,
> My body and my soul and all I have, all is Rām's.
> If you sell me, O Rām, who will keep me?
> If you keep me, O Rām, who will sell me?

Rām is not only the companion and friend; He is more than a father—He is a mother:

> Whatever fault a son commits,
> His mother will not have a grudge against him:
> O Rām, I am your little child,
> Will you not blot out all my faults?

Similar prayers and the sentiments which they express are not rare in the Bhakti literature, even before Kabīr. But the latter spoke of a completely spiritual Being, which he endeavored to discover in the depths of his own soul. Kabīr's devotion differs from Vishnuite Bhakti not only in its object but also in its character. Indeed, it does not consist only of the sentiments of tenderness, trust, and abandon, of which the entire Bhakti

literature provides so many examples: it is also—and above all—an ardent quest, a heroic adventure in which he is completely involved, at the peril of his life. Kabīr's conception of divine love seems to be an original synthesis of the traditions of Yoga and of Sufīsm, the former exalting man's effort, the latter making of the yearnings, of the torments suffered by the exiled soul in its mortal condition, the necessary condition for every spiritual ascension. For Kabīr, Bhakti is no longer the "easy path," but the precipitous path where the lover of God risks his life:

> Bhakti is the beloved wife of Rām, it is not for cowards:
> Cut off your head and take it in your hands, if you want to call upon Rām!

Rām is the inestimable "Diamond" that one buys only with his life, and the love of Rām is "cutting as the edge of the sword," terrible as the fiery furnace; in the "tavern" of Love, the Tavernkeeper demands the blood price. Many are the verses which seem to paraphrase the Scripture: "*fors sicut mors dilectio, dura sicut infernus aemulatio, lampadae ejus lampadae ignis atque flammarum.*"

The path which leads toward God is, then, a path of suffering, vigils, and tears, and there is no other. This suffering has its source in the separation—at least apparent—of the soul from its Beloved. As the wife whose husband is on a distant journey, she languishes in sorrowful and faithful vigil. This mysterious suffering that Kabīr calls *viraha*, "separation," is one of his favorite themes:

> I cannot go to You and I cannot make You come:
> So You will take my life, burning me in the fire of separation!

> Kabīr, painful is the wound, and suffering continues in the body:
> This unique suffering of love has seized my entrails. . . .

This suffering is itself a mystery, hidden from profane eyes. Nothing of it appears externally. He who loves "bleeds silently in the depths of his soul, as the insect devours wood." Only the Lord can understand it: "He who has opened the wound understands this suffering and he who suffers it."

He who loves does not, however, seek to avoid this torment, for he knows that this torment is the mark of divine election. The soul which has not known it will not have access to the true life:

> Do not revile this suffering: it is royal,
> The body in which it is not found will ever be but a cemetery!

It seems that Kabīr, like certain Sufīs, such as the celebrated Mansur Hallāj, has come to love suffering itself, as a privileged path to God:

> Kabīr, I went out searching for Happiness and Suffering came to me,
> Then I said: "Go home, Happiness—I no longer know anything but Truth and Suffering!"

The Yogis called the "living dead" (*jīvanmukta*) the ascetic who had succeeded in "conquering the mind" and thus freeing himself from his empirical self. Kabīr borrows this idea of the "living dead" from them and applies it to the mystic engaged in the Way of Love, who has sacrificed his earthly life. But this "death" is, in reality, the condition for the true "life" in God:

> If I burn the house, it is saved, if I preserve it, it is lost,
> Behold an astonishing thing: he who is dead triumphs over Death!
> Death after death, the world dies, but no one knows how to die,
> Kabīr, no one knows how to die so that he will no longer die!

This astonishing synthesis of such disparate elements shows the originality of Kabīr. Whatever the systems from which he was able to borrow, it is evident that all of his religious thought is ordered by an intimate experience, which may be properly called "mystical." If Kabīr happens to speak the language of Yoga, indeed, of Vedanta monism, it is difficult to misapprehend the import of some affirmation apparently tainted with monism or pure idealism. If Kabīr has a dogma, it is that of the immanence of the divine. God is the "milieu" of the soul, as water is the milieu of the water lily:

> Why do you wither, O Water Lily?
> Your stem is full of water!
> In the water you were born, in the water you live,
> In the water, you have your dwelling, O Water Lily.

The mystery is not that the "water lily" lives but that it dies. Death is the only true scandal; it is the perpetual defiance thrown in the face of God. The attitude of Kabīr with regard to the mystery of human destiny is essentially pragmatic, as that of the Yogis and of the Buddha himself: he seeks less to pierce the mystery than to triumph over death, in which he recognizes the fruit of a monstrous *separation* between the soul and its divine milieu. A man without culture but profoundly intuitive, when Kabīr tries to speak of this ineffable Reality that he has discovered in the depths of his soul, he quite naturally borrows a language of pure immanence which is that of the Yogis and Sufīs of his time. However, guided by his own intimate experience, Kabīr seems to presume the existence of a God who is *both* immanent and transcendent. While he is incapable of reconciling these two aspects, he holds firmly "the two ends of the chain," preferring the obscurity of paradox to the false clarity of a superficial systematization—and he keeps repeating that God is the Wholly Other, the Unknowable, the Ineffable, whose nature remains always inaccessible to created intelligence: "You alone know the mystery of your nature: Kabīr takes his refuge in You!"

For Kabīr, God is "the One," "the True," "the Pure," "the Mysterious." He feels only contempt for all those "makers of pious discourses" who pretend to speak of Him without having seen Him! Where is the truthful witness? What credence is to be given to these sages, to these prophets? All are dead and their bodies "burn with fire." And the gods also are dead! Who has ever defied Death? This world is only a see-saw on which swing myriads of beings given up to their ruin:

> Myriads of living beings swing while Death meditates:
> Thousands of ages have passed and it has never suffered a defeat.

For Kabīr, only God himself can meet the challenge of death. It is He, the "perfect Guru," who instructs his disciple in the depths of the soul and opens in him that mysterious wound from which life will emerge; the "Word" of the divine Guru is "the single arrow" which pierces the depths of the soul:

> When I found grace with the Perfect Guru, He gave me a unique revelation,
> Then the cloud of love burst with rain, flooding my limbs.

Then Kabīr, having unmasked the immense imposture of the false prophets, remains alone before his God, the unfathomable Being, at the same time near and far, immanent and inaccessible to the soul:

> O Madhao! You are the Water for which I am consumed with thirst.
> In the midst of this Water, the fire of my desire grows!
> You are the Ocean and I am the fish
> Which dwells in the Water and languishes with its absence.

Toward Him, there is no marked trail, no "way" other than the painful and faithful awaiting of an unforseeable illumination. God speaks only in the secret of the soul—but most men are incapable of hearing Him, and they run in crowds to their ruin "in the way of the world and of the Veda." This spiritual quest, this heroic effort toward a purely interior religion ends on a note of infinite despair. Through the grace of Rām, Kabīr and some "saints" have been able to cross "the Ocean of Existence," but the world is not saved, and will not be, for death remains unconquered and continues to reign over it.

"O Death, where is your victory?" This triumphant cry of St. Paul did not reach the ears of Kabīr. For him, hope is dead and no light can ever rise upon this world. The saint is he who does not yield, who does not resign himself, and who goes out alone, gropingly, in search of the true life, illumined by that unique Lamp which burns in the depths of his heart.

Notes

1. The Tantric Yoga tradition seems to have profoundly impregnated the lower layers of society in North and Central India from the tenth century. In the north the most famous sect is that of the *Nāth-Panthīs* or *Kānphaṭa-Yogīs* ("the Yogis with pierced ears") who claim as a founder the fabulous Yogī Gorakhnāth. Besides the innumerable wandering Yogis, who were usually celibate and "unattached" (*Yogī bairāgī, avadhūtas*), there were numerous castes of married Yogis, called *Yogīs grhastīs* (also called *Jogīs, Jugīs*) and considered as beyond the pale of Hindu society, properly speaking. The majority of these Jogis seem to have been musicians, cotton-carders, and weavers. Many of these castes were superficially Islāmicized during the fourteenth and fifteenth centuries. Such seems to have been the case with the Julāhas of Banaras in the fourteenth century (cf. Ch. Vaudeville, *Au cabaret de l'Amour, Paroles de Kabīr* [Paris: UNESCO, 1959], Introduction, p. 24).

Isaac Ezekiel (essay date 1966)

SOURCE: Ezekiel, Isaac. "Literary Style." In *Kabir: The Great Mystic*, pp. 62-74. Punjab, India: Radha Soami Satsang Beas, 1966.

[*In the following essay, Ezekiel explores the daring simplicity of Kabīr's style and the directness and vigor with which he set forth his unorthodox ideas.*]

> Both Muslims and Hindus will go to hell,
> With Qazis and Brahmins leading them there.
> Both deserve nothing better.
>
> Kabir

> There is probably no Indian author whose verses are more on the lips of North India than those of Kabir, unless it be Tulsidas.
>
> Rev. Keay

No Indian Saint has displayed such strength of language, such vitality, such ruggedness and down-to-earth assertion of facts and views as the weaver Saint of Benaras. This serene and saintly personality breathes scorn and disgust, uses frowns and sneers, generates thunder and wrath—all so contrary to his inward peace and compassion towards erring humanity. They are his weapons; not part of his mental make-up.

Banter, ridicule, sarcasm, wit and humour—these are the weapons he wields! Nor does he hesitate to hit straight-from-the-shoulder, hitting hard, ceaselessly and without stop, till the face of false piety and hypocrisy is battered out of shape and exposed to the view of the general public for general laughter.

He summons the entire zoo to portray human beings of different sorts. Donkeys and dogs, foxes and wolves, snakes and vipers, lions and tigers, fishes and fowls, camels and elephants, cranes and herons, swine and scorpions—march past before us as representations of human beings, who thus properly labelled, carry the labels wherever they go—for the labels stick so fast in the reader's mind that nothing can remove or destroy them.

Kabir specialises in deflation—deflation of our mind, our ego. He deflates the high and mighty and shows them their proper place both on this earth and in the nether worlds.

Royalties and aristocracies, mighty mansions and magnificent palaces lie in dust before his withering banter. He punctures the pretensions of the pious, pierces holes in the learning of the learned, atrophies the ambitions of the wealthy, grinds to dust the pride of youth and beauty, files and chisels the wrath of the haughty, crushes the showmanship of the sadhus and fakirs, and diminishes the height of yogis and yogeshwars.

Above all, he is concerned with the ordinary man, the landless labourer and the hand-to-mouth peasant who toils from morn to night in sweltering heat and blistering cold, but does not have food enough to fill his empty stomach when alive, and cloth enough to cover his nakedness when dead.

He sees with his own eyes how long and how deeply the peasant suffers—suffers at the hands of his exploiters and at the hands of his spiritual leaders. He has nothing but compassion for the poor.

But mere compassion would not have abolished their spiritual subjection. And so he narrates interesting stories to expose what simpletons they are, and how they are fooled and humbugged by the charlatans; defrauded and cheated by the guardian angels of temples; blinded and hoodwinked by cheats and thugs; bluffed and bamboozled by highwaymen of the spiritual path.

These stories are very simple and naive, but very easy to understand and so easy to remember. The proud intellectual may not think much of them, but they remain in the mind and pierce the heart like an arrow.

They project the spiritual purpose of life; they pitch and toss the spiritual idea that keeps working in the mind; they heave aside age-old traditions and unthinking submission to the past. In that sense Kabir is a most daring modernist; and the modernist of today seems to be tattered and out-of-date before him.

Within the range of reason, Kabir is a most uncompromising rationalist. In the intellectual field, he is the most clear-brained intellectual. Among the learned, he is the most learned—though he is ignorant of the alphabets. He quotes the Shastras, the Puranas and the Vedas with an authority before which the learned shiver and the traders in holy lore call for the hangman's rope.

Kabir's songs seek nobody's approbation. They seek no sanction, ask for no approval, search for no popularity, invite no commendation, crave no compliment. They stand independent of these considerations, and they constitute the most uninhibited literature, the freest of free writing ever produced by a Saint. They are the most fearless of fearless hymns, for they launch assaults on the very foundations of institutional religion and the self-appointed customs officers of the Gates of Heaven.

Kabir wields the scalpel and the forceps with the dexterity of a skilled surgeon. He manipulates the lancet and the knife with the facility of a specialist out to lay bare the putrefication within us. "Are you old and respectable?" he asks, and replies, "But your lustful hunger has sharpened, not diminished, with age, and hardly makes you worthy of respect." "Have you abandoned the world?" he asks, and replies, "But your mind clings to the worldly dross with rapacious greed and nauseating egotism."

He divests us of our affectations, uncovers our prudery, lays bare our charlatanism, undrapes our moral skeleton to expose its death-like ugliness, and he slits open our skin-deep beauty to reveal the sores within.

The most daring of Kabir's songs are those that uncover the true nature of the gods and goddesses we worship.

"Who are these gods?" he asks, and replies that "their prime purpose is to keep us away from the Lord, and you go to them for salvation." "Who are these gods?" he asks again, and quotes the Puranas to prove their many delinquencies. He recalls the stories of their hysterical fits of temper unworthy of any cultured gentleman; their cunning devices of greed that surpass the records of fraudulent company promoters and practised racketeers; their unquenchable ego that would put to shame dictators and 'conquerors of the world'; their crimes of lust—kidnapping, adultery, fornication, rape, incest—crimes that would rock a civilised society if committed by men at the top, crimes that would invite heavy sentences of imprisonment if committed by any ordinary mortal and condemn him for life as unworthy of decent company.

"How can these gods, themselves wallowing in passions, free you from their fury?" he asks. "How can these gods, themselves submerged in suffering, redeem you from its anguish? How can these gods, themselves beset with gnawing anxiety, liberate you from its distractions? How can these gods, themselves encompassed by fear, release you from its stranglehold? How can these gods, bound hands and feet to Duality, free you from Illusion? How can these gods, themselves entangled in transmigration, deliver you from the Eternal Wheel?"

Kabir uses the language of the common man, simple, direct, terse, pithy. Metaphors and similies drawn from the life of the villager, pour out with an ease and beauty that amaze the reader. His simple figures of speech carry conviction where pages of argument would be unconvincing. The precision with which he conveys profound ideas and the simplicity with which he propounds the Eternal Truth, remain the crowning glory of Indian bhakti (devotional) literature. His plays on words and elliptical structures are such as only disciples of mystics can understand.

The **Bijaks** constitute the most authentic works of Kabir. They are written in Eastern Uttar Pradesh Hindi, for he himself writes, "My speech is of the east." It is a dialect of Hindi somewhat different from the Hindi used in Western Uttar Pradesh, Bihar or Rajasthan. The name *Bijak* needs explanation.

A practice prevailed during Kabir's days of burying gold and silver and other valuables in some secret place which was not known to anybody except the master of the house. A chart of how to locate the place was made, sealed and handed over to the inheritor of the treasure. The chart itself was made in a mysterious language which only some members of the family could unravel. This chart was known as a 'bijak'. The **Bijaks** of Kabir are, therefore, a document which discloses the way to Spiritual Treasure only to those initiated. 'Bijak' also means essence or invoice, and Kabir's **Bijaks** are an essence or invoice of spiritual teachings.

Kabir's poems contain a number of words of Arabic and Turkish origin; words which were current in those days. He also uses some words and phrases which only the common man from Benaras and surrounding areas can appreciate. He is no purist and is concerned only with driving his teachings home.

Kabir himself did not write a single line. He was utterly illiterate and says, "I have never touched ink to paper." All his songs were written down by his immediate followers, some during his life-time, and many a little later. He resorted to the poetical form of expression whenever any question on a spiritual subject was put to him. This method was more effective than an explanation in prose. The rhythm and terseness of the language made it easier to remember the teachings, so concise, so simple and so clear.

Kabir's poetical collection runs into some thousands of verses. Yet he was not a poet in the ordinary sense of the word. He did not sit down to compose his poems. They were *extempore* expositions. Nor was he bound by any poetical technique. He invented his own metre, or rather a variety of metres, each suited to the occasion. To give first importance to him as a poet and second to his teachings is to mistake the means for the end.

Kabir was a pioneer in using Hindi, instead of Sanskrit, for conveying spiritual knowledge. In doing so, he and other Saints of the time had to face fierce opposition. Just as in medieval Europe, Latin was the church language and Latin the language of spiritual books, so in India we were wedded to Sanskrit. Just as the prayers and services were conducted in Latin in Roman Catholic churches, so was Sanskrit used in India. And just as the Protestant Church had to wage a struggle to introduce the national languages of various countries for spiritual books and prayers, so also had medieval Indian Saints to face opposition in introducing the use of regional languages. But Kabir was no anti-Sanskritist. It was all a matter of taking a practical view of things. The masses did not know Sanskrit; nor did he.

The exact texts of the *Bijaks* vary from region to region. This needs to be explained. No printing presses then existed and every copy of the *Bijaks* had to be written by hand. As a result, copyists of the *Bijaks* in Western Uttar Pradesh, the Punjab, Rajasthan and Bihar have sometimes replaced original words with their own regional words, but these copies are faithful to the original in maintaining the meaning and purpose of the songs. These changes are verbal and none has resorted to distortion.

There are copies of *Bijaks* that belong to another category. As has happened in the case of all medieval Indian Saints, a number of forged songs composed long after Kabir had passed away are also to be found; but their language is different and they propound thoughts and ideas contrary to the teachings of Kabir.

Many songs are also composed by genuine disciples of Kabir in the name of their Master and are consistent with his teachings. This is done out of sheer love for the Master; but their language is somewhat different and more modern, and Kabir's terseness and figures of speech are either not found in them at all or are far less effective. These can be easily distinguished from the original poems.

The practice of disciples writing in the name of their Master is by no means rare. Everything that a good disciple does is done in the name of his Master. The po-

ems written by the successors of Guru Nanak and included in the *Granth Sahib* are written in the name of Guru Nanak. These cannot be called forgeries. They are the product of love for Guru Nanak, with whom succeeding Gurus had completely identified themselves.

The genuine poems of Kabir can be distinguished from the real forgeries by the facts that:

1. Kabir condemns idolatry, asceticism, rituals and outward forms of worship as useless for salvation.

2. Kabir emphasises the need for a Guru to pursue the higher path, and gives fixed and unalterable qualifications of a Guru.

3. Kabir opposes the caste system and never speaks of the Brahmins or any other caste as especially holy.

4. Kabir does not accept the Vedas and the Quran as the highest revelations.

5. Kabir stands for complete vegetarianism and against the use of drugs and drinks.

Any poems not consistent with these teachings can be easily classed as the works of someone other than Kabir.

In this respect Kabir is lucky. He has largely escaped from the forgeries that go contrary to his teachings. Many other Saints have been less fortunate. In the name of Tukaram, for example, poems have been composed in which the caste systems and the Brahmins, rites and rituals and outward forms of worship are lauded to the sky and sometimes placed in close juxtaposition with poems condemning all these. Obviously, they are shameless and unscrupulous forgeries committed by supporters of religious vested interests.

The Rev. F. E. Keay considers that the collection of Kabir's poems in the *Granth Sahib* are not "so authoritative as those in the *Bijaks*", but he himself in practice refutes the idea by quoting mostly from the *Granth Sahib* in his chapter on "Historical Kabir", and from other sources in the chapter on "Legendary Kabir". The collection of Kabir's poems in the *Granth Sahib* may have, in some cases, local words to suit the Punjabi readers, but there can be no doubt about their genuineness. They have been incorporated in the *Granth Sahib* by Perfect Masters themselves. The Rev. Keay himself says, "The language and spirit of the two collections (in the *Granth Sahib* and in the *Bijaks*) are the same, and there seems no reason to doubt that they both contain a large majority of poems which are the genuine works of Kabir."

The collection in Kabir's *Bijaks* is undoubtedly authentic. Most writers are agreed on the point.

To return to the literary style, the directness and vigour with which Kabir expounds unorthodox views may be illustrated with a few examples. Emphasising that even gods such as Brahma, Vishnu and Shiva are not free from the grip of Maya (Illusion) and passions, Kabir writes:

> The woman (Maya) hath conquered the three worlds;
> She hath made the eighteen Puranas
> And the places of pilgrimage love her;
> She hath pierced the heart of Brahma, Vishnu and Shiva,
> And infatuated great kings and sovereigns.

Condemning wealth and pride in physical beauty, Kabir writes:

> The limbs that are anointed
> With ground aloe-wood, sandal and fragrant soap,
> Shall be burnt with wood.
> What is there to be proud of in this body and in wealth?

In a single sweep Kabir smashes the whole lot of devotional devices of Hinduism and condemns the Vedas and the Quran as "cloaks of falsehood". No modernist has dared to classify the Vedas and the Quran thus:

> Ceremonial devotion, sacrifice and rosary,
> Piety, pilgrimage, fasting and alms,
> The nine bhaktis (devotions), the Vedas, the Book (the Quran)—
> All these are cloaks of falsehood.
>
> If union with God be obtained by going about naked,
> All the beasts of the forests should be saved.
> If perfection be obtained by shaving the head,
> Why should not sheep obtain salvation?
>
> Kabir says: Hear, O my brethren,
> Who hath obtained salvation without the Name of God?

Kabir declares that even Brahma, Vishnu and Shiva are not free from transmigration:

> Who of men did not die? O pandit, speak and make this plain to me;
> Dead is Brahma, Vishnu, Mahesha;
> Dead is Ganesh, the son of Parvati;
>
> Dead is Krishna, dead is the Maker (Kal);
> Only one did not die—the Lord.
> Kabir says, He alone dies not,
> Who is not held fast in coming and going
>
>   (transmigration).

The Vedas, the Smritis, the Puranas (three Hindu scriptures) are exposed in a single, short verse as works that know nothing of the Supreme Lord:

> Indra and Brahma know not Thy attributes;
> The four Vedas, the Smritis and the Puranas,
> Vishnu and Lakshmi know them not.
>
>   Kabir Granth

The Brahmins are denounced in language that they cannot easily forget:

> If birth from a Brahmin makes you Brahmin,
> Why did you not come another way?
> If birth from a Turk makes you a Turk,
> Why were you not circumcised in the womb?

It is quite a widespread practice in India to keep repeating "Ram, Ram" as a devotional device for salvation. Kabir reveals its ineffectiveness in a single, short verse by a simple comparison. Can one's mouth be sweetened, he asks, by repeating the word "sugar"? The true mystic "Name" of God or "Ram Nam" is something totally different from the mere repetition of "Ram, Ram". How that devotion is to be done is indicated in the second verse below:

> If by repeating Ram's name, the world is saved,
> Then by repeating the word 'sugar', the mouth is sweetened.

The path of salvation lies through the body, to be pursued by devotion to the Divine Word:

> Make thy body the churn, thy heart the churning staff;
> Into the churn put the Word instead of milk.

. . . Kabir always makes a direct approach to the subject and discards abstractions and speculation as utter nonsense. He was not, as imagined by some, a Vedantist, nor a Vaishnavite, nor a pantheist, nor yet a transcendentalist. He was not influenced by Persian or Arabian mystics. He stood independent of them all, and he certainly never sought to reconcile "the intense and personal mysticism of Islam with the traditional theology of Brahminism". There is not a word in his ***Bijaks*** to support the theory that he sought to bring Hindusim and Islam together in any ordinary, social or political sense of the word.

Nor are his ***Bijaks*** an attempt to bring about a compromise between "the simplicity of Islamic practice and the complications of Brahminical ceremonialism". He was not concerned with either.

It is also fantastic to imagine that he was influenced by Christian thought or teachings. Saints may quote any other Saints and scriptures and use them for driving their message home to their followers, but they do not have to learn their message from books. They teach what they have seen with their own spiritual eyes.

The teachings of all Saints are the same in all essentials. They are not derived from scriptures, but from direct knowledge of the higher path and the ways and means to traverse it. They can write their own scriptures.

Kabir was not "essentially a poet and a musician." Speaking in poetical form was an incidental part of his work, and it is doubtful if he ever sang his songs.

However great and original his poems—and about their grandeur and beauty there can be no dispute—and however soul-stirring the tunes to which subsequent musicians have set his songs, we must never forget that his poems were only a means. Their end always was to call upon the reader to search for a Perfect Master and thus go back home to his Heavenly Father.

Finally, it must be mentioned that the Bhakti or Devotional School of spiritual practice, of which Kabir was such an outstanding champion, was not the product of the Islamic impact on Hinduism. Perfect Masters explain over and over again that the Bhakti Marg (Devotional Path) for God-realisation came into being along with the creation of the world, and always and ever there is at least one Perfect Master on this earth to show seekers the Homeward Path. Kabir's poems are great because they are the product of a Param Sant Satguru pointing to the Homeward Path. Their literary style, however fascinating, is of secondary importance.

Prabhakar Machwe (essay date 1968)

SOURCE: Machwe, Prabhakar. "Poetry." In *Kabir,* pp. 35-43. New Delhi: Sahitya Akademi, 1968.

[*In the following essay, Machwe argues that Kabīr's originality—evident in the language, meter, paradoxes, and ideas in his works—marks him as more than merely a "mystic poet" but a poet in the broadest and deepest sense of the word.*]

> Search the word and know the word
>   Follow the word by word
> Word is sky and word is underworld
>   Word pervades the core and the cosmos
> Word is in speech and in hearing
>   Word makes the image and the form
> Word is Ved and word is the sound
>   Word is the scripture sung variously
> Word is the visible and the invisible
>   Word creates the entire universe
> Kabir says you test the word
>   Word is God, O brother!

> [*Kabir Vachanavali,* p. 189]

Whether mystic poetry should be judged by the same poetic norms as are applied to pure poetry is the subject of a long-drawn debate amongst Sanskrit rhetoricians and Western aestheticians. Partly it is the age-old distinction between the sublime and the beautiful. The Indian eclectic writers on poetics in Sanskrit resolved the conflict by calling the joy derived from poetry as akin to divine bliss (*Brahma-ananda-sahodarah*)—the two being twin brothers. On the other hand, there are not a few orthodox and conservative critics in Hindi, even today, who do not consider Kabir as a poet, but count him among the saints and devotees who also indulged

in some sort of uneven versification. Such critics perhaps put undue premium on polish in technique and perfection of style, etc. But if individuality is one of the characteristics of a major poet, Kabir is without doubt one.

He uses images and symbols that are at times obscure, though not more obscure than the private imagery of some modernist poets. Like Blake or Rilke, he has many passages which sound simple and yet are deeply charged with metaphysical meaningfulness. The truth is that Kabir was much more than a mere poet. He lived in two dimensions at the same time. For him God-consciousness and poetry were not two analysably separate states of mind. As the mystic Meister Eckhart rightly pointed out, 'For a man must himself be One, seeking unity both in himself and in the One, which means that he must see God and God only. And then he must "return", which is to say he must have knowledge of God and be conscious of his knowledge.' Kabir seemed to be possessed of the same frenzy and so he questions: 'O lotus, why did you fade? The water of the pond was at your stem. You were born in water, lived in water, all the time surrounded by water. No fire was there nearby. And yet why did you die?'

LANGUAGE

One of the important keys to this problem of extra-poetical sensibility communicated through poetry is the language used by the poets. Every poet chooses his own idiom, and addresses his own imaginary audience. The greatness of Kabir lies in the fact that he did not care for the language of the sophisticated in those days, namely Sanskrit or the court-language Persian, but composed his verses and songs in a mixed language of his own, which is now called by Hindi scholars *Sadhukkari* (language of the *sadhus*). As Dr Govind Trigunayat says in his *Kabir ki Vichardhara,* 'Kabir did not use one language. In his *bani,* one comes across a mixture of Hindi, Urdu, Persian and many dialects like Bhojpuri, Punjabi, Marwari and so on. The first authentic collection of Kabir's works is ***Kabir Granthavali,*** edited by Dr Shyamsundar Das on the basis of two manuscripts dated Samvat 1561 and 1881 (A.D. 1508 and A.D. 1828); the other is ***Sant Kabir*** by Dr Ramkumar Varma which contains Kabir's writings in the *Granth Saheb* too. In both these works we find (1) Punjabiness, (2) noun and verb forms of Bhojpuri, (3) some Khari Boli forms, (4) language according to subject-matter, (5) many words from regional languages, (6) simple and direct expression, (7) symbolism and technical allusiveness, (8) no adherence to any one standardised form.'

Acharya Ramachandra Shukla writes in his *Hindi Sahitya ka Itihas* that the saint-poets of Hindi used Khari Boli which they received as a legacy from the

Siddhas. But Dr Trigunayat differs from this opinion and maintains that Kabir did not confine himself to *Purbi* (eastern U.P. dialect of Banaras) only but made use of many other dialects so as to make himself more communicable to saints coming from other regions. Kabir uses Persianized Hindi when he talks of Hindu Pandits. In his language one comes across Bengali verb forms like 'achhilo'. There are also words from Rajasthani and Lahanda. His language has a peculiarity that it is at once simple and yet difficult to interpret. Added to it is the great difficulty which scholars have to contend with, namely, the different forms of the same text—due, maybe, to oral transmission. Many words have undergone such transformation and even corruption that it is difficult to decipher and excavate the correct original form. Kabir's language in *Ult-bansiyan* is also called, on account of its obscurity and vagueness of meaning, *Sandhabhasha* (according to Vidhusekhara Bhattacharya) or *Sandhya Bhasa,* the language of the meeting-point or the language of the evening. Dr Das Gupta has discussed it in his *Obscure Religious Cults,* and given different reasons for such riddle-like usages. Either they were deliberately done to confound the opponent, or because of the mixture of Apabhramsa and Hindi, or such was the language on the borders of Bengal and Bihar. In Sanskrit 'Sandhi' is used even for an allegorical language and, maybe, poets like Kabir used it consciously, as the Tantriks did, to hide some secret notions or esoteric practices not considered proper in ordinary society. Whatever the reasons, in Kabir one comes across many such poems which apparently seem to be contrary to all rational meaning. Maybe, Kabir did it in fun to confound the Pandit who took recourse to very intricate Sanskrit. Some examples of this kind of Sandhabhasha are given below under 'paradoxes'.

PARADOXES

These *padas* of Kabir are also called *Ult-bansiya* or *Ult-batiya* (inverted bamboos or inverted talks). One example is in ***Kabir Granthavali*** (p. 14):

> Such wonderment did the guru tell
>   I remained stunned
> The mouse fought the elephant
>   one rarely sees
> The mouse entered into a hole
>   serpent afraid ran
> Contrarily, mouse devoured the serpent
>   it was a great wonder
> The ants uprooted the mountain
>   and brought in open
> The cock fought the human
>   the fish ran after water.
> The cow was milking the calf
>   the calf was giving milk
> Such wonderment happened
>   the deer killed the tiger
> The hunter hid himself in the thicket
>   the rabbit shot arrows

> Kabir says make him a guru
>   who tells you the meaning of this poem.

Dr Hazari Prasad Dwivedi discusses these poems in a chapter entitled 'Yogic Allegories and *Ult-bansiyan*', and quotes from ***Kabir Granthavali*** another passage, given below, and gives a chart of the three different interpretations by Vishvanath, Vichardas and the traditionalists of 23 such symbolic terms in this *pad*:

> [Santan jagat neend na kyai . . .]

> Saints don't sleep while awake
> Death does not eat, epochs don't cover
>   the body is not eroded by old age
> Contrari-wise the Ganges absorbs the ocean
>   and darkness eclipses the sun
> The sick man kills nine constellations
>   the reflection in water gives light
> Without feet one runs in ten directions
>   without eyes sees the world
> The rabbit devours the lion, such wonder who can
>   solve?
> The inverted pitcher does not sink in water
>   the straight one is filled with it
> The reason why men are different
>   with guru's grace they get through
> Inside the cave one sees the whole world
>   outside nothing is seen
> The arrow upturned and killed the hunter
>   only the brave can follow
> The singer when requested cannot sing
>   the dumb sings always
> The juggler's game is seeing the onlookers
>   *Anhad* cause is increased
> The statement inspects itself
>   all this is an inexpressible tale
> The earth enters into the sky
>   this is the word of a man
> Without glasses nectar oozes
>   the river keeps away the water stored
> Kabir says he alone is immortal
>   who drinks *Ram-rasa.*

Obviously in their first reading such compositions sound very much like irrational mutterings. But all these words have some symbolic meanings: the mind is generally compared with fish, weaver, hunter, elephant, *niranjan*; the soul is referred to as son, calf, hunt, lion, mouse, bee, yogi; the *maya* is harlot, woman, she-goat, cow and cat; the world is like a forest or an ocean; the senses are the five maidens and friends and so on. Such songs also refer to certain numbers: five stands for elements or senses; three for qualities or three tenses or worlds; eight for the Hathyogi's eight centres in the body, more or less like the glandular endocrinic seats secreting hormones. In a *doha* like—

> Sixty-four lamps lighted in fourteen moons
> What moon is there in the house where Govind is not

sixty-four stands for arts and fourteen for Vidyas or achievements.

Such paradoxes have a long tradition dating from the Upanishads. The inverted tree and the two birds are well known. In Taittiriyopanishad there is a passage which says, 'the sky rests in the earth and the earth rests in the sky.' It was carried further by Vajrayana Buddhists. Perhaps Kabir got it through them.

METRES

One does not come across a variety of metres or any virtuosity in their use in Kabir. He uses the common metres like *doha* or *sakhi*, *sabad* and *Ramaini* which were *chaupais* or *chaupai-dohas*. Mainly they are two-line pithy couplets or longer *pads* set to music. Many tunes are taken from folk-songs. It is possible that community singing was responsible for the many repetitions that occur in them. None of the metres used are bound by any rigid rules of prosody. They seem to have their own rules and Kabir follows his own pattern of internal rhymes.

M. A. Ghani wrote in his *History of the Persian Language at the Moghul Court* that the six lines beginning with *Haman hai ishk mastane haman ko hoshiyari kya* might be deemed as the first Urdu ghazal ever composed. But this statement is not verified. There are earlier ghazals in the Dakhni variety of Urdu and a ghazal by a Brahmin named Chander is mentioned in *A History of Urdu Literature* by Rambabu Saksena. Though Urdu or Persian metres were not adopted by Kabir, it seems that he had heard the poetic compositions of Sufis and many allusions to love and divine intoxication in Kabir seem to be patterned on them.

Kabir was not a conscious urbane poet. He wanted to communicate his ecstasy and agony in any language which came handy to him. He did not wait for the chiselled word or care for the applause of the connoisseur. So there is a roughness and ruggedness about his writing which lends it a rare charm. His verse-pattern is very simple and yet haunting. Most of his *dohas* and *pads* end with the composer's name woven in it. It was a kind of copyright in those days, as there were innumerable imitators and plagiarists. The seal of originality was necessary and so in the medieval songs of saint-poets one always comes across such lines as 'Mira says, O Girdhar Nagar' or 'Tulsidas says . . .' or 'Surdas remembers Shyam . . .' and so on.

Kabir's *dohas* should be given a special mention as later Hindi poets have written several compilations of 700 *dohas* called *satsais* on the lines of the medieval Arya-saptashatis, though Kabir did not care for the magic number 700.

OTHER POETIC QUALITIES

Marathi poet Namdev, Punjabi poet Nanak, Telugu poet Vemana, Kannada poet Basaveshwar and Gujarati poet Akho share with Kabir a rare kind of catholicity and humanism which broke all conventions of caste, creed or cult. This was all the more difficult in that age when orthodoxy had a firm hold over the minds of the people. Kabir is being re-evaluated as the first rebel poet and the earliest modernist in Hindi criticism (see in *Purbi Times,* Kabir Special Number, June 1966, articles by Yashpal, Sampurnanand, Amritlal Nagar, Ali Sardar Jafri, Firaq Gorakhpuri, Prakashchandra Gupta, E. Chelyshev and others). One young critic has in all seriousness gone to the extent of calling Kabir the grandfather of Beat poetry in Hindi.

All these articles referred to above emphasise on the way Kabir takes the reader or listener almost by storm. The impression left after reading Kabir is that of a person who is transformed or touched to the core. This Kabir achieves by drawing from his own personal experience as a weaver or as a person persecuted by high-caste Hindus or conservative Muslims, and transforming his material into a universal and deeply moving concern. His personal protest becomes the voice of the dumb millions.

According to Firaq Gorakhpuri, Kabir charged the language of the rural masses of eastern U.P. with a new meaning. He electrified their dialect. Firaq cites various examples of this metamorphosis wrought by Kabir, who was formally unlettered and yet one of the greatest contributors to Indian literature. Kabir regarded human life as a passing phase and so was aware of the 'horror in the handful of dust', as T. S. Eliot would have said. The feeling of this 'worm within the rose' is well expressed in such *dohas* as—'We know not what the quarter of a second may bring and yet we make plans for the morrow; death comes suddenly as the hawk pounces down on the partridge.' 'The gardener comes to the garden and seeing him the buds cry out: the full-blown flowers are culled today, tomorrow our turn will come.' 'The earth said to the potter, why do you trample on me? The day will come when I shall trample on you.' A similar *rubai* is found in Omar Khayyam's Kuza-namah.

Gandhiji included the following song of Kabir in his daily prayer book—(*Jhini jhini bini chadariya . . .*)

> What is the warp and what is the woof
>   what are the threads from which the *chadar* is woven?
> *Ingla* and *Pingla* are the warp and woof
>   *Sushaman* are the threads from which the *chadar* is woven.
> Eight are the lotuses and ten are the spinning wheels
>   five are the elements and three the qualities of the *chadar*.
> The Master required ten months to weave it
>   and made it well-woven by hitting it and beating it.
> This *chadar* the gods, men and sages used
>   and used and soiled the *chadar*.
> Kabir Das has used it very carefully
>   and kept the *chadar* back as it is.

Weaving was the profession of Kabir. Gandhiji also gave much weight to spinning and weaving. In several matters there is great similarity in these two great men of India, though functioning in different periods of history and in different circumstances.

Kabir's poetry has another great quality: it does not stale. Kabir tried to put his finger on the basic yearnings of man, the eternal quest for internal peace, the 'angst' of a person functioning in a maladjusted society. Where religions turn into hidebound ritualistic codes, where philosophies turn into mere verbal jugglery and linguistic labyrinths, where there is a crisis of conscience and the leadership is lame, Kabir's poetry serves as a great inspiration. At times he seems to shock us by ripping open the shams and exposing the double-talk and double-think of the so-called respectable learned; yet there is no note of despair. Kabir's poetic world is not a vale of tears, not merely a dark night of separation, not an abyss which can never be crossed. He has the robust and rebellious spirit of a rustic. He has always a Hope Beyond. No doubt the springs of this Hope are spiritual and it may be argued that today in an age of 'no values', all that sounds unreal. But Kabir has much left in his poetry, even when one does not agree with his theism, and so to enjoy Kabir one need not be a Kabir-panthi. Herein lies the secret of his ever-continuing greatness as a poet: he transcends time and place. His poetic vision is larger and higher. He did not bother about what kind of political set-up was in Hindustan in the thirteenth or fourteenth century; he did not even care for the literary heresies or traditional tentacles of his times. He just did what Nietzsche would have said, his 'Yea-saying'. This requires great courage in any age. Kabir had that daring to say the truth and the heroism to suffer its consequences. Kabir's poetry, therefore, stands in a very different category, as it breaks through many conventional bondages. It is the poetry of a Free Spirit.

Robert Bly (essay date 1971)

SOURCE: Bly, Robert. "Some Rumors about Kabir." In *The Kabir Book: Forty-Four of the Ecstatic Poems of Kabir*, adapted by Robert Bly, pp. 61-9. Boston: Beacon Press, 1977.

[*In the following essay, originally published in 1971, Bly recounts some stories about Kabir's life, discusses his status as a Bhakti poet, and offers brief comments on what he regards as the poet's intensely spirtual and controversial verse.*]

1

No one knows much about Kabir. A few life details and a few stories are told over and over. He was evidently not a monk or ascetic, but was married, had children,

and made his living by weaving cloth at home. Some say he was the son of Moslem parents, others that he was found on the streets and brought up by a Moslem couple. There may have been in the house books of the great Sufi poets of two hundred years before, such as Rumi. So it is possible Kabir knew the eccentric energy of the Sufis, the heretical or rebellious branch of the Mohammedans, by the time he was sixteen or seventeen. It is said he then asked Ramananda, the great Hindu ascetic, to initiate him. Ramananda had experienced the ecstatic power of the male god Rama, and took the name "the glad joy of Rama" as his name. Ramananda refused, saying, "No, you're a Moslem." Kabir knew which temple Ramananda meditated in each day before dawn, and Kabir lay down on the steps outside. Ramananda walked out in the half dark, and stepped on the boy's body. Astonished, he leaped up, and cried, "Rama!" Kabir then jumped up, and said, "You spoke the name of God in my presence. You initiated me. I'm your student!" Ramananda then, it is said, initiated him. Kabir became a powerful spiritual man and poet. His poems are amazing even in his wide tradition for the way he unites in one body the two rivers of ecstatic Sufism—supremely confident, secretive, desert meditation, utterly opposed to orthodoxy and academics, given to dance and weeping—and the Hindu tradition, which is more sober on the surface, coming through the Vedas and Vishnu, Ram, and Krishna.

Here's another Kabir story. At one time about fifteen hundred meditators came down from the hills and sat together in a big hall in north India. The number of people doing hard inner work in that century was large. They asked Kabir to read to them, but had not asked Mirabai. Mirabai composed ecstatic bhakti poems; her whole life flowed in the stream of Radha-Krishna intensity. She walked from village to village with holy men singing her poems "for the Dark One," and dancing; she was much loved. Kabir entered the hall, and said, "Where is Mirabai? You know what I see in this hall? I see fifteen hundred male egos." He refused to read until Mirabai came. So someone went for her—she was miles away—and they waited in silence, maybe one day or two. Mirabai at last arrived. She read for thirty-five minutes. At the end of that time it was clear that her bhakti was so much greater than anyone else's in the room, that the gathering broke up, and all the meditators, reminded of how much they had to do, went back to their huts.

Mirabai wrote her poems in Rajasthani, and about two hundred of them have survived. A later book in this Beacon Press series will include Mirabai poems. This story of Mirabai and Kabir is lovely, and as the Sufis would say, in the spiritual world it happened. In chronology there is a problem. When my first small group of Kabir versions was printed in Calcutta, the publisher set down firmly the birth date of Kabir as 1398, and the death date as 1518. That means he lived 120 years. That's possible. Most scholars guess Mirabai's birth date as 1498. That means Kabir was a hundred years old the day she was born. So if both dates are true, then she could have been 18 when she arrived at the hall, and he would have been 118 years old. That's possible; anything is possible. Or since dating is difficult, both birth dates may be wrong. We do know that both poets lived—accounts of people who met them have survived. Mirabai does mention Kabir in one of her poems, as well as another poet, Namdev, born earlier, around 1270. Mirabai says, speaking to Krishna:

> Oh you who lift mountains, stay with me always!
> You brought a full ox to Kabir's house,
>   and mended the hut where Namdev lived.

So there was a flow between the two, and the story suggests that very well.

2

Most of the observations a critic could make about Kabir's poems you can deduce by reading them. He does mention several times that his poems belong in the bhakti tradition, and I've decided to leave their word as it is. There's very little one can say about the bhakti tradition that doesn't diminish it. Perhaps we could see it more clearly by comparing it with a contrasting road. Some of the European saints of the Middle Ages, such as Tauler, walked the opposite path, they said no to the body and meant it. On this path the link between the ego and the body is emphasized, and the ego is then dispersed through humiliation of the body. The humiliation is a long process associated with hatred of the senses. The practicer tries to imagine how disgusting his or her body will be when it's dead, hair shirts and whips are used to humiliate the skin, attachments are dispersed, the practicer tries to free his spiritual energy from sexual energy by repulsion. Blake wrote the most powerful criticism of this path: "Better murder an infant in its cradle than nurse unacted desires." "Priests in black gowns are walking their rounds, and binding with briars my joys and desires." The road was called the "via negativa," and Eliot in his religious life consciously followed it.

The bhakti path is not peculiar to India, is no one's invention, and I'm sure existed in Ras Shamra and among the Etruscans. Some of the Odin myths and Babylonian myths that seem to us quaint will be seen to refer to it. In the Indian subcontinent a vast rise of bhakti energy began in the eighth or ninth century, as if ocean water had suddenly reappeared in the center of a continent. Sometime during those centuries an alternative to the Vedic chanting began. The Vedas were in Sanskrit, and the chanting done for others by trained priests, by what we might call "religious academics." The new bhakti

worship involved heart-love, feeling, dancing—Mirabai evidently used castanets and ankle rings—love of color, of intensity, of male-female poles, avoidance of convention, a discipline which is shared by Tristan and Isolde. Bhakti worship involves the present tense, and in contemporary language, rather than the old "classical" tongue, as when Dante decided to write *La Vita Nuova* in Italian rather than in Latin. The poets of India began to write ecstatic poetry in their local languages, and so refreshed the bhakti experience "from underneath." Some poems were written specifically for the long bhakti sessions, which lasted three or four hours in the middle of the night, and were guided through their stages by chanted and sung poems.

In north India, the bhakti experience became associated with Krishna as a visualization of the right side of the body, and Radha as a visualization of the left. Jayadeva gave a great gift around 1200 with his *Gita Govinda,* and its ecstatic passages of Radha and Krishna lovemaking. "Great circle" dances appeared, and marvelous paintings, where Radha and Krishna look at each other with enormous eyes. "The joy of looking for him is so immense that you just dive in and coast around like a fish in the water. If anyone needs a head, the lover leaps up to offer his. Kabir's poems touch on the secrets of this bhakti." The male poets usually describe Radha and Krishna from outside, or evoke her feelings when separated. Mirabai never mentions Radha, just as Christ never mentions the Essenes, because he is the Essenes, just as she is Radha. Kabir sometimes speaks as a man, sometimes as a woman.

> This woman weaves threads that are subtle,
> and the intensity of her praise makes them fine.
>
> Kabir says: I am that woman.
> I am weaving the linen of night and day.
>
> When my lover comes and I feel his feet,
> the gift I will have for him is tears.

The ecstatic meditator, Shri Caitanya, traveled for a while around 1510-1530 from village to village in Bengal, teaching the villagers what bhakti experience looked and felt like, bringing dances with him, and the intensity rose higher. Namdev, Jnaneshwar, Chandidas, and Vidyapati wrote marvelous poems, all virtually unknown to us, in the years before Kabir. Mirabai, Kumbhandas, and Surdas are a few of the intense poets that followed.

3

Kabir in his joyful poems delivers harsh and unorthodox opinions. He enters controversies. For example, when Christ says, "The Kingdom of the Spirit resembles a cottonwood seed," the translators of the time found themselves dealing with three sets of opposites, familiar also to Chinese thought, of Spirit-Body, sky-earth, and Heaven-this world. The translator must choose among them. St. Paul, with other early fathers, committed the Church to translating the phrase as "the Kingdom of Heaven." The opposite state then is this life. Salvation is then driven into the next life. Kabir says a simple error of translation like this can destroy a religion. This throwing of intensity forward is a destructive habit of both Hindus and Moslems, and Kabir, attacking both, writes of that in his terrifying poem:

> If you don't break your ropes while you're alive,
> do you think ghosts
> will do it after?
>
> What is found now is found then
> If you find nothing now, you will simply end up
> with an apartment in the city of death.

The best known religious poetry in English, of Vaughn and Traherne, for example, contains rather mild and orthodox ideas. Such harsh instruction as Kabir gives we are unprepared for. In Vaughn the thought and feeling swim together under the shelter of a gentle dogma. In Kabir one leaps ahead of the other, as if jumping out of the sea, and the reader smiles in joy at so much energy. It is as if both thought and feeling fed a third thing, a rebellious originality, and with that tail the poem shoots through the water. We feel that speed sometimes in Eckhart also. Kabir says that when you work in interior work, the work is not done by the method, but by the intensity. "Look at me, and you will see a slave of that intensity." The word "intensity" widens to its full range here. We understand that such intensity is impossible without having intense feeling, intense thinking, intense intuition, and intense love of colors and odors and animals. He hears the sound of "the anklets on the feet of an insect as it walks."

In Kabir's poems then you see the astonishing event—highly religious and intensely spiritual poems written outside of, and in opposition to, the standard Hindu, Mohammedan, or Christian dogmas. Kabir says, "Suppose you scrub your ethical skin until it shines, but inside there is no music, then what?" He also attacks the simple-minded Yoga practices and guru cults, such as we see growing up all around us in the United States. It's valuable to have these practices discussed by an Indian, not a Westerner. Kabir says, "The Yogi comes along in his famous orange. But if inside he is colorless, then what?" To Kabir, the main danger is spiritual passivity. Kabir is opposed to repeating any truth from another teacher, whether of English literature or Buddhism, that you yourself have not experienced.

> The Sacred Books of the East are nothing but words.
> I looked through their covers one day sideways.
>
> Kabir talks only about what he has lived through.
> If you have not lived through something, it is not true.

Kabir mocks passivity toward holy texts, toward popular gurus, and the passive practice of Yoga, but we must understand that he himself is firmly in the guru tradition and that he followed an intricate path, with fierce meditative practices, guided by energetic visualizations of "sun" and "moon" energies. In poems not translated here—I don't have the language for it, nor the experience—he dives into the whole matter of Sakti energy, ways of uniting right and left, and going upward with "the third". . . . These labors have not been experienced yet in the West, or have been experienced, but discussed at length only in alchemy. He has, moreover, enigmatic or puzzle poems that no contemporary commentator fully understands. I love his poems, and am grateful every day for their gift.

Baidyanath Saraswati (essay date 1977)

SOURCE: Saraswati, Baidyanath. "Notes on Kabir: A Non-literate Intellectual." In *Dissent, Protest and Reform in Indian Civilization,* edited by S. C. Malik, pp. 167-84. Simla, India: Indian Institute of Advanced Study, 1977.

[*In the following essay, Saraswati explores Kabīr's poetry and describes the poet as a non-literate genius who criticized institutional religion and religious and intellectual elitism, while making spirituality accessible to common people. The critic goes on to point out the irony of the attempt by scholars and some of Kabīr's followers to make his ideas acceptable and in line with orthodox philosophy and religion.*]

The first historical event of protest in Indian civilization occurred in the sixth century BC when Jainism and Buddhism repudiated the authority of an elitist culture called Brahminism.

THE TRADITION OF NON-CONFORMITY

In denying the authority of the Vedas, Jainism is perhaps the oldest form of non-conformity in India. It revolted against the Vedic sacrifices—excited pity for the protection of dumb animals—and in doing so, for the first time in the history of religion, called social forces to its aid. It also socialized the notion that 'man's religious consciousness must be the result of his own private realization of truth.' This gave impetus to the evolution of the idea of sect, and Jainism became the first organized sect in India. Jainism was followed immediately by Buddhism; in fact, both flourished contemporaneously. Gautama, the Buddha, accepted from Jainism its denunciation of Vedic sacrifices and its compassion for dumb animals; he, of course, extended this compassion to man himself suffering from the bondage of birth, old age, sickness and death. But in all essential respects his teachings were identical with those of the Upanishads; he acted at best as a bridge between the Vedic Brahminism and the non-Vedic Jainism. However, in socializing religious ideas both Jainism and Buddhism followed the same path—both took up the cause of the common people wandering in ignorance, asserted a common spiritual right for all men, sought compassion and love for all life, preached in the language of the common people, and rejected the authority of the arrogant brahmans dividing the society into high and low. As a consequence of this challenge, the unorganized non-Jains and non-Buddhists now held themselves in some sort of unity round the brahman priesthood which allowed religion to be cultivated by a special class of people using a special language, performing expensive rites, sacrificing dumb animals for transient desires, and enforcing its superiority over the rest of mankind. In sociological terms, the *dharmayuddha*—the righteous war—which Jainism and Buddhism waged against Brahminism was a struggle between the forces of egalitarianism and elitism.

In course of time the organization of Jainism and Buddhism got weakened, but what came out as a result of their struggle with Brahminism proved itself a more effective leaven to the growth of egalitarianism in Indian society. This was Hinduism. Though Buddhism died out in India, we believe that the memory of the compassionate Buddha was scrupulously preserved in the cult of Shiva. The Shiva and the *dhyani* Buddha share many elements in common in their form and character—their compassion and love for all, their renunciation and purity of life, and their involvement in the conception of death as the giver of *moksha* or *nirvana*. The influence of Buddhism on the early Saivism cannot possibly be ruled out. Perhaps the image of Shiva evolved in the *stupa*, and it is not without significance that Varanasi which was the principal seat of Buddhism subsequently became the most important centre of Saivism for the whole of India. The egalitarianism of the Buddha must have prevailed upon the Saivite saints of South India, who like the Buddha, preached in the language of the common people, gave up the distinction of high and low, and waged a war against elitism. Later on the Vaishnava saints of North India joined them in their struggle and intensified it greatly. Indeed, it is this 'santa tradition' which has made Hinduism richer and progressive by waging a righteous war for the redemption of the common man.

The outstanding characteristics of the 'santa tradition' which emerged as a protest against the orthodox traditional theology promoting elitism and religious exclusivism are as follows:

(*i*) rejection of intense intellectualism in favour of the religion of the heart, i.e., the religion of love;

(*ii*) taking recourse to a *guru* for spiritual guidance—considering words of the *guru* more valuable and authentic than the cannons of traditional scriptures;

(*iii*) treating all men as children of God and hence equal in social life;

(*iv*) using the language of the common man in place of Sanskrit—the language of the elite; and

(*v*) preaching righteous way of life instead of complex ritualism, and hence emphasis on *satya, ahimsa* and *kshama*. In brief, 'santa tradition' is the harbinger of egalitarianism in Hindu society and civilisation.

THE ENVIRONMENT OF KABIR

Among the luminaries who built up the 'santa tradition', Kabir (AD 1440-1518) occupies a distinct position as a ruthless critic of the weaknesses of institutional religions, a religious teacher whose feet were firmly planted upon the earth, and a non-literate genius who instead of philosophising religion made it easily accessible to the common man. His task was, of course, more difficult than that of his predecessors in the 'santa tradition'. For, he was almost like a rudderless ship in his personal life and social environment; he had to open war on several fronts against two mighty forces—orthodox Brahminism and Islam. Kabir was disowned both by the Hindus and the Muslims. He was believed to be born of a Hindu mother who deserted him in infancy and was brought up by a Muslim weaver Niru and his wife Nima who lived in abject poverty. In his age Brahminism was invigorated by its triumph over Buddhism, and Islam was enjoying the patronage of bigotted Muslim rulers who were hostile to Hinduism. He lived and preached in Banaras—the citadel of orthodox Brahminism. There are various legends about his persecution, and it is said that on receiving complaints from brahmans and *maulavis* the Emperor Sikander Lodi banished him from Banaras late in his life. But Kabir was not a person to be shaken by such external forces.

According to tradition, Kabir somehow managed to become the disciple of Ramananda—a Vaishnava ascetic who was at that time at the height of his fame as the propounder of absolute loving faith in a personal god who could be approached through personal devotion by all, regardless of one's status in social life. It is said that Ramananda had admitted among his disciples persons belonging to the so-called low-caste, such as Sena, the barber, Dhana, the Jat, and Rai Das, the cobbler. He regarded Kabir, the Muslim weaver, as foremost among his disciples. Ramananda was undoubtedly a large-hearted saint, a liberal in social behaviour, but in his personal life he could perhaps never completely free himself from Brahminic influences; he did not give up his belief in the old mythology of the Hindu pantheon and in no way minimized the privileges granted to brahmans. After all he was a brahman by birth, and a disciple of an orthodox Ramanuji ascetic. With this background he could not have done more than what he did. But Kabir had the advantage of being brought up in a Muslim family and having been initiated by a liberal *guru* like Ramananda. As the legend has it, he also received instructions from Shaikh Taqqi who belonged to the Suhrwardi order of Sufis. He was thus connected with both Hinduism and Islam, and yet he was not firmly rooted in the orthodox cult of any of these religions. It is because of his unusual personal situation that Kabir could point out with considerable boldness and independence the weaknesses of Hindus and Muslims alike.

KABIR AS A CRITIC OF TRADITION

From the point of view of orthodox Hinduism and Islam, Kabir was a heretic. He rejected the authority of the traditional scriptures and ruthlessly criticized the injurious beliefs and practices of both Hindus and Muslims. While deprecating idol worship he said:

> If by worshipping stone one can find God,
>   I shall worship the mountain;
> Better than these stones are the stones
>   of the flour mill which grind men's corn.

He denounced all external observance:

> Hindus keep fast on Ekadasi,
>   they eat only singhara and milk.
> They abstain from grain,
>   but do not control the mind's desire.
> Next day they eat the flesh of beasts.
>
> Turks keep fast and hours of prayer;
>   they cry aloud in the name of God.
> How will they find paradise?
>   When evening comes they slaughter fowls.
>
> Devotion, sacrifice, and rosary, piety,
>   pilgrimage, fasting and alms.
> Nine bhaktis, Vedas, the Book (the Quran),
>   all these are the cloaks of falsehood.
>
> If by immersion in the water salvation be obtained,
>   the frogs bathe continually.
> As the frogs so are these men,
>   again and again they fall into the womb.
>
> O mind, you make your gods and goddesses,
>   and kill living creatures to make offerings to them;
> But if your gods are true,
>   why do they not take them when grazing in the fields.
>
> If it is God that makes thee to be circumcised,
>   why came not this cutting of itself?
> If by circumcision one becomes Turk,
>   what then will be said of your woman?
> 'Half the body', so the wife is styled;

then you will remain Hindu!
> By putting on the sacred thread,
>   does one become a brahman?
> What hast thou given to women to wear?
> She from birth is but a Sudra!
>   Why dost thou eat the food she brings, O Pande?

Kabir condemned the display of *siddhis* by *yogi* ascetics and ridiculed some of their practices:

> Some shave men's locks,
>   and hang the black cord on their necks;
> And pride themselves on the practice of yoga.
> What credit is there in causing your seat to fly?
>   crow and kite also circle in the air.
> O Brother, never have I seen yogi like this!
>   Puffed up with pride he walks, caring for nothing;
> He teaches the religion of Mahadeva,
>   and therefore is called a 'great mahant'.
> In market and street he sits in the posture of a yogi;
>   He is an imperfect siddha, a lover of maya.
> When did Dattatreya attack his enemies?
> When did Sukdeva lay a cannon?
>   Or Vasudeva wind a horn?
> They who fight are of little wisdom.
>   Shall I call such ascetics or bowmen?
> They have renounced the world,
>   Yet covetousness rules their minds;
> They wear gold and disgrace their order,
>   They gather horses and mares.
> They acquire villages and go like millionaires,
>   A beautiful maiden is not fitting in the company of
> Sanak and his kind.
> He who carries a blackened vessel,
>   will one day be fouled.

His outright rejection of the Brahminic caste system came out in strongest words:

> If birth from a brahman mother makes you a brahman,
>   why did you not come by another way?
> If birth from a Turk makes you Turk,
>   why were you not circumcised in the womb?
> If you milk black and yellow cows together
>   will you be able to distinguish their milk?

He dismissed the artificial division of men by caste and sect by saying:

> I and you are of one blood,
>   and one life animates us both.
> From one mother is the world born.
>   What knowledge is this which makes us separate?
> All have come from the same country
>   and have landed at one ghat;
> But the evil influence of this world
>   has divided us into innumerable sects.

It is said that once a brahman drank water from the hands of a young woman named Kamali and was later horrified to learn that she was the daughter of a Muslim weaver, Kabir. He went to Kabir to express his sorrow at losing caste. To him Kabir gave the following answer:

O Pandit, think, when thou drinkest water in the mud-
dwelling,
    wherein thou sittest the universe is contained;
Where fifty six kotis of Yadavas perished,
    eighty eight thousand men and munis;
At every step prophets are buried,
    they decayed to dust therein.
Fish, tortoise, and crocodile there gave birth,
    the water is filled with blood.
The water of the river flows in through its channels;
    men and cattle dissolve in it.
The bones are dissolved and the marrow melted;
    how else comes the milk?
Thou O Pandit, thou didst sit down to drink;
    yet the earthen pot thou accountest defiled.
Renounce the Vedas and the Book (the Quran),
O Pandit: all these are fictions of the mind.
Kabir says, hear, O Pandit,
    these are your pious deeds.

Kabir vehemently denounced untouchability and despised the brahmans for perpetuating such an unjust and
evil practice:

By the touch of others you brahmans
    consider yourselves polluted.
Great pride never produces any good.

How will he, who is called the vanquisher
    of the proud
bear with your pride?

Do not oppress the weak;
    their sighs have great power,
By the puffs of the bellows
    iron is converted to flames (or is utterly consumed).

Here Kabir speaks as a rebel. He warns the oppressors
of dire consequences, for if puffs from the skin of the
dead animal can do so much, how much more the sighs
of the living effect. When he announces, 'Kabir is standing in a market place with a burning stick in his hand',
he obviously appears as an anarchist threatening bloody
revolution.

Kabir not only preached non-conformity but actually
lived up to it. When he knew that his death was near-
ing, he left Banaras and went to Maghar. According to
Brahminic tradition one who dies at Banaras gets salvation but the death at Maghar makes one to be born
again as an ass. When his disciples urged him not to go
to Maghar in the last stage of his life he told them:

One who dies at Maghar becomes an ass!
    A fine thing, you have lost your confidence in
Rama!
What is Banaras, what the waste land of Maghar,
    If Rama dwells in my heart?
If Kabir leaves his body in Banaras,
    what credit will it be to Rama?

Kabir did pass away at Maghar in perfect peace.

While Kabir was highly critical of the outward form
and superstitions of age-old tradition, he himself did

not create a new system. He preached and emphasized
on the unity of god, but his doctrine cannot be accurately placed in any of the six recognized Hindu systems of philosophy. For, he was not a philosopher, he
was a practical teacher who wanted to make people realize the futility of institutional religion and sectarian
and social differences. Philosophers and scholars of religion may find him logically inconsistent in his conception of God and the divine reality; but in the social
context his views were unmistakenly consistent, bold
and original; he systematically denounced everything
that seemed to him unreal and meaningless. And it is
this aspect of Kabir's life and teaching that can help us
understand the tradition of non-conformity in Indian
civilization.

KABIR AS A NON-LITERATE INTELLECTUAL

In my opinion the egalitarianism of the 'santa tradition'
finds its fullest fruition in Kabir, for Kabir had struck at
the very root of elitism—the booklore which the *pandits*
and the *maulavis* had monopolized.

As is clear from the following verse, Kabir was a non-
literate:

I touch not ink nor paper,
    nor take pen in my hand;
Of the greatness of the four ages
    Kabir has given instructions with his lips.

Or again,

I am not skilled in book knowledge,
    nor do I understand controversy.

Kabir spoke in the dialect of the non-literate masses,
and considered Sanskrit as a dead language:

Sanskrit is like the water of a well;
    Bhasa (the vernacular) is like the
flowing waters of the river.

He taunted the *pandits* and the *mullas* for their pride in
booklore:

The pandits are in error by reading the Vedas.
    They have no commonsense.

O Qazi, what book is expounded by thee?
    All such as are pondering on the book are killed;
No one has obtained true knowledge;
    Give up the book, adore Ram, O foolish one.

O maulavi, what books are you explaining?
    Although day and night you remain babbling and
jabbering
you have not found the one (true religion).

According to Kabir,

A man may read many books
    before he dies and yet not be a pandit;

He is a pandit who understands the two-and-a-half letters
   (prema) which form the word love.

He is a mulla who struggleth with his heart,
   who by the instruction of the guru contendeth with Death,
And crusheth Death's pride.

In emphasizing the importance of personal experience he reproached the *pandits* by saying:

You say what is written on paper;
   I describe what my eyes have seen.

For, he believed that

Should all the earth be turned into paper
   and all the trees into pens;
Should the seven seas be turned into ink,
   yet could not an account of God be written.

Kabir wanted to impress upon the common people that booklore is not at all necessary for experiencing true knowledge or for establishing fellowship with God. In support of this he cites his own example:

When the pandits and the mullas prescribed for me,
   I have received no (advantage) from, and have abandoned.
My heart being pure, I have seen the Lord;
   Kabir having searched and searched himself,
hath found God within him.

Scholars of Hindi literature have laboriously unravelled the mysticism contained in the poems of Kabir. But my personal opinion is that most of them have failed to appreciate the real character of Kabir's poetry. Kabir did not compose poems for the elite—the professionals in theology; he addressed his poems to common non-literate people, and accordingly employed simplest imagery and metaphors which could be understood by all men. Being himself a weaver he employed the language of his trade frequently in the description of God:

Weaver, weave the name of Hari,
   On which Gods, men and munis (sages) are meditating.
He stretched the warp and took the shuttle.
   The four Vedas are the wheel.
One beam is Rama Narayana,
   fulfilling the proposed work.
He made the ocean of the world a trough;
   therein he kneads the starch.
The body of that starch is stiffened;
   Few know that it is starch.
Moon and sun, they are two treadles;
   in mid-ocean the warp is made.
As the lord of the tribhuvan (three worlds)
   brushed on the starch, Syama joined the broken ends.
He set the pegs, and when he took the reed,
   then was Rama bound.

As the reed beat up the warp,
   the three lokas were bound: none he left free.
The three lokas were made one loom;
   the warp worked up and down.
The Eternal Purusha bade me to sit beside him;
   Kabir entered into Light.

Or again,

No one knew the mystery of that weaver,
   who came into the world and spread the warp.
The earth and the sky are two beams;
   the sun and the moon are two filled shuttles.
Taking a thousand threads,
   he spreads them lengthwise.
today he weaveth still,
   but hard to reach the far-off end.
Says Kabir, joining karma with karma,
   woven with unwoven threads,
Splendidly the weaver weaves.

In explaining the nature of truth Kabir used the incidents of common experience:

Upside down the pitcher does not fill with water;
   But upright the vessel fills.
For one object, men have tried this way and that;
   Only by the Guru's gift will they cross safely.

To drive home the idea of the nature of relationship between man and god he drew his imagery from day-to-day life using kinship terms—the bridegroom and the bride, the *guru* and the *shishya,* the father and the son and all relationships involving deep personal emotions. When he was about to die, it is said, he sang the following verse:

Sing, O Bride, the bridal song of blessing,
   to my house has come Raja Ram my husband.
My body, my soul, are transported with delight.
   The five elements form his bridal canopy.
Ram Deva has come to be my guest;
I am inebriated with the joy of youth.

From the foregoing illustrations there remains no doubt that Kabir did not intend to pronounce mysticism; he wanted to speak the language of the divine in simplest words understandable to illiterate farmers, craftsmen, and shopkeepers. He belonged to the common folk and lived a simple life:

Kabir says, I have neither
   a thatched roof, nor hut;
Neither have I a village nor a house.

Kabir earned his livelihood at the loom, and he had hard days all his life. (Even today the weavers of Banaras live in abject poverty). He asked God to provide him with the necessities of life:

A hungry man cannot perform service,
   take back this rosary of thine.
I ask only for the dust of the saint's feet;

since I owe not any man.
O God, how shall I fare
  if I am shamed before thee?
If thou give me not (of thine own accord),
  I will beg for it.
I beg for two seers of flour,
  a quarter of a seer of clarified butter with salt;
I beg for half a seer of dal,
  which will feed me twice a day.
I beg for a bed with four legs to it,
  a pillow and a mattress;
I beg for a quilt over me;
  and then thy slave will cheerfully serve thee.
I have never been covetous;
  thy name alone becometh me.
Saith Kabir, my soul is happy;
  and when my soul is happy then I recognize God.

These verses illustrate Kabir's practical approach to life. Unlike ascetics of the orthodox tradition, he did not give up the work of his livelihood to devote himself to the exclusive pursuit of religion. As Underhill (1945: XIII-XIV) has rightly pointed out:

> . . . he (Kabir) knew how to combine vision and industry; the work of his hands helped rather than hindred the impassioned meditation of his heart. Observing mere bodily austerities, he was no ascetic, but a married man, the father of a family—a circumstance which Hindu legends of the monastic type vainly attempt to conceal or explain—and it was from out of the heart of the common life that he sang his rapturous lyrics of divine love. Here his works corroborate the traditional story of his life. Again and again he extols the life of home, the value and reality of diurnal existence, with its opportunities for love and renunciation; pouring contempt upon the professional sanctity of the *yogi* who 'has a great beard and matted locks, and looks like a goat', and on all who think it necessary to flee a world pervaded by love, joy, and beauty—the proper theatre of man's quest—in order to find that One Reality who has spread His form of love throughout *all* the world.

Kabir lived in an age and at a place where the Hindu logicians (*Naiyayikas*) were engaged in hair-splitting interpretations of the *shastras*. The *shastrarthas* of the *pandits* did not impress him, but if he were to establish his radical ideas he could not have possibly avoided the language of logic in answering the complex theological questions put to him by his opponents. In his condemnation of the prevailing customs supported by brahmans he used the weapon of satire, plain logic, and traditional explanations which could easily attract the unsophisticated. Sometimes he seems to have no restraint on his language while asserting his point of view:

> If birth from a brahman mother makes you a brahman,
>   why did you not come by another way?

Or again,

> The brahmans of this age are objects of ridicule;
>   give not to them alms;

They with their families will go to hell,
  and take with them their employers (those who give
    them fees or alms).
If union with God be obtained by going about naked
  All beasts of the forest shall be saved!
What mattereth it whether man goeth naked or weareth
  a deer skin,
  If he recognizes not God in his heart.
If perfection be obtained by shaving his head,
  Why should not sheep obtain salvation?
If, O brethren, the continent man is shaved,
  why should not a eunuch obtain the supreme reward?

Both in perception and presentation Kabir emphasized on the wisdom gained through personal experience—the oral tradition; he used the incidents of common life to explain his ideas. Knowing well the consequences of the *indrajal* of the textual knowledge which the *pandits* and the *maulavis* used in bewitching the masses, he denounced booklore and exalted the importance of the guru with whom one may communicate intimately through the words of the mouth. Describing the importance of the guru he says:

> The guru is the potter and the disciple the vessel;
>   he removes all defects.
> He first places the support (sahara) within,
>   then with blows he fashions the vessel into shape.
>
> Regard your guru as a knife grinder,
>   let him grind your heart;
> Cleansing the heart from all impurity,
>   let him make it bright as a mirror.

As a poet of the non-literates Kabir composed such songs as may easily be remembered and sung by the folk surrounding him. To those who are fond of grammatical accuracy or what is called literary style, the colloquial and unpolished poetry of Kabir may not be impressive. But in every village, in every home and, on all such occasions when abstract logic fails, the words of Kabir are on the lips of the non-literates all over North-India. For, Kabir was after all a people's poet.

THE MATCHLESS KABIR

To sum up, Kabir's contribution to the tradition of non-conformity in Indian civilization we may list as follows:

(1) Outright rejection of the caste system, the practice of untouchability and all social distinctions;

(2) denial of brahmans and the *mullas* as the ones having special religious functions or as being specially holy;

(3) refusal to recognize the authority of the six Hindu schools of philosophy;

(4) denunciation of booklore that promotes pride;

(5) disapproval of sectarian distinctions between the Hindus and the Muslims—no preference for either religion; and

(6) condemnation of such beliefs and practices as idolatory, polytheism, mythology of divine incarnation, fasting, ceremonial purification, pilgrimage, asceticism and severe austerities, circumcision, prayer in a mosque, and all externals of religion.

In his positive approach to tradition Kabir emphasized the unity of men, truth, non-violence, tolerance, love, compassion, and belief in one God.

But these negative and positive approaches to tradition were no speciality of Kabir. Many of his predecessors and successors have said the same thing again and again. What makes Kabir different from all others is his mode of protest—the language and the logic of condemnation. Our image of Kabir is not the same as that of Mahavir, or the Buddha, or Chaitanya, or Jnaneshwara, or Gandhi. Kabir preached tolerance, when he says:

> For him who sows thorns for thee,
>   do thou sow flowers;
> For thee the harvest will be flowers;
>   but for him sharp pains.

From these verses we do not however get the same feeling as we get from Christ's saying:

> That ye resist not evil: but whosoever shall strike thee on thy right cheek, turn to him the other also. Love your enemies, bless them that curse you, do good to them that hate you, and pray for them which despitefully use you and prosecute you.
>
> (Matthew: V. 39, 44)

In the lines of Kabir the idea of vengeance is implicit, for the offender will be punished. Indeed, such saintly traits as a compassion, tenderness, and fervent love are not generally attributed to Kabir's intrinsic character. Kabir appears as a rugged poet, earnest and vigorous in his message, exposing with merciless severity the weaknesses of both the Hindus and the Muslims. As has been quoted earlier, he even used invectives in his denunciation of brahmans and *mullas*. But must we not forget that Kabir was after all a non-literate poet who used the language of his heart which may sometimes appear rugged and unsophisticated, particularly to those who are not used to hearing plain truth. Kabir's attack on tradition was direct and frontal; he spoke fearlessly and he never said anything in a roundabout way merely to please his hearers. In the cultural language of Banaras he was *akkhara* and *phakkar*.

Looking at Kabir's personal life as that of one who is disowned both by the Hindus and by the Muslims and lives in abject poverty, we are not surprised at the ruggedness of his expressions. His voice was that of a downtrodden who rebels openly against social inequalities and injustices, and seeks social reordering. His was the insider's view of the commoners' expectations of social change, and hence he spoke differently from the soft clamourings of literate intellectuals, and saints coming from the privileged class and caste. It is in this context of the non-literate movement in Indian tradition that Kabir is matchless. We believe he occupies the highest place among the non-conformists in Indian tradition. And from the fact that amongst his more than one million followers, the Sudras are most numerous we can easily say that his influence on the non-literates was not only great in his life-time but has continued to the present day.

THE PANTH OF KABIR

It has already been pointed out that Kabir did not try to build up a new system, did not give up the life of a householder in favour of asceticism, and did not approve the authority of the scriptural booklore. But, from what I have so far gathered, it appears to me that the followers of Kabir have undone everything which Kabir did in building up a non-literate cultural tradition.

One does not know how many disciples Kabir made during his life-time; many persons must have been influenced by his message, but there is no evidence that Kabir organized a sect or formally initiated disciples. The sect which is now known as Kabirpanth seems to have come much later. Nevertheless it is true that a large number of sects owe their origin to the ideas which Kabir promulgated. Of these sects, the most important ones are the Sikhs whose founder Nanak (1469-1538) was greatly influenced by Kabir, a large number of verses of Kabir are included in the *Adi-Grantha*; the Dadupanth whose founder Dadu (1544-1603), a cotton carder by caste, followed the teachings of Kabir; the Laldasi whose founder was Lal Das (—1648) a member of the Meo tribe of Rajasthan, was greatly influenced by Kabir; the Baba Lalis whose founder was one Baba Lal(—1649) and which survives in parts of Gujarat; the Sadhs whose founder Birbhan(—1543) drew most of his ideas from Kabir; the Dharnidasi whose founder was one Dharni Das (—1656), a Kayastha of Chhapara in Bihar; the Charandasi whose founder Charan Das (1703-1782) was a Baniya by caste and whose teachings are very much the same as that of Kabir; the Shiva-Narayanis which was founded in 1734 by a Rajput named Shiva Narayana; the Garibdasis whose founder was Garib Das (1717-1782), and whose scripture *Guru Grantha Sahib* contains twenty-four thousand verses out of which seven thousands are taken from Kabir; the Ramsanehis whose founder Ramcharan (1718) lived in

Rajasthan; the Paltupanthis whose founder Paltu Sahib lived sometime in the eighteenth century in the Azamgarh district in Uttar Pradesh; the Satnamis which was founded before the middle of the seventeenth century by Jagjivan Das and subsequently reorganized by Ghazi Das; the Prannathis whose founder lived in Panna in Madhya Pradesh during the early eighteenth century; and the Radhaswami Satsanga which was founded by Tulsi Ram (1818-1878) of Agra in U.P. All these sects owe to Kabir; in some cases the influence is direct, in others indirect. Though they differ in many important details they all have something in common—the need of a Guru, denunciation of idolatrous practices, and preachings in the vernacular.

The modern Kabirpanthis recognize two main divisions (there are also several minor sections) of their *panth*—one with its headquarters at the Kabir Chaura matha in Banaras, and the second founded by Dharam Das in the Chhatisgarh districts in Madhya Pradesh. The Kabirchaura matha, called *mulagaddi,* is headed by an ascetic *bairagi.* The Dharmadasi section is called *banshagaddi.* The *mahantha* of this section has to marry, and ideally live with his wife till a son is born; after the son is born the wife should become a *bairagi.* Traditionally, the *mahantha* should also hold the office for 25 years and 20 days and is then succeeded by his son. But these ideal situations are not always followed now in actual practice.

From what has so far been gathered the historical Kabir has been mythicized by his followers and numerous legends are now in existence with regard to his birth, life, and death:

> Kabir was born of a virgin brahman widow whom the great saint Ramananda without knowing that she was a widow wished her the blessing of a son.
>
> Kabir descended on a lotus flower, and was picked up by Niru and Nima, the Muslim weavers, who in previous birth had been brahmans and whom Kabir had then promised to be born in their house to deliver them from transmigration.
>
> At the instance of the *Qazi,* Niru tried to destroy the child Kabir, but he was terrified to see that though he plunged a knife into him there was not a drop of blood and the child was unharmed.
>
> One day a cow was sacrificed; Kabir reproached the *Qazi* for his sin in killing a cow and having raised it to life again disappeared.
>
> Sikander Lodi gave orders for Kabir to be bound with chains and put into a boat full of stones which was then pushed out into the river Ganges and sunk, but a moment later Kabir was seen seated on a deerskin on the water and floating up against stream.
>
> Kabir was then bound in a basket and the fire heaped round him, then he was brought to be trodden under foot by an infuriated elephant and a lion. But all these failed, and then the Emperor prostrated himself at the feet of Kabir and asked pardon for his fault.
>
> When Kabir was dying a dispute occurred between his Hindu and Muslim followers as to whether he should be cremated or buried. Kabir asked them not to quarrel and wait for the event to follow. He laid down and spread the sheets over himself and told the disciples to close the door and leave him inside, which they did. After a few minutes a sound came from the room, and when the room was opened nothing was to be seen except two sheets and some flowers in them. One sheet and half the flowers the Hindus took, and the other sheet and the remainder of the flowers were taken by Muslims; and both performed the ceremony of disposal according to their respective custom.

These myths and legends are transmitted orally among the non-literate followers of Kabir. Some of these have now been published by the Kabirpanthi scholars.

Although Kabir transmitted his message orally and denounced booklore, his followers could not help writing down his poems soon after his death. A collection of his poems, called **Bijak** (which means, essence or seed), has come down in various editions which differ considerably one from the other; it is difficult to say what the true text of the **Bijak** is. Perhaps, the first edition of the **Bijak** was printed at Banaras in 1868. Besides the **Bijak,** which is the sacred scripture of all the Kabirpanthis, there is a vast sectarian literature on Kabir—both published and unpublished. To give the idea of what Kabirpanthi literature is like, the book *Kabir Mansoor* may be referred to by way of example. This book was written by Sadhu Parmananda, a Kabirpanthi of Ferozepur and published in Urdu in 1857. It was subsequently translated into Hindi by Makanji Kuber of Bombay, a painter by profession and a Kabirpanthi by religion, and published in 1903 by the Venkateshwar Steam Press, Bombay. The book contains 1493 pages (texts) and a large number of line drawings of the various Hindu gods and goddesses. It is a sort of anthology of the Brahminic, Christian, and Islamic scriptures. The major portion of the book is however devoted to the description of Hindu mythology, and is written in the style of the *Puranas.* The book describes Kabir as having appeared in all the four yugas—in the Satyayuga Kabir was known as Satya Sukritajee, in the Tretayuga he was famous as Munindrajee, in the Dwapara he was called Karunamaya, and in the Kaliyuga he appeared no less than fourteen times as Musa, Daud, Suleman, Issa, Mohammad and several others. Similarly, in the Tretayuga he is described as having taught Ramachandra the techniques of *yoga* and preached to Ravana of Lanka; in the Dwapara, Krishna requested Kabir to come to his rescue in the Kaliyuga when he will take the form of Jagannath, and the god of the sea will threaten to destroy his temple at the sea-shore in Puri. Kabir is described also as the author of the *Svasamveda* from which, according to the *Kabir Mansoor,* the four Vedas have originated. The book describes the various *leelas* or the miracle-plays of Kabir and extols him as the *Parabrahman.*

Thus in the processes of myth-making the men of letters have tried to link Kabir with the Pauranic Hindu gods and goddesses and have made him an *avatar*—a thing which Kabir himself denounced all his life. The manner in which the book *Kabir Mansoor* shows the affinity of Kabir with Islam and Christianity is also the vulgarization of the Kabir's doctrine of making no distinction between Hindus and Muslims, Rama and Raheem. The mythologists may have good reasons for making Kabir a mythical figure and such myths might also easily catch the imagination of the non-literate masses, but thereby the historicity of Kabir is destroyed and the social aims with which Kabir began his movement obviously get distorted and wavered.

Perhaps the Kabirpanthi men of letters have now realized that the kind of mythomania which books like *Kabir Mansoor* want to perpetuate no longer appeals to the masses, much less to the literate devotees. Hence, the recent trend to systematize and philosophize the doctrines of Kabir and to establish him as equal in position to the Vaishnava *acharyas*. In Varanasi (Banaras) practically all the Kabirpanthi students in Sanskrit *panthasalas* and at the Varanaseya Sanskrit University are studying Vedanta. It is their hope that 'if they could prove that the doctrines of Kabir in its pristine purity are the essence of the Vedantic system, then their *pantha* will spread rapidly among the orthodox Hindus.' Some of them hold that the teachings of Kabir have close parallels in the Vedas and the Upanishads.

To make the doctrines of Kabir acceptable to the orthodox Brahman philosophers the modern Kabirpanthis are publishing their works also in Sanskrit, such as the *Dasmatra,* the *Kabirsatakam,* and the *Brahmanirupana.* The *Bijak* has also been translated into Sanskrit.

In their religious observance, rites and ceremonies (particularly the *Chauka*-rites), modern Kabirpanthis do not seem to be different from the orthodox Vaishnavites. They are guided by the Brahminic *paddhaties*: they worship the idol of Kabir, and wear sacred-thread, sandalwood paste and a rosary made from the *tulsi* plant or *Bela*-wood. In the Kabirchaura matha in Varanasi there is a regular discourse on the *Gita* and the *Puranas.* A brahman Kathabachaha from Bihar is appointed for this purpose. In some of the Kabirpanth-*maths* the devotees visiting during the day receive three spoonfuls of *charnamrita* together with three leaves of the *tulsi* plant which is sacred to Vishnu. When Kabir spoke of Rama, he did not mean the incarnation of Vishnu; his Rama was the Supreme Being. The Kabirpanthis have not given up the caste system. Even among their ascetics the influence of caste is easily noticeable; the concept of purity and pollution is also deeply rooted in their social interaction. At the time of *bhandara* (community feast) the ascetics from the so-called untouchable castes announce *on their own* that they will sit in a separate row (or what they call *hamari panghati alag lagi*).

We have not yet met any Muslim Kabirpanthi anywhere in Bihar and eastern U P, not even in Banaras, the hometown of Kabir. The Hindu Kabirpanthis do not feel happy on the question whether Kabir was a Muslim weaver. Several pamphlets published from Gujarat and Madhya Pradesh make Kabir the legitimate son of a brahman couple. Although today among the followers of Kabir the Sudras—Ahirs, Kunbis, Dhanukas, Manjhis, Dusadhas, Suris, and Telis—are most numerous, the brahmans are given great importance in the *pantha*. Some of the Kabirpanthi-*mathas* in eastern U P are headed by brahmans.

These illustrations clearly show that the modern Kabirpanthis are becoming brahman-minded, a phenomenon which might be called *virprachitti*.

Although, we wish to avoid generalization at this stage of this work which has yet to be completed, in conclusion we may observe that in the course of five hundred years the message of Kabir has been thoroughly and systematically distorted by men of letters. What has been presented in this essay is a case history of how a non-literate movement deviates from its cultural goal as soon as it changes its mode of transmission. In other words, when a non-literate group concedes to the Brahminic scriptural lore the *virprachitti* syndrome becomes operative. In brief, it seems the Kabir movement is no longer a movement, it has become *pravaha patita*—fallen into the mainstream of Brahminism. In other words, it has turned into a system against which Kabir had fought all his life.

Select Bibliography

Underhill, Evelyn (1945); "Introduction," in *One Hundred Poems of Kabir* by Rabindranath Tagore; Calcutta, Macmillan & Co. Ltd.

The English rendering of the poems of Kabir is based on the following books:

Keay, F. E. (1931); *Kabir and His Followers*; Calcutta, Association Press (YMCA).

Westcott, G. H. (1907); *Kabir and the Kabir Panth*; Cawnpore, Christ Church Mission Press.

Ashok Kumar Jha (essay date May-June 1986)

SOURCE: Jha, Ashok Kumar. "Kabir in Tagore's Translation." *Indian Literature* 29, no. 3 (May-June 1986): 48-60.

[In the following essay, Jha analyzes the influence of Rabindranath Tagore's own poetry on his translations of Kabīr's verse.]

As if conscious of the limitation of translating a text, Evelyn Underhill, in her introduction to *One Hundred Poems of Kabir,* points out that Kabir is able to dramatize his symbols, and that he uses all the senses in communicating his experience. To state in advance to the reader what a text appears to lose in taking to the medium of another person, Underhill takes pains to mention Kabir's use of popular Hindi to his purposes, the closeness of the language of his songs to common life and a poetic use of material from popular Hinduism of his time as he draws upon symbols and images from contemporary life. Tagore's attempt with Underhill at introducing Kabir to the western world could be taken to be largely successful.

And yet, in spite of the success a translation may have, there are certain questions that inevitably follow. For example, there is the important question of the relation of a secondary creation to the original. Sometimes the gap between the original and its translation may be a little too wide as is the stand of T. S. Eliot in respect of Gilbert Murray's translation of the Greek plays. That in the case of a translator so gifted as Rabindranath, the limitation proceeds from a difference of what his own verse is and what it can be in relation to Kabir has been stated by Edward Thompson. What concerns us here is what Kabir may lose in being translated. As if conscious of a possible loss in such an effort, Underhill says:

> The constant insistence on simplicity and directness, the hatred of all abstractions and philosophizings . . . are amongst his most marked characteristics.

This is mainly a statement about the nature of experience, what Richards calls the 'critical' part in a work of art. It is because of the directness of an approach to reality with the kind of monism which is implicit in his attitude of protest and rejection that Kabir is acceptable to people:

> God is that Root where all manifestations, 'material' and 'spiritual', alike proceed; God is the only need of man—'happiness shall be yours when you come to the Root'.

On the philosophical side, such 'eclecticism' implies 'vedantist and vaisnavite, pantheist and Transcedentalist, Brahman and Sufi' ideas and beliefs. That Tagore himself was under the influence of some of these ideas and beliefs and his almost constant preoccupation with the poet's craft make him an ardent translator of Kabir.

But there are differences between Kabir, the humble weaver, who passes into a sect because of his life and songs, and Rabindranath, the versatile experimenter of many forms and genres, for whom the translation could not have been more than an important side-affair. This is not to lessen the value of the translation, but to set

limits within which it can be judged, in spite of its success, against the original. Thompson is close to to what Tagore and Kabir can be together. But he seems to undermine the value of the derived in the making of a poet, when he attributes the liveliness of Kabir's verse to a mere relation to its time.

For a person so keen of mind and sharp of speech as Kabir, the ignorance of the written word became a regulating compulsion that made his speech the sharper in verse. In Rabindranath, the area of experience on which his poetry draws as well as awareness of the past behind such a practice is wider. By constant exercise of himself, he has disciplined his wide awareness of literature in several traditions to serve his particular needs as a poet. While his training in the poet's craft or his discipline as a poet does not affect the ease of his utterance as a poet, he does bring into effect part of his beliefs and training in translating Kabir.

What has he, then, in common with Kabir that impels him to present Kabir to the western world? Writing much later, Rabindranath is appreciative of the Bauls of Bengal for what they offer. He thinks they have, as religion, a framework of beliefs without the formal framework of a religion.

Like Kabir, there is a protestant element in Tagore's stand in respect of sanctioned values of the traditional religion. His admiration for Buddhism cannot be concealed. A protestant belief close enough to the traditional fold to be a worthwhile offshoot, and yet distant enough to reject much of what is orthodox, can be seen at work in what Tagore inherits from his father. Also what comes from the Upanishads, Kabir and Raja Rammohun Roy may have blended into one as an influence behind Tagore's protestant zeal to bypass the demands of a stratified society and the external authority of religion.

It is a falsehood often practised in our discussion of 'uneducated' men like Kabir or Ramakrishna that the extent of their reliable knowledge could not be of much value for consistent academic investigation. What Shakespeare could absorb out of one page of Plutarch, Kabir could glean from his associations with Ramananda and the ethos around him in Benares. Like Ramakrishna's use of the Vedantic ideas, Kabir's use of such ideas is considerable, leading one from their popular sources to Ramananda and Ramanuja and the Upanishads themselves.

In the more educated personality of Rabindranath, the Upanishads become more of a derived influence. Under such influences as those of Kabir and Buddhism, it may appear for a time that the preparation of life—as far as it consists of the common experience of living—is limited in view of that awareness of an ineffable source of

Reality. But more than Kabir, perhaps under Chaitanya's latest influence in Bengali tradition, he is led to an affirmation on the side of joy in faith even through the senses which may be close to the explicit intention of his prose works.

And yet like the Bauls, Kabir attracts him as the example of a use of religion outside its authoritative fold. Kabir's language must have been an impediment to him. Even Vidyapati, whom he used as a model in *Bhanusingher Padavali,* offered him some difficulty:

> Vidyapati's quaint and corrupt Maithili language attracted me all the more because of its unintelligibility.

That the verse which could have been archaic for him could be adapted and absorbed into his needs was possible because of an existing influence of this kind in the Bengali language and literature earlier to him. The mastery of a technique in modern Bengali coming of the practice of the poets from the west was, properly speaking, a use of the Brajabuli influence to a new purpose in the verse of a modern poet. This brought with it also a cultural awareness:

> Those who have studied the lives and writings of our medieval saints, and all the great religious movements that sprang up in the time of the Muhammadan rule, know how deep is our debt to this foreign current that has so intimately mingled with our life.

There is a difference between a correct translation of verse into equivalent prose by a scholar and the translation by an amateur scholar and craftsman of verse. An able translator will, as often as not, eschew the merely literal. But he may in the process lose something of the freshness and appeal of the original. If the translator is not a poet himself, which means that the translated work must be dependent on his use of language and diction elsewhere, and if he wants to keep to verse patterns that he wants to translate, it is most likely that he will draw on the available rhetoric and diction of verse in his time. In doing so, although handicapped by what is the creation and convention of other men, he is yet useful to them in extending the apparatus of communication they had created in respect of new things.

But, if like Rabindranath, he is a master of his own craft, what he puts into English is not only a correct translation, but it becomes some sort of a valuable translation of the original into a new form available to a foreigner now in his own language. For the language into which it has been translated, it brings something new into existence. As Kabir goes by a dependence on the high and intense rhythms of a song, which are essentially untranslatable in any other tongue, it is safer to try get to Kabir in trying to put his songs into a form devoid of that ingredient poetic form and its necessary accompaniments that constitute a song of Kabir. Tagore

himself is capable of high and intense rhythms in poetry in Bengali, but trying to translate into English the Hindi songs of Kabir, he takes to the more sober medium of prose. Thus the translation of:

> Pīle pyālā ho matwālā pyālā nām amīrasa kā re
> bālpanā sab khel ganvāyā tarun bhayā nārī bas kā re
> Biradh gayā kaph vāyu ne gherā, khāt paṛā na jāya khasakā re
> nābhi kamal bich dai kastūrī, jaise mirag phirē ban kā re
> Bin satgur itnā dukh pāyā, vaid milā nahi is tan kā re
> mātu-pitā-bandhu-sut-tiriyā, sang nahīn koi jāv sakā re
> Jab lag jīve guru gun legā, dhan jīvan hai din das kā re
> chourasī jo ubarā chāhe chōri kāmini kā chasakā re
> Kahai kabīr sunāu bhai sādhau, nakh sikh pūrā rahā bisakā re

shows how he takes recourse to simple English to express what is unique in a literature. The expression, 'Empty the cup! O be drunken.' for *'pīle pyālā ho matwālā'* is hardly just to the export of feeling in the spoken idiom of native speech in Kabir, which is hard to get to even for a poet like Rabindranath. The other half of the verse line, *pyālā nām amīrasa kā re,* is translated easily into a sort of prose, "Drink the divine nectar of his Name!" that tries its best to reach up to the intensity of the original in terms of a foreign idiom.

Sometimes, in Kabir, the verve and vigour of a localized idiom—within the diction available to him—becomes so adequate in terms of the communicated effect that a translation appears to be begging the issue. It is perhaps because of such a difficulty that the lines that follow have been left out. The translation is completed by merely expressing in English "Kabir says: Listen to me, dear Sadhu! / From the sole of the feet to the crown of the head this mind is filled with poison", what the last line in the poem itself says so deftly, at the head of all that precedes *'Kahai kabīr sunāu bhāi sādhau nakh sikh pūrā rahā bisakā re!'*

Tagore is happiest at translating verse lines that are less localized to their idiomatic vigour and sharpness, or in any case verse lines or poems that are closer to his own sympathies as they express the infinite. Thus, for:

> Sunatā nahīn dhun kī khabar anhad kā bājā bājathā
> rasa mandir bājatā bāhar sune to kya huā

we have:

> Have you not heard the tune which the unstruck Music is playing? In the midst of the chamber the harp of joy is gently and sweetly played; and where is the need of going without to hear it?

The more literary as well as sophisticated approach to the original in translation is the gift of an educated sensibility. At his best, the translator makes his English come beyond the stereotyped syntax and idiom of his contemporaries to the largely self-educated needs of a man of letters to communicate what could be of a foreign culture and language. In this, he had his forerunners who had popularized vedantic ideas in the west but the inherence of these ideas in terms of the manifest personality of a poet and his songs could very well be the preoccupation of a gifted translator. A perception of a lack of reality beneath the appearance, thus, is the main preoccupation in the original in these lines:

> *Jogī digambar sevaṛā kapaṛ ā range lāl men!*
> *wākif nahin us range se kapaṛā range se kyā huā!!*

A translation of these lines has to be more even against the uneven and irregular tone of the original:

> The Yogi dyes his garments with red: but if he knows naught of that colour of love, what does it avail though his garments be tinted?

What Tagore contributes in spite of his handicaps is a clear communication of the experience and intention of the original. What he lacks by way of tone and rhythm, he tries to compensate by supplying us with what he has himself created. Even in his prose, particularly in his short stories, he uses a broad and persuasive tone to carry his reader along to the end of the piece. His prose acquires a more durable value by an evasion of the sordid, the commonplace, the merely factual and the statement-like by a subtle interplay of tone he has learnt to use as a professional writer. If it is such a language that is the staple basis of his dependence in translating verse he can even give his sentence an implicit rhythm, which he is capable of, even as he uses it to a different purpose in the prose that is created.

To understand his translation better, perhaps it will be more just to bring in a partial consideration of his verse. In Sanskrit, it is a suggestive sentence that has been called to be a unit of verse and, in a sense, the idea bears on his practice as a craftsman of prose and verse. When he chooses to write beyond the limitation of traditional forms, Rabindranath flattens the rhetoric of his verse:

> Where words come out from the depth of truth:
>   . . . . .
> Where the clear stream of reason has not lost
> its way into the dreary desert sand of dead habit;
> Where the mind is led forward by thee
> into ever-widening thought and action—
> Into that heaven of freedom,
> my Father,
> let my country awake.

Here he uses the sheer value of a generalized poetic experience to poetic purposes. To reach the impersonal effect of a poem through the self-created rhetoric is an exercise of a poetic power at the other extreme of a self-involvement in experience typical of the subjectively romantic. It is through this that Rabindranath came to influence the technique of some of his contemporaries and even younger men in Europe and America. It is a technique close to that of Whitman and is at the same time neater and more controlled than Whitman could ever be.

It is such a technique in expression together with a rhetoric that seems to be in keeping with this kind of expression which seems to account for his translation of Kabir from Hindi.

As for the content of Kabir's poetry, although Rabindranath understood Shaktism in its essentials as such a tendency had become part of the tradition in Bengal, he was not a Shakta himself. Participation in life and activities that he stood for were not of that sort.

As it was, Kabir and his followers were averse to Shaktism as it meant allowing the senses to participate while trying to control and sublimate them, using partly the Yoga discipline to its end. Hindered by Buddhism in a full participation of the senses, the Shakta took to a fulfilment of such cravings by taking resort to more primitive archetypes of a compelling elemental sort in his effort to reassert vital participation. In this, he mixed the value of the 'mother' image toward a sublimation even from Buddhistic sources.

Coming from a fresh approach to the Upanishads in the wake of the new consciousness of the Brahmos, Rabindranath is able to understand together the Shakta on the one hand and the Buddhist on the other.

It is in such a light that one should view his translation of such poems of Kabir in which there is a blend of an apprehensive of the real in one of the ways as the *Brihadaranyaka* understands it. Left to himself, Tagore can communicate such simple and naked states of the soul at their keenest in poetry. But trying to imitate a past mode in expression in such an apprehension of the real, he appears at times to be grappling with a derived influence and a somewhat outdated convention.

In Kabir, this urgency is often and unmistakably expressed in the figure of a beloved yearning for her lord:

> *Hai kōi āisa par upagahi Hari saun kahai sunāi re*
> *ab tāu behal Kabīr bhaye hāin dekhen jiu jāi re*

Tagore's familiarity with such yearning for God as the infinite coming to him from several sources makes him naturally sympathetic to such an experience, and thus he is able to transmute the former adequately into English:

> My body and my mind are grieved for the want of Thee;

O my Beloved! Come to my house.
When people say I am thy Bride, I am ashamed; for I
   have not tou-
ched thy heart with my heart.
Then what is this love of mine? I have no taste for
   food, I have no
sleep; my heart is ever restless, within doors and without.
As water is to the thirsty, so is the lover to the bride.
   Who is there
that will carry my news to my Beloved?
Kabir is restless: he is dying for sight of him.

A transmutation of the physical to the process of faith, which comes of a view of the Real is characteristic of the devotional literature of mediaeval India, and in Kabir such an experience finds a poet capable of expressing the same. A complete subservience of the self in faith to God is born of a feeling of humility of the loved one for the lover. This submission of the subject to God is the result of a high sense of priority in value which is attested by the evidence of the humming, pulsating states of feeling of the sense in what they apprehend as truth in conceiving of such a likeness. The bare commonsense of the weaver, as he registers a view of human relation in the society around him, is used as a point of likeness for expressing a very different experience.

The complex wholeness of two separate experiences is grappled at some remove from the original, as it is couched in expression by a partly romantic poet, in the language of the cultivated, as in "O my Beloved! Come to my house . . ." etc. above.

That even the given relation between a lover and his bride is more than mere love of such a relation, *jyōn kāmin ko kāmini pyāri* is expressed with the help of what is basic to the relation itself. The nature of a desire for which a different kind of a feeling for physical love is the point of correlation between the subject and the object communicates the urgent and necessary character of the referent, *jyōn pyāse ko nīr re*. Tagore, however, simplifies such suggestions as he expresses the full line together in English, "As water to the thirsty, so is the lover to the bride."

Kabir finds it convenient to express his urgent cravings through the beloved symbol. His humility is unusual if one takes into account the manly vigour of his speech as well as its sharpness. That his humility comes in spite of his keen intellect and his full grasp of a vital speech in all its liveliness becomes possible because of a dramatization of the sensibility with that peculiar vantage that is his as a mystic. Whereas Tagore is happier at translating such a poem:

> Is there any wise man who will listen to that solemn
>   music which arises in the sky?

For He, the Source of all music, makes all vessels
   fraught and rests in fullness Himself.
He who is in the body is ever athirst, for he pursues
   that which is in part.
But ever there wells forth deeper and deeper the sound
"He is this—this is He", fusing love and renunciation
   into one,
Kabir says: "O Brother! that is the Primal word".

His translation of a more complex verse as:

> *Nāihar te jiyarā phāt re*
> *Nāihar-nagarī jisakī bigarī, uskā kyā ghar bār re*
> *tanik jiyarabā mōr na lāge, tan man bahut uchāt re*
> *Yā nagari men lakh darwājā, bīch samandar ghāt re*
> *kaise ke pār utari hain sajanī, agam panth kā pāt re*
> *Ajab tarah ka bana tambūra, tār lage man māt re*
> *khūṇtī tūtī tār bilgāno, kōun pūchat bāt re*
> *Hansi-hansi pūchāi māt pitā sāun, bhōre sasur jawa*
>   *re*
> *jo chāhen so vāhī karihen, patvāhī ke hāth re*
> *Nhāya-dhōya dulhin hoya bāithī, johe piyā kī bāt re*
> *tanik gūṇghatwā dikhaw sakhī ri, āj sōhhāg kī rāt re*

becomes possible because of an undue simplification of some of the actual verse lines. Thus, "My heart cries aloud for the house of my love" is hardly the proper translation of, *Nāihar te jiyarā phāt re*. In his failure to translate the more localized element in Kabir's use of a native tongue, "*Nāihar-nagarī jisakī bigarī uskā kyā ghar bār re*", the translator uses a language that communicates a more consistent sense in relation to the intention of the poem at the close. But, in fact, it leads one away from the effect of the original. That *Nāihar-nagari* is not all right to the beloved figure in the poem means a deeper disturbance than Rabindranth's translation evokes:

> My heart cries aloud for the house of my lover; the
> open road and the shelter of a roof are all one to her
> who has lost the city of her husband.

The ultimate sense of the poem is brought a little too soon in translation at the cost of the verse lines in the original. The confounding nature of an ecstasy that results of an experience of the variety and grandeur implicit in the infinite is expressed in terms of a place with a large number of gates. But it is still the feeling of most humane kind as it is made real in terms of how a beloved craves for entry into her lover's house.

Sometimes the poet achieves his objective correlative in terms of the familiar and the homely, *Hansi-Hansi pūchāi māt pitā sāun* which dramatizes what is essentially the indefinable nature of his ecstasy. In translating it in explicit terms, Tagore being a poet himself is perhaps conscious of the fact that such verse can only be translated in the manner he does it. The indefinable nature of the feeling involved in communicating ecstasy comes naturally to expression after such a dramatization of the basic content in the original text:

*Hansi hansi pūchāi māt pitā sāun bhore sāsur jawa re
jo chāhen so vāhī karihēn, patvāhi ke hāth re
Nhāya-dhoya dulhin hoya bāithī, johe piyā kī bāt re*

(which the translator thinks best to achieve in terms of direct speech) becomes possible through simple and direct presentation in another language:

I tell my parents with laughter that I must go to my Lord in the morning;

They are angry, for they do not want me to go, and they say: "She thinks that she has gained such dominion over her husband that she can have whatever she wishes; and therefore she is impatient to go to him."

The rhetorical power that Tagore can build up for a sustenance of the personal and the general in experience in verse comes to help him in expressing that community sense basic to Kabir and his followers in a poem like:

*Abadhū begam desa hamārā
rājā rang phakīr bādsā, sabse kahāun pukārā
Jo tum chahō param pad kō, basihō desa hamara
jo tum āye jhīne hoke, taj do man kī dhārā
Aise rahan rahōre pyāre, sahajāi utār jāwō pārā
dharan akās gagan kachu nāhin, nahīn chandra nahīn
   tārā
Sant dharma kī hai mahatābe, sāheb ke darbārā
kahāi Kabīr sunō ho pyāre, sant-dharm hāi sārā*

That Kabir also passes into a sect is possible because of the way in which he masters a common participation of the kind possible for others as well. In Rabindranath, with all his reformer's zeal, it becomes difficult to translate that sense of a live human participation together achieved in a poem that bases itself wholly on the power of a song to go by way of mouth. A literary craftsman like Rabindranath is up against an unusual mode in spite of his close familiarity with such ways of expression in the religious literature of Bengal. Thus, in spite of his unusual deftness in the use of the verse-craft, he can hardly recapture the full tone and effect of "*Abadhū begam desa hamara*", translating it as "Sadhu! My land is a sorrowless land."

Charlotte Vaudeville (essay date 1993)

SOURCE: Vaudeville, Charlotte. "Kabīr's Language and Languages." In *A Weaver Named Kabīr: Selected Verses With a Detailed Biographical and Historical Introduction*, pp. 109-30. Delhi, India: Oxford University Press, 1993.

[*In the following essay, Vaudeville explores the complex subject of the language of Kabīr's poems, discussing the languages in which the verses were written, his own spoken language, the language of the literate versus the non-literate people of his day, and the poet's spontaneous style.*]

There is no evidence that Kabīr ever composed a single work or even wrote a single verse—though a large number of works has been attributed to him by the *Kabīr-panthīs,* Kabīr's followers. The list of works attributed to Kabīr varies from forty to eighty or more. Though Kabīr's followers believe that *Sat Kabīr* was omniscient from the age of five, they do not assert that the Prophet himself wrote down the numerous compositions ascribed to him. They hold that he composed them orally and that they were subsequently written by his immediate disciples, among whom they name Surat-Gopāl, Dharmadās and Bhaggojī.

Moreover, Kabīr's social background as a low-caste weaver makes it likely that he was more or less illiterate, or at least that he had no formal teaching in reading and writing. In a couplet found in the *Bījak,* Kabīr says that he never touched a pen:

Ink or paper, I never touched, nor did I take a pen in
   hand—
The greatness of the four ages, I have described by
   word of mouth.

Bī. [*Bījak*], *sā.* 187

The written word, holy scriptures in general, be they Veda or Qur'ān, he cordially despises:

Reading book after book the whole world died
   and none ever became learned:
He who can decipher just a syllable of Love,
   he is the true Pandit!

KG[*Kabīr Granthāvalī*], *sā.* 33.3

Kabīr's contempt for scriptural authority and contempt for the written word is rooted in the medieval Tantric tradition, especially the Sahajiyā Buddhists and the Nāth-Yogīs, disciples of the famous Master Gorakhnāth.[1] From the early middle ages, perhaps as early as the eight or ninth century, Siddhas and Yogīs, mostly low-caste people, had been preaching their Gospel in the common tongue, *bhāṣā,* in some form of Western Apabhramsha or old Bengali. Kabīr shared the Siddhas' contempt for the sacred Brahmanical language, Sanskrit, as expressed in a couplet traditionally ascribed to him:

Kabīr, Sanskrit is like well-water
   and the *Bhāṣā* like the live water of the brook!

Like the *bāṇīs* (*vāṇīs*) 'utterances' of the Siddhas and Nāth-yogīs, Kabīr's *bāṇīs* are mostly short, pithy utterances, whose terseness is often not exempt from obscurity. The metrical forms in which they are couched are the same as those used by the Siddhas and Nāth-Yogīs of old: essentially distichs called *dohās* and short rhymed poems known as *pads* or *ramainīs*.

The *dohā* (Skt *dogdhaka* or *dodhaka*) appears as the most typical form of Apabhramsha literature. It differs from the Prakrit *gāthā*, which it has replaced, as the last syllable or each line (*ardhalī*) is short, whilst it is long in the *gāthā*, and also because it introduces the rhyme.[2] This type of rhymed couplet is the principal metre used in the *dohā-koṣa*s composed by the Sahajiyā Buddhists.[3] It was equally popular with the Jain Munis in the middle ages, as shown by the *Pāhuḍa-dohā* of the Jain ascetic Rāmasimha Muni.[4] In ascetic literature, the *dohā* appears exclusively in a didactic form—but it has also been used in lyrical compositions in *grāmya* popular Apabhramsha and in Old Western Rajasthani. The most ancient version of the famous Old Western Rajasthani folk ballad *Ḍholā-mārū-rā dūhā* includes a number of popular lyrics entirely composed in such *dūhā*s.[5] Kabīr himself must have memorized an indefinite number of such *dūhā*s or *dohā*s in the vulgar tongue, which were freely sung and quoted by the common folk. In the *Gurū Granth* collection of Kabīr's sayings, the *dohā*s attributed to Kabīr and the other Bhagats are called *saloku* (Skt *sloka*) i.e. witnesses: one should understand that the couplet is a pithy utterance, 'witnessing' to the ultimate Truth. At the same time, the *sākhī* itself is conceived as the Word (*śabda*) fallen from the guru's mouth—Himself the true and only Witness to the supreme Reality.[6]

The custom of invoking the witness of a great saint of yore in the last line of a stanza is well-established. It is already found in the *Dohā-koṣa*s and the *Caryā-pada*s composed by the Sahajiyā Siddhas and in the *Bāṇī*s of the Nāth-panthīs. In the *Caryā-pada*s, Kāṇha or Kāṇhupa, who calls himself 'naked Kāṇhila', invokes the famous Siddha Jālandhari as his witness. The Siddha invoked as witness may or may not be the poet's own guru, but he is conceived as endowed with perfect knowledge: he embodies the 'Perfect Guru' (*satguru*) who is identical with the supreme divinity or essential Reality. Every *sākhī*, therefore, implicitly refers to the witness of the *Satguru*. The last couplet in the **Bījak** collection says:

> The *sākhī*s are the eyes of Wisdom: understand it in your mind—
> Without the *sākhī*s, there is no end of strife in this world.

Bī. sā. 353

Being the true fountain of wisdom, the 'witness' of the Satguru abolishes the need for all the other *pramāṇa*s or proofs: it puts an end to vain disputes and arguments, as it substitutes direct evidence transmitted by word of mouth for scriptural evidence. Though *sākhī*s may be written, a *sākhī*, by its very nature, is meant to be memorized: it lives in the heart of those whom it has struck and who have been penetrated by its message. Even when couched in the well-defined metrical form of a *dohā,* the *sākhī* is not merely a literary genre, but a privileged form of expression—or rather the evocation of the highest truth.

Kabīr is known all over India essentially as a composer of *sākhī*s and all the main compilations of his verses contain a large number: the Sikh *Gurū Granth* has 243 *sākhī*s, the **Kabīr-granthāvalī** has 811; various editions of the **Bījak** have from 353 to 445 *sākhī*s. The smallest collection is that of the *Sarbāngī*, which includes 181 *sākhī*s out of a total 337 verses attributed to Kabīr.[7] But the number of *sākhī*s attributed to him is much greater. Their number is said to be infinite, as suggested by a verse found in the **Bījak** itself:

> Like the leaves of a great tree, like the grains of sand of the Ganges
> Are the words which have come from Kabīr's mouth
> . . .

Bī. sā. 261

1. KABĪR'S CRYPTIC LANGUAGE

Besides Old Avadhi, the ubiquitous *Nāth-panthī*s, who considered themselves as the disciples of the ancient Yogī Gorakhnāth, made use of various dialects: especially the Dingal (old Rajasthani) and the Pingal impregnated with old Braj-Bhāṣā. It seems that, in Kabīr's time, Dingal was dominant, as the language of the Buddhist Siddhas. On the other hand, before Kabīr, many Sufis had made use of the old Hindui dialect, mixed with Panjabi and Arabo-Persian vocabulary. It is certain that Kabīr used more than one of those languages, according to his audience and to his own fancy. We must also account for Kabīr's polemicist talent—an extraordinary virtuosity in adapting himself to his audience and in borrowing his adversaries' jargon. We give here a specimen of such blasting, for which he was famous:

> O *Miyān!*[8] Your order is not just:
> We are the poor servants of God—and You just seek glory!
> Allah is the Master of Religion, He did not order to oppress the poor:
> Your *Murshīd* and your *Pīr,*[9] tell me, where did they come from?
> You observe the *Ramzān*[10] and you keep spelling prayers—
> but that Kalimā[11] won't earn you heaven:
> He who knows Him through the Experience, his soul possesses seventy Kaabas[12]

In Kabīr's words, the technical terms of Tantric Haṭh-yoga are already detached from ancient traditional meaning. Tantric Yoga practices, while passing from the ancient Buddhist Siddhas to the Shaivite Nāth-panthīs, have been considerably modified. The mythical founder of the sect, Matsyendra (or Macchendra), followed by the ancient Master Gorakhnāth, appear as reformers. In the writings attributed to him, Gorakhnāth himself does away with exterior practices. He rejects the cult of fancy deities as well as the distinction of castes, and he preaches detachment, chastity and sobriety.

The Goal is to accede to a state of 'non-conditionment', 'pure spontaneity', leading to Immortality. That mysterious state, or'Country' described in paradoxical terms, is the *sahaj* state itself. The word has been variously translated by scholars. Shahidullah chooses 'l'Inné', Snellgrove 'The Innate'; Kwaerne adopts Guenter's translation, 'The Co-emergent', based on the literal sense of *sahaj*.[13] Essentially, it refers to 'Transcendence and Immanence, Subject and Object, indivisibly blend'. The Co-emergent is an ontological category: it is the true nature of 'the World'—all that which can be experienced. It is also that infinite Bliss which the Yogī finally obtains as a permanent condition.

The mysterious Reality which is at the centre of Kabīr's practice or *sādhanā* is expressed in a rich variety of terms. Some are Islamic terms, such as Allah, Khudā, Hazrat, Pīr and so on. A few come from the Vedantic tradition, negative epithets such as Alakh, Nirākār, Anant, Guṇātīt; a few are philosophical notions, such as Brahman, Ātman, Āp, Sār. Other terms are directly borrowed from the Haṭhayoga language and practice, such as Śabda, Anāhad, Sahaj and Śūnya, the last two being key-words:

> O *Avadhūt!* The true Yogī is detached from the world,
> He has his dwelling in the sky, He does not see the world,
>   seated on the seat of Conscience:
> Outwardly, He wears the frock,
>   but His soul contemplates the Mirror.
> His body, he has burnt in the Fire of Brahman
>   and He remains awake in the triple Confluent:
> Says Kabīr, such is the King of Yogīs,
>   who has immerged Himself in the *Sahaj-śūnya.*

Sahaj is realized when duality is abolished and the Yogī accedes to transcendental Oneness, in the *sahaj-samādhi.*

The term *Śūnya,* the Void, also belongs to the Buddhistic tradition. Without going back as far as the philosopher Nāgārjuna, *Śūnya* is often mentioned by the *Vajrayānī* Siddhas. In the Haṭha-Yoga, *Śūnya* becomes an equivalent of Keval, Brahman, Sahaj, Nirañjan to call the supreme Reality: as in the *Gorakh-bānīs:*

> *Śūnya* is my Mother, *Śūnya* is my Father,
> *Śūnya* is Nirañjan, the own of my Own!

For Kabīr and the Nāth-Yogīs, *Śūnya* is an equivalent of *Sahaj*—and the two terms are often associated. *Śūnya* means both the supreme Reality and the'Place' where the human being (*jīvātmā*) operates its junction with that Reality:

> *Kabīr,* the Pearl germs in the Fortress whose summit is the Void.

Potions of Immortality play a great part in Tantric theories. *Amṛt* (ambrosia) is conceived as a Liquor flowing from the Moon, i.e. the *sahasradal* formed by 'a thousand petals'. The Nāth-yogīs believe that, from the *sahasradal,* flows a wonderful Liquor: by the blockade of the breath, the Yogī forces the liquor along the *suṣumnā-nāḍī* into the *sahasradal,* where it is drunk by the *jīvātmā,* the living Soul which then obtains Immortality. Kabīr apparently makes use of that language—but he gives another meaning to words such as *rasa, amṛta, sahajaras*: those terms are now taken in the sense of Rām's Love, or of Rām Himself. The Tantric interpretation is rejected: for the true Saint, Rām himself, is the only Drink of Immortality:

> The Shāktas die, and the Saints live
>   as their tongue drinks Rām's Liquor!

and:

> He got absorbed in Sahaj-rām.

Though the alcoholic practices of the Shāktas are negated, Kabīr enhances the spiritual intoxication produced by that Liquor:

> He who has drunk of Rām's Liquor,
>   is intoxicated for ever . . .

The word *khumār,* or intoxication is borrowed by Kabīr from the language of the Sufis, who have often described that 'Intoxication of Love'. But the Sufis themselves had borrowed from the Tantrikas such terms as *ras* and *varuṇī,* which they interpret as *prem-ras,* mystical Love:

> He is the true Yogī, who wears his ring in Spirit:
>   Night and day, He keeps watch:
> In spirit is his posture, in spirit his practice,
>   in spirit his litanies, his asceticism, in spirit his words;
> In spirit his skull, in spirit his whistle—
>   blithely he plays on the flute the silent Music.
> He who has reduced his five senses to ashes,
>   That One will conquer Lanka, says Kabīr.

Surati is a difficult word to interpret—probably derived from *śruti,* 'audition' (of the unspoken Word). In the **Kabīr-granthāvalī,** the *surati* is compared to the Well from which the Water of Love springs up:

> Surati is the balancing pole, Absorption is the rope,
>   and the Spirit rocks the pulley—
> In the Well of the Lotus,
>   the Yogī keeps drinking the Liquor of Love.
> The Ganga and Yamuna are within the heart,
>   and the Yogī has merged in the *Sahaj Śūnya*—
> There Kabīr has built his hideout,
>   while holy men look for a Path!

2. KABĪR'S OWN LANGUAGE

Kabīr's own language and the languages in which his 'Sayings' were originally composed have long been a matter of controversy. According to Ahmed Shah, who translated the **Bījak** into English, Kabīr composed his poetry in the language spoken in his own area, i.e. in Benares and its neighbourhood, in Mirzapur and Gorakhpur.[14] In Gorakhpur, the regional language is Bhojpuri, an Eastern dialect of Hindi, spoken from the Easternmost part of present Uttar Pradesh to the Westernmost part of Bihar and spreading to the North up to the Himalayan border. Grierson argues, however, that there is hardly any trace of the Bhojpuri language in the **Bījak**.[15] For Grierson, the basic language of the **Bījak** is old Avadhi, which seems to fit in with an often-quoted *sākhī* of Kabīr:

> *bolī hamārī pūraba kī, hami lakhai nahī koī*
> *hama to to soi lakhai, dhura pūraba kā hoy*

> My language is of the East—none understands me:
> He alone understands me who is from the farthest
>   East.

Grierson however remarks that any dialect spoken east of the Braj Bhāṣā area is called 'Eastern' in Northern India, and that Avadhi itself is often referred to as *pūrbī*.[16] Yet the meaning of the above-quoted *dohā* which both Grierson and Ahmed Shah have taken literally, is far from obvious. A literal interpretation appears hardly plausible: the idea that no one (in the West?) understands Eastern Hindi is a rather flat statement. P. Chaturvedi argues that *purab dīsā*, 'the Eastern region', symbolizes the ultimate spiritual stage which is the aim of the Yogis.[17] Kabīr's 'Eastern' languages, therefore, means a cryptic language, understandable only to the Yogis and Siddhas who are the dwellers of that mysterious country. Actually, in the **Bījak** itself, another mention of that far-away land confirms Chaturvedi's interpretation: *pūraba dīsā hamsa gati hoī*, 'The Eastern region is the resort of the Hamsa.'(Bi. ra 5.5).

Following R. C. Shukla, most Indian scholars have stressed the heterogeneous character of Kabīr's language, which seems to borrow freely from a variety of dialects. Shukla, however, draws the conclusion that Kabīr's nondescript idiom is essentially based on the idiom used before him by the Nāth-panthī Yogis and other itinerant preachers, and he proposed to call it *sādhukkarī bhāṣā*, lit. Sādhus' jargon.

The first editor of the **Kabīr-granthāvalī**, S. S. Das, also stresses the composite character of Kabīr's language, giving examples, in his Introduction, of *vāṇī*s composed in Khari Bolī, i.e. old Hindī, and also in Rajasthani and Panjabi, besides Avadhi. For S. S. Das Kabīr's language is *panchmel kichrī*, 'a hotch-potch.'[18] Other Indian authors do not give up so easily. The editor of the old Rajasthani ballad, *Dholā-Mārū-rā Dūhā*, thinks that Kabīr's language is mostly Rajasthani.[19] S. K. Chatterji's opinion is that 'Kabīr's poems are composed in mixed Hindi (so-called Hindustani) and *Braj-bhākhā*, with occasional Eastern Hindi (Kosali) and

even Bhojpuri forms'.[20] The difficulty of the problem is largely due to the uncertainties of the textual tradition: the various recensions of a single verse often exhibit dialectical variations. P. Chaturvedi has shown that the same *pad* may be found with characteristic Avadhi forms in the **Bījak,** with more Kharī Bolī in the *Guru Granth* and with a few Braj forms in the **Kabīr-granthāvali,** the latter representing the *Dādū-panthī* tradition. None of the three main recensions, however, is wholly consistent: all show dialectical variations.

Given the complex linguistic pattern which prevailed in Northern India at the time, it cannot be taken for granted that Kabīr preached only in his own dialect. What could have been Kabīr's dialects? As a resident of Benares and a Muslim, he must have been familiar with at least two idioms besides Hindui: the two regional languages, Avadhi and Bhojpuri. Bhojpuri probably was his home language—but he must also have been familiar with Avadhi or *Pūrbī*, the language of the Muslim kingdom of Jaunpur, which included Benares. Houlston notes that "in the Eastern Patna and Gaya districts, where the regional language is Magahi, the dialect of South Bihar, Avadhi is used by many Muslims and Kayasthas, who were scribes in the service of the Moslem rulers; also that, in part of Eastern Uttar-Pradesh, where the regional language is Bhojpuri, the Muslims and Kayasthas do speak Avadhi". But there are good reasons to believe that, in Kabīr's time, the illiterate crowds already used, as a *lingua franca,* the ancient composite idiom known as Hindui: the language of the bazaar.

The language of the *dohā*s differs from that of the *pad*s and *ramainī*s. As noted by Barthwal, "the style is more archaic in the *dohā,* a metre natural to Apabhramsha". Western dialectal forms (Kharī Bolī, Rajasthani, and some Panjabi forms) are more numerous in the *sākhī*s, whereas Braj tends to dominate in the *pad*s. The latter can be explained by the very nature of the genre: the *pad*s are lyrics and, already by Kabīr's time, Braj (or *pingal*) had become the lyrical language *par excellence.* As to the Rajasthani and Panjabi forms in the *sākhī*s, Barthwal, like Shukla, is of the opinion that they reflect "the language of renunciates" discourse (*sādhukkarī bhāṣā*), prevalent at the time. Actually the language of Kabīr's *sākhī*s resembles the language of the *Gorakh-bānī*s, the sayings attributed to Gorakhnāth by the Nāth-panthīs.[21] This nondescript Western idiom is probably inherited from the *dohā-kos*as described by Chatterji as popular (*grāmya*) Apabhramsha. An interesting point is that the dialectical difference between the *dohā*s and *pad*s attributed to Kabīr corresponds to the difference noted between the language of the *Dohā-kos*as and *Caryā-pad*as composed by the Sahajiyā Siddhas.[22]

Though agreeing with Shukla and Barthwal about the influence of the Nāth-panthī language and style on the language of Kabīr's *sākhī*s, Chaturvedi remarks that many such *sākhī*s appear directly influenced by folk-songs and ballads in dohās.[23]

As a matter of fact, the language used by Sant poets, whose works are preserved in the *Granth,* such as Senā, Pīpā and Ravidās, who may have been Kabīr's younger contemporaries, are composed in a very similar language. Even Nāmdev, who lived in the fourteenth century and hailed from Maharashtra, used this mixed Western dialect in his Hindi hymns recorded in the *Granth.*[24] During the course of the fourteenth to the fifteenth centuries, old Hindui or Kharī Bolī had become to be recognized as a *lingua franca* fit for the propagation of popular religious teaching—mostly unorthodox and anti-Brahmanical: one may say that Hindui was the language of the Indian 'Reformation'.[25]

Kabīr himself being an Easterner, would naturally have mixed some forms of his native dialect into his verses. With Benares situated in the Bhojpuri linguistic area, one would expect to find an admixture of Bhojpuri forms in his *sākhī*s; actually such forms are rare, whilst there is general evidence of the Avadhi influence. The reason seems to be that the Bhojpuri language was then, and had remained since, merely a spoken dialect without any written literature, a rural idiom to which the dominant Muslims do not seem to have paid attention. It was not so with Avadhi or *Pūrbī,* which had become, after Persian, the language of the Muslim kingdom of Jaunpur under the Sharqī, (Eastern) dynasty. Like Hindui in the West and in the Deccan, Avadhi, which was already a written language before the time of the Muslim conquest, had begun to be cultivated by the Eastern Sufis, as a means to propagate their own doctrines. Born as a Muslim Julāhā and living about Benares, Kabīr certainly was conversant with the dominant provincial language, Avadhi, and he was probably more familiar with it than with rural Bhojpuri. But there is no reason to suppose that he composed his *sākhī*s in *theth* (pure) Avadhi: he more probably used a composite language, Hindawi or Hindui. Amīr Khusrau, in his *Masnavī,* defines the language of the time:

> Now in India, every province has a peculiar dialect of its own: There is, for instance, Sindhi, Lahori, Kashmiri, Canarese, (. . .) and Oudhi (Avadhi). But in Delhi and all around it, the current language is the same Hindawi that has been used in India from ancient times and has been used for all forms of speech.

The language of the aristocratic Khusrau, like that of the poor Julāhā Kabīr, must have been basically the same: good old Hindui, the language of the bazaar, though the language of the heart may still have been Avadhi.

3. The Conclusion or 'Signature'

The *dohā*s and *pad*s being, by their very nature, *muktak,* i.e. detached, independent verses, their authors often claim ownership by the simple device of introducing their own name in the verses themselves in the last line. This practice, which constitutes a kind of signature, is ancient. It appears already established in the *Dohā-koṣ* and *Caryāpad* of old, composed by the 'Sahajiyā Siddhas' and the 'Nāth-panthīs'. In the *Dohā-koṣ,* we find formulas such as *sarahapa bhaṇanti* or '[the Master] Saraha says'. The formula is called *bhanitā* or 'what is said'. In the Tantric Sahajiya and Nath-panthī literature, the *bhanitā* is not regularly found. In the *Caryā-padas,* it is found in a more developed form such as 'Kanha says', 'Sarahpā says'. Often, the name of the poet, who is a Siddha, is directly introduced in the line as the subject in a clause, such as: *kāṇha vilasiā āsava-mātā,* '[The Master] Kāṇha sports, drunk with liquor'.[26]

The use of the *bhanitā,* also called *mudrikā,*'stamp', seems to have become generalized in Northern and central India from the fifteenth century onwards, before Kabīr. It is found in the so-called *abhanga*s in archaic Marathi, as well as in the *pad*s of the Northern saint-poets. In the *sākhī*s, however, the full *bhanitā* is rarely found: either there is no signature at all, or else the single word *kabīr* is used at the beginning of the first line of the *dohā,* rarely of the second.[27] It is then used as a 'stamp' without having any syntactic function in the clause, which then becomes susceptible of a double interpretation.

4. The Literary Languages of the Muslim Medieval Period

Between the 14th and the 16th centuries A.D., under the influence of the Sufis, especially the Chishtiyas, two Indian vernaculars had emerged as literary languages in Northern and Central India: the highly persianized Dakhani in the Bijapur-Golconde area of the Deccan and the 'pure' (*theth*) Avadhi in Eastern Uttar Pradesh—an idiom practically free from Arabo-Persian vocabulary. The former reflected the language of the literate Muslims, the latter was attuned to the ear of educated Hindus. The works composed in those literary dialects had an ecumenical ring, as their Sufi authors were eager to build a bridge between 'the Two Religions', Hinduism and Islam, to unite rather than divide. All those works were written in the Persian script, with which literate Hindus, especially the Kayastha caste, had long been familiar.

Meanwhile the uneducated masses of Northern India went on with their own provincial languages and dialects, to which a *lingua franca* was superposed out of the necessities of common intercourse, especially between low-caste Hindus and equally low-caste Muslim converts: as we have seen, that *lingua franca* was *Hindui,* whose origin was probably anterior to the Muslim conquest and the Muslim predication: a mixed language of Northwestern origin, used by itinerant holy men of various denominations, mostly by the ubiquitous *Gorakhnāthi* or *Nāth-panthī* Yogīs. A hybrid language from the start, Hindui easily absorbed the Arabo-Persian vocabulary, with any amount of phonetic variations and deformations. Persianized Hindui, later called'Hindustani' seems to have been spoken—or at least understood—all over Northwestern India and the Ganges valley, including Bihar and Central India, and also in part of Maharashtra—all regions where the Nāth-panthī propaganda had been active from the tenth century onwards. The very plasticity of old medieval Hindui made it the perfect medium for the spreading of new ideas and new religious values among the downtrodden masses of India: it was the privileged idiom of the anti-Brahmanical propaganda carried on by the Nāth-panthīs and the Sufis with equal fervour. In the Deccan, the Hindui language appears to have been familiar to the unorthodox, bitterly anti-Brahmanical Manbhau (*mahānubhāv*) sectarians, themselves indebted to the Nāth-panthī predication, though antagonistic to their cult. This is confirmed by the *Caupaḍī*s (i.e. *caupāī*) verses of Dāmodar Paṇḍit, a Manbhau author belonging to the 13-14th century (1237-1316) whose verses were composed as a retort to the philosophy of the Nāth cult.[28] According to V. D. Kulkarni, out of 60 verses (*caupadī*) in that work, 35 are composed in a language which is predominantly the regional language, *Marāṭhī*—whereas the other 25 represent the language of the Nāth-Siddhas—a language that the author describes as "a harmonic blending of Hindi and Marathi words, without any Arabic or Persian element".[29]

The Caupaḍīs of Dāmodar Paṇḍit testify to the extraordinary plasticity of 'Hindui', as used by unorthodox preachers. V. D. Kulkarni notes that the language of the Caupaḍīs is close to the language of the Gorakh Bānīs. Apparently, as a Sādhus' jargon, Hindui could include and assimilate any amount of words borrowed from other Indo-Aryan dialects. The fact that the Caupaḍīs of Dāmodar Paṇḍit contain no Arabo-Persian vocabulary, suggests that their origin goes back to the pre-Muslim period. Later Manbhau literature is entirely and exclusively composed in Marathi. In spite of its strongly monotheistic trend, the literature of the Marathi *abhang*as appears more akin to Krishnaite Bhakti than to the religion of the Northern Sants, including the old saint-poet Nāmdev from Maharashtra. Nāmdev, who probably belongs to the fourteenth century, is the author of a large number of *abhang*as, short devotional poems in medieval Marathi. Though Nāmdev is not a northerner, the Sant tradition invariably names him as Kabīr's predecessor—and the *Dādū-panthī* themselves name him as the first (i.e. the earliest) of the Northern Sants. He is known to have expressed himself in the *lingua franca* of the time: old 'Hindui'. The inclusion of the old saint Nāmdev among the Sant poets of Northern India is based on the sixty-one Hindi hymns attributed to him in the *Gurū Granth* of the Sikhs. Some poems attributed to Nāmdev are composed in a queer

mixture of Hindi and Marathi;[30] moreover, a number of *pad*s attributed to Nāmdev in other collections also include Marathi grammatical forms. Nāmdev is the oldest poet in the Sant *paramparā*: after him, the tradition diverges. The Maharashtrian Sants become more devotional and more vaishnavized, while the old Nāth-panthī, anti-brahmanical trend of thought and Tantric vocabulary is on the wane. The case of Dāmodar Paṇḍit as well as that of Nāmdev suggests a strong link between the old Hindui language and the rejection of Brahmanical orthodoxy and social establishment. First used as a *lingua franca* by the Nāth-panthīs to spread their gospel of religious and social rebellion, Hindui remains in use in vast areas in which more developed literary languages already existed, as in Eastern India and in Maharashtra: old Hindui emerges as essentially the language of non-conformity and the Indian medieval Reformation. The Arabo-Persian script becomes the only script available to all, Hindus as well as Muslims, for mundane affairs as well as religious expression—as seen in the *premākhyān* love tales, in old Avadhi. The ancient *devanāgarī* script remains the privilege of the Pandits, and the *Kaiṭhī* script that of the Kayastha scribes, who use it concurrently with the Arabo-Persian script. If the poor Julāhā Kabīr was somewhat acquainted with any script, it could only have been with that Arabo-Persian script.

5. KABĪR'S STYLE

Much has been said and written about Kabīr's style. All critics, especially modern ones, have emphasized its extraordinary vigour—a quality in which his verses stand supreme in the Hindi language and perhaps in the whole Indian tradition—as well as its abrasive roughness. Indifferent to 'literature', unskilled in the delicate art of ornate poetry, Kabīr cannot be called a *kavi*, 'poet', in the traditional Indian sense. Some Indian scholars would rather consider him as a social reformer and a mystic than as a poet. Not only are Kabīr's verses devoid of all literary ornaments (*alamkāra*) and figures of speech, but the very bluntness of his expressions, the triviality of his comparisons and his scoffing, are likely to shock the reader or listener whose ears are attuned to the refinements and intricacies of *kāvya* poetry.

H. P. Dvivedi is not wrong when he argues that "Kabīr found the Hindi language still in infancy, yet put it to severe trial and somewhat attempted to bend it to his needs". The same scholar calls Kabīr "a dictator of language"; "Language trembles before him, unable to serve him and to comply to his will . . ." Actually, no scholar who ever read Kabīr in the original could fail to be struck by the unique forcefulness of his style. As noted by W. G. Orr, "for sheer vigour of thought and rugged terseness, no later bhakti writer can be brought into comparison with him".

More so with Kabīr than with any other Indian author, the peculiar quality of the style seems to reflect an outstanding and somewhat mysterious personality. Indifferent or opposed to traditional beliefs and values, apparently unconcerned with the pleasure or displeasure of his audience, Kabīr fearlessly voices his inner conviction. His blunt language, his bitter irony bespeak ardent indignation—but also a desperate effort to awaken his dumb, sleepy fellow men, unaware of their impending doom.

The heroic striving of the soul awakened by the 'Satguru's arrow' to reach the unseen, inaccessible Beloved, the dangers and torments of the spiritual Path, inspire him with stirring words, revealing the depth of his own suffering and despair. On the other hand, the ineffable bliss of Union in that far-away 'land', beyond the'impassable Pass'—yet hidden in the depth of man's own soul—the ecstasy of the secret, silent merging into the One, in which all duality is abolished, are evoked in strange, often obscure words, yet endowed—at least for the Indian ear—with an extraordinary power of suggestion.

Even when chaotic and somewhat obscure, Kabīr's style, at least in his well-established sayings, is never dull, never lacking in naturalness and spontaneity, which gives it its inimitable charm. Dvivedi has found suggestive words to evoke Kabīr's style: 'Tender as a flower, hard as a diamond'. And it is true that Kabīr's best utterances are endowed with a diamond-like quality, the transparency, multi-faceted brilliancy and mysterious glow of pure diamond. If not a learned poet, a *kavi* in the traditional sense, the little weaver of Benares was indeed a great poet, one of the greatest known in India and elsewhere.

Notes

1. The Sahajiyā Master Kāṇha says in one of the *Caryā-pad*s: *jo managoara ālājālā, āgama pothi iṣṭam ālā.*

   "What the mind perceives is mere humbug and so are the *āgamas* (scriptures), the books and the bead-telling".

   Shahidullah, *Les Chants mystiques de Kāṇha et Saraha: le Dohā-koṣa et les Caryā,* Paris, 1928, p. 115, 10.

2. According to the scholar H. P. Dvidevi, *Hindī sāhitya kā ādikāl,* Patna, 1952, p. 93, the *dohā* is the first *chand,* i.e. prosodical form, in which the rhyme was introduced.

3. The Buddhist Saraha himself praises the *dohā-chanda* in these terms: *ṇaü ṇaü dohā-saddena ṇa kahabi kimpi goppia.*

   "Through ever new *dohā*s, nothing remains hidden" (i.e. all spiritual truth can be expressed in *dohā*s); cf. Shahidullah, op.cit., p. 160, *dohā* 94.

4. *The Pāhuḍa Dohā of Rāmasimha Muni, An Apabhramśa work on Jaina mysticism,* ed. Hiralal Jain, Karanja, 1933.

5. On lyrical *dohā*s in late Apabhramsha and in Old Western Rajasthani literature, cf. Ch. Vaudeville, *Les Dūhā de Ḍholā-Mārū,* Pondichery, 1962, pp.46-7 and 116-18.

6. Barthwal (*NSHP,* pp. 223-4) remarks that the terms *sākhī* and *sabad* (*śabda*) meaning 'witness' or 'authoritative word' (of the Guru) seem to have been originally used as synonyms.

7. According to Tiwārī (*KG,* Preface, pp. ii-iii), there are no less than 1.579 *pads,* 5.395 *sākhīs* and 134 *ramainīs* attributed to Kabīr in various compilations—and research could probably uncover more!

8. 'Sir', addressed to a Muhammedan.

9. 'Murshid': a leader, an eminent person.'Pir': a Muhammedan Saint, a holy man.

10. Ramzān: the ninth month of the Muhammedan year, in which fast should be observed from early dawn, to sunset.

11. Kalimā: the sacred formula of the Muslim faith: Allah is God and Muhammad is his Prophet.

12. Kaaba: the sacred square building at Mecca, visited by all Muslim pilgrims.

13. 'Co-emergent' may also be interpreted as'Essential'.

14. Ahmed Shah, [ed., *The Bījak of Kabīr,* Baptist Mission, Cawnpore, 1911], p. 29.

15. G. Grierson, *The Bijak of Kabir,* JRAS, 1918, p. 152.

16. B. R. Saksena's opinion in the matter is cautiously stated: '*Pūrbī* means "Eastern" and is sometimes used for Avadhi and at others for Bhojpuri. It may well be a suitable name of Eastern Hindi to distinguish it from Western Hindi.' *Evolution of Avadhi,* Allahabad, 1937, p. 2.

17. P. Chaturvedi, *KSP,* pp. 209-10; see also D. V. Bharati, *Siddha-sāhitya,* Allahabad, 1965, pp. 447-8.

18. *KG* I, Intr., pp. 71-75.

19. *Dholā-mārū-rā-dūhā,* eds. Ram Simha, S. K. Parik and N. D. Svami, Benares V. S. 1991 (1934), pp. 167-8.

20. A review of conflicting opinions about Kabīr's language is found in P. Chaturvedi, *KSP,* pp. 208ff.

21. Cf. *Nāth siddho kī bāniyå,* ed. H. P. Dvivedi, Benares, Vi.S. 2014, 1957 A.D.

22. S. K. Chatterji (*ODBL*, vol. 1, Calcutta, 1926, pp. 112-13) characterizes the language of the *Dohā-koṣa*as as a king of Western (Sauraseni) Apabhramsha and the language of the *Caryā-pad* as "a form of old Bengali".

23. Among those Southern Indian Sufis, Shah Burhanuddin, who flourished at Bijapur and who might have been Kabīr's contemporary, wrote a short work called *Sukh-sahelā* which had the vocabulary and metres of 'Hindu Hindi'. S. K. Chatterji (*Indo-Aryan and Hindi* [Calcutta: Firma K. L. Mukhopadhyay, 1960], p. 206) writes that the Hindi found in the *Sukh-sahelā* "is very like the Hindi we find in Kabīr's poems and in the works of the Saints".

24. The dates of Nāmdev, who in the North is given as Rāmānand's disciple and in Maharashtra as a contemporary of Jñāneshvar, remain uncertain. Besides, the Maharashtrian tradition knows more than one 'Namdev'; cf. P. Machve, *Hindī aur marāṭhī kā nirguṇ sant-kāvya*, Benares, 1962; see also Bhandarkar, VS, pp. 124 ff. The Hindi hymns of Nāmdev have been edited, in Hindi, with a substantial Introduction by Bhagirath Mishra and R.N. Maurya: *Sant Nāmdev kī hindī padāvalī*, Poona, 1964. A critical edition and English translation has been prepared by Winand M. Callewaert & Mukund Lath, *The Hindī Songs of Nāmdev*, Leuven, 1989, 432 p.

25. Vaudeville, *Kabīr's language and languages: Hindui as the Language of Non-conformity*, Madison University, 1987.

26. Quoted in R. Sankrityayan, *Hindī kāvya dhārā*, Allahabad, 1945, p. 151.

27. In the *Gurū Granth*, the word *kabīra* is regularly added at the beginning of each *saloku* (śloka) without consideration for the rhythm. We have omitted it in translation.

28. V. D. Kulkarni, 'The *Caupaḍī*s of Dāmodar Paṇḍit'.

29. A few Arabo-Persian words, however, are found in the Hindi *pad*s and also in the Marathi *abhang*as, attributed to saint Nāmdev.

30. The Hindi hymns of Nāmdev have been edited with a substantial Introduction by Bhagirath Mishra and R. N. Maurya: *Sant Nāmdev kī hindī padāvalī*, Poona, 1964; for the mixed language, see *pad*s 15, 20, 31, 34. See also Callewaert-Lath:1989.

Abbreviations

JRAS: *Journal of the Royal Asiatic Society*

KG: *Kabīr Granthāvalī*, ed. P. N. Tiwari, Prayāg, 1961.

KSP: P. Chaturvedi, *Kabīr sāhitya kī parakh*, Prayāg, Vi.S. 2011.

NSHP: P. D. Barthwal, *The Nirguna School of Hindi Poetry*, Benares, 1936.

ODBL: S. K. Chatterji, *The Origin and Development of the Bengali Language*, 2 vols., Calcutta, 1926.

VS: R. G. Bhandarkar, *Vaiṣṇavism, Śaivism and Minor Religious Systems*, Collected Works, iv, Poona, 1929.

FURTHER READING

Biographies

Bahadur, Krishna Prakash. *A New Look at Kabir*, New Delhi: Ess Ess Publications, 1997, 288 p.

Detailed study that covers Kabīr's life, philosophy, poetry, and language; the social and religious context in which he lived and wrote; and traditional beliefs about his life and contributions.

Varma, Ram Kumar. *Kabir: Biography and Philosophy*, New Delhi: Prints India, 1977, 152 p.

Reconstruction of Kabīr's biography and philosophy based on his utterances.

Criticism

Callewaert, Winand M. "Kabir. Scholarly Commentaries on Un-Critical Texts?" *Annali Istituto Universitario Orientale, Napoli: Rivista del Dipartmento di Studi Asiatic* 56, no. 1 (1996): 88-98.

Discusses the authenticity of the songs attributed to Kabīr.

Ram, K. S. "Kabir, Surdas and Mirabai: A Note on Bhakti Poetry in Hindi." *The Literary Criterion* 24, no. 1 (1989): 147-52.

Examines common features of the Bhakti, or devotional, poetry of three of the four most important Bhakti poets in Hindi.

Schomer, Karine. "Kabir in the *Guru Granth Sahib*: An Exploratory Essay." In *Sikh Studies: Comparative Perspectives on a Changing Tradition*, edited by Mark Juergensmeyer and N. Gerald Barrier, pp. 75-86. Berkeley, Calif.: Berkeley Religious Studies Series, 1979.

Compares the Kabīr traditions preserved in the Sikh scriptures, *Guru Granth Sahib*, with those preserved elsewhere to shed light on Sikhism.

Vaudeville, Charlotte. "Kabir's Language and Languages, Hindui as the Language of Non-Conformity." *Indo-Iranian Journal* 33, no. 4 (October 1990): 259-66.

Discussion of Kabīr's own language and the use of the languages in which his sayings were originally composed.

Additional coverage of Kabīr's life and career is contained in the following sources published by Thomson Gale: *Literature Resource Center; Poetry Criticism,* **Vol. 56;** *Reference Guide to World Literature,* **Eds. 2, 3.**

The Literature of the Counter-Reformation

INTRODUCTION

The Counter-Reformation refers to a movement dominated by Catholic reaction to the challenge of Protestantism for a period from the mid-sixteenth to mid-seventeenth century, from approximately the reign of Pope Pius IV to the end of the Thirty Years' War in 1648. Literature of this period includes some of the most highly acclaimed works in theology. The term "Counter-Reformation" traditionally has been rejected by Catholics because it implies that the Church was motivated to fight internal corruption only because Protestant actions demanded it. Catholics note that reform had a long history in the Church before Protestantism and continues to the present day; to Catholics, their view is better rendered by the term "Catholic Reformation." Hubert Jedin has examined the complex history of the words and concepts involved, particularly the differences between "reformation," "reform," and the Latin "*reformatio,*" and whether "internal renewal" or "radical reconstruction" is the more appropriate descriptor for the changes that occurred in the Church. Ultimately Jedin has found the use of both terms essential: "Catholic Reformation" to emphasize continuity, "Counter-Reformation" to emphasize reaction.

When discussing the Counter-Reformation, scholars generally find it useful to give background on the Reformation to which the movement was a reaction, and on the state of Church practices that preceded the Reformation. John C. Olin has traced the history of Christian reform in his study of the background to the Catholic Reformation, including Church abuses and Martin Luther's demands for the end of the sale of indulgences. Olin notes that the concept of reform developed over time, from signifying personal change on an individual basis to eventually encompassing the restoration of the Church at large; but he adds that institutional and personal reforms are closely related. He cites *The Imitation of Christ,* a 1411 work by Thomas à Kempis, as one of the most influential books of spiritual ideals. A. G. Dickens has also credited *The Imitation of Christ* for inspiring numerous religious writers who followed. Dickens's survey of some of the more influential literature leading up to the Counter-Reformation explores the conflicts between traditional ways of undertaking spiritual studies and newer, more intellectual approaches, and further discusses how meditative and mystical methods fused into *devotio moderna* ("Modern Devotion"). H. Outram Evennett has explored the genesis of the most important work in the Catholic Reformation, the *Spiritual Exercises* (c. 1522-23) by Ignatius of Loyola, the founder of the Society of Jesus. Evennett discusses how the society's members, referred to as Jesuits, empowered by the *Spiritual Exercises,* promoted active, good works. He credits them for "transforming and enormously quickening the spiritual life-blood of Catholicism." Church leaders throughout Europe had met in council for many years but had always failed to reach an accord. Finally, in 1561, at the Council of Trent, a breakthrough came and pronouncements and decrees were agreed upon. With its new unity, the Council of Trent greatly strengthened the orthodox faith at the same time that internal disputes among Protestants led them to split into numerous sects, thereby decreasing their power.

Significant scholarly interest is directed to the responses elicited by the Counter-Reformation. Phebe Jensen has discussed how the Elizabethan government dealt with Catholic challenges to its authority, censoring Catholic writings at a time when much of the public supported the expression of religious speech and conscience. Michael A. Mullett has examined how religious leaders sought acceptance of their message by employing a new style of art; he describes how the concept of the baroque dominated all art forms in seventeenth-century Europe, and explains that the Jesuits favored the utilitarian and that "instruction through delight" was one of the chief aims of Catholic baroque art and literature.

REPRESENTATIVE WORKS

Robert Bellarmine
The Book of Controversies (essays) 1586-89

Louis de Blois
A Book of Spiritual Instruction (handbook) 1551

Edmund Campion
Ten Reasons (essays) 1581

Peter Canisius
The True Evangelical Life (sermons, essays, letters, songs) 1543

The Council of Trent
Canons and Decrees (manifesto) 1566

Ignatius of Loyola
Spiritual Exercises (handbook) c. 1522-23

William Peryn
Spiritual Exercises (handbook) 1557

Dionysius Petavius
Dogmata theologica (essays) 1643

Teresa of Avilia
Life Written by Herself (autobiography) 1565

OVERVIEWS AND GENERAL STUDIES

John C. Olin (essay date 1969)

SOURCE: Olin, John C. "Introduction: The Background of Catholic Reform." In *The Catholic Reformation: Savonarola to Ignatius Loyola: Reform in the Church, 1495-1540,* pp. xv-xxvi. New York: Harper & Row, 1969.

[*In the following essay, Olin examines the long history of religious reform and explains how the efforts of Renaissance humanists to lessen the disparity between the ideal and reality influenced Church reform.*]

The Church in the late Middle Ages endured what may be called a "time of troubles"—a time marked by challenge and dissent, manifesting the symptoms of spiritual and institutional decline, climaxed by the great crisis and disruption that broke in the sixteenth century. The pattern is large and complex and its texture is uneven, but the observer can hardly fail to perceive that trial and peril beset the vast ecclesiastical structure of the West in the fourteenth and fifteenth centuries. Its organization and authority as well as the integrity of its inner life and mission seem to have been placed in prolonged jeopardy by the events and currents of that age. And it was not simply a matter of external forces beating against the Church and taking their toll of its power and substance. Within the religious community itself there were ominous signs of weakness and disorder: the schism resulting from the double papal election of 1378 and continuing down to 1417, the exaggeration of papal power and a concomitant opposition to it both in practice and in theory, the worldliness and secularization of the hierarchy that reached to the papacy itself in the High Renaissance, ignorance and immorality among the lower clergy, laxity in monastic discipline and spiritual decay in the religious life, theological desiccation and confusion, superstition and abuse in religious practice.

The picture should not be overdrawn (there were many instances of sanctity, dedication, and even spiritual renewal during this time), but in general, Catholic life in the late Middle Ages seems grievously depressed—hollowed out, to use Lortz's image[1]—and the evidence of deep-seated trouble is inescapable.

A considerable body of contemporary comment and observation can be cited to this effect, and indeed the texts presented in this volume bear frank witness to the ills that afflicted the Church. But at the outset two voices may be allowed to speak to lend credence and confirmation to the state of affairs we have described. Lorenzo de' Medici, *Il Magnifico,* wrote a letter of paternal advice in early 1492 to his son Giovanni, who at the age of sixteen was about to go to Rome and take up his residence as a cardinal. The youth is the future Pope Leo X. Lorenzo urged him to virtue and an exemplary life, and he added: "I well know, that as you are now to reside at Rome, that sink of all iniquity, the difficulty of conducting yourself by these admonitions will be increased. . . . You will probably meet with those who will particularly endeavor to corrupt and incite you to vice."[2] From north of the Alps the German scholar and versifier Sebastian Brant gave a broader and more public warning. In his moralistic poem *Narrenschiff,* first published in Basel in 1494, he wrote the following quatrain:

> St. Peter's ship is swaying madly,
> It may be wrecked or damaged badly,
> The waves are striking 'gainst the side
> And storm and trouble may betide.[3]

Such voices can be multiplied, and it must also be stressed that the plight of the Bark of Peter evoked a fuller response than the mere advertisement of its fitful course or the castigation of its crew. There arose the call for remedying the evils that had come to pass. There was counsel and advice on restoring the vessel to its former efficiency and its original progress. Nor were efforts lacking in the attempt to achieve these goals. This response, constructive and restorative, to the condition of the Church is generally what we mean when we use the words reform and reformation. And it is of course the subject of our study.

Basically the two terms reform and reformation mean a return to an original form or archetype or ideal and imply the removal or correction of faults which have caused deformation. The object of reform is restored to its original character, its essential mode of being. Applied to the Church and to religious faith and practice, the significance of these words is obvious. They mean a return to the original purity and splendor of Christ's Church and indeed to Christ himself, the model of Christians and the very *form* of the Church. Dante's words in *De Monarchia* come to mind:

Now the form of the Church is nothing else than the life of Christ in word and in deed. For his life was the idea and pattern of the Church militant, especially of its shepherds and most especially of its chief shepherd, whose duty it is to feed the sheep and lambs. He himself said, in John's Gospel, as he bequeathed the form of his life to us, "I have given you an example that as I have done to you, so you do also." And specifically to Peter, after he had assigned him the post of shepherd, he said, "Peter, follow thou me."[4]

The call for such reform may be said to arise from the nature of things—from the disparity between the ideal and the reality that to a lesser or greater degree is ever present in man's history. With respect to the Church, as Jedin points out, it "originated in the consciousness that Christ's foundation, as historically realised in its individual members, no longer corresponded to the ideal—in other words, that it was not what it should be."[5] And so the disparity must be ended and the historical Church brought into conformity with the ideal. It must strive to be what it should be—faithful to Christ and the mission He enjoined, drawing close to that glorious Church of which St. Paul speaks, "without spot or wrinkle or any such disfigurement."[6]

Because of conditions in the late Middle Ages the consciousness of a contrast between the contemporary Church and the primitive form and ideal was particularly acute. Dante is expressing it in the chapter we have quoted from the *De Monarchia,* and in several striking passages of the *Paradiso* he observes the grave discrepancy between the Church of his day and that of Christ and the Apostles and the saints.

> Barefoot and lean came Cephas, came the great
> Vessel of the Holy Ghost; and they would sup
> At whatsoever house they halted at.
>
> Pastors today require to be propped up
> On either side, one man their horse to lead
> (So great their weight!) and one their train to loop.
>
> Over their mounts their mantles fall, full-spread;
> Two beasts beneath one hide behold them go!
> O patience, is thy meekness not yet fled?[7]

Thomas à Kempis in his *Imitation of Christ*—the title of which is a reform program—also marks the difference, though in more personal moralistic terms. "Behold the living examples of the old fathers in which shineth true perfection, and thou shalt see how little it is and almost naught that we do. Alas, what is our life compared to them?" And, after describing their life of sanctity and virtue, he exclaims: "O how great was the fervor of religion in the beginning of its institution!"[8] Savonarola is likewise deeply conscious of the discordance between present ways and the model of the early Church. "In the primitive Church the chalices were of wood, the prelates of gold; in these days the Church hath chalices of gold and prelates of wood."[9]

Given this awareness, the task then was correcting what was wrong and restoring the Church to her pristine state. However, we have perhaps said enough in general terms about the nature and occasion of Catholic reform in the late Middle Ages. Let us now look briefly at the historical development of the notion of reform and at some of its specific manifestations in the life of the Church. Our perspective on the Catholic Reformation in the sixteenth century will thereby be enlarged.

The original concept of Christian reform is one of the reform of the individual—of his personal renewal and the restoration in him of the image of God, the *form* of his creation. It is the concept found in Holy Scripture and in the Fathers of the early Church, and it has been studied very thoroughly by Gerhart Ladner in his work *The Idea of Reform.*[10] The Church as such was not the object of a reform endeavor, but rather the inner man who was to be remade *ad imaginem et similitudinem Dei.* This original and fundamental concept never disappears, for it is an integral part of the Christian message. "If then any man is in Christ, he is a new creature: the former things have passed away; behold, they are made new!"[11] Erasmus underlined this doctrine in the introduction to the New Testament he published in 1516. "What else is the philosophy of Christ," he asks, "which He himself calls a rebirth, than the restoration of human nature originally well formed?"[12] Rebirth (the Latin term Erasmus used is *renascentia*), restoration, and reform refer then to the very basic personal renewal that Christianity entails.

By the eleventh century, however, the idea of reform had also come to include the correction and renewal of the Church at large. This expanded concept found expression in the Gregorian reform of that time.[13] So-called because Pope Gregory VII (1073-85) was its leading figure, it sought to end the feudal lay domination of the Church and restore her freedom and her spiritual mission. It centered chiefly on the clergy or *sacerdotium,* and its thrust was what we would call institutional. Papal primacy and authority were forcefully asserted; elections to ecclesiastical office were to be freely and properly conducted; old canons governing the Church were renewed; bad customs and practices were to be abolished. The Church, in short, was to be reformed in line with its original and authentic constitution so that its true apostolate might be realized.

But such institutional reform is not to be conceived apart from the reform of the individual Christian. "Gregory VII and the Gregorians," writes Dom Leclercq, "many of them monks and all of them influenced by St. Augustine, conceived of reform as an essentially spiritual matter. For them, as for their master, there could be no reform of the Church without reform of the Christian."[14] The latter is the primary goal, and the Church reformed is actually the Church made more effective in the *cura animarum*—in the work of teaching, guiding, and sanctifying her members. Vatican II formulated that in a memorable way when it declared that "every renewal of the Church essentially consists in an increase of fidelity to her own calling."[15] Her reform and renewal, however, must come in some way through her members, and this presupposes their own personal conversion and commitment. The institution per se does not reform itself but is reformed by men who are reformed. In this sense the Church needs saints, that is, men who truly are reformed and whose example and efforts are the means for further reformation.

The life of St. Francis of Assisi (1181/2-1226) is particularly instructive in this regard. His own conversion was accompanied by those symbolic words he heard in the chapel of San Damiano: "Repair my house which, as you see, is being totally destroyed." And his remarkable life was lived in such close imitation of Christ that it became an inspiration and strength for the whole Church. Of him the Cardinal of Santa Sabina reported to Pope Innocent III: "I have found a man of most perfect life, that is minded to live conformably with the Holy Gospel, and to observe in all things Gospel perfection: through whom, as I believe, the Lord is minded to reform throughout the whole world the faith of Holy Church."[16] The Pope himself saw in Brother Francis "the holy man by whom the Church of God shall be uplifted and upheld."[17]

The two kinds of reform—institutional and personal—thus are closely related, and, as Ladner suggests, the Gregorian and Franciscan movements are complementary phases and aspects of the same idea.[18] It is also clear that St. Francis moves at the deeper level, more in keeping with the original and fundamental concept of Christian renewal. Yet thereby the Church and Christendom were renewed.

> He'd not long risen when the earth was stirred
> By touches of invigorating power
> From his great strength . . .[19]

The expanded concept of reform is also in a sense expressed in the formula *reformatio in capite et in membris* which gained currency in the late Middle Ages. Attributed to William Durandus at the time of the Council of Vienne (1311-12), its most famous usage perhaps is in the decrees and pronouncements of the Council of Constance (1414-18).[20] The decree *Sacrosancta* of 1415, for example, declares the Council's purpose to be the ending of the great schism which had rent the Church since 1378 and the Church's reformation in its head and members. Thus used, the phrase became linked with the conciliar movement that was born of the Western Schism and the plight of the Church at that critical time, and it serves to underline the fact that conciliarism was essentially a reform movement. Asserting the su-

premacy and active role of the General Council in the government of the Church, the conciliarists sought to limit papal authority and end the abuses connected with papal appointments and papal taxation.[21] This was the heart of their *reformatio in capite* and the first principle of the more general reformation that must follow, for, as Durandus himself had pointed out, "when the head languishes, all the members of the body suffer pain."[22]

The Council of Constance did resolve the Western Schism, but it was not eminently successful in its reform endeavors. Nor did the subsequent Councils of Pavia-Siena (1423-24) and of Basel (1431-49), as provided for by the decree *Frequens* of 1417, achieve that reform and renewal that so many sought. Basel featured from beginning to end a bitter struggle between the conciliarists and the Papacy and climaxed its antipapal legislation in 1439 by deposing the reigning Pope Eugenius IV and electing an antipope Felix V. In this instance a Council had led to schism, and the spectacle thus afforded contributed decisively to the defeat of the conciliar movement and the victory of the papal monarchy in the fifteenth century. The hope too of achieving a *reformatio in capite et in membris* through the agency of a General Council was also ended.[23] It was now incumbent on the Papacy whose primacy had been reasserted and confirmed to give leadership in that cause.

In this heavy responsibility the Papacy failed. Neither its own reform nor that of the Church at large was sufficiently promoted, and therein lies one of the darkest features of the religious scene at the close of the Middle Ages. A deeply moving page of Gordon Rupp's *Luther's Progress to the Diet of Worms* is recalled: "What are the inexorable consequences of the sins of the New Israel? . . . What happens when the successors of the Apostles betray, deny, forsake their evangelical vocation?"[24] Stern judgment will be rendered, and Rupp, evoking the tremendous vision of Michelangelo in the Sistine Chapel of a Christ risen in wrath, sees the Reformation as an ordeal, the Doomsday of the late medieval Church. Yet an awareness of the need for reform was not lacking in the Roman Curia following its triumph over the rebellious Council of Basel.[25] The *Advisamenta* of Cardinal Capranica during the pontificate of Nicholas V (1447-55)—it "reads like a complete programme of the Catholic reformation," says Jedin[26]—and the reform memorials of Domenico Domenichi and Nicholas of Cusa in the days of Pius II (1458-64) are witness to this fact. And even the notorious Alexander VI, struck by remorse over the assassination of his son, the Duke of Gandia, in 1497 appointed a reform commission which seriously and competently reported on the state of the Church and drafted comprehensive reform measures. But these were all dead letters. Nothing was accomplished, nothing gained. In fact, the Papacy itself in the later decades of the fifteenth century—the "Papacy of Princes," as Father Hughes has called it—

entered a period of moral disintegration which culminated in the most scandalous venality and secularization.[27] The *deformatio in capite* was most acute as the hour of judgment began to strike.

But if Council and Pope had eliminated themselves from the quest for reform in the actual circumstances of the time, what other avenues or agencies for Christian renewal and the Church's reformation remained? Here the picture is not quite so dreary; here the signs of regeneration may be discerned. For this perspective, however, we must turn for the moment from our concern with institutional reform, that is, from the *reformatio in capite* which had been obstructed and denied, to the matter of personal reform, that is, to the *reformatio in membris* which could and did have a spontaneous life. The two reformations, as we have said, must be joined in the Catholic concept, and they are of course closely related in their mutual interaction, but there is an obvious difference in their proximate goals and in their spheres of activity and effective means. We must turn then to the reform of the members if we would observe the beginnings—and the wellspring in the immediate sense—of the Catholic Reformation of the sixteenth century. The documents in this volume and the development they represent by the same token are linked very closely to these endeavors.

There are many examples of personal renewal and partial reform in the late Middle Ages. Jedin has given clear indication of this in a substantial chapter in his *History of the Council of Trent.*[28] The Church was not without religious communities or prelates or zealous men and women who sought to live by the highest spiritual ideals. The Charterhouse of Cologne, the Augustinian Canons of Windesheim, Jean Gerson, chancellor of the University of Paris, the scholarly Cardinal Nicholas of Cusa, St. Antoninus, Archbishop of Florence, Thomas à Kempis, the great preacher St. Bernadino of Siena are but a few of the examples—notable ones, to be sure—the fifteenth century affords. And these are characterized not only by their own individual virtue and dedication but by the wider influence their labors bore. A movement broader than any single individual or community can also be cited as witnessing and in turn contributing to the religious renewal so needed at this time. This was the *Devotio moderna,* originating in the Netherlands and associated primarily with the Brothers of the Common Life and the congregation of Windesheim, but casting wide its net of inspiration and revival. It was, to quote Margaret Aston, "probably the most generative religious movement of the whole century," and it forms a major source of Catholic reform in the following era.[29]

The *Devotio moderna* was a spirit of personal piety, based above all on the following of Christ and the cultivation of a simple and fervent interior life. It centered

its doctrine on Christ and the Gospels; it stressed meditation and methodic prayer; it aimed at a life of practical virtue. Gerard Groote of Deventer (1340-1384) was its father, and his life and preaching—*docuit sancte vivendo*—were the inspiration for two religious societies—the Brothers of the Common Life and the Canons Regular of Windesheim—that continued and expanded its spiritual ideals. Florence Radewijns was Groote's most important disciple and the actual founder in 1387 of the Windesheim congregation. A canon in the monastery of Mount St. Agnes near Zwolle, Thomas à Kempis, wrote (*c.* 1411) its most celebrated and characteristic work, *The Imitation of Christ.* From the end of the fourteenth century on, the influence of this new spirituality spread widely in Europe. Its schools and convents multiplied, and its writings circulated everywhere (more than 600 manuscripts and 55 printed editions of the *Imitation* date from the fifteenth century). Nicholas of Cusa and Erasmus were its pupils; Jacques Lefèvre and St. Ignatius Loyola came within its orbit.[30] There is no question that we are in the presence of a reform current of the utmost importance.

It is also frequently pointed out that the *Devotio moderna* represents, at least to some extent, a "lay" spirituality, an assertion of the layman's need for spiritual life and renewal in the face of an ecclesiasticism that had become decadent and corrupt.[31] Too much of a thesis or dichotomy should not be made of this, but there seems little reason to doubt that the *Devotio* does signalize a quest for a more personal religious experience on the part of laity and clergy alike as against the merely formal or traditional practices of piety and prayer. Evennett's judgment that "we see here the individualism of the age taking its appropriate form in Catholic spirituality" would seem to go the heart of its particular historical derivation and significance.[32] And at this juncture and in this sense we can also connect the *Devotio moderna* with other efforts toward personal sanctification and renewal during this time—with the revival preaching of St. Bernadino, St. John of Capistrano, and Savonarola, with lay confraternities like the Oratory of Divine Love, with the devout humanism of so many of the scholars of the Renaissance. The age itself served to stir the need, mold the shape, and impel the surge of religious reform.

Our reference to humanism brings us to another important movement, parallel to the *Devotio moderna,* different in character and spirit from it but nevertheless manifesting basic reform features and certainly contributory to actual Catholic reform in the sixteenth century. Humanism is the name given to the so-called classical revival in Renaissance Italy. There are controversies regarding its origins, nature, significance, and influence, but the view that it was a pagan or anti-Christian movement is no longer tenable.[33] Indeed a contrary evaluation seems much closer to the mark. As a literary and scholarly movement it bore from the beginning a very prominent ethical character and a lively awareness of the problem and task of reconciling an authentic classicism with Christian values and beliefs. In fact, there are signs that in its origin and impulse humanism was a profound regenerative movement within the context of the classical and Christian tradition, that it was, in short, what we can at least loosely call a reform.[34] Its emphasis on rhetoric or philology or classical learning should not blind us to its deeper hopes and implications. The important humanists were convinced that the study of classical letters, the *studia humanitatis,* was the foundation for the education and development of the whole man, and they held this conviction as Christian scholars and Christian educators.[35] And they believed too that this heralded a new day, a return to a golden age.

In quite a different way humanism also had very great bearing on religious renewal and reform. This relates to its scholarly approach and method. The humanists sought to discover the authentic texts of the ancient classics, to read them in their original language, and to understand them in their original context and meaning. When this "return to the sources" together with the critical scholarship and the historical perspective such a "return" entailed were applied to the Christian classics, that is, to Holy Scripture and the early Fathers, the way was opened for a theological and religious reorientation, the dimensions of which encompass both Catholic and Protestant reform in the sixteenth century. "To be able to read the book of God in its genuine meaning is to be a genuine theologian."[36] This extension of classical humanism we are accustomed to call Christian humanism and to associate with the northern humanists—Colet, Erasmus, Lefèvre—but it must be remembered that biblical and patristic study was "a real and very extensive phenomenon" in the Italian Renaissance.[37] Lorenzo Valla's *Adnotationes in Novum Testamentum* (*c.* 1444), the first printing of which Erasmus arranged in 1505, Gianozzo Manetti's Latin translations of the New Testament and the Psalms (*c.* 1450?), and Pico della Mirandola's Genesis commentary called the *Heptaplus* (1489) are monuments to this scholarly endeavor. Nor must one forget the related contribution—indeed the life's work—of the great Florentine Platonist Marsilio Ficino (1433-1499), who sought to restore a *docta religio* in the guise of a Neoplatonic Christian theology.[38] His mission and purpose at least were primarily religious, apologetic, and reformative.

By the turn of the sixteenth century Renaissance humanism was beginning to have a galvanizing effect throughout Europe. *Ad fontes* was becoming more and more a guiding principle for those who sought religious renewal and reform, and the return to Scripture and the Fathers was seen as the means of reforming theology and revivifying Christian life. Erasmus is usually cited as the leader and exemplar of this European-wide humanist reform movement.[39] There is no need to challenge his preeminence in this regard, but it should be pointed out that just as Erasmus was not the first to move in this direction, so humanism's influence on reform can be observed in many other instances and in many diverse ways. Not a few of the documents in this volume bear this out, though they do not by any means exhaust the subject. Its spectrum is vast indeed, and Protestant reform as well as Catholic reform comes within its range.[40] There is, however, a striking example which we have not otherwise recorded of actual reform within the Church in the early sixteenth century closely associated with the expansion of humanism. This is the undertaking and achievement of the great Cardinal of Spain, Francisco Ximenes de Cisneros (1436-1517).

From 1495 on, this remarkable man, the most important figure perhaps in the reign of Ferdinand and Isabella, held the primatial see of Toledo.[41] From that post and in close cooperation with the Catholic monarchs he pursued the task of reforming the Spanish Church and restoring its discipline and spiritual zeal. In his synods of Alcalá (1497) and Talavera (1498) he set down the program his priests must follow in their own consecrated lives and in preaching the Gospel and caring for the souls entrusted to them.[42] Soon afterward he founded the University of Alcalá—the original college of San Ildefonso was opened in 1508—for the education of a clergy who would constitute, in the words of Bataillon, "the cadres of a Church more worthy of Christ."[43] Alcalá was from the start the center of humanism in Spain. The greatest humanist scholars were invited there; the three languages—Latin, Greek, and Hebrew—were studied; Scripture and the Fathers as well as the pagan classics were engaged, though there were also chairs in Thomist, Scotist, and Nominalist theology. Unquestionably the crown of this enterprise was the preparation of the famous Complutensian polyglot Bible by the scholars Ximenes had gathered at Alcalá. Begun in 1502 under the Cardinal's direction and printed in the years from 1514 to 1517, its six large volumes are "the greatest achievement of early Spanish humanism."[44] They are also a witness of the orientation and the increasing momentum of the early Catholic Reformation.

There was much amiss within the Church and within Christendom at the close of the Middle Ages. There was serious and urgent need for religious reform. But there were attempts also to achieve it in various places and in various ways. These efforts in turn form the background—the preliminaries, so to speak—of the movement we seek to document in the pages that follow. A most serious crisis within the Church, however, was destined soon to intervene. Involving basic questions of doctrine, practice, and authority, this severe trial was to put in jeopardy the very life of the existing Catholic Church. Needless to say, it had major, nay decisive, effect on the course of reform in the Catholic Church. The pattern of that reform nevertheless had been indicated, the foundations laid.

Notes

1. Joseph Lortz, *How the Reformation Came,* trans. O. M. Knab (New York, 1964), pp. 105, 111. See also the judgment of Ludwig Pastor in *The History of the Popes from the Close of the Middle Ages,* trans. F. I. Antrobus, R. F. Kerr, *et al.* (40 vols.; St. Louis, 1891-1953), V, 226, and VII, 292 ff.

2. William Roscoe, *The Life of Lorenzo de' Medici* (10th ed.; London, 1851), pp. 285-86. Lorenzo's low estimate of the College of Cardinals was "unfortunately only too well founded," says Pastor, *op. cit.,* V, 361.

3. Sebastian Brant, *The Ship of Fools,* trans. Edwin H. Zeydel (New York, 1944), p. 333.

4. Dante, *On World Government (De Monarchia),* trans. Herbert W. Schneider (2d ed.; New York, 1957), p. 76. The quote is from Bk. III, Chap. 15, of *De Monarchia.*

5. Hubert Jedin, *A History of the Council of Trent,* trans. Dom Ernest Graf (2 vols.; St. Louis, 1957-61), I, 6-7.

6. Ephesians 5, 27.

7. *Paradiso,* XXI, 127-35, quoted from the Dorothy L. Sayers and Barbara Reynolds translation (Penguin Classics; Baltimore, 1962), pp. 244-45.

8. Thomas à Kempis, *The Imitation of Christ,* Pt. I, Chap. XVIII (Everyman's Library ed.; London, 1910), p. 30.

9. Savonarola's Advent sermon XXIII of 1493, quoted in Pasquale Villari, *Life and Times of Girolamo Savonarola,* trans. Linda Villari (London, 1896), p. 184.

10. (Cambridge, Mass., 1959; Harper Torchbook ed., 1967.)

11. II Corinthians 5, 17.

12. From the *Paraclesis,* in *Christian Humanism and the Reformation: Selected Writings of Erasmus,* ed. John C. Olin (New York, 1965), p. 100.

13. Ladner, *The Idea of Reform,* pp. 277, fn. 147, 401-2, 423-24; *idem,* "Reformatio," in *Ecumenical Dialogue at Harvard: The Roman Catholic-Protestant Colloquium,* eds. Samuel H. Miller and G. Ernest Wright (Cambridge, Mass., 1964), pp. 172 ff.; and Jean Leclercq, "The Bible and the Gregorian Reform," in *Historical Investigations* (Vol. 17 of *Concilium;* New York, 1966), pp. 63-77.

14. *Ibid.,* p. 74.

15. From the Decree on Ecumenism, in *The Documents of Vatican II,* ed. Walter M. Abbott (New York, 1966), p. 350.

16. *The Legend of Saint Francis by the Three Companions,* trans. E. G. Salter (London, 1905), p. 78.

17. *Ibid.,* p. 82.

18. Ladner, "Reformatio," pp. 172, 190. See also David Knowles' portrait "Francis of Assisi," in his *Saints and Scholars* (Cambridge, 1962), pp. 86-87.

19. Dante's *Paradiso,* XI, 55-57 (Sayers and Reynolds translation).

20. William Durandus the Younger, *Tractatus de modo generalis concilii celebrandi* (Paris, 1671), Pt. I, Chap. I. For the decrees of Constance, see *Readings in Church History,* ed. Colman J. Barry (Westminster, Md., 1960), I, 504-5. See also Cardinal D'Ailly's reform proposal, *De reformatione ecclesiae,* presented at Constance in 1415 (in the volume containing Durandus' *Tractatus* cited above).

21. Jedin, *op. cit.,* I, 9 ff.; E. F. Jacob, *Essays in the Conciliar Epoch* (2d. ed.; Manchester, 1953), pp. 18-23; and Paul de Vooght, *Les Pouvoirs du concile et l'autorité du pape au concile de Constance* (Paris, 1965). See also Joseph Gill, S.J., *Constance et Bâle-Florence* (Paris, 1965), for a general history of the fifteenth century Councils.

22. Durandus, *op. cit.,* p. 241.

23. This must be understood only with reference to the conciliar movement in the fifteenth century. A General Council might still be deemed a necessary and essential means for achieving reform, as indeed the address of Egidio da Viterbo at the Fifth Lateran Council in 1512 clearly shows (see Chap. IV *infra*). As for the consequences of conciliarism on reform in the Church, the argument is tangled. J. N. Figgis, in his *Studies of Political Thought from Gerson to Grotius, 1414-1625* (Cambridge, 1916), pp. 31-32, views the failure of the conciliar movement as making the more violent Protestant Reformation inevitable. Philip Hughes, in *A History of the Church* (3 vols.; New York, 1935-49), III, 282-84, 306-7, 330-33, comes down hard on conciliarism as sponsoring inadequate and misdirected reforms and as creating conditions which made the needed reforms all the more difficult to achieve. Jedin, in the opening chapters of his *History of the Council of Trent,* I, gives the fullest and most nuanced treatment of this difficult question.

24. (New York, 1964), p. 49.

25. Jedin, *op. cit.,* I, Bk. I, Chap. VI; Pastor, *op. cit.,* III, 269 ff. (for Pius II), V, 500 ff. (for Alexander VI); L. Celier, "L'Idée de réforme à la cour pontificale du concile de Bâle au concile du Latran," *Revue des questions historiques,* LXXXVI (1909), 418-35; and *idem,* "Alexandre VI et la réforme de l'église," *Mélanges d'archéologie et d'histoire,* XVII (1907), 65-124.

26. Jedin, *op. cit.,* I, 121.

27. Hughes, *op. cit.,* III, 386 ff., and H. O. Evennett, *The Spirit of the Counter-Reformation,* ed. John Bossy (Cambridge, 1968), pp. 103-5.

28. Vol. I, Bk. I, Chap. VII.

29. Margaret Aston, *The Fifteenth Century: The Prospect of Europe* (New York, 1968), p. 157; Evennett, *op. cit.,* pp. 9, 18, 33; and L.-E. Halkin, "La *'Devotio moderna'* et les origines de la réforme aux Pays-bas," in *Courants religieux et humanisme à la fin du XVe et au début du XVIe siècle* (Paris, 1959), pp. 45-51. On the *Devotio moderna,* see Albert Hyma, *The Christian Renaissance, a History of the 'Devotio Moderna'* (2d ed.; Hamden, Conn., 1965); Jacob, *op. cit.,* Chaps. VII and VIII; R. R. Post, *The Modern Devotion* (Leiden, 1968); and *Dictionnaire de spiritualité,* III, cols. 727-47 (article *Dévotion moderne,* by Pierre Debongnie).

30. On the very interesting question of the influence of the *Devotio moderna* on St. Ignatius Loyola, see I. Rodriguez-Grahit, "La *Devotio moderna* en Espagne et l'influence française," *Bibliothèque d'Humanisme et Renaissance,* XIX (1957), 489-95, and *idem,* "Ignace de Loyola et le collège Montaigu. L'influence de Standonck sur Ignace," *ibid.,* XX (1958), 388-401. One of Evennett's main themes in *The Spirit of the Counter-Reformation* is this influence; see Chaps. II and III and John Bossy's comments in the Postscript, pp. 126-28.

31. Aston, *op. cit.,* pp. 157-61. See also the closely related view in Friedrich Heer, *The Intellectual History of Europe,* trans. Jonathan Steinberg (2 vols.; New York, 1968), I, 260, 274-75.

32. *Op. cit.,* p. 36.

33. P. O. Kristeller, *Renaissance Thought* (New York, 1961), Chap. IV. On the interpretation of humanism, see William J. Bouwsma, *The Interpretation of Renaissance Humanism* (an A. H. A. pamphlet; Washington, 1959), and P. O. Kristeller, "Studies in Renaissance Humanism during the Last Twenty Years," *Studies in the Renaissance,* IX (1962), 7-30. On humanism, see also *idem, Renaissance Thought II* (New York, 1965); Eugenio Garin, *Italian Humanism,* trans. Peter Munz (New York, 1965); R. Weiss, *The Spread of Italian Humanism* (London, 1964); and A. Renaudet, "Autour d'une définition de l'humanisme," in his *Humanisme et renaissance* (Geneva, 1958), pp. 32-53.

34. Garin lays great stress on this, as do Federico Chabod, *Machiavelli and the Renaissance,* trans. David Moore (London, 1958), pp. 191-95, and Heer, *op. cit.,* I, Chap. XII.

35. This seems clear enough from W. H. Woodward, *Vittorino da Feltre and Other Humanist Educators* (Cambridge, 1897; repr., New York, 1963).

36. Garin, *op. cit.,* pp. 70-71. On scriptural humanism in its late medieval and Reformation context, see Werner Schwarz, *Principles and Problems of Biblical Translation* (Cambridge, 1955), and Henri de Lubac, S.J., *Exégèse médiévale,* Second Part, II (Paris, 1964), Chap. X.

37. P. O. Kristeller, *Le Thomisme et la pensée italienne de la renaissance* (Montreal, 1967), pp. 65-66. See also Raymond Marcel, "Les perspectives de l'apologétique de Lorenzo Valla à Savonarole," in *Courants religieux et humanisme à la fin du XVe et au début du XVIe siècle* (Paris, 1959), pp. 83-100, and E. Harris Harbison, *The Christian Scholar in the Age of the Reformation* (New York, 1956), Chap. II.

38. Kristeller, *Renaissance Thought II,* Chaps. IV and V; Garin, *op. cit.,* pp. 88-100; and Nesca A. Robb, *Neoplatonism of the Italian Renaissance* (London, 1935), Chap. III.

39. See Chap. VI *infra.*

40. For an introduction to at least part of that spectrum, see Lewis W. Spitz, *The Religious Renaissance of the German Humanists* (Cambridge, Mass., 1963), and Alain Dufour, "Humanisme et Réformation," in *Histoire politique et psychologie historique* (Geneva, 1966), pp. 37-62.

41. The major study is L. Fernandez de Retana, *Cisneros y su siglo* (2 vols.; Madrid, 1929-30). There are several works in English, including Reginald Merton, *Cardinal Ximenes and the Making of Spain* (London, 1934), and Walter Starkie, *Grand Inquisitor* (London, 1940). Marcel Bataillon, *Erasme et l'Espagne* (Paris, 1937), Chap. I, is devoted to Ximenes' reforms. On the role of Ximenes and the development of a "Spanish thesis" concerning the origins of the Catholic Reformation, see the discussion in Evennett, *op. cit.,* Chap. I.

42. Cisneros, *Sinodo de Talavera* (Madrid, 1908). The parallel with Giberti's regulations at Verona (see Chap. XI *infra*) is striking.

43. Bataillon, *op. cit.*, p. 14.

44. *The New Cambridge Modern History,* Vol. I: *The Renaissance, 1493-1520* (Cambridge, 1964), p. 124.

Michael A. Mullett (essay date 1999)

SOURCE: Mullett, Michael A. "The Catholic Reformation and the Arts." In *The Catholic Reformation,* pp. 196-214. London: Routledge, 1999.

[*In the following essay, Mullett examines how the Catholic Reformation influenced baroque art, including architecture, poetry, drama, and music.*]

In this final chapter we shall consider the relationship between the Catholic renewal of the sixteenth and seventeenth centuries and the arts used as media for purposes of doctrinal instruction and the raising of religious consciousness. We shall review the art forms of architecture, painting, literature, theatre and music—looking very selectively at a few representative architects, painters, authors and musicians, and we shall consider the question of the baroque as, so to speak, the 'house style' of the Catholic Reformation.

The concept of the baroque, deriving in the first instance from architecture, has been extended to cover all the arts, and even lifestyle or the wider *zeitgeist* of seventeenth-century Europe: what Skrine calls 'baroque culture in its broadest sense', and including, in Friedrich's definition, moral excess and extremism of behaviour. Indeed, excess, distortion and fantasy have often been seen as the essence of baroque building and the characteristics of some of its best-known practitioners: 'dramatic fantasy', for example, is said to have been the hallmark of the architect Francesco Borromini (1599-1667), while the German and Austrian masters of baroque architecture such as Johann Bernhard Fischer von Erlach (1656-1723), the brothers Cosmas Damian Asam (1686-1739) and Egid Quirin Asam (1692-1750) and Balthasar Neumann (1687-1753) are said to have exhibited 'reckless extravagance' (Friedrich). The identification of irregularity as the guiding feature of baroque is, indeed, implicit in the very etymology of the word, which may have been derived from the Portuguese term for a rough-shaped pearl. If baroque represents distortion, though, from what standards is it supposed to have been an aberration? A common view is that baroque means a radical, indeed a revolutionary, departure—Beny and Gunn call Borromini the exponent of a 'revolutionary' art—from the canons of geometric regularity and rational beauty upheld above all in the classicist art of the Renaissance and in its acknowledged masters such as the primary architect of St Peter's, Donato Bramante (1444-1514), and the theorist of

neo-classical architecture based on ancient Roman models, Andrea Palladio (1518-80). In the eighteenth century hostile critics of the baroque led by the ardent classicist Johann Joachim Winckelmann (1717-68) employed the term baroque, as Friedrich says, 'to describe works of art and architecture which did not meet the standards they believed to have eternal validity as "classic" forms of beauty'. Further, baroque in its a-rationality has represented in the minds of its critics a flight from reason and indeed from reality itself and a 'highly emotional escape from the miseries of the world' (Cooper). Then, too, while classical architecture has been seen as maintaining the self-evident truth of rational, stable and orderly principles, especially symmetry of design, suspicion hangs over baroque, and above all over baroque architecture, as an art, if not of deception, through techniques such as *trompe l'oeil,* then, as Norman writes, of 'illusion to transport the spectator into a visionary world'. Baroque, then, has been accused of radical departure from the principles of mathematical order associated with the classical architecture of the Renaissance. In other terms, whereas the straight lines of the classical have been seen as representing the veracity of a geometric axiom, baroque, with its kinetics, has been deemed the epitome of subjective and emotional circularity—and of deceit.[1]

If baroque was an innovatory or revolutionary architecture, eschewing the guiding principles of the preceding dominant style, then it might be thought to have abandoned a stylistic canon that was inseparably connected with the dictates of rational regularity, simplicity and severity associated originally with the first-century Roman architect, Marcus Pollio Vitruvius. Palladio was Vitruvius's most influential sixteenth-century disciple in the quest for harmony of form. As iterated by Jacopo Barozzi da Vignola (1507-73) in the *Regole [or Regola] delli cinque ordini d'architettura* (*The Rules of the Five Orders of Architecture*) (1562) Vitruvianism was the application of a geometry in which all proportions were precisely calculated in ratios, for *ratio* means reason, as well as truth and the antithesis of illusion. Geometry was a branch of mathematics, and mathematics were incontestable: according to Aristotle mathematics provided the provable basis of veracity, not of illusion. Above all, the fixed, straight line and the right angle, drawn by the set-square of reason, prevailed in Renaissance classical architecture. They did, for example, in Vignola's designs incorporated in an architectural textbook of which a late eighteenth-century edition carried a frontispiece showing an uncompromisingly severe and geometrical classical arch whose straight verticals and horizontals were capped with a scroll celebrating the partnership of *Matematica* and *Architettura*. In apparent contrast to this Renaissance classical Vitruvian architecture which, Norman says, 'embodied clarity and order' and in which 'the humanist strand was geometry'—with which discipline Renaissance minds were 'in love'—the baroque architecture of the seventeenth century might, from one point of view, be claimed to have espoused riot, circularity and the primacy of effect and emotion over truth and reason, the more so as it grew to maturity and fulfilled its own inner logic. Thus the *Cathedra Petri* (Throne of St Peter) undertaken in 1656 by the master of the Roman baroque Gian Lorenzo Bernini (1598-1680) may appear to be a product of 'stagecraft' (by the 'greatest master of baroque illusionism': Norman) rather than of mathematics. To take another Roman example, Borromini's spire of San Ivo alla Sapienza (1642-60)—said to resemble the twisted horns of a Sicilian goat—seems the epitome of circularity and the antithesis of rational geometry, from the design of the architect who said that the corner— literally the base of geometric building—was 'the enemy of architecture'. Borromini's San Carlo alle Quatro Fontane (Rome, 1638-67) seems likewise to represent the triumph of the anti-geometric, of convex and concave discs in place of 'true' and fixed angles, lines and squares. And as baroque expanded its geographical range within Europe into the eighteenth century, it seemed to fulfil an anti-geometric dynamic within itself. In Turin the creations of the Theatine architect Guarino Guarini (1624-83), such as the church of San Lorenzo (from 1668), celebrate whorls and vortices; as the later baroque flourished in Bohemia, it exhibited, writes Blazicek, 'the intersection of circular shapes', the 'concave curve' 'undulating walls' 'sinuous . . . flowing, undulating form'. The 'dynamic' pulpit seemingly 'blown into ecstasy', executed by Dominikus Zimmermann (1685-1776) in Die Wies in Bavaria (1746-54) eschews straight lines, and actually appears to defy geometry and indeed gravity. And whereas Vitruvian mathematical architecture proved its rational truth through the axioms of straight lines and fixed angles, baroque, it might be claimed, asserted its emotional power through the dazzlement of circular, fluid and kinetic forms, so that, for example, Bernini's *Cathedra Petri* has been seen as a triumph of a-rational illusionism, a 'theatrical *tableau vivant* before which the devout spectator surrenders, while the agnostic connoisseur turns silently away'.[2]

Perhaps, though, we ought to exercise a little caution in making statements about the non-rational appeal of baroque, about its innovatory or revolutionary departures from Vitruvian-Palladian principles or about its alleged violations of geometry or its anti-rationality. If we stay with our subjects, the arch-rivals Bernini and Borromini, we shall see that they operated to a large extent in the Vitruvian tradition. Borromini is often considered the most baroque—in the sense of the most extravagant—of the seventeenth-century Roman architects, yet in his commission for the Roman Oratory, completed in 1640, for example, although the façade is curvilinear, the architect allowed himself to be constrained into classical restraint by the austere spirit of that 'Congregation of

souls so meek that in the matter of ornament they held my hand'. In point of fact, Borromini's whole architecture was one of strict control. For example, underpinning the balletic quality of San Ivo alla Sapienza is a very precise mathematical engineering, and if Borromini was 'revolutionary', it was not because he eschewed geometry or proportion in themselves but because he rejected the specific human-centred geometry of the architectural masters of the Renaissance, including Bramante. Beny and Gunn write:

> The apparently wilful and aimless undulations or meanderings that have disturbed many people who have seen Borromini's buildings are in fact coherent and logical elements in the architect's highly original and brilliantly executed inventions, and there are reputable precedents for all of them.[3]

If Borromini was basically more conventional and, in his massive contribution to the evolution of baroque, less revolutionary than is sometimes assumed, Bernini operated largely within the Vitruvian tradition, to the extent that Carunchio speaks of his classicism, and Thoenes refers to his indebtedness to Palladio and to the genius of Roman classical form in sixteenth-century Rome, Michelangelo. Bernini's high altar for the Barnabite church in Bologna, with its vertical, Corinthian-capped columns and geometrical assemblage, resembles Bramante's *tempietto* (1502)—itself based on the pure, harmonious form of an ancient Roman temple—at San Pietro in Montorio in Rome. The Bologna high altar is in fact a masterpiece of Palladian-Vitruvian classicism, and equally classical in its symmetry, severity and sense of geometry is the chapel of the Palazzo de Propaganda Fide by Bernini (1634), rebuilt by Borromini in 1662. Thus Bernini and Borromini should, along with other accomplished practitioners of baroque architecture, such as the designer of the façade of St Peter's, Carlo Maderna (1556-1629), and Pietro Berrettini da Cortona (1596-1669), be considered as belonging well within the Renaissance-classical legacy and to have been part of an architectural sequence and tradition going back to Bramante's arrival in Rome in 1499. That in turns tells us that the baroque architects of the seventeenth century manifested stylistic evolution rather than revolution, because they were contributing to a long-term project, the restoration and glorification of the papal city of Peter. The summit of that project was the completion of St Peter's begun by Bramante but completed by Bernini in the sense that he put in place the crucial finishing touches, such as the *Cathedra Petri,* that hammered home the message of the meaning of Rome, of its churches and above all of its basilica. As we saw in Chapter 4, the reaffirmation of Rome's role as the Petrine centre of the Catholic world was a protracted and ambitious scheme. Crucial to its success was a unified architectural conception, as continuous in its styling as the project of Rome was itself a unity. Any revolutionary eruption into the classical models of Bramante and Michelangelo of a radically non-classical style would certainly have disrupted the essential sequence of the Roman building project. Bernini's and Borromini's baroque represented, then, a development and an evolution on what had gone before, as with Bernini's colonnade at St Peter's (from 1656), a perfect completion of the conceptions of his predecessors of what the basilica represented—in this case the church of the Apostle embracing the globe.[4]

Much of Bernini's Roman work was indeed concerned with the setting out of a pedagogy about Rome and its papal and Petrine significance, centred on St Peter's. How much this instruction had to do with 'baroque illusion' is what we should next consider. Sometimes viewed as the 'greatest master of baroque illusionism', a conjurer of dazzling prestidigitation, amazing the stupefied beholder with his conquest of self-imposed challenges, Bernini might seem at his most histrionic in the *baldacchino* (1624-33), the sculpted canopy over the high altar in St Peter's believed also to cover the tomb of the Apostle. Surely this work, with its apparent defiance of the classical disciplines, its spiralled columns, circularity, plasticity, dynamic motion and apparent abandonment of regularity, must be regarded as both the 'frontispiece of the baroque' (Kirwin) and a high point of baroque emotionality, deception and 'fantasy'. Yet this is no work of mere decorative virtuosity or of grand illusion, but rather of a carefully thought-out and in fact rather academic set of propositions based on a coherent reading of sacred history. The columns of the *baldacchino* are indeed twisted, in a way that seems totally foreign to the Bramantian classicism that Bernini had adopted in his Bologna Barnabite commission. However, the belief prevailing in Bernini's day was that the twisted pillars in the older Roman basilica of St Peter had come from Solomon's Temple in Jerusalem. Bernini's statement in the bronze of the *baldacchino* is thus that the pope's basilica was the centre of the Church as the temple of the New Covenant. Similarly, the bronze cover of the *baldacchino* is represented as a textile canopy, and if this is 'illusion', then it is a highly didactic form of that art, for a canopy is the covering placed over a living dignitary, in this case Peter who, for Bernini, lives in the person of his successor in office, the pope who sponsored his work, Urban VIII (Maffeo Barberini, pope 1623-44). Likewise, Bernini's *Cathedra Petri* is undeniably emotive and 'theatrical' in its effect but the message of the ensemble is profoundly serious and doctrinal as well as affective, for the spectacular throne in bronze contains an ancient relic believed to be St Peter's wooden chair, and the whole is sustained by four Fathers of the Church, Catholicism's mentors.[5]

Despite all the traditionalism of style we have so far considered, baroque was undeniably a novel mode of architecture. The primary model for the style through-

out Europe was the Jesuit church, Il Gesù in Rome, begun in 1568 by Vignola with Cardinal Alessandro Farnese as patron, and continued from 1573 by Vignola's pupil Giacomo della Porta (c. 1540-1602)—a church of the new age of the Catholic Reformation, though initially designed by a conservative and classicist architect. Indeed some of the Gesù's features, especially the elimination of columned aisles so as to open up the interior as a huge auditorium for preaching, were novel, in Wittkower's words, not as an outcome of a 'new aesthetic of architecture' but from 'a new concept of the role of the church', one aimed at involving greater frequency of lay attendance at Mass and the Sacraments. Simultaneous Masses were provided for on various altars but there was also a focused concentration of reverence on a high altar, for solemn Masses and also for veneration of the Blessed Sacrament in Benediction and *Quarant' Ore*. In the baroque age the main altar was to be the single most magnetic internal feature of churches, with vision of it maximised by the same openness of space demanded by emphasis on preaching. The drama of the high altar was certainly brought out in Bernini's superb execution in the Barnabites' church in Bologna. Considerable discussion has arisen over the extent to which churches built in the style that emerged in the period of the Catholic Reformation represented a 'Jesuit architecture'. It may be the case, though, that a common stylistic currency, one dictated by considerations of lay use, was evolved for the churches of the orders of clerks regular at large. Orders including the Barnabites, as well as the Theatines and the Oratorians, shared a stress on a mission to the laity and thus on the employment of churches as worshipping halls. Goals common to orders of clerks regular dictated, then, much of the lay-out of the churches of the baroque age. Interior art work was intended to be instructive by means of impact, calling for the force, the movement and the stupendous effect of paintings such as *The Adoration of the Name of Jesus* (1674-9) by Giovanni Battista Gaulli ('Il Baciccio, or 'Baciccia', 1639-1709), placed in the ceiling of the nave of the Gesù. At the same time, the clerks regular focused their missions on towns, and space was often at such a premium that new churches were squeezed into confined quarters, as was, for example, the Barnabites' San Barnaba, substantially the work, from 1561, of Galeazzo Alessi (1512-72), which is fitted into a humdrum terrace in the old centre of Milan and whose façade has a suggestion of a false front. In crowded townscapes the new urban churches of the Catholic Reformation had to establish themselves and advertise their presence as effectively as possible through their architecture. Spectacular façades, perhaps the feature of the baroque that we most immediately associate with the style, could be highly effective in solving this problem of maximising the presence of a church. Thus in 1656, for example, da Cortona added the 'magnificently spectacular' façade and portico of

Santa Maria della Pace, which is encountered as a splendid surprise 'in a maze of narrow streets' (Beny and Gunn) in Rome. The grandeur and mass of della Porta's 1575 facade of the Gesù asserted the position of the building in a highly competitive Roman scenery of churches. The architecture of such churches of the Catholic Reformation were designed to express the needs and purposes of orders of clerks regular, including the Jesuits.[6]

The Jesuits certainly propagated the baroque building style, and did so in an entirely utilitarian fashion, conforming to the Society's principle of the subordination of form to purpose, as set out, for example, by the Jesuit poet Gerard Manley Hopkins (1844-89): 'Our Society values . . . and has contributed to . . . culture, but only as a means to an end'. The Jesuit purpose of communicating with people might dictate the extensive modification of what has been viewed as the Society's 'house style', the baroque. Thus the Jesuit church of Dillingen (1610-17) in Bavaria (Hans Alberthal/Alberthaler, originally known as Giovanni Albertalli, d. c. 1667), a model of Jesuit architecture in German-speaking Catholic lands, falls partly into line with the predominant late medieval gothic German architectural habit and with 'local taste' (Bourke) and tradition. Again, and given that the Jesuits were in the business of teaching and of highlighting their messages through every means at their disposal, we should appreciate that their use of the arts to 'adorn' their churches was inspired by pedagogic and promotional considerations and their urge to publicise the importance of the Society, in part through harnessing the value and power of their founding saints. Such considerations defined the representations of themes in Jesuit art. This was particularly the case with depictions of Ignatius Loyola.[7]

Images of Loyola were strongly promoted in Jesuit churches, as, for example, they were by Rubens in his 1617 *Miracles of St Ignatius* in the Jesuit church of St Carlo Borromeo (St Carolus Borromeüskerk) in Antwerp. For mass distribution, monochrome engravings produced in Brussels in 1609 on the occasion of Loyola's beatification featured key scenes in his career and related his life in popular pictorial form. Loyola's beatification in fact produced a flurry of Jesuit-sponsored art works in commemoration of him, including a scene of his writing the Rules of the Society attributed to the Spanish-born artist Jusepe de Ribera (1588-1656). A depiction of the *Death of Loyola* in the style of the Italian-born Spanish artist Bartolomé Carducho (or Bartolomeo Carducci, c. 1560-1608) shows him in the posture of the 'happy death', a genre scene of late medieval origin in which the Christian in his or her last moments is surrounded by relatives. The Loyolan 'family' on this occasion are the founding fathers of the Society of Jesus. A growing trend evident in a selection of renditions of Loyola is that of presenting him as heroic and dramatic. In the porch of the sacristy of the Gesù, a work from the seventeenth century showing Loyola presenting the Jesuit Rule to Paul III centres on the pope, with Loyola in a subordinate kneeling position. However, a painting after the Italian Jesuit artist Andrea Pozzo (1642-1709) showing Loyola commissioning Francis Xavier to go on the missions, has the Jesuit founder in the dominant position, standing, with Xavier submissively half-genuflecting. The trend towards glamorising Loyola may have reached a new level at around the time of his canonisation in 1622. A 1609 *Loyola's Vision of the Trinity* shows a swarthy individual, somewhat coarse-featured. However, in a post-canonisation portrait (1625-6) by Gian-Francesco Barbiero Guercino (1590-1666), Loyola, balding, lightly bearded, fine-featured, has been made handsome. He is partnered by a dashing Francis Xavier but the papal involvement with the Jesuits is not now that of Paul III's condescending to a suppliant Loyola: instead, the latter and Xavier flank, in a posture of parity, one of the greatest of the popes, St Gregory the Great. In this version, the new-minted saints Loyola and Xavier are upgraded by placing them in close association with one of the most venerable saints of the Church. The pictorial enhancement of Loyola upgraded him in an iconography of promotion designed not only to project a powerful image of the saint himself but also to advertise the Society he founded in the most spectacular light possible. The apotheosis of Loyola in his inseparable association with the founding and launching of the Society of Jesus is caught in the silver statue of him by Francisco de Vergara the younger, in the basilica of Loyola. Here a powerful, muscular Loyola, in flowing, jewel-encrusted chasuble and with dominant features and gaze, points to the text he is holding which bears the Jesuit motto, *Ad majorem Dei gloriam*—'To the greater glory of God'. The magnification of Loyola reached an even higher level with the silver statue (1697) by Pierre Legros the Younger of the saint above his burial altar and grave in the Gesù. Sited so as to place Loyola above the Mass altar and immediately below the Trinity, this representation went as far as it could in putting forward a suggestion that the Jesuit founder was the greatest of saints. Such work, though, with all its hyperbole, is part of a systematic artistic campaign of promotion of the greater glory of the Society of Jesus. While such baroque images incorporated elements of exaggeration, yet this art of hyperbole was conceived with the instructional and promotional functions of publicity in mind.[8]

There remains widespread agreement that the salient features of baroque are violence and brutality, as in the pronounced realism of the Italian Michel Angelo Merisi [or Amerighi] da Caravaggio (1569-1609). Artemesia Gentileschi (1590-1642) if anything outdid Caravaggio in the unflinching immediacy of her scenes of blood and gore, for instance in her two versions of *Judith Slaying Holofernes* (1612-13, c. 1620). If there were, though, a baroque love-affair with the brutal, it also had a didactic purpose. In a work such as Gasparo Celio's (1571-1640) *Christ Carrying the Cross,* there is certainly no shrinking—quite the reverse—from representing the pain of the experience, nor was there any novelty in Western Christian art in bringing to bear a deliberately horrifying realism in Crucifixion scenes, for the depiction of the human agony of the Passion was part of an essential homiletic purpose in iconography. As for renderings of martyrdom, medieval hagiographic art had depicted the widest range of forms of torment in the fullest detail. Some baroque art brought this martyrological realism, as it were, up to date, for example with the frescoes (1583) in the English College, Rome, by Niccolò Circignani (called Il Pomarancio, *c.* 1516-96) featuring with the closest anatomical observation the horrific scenes of the disembowelling of Edmund Campion (b. 1540) and other English martyrs in 1581. If this is to be regarded as a further example of a predilection towards violence in some way typical of baroque, then at least we should bear in mind the utilitarian instructional purpose of this art-work, for it was, wrote Émile Mâle, 'intended to assist the instructors in the tempering of souls, and the images of torture scenes were used as a preparation for martyrdom'. Once more it becomes evident that it was a goal of instruction that set the tone of much of what we think of as being typical of Catholic baroque.[9]

Spanish art of the period of the Catholic Reformation discovered, or rediscovered, the value of simplicity and realism, including the realistic rendition of violence, in religious painting. Religious painting in sixteenth-century Spain had received the impact of two features of Renaissance aesthetics, a cult of the recondite and the celebration of physical beauty. The former tendency can be seen in *Holy Family* (1562-9) by Luis de Morales (known as 'El Divino', 1509-86) which contains arcane allusions and devices such as a basket of eggs (a coded symbol of new life in Christ) and, representing a typical Renaissance classicist amalgam of pagan astrology and Christian doctrine, Christ's horoscope. It was significant of a shifting mood in Spain, and specifically of abandonment of attempts to merge classical-pagan and Christian cultures, that Gerolamo Cardano (1501-76), the original author of the horoscope conceit, was arrested by the Inquisition in Italy soon after Morales's *Holy Family* was completed. A further feature of religious art of the Spanish Renaissance is the glorification of the physical, achieved in part through the deletion of the reality of suffering in favour of the celebration of the human body. The suppression of truth involved in this sort of exercise can be seen, for example, in Pedro Machuca's (1490s-1550) *Deposition* of 1520-5 in which a virtually unmarked Christ is brought down from the Cross: the conception resembles that of the serene and painless Deposition (1507) by Raphael (Rafaello Santi, or Sanzio, 1483-1520), a glorification of physical per-

fection. As late as 1592 the Italian artist, Pellegrino Tibaldi (called Pellegrino de Pellegrini, 1527-96), was continuing in the vein of celebrating physical athleticism with his pain-free *Martyrdom of St Lawrence.* However, Morales who painted the recherché *Holy Family* in 1560-70 also carried out an agonised *Pietà* for the Jesuit church in Córdoba. Not only does this work reveal the return to realism in the depiction of the Passion but, deriving perhaps from Flemish influences on Spanish art, it must also reflect an even more immediate Ignatian spirit of meditation through the insistence in Loyola's *Spiritual Exercises* on absolute reality in contemplations of the Gospel narrative. Realism and simplicity were now once more the guiding principles of form and content in Spanish religious art. In the year after Tibaldi's *Martyrdom of St Lawrence,* in which the focus of devotion could be said to be the idealised nude human body, the starkly un-sensuous rendition in 1593 of the death of another saint, St Francis, by Carducho, in a study in Franciscan brown, features clothed figures and exalts holy poverty and simplicity. The devotional emphasis of Trent in its treatment of the arts, along with Catholic and counter-humanist suspicion of the nude, plus the influence of Ignatian meditation—which itself drew on medieval wells—was dictating a major change in the themes and modes of Spanish art before the end of the sixteenth century. Under Philip III the leading minister Lerma gave his favour to the artistic 'reformers' who restored a spirit of simpler piety, directness and realism to Spanish art.[10]

Reflecting the enormous importance of the Mendicant orders—not least as patrons of artists—the Dominican scenes of the protégé of the Ávila convent Pedro Berruguete (1450s-1503/4) had exalted the Order of Preachers, in *The Temptation of St Thomas Aquinas* and *St Dominic Pardons a Heretic.* To set alongside this promotion of Dominican themes, the Franciscans come off poorly in Juan de Flandes's (d. *c.* 1519) *Temptation of Christ* (*c.* 1500) in which the devil is garbed as a Franciscan. Spain, seemingly, was not exempt from the hostility to the traditional religious orders which characterised the age of Erasmus. The Greek adoptive Spaniard, El Greco (Domenico Theotocopouli, 1541-1614), though, manifested an intense respect for the Franciscans. In the *Burial of the Count of Orgaz* (1586-88) it is the two friars present, dressed in simple contrast to the beruffed nobles and vested saints, who point out and preach the message of the life and death of the charitable count. The doctrine being drawn out is an anti-Lutheran one, to the effect, as Trent had declared, that the just are saved by their good deeds as well as by faith. Increasingly, too, depictions of Francis himself reflected Tridentine Christocentricity, for Francis was celebrated in Spanish religious art of the Catholic Reformation as Christlike, and as being in close association with Christ. *St Francis Embracing the Crucified Christ* (1620-01), by Francisco de Ribalta (1565-1628), forms an audacious artistic adventure in which Christ lowers an arm from the Cross to clasp Francis. Versions (1656-9, 1657) of the *Stigmatization of St Francis* by Juan Rizi (or Ricci, 1600-81) and by Francisco 'El Mozo' de Herrera (1622-85) honour the moment when Francis's imitation of Christ was perfected.[11]

In Italy, de Maio claims, Naples 'can be regarded as the real capital of the Counter-Reformation . . . [,] the mirror of its successes, its ambiguities and of its failures'. It was certainly a most religious city, with its thirty canonised saints, eight patron saints, seven miraculous crucifixes, seventeen thorns from the Crown of Thorns, and its 504 religious houses in 1692. However, if the claim that Naples was the capital of the Counter-Reformation threatens Rome's title, it may at least be possible to consider the southern city as the heart of what de Maio calls the 'rhetorical' Counter-Reformation. Is it possible, for example, that rhetoric, in the sense of evasion of reality, of claims that what is said to be the case *is* the case, is implicit in such a work as Caravaggio's *The Seven Acts of Mercy* (1607) and might this work even be read as presenting an artistic alternative to performing those deeds of charity, in this city where fifty per cent of the population was destitute? Yet Gregori argues that Caravaggio's painting carried out for the Monte della Misericordia which was founded in 1601 specifically for the practical implementation of the Seven Works of Mercy set out in Matt., 25: 35, 36 and elsewhere in Scripture should be read as a clear, and not (as de Maio suggests), 'obscure', mandate to carry out the deeds of mercy—visiting the sick and the imprisoned, feeding and giving drink to the hungry and thirsty, clothing the naked, harbouring strangers, and burying the dead. As Gregori writes, 'The support for the needy demanded by the Church is transformed in [Caravaggio's] painting into a moving participation in tragedy, evoked by the text of Matthew'. If, then, Caravaggio's *Seven Works of Mercy* represents 'rhetoric', it should be seen as a didactic rhetoric in favour of practical action in the direction of the meritorious good works recommended by Trent. Again, it may be possible to see the Naples of the Catholic Reformation as a place of exploitation, of political deference and social conformity, in which the appalling poverty of the many was insulted by the opulence of the city's cathedral, by the elaborate chapel of the city's favourite saint, San Gennaro and by the ornate tabernacles in the Franciscans' churches. From one point of view, the Naples of the Catholic Reformation was a place where 'obedience was the supreme quality' (de Maio), where the Jesuits used the arts and artists for purposes of thought-control and indoctrination in the arts of subordination. On the other hand, we ought at least to be aware that the image of the Virgin of the Carmine, the iconic inspiration for the plebeian anti-state, anti-tax revolt led by the fisherman Masaniello (Tomasso Aniello, 1623-47) in 1647, was one of the city's two Madonnas

splendidly rehoused in the 1620s and 1630s: religious images in baroque Naples were capable of fuelling dissidence and revolt as well as 'obedience'.[12]

The same teaching purpose that was to the fore in Catholic baroque religious painting inspired the religious theatre of the Catholic Reformation from the sixteenth century onwards. In fact, this theatre had its roots in the late medieval religious drama that continued to thrive in the earlier sixteenth century in Paris, for example, where the Confraternity of the Passion 'played and acted many fine mysteries for the edification and entertainment of the common people'—though it may have been a changed attitude to the propriety of sacred representation that induced the municipality in 1548 to forbid the Confraternity to enact the Passion or 'any other sacred mysteries'. The medieval roots of the religious theatre which the Jesuits introduced as part of their religious pedagogy are likewise clearly evident from the *perioche,* or plot outline, of a Jesuit play put on at the Jesuit *Gymnasium* (grammar school) in Ingolstadt in Bavaria in 1606. Even the title of this work betrays its essentially medieval character: *Vonn dem Todt oder Todtentanz,* 'All About Death, or the Death Dance', a traditional dramatic representation of the medieval theme of *memento mori,* of the universality of death and of the *danse macabre.* As with most medieval religious theatre, the basic sources of the material are scriptural, rather than classical, in this particular case a text from Isaiah, (40: 6) which, again in entirely medieval theatrical fashion, delivers the message which was to the fore in the morality plays of the middle ages, concerning the certainty of death, regardless of rank: 'All flesh is as grass. . . . In confirmation of this he [Isaiah] finds a skull which answers him saying: "Everyone, great or small, rich or poor, noble or common, must die."'.[13]

Produced in Munich only two years after the Ingolstadt play, a drama by the Jesuit preacher to the court of Maximilian I of Bavaria, Jeremias Drexel (1581-1638), on *Julian the Apostate,* about the Roman Emperor (*c.* 331-63) who abandoned Christianity and reintroduced paganism, has an entirely different feeling from the medievality of *Vonn dem Todt,* for it incorporates the classicism of the Renaissance which the Jesuits utilised for their purposes and which they integrated into their educational programme. *Julian* is based on Roman rather than scriptural history and, in a regularised, classical five-act structure, focuses, as ancient Greek tragedy had, on the central character who gives unity to the action and lends his name to the title of the work. Drexel's *Julian* is in fact presented as a complex and, indeed, almost tragic human being, rather than as a stereotypical figure of vice as in a medieval morality play: Drexel depicts Julian as a learned and virtuous philosopher. Himself a convert from Protestantism, this Jesuit dramatist had every reason to reflect on the theme of change in a person's religious convictions, for conversion of religion was a *leitmotif* of public life and of Jesuit endeavour in Germany in the pre-Thirty Years' War period. Also crucial in the religious make-up of the *Reich,* under the principle of the 1555 Peace of Augsburg summarised as *cujus regio, ejus religio* ('A ruler decides his subjects' religion') was the religious orientation of the prince. Whereas in the Roman Empire of Julian, the emperor's preferences threatened to halt the whole progress of Christianity, in the early-modern Holy Roman Empire of the German Nation the promotion of 'true' religion by regional princes such as the Wittelsbach rulers of Bavaria was vital to the whole success of the Catholic counter-offensive against the Reformation. Classical and medieval history, and especially the issue of religious allegiance under the state, provided the theme of a series of German Catholic dramas of the Catholic Reformation period. England's two saints Thomas—Thomas Becket (1118-70) and Thomas More (1478-1535), both martyred by royal autocrats—were the subjects of such German plays as *S. Thomas Cantuariensis Archiepiscopus & Martyr* (*St Thomas of Canterbury, Archbishop and Martyr*) and *Tragoedia Vom König Henrico II* (*A Tragedy Concerning King Henry II*), both featuring St Thomas Becket, and *Thomas Morus ex Anglie* ('Thomas More of England') in which More's position within the Reformation of the sixteenth century was recalled in extensive historical detail under the thematic caption of the conflict of duties. Classical martyrdom themes fed Jesuit theatre in France, leading eventually to the theatrical masterpiece of the Jesuit pupil Pierre Corneille (1608-84). Janelle comments: 'Corneille may . . . justifiably be considered as the greatest tragic poet of the Jesuit school, and his *Polyeucte* [1643] as the direct consequence of the Catholic Reformation, and the highest point reached by it in the field of literature'.[14]

In Germany, Drexel's fellow Jesuit Friedrich von Spee (1591-1635) composed poetry in which personal love for Jesus was mingled with themes from nature in works such as *Die Gespons Jesu seufftzet nach jhrem Bräutigam* (*The Bride of Jesus [the Church] Longs for Her Groom*). The note of personal, almost romantic, love for Jesus characteristic of von Spee was captured in the Spanish Netherlands in the *Triumphus Iesu oft Godliicke Lof-Sangen* (*The Triumph of Jesus, or Holy Songs of Praise*) (1633) by an anonymous woman member of the Third Order of St Francis in the Sion cloister in Lier, a town near Antwerp with a tradition of female religious lyricism in Dutch going back to the Beguine Beatrice van Nazareth in the thirteenth century. (There is additional verse material in *Triumphus,* including a 'spiritual pastoral' in the form of a dialogue between a shepherd and a shepherdess, by the Reverend Mother of the Sion cloister, Maria van Etten: the Lier house, 'Sion', is alluded to in the verses of one of the holy poems, one based on a song of the Holy Land).

The title of the collection *Triumphus Iesu* is also an allusion to a near-contemporary poem in praise of love, *Triumphus Cupidinis* (*Cupid's Victory*) (1628), by an Antwerp poet, Joan Yselmans (1590-1629). The spiritual lyrics of *Triumphus* are set to well-known popular songs, including ballads of love and fashion, such as *La picarde* (*The Girl from Picardy*) and *Van de nieuw Balette* (*The New Dance*). Reflecting Spanish cultural influences in the southern Netherlands, one of the Jesus poems is set to a popular Spanish tune. However, despite the collection's employment of the devices of popular culture and romance, of 'little songs' and verses to aim its message at youth, the underlying theme was a profoundly spiritual one, aiming, as the title of *Triumphus* says, to banish worldly and trivial verses, by which the *Triumphus Cupidinis* was clearly intended. The message was that religious love was superior to carnal and romantic affection and that the everlasting crown and sceptre of Jesus reigned supreme over the transitory triumphs of the god and goddess and love, Cupid and Venus.[15]

The subtitle of this collection, *Holy (or Godly) Songs of Praise, Godliicke Lof-Sangen,* reiterates its central spiritual message, along with its insistence on the meditation of God and Christ. *Godliicke Lof-Sangen* also reflects specific indebtedness to a Jesuit source, the collection (1620) of the Netherlands Jesuit Justus de Harduwijn (1528-1641). The saints feature in the text in the persons, for example, of Augustine as victor over an heretical sect, of Dominic, of the Seven Doctors of the Church, of the Apostle Philip, of Mary Magdalene, of Francis, of St Louis IX as a member of the Third Order of St Francis and of Loyola in two tributes. Naturally, Mary is included, for instance, as 'advocate' and 'fair queen', but the emphasis is on her role *vis-à-vis* Jesus, as in a poem on the Annunciation. Christ, then, is central in this work, as is indicated in the repetition of the device *IHS,* the abbreviation of *Jesus Hominum Salvator,* 'Jesus Saviour of Mankind'. His nativity from a virgin is approached with the kind of simple astonishment at the apparent paradox of the maiden-mother that was recurrent in medieval religious lyrics in Europe:

> *O Wonderbaer vertoogh! ò wonderbaere Min!*
> O wonderful sight! O miraculous love
> *Die sonder eynde is, en noont en had begin,*
> Quite without beginning or end,
> *Wi'ns Vader daer was Godt, Wi'ns Moeder was een Maeghet*
> Whose father was God, whose mother a maiden!

The meditation in *Triumphus Iesu* certainly has its roots in the medieval contemplative tradition and especially in the Netherlands heritage that, through the *Imitation of Christ,* had inspired Loyola and through him Jesuit meditative techniques. However, as well as being the product of a long-standing tradition of piety, *Triumphus* was very much a work of its time, not least in its poignant allusions to the agony of Lier's province, Brabant, amidst plague and hunger, with a heartfelt cry for peace at that mid-point of the Thirty Years' War. The collection also had the most direct bearing on the progress of the Counter-Reformation in the Spanish Netherlands, for it was dedicated to one of the most earnest promoters of Catholic renewal in the provinces, the bishop of Antwerp, Jan Malderus (1563-1633), official visitor of the Lier Sion convent. Malderus, himself a renowned author on Aquinas, on issues of the Confessional, law, justice, Scripture and synodical regulations, who died in the year of the collections' publication in Antwerp, must have been aware of the potential utility of published Dutch-language texts of the sacred songs of *Triumphus Iesu,* which were probably designed in the first instance for use in the cloister in Lier. However, the adoption of the lyrics for 'official' ecclesiastical use required some editorial discussion of their female authorship, which came in the form of a prefatory explanation that the work, dedicated to Malderus, was not an elevated scriptural commentary out of the University of Leuven but had its precedents in the use that Moses had made of the humbler gifts of women to protect the tabernacle of the Lord.[16]

Whereas the author of *Triumphus Iesu* deployed the 'profane' art of popular song to propound piety, in Spain theatre—an art form that was sometimes regarded in Europe as the antithesis of the sacred—was deployed to promote Catholicism. In the Spain of the 1640s, military disaster at Rocroi (1643), and the deaths of the queen and the heir to the throne gave rise to a Lenten mood of national recollection in which the theatres were closed for lengthy periods. It is against that background that we should consider the career of the dramatist Pedro Calderón de la Barca Henao y Riano (1600-81). Educated at the Colegio Imperial of the Jesuits, with his brothers he had led a violent and disorderly life involving the break-in of a convent. The death of one brother and the murder of another were followed by his ordination to the priesthood in 1651. As a writer Calderón turned to resolve a widely sensed contradiction between religion and priesthood on the one hand and secular literature, especially theatre, on the other. His Corpus Christi plays, *autos sacramentales,* composed for the city of Madrid—over seventy of them—present the values of the Spanish Catholic Reformation and harmonise theatre with piety. It may be true, as Greer writes, that Calderón has been typecast as 'the dramatist of Catholic orthodoxy', more 'doctrinal and didactic' than his great contemporary Lope de Vega (1562-1635). However, the latter's output included *Rimas sacras (Sacred Verses)* (1614) and *El Isidro* (1599) in honour of Madrid's patron saint, St Isidore, as well as celebrations of Spanish crusading ardour, such as a version of the Italian Torquato Tasso's (1544-95) *Gierusalemme Liberata* (1575), *La Jerusalén conquistada (Jerusalem Conquered)* (1609). With Calderón,

though, there is no doubting the specific Jesuit inspiration behind much of his work or the likelihood that 'those close-knit speeches, with elaborate analogies, continued metaphors, conceits, and rhetorical colours . . . originated in the Jesuits' classrooms and the works he studied there'. Calderón's Jesuit education in the classics gave him the material for *Los encantos de la culpa (The Delights of Sin)* (1649) in which he reinterpreted the Greek legend of Ulysses and Circe, with Ulysses representing mankind and his ship the Church. Specific Jesuit themes in Calderón include a verse romance, on Loyola's experiences at Manresa; the pro-Jesuit *Don Baltasar de Loyola* (1585) concerned a Moorish convert. In an *auto* composed for the feast of Corpus Christi in Toledo, *El mágico prodigioso (The Amazing Wizard)* (1637), Calderón's source was the one that had influenced Loyola's conversion, the *Golden Legend.* Not surprisingly, then, it was a Jesuit who made one of the most favourable of comments on Calderón, his style and the 'sweetness' of his verses as well as the correctness of his theology, all features to be found in *El nuevo palacio del Retiro* (1634). (The title contains a play on words—'The New Palace of Withdrawal from the World' and 'The New Royal Palace Called 'El Buen Retiro'.) The Jesuit commentator 'viewed this play with great admiration. . . . It contains well-regulated doctrine'. Focusing on such well-regulated doctrines, *La devoción de la cruz (The Devotion of the Holy Cross)* (1634, 1640) presented, in an intense drama of violence, sex and crime, the Council of Trent's strictures on the necessity for freedom of choice in marriage and the religious life. Freedom in a wider sense, the freedom of the will and its co-operation in opting for virtue—the viewpoint that the Jesuits made their own—is the theme of *La vida es sueño (Life's a Dream)* (1635), with its self-reforming central character Segismundo. Calderón, in Parker's words 'a theological poet', was, in the theatre, the great master of a chief aim of Catholic baroque art and literature, that of instruction through delight.[17]

A distinctive theology of grace and the will suffused a drama by a playwright whom Calderón greatly admired, the Mercedarian friar and artistic disciple of Lope de Vega, Tirso de Molina (Fray Gabriel Téllez, known as El Mercedario, 1571-1648). The subject of sin haunted a play attributed to Tirso, *El Condenado por desconfiado (Damned for Despair)* (c. 1624), a work whose composition is said to have been triggered by the author's discovery that a member of his order had turned bandit. The theology of forgiveness in this play is nuanced but leans towards the comforting views of the Jesuit Luis Molina (1535-1601) on the availability of God's forgiveness in accordance with the sinner's willed desire for grace. Indeed, sympathy with Molina's interpretation may have inclined Téllez to adopt part of the name of the theologian. The entry in the *Oxford Companion to Spanish Literature* explains that a 'brilliantly dramatised' Molinist soteriology underpins his play. This doctrine of salvation is conveyed through the sensational use of realism, violence and the depiction of vice by this dramatist who introduced the character of Don Juan to the stage. The central character in *El condenado desconfiado,* who 'lives by gambling, blackmail, contract killings, and the immoral earnings of his mistress', introduces his immorality in a narrative of his malevolence which is intense, high-powered, melodramatic and horrifically gripping in its hasty, excited diction:

> Once, when I was struck
> on some rich man's wife, and I'd gone
> into the house, determined
> to get what I'd wanted from her
> the bitch called out, and her husband
> came into the room. I was mad!
> I took a grip of him
> and lifted him off the ground,
> and once I'd got him like that
> I ran to the open window
> and threw him out, and he died
> where he fell. She began screaming,
> I had my knife; I stabbed her
> five or six times in the breasts.
> Snow white they were, and the blood ran down
> like rubies over the slope,
> and her life ran out with it too.

Divine forgiveness and grace were available to human beings even amidst such stark realisations of evil, but the theological message—which Tirso de Molina claimed was derived from the writings of the Jesuit theologian Bellarmino—was presented with the utmost realism and entertainment value, in precisely the way that baroque religious art taught Catholic doctrine through every resource of diversion that could be summoned.[18]

Instruction through the heightening of effects was also sought by means of deliberate affronts to sensibility through an audacity that was intended to grip the imagination by its power to shock. The Spanish Jesuit writer, Baltasar Gracian (1601-58), for example, imaged the Eucharist as a banquet at which was served 'a Lamb fed with virgin's milk, seasoned with the fire of His love. Oh! what a luxurious dish. Here a heart in love with souls; what a tasty dish!' A boldness of metaphor that ventured up to and beyond the bounds of what a later generation would decree were the limits of taste often characterised baroque literature and forms of artistic expression which included Bernini's representation of the mystical ecstasy of St Teresa as an orgasm. The reason, I suggest, for such artistic boldness in the description of the spiritual through the use of shock tactics by reference to the mundane was a desire to convey the familiar lineaments of Catholicism in novel terms, for teaching purposes.[19]

In the field of music the Council of Trent laid down the clearest canons for composition—restraint, solemnity, the avoidance of secular and romantic motifs. The dominant musical mode in the early sixteenth century in Europe was the complex polyphonic and contrapuntal style of the northern Franco-Flemish school associated with such masters as Josquin des Prés (1440-1521). The characteristics of this school included enormous elaboration of musical complexity, a subordination of the meaning of the words to the aesthetic demands of the music and a free adoption of secular tunes and love songs to furnish tunes for choral Masses. The Mass known as '*L'Homme Armé* (1502) by the greatest composer of polyphony in the Flemish tradition, des Prés, provides a powerful example of the borrowing of music for the Mass from the world of popular song. The Netherlander Orlando di Lasso (Roland de Lassus, *c.* 1532-94) was a composer, on a massive scale, of secular and romantic works as well as of Masses and motets. His Mass known as *Bell'Amfitrit altera* (posthumous, 1610) provides a clear example of the absorption by Church music—even in the Tridentine age—of the worldly themes and the pagan cultural allusions of the Renaissance: 'Bell' Amfitrit', 'Beautiful Amphitrite', was the wife of Poseidon, goddess of the sea (and also the symbol of the maritime Republic of Venice). The di Lasso Mass is a work of intricate complexity, sophistication and ravishing beauty, though with little relationship to the Mass as the Council of Tent had viewed it as being, and it embodies a potentially blasphemous dedication to a pagan goddess.[20]

Catholic reformers detested this kind of music. Savonarola was typical in his criticism that 'figured music does nothing but charm the ear and the senses'. Erasmus took up the theme—'We have introduced an artificial and theatrical music into the church, a bawling and agitation of various voices'—and he condemned, as Savonarola did, 'the sensuous charm of the ear'. From the time of the reforms of Giberti in Verona worldly music was banned in church and in his Modena diocese Morone legislated against what Savonarola had called 'figured' music. Before the Council of Trent met, then, a body of reformist complaint had built up about the kind of music that had been in vogue for church use in the decades up to the inception of the Catholic Reformation. However, the golden age of polyphony coexisted, especially in Italy, with a strong survival of the pre-polyphonic tradition of 'plain song', 'plain chant' or 'Gregorian chant', an ancient simpler rhythmic mode in which the Office of the Church was sung in monasteries and convents and whose stately pace and apportionment of syllables to notes made for clear hearing of the text. As Sherr writes, 'singing Gregorian chant was the major task of all the singers and composer singers of the Renaissance', and perhaps Italian singers understood only imperfectly the basic techniques of singing 'figured' polyphonic music. Though polyphonic complexity held sway in much of late medieval northern Europe, in Italy the greater simplicity of the older Gregorian form does not seem to have been buried under polyphonic fashion. The revival of religious priorities in the music of the Mass, as demanded by the Council of Trent, can be seen to have had roots in an unbroken Italian musical-liturgical tradition. Particular attention seems to have been given in the Italian attitude to church music to the careful enunciation of the words of the service, as an English visitor to Rome in 1576-8 commented: 'and everie syllable [is sung] so distinctly, so cleare, so commodiously, so fully, that the hearers may perceave all that is done'.[21]

Clarity of enunciation dictated a measured pace, as did the requirement of solemnity. As an Italian bishop wrote in 1549:

> *Kyrie eleison* [a prayer for mercy and forgiveness sung near the beginning of Mass] means 'Lord, have mercy upon us'. The ancient musicians would have expressed this affection of asking the Lord's pardon by using the Mixolydian mode [the mode thought suitable for tragedies] which would have evoked a feeling of contrition in the hearts and souls.

Likewise, audibility and dignity in the musical setting of the Mass were the goals that Trent gave itself: 'All things should be so ordered that the Masses, whether they be celebrated with or without singing, may reach tranquilly into the ears and hearts of those who hear them, when everything is executed clearly and at the right speed'. Tropes should be sung, the Council ordered, 'in a simple clear voice beforehand, so that no one will miss any parts of the eternal reading of the sacred writings'. However, this insistence should be seen as arising out of an emphasis, continuing to concern the Italian school of liturgical music, on religious meaning rather than aesthetic pleasure.[22]

Though a keen student of the Franco-Flemish form of polyphony, the Italian Palestrina carried a heavy debt to plain song and achieved, in his *Missa Papae Marcelli* (*The Requiem Mass for Pope Marcellus*) (1555, published 1567) the sobriety, clarity and grave suitability of tone to occasion which Trent demanded, while at the same time achieving a compromise with polyphony in what Palestrina termed his 'new stylistic approach' (*novo modorum genere*). In 1567, the same year, that Palestrina published the *Missa Papae Marcelli,* his friend Giovanni Animuccia claimed to have achieved a new level of austerity in the musical accompaniment of the Mass—'to adorn these divine prayers and praise of God as little as possible'. The issue of the decrees of the Council and of the Breviary gave Animuccia standards by which to compose, and the move in the direction of plainer musical settings gained momentum from the powerful backing of Carlo Borromeo: one of the composers of the Tridentine musical style, Vicenzo Ruffo (1508-87) cited the commission:

> which Cardinal Borromeo had formerly imposed on me that in accordance with the decrees of the Council of Trent I was to compose some Masses that should avoid everything of a profane and idle manner in worship. . . . Accordingly . . . I composed one Mass in this way; so that the number of the syllables and the voices and tones together should be clearly and distinctly understood by the pious listeners.

Nevertheless, the force of the movement in favour of musical austerity in Borromean Lombardy, where Ruffo contributed to the reordering of the music of the Ambrosian rite, should not be exaggerated—though it is true that Borromeo directed a drive against erotic madrigals in Cremona in the Jubilee year, 1575. However, Niccolò Sfondrato (1535-1591), bishop, from 1560, of Cremona—the second city of the province, its musical centre and the birthplace of Claudio Monteverdi (1567-1643)—was committed to a strongly popular form of Catholic Reformation, designed in part to halt the spread of Protestantism in his border diocese. Sfondrato (subsequently pope as Gregory XIV), who attacked the privileges of the cathedral clergy, who developed public schooling, welfare and confraternities and brought in Theatines, Somaschi and Barnabites, could hardly afford to dispense with the extant rich and much-loved musical traditions of the Church as an asset in his campaign to consolidate the orthodoxy of his diocese. Animuccia, one of the new breed of Tridentine composers, sought a reconciliation in which 'the music may disturb the hearing of the text as little as possible, but nevertheless in such a way that it may not be entirely devoid of artifice and may contribute in some degree to the listener's pleasure'. The series of Masses in four, five and six parts by Monteverdi's teacher, Marco Antonio Ingegnero (*c.* 1545-92) represent a new compromise between Tridentine principles and the beautiful legacy of polyphony from the late fifteenth and early sixteenth centuries. This was the musical half-way house that remained in place into the age of Claudio Monteverdi (1567-1643), especially in Rome, where the large choirs needed for the performance of polyphony (*stile antico* or *prima prattica,* both phrases betokening a superseded style) remained available in the early seventeenth century. Monteverdi's own Mass *Il illo tempore* (1610) is set for six voices and deliberately incorporates what a contemporary called 'great seriousness and difficulty', that is to say both liturgical propriety and pleasurable elaboration. His 1610 Mass of the Blessed Virgin Mary has, it is true, strong Gregorian features, but the vespers accompanying it are indebted stylistically to the sixteenth-century Flemish polyphonist Nicholas Gombert (*c.* 1495-1560) and, indeed, introduce a novel operatic method. In such ways, the music, like the other arts of the Catholic Reformation, represented compromise, between an official aesthetic and the need to please a public with its own tastes, formed by the accretions of artistic tradition.[23]

We seem to have ended our survey on an 'upbeat' note of optimism over the Catholic Reformation as a popular or even kindly set of processes. It was far from being entirely that. Whatever revisionisms are conducted over the scale of the Inquisition's cruelties, it was, wherever it extended its reach of operations, an engine of appalling terror. The Counter-Reformation involved a worsened outlook for dissidents and minorities, especially Jews, who were consigned to the ghetto, especially in Italy. The prosecution of Galileo Galilei (1564-1642) epitomised an underlying and lasting Catholic suspicion of scientific research. Large numbers of women accused of witchcraft were executed, particularly in the period from the 1580s to the 1630s and, in Spain especially, women's religious charisms were subjected to intense scrutiny and hostility. Catholic militancy was more than a metaphor, in an age when the papacy rejoiced in the St Bartholomew massacre of the Protestants of France in 1572 and when, in the following century, the Catholic cause in Germany and in Europe at large was upheld through the terrible barbarities of the Thirty Years' War. Above all, in the Czech lands of Bohemia, Catholicisation was the religious accompaniment to political enslavement to Austria. The division of large parts especially of central Europe into reciprocally antagonistic slabs of territory through the processes of 'confessionalisation' left Catholics deeply hostile and suspicious towards other Christians. Through the policing activities of Catholic magistrates and busybody parish priests encouraged by episcopal visitations, much of the rare enjoyment that European peasants took from gruelling lives was proscribed. Indeed, the Counter-Reformation Catholic Church often imposed a puritanism sometimes even more stringent than the Protestant variety, leaving generations of Europeans fearful and guilty over sex, as well as driven by the intense work ethic inculcated by teaching orders such as the Jesuits and the de la Salle Brothers. The majority of modern Europeans, especially in the countries of the European Union, come from backgrounds strongly tinged by the influences of Catholic Reformation Catholicism, and modern Europe, for good or ill, simply cannot be understood without some insight into the processes described in this book.

Notes

1. Peter N. Skrine, *The Baroque Literature and Culture in Seventeenth-Century Europe,* London, Methuen, 1978, p. 83 *passim*; Carl J. Friedrich, *The Age of the Baroque 1610-1660,* The Rise of Modern Europe, William L. Langer (ed.), New York, Harper & Row, Harper Torchbooks, The University Library, 1962, pp. 38, 68, Chapters 2 and 3; Oldrich J. Blazicek, *Baroque Art in Bohemia,* trans. Slavos Kadecka, Feltham, Middlesex, Paul Hamlyn, 1968, p. 48; Roloff Beny and Peter Gunn, *The Churches of Rome,* London, Weidenfeld and Nicolson, 1981, p. 186; J. P. Cooper, 'General Introduction' in Cooper (ed.), *The New Cambridge Modern History,* vol. IV *The Decline of Spain and the Thirty Years' War,* Cambridge, Cambridge University Press, 1970, p. 9; Edward Norman, *The House of God: Church Architecture, Style and History,* London, Thames and Hudson, 1990, p. 176.

2. Alberto Pratelli (ed. and intro.), *Architettura del Barocco da Vignola Concernete i Cinque Ordini. La 'Regola' del Vignola in una edizione de XVIII secolo,* Bologna, Editrice CLUEB, 1984, pp. xxiv, 14-15, 38-9, 22-3 and frontispiece; Edward Norman, *The House of God,* pp. 76, 217, plates 44-5; Blazicek, *Baroque Art in Bohemia,* p. 48; Beny and Gunn, *The Churches of Rome,* pp. 208, 255; John Bourke, *Baroque Churches of Central Europe,* London, Faber and Faber, 1978, pp. 89-91.

3. Joseph Connors, *Borromini and the Roman Oratory,* New York, The Architectural History Foundation, Cambridge, MA, and London, MIT Press, 1980, p. 3, plate 3; Friedrich, *The Age of the Baroque,* p. 70; Beny and Gunn, *The Churches of Rome,* p. 186.

4. Tancredi Carunchio, 'Ipotesi "barocche"' in Sebastiano Serli, Gianfranco Spagnesi and Mariello Fagiolo (eds), *Gian Lorenzo Bernini e l'architettura europea nel Sei-Settecento,* Rome, Istituto della Enciclopedia Italiana, 1983, p. 35; Christof Thones, 'Bernini architetto tra Palladio e Michelangelo' in ibid., pp. 105-34; Stefano Ray, 'Bernini e la tradizione architettonica del cinquecento romano' in ibid., pp. 13, 17; Klaus Güthlein, 'Bernini architetto e gli Spada: l'altare maggiore et la facciata di San Paolo a Bologna' in ibid., pp. 81-104; Norman, *The House of God,* p. 190; Beny and Gunn, *The Churches of Rome,* pp. 142-3, 145, 139-40, 244-5.

5. W. Chandler Kirwin, 'L'illusionismo del Baldacchino' in Spagnesi and Fagiolo (eds), *Gian Lorenzo Bernini,* pp. 53-80, plates 1, 2, 12; Michael Kitson, 'The age of baroque' in Bernard S. Myers and Trewin Copplestone (eds), *Landmarks of Western Art: Architecture, Painting and Sculpture,* Feltham, Middlesex, Hamlyn Publishing Newnes Books, 1985, pp. 627-8.

6. James S. Ackerman, 'The Gesù in the light of contemporary church design' in Rudolf Wittkower and Irma B. Jaffe (eds), *Baroque Art: The Jesuit Contribution,* New York, Fordham University Press, 1972, pp. 15-28; Wittkower and Jaffe (eds), *Baroque Art,* plates 15c, 14a; Beny and Gunn, *The Churches of Rome,* pp. 192, 267.

7. Wittkower, 'Problems of the theme', in Wittkower and Jaffe (eds), *Baroque Art,* pp. 4-5, 10; Bourke, *Baroque Churches of Central Europe,* pp. 30, 32-3, 119.

8. Wittkower, 'Problems of the theme', p. 10; Karl Rahner, SJ, and Paul Imhof, SJ, *Ignatius of Loyola,* trans. Rosaleen Ockenden, London, Collins, 1979, pp. 48-62, plates, 37, 48, 38, 45, 34, 36; Howard Hibbert, '*Ut picturae sermones*: the first painted baroque decorations in the Gesù' in Wittokower and Jaffe (eds), *Baroque Art,* pp. 29-41.

9. Mary D. Garrard, *Artemesia Gentileschi: The Image of the Female Hero in Italian Baroque Art,* Princeton, NJ, Princeton University Press, 1989, plates 4, 8; Wittkower and Jaffe (eds), *Baroque Art,* plate 28; Michael E. Williams, 'Campion and the English Continental seminaries' in Thomas McCoog, SJ, *The Reckoned Expense: Edmund Campion and the Early English Jesuits. Essays in Celebration of the First Centenary of Campion Hall, Oxford (1896-1996),* Woodbridge, Suffolk, The Boydell Press, 1996, pp. 293-4; Émile Mâle, *Religious Art From the Twelfth to the Eighteenth Century,* London, Routledge & Kegan Paul, 1949, p. 175.

10. Jonathan Brown, *The Golden Age of Painting in Spain,* New Haven and London, Yale University Press, 1991, plates 78, 62, 48, 47, pp. 50, 90-2; Myers and Copplestone (eds), *Landmarks of Western Art,* plate 50; for Cardano see *Dizionario Biografico degli Italiani,* Rome, Istituto della Enciclopedia Italiana, vol. 19, p. 760.

11. Brown, *The Golden Age of Painting in Spain,* pp. 12-14, 80-3, plates 6, 7, 3, 63, 24b, 138, 231.

12. Romeo de Maio, 'The Counter-Reformation and Painting in Naples' in Clovis Whitfield and Jane Martineau (eds), *Painting in Naples 1606-1705: From Caravaggio to Giordano,* London, Royal Academy of Arts in association with Weidenfeld and Nicolson, 1982, pp. 31-5; Mina Gregori, 'Caravaggio and Naples' in ibid., pp. 125-7; Peter Burke, 'The Virgin of the Carmine and the Revolt of Masaniello', *Past and Present,* 1983, No. 99, pp. 3-21.

13. William D. Howarth, *French theatre in the neoclassical era, 1550-1789,* Theatre in Europe: a Documentary History, General Editors Glynne Wickam *et al.,* Cambridge, New York, Melbourne, Cambridge University Press, 1997, pp. 11-12; George W. Brandt, *German and Dutch Theatre, 1600-1848,* Theatre in Europe, Cambridge, New York, Melbourne, Cambridge University Press, 1993, pp. 54-5.

14. Elida Maria Szarota, *Geschichte, Politik und Gesellschaft im Drama des 17 Jahrhunderts,* Bern, Munich, Francke Verlag, 1976, pp. 12-13; Curt von Faber du Fauv, *German Baroque Literature: A Catalogue of the Collection in the Yale University Library,* New Haven, CT, Yale University Press, 1958, pp. 247ff.; Pierre Janelle, *The Catho-*lic Reformation, London, Open University Set Book, Bruce Publishing, Milwaukee, Collier-Macmillan, 1971, pp. 155-8.

15. A. Closs and W. F. Maitland (eds), *German Lyrics of the Seventeenth Century,* London, Gerland Duckworth, 1949, pp. 61-5; *Trivmphvs Jesv oft Godliicke Lof-Sangen Verciert met Gheestlijcke Liedekens ende dichten, tot voortganck vande Ionckheyt, recreatie voor de blygeestige: om daer te verdryven alle fabuleuse en lichtveerdighe weireltsche dichten,* Antwerp, Geeraerdt van Wolsschaten, 1633, pp. 12, 17, 19, 25, 26, 33, A3 *passim*: see the edition by Peter Roelens, and Edward Vanhoutte (who most generously made the original available to me), Leuven, Katholieke Universiteit, 1994; Benny de Cupere, *Of Seven Ways of Holy Love: An English Edition of the Middle Dutch Mystical Treatise by Beatrice of Nazareth, With an Historical Discussion,* unpublished MA thesis, University of Lancaster, 1997.

16. *Trivmphus Jesv,* 12, 15, 25, 27, A1-A2 *passim*; Roelens and Vanhoutte (eds), *Trivmphvs Jesv,* intro., pp. 3-6; J. Fr Michaud, *Biographie Universelle Ancienne et Moderne,* 45 vols, Paris, C. Desplaces and M. Michaud, 1854, reprinted Graz, Austria, Akademische Druck-u. Verlagsanstalt, 1968, vol. XXVI, p. 218.

17. Edward M. Wilson, "Calderón", in Edward M.Wilson and Duncan Moir, *The Golden Age of Spanish Drama 1492-1700,* A Literary History of Spain, General Editor R. O. Jones, London, Ernest Benn, New York, Barnes & Noble, 1971, pp. 85-7, 101-3, 110-11, 116; Philip Ward (ed.), *The Oxford Companion to Spanish Literature,* Oxford, Clarendon, 1978, pp. 85-7, 598-9, 353, 154, 263-4; Margret Greer, 'Bodies of power in Calderón: *El nuevo palacio del Retiro* and *El mayor encanto, amor*', in Peter W. Evans (ed.), *Conflicts of Discourse: Spanish Literature in the Golden Age,* Manchester and New York, Manchester University Press, 1990, pp. 145-65; Calderón de la Barca, *La Vida es Sueño y El Alcalde de Zalamea,* ed. Augusto Cortina, Clásicos Castellanos, Madrid, Espase-Calpe, 1964, pp. xxv-xxvi; Phyllis Hartnoll, *A Concise History of the Theatre,* London, Thames and Hudson in association with Book Club Associates, 1968, pp. 95-6.

18. Ward (ed.), *The Oxford Companion to Spanish Literature,* pp. 130, 393, 565; Tirso de Molina, *Damned for Despair,* intro., ed. and trans. Nicholas G. Round, Warminster, Wilts, Aris & Phillips, 1986, pp. xxxviii-xliv, 59-60.

19. Adolphe Coster, 'Baltasar Gracian, 1601-58', *Revue Hispanique,* 1913, pp. 447-8. The same kind of intrepid use of temporal material as an allegorical basis for spiritual descriptions characterised

the English Protestant religious writer John Bunyan (1628-1688) whom Dr Skrine considers an artist with baroque affinities (Skrine, *The Baroque*, p. 159): in Part II of *The Pilgrim's Progress* (1684), for example, Bunyan has his character Matthew cured of stomach cramps by the application of the medicine of the flesh and blood of Christ: Michael A. Mullett, *John Bunyan in Context*, Studies in Protestant Nonconformity, editor Alan P. F. Sell, Keele, Keele University Press, 1996, pp. 258-9.

20. e.g., Josquin des Préz, 'Missa "L'Homme Armé"', Stereo Supraphon, Music Antiqua, Prague.

21. Tim Carter, *Music in Late Renaissance and Early Baroque Italy,* London, Batsford, 1992, pp. 13; 303, 103, 102, 104; Janelle, *The Catholic Reformation,* pp. 178-9; Richard Sherr, 'The performance of chant in the Renaissance and its interactions with polyphony' in Thomas Forrest Kelly (ed.), *Plainsong in the Age of Polyphony,* Cambridge Studies in Performance Practice, 2, General Editor Peter Williams, Cambridge, New York, Port Chester, Melbourne, Sydney, 1992, pp. 178, 182, 184-5.

22. Janelle, *The Catholic Reformation,* p. 180; Jerome Roche, *Palestrina,* Oxford Studies of Composers, No. 7, General Editor Colin Mason, London, New York, Toronto, Oxford University Press, 1971, pp. 7, 51; Carter, *Music in Late Renaissance and Baroque Italy,* pp. 105, 106.

23. Paolo Fabbri, *Monteverdi,* trans. Tim Carter, Cambridge, New York and Melbourne, 1994, pp. 9-10, 110-11, 114-15; Carter, *Music in Late Renaissance and Baroque Italy,* pp. 105, 228; Jerome Roche, 'Monteverdi and the prima *prattica*' in Denis Arnold and Nigel Fortune (eds), *The New Monteverdi Companion,* London and Boston, Mass., Faber and Faber, 1985, pp. 159-60.

INFLUENTIAL FIGURES

H. Outram Evennett (essay date 1951)

SOURCE: Evennett, H. Outram. "St. Ignatius and the Spiritual Exercises." In *The Spirit of the Counter-Reformation: The Birkbeck Lectures in Ecclesiastical History Given in the University of Cambridge in May 1951,* edited by John Bossy, pp. 43-66. London: Cambridge University Press, 1968.

[*In the following essay, originally presented as a lecture in May 1951, Evennett analyzes the* Spiritual Exercises *St. Ignatius had developed as a technique for conversion and describes their influence.*]

I attempted in my last lecture the somewhat formidable task of trying to convey what seem to me to be the main characteristics which marked the reinvigoration of Catholic spiritual life during the Counter-Reformation: the main traits of that teaching in regard to spirituality which gradually prevailed in the formation of new generations of parochial clergy in the Tridentine seminaries, in the pastoral activities of religious orders and new congregations of priests, and which was passed down to the laity in multiple ways throughout the sixteenth and seventeenth centuries, to the general moral reform of the Church in head and members. Among these agents of spiritual renewal, for both clergy and laity, the Society of Jesus was of outstanding and, in the true sense of the word, peculiar importance; and its teaching and influence in the spiritual sphere show almost all the characteristic counter-reformation marks to the highest degree. The Tridentine decree on Justification had shut out the Augustinian, or if you like, semi-Lutheran tendencies evinced by Contarini, Seripando, Pole, Gropper and others: the Jesuits developed a theological school concerning the relations of free will with Grace which, with the great controversy with the Dominicans over Molina's work, brought upon them the reproach of swinging to the near verge of Pelagianism. Bound up with this was their constant stress on activity of all kinds; the active use of the mind and intellect, with all their powers, in prayer, and especially in pictorial meditation, as against contemplative trends; their doctrine of the insufficiency of purely passive resistance to temptation with its corollary of the necessary counter-attack, the principle of *agendo contra*; the development of their casuistry in a humane and accommodating direction; their respect for each individual and his 'special case', seen in the flexibility of their general spiritual direction; their reaction from excessive corporal mortifications, either for themselves or their penitents. Active struggle against self; activity on behalf of others; frequent recourse to the sacraments; prayer found in work and action in the world rather than in eremetical retirement from it: these were some hallmarks.

Within the Counter-Reformation, however, the Jesuits were themselves a 'special case' in that, while breathing the same general spiritual atmosphere as others in the movement, they nevertheless depended immediately, for their formation, on a personality and a teaching about both of which there was something of the unique, and as a result of which the Society of Jesus, while generating and retaining its own peculiar exclusiveness of spirit, nevertheless became the most powerful, active, modernising, humanistic, and flexible force in the Counter-Reformation, impressing, in the long run, so much of its outlook and even to some extent the principles of its structural form on the life and organisation of Catholicism as a whole.

The small international society of the first nine—'Haec minima congregatio'—which was approved by the papacy in 1540 and which took up its headquarters in Rome, putting itself at the special disposition of the papacy because of its international character, had as its object the salvation and perfection not only of its own members, but equally those of other men. It was a society of reformed and apostolic priests. It had two special and outstanding assets, apart from the high qualities of all its original members: they were the remarkable history and gifts of its founder, Ignatius of Loyola; and the Spiritual Exercises which he had constructed and worked out as a technique for conversion. Applied first to his own original companions, they were soon to reach a much wider public, and to become the foundation of Jesuit pastoral activity, in preaching, missions, retreats, personal direction and otherwise. Not every point in the formation and early history of the Society, and the place of the Exercises in it, is by any means historically crystal-clear; but that the Exercises are inextricably linked up with St Ignatius's personality and evolution and with the foundation and development of the Society is hardly open to question.

Let us look then, first, at these 'Exercises'—the full title, in English, is: *Spiritual Exercises whereby to conquer oneself and order one's life without being influenced in one's decision by any inordinate affection.* The text of the *Spiritual Exercises* of St Ignatius does not constitute a continuous book intended to be read through as such and used by the individual who hopes to profit by them. The work is not a literary treatise on the spiritual life, or even a special didactic treatise on meditation, to be consulted at her own fireside, as it were, by the fervent soul seeking light on the amendment of life and the approach to God. The Spiritual Exercises are a special experience to be undergone, a shock-tactic spiritual gymnastic to be undertaken and performed under guidance, at some particular moment—perhaps of inward crisis—when new decisions and resolutions in life are called for or held to be desirable. But the written text is not—so to speak—a work in the *Teach Yourself Series*: it is the gymnastic instructor's handbook—the manual of direction for the spiritual guide who 'gives' the Exercises to him who performs them. The individual performing the Exercises not only need not but, in the early days before the text was available publicly, did not and probably could not himself have access to it. This is a point of great importance. The Jesuits 'gave' the Exercises: they did not give them to be read. This was from the start, even the false starts—if the expression be permitted—at Alcalá and Salamanca, the technique of St Ignatius himself; and the Exercises not only formed the instrument by which he first achieved the conversion, and then assured the life-long co-operation, of his first companions who formed the original Society of Jesus, but they remained—some would perhaps prefer to say, eventually became—the main permanent

spiritual inspiration in the Society in perpetuity. They were in a sense the systematised, de-mysticised quintessence of the process of Ignatius's own conversion and purposeful change of life, and they were intended to work a similar change in others. Conversion, and the consequent taking of new and appropriate resolutions for the future: these are the simple, straight-forward evangelical purposes of the *Spiritual Exercises.* There is nothing in them, says an Anglican commentator, 'which goes beyond the simplest and most fundamental truths of the Gospel'.[1] Their remarkable efficacy, their undoubted power, proved many times over, to 'change' men permanently, sprang from the extraordinary way in which they combined, by the instinct of spiritual genius, the accumulated spiritual wisdom of the past Christian centuries with the direct lessons learned by the saint himself in his own, in so many ways exceptional, spiritual experiences. The *Exercises,* as eventually made use of by the Society of Jesus in its wide general apostolate, and especially the development of retreats, spelt the formation of a new high-powered spiritual weapon capable of being applied with almost explosive results to men at all levels of spiritual need. For the 'conversion' and consequent 'election' of a new manner of life by the exercitant might operate—so to say—anywhere along the line of spiritual advance. It might work a change from indifference to regular Christian life; or from regular but tepid Christian life to a new purposeful fervour; or from fervour in the lay state to the embracing of the regular life in some religious order; or, indeed, again, from a normal regular observance within a religious order to a higher pitch of fervour and determination. The Exercises were—or at any rate soon became in the hands of experienced directors—infinitely flexible, capable of being modified according to the patient's character, or intellectual capacity, or his social condition of life, or the diagnosis of his inward condition by the discretion of the spiritual doctor. The medicine could be given in larger or smaller, in stronger or weaker, doses as required. But it was a medicine containing, like Alice's, so many good things that some mixture or other of it was always applicable. Here indeed was a weapon of unprecedented power: St Ignatius himself in tabloid form.

I do not think that this is the language of exaggeration. The pastoral efficiency of the Jesuits has had an enormously wide range and has comprised a great variety of approaches. But the principles arising out of the *Exercises* have underlain all. Though there are some obscurities in the early story, I think myself that the history of St Ignatius and of the early society does in fact point to the central importance of the Exercises from the start both for the spiritual formation of the Jesuits themselves—at any rate in Italy—and for their influence on others.[2] Recent Jesuit work, especially that of Padre Iparraguirre,[3] strengthens the evidence for this. It was not only that frequently through the Exercises, as was perhaps their original historical purpose, men became Jesuits: some, like Nadal—whose name despite his very great importance never gets into the textbooks—only at long last after refusing the ordeal for many years.[4] But men in all walks of life, in high and low places, laymen and ecclesiastics, were found amenable to them; and many not only found their own lives changed permanently but became themselves thenceforward, sometimes from doubters, enthusiastic supporters of the society. Such, for example, were Contarini, Tolomeo Gallio, Ortiz, three men of high influence in Rome, to whom the society owed much in the facilitation of its recognition by Paul III in 1540, in circumstances of considerable difficulty and delicacy.

In analysing what the Exercises demand and involve, two elements can be picked out as central: first, the examination of conscience, which is stressed most of all at the beginning; and secondly, the method of meditation and the practical fruits to be culled from it, which runs throughout the whole and forms the core of the method. The systematic examination of conscience is done in two forms, first, the general examination and then the particular examination; this is a special and continuous technique, to be continued as long as necessary, in which the attack on special besetting sins is remorselessly pursued. It is interesting to compare the energy, vitality and pithiness of this famous technique of the particular examination—examining oneself two or three times daily—with the somewhat cumbrous recommendations characteristic of the medieval manuals for penitents. Here St Ignatius is concerned not so much with the classification of sins, for use in the confessional, but with the psychology of eradicating them. In the Ignatian meditations the whole developing tradition of the fifteenth-century teachers comes to a powerful climax. Meditation is not just a vague devotional 'thinking about' some biblical scene or religious consideration. It is the systematic concentration upon it of the whole attention of the mind. A certain preparation is each time necessary, with preludes in the form of prayers and recollection of purpose. Then comes the formation of the mental picture, followed by the application of the senses, the affections, and the will, point by point; and, finally, what St Ignatius calls the colloquy—the free prayer in converse with God, after the meditation proper, as each individual finds it comes to him to do, in order to concentrate and harvest the result in the taking of some definite determination. Every effort, in effect, must be made to bring every detail of an imagined scene vividly to one's mind, as if one were present, and then to draw fruit and grace in prayer and new resolutions. No stylised presentation, for example, of the Passion but the stark realities are to be imagined, with each sense.

The four weeks into which the *Spiritual Exercises* are divided are fixed and equal periods only by courtesy, like the days of creation. Each 'week' represents a stage—a true week being the optimum duration. But each week can be prolonged or shortened, and some of them even omitted, according to the decision of the director. The first week, purgative in nature, deals with the examination of conscience, confession and eradication of faults, the start of the struggle against self: the meditations concern sin and hell; and in this first week a preliminary election or choice of God, as against sin, is in fact tacitly made. But it is the second week that brings the climax of the specific election, or choice, with the famous opening meditations on the kingdom of Christ and the choice of standards, followed, before the election itself, by a series of meditations on the main events of our Lord's life from the Nativity to Palm Sunday. The election itself is a determination not merely to avoid sin—that has already been done in the first week—but actively to promote the kingdom of Christ in the state of life to which one is called, or to which one now decides that the call comes. The third week, illuminative we may say, following the traditional threefold conception of the stages of spiritual advance, strengthens the resolves already taken by a series of further meditations, mainly on the Passion. The fourth week, unitive in spirit, is based on meditations on the risen Lord, his glory, his love, which we are called upon to share. The complete series of meditations, after the preliminary ones in the first week on sin and hell and the opening one of the second week on the kingdom of Christ, cover the gospel story from the Nativity to the Resurrection; it has often been commented upon that neither here nor in the appended list of supplementary meditations is the divine history carried on further to the Ascension or to Pentecost.

In addition to the four groups of meditations proper, each with its accompanying outcome of personal resolve, the text of the *Exercises* contains in pithy, carefully phrased terms a number of other elements upon which the director can draw from time to time to assist his exercitant as may seem advisable, according to his character, his progress or his lack of progress, or the exact number of 'weeks' which are being undertaken. For it is possible—and indeed common—to do the Exercises only in part, though the election at the end of the second week is usually vital. The list of these other elements is quite long. First, the twenty annotations, or rules for the director, which open the text; secondly, the famous section known as the Principle or Foundation, a short but masterly summary of the end of man, his proper use of created beings, and his attainment of indifference to worldly conditions. This is placed at the beginning of the first week and is a nodal point in the whole scheme. Then there are special considerations to be made use of, to be brought to the notice of the exercitant, during the crucial second week, on different states of life, different classes of men, different degrees of humility. Then, coming after the end of the fourth week's meditations and fruits to be garnered, are, first, an additional series of mysteries of the life of our Lord, divided into points for meditation according to the plan of the four weeks; then twenty 'rules for the discernment of spirits', that is, tests for the genuineness of religious claims or emotions, again according to the way in which they may be useful during the experiences of the weeks; four rules for the distribution of alms; six observations concerning scruples; the famous eighteen rules for 'Thinking with the Church'—safeguards, that is, of orthodoxy—and lastly seventeen additional notes applicable to various points throughout the text. This curious literary form, in which the main expositions of the meditations and fruits to be sought in the four weeks are accompanied and followed up by a rich variety of running comments, as it were, in the way of rules for guidance, observations, considerations, analyses and so forth, shows clearly the nature of the whole; that it is designed for the director giving the Exercises, and not as a continuous text to be read by the exercitant. And, as if all this were not enough to ensure sufficient guidance and flexibility, there came into existence, first drawn up by St Ignatius and perfected later in the century under Acquaviva (1581-1615), forty further chapters of detailed advice to givers of the Exercises, known as the *Directory*.[5] Flexibility, indeed, was to be the main concern of the giver, who was to adapt the technique and the general plan to the particular needs, state, psychology, character, intelligence, stamina, of each individual concerned, without, however, altering the actual method of making what meditations were included: the composition of the mental scene, the application of the senses, the subsequent prayer and resolution. This recognition of the separateness and difference of each individual person is surely a high tribute to the perceptive humanity of St Ignatius. It runs not only through the *Exercises,* but also, despite the stress on implicit obedience, in the constitutions of his society as well.

Those who wish for a closer acquaintance with the *Exercises* may be referred, from among a multitude of works, to the definitive edition of the text—or more accurately, the texts—made by the Spanish editors of the *Monumenta Historica Societatis Jesu,*[6] to the various, and all masterly, recent works of Père de la Boullaye, S.J.,[7] and to the useful and understanding English edition by the late Rev. W. H. Longridge of the Anglican Society of St John the Evangelist.[8] Here, I pass on to ask how it was that St Ignatius came to contrive this instrument, this finely adaptable spiritual mangle, through which men were passed to be brought out new.

Much has been written and continues to be written on the history of the *Exercises* and the problem of their genesis and sources. It seems clear that in the main they originate from and are in fact a synthesised, as it were dehydrated, form of at least parts of St Ignatius's own experiences of conversion and subsequent development,

from the first conversion on his sick-bed, through the formative stages of the pilgrimage to Montserrat, the vital experiences of Manresa, the pilgrimage to Jerusalem, the subsequent periods at Barcelona, Alcalá and Salamanca, right up, indeed, to the important time at Paris. The main substance of the *Exercises,* with practically all the most important elements and meditations, would seem to date from the end of the time at Manresa—1522-3. Some first retouches were no doubt made in the experimental period when, as a student at Barcelona, Alcalá and Salamanca, St Ignatius began to attract and teach followers and was obliged to submit his text to the Inquisitorial authorities. In this period, 1524-8, or perhaps even later, at Paris, the important section known as the Principle or Foundation was probably added. Then at Paris, where St Ignatius first began seriously to study philosophy and theology, and to attract as his disciples men who were also students, the *Exercises* seem to have undergone general revision. Various additions and annotations were added which show traces of the new intellectual environment, of an awareness of scholasticism, and of the wider ranges of human types who now came into the saint's purview; possibly also, for the first time, of an awareness of Protestantism. It was at Paris, apparently, that the famous rules for orthodoxy were formulated, also the well-known sections on the degrees of humility and on the three classes of men. At Paris, too, there seems to have been a recasting of the rules for the discernment of spirits—so important in an age of novelties and uncertainties and new claims—and a certain revision of the central point of the election, or choice of a state of life.

While, therefore, the main substance and structure of the *Exercises* were firmly laid down at a very early stage after, or even during, the experiences at Manresa—there are those who cull some satisfaction from reflecting that they may well have been written in a cell in the Dominican priory there!—they nevertheless underwent expansion and adaptation during the next dozen years or so until reaching their final form. I follow here Père Pinard de la Boullaye's brilliant little book *Les étapes de rédaction des Exercices de S. Ignace*[9] which, together with Padre Leturia's similar conclusions, would seem definitive. Behind this question, however, there lies a further important issue. How much did the teaching and influence of St Ignatius derive directly and independently from his own extraordinary experiences, mainly those undergone at Manresa in 1522-3, and how much from the spiritual traditions which surrounded him on all sides: the spiritual literature then influential in Spain, and Paris, the various external influences which came upon him in the course of his evolution—in a word, the whole historical, literary and spiritual atmosphere of the day which his *Exercises,* their method, spirit and purpose, seem to have caught up and so brilliantly synthesised and focused? There is indeed a sense in which St Ignatius may be seen as the St Paul of the Counter-Reformation, and the problem of his influence upon it as similar to the analogous Pauline problem. Here was a man subject to a more or less sudden conversion, to special privileged illuminations (no historian, I think, could wholly discount Ignatius's own story of an extraordinary illumination on the banks of the River Cardoner at Manresa—to mention no other incidents), and destined to give new definition, impetus and modernity to the religious movement with which he was associated, and to carry it far and wide across the earth. Yet, on the other hand, as those of his followers are not slow to claim who emphasise most strongly the extent of his dependence on God's own direct private dealings with him, St Ignatius in no wise invented a new religion—any more, shall we say, than did St Paul?—and his spirituality, though conveyed through the *Exercises* in a practical technique that was brilliantly new and brilliantly successful, was nevertheless in full accord, when properly seen, with the dominant Catholic tendencies of his day and therefore drew undeniably upon a legacy from predecessors.

There is first of all a purely literary problem. Can any direct literary dependence on earlier texts be detected in the *Exercises*? In 1919 the able Spanish Jesuits who edited the texts of the *Exercises* in the *Monumenta Historica*[10] went very fully into this question in their introduction, referring learnedly to a large preceding literature. They concluded that no direct borrowing of phrases could be traced from the three books which so much influenced Ignatius in his earliest stages of conversion: the *Flos Sanctorum* (or Golden Legend), the *Vita Christi* of Ludolph the Carthusian, the *Imitation of Christ,* though they conceded that the author must have made considerable use of the multitudinous notes that he is known to have made on these works. In regard to a possible influence of Abbot Cisneros's *Ejercitatorio de la Vida Espiritual,* which may have become known to St Ignatius during his short time at Montserrat, they concluded that here too there is no single instance of textual reproduction. In the actual *Exercises* themselves, as distinct from the various additions, they admit only seven or eight passages of real resemblance, all of which, however, are passages that might just as well derive from Ludolph or à Kempis. Furthermore, they point out, and the point has cogency, that the form and object of the *Exercises* is quite different from that of the *Ejercitatorio.* The latter is a work for the general deepening of the spiritual life of monks; it is based upon, and assumes, the monastic horarium of liturgical prayer throughout the year. The Exercises, on the other hand, are, as we have seen, a special 'occasional' technique aimed primarily at effecting a change of life and possibly also a change of state of life. Commentators who have tried to find direct literary sources for the *Exercises* in a number of various quarters—the works of St Bernard, St Anselm, Gerard of Zutphen, Raymond Lull,

Abbot Werner, Savonarola, Jan Mombaer, even Erasmus's *Enchiridion*—are similarly dealt with by the editors of the *Monumenta.* Possible parallels and resemblances turn out to be largely on points which, however important, are in fact commonplaces that might have one or more of any number of various inspirations; the textual similarities are never so close as to be completely convincing; moreover, St Ignatius could not, at the early time of the first writing of the *Exercises,* have read at all widely in patristic and medieval spiritual literature. He was still for all practical purposes a layman—and his early movement of apostolate, a lay one.

The findings of these editors in regard to direct literary dependence, though expressed in terms of perhaps undue asperity, are to my mind, on the whole, convincing, and would seem to have been very generally accepted. From a literary point of view, the *Exercises* are not just a patchwork from earlier writers—they are as original in expression as in general concept and design. And yet this is not the end of the problem. It is only the beginning of another, more difficult one. Granted that in detailed form, in elaboration of technique, in clarity and unity of purpose, the Ignatian *Exercises* are *sui generis,* different somehow from all the 'Exercises' and 'Scalae' and didactic treatises on meditation of the previous hundred and fifty years—in that everything in them is drawn up, as it were, in masterly battle-array under a skilled commander—yet it remains that their author lived in a certain historical setting; that he was part and parcel of an age; and that the expression of his perhaps unique spiritual gifts and perceptions and wisdoms was necessarily in the mode of his time. For all his uncovenanted privileges of special insight and understanding, which I for one would certainly not wish to question, St Ignatius was not, and could not be, a stained-glass figure abstracted from his environment and its influences. In recent decades, in fact, the history of St Ignatius, of his personal evolution and of his work has been much illuminated—not to say modernised—by able Jesuit scholars such as Padre Leturia, Père Pinard de la Boullaye, Père Watrigant, Père de Grandmaison, Père Dudon,[11] and others, who have understood and met this problem of envisaging St Ignatius in his historical setting, and who have had the enormous volume of materials in the *Monumenta Historica Societatis Jesu,* first published in Madrid, now being continued from Rome, from which to quarry. If so many critics have thought to find the 'origin' of various of the main ideas of the *Exercises* in previous writers it is because these ideas, however acquired by St Ignatius, are not in themselves, intrinsically and separately, new. Take the meditation on the kingdom of Christ, the famous choice of standards and the resolve to follow the standard of Christ rather than of his enemy—dramatic opening and climax, as it were, of the second week of the *Exercises*; all this is not just the colourful imagery of an old soldier turned evangelist, it is an age-old traditional concept of the spiritual writers, closely paralleled indeed in so un-Ignatian a book as Erasmus's *Enchiridion Militis Christiani*: paralleled there so closely that even Jesuits like Padre Leturia, Père Watrigant, and Père de Grandmaison will not follow the editors of the *Monumenta* in ruling it out utterly as a possible direct influence—whether Ignatius actually finished reading this work of Erasmus or no![12] And indeed what else, at bottom, is the concept of the choice of standards than the classic one of the two allegiances, two communities, two cities—of the righteous and unrighteous—of God and the devil—Babylon and Jerusalem—what you will—which we find not only in St Augustine but in a host of other writers. Similarly, precedents can be found in plenty for the Ignatian doctrine of the three powers of the soul—memory, understanding, will; for some points in the method of meditation, of imagining ourselves actually present with each sense in turn at the scenes of our Lord's life and passion (made easier in St Ignatius's own case by his having actually visited Jerusalem); for the whole question of spiritual discernment, as well as for other less central points such as the regulation of the appetite in eating and drinking, the use of sleep etc. The *Exercises,* in fact, are at one and the same time uniquely new as a whole and in their method of activating men—but full of traditional spirituality in their particular points. The old wine in a new bottle—and brought to a new ferment. How did this come about? How did St Ignatius receive this deep understanding, practical wisdom, and succinct expressive power on paper, before he was either a wide reader of spiritual books or a scholar in the universities? Was it *all* infused at Manresa? Or did St Ignatius in fact undergo something which we could in the normal sense call a 'spiritual formation' at the hands of men?

That before his wound and conversion in 1521 Ignatius, though not an enthusiast in religious matters, had had close contact with them would seem evident from the fact that he was originally destined by his family for the Church, and indeed was a tonsured cleric of the diocese of Pamplona from early years. But it would appear that he must have turned away to the pursuit of the knightly and courtly life, with all its romantic self-indulgences; that he had made a deliberate 'election' of a state of life, as it were, but one turning away from God's service to that of an earthly prince. If this be so, there must always have been the recollection of it at the bottom of his mind. As a young page and then a knight at Tordesillas and at Arévalo contrasting examples of sin and piety would come his way plentifully: the easy relations of sensual people on the one hand; the atmosphere of official court piety on the other. On one side, duels, women, gaming; on the other, the ideals of chivalry, devotion, obedience, discipline in the service of a Lord. Doubtless Ignatius was no better than he should have been. But Arévalo was at this time one of the centres of the reviving Franciscanism in Spain so much

promoted by Cardinal Jiménez de Cisneros. The influence of the Franciscan Ambrosio Montesino, whose translation of Ludolph's *Vita Christi* Ignatius later read on his sick-bed, was at work at Arévalo, where Ignatius may well have read his *Itinerario de la Cruz* dedicated to the Duchess of Nájera, wife of Ignatius's patron. There is reason, too, to suppose that he read at this time the *Triunfo de los Apóstoles* by the Franciscan poet Juan de Padilla, with its references to the Charterhouse of Seville, to which (and not to the nearer Charterhouse of Miraflores at Burgos) the saint at a later time once expressed a wish to retire. Add to all this early impressions of piety derived from the family circle, and it is clear that from a spiritual point of view Ignatius could not have been a complete *tabula rasa* when, on his sick-bed after Pamplona, the romances gave out and he was fain to turn to Montesino's translation of Ludolph and the lives of the saints. But at this period of what we may call his first 'conversion' these books of Germanic piety seem to have been the only religious books that he had by him and which inspired or at least accompanied his change of life. Under their aegis Ignatius made a new 'election'; the resolve to change his state of life from a knight of the world to that of a knight of Christ; to become a humble, poorly clad, penniless pilgrim. And it was as a preparation for a pilgrimage to Jerusalem, to set his eyes upon the exact sites of our Lord's life and sufferings, that he set out, when healed, across the north of Spain for the famous pilgrimage-shrine of our Lady of Montserrat, there to do vigil before the Madonna, to take, as it were, his new vows, and to exchange the rich garb of a knight for the coarse sackcloth of a pilgrim.

What really happened to Ignatius at Montserrat? It would be most interesting to know for certain! Was it simply a matter of three days of high generous religious emotion, marked by the—dare one suggest it?—slight exhibitionism of the famous vigil and discarding of knightly costume as well as by the more searching ordeal of a three days' general Confession? Or did St Ignatius at Montserrat, through his confessor the French monk Dom Chanones, come into touch, unexpectedly, with a powerful force of organised spirituality that was to supply him with the groundwork of something the need for which he had not previously understood but which he now saw that he must acquire—a solid spiritual formation at the hands of experienced guides? That this is in fact what occurred is the broad thesis of Dom Anselmo Albareda's extremely ingenious book *Sant Ignasi a Montserrat* (written, regrettably, in Catalan).[13] Dom Albareda, a monk of Montserrat, now librarian at the Vatican Library, maintains that it was this realisation of the need of formation which deflected Ignatius from his original purpose of proceeding immediately to Jerusalem (not any question of practical difficulties—plague in Barcelona, robbers on the road) and which sent him instead into unpremeditated retirement at the neighbouring town of Manresa where the Hospice of Santa Lucía could house him. Furthermore, Dom Albareda maintains that Ignatius did not stay merely three days on the holy mountain but that he lived there for some weeks as a penitent in a cave higher up than the monastery, receiving alms and spiritual advice; and that even when he finally betook himself to Manresa he came back frequently for conferences with Dom Chanones and others. This whole thesis has been severely criticised on every point by Jesuit authors, and I must confess that it seems to me very difficult to maintain in its entirety. The theory of the prolonged stay on the mountain and the frequent revisits rests only on the traditions of the monastery, and on late and circumstantial evidence, some of it hearsay and given by very old men at the beatification enquiries in the 1590s; moreover—and this seems to me extremely significant—St Ignatius himself gives no ground for it in the autobiography of his spiritual evolution which in his later years he dictated to Father Luis Cámara.[14] It is admitted on all hands that the claims of some seventeenth-century and even of certain more modern Benedictine writers, who maintained that St Ignatius owed everything to the Benedictines and that the *Exercises* flow directly from Abbot Cisneros's *Ejercitatorio,* cannot possibly be maintained; that such an extreme thesis is riddled with major misconceptions and critical impossibilities. Yet, despite the difficulties in maintaining Dom Albareda's less drastic thesis to the full, it seems to me nonetheless highly probable that Montserrat may have been a real turning-point and a step forward in the saint's spiritual evolution, bringing him into contact with a new force in organised religion and the realisation of how much he had to learn. It is highly plausible, to my mind, to suggest that this realisation turned him aside from the project of an immediate pilgrimage to Jerusalem, in order to retire, for the purpose of an intenser spiritual cultivation now seen to be necessary, to Manresa nearby. The possibility of this having happened, it seems to me, is underestimated by Dom Albareda's critics. Later relations of St Ignatius and the Jesuits with Benedictines were always especially cordial, so much so as even to suggest some kind of acknowledged debt.

But then what happened at Manresa? Normal formative influences were no doubt present—and, on his own admission, sought by the saint: the local Dominicans where he lodged for a time, a nearby Cistercian, certain pious women; he does not in his spiritual autobiography mention Montserrat or the Benedictines again. But all these now become secondary: indeed he records in his spiritual autobiography that no one could now give him any help in the extraordinary crisis of experiences which came upon him and out of which he emerged a new man (not this time by his own but by God's election) rich with mystical knowledge of God, mature in spirit after passing in a few weeks through a whole gamut of spiritual experiences which with others have been the

spun-out story of a lifetime. It was now that he first read the *Imitation of Christ,* which he declared made every other spiritual work seem superfluous; now that he put down on paper the main points of the *Exercises,* before, the ordeals and enlightenments over, he set out, via Barcelona, for Jerusalem—now at last prepared for the deferred pilgrimage. Now he was, as it were, the mystic; illuminated, and in an interior sense changed and formed; but he was also the incipient apostle, beginning to sense that his call was not to the Carthusian cloister at Seville, nor to the reform of some lax order, not indeed to retirement, but to apostolic work for the greater glory of God and the good of souls; that, in a sense, he must hand on to others the fruits of the cleaning fires through which he had himself just passed. The Society of Jesus, not yet in his mind as such—not to take definite shape there for about another fifteen years or so—was nonetheless in principle conceived.

Jerusalem was a further climax; but one which served still further to clarify the future. His experiences in the Holy Land finally taught Ignatius that he was not destined to be an obscure hermit, either there or in his native land. With his return from Palestine there may be said to end the early ecstatic—mystic—stage of his religious evolution; the stage comparable with St Philip Neri's early quasi-Franciscan life in the catacombs and ruins of Rome, before he learnt that he must in the end give order and outward respectability to his way of life. The emotions and the will were now in harness. There remained the intellect. Education was required for the coming apostolate to be fruitful. Now well over thirty years old, Ignatius sat with mocking boys on hard benches in the lecture rooms at Barcelona, Alcalá and Salamanca successively, acquiring the rudiments of Latin. But always the pull was in two ways: to study, the immediate necessity; to the apostolate, the long-term basic urge. Early disciples gathered around; the Exercises began to be given, the Inquisition to be aroused. Was this strange errant cleric without Holy Orders an impostor? Another *alumbrado,* claiming direct light and ready to ignore the authorities of the Church—in contact perhaps with suspect circles? The Inquisitors saw that he was not; but they declared that he must not guide souls nor teach the difference between mortal and venial sin without further study. No doubt a sensible and salutary decision; one, certainly, which contributed to the saint's decision to leave Spain and go straight to the recognised fountain-head of traditional European scholastic learning, whither so many Spaniards had preceded him. In 1528 he was in Paris.

The effect upon St Ignatius of his years in Paris was profound. Here, in more ways than one, his whole outlook was widened and made more practical. A growing scholasticism of action, if we may use the phrase, accompanied the studies of scholastic philosophy and theology. A deeper sense of prudence and caution, of the practical, made themselves manifest, both in his dealings with men and in the additions and modifications to the *Exercises* which he now made, no doubt with new types of convert in mind. It was in Paris too that, if ever, he came into direct touch with the influence of the *devotio moderna,* for the whole religious atmosphere of the Collège de Montaigu at which he spent his first year had been formed by Mombaer and Standonck, and many monastic and other reforms had been attempted in Paris by representatives of the religious fervour from the Low Countries. Other influences in plenty, of course, were at work in Paris: spiritual, intellectual and humanist; the new biblical ardour of a Lefèvre as well as the strong conservatism of a Noël Beda. Paris was a centre of powerful forces and ideas such as Ignatius had not known before. Did all this pass him by in his campaign of choosing new disciples for his future work from among his fellow university students? Did he become here more aware of Protestantism and events in Germany and Switzerland? It can hardly have been otherwise. The vows on Montmartre—nearly contemporary with the *placards*—mark a further step in the evolution towards the foundation of the Society of Jesus. Ignatius is becoming a churchman as well as an apostle; the practical common sense, the genius for reality, the matter-of-factness of the future society are rising upon the basic spiritual foundations. If the nine—drawn from several nations—cannot visit Jerusalem together, they will put themselves at once at the disposition of the Pope. Six years more, after mission work in Italy, and the frustration of a joint pilgrimage to Jerusalem, would see the society established in Rome.

How insufficient, in view of all this history, it is to regard St Ignatius as simply an ardent Spaniard who brought medieval ideals of chivalry and a military outlook into his band of followers! The word *compañía* has no more necessarily military connotation than when applied in the Italian ten years earlier to St Angela's first group of pious lady-helpers. Translated into Latin, it is *societas,* not, for example, *cohors.*[15] In fact, St Ignatius and his Society of Jesus are the richest amalgams, formed by the successive influences which operated upon him in Spain, France and Italy, as well as being based upon his personal sanctity and the secrets of his direct knowledge of God.

The problem of the forces acting upon the origins of the society is in one aspect only part of a larger problem—that of foreign religious influences in the Spain of the early sixteenth century. The notion of a spiritually and intellectually isolated Spain at this period is a misconception formed by the casting-back of later views of Spain as a land impermeable to foreign influences. The new Spain of 1450 to 1550, which was so closely related, politically, to Italy, and subsequently to the Netherlands and to England; which was creating for herself a new empire in strange lands beyond the Atlantic, and

which bore within herself the rich strains of Arab and Jew, Castilian and Basque, Catalan and Aragonese, could hardly form a solid watertight cultural entity. Today, specialists are perhaps more concerned to vindicate Spanish originality, or at least to disentangle the different strands of influence. I have already spoken of the Dominican influences passing between Italy and Iberia; and of what Fr Beltrán de Heredia has called the Savonarolian invasion of Spain, indicated by both direct and circumstantial evidence; though in respect of the Dominicans one must remember at the same time that the Castilian Preachers, for all their traditional intellectual contacts with Italy and Paris, had never succumbed to the all-powerful nominalism of the fifteenth century, and that the rise of the Thomist school of San Esteban at Salamanca, clinched though it was by the work of Vitoria after his return from Paris, was nonetheless largely indigenous. While Boehmer in his books on Ignatius studied the possibility of German mystical influences having played, in the ultimate analysis, a prominent part in his formation,[16] Altamira contended that all Spanish counter-reformation mysticism could be regarded as an importation from Germany and the Netherlands at the time of the Reformation.[17] Similarly, while a German called Muller could write a book trying to show that Ignatius copied the form and structure of his society from the example of certain Moslem societies,[18] it could also be asserted by others that Spanish medieval mysticism was rooted in Moslem philosophy.[19] Whatever we may think of this from the purely spiritual point of view, it is surely not absurd from the intellectual or literary standpoint. When Moslem influence has been detected by Asín and others in even Dante,[20] can any branch of *Spanish* thought or literature claim, *a priori,* to be exempt? Thinking of Erasmus's wide popularity in Spain up to the suppression of his works there, a popularity wider than he ever had in Italy, and studied in so masterly a way in Bataillon's big book, we remember that Erasmus is himself but one form of a Netherlandish influence coming south—an ex-Canon Regular of Windesheim; while any reader of the valuable and interesting work on Erasmus's early period by Paul Mestwerdt, a young German scholar killed in the first World War, will not underestimate the influence of the *devotio moderna* upon him.[21]

More research needs to be done, perhaps, before the real nature and extent of Germanic influence on the sixteenth-century Spanish mystics can be adequately gauged; Groult's book on the subject is inconclusive[22] and I have not yet been able to see a recent general work on this point, by a Spanish Franciscan.[23] But it is noteworthy that the late Padre Crisógono, O.D.C., an outstanding Carmelite scholar who died all too young, wrote of St John of the Cross and Tauler that 'the history of mysticism knows of no two mystics who resemble one another more closely',[24] and very recently another Spanish Carmelite scholar has seen a probable literary influence on St John in Ruysbroeck. Professor Allison Peers, though not subscribing to all Padre Crisógono's views on St John, is nevertheless concerned to indicate adequately the foreign influences in Spanish mysticism—especially Tauler, Ruysbroeck and Gerson. But in estimating the real originality of St Teresa and St John, who quote so little from other writers, we are up against the same sort of problem as we are in regard to the originality of St Ignatius. Behind all three lie centuries of tradition, and influences both Latin and Germanic. All are creative in a real sense, in that they fashion out of their materials—their experiences and their literary sources—something new. But it is undeniable that Germanic mysticism, like the Germanic *devotio moderna* with its large contribution to the systematised meditation of the Ignatian Exercises, like, again, the Germanic devout humanism of an Erasmus, were among the many influences present in renaissance and counter-reformation Spain.

Let me here, in conclusion, enter this *caveat*. In suggesting the existence of similar problems of derivation or influences undergone, in respect of the Spanish mystics and of St Ignatius's *Exercises,* I must not be taken as implying that I equate the two. Mystic, in a real sense, St Ignatius himself undoubtedly was; favoured, at Manresa principally, and then again later in life while composing the constitutions of his society in 1544-5, with special illuminations, special understandings, special and no doubt lasting intimacies with God. But despite the comparisons which can be and have specifically been made, recently again by Padre Larrañaga, between Ignatius's experiences of 1544-5 as recorded in his *Spiritual Diary* and the autobiography and other works of St Teresa,[25] it is surely plain that it must be difficult, by and large, to fit St Ignatius's case into the normal 'main-line' framework of Catholic mysticism and the development of contemplative prayer as we see it in the Spanish Carmelites, St Teresa, St John of the Cross, and other sixteenth-century Spanish mystics. Moreover, however this may be, it remains the fact that the *Spiritual Exercises,* this recipe for conversion, written substantially at Manresa itself, is not a work of mysticism or contemplation in the technical sense—despite St Ignatius's employment of the word 'contemplation' to denote a certain mode of imaginative discursive meditation. Indeed, nothing is so astonishing as the outcome of the raptures and visions of Manresa in this very unmystical, almost matter-of-fact, technique of the *Spiritual Exercises.* There is, of course, nothing in the *Exercises* either to suggest or to discourage the idea of the converted man being able eventually to reach the attainment of contemplative prayer as Grace develops in him, a prayer rising above vocal utterances, mental images or discourse of reason; and there are those who have maintained that in the meditations of the fourth week there are direct preliminaries, if not invitations, to the contemplative state. The *Exercises,* remember, are not a general philosophy of prayer or the spiritual life as a whole. They are a way of conversion—usually a *première,* not Lallemant's *deuxième conversion.* But in fact, whether this happened according to the mind of St Ignatius or not, there developed in the society, especially under the generalships of Mercurian and Acquaviva, a view that contemplation proper was an inappropriate form of prayer for members of an institute whose life was devoted to activity.[26] There have, of course, been true Jesuit contemplatives in the normally accepted sense of the word—Balthasar de Álvarez, confessor of St Teresa (who was commanded, however, by Mercurian to return to the methods of the *Exercises*), Álvarez da Paz, Provincial of Peru, Lallemant and Surin in early seventeenth-century France, and others. Yet on the whole, in the society's own life and therefore also in its pastoral activities it has not promoted this higher way of prayer even in those who feel called to it—this prayer which doubtless St Ignatius knew and experienced, but which he did not deal with in the *Spiritual Exercises.* The mystic and the active man merged naturally in St Ignatius himself. They were not encouraged to do so in the society. What difficult theological problems in regard to Grace and the nature of prayer are involved herein, I cannot here discuss.

Notes

1. W. H. Longridge (ed.), *The Spiritual Exercises of Saint Ignatius of Loyola, translated from the Spanish with a commentary and a translation of the* Directorium in Exercitia (London, 1930; 1st ed. 1919), p. xxxiv.

2. The opposite view was maintained by Bremond, *Histoire littéraire du sentiment religieux,* VIII (1928), 185 f., where he argued for a 'réaction ascéticiste' and a 'crise des Exercices' around 1580; note the attack on Watrigant, pp. 186, 229, and cf. J. de Guibert, *La spiritualité de la Compagnie de Jésus* (Rome, 1953), p. 3.

3. I. Iparraguirre, *Historia de la práctica de los Ejercicios espirituales de San Ignacio de Loyola*: I, *Práctica de los Ejercicios . . . en vida de su autor (1522-56)* (Bilbao/Rome, 1946), with fine bibliography.

4. See M. Nicolau, *Jerónimo Nadal (1507-80), sus obras y doctrinas espirituales* (Madrid, 1949).

5. I. Iparraguirre (ed.), *Directoria exercitiorum spiritualium, 1540-99* (Monumenta historica Societatis Jesu: Monumenta Ignatiana, series II, nova editio, vol. II, Rome, 1955): a new edition of the relevant part of the next reference.

6. *Exercitia spiritualia Sancti Ignatii de Loyola et eorum directoria* (Monumenta Ignatiana, series II, Madrid, 1919).

7. H. Pinard de la Boullaye, *Saint Ignace de Loyola, directeur d'âmes* (Paris, 1947); *La spiritualité ignatienne: textes choisis et présentés par H.P.* (Paris, 1949); *Les étapes de rédaction des Exercices de S. Ignace* (Paris, 1950). None of these works is in the British Museum.

8. See above, n. 1.

9. See above, n. 7; P. Leturia, 'Génesis de los ejercicios de San Ignacio y su influjo en la fundación de la Compañía de Jesús (1521-40)', *Archivum historicum Societatis Jesu,* X (1941), 16-59, repr. in Leturia, *Estudios ignacianos,* ed. and rev. I. Iparraguirre (2 vols., Rome, 1957), II, 3-55.

10. See above, n. 6.

11. See above, n. 7, n. 9; P. Dudon, *Saint Ignace de Loyola* (Paris, 1934). I do not know which work of Père de Grandmaison is referred to.

12. Leturia, on page 23 of his article cited in n. 9, refers the matter to Watrigant, *La méditation fondamentale avant S. Ignace* (Enghien, 1907), p. 71, and R. García Villoslada, 'San Ignacio de Loyola y Erasmo de Rotterdam', *Estudios eclesiásticos,* XVI (1942), 244-8. Gonzáles de Cámara says that humanist friends at Alcalá suggested that Ignatius should read it, and that he refused; Ribadeneira, that it was at Barcelona, and that he read but did not finish it because it 'lui faisait perdre sa dévotion' (Guibert, *Spiritualité de la Compagnie de Jésus,* p. 155).

13. Monestir de Montserrat, 1935.

14. Leturia, '¿Hizo San Ignacio en Montserrat o en Manresa vida solitaria?', in *Estudios ignacianos,* I, 113-78, especially 175-8.

15. Cf. the remarks to a similar effect in G. R. Elton, *Reformation Europe, 1517-1559* (London, 1963), p. 203; O. Chadwick, *The Reformation* (Pelican History of the Church, III, Harmondsworth, 1964), p. 259; A. Guillermou, *Saint Ignace de Loyola et la Compagnie de Jésus* (Coll. *Maîtres Spirituels,* Paris, 1960), p. 50.

16. H. Boehmer, *Loyola und die deutsche Mystik* (Sächsischen Akademie der Wissenschaften, phil.-hist. Klasse, Bd. XXIII, Heft 1, Leipzig, 1921), p. 21, etc.

17. I have not found the reference. In *Historia de España y de la civilización española,* III (3rd ed., Barcelona, 1913), 554, Altamira describes the mystics as being 'sí influídos por los alemanes contemporáneos [sic], diferentes de ellos por su ortodoxia y su repulsión a las extravagancias . . .'

18. Herrmann (sic) Muller (presumably pseud.), *Les origines de la Compagnie de Jésus: Ignace et Lainez* (Paris, 1898).

19. Altamira, *Historia de España,* I, (2nd ed., 1909), 570, *à propos* of Ramón Lull.

20. M. Asín Palacios, *La escatología musulmana en la Divina Comedia* (Madrid, 1919): see U. Cosmo, *A handbook to Dante studies* (Oxford, 1950), p. 149.

21. *Die Anfänge des Erasmus: Humanismus und 'Devotio Moderna'* (Leipzig, 1917).

22. P. Groult, *Les mystiques des Pays-Bas et la littérature espagnole du seizieme siècle* (Louvain, 1927).

23. J. Sanchís Alventosa, *La escuela mística alemana y sus relaciones con nuestros místicos del Siglo de Oro* (Madrid, 1946): no. 2005 of bibliography in E. Allison Peers, *Studies of the Spanish mystics,* III (London, 1960).

24. Quoted, with dissent, by Allison Peers, *St John of the Cross and other lectures and addresses* (London, 1946), p. 41, from Crisógono de Jesús Sacramentado, *San Juan de la Cruz* (2 vols., Madrid, 1929), I, 51. I do not know who the 'other Carmelite scholar' is.

25. V. Larrañaga, *La espiritualidad de S. Ignacio comparada con la de S. Teresa de Jesús* (Madrid, 1944). Larrañaga is the author of the introduction to the *Obras completas de San Ignacio de Loyola* in the *Biblioteca de autores cristianos,* LXXXVI (Madrid, 1952). Neither of these is in the British Museum.

26. Bremond, *Histoire littéraire,* VIII, 228 f.; J. de Guibert, 'Le généralat de Claude Aquaviva (1581-1615): sa place dans l'histoire de la spiritualité de la Compagnie de Jésus', *Archivum historicum Societatis Jesu,* X (1941), 59-93, and *La spiritualité de la Compagnie de Jésus,* pp. 219-270; Allison Peers, *Studies of the Spanish mystics,* III, 181.

Works Cited

Altamira y Crevea, R. *Historia de España y de la civilización española.* Various editions, Barcelona, 1900-.

Asín Palacios, M. *La escatología musulmana en la Divina Comedia.* Madrid, 1919.

Beltrán de Heredia, V. *Historia de la reforma de la Provincia [O.P.] de España.* ?Madrid, 1939.

———. *Las corrientes de espiritualidad entre los Domínicos de Castilla durante la primera mitad del siglo XVI.* Salamanca, 1941.

Boehmer, H. *Loyola und die deutsche Mystik.* Sächsischen Akademie der Wissenschaften, phil.-hist. Klasse, Bd. XXIII, Heft 1, Leipzig, 1921.

Bremond, H. *Histoire littéraire du sentiment religieux en France depuis la fin des guerres de religion jusqu'à nos jours.* 12 vols., Paris, 1916-36.

———. *A literary history of religious thought in France.* English translation of first 3 vols. of above, London, 1928-36.

Chadwick, O. *The Reformation.* Pelican History of the Church, III, Harmondsworth, 1964.

Dudon, P. *Saint Ignace de Loyola.* Paris, 1934.

Elton, G. R. *Reformation Europe, 1517-59.* London, 1963.

García Villoslada, R. 'San Ignacio de Loyola y Erasmo de Rotterdam', *Estudios eclesiásticos,* XVI (1942), 244 ff.

Groult, P. *Les mystiques des Pays-Bas et la littérature espagnole du seizième siècle.* Louvain, 1927.

Guibert, J. de *La spiritualité de la Compagnie de Jésus.* Rome, 1953.

Guillermou, A. *Saint Ignace de Loyola et la Compagnie de Jésus.* Collection *Maîtres Spirituels,* Paris, 1960.

Ignatius of Loyola, St. *Obras completas de S. Ignacio de Loyola.* Ed. V. Larrañaga, *Biblioteca de autores cristianos,* LXXXVI, Madrid, 1952.

———. *Spiritual Exercises. See* Longridge; Monumenta Historica Societatis Jesu. Iparraguirre, I. *Historia de la práctica de los Ejercicios espirituales de San Ignacio: I, Práctica de los Ejercicios . . . en vida de su autor, 1522-56.* Bilbao/Rome, 1946.

Larrañaga, V. *La espiritualidad de S. Ignacio comparada con la de S. Teresa de Jesús.* Madrid, 1944.

Leturia, P. 'Génesis de los ejercicios de San Ignacio y su influjo en la fundación de la Compañía de Jesús (1521-40)', *Archivum historicum Societatis Jesus,* x (1941), 16 ff.

Longridge, W. H. (ed.) *The Spiritual Exercises of Saint Ignatius of Loyola, translated from the Spanish with a commentary and a translation of the* Directorium in Exercitia. London, 1919; Everyman's Library, 1930.

Mestwerdt, P. *Die Anfänge des Erasmus: Humanismus und Devotio Moderna.* Leipzig, 1917.

Monumenta Historica Societatis Jesu. *Exercitia spiritualia Sancti Ignatii de Loyola et eorum directoria.* Monumenta Ignatiana, series II, Madrid, 1919.

———. *Directoria exercitiorum spiritualium, 1540-99.* Ed. I. Iparraguirre, Monument Ignatiana, series II, nova editio, vol. II, Rome, 1955.

Muller, H. (?pseud.) *Les origines de la Compagnie de Jésus: Ignace et Lainez.* Paris, 1898.

Nicolau, M. *Jerónimo Nadal (1507-80), sus obras y doctrinas espirituales.* Madrid, 1949.

Peers, E. Allison *Studies of the Spanish mystics.* 3 vols., London, 1927-60. *St John of the Cross and other lectures and addresses.* London, 1946.

Pinard de la Boullaye, H. *Saint Ignace de Loyola, directeur d'âmes.* Paris, 1947.

———. (ed.) *La spiritualité ignatienne: textes choisis et présentés par H.P.* Paris, 1949.

———. *Les étapes de rédaction des Exercices de S. Ignace.* Paris, 1950.

Sanchís Alventosa, J. *La escuela mística alemana y sus relaciones con nuestros místicos del Siglo de Oro.* Madrid, 1946.

Watrigant, H. *La méditation fondamentale avant S. Ignace.* Enghien, 1907.

A. G. Dickens (essay date 1968)

SOURCE: Dickens, A. G. "The Medieval Sources of Catholic Revival." In *The Counter Reformation,* pp. 19-28. New York: W. W. Norton, 1979.

[*In the following essay, first published in 1968, Dickens discusses some of the prominent fifteenth- and sixteenth-century writers of the Catholic Reformation.*]

The period of decline in medieval Catholicism nourished many of the seedlings of Catholic Reformation. Among the features of the latter stands a notable revival of scholastic philosophy and especially of Thomism. Yet this revival had in fact begun among the Dominicans over half a century before the birth of its greatest figure Francisco de Suarez (1548-1617). Thomas de Vio, later famous as Cardinal Cajetan (1469-1534), composed his treatise on the *De Ente et Essentia* of Aquinas while teaching at Padua in 1494-7. His famous commentaries on the *Summa Theologica* followed between 1507 and 1522: the first great monument of this neo-Thomism, they remain among the classics of the revival. Between 1520 and the rise of Thomist theory throughout the Council of Trent, the movement was defended by Domingo Soto and others against the attacks of biblical humanism. As the Dominicans had resuscitated Thomism, so in the fifteenth century the Franciscans had fostered Scotism, a less powerful and integrated tradition, yet one which was to inspire a succession of philosophers into and even beyond the seventeenth century. Today its points of divergence from Thomism may well seem to non-specialists quite marginal, yet they served to give life to the scholasticism of the sixteenth century and to prevent it from becoming monolithic. Alongside these revivals stood the classical or humanist tradition, literary, philological, historical and antiquarian, which so powerfully influenced many aspects of Catholic reform from the decrees of the Council of Trent to the education provided by the Jesuits. Like the Protestant Reformation, that of Catholicism made a distinctly selective approach to the work of the humanists, yet the latter did much to shape it, and they represented a tradition already—at least in Italy—some two and a half centuries old by the time of Trent.

Such were among the main intellectual foundations of the new Catholic world, and its spirituality was equally deep-rooted in tradition. Devotional books and concepts emanating from the fourteenth century were still lively in some circles during much of the seventeenth. Even the great figures in whom we find more originality and personal inspiration were nevertheless dependent at some phases of their development upon medieval instruments of devotion. At innumerable points, the new growth was firmly grafted upon the old. While recovering in 1521 from his painful wound at his father's castle of Loyola, the young Ignatius had exhausted the romances of chivalry when his thoughts were led into more serious channels by chance encounters with *The Flower of Saints,* a Spanish adaptation of *The Golden Legend,* and with the famous *Life of Christ* by the fourteenth-century Carthusian Ludolph of Saxony. These and similar books later left their marks upon Loyola's *Spiritual Exercises.* A more debatable inspiration came from the *Exercises of the Spiritual Life,* composed for monks as recently as 1500 by García de Cisneros, the Benedictine abbot of Montserrat. Yet undoubtedly the chief medieval influence upon Loyola's spiritual life was the *Imitation of Christ* (c. 1418), the great monument of the 'new piety', the *devotio moderna* of the Netherlands. This famous book Ignatius first read at Manresa: in his own words, he 'preferred it ever afterwards to any other book of devotion.' The *Exercises* of St Ignatius are of course predominantly meditative rather than mystical; they lead the mind through an ordered sequence of holy themes and images; they do not seek to empty the mind of images in order to make way for the indescribable 'states' of the mystic. Yet the two methods are not mutually exclusive; they had fused together in the *devotio moderna,* and, as we shall shortly argue, Ignatius and some other Jesuits were to retain more of the old mystical tradition than is commonly supposed.

Among the greatest names in Jesuit history is that of the Dutchman Peter Canisius, who soon after joining the Society published (1543) *The True Evangelical Life: Divine Sermons, Teachings, Letters, Songs and Prophecies.* These are taken partly from the works of Johann Tauler, the fourteenth-century mystic who had so deeply influenced Luther, but they also incorporate a number of other old Rhenish and Netherlandish writings, including important extracts from Ruysbroeck. Again, as

St Teresa of Avila strove to discipline her spiritual impulses, she learned much from the recent Spanish mystics, Laredo, Osuna and her personal counsellor St Peter of Alcántara; yet she was also very familiar with the *Imitation of Christ* and with St Augustine's *Confessions,* while in her autobiography she also cites St Vincent Ferrer (d. 1419) and Ludolph of Saxony. A Spaniard among Spaniards, she nevertheless derived far more than she can have realized from Netherlanders of former generations, since in the *Third Alphabet* of Francisco de Osuna she was in fact imbibing mystical ideas derived from Thomas à Kempis, Ruysbroeck and Jan Mombaer. Still more striking are the continuities observable in the religious life of Italy. The Oratory which grew around St Philip Neri in Rome during the 1550s and 1560s lies at the very heart of the Catholic Reformation, and we know in detail what books were used as starting-points by his famous discussion groups. The list, highly traditional in character, forms a select bibliography of medieval devotional authors: Richard of St Victor, Innocent III, Denis the Carthusian, St Catherine of Siena, various Franciscan writers and the hymns of Jacopone da Todi (d. 1306), reputed author of the *Stabat Mater.*

In the Netherlands the continuity of the *devotio moderna* is especially impressive. During the later sixteenth century few devotional writers became more popular in the Catholic areas than François-Louis de Blois (Blosius, 1506-66) the Benedictine abbot of Liessies in Hainault. A reformer in his Order, he wrote with exceptional clarity 'for simple but earnest people', and his *Institutio Spiritualis* (1551) has long been accepted as a classic of its school. But despite its date the book belongs wholly to the *devotio moderna.* The favourite author of Abbot Blosius is Johann Tauler, and he is closely followed by Suso, Ruysbroeck, the Victorines and a number of twelfth- and thirteenth-century mystics. In this old tradition Blosius gently conducts his readers up the ladder of mystical prayer. Though he accepts the meditative technique ('picture-making') as helpful in the earlier phases, he looks forward to the stage when the devout man or woman will be able to abandon these crutches. Meanwhile, in France, the translation and printing of the late medieval mystics began with Lefèvre of Étaples (c. 1455-1536), the famous biblical humanist and student of mysticism who stands so ambivalently between Catholic and Protestant reform. Between 1570 and 1620 there followed very numerous editions both in French and Latin. They included not only modern contemplatives like St Teresa and Luis de Granada, but also Denis the Carthusian, Suso, Tauler, Catherine of Genoa, Angela of Foligno and others of the earlier age. From this stage, as Frenchmen made their most weighty contributions to the revival of Catholic spirituality, their debt direct and indirect to medieval tradition remains clear enough.

Similar things may also be said of the persecuted Catholics in Elizabethan and early Stuart England; still more of the many English Catholics then exiled on the Continent. The martyr of York, Margaret Clitherow (d. 1586), was a convert from Anglicanism and by that fact a significant figure of the Counter Reformation. During the 1570s her main reading was in the *Imitation of Christ* and in the recent *Spiritual Exercises* (1557) of the Dominican William Peryn, who derived both from Loyola and from medieval sources. The *Imitation* is again prominent among the books of Catholics who built up a community life in their prisons, like Father William Davies and his companions of the early 1590s in Beaumaris Castle. By this time the chief surviving master in the mystical tradition was an English exile; the Capuchin Benedict Canfield (d. 1611). Through him this tradition descended to numerous continental disciples including his fellow Capuchin Père Joseph, the *éminence grise* of Richelieu. Amongst the English their own native mystical heritage had also survived. During the reign of Mary Tudor pious Catholics like Richard Whitford and Robert Parkyn were writing devotional essays with close affinities to Richard Rolle and to that greater contemplative Walter Hilton. Even in the seventeenth century Father Augustine Baker (d. 1641) was introducing his English nuns at Cambrai to these old mystics, and observing that by this time a Latin translation might help them with the antiquated English. Even after the Restoration of 1660 these same writings were still being studied by Serenus Cressy in the household of Queen Catherine of Braganza.

Since Spanish mysticism stands among the most striking phenomena of the Catholic Reformation, the problems surrounding its origin assume a special importance at this stage of our inquiry. The interest of Spaniards in this approach to religion was not limited to a handful of choice spirits: it became almost a literary mass-movement. Menendez y Pelayo calculated the number of mystical works in print or in manuscript as amounting to some three thousand. Mystical authors can be numbered in hundreds between 1500 and 1675, around which latter date the school went into steep decline with the Quietist Miguel de Molinos. Many of these writers, it is true, were analysts of mysticism, or even sentimental romantics, rather than first-hand practitioners. 'No one', writes Allison Peers, 'can appreciate the depths to which they can descend who has not read some of the worst.' Interest has nevertheless tended to centre unduly upon the towering figures of St Teresa and St John of the Cross, before whom at least half a dozen major contemplative writers, mostly Franciscans, were active. The two great Carmelites should indeed be seen not in isolation but as the highest peaks in an impressive mountain range which also included such figures as Luis de Granada (d. 1585), St Peter of Alcántara (d. 1562) and Luis de Leon (d. 1591).

This school emerges with dramatic suddenness in the year 1500 with the works of Gómez García and García de Cisneros, all the more dramatically since during the previous two centuries, the contribution of Spaniards to mystical literature had proved almost negligible. For the sudden flaring of this experience and literature no single factor can account. Several specialist scholars and historians of literature have frankly ascribed it—especially in the case of Cisneros—to belated Netherlandish and German influences from the worlds of Tauler and the *devotio moderna*. Even where overt links do not appear, the close similarities of theme and method cannot be wholly due to coincidence. Again, some of the Spanish mystics show obvious debts to the neo-Platonism of Ficino, Pico and other Italians of the High Renaissance. On the other hand, it seems equally clear that about 1500 the Spanish mind stood prepared not merely to accept these foreign influences but to develop them further than they had hitherto been developed in the West. In examining the writings of the great Carmelites one finds more inducement to stress their independence than their traditionalism. Nevertheless, the Castilian temperament with its strange blend of morosity and ardour is a factor which no one who knows this people will ever take lightly. Even in the Spain of our own day it is impossible to avoid being struck by a capacity for ecstatic worship, an idealism which counts the world well lost for a cause. Medieval Spain had infused these qualities of mind into the harsh tasks of warfare against the infidel, and after the conquest of Moorish Granada they flowed into new channels: into the interior life, into military adventure and imperialism. There seems to have occurred a cultural release comparable with that which occurred in the northern Netherlands a century later, when the Dutch first savoured their newly-born independence and nationhood. Yet again, the Spanish Church was the first to experience rigorous reform; and while the accidents of individual genius must not be discounted, the growing host of monks, friars and nuns provided seed-beds incomparably larger than those of any other European nation.

Despite the remarkable phenomena of Protestant 'spiritualist' religion, it must be acknowledged that the Western mystical tradition has in general been closely linked with monasticism, which alone afforded conditions making for the higher degrees of mental concentration. And if one Order be singled out as a special nurse of this tradition, it should certainly be that of the Carthusians, whose external influence—considering the enclosed character of their rule—proved surprisingly widespread and extended to many members of other Orders. Even so, it would seem unrealistic to 'explain' the Catholic revival chiefly by reference to spiritual enterprise on these exalted levels. The Netherlandish *devotio moderna* and its parallels elsewhere in Europe owed much to the high mystics, yet it nurtured in its offspring a mild and beneficent pietism, a spiritual integrity rather than a sense of close union with the divine. These people were mostly literate, middle-class laymen and laywomen, or else secular priests also living the 'active' life. As they read the *Imitation of Christ* and the numerous guides written in its spirit, they did not very seriously aspire to scale the pinnacles of religious experience. But alongside the immense output of hagiographical and other books catering for the mere popular cults, there grew throughout the early and middle decades of the sixteenth century an extensive literature dealing with the interior life and largely intended for the use of people in the world as distinct from the cloister. These range from simple primers to sophisticated guides, mostly in fact by members of religious Orders. They include the works by Cisneros and his Spanish successors, those of Giovanni Battista Carioni (d. 1534) and Serafino Aceto da Pratis (d. 1534) in Italy, of William Bonde (*fl.* 1500-30), Richard Whitford (d. *c.* 1555) and William Peryn (d. 1558) in England, together with a long succession of Netherlanders in the Ruysbroeck tradition from Henry Herp (d. 1477) to Francis Vervoort (d. 1555) and Nicholas van Esch (d. 1578). Little is known about some of these authors. The long-popular *Gospel Pearl* went through a dozen Netherlandish editions and several foreign translations; it was ascribed by van Esch merely to a 'holy woman' who died in 1540 at the age of seventy-seven.

Unquestionably this voluminous literature did much to fortify Catholicism in the minds of the middle ranks of European society, and to prepare the way for religious education as methodized by the Jesuits and other teaching Orders. Amongst its authors there figure numerous friars, and no account of the earlier phases of Catholic revival would be complete without a distinct emphasis upon the living spirit of St Francis. Needless to add, this is especially true of the Italian revival. We tend perhaps too often to imagine the Catholic Reformation against a backcloth of harsh sierra and tableland in Castile. At least equally may an imaginative traveller sense its lingering spirit along the shores of Maggiore and Garda; better still in the Franciscan homeland itself, as he gazes from the crest of Assisi across the gentle, velvet distances of Umbria.

Phebe Jensen (essay date summer 1998)

SOURCE: Jensen, Phebe. "Ballads and Brags: Free Speech and Recusant Culture in Elizabethan England." *Criticism* 40, no. 3 (summer 1998): 333-54.

[*In the following essay, Jensen discusses how the religious censorship practiced by the Elizabethan government was challenged in a sermon by Bishop John Jewell and a manuscript by Edmund Campion.*]

Writing to a friend in 1586, the English Catholic exile Sir Francis Englefield described the attempt to reconvert England to the old faith: "In stede therfore of the sword, which we cannot obtayne, we must fight with paper and pennes, which can not be taken from us."[1] Although the Counter-Reformation in England is usually characterized by those few dramatic episodes of violence—the Rising of the Northern Earls, the Spanish Armada, the Babington and other conspiracies to assassinate Elizabeth—which were successfully used by the government to galvanize public opposition to Catholicism, in fact the Catholic assault on England was primarily, as Englefield's letter suggests, linguistic rather than violent. Certainly the most radical fringe of the movement, the seminary priests, fought "with word & not with sword."[2] According to traditional understandings of Elizabethan attitudes toward Catholicism, we could assume that most of the Queen's subjects responded to the invasion of Catholic writings rolling secretively from mobile, hastily erected presses or smuggled from continental sources as Spenser clearly means his audience to react to the "bookes and papers" comprising the vomit of the hideous monster Error in Book I of *The Faerie Queene*: with instinctive loathing and disgust. We could also assume widespread popular support for the series of acts and proclamations controlling seditious speech, writing, books, and libels.

But if we analyze some of the public events that comprised this Catholic invasion along with the language of contemporary pamphlets, ballads, and polemic involved in promoting and resisting the English Counter-Reformation, a sense of deep cultural contradiction emerges. For alongside increasingly draconian attempts to control both theological and political Catholic writings was a cultural ideology that championed the idea of freedom of religious thought—including the principle that open disputation and debate was the best way to arrive at religious truth. The contradiction between practice and ideology, between censorship on the one hand and the principle of freedom of conscience on the other, is one way to understand the Elizabethan government's need to claim that it prosecuted Catholics for treason, not religion. For in the face of the powerful cultural idea that denying subjects freedom of conscience in religious matters was wrong—an idea born largely out of the Marian prosecutions of the 1550s— the government had to provide an alternative explanation for the executions of seminary priests, secular priests, and lay recusants that took place throughout the 1580s and '90s.[3]

As the outlaw publications surrounding the execution of Edmund Campion in 1582 particularly suggest, the paradoxes of a culture in which censorship is accompanied by rhetoric championing freedom of thought helped open up a conceptual space in Elizabethan culture within which could develop the principle of free speech. Such a broad claim for the political efficacy of ideas originating in Catholic practice can only be made in the wake of recent studies that have underlined "[t]he relative impunity with which Catholics went about their business, the allegedly chaotic, corrupt and uneven administration of the recusancy statutes, and indeed the ideological and political disagreements and incoherences which lay behind both the drafting and the enforcing of those laws."[4] In the light of recent scholarship, Catholicism can no longer be dismissed as "the great unifying Other for the English state and nation."[5] Rather, it must be seen as one source of the political language which comprised the "strands of thoughts, congeries of concerns, catchwords and symbols in and through which contemporaries could view, describe and shape their political experience."[6] Trained by the official rhetoric of the government, Elizabethans in the last two decades of the reign may have distrusted Catholicism, hated the pope, and despised the Jesuit seminary priests, but some of the ideas produced by the peculiar situation of recusants in England were nevertheless congenial to the broader political culture.

In words and actions, Elizabethan Catholics made the argument that they asked only the "liberty" to engage in open debate and disputation on matters of religion.[7] Especially during the events surrounding the arrival of Campion and Parsons in England in the early 1580s, Catholic writers attacked censorship, in almost Miltonic language, as an obstacle to the discovery of God's will in the world. Of course these arguments were self-interested, but they also packed a cultural punch, largely because they fed into the claims of other constituencies (some equally self-interested) urging the right of freedom of expression. As Frederich Siebert argued in 1952, Catholic pleas for freedom of "the press" circulated in Elizabethan England alongside very similar claims being made by Peter Wentworth in Parliament, by printers interested in the economic fruits of less tightly controlled printing, and by the Godly. Together the rhetoric of these groups creates, by the end of the Elizabethan reign, a cultural climate within which could flourish a widespread belief in the value of free expression.[8]

JEWELL'S CHALLENGE

At the start of the Elizabethan age, the strategies used to convince the English nation to accept the Anglican compromise suggest a commitment to the principle that truth in theological matters should be arrived at through open disputation. Such a commitment is hardly surprising, for disputation was associated not only with the rich scholastic tradition of the late medieval church, but also with Martin Luther's religious revolution. As G. R. Evans argues in a recent study of sixteenth-century theological debates, "Luther's career as a reformer began with a series of more or less formal disputations"; in addition, the rhetorical forms provided by scholastic debate provided a conceptual structure within which he began his inquiry into problems of contemporary church authority. Luther's *Disputation Against Scholastic The-*

ology (1517) "was written as a set of theses for the degree examination of Franz Gunther, at which Luther presided as Dean of the Faculty of Theology"; the more radical Ninety-Five Theses are also constructed rhetorically as a set of propositions to be disputed in formal debate.[9] In the published version of the Theses, Luther challenges hostile readers to debate, a challenge partially fulfilled in Heidelberg in 1518 and Leipzig in 1519.[10] The central concepts of Protestantism were in this sense born out of the processes of formal debate, and the founder of the movement encouraged the open airing of theological disagreement in public forums: "[W]e are accused of heresy and of being authors of new doctrine," wrote Luther, "So we must defend ourselves in public disputation."[11]

So a government intent on restoring Protestantism to England in 1558 was to a certain extent intellectually beholden to a tradition of theological debate and disputation that was as much Lutheran as scholastic. And indeed, one of the ways in which Elizabeth and her councilors attempted to garner public and parliamentary support for the Acts of Supremacy and Uniformity was to stage an allegedly open debate at Westminster between divines from either end of the religious spectrum. The contest was over almost before it began, for "during arguments on the first proposition . . . the parties began quarreling about the rules and the Catholics refused to proceed."[12] To be sure, by the 1560s discussions between the two sides had become all but impossible since Protestants and Catholics could no longer agree about what constituted allowable authorities and evidence.[13] But the arrest of the recalcitrant bishops immediately following the dissolution of the debates suggests that the government's true motives were not to encourage but to stifle disagreement. The Westminster debates represent the Elizabethan government's interest in creating the useful fiction that it was willing to submit ecclesiastical policies to free and open disputation.

This double-edged approach to debate comes into sharper focus in the wake of Bishop John Jewell's "Challenge" sermon, first delivered in November 1562.[14] The sermon ends with this appeal: "If any one of all our adversaries be able clearly and plainly to prove, by such authority of the scriptures, the old doctors, and councils . . . I am content to yield unto him, and to subscribe. But I am well assured that they shall never be able truly to allege one sentence."[15] Jewell's challenge set off a written debate that continued until the 1570s. Epistolary responses from Dr. Henry Cole soon provoked Jewell's *Apologia Ecclesiae Anglicanae*, the book that "gave the Church of England a doctrinal form that it had lacked";[16] in this way the articulation of Anglican doctrine could be said to have been partially determined in the context of polemical debate. But although Jewell's Challenge seemed to embrace the concept of public disputation, the fight was, not surprisingly, rigged from the start. For one thing, speaking out in favor of Catholicism was punishable by law; even though the controversy began in the early Elizabethan "period of tolerant confusion" on religious matters, the imprisonment of the bishops had shown it was dangerous even in the early 1560s to support the old faith too enthusiastically.[17] Secondly, almost all the books on the Catholic side of the controversy had to be printed on the Continent and smuggled into the country, a system which not only limited the distribution of Catholic responses to the well-circulated Anglican side of the dialogue, but could result in delays of up to four years between the writing of a Catholic tract and its appearance in print.[18] The distribution difficulties encountered throughout the 1560s by Catholic writers were legally solidified by the first of the Elizabethan proclamations controlling seditious writing, issued in March 1569, in which subjects were called upon to "forbear" the "use or dealing with any such seditious books impugning the orders and rites established by law for Christian religion and divine service within this realm, or otherwise stirring and nourishing matter tending to sedition."[19] The proclamation followed upon (and referred to) the trial in Star Chamber of a group of men convicted of "receiving, buying, reading, keeping, commending, and sending abroad seditious books, set forth beyond the seas in the name of Harding, Dorman, Staphilus, Stapleton, Sanders, Smith, Rastell, and others, enemies to God's truth and the quiet government of the Queen."[20] With the exception of Smith and Staphilus, all the writers listed in this conviction were involved in the controversy set off by Bishop Jewell in 1562. So although Jewell's Challenge seemed to embrace the concept of free and open disputation, it was clearly the impression of religious freedom, and not the reality, that the Elizabethan government was after. The government continued to engineer a series of false debates in the years leading up to the Jesuit influx of the early 1580s, including the written disputation inaugurated by the Bishop of Silves by the 1563 tract, *Epistola ad Elizabetham Angliae Reginam de Religione* and the "disputations" used in an attempt to bring the Abbot of Westminster to accept the Anglican settlement.[21]

On the one hand, then, it was important for the Elizabethan government and its chief apologists to display a willingness to subject Anglican doctrine to disputation. On the other hand, truly open debates, whether in person or in print, were not to be risked in the vulnerable early years of the Elizabethan settlement. Following the Northern Rising and the 1570 papal bull excommunicating Elizabeth and releasing English Catholic subjects from allegiance, the increased governmental emphasis on censorship can be tracked in a series of proclamations and statutes which steadily increased the penalties for airing unorthodox religious opinions.[22] But even while Catholic written and spoken expression was being curtailed by acts and proclamations, the government

continued to insist it allowed freedom of conscience in religious matters. The lengthiest official statement of the Elizabethan position was Burghley's *Execution of Justice in England,* published in response to the literature of martyrdom produced after Campion's execution. Burghley distinguished between the executed priests who had been convicted of treason, and the "many subjects known in the realm that differ in some opinions of religion from the Church of England . . . yet in that they do also profess loyalty and obedience to her Majesty . . . none of these sort are for their contrary opinions in religion prosecuted . . . nor yet willingly searched in their consciences for their contrary opinions that savor not of treason."[23] Even in the relatively drastic proclamation "Establishing Commissions against Seminary Priests and Jesuits" (1591), which obligated all Englishmen and women to report any knowledge of seminary priests "upon pain that the offenders therein shall be punished as abettors and maintainers of traitors," the government still claimed that attacks on Catholics were made "not for any points of religion."[24] It was not impossible for Elizabethans, Catholic as well as Protestant, to see the absurdity couched between the avowed principles of freedom of conscience and debate, and the practice of Elizabethan policy toward Catholics. For despite Burghley's accurate claim that few Elizabethans were executed for religion, it was difficult to claim that Catholic belief was tolerated when any *expression* of that belief, in speech, writing, or practice, was punishable by increasingly severe laws.[25] It was this illogic at the heart of the governmental rhetoric surrounding the censorship of religious expression that was most effectively exploited by the seminary priests as they claimed the right to make their case for the old religion in public disputations.

CAMPION'S BRAG

Edmund Campion's arrival in England in the fall of 1580 posed a serious challenge to the delicate balance the Elizabethan government had constructed between its claims to tolerate freedom of thought on religious matters and the increasingly strict control of Catholic expression. For the primary source of Campion's intellectual reputation lay in his rhetorical talents, talents widely and publicly recognized from his youth. Even as a grammar school pupil Campion had been identified as a gifted speaker when he was chosen to welcome Queen Mary to London "a representative of London Scholarship"; thirteen years later, during Elizabeth's state visit to Oxford in 1566, he was selected to greet the monarch and participate in a showcase public debate.[26] Campion so impressed the Queen on this visit that she recommended him as a protégé to her companion, the Earl of Leicester, then chancellor of the university.[27] Given Campion's well-known eloquence, coupled with the government's increased repression of Catholic written and spoken expression, as news of his return to

England as a Jesuit missionary spread through the country in 1580, the threat he represented to the English government was as much rhetorical as ideological.[28]

And Campion immediately began to fulfill these fears when one of his first acts upon arrival in England was to pen a challenge to disputation analogous to Jewell's challenge of 1560. Upon encouragement by one of his London hosts, both Campion and Parsons agreed to write down, against the possibility of their future arrest, "a brief declaration of the true causes of [their] coming."[29] Campion's manuscript incidentally responds to official Elizabethan policy by making the claim that the purpose of his mission to England is spiritual, not political, but primarily the "Letter to the Lords of the Council," popularly known as Campion's "Challenge" or "Brag," is a plea for the Elizabethan government to allow an open theological debate. Campion requests that he be allowed to dispute before the Council itself, "before the Doctors and Masters and chosen men of both Universities," and "before the lawyers, spiritual and temporal"—that is, in the political, scholarly, and legal argumentative arenas.[30] He wants only, he claims, to have the "questions of religion opened faithfully."[31] There is plenty in the tone of the letter to offend the Elizabethan authorities, but its primary source of irritation is the way in which it challenges the government's policy of censorship.

Soon copies of Campion's Challenge were circulating through Catholic channels in England: in a November letter William Allen comments that the declarations of both Campion and Parsons "pass from hand to hand everywhere among people in England and are a source of strength to many."[32] Both William Charke and Meredith Hanmer produced books confuting Campion, Hanmer's book further publicizing the Brag by reprinting it in its entirety.[33] The difficulties into which Campion's Challenge put the government were clearly articulated in Robert Parsons's early contribution to the dispute, *A brief discours contayning certayne reasons why Catholiques refuse to goe to Church,* published under the pseudonym John Howlet. Here, Parsons makes an impassioned plea that an "indifferent triall" of Catholicism and Protestantism, "by publique disputation or otherwise," be permitted in the name of "Gods cause, and the love of his truth."[34] Parsons explicitly connects the recent petition of Campion (and, he claims, "sundry" others) to Jewell's challenge, which he claims was never allowed to be answered openly. Catholics have repeatedly submitted "most humble petitions that, seeing those men, which first challenged at Poule's Crosse, all the learned of our side that might be found, either to writing, or disputing: afterward procured your Majesties prohibition by proclamation, that no books should be written or read of that part in England: their petition was (I say) that at the least, there might some public

disputation be admitted, whereby men's doubts might be resolved." Not only does Parsons imply that a theological disputation would be in the service of discovering "God's truth," but he articulates the impression being created by the refusal of the Elizabethan authorities to let the Catholic side be heard: "If our adversaries refuse this offer, they shall show too much distrust in their own cause."

An unpublished ballad appended to a manuscript copy of the Life of Ignatius Loyola can further illustrate the ways in which Catholics used the example of Campion to support the concept of freedom of speech. The major polemical argument of this poem is that Catholics have not been allowed to try their cause in open debate.[35] Among the deluded souls who "know not gold from Drosse" the poet asks us to "specially . . . note" Hanmer and

> the fondlings Fulke and Charke
> Whose peevish pride against the truth
> was published late in print.

These men only state their positions so boldly, the poet claims, because they know they need not fear a Catholic response: "They play upon advantages which makes them be so stoute, / They know what is against them sayde shall not be published out." The poem also responds to calls for the Jesuits to come out of hiding such as Hanmer's exhortation to Campion to "yield yourself, become a good subject, and pray unto God that your Eyues may be opened."[36] The poet of "You Catholics that Protestants" analyzes Hanmer's challenge and pronounces it deceitful, for if Campion agrees to debate without "safety," "Ere disputation should be had first Tyburne should him beare." Campion is better off, the poet suggests, going to work "discreetely," for the conditions of censorship and threat under which he must write are insupportable:

> They cuff his wing and bid him flyth
>   they bid him fight but how,
> His weapon must be taken away
>   such odds they do allow,
> They blame the hiding of his head
>   their penal lawes do urge him . . .

The reason Campion has been disarmed of his weapon, the pen, is that Hanmer and Charke and the other Protestant controversialists know that if allowed to dispute Campion would win:

> They would and do persuade the world
>   such conference were vain
> Foreseeing what should happ thereby
>   the ruin of their raigne.

After Campion's capture in the summer of 1581 and before his trial, his Challenge was nominally taken up when the Elizabethan government, implicitly acknowledging the potency of Jesuit calls to open debate, arranged a series of four disputations between Campion on the one side, and leading Anglican ecclesiastical authorities and controversial writers on the other. But, if these debates were meant to prove the government's open-mindedness, the strategy apparently backfired. During the first debate, Campion drew the audience's attention to his mistreatment when he asked whether it were "an answer to his challenge to rack him first, then to deprive him of all books, and to set him to dispute."[37] The inequities of the situation were also readable in the physical set-up of the room: the racked and weakened Campion, unable to lift his arms, stood without the support of a table holding only a bible, while across from him sat two adversaries comfortably seated behind a table covered with books.[38] The Tower debates were clearly engineered to make sure the right side won, but there is evidence that the crown was less than pleased with the outcome. Bishop Aylmer objected to Lord Burghleigh that "so many [spectators] were admitted" to the first debate; for this reason he "sent to stay it."[39] The second, third, and fourth debates were moved to smaller rooms that precluded large audiences. The debates were ended altogether after one of the disputants reported in a letter to the Privy Council that "the course hitherto taken, either by lack of aid or of moderation or convenient respect of admitting men to be hearers, hath been both fruitless and hurtful, and subject to great harm by reports."[40] Anecdotal evidence also suggests that the maltreatment of Campion perversely contributed to his victory. According to the biographer of Philip Earl of Arundel, the earl converted to Catholicism as a result of his attendance: "by what he saw and heard then, he easily perceived on which side the truth and true religion was."[41] A man named Cawood got himself into trouble with Bishop Aylmer by "talk[ing] very liberally, extolling Campion's learning, and attributing the victory to him"; another man, Oliver Pluckett, "affirmed that Campion was both discrete and learned, and did say very well, and would have convinced them if he might have been heard with indifference."[42]

That the government would only hazard a debate with Campion when he was racked, unprepared, and bookless became an important theme in Catholic challenges to governmental censorship. But it was also possible for non-Catholics to perceive the weakness implicit in the government's refusal to debate the Jesuit fairly. Before the September debates public opinion had evidently turned against Campion with rumors—some substantiated—that the priest had betrayed fellow Catholics on the rack. But Campion's reputation was restored in the wake of reports of the four Tower debates.[43] A ballad preserved in the State Papers acknowledges from a Protestant point of view the danger posed by the treatment of Campion:

> If instead of good argument,
> We deal by the rack,
> The Papists may think
> That learning we lack.

This ballad encourages the government to engage Catholic calls to dispute head on:

> Come forth, my fine darling,
> And make him a dolt;
> You have him full fast,
> And that in strong holt.

Although confident that Campion could be successfully disputed, this ballad does not differ substantially from Catholic claims that Campion's views were assessed, not by a free and fair trial, but by the rack.[44]

BALLAD DEBATES

In the wake of Campion's execution in February 1582, the disputation that was in his English career repressed from the scholarly sphere reappears in the language of popular ballads. To a 1582 account of the execution of Campion published by the Catholic printer Richard Verstagen were appended four pro-Catholic ballads;[45] when Anthony Munday responded to this pamphlet with *A Breefe Aunswer made unto two seditious Pamphlets* (1582), he reprinted the poems but added four new compositions of his own, each one refuting the arguments of the original poems in the same meter and style. These eight poems rehearse, in the idiom of the popular ballad, the debate disallowed in scholarly or political venues. In the process of being expressed in this medium the quarrel between Catholicism and Anglicanism is simplified, but for this reason the ballad form of the debate reveals the images and rhetoric through which popular culture processed the issues of language, censorship, freedom of thought, and freedom of debate raised by the Catholic martyrs.[46]

The first pro-Campion ballad and Munday's poetic rejoinder are the two poems in the collection that most clearly thematize the centrality of linguistic expression and its restriction to the Campion story.[47] The Catholic version of the poem "Why do I use my paper, inke, and penne?" begins by counterpoising the poet's feeling of linguistic inadequacy with a description of Campion's language skills. Immediately the theme of censorship is introduced when the poet considers censoring himself because his subject "exceedes the compasse of my skill" (9); it returns as a central theme in the subsequent account of the Tower debates. There, as the poem repeats contemporary descriptions of the contest, Campion is described as having been effectively censored by being brought in "[f]rom rack in Tower," "bookless, alone, to answer all that came" (44). Campion's execution is next interpreted as the government's most drastic form of censorship, but this censorship is transcended as Campion's death inspires the creation of several alter-

native mediums that will evade such governmental suppression. First, the execution is described as itself an
act of writing that will be interpreted differently than
was originally intended: "You did not know how rare
and great a good / it was to write his precious gifts in
blood" (113). Campion's martyrdom engenders a new
language even more powerful than the earthly one:

> his pen must cease, his sugared tongue be still;
> but you forgot how loud his death it cries,
> how far beyond the sound of tongue and quill.
>
> (110-12)

Alive, Campion was only able to speak "to them that
present were," but now, in defiance of print censorship,
"fame reports his learning far and near / and now his
death confirms his doctrine true" (117-18); "All Europe
wonders at so rare a man; / England is filled with rumor
of his ende . . ." (121-22). A second newly articulate
medium is London itself, as "the streets, the stones, the
steps you hailed them by / proclaim the cause for which
these martyrs die" (125-26). As the poet interprets the
speech of the dumb streets of the city, the language of
Campion infuses itself into the streets and buildings of
England's capital:

> The Tower saith, the truth he did defend;
> the barre beares witness of his guiltles minde;
> Tiborne doth tell he made a pacient ende;
> on every gate his martirdome we find.
> in vaine you wroght yet would obscure his name,
> for heaven and earth will still record the same.
>
> (128-32)

Even "heaven and earth" are now graced with the
speech denied Campion: "his virtues now are written in
the skies, / and often read with holy inward eyes" (115-
20). The final medium which speaks in the poem is
Campion's martyred body. The sight of Campion's
'partid quarters' teach observers

> to play the constant Christian's parts;
> his head doth speak, & heavenly precepts give,
> how we that look, should frame ourselves to live.
>
> (160-62)

Now the example of Campion's life has become a more
eloquent testimony to the Catholic faith than any words
even Campion himself could have uttered. The argument that should, the opening of the poem suggested,
have been heard openly in the Tower debates and in
Campion's preaching, is now expressed by the example
of Campion's life:

> His youth enstructs us how to spend our daies;
> his flying bids us how to banish sinne;
> his straight profession shews the narrow waies
> which they must walk that looke to enter in;
> his home returne by danger and distresse,
> emboldens us our conscience to professe.
>
> (163-68)

Ultimately, imagery of "speaking" in "Why do I use my
paper, inke, and penne?" coalesces to suggest that censorship of Campion, and indeed of Catholicism generally, is self-defeating. In a world where Catholics are
not allowed to speak publicly, publish in safety or debate openly, the message of Catholicism has been dis-
placed into other mediums: rumors and news, the sacred sites of martyrdom, the hagiographic life stories of
martyred priests, and most powerfully in the visual
signs of the martyred body. By rereading Campion's
execution from a Catholic point of view, the poem confirms that the execution of Catholic traitors "opened
spaces for Catholic agency and speech at the very centre
of the persecutory state which was supposedly crushing
Catholic treachery into silence and oblivion."[48]

The companion poem Munday writes as an accompaniment to "Why do I use my paper, inke and penne?" directly refutes the original poem, but the attempt to re-
impose the official interpretation of Campion's
execution inadvertently reveals the difficulties the government faced in defending both its treatment of the
missionary priests and its policy of censorship. To begin with, in order to refute the claims of the first poem
Munday must blatantly rewrite well-documented facts.
Gone are any references to the use of the rack before
the Tower debates: the prisoner is called to dispute only
"After long delay," a phrase which suggests Campion
was told beforehand of the debates, and Campion is
said to have been given "Bookes as many as he could
demaund" (43-44). In Munday's account, the Anglican
disputants "quickly did confute" Campion's "chiefest
cause":

> His proofe layd downe, reprooved out of hand.
> So that the simplest present there could say,
> That Campions cause did beare the shame away.
>
> (46-48)

Though either side could (and did) claim victory in the
contest, when Munday must change the facts of the
case in order to insist on the government's triumph, he
reveals the weaknesses of his claim.

More subtly, Munday's main rhetorical tactic in this response poem also suggests the vulnerability of his position. For here Munday simply—and crudely—reverses
the images of the original poem in an attempt to
recharacterize Campion as villain rather than hero. For
example, the first poet's opening statement of linguistic
inadequacy in the face of Campion's glory becomes
Munday's reticence to repeat the horror of Campion's
treason (25-30). Munday also denies claims made by
the first poet for the final expressiveness of Campion's
death and martyrdom by repeating the original words

with just enough changes to reverse the meaning: "The streets, the stones, the steps they hauled him by," instead of proclaiming "the cause for which these martyrs die" now "Pronounst these Traitours woorthy for to die":

> The Tower sayeth he Treason did defend;
>   The Barre beares witnesse of his guilty minde;
> Tiborne dooth tell he made a Traitours ende;
>   On every gate example we may finde.
>   In vaine they work to laude him with such fame,
>   For heaven & earth beares witnes of his shame.
>
>   (169-74)

Munday reads the death of Campion as the Elizabethan government meant it to be read, but in several ways the relationship between these two poems elucidates the central conceptual problem facing the Elizabethan authorities in their quest to restrict the expression of Catholic belief. Just as Hanmer reprinted Campion's challenge in the course of refuting it, just as Burghley restated the Catholic claim that Jesuits were being executed for religion not treason as he attempted to contradict it, so Munday's attempt to reinterpret Campion's death cites the Catholic position—and in the process inevitably indicates the centrality of disagreement and debate to social, political, and religious meaning. Repeating the words of the opponents both underscores the censorship to which they have been subjected, and also gives the lie to the claim (made, for example, by Hanmer) that debate on theological issues was closed. By attempting to impose an official reading on Campion's death, Munday also inevitably demonstrates that his is only one of a number of different readings. In this way these dueling ballads rehearse linguistically what Peter Lake and Michael Questier have argued about the executions of the seminary priests: that the failure of the government to control the meaning of these spectacles was not the result of "administrative weakness" but was inevitable given the "essentially theatrical way of dispatching the felon and embodying the power of the state."[49] Not only does Munday's poem inevitably broadcast the Catholic case in the act of refuting it, but the language that makes the government's case is, like the bodies of Jesuits at the site of execution, always vulnerable to a range of interpretations.

PROTESTANTS, PURITANS, PRINTERS, AND THE FREE SPEECH PRINCIPLE

The 1587 *Holinshed* engineers a significant juxtaposition between the prosecution of Elizabethan Catholics, the trial of Campion, and another contemporary political event, one which occasioned an equal amount of governmental concern about printed opposition to official policy:

> At the same sessions were brought from the Fleet, the Gatehouse, Newgate, and the Counters, sundrie prisoners, indicted for refusing to come to church; all which

being convicted by their owne confession, had judgement according to the statute, to paie twentie pounds for every moneth of such wilfull absence from the church. The first of November, monsieur Francis duke of Anjou, the French kings brother, and other nobles of France (having lately arrived in Kent) came to London, and were honorably received, and retained at the court with banqueting, and diverse pleasant shows and pasttimes, of whom more hereafter in place convenient.

> On mondaie being the twentieth of November, Edmund Campion, Rafe Sherwin, Lucas Kerbie . . . were brought unto the high barre at Westminster. . . .[50]

Although chronology might have determined the proximity of Monsieur and Campion in this passage, because the main description of the French visit is deferred there seems no pressing narrative need to sandwich it here between two different legal actions taken by the government against Catholics. The effect of this seemingly gratuitous juxtaposition is powerfully ironic, because it underscores that foreign policy imperatives were leading the Queen close to marriage with a Catholic duke even as Catholics on the domestic front were being defined as enemies of the English state. Since these marriage negotiations sparked a series of unwelcome written attacks from Protestants, in the early 1580s the mechanism of censorship was being used simultaneously against adversaries from opposite ends of the religious spectrum.

To what extent were the ironies of this fact widely observable by contemporary Elizabethans? In light of similar restrictions on freedom of debate experienced by both English Catholics and opponents of the Anjou marriage, did these groups, in many ways adversarial, perceive any affinity on the issue of censorship? It is true that those pressing for freedom of expression in the Elizabethan reign—Puritans, printers, Parliamentarians, and Papists—did not generally extract "intellectual principles of freedom" from their own singular claims for free expression: "their attacks were directed not against the theory underlying the restrictions but against the application of these restrictions to themselves."[51] But the absence of such statements of principle is hardly surprising given the treatment accorded those few who did express them: Peter Wentworth, for example, who claimed that only through free inquiry could "falsehood and all subtilties that should shadow and darken [Truth] be found out," was imprisoned in the Tower for these opinions even though they were spoken in the relatively privileged venue of the House of Commons.[52]

Some of the evidence for the claim that Catholic attacks on the curtailment of debate resonated widely in Elizabethan society have already been suggested: the Protestant ballad which urged open disputation with the Jesuits from a Protestant point of view; the anecdotal evidence of men who were appalled by the government's treatment of Campion in the Tower debates; the attempts of the government throughout the reign to create the illusion of free debate and claim the existence of freedom of conscience, despite evidence to the contrary. The possibility of solidarity between Catholics and Protestants on the issue of censorship in the 1580s is also richly suggested in the clues we have of the relationship between Sir Philip Sidney and Campion, two men who can represent the two constituencies most touched by governmental restrictions on debate in the early 1580s. Sidney almost certainly knew Campion in the 1560s and early 1570s, since Campion had been under the protection of his uncle Leicester in England and his father Sir Robert in Ireland; he also probably encountered the older man at Oxford, both at the state visit of Elizabeth in 1566 and when Sidney was an undergraduate and Campion one of the university's intellectual luminaries. At any rate, Sidney certainly visited Campion in Prague in 1577 during his European tour.[53] As Katherine Duncan-Jones has observed, Sidney biographers have gone to great lengths to dismiss Campion's description of Sidney as a "wavering soul," "most eager" to hear the conversation of a Catholic. But if we loosen our grip on both the traditional image of Sidney "as a Protestant hero, whose whole life supposedly declared his commitment to the Reformed faith" and on the belief that Catholics and Protestants shared few common assumptions about politics and religion, it becomes possible to see in Sir Philip's receptivity to Campion an adherence to the principle of informed debate and disputation. As Duncan-Jones argues, Sidney's attitude toward free debate is congenial with Campion's; reared in the same academic culture, the two had had instilled in them a similar belief in "[c]hallenge and disputation, conducted on lines partly academic, partly chivalric."[54] Certainly Sidney acted in accordance with this belief when, in the early 1580s, he wrote an unpublished but widely circulated letter to the Queen objecting to the match with Anjou. Since the letter resulted in his temporary loss of favor at court and banishment to Wilton, Sidney felt firsthand the frustrations occasioned by censorship. In writing and delivering the letter, Sidney seemed to register his own belief in the importance of disputation; the visit to Campion suggests Sidney extended this belief in the value of open debate to include the views of Jesuits.

The censorship of opposition to the Anjou marriage represented restrictions on the speech of mainstream Protestants; the more radical religious reformers constituted another group whose experiences with censorship led them to denounce the Elizabethan government. In the 1570s, the controls on Catholic books inaugurated by the March 1569 Proclamation was expanded to target Puritan opposition as the government took aim against the authors of the *Admonition to Parliament*.[55] From this point on, Puritan printers operated as the Catholics did, using secret and often transported presses, surreptitiously distributing hastily assembled publications. In the early 1590s, by a political irony that was lost neither on the Elizabethan authorities or religious nonconformists, the participants in the Martin Marprelate affair were prosecuted under laws first enacted to hinder the publication of Catholic writings. By this time the Godly were apparently capable of expressing solidarity with recusants on the issue of freedom of thought and expression. When Morris Udall was examined in Star Chamber by Solicitor Egerton he admitted political kinship with Catholics who also claimed freedom of conscience:

EGERTON:

> Mr. Udall, I am sorry that you will not answer, nor take an oath, which by law you ought to do: I can assure you, your answers are like the seminary priests answers; for they say, there is no law to compel them to take an oath to accuse themselves.

UDALL:

> Sir, if it be a liberty by law, there is no reason why they should not challenge it; for (though they be very bad ones) they are subjects, and until they be condemned by law, may require all the benefits of subjects; neither is that any reason, that their answering so, should make the claim of less value for me, seeing that herein we are subjects alike.[56]

Remarkably Udall, passionate reformer and ideological archenemy to the papists, is capable here of detaching religious issues from the legal and political ones that were at stake in the government's attempts to control Catholicism. Neither the theological errors of the priests, nor the fact that they are "very bad subjects," could for Udall taint the legal principle that they were entitled to withhold certain information about the content of their consciences from the government.

Finally, a principled belief in freedom of speech was also expressed, albeit implicitly, throughout *Holinshed's Chronicles*. As Annabel Patterson has recently argued, the editors of the book "continually *thematized* the problem of censorship as the obverse of their belief in freedom of the press, the right to know, and liberty at least of conscience."[57] In the uncensored 1587 edition of the *Chronicles*, Anthony Munday's *Discoverie of Edmund Campion, and his Confederates*, Holinshed's major source for the account of the Jesuits' trial, is edited and repositioned in such a way that the issue of censorship becomes the trial's dominant theme. In the absence of hard evidence against the defendants, Campion and the other Jesuits were charged primarily with having owned, read, and maliciously interpreted Nicholas Sander's *De Visibili Monarchia*, Bristow's *Motives*, and a Jesuit handbook on prevarication.[58] By cutting from the *Discovery* the case put forth by

Munday that these books were part of the papist plot to overthrow the Elizabethan government, the *Chronicles'* editors foreground the epistemological and moral difficulties raised by censorship. For how can the Jesuits fairly be condemned for their alleged familiarity with certain disallowed books? Some defendants deny ever having seen the books; all deny that "they were commanded to be used amongst them both at Rome and at Rheimes."[59] When Campion himself argues that the books were "not so ill as they tooke it for, nor deserved anie such iudgement of prejudice," he suggests unstable processes of interpretation were the basis of the government's case.[60] Campion's trial in Holinshed, then, endorses in its own way the claim of the clearly Catholic ballad, "You Catholics that Protestants" by suggesting that the underlying purpose behind the execution of Campion was to control the expression and circulation of unorthodox religious ideas. Judiciously edited, and put into the context of a book "peppered with telling instances of freedom and speech denied and punished," the allusions to censorship incidental in the original account of Campion's trial become readable as implicit support for Catholic pleas for open disputation and debate.[61]

One of the unwitting side-effects of rapid changes in religion legislated in the middle of the Tudor century seems to have been the creation of a climate within which a belief in tolerance, freedom of conscience, and even freedom of the press in theological matters was able to flourish. One important source for this belief was the experience of Catholics attempting to have their voices heard in the wake of the Elizabethan settlement, especially after the relatively open early days of the reign had given way to increasingly strict censorship. The inconclusive conclusion arrived at by John Donne's Satire III about the search for "true religion" in the post-Reformation world suggests how and why the principle of free speech was so congenial to this historical and intellectual moment. "Doubt wisely," the poem suggests, "in strange way / To stand inquiring right, is not to stray; / To sleep, or run wrong, is" (77-78). In the wake of the splintering of the church, "doubting wisely" and "inquiring right" become the way to climb the "Cragged and steep" hill on which Truth sits; these processes were fed by the open disputation and debate which was as much a part of the Protestant and humanist tradition of inquiry as it was of Catholic scholasticism. The illogic of the Elizabethan government's attempt to square this increasingly important cultural ideology with a contradictory policy of escalating repression helped the political concept of free speech to thrive. For this reason, recusant culture should be seen as one important source for the rhetoric of free expression which ultimately served a number of the religious, social, economic, and political agendas of early modern England.

Notes

1. Letter from Sir Francis Englefield, March 9, 1586, PRO SP 53/15/552, quoted from D. C. Peck, "Government Suppression of Elizabethan Catholic Books: The Case of *Burleigh's Commonwealth*," *The Library Quarterly* 47 (1977): 164.

2. From a ballad first published appended to *A True Reporte of the Death and martyrdom of M. Campion, Jesuite and Priest* by an anonymous "Catholike preist" (1582), reprinted by Hyder Rollins, ed., *Old English Ballads, 1553-1620, Chiefly from Manuscripts* (Oxford: Clarendon Press, 1920), 178.

3. On the roots of this idea in the Marian reign see Peter Lake and Michael Questier, "Agency, Appropriation and Rhetoric under the Gallows: Puritans, Romanists and the State in Early Modern England," *Past and Present* 153 (1996): 69-70; on the gradual development through the reign of the claim that Catholics were prosecuted for treason, not religion, see Gillian Brennan, "Papists and Patriotism in Elizabethan England," *Recusant History* 19 (1988): 1-15.

4. Lake and Questier, 66.

5. Ibid., 66.

6. Kevin Sharpe and Peter Lake, "Introduction" to their edited volume of essays, *Culture and Politics in Early Stuart England* (Stanford: Stanford University Press, 1993), 12.

7. See Thomas M. McCoog, S.J., "Playing the Champion: The Role of Disputation in the Jesuit Mission," in McCoog, ed., *The Reckoned Expense: Edmund Campion and the Early English Jesuits* (Woodbridge, Suffolk: Boydell, 1996), 119-40; my narrative of the role of disputation in Jesuit and Elizabethan culture is indebted to McCoog.

8. Frederich Seaton Siebert, *Freedom of the Press in England, 1476-1776* (Urbana: University of Illinois Press, 1952), 89; see also David Loades, "Censorship in the Sixteenth Century," in *Politics, Censorship and the English Reformation* (London and New York: Pinter Publishers, 1991) and Annabel Patterson's recent argument that the arrangement of *Holinshed's Chronicles* expresses a belief in "freedom of the press," in *Reading Holinshed's Chronicles* (Chicago: University of Chicago Press, 1994), 234-63.

9. Evans, *Problems of Authority in the Reformation Debates* (Cambridge: Cambridge University Press, 1992), 103.

10. Ibid., 105-7.

11. Ibid., 103-11. See also McCoog, 119-20.

12. Norman L. Jones, *The Birth of the Elizabethan Age* (Oxford: Blackwell, 1993), 23.

13. Ibid., 24; see Evans, passim, on the nature of authority and evidence in Reformation debates.

14. On Jewell's sermon and its aftermath, see Jones, 69-71 and A. C. Southern, *Elizabethan Recusant Prose, 1559-1582* (London: Sands, 1950), 60-118. Southern, who dubs the ensuing debate "The Great Controversy," provides a bibliography of 64 titles he includes as part of the disputation.

15. John Ayre, ed., *The Works of John Jewell*, 4 vols. (Cambridge: Cambridge University Press, 1845-50), 1:1-25, quoted in McCoog, 119.

16. Jones, 69.

17. Ibid., 69; McCoog, 121-22.

18. See Southern's bibliography of the controversy, 61-64.

19. Paul L. Hughes and James F. Larkin, *Tudor Royal Proclamations* (New Haven and London: Yale University Press, 1969), 2:312-13.

20. Huntington Library MS Ellesmere 2768, 23, quoted in Hughes and Larkin, 2:313n.

21. Southern, 125-26.

22. On these proclamations see Hughes and Larkin, 2:341-43, 347-48, 376-79, 506-8, and 3:13-17. See also Peck's discussion, 166-67.

23. Robert M. Kingdon, ed., *The Execution of Justice in England. . . .* (Ithaca: Cornell University Press, 1965), 9-10.

24. Hughes and Larkin, 3:88, 92.

25. On responses to the so-called Bloody Questions see Patrick McGrath, "The Bloody Questions Reconsidered," *Recusant History* 20 (1991): 307, and Leslie Ward, "The Treason Act of 1563: A Study of the Enforcement of Anti-Catholic Legislation," *Parliamentary History* 8:2 (1989): 298; on the rate of imprisonment of English Catholics for the offenses of harboring seminary priests, refusing to go to church, speaking against religion, and being caught with Catholic written material, see Patrick McGrath and Joy Rowe, "The Imprisonment of Catholics for Religion under Elizabeth I," *Recusant History* 20 (1991): 419-20.

26. Richard Simpson, *Edmund Campion: A Biography* (London: J. Hodges, 1896), 3, 14.

27. Katherine Duncan-Jones, "Sir Philip Sidney's Debt to Campion," in McCoog, ed., *The Reckoned Expense*, 88.

28. On this concern see Simpson, 169-76.

29. Ibid., 225.

30. This version of Campion's *Letter to the Lords of the Council* is taken from Southern, 154.

31. Ibid., 155.

32. Patrick Ryan, S.J., ed., "Some Correspondence of Cardinal Allen, 1579-85," *Miscellanea VII*, Catholic Record Society 9 (London: Catholic Record Society, 1911), 31.

33. See Meredith Hanmer, *The Great Bragge and Challenge of M. Champion a Jesuite . . . confuted & aunswered* (London, 1581), 21[v].

34. Douay 1580. These passages are part of an introductory Epistle "To the Most Highe & Mightie Princesse Elizabeth," unpaginated.

35. Bod. MS Rawl. D. 10, f. 134[v]-5[v]. The poem is written in the context of the controversy set off by the publication of Campion's "Challenge" in 1580, probably after the publication of the Charke and Hanmer's responses in early 1581, but before Campion's capture and execution.

36. Hanmer, 27.

37. Simpson, 366.

38. Ibid., 363-64.

39. Letter from Bishop Aylmer to Lord Burghley, 29 September 1581, BL Lansdowne MS 33, art. 24, quoted in Simpson, 377.

40. Ibid., 377, quoting from Lansdowne MS 33, art. 61.

41. Quoted in Simpson, 369.

42. Strype, Aylmer, c. iii; quoted in Simpson, 379. Lansdowne MS 33, art. 63, 28 December 1581, quoted in Simpson, 379.

43. Simpson, 378.

44. Quoted in ibid., 378.

45. *A True Report of the Death and Martyrdom of M. Campion Jesuit and Priest, & M. Shwerwin, & M. Bryan priestes, at Tiborne the first of December* (1582); on controversy over the authorship of this pamphlet, see Southern, 376-79.

46. That these poems circulated relatively widely in manuscript is suggested by the survival of the longest of them, "Why doe I use paper, pen and inke," in at least five extant commonplace books of the sixteenth century. See Margaret Crum, ed., *First Line Index of Manuscript Poetry in the Bodleian Library* (New York: MLA, 1969), 2:1132.

47. The pro-Campion version of this ballad is entitled "Upon the death of M. Edmund Campion, one of the Societie of the holy name of Jesus"; Munday's poem is "Verses in the Libell, made in prayse of the death of Maister Campion." Citations to the poems are given in line numbers, and are to the printed versions in Rollins, 66-172.

48. Lake and Questier, 66.

49. Ibid., 65.

50. *Chronicles of England, Scotland and Wales,* ed. Raphael Holinshed et al. (London, 1587), 3:1332.

51. Siebert, 89.

52. Ibid., 89.

53. Duncan-Jones, 87.

54. Ibid., 96.

55. Patterson, 254-55.

56. Thomas Bayley Howell, *Cobbett's Complete Collection of State Trials* (London: R. Bagshaw, 1809-26), 3, col. 1275.

57. Patterson, 234.

58. These works provide the content of so-called Bloody Questions. Another anti-Jesuit pamphlet which reprints questions based on the books of Sanders and Bristow, *A Particular declaration . . . of the undutifull and traiterous affection borne against her Majesty by Edmund Campion . . .* (1582), further highlights the centrality of reading and interpreting to the Jesuit prosecutions.

59. Holinshed, 3:1323.

60. Ibid., 3:1323.

61. Patterson, 238-39.

FURTHER READING

Criticism

Bireley, Robert. *The Counter-Reformation Prince: Anti-Machiavellianism or Catholic Statecraft in Early Modern Europe.* Chapel Hill: University of North Carolina Press, 1990, 309 p.

Analyzes the political thought of the greatest anti-Machiavellian writers of the sixteenth and seventeenth centuries and their relationship to the Counter-Reformation.

Cameron, Euan. "'Civilized Religion' from Renaissance to Reformation and Counter-Reformation." In *Civil Histories: Essays Presented to Sir Keith Thomas,* edited by Peter Burke, Brian Harrison, and Paul Slack, pp. 49-66. Oxford: Oxford University Press, 2000.

Discusses the influence of Renaissance thinkers on civil conduct and education and considers some fundamentally different attitudes of Catholics and Protestants.

Clancy, Thomas H. "Ecumenism and Irenics in 17th-Century English Catholic Apologetics." *Theological Studies* 58, no. 1 (March 1997): 85-89.

Outlines attempts by writers to bring Catholics and Protestants into agreement over Christian doctrines.

Davidson, N. S. *The Counter-Reformation.* Oxford: Basil Blackwell Ltd, 1987, 87 p.

Explores Catholic doctrine before and after the Council of Trent and the role of the laity in reform.

Evennett, H. Outram. "Counter-Reformation Spirituality." In *The Counter-Reformation: The Essential Readings,* edited by David M. Luebke, pp. 48-63. Malden, Mass.: Blackwell Publishers Ltd, 1999.

Discusses the development of writings that took a new approach to spirituality, one which emphasized mental prayer, the holy Eucharist, and good works.

Houliston, Victor. "St. Thomas Becket in the Propaganda of the English Counter-Reformation." *Renaissance Studies* 7, no. 1 (March 1993): 43-70.

Describes how the legend of Thomas Becket was used for propaganda purposes in the Counter-Reformation.

Jones, Verina R. "Counter-Reformation and Popular Culture in *I Promessi Sposi*: A Case of Historical Censorship." *Renaissance & Modern Studies* 36 (1993): 36-51.

Assesses the influence of Alessandro Manzoni's novel on the attitudes of Italian readers towards the Counter-Reformation.

Monahan, Arthur P. "Richard Hooker: Counter-Reformation Political Thinker." In *Richard Hooker and the Construction of Christian Community,* edited by Arthur Stephen McGrade, pp. 203-17. Tempe, Ariz.: Medieval & Renaissance Texts & Studies, 1997.

Contrasts the views of Richard Hooker with those of Martin Luther and John Calvin.

Parente, J. A., Jr. "Counter-Reformation Polemic and Senecan Tragedy: The Dramas of Gregorius Holonius (1531?-1594)." *Humanistica Lovaniensia: Journal of Neo-Latin Studies* 30 (1981): 156-80.

Discusses how the sixteenth-century martyr plays of Holonius reflected concerns addressed by the Counter-Reformation.

Voss, Paul J. "The Making of a Saint: John Fowler and Sir Thomas More in 1573." *Journal of English and Germanic Philology* 99, no. 4 (October 2000): 492-512.

Examines the publishing history and structure of More's *Dialogue of Comfort,* which helped sustain members of the Catholic community.

Nahum Tate
c. 1652-1715

(Born Nahum Teate; also known as Nathaniel or Nat Tate; wrote as N. Tate) Irish playwright, poet, essayist, and librettist.

INTRODUCTION

Tate's *History of King Lear* (1681) is widely considered the best-known, most successful, and most maligned adaptation of a Shakespeare work. For 150 years after its first production, Tate's adaptation dominated the stage, and contemporary audiences preferred it to the original. Nevertheless, the term "Tatefication," coined in the nineteenth century, describes the practice of attempting to improve upon, but actually harming, Shakespeare's texts. Modern critics have shown interest in Tate's work mainly because of the insight it offers on the stage history of *King Lear*—much contemporary staging of Shakespeare's *Lear* is indebted to Tate's version. While Tate produced an enormous body of work in many genres, only his adaptations of Shakespeare have garnered critical attention—Tate's adaptations of Shakespeare provide insights into seventeenth-century tastes and the stage history of Shakespeare's plays.

BIOGRAPHICAL INFORMATION

Tate was born in Dublin in 1652, the son of Faithful Teate, a clergyman, and Katherine Kenetie Teate. Faithful Teate was rector of Castleterra, Ballyhaise, until the Catholic rebellion of 1641; when Teate informed on a group of rebels, they responded by plundering the Teates' home, resulting in the deaths of three of their children. Tate probably spent his early childhood in both England and Ireland, although details of his life before 1672 are uncertain. He likely entered Trinity College, Dublin, in 1668, and in 1672 moved to London to become a writer. It was at this time that he changed his name to Tate. He began publishing poems in 1676, issuing a volume of collected verse in 1677. The following year, his first play, *Brutus of Alba; or, The Enchanted Lovers* was produced. It was by all accounts a critical and commercial failure. After the failure of his second dramatic effort, *The Loyal General* (1679), Tate turned from composing original dramatic works to adapting Renaissance texts. In 1681 his adaptations of Shakespeare's *King Lear, Richard II,* and *Coriolanus* were produced for the stage. Tate's *Lear*

was a success, but his *Richard II* was banned after two performances and his version of *Coriolanus* failed to attract audiences. Tate continued to compose and adapt plays, but apart from the modest popularity of the farce *A Duke and No Duke* (1684), they failed to achieve popular success. In 1692 Tate was appointed poet laureate, and spent much of the rest of his career writing poetry to commemorate birthdays and other occasions for noble personages. He also collaborated with his mentor John Dryden, among others, on translations of Latin classics, edited various collections of poetry, and wrote literary criticism. He produced two important works during this period, *A New Version of the Psalms of David* (1696) in collaboration with the clergyman Nicholas Brady, and the mock-heroic *A Poem Upon Tea* (1700). Despite his appointment as laureate, Tate was plagued with financial problems during his last years. In 1713 he founded a poetry journal, *The Monitor,* but it published only a few issues. Tate died at the Mint, the area of London where debtors could stay without fear of arrest, on July 30, 1715.

MAJOR WORKS

Tate produced an enormous body of work, but little of it is thoroughly studied by modern critics. The work for which he is best known is *The History of King Lear.* In his preface to the play, Tate describes Shakespeare's text as "a Heap of Jewels, unstrung and unpolisht, yet so dazling in their Disorder, that I soon perceiv'd that I had seiz'd a Treasure," and explains the principles underlying his changes, which he would later apply to his other adaptations of Renaissance texts. Tate rejects Shakespeare's disregard for poetic justice, and thus provides the play with a happy ending: Cordelia and Edgar marry, and Lear leaves his kingdom to them. Tate also adapted Shakespeare's language for the more refined taste of the late seventeenth century, and clarified the motivations for characters' actions. One of the most significant omissions in Tate's version is the character of the Fool, who brings an element of levity to Shakespeare's play. The changes Tate made in his version of *Lear* were intended to bring the play closer to seventeenth century tastes in tragedy. Although the work has been maligned by critics through the ages, it has also been the most successful Shakespearean adaptation of all time. For 150 years, well into the eighteenth century, audiences preferred it to the original; as Johnson noted, "In the present case, the publick has decided." In the late eighteenth and early nineteenth centuries, theaters returned to Shakespeare's originals, and there was considerable resentment against the many Restoration writers who had attempted to improve on the Bard's works. The word "Tatefication" was coined to describe such revisions. However, Tate's *Lear* continued to play a such major part in the performance history of Shakespeare's play that elements of his version are retained in stagings to this day.

King Richard II, Tate's second Shakespeare adaptation, did not enjoy the same success. Tate's Richard II is a far more sympathetic character than Shakespeare's, as he tries to spare his subjects from civil war. Plays about usurpation were never popular with the crown, however, and the timing of Tate's *Richard II* was particularly bad—the play appeared during the Exclusion Crisis, when political parties were divided over whether to exclude the duke of York from the royal succession. The play was banned after two performances, but Tate reissued the play after changing the names of the characters, moving the location to Sicily, and retitling it *The Sicilian Usurper* and *The Tyrant of Sicily.* However, the changes made were not significant enough, and the authorities reimposed the ban. *The Ingratitude of a Commonwealth,* Tate's version of Shakespeare's *Coriolanus,* is a melodramatic work of political intrigue. The central character represents the duke of York, and the play is an apology for Tory political ideas. Although the authorities did not ban the work, it failed to become a popular success.

Tate's original dramatic works, *Brutus of Alba,* a reworking of the story of Dido and Aeneas, and *The Loyal General,* about a weak king opposed by his adulterous queen, were not popular during their own time and are of scant interest today. Tate's libretto for the opera *Dido and Aeneas,* a collaboration with composer Henry Purcell, has achieved some measure of critical success. The work was adapted from part of Virgil's *Aeneid. Dido and Aeneas,* was the first true English opera and is generally considered a masterpiece. Although the significance of Tate's contribution to the work is considered minimal by many, some critics have argued that he deserves credit for writing one of the great librettos in English. Tate's other adaptations of dramatic tragedies were failures, but his comic farce *A Duke and No Duke* (1684), adapted from *Trappolin Supposed a Prince* by Aston Cokain, was well liked by audiences. Tate's "Preface Concerning Farce"—the introduction to the 1693 edition of *A Duke and No Duke*—was one of the first attempts in English to explain and defend the genre.

CRITICAL RECEPTION

Despite his status as poet laureate and the enormous popularity of *The History of King Lear,* critics have generally considered Tate a poor writer. Alexander Pope

attacked his poetry in the *Dunciad,* and Sir Walter Scott said of him: "He is one of those second-rate bards who, by dint of pleonasm and expletive, can find smooth lines if any one will supply ideas." There has been general critical agreement that Tate was not an original writer or thinker, and that his strongest efforts were produced in collaboration with those who supplied the creative ideas. The first full-length study of Tate's life and career, by Christopher Spencer, appeared in 1972, and acknowledged the inferior quality of the laureate's writing. The vast majority of critical studies on Tate have centered on his adaptations of Shakespeare, particularly his *King Lear.* The interest in the work is less a testament to Tate's abilities as a playwright than an abiding interest in Shakespeare. Critics have noted that Tate's adaptation has had a significant impact on the reading and staging of Shakespeare's work. It is argued by some critics that the interiority of King Lear as he is presented by most actors is not so much a product of Shakespeare's script as audiences' and actors' familiarity with the character as he is presented in Tate's version. The "heath" on which so much of the important action in stagings of Shakespeare's play takes place is also a construct credited to Tate. Some critics have maintained that Tate's adaptation is better than it is often assumed to be. They claim that the play must be read as an individual work, not merely in relation to Shakespeare's original. Tate is also praised by several scholars for his talent as a librettist. They argue that while the verse dialogue in *Dido and Aeneas* is not particularly interesting if read as poetry, Tate's words are appropriate for a musical drama. In general, critics regard Tate as a mediocre writer, but continue to take interest in his works because of the light they shed on those he imitated and collaborated with.

PRINCIPAL WORKS

Poems (poetry) 1677; revised and enlarged as *Poems Written on Several Occasions,* 1684

Brutus of Alba; or, The Enchanted Lovers (play) 1678

The Loyal General (play) 1679

*Ovid's Epistles, Translated by Several Hands [cotranslator] (poetry) 1680

The History of King Lear [adaptor; from *King Lear* by William Shakespeare] (play) 1681

†*The History of King Richard II* [adaptor; from *Richard II* by William Shakespeare] (play) 1681

The Ingratitude of a Commonwealth [adaptor; from *Coriolanus* by William Shakespeare] (play) 1681

The Second Part of Absalom and Achitophel [with John Dryden] (poetry) 1682

A Duke and No Duke [adaptor; from *Trappolin Supposed a Prince* by Aston Cokain] (play) 1684

Cuckold's Haven [adaptor; from *Eastward Ho!* by Ben Jonson, John Chapman, and John Marston] (play) 1685

Poems by Several Hands, and on Several Occasions [editor and contributor] (poetry) 1685

‡*The Æthiopian History of Heliodorus. In Ten Books* [co-translator; from *Æthiopics* by Heliodorus] (prose) 1686; also published as *The Triumphs of Love and Constancy,* 1687

Syphilis: or, A Poetical History of the French Disease [translator; from Girolamo Fracastoro's poem] (poem) 1686

The Island Princess [adaptor; from an anonymous adaptation of John Fletcher's play] (play) 1687

Dido and Aeneas (libretto) 1689

The Life of Alexander the Great [editor and co-translator; from Quintus Curtius Rufus's biography] (biography) 1690

A Pastoral Dialogue (poem) 1690; also published as *A Poem Occasioned by the Late Discontents & Disturbances in the State. With Reflections Upon the Rise and Progress of Priest-Craft,* 1691

"A Present for the Ladies: Being an Historical Vindication of the Female Sex" (essay) 1693

§*The Satires of Junius Juvenalis. Translated into English Verse. By Mr. Dryden, and Several Other Eminent Hands. Together with the Satires of Aulus Persius Flaccus Made English by Mr. Dryden. With Explanatory Notes at the End of Each Satire. To which Is Prefix'd a Discourse Concerning the Original and Progress of Satire. Dedicated to the Right Honourable Charles Earl of Dorset, &c.* [co-translator] (poetry) 1693

The Four Epistles of A. G. Busbequius, Concerning His Embassy into Turkey, Being Remarks Upon the Religion, Customs, Riches, Strength and Government of That People [translator] (travel essays) 1694

Miscellanea Sacra; or, Poems on Divine & Moral Subjects [editor and contributor] (poetry) 1696

A New Version of the Psalms of David, Fitted to the Tunes Used in Churches [translator, with Nicholas Brady] (songs) 1696

‖*Ovid's Metamorphosis. Translated by Several Hands. Vol 1. Containing the First Five Books* [co-translator] (poetry) 1697

Panacea: A Poem Upon Tea: In Two Cantos (play) 1700; revised as *A Poem Upon Tea,* 1702

#*Injur'd Love; or, The Cruel Husband. A Tragedy, Design'd to Be Acted at the Theatre Royal* [adaptor, from *The White Devil* by John Webster] (play) 1707

The Celebrated Speeches of Ajax and Ulysses, for the Armour of Achilles. In the 13th Book of Ovid's Metamorph [translator, with Aaron Hill] (speeches) 1708

***Ovid's Art of Love. In Three Books. Together with His* Remedy of Love. *To which Are Added,* The Court of Love, *a Tale from Chaucer. And* The History of Love [co-translator] (poetry) 1709

"An Essay for Promoting of Psalmody" (essay) 1710

††*The Fourth and Last Volume of the Works of Lucian* [co-translator] (poetry) 1711

*Tate translated "Leander to Hero," "Hero to Leander," and "Medea to Jason."

†Usually performed under this title but some early stagings were called *The Sicilian Usurper* or *The Tyrant of Sicily.*

‡Tate translated books 6-10.

§Tate translated satires 2 and 5.

‖Tate translated most of book 4.

#This play was never performed. The date is that of its publication.

*Tate translated *Remedy of Love.*

††Tate translated "Dialogues of the Gods: To Ridicule the Fables About Them."

CRITICISM

Wiltshire Stanton Austin and John Ralph (essay date 1853)

SOURCE: Austin, Wiltshire Stanton, and John Ralph. "Nahum Tate." In *The Lives of the Poets-Laureate: With an Introductory Essay on the Title and Office,* pp. 196-222. London: Richard Bentley, 1853.

[*In the following essay, Austin and Ralph offer an overview of Tate's life and literary career, suggesting that while his literary merit is limited, he has been misrepresented and deserves more respect than he has received.*]

It is amusing, if not edifying, to observe the manner in which all works of general reference, save a very few, repeat in regular succession the idlest inventions, and the clumsiest distortions of fact. In literary history this is especially the case, and we can trace in dictionary after dictionary, life after life, note upon note, some blunder copied with slight variations by book-makers, who lacked the honest industry to investigate, or the ingenuity to detect falsehood.

So because Tate was put into the *Dunciad,* and Warburton sought to crush him, he has ever since been treated as a malefactor and impostor. In *The Pictorial History of England* he is described as "the author of the worst alteration of Shakespeare, the worst version of the Psalms of David, and the worst continuation of a great poem." Now it nevertheless does so happen, that his alteration of *King Lear* kept possession of the stage for nearly a century, and that Dr. Johnson admits that when an attempt was made to play the tragedy as Shakespeare wrote it, the public decided in favour of Tate;

that in seeking to dwarf the sublimity of Hebrew poetry by English rhyme and metre, he has only failed where every one else has done so; that his Version of the Psalms has for more than a hundred and fifty years been used in our Churches; that it was in itself no small thing to be Dryden's coadjutor; and that the parts of the continuation contributed by Tate have such merit, that Sir Walter Scott, not prone to be charitable towards him, is compelled to conjecture that they underwent the revision of Dryden.

He was doubtless only a second-rate man; but does he deserve to be damned in one sentence as a tenth-rate scribbler by those who very probably have read but a small portion of his works? In another compilation,[1] full of inaccuracies, he is assailed with acrimony, and treated with contempt. That he was the friend of Dryden, the *protégé* of Dorset, and Laureate for a quarter of a century, even those writers so hasty and indiscriminate in their censures will not deny. We may perhaps show that, however extravagant in tragedy, he was as a dramatist tolerably successful in comedy, farce, and opera; that he has done some good service as an English Psalmodist, and that he is not utterly unworthy of a brief, if not a eulogistic memoir.

Nahum Tate's grandfather and father were both clergymen. It is to be regretted that he did not adopt the hereditary profession. Coleridge[2] has declared that all literary men should have some source of income besides the pen; and there is no lack of instances to show that first as well as second-rate men of letters may live and die in indigence; and that in one age refuge may be sought in the Mint, in another in the Insolvent Court. His father, Dr. Faithful Teat, (for in this way was the name spelled until Tate adopted the English orthography of the Irish mal-pronunciation) was minister of Ballyhays. He was educated at Winchester, but expelled from that school; and became the author of some poems and theological works. During some disturbances in Ireland, he gave information against a party of rebels, who wreaked their vengeance by robbing him on his way to Dublin; while a part of the gang simultaneously plundered his house, and treated his family with such severity that three of his children died from the cruelties inflicted on them. After residing some time in the lodgings of the Provost of Trinity College, Dublin, he was appointed to preferment in Kent, but finally returned to Dublin. He is supposed to have been inclined to Puritanical opinions; but the surmise may have arisen from the fact of his giving his children (which was the fashion with this party) scriptural names.

Nahum was born at Dublin in 1652. He was for some time at Belfast under the tuition of a master whose name was Savage, and he matriculated at the age of sixteen, at Trinity College, Dublin. Of his university ca-

reer nothing whatever is known. He appears to have determined on not adopting a profession, and came up to London to seek his fortune as a literary man. He was so fortunate as to gain the friendship of Dryden and the patronage of Dorset. His earliest production was a volume of poems in 1677. It consists of a great many verses on subjects the most heterogeneous. One composition laments "the present corrupted state of Poetry," and is, doubtlessly, a striking example of the decay of which it complains. There are some erotic lays replete with the quaintest and most elaborate conceits. The last stanza of a poem called **"The Tear,"** reminds us, of (but we must not compare it with) Mr. Rogers' simple and beautiful lines on the same subject. Tate's are:

> It shall be so. I will convert
> This tear to a gem—tis feasible;
> For laid near Julia's frozen heart
>   'Twill to a diamond congeal;
>   And yet, if I consider well,
> These tears of Julia can forbode no ill—
> The frost is breaking, when such drops distil.

But the booksellers who catered for the taste of the small reading public of that day did not remunerate our poet very liberally for these effusions; so he betook himself, at once, to the stage, then the best source of income to authors.

His first production was **Brutus of Alba, or the Enchanted Lovers,** a tragedy. It was dedicated to the Earl of Dorset with the usual amount of flattery, and the poet tells his patron that to lay this tragedy at his feet transports him more than the greatest success on the stage could have done. The play was originally to have been called *Dido and Æneas,* but Tate with much modesty feared to attempt "any character drawn by the incomparable Virgil." The plot is founded on an old story told by Geoffrey of Monmouth, who gives the descent of the Welsh Princes from Brutus the Trojan. This Brutus, according to him, came from Troy to Albion, killed a race of giants who occupied this country, and then built London. Tate applies the incidents of the fourth book of the Æneid to this fabulous hero; and as it is his first and most original drama, the reader may be amused by a short account of the plot, which is interesting from its daring absurdities. The scene is laid at Syracuse. Brutus, Prince of the Dardan forces, has been cast by a storm on the shore of Sicily. He is brought into the presence of the Queen of Syracuse, who at once falls hopelessly in love with him. With him is his son Locrinus, who signalizes himself by slaying in a quarrel a young Syracusan, the son of Soziman. Brutus, with much magnanimity, gives up his son to justice; but upon the youth explaining to her Majesty that he was entirely in the right, and the dead man entirely in the wrong, she instantly pardons him, and makes Soziman, who is described as a designing lord, her secret enemy. Brutus is so much distracted with grief for the loss of his friend Assaracus, who has on his voyage suffered shipwreck, that he cannot at first reciprocate the royal regard. Meanwhile, two ambassadors arrive from Agrigentum to demand the Queen in marriage for their lord and master, offering the alternative of war in case of a refusal. Her Majesty valorously and haughtily spurns the proposal. Soziman, however, resolves in a soliloquy that the tyrant of Agrigentum shall have the Queen's person while he allots to himself the sceptre of Syracuse. In the midst of all this, the lost friend, Assaracus, arrives. Brutus is in ecstasies of joy. Then ensues a tender scene between the Queen and her confidante Amarante, in which the royal lady confesses the soft impeachment of being over head and ears in love with Brutus. So ends Act I.

In Act II., the Agrigentine ambassadors and Soziman intrigue, and a plan is arranged by which Soziman is to be put in possession of the throne of Syracuse, on the condition of the Queen being delivered up into the hands of the King of Agrigentum. Meanwhile, her charms have won her another lover in Assaracus, who declares his passion in a very rough and blustering style, informing her that he has been so unfortunate as to have become enamoured of her, that he is very sorry for it, and hopes she will in no way encourage his advances. She replies that she will endeavour to be as reserved as he wishes, but confesses in a soliloquy that she cannot but admire the odd grace of his surly passion. Brutus and Assaracus are both invited to join her Majesty in a hunting expedition. Next follows an interview between Brutus and the Queen, who is surprised by him while doing homage at the tomb of her departed husband. Brutus declares his passion. She is irresolute, and exclaims:

> What can I give, when charity to you
> Is perjury to my deceased Argaces?

In Act III., Ragusa, a sorceress, is in league with Soziman to ruin the virtue and constancy of the Queen. She has four female attendants, who are coarse imitations of the witches in *Macbeth*. In this act, the supernatural element is introduced to a terrific extent. Ragusa and her haggard satellites conspire with Soziman, and it is agreed that the Queen and Prince shall be driven to seek refuge from a storm in the same cavern, and that then a philtre, administered by Soziman, shall work its dread effects. The sports begin, the storm is raised, they fly for shelter to the same cavern, and with, of course, the same result as in the case of Dido and Æneas—

> Prima et Tellus et pronuba Juno
> Dant signum; fulsere ignes, et conscius æther
> Connubiis; summoque ulularunt vertice Nymphæ,
> Ille dies primus leti primusque malorum
> Causa fuit.

Act IV. The Queen pours out her grief to Amarante, and informs her of her ruin. She holds a dagger in her hand, with which, she informs her confidante, she contemplates stabbing Brutus. He, however, enters and succeeds in soothing her. She throws away the dagger, and there ensues much kneeling, weeping, and fainting. Assaracus, meanwhile, having overcome his passion for the Queen, reproaches Brutus with his delays, reminds him of the oracle which urged him to go to Albion, and pleads the cause of his son Locrinus, whom he represents as cheated out of his hopes of an empire. A stormy interview is ended by Assaracus stabbing himself to prove the sincerity of his sentiments. Brutus is so affected by this desperate act, that he gives orders for the sailing that night. The Queen enters, and asks whether it is his intention to fly from her, observing, that although he may leave her without destroying his peace of mind, that her's is gone for ever. He answers:

> You call him happy whom the damn'd would pity!
> Despairing ghosts that yell in lightless flames
> Would stand aghast to hear my sufferings told.
> Reflect, and grow more patient of damnation!

He then adds that go he must, and she, as a matter of course, swoons.

In the last act, the Queen raves about the perjury of Brutus. Amarante requests her Majesty to be tranquil, and declares that if she is not, she will commit suicide. The Queen is quieted. A conference next takes place between Ragusa and Soziman. She gives him a bracelet to wear which she has previously poisoned. To Ragusa it is announced by a spirit, whom she summons from the vasty deep, that she is doomed to perish that night, but she is consoled by the additional intelligence that it will be one of horrific deeds and disasters. Brutus is driven back by a storm, and there is another terrible parting scene between himself and his royal innamorata. Soziman has, in the interval, discovered that he has been poisoned by the bracelet. He goes off the stage in a fury, tearing his hair. The Queen is in agonies of grief, but is soothed by music, and dies. Amarante at this, stabs herself and dies also. The venom of the poisoned bracelet racks the frame of Soziman, and he rushes on, tearing his clothes, stabs himself, and, to use his own language, plunges "headlong to eternal deeps." At this conjuncture of affairs, the ambassadors from Agrigentum again arrive. They find all their plans frustrated. One exclaims "Prodigious!" while the other confesses that he is "lost in confusion." It is really a very bustling tragedy. There are in it only

1 Natural death,

1 Murder,

1 Poisoning,

3 Suicides,

And there is much thunder and lightning, rage, fury, and bombast throughout. There are horrors enough for a French novel, and it might be revived at a transpontine theatre with great effect. To speak of it in language applied to a different kind of composition: daggers, flames, and poison "dance through its pages in all the mazes of metaphorical confusion. These are the companions of a disturbed imagination—the melancholy madness of poetry without its inspiration."[3]

In 1680, he produced *The Loyal General,* the prologue to which was written by Dryden. Like that great poet, he prefixes to his plays dissertations, which are rather essays on some questions of criticism than prefaces properly so called. The introduction to *The Loyal General* contains some remarks on Shakespeare, which, though they may seem to possess little novelty now that the subject is exhausted, yet show that it was out of no want of respect and admiration for Shakespeare that Tate ventured to alter some of his plays. On the question of the amount of Shakespeare's learning, he asserts that he possessed more than by common report is granted him. He adds: "I am sure he never touches on a Roman story, but the persons, the passages, the manners, the circumstances are all Roman. And what relishes yet of a more exact knowledge, you do not only see a Roman in his hero, but the particular genius of the man without the least mistake of his character, given him by the best historians. You find his Antony, in all the defects and excellencies of his mind, a soldier, a reveller, amorous, sometimes rash, sometimes considerate, with all the various emotions of his mind. His Brutus, again, has all the constancy, gravity, morality, generosity imaginable, without the least mixture of private interest or irregular passion. He is true to him even in the imitation of his oratory, the famous speech which he makes him deliver, being exactly agreeable to his manner of expressing himself; of which we have this account: 'Facultas ejus erat militaris et bellicis accommodata tumultibus.'"

The Loyal General was succeeded by *The Sicilian Usurper,* which is an alteration of *King Richard II.* of Shakespeare. It was on political grounds suppressed. Tate some years afterwards published it; and in a prefatory epistle in vindication of himself, he says: "I fell upon the new modelling of this tragedy (as I had just before done on the history of King Lear), charmed with the many beauties I discovered in it, which I knew would become the stage; with as little design of satire on present transactions as Shakespeare himself, that wrote this story before this age began. I am not ignorant of the position of affairs in King Richard II.'s reign: how dissolute the age, and how corrupt the court, a season that beheld ignorance and infamy preferred to office, and power exercised in oppressing learning and

merit; but why a history of these times should be suppressed as a libel on ours, is past my understanding. 'Tis sure the worst compliment that was ever paid to a prince."

As Tate has here alluded to his alteration of *King Lear,* a few words may be here said on that subject. The crime of mutilating the works of Shakespeare cannot be magnified; but we must impute this seeming arrogance rather to the age than to the individual who attempted it. There appears to have been an impression at this time, that in taste and refinement they had so outstripped the cultivation of the Elizabethan era, that it was necessary to tame the extravagancies of Shakespeare's rude imagination. Davenant and Dryden had both set Tate the example. In altering *King Lear,* Tate omitted the part of the Fool and introduced a love plot between Edgar and Cordelia. Tate's alteration, as has been before observed, maintained possession of the stage for a considerable time. Colman rejected most that Tate had added. Garrick did the same. When Kemble remodelled it in 1809, he reintroduced many of Tate's lines which had been rejected by Colman and Garrick. In speaking of this, the author of *The History of the English Stage,* remarks, "When Shakespeare met John Kemble in the Elysian fields he said to him, 'I thank you heartily for your performance of my Coriolanus, Hamlet, Brutus, &c.—but did you never hear the good old proverb: The cobbler should not go beyond his last? Why would you tamper with the text of my plays? Why give many of my characters names which I never dreamed of? Above all, what could induce you to restore such passages of Tate as even Garrick had rejected when he revised King Lear. St. Laurence never suffered more on his gridiron than I have suffered from the prompt-book.'" Whatever alterations and restorations were occasionally made, it was not until at Drury Lane, in 1823, that the entire fifth act was played as Shakespeare wrote it. Here an unfortunate accident for a time baffled its success. Cordelia was impersonated by Mrs. West. Kean, who played Lear, was scarcely strong enough to carry her. This tempted the risibility of the house, and pit, boxes, and gallery joined in a laugh which lasted until the curtain fell.

Tate in his dramatic compositions has manifested no great desire to win the praise of originality. One successful play was more remunerative than many fulsome dedications. To amuse the theatre-goers, therefore, was the object of Tate and others—and they accordingly plundered the plots of their predecessors as unblushingly as we now prey on those of our Gallic contemporaries. In the nine dramatic pieces which he has left behind him, he borrowed from Ben Jonson, Fletcher, Dekker, and others—besides his alteration of Shakespeare. They had no brilliant success—more than one was a decided failure, but others were frequently played and remained stock pieces. His *Duke and no Duke,* was last played at the Haymarket, in 1797. Into his ***Richard II.*** Tate introduced some songs, one of which is the following:

> Retired from any mortal's sight,
> The pensive Damon lay,
> He blest the discontented night,
> And cursed the smiling day:
> The tender sharers of his pain,
> His flocks no longer graze,
> But sadly fixed around the swain,
> Like silent mourners gaze.
>
> He heard the musick of the wood,
> And with a sigh reply'd;
> He saw the fish sport in the flood,
> And wept a deeper tide.
> In vain the summer bloom came on,
> For still the drooping swain,
> Like autumn winds was heard to groan,
> Outwept the winter's rain.
>
> Some ease, said he, some respite give.
> Ah, mighty powers! Ah, why
> Am I too much distress'd to live,
> And yet forbid to die?
> Such accents from the shepherd flew,
> Whilst on the ground he lay,
> At last so deep a sigh he drew,
> As bore his life away.

A song in ***Cuckold's Haven*** supplied Charles II. with a quotation, on an occasion mentioned by Mr. P. Cuningham in his charming story of "Nell Gwynne." The King was dining at the Guildhall. The courtiers and citizens drank as deep as was then the fashion. The Lord Mayor in his cups waxing practically facetious, Charles dismissed his suite without ceremony, and sought to extricate himself from the wine-inspired familiarities of the civic dignitary by stealing off to his coach. He was pursued; his Lordship seized him by the hand and said, "Sir, you shall stay, and take another bottle." The merry Monarch quoted from Tate:

> He that is drunk is as great as a king.

and went back to finish the wine.

In the play, at the end of Act II., there is another song equally in praise of Bacchus, which illustrates the political influence of the theatre, and the support that it strove to give to the throne.

> How great are the blessings of Government made,
> By the excellent rule of our Prince,
> Who, while trouble and cares do his pleasure invade,
> To his people all joy does dispense:
> And while he for us is carking and thinking,
> We have nothing to mind—but our shops and our
>   trade,
> And then to divert us with drinking.
>
> For him we derive all our pleasure and wealth,
> Then fill me a glass; nay, fill it up higher,

> My soul is athirst for his Majesty's health,
> And an Ocean of drink can't quench my desire;
> Since all we enjoy to his bounty we owe,
> 'Tis fit all our bumpers like that should o'erflow.

No materials exist, or if they do the authors of this work have failed to discover them, which would enable us to give any accurate or trustworthy account of the incidents of Tate's life. As dramatist we have spoken of him. Let the reader next look at him under the aspect of Laureate and psalmodist.

Tate succeeded on the demise of Shadwell in 1692. His appointment by Lord Jersey, after the accession of Queen Anne, is recorded in the following form of words:

> These are to certify that I have sworn and admitted Nahum Tate into ye place and quality of Poet-Laureate to her Majesty in ordinary, to have, hold, and exercise and enjoy the said place together with all rights, profits, privileges, and advantages thereunto belonging, in as full and ample manner as any Poet-Laureate hath formerly held and of right ought to have held and enjoyed the same.
>
> Given under my hand this 24th day of Decr. in the first year of her Majesty's reign.
>
>   JERSEY.

During this reign the appointment was placed in the gift of the Lord Chamberlain, and Tate was re-appointed in 1714.

In his position as Laureate little can be said to his honour. His excuse we find in what we know of the literary men of that era. He was, as Mr. Macaulay says, in morals something between a beggar and a pander. In times of sudden change, it is scarcely probable that we should find the life of a necessitous man of letters, free from the inconsistency which blemished the careers of even the rich and noble. Tate was nearly five-and-twenty years a Poet-Laureate. He eulogized the memory of Charles II.; hailed the accession of James; welcomed William more enthusiastically; panegyrised Mary and Anne, living and dead; and wrote one official ode for George I. Dryden and Waller, however, before him, had exhausted fancy in lauding Cromwell, and at the Restoration were lavish of their praise on the Merry Monarch. To say good things on a great occasion, was all they aimed at. Conscience and consistency were quite out of the case.

It is difficult to discover by what interest Tate gained the appointment, for he had eulogized Charles and James, and had been the friend and coadjutor of the deposed Dryden. His Christian name may possibly have recommended him—or his father's puritanical leaning have been remembered. It seems more likely, however, attributable to the fact that his poverty was known, that he had a little interest, that he possessed the necessary amount of pliancy for a court poet, and that there were no formidable rivals in the field.

Pope was only at this time four years old, and even with his precocity had not yet "lisped in numbers." Swift had written one or more of his Pindaric Odes, but they had merited the discouraging remark of his relation Dryden, and had been sufficiently rewarded by the King teaching him in Sir W. Temple's garden, how to cut asparagus in the Dutch way. Handsome provision had been made for Montague and Prior. Garth had only just passed his examination, and become a fellow of the College of Physicians, and the world had not yet seen the Dispensary. Butler had died in poverty twelve years before; and that poverty, in Tate's words, was a greater satire on the age than his writings. Otway had shared the same wretched fate. And the sweet numbers of Waller were silent. Tate was as good as any of the poetasters of the day, and as a voluminous versifier, and an industrious dramatic author, had been much before the public. Any detailed account of his laureate lucubrations would be superfluous. They are very numerous, and may be found in the library of the British Museum with much pomp of large type and gorgeous binding. The brevity of each poem is its chief recommendation. He flattered the throne, rejoiced in all court appointments, wrote elegies when great men died, advised the Parliament, and celebrated the victories of Prince George of Denmark, and of Marlborough. There is a couplet in his poem on the "sacred memory" of Charles II., which is worthy of one of his successors, Eusden. The grief is terrific.

> To farthest lands let groaning winds relate,
> And rolling Oceans roar their master's fate.

"The death of Queen Mary," says Johnson, "produced a subject; perhaps no funeral was ever so poetically attended." Tate is not mentioned by the Doctor as one of the tuneful mourners, but his strain is louder and loftier than usual. He apotheosizes her in these lines.

> With robes invested of celestial dyes,
> She tow'rs, and treads the Empyrean Skies;
> Angelick choirs, skill'd in triumphant song,
> Heaven's battlements and crystal turrets throng.
> The signal's given, the eternal gates unfold
> Burning with jasper, wreath'd in burnish'd gold,
> And myriads now of flaming minds I see—
> Pow'rs, Potentates, Heaven's awfull Hierarchy
> In gradual orbs enthron'd, but all divine
> Ineffably those sons of glory shine.

By one of his official poems, written at a particular crisis in the reign of William III. he excited much bitter attack from opponents. Many of our readers will remember the history of the Kentish Petition. This bold document requested the Parliament then sitting to at-

tend to public affairs and not their "own private heats," and besought them to turn their attention to the supplies, and enable the King to defend the country, and protect our allies. The gentlemen who presented it were Justinian Champneys, Sir Thomas Culpepper, William Culpepper, William Hamilton, and David Polhill. The House of Commons felt that so bold a measure must be as boldly resisted. They treated this document as a libel, and gave these five gentlemen into the custody of the sergeant-at-arms. On their remonstrating with him on the illegality of the arrest, that officer informed them in language highly indecorous, that he did not care for the law. They remained under his charge for five days, and were then lodged in Gate House Prison. This arbitrary act occasioned much discontent and disturbance. Many pamphlets were written on both sides of the question, De Foe being one of the ablest advocates of the petitioners. The popular feeling was against the Parliament, and they were at length liberated. Tate took the royal and popular view of the case against the House of Commons, and wrote a poem called **"The Kentish Worthies."** For this he was severely assailed. In *The History of Faction,* we read: "Nor had they reason to think that the court would discountenance them in such practices; for the Poet-Laureate, who is a sworn servant to the Crown, was ordered to write a poem called **'The Kentish Worthies,'** which he otherwise durst not have done." Another writer tells us:[4] "And to complete the show (the liberation of the petitioners), that it might look somewhat majestic, the ballad-maker of Whitehall was ordered to compose some lines to the laud and praise of the five Kentish Worthies, which he did with like success as when he and the parson (Dr. Brady), rebelled against King David, and broke his lute, and murdered his psalms."

Tate's Laureate Odes are not more meritorious than his other official poetic offerings. The one for the year 1705 is preserved. It was performed to music before her Majesty, on the 1st of January. The grand chorus with which it concludes runs thus:

> While Anne and George their empire maintain
> Of the land and the main,
> And a Marlborough fights
> Secure are the rights
> Of Albion and Europe in Piety's reign.

Whatever envy among contemporaneous, or contempt among later writers, Tate's official eminence provoked, he had his share of eulogy as well. In some lines prefixed to his *Miscellanea Sacra,* the writer thus addresses him:

> Long may the laurel flourish on your brow,
> Since you so well a Laureate's duty know,
> For virtue's rescue daring to engage
> Against the tyrant vices of the age.

In contrast to such writings as called forth this praise, Tate has been guilty of some offences. The fact that he rendered into English the second Satire of Juvenal, in what is called "Dryden's Translation," should perhaps screen Dryden from some of the censure which has been cast on him for coarseness. Tate contributed also to *Miscellaneous Poems,* published by Tonson, and edited by Dryden, an English version of one of Ovid's loosest elegies. This publication chiefly consisted of poems, original and translated, by "the most eminent hands." The nature of some of its contents, is quite sufficient to show that the taste of the reading public was not a whit purer than that of the *habitués* of the theatre. At the end of the fourth volume, there is a long translation by Tate of a composition of a very singular kind. It is the celebrated Latin poem on a medical subject by "that famous Poet and Physician, Fracastorius, Englished by Mr. Tate." There are some prefatory lines to Dr. Thomas Hobbs, and a life of the renowned medico-poet-philanthropist. In this memoir, the world is informed that Fracastorius was born at Verona, that he was specially and providentially preserved in childhood to write his great poem, for that while in his mother's arms, she was struck dead by lightning, while he remained unscathed; that he lived to rival Pliny and Catullus, and outstrip all his contemporaries in learning and poetry; that he studied under Peter Pomponatius, and became so devoted a student that Polybius and Plutarch were scarce ever out of his hands; that when not employed in literary avocations he was occupied in curing disorders, and that in the intervals of his professional exertion, while the pestilence he so vividly describes, was raging in the city he found leisure to compose these undying verses, which no less a man than Sanazarius is driven in despair to admit excelled his own poem "De Partu Virginis," which was a labour of twenty years. It is also recorded that Fracastorius died of apoplexy at seventy, having contracted many friendships, and having deservedly no enemy.

To criticise either the Latin or English would take us beyond our limits. Tate appears to have been compelled to work for the booksellers, as a translator of prose as well as verse. In 1686, he published, under the title of *Triumphs of Love and Constancy,* a translation of the *Æthiopics* of Heliodorus. This work is the earliest and best Greek romance, and narrates what are called *The Heroic Amours of Theagenes and Chariclea.* Its author was born at Emesa, in Syria, and lived at the end of the fourth century, under the reign of Theodosius and his sons. He wrote the *Æthiopics* in his youth, and upon his being appointed Bishop of Tucca, it is said, that a provincial Synod decreed that the author must burn his romance or lay down his bishopric. Heliodorus chose the latter alternative. The whole story, however, sounds very apocryphal; and its improbability is heightened by the fact that, although as a love story it offends against modern notions of delicacy, its tendency is to exalt vir-

tue. It was twice translated into English before Mr. Tate and his coadjutor, who is described as a person of quality, undertook it. A version has since been given by Mr. Payne in 1792. The Greek manuscript was strangely preserved. Although well known in earlier, it was in modern times, almost forgotten, until, at the sacking of Ofen, in 1526, the manuscript was found in the library of Matthias Corvinus, King of Hungary, and as it was decorated and illuminated it attracted the cupidity of a soldier who brought it into Germany, where falling into the hands of Vincentius Opsopæus, it was printed at Basil in 1534.

Tate also published a translation from the French of *The Life of the Prince de Condé.* We must, however, forget what he had meanwhile been doing in his poetical capacity. In 1697, he produced a short poem called **"The Innocent Epicure, or the Art of Angling."** It is of the didactic kind, and lays down minute directions for fishing. It is tedious and prosaic, and the rhymes are careless and faulty. *Panacea,* a poem on tea, in 1700, was a more successful effort of his Muse. The subject may appear to us a strange one, but tea was then a novelty and a luxury. It was sold in a liquid state. In Dryden's *Wild Gallant* it is spoken of as a morning draught for those who had drank too deeply overnight. Pepys tells us: "I sent for a cup of tea (a Chinese drink), of which I had never drank before." In 1664, the East India Company purchased two pounds and two ounces to present to the King. Its virtues were then very highly estimated, and they are celebrated in this poem with Tate's utmost power. The versification is excellent, but as a whole, from its plan and subject, it is uninteresting.

This effort, his partnership with Dryden, his translations, and the success of one volume of poems, which had gone through two editions, seemed to have increased the fame of the Laureate. By a poetical friend he is thus addressed:

> The British Laurel by old Chaucer worn,
> Still fresh and gay did Dryden's brow adorn,
> And that its lustre may not fade on thine,
> Wit, fancy, judgment, Tate, in thee combine.

It remains that we should look on Tate as Psalmist. And we shall see that he made much recompense for his few former offences against morality in pandering to the taste of the age, by his later writings, which tend to support the cause of religion and virtue. The times were mending a little, and some check seems to have been given to the open profligacy which characterized the period of the Restoration. In the Reformed Churches abroad, Protestantism and Psalmody had gone hand in hand together. A want was now felt in the English Church. The Old Version, written by Sternhold, and altered by Hopkins and others, sometimes for the better, oftener for the worse, had been in general use from the time of its publication. It was now thought that the advance our language had made, demanded a version more in accordance with the taste of the age, and that smoothness of versification which was more and more aimed at by our poets. Hence we exchanged the rugged strength and occasional doggerel of Sternhold and Hopkins for the more level mediocrity of Brady and Tate.

What brought about the literary partnership, which has been so often made a target for the shafts of sarcasm, we have no means of ascertaining or conjecturing, unless it were the tie of a common nationality. Dr. Nicholas Brady was Tate's fellow-countryman. He was educated at Westminster, and showed very early a talent for writing verse. He was an active politician and a popular preacher, and took a busy part in the Revolution of 1688, for which at the time he severely suffered. He lived, however, to be rewarded for his exertions, for at his death, in 1726, he was the incumbent of three benefices. He outlived his coadjutor eleven years, and could, with a better grace, have preached the funeral sermon of the unfortunate Psalmodist than that of sack-drinking Shadwell, whose name, until heard from the pulpit, had been mainly associated with taverns and theatres. Dr. Brady, however, could have quoted a precedent for his funeral oration; for the praises of Nell Gwynne had been sounded from the pulpit.

They at first printed a version of twenty Psalms, as an "Essay," as they termed it, and in the following year appeared the completed work, *A New Version of the Psalms of David,* fitted to the tunes used in churches, by N. Brady, D.D., Chaplain in Ordinary to Her Majesty, and N. Tate Esq., Poet-Laureate. In a pamphlet entitled: "A brief and full account of Mr. Tate and Mr. Brady's *New Version of the Psalms,* by a true son of the Church," the Royal Sanction is copied. "At the Court of Kensington, Decr. 3rd, 1696. Present, the King's most excellent Majesty in Council. Upon the humble petition of Nicholas Brady and Nahum Tate this day read at the Board, setting forth that the Petitioners have, with their utmost care and industry, compleated a New Version of the Psalms of David in English Metre, fitted for publick use; and humbly praying His Majesty's Royal allowance that the said Version may be used in such congregations as shall think fit to receive it; His Majesty, taking the same into his royal consideration, is pleased to order in Council that the said New Version of the Psalms in English Metre be, and the same is hereby allowed, and permitted to be used in all Churches and Chapels and Congregations as shall think fit to receive the same."

Dr. Compton, Bishop of London, sent out circular letters of recommendation to all the clergy of his diocese. The version has been eulogised by Basil Kennet and others; but Bishop Beveridge has censured it for faults

which it would *now* be difficult to discover. "There are," he says, "many such new phrases and romantic expressions in the new version, which are taken up by our present poets, and being now in fashion may serve well enough in other places, but can by no means suit with a divine poem, much less with one inspired by God himself." It encountered much prejudice and provoked some controversy. Tate undertook its defence, and published, in 1710, **"An Essay for Promoting Psalmody."** It is dedicated to Queen Anne. The style is quaint and florid. Psalmody is boldly personified and apostrophized as a goddess, a princess, a charmer. Parts of the treatise are written in a strain of rapture, and with the tone of a man of warm and sincere piety. He complains that while psalmody has been much cultivated in all the Reformed Churches it has been neglected in ours, and he attributes the decay into which it has fallen very much to the apathy "of our quality and gentry." "You may hear them," he says, "in the responses and reading psalms; but the giving out a singing psalm, seems to strike 'em dumb." He next extols Praise in occupying a devotional rank higher than Prayer, and supports his view by some beautiful lines from the "Gondibert" of his Laureate predecessor Davenant.

> For Prayer the Ocean is, where diversely
> Men steer their course, each to a different coast,
> Where oft our interests so discordant be,
> That half beg winds by which the rest are lost.
>
> *Praise is devotion fit for mighty minds,*
> *The diff'ring World's agreeing sacrifice.*

These raptures about the superior nature of Praise from one who had written a version of the Psalms, remind us forcibly of the clerk of a small country church in Wales, who, inasmuch as by playing a violoncello and singing lustily, he produced what is called in the 100th psalm "awful mirth," was so gratified with the success of his musical efforts, that he informed the rector one Sunday with an air of cheerful confidence, that although prayer and preaching were perhaps necessary, praise was the noblest part of divine worship. The rector's reply is an answer to Tate and to the rural musician, and is a good comment on the lines of Davenant: "If your prayers are not accepted, your praises will never be heard."

Tate then proceeds, in his treatise, to show what were the faults of the old version, and to lament the prejudices which obstruct the attempt to produce one better fitted for purposes of devotion. "You must," he writes,

> expect the first outcry against any new version of the Psalms from the ignorance amongst some of our common people, who, because they found the old singing psalms bound up with their Bibles, take it for granted that these English metres, as well as the matter, were compiled by King David. Nay, some have supposed a greater person was the composer of these metres. For

instance, the late Bishop of Ely upon his first using of his brother Dr. Patrick's new version in family devotion, observed (as I have heard himself relate the passage) that a servant maid of a musical voice was silent for several days together. He asked her the reason, whether she were not well or had a cold, adding that he was much delighted to hear her, because she sung sweetly and kept the rest in tune. "I am well enough in health," answered she, "and have no cold, but if you must needs know the plain truth of the matter, *as long as you sang Jesus Christ's psalms, I sung along with ye, but now you sing psalms* of your own invention, you may sing by yourselves."

Tate concludes his essay with a rhapsody, from which we give a brief extract.

> O Queen of Sacred Harmony, how powerful are thy charms. Care shuns thy walks, Fear kindles with courage, and Joy sublimes into ecstasy. What! shall stage syrens sing and Psalmody sleep! Theatres be thronged, and thy temples empty! Shall thy votaries abroad find heart and voice to sing in the fiery furnace of persecution, upon the waters of affliction, and our Britons sit sullenly silent under their vines and fig-trees?

To expend any criticism on this version of the Psalms would scarcely be less absurd, than to gravely endeavour to discover by internal evidence which were contributed by Brady and which by Tate. In **Miscellanea Sacra,** published in 1698, there is a rendering of the 104th Psalm by him which is excellent. Nothing but want of space prevents our inviting criticism to it by a long quotation. To sum up his merits as a psalmodist, it may be said of him that he has only failed where others have done so; for are not all attempts, save a few by eminent poets, scattered here and there in literature, rather parodies than paraphrases?

The sorrow and the triumphs which shook the strings of the royal harp are breathed in such strains of poetry as speak with divine eloquence in the unfettered rhythm of our version; but the sublimity is dwarfed by the exactments of metre, and the music faintly and falsely echoed by the jingle of rhyme.

In 1713, Tate undertook the management of a well-meaning publication, which was as short-lived as many such have been, and, strange to say, as one of the same name started in London within the last four years. *The Monitor,* for so was it called, was to appear on alternate days, and the first number was issued on March 2nd, 1713. It was "intended for the promoting of Religion and Virtue, and the suppression of vice and immorality, in pursuance of Her Majesty's most gracious Direction."

The undertaking not only enjoyed royal patronage, but was encouraged by many of the nobility, bishops, and clergy. But in spite of all this, and the moderate price (one penny per number), it struggled unsuccessfully for but a short time. They were sent to the subscribers' houses on the terms of twelvepence a month, "sixpence on the receipt of the first paper, and sixpence more when the twelfth paper is delivered."

We are informed that through the contribution of some pious persons, some schools were to be supplied with them, "the masters of which will oblige their scholars to get the Poems by heart as part of their exercise." These scholars merit our sincerest sympathies. The publication commences with an "Essay on Divine Poesie." Then follows an exhortation to the youth of Great Britain, which endeavours to carry out the principle which the paper professed, viz., "to establish them in the principles of Religion and Virtue, and fortify them against the attacks of Vice." The swearer and the gambler are denounced in two separate numbers. "The Witch of Endor" is the subject of a sublime dialogue, full of pious profanity. Another is a description of "The Upright Man," and is a bombastic paraphrase of Horace's "justum et tenacem propositi virum." The stern stoicism of the character is depicted in a couplet, which prophetically expresses a phrase of modern slang—

> Though whirl'd by storms the racking clouds are seen,
> His unmolested breast is *all serene.*

In the number for April 6th, a prose notice is added, which contains an anecdote not in the least *à-propos* to the subject of the paper, but referring to a matter which has been alluded to in a former part of this work. "We shall beg the reader's pardon for mentioning a passage told us by a gentleman of our society, almost forty years since, by Mr. Dryden, who went, with Mr. Waller in company, to make a visit to Mr. Milton, and desire his leave for putting his *Paradise Lost* into rhyme for the stage. 'Well, Mr. Dryden,' says Milton, 'it seems you have a mind to tagg my points, and you have my leave to tagg 'em; but some of 'em are so awkward and old-fashioned, that I think you had as good leave 'em as you found 'em.'" In the last number but one, we are told that those "who particularly approve of these Divine subjects, seem anxious that entertaining ones may be mixed with them, and that to meet this want, some gentlemen of the brightest parts are setting upon such a work." Whether "The Oracle" ever appeared, we know not; but next day *The Monitor* died.

And so ends the literary career of Nahum Tate.

Of his private life and habits, little can be ascertained. He was, we are told, of a downcast look, and very silent in company; but he has also been described as a "free and fuddling companion." He has been praised for his integrity and modesty.

There is nothing to justify Dr. Johnson's surmise that he was ejected from his office at the accession of George

I. The date of Rowe's appointment is 1715, and it was in this year that Tate died in the Mint, Southwark, where he had taken refuge from his numerous creditors.

He appears to have been very industrious with his pen, but in worldly matters imprudent and unfortunate. His case is one among a thousand which prove the necessity of such institutions as the Athenæum Institute and the Guild of Literature and Art. Patronage was of some avail to Tate and other necessitous men of letters; but when improvidence has not even patronage to fall back upon, as is now the case, there would seem to be greater need for co-operative providence.

Had Tate lived in these days, his life would doubtless have been very badly written by a near relative, and the minutest details of his existence chronicled with precision. There was no such lust for biography when he died in the Mint. But gibbeted by the sarcasms of Pope, he has been much misrepresented by those who copied the sarcasms without reading his works. Sir Walter Scott, who doubtless knew them, gives a mention of him, severe, but fairer than that of many other writers. "He is one of those second-rate bards," he says, "who, by dint of pleonasm and expletive, can find smooth lines if any one will supply ideas."

Neither he nor Shadwell deserve the treatment they have suffered even at the hands of recent writers. Miss Strickland calls the latter "the loathsome Laureate." Religious and political prejudice can see nothing but what is detestable in the poet of the court of William and Mary. We are more surprised to read in Southey's *Life of Cowper*—"Nahum Tate, of all my predecessors, must have ranked the lowest of the Laureates if he had not succeeded Shadwell." Could Southey, with all his varied book lore, have been ignorant of the verses of Eusden? and is he not in this estimate somewhat polite and merciful to his immediate predecessor, Pye?

Notes

1. "Lives of English Dramatists." *Lardner's Encyclopædia.*

2. *Biografia Literaria.*

3. Letter of Junius to Sir W. Draper.

4. "Account of some late designs to create a misunderstanding between the King and the people," quoted in [Walter] Wilson's *Life of De Foe.*

Hazelton Spencer (essay date 1927)

SOURCE: Spencer, Hazelton. "Tate's Adaptations." In *Shakespeare Improved: The Restoration Versions in Quarto and on the Stage,* pp. 241-73. Cambridge, Mass.: Harvard University Press, 1927.

[In the following excerpt, Spencer presents an analysis of Tate's adaptations of Shakespeare, detailing how his versions of King Lear, Richard II, *and* Coriolanus *differ from the originals.]*

1. KING LEAR

For half a century after the death of Sir William D'Avenant, every one of the poets laureate took a hand in improving Shakespeare. . . . The name of [Nahum Tate] lives in the hymnals. His treatment of Shakespeare's lines is even worse than his doggerel rendering of David's—the pompous substantive, "Tatefication," has been coined expressly to describe his bungling.[1]

Though apparently not the first acted, Tate's **Lear** was the first written of his adaptations; this is evident from the epistle dedicatory to his **Richard II.** It was printed in quarto in 1681, the year of its production at Dorset Garden.[2] The epistolary dedication is one of a number of documents in which the Restoration adapters explain their mental processes. Tate confesses to embarrassment in finding it necessary to provide dialogue for the old characters in his new scenes. But this humility is not evident as he deals with structure:

> I found the whole . . . a Heap of Jewels, unstrung and unpolisht; yet so dazling in their Disorder, that I soon perceiv'd I had seiz'd a Treasure. 'Twas my good Fortune to light on one Expedient to rectifie what was wanting in the Regularity and Probability of the Tale, which was to run through the whole A Love betwixt Edgar and Cordelia, that never chang'd word with each other in the Original. This renders Cordelia's Indifference and her Father's Passion in the first Scene probable. It likewise gives Countenance to Edgar's Disguise, making that a generous Design that was before a poor Shift to save his Life. The Distress of the Story is evidently heightned by it; and it particularly gave Occasion of a New Scene or Two, of more Success (perhaps) than Merit. This Method necessarily threw me on making the Tale conclude in a Success to the innocent distrest Persons: Otherwise I must have incumbred the Stage with dead Bodies, which Conduct makes many Tragedies conclude with unseasonable Jests.[3] Yet was I Rackt with no small Fears for so bold a Change, till I found it well receiv'd by my Audience; and if this will not satisfie the Reader, I can produce an Authority that questionless will. *Neither is it of so Trivial an Undertaking to make a Tragedy end happily, for 'tis more difficult to Save than 'tis to Kill: The Dagger and Cup of Poyson are alwaies in Readiness; but to bring the Action to the last Extremity, and then by probable Means to recover All, will require the Art and Judgment of a Writer, and cost him many a Pang in the Performance.*
>
> *Mr. Dryd. Pref. to the Span. Fryar.*

In seeking to motivate Cordelia's failure to speak out, Tate recognizes the structural weakness of Shakespeare's play from a realistic point of view, which, of course, is precisely the point of view it is fatal to adopt. Nor does his happy ending bring aught but outrage to King Lear, whose bitter cup seemed less significant to the adapter than the billing and cooing of Cordelia and Edgar.

In the prologue Tate announces his ethical purpose, anticipating Mr. Bernard Shaw's prediction that the theatre must replace the church as the custodian of morals. The clergy are accused of plotting in the Whiggish interest; thus *Lear,* like Tate's other alterations, is linked with the political troubles.

ACT I[4]

The play begins with Edmund's soliloquy (I, ii, 1-22), Gloster having already been apprised of Edgar's apparent disloyalty, as is explained in an original scene between Kent and Gloster. Then comes the partition scene (I, i, 32 f.). As the court enters, Edgar and Cordelia exchange amorous speeches. Shakespeare's dialogue is then employed, though in mangled form. France does not appear in this version. Cordelia's motive is now her desire to offend Lear in order that Burgundy may reject her. The King knows of her love affair; he supposes Edgar a bad lot. Kent is banished, and Burgundy refuses Cordelia.

Thus, to line 207, the action runs as in Shakespeare. At that point all go out except Edgar and Cordelia. Edgar then woos her with some assurance, but Cordelia will not hear him. Her answer is typical of Tate's idiom; notice also his tripping measures:

CORD.

> When, Edgar, I permitted your Addresses,
> I was the darling Daughter of a King,
> Nor can I now forget my royal Birth,
> And live dependent on my Lover's Fortune.
> I cannot to so low a fate submit,
> And therefore study to forget your Passion,
> And trouble me upon this Theam no more.

EDG.

> Thus Majesty takes most State in Distress!
> How are we tost on Fortune's fickle flood![5]
> The Wave that with surprising kindness brought
> The dear Wreck[6] to my Arms, has snatcht it back,
> And left me mourning on the barren Shore.

CORD.

> This Baseness of th' ignoble Burgundy [*Aside*
> Draws just suspicion on the Race of Men,[7]
> His Love was Int'rest, so may Edgar's be
> And He but with more Complement dissemble;
> If so, I shall oblige him by Denying:[8]
> But if his Love be fixt, such Constant flame
> As warms our Breasts, if such I find his Passion,
> My heart as gratefull to his Truth shall be,
> And Cold Cordelia prove as Kind as He. [*Exit.*]

Now the Bastard bustles in, warns his brother, and shoves him out. Gloster then appears and we have the scene of the forged letter (the remainder of I, ii, 30 f.). Though the heroic play was supposed to be defunct, Drawcansir was still at large; he appears for a moment in Gloster's speech urging Edmund to "wind me into him." Tate's addition gives a specific reason for this injunction:

> That I may bite the Traytor's heart, and fold
> His bleeding Entrals on my vengefull Arm.

Gloster makes his exit after line 111, as in Shakespeare; but instead of Edmund's cynical comment on his father's credulity we have more exposition: the villain plans to deceive his father again by placing him where he can overhear an interview with Edgar. Edmund then goes, and the disguised Kent comes in for Shakespeare's I, iv, his engagement by Lear; this is greatly reduced, though not much altered. Oswald is haled back by Kent. The Fool is entirely excised from Tate's version. For the most part the action runs as in Shakespeare, though with great condensation and the omission of many speeches. Lear departs shortly after Albany's appearance and does not reënter. Except for the brief comments of Goneril and Albany, the act ends on Lear's curse. Thus we do not learn of the message to Regan.

ACT II

The second act begins as in Shakespeare with the beguiling of Edgar and Gloster. Curan does not appear. Kent and Oswald enter before Regan and Cornwall: thus Shakespeare's II, i, and II, ii, are telescoped. Kent chases Oswald off the stage to make way for the entrance of the ducal party. Cornwall gives no reason for their visit to Gloster; instead he commands sports and revels. Oswald (who is called simply a Gentleman) now rushes back, pursued by Kent, and we pass to Shakespeare's II, ii, 43 f.

Shakespeare's scenes iii and iv follow at once, as in the original. As he tells us in the dedicatory epistle, Tate thinks Edgar's assumption of his rags unjustified by the sordid instinct of self-preservation. Accordingly, Edgar heroically meditates suicide, but refrains because Cordelia is in distress. To preserve himself for her service he condescends to assume a disguise. When Lear inquires for his daughter we learn that she is at a masque. He does not leave the stage. The action runs along as in Shakespeare, with the speeches much reduced, up to line 285; the act ends with Lear's departure into the storm.

ACT III

Act III begins with Shakespeare's III, ii, Lear on the heath, scene i being omitted. This great passage is grievously reduced and altered; without the Fool it is but a faint echo of its original. It is followed by a new scene in Gloster's palace; Edmund soliloquizes and reveals his lust for the "proud imperial Sisters." Tate, albeit he dabbled in pious psalmody, emphasizes this feature of the story and writes it up *con amore*. "Two Servants from several Entrances deliver him each a Letter."

Gloster then comes in, announces his intention of revolting, and entrusts Edmund with despatches. The Bastard declares, in a long aside, his purpose of betraying his father, and at a distance overhears him interview Cordelia, who wants to die with the King. Gloster informs her of his rebellion, and departs. Still overheard by Edmund, she bids Arante, a colorless confidante, to get her a disguise, that she may seek her father on the heath. It is there that she occupies the interim which in Shakespeare's play she spends in France. Edmund is a heavy villain, and has designs on everyone:

> Provide me a Disguise, we'll instantly
> Go seek the King:—ha! ha! a lucky change. . . .
> I'll bribe two Ruffians that shall at a distance follow,
> And seise 'em in some desert Place, and there
> Whilst one retains her t'other shall return
> T' inform me where she's Lodg'd; I'll be disguis'd too.
> Whilst they are poching for me I'll to the Duke
> With these Dispatches, then to th' Field
> Where like the vig'rous Jove I will enjoy
> This Semele in a Storm, 'twill deaf her Cries
> Like Drums in Battle, lest her Groans shou'd pierce
> My pittying Ear, and make the amorous Fight less fierce.

No wonder this play was popular, with a program of villainy like that.

We next return to the heath, for the scene before the hovel (III, iv). This is telescoped with a badly mangled version of III, vi, the scene in the farmhouse. The fantastic trial of the sisters is excised. Finally Edgar withdraws, while Gloster and Kent take the King away to shelter. Cordelia and Arante[9] now arrive (luckily for them) before the hut, followed by the two ruffians, who seize them. At their shrieks, Edgar rushes out and drives away their captors. He reveals his identity, and is rewarded by Cordelia with the declaration of her love. I quote a few speeches as a fair sample of the curious mixture of extravagance and bathos that composes Tate's style.

CORD.

> Come to my Arms, thou dearest, best of Men,
> And take the kindest Vows that e're were spoke
> By a protesting Maid.

EDG.

> Is't possible?

CORD.

> By the dear Vital Stream that baths my Heart,
> These hallow'd Rags of thine, and naked Vertue,
> These abject Tassels, these fantastick Shreds,
> (Ridiculous ev'n to the meanest Clown)
> To me are dearer than the richest Pomp
> Of purple Monarchs.

The scene now changes to the palace and Gloster's punishment (III, vii). Edmund pretends to more sensibility than in Shakespeare, since before he goes he sheds a few tears over his father's plight. Goneril does not appear in this scene. To spare his feelings, Cornwall orders Edmund to withdraw, and in an aside Regan bids him seek a certain grotto. The action of Gloster's punishment runs as in Shakespeare, though it is shortened. The scene ends in a long soliloquy by the blinded man; he determines to show himself to the populace, arouse them against the Duke, and then throw himself from some precipice,

> Whence my freed Soul to her bright Sphear shall fly,
> Through boundless Orbs, eternal Regions spy,
> And like the Sun, be All one glorious Eye.

ACT IV

We now see the grotto of dalliance. The scene being drawn discloses "Edmund and Regan amourously Seated, Listning to Musick." Their conversation signifies terms of complete intimacy. Regan gives her lover a ring, and he reciprocates with a picture of himself. In pulling it from his pocket, he inadvertently drops a note, which is read by Regan after he goes. Of course it is from Goneril. An officer arrives with news of the rebellion.

The next scene shows the meeting of Edgar and Gloster (IV, i). As they set out for Dover, they are met by Cordelia and Kent, who seek the King. Gloster urges Kent, whose identity is now revealed, to lead the rebellion.

The scene changes to Goneril's palace. We learn that Edmund is still with Regan, that Goneril has taken her affairs out of her husband's hands, and finally that Cornwall is dead.

the next scene is tagged "Field Scene." It begins with Shakespeare's IV, vi, the supposed ascent of Dover cliff. This whole scene, including the appearance of Lear, and the killing of Oswald, is somewhat reduced but not greatly altered. It is followed by IV, vii, both altered and reduced; the place is of course not the French camp, since there is no foreign invasion. Following Lear's exit the act closes with a warlike speech by Cordelia.

ACT V

The last act opens with an original camp scene in which the plot thickens desperately. Goneril instructs an attendant to prepare a poisonous draught for her sister, who is soon to arrive as Goneril's guest at a banquet. We next hear Edmund's speculation (altered from his soliloquy, V, i) on the future course of his amours. He has already enjoyed Regan, and Goneril thus becomes more attractive. The next scene, in "a Valley near the Camp," is Shakespeare's V, ii. After Edgar leaves, his father soliloquizes, regretting that he is no longer able to take his customary share in the bloody work. The rest of the scene remains practically unchanged.

Next comes an altered version of V, iii. It begins with the entrance of Albany, Goneril, Regan, and Edmund, with Lear, Cordelia, and Kent as prisoners. Albany gives strict injunctions for their good treatment; but in an aside Goneril directs their execution. Edmund, accordingly, instead of telling what he has done with them, as in Shakespeare, begins to argue for their despatch; and, as in Shakespeare, is snubbed by the Duke. The first speeches of the royal ladies are left, but their controversy is then halted; Albany does not reveal his knowledge of the true situation. He is a much less interesting character in Tate than in Shakespeare.

The quarrel over Edmund's affections is terminated by the entrance of the disguised Edgar with his challenge (V, i, 38 f.). This he delivers orally, and the trial is appointed at once. All go out except the prisoners and their guards. We now have the identification of Kent with Caius, and an altered version of Lear's speech (V, iii, 9-17);

> We too alone will sing like birds i' th' cage.

Goneril orders their immediate execution. With the other dignitaries she has come in for the trial. Edgar is recognized as soon as he enters, and his guilty brother is terrified. Their speeches of defiance are greatly altered; Edmund's bastardy is the chief theme. After his fall, and Albany's denunciation of Goneril, Edgar and the Duke go out, while Goneril and Regan remain to quarrel over their dying lover. Regan's boast that she has enjoyed him maddens her sister, who retorts by revealing the poisoning. But Regan announces that she has poisoned Goneril. Edmund declares he loved them both, and dies happy.

The final scene shows a prison. Lear is asleep with his head in his daughter's lap when the assassins enter. Cordelia begs to be strangled first, but as the soldiers begin their task, Lear "snatches a Partizan, and strikes down two of them; the rest quit Cordelia, and turn upon him. Enter Edgar and Albany"—in the nick of time. The former's remarks would cause almost anyone to desist from murder:

EDG.

> Death! Hell! Ye Vultures hold your impious Hands,
> Or take a speedier Death than you wou'd give. . . .
> My dear Cordelia, Lucky was the Minute
> Of our Approach, the Gods have weigh'd our Suffrings;
> W' are past the Fire, and now must shine to Ages.

Albany assigns the whole kingdom except his marriage-portion to Lear, who gives it to Cordelia. Edgar brings the news of her sisters' deaths. Lear bestows his blessing on the lovers, and proposes to retire with Gloster and Kent to some cool cell where they may cheerfully pass in calm reflection the little remainder of their lives. The play ends with a mealy-mouthed speech by Edgar:

> Divine Cordelia, all the Gods can witness
> How much thy Love to Empire I prefer!
> Thy bright Example shall convince the World
> (Whatever Storms of Fortune are decreed)
> That Truth and Vertue shall at last succeed.

Before reviewing the play as a whole, let us notice a few samples of the verbal alteration. Tate worked more freely than either D'Avenant or Dryden; where the earlier adapters would have been content to change a word or two, Tate would often cut loose and retain practically nothing of Shakespeare's. On the other hand, when he did retain Shakespeare's diction he was less apt than either of his predecessors to tamper with it.

Yet that is not saying much. There are many cases of such tampering, a few of which I shall now cite. The text first quoted is in each case that of the Quarto of 1681.[10] Lines are numbered to agree with Dr. Furness's New Variorum Edition. Words replaced are cited from the Praetorius facsimile (London, 1885) of Q 2 (Butter, 1608). Tate's source is certainly the text of the Quartos, not of the Folios, and seems to be Q 2, but there are many exceptions, including Folio corrections, which point to some attempt at collation or to the existence of another text in the theatrical library.[11] This may be a good point for Professor Nicoll. The reason why Quarto 2 was not exclusively used is, of course, its archaic character.

Grammatical corrections are fairly numerous. Example:

> II, ii, 111 (Q 1681, p. 16): "lately." For: "late."

Many changes are modernizations. Examples:

> II, iv, 54 (Q 1681, p. 19): "Spleen." For: "mother."

> II, iv, 180 (Q 1681, p. 21): "confirms." For: "approues."

> III, ii, 44 (Q 1681, p. 24): "Frightens." For: "gallow."

A zeal for clearness accounts for many others. Examples:

> I, i, 54 (Q 1681, p. 3): "more than words can *utter.*"

For: "wield the matter."

I, i, 122, 123 (Q 1681, p. 5):
            "and in her tender Trust
            Design'd to have bestow'd my Age at Ease!"

For: "and thought to set my rest
            On her kinde nursery."

Elegance seems to have been cherished less by Tate than by either of his laureate predecessors. Yet there are some changes which seem due to it. Examples:

I, i, 90, 91 (Q 1681, p. 4): "I can't dissemble."

For: "I cannot heaue my heart into my mouth."

III, ii, 14 (Q 1681, p. 24): "Rumble thy *fill*."

For: "belly full."

The literalization of figurative language and the toning down of impassioned flights could not, of course, operate extensively in a play dealing with madness. Tate frequently refigures, however, and there are occasional cases of literalization. Example:

II, ii, 15 (Q 1681, p. 14): "white liver'd."

For: "lilly liuer'd."

Scores of changes seem to be purely capricious. Examples:

I, i, 121 (Q 1681, p. 5): "Rage."

For: "wrath."

IV, i, 74 (Q 1681, p. 43): "Poverty."

For: "misery."

Tate's version held the stage for a century and a half. Even Dr. Johnson defended his changes, on the ground that the original tragedy is too terrible and that innocence is better rewarded on the stage than afflicted. In vain the voice of Addison was raised in advocacy of the original play; he believed that in Tate's version it had "lost half its beauty."[12]

In the light of the critical canons, this adaptation is a curious hodge-podge. The unities of time and place are disregarded, but the action is more closely knit by the Edgar-Cordelia love story. The excision of the Fool recognizes the principle of strict separation. Like Dryden, Tate cared nothing for the dictum against scenes of violence; we shall find in his version of **Coriolanus** no horror too gory for him. Contrary to the neo-classical rule that love should be kept out of tragedy, it becomes

in Tate's **Lear** the chief motivating force. In Shakespeare we catch glimpses of the sinister affections of the two elder sisters—enough to show us that other dark currents of passion are seething past. Tate not only amplifies these hints, but creates a new love story, equal in importance to the fortunes of Lear. These are not happy changes. The scenes dealing with the Edmund-Goneril-Regan triangle are highly voluptuous; and Cordelia's more decorous passion does not improve her character. She becomes, in fact, almost a Lydia Languish, as in the over-refinement of her feelings in her feigned indifference to Edgar (Act I).

Worst of all is the so-called happy ending. In Tate's alteration the principle of poetic justice receives the most pitiable sacrifice in all the English drama. The preservation of Lear is best condemned in the very words of Shakespeare: "Vex not his ghost," cries Kent, as that tormented spirit languishes,

Vex not his ghost, O let him passe,
he hates him much, that would vpon the wracke
Of this rough world stretch him out longer.

2. *KING RICHARD THE SECOND*

Tate's second revision of Shakespeare was also printed in 1681;[13] there was a second edition ten years later. The play lived, as we have seen, but two days on the stage. In his epistle dedicatory Tate gives rein to his resentment:

I am not ignorant of the posture of Affairs in King Richard the Second's Reign, how dissolute then the Age, and how corrupt the Court; a Season that beheld Ignorance and Infamy preferr'd to Office and Pow'r, exercis'd in Opressing, Learning and Merit; but why a History of those Times shou'd be supprest as a Libel upon Ours, is past my Understanding. 'Tis sure the worst Complement that ever was made to a Prince. . . .

In depicting King Richard, Shakespeare, says Tate, was faithful to history, but the adapter has been at pains to "elevate" him:

I have every where given him the Language of an Active, Prudent Prince. Preferring the Good of his Subjects to his own private Pleasure. . . . Nor cou'd it suffice me to make him speak like a King (who as Mr. Rhymer says in his Tragedies of the last Age considered, are always in Poëtry presum'd Heroes) but to Act so too, viz. with Resolution and Justice. Resolute enough our Shakespear (copying the History) has made him, for concerning his seizing old Gaunt's Revennues, he tells the wise Diswaders,

Say what ye will, we seize into our Hands
His Plate, his Goods, his Money and his Lands.

But where was the Justice of this Action? This Passage I confess was so material a Part of the Chronicle (being the very Basis of Bullingbrook's Usurpation) that I cou'd not in this new Model so far transgress Truth as to make no mention of it; yet for the honour of my Heroe I suppose the foresaid Revennues to be Borrow'd onely for the present Exigence, not Extorted. . . .

My Design was to engage the pitty of the Audience for him in his Distresses, which I cou'd never have compass'd had I not before shewn him a Wise, Active and Just Prince. Detracting Language (if any where) had been excusable in the Mouths of the Conspirators . . . but I wou'd not allow even Traytors and Conspirators thus to bespatter the Person whom I design'd to place in the Love and Compassion of the Audience. . . .

Further, to Vindicate ev'n his Magnanimity in Regard of his Resigning the Crown, I have on purpose inserted an intirely new Scene between him and his Queen, wherein his Conduct is sufficiently excus'd by the Malignancy of his Fortune, which argues indeed Extremity of Distress, but Nothing of Weakness.

Yet, complains Tate, "a positive Doom of Suppression *without Examination*" ended the play's run on the third day. And this despite the fact that "Every Scene is full of Respect to Majesty and the dignity of Courts, not one alter'd Page but what breaths Loyalty."

Turning from political to aesthetic considerations, the adapter excuses his introduction of comic relief, which he

> judg'd necessary to help off the heaviness of the Tale, . . . though less agreeable to strictness of Rule; [this change is] confirm'd by our Laureat's last Piece, who confesses himself to have broken a Rule for the Pleasure of Variety.* The Audience (says he) are grown weary of melancholly Scenes, and I dare prophesie that few Tragedies (except those in Verse) shall succeed in this Age if they are not lightned with a course of Mirth.
>
> *Epst. Ded. to the Span. Fryar.

ACT I

Tate begins with Shakespeare's opening scene, which is not greatly altered, though speeches are reduced and rearranged and there is a good deal of minor tampering with diction. Scene ii follows, as in Shakespeare; it begins with an original soliloquy by the Duchess. Gloster's opening speech is transposed and follows the Duchess's lamentation. Immediately after, York comes in. Only slightly comic in Shakespeare, he is broadly so in Tate; he is simply a funny fat man. Like his brother, he refuses to take up the Duchess's cause.

The third scene shows the pavilion at the lists.[14] It is little altered. The speeches are cut down and there is some verbal tampering, but not much. Richard's exit speech is taken from Shakespeare's next scene (I, iv, which Tate omits); it is composed of lines 38-40 of Green's advice to prosecute the war in Ireland, and line 42 of Richard's decision to go there in person. The parting of Gaunt and Bolingbroke is cut down to 20

lines from 57; it is largely original with Tate and is a deplorable change, for instead of the emphasis on the human side of the parting Tate allows Bolingbroke to express his already meditated designs on the throne. But with this exception there is no serious structural alteration.

ACT II

Omitting Shakespeare's I, iv, in which Richard actually expresses his longing for his uncle's death, a species of royal turpitude that was too much for Tate's loyalty, Act II opens as in Shakespeare at the deathbed of John of Gaunt. The old lion's eulogy of England is nearly all excised, I suppose because it contains serious charges against Richard; eight lines of it are introduced later, in the King's presence. In its stead, the comic York expresses forebodings of disaster. Tate gives him Richard's lines in the preceding scene (I, iv, 24-34) descriptive of Bolingbroke's cultivation of the commons. York's part is also fattened with exposition of the rebellion in Ireland, and includes what looks like a topical hit on the court of Charles II:

> all goes worse and worse in Ireland, Rebellion is there on the Wing, and here in the Egg; yet still the Court dances after the French Pipe, Eternal Apes of Vanity: Mutiny stirring, Discipline asleep, Knaves in Office, all's wrong.

Gaunt's warning to the King is echoed by York; Richard meekly accepts their correction, thanks them for it, and puts up a pious petition for his uncle's long life. As Tate points out in his preface, the King seizes the revenues only temporarily:

> Be Heav'n our judge we mean him nothing fowl
> But shortly will with interest restore
> The Loan our sudden streights make necessary.

Piercy, that is, young Hotspur, is added to the group of lords who remain to plot, and is given some original lines and some stolen from those of his associates.

Scene ii (not so marked) corresponds to Shakespeare's II, ii, 67 f.; the Queen's conversation with the King's favorites and the exposition there given of the rebellion are omitted. The scene begins with Bushy's line, "Despair not Madam," which is spoken by a lady in waiting. York cuts a ridiculous figure; to the Queen's demand that he "speak comfort," he replies (in prose):

> Comforts in Heav'n, and we are on the Earth, nothing but crosses on this side of the Moon; my heart stews in Choller, I shall dissolve to a Gelly. That your Husband shou'd have no more wit than to go a Knight Erranting whilst Rogues seize all at home, and that I shou'd have no more wit than to be his Deputy at such a proper time: to undertake to support a crazy Government, that can scarce carry my own Fat.

The scene ends with his exit, since Bushy, Green, and Bagot do not appear in Tate's version. This reduction of casts is typical of the altered versions.

Scene iii follows in reduced form. It begins seven lines before the arrival of Ross and Willoughby, who according to Tate bring the news of the dispersal of the Welsh royalists. Berkeley is not among Tate's characters. York enters eight lines after Ross and Willoughby, and addresses his hypocritical nephew in excellent (Shakespearean) blank verse, which is highly inconsistent with his previous utterances. To Bolingbroke's protest against the confiscation York reiterates Tate's palliation:

> Thy words are all as false as thy Intents,
> The King but for the Service of the State,
> Has Borrow'd thy Revenue for a time,
> And Pawn'd to me his Honour to repay it,
> Which I as Gaunt Executour allow'd.

This explanation fails to satisfy the heir; he arrests his uncle, and the scene closes with York's reproaches.

Scene iv is an original low comedy scene in which the rabble, consisting of "a Shoomaker, Farrier, Weaver, Tanner, Mercer, Brewer, Butcher, Barber, and infinite others with a Confused Noise" debate the respective merits of a republic and a commonwealth, and then engage in a free-for-all fight, some shouting "no Laws, no Laws, no Laws," and others, "Laws, Laws, Laws." Bolingbroke and his forces come in. Young Piercy is all for sweeping the rabble aside. But Bolingbroke is too politic for such methods; the mob is easily swayed by his flattery. He makes the mistake of pretending not to desire the crown; but when he sees the temper of the crowd, quickly retrieves himself and professes his readiness to "take the burden of the State." The leader of the mob counsels him not to be chicken-hearted, and, now secure in his ascendency, Bolingbroke exemplifies this advice by ordering the leader hanged; the act ends with the shouts of the rabble for their new hero.[15]

ACT III

Shakespeare's II, iv, the dispersal of Salisbury's Welsh troops, is omitted by Tate, the necessary exposition having been given. Shakespeare's III, i, is also omitted, since the King's favorites do not appear in Tate's version. The third act begins, therefore, with Shakespeare's III, ii, Richard and his adherents before Berkeley castle. The scene is greatly cut down. After Richard's prediction that the rebels will melt away, Carlile speaks two lines from the same speech (III, ii, 54, 55), and the fatuous Richard closes the scene with a new couplet:

> Move we secure then in our Royal Right,
> To th' Traytors Executions, not to Fight.

The bad news brought by Salisbury and Scroop is postponed by Tate in order to introduce the Queen's scene in York garden. This it is necessary to move forward,

since Tate intends to bring the Queen to Richard's side while he is still in the field. The second scene, then, of this act is a grievously abridged version of Shakespeare's III, iv, the Queen and the Duchess of York exchanging original speeches of apprehension. The whole scene is verbally altered.

Scene iii takes us back to Shakespeare's III, ii, where Tate's III, i, ended. The place is a heath, where Richard is met successively by Salisbury and Scroop with their news of disaster. Richard's great speech of despair, beginning

> No matter where, of comfort no man speake,

is cut from 34 to 24 lines, and badly garbled besides. The scene is prolonged after the news of York's capture (as it becomes in Tate), by the entrance of the Queen, the Duchess of York, and their train. The scene then turns into a love passage between the unhappy monarch and his consort, who assures him:

> This Kingdom yet, which once you did prefer
> To the worlds sway, this Beauty and this Heart
> Is Richards still, millions of Loyal thoughts
> Are always waiting there to pay you homage.
> That glorious Empire yields to you alone,
> No Bullingbrook can chase you from that Throne.

At this tender invitation, Richard incontinently orders:

> We'll march no farther, lead to th' Castle here,

a change of plan which, in view of the King's political situation, reminds us of the celebrated simile of Mr. Bayes in *The Rehearsal*.

Scene iv continues with Shakespeare's III, iii, Bolingbroke's appearance before Flint castle, and Richard's surrender. Piercy is already present with his father; it is Ross who comes with the report of the castle's strength. York is much more loyal and defiant in Tate's version than in the original. Speeches are reduced and altered; otherwise the scene is little changed.

ACT IV

In place of the accusation of Aumerle as guilty of Gloster's death, and the subsequent quarrel between him and Surrey, Fitzwater, and Piercy, Tate gives us several short scenes emphasizing the new interests he has brought into the plot. The first is between Aumerle and his father. Both are hostile to Bolingbroke, York in prose and Aumerle in blank verse. The usurper has sent for York to seek his counsel, but the old man refuses to go. He retires, and the Duchess comes in, and urges her son to restrain his father's rashness.

Next the Queen appears, "supported by Ladies." She is evidently the only person unaware of the King's decision to abdicate, but she prophesies evil none the less.

The King now enters, dressed in mourning. The attendants are dismissed, and he tells the Queen of his decision. She implores him to die rather than yield the Crown. He answers in typical Tatese:

> Permit me briefly to recount the steps,
> By which my Fortune grew to this distress.
> Then tell me, what cou'd Alexander do
> Against a Fate so obstinate as mine.

The Queen "Weeps over him," and inquires whether none will strike for "an injur'd King." Richard will not hear of further attempts, and the loving couple sadly separate.

Scene ii is Shakespeare's IV, i, beginning with line 107. York's announcement of Richard's willingness to abdicate is given to Northumberland. There is little other alteration, except in diction, to the end of the scene. York then draws a fine distinction, in terms of current political philosophy, between royalty and the King's person. He is thus able to promise obedience to King Henry IV, though he reserves the right to pity Richard. The latter remains on with Carlile, to whom he counsels patience. There is no suggestion of a counter-revolution.

Act V

The first two scenes of this act are transposed by Tate. The first is Shakespeare's V, ii, beginning with the description of the contrasting receptions of Richard and Henry by the populace. This is assigned to Aumerle, not to York. The latter comes in and protests he cannot blame his son for grieving. On top of that profession, and most inconsistently with York's position during the whole play up to this point, his discovery of his son's complicity is as in the original. The scene as altered is played in a much lower key. To the Duchess's passionate remonstrance,

> Hadst thou groan'd for him, York, as I have done,

the fat man cleverly replies,

> And art e'en like to groan for him again. Away.

The transposition of this scene with Shakespeare's V, i, gives longer suspense for the fate of Aumerle, since that scene intervenes between his discovery and his pardon.

Scene ii follows Shakespeare structurally, but the dialogue is rewritten. The Queen has put on mourning; for

> Thus dead in Honour, my Lord and I[16]
> Officiate at our own sad Funeral.

Instead of strengthening her dejected Lord, Tate's Queen invites him to

> Lean on my Brest whilst I dissolve to Dew,
> And wash thee fair agen with Tears of Love.

The height of the ridiculous is scaled in Richard's last speech before Northumberland and the Guards tear them asunder:

RICH.

> Now Heaven I thank thee, all my Griefs are paid!
> I've lost a single frail uncertain Crown,
> And found a Virtue Richer than the World:
> Yes, Bird of Paradise, wee'll pearch together,
> Sing in our Cage, and make our Cell a Grove.
> *Enter Northumberland, Guards.*

NORTH.

> My Lord, King Bullingbrook has chang'd his Orders,
> You must to Pomfrett Castle, not to th' Tower;
> And for you, Madam, he has given Command
> That you be instantly convey'd to France.

KING.

> Must I to Pomfrett, and my Queen to France?
> Patience is stale, and I am weary ont 't [*sic*],
> Blood, Fire, rank Leprosies and blewest
>   Plagues. . . .

Permit is a favorite verb with Tate; he begins Richard's concluding speech with it:

> Permit yet once our Death-cold Lips to joyn,
> Permit a Kiss that must Divorce for ever,
> I'll ravish yet one more, farewell my Love!
> My Royal Constant Dear farewel for ever!
> Give Sorrow Speech, and let thy Farewell come,
> Mine speaks the Voice of Death, but Thine is dumb.

Critics (like Mr. Shaw) of Shakespeare's romantic incorrigibility should study the Restoration versions to learn, not that Shakespeare was unromantic, but that his good sense usually restrained his romanticism. Compared with the tragic writers of the Restoration, and for that matter with the nineteenth-century romantics, Shakespeare seems severely realistic, austere, and classical.

The third scene is Shakespeare's V, iii, the pardoning of Aumerle. York is even more disgusted with the King's clemency than is Shakespeare. In the speech with which he ends the scene Henry includes his hint that the murder of Richard would be acceptable. Thus Shakespeare's brief scene of exposition (V, iv) becomes unnecessary; its omission is doubtless an improvement.

The last scene begins, like Shakespeare's V, v, with Richard's long soliloquy, though this is curtailed. An amazing example of Restoration taste is incorporated in this passage:

A Table and Provisions shewn.
What mean my Goalers [*sic*] by that plenteous Board?
For three days past I've fed upon my Sighs,
And drunk my Tears; rest craving Nature, rest,
I'll humour thy dire Need and tast this food,
That only serves to make Misfortune Live.
Going to sit, the Table sinks down.

Apparently the patrons of Dorset Garden insisted that some use should be made of the mechanical features of that stage, whatever the subject of the play. It is difficult to see why else table-sinking should be introduced here. Its employment in *The Tempest* must have scored a tremendous hit, the delight of which lasted long after it had ceased to be a novelty.

The interview with the trusty groom (V, v, 67-94) is omitted in favor of the arrival of letters from the Queen. The King is in the seventh heaven and sits down to answer them when

Enter Exton and Servants.

[RICHARD].

Furies! What means this Pageantry of Death?
Speak thou the foremost Murderer, thy own hand
Is arm'd with th' Instrument of thy own Slaughter,
Go thou and fill a room in Hell,
Another Thou.   [*Kills 4 of them.*]

But, despite this extraordinary prowess, the scene ends as in Shakespeare with Richard's death and Exton's repentance.

Scene v is Shakespeare's V, vi; York does not appear in it. Henry's remorse is more outspoken, and so more "loyal."

Structurally Tate has made few serious alterations. The most important is Bolingbroke's winning of the rabble. This is amusingly done and probably acted well enough. More serious is the "elevation" of Richard's character, a feat on which Tate plumes himself in his preface. As a matter of fact, it spoils the play. The fall of Shakespeare's Richard would not be so tragic if he were only a weakling; his energy in the earlier scenes makes his collapse more striking. We cannot sympathize greatly with Tate's Richard, whose only virtues are negative. The adapter tries to engage our sympathy for the lover, but the picture is overdrawn and Richard becomes uxorious. The Queen, instead of being his foil in the last act, is merely a feminine counterpart of her husband. York is the only other character that suffers alteration. He is not elevated, but degraded to a buffoon.

Of verbal tampering there is a good deal, yet not so much as in either D'Avenant's or Dryden's alterations. Here again Tate works with a freer hand. The following illustrations of his changes are characteristic. The text first cited is in each case that of the Cambridge edition

(Clark and Wright, vol. iv, 1864). Lines are numbered to agree with this edition, on which I have relied for variant readings except in the case of Q 5, which I have collated by means of the Praetorius facsimile (1887). Words replaced are cited from the latter text.

That Q 5, issued in 1634, is Tate's source I cannot state certainly, not having made an exhaustive collation. The pre-Wars texts of **Richard the Second** fall into two groups: (1) Q 1, 2, 3, 4; (2) Fs, Q 5. Q 5 is printed from the Folios text. Tate's alteration was printed in 1681; its source is certainly group (2), and probably Q 5.[17]

Tate was no such man of parts as Dryden or even D'Avenant, and his changes were not guided by principles so clearly distinguishable. Yet some categories can be set up. Modernization accounts for many of the adapter's changes. Examples:

I, i, 4 (Q 1681, p. 1): "th' Impeachment lately charg'd."

For: "the boysterous late appeale."

III, ii, 36 (Q 1681, p. 25): "*Desponding* Cousin."

For: "Discomfortable."

Metrical considerations account for other changes. Example:

IV, i, 148 (Q 1681, p. 41): "Prevent [it], resist it, stop this breach in Time." Om. Q 1681, followed by Pope.

Efforts to clear up the meaning are less numerous in Tate than in either D'Avenant or Dryden, but I have noticed a few changes which appear to have that object. Examples:

II, iii, 84 (Q 1681, p. 19): "feign'd." For: "deceivable."

V, iii, 35 (Q 1681, p. 50): "To win thy *future* Love I pardon Thee."

For: "after—."

The same is true of elegance. Tate's was not an elegant mind. But the following passage seems to be a feeble attempt to rise above earthly diction:

IV, i, 184, 185 (Q 1681, p. 41):
"Now is this Crown a Well wherein two Vessels
That in successive Motion rise and fall."

For: Now is this Golden Crowne like a deepe Well,

That owes two Buckets filling one another."

But by far the greatest number of Tate's changes appear to be simply capricious. Examples:

I, i, 8: "sifted." For: "sounded."

I, i, 12: "sound." For: "sift."

I, i, 92 (Q 1681, p. 3): "Combate." For: "battel."

III, ii, 39 (Q 1681, p. 25): "Then Thieves and Robbers *do securely Range.*"

For: "raunge abroad unseene."

III, ii, 45, 46 (Q 1681, p. 25): "Dismantled from the Cloak of Night, stand bare, And Tremble at their own Deformity!"

For:

"(The Cloake of Night being pluckt from off their backes) Stand bare and naked, trembling at themselves."

Cf. Tate's second line with Shakespeare's *Richard III*, I, i, 27:

"And descant on mine own deformity."

III, iv, 29 (Q 1681, p. 26): "Peaches." For: "Apricocks."

III, iv, 34 (Q 1681, p. 26): "Sprigs." For: "sprayes."

Many other examples might be cited. Trifling of this sort is not so serious as the bold mangling of D'Avenant and Dryden, but it is hardly less discreditable.

Taking the play as a whole, Tate's structural changes seem to be motivated, chiefly, by his desire for "elevation." The unities are no more observed than in Shakespeare; there is more comedy; and there is no attempt to dodge scenes of violence. Tested by the canons Tate's version is a wretched failure; it conforms only in its elevation of its hero's character; and this in fact degrades him no less than the elevation of Cleopatra and Cressida at the hands of Dryden. As in his *Lear,* Tate emphasizes the love motive above all else, and here the sinister influence of the heroic play is once more visible.

A cleverer policy on the part of the court would have allowed Tate to produce his play unmolested, for it would undoubtedly have died as speedy a natural death as did his next Shakespearean venture. But censors have rarely been distinguished for their cleverness.

3. THE INGRATITUDE OF A COMMONWEALTH, OR THE FALL OF CAIUS MARTIUS CORIOLANUS

Tate's third and last attempt to improve a Shakespearean drama also had a political inspiration. *Coriolanus,* Professor Odell points out, "seemed destined to be launched, with new trimmings, during or after each of England's successive politico-civic upheavals; Dennis so set it forth after 1715, and Thomson, after the '45."

The Ingratitude was printed in quarto in 1682.[18] Tate's dedicatory epistle to this play is much briefer than those to his *Lear* and his *Richard II.* He owns that he has again

launcht out in Shakespear's Bottom. Much of what is offered here, is Fruit that grew in the Richness of his Soil; and what ever the Superstructure prove, it was my good fortune to build upon a Rock.[19]

This time, he carefully points out, the satire is unmistakably for the Whigs.

Upon a close view of this Story, there appear'd in some Passages, no small Resemblance with the busie Faction of our own time. And I confess, I chose rather to set the Parallel nearer to Sight, than to throw it off at further Distance. . . . Where is the harm of letting the People see what Miseries Common-Wealths have been involv'd in, by a blind Compliance with their popular Misleaders: Nor may it be altogether amiss, to give these Projecters themselves, examples how wretched their dependence is on the uncertain Crowd. Faction is a Monster that often makes the slaughter 'twas designed for; and as often turns its fury on those that hatcht it. The Moral therefore of these Scenes being to Recommend Submission and Adherence to Establisht Lawful Power, which in a word, is LOYALTY.

As always in these alterations, the number of characters is greatly reduced; in this case, to eleven.

ACT I

There is no structural alteration up to the point of the entrance of the Messenger with news from the Volscian war. The senators do not come in; the Messenger announces Martius's appointment as Cominius's second, in place of Titus Lartius, who is supposed to be dead and does not appear in Tate's version. The reluctance of the citizens to go to war is emphasized rather deftly by Tate. The colloquy of the tribunes is reduced from 28 lines to 11.

Shakespeare's I, ii, in which Aufidius makes his first appearance, is omitted by Tate, who passes directly to Shakespeare's I, iii, the Roman women. The prose of the opening speeches is rewritten as blank verse. Thus Shakespeare:

Then his good report should haue beene my Sonne, I therein would haue found issue. Heare me professe sincerely, had I a dozen sons each in my loue alike, and none lesse deere then thine, and my good Martius, I had rather had eleuen dye Nobly for their Countrey, then one voluptuously surfet out of Action.

But Tate:

Then—

His Glory shou'd have been my Darling Son:
Now by Minerva, had the Indulgent Gods
Blest me with Twenty Sons, as much Belov'd
As my brave Martius; I had rather Lose them All
In Chase of Glory, and their Country's Cause,
Than One, i' th' Surfeit of voluptuous Peace.

Tate's Virgilia is more outspoken in her pacifism than Shakespeare's. Valeria turns out to be a Restoration coquette. She enters "Gawdily and Fantastically Drest, follow'd by Six or Seven Pages." Her airs and graces are amusing enough, but hardly suit their surroundings. No mention is made of Young Martius, though the lad is introduced by Tate later on in the play.

Scene iii is Shakespeare's I, iv, 8 f. (I number with Neilson's Cambridge edition), the attack on Corioli, the wager being omitted. It is followed by Shakespeare's I, v, the spoil-laden soldier. I, vi, the arrival of Martius at the camp of Cominius, is left out by Tate, who also omits I, vii, at the gates of Corioli. He goes instead to I, viii, the encounter of Martius with Aufidius. This is followed by Shakespeare's I, ix, the entitling of Martius. Tate seems to have missed Shakespeare's effective stroke of characterization near the end of the scene, when the lordly Martius so lightly lets go by the name of his former host. Yet it seems incredible that this should have gone over Tate's head; perhaps he excised it as a means of elevating his hero's character. Shakespeare's last scene, showing Aufidius's hatred, is also cut by Tate. This compression of the events of the fighting into two scenes instead of six is justifiable, and, on a picture stage, perhaps necessary. Tate has omitted nothing essential to his story, though his tampering with the phrasing is constant and deplorable.

Act II

The second act opens directly with the return of Coriolanus to Rome (Shakespeare's II, i, 179 f.), omitting Menenius's skirmish with the tribunes and the proud and anxious talk of the women. The triumphal entry is thus much less effective than in Shakespeare, since no suspense is created. The conspiracy of the tribunes is abbreviated. Immediately after their resolution (at Shakespeare's II, i, 275) the scene opens and shows the Senate sitting (II, ii); the preliminaries between the officers are omitted, and the scene begins with Coriolanus's remonstrance against the eulogies of his wounds (II, ii, 71 f.). Typical of Tate's condensation is the reduction of Cominius's speech from 41 lines to 25.

The final scene is Shakespeare's II, iii, the solicitation of votes. The debate before Coriolanus's entrance is shortened, and there is much verbal alteration throughout the whole scene.

Act III

The third act begins as in Shakespeare, with the tribunes' warning (III, i, 24 f.) and the broil between the parties. It is followed by III, ii, much altered. This takes place, not in the house of Coriolanus, but in a street, where Volumnia is met "by Valeria, passing by in a Chair." This talkative dame babbles not unamusingly, and goes on her way rejoicing. Then the patricians appear and we have III, ii. It is immediately followed by Shakespeare's III, iii, 39 f., the people entering the street.

The next scene, Coriolanus's parting from his family and friends (IV, i), is not tagged by Tate; probably the scene did not change and the farewell was said in the street. The adapter possessed a remarkable facility in the invention of imprecations, and Volumnia is assigned in this scene a number of mouth-filling curses. Tate brings in, rather effectively, the young son of Martius, who begs to accompany his father into exile.

Act IV

We now pass directly to the arrival of Coriolanus at the enemy's city (IV, iv). Both Shakespeare's intervening scenes, Volumnia baiting the tribunes (IV, ii), and the expository scene on the highway (IV, iii), are omitted. In Tate, however, it is to Corioli, not to Actium, that the exiled general goes. He recognizes Aufidius's house without assistance, and (presumably) the scene draws and reveals its interior. We then have Shakespeare's IV, v. The dispute with the servants is much shortened. Immediately after the conclusion of the scene, we are introduced to Nigridius, a broken Roman officer in the service of Aufidius, whom he inflames with jealousy at the warmth of Coriolanus's reception.

The next scene is Shakespeare's IV, vi, the arrival of the news of Coriolanus's treachery. It is greatly abbreviated, though it is telescoped with a reduced version of Shakespeare's V, i, in which Menenius consents to visit the renegade.

Next comes V, ii, the repulse of Menenius, considerably altered. The sentinels are omitted. On the other hand, Tate manages to crowd into this scene all the Roman efforts to soften Coriolanus. The first of these are in dumb show. Menenius's plea is shortened and turned from prose into blank verse.

After his repulse, the invaders are about to attack the walls, but are met by the family of Coriolanus. The scene is, of course, Shakespeare's (V, iii), but how differently phrased! It begins:

Cor.

Look there, my Mother, Wife, and little Darling,
Are come to Meet our Triumph on its way,
And be Spectators of our keen Revenge. . . .

He greets his wife:

Life of my Life, Fly to me? O a Kiss.

For several speeches the unthinkable proposition is implied that Coriolanus does not know why the women have come. Thereafter Shakespeare's structure is retained, though his diction is mutilated.

ACT V

Tate's last act is brief, but he packs it full of surprise and violence. Shakespeare's V, iv, the arrival of the news of peace, is omitted. On the other hand, Shakespeare's V, v, the honored return of the ladies, furnishes Tate with another excuse for Valeria's babbling; she did not join their mission, and now affects the rôle of committee of welcome. Virgilia receives a letter from Menenius warning her that Nigridius is plotting her husband's ruin. The women determine to return and save him, though how that could possibly have been accomplished Tate does not trouble to suggest.

The next scene is original with the adapter. In voluptuous accents Aufidius confides to Nigridius his passion for Virgilia. News comes that with Volumnia and Young Martius she has entered Corioli. Aufidius orders them seized.

The final scene is in the palace, where the Volscian lords are met in council. It follows Shakespeare's V, vi (though it is much condensed) up to the assassination of Coriolanus, who manages to wound Aufidius. Nigridius comes in with news of an imminent battle between the legions of the two generals.

All rush out except Aufidius, Nigridius, and Coriolanus. The first now tells the dying Roman that Virgilia is in his power. I quote his speech despite its brutality, because it affords a curious view of the pious Tate.

> I charge thee Dye not yet, till thou has seen
> Our Scene of Pleasures; to thy Face I'll Force her;
> Glut my last Minuits with a double Ryot;
> And in Revenges Sweets and Loves, Expire.

Virgilia is brought in wounded; the piteous sight is too much for the ravisher and he dies. Coriolanus now inquires:

> What means that purple Dew upon thy Breast?

Virgilia replies:

> 'tis a Roman Wound,
> Giv'n by Virgilia's Hand, that rather chose
> To sink this Vessel in a Sea of Blood,
> Than suffer its chast Treasure, to become
> Th' unhallowed Pyrates Prize.

With a tender farewell she dies, and Coriolanus begs that "Some kind God descend t' inform me" where Volumnia and his son may be.

Nigridius responds, gloating over his former commander's plight, that the boy has been "Mangled, Gash't, Rack't, Distorted." Coriolanus asks how the torturer disposed of him: "Didst eat him?" Nigridius answers:

> Having kill'd your old Menenius,
> Off'ring his feeble Vengeance, streight I threw
> The Tortur'd Brat, with Limbs all broke . . .
> Into Volumnia's Arms, who still retain'd
> Her Roman Temper; till with bitter Language,
> And most insulting, added to her Suff'rings;
> I rous'd her silent Grief, to loud Disorder. . . .

Mark Coriolanus's phrasing of his agony:

> Convultions! Feavers! blewest Pestilence!
> Sleep on Virgilia. . . .
> *Enter Volumnia Distracted, with Young Martius under
> her Arm.*

We now witness a mad scene, in which Volumnia raves at great length (one of her speeches contains 23 lines), but certainly does not turn thought and affliction, not to mention passion or hell, into either favor or prettiness. At last she snatches a partisan from one of the guards, kills Nigridius with it, and runs off.

But she has dropped the boy. And now succeeds a really "sweet bit," as Mr. Odell calls it, between Coriolanus and his son. The pathos is artificial, and the insistence on physical torture is too painful; but the little scene is affecting, none the less. At last the boy dies and so does Coriolanus, who clasps with one arm the body of his wife, and with the other his son's.

Naturally, the Epilogue is spoken by Valeria.

The verbal changes made by Tate are of the same order as those we have noticed in his ***Lear*** and his ***Richard II.*** It hardly seems worth while to list further examples. Tate worked less on a principle than either D'Avenant or Dryden. Consequently more of his changes seem made without rhyme or reason, while on the other hand he frequently retains phrases which his predecessors would almost certainly have altered.

His play follows Shakespeare's with a reasonable degree of fidelity up to the catastrophe. Tate then cuts loose completely and turns a respectable tragedy into an unpleasant reminder of the old tragedy-of-blood. He evidently aimed at giving his audience a last act they would not easily forget; accordingly he works in a sword combat with the death of both the principals, an attempted rape, a suicidal demise, a mad scene, and a juvenile expiration.

Like Shakespeare's play, Tate's violates all the canons. The unities of time and place are disregarded by both. The unity of action is more observed by Shakespeare than by Tate, whose Valeria scenes are irrelevant to the plot. These also go a long step beyond Shakespeare's in permitting the mingling of comic with tragic. The last scene is one of horrid violence. Poetic justice is flouted by Tate even more than by Shakespeare. Again the love motive is emphasized. Rape is a favorite device with Tate; he uses it in both *Lear* and *The Ingratitude* without the slightest warrant in either source. In spite of this morsel the latter play was a failure; but in the former the poetaster scored a success which more than compensated. Shakespeare's *Coriolanus* seems never to have appeared on the Restoration stage.

Notes

1. Ward [Adolphus William. *A History of English Dramatic Literature to the Death of Queen Anne,* new and revised ed., 3 vols., London, 1899.] (*Camb. Hist. Eng. Lit.,* viii, 41) describes Tate as "a painstaking and talented writer who, with enduring success, adapted *King Lear.*" The *D. N. B.* bluntly calls him a poetaster.

2. It appears in the *Term Catalogue* for May, 1681 (Arber's ed., i, 440).

3. Had the audience indulged in witticisms over Dryden's corpse-paved ending for *Troilus and Cressida,* two years before?

4. For elaborate tables showing Tate's use of Shakespeare's lines, see R. Erzgräber, *Nahum Tate's und George Colman's Bühnenbearbeitungen des Shakespeare'schen King Lear,* Weimar, 1897, pp. 40-44.

5. Shades of Pyramus and Thisbe!

6. An exquisite trope for Cordelia!

7. In spite of the fact that she has counted on it, and has directed her conduct accordingly!

8. A rather casuistical paradox.

9. Erzgräber (p. 52) points out that the introduction of the confidante was probably due to French influence. Certainly it was more decorous for Cordelia to make her sweet avowal in the presence of a chaperone.

10. This was reprinted in 1689, *c.* 1690, 1699, *c.* 1710, 1712, 1717, 1729 1733, 1745, 1749, 1750, 1756, 1757, 1759, 1760, 1761, 1763, 1767, etc. etc. See Jaggard, [William. *Shakespeare Bibliograpohy,* Stratford-on-Avon, 1911,] pp. 356 f. It has recently been reprinted by Mr. Montague Summers in his *Shakespeare Adaptations,* [London] 1922.

11. Erzgräber (p. 14) concludes that Tate's sources are Q 2 and F 3.

12. *Spectator,* No. 40 (April 16, 1711). Cited by Furness, v, 477.

13. It appears in the *Term Catalogue* for June, 1681 (Arber's ed., i, 451). William Allwardt (*Die englischen Bühnenbearbeitungen von Shakespeares King Richard II*; Rostock dissertation, Doberan, 1909, p. 11) concludes that Tate's sources were F 1 and F 3.

14. Professor Odell errs in stating that this scene is omitted (Odell, [George C. D. *Shakespeare from Betterton to Irving,* 2 vols., New York, 1920,] i, 58).

15. Allwardt (p. 20) suggests that Tate's reason for interpolating this scene was to show Bolingbroke in an unfavorable light, thus preparing the audience for his treachery to Richard. It was, rather, chiefly to portray the fickleness of the mob, a favorite theme of "loyal" writers at this time.

16. Tate had a positive genius for falling into tripping measures at solemn moments.

17. For the evidence see my unpublished Harvard dissertation (1923), pp. 457, 458.

18. *Term Catalogue,* Feb. 1682 (Arber's ed., i, 473).

19. Another instance of Tate's genius for absurd metaphor.

H. F. Scott-Thomas (essay date December 1934)

SOURCE: Scott-Thomas, H. F. "Nahum Tate and the Seventeenth Century." *ELH* 1, no. 3 (December 1934): 250-75.

[*In the following essay, Scott-Thomas argues that Tate's work clung to the Elizabethan past, that he struggled unsuccessfully to explore in his writings newer ideas and modes, and that his psychological and intellectual preoccupation with the past resulted in a superficial quality in his writing.*]

> The Restoration contains an appreciable quantity of literary expressions irreducible to the dominant forces at work in the epoch. . . . The Restoration is unable to forget the Renaissance. Not only does it preserve in its innermost self this subconscious remembrance, but it also possesses the other's creative faculties in a latent state, inhibited but always ready to reawaken; and under one form or another, through the artistic expressions of the moment, this secret quality allows itself to be seen or divined.[1]

The work of the Laureate, Nahum Tate, was the product of this quality. He stands, Janus-like, with one face turned towards the past and the other looking to the future. Psychologically, he was entirely out of sympathy with the popular modes. Limited intellectual power put rationalism, neo-classical ideals, and the new scientific method almost entirely beyond his reach, and left him bathing himself in the tepid waters of his own equally limited emotions. Indeed, it is into bourgeois conscientiousness, sentimental virtue, and ready "sensibility," such as his, that the eighteenth century struck its roots and first drew feeble warmth and thin nutriment for the earliest indications of the recrudescence of Elizabethan spirit which was to flower in the Romantic movement, a century later. Yet Tate constantly strove to tickle the palates of his own generation with the fare to which they had become inured. The exigencies, first of his economic situation, and then of his official post, compelled him to grapple with materials and modes which were far beyond his strength, and which were utterly distasteful to him, in an unceasing effort to wring from their stubborn fibres a bare sustenance; and only a death in the Mint[2] released him at length from the dreary struggle. It is to this effort that the superficial, occasional, and generally journalistic character of his work is to be attributed, as well as the all-pervading atmosphere of relaxation and lassitude which hangs over it like a dark cloud.

Two additional circumstances aggravated the situation: Tate was a man of congenital weakness of constitution,[3] which probably left him tired at the start; and he was an Irishman,[4] to whose natural, racial sentimentality and emotionalism all that smacked of the cold, cynical realism of the Restoration must have been particularly discouraging and repellent.

Tate's relation to his period will be rendered the more intelligible if the main tendencies of the era are examined in turn, and duly associated with him. The first of these is neo-classical. With the passing of all the fine careless rapture of the Renaissance, the exhaustion of the inventive faculty, and the satiety of the imagination and of the emotions, a longing had arisen for the equilibrium, rest, peace, tranquillity, and precision which only law and order could give. A suitable and satisfactory code had been found in the literature and culture of the ancient worlds, and behind the massive shoulders of Ben Jonson, an important faction in the English realm of culture had begun to move toward the neo-classical goal.

The march was accelerated, though not inaugurated or directed, by French influence. France had emerged from the Thirty Years' War with the hegemony of Europe in her grasp. She was one. Richelieu and Mazarin had crushed Protestantism at home, even while supporting it abroad, and had established a strong central government. A similar organization shaped the course of the national literature. The Pléiade had promulgated a definite code, and in 1635 the Academy had been organized under Richelieu. France had gone over to classicism under Molière and Boileau.

Even before the civil war, England had felt the influence of France. The French marriage of Charles I and the fondness of the Cavaliers for Gallic manners and customs had drawn the two kingdoms together. Now, the English King and his nobility had lived at the French court, and had returned more strongly imbued with the French influence than would have been possible had the Channel always flowed between them. The Restoration, therefore, represents no sharp break with the past, but rather a quickening under the French stimulus, of movements, English in their origin, but analogous to similar movements on the continent. Even without the Restoration, England must have moved, eventually, toward neo-classicism.

The whole movement was based upon a theory, and looked toward an ideal, both entirely external and objective. It was the calm, tranquil, open-eyed attitude toward life, which refused to allow itself to be hurried or to become irritated or confused by ambition, contradiction, or complexity; It was the balanced, practical, realistic simplicity of matter and of form, that fascinated an age whose eager, ambitious idealism, nascent imagination, and tingling emotions had brought only confusion, bitterness, and repletion. In short, it was an even proportion, a regular organization, a perfection of form, which came to be the ideal of the neo-classical group.

All that was strange, unusual, singular, particular, or exotic, apart from the accepted extravagances of a few *genres* like the heroic tragedy, all that could not be brought into harmony with the whole, or catalogued and classified according to rule, law, and precedent, was to be viewed with distrust, if not with actual dislike and contempt. Conformity, regularity, convention, rule, and discipline, were to be observed and followed. Elegance and deftness were highly esteemed.

Rule, law, and precedent could be found and examined in the works of the ancients, Aristotle, Horace, and a host of lesser lights. These ancients were the rule, law, and order, more remotely, of a sovereign and inviolable code, the code of nature; and more immediately, of the French exponents of classicism, Boileau, Molière, Corneille, and Racine. It was unnecessary to appeal from the ancients, however. They had rendered the laws of nature accessible and intelligible. They had done their work better than the French exponents of classicism. Indeed, so perfectly had they wrought, that to follow them was to follow nature, and never again would it be either necessary or possible for others to perform the same task. It was perfect, complete, final.

To attain to the ideal with any measure of perfection was always quite beyond the comparatively muddled mind of an Englishmen, so incurably Gothic in its very timbre; but the national taste could move in the desired direction, as the Restoration and post-Restoration periods were to show. Accordingly, the group were closely intent upon organization; and after them came Tate, hobbling along, handicapped by his natural limitations and his Irish birth and education, striving to do what they were striving to do, the shadow of shadows.

Throughout his dramatic works[5] he has observed, at least formally, the unities of time and of place, his most marked failure, apart from his Shakespearean adaptations, being in *Injur'd Love,* where his feeble powers made it impossible for him to mould Webster's firmer and more twisted material along the desired lines.[6] Unity of action was always beyond his grasp, just as it is almost always beyond the grasp of any Englishmen. Yet he strove for it in his own vague and indirect way by processes of consolidation and compression, and in some instances by a more direct motivation. To this circumstantial evidence must be added his formal statement in the preface to *King Lear*: "I found the whole . . . a Heap of Jewels, unstrung and unpolisht. . . . 'Twas my good Fortune to light on one Expedient to rectifie what was wanting in the Regularity and Probability of the Tale. . . ." He had laid hold of the classical and neo-classical ideas of organization, even if he had not the strength or genius to give them a more complete and successful application.

To the neo-classical vogue must be ascribed also the polish and regularity of his versification. It is true that in his early plays, following in the steps of Dryden, who in *All for Love* (1677) had abandoned the rhymed couplet, he too sets aside rhyme; but his verse is done consistently with regularity and precision.[7] Such regularity and precision did not come naturally to the man; yet he felt the demand for it, and strove by various devices to attain it, at least formally. Between the years 1677 and 1684, moreover, he was moving steadily towards greater regularity in his poems,[8] and after 1684 his homage to the couplet is almost unbroken, the official occasional poems presenting, except for an odd "Pindaric" ode, an almost unvaried succession of rhymed pentameters. That his heart never was in it, however, is obvious. The early diversified lyrics are, undoubtedly, what came more naturally to him.

Neo-classical "good taste" is evident in his selection of words. Indeed, part of the ludicrous effect of his and Brady's renditions of the Psalms[9] may be traced to the very precision and aptness with which they have chosen their language, such precision and aptness giving an effect of superficial sprightliness and dexterity wholly out of harmony with the dignity and strength of the originals. There is direct evidence, too. Turning again the leaves of the introduction to *Lear,* one comes upon Tate's formal assertion:

> I have one thing more to apologize for, which is that I have us'd less Quaintness of Expression even in the Newest Parts of the Play. I confess, 'twas Design in

me, partly to comply with my Author's Style, to make the Scenes of a Piece, and partly to give it some Resemblance of the Time and Persons here Represented.

In organization, language, and style, therefore, Tate felt and responded to the neo-classical stimulus. It was always unnatural to him, however, and though he practised the tenets with some degree of formal success, his heart never moved with his hand, and he never succeeded in acquitting himself with ease, spontaneity, or brilliance.

Closely allied to neo-classicism, but broader in its scope, was the rationalistic movement. Indeed, in so far as neo-classicism is fundamentally the application to the realm of fine art of the principles of science which are inviolable because they are "nature's," the whole movement may be regarded as essentially only one phase of the general vogue of rationalism which was sweeping over England and permeating the life of the nation in all its various aspects. Rationalism disliked extravagance, imagination, fancy, and emotionalism. It sought order, simplicity, and the universal assent of common intelligence. In short, it did for manners, philosophy, religion, and all else, what neo-classicism was doing for esthetics. It had this, also, in common with neo-classicism: both were based upon a final authority. Here, however, there was a sharp difference; for neo-classicism was founded upon a sanction which was, immediately at least, external and objective, while the rationalist's criterion was internal and subjective, that portion of the intellect which was marked by its very sanity as common to, and equal in, all men. The two could be merged, therefore, rationalism being in a certain sense the potential activity of a faculty, and neo-classicism a code, a channel, into which rational performance might be directed, as, indeed, it came to be directed in such a man as Pope. Such merging was, of course, facilitated and expedited by the fact that both neo-classicism and rationalism were inherently "primitive" and universal in their character. Neo-classicism looked back to a time when men's minds had been unclouded by all the anxieties and perplexities which had arisen with the development of new and different theories and manners in the realm of art and literature; and rationalism strove to regain a position such as it had when the clear light of reason had burnt brightly within the brain of primitive men, before a confused philosophy and theology had half-choked intellectual interpretation, control, and direction.

Historically, Restoration rationalism took its rise in the Renaissance rebellion against scholasticism. Bacon had mapped out the program. But no one had risen to succeed Bacon, and English rationalists had turned aside to examine the manner and nature of Descartes' work before coming under the more congenial direction of Thomas Hobbes. Hobbes had applied the rational faculty to philosophy, theology, and manners, in a radically empirical, and therefore characteristically English, manner. Rationalism languished under the reactionary and pre-Baconian thought of the Puritan tyranny, but blossomed anew, naturally, under the benign rays of the Restoration.

To follow the movement further into all its ramifications and the reactions which it engendered, is clearly beyond the scope of this article; moreover, it was almost entirely beyond the scope of Tate. Pyrrhonism, the Platonism of Cambridge, deism, libertine naturalism, empiricism, and all the other rationalistic and semi-rationalistic movements of the age in their formal and technical aspects left him undisturbed. He was incapable of appreciating them or of modifying his conduct materially under the influence of their rational validity. It was impossible for him to remain completely unaffected, however, and to such traces of the rationalistic method I now turn.

On the positive side, rationalistic method centres about three separate foci. I have said that Tate's whole attitude toward the drama was determined by neo-classical modes. It should now be evident that such an attitude is essentially, if more remotely, rationalistic. To support this general statement we may cite the "happy" ending of *Lear*. Rationalism was held to entail poetic justice. Tate also applied, in a feeble and child-like manner, the rationalistic method to morality. He inveighs against profanity. Why? Because, if there be a God, it is not rational for a mere man to invoke him carelessly; and if there be no God, the whole thing is senseless. Similarly, gambling is rejected because it, too, is irrational, though here there is also a trace of the utilitarian ethics of Locke: If you lose at gaming, it is not sensible to deprive yourself thus; if you win, it is only a matter of time until you lose and are back at the original starting point; and if you do not lose in the second instance, you have simply deprived another of what he ought to have and requires.[10] And so on. Finally, Tate's attitude towards religion is a rationalistic one. Theoretically, it makes him broadly tolerant, with a cosmopolitanism that is fundamentally rationalistic. Religious differences must be respected, but only that they may be compounded by a rationalistic appeal to common sense, which is first to be stimulated and then convinced.[11] It must not be imagined that Tate ever was willing to compromise "orthodox" doctrine.[12] He was merely prepared to be patient until the intelligence of men could be convinced of the reasonableness of Christianity. Once again we hear the echo of the foot-steps of Locke.

On the negative side, Tate's antipathy to atheism on the one hand, and to libertine naturalism on the other, both logical outcomes of a fearless and thoroughgoing application of the rationalistic method to life, brought him into violent opposition to these extreme forms of rationalism. He employs against them the "orthodox" rationalistic method, combined with, once again, the utilitarian ethics of Locke. Atheism is denounced because it is not sensible, but also because it proves of no practical utility in the face of the early physical disintegration of death.[13]

Such is Tate's connection with rationalism. It is easily exaggerated. The method is often rationalistic or semi-rationalistic, but it is clear that the attitude never is. It is, rather, the attitude of vulgar and bourgeois middle-class morality and Christian "orthodoxy," modified by an unedifying utilitarian ethic, which employs the rationalistic method for its own ends.

A third movement of the period is the growth of the scientific spirit. Like neo-classicism, this development has much in common with rationalism, being in some measure the application of the rationalistic principle within the realm of objective phenomena. It takes its departure from both neo-classicism and rationalism, however, in that it does not seek for a single, final authority. Its method is experimental and inductive, Socratic rather than Aristotelian. The fundamental assumption is that sense errs, so that the end sought becomes a principle which will compound all former mistakes and weaknesses. Doubt becomes a necessity, and a pessimistic emphasis upon the weaknesses of men a duty. Science is divorced from rationalism and seems to join hands with scepticism. There is this difference, however: with the sceptic, agnosticism is the result of his effort; with the scientist, it is the beginning. With the scientist, confessed ignorance is the required antecedent condition of a subsequent degree of certainty. Moreover, the scientist holds the positivistic and optimistic belief that sense can be corrected and strengthened. The mind must first be cleared of all earlier errors and prejudices of sense, to prepare the way for natural experiment and accurate observation. Such a complete expunging is, of course, neither possible nor desirable; but it was held to be both, even by such men as Descartes, Bacon, and Boyle. A science of causes thus becomes practically impossible, the scientist seeking only to observe and to record the course and result of experiment, and from such observation to arrive at plausible hypotheses.

Quite obviously, it would be a work of supererogation to follow up the scientific development into all its ramification of Cartesian and Baconian method and psychology. It is evident that with such developments, Tate had but slight formal connections. His most direct contact is through the little scientific and pseudo-scientific miscellany which he edited,[14] and this is supplemented by his translation of Cowley's Latin botanical poem,[15] which introduces him to the science of plants. The Latin poem of Frascatorius on syphilis[16] gives him some insight into the history of venereal disease and its current materia medica. What is more important is the future Laureate's response to the scientific spirit and his occasional adoption of the scientific method.

It is clear that the employment of neo-classical and rationalistic criteria is, in itself, a modified scientific process. These two are based upon the application of general formulae and common hypotheses such as it is the purpose of the scientist to establish. In addition to these, however, Tate's consistently applied taste for collecting and for convenient epitome is basically experimential and scientific. There are occasions, moreover, when he goes even farther and attempts a systematic application of the scientific method, followed by regular estimation and interpretation. The most sustained example occurs in the prose work, **"A Present For the Ladies."**[17] Here Tate begins with a preconceived thesis, and is, accordingly, thus far unscientific. But once the thesis is set aside, the method becomes essentially one of empirical example and careful observation, the conclusions proving to be identical with the presupposed thesis. It must be confessed that the selection of examples is not unprejudiced, nor are the observation and interpretation accurate or intelligent, but these are secondary considerations. Primarily the method is scientific.

A less prejudiced application is to be observed in the life of Horace and the analysis of the prosody of the *Carmina.* Here Tate's method is properly scientific. He presents us with an early bit of research carefully executed. The biographical section is thoughtfully built up, each statement emerging from definite statements by the Latin poet himself, culled directly from the poems. The discussion of the prosody is clear, deliberate, systematic, and equally experimental. Tate never was a scientist in any real sense of the word; but he understood, and was not averse to, scientific method. On occasion he could apply it, although only to comparatively superficial material, with a considerable degree of thoroughness and success.

Tate's prose style was fused in a scientific furnace. This was the age which developed the modern mode, vigorous and non-rhetorical. Rational inquiry of the early Renaissance had found prevailing styles inadequate, and had supplemented the Ciceronian cult and the manner of the Greek orator with the more satisfactory medium of "Attic prose," founded upon the literary monuments of the silver age of ancient literature. In time, however, both "curt" and "loose" styles had run to seed in ornament and wit. The Ciceronian manner had persisted throughout the seventeenth century, but the Attic development had stimulated a close criticism of it. The struggle was against obscurity.

In England the cry became more compelling after the Restoration. Scientific complaint of the inadequacy of both styles was met by scholastic emphasis upon form.

Science demanded simplicity in vocabulary and mathematical accuracy of arrangement. It is easy to stress the scientific protest too highly, however. Dissatisfaction was rife outside scientific circles, and scientists themselves recognized that a close mathematical manner could be required in science and philosophy alone. The racial idea of the *honnête homme* strove against a style which manifestly had been developed for the Court. Boyle thought it proper for a gentleman to write and speak plainly, though differently from a scientist. Sermonizing had its effects, too. The enthusiastic excesses of Dissent provoked a more controlled manner in the Establishment, but the Establishment, in its turn, was moved by Dissent to ways, plain, practical, and affectionate. Commerce made its demands for brevity and simplicity; but most important of all was the complete change in literary taste, in harmony with the Augustan spirit of the age and its stress upon the regularity and uniformity of nature.

It was in the midst of these demands, cultural, ecclesiastical, rational and practical and therefore scientific, that Tate's prose style was forged. The result was terse, plain, and unaffected. He seldom writes at length. His sentences are consistently brief. His arrangement is straightforward and logical, and his selection of words, simple, adequate, and familiar.

Tate's immediate connection with the scientific movement, then, was small; but indirectly, he owed much to its attitude, outlook, and method, which frequently modified and shaped his work.

With neo-classicism, rationalism, and science, therefore, Tate had formally but slight contacts. It is when we turn to tendencies less severely logical and intellectual that we find him more closely subjoined. The moral trend of the period could claim him as one of its own. It is true that it had its rationalistic aspects, in that rationalism held that sound morality was based upon good sense, and in that morality, up to a point, employed the rationalistic method; but morality was not satisfied to remain merely within the limits of the intellect, and once outside these limits, it became essentially passionate or emotional, and, accordingly, irrational. With the progressive drying up of the springs of the emotions beneath the ascending sun of the Restoration, emphasis was laid more and more upon ethics and morality. In the smartest and most brilliant circles, religious enthusiasm and sentiment died, and in their places came moral dialectic and ethical discussion. That was as far as the sprightly and disillusioned members of those circles could go. Moralists had always been numerous, but now expression began to be clear, pleasant, and elegant. What had been consistently marked by the heavy seal of scholasticism and Church teaching, and shaped by tradition and orthodoxy, now became the legitimate and common possession of all educated people. It was out of such discussion that the generally accepted dictum emerged that poetry should have at its heart a moral. There was a classical precedent for it, and in this way morality and neo-classicism were drawn closely together. Aristotle had said that poetry should present phenomena not as they are but as they ought to be. For this reason he had held poetical fiction greater than historical truth. It could be more easily moulded, and in a philosophic sense, it was even truer than history; for it could be given a more general significance and a wider application. Moreover, through the potential novelty of fiction, a pleasure could be added to literature, impossible to the mere recording of temporal fact. The sequence was normal and logical. Without a fable, there could be no epic or tragedy, and without a potential moral application, there could be no fable. Once this point had been attained, it took but a moment for less carefully-balanced and hard-headed individuals to take the final step pointed out by emotion and sentiment and to insist, as Dennis came to insist, that all great poetry must be religious. With such a theory and with such a position Tate was bound to be in sympathy, and the stupendous achievement of Milton overshadowing the more characteristic work of the period was an inexhaustible treasure-house of illustration and argument.

That Tate *was* influenced by Milton has already been demonstrated by Professor Havens, and it is now possible to supplement Professor Havens's material with additional citations. Most significant is a poem published in 1691 and entitled ***A Poem Occasioned by the late Discontents & Disturbances in the State. with Reflections upon the Rise and Progress of Priest-craft*** . . . Here, *Lycidas,* which up to this time had made scarcely any impression on English literature, is the work that Tate has in mind. The ecclesiastical situation in which he wrote was not basically different from that in which Milton had found himself fifty-four years before. Milton had found the clergy idle, indifferent, and dissipated; Tate thought that he found them stubborn, malicious, treacherous. The recent settlement under William had left many knotty problems unsolved. Not the least formidable of these was the difficulty of the non-juring High Churchmen who, having taken an oath of allegiance to the House of Stuart, now declared themselves unable conscientiously to take a similar pledge to the House of Nassau, and were even ready for the return of James from the continent. Tate inveighs in the preface against this faction in a manner which smacks strongly of the splendid outbursts and sweeping prose denunciations of the outraged Milton:

> . . . After so happy and wonderful a Revolution as we have seen, when our Hopes were grown desperate, and our Liberty reduc'd to its very last gasp. to have the only Remedy in Nature so effectually apply'd, so Miraculous a Recovery perform'd; after all this to find Englishmen, and such as pretend to no other Interest or Religion but That of their Country; to find Them ex-

> pressing Dissatisfaction, everywhere Busie in sowing Dissension, obstructing, as far as in them lies, the Progress of Affairs, and unhinging the present Settlement (upon which alone depends the Safety of these Nations, and common Quiet of Europe). . . .

> In tracing the Occasions of the late Disturbances and Discontents of the State, I was unwillingly brought within the Verge of the Church. There is no Man that has a greater Veneration for the Sacred Function and Order or the Discipline and Worship by Law establish'd; neither does the Passive Principle itself, that has so nearly endanger'd the Shipwreck both of State and Church; derive its Source from the pure Foutnain of our Reformation: 'Twas a new-sprouted Tail of the Dragon, that swept many of our Stars, tho' but few of the First Magnitude; most whereof recover'd themselves as soon as they were sensible of the Consequence. . . .

> There is no Person so obscure or inconsiderable but might have observed our most zealous Protestants, both Church-men and Dissenters, to have been all along Properties to the common Enemy; so visible have been the Triumphs and Insultings of Roman Emissaries upon the Animosities they have sown amongst us, and of which they reckon'd shortly to reap the Harvest.

After the manner of *Lycidas,* the poem, itself, as the complete title indicates, is cast in the pastoral mould. The usual pastoral dialogue is carried on between two shepherds, Palæmon and Philander. The national life during the period of Roman domination in the Church is described thus (p. 4):

> The vile Remembrance we can scarce support,
> How Vermin to our Palace did resort,
> And Nations purg'd their Scum into our Court.
> The Rogue was qualify'd for Magistrate,
> Tribunals then were Shambles of the State.

Of course, in 1691, the whole history of the trouble may be traced to the one and only possible source, Rome; and it is in this passage that Tate shows most definitely his debt to Milton. For purposes of convenient comparison Milton's lines may be set down too:

Tate

> Mark the whole Chain of Publick Woes, you'll find
> The last Link still to the Priest's Girdle join'd.
> *Pan* prosper me, as I the Function hold
> Most Sacred, and the Watchman of the Fold;
> But hate the Shepherds who their Labour spare,
> To Hirelings leave their Flocks, their only Care
> To call at Sheering-time for an ungodly Share
> Fleece-worn, and with an Amaryllis sped,
> They Pipe and Feast, and jocund Measures tread,
> While their lean Sheep look up, and are not fed.
> Nor care which way, make but the stipend large,
> Through Door or Breach they climb into the Charge.
> Profit with them is Grace's loudest Call;
> Preferment's Sacred, let the Blessing fall
> From a Court-Mistress, or a Priest of Baal.
> From hence, from this corrupted Fountain's Head,
> The poyson'd Stream of *Passive Nonsense* spread:
> . . .

Milton
Of other care they little reckoning make,
Than how to scramble at the shearer's feast,
And shove away the worthy bidden guest; . . .
To sport with Amaryllis in the shade, . . .
What recks them? What need they? They are sped;
And when they list, their lean and flashy songs
Grate on their scrannel pipes of wretched straw;
The hungry sheep look up, and are not fed, . . .
Enow of such, as for their bellie's sake
Creep, and intrude, and climb into the fold? . . .
But swoln with wind and the rank mist they draw;
Rot inwardly, and foul contagion spread: . . .

The poem concludes with a short history of the Church of England.

This is, perhaps, as ambitious an occasional poem as Nahum ever achieved. It is of a length which is unusual in our poet, and there is a solidarity and a fixity of purpose about it, even in the introductory remarks, which can be found but seldom elsewhere in his work and which may very well be the result of the obvious transfusion of Miltonic blood which he had just undergone. Changing opinions and the mitigation of ancient suspicions and animosities have made many of the lines obscure and much of the phraseology irrelevant, as has been the case with Milton himself; yet the work stands easily as one of the strongest accomplishments in the realm of the poetry of Tate's younger manhood.

The influence of Milton seems to appear again in a pastoral poem published the same year and entitled *A Poem occasioned by His Majesty's Voyage to Holland, the Congress at the Hague, and Present Siege of Mons.* . . . The shepherd Philander dreams that he is carried away to Elysium. There he is met by Cowley, who shows him a vision of all the great poets of England, among them, Milton himself. The other poets are singing the glories of Edward and Henry, the heroes of Crecy and Agincourt, so naturally, Milton sings William and the Boyne (p. 5):

Behold where *Milton* Bower'd in Laurel Groves.
A Task beyond his warring Angels moves,
Himself a Seraph now with sacred flame
Draws Schemes proportion'd to great *William's* Fame;
(For Commonwealth no more his Harp he strings,
By *Nassau's* Virtue Reconcil'd to Kings)
Ere long the Sacred Numbers He will joyn
And bring his Heroe thund'ring to the Boyne.

Philander is now given a supplementary vision of William's present and future activities, and a detailed description of the Boyne brings the poem to a close.

The general influence of Milton is marked throughout the work. The whole fiction of the vision of the future is Miltonic, though certainly not only Miltonic, and the direct references indicate that Tate had in mind the great English epic.

The name and work of Milton were further exploited by the Laureate, in the interests of his ill-starred *Monitor.* In the thirteenth number, p. [2], he apologizes for his prosody thus:

We have presented the Two first Copies in their own Antique Dress, Antiquity in Expression, as well as on Other Accounts, being, on some Persons Sentiments, venerable; and this was our great *Milton's* Persuasion and Practice.

And in a later number (20) Milton's glorious invocation of the Heavenly Muse has been rewritten by a sincere but mediocre man as follows:

Thou sacred Spirit, thou alone,
Who know'st th'Arcana of Heav'n's shining Throne
And with expanded Wing
Sat Brooding on the *Universe,*
Reducing *Chaos* unto Form
And into Amity its Hetrogenial Storm; . . .

And chiefly thou, O Spirit, . . .
. . . thou from the first
Wast present, and with mighty wings outspread
Dove-like sat'st brooding on the vast abyss,
And mad'st it pregnant: . . .

Historically, the moralistic movement took its more immediate rise, like the other movements of the century, in the Renaissance. Against the classical and neoclassical use of the Olympic pantheon in epic and tragedy had come the literary protest of Tasso and of Spenser. The struggle had gone on in France until the all-powerful name of Boileau carried the day—appended to a rationalistic argument that Christianity, with its doctrines of divine justice, repentance, and punishment, was wholly unsuitable for tragic development.

In England, D'Avenant and Cowley espoused the positive side of the question, the former defending his action on utilitarian grounds. Dennis and Dryden followed, Dryden having the temerity to take issue with Boileau, pointing out that in the Christian doctrine of an angelic hierarchy lay a more valuable poetical machinery than the whole supernatural economy of the Greeks. Out of such assertions and the unrecognized influence of Miltonic achievement and argument were developed Dennis's official pronouncements. They were formally rational. Through the fall came a conflict of reason and passion. Christianity reconciled the two, recognizing the passions but seeking to exalt them. Thus it comes into harmony with poetry which seeks the same end. Divine poetry raises the purest and most sublime emotions, and is, accordingly, far in advance of the more commonplace possibilities of classical themes. Dennis became the leading exponent of the theory, and with the position of Dennis, Tate was heartily in accord. Indeed, his own words, that both morality and religion are material for the best poetry, were set down some five years before the formal declaration of Dennis.[18] Unfortunately, however, Tate never wrote the best poetry; and he never forgot his religion and morality. He could apply the rationalistic method to his morality, but once again it is necessary to keep in mind his highly emotional Irish temperament and his Puritan parentage and discipline. His early work was coloured—or stained—by his overcharged religious poems, and though these were set aside subsequently for the more purely moral projects of the eighties and nineties, the religious note becomes dominant in the version of the *Psalms* and in the poems of 1696. It is marked in his last play (1707), and it culminates in the impossible stuff of the *Monitor,* which is wretched material, badly expressed and comparable only to the worst effusions of Isaac Watts. Whatever views we may hold about the possibility of wedding religious fervour to poetry, Tate was certainly not the one to perform the ceremony, since he had little fervour and less poetry. His work is interesting historically, however, for, strange as it may seem, it was through such humble entrances as these that imagination and feeling were to creep back to their dominant position in the Romantic poetry of the third and fourth generation.

With the social and academic controversy of the day over education, Tate properly had no connection. Sympathetically and socially, however, he belonged to the group which put forward the ideal of the *honnête homme* in opposition to the exponents of a scientific education. In his earlier poems he continually stresses the difficulty and importance of the classics, and all his life he was constantly at work upon his own classical hobbies. Moreover, as time went on, he emphasized morality and culture in education. It was the contention of the scientist that science taught morality and religion and had a distinct cultural value, but of these reasonable claims Tate has nothing to say. Of the current theories of esthetics, also, he seems to have taken no cognizance.

It is clear, therefore, that Tate was, psychologically, almost entirely out of harmony with the major movements of his own day and generation. It remains to be shown whence he came, whither he was going, and in what manner he paid lip service to the more fashionable and superficial modes of his fellows.

Beside post-Renaissance "orthodox" striving for law and order, there develops a "heterodox" effort to prolong a period actually drawing to a close. Imagination, exhausted by sustained activity, and emotions, jaded and capricious from continual exhilaration, are to be roused to new responses by appeals necessarily artificial and strained. The result is a literature marked by strange and sometimes morbid imagery, comedy which has become sentimental, flushed, and sensational, and tragedy which has moved into the realm of exotic horror and melodrama. As time goes on and literary fabric becomes increasingly fragile, this exotic character becomes more and more pronounced and more and more extreme. The imaginative and emotional response changes, too. Starting out sudden, intense, erratic, it becomes feebler and feebler until the iron hand of the Protector closes the theatres, and the rule of the army takes the attention of the nation. But even in literature imagination never quite dies, emotions are never completely dried up, and after the Restoration they still thread their tortuous and precarious way among the gigantic piles erected by victorious science and rationalism; and behind the "heterodox" stand the people as a whole, never forgetting the spirit of the Renaissance and remaining persistently loyal to the congenial moods of English romanticism.

Tate belongs to this heterodox remnant. His first volume of poems is marked by an irregularity and variety of technique, still partially free of the "tyranny of the couplet." His themes are diversified, and when he has shaken off fashionable modes, his approach is, in intention, mildly emotional and moderately imaginative. His pure lyrics are directly in the succession of Jonson and Herrick. In the drama, after an unsuccessful attempt to meet the recently popular taste for the heroic play, he turns back to the immediately post-Elizabethan vogue for Shakespeare, Jonson, and Beaumont and Fletcher. In Shakespeare's work he sees a "heap of jewels." *Coriolanus* and *Richard II* are damned because in each he tries to meet the exigencies of an occasion; but in *Lear* he scores a marked success. With the "orthodox" and neo-classical Jonson, he can do but little, his work never rising above the level of poor farce. The "heterodoxy" of Beaumont and Fletcher is more congenial, however, and he revels in the light of its sustained sentiment and colourful trappings. Throughout his career he turns constantly with pleasure to other Elizabethans, working sporadically upon their work; and over all, his emotion and imagination find outlet and scope in the preparation of overcharged and highly coloured religious exercises, which culminate in the imaginative and emotional extravagances of the *Monitor.* Tate is the child of the Renaissance; but he belongs to the third and fourth generation, and in him the once fine pulse of the Elizabethans throbs but feebly. By this time, the pure blood of a golden age has been diluted by many tributary streams.

Like all survivors of that lost generation, however, Tate belongs as much to the future as to the past. His vulgar and bourgeois religious attitude and emotion, engendered though they may have been in the Puritanism of pre-Cromwellian days, point the way to the emotional revival and excesses of the Wesleyan agitation which will shake England and provoke strong repercussions even within the rationalistic and Platonic bosom of the Established Church. His weariness with the town, his nausea at the convention and chicanery of Court life, and his longing for the unaffected modes and simple sincerity of the country[19] may look back to the more spacious days of a merrier England, but they will be emphasized, magnified, and developed in another generation by the whole tribe of primitivists and semi-primitivists. His benevolent attitude towards his fellows and his ready emotional response to anxiety and unhappiness take their rise in a day which gave light to a Sir Philip Sidney and a Sir Walter Raleigh, but they will flow onward, also, into a society which will have for its ideal a Charles Grandison and a "man of feeling." His melancholy[20] and his preoccupation with death[21] which look back to the ancient civilizations of Greece and of Rome and more immediately to the exotic Robert Burton, will be reflected in Young, Blair, Goldsmith, Gray, and Sam Johnson. In the realm of the drama, he has already helped to undo the rationalistic and cynical work of the Restoration by his constant emotional effort to sentimentalize, purify, and moralize. He has taken his place beside Collier, and has even advanced his own program[22] for the reform of the stage. His last tragedy—never produced, alas (!)—announces an extra-rational moral purpose, and in its emphasis upon a domestic situation and conjugal affections, it is close to the work of Steele, pointing the way to the sentimental theatre which ensued.

It is now evident that historically and psychologically Tate's connection with the major intangible movements of the Restoration and post-Restoration periods is a slender one. The past and the future were his, but the present belonged to others. With the more superficial and fluctuating fashionable tastes of society, however, the relation is a much more direct and manifold one. For Tate was to his very finger-tips a thoroughgoing and unrepentant opportunist—he had to be! Within the realm of the drama, coming into the field late, he first modelled his work upon that of the successful exponents of the popular heroic manner. Failing here, he turned to the recently increased vogue for adaptations from Shakespeare. His first adaptation is a success, but two subsequent failures drive him into discipleship to Ravenscroft, whose successful farces must have made the hungry mouth of the poverty-stricken playwright to water copiously. The second time he tastes both victory and defeat before he turns to the third hope of the Restoration, Beaumont and Fletcher. Two successes and six failures turn him away from the stage until a new and definitely moral Sovereign, Queen Anne, and a changed taste in society seem, after the lapse of twenty years, to point the way to a late triumph. His efforts in the realms of poetry and of journalism are similar. He sets aside the pure lyrics and the prosody which seems to have come most natural to him, he shackles himself with the heroic couplet and tries his hand at all the fashionable and unfashionable exercises of the day, at everything that seems to hold out the slightest prospect of monetary remuneration—occasional poems, translations,

pastorals, satire, collections, paraphrases, prologue, epilogue, magazines, and journals, the historical, scientific, neo-classical, moral and religious modes, personal joys and sorrows—with anxious hope and wistful longing, but without intelligent discrimination, all are exploited shamelessly for what they will bring in pounds, shillings, and pence. The man is tired, the work is uncongenial, recognition is slow, and life becomes a burden. Yet he does not dare to rest—he cannot afford to. His work becomes superficial, journalistic, objective, dull, without sparkle and animation, but from time to time it does meet the popular demand, and with opportune assistance from Dorset, and the royal pension, it does serve the purpose of keeping body and soul together for over thirty years. Literature, indeed, proved for him a bad crutch.[23]

It is not surprising, therefore, that he should have been almost entirely neglected by critics and historians, or referred to only with expressions of pity and contempt. The faithful Dunton was found to praise him; one, Pittis, and a few others were equally well disposed; but all the great men scorned him. Pope refers to him with characteristic satire:

Dunciad, 1. 105:

> She saw slow Philips creep like Tate's poor page,

Ibid., 238:

> O! pass more innocent, in infant state,
> To the mild limbo of our father Tate

Epistle to Doctor Arbuthnot, lines 179-90:

> The bard whom pilfered Pastorals renown,
> Who turns a Persian tale for half a crown,
> Just writes to make his barrenness appear,
> And strains from hard-bound brain, eight lines a year;
> He, who still wanting, though he lives on theft,
> Steals much, spends little, yet has nothing left:
> And he, who now to sense, now nonsense leaning,
> Means not, but blunders round about a meaning:
> And he, whose fustian's so sublimely bad,
> It is not poetry, but prose run mad:
> All these, my modest satire bade translate,
> And owned that nine such poets made a Tate.

Swift employs delightful irony (*The Tale of a Tub,* "Dedication to Prince Posterity"):

> There is another, called Nahum Tate, who is ready to make oath, that he has caused many reams of verse to be published, whereof both himself and his bookseller (if lawfully required) can still produce authentic copies, and therefore wonders why the world is pleased to make such a secret of it.

Southey is content to mention him thus in passing (*Life of Cowper,* pp. 293-4):

Nahum Tate, who of all my predecessors must have ranked lowest of the laureates,—if he had not succeeded Shadwell,—adapted Coriolanus, Richard the Second, and King Lear to his own notions of dramatic propriety . . . poor Nahum may be excused for fancying that he could fit Shakespeare's tragedies to the stage.

Macaulay only damns with faint praise (*Critical and Miscellaneous Essays* 4. 28):

Had he [Wycherley] devoted himself to the making of verse, he would have been nearly as far below Tate and Blackmore as Tate and Blackmore are below Dryden.

These and a few similar meager comments, tell all that contemporaries and posterity have thought of poor Nahum Tate. That he was a poverty-stricken man lacking physical vigour and wanting great talents, and that he spent his life in an almost vain and heart-breaking pursuit of popular favour, without pride, self-respect, or dignity, it is useless to deny. The evidence appears on nearly every page that he has written. But it is less than good sportsmanship to vilify him for his physical and intellectual limitations, whatever these may have been, and poverty often entails the sacrifice of an appropriate independence and self-esteem. Moreover, his actual place in the world of letters is not a totally insignificant one. He had the honour of collaborating more than once with Dryden, the greatest man of letters of his age; he prepared a version of **King Lear** which took precedence in the theatre over Shakespeare's own version for more than a hundred and fifty years; and with Doctor Brady, he furnished the National Church with a version of the **Psalms** which was still in use in the days of our grandfathers. The history of an age is never adequately told by an examination of only its outstanding men. Conclusions can never be accurate when they are based upon preconceived notions and a deductive method. It is only when an age is seen singly and whole that evaluation can be intelligent and discriminating, and then it will be found that obscure and despised third-rate individuals are sometimes of greater significance than more brilliant and energetic men, who, shaped only by popular fashions, move constantly in the limelight. The brilliant and reckless carnival of the Restoration, with its Etherege and its Wycherley, its Shadwell and its Congreve, went on to a close, and with the passing of the gay regalia, the loud trumpets, and the witty chatter, came the sound of the stiller and smaller voices of men like Tate, humble but not entirely insignificant links in the long chain of English literature, firmly attached to the more enduring elements which had gone before and reaching forward, also, to a new day which should carry out and bring to completion the slower, more thoughtful, and therefore, more permanent, developments in the language and literature which they had helped to mould and to create.

Notes

1. Cazamian, *A History of English Literature*, New York, 1928, 2. 8.

2. *Notes and Queries*, Fifth Series, 11. 100.

3. In the preface to his *A Poem upon Tea*, 1702, p. [8], Tate writes: ". . . I must honestly acknowledge, 'tis to This (despicable) Tea-Leaf that I owe Recovery out of a weakly Constitution from the very Cradle. . . ."

4. *Biographia Dramatica*, 1812, 1. 2. 703.

5. Tate wrote nine plays: *Brutus of Alba*, 1678; *The Loyal General*, 1680; *The History of King Lear*, 1681; *The History of King Richard the Second*, produced 1680, printed 1681; *The Ingratitude of a Commonwealth, or Coriolanus*, 1682; *A Duke and No Duke*, produced 1684, published 1685; *Cuckolds-Haven*, 1685; *The Island Princess*, 1687; *Injur'd Love*, 1707.

6. *Injur'd Love* is an adaptation of Webster's *White Devil*. See Professor Spencer's article in this issue.

7. For example (*The Loyal General*, 1. 1, p. 3):

Could I give Being to a thing so Tame!
Rouse, rouse, thyself, Edraste, nor permit
My active Blood to freeze within thy Veins;
If thou want'st Heat, come, to my Bosom fly,
For I have yet enough of Warmth to spare.

(*Ibid.*, 2. 1, p. 11):
What, mar these eyes with Penitential Tears,
Fond Youth? They have too much of fire to weep.
Their glances cou'd Create a Day in Cells,
And kindle freezing Hermits into Dalliance.

(*Ibid.*, 3. 6, p. 31):
I'll make those Mansions fairer than those Bow'rs
And in a Scene of thought repeat these Joys,
So oft within these rev'ling Shades Possesst.
See there thy rival, King, how lovelier far
In Death than thou are Breathing? Fear him still,
Be jealous of his Memory, and live
Till ev'ry Subject scorns thee as I do,
And Vermine like o'r-leap their Wooden King.
State, Tempests, shake thee into Dust—Fates catch
My Curse, and stamp it in their brazen Volumns.

8. *Cf. Poems*, First edition, 1677, and Second edition enlarged, 1684.

The devices are numerous by which this desire for regularity is wrought out:

I. The length of the line is changed:
   A. Long lines are often shortened:
      1677 That Rings *my Own*, or dearer Friends untimely Knell (p. 2).
      1684 That Rings my dearest *Friends* untimely Knell (p. 7).
   B. Sometimes a very long line may even be divided into two lines:

1677 But now, forgetful of thy high Descent, meanly thou labour'st to foment . . . (p. 14).

1684 But now forgetful of thy Bright Descent, / Thy prostituted Pains foment, / And feed the Vices of the Age . . . (p. 17).

C. A short line is lengthened:

1677 Ev'n *Hurricanes* abroad are found . . . (p. 3).

1684 From Hurricanes abroad less harm is found . . . (p. 7).

1677 To guild thy Theam . . . (p. 11).

1684 To guild the darkest Theam . . . (p. 14).

D. Rarely, short lines may be combined into a long line:

1677 Th' Enormities / Of these Apostate votaries / But them and their Confæd'rates too, with signal Rage pursu'd (p. 18).

1684 But with a signal Rage their Crimes pursu'd . . . (p. 20).

II. There are changes within the line:

A. Words are often changed in order to do away with hypermetrical syllables:

1677 And act thy Miseries o're agen . . . (p. 5).

1684 And act thy Troubles o'er agen . . . (p. 8).

1677 Th' Unfortunate Man, whom any *Muse* befriends (p. 18).

1684 The wretched Man, whom any *Muse* befriends (p. 20).

B. Changes in vocabulary are sometimes made to regularize stress:

1677 Which the *offending Pair* did frame . . . (p. 13).

1684 The first offending Pair did frame . . . (p. 16).

1677 By the important Labours of Mankind . . . (p. 20).

1684 By never-ceasing Labours of man-kind . . . (p. 21).

C. Occasionally, merely the order of the words is altered for the sake of smoothness:

1677 Is *Folly,* not to be forgiv'n, in ev'n thy *Doating Age* (p. 5).

1684 Is *Folly,* not to be forgiv'n, ev'n in thy *doating Age* (p. 8).

9. [Brady and Tate] tr. and ed., *An Essay of a New Version of the Psalms of David,* 1695.

10. *The Monitor,* 1713, nos. 1-21.

For example ("The Swearer," no. 4, p. 1):

But He that Practises this Odious Vice
Sells for an empty Sound his Paradise.
. . . . .
If he believes a God, how void of Sense
Are Pigmies to defy Omnipotence?
If not, Himself an Idiot he proclaims
Who Swears by Pow'rs that are but any Names.

11. *A Pastoral Dialogue,* 1690, p. 17:

Brand such as wou'd to Truth reveal'd agree,
But Penalties on such as cannot see
What others can, is Breach of Charity.
Had Charity in Synods interpos'd,
The Seamless Garments Breach had soon been clos'd.

Ibid., p. 14:

. . . first you must convince the Reason's Light,
That They *mistake,* and You are in the right:
Where you mistake, and They the Truth may hit,
Will you to your own Rule of Force submit?
You'll plead the Privilege They urg'd before,
Conviction crave, and They demand no more.
Conviction clear the Soul can only win;
With Club or Hammer try to force the Pin,
The Brains you may beat out, ne'r drive the Notion in.

12. *Ibid.,* p. [2] of the Preface:

There is no Man that has a greater Veneration for the Sacred Function and Order, or the Discipline and Worship by Law establish'd; neither does the Passive Principle itself, that has so nearly endanger'd the Shipwreck both of State and Church, derive its Source from the pure Fountain of our Reformation: 'Twas a new-sprouted Tail of the Dragon, that swept many of our Stars, tho' but few of the First Magnitude; most whereof recover'd themselves as soon as they were sensible of the Consequence. . . .

13. "The Mid-Night Thought," in *Poems,* 2nd ed., 1684, lines 13-7, 29-32, 37-8, pp. 101-3:

How long since I did meditate
Of Life, of Death, and future State?
Approaching Fate his Pace will keep,
Let Mortals watch, or let them sleep.
What Sound is that?—a Passing Bell! . . .

Now, wakened Conscience, speaks at large,
And envious Friends enhance the Charge!
Let the bold Atheist now draw near,
And try the drooping Heart to chear; . . .

Who hopes for Rescue here, will fail,
And the grim Serjeant takes no Bail.

14. J. D., *A Memorial for the Learned; or Miscellany of choice collections from the most eminent authors,* 1686.

15. "The Book of Plants, General Int. and Dedication to Charles, Duke of Somerset by Tate; Book 4, Of Flowers and Book 5, Of Trees tr. by Tate," in *The Poetical Works of Cowley,* Edinburgh, 1777.

16. Tate, tr., "Syphilis," in *Examen Poeticum,* ed. John Dryden, 1693, p. [469].

17. Tate, *A Present For the Ladies; Being an Historical Vindication of the Female Sex,* 1692.

18. Tate says (Tate, ed., *Miscellanea Sacra; or, Poems on Divine and Moral Subjects,* 1696, 1, p. 1 of Preface): "That Religion and Morality are capable of all the Embellishments of Poetry has been confirmed by the Suffrage and Performance of best Poets in all Ages."

19. "Strephon's Complaint," in *Poems,* 2nd ed., 1684, pp. 70-3:

Business!—Oh stay till I recover Breath,
The dreadful Word puts all my Sense to flight;
Business to me sounds terrible as Death;

. . . . .

But Business to Preferment will direct,

. . . . .

Ah! have I then no more than *this* t'expect?

. . . *Content* I crave,
And wildly you of Greatness rave!
If Life's at best a tedious rugged Road,
What must it be with State's encumbring Load?

Condem'd to Town, Noise and Impertinence,
Where *Mode* and *Ceremony* I must view!
Yet were the Sight all, *Strephon* cou'd dispense;
But he must there be *Ceremonious* too.

20. "To a desponding Friend," in *Poems,* 2nd ed.,
1684, p. 107:

Repine not, pensive Friend, to meet
A Thorn and Sting in every Sweet;
Think it not yours, or my hard Fate,
But the fixt Lot of Humane State.

"Disappointed," in *ibid.,* pp. 76-7:
From Clime to Clime with restless Toyl we Roam,
But sadly still our old Griefs we retain,
And with us bear beyond the spacious Main
The same unquiet *selves* we brought from Home!

"The Search," in *ibid.,* pp. 21-6:
Ev'n in this vale of Misery,
Some Rivulets of Bliss we taste;
But Rivulets half *dry,*
And *tainted* with the *Soil* through which they past.

21. See p. 259, n. 13, above.

22. [Tate], *A Proposall for Regulating of the Stage
and Stage-Plays,* Lambeth MS. 933, no. 57, The
Gibson MS.

23. "The Match," in *Poems,* 2nd ed., 1684, pp. 66-7:

By what wild Frenzy was I led,
That with a *Muse* I must needs wed?
Whose *Dow'r consists of empty Fame,*
Yet with that Trouble and Debate
The owner holds this poor Estate;
Where after long Expence and Toil
He *starves* on the ungrateful Soil.
The Fields and Groves which Poets feign
The curious Fancy entertain,
But yields no timely Grain or Fruit,
The craving Stomach to recruit.

Christopher Spencer (essay date winter 1963)

SOURCE: Spencer, Christopher. "A Word for Tate's
King Lear." Studies in English Literature, 1500-1900 3,
no. 1 (winter 1963): 241-51.

[*In the following essay, Spencer claims that Tate's* King
Lear *should not be dismissed as hackery and a mutila-
tion of Shakespeare's version, arguing that the play is
coherent, entertaining, and has its own plan.*]

In 1959 Kenneth Muir remarked of Tate's **King Lear,**
"The beautiful scene in which the King of France receives the despised and rejected Cordelia is cut, presumably because there was no room for a rival to her
affections. . . . [And Tate] provides a scene with Lear
and Cordelia in prison, lest we should be unable to
imagine it from Lear's words before and after the death
of Cordelia."[1] Whatever the value of this criticism for
Shakespeare's play, it is irrelevant to the adaptation.
Since Cordelia is pursued and won by Edgar in Tate's
version, what happens to France is not a question of
"room" but of relevance: France's presence in the adaptation would be absurd. And since Cordelia does not die
in Tate's play, the scene we are to "imagine" is not suggested by "Lear's words before and after the death of
Cordelia" (which does not take place). The critic is obviously thinking only of Shakespeare's play; yet at stake
here is the taste of about five generations of our theater-
going ancestors, who supported the adaptation on the
main London stages from 1681 to 1838.[2]

A similar irrelevance, as I hope to show later, exists in
Lamb's eloquent denunciation of the happy ending:

A happy ending!—as if the living martyrdom that Lear
had gone through,—the flaying of his feelings alive,
did not make a fair dismissal from the stage of life the
only decorous thing for him. If he is to live and be
happy after, if he could sustain this world's burden after, why all this pudder and preparation,—why torment
us with all this unnecessary sympathy? As if the child-
ish pleasure of getting his gilt robes and sceptre again
could tempt him to act over again his misused sta-
tion,—as if at his years, and with his experience, anything was left but to die.[3]

Since Lamb wrote, few criticisms of Tate's adaptation
have been kind: A. W. Ward's unexpanded reference to
Tate as "a painstaking and talented writer who, with enduring success, adapted *King Lear,*"[4] stands almost alone
against a commentary which, Odell observed in 1920,
had made Tate "perhaps the most universally execrated
of the daring souls who violated the precious shrine of
[Shakespeare's] plays."[5] Hazelton Spencer, with his eye
constantly on Shakespeare's play, was only a little less
unsympathetic.[6] More recently, Moody Prior has studied
Tate's **King Lear** as "a curious example of how far the
heroic play had altered the current conception of the
tragic pattern," and his observations lead to a somewhat
better understanding of what Tate was trying to do.[7] Another approach, which George C. Branam has used with
eighteenth-century adaptions, is to examine the play
against the background of neo-classic theory. However,
this avenue would not lead us very far toward really
understanding what Tate was trying to accomplish: as
Branam observes, "The adapters of Shakespeare . . .
seldom felt constrained to obey a 'rule' to the letter.
They demonstrated a generalized awareness of critical
principles rather than a well-memorized knowledge of a

rule book."[8] Instead, I wish to approach Tate's adaptation as a play with its own plan and to study its parts in relation to each other with the intention of arriving at a better knowledge of Tate's—not Shakespeare's—**King Lear.** Such a study will show, I believe, that Tate's play is coherent and entertaining—in other words, that our ancestors did not show such bad taste as they are thought to have shown in supporting it and that there is even something in the play for the modern reader.

The adapter seems to have considered the added love plot to be the most important of his alterations. In his Dedication he remarks that he found Shakespeare's play "a Heap of Jewels, unstrung, and unpolish'd; yet so dazling in their Disorder, that I soon perceiv'd I had seiz'd a Treasure"; he then explains the addition of the love plot:

> 'Twas my good Fortune to light on one Expedient to rectifie what was wanting in the Regularity and Probability of the Tale, which was to run through the Whole, as *Love* betwixt *Edgar* and *Cordelia*; that never chang'd Word with each other in the Original. This renders *Cordelia's* Indifference, and her Father's Passion in the first Scene, probable. It likewise gives Countenance to *Edgar's* Disguise, making that a generous Design that was before a poor Shift to save his Life. The Distress of the Story is evidently heightened by it; and it particularly gave Occasion of a new Scene or Two, of more Success (perhaps) than Merit. This Method necessarily threw me on making the Tale conclude in a Success to the innocent destrest Persons: Otherwise I must have incumbered the Stage with dead Bodies, which Conduct makes many Tragedies conclude with unseasonable Jests.[9]

By "what was wanting in the Regularity . . . of the Tale" Tate surely means the lack of ties between the Lear and Gloucester plots; his remedy, the love affair, is the *raison d'etre* of most of the passages he adds. These are as follows: 1) in I.i, a 9-line addition just before Lear divides his kingdom introduces the lovers and gives Cordelia a chance to state the motive for her "indifference"; 2) a 46-line passage after Cordelia's rejection and Lear's angry departure enables Edgar to rejoice that Burgundy is no longer a rival, but Cordelia turns away from her lover and resolves to test his faithfulness; 3) in 65 lines added to III.ii Cordelia begs Gloucester for aid in finding her father and, with her maid Arante, disguises herself to search for him, unaware that Edmund has eavesdropped and is determined to ravish her; 4) in 111 lines Poor Tom rescues Cordelia from ruffians sent after her by Edmund; when her rescuer unmasks, Cordelia confesses her love for him; 5) in Act IV just after Poor Tom and the blinded Gloucester have met, they encounter Kent and Cordelia (46 lines); 6) the happy ending calls for much rewriting in Act V, including a tournament between Edgar and Edmund followed by the indecorous quarreling of Goneril and Regan over Edmund's body, together with the an-

nounced retirement of Lear, Gloucester, and Kent, and the elevation of Cordelia and Edgar to the throne. The other lengthy addition—the only one outside of Act V that does not involve at least one of the two lovers—is a 48-line scene at the beginning of Act IV located in a "Grotto," "Edmund *and* Regan *amorously Seated, listening to Musick*." Thus, the adapter increases the meetings of the two families: to Edgar's encounter with Cordelia's father in Act III Tate adds two passages that bring together Cordelia and Edgar's father; and in five passages Edgar and Cordelia meet. Edmund's lust for Cordelia early in Act III enables Edgar to perform the "heroic" deed that brings Cordelia and her lover together. Edgar nearly becomes the hero, and the love story becomes almost as important as the main plot.

By these same additions Tate felt that he had improved the "probability" of the tale in motivating Cordelia's "indifference" toward Lear: she tells us in advance that since she detests the "loath'd Embraces" of Burgundy and prefers "her *Edgar's* Arms," she will "with cold Speech tempt the Chol'rick King." Shakespeare does not supply an explicit motive for Cordelia's reticence, though it is not hard to find a reason for her behavior if one feels it to be natural or if one emphasizes her symbolic value. However, there is still room to question her motivation, and from the Augustan point of view her act must have seemed abnormal—a violation of probability—and in need of an explanation that would make it normal and probable.[10] In Tate, moreover, Cordelia is not Truth itself, nor is she rigorously honest: she deliberately misleads both her father and Edgar in this very scene. The change in Cordelia's behavior and character in Tate makes explicit motivation more desirable.

However, Cordelia's motive has the still more far-reaching effect of relieving Lear of some responsibility for his error. Since Cordelia, like her sisters, deliberately misleads her father, Lear is presented with a choice not between Falsity and Truth but between two kinds of Falsity: he is more misled than self-misleading, and Cordelia must share the responsibility for the results. Yet Cordelia should not be harshly judged either; her lie is meant to be for everyone's good and is conventionally "good" in that the younger generation is trying to realize its true love in opposition to an autocratic parent and can succeed only by tricking the latter until he can be brought to see his mistake. It is not that Lear does not know himself, Cordelia, and the truth, but that he is *like many other parents* in not knowing himself, his child, and the wisest course of action—a typical Augustan metamorphosis. Lear's Error, then, is reduced in stature to a very common sort of misunderstanding and is not entirely his fault. Accordingly, his punishment and suffering are reduced, and the happy ending follows more naturally.

Lear's punishment is made to seem less by heavy cutting in Act III and by the omission of the Fool. Not only are the great speeches of Lear in the storm short-ened, but some of the more moving figures are omitted from the speeches, with the consequence that, like the hero of the heroic play, Lear tends to rant, to express himself in language which—cut though it is—still seems to exceed the actual emotion. After comparing Tate's version of the "Blow winds" speech with Shake-speare's, Prior remarks, "In short, most of the figures which [in Shakespeare] relate this passage to the large scheme of images which runs through the play, to the immediate turmoil of Lear's mind, and to the thought which lies at the heart of it are either weakened or de-stroyed, and all we have is the expression of violence of feeling and rage."[11] III.i and ii, 150 lines in Shake-speare, are condensed to 44 in Tate; III.iv, 189 lines, is shortened only slightly to 168 lines, but includes a few passages from Shakespeare's III.vi (122 lines), which is otherwise omitted entirely. Furthermore, excluding the Fool and his conversations with Lear diminishes our awareness of the depth of Lear's suffering; we do not see the Fool rubbing salt in his master's wounds. In fact, some of the interest in Act III is shifted from Lear's sufferings to Edgar's. This diminution of the King's agony—both quantitatively, his time on the stage and sharing his suffering with others, and qualitatively, the thinner language and the missing dimension of the Fool—plus the King's lesser responsibility, and, of course, the survival of Cordelia make Lear's continuing to live the better ending in Tate's play. Lamb, like many modern readers, was reading Shakespeare between the lines.

Critics generally assume that the Fool does not appear in Tate's version because of the neo-classic objection to mixing comedy with tragedy. Perhaps so, but there would seem to be every other reason for omitting the Fool as well. His remarks are frequently obscure and indirect in a play Tate was making more obvious and direct. The Fool deepens the experience of *King Lear* without contributing to its rhetoric, but characters and actions were doubtless justified to Tate in terms of the play, not in terms of what they might reveal about hu-man nature.[12] Hazlitt suggested that the Fool was a safety-valve, and Keats commented that "the Fool by his very levity give[s] a finishing-touch to the pathos."[13] Paradoxically, he does both, but in Shakespeare's play: in Tate's a safety-valve would be superfluous, and Tate's kind of pathos—ladies in distress and angry men in storms—would not be enhanced by the Fool. Tate makes *Lear* more rhetorical and less poetic, more worldly and less cosmic (the people are not Titans, or are less titanic); the situations are more conventional and more artificial. The Fool belongs with none of these. Finally, if the Fool serves to make clear to the King the magni-tude of his Error, he is correspondingly less necessary as the Error dwindles into a mistake.

It might seem that reducing Lear's suffering does not fit well with the interest Tate has in the "distress" of his story, but the adapter is thinking of the "distress of lov-ers caught in unhappy crises, of virtue exposed to inju-ries that asked for pity, of noble heroism restrained from exercise of its strength—in short, the kinds of dis-tress which the plots of Restoration heroic drama had made the familiar stock in trade of the serious drama-tist."[14] As Lear is less tragic, so is Gloucester, though the latter's suffering is given a "distressing" twist. Gloucester exhibits himself publicly, intentionally stirs up a rebellion, and then, seated under a tree during the battle, becomes a portrait of heroism in distress:

> The Fight grows hot; the whole War's now at work,
> And the goar'd Battle bleeds in every Vein.
> Whilst Drums and Trumpets drown loud Slaughters
>   Roar;
> Where's *Gloster* now that us'd to head the Fray,
> And scour the Ranks where deadliest Danger lay?
> Here, like a Shepherd, in a lonely Shade,
> Idle, unarm'd, and listning to the Fight;
> Yet the disabled Courser, maim'd and blind,
> When to the Stall he hears the ratling War,
> Foaming with Rage, tears up the batter'd Ground,
> And tugs for Liberty.
> No more of Shelter, thou blind Worm, but forth
> To th'open Field; the War may come this Way
> And crush thee into Rest.—Here lay thee down,
> And tear the Earth, that Work befits a Mole.
> Or dark Despair! When, *Edgar,* wilt thou come
> To pardon, and dismiss me to the Grave?

Moreover, Gloucester is made less credulous in Tate than in Shakespeare, for Edmund reveals at the end of the first speech of the play (his "Thou, Nature, art my goddess" soliloquy) that his father already believes Edgar a villain. (Tate is even ingenious enough to have Lear reproach Cordelia a few minutes later for her friendship with "the Rebel Son of *Gloster.*") If Gloucester is the old "Courser" of the heroic stable, Edgar is the younger and, to be worthy, must disguise himself not as "a poor Shift to save his Life," but for the acceptably heroic motive of protecting Cordelia. It is Edgar who steps forward to speak the edifying moral of the adaptation:

> Our drooping Country now erects her Head,
> Peace spreads her balmy Wings, and Plenty blooms.
> Divine *Cordelia,* all the Gods can witness
> How much thy Love to Empire I prefer!
> Thy bright Example shall convince the World
> (Whatever Storms of Fortune are decreed)
> That Truth and Vertue shall at last succeed.

Thus, the suffering of the royal family is lessened, the heroism of the noble family is raised, and the two fami-lies are united by a third strand of love and marriage. For Shakespeare's two plots, Tate gives us three in one.

Virtue succeeds but Vice, of course, fails. Goneril, Regan, and Edmund are portrayed by Tate as more lustful—or, at least, more explicitly lustful—than they were in Shakespeare. This contrast of Virtue and Vice is heightened by a family resemblance: Like Edgar, Edmund belongs at moments to the heroic world, and when he is challenged by the disguised Edgar, he replies instantly,

> What will not *Edmund* dare! my Lord, I beg
> The Favour that you'd instantly appoint
> The Place where I may meet this Challenger,
> Whom I will sacrifice to my wrong'd Fame;
> Remember, Sir, that injur'd Honour's nice,
> And cannot brook delay.

And as Goneril and Regan snarl at each other over his mortally wounded body, he remarks,

> Now, *Edgar,* thy proud Conquest I forgive;
> Who wou'd not choose, like me, to yield his Breath
> T' have Rival Queens contend for him in Death?

Edmund's lust for Cordelia increases her "distress," and the "love" interest is provided for an audience that expected it. Furthermore, as J. H. Wilson and Lucyle Hook have emphasized, places had to be provided for the actresses. By developing the parts of the sinful sisters—and the star part of Cordelia—Tate was adjusting the play to the theater situation of his time. Wilson suggests that the parts of Regan and Cordelia were planned for Mary Lee, who was "the leading tragedienne and villainess," and Elizabeth Barry, her "ambitious young rival."[15]

Tate was not a distinguished poet, and few compliments can be paid the style of the adaptation; however, the worst is usually what is quoted. Tate has trimmed Shakespeare's lines throughout as part of the general pruning, clarifying, and surface emphasis of this as of other Augustan adaptations of Shakespeare. Edgar and Cordelia speak a language that is highly conventional at one moment, as

> . . . Do I kneel before thee,
> And offer at thy Feet my panting Heart?
> Smile, Princess, and convince me; for as yet
> I doubt, and dare not trust the dazling Joy.

Then seventeen lines later Cordelia speaks what is hardly more than prose:

> When, *Edgar,* I permitted your Addresses,
> I was the darling Daughter of a King,
> Nor can I now forget my Royal Birth,
> And live dependant on my Lover's Fortune;

Gloucester, just blinded and imagining his suicide, is bathetic:

> Whence my freed Soul to her bright Sphear shall fly,
> Through boundless Orbs, eternal Regions spy,
> And, like the Sun, be All one glorious Eye.

On the other hand, much of Act V is successfully written. After Lear has killed two of the guard, Albany and Edgar enter. Lear assumes that they have come to carry out the sentence the guards failed to execute, and when his chains are removed, his language is firm:

> Com'st thou inhumane Lord, to sooth us back
> To a Fool's Paradise of Hope, to make
> Our Doom more wretched? Go to, we are too well
> Acquainted with Misfortune to be gull'd
> With Lying Hope; no, we will hope no more.

Kent, befitting his character, is more willing to listen to Albany: "What wou'd your Highness?" he asks; but Albany is slow to explain, and Lear interrupts raspingly, "And whether tends this Story?" Then he is silent for some lines as Albany, Kent and Cordelia remark on Edmund's death; recovering, he exclaims over his own return to power (he retracts a few minutes later) and over Cordelia's:

> *Cordelia* then shall be a Queen, mark that:
> *Cordelia* shall be a Queen; Winds catch the Sound
> And bear it on your rosie Wings to Heav'n.
> *Cordelia* is a Queen.

If only the wings had not been "rosie," these lines too would convey their enthusiasm forcefully.

Tate's work is spotty—sometimes fairly good, sometimes bad—but doubtless his contemporaries, like ours, were attracted to the theater less by the consistency or quality of style than by adequately written scenes of the kinds they liked to see, hung together on an interesting story line. To scenes of rage and horror, made brief and shorn of much of their power, Tate adds passages of distressed love, heroic rescue, joyful reunion with happy prospects, and adulterous lust. For the depth of Shakespeare's play he substitutes speed and a quick succession of moving situations.[16] His play has an inner consistency of its own, but it is a play rather than an experience, bringing several groups of characters through a series of complications to a resolution consisting of punishment for the wicked and reward for the good and the regenerate.

It is not surprising that Restoration and eighteenth-century audiences preferred this lively adaptation to the original. Shakespeare's *King Lear* is an unconventional play by the standards of any age and especially so by the comparatively brittle criteria of the neo-classic theater. Although the Augustans saw enough in Shakespeare to establish his popularity firmly, they were often not interested in the method or direction his plays took: the manner and moral of the Jacobean *King Lear* must have seemed as much the opposite of what the Restoration admired in art as Tate's making the play more superficial seems inartistic to us. Since the adapters felt no obligation to keep what they did not like, they sometimes used the Shakespearean material for other ends which interested them. The enduring success of the adaptation was probably due to both playwrights: to what was left of Shakespeare's matter and to the skillful and canny alterations made by Tate in an extraordinary literary experience as he changed it into an ordinary literary work.

Our own inability to appreciate Tate's adaptation seems to result largely from the radical disappointment of our expectation that Tate will remain as faithful as he can to Shakespeare's purposes as we conceive them, and that his adaptation can be treated as an Augustan equivalent of the early Jacobean play. We expect Tate to value Shakespeare's variety, richness of suggestion, and deep analysis of the human spirit; and, of course, he does not do so. Since both our comprehension of Shakespeare's play and our expectations of a reworking of it differ greatly from those of the Augustans, we can best read Tate's *King Lear* as a new play with its own purpose and thus avoid judging it in terms of expectations it was never intended to satisfy. Read in this fashion, it is both coherent and entertaining.

Notes

1. "Three Shakespeare Adaptations," *Proceedings of the Leeds Philosophical and Literary Society,* Literary and Historical Section, VIII (1959), 238-239.

2. Actually, more and more of Shakespeare's play was restored beginning about 1756, but Tate's version was played along with other adaptations at least until 1800: see G. W. Stone, Jr., "Garrick's Production of *King Lear,*" *SP,* XLV (1948), 89-103; G. C. D. Odell, *Shakespeare from Betterton to Irving,* 2 vols. (New York, 1920); and C. B. Hogan, *Shakespeare in the Theatre, 1701-1800,* 2 vols. (Oxford, 1952-57). According to Odell (II, 154), the tragic ending was restored at Drury Lane on February 10, 1823.

3. *The Works of Charles Lamb,* ed. Thomas Hutchinson (London, 1924), I, 137. This and several other well-known comments on Tate's *Lear,* including the remarks of Charlotte Lennox, Dr. Johnson, Hazlitt, and A. C. Bradley (Addison's are not included), are in *The King Lear Perplex,* ed. Helmut Bonheim (San Francisco, 1960). What Lamb saw on the stage may have been Tate's *Lear* with some of Shakespeare's restored, but his words are often cited as final condemnation of Tate's play itself—by Muir, for example ("Three Shakespeare Adaptations," p. 238).

4. In *The Cambridge History of English Literature,* VIII (Cambridge, 1934), p. 41.

5. Odell, I, 51.

6. *Shakespeare Improved* (Cambridge, Mass., 1927), pp. 241-252.

7. *The Language of Tragedy* (New York, 1947), pp. 180-185.

8. *Eighteenth-Century Adaptations of Shakespearean Tragedy,* University of California Publications, English Studies, No. 14 (Berkeley, 1956), p. 66.

9. Quotations are from *Shakespeare Adaptations,* ed. Montague Summers (London, 1922).

10. H. Spencer remarks (p. 242), "In seeking to motivate Cordelia's failure to speak out, Tate recognizes the structural weakness of Shakespeare's play from a realistic point of view, which, of course, is precisely the point of view it is fatal to adopt." It is "fatal" for Shakespeare's play, but necessary for Tate's: again, the critic is thinking only of Shakespeare.

11. Prior, p. 184.

12. The difference appears in the following remark by Dr. Johnson on Hamlet: "Of the feigned madness of Hamlet there appears no adequate cause, for he does nothing which he might not have done with the reputation of sanity." (*Samuel Johnson on Shakespeare,* ed. W. K. Wimsatt, Jr. [New York, 1960], p. 112.) To find the "cause" of behavior, modern readers look less to the action the characters must perform or to the action's demands upon the playwright than to the character himself and his past. A playwright asking himself which of the actions in *King Lear* "might not have been done" without the Fool might well conclude that there were none.

13. Quoted together by Kenneth Muir in his introduction to the Arden edition of *King Lear* (London, 1955), p. lxiv.

14. Prior, p. 181.

15. J. H. Wilson, *All the King's Ladies* (Chicago, 1958), p. 104; Lucyle Hook, "Shakespeare Improv'd, or A Case for the Affirmative," *SQ,* IV (1953), 289-299.

16. Also, W. M. Merchant, *Shakespeare and the Artist* (London, 1959), p. 24, remarks that Tate's *Lear* "has more visual interest than any other of the non-operatic adaptations."

James Black (essay date summer 1967)

SOURCE: Black, James. "The Influence of Hobbes on Nahum Tate's *King Lear.*" *Studies in English Literature, 1500-1900* 7, no. 3 (summer 1967): 377-85.

[*In the following essay, Black examines the influence of the philosopher Thomas Hobbes on Tate as he was writing his* King Lear, *maintaining that Hobbesian ideas are seen most clearly in the character of Edmund.*]

Nahum Tate's famous adaptation of Shakespeare's *King Lear* has recently been the object of renewed critical attention.[1] Up to now, however, no one has commented upon the decided influence which the writings of Thomas Hobbes appear to have had upon Tate at the time[2] when he undertook to reduce Shakespeare's great tragedy into his own ***History of King Lear.*** This influence shows up most clearly in the modifications made by Tate in the character of Edmund, who is the one figure of real literary interest in the adaptation.

There are indications that Tate had studied at least Hobbes's aesthetic ideas, perhaps following in the intellectual path of his friend and mentor Dryden, who was a friend and keen student of Hobbes. For example, Tate's use of Hobbesian aesthetic ideas has been observed by Clarence Thorpe: "Writing [in 1689] in praise of Cowley's *Six Books of Plants,* Nahum Tate uses the terms 'wit,' 'fancy,' and 'judgment' in a quite Hobbian manner."[3] Thorpe's analysis of Tate's description of Cowley as a creative writer leads him to the conclusion that Tate's critical approach "readily bring[s] to mind Hobbes's notion [s of wit, fancy and imagination]."[4] But Tate had been using this approach long before his essay on Cowley: in the **"Epistle Dedicatory"** to ***The History of King Lear*** he writes of the play as he had found it:

> *Lear*'s real, and *Edgar*'s pretended Madness have so much of extravagant Nature (I know not how else to express it) as cou'd never have started but from our *Shakespear*'s Creating Fancy. The Images and Language are so odd and surprizing, and yet so agreeable and proper, that whilst we grant that none but *Shakespear* cou'd have form'd such Conceptions, Yet we are satisfied that they were the only Things in the World that ought to be said on those Occasions.

His use of the terms "extravagant Nature" (referring in this case to language which is outlandish yet appropriate to the circumstances in which it is spoken) and "creating Fancy" indicates a knowledge of Hobbes's discussions, in *Leviathan* and the *Answer to D'Avenant's Preface to "Gondibert,"* of the roles of fancy and judgment in poetical creation. In *Leviathan,* Hobbes had said that "In a good Poem, whether it be *Epique,* or *Dramatique;* as also in Sonnets, Epigrams, and other Pieces, both Judgement and Fancy are required; but the Fancy must be more eminent; because they please for the Extravagancy" (I,viii). Hobbes defines fancy as the inventive faculty: "He that hath [fancy] will be easily outfitted with similitudes that will please . . . by the variety of their invention" (I,viii). Thus Tate, in attributing to Shakespeare a fancy which is "creating" and owes nothing to memory, is following Hobbes, and he also followed Hobbes in praising Shakespeare's judgment. "If the defect of Discretion be apparent, how extravagant soever the Fancy be, the whole discourse will be taken for a signe of want of Wit," Hobbes had said

(I,viii), and Tate accordingly adds that Shakespeare's extravagance is "extravagant Nature" and his images "agreeable"—that is, with the madman's vision—and "proper" in the mouth of a madman. Certain parts of Shakespeare's *King Lear* thus qualify as art from a Restoration point of view, and Tate makes few alterations in the mad speeches.

If Hobbes's aesthetic ideas provided a standard by which Tate could judge certain passages of *King Lear,* the political ideas of the Malmesbury philosopher gave the adaptor a design for a modified characterization of the villain. Practically all of Shakespeare's characters have been simplified in ***The History of King Lear,*** to make them conform to recognizable stage patterns. Lear is a stage representation of the typical bewildered parent;[5] Cordelia is the standard virtuous heroine of the Restoration theater, Edgar is her male counterpart; Gloster has become another edition of Lear—the grievously misled and abused father who is more sinned against than sinning; Kent epitomizes loyalty and rough virtue. While these "good" characters invariably act impulsively, Tate's villainous people, Gonerill, Regan, and Edmund, are contemplative: they scheme, write and forge letters, devise "projects," plan rapes and murders, and resolve the most appropriate times for administering poison. They carouse at a masque while the good people are suffering in the storm. The impulse to categorize the characters and to place them in niches for easy identification by the audience is strongest of all in the portrayal of Edmund, who as the most villainous character in the play has been made to correspond in many details to the popular contemporary idea of the "Hobbist."

As Louis Teeter and Samuel I. Mintz have shown, Hobbes's materialistic and deterministic ideas, as expressed chiefly in *Leviathan,* were widely read and widely misunderstood.[6] Most misconstrued of all were his propositions concerning the "state of nature" and "liberty."

> The Right of Nature . . . is the liberty each man hath to use his own power, as he will himself, for the preservation of his own nature, that is to say, of his own life, and consequently, of doing any thing, which in his own judgment, and reason, he shall conceive to be the aptest means thereunto.

> By Liberty, is understood . . . the absence of external impediments: which impediments, may oft take away part of a man's power to do what he would; but cannot hinder him from using the power left him, according as his judgment, and reason shall dictate to him.[7]

These and other passages, read out of their context, were widely interpreted as announcing a programme for libertinism, irreligion, and free-thinking—a code for the Restoration rakes for whom Hobbes "erigeait le manuel de leur conduite, et redigeait d'avance les axiomes qu'ils allaient traduire en actions."[8] "Irreligion 'tis true in its practice hath been still the companion of every Age, but its open and publick defence seems the peculiar of this," wrote Charles Wolseley in 1672, and went on to blame Hobbes: "'Tis but of late that men come to defend ill living and secure themselves against their own guilt, by an open defyance to all the great Maxims of Piety and Virtue . . . ; and most of the bad Principles of this Age are of no earlier a date than one very ill Book, are indeed but the spawn of the Leviathan."[9] Samuel Mintz, quoting Wolseley, shows that this tirade accurately reflects the general conception of Hobbes's ideas.[10] The general idea of Hobbism was encouraged by the well-publicized career of John Wilmot, Earl of Rochester, who professed to be a Hobbist, and who died in 1670 at the age of thirty-three after acquiring the reputation of the most notorious libertine of his time. Rochester's dying confession was as misleading as his lifetime's example, for he was reported to have said that "that absurd and foolish Philosophy, which the world so much admired, propagated by the late Mr. Hobbs, and others, had undone him."[11]

It was inevitable that the ideas—or what were thought to be the ideas—of Hobbes should eventually be given dramatic expression. The Restoration stage was often an extension of the real-life political and philosophical milieu and, as Louis Teeter observes, "the very notoriety of [Hobbes's] ideas made them valuable to the dramatists who wished to have their political villains up to date."[12] The "modern" villain was Hobbes's "natural" man, as popularly conceived: cynical, treacherous, lustful and cruel, judging the rightness of a cause by its success, and recognizing no power beyond his own strength. Settle's Crimalhaz (*The Express of Morocco,* 1673), Dryden's Zempoalla (*The Indian Queen,* 1663), Maximin (*Tyrannic Love,* 1669) and Morat (*Aureng-Zebe,* 1675), and Otway's Don John (*Don Carlos,* 1675) are five of the major characters of Restoration tragedy whose outstanding quality is their disregard of any ethical criterion but success. Tate's Edmund could be modelled upon any or all of these characters, or simply made to conform to the popular idea of the Hobbist. There are, however, indications that Tate was as closely acquainted with the political and moral ideas expressed in *Leviathan* as with Hobbes's aesthetic theories. His modification of the character of Edmund reveals a desire to do more than simply make the Bastard vaguely Hobbist. Rather, he attempts, through the use of echoes of Hobbes's own words and of important criticisms and interpretations of those words, to create definite points of correspondence between Edmund and the "natural" man.

One of Tate's changes in the structure of *King Lear* consists of moving the famous soliloquy "Thou, Nature, art my goddess . . . ," from Act I, Scene ii to the very beginning of his version, a modification which seems to

represent an attempt to capture the audience's immediate interest through the initial presentation of a well-known type. Not only does Edmund announce at once that he is a villain; he goes further than his Shakespearean counterpart to point out that he is a successful villain, and later announces that he means to be even more successful:

> With success
> I've practis'd yet upon their easie Natures
>
> (I.i.14-15)
>
> . . . . .
>
> What Saint so divine
> That will successful Villany decline?
>
> (I.i.298-299)

The last-quoted lines, especially, are designed to be immediately recognized as embodying the Hobbist idea that the success of an enterprise made that enterprise just. Hobbes's observation that "Good success is power,"[13] had been taken so literally that Oxford University, in a *Judgement and Decree of the University . . . passed in the Convocation, July 21, 1683,* was to attribute to Hobbes and condemn as a "damnable doctrine" the proposition that "Possession and strength give a right to govern, and success in a cause or enterprise proclaims it to be just."[14]

It was believed that the true Hobbist had no other motive but self-interest for undertaking any course of action. One of the wittiest attacks on Hobbes, John Eachard's *Mr. Hobbs's State of Nature Consider'd, In a Dialogue between Philautus and Timothy* (1672), is also an excellent source for estimating the extent to which narrow interpretations of Hobbes's ideas were current. A section of the dialogue is devoted to showing the attempts of Philautus (Hobbes) to defend the principle of "self-interest."

PHILAUTUS.

> I do not at all question but that thou wilt fully believe what I have taught thee to be true; namely, that the world is wholly dispos'd of, and guided by *self-interest.*
>
> My main reason that self-interest is to be looked upon as the first *Principle of Nature* was, because I found that every man was desirous of what was good for him, and shun'd what was hurtful and evil: and this he did by a certain impulsion of Nature, no less than that whereby a stone moves downward.[15]

Tate's Edmund, a "natural" man, clearly proclaims that for him the choice between good and evil depends upon self-interest: "Be Honesty my Int'rest and I can / Be honest too" (I.i.297-298). "Interest" is, in fact, an important word in the adaptation: Burgundy seeks Cordelia's hand in order to consolidate an "alliance" with Lear's kingdom (I.i.), and Cordelia attributes his affection to "interest" (I.i.). On the other hand, Tate holds up Edgar, Kent, and Cordelia for admiration as examples of disinterested service to others.

At one of the high points of the adaptation, during an exchange of defiances before the duel in Act V, Edmund labels himself with a word not used in the original: "I / Was born a Libertine, and so I keep me" (V.i.18-19). To use such a word as "libertine" is to summarize the traits already exhibited to the audience. Tate's Edmund is a libertine not simply in the sense that he recognizes no moral restraint in his relations with women, but also in his character as a free-thinker. The word was strongly associated with the idea of Hobbism, for, as Mintz has shown,[16] both of these meanings—rake and free-thinker—were combined after the Restoration in the attacks upon Hobbes, whose critics tried to show that the libertinism which manifested itself in dissolute living resulted directly from the libertinism of free-thought and denial of religion. This movement from free-thinking—the rejection of any deity but "Nature"—to dissolute living is, of course, the sequence of Edmund's moral career in both Shakespeare and Tate. It remained for Tate to mark Edmund as a topical villain by appending the label of Libertinism. This libertinism of Edmund's extends in Tate's version of *King Lear* to a love of luxury, which Edmund shares with Gonerill and Regan. His inclinations are clearly stated during an interval of the "masque," the revels which the villains enjoy during Act III: "The Storm is in our louder Rev'lings drown'd. / Thus wou'd I reign cou'd I but mount a Throne" (III.ii.1-3). He thoroughly enjoys the sensual luxuries of a grotto where he makes love to Regan in Act IV. With leanings such as these, Edmund is associated with Gonerill, Regan, Cornwall, and the Gentleman-Usher (Shakespeare's Oswald metamorphosed for Restoration audiences) in a luxuriousness which, was thought to go hand-in-hand with a belief in Hobbes. In *Leviathan,* (I.xi), Hobbes explains that after the securing of power "there succeedeth a new desire; in some, of fame from new conquest; in others, of ease and sensual pleasure," and there were critics who accused him of advocating the pursuit of such pleasure. One of these critics, Robert Sharrock, writing in 1673, outlined some "Principles of Baseness" which are practically a summary of the conduct of the villains in Tate's *King Lear*:

> Fill yourselves with costly Wine and Oyntments and let none of you go without some part of his voluptuousnesse . . . ; oppress the poor righteous man, spare not the Widow and (which is perfect Hobbisme) Let your strength be the Law of Justice and what is feeble count it little worth. Lay wait for the Righteous man. . . . Examine him with Despitefulnesse . . . know his meeknesse . . . prove his Patience. Do not only make your scoffs at Vertue, but . . . destroy it and root it out and then fear not to venture upon any acts of Impiety or Insolence.[17]

When, in Tate's third act, Edmund plans to rape Cordelia, he proposes to seize her in "some desert place." Cordelia has departed to search the heath for her father, and Edmund rejoices that her virtue is delivering her into his hands. Away from the palace, in a wild place, there will be no restraints. This is not to force a melodramatic plan for a rape into a philosophical context, nor to overlook the fact that Cordelia's subsequent capture on the heath near the hovel which shelters Edgar is designed to give the latter an opportunity to rescue her: Tate knew that his audience would recognize the appropriateness of the "natural" man's proposing to seize his victim in a "natural" setting, where all inhibitions and barriers set up by decorum, rank, and morality would be nullified. In this setting, Edmund proposes to prosecute "the amorous Fight" while the thunder drowns Cordelia's cries "like Drums in Battle." The images here are suited to Edmund's aggressive temperament and, taken with what he proposes to do, and where, they are also reminiscent of the Hobbesian law: "The condition of mere nature . . . is a condition of war."[18]

Tate's Edmund has one more trait which is carried over from Shakespeare, is shared with Gonerill and Regan, and which may, when contrasted with a marked feature of Albany's character, be seen as consciously "Hobbist." As in the original, he has designs upon the lives of Lear and Cordelia, and though in Tate's version the most systematic malice toward the King comes from Gonerill, Edmund still advises Albany to execute Lear. His reasons are, like Gonerill's, political. Lear alive would always be an inducement to rebellion among the commons. However, in the adaptation their vindictiveness is made to contrast sharply with Albany's pronouncement (added by Tate) at the opening of Act V, scene iv: "It is enough to have Conquer'd, Cruelty / Shou'd ne're survive the Fight." To Albany the battle is over, and with its cessation the passions which it aroused should abate. As in Shakespeare (V.iii.42-46), he appears to have in mind some plan for releasing Lear and Cordelia. In Tate's version, Albany has not appeared since Act I, scene i, where he was a neutral character. He is now to play a large part in the unravelling which leads up to the happy ending, and it would appear that Tate expended some thought upon the problem of instantly stamping Albany at his reappearance as a "good" or at least a hopeful character. Albany's opening lines are more than vaguely humanitarian; they are meant to be taken as a pointed denial of the strongly-deprecated Hobbesian doctrine of a perpetual state of war, a state which "consisteth not in battle only, or the act of fighting; but in a tract of time, wherein the will to contend by battle is suficiently known."[19] This "will to contend" is short-lived in Albany, and all the more conspicuously present in Edmund and Gonerill. Indeed, it is a prominent feature of Edmund's character both in Shakespeare and in Tate.

Tate's addition of Hobbesian dress to a Shakespearean character seems, therefore, to go beyond a mere catching at certain popular notions of Hobbes's doctrines. It suggests rather that Tate was familiar with the letter of Hobbes's works as well as with the general spirit of distrust and fear in which Hobbes's ideas were held. Tate saw in Shakespeare's Edmund an adumbration—if not an actual type—of the Hobbesian "natural" man[20] and took pains to make the Shakespearean villain more exactly Hobbesian than he found him to be. It is paradoxical—though not untypical of the work of the Restoration dramatists—that while Tate's treatment of Edmund grows out of a close familiarity with Hobbes's works, the result tends towards a perpetuation of the misconceptions about the philosopher's ideas.

Notes

1. Margareta Braun has deplored many of Tate's alterations in "'This is Not Lear.' Die Leargestalt in der Tateschen Fassung," *Shakespeare Jahrbuch,* XVIX (1963), pp. 30-50; Christopher Spencer has carefully appraised the adaptation to show that Tate's changes are often "skillful and canny" ("A Word for Tate's *Lear,*" *Studies in English Literature,* III (Spring 1963), 241-252.

2. 1680. *The History of King Lear* was the first of Tate's three Shakespearean adaptations: he went on to new-model *Richard II* and *Coriolanus.* The adaptation of *Richard II* was undertaken just after the version of *Lear,* as Tate says in the Prefatory Epistle attached to *Richard II*: "I fell upon the new-modelling of this Tragedy (as I had just before done on the *History of King Lear*). . . ." *Richard II* was first produced on 11 December 1680 (Allardyce Nicoll, *A History of Restoration Drama 1660-1700* [Cambridge, 1952], p. 434), and *The History of King Lear* shortly afterwards. Tate's *Lear* was entered in the *Term Catalogues* under May 1681.

3. *The Aesthetic Theory of Thomas Hobbes* (Ann Arbor, 1940), pp. 280-281. Tate wrote an epistle "To the Reader" which was affixed to the 1689 edition of the *Six Books of Plants.*

4. *Aesthetic Theory,* p. 281.

5. Cf. Christopher Spencer, *SEL,* III (1963), 245.

6. Cf. Louis Teeter, "The Dramatic Use of Hobbes's Political Ideas," *E.L.H.,* III (1936), 140-169; and Samuel I. Mintz, *The Hunting of Leviathan* (Cambridge, 1962), Ch. VII.

7. *Leviathan,* I.xiv.

8. Hippolyte Taine, *Histoire de la Littérature Anglaise* (Paris, 1899), III, 34.

9. *The Reasonableness of Scripture Belief* (London, 1672), sigs. A3-4.

10. *The Hunting of Leviathan,* p. 135.

11. Robert Parsons, *A Sermon Preached at the Funeral of the Rt. Honorable John Earl of Rochester* (Oxford, 1680), p. 26.

12. Teeter, *E.L.H.,* III (1936), 168.

13. *Leviathan,* I.x.

14. Quoted by Teeter, *E.L.H.,* III (1936), 148.

15. English Reprints Series, ed. Peter Ure (Liverpool, 1958), pp. 89-90.

16. *The Hunting of Leviathan,* p. 134.

17. R[obert] S[harrock], *De Finibus Virtutes Christianae* (Oxford, 1673), pp. 195-196.

18. *Leviathan,* I.xv.

19. *Leviathan,* I.xiii.

20. John F. Danby has argued that Hobbes originally "took over Edmund and made him his basic pattern [for the natural man]": cf. *Shakespeare's Doctrine of Nature* (London, 1949), pp. 38-43, 47.

Peter L. Sharkey (essay date December 1968)

SOURCE: Sharkey, Peter L. "Performing Nahum Tate's *King Lear*: Coming Hither by Going Hence." *Quarterly Journal of Speech* 54, no. 4 (December 1968): 398-403.

[*In the following essay, Sharkey examines a 1967 staging of Tate's* King Lear, *revealing the influence of stage history on modern versions of Shakespeare's* Lear.]

Producing Nahum Tate's seventeenth-century adaptation of Shakespeare's *King Lear* illustrates how much past stage history affects our modern view of *Lear.* Over the years popular tragedians of the English and American stages developed a declamatory acting style that was born of Tate's modifications, and their success profoundly influenced the philosophy of producing Shakespearean tragedy. Neither the restoration of Shakespeare's text nor a change in rhetorical fashion could reverse a trend started by Tate and fully realized in the radical internalization of Shakespeare's dramaturgy in the modern theatre. The experimental production by students at the University of California, Berkeley, traces another source of the narrowness of the historically influential concept that the generative kernel of each Shakespearean tragedy is to be found solely in the pathology of the central character.

The revival of Tate's operatic version at Berkeley last year was probably the first in over a century. Perhaps it has taken that long to forgive those who preferred Tate to Shakespeare and who demanded exclusively to see the "restored" version on their stage in the 150 years from 1681 to 1837. The experiment helped surprisingly to identify and clarify Tate's lingering, curiously stubborn influence upon modern views of the play, especially in regard to structure and psychological coherence. Although the last age has tried to forget Tate, modern productions of *Lear* as an existential-psychological drama stem, in fact, in a greater part than we realize from the exaggerated style of elocution of that period. In retrospect, the tonal similarities between Tate's "improvement" and modern renditions of the original provoke more thought than the quaint differences in the respective texts.

Two critical events connected with the Shakespeare Quadricentennial inspired and shaped the Berkeley experiment: in 1964 Professor Maynard Mack as Beckman Lecturer delivered three talks on the history of *Lear* criticism and production,[1] and in 1965 Professor Christopher Spencer edited, and the University of Illinois Press published, a collection of redactions entitled *Five Restoration Adaptations of Shakespeare*. Professor Spencer supplied a bright new copy of Tate's obscured heroic text, and Professor Mack, weighing with great wisdom the history of redactions, put Tate's "restoration" in a new and attractive light.[2]

Professor Mack emphasizes Tate's direct and honest efforts to solve the Lear dilemmas for Restoration taste, devoted as it was to formal order and realism in dramatic art. As a result, he has demonstrated the need to estimate the extent to which contemporary productions build upon the partial solutions and compromises of past performances and to evaluate this legacy of interpretation as a phenomenon apart from the directions implicit in the text. The stage success or failure (for example) of the blinding of Gloucester, or the imaginary plummet over the cliff have traditionally served as critical points of departure in judging productions. The verisimilitude of the King's insanity on stage has too often been the unfortunate measure of an actor's handling of the complex role, and this has had a pernicious effect upon the stage tradition. Thus, problematic *loci* in the text have become, through the memorable performances of individuals, the histrionic *foci* of director and actor.

An excellent case in point is David Garrick's brilliant modification of Tate's King to fit his own talent. By restoring to the role more and more of Shakespeare's lines over the years, his performances soared in pathos. Eighteenth-century listeners flocked to his performances in the role of the "ill-used" old man, and their tears flowed. So lachrymose was the atmosphere of those productions that the very actresses who played the obdurate, evil sisters could not refrain from weeping during Garrick's pyrotechnical declamations of the curses against them. Did the contrastive rhetoric of Shake-

speare's lines within the melodramatic setting radically increase the pathos, or did the tears result from the actor's sheer sympathetic talent?[3] How did this affect the Lear role when Shakespeare's text was restored completely in the next century? Mack suggests that we have been so influenced by the productions and actors of the past that our dramatic expectations have been shaped in a way that no purely historical, textual analysis could, or should, supersede.

Taking its cue from Mack, the Berkeley production attempted to present seriously Tate's radical solution to problems inherent in Shakespeare's play. By writing into the play a psychology of "ruling passions," Tate conveniently managed to dispose of such familiar problems as the lack of any apparent motivation for the ancient King's precipitous, destructive actions, or for the otherwise dutiful Cordelia's refusal to conform to her obsequious sisters, or for Edmund's evil machinations, or for Edgar's disguise and his persistent virtue. Tate changed Shakespeare's plot in these particulars: He invented a love affair between Cordelia and Edgar, omitted France and the Fool, and gave Cordelia a lady-in-waiting to accompany her across the blasted heath in search of her father throughout the middle of the play. Edmund intends to rape Cordelia and follows her hence, but his plan is foiled when his ruffians are dispersed by the lover-hero Edgar, a miniature Hercules dressed as Tom-O-Bedlam. Through Edgar's, Gloucester's and Lear's heroic acts the play ends happily "at the seashore" (Dover) with the virtuous characters restored to power and the others destroyed by their foul devices. Thus, "Vice is punished and Virtue rewarded," poetic justice is established, and natural probability abandoned.

Lear's curses and his ravings in the mad scenes, Gloucester's and Edmund's oaths of revenge, and Edgar's and Cordelia's love complaints and vows constitute the heart of Tate's play; each is a rhetorical cameo or locket of the single passion ruling the corresponding character, and the scenes in which they appear are essentially rhetorical frames. This results in a kind of declamation contest between good and evil. By putting passionate hymns to love and duty in Cordelia's mouth Tate arrests the momentum of the horror that is the essence of his model. He gives Cordelia, thereby, an interest in the total plot not just equal to her sisters', but comparable to her father's. Each scene is built around an emotional high point. Elocution is the name of this interpretative game; to perform Tate, the cast must build from this simple rhetorical schema. The great speeches, soliloquies as well as exhortations, which in Shakespeare throw so much light in all directions at once, in Tate become isolated from the tone and content of the surrounding discourse; they are freed from the figurative, allusive diction which originally functioned in Shakespeare to keep the subplots alive in the minds of the audience and actors and to expand the meaning vigorously on many levels of thought at once. In Tate this tumult of sound and sense has been quieted so that the single revealing speech stands alone as a paradigm of its passion. The Fool has been eliminated altogether, not only because his medicine is too harsh for Tate's audience, but because he is a constant distraction from the stark effect of the King's declamation. Consequently, much of Lear's speech sounds like dramatic monologue. The dialogues throughout the play merely lead up to and down from the great bursts of tears and ravings.[4]

In his dedicatory letter Tate expressed admiration for Shakespeare but qualified it by noting that the master had left behind a "heap of Jewels, unstrung and unpolished." By "Jewels" Tate meant specifically a number of noble speeches whose moral impetus was unclear because the motivation of the characters who spoke them was obscured in the confusion of plots. As he found the play, the action did not conform to Restoration standards of dramatic unity, and the mixed style failed the test of genre. Tate was determined to make the action more probable and the dilemmas more obviously moral. Thus in the first sixty-five lines of his improved version, each character, except the King, tells us directly why he is going to do what he does. The fact that Lear does not know his own nature or intentions sets him apart. He is intended to become the potentially "tragic" character who, by learning and adjusting to his fate, will, in the last analysis, live and thrive. He is tragic in this context because his rational faculty is inoperative while he continues to perform his regal functions. King Lear possessed no "tragic flaw" until Tate endowed him with one. In itself this modification in the King's characterization would not have led future generations so far astray. Tate's mistake was that he tried to make too much of a good thing and over-developed the psychological motivations of all his major characters somewhat mechanically. Certainly Tate cannot be held wholly responsible for the endless, hopeless search of critics for the tragic flaw of all of Shakespeare's heroes. The germ of inquiry into Lear's pathology, however solidly planted by Tate, had to be nourished by the directors and actors from Tate to the present day to make it grow into its maturity on our contemporary "subjective" stages.

Listen to Edmund who opens Tate's play:

> Thou Nature art my Goddess, to thy Law
> My Services are bound, why am I then
> Deprived of a Son's Right because I came not
> In the dull Road that Custom has prescribed?
> Why Bastard, wherefore Base, when I can boast
> A Mind as generous and a Shape as true
> As honest Madam's Issue? Why are we
> Held Base, who in the lusty Stealth of Nature
> Take fiercer Qualities than what compound
> The scanted Births of the stale Marriage-bed?

> Well, then, legitimate Edgar, to thy Right
> Of Law I will oppose a Bastard's Cunning.
> Our Father's Love is to the Bastard Edmund
> As to Legitimate Edgar: with Success
> I've practis'd yet on both their easie Natures:
> Here comes the old Man chaf't with th'information
> Which last I forged against my Brother Edgar,
> A Tale so plausible, so boldly uttered
> And heightened by such lucky Accidents,
> That now the slightest Circumstance confirms him,
> And Base-born Edmund spight of Law inherits.

Tate has added a key causational concept in the terms "plausible," "lucky accidents," and "opposed." Edmund's place in nature and his moral capacity are never in doubt. There is no hesitation and intellection, no frustrated introspection. For contrast, here are the crucial lines from the original speech in Shakespeare:

> Why brand they us
> With base? With baseness? bastardy? base, base?

From here Tate's plot moves swiftly and deliberately. A few lines later Kent and Gloucester expatiate upon the King's "ruling passion":

KENT:

> I grieve to see him
> With such wild Starts of Passion hourly seized
> As renders Majesty beneath itself.

GLOS:

> Alas 'tis the Infirmity of his Age,
> Yet has his Temper ever been unfixt,
> Cholerick and suddain.

Thus the audience is prepared for the suddenness of Lear's change of heart in the ensuing testimonial scene. Also antecedent to that scene is the following exchange between Edgar and Cordelia:

EDGAR:

> Cordelia, royal Fair, turn yet once more,
> And e're successfull Burgundy receive
> The Treasure of thy Beauties from the King,
> E're happy Burgundy forever fold thee,
> Cast back one pitying Look on wretched Edgar.

CORD:

> Alas what would the wretched Edgar with
> The more unfortunate Cordelia;
> Who in obedience to a Father's Will
> Flys from her Edgar's arms to Burgundy's.

In her preference for Edgar over Burgundy she reveals further grounds for Lear's sudden outrage at her disobedience. Then comes a very abbreviated testimonial scene in which the traditional, rhetorical speeches on merit and value by the sisters have been truncated in order to avoid comparison with Cordelia's expanded, idealistic remarks. This strategy reverses Shakespeare. It is the anti-rhetorical bias of Cordelia there which focuses our attention on true value. In Tate, the overall effect of this opening is that a clear geometry of moral interests is presented with its matching hierarchy of rhetoric: love is on the top and hate and distrust are on the bottom. The love tryst simplifies the dependence of Lear, Cordelia, and Edgar upon each other and encloses the physical and psychological space they inhabit and share with the audience. This serves to meld the subplot into the main action, bringing the play in line with classical models. Lear's malady is diagnosed according to the familiar formula of humours identifying him with those reasonable, but occasionally choleric gentlemen in Tate's audience. Thus, by polarizing the elements of love and hate, and identifying the protagonist's natural affliction, Tate neutralizes the debate on the preeminence of cosmic and natural accident which he had found infecting the tone of Shakespeare's opening act. This allows him to establish the theme of *amor vincit omnia* and to evade the poignancy of the coincidence of Lear's and Gloucester's misfortunes which is the essence of Shakespeare's tragedy.[5]

Quite naturally, therefore, when the student readers came to realize that passionate exaggeration was indeed the intended effect of the rhetoric they were interpreting, the first crisis of the production arose. How could they possibly read without irony the patriotic ravings of the blind Gloucester, or the love-longing of Edgar, or the exhortations of Cordelia as she wanders the heath in search of her lost father? Could the production be saved from sick laughter and high camp sneers? This drew their attention directly to the more central matter of how to sustain the action, create continuity of character, and develop a recognizable tone which would modulate a steadily rising vocal intensity and increasing rhythm until the very end. It was quickly settled that, since the ideal of melodrama is to keep the audience on edge in a state of emotional uncertainty, they must not be allowed to laugh or cry in relief, but they must be kept just at a breaking point for the maximum effect. True success depended upon the control of tension up to the concluding reconciliation scene, when, having at last swept aside the forces of evil, and relaxed at the seashore, the happy, healthy, restored King would pronounce to the relief and joy of the audience that:

> Cordelia then shall be a Queen, mark that:
> Cordelia shall be Queen: Winds catch the Sound
> And bear it on your rosie Wings to Heaven.
> Cordelia is a Queen.

The actor who lapses into eye-rolling parody of this kind of hyperbolic discourse before the climax destroys the ambiguous melodramatic tension and deflates his characterization.

Notice here that the modern actor who lacks schooling in the grand manner of elocution will find it much harder to sustain Tate's characterization of Lear than Shakespeare's simply because there exist practically no clues in Tate for developing psychological continuity in the valleys between the emotional outbursts; when the character is not revealing his ruling passion in a set speech, he is usually speaking rationally in rather polished blank verse and periodic prose. The actor is required suddenly to leap to the heights of passion.[6]

In this interpretive dilemma the Tate production touches modern portrayals of *Lear*. In modern performances of Shakespeare's play this legacy of grotesque histrionics often results in aberration and breakdown of tone, usually caused by the actor's over-regard for the portrayal of Lear's pathology which was Tate's interest far more than Shakespeare's. Also, because of a failure to appreciate and control the profound stress pattern of the bass drum beat in the rhythm of Lear's preliminary speeches, the modern actor is often swept too far along in the first waves of Lear's oncoming madness, and he often reaches an unfortunate, premature crescendo in the first curse at the end of Act I that cannot be topped again. Thus he may spend the rest of the play trying to convince himself and his audience that madness, once it has begun, has the same tonal consistency throughout its run.[7] At this point "method" acting takes over.

When we return at last to imagine the quality of the famous eighteenth- and nineteenth-century performances of Lear we cannot help but be impressed by the strength of the tradition of elocution and declamation in that period. The success of those performances can be said to be "immortal" in a number of senses, a few of which we still fail to understand. Naturally, the pathetic renditions of Lear did not end with the restoration of Shakespeare's text near the middle of the last century; and although most teachers would deny it, the ability to declaim a set speech from Shakespeare often persists today as the tacit goal of an education in oral interpretation. The search for ourselves in Lear's pathology is the bias which conserves wrongly a mental landscape for the play's context despite the fact that the grand declamatory style which originally grew up in response to this view has long since dried up, cracked, and fallen away from the kernel. One consequence of this phenomenon is the fact that in most *Lear* productions the prose passages bear very little tonal relation to the rhapsodic verse speeches. Too often in a modern production we fail to hear the poetry in the heath scenes because of the special "psychedelic" sound effects and music which drown out the actors.[8] What are we to think of the now-accepted renditions of the Fool as Lear's partially cracked psychiatrist who never directs a word out to the audience? And perhaps worst of all, what are we to feel when we are suddenly plunged into darkness and the action completely halts following each scene? If we too are left darkling, and all the world is madder than Lear, then who will be left to speak the final admonitory speech? Through psychological reductions most modern directors lead us to premature conclusions about the play that differ little from Tate's view. They present a skillful dramatization of Lear's tortured psyche, but never a drama of all the forces of nature working together simultaneously on all the characters on the stage. In today's productions, as in the heyday of Tate's adaptation, we continue to suffer the presentation of a sick, dotty old man, not a great tormented king.

Notes

1. Since published as *King Lear In Our Time,* University of California Press (Berkeley and Los Angeles, 1965).

2. This is the first comprehensive analysis of the play's stage history to appear since George C. D. Odell's classic *Shakespeare from Betterton to Irving* (2 vols., New York, 1920, 1966). Modern scholarship on the tradition of Shakespeare redactions begins with Hazelton Spencer's invaluable study, *Shakespeare Improved, The Restoration Versions in Quarto and on the Stage* (Cambridge, Mass., 1927).

3. George Winchester Stone, Jr., describes the contemporary controversy concerning the presentation of passion on the stage stirred by Garrick's Lear in "Garrick's Production of King Lear: A Study in the Temper of the Eighteenth Century Mind," *Studies in Philology,* XLV (January 1948), 89-103. Evidently, the strong audience reaction discouraged Garrick from abandoning Tate's structure even though he was inclined to do so on numerous occasions.

4. Throughout the play Tate regularized the blank verse without regard to the dramatic context. By smoothing out Lear's speeches and yet retaining Shakespeare's diction he presents the King basically as a man of reason who suddenly runs off his trolley. This is disturbingly noticeable in the heath scenes where his own descriptive speeches seem emotionally similar to Kent's, while his ravings and curses are sudden and "epileptic" compared to either. The absence of the Fool in these scenes places a monstrous burden upon the actor.

5. Even though many critics following Addison had judged Tate's text inferior to Shakespeare's, by the mid-eighteenth century his psychology remained in vogue and seemed to be dominating the best criticism.

6. Faced with the same problem. Garrick gradually restored the lines of Shakespeare's King without changing Tate's context. See *Stone,* p. 101.

7. Hazelton Spencer speculates that Tate may have seen one of Davenant's rare productions of Shakespeare's *Lear* in the late 1670's, which, if true, might begin to explain his extraordinary interest in the King's pathology.

8. Addison complained of the growing vogue of spectacle on the English stage in his time in *The Spectator,* No. 44. He pointed particularly to distractive, ill-conceived "special stage effects" such as bells, thunder and ghosts. For further discussion of the neoclassical critical approach to Shakespeare see Robert Witbeck Babcock, *The Genesis of Shakespeare Idolatry, 1766-1799* (New York, 1964), especially Chapter XII, "The Psychologizing of Shakespeare."

Lawrence D. Green (essay date spring 1972)

SOURCE: Green, Lawrence D. "'Where's My Fool?'— Some Consequences of the Omission of the Fool in Tate's *Lear." Studies in English Literature, 1500-1900* 12, no. 2 (spring 1972): 259-74.

[*In the following essay, Green argues that the omission of the Fool in Tate's* King Lear *resulted in more focus on the internal workings of Lear's mind, an element that has been retained in productions of Shakespeare's play.*]

The major differences between Shakespeare's *King Lear* and Nahum Tate's redaction of it in 1681 are often viewed with either amusement or horror, and then dismissed as long-gone aberrations of little consequence. Tate's substitution of a happy ending for the play and his addition of a romance between Edgar and Cordelia have shared most of this attention, but his omission of the Fool may be his most enduring influence on *King Lear.* The Fool has almost all his scenes with Lear, and many of Lear's lines develop as direct or indirect responses to the Fool's dialogue or actions. The omission of the Fool would seem to require considerable alterations of these lines, but comparison of Tate's text with Shakespeare's shows that Lear's lines are substantially intact. The isolation of these lines from their context suggests strange changes for both Lear and the play.

In actual productions actors found it necessary to reconstruct for themselves the context that was omitted with the Fool. Tate's additions, the happy ending and the romance, had little effect on the situation, so the individual actor was left to his own imagination. This reliance on personal insight, rather than interplay with other characters, often had spectacular results. In time the actor's freedom in interpreting Lear became a dramatic tradition, and not even the restoration of Shakespeare's text and Fool could control this obsession with the inner workings of Lear's mind. A number of modern productions indicate that the concept of an internalized Lear has persisted, even though his context has been supplied once more by the Fool. This study into Lear's pathology as a basis for interpretation has lasted beyond the necessity of Tate's text and continued into more recent interpretations of Shakespeare's text.

The nature of the interpretive problem with Lear can be seen in the way Tate approached the entire play and his new romance in particular. Tate was more interested in plot than in characterization, and when he felt that motivations were needed, he turned to sentimentality. The romance at the center of the play was intended simultaneously to provide reasons for unexplained actions and to bind explicitly the plots of Lear and "Gloster" together. Tate evidently felt that the entire play, Fool and all, was too unrefined for Restoration tastes. In his **"Epistle Dedicatory"** Tate describes Shakespeare's play as a "Heap of Jewels, unstrung and unpolisht" and goes on to explain that "'Twas my good Fortune to light on one Expedient to rectify what was wanting in the Regularity and Probability of the Tale, which was to run through the whole A Love betwixt Edgar and Cordelia, that never chang'd word with each other in the Original."[1] In Act I, Tate's "Expedient" has Cordelia and Edgar declare their love for one another before the testimonial begins, and while it is in progress, she tells the audience she would rather make the king disown her than be forced to marry Burgundy (France has been omitted completely). The king does get angry and she does not marry Burgundy, but the king suspects the reason for her cold speech—"Thy Fondness for the Rebel Son of Gloster" (I, p. 4). After this Lear divides his kingdom and banishes Kent, but as the Court leaves, Edgar rejoices that Cordelia may be left to him and he offers her his panting heart. She rebuffs him, reasoning in an aside that Edgar, like Burgundy, may only be interested in her for her royal property, and that she will wait for proof of love before committing herself. In Act II, when Edgar realizes he is being sought, he decides to stay around in disguise since he feels that "Cordelia's in destress" and "Who knows but the white minute yet may come / When Edgar may do service to Cordelia" (II, p. 17). Fortunately for Edgar, Tate has packed the play with white minutes. In Act III Cordelia seeks Gloster's help for her father who is lost on the heath, and Edmund, overhearing their conversation, decides to rape her on the way. Just as his henchmen are about to seize her, Edgar, dressed as Poor Tom, beats the ruffians off with the ringing words "Is this a Place and Time for Villainy? / Avaunt ye Bloud-hounds" (III, p. 34), and the two lovers confess their feelings with heartfelt sighs and exclamations. In Act V Edgar saves Cordelia again, and after they are gloriously re-united, Edgar ends the play with the pronouncement that "Truth and Vertue shall at last succeed" (V, p. 67).

This expedient of Tate's supplies the regularity the play wanted, but it also indicates the type of jewels he was

stringing together. Almost all his dramatic high-points and turns in the plot occur either at the end of a long speech or in a sudden action on stage. As a result Lear's dramatic moments of self-realization are reserved for the ends of speeches. The speech must include all the necessary information and at the same time build emotionally to the desired brilliance. Polishing these dramatic moments is difficult with Lear because they usually occur in Shakespeare after a series of fast exchanges with the Fool. The Fool's language itself is highly figurative and simultaneously points to several different levels of meaning. The manner in which he jumps around from one line to the next perhaps baffled Tate's impulse towards regularity and probability, but it is a very efficient manner of revealing what is troubling Lear. The Fool is continually focusing on Lear from different directions which shift as quickly as Lear responds to them. In the longer speeches which follow these fast exchanges, Lear is free to give vent to his emotions. His feelings have already been exposed by the Fool, so Lear is under no burden to explain them within the speech itself. He needs only to express them in the intensity the Fool aroused. These are the noble speeches which interested Tate, and despite some condensation and rearrangement,[2] they remain substantially intact. The Fool's end of the conversation, however, has been excised. This turns both Lear's dialogue and his extended responses into dramatic monologue. After three acts of monologue the isolation of Lear from his Fool becomes the isolation of Lear's character. A comparison of the relevant scenes from Shakespeare and Tate indicates the extent of this isolation and its consequences for the interpretation of Lear.

The Fool first appears in Act I, scene iv,[3] as Lear and Kent finish tripping-up Oswald. Lear is accustomed to being treated as a king, and the Fool's constant flow of songs, coxcombs, and pared crowns makes both Lear and the audience more conscious of the enormous change in Lear's state. Goneril breaks in upon them, and the Fool comments on Lear's new-found concern for his daughter's frowning. His remarks make Lear more sensitive to any affront, and at the same time they let Goneril frame her attack around the insolent, all-licensed Fool. Before Lear can respond to her argument, the Fool interjects with a song that likens her to a killer-cuckoo and further focuses Lear's attention on her attitude instead of her words. Lear cannot believe such a speaker could be his daughter or that such a listener could be Lear. His incoherent questioning is disoriented even more by the Fool's interjections. Lear is unable to understand or to respond, and when Goneril contemptuously ignores his anger and pain, he explodes into "Darkness and devils!—"

In Tate's revision (I, p. 10) there is no preliminary exchange between Kent and the Fool on status and employment, so that Goneril's instructions to her servant and his subsequent affront to Lear both lose much of their irony. The entire scene is less an inversion of the hierarchy in Lear's confused public and private lives, and more a spiteful, gratuitous action on Goneril's part. She enters while Lear and Kent are still tripping-up her servant, and her verbal attack responds directly to this act. When Lear asks "Now, Daughter, why that frontlet on? / Speak, do's that Frown become our Presence?" this situation makes the first question sound sheepishly guilty and the second one an indignant return to decorum. Her accusation reads more like a routine administrative announcement than a violation of a king's decree. Lear's response "Are you our Daughter?" seems a rather odd reply and unrelated to either his previous style of speaking or to Goneril's announcement. She resumes in the same manner, but Lear replies with a series of questions about himself and his identity. Goneril's final speech ("Come, Sir, this Admiration's much o' th' favour / Of other your new humours . . .") is then a reply to disconnected questioning. At no time does Lear appear to be saying anything relevant to what Goneril is saying nor is there any indication of his state of mind that might relate his speeches to the scene. When he suddenly bursts into "Darkness and Devils!," there seems to be little basis for his conduct or speech.

Lear's incoherent questions become incomprehensible and are unable to stand by themselves without the Fool to interpret both Goneril's speech to Lear and Lear's speech to the audience. Prior to the cursing of Goneril the Fool establishes the image of the rod simultaneously as the sceptre, the whip, and Lear's manhood:

LEAR:

> When were you wont to be so full of songs, sirrah?

FOOL:

> I have used it, nuncle, e're since thou madest thy daughters thy mothers; for when thou gavest them the rod and puttest down thine own breeches. . . .

> (I.iv.164-167)

This provides a basis for a steady rise to a level from which Lear can appeal to Nature to curse Goneril's womb, and from that new level he can threaten her for shaking his manhood. Tate does not establish this basis, nor does he have the lines with the Fool to serve as stepping stones for this rising passion. Tate, instead, reverses the order of Shakespeare's two speeches (the curse and the threat) and avoids the references to Lear's manhood. Tate's Lear presents himself as a wronged father and curses her, then calls on Nature for Goneril to have an ungrateful child who will make her "curse her Crime too late" (I, p. 12). The language of the final curse is substantially Shakespeare's, but Tate's previous lines do not provide an adequate spring-board to its intensity. Lear's total response to Goneril has been largely

generated by the Fool's remarks, and the irony of his outbursts has been increased by framing them with references to the Fool and foolishness. Without the Fool, Tate's Lear must generate the effect of those remarks himself if he is to fill out Shakespeare's language. The cues and the path for rising passion have been built into Shakespeare's lines. They are not present in Tate's lines, and it is much more difficult to reach the power the speeches demand. At this point it is necessary for the individual actor to supply his own cues, either through voice, expression, or gesture, and to create for himself the context for these speeches.

In Shakespeare's play the Fool is with Lear almost continually during the first three acts, so that the Fool establishes both the literal context in which Lear speaks as well as the broader figurative context for both Lear and the play. Kent, Goneril, Edmund, and Lear all refer to foolishness in the beginning of Shakespeare's play, and their differing ideas contribute to the audience's sense of conflict.[4] Shakespeare develops this further as Lear, Kent, and the Fool prepare to leave for Regan's palace. The Fool tells Lear he is deluding himself to think his other daughter will use him kindly and that he was foolish to part his kingdom so. Lear responds by thinking simply of Goneril's monstrous ingratitude, and the Fool tells him that he would make a good Fool. When Lear was master, or thought he was in control, he could threaten the Fool to take heed of the whip, but more than that has changed now:

FOOL:

> If thou wert my Fool, nuncle, I'd have thee beaten for being old before thy time.

LEAR:

> How's that?

FOOL:

> Thou shouldst not have been old till thou hadst been wise.

LEAR:

> Oh let me not be mad, not mad, sweet heaven! Keep me in temper; I would not be mad!—

> (I.v.38-44)

Tate has completely omitted this dialogue so that the sense of irony Shakespeare built into the lines as a basis for Lear's speeches is missing. It must be developed by Lear himself, if he is to retain his later language. The basic context of inverted relationships and unsteady standards is particularized and controlled in Shakespeare through Lear and his Fool. The differing attitudes of Goneril, Kent, and Lear towards hierarchy, their differing values and conceptions of foolishness, are all measured against the Fool and his relationship with Lear. Thus this relationship both defines Lear to the audience and controls the discrepancy between this view and Lear's own opinion of himself. With the loss of the Fool and many of the references to foolishness this basic irony is missing, so that Lear himself must somehow supply the sense of continual cross-reference his language calls for. The sharp focus the Fool provided on this shifting context is gone, and Tate's actor can provide it only by responding to a shifting image of Lear that exists solely in his own mind.

Lear perceives the broader dimensions to the stocking of Kent only after the Fool's interjections. The Fool replies to Kent's narrative by telling Lear he shall see his children kind only as long as he still bears bags for them. Lear's climbing sorrow is as much an impassioned response to the Fool's interpretation as to Kent's story. The depth of sorrow brought out in Lear by the Fool provides the basis for the terrible and erratic curses upon the sisters. The Fool's constant presence is a visual reminder of this, and Lear ends his curse with "—O Fool, I shall go mad!" (II.iv.283)

Tate has no pause between Kent's story and Lear's response to it. There is no time for his thoughts and speech to gather the dimensions that would have been interjected by the Fool, although the language remains. Tate's Lear replies directly to Kent's stocking with "climbing Rage." Where Shakespeare's Lear is starting to climb to a sorrow that will embrace far more than just his daughters, Tate's Lear is furious about a personal insult. Before Regan's entrance in Shakespeare, Lear struggles with his rising heart, only to have the Fool tell him a tale about beating down wanton eels who resisted being cooked alive. Lear's forced restraint bubbles through the scene with the sisters, until it breaks into passion bordering on madness. Tate has no such dialogue or pause before Regan's entrance. Instead he requires the actor to generate his own pressure for the scene. With the loss of depth and power that the Fool released, the actor now has the necessity as well as the opportunity to respond freely to whatever he thinks it is that makes Lear tick. There is no control on Lear's diction now. The Fool no longer pulls Lear's language back into reality or serves as a standard to measure the changes in that language.

Shakespeare describes the physical scene of the storm on the heath before we see it. A gentleman tells Kent that Lear is contending with the elements, and the Fool is with him trying to outjest his pains and sorrows. Thus Lear himself is free to respond to the storm with pounding apostrophes, and the Fool to respond to both Lear and the storm. Even a Fool knows when Lear should come out of the rain and ask his daughter's blessing, but Lear's mind is on greater things. When he alludes to generation and all creation, the Fool is still singing about Lear's earlier choice of his toe over his heart. It is during the Fool's song of self-control, wisdom, and folly that Lear regains his own control, or at least subsides. When Kent enters, the Fool ironically points out in summation "Marry, here's grace and a cod-piece; that's a wiseman and a fool" (III.iii.40-41).

Tate's heath scene has Lear raging against the storm, while his only companion, Kent, tells the audience what is going on. Instead of a contrast between the Fool and Lear, between their different attitudes toward the storm and one another, there is only Lear delivering orations to the rain, while Kent asks him to consider the pros and cons of what he is doing. Where Shakespeare's Lear thinks of the universe and says "No, I will be the pattern of all patience," Tate's Lear grabs a line that had expressed an earlier, supposedly superseded emotion: "I will forget my Nature, what? so kind a Father, / I, there's the point" (III, p. 24). Again Tate has left much of the language of Shakespeare, despite alterations, but he has removed the context of it that was developed by the interplay of Lear and his Fool. Tate's Lear has an essentially uninterrupted speech on the heath, and Kent's explanatory speeches simply confirm that the old king deserves compassion—indeed, pathos is about all that an actor can develop from this vestigial scene. Lear is even robbed of his awareness and compassion for his Poor Fool, since "how dost my Boy? art cold?" is addressed to the stalwart Kent, making this speech sound somewhat silly and sentimental.

The scene before the hovel and Lear's mock-trial of daughters have both been telescoped and rearranged in Tate to form one scene, and the Fool's soothing effect on Lear in his madness has been completely lost. When Shakespeare's Lear starts to unbutton, the Fool cries "Prithee, nuncle, be contented" (III.iv.106), while in Tate, all Kent can say is "Defend his Wits, good Heaven!" (III, p. 31)

This scene indicates the great difference in the characters of Shakespeare's Lear and Tate's. Just as the Fool's ironies previously pointed to a significance greater than the immediate situation, now Lear's lines refer to matters greater than himself. He is losing his capacity to reason, and the speed with which his images follow one another outstrips even the Fool's scope. The Fool's relationship to Lear continues to define Lear to the audience, at the same time serving as the measure of his madness. Tate's Lear, however, is essentially a rational man who temporarily loses his reason. Without the Fool to help supply the context he is not free to rage. Instead he must explain to the audience that he is raging ("Blow Winds and burst your Cheeks, rage louder yet"). He is never too far from rationality, and even Kent thinks Lear simply is not thinking clearly tonight; he says, "Consider, good my Liege. Things that love Night / Love not such Nights as this" (III, p. 24). Here the second sentence is offered to Lear as a new approach to a logical problem. In Shakespeare Kent is more concerned about Lear's safety and ability to reason at all, and the same anti-thesis is more of a confirmation by Kent to himself that it is dangerous on the heath: "Alas, sir, are you here? Things that love night / Love not such nights as these" (III.ii.42-43). The rhetorical question is one of concern, but the situation is not quite this serious in Tate, where Kent is still trying to reason with Lear. Kent does not supply the contrastive presence that the Fool did, so that when Lear flashes from rationality to madness there is no way to grade the difference. The actor must single-handedly convey both Lear's madness and the reasons for it, all without textual guidelines.

The possibility remains that within the heroic context of Tate's play the remnants of Shakespeare's lines took on dimensions omitted with the Fool, but the testimonial scene is the only point of contact in the first three acts between Lear and Tate's "Expedient." In a discussion of the effects of Tate's concerns for probability, Christopher Spencer has noted that this single contact diminishes Lear.[5] All three sisters are scheming against their father in the first scene—Goneril and Regan to obtain power and Cordelia to avoid marriage with Burgundy. Lear seems simply to have chosen the worse of two deceits, and if the purpose of the Fool is to make clear the magnitude of Lear's error, he is not necessary for Tate's family misunderstanding.

The problem seems to lie in Tate's overall structure. He used probability and a love-theme to tie the parts together in a more emotional manner ("The Distress of the story is evidently heightened by it"), and he placed Lear in reasonably defined situations. Unfortunately, Tate placed Lear's speeches in a context of plot and probability, when they were meant to function in a context of allusion and metaphor. The Fool's stream of paradoxes, references, and ironies all reverberated with a universe beyond just Lear, at precisely those moments when Tate wanted to make the play easy to comprehend.[6] In addition to the confusion he caused, the Fool also appeared somewhat coarse to Restoration minds. Although there is very little about the Fool's speech that is actually comic, perhaps he was also omitted because of his name, as a sort of lipservice to the neoclassical theory that decreed separation of comedy and tragedy. Certainly some of Kent's speeches and his activity with Oswald would indicate that comedy was really acceptable as long as it was not called comedy.

With the omission of the Fool the metaphoric context for Lear's speeches was gone. Despite the probability and the plot machinations surrounding Lear's speeches, there was not enough energy to fill out his language. With the reduction of Lear's lines to speeches and the isolation of those speeches from their context, Lear's character also became isolated. The only way left around this was for the individual actor to create a metaphoric context outside of the lines themselves, to have a private understanding of what gave rise to Lear's speeches and actions, since the play itself did not supply such an understanding. In short, Tate's text required the actor to create an internal reality for Lear apart from the play. In actual productions of *King Lear* after 1681 this is precisely what happened.

The first actor to play Tate's Lear was Betterton. His response to this problem of context in 1681 was symptomatic of almost all subsequent interpretations. Something had to be wrong with Lear's mind, since what he said did not make sense with the play around him. Betterton concluded that Lear's speeches "must be spoke with an elevated Tone, and enraged Voice, and the Accents of a Man all on Fire, and in a Fury next to Madness."[7] Thus this need in Tate for a new context would seem to be the source of elaborate study of Lear's pathology to find a basis for creating a role. From this study it is not far to the critical attempt to understand the play by understanding Lear's mind. Despite Betterton's near-madness and Tate's own claim that "I found it well receiv'd by my Audience," *King Lear* does not appear at first to have been as popular as *Hamlet* or *Othello*.

Apparently a superlative Lear was required to save the play from oblivion. Conversely, Tate's play provided the background from which such a Lear could appear. *King Lear* was the only one of Shakespeare's tragedies during the Restoration to present this dual requirement and opportunity. In the period from 1700 to 1750 there were several surges of interest in Shakespeare, but the London box-office success of Tate's *King Lear* was independent of the mutual fortunes of *Hamlet, Macbeth,* and *Othello,* even when the latter plays were adaptations or refinements. The play had two periods of popularity during this time, and each coincided with the emergence of a new actor: Boheme appeared in the 1720's and Garrick in the 1740's.[8] Actors soon realized how few restrictions Tate's plot had placed upon their imaginations and how much the play needed a context for Lear. The combination of such freedom and need resulted in a very attractive challenge to an ambitious actor. The taste of the 1720's ran towards sentimental, tear-strewn drama, and Boheme accordingly emphasized the unhappy, grief-stricken side of Lear. After his death in 1731 the play fell into a slump. Despite a succession of popular actors in the heroic roles of Edgar and Cordelia, Tate's romantic play was not able to sustain itself without a superlative Lear. Garrick first appeared as Lear in 1742, after his debut in *Richard III*, and single-handedly brought the play to the forefront of the London stage again. After 1745 *King Lear* became almost Garrick's private property, and the play continued to be performed only by theaters at which he happened to be acting.

Garrick recognized the magnificent opportunity for solo performance in the vacuum left by the Fool. He made no changes in Tate's version until 1756, although G. W. Stone believes he was continually adding lines from Shakespeare throughout his career.[9] Garrick expanded on Tate's possibilities by enlarging the role, and his versions printed in 1774 and 1786 show extensive restorations. Despite his expurgations of Tate from the text, he kept the romance and the happy ending, and kept out the Fool. Still there were restrictions on Garrick's seemingly free-handed creation. The omission of the Fool omitted the sense of continual cross-reference and "cosmic" reverberations, so that the possibilities for Lear's universe were limited. An account of Garrick's last performance is an indication of how Lear was portrayed as the "ill-used" old king:

> The curse at the close of the first act, his phrenetic appeal to heaven at the end of the second on Regan's ingratitude, were two such enthusiastic scenes of human exertion, that they caused a kind of momentary petrifaction thro' the house, which he soon dissolved universally into tears. Even the unfeeling Regan and Goneril forgetful of their characteristic cruelty, played through the whole of their parts with aching bosoms and streaming eyes. . . .[10]

The depths and range of sorrow that the Fool set free in Lear have here been replaced by soaring pathos as Garrick seized his opportunity for an operatic cadenza. After Garrick's spectacular interpretation the role became the test of an actor's talents.

By this time almost all alterations, adaptations, and interpretations were directed towards improving the solo performance of Lear. Colman, Garrick's contemporary, produced a short-lived version that crossed Shakespeare's language with Tate's structure and kept the Fool out of Lear's way: "I had once some idea of retaining the Fool, but after the most serious consideration I was convinced that such a character in a tragedy would not be endured on the modern stage" (Odell, I, 380). Barry, Garrick's understudy, returned to the purity of Tate's adaptation in 1774. This was kept by Kemble until 1810, when he restored some of the language.

Edmund Kean concentrated upon the workings of Lear's insane mind and presented Lear on the heath as a dream-like recollection. The need for a speaking context independent of the text allowed Kean to create a Lear who responds to a mysterious influence or inspiration rather than to immediate feelings and faculties (Furness, pp. 440-443). Again the requirements for Lear's speeches has led to two plays—the one in the text and the second in Lear's mind. Again Lear's response to the missing Fool has created a dramatic monologue that tends towards a confused soliloquy. Kean produced the Tate version until 1823, when he restored the tragic ending, although it was not Shake-speare's ending. Odell hails this as a revolutionary breakthrough (II,155), but in fact the production was a disaster: "Kean could not carry Mrs. W. West without difficulty—this is said to have set the audience into a laugh, which continued till the curtain dropt" (quoted in Black, p. 46).

By the time of Macready the tradition of the self-sufficient Lear was so firmly established that even the restoration of the Fool could not alter it. The tradition instead altered the Fool when he appeared. In 1834 Macready restored nearly all of Shakespeare's text, but still left out the Fool. In preparing for a production in 1838 he wrote that the Fool was such a terrible contrast that "in acting representation it will fail of effect; it will either weary and annoy or distract the spectator" (Odell, II,195). At the last minute Macready conceived of the Fool as a "sort of fragile, hectic, beautiful-faced boy" (Furness, pp. 67-68). He finally settled on having a woman play the poor fool and knave in the Fool's first appearance since 1681.

Two pages later Odell piously intones that "With this production the ghost of Nahum Tate—so far as England, if not America, was concerned—was laid forever." Unfortunately, his ghost, if not his text, may remain with us considerably longer. The element of pathos which has always existed in Lear was kept in check by the Fool, whose lines would continually undercut sloppy sentiment, but when the Fool was taken away this element ran wild. Coupled with the loss of dimension and language, the omission of the Fool led to extravagant deliveries of Lear's speeches and extensive explorations into the causes of his pathology. Those few times that Lear actually does talk in a situation that exists only in his mind, as with Goneril's ingratitude (I.v.20-40), have the impact of the internal shift obliterated by the successive cadenzas. The Fool's restoration after 150 years of stage tradition and criticism has not in itself been enough to cause actors and directors to abandon their dramatic field day. Maynard Mack has traced the production of *King Lear* through recent times, and concludes that most of the nineteenth-century Lears after Macready were senile, old, pathetic men.[11] Charles Laughton's interpretation, as recent as 1959, portrayed Lear as a diminutive, sympathetic "representative of the common man" and was intended "to put the play within the scope and comprehension of a mass Shakespearian audience" (Mack, p. 27), playing upon emotions which are considerably less in scope than Shakespeare's play, with the Fool, would seem to call for. Herbert Blau's production in 1961 treated the storm on the heath as an extension of Lear's mind, complete with a cacophonic electronic score and improvised ballet between Lear, the Fool, and Poor Tom—"one felt the storm as a nightmare; one saw the descent to absolute dispossession on the part of the King."[12] The entire production was based upon a "sub-text" (the play behind the text) taken from

Cordelia's response "nothing." Thus the creation of an internal reality for Lear continues long after the Fool's return to the stage, and modern productions can deliver that "nightmare" directly to the audience without any interference from the text.

What began as a side-effect or corollary to Tate's major alterations may well prove to be his most long-lasting effect. Tate's adaptation in 1681 produced a play that appealed to contemporary dramatic tastes, and it took over 150 years for his love-theme to be discarded. It is unlikely that the modern audience will ever encounter this particular love story. Some current stage ideas, however, continue to have Lear responding in isolation to a world largely of his own creation, and this leaves the Fool scampering along side him, uttering unneeded paradoxes. Perhaps this would have been Lear's fate on the modern stage without Tate's help, but his redaction made it all but unavoidable. Instead of presenting a Lear who can build only on the context provided by the Fool, there is an internalized Lear with diminished proportions. It may take some time for the Fool to reassert himself on stage and restore the needed interplay with Lear. Until then we can cry out with Lear "And my poor fool is hang'd! No, no, no life!"

Notes

1. Nahum Tate, *The History of King Lear* (London, 1681), "The Epistle Dedicatory." All further citations from *The History of King Lear* are to this edition, referenced by act number and page number.

2. Tate made numerous stylistic changes as well. Hazelton Spencer has examined a number of these in *Shakespeare Improved* (Cambridge, 1927), pp. 250-251. They result from grammatical corrections, modernizations, prosaic clarity, literalization of figurative language, and often pure capriciousness.

3. William Shakespeare, *King Lear*, ed. H. H. Furness, A New Variorum Edition of Shakespeare (New York, 1880). All further citations from *King Lear* are to this edition.

4. The entire subject of majesty falling to folly is first brought up in the testimonial scene by Kent. When he reappears disguised in Act II his earlier words are literally expressed in the inverted roles of the king and his Fool. Shakespeare uses this broader subject of foolishness as a tool in exploring the problem of how to deal with experience and as an indication within the play of the different characters' attitudes towards the problem. For a fuller discussion of this aspect in Shakespeare, see R. B. Heilman, *This Great Stage—Image and Structure in "King Lear"* (Seattle, 1963), pp. 182-192.

5. Christopher Spencer, "A Word for Tate's *Lear*," *Studies in English Literature*, III (Spring, 1963), p. 246. Spencer argues that this diminution of Lear is irrelevant to an appreciation of Tate's *Lear*, and that such a judgment must be based on Restoration standards rather than those applied to Shakespeare's plays.

6. Tate thought the problems the play posed were best understood as moral choices. This ultimately resulted in a triumph for Lear, since truth and virtue had to succeed. For an account of the production difficulties and critical repercussions of this concern with moral motivations, see Peter L. Sharkey, "Performing Nahum Tate's *King Lear*: Coming Hither by Going Hence," *Quarterly Journal of Speech*, LIV (December, 1968), pp. 398-403.

7. James Black, "An Augustan Stage-History: Nahum Tate's *King Lear*," *Restoration and Eighteenth Century Theatre Research*, VI (May, 1967), p. 40. Tate wrote for both the individual actors' interest in the roles and the theater's capabilities. In 1681 the Duke's Theatre held exclusive rights to any production of Shakespeare's *King Lear*, and if the theater decided not to accept Tate's play, it could not be produced at all. The theater had both prison and grotto sets. Tate wrote one scene showing Lear and Cordelia actually in prison, and another with Edmund and Regan amorously engaged. The two lead actresses, Elizabeth Barry and Mary Lee, were vying with one another, and research by Black suggests the grotto love-scene was written primarily for the second actress.

8. Max F. Schulz, "*King Lear* A Box-Office Maverick Among Shakespearian Tragedies on the London Stage 1700-01 to 1749-50," *Tulane Studies in English*, VII (1957), pp. 83-90.

9. G. W. Stone, Jr., "Garrick's Production of *King Lear*: A Study in the Temper of the Eighteenth-Century Mind," *Studies in Philology*, XLV (January, 1948).

10. George C. D. Odell, *Shakespeare—From Betterton to Irving* (New York 1920), I. 454.

11. Maynard Mack, "*King Lear*" *in Our Time* (Berkeley, 1965), p. 2.

12. Herbert Blau, "A Subtext Based on Nothing," *Tulane Drama Review*, VIII (1963), p. 130.

Christopher Spencer (essay date 1972)

SOURCE: Spencer, Christopher. "Short Poems and Translations of Ovid and Juvenal" and "*A Poem upon

Tea." In *Nahum Tate,* pp. 41-53; 141-45. New York: Twayne Publishers, 1972.

[In the following essay, Spencer discusses the two editions of Tate's Poems *and his translations of Latin classics, which the critic says show that Tate was not particularly creative or original but had considerable talent for collaboration. The critic then examines Tate's mock-heroic poem,* A Poem upon Tea, *and offers a brief assessment of the author's place in English literary history.]*

SHORT POEMS AND TRANSLATIONS OF OVID AND JUVENAL

Of the sixty-nine pieces in the first edition of Tate's **Poems** (1677), about half belong to the tradition of melancholy verse that reaches back to the early years of the seventeenth century and forward to the period of Tate's laureateship around 1700, a time whose "widespread fondness for melancholy subjects in literature" and for funeral elegies has been emphasized by Amy Reed and by J. W. Draper.[1] The publication of Robert Burton's *Anatomy of Melancholy* in an eighth edition the year before Tate's poems appeared testifies to the continuing interest in the subject. However, the most respectable and most talented writer of this kind of verse during the 1670's was Tate's friend Flatman, who wrote of death so often that, when he composed an elegy on his brother, he could begin with the thought that he had nothing on the subject left to say.[2] Tate commented on Flatman's common theme in his first published poem from the point of view of the admiring apprentice:

> Strange Magick of thy Wit and Stile,
> Which to their Griefs Mankind can reconcile!
> While thy Philander's tuneful Voice we hear,
>   Condoling our disastrous State,
>   Toucht with a sense of our hard Fate,
>   We sigh perhaps, or drop a Tear;
> But he the mournful Song so sweetly sings,
> That more of Pleasure than Regret it brings, . . .[3]

In another poem, **"Ode. To my Ingenious Friend, Mr. Flatman,"** Tate emphasized his apprenticeship as Icarus to Flatman's Daedalus.[4]

Especially interesting are the melancholy poems which seem to look forward to the eighteenth century or beyond. Tate's **"Mid-Night Thought,"** for example, seems to anticipate Edward Young's *Night Thoughts* (1742), two-thirds of a century later:

> Now that the twinkling Stars essay
> A faint Resemblance of the Day,
> Shewn fairer now for being set
> In Night (like Diamonds in Jett)
> Let me (repos'd within this Grove)
> The solemn Season once improve.
> Restless, Alass! from Sun to Sun,

> A Round of Business I have run:
> Whilst others slept, projecting lay,
> My Night as thoughtful as my Day;
>
>   . . . . .
>
> How long since I did meditate
> Of Life, of Death, and future State?
> Approaching Fate his Pace will keep,
> Let Mortals watch, or let them sleep.
> What Sound is that?—a Passing Bell!
> Then to Eternity farewell! . . .[5]

And in **"Disappointed"** Tate seems to anticipate the mood of Matthew Arnold:

> From Clime to Clime with restless Toyl we Roam,
> But sadly still our old Griefs we retain,
> And with us bear beyond the spacious Main
> The same unquiet selves we brought from Home.[6]

Tate's melancholy is not the "divinest Melancholy" that Milton hails in "Il Penseroso," but rather the Burtonian disease which, in **"Melancholy,"** Tate calls the "Malignant Humour, Poyson to my Blood," from which he wants to escape.[7] Usually, his melancholy poems have a strong moral emphasis. **"On a Diseased Old Man, Who Wept at thought of leaving the World,"** for example, and **"Disswasion of an Aged Friend from leaving His Retirement"** argue—one harshly, the other gently—the worthlessness of mundane concerns.

The longest poem in the 1677 volume, **"The Vision. Written in a dangerous Fit of Sickness,"** is of this kind. Dreaming that he enters "Death's sad Courts," the poet comes to a cave filled with tablets hung on threads, each giving the story of a life. He finds one with his name on it and learns that he is about to die. When Death enters with his dart, scepter, skull, bloody attendants, and assistant diseases, the Dreamer pleads for his life on the grounds that, though he has been sinful, he should be allowed time to repent. His plea is denied, but, as the Demons are about to seize him, his Guardian Angel disperses them. Observing that the Dreamer is indeed close to death, the Angel gives him a vision of his own body, which the Dreamer addresses with disgust and loathing. Momentarily, he is given a vision of Heaven, and then he awakens to life—which seems to be Hell.[8]

The moral emphasis appears also in his **"On the Present Corrupted State of Poetry"** in the 1677 volume:

> Write thy own Elegy Apostate Art,
> Thou Angel once of Light;
> But, since thy Fall, a Friend of Night,
> Mankind endeav'ring to pervert.

The poet contrasts the noble religious origins of poetry, the support it has received from wise and potent kings, its dignity in more virtuous ages when it was used "t'embalm some Worthy Name," and its freedom from mercenary concerns in the past with its present tendency to encourage "The Vanity and Vices of the Age; / Flatt'ring in Courts, and Rev'lling on the Stage.'"[9] He laments the poverty that befalls "Th'Unfortunate Man, whom any Muse befriends."

I Other Models

The 1677 *Poems* was a typical first effort in that it contained many experiments and imitations of various recent or contemporary writers. One of these was Milton, who had died only three years earlier. As Raymond D. Havens has pointed out, Tate's poem **"On Snow fall'n in Autumn, and Dissolv'd by the Sun"** is an imitation of two stanzas of Milton's *Nativity* Ode.[10] *Lycidas,* from which Tate also borrowed in **A Pastoral Dialogue** (1691), is echoed at the end of **"Melancholy,"** in which Tate answers his own questionings of the "Book of Fate" as follows:

Who seeks for Happiness with nicest Care
Must watch its Seasons, and frequent its Haunt.
    Delight is a rich tender Plant
That Springs not in all Soils, and all the Year:[11]

Phoebus had replied similarly to the poet's question in *Lycidas* (11. 78-80): "Fame is no plant that grows on mortal soil, / Nor in the glistering foil / Set off to th'world, . . ."

Later, Tate expressed his admiration for Milton's style and occasionally even imitated it. Although he seems never to have published a poem in blank verse, he referred in 1688 to the "Majestic Plainness" of Milton's style, "just" but "Subservient to the Thought."[12] In his epigram **"On the Spectator,"** published at the end of an essay by Addison in *The Spectator* for September 19, 1712 (No. 488), Tate imitates Milton's manner:

When first the *Tatler* to a Mute was turn'd,
Great Britain for her Censor's Silence mourn'd.
Robb'd of his sprightly Beams she wept the Night,
Till the *Spectator* rose, and blaz'd as bright.
So the first Man the Sun's first Setting view'd,
And sigh'd, 'till circling Day his Joys renew'd;
Yet doubtful how that second Sun to name,
Whether a bright Successor, or the same.
So we: but now from this Suspence are freed,
Since all agree, who both with Judgment read,
'Tis the same sun, and does himself succeed.

The Miltonic effect of the four-line metaphor describing the "first Man" is conveyed principally by the phrase "circling Day" and by the omissions of both subjects and verbs in lines 7 and 8 and of the verb in line 9. It seems surprising that Tate did not imitate Milton more than he did, for he seems to have regarded his predecessor as England's greatest poet; and, as the son of a Puritan minister, as a man with some scholarly attain-

ments and an interest in education, and as a supporter of the poet's important role in encouraging moral reform, Tate must have found much of Milton's thought and attitude congenial. In part, the explanation of Tate's independence of Miltonic influence probably lies in the very different kinds of poems the two men were called upon to write.

About one-third of the poems in Tate's 1677 collection are love lyrics. Most are short and are set in a pastoral background in which shepherds—usually anonymous but sometimes named Strephon, Thirsis, Alexis, or Damon—discourse with or about shepherdesses, Laura, Sylvia, Larissa, Fanarett, Olinda, or Julia. Love is generally painful for Tate's shepherds. In **"The Escape,"** in fact, the lady fisherman hooks her lover; but, in her eagerness to land her catch, she lets him escape with a permanently painful jaw. One of Tate's more successful "love poems" is **"Laura's Walk,"** in which the lady is blended with the flowers in a manner reminiscent of Robert Herrick:

I.

The Sun far sunk in his Descent,
    Laid now his Tyrant Rays aside,
When Laura to the Garden went,
    To triumph over Natures Pride.

II.

The Rose-Buds blusht with deeper Dye,
    Envying Lillies paler grew;
The Violets droopt with Fear to spie
    On Laura's Veins a richer Blew.

III.

She stoopt and gather'd as she went,
    But whilst she slaughter'd sweetly Smil'd;
As Angells tho' for Ruine sent,
    Appear with Looks serene and mild.

IV.

But now grown weary with her Toyl,
    A Garland for her Brow she frames:
Thus with proud Trophies made o'th' spoil,
    Her Conquest o'er the Spring proclaims.[13]

Of the more intellectual variety of love lyric, Tate attempted a few examples; but his development of the subject was usually slight. In **"The Tear,"** the rich drop on Julia's face will die whether or not it falls to earth; but it can be preserved in a vial and will even be frozen—converted to a diamond—if it is put close to Julia's heart. But this last thought leads to the reflection that there is hope, for the very existence of the tear shows that the frost of Julia's heart is breaking. In **"The Politicians,"** the title is witty; for the poem begins with the idea that, like politicians, lovers find that quarrels make the heart grow fonder; but Tate fails to develop the deeper possibilities of the metaphor. In "The Wish," Abraham Cowley had asked for his mistress, few friends, and many books; more modestly in **"The Choice,"** Tate longs only for "a rurall Seat" and

> A private, but an active Life.
> Conscience bold, and punctual to his Charge;
>   My Stock of Health, or Patience large.
> Some Books I'd have, and some Acquaintance too,
>   But very good, and very few.[14]

One of the most individual poems in the 1677 volume is **"Sliding on Skates in a hard Frost,"** in which Tate maintains a suitably mock-heroic attitude toward his rather unconventional subject:

> How well these frozen Floods now represent
> Those Chrystal Waters of the Firmament!
> Tho' Hurricanes shou'd rage, they cou'd not now
> So much as curl the solid Water's Brow;
> Proud Fleets whose stubborn Cables scarce withstood
> The Fury of the late tempestuous Flood,
> In watry Ligaments are restrain'd,
> More fast than when in binding Ooze detain'd.
> But tho their Service does at present fail,
> Our selves without the aid of Tide or Gale,
> On Keels of polisht Steel securely sail;
> From ev'ry Creek to ev'ry Point we rove,
> And in our lawless Passage swifter move
> Than Fish beneath us, or than Fowl above.[15]

Other distinctive poems in the collection include **"The Hurricane,"** a dramatic monologue describing a ship-wreck, and **"The Beldam's Song,"** which is the spell of a witch as she stirs her pot. In these two poems Tate may well have been imitating the two "operatic" versions of Shakespeare that were highly popular during the 1670's, *The Tempest* and *Macbeth*.[16]

II THE SECOND EDITION (1684)

Most of the poems underwent considerable revision for the second edition, published in 1684.[17] Some of the changes seem to be mere tampering, but most are improvements, smoothing out awkward wording in the earlier version or making the meter more regular. The last five lines of the first stanza of **"The Installment,"** for example, had been extremely rough in meter and diction. The whole stanza originally read as follows:

> Long have I Languisht in the Fire
>   Of an unquenchable Desire;
> And will it not suffice thee Love,
>   That I thy patient Martyr am,
> Unless thy Worship I promove,
>   And proselyte others to thy Flame?
> If as a Laick-Lover ought I act,
>   What canst thou more from me expect,
> Who am not gifted for a Teacher in the Sect?

In 1684 the last five lines were altered to read:

> Unless thy Worship I improve,
>   Converting others to thy Flame?

> If I the Practise not neglect,
>   Thou canst no more from Me expect:
> Not gifted for a Teacher in the Sect.[18]

The thirty-three poems added in 1684 are a miscellaneous collection: a few are political or occasional; some are complimentary verses to Dryden and other friends on the publication of various works; some are songs, prologues, or epilogues for the plays Tate had written between 1677 and 1684; and more than a third are translations of Roman poets. One distinctive poem is **"The Battle of the B[aw]ds in the Theatre Royal, December the 3d 1680,"** which begins:

> Give ore ye Tilters of the Pit, give ore,
> Frighten the Boxes and your selves no more:
> Two Amazons of Scandalous renown,
> Have with dire Combat made this Field their own.

The method is that of the amused mock-heroic, not unlike the battle that concludes Pope's *Rape of the Lock*; Tate continued:

> Strong Sarcenet Scarf with Hood of Gause more slight,
> Promiscuously lay scatter'd in the fight:
> Necklace and Pendants perish't in the fray,
> And rev'rend Point that did the Art display,
> Of Ages past had now its fatal Day.[19]

Bellona finally stops the fight, "And Drury-lane all loyal Wh———es resound."

In form, the additions in 1684 are more conservative than the poems of 1677. Almost half those in the earlier volume are in couplets, about equally divided between tetrameter and pentameter. Five poems, including **"Advice to a Friend"** quoted above, are in couplets with alternating pentameter and tetrameter lines. Elaborate repeated stanzas appear in some of the love poems with the more extravagant conceits, such as **"The Usurpers"** and **"The Tear."** Several poems are in quatrain stanzas, and several are in stanzas made up of unequal lines after the manner of Cowley's and Flatman's odes, although in only one of these poems—the **"Ode. To my Ingenious Friend, Mr. Flatman"**—does Tate use the word in the title. The ode was regarded as a noble form, and Tate's restraint may be the result of the same excessive modesty that later in 1677 led him to change the names in his first play. Of the poems added in 1684, twenty-six are in pentameter couplets, three in tetrameter couplets, two in quatrains, and two in irregular stanzas.

Many of the verses in the first edition show a poet in his early twenties feeling his way and experimenting with models from the recent past. But they demonstrate a sense of poetic form and often a felicity and smoothness of expression. It is not surprising that Dryden took an interest in the young poet, collaborating with him in translations and offering him *The Second Part of Absalom and Achitophel*. The second edition of the

Poems shows more confidence; a preference for the pentameter couplet, in which Tate was to write almost all the rest of his nondramatic verse; and an inclination toward translation.

III TRANSLATIONS OF OVID AND JUVENAL

In 1680 Tate joined with Dryden and Flatman, as well as Thomas Rymer, Elkanah Settle, Thomas Otway, Samuel Butler, and at least ten other poets in a translation of Ovid's *Epistles*. Although Dryden wrote the Preface ("Ovid and the Art of Translation"), translated two Epistles himself, and collaborated with the Earl of Mulgrave on a third, the project was probably that of the publisher, Jacob Tonson.[20] Tate translated **"Leander to Hero," "Hero's Reply to Leander,"** and **"Medea to Jason,"** of which the best is certainly the third—as Tate recognized, for he printed it but not the other two in the second edition of his *Poems.*

Ovid, a favorite in Restoration times, was admired especially for his "polite" and civilized style—"tenderly passionate and courtly," according to Dryden.[21] As the editors of the California edition point out, Dryden attempted to reproduce this style partly by omitting synaloephas (cutting off the vowel at the end of a word when the next begins with a vowel, as "th' are"); by omitting triplets; and, in "Dido to Aeneas," by composing individual couplets that are not only end-stopped but are complete units, ending with a period or its equivalent and not built in clusters of several together. Ovid's verse, Dryden would remark in 1685, has "little variety of numbers and sound"; it "is always as it were upon the Hand-gallop, and his Verse runs upon Carpet ground."[22] Dryden ended about 72 percent of the couplets in "Dido to Aeneas" with final punctuation, as opposed to about 41 percent in "Canace to Marcareus" and 47 percent in "Helen to Paris."[23] Tate used final punctuation at the end of over 80 percent of the couplets in **"Hero to Leander,"** almost 90 percent in **"Leander's Answer to Hero,"** and about 70 percent in **"Medea to Jason."** A comparison with Tate's longer couplet poems written nearest to 1680 shows that he, too, was deliberately trying to imitate Ovid's style: in **"The Vision, Written in a Dangerous Fit of Sickness"** (1677), only 50 percent of the couplets end with final punctuation, and final punctuation is so employed in just under 50 percent in *The Second Part of Absalom and Achitophel* (1682).[24]

Tate and Dryden shared an enthusiasm for Ovid. In Dryden's Dedication of *Examen Poeticum* (1693), he declared that he thought his best translations were those of Ovid; his total has been estimated at more than seven thousand lines.[25] Tate, too, had high praise for Ovid and his adaptability: in 1697, he observed that "Some of our greatest Judges of Poetry have declared their Sentiments of this Author, That he is the fittest amongst the Classick Poets to be Translated into English. Indeed, he is so Natural a Writer, that he cannot fail of being agreeable in any Language he shall be made to speak."[26] About two hundred lines of Book VII of the *Metamorphoses* had appeared in Tate's 1684 *Poems*; and Tate was apparently working on a translation of more of this work as early as 1692, when Dryden wrote of "spoyl[ing] Tate's undertakings" in a letter to Tonson.[27] The first five books of the *Metamorphoses* were published under Tate's editorship in 1697 (Tate himself contributing part of Book IV) with the assurance that the remaining books were "preparing for the Press, and will be Published with all convenient Speed."[28] Although the other books were apparently never issued, Tate's remark shows that more of the translating may have been done.

In 1708 Tate collaborated with Aaron Hill in **The Celebrated Speeches of Ajax** (translated by Tate) **and Ulysses** (by Hill) from Book XIII of Ovid's *Metamorphoses*. Dryden himself had translated these speeches for his *Fables* (1700), and the sense of rivalry between the poets, suggested by Dryden's earlier letter to Tonson, appears again in the Dedication by Tate and Hill in which they express their confidence that a "Genuine Translation" will be useful. They refer to the criticism advanced against Dryden, "the Great Master of the Muses," that he mistook Ovid's manner; and, although they do not say that they subscribe to this view, they insist that at least they are not guilty of a similar error. In the following year, Tate published his translation of Ovid's *Remedy of Love,* along with an English version by others, including Dryden, of *The Art of Love.* Although Tate published fewer lines of Ovid in English than Dryden, he nevertheless had an important role in the age's translation of the Roman poet.

In 1692, Tate contributed to Dryden's translation of the *Satires* of Juvenal and Persius, which Gilbert Highet in 1954 called "still the best verse translation of Juvenal in English."[29] It is from Tate's version of Satire XV that Samuel Richardson's *Clarissa* quoted with praise.[30] Dryden wrote the Dedication to Dorset, the "Discourse Concerning Satire," and translated all six of Persius's and five of Juvenal's fifteen satires. He made the other assignments and, apparently, supervised the work, his collaborators being his sons, Charles and John, and Bowles, Stepney, Hervey, Congreve, Power, and Creech, each of whom did one satire, and Tate, who did Satires II and XV.[31]

Satire II begins as an attack on hypocrisy, but it soon becomes an attack upon homosexuality. From the Argument, it appears that Tate intended to gloss over some of its cruder passages: "The Poet, in this Satyr, inveighs against the Hypocrisie of the Philosophers, and Priests of his Time: the Effeminacy of Military Officers, and Magistrates. Which Corruption of Manners in General, and more Particularly of Unnatural Vices, he imputes to the Atheistical Principle that then prevail'd." Actually, however, Tate translated frankly lines that the translator in the Loeb edition, for example, thought were better left as ellipses. The high percentage of closed couplets is well suited to vigorous, forceful expression of Juvenal's wrath. The fidelity of Tate's translation of Juvenal can be judged from the relatively decorous opening lines of Satire II. The literal Loeb translation is as follows:

> I would fain flee to Sarmatia and the frozen Sea when People who ape the Curii and live like Bacchanals dare talk about morals. In the first place, they are unlearned persons, though you may find their houses crammed with plaster casts of Chrysippus; for their greatest hero is the man who has bought a likeness of Aristotle or Pittacus, or bids his shelves preserve an original portrait of Cleanthes. Men's faces are not to be trusted; does not every street abound in gloomy-visaged debauchees? And do you rebuke foul practices, when you are yourself the most notorious delving-ground among Socratic reprobates?[32]

Tate translated the passage thus:

> I'm sick of Rome, and wish myself convey'd
> Where freezing Seas obstruct the Merchants Trade,
> When Hypocrites read Lectures, and a Sot,
> Because into a Gown and Pulpit got,
> Tho surfeit-gorg'd, and reeking from the Stews,
> Nothing but Abstinence for's Theam will chuse.
> The Rakehells too pretend to Learning—Why?
> Chrysippus Statue decks their Library.
> Who makes his Closet finest is most Read:
> The Dolt that with an Aristotle's Head,
> Carv'd to the Life, has once adorn'd his Shelf,
> Streight sets up for a Stagyrite himself.
> Precise their Look, but to the Brothel come,
> You'll know the Price of Philosophick Bum.[33]

The one hundred and seventy lines of Latin become two hundred and forty-five in Tate's version.

Of the three sorts of translation that Dryden distinguished in his Preface to Ovid's *Epistles,* metaphrase (word-for-word translation), paraphrase ("translation with latitude, where the author is kept in view by the translator, so as never to be lost, but his words are not so strictly followed as his sense"), and imitation (which often departs from both words and sense),[34] Tate generally paraphrased, though he occasionally imitated. An example of imitation is a couplet near the end of Satire II (11.217-18) for which there is no justification in Juvenal and which directs the Satire as a whole against atheism (as Tate had indicated in the Argument): "To what dire Cause can we assign these Crimes, / But to that reigning Atheism of the Times?" Juvenal does not mention atheism. Similarly, in Satire XV, "against the Superstition and Cruelty of the Egyptians," Tate indulged in a six-line parenthesis, criticizing English bor-

rowing of false rhetoric from the French. Just a few years later such departures from the text in his translation of the Psalms provided his enemies with an opportunity to attack him.

In November, 1693, about a year after the translation of Juvenal had appeared, Tate published his own satire in *The Gentleman's Journal.*[35] Although the Juvenalian attitude was not really congenial to him, the poem succeeds fairly well as a mild imitation of it. The satire is addressed to Richard Baldwin, the publisher of Motteux and Sir Thomas Urquhart's translation of Rabelais, whom Tate familiarly calls "Dick." The poet first asserts the futility of satire, for even Rabelais, Cervantes, and Quevedo together have not reformed society. Lawyers and doctors still prey upon their clients, and clergymen profit, too:

> Has Biggottry to make a Man turn Sot,
> Or Priest-craft how to menage Fools forgot?
> Or is not, when a Pastor shifts his Place,
> A fatter Benefice the Call of Grace?
> Have you ne'er seen a Drone possess at ease
> What would provide for Ten Industrious Bees?

Tate continues with the "Plodding Citt" who becomes rich while "his graceless Son Turns Wit and Beau, drinks, whores, and is undone." Refinement of manners and speech has brought no improvement, and "Science is made Cant, and Nonsense Mystery." "Half the Gallamaufry of Mankind" consists of "Pimps, Pandars, Stallions, Buffons, Parasites, / Setters, Suborners, Sharpers, Pillory-Knights, / Cheats, Cullies, Bravoes, Cowards, Hypocrites. . . ." The poem turns finally to the vanity of human desires, and then lightly back to Rabelais: "Yet—As by witty Rabelais 'tis Exprest, / Life's Idle Droll's an entertaining Jest."

Translation and imitation seem to have been congenial occupations for Tate. His mind was not especially creative either of new ideas or of really fresh means for developing them; and he did better when the central idea and the main lines of development were suggested or laid out for him. Evidently, Dryden recognized his ability; for, when Dryden worked with a collaborator, he often chose to work with Tate.

· · · · ·

A POEM UPON TEA

It is sometimes said that Tate's best poem is **Panacea: A Poem upon Tea: In Two Canto's,** first published in 1700 and republished as **A Poem upon Tea** in 1702.[36] It appeared the year after Dr. Garth's successful mock-heroic poem *The Dispensary,* and it heralded a spate of early eighteenth-century mock-heroic poems on beverages, including John Philips's *Cerealia* (1706) in praise of ale and John Gay's *Wine* (1708).[37] Tate's friend Motteux wrote another *Poem upon Tea* (1712).[38] Although ***Panacea*** is mock-heroic, the burlesque element is much lighter in Tate's poem than it is in the Miltonic burlesques of Philips and Gay.

I The Celebration of Tea

Tea had come to England near the middle of the seventeenth century. At first it was drunk only by the very wealthy, but in 1657 Thomas Garway began underselling the market at his coffeehouse, and tea soon became popular. It was supposed to have many virtues, twenty of which are listed in a manuscript in the British Museum dated 1686 and allegedly translated from the Chinese by Thomas Povey, M. P. The twenty virtues include some that are physical (tea "Prevents the Dropsie" and "Clenseth and Purifieth adult humours and a hot Liver") and some that are mental or ethical (it "Sharpens the Will and Quickens the Understanding" and encourages "the use of due benevolence").³⁹ In the Preface that Tate added to the second edition of his poem, he observed: "I must honestly acknowledge, 'tis to This (despicable) Tea-Leaf that I owe Recovery out of a Weakly Constitution from the very Cradle: and make no Doubt of the like Benefit to Others (in most Infirmities) with right Knowledge of this Panacea, and different Preparation and Use of it's Infusion, for the purpose of Pleasure Only, or for Health."

The speaker of Tate's poem is the shepherd Palaemon, who leaves the Avon to visit "Foreign Climates":

> Most strict Survey in every Realm he made
> Of Men and Manners, Policy and Trade;
> But none he found, his gentle Soul to please,
> Like the Refin'd and Civiliz'd Chinese.⁴⁰

On returning home, he introduces his fellow shepherds to tea and then tells his astonished listeners the story of its origin. China had enjoyed a Golden Age until the time of Emperor Ki, who had ruined the country to support his own luxury. He was eventually overthrown, but the diseases that had come with him would not leave. Finally, the new emperor went with his court to consult with Confucius, and growing in front of Confucius's cave they discovered three kinds of tea—Soumblo, Imperial tea, and Bohea—given to Chinamen in compensation for their "Publick Grief." The first canto closes with an announcement of the subject of the second:

> Next, how their [China's] Poets sing (in bolder Verse)
> The Virtues of this Plant—I shall rehearse
> How happily their Art they have Express'd,
> With useful Truth in pleasing Fable drest;
> That sickly Mortals, by the Tempting Lure
> Of Fiction, may be drawn to certain Cure.⁴¹

In Canto II Palaemon sings the virtues of the plant in terms of a competition among the Goddesses before Jupiter and the "Gods in Council" to see who should be the "Patroness and Guardian" of tea. Speaking first,

Juno demands the right to sponsor the "Queen of Plants"; she urges Jove to assert the rights of royalty. Minerva retorts that "Merit" should not give way to "Majesty" and claims the privilege of sponsoring tea for herself in the name of Athens, Isis, and Cam; for tea is especially the reward of scholars, who have surrendered the "Life of Pleasures" to devote themselves to study. It is also the reward of poets:

> From this Pirene, this Castalian Spring,
> Exclude the Muses, And what Muse will sing?
> And when no Poet will vouchsafe to write
> What hardy Hero will vouchsafe to fight[?]
> 'Tis Tea sustains, Tea only can inspire
> The Poet's Flame, that feeds the Hero's Fire.⁴²

Venus appeals in the name of Beauty, which, she urges, inspires both soldier and poet; and she points to the tea-drinking British ladies to show the close connection between tea and beauty. Cinthia promptly claims the British ladies (and therefore tea) as her own, for they are particularly famed for their virtue. She is followed by Thetis, who pleads the sea's support of Albion and the tea trade, and then by Salus, the Goddess of Health. Somnus awakens long enough to praise tea as the inspiration of man's happy dreams: "Thus Human Life in cruel Fate's despight, / May have its Sorrows checquered with delight." When the deities quarrel, Jove finally finds the solution in accepting all the goddesses as patronesses of the plant and giving it the name of "Goddess" or "Thea."

At the end of Canto II is **"The Tea-Table,"** a brief poem celebrating tea over strong drink:

> To Bacchus when our Griefs repair for Ease,
> The Remedy proves worse than the Disease:
> Where Reason we must lose to keep the Round,
> And drinking Others Healths, our Own confound:
> Whilst Tea, our Sorrows safely to beguile,
> Sobriety and Mirth does reconcile:
> For to this Nectar we the Blessing owe,
> To grow more Wise, as we more chearful grow.
> Whilst Fancy does her brightest Beams dispense,
> And decent Wit diverts without Offence.
> Then in Discourse of Nature's mystick Pow'rs
> And Noblest Themes, we pass the well-spent Hours.
> Whilst all around the Virtues Sacred Band,
> And list'ning Graces pleas'd Attendants stand.
> Thus our Tea-conversation we employ,
> Where With Delight, Instruction we enjoy;
> Quaffing, without the wast of Time or Wealth,
> The Sov'reign Drink of Pleasure and of Health.

The practical purpose of the poem was supported in the second edition with a handbook for tea drinkers, containing sections headed "An Account of the Nature and Virtues of Tea: With Directions in the Use of It for Health. Collected from Treatises of Learned and Skilful Physicians upon That Subject," "Directions in the Use of Tea," "The several Kinds of Tea," "Observations for Making of Tea," and "For Preserving the Tea-Leaf."

Except for an extravagant dedication to Charles Montague, *A Poem upon Tea* was written without the usual pressures: there was no king or other dignitary to celebrate in heroic verse, no high standard of elegance to strive for, no laureate duty, no musician to satisfy, and no responsibility to sacred text. Tate was able to relax and enjoy himself, and the result is an entertaining poem written with the amused awareness of the relatively trivial nature of his subject that had appeared in such early poems as **"Sliding upon Skates."**

II FINAL ESTIMATE

In his frequent lack of confidence and vigor, Tate differed from his leading contemporaries, Dryden, Defoe, Swift, and Pope; but in many other respects he was very much of his age. At the same time, his broad literary sympathies linked him with both earlier and later periods, though it is a mistake to think that he belonged more to the other eras than to his own. He combined a Puritan heritage with a modestly successful literary life at the courts of the later Stuarts, William and Mary, and Anne; and his works have affinities with many types of verse and drama from Spenser and Shakespeare to Cibber and Young. As Polonius might say, he wrote verse that is melancholy, moral, panegyrical, satiric, and mock-heroic; and his nine plays and adaptations include at least one in each of the categories of heroic tragedy, sentimental tragedy, history, tragicomedy, realistic comedy, and farce.

Tate also made important contributions to the reestablishment of Shakespeare in the theater, to the early growth of English opera, to the early development of the English hymn, and to the translation of the classics in a style suited to the eighteenth century. He wrote a large number of works, many of which succeeded in their own day, and several of which outlasted the age for which they were written. He was suitably the poet laureate of his time; and, although poverty and failing health seem to have limited his activity after 1702, he carried out what he felt to be the duties of his office with dignity and with responsibility.

Notes

1. Amy Reed, *The Background of Gray's Elegy* [New York: Columbia University Press, 1924], p. 27; Draper, *The Funeral Elegy and the Rise of English Romanticism* (New York, 1929).

2. "On the Death of my Dear Brother Mr. Richard Flatman," *Poems and Songs*, 4th ed. (London, 1686), p. 193.

3. *Poems*, 2nd ed. (London: B. Tooke, 1684), pp. 11-12.

4. *Ibid.*, pp. 64-65.

5. *Ibid.*, pp. 101-2. The resemblance to Young (and the resemblance to Arnold in the next example)

are pointed out by Scott-Thomas, "The Life and Works of Nahum Tate," [doctoral dissertation, Johns Hopkins, 1932] I, 325, 327.

6. *Poems*, 2nd ed., p. 76.

7. *Ibid.*, p. 81. In the list of errata (sig. A7v), the misprint "Honour" is corrected to "Humour."

8. *Ibid.*, pp. 56-64.

9. This poem is quoted from the first edition of *Poems* (London: B. Tooke, 1677), pp. 14-15. It was heavily revised in the second edition, although the only revision of significance in the lines quoted was the unfortunate substitution of "(alas too prone.) contriving" for "endeav'ring" in the fourth line. Scott-Thomas, "The Life and Works of Nahum Tate," I, 9, says that Dryden admired this poem, but he gives no evidence for his statement.

10. *The Influence of Milton on English Poetry* (Cambridge, Mass., 1922), p. 566, and note, where he quotes Tate's poem in full. Tate's use of the phrase "Wood-wild Notes" in "To the Athenian Society" (cf. Milton's "L'Allegro," l. 134, "wood-notes wild") seems to have been first noticed by George Sherburn in "The Early Popularity of Milton's Minor Poems," *Modern Philology*, XVII (1919), 522.

11. *Poems*, 2nd ed., p. 83.

12. Complimentary verses by Tate accompanying Francis Fane's *The Sacrifice* (London, 1686).

13. *Poems*, 2nd ed., pp. 31-32.

14. *Ibid.*, p. 105.

15. *Ibid.*, p. 69.

16. Scott-Thomas, "The Life and Works of Nahum Tate," I, 330, points out the resemblance of "The Hurricane" to *The Tempest*.

17. *Ibid.*, I, 332-36; II, 205-33, includes many examples of Tate's revisions for the second edition.

18. *Poems* (1677), p. 27; *Poems*, 2nd ed., p. 28.

19. *Poems*, 2nd ed., pp. 153-54.

20. *Works of John Dryden*, ed. Edward IV. Hooker (Berkeley, 1956), I, 324; Ward, *Life of John Dryden* (Chapel Hill, 1761), p. 143.

21. *Essays of John Dryden*, ed. W. P. Ker (Oxford, 1926), I, 236.

22. *Ibid.*, p. 255.

23. *Works of John Dryden*, ed. Hooker, I, 326-28.

24. The text of the *Second Part of Absalom and Achitophel* that I have used is the one in the second edition of Noyes's *Poetical Works of Dryden*.

25. *Essays,* ed. Ker, II, 9. The estimate was made by David Nichol Smith, *John Dryden* (Cambridge, England, 1950), p. 68.

26. *Ovid's Metamorphosis. Translated by Several Hands,* Vol. I (London, 1697), sig. A6.

27. *Letters of John Dryden,* ed. Charles E. Ward (Durham, N.C., 1942), pp. 50, 162. See also Hugh Macdonald, *John Dryden: A Bibliography of Early Editions and Drydeniana* (Oxford, 1939), p. 67, note.

28. *Ovid's Metamorphosis,* I (1697), sig. A7.

29. *Juvenal the Satirist* (Oxford, 1954), p. 214.

30. *Clarissa* (Oxford, 1930), IV, 339.

31. Ward, *Life of John Dryden,* p. 364.

32. *Juvenal and Persius,* tr. G. G. Ramsay, rev. ed. (Cambridge, Mass., 1950), pp. 17-19.

33. *The Satires of Decimus Junius Juvenalis. Translated into English Verse. By Mr. Dryden and Several Other Eminent Hands* (London, 1693), p. 19.

34. *Essays,* ed. Ker, I, 237.

35. *The Gentleman's Journal* (November, 1693), pp. 380-82.

36. Those who have preferred it to the rest of Tate's work include Edmund K. Broadus, *The Laureateship: A Study of the Office of Poet Laureate in England* (Oxford: Clarendon Press, 1921), p. 101, and W. Forbes Gray, *The Poets Laureate of England* (New York, 1915), p. 108, who calls it his "masterpiece."

37. See Richmond P. Bond, *English Burlesque Poetry 1700-1750* (Cambridge, Mass, 1932), esp. pp. 108-9, 163-64, 238-39.

38. Motteux's poem was dedicated to the *Spectator,* and was acknowledged by Steele on December 3, 1712 (No. 552); it was reprinted in *The Bee,* Part III (London, 1715), pp. 38-46.

39. William H. Ukers, *All About Tea* (New York, 1935), I, 39-40.

40. *A Poem upon Tea,* 2nd ed. (London, 1702), p. 2.

41. *Ibid.,* p. 16.

42. *Ibid.,* pp. 21-22.

Ruth McGugan (essay date 1987)

SOURCE: McGugan, Ruth. Introduction to *Nahum Tate and the Coriolanus Tradition in English Drama, with a Critical Edition of Tate's* The Ingratitude of a Common-Wealth, pp. v-cvii. New York: Garland Publishing, 1987.

[*In the following excerpt, McGugan comments on Tate's life and reputation, and discusses his adaptations and scholarly responses to his works.*]

NAHUM TATE'S LIFE AND REPUTATION

Perhaps the most striking similarity between Tate and Shakespeare is the paucity of intimate biographical details that historians can provide for either man. Official documents contain some vital statistics, and their publications testify to how they spent their working time, but of their private lives, little is known. The popular conjecture is that anyone whose literary work is as vital as Shakespeare's must have been a lively personality, and the process of reconstructing it has been a fascinating and creatively fruitful project for such researchers as Spurgeon. The case is quite different with Tate. Few have ventured beyond, the *DNB* account, and only Samuel A. Golden has produced substantial amplification of it. However, after reviewing "the scant material available," Golden concludes that "the conception of Tate need not be indistinct . . . [but is] rather, the clear impression of a man who led a dull, hard life with few moments of happiness as he laboured to exchange his literary work for money."[1]

The standard accounts begin with a summary of the lives of Tate's father and grandfather, both clergymen who went by the name of Faithful Teate. Since the first son in Nahum Tate's generation had already received the name of Faithful, the birth of a second son (in Dublin in 1652) forced the parents to turn to his maternal grandfather for "Nahum," a name that never appeared in his published works;[2] apparently he preferred the simplicity of the solitary initial N. Citing the *Entrance Register (1637-1725),* Trinity College, Dublin, I, 58, Golden supplies the names of a Mr. Savage, who served as Tate's tutor in Belfast before he matriculated at Trinity College in June, 1668, and of George Walker, who was his tutor at the University in Dublin.[3] For the period between Tate's graduation with a B. A. in 1672 and the appearance of his first published work, a single contribution to the second edition of Thomas Flatman's *Poems and Songs* (London, 1676), even Golden supplies no details.[4] He does, however, fix the dates between which the change in the spelling of the surname must have occurred as April 10, 1674 (the licensing of Flatman's *Poems and Songs*) and November 27, 1676 (the licensing of the first edition of Tate's own **Poems**).[5]

There were the editions of Tate's **Poems,** the first (London, 1677) and the second, "enlarged" and extensively revised, (London, 1684). They are of particular relevance to this study because of what they reveal about Tate's technique as a poetic workman. The "reworking" of his own lines between the two editions is analogous to the "tampering" he did with other men's lines when he adapted old plays to new audiences.[6]

Announcements in the *Term Catalogues* and the title pages and dedications of his published works constitute the bulk of the evidence for how N. Tate spent the rest of his life.[7] Between 1678 and 1687 he obviously concentrated on drama.[8] By 1686 he had begun to publish a series of translations which constitute evidence of his ability to use Latin and Greek sources. The first of these was **Girolamo Fracastoro's Syphilis, A Poetical History of the French Disease, Attempted in English by N. Tate** (London, 1686). In the same year he dedicated a one-volume edition of **The Aethiopian History of Heliodorus** to the Duke of Beauford. In the dedication he described his discovery of the first five books translated "by a Person of Quality and Judgement," who had not lived long enough to complete the task, and his own decision to translate the last five.[9] Presumably Tate could also have used French sources,[10] although evidence is not conclusive. He did edit **The Four Epistles of A. G. Busbequius** (London, 1694) because, as he explained in the dedication, he had found yet another valuable translation made by someone who had not lived to see his work through the press.[11]

Translating, editing, and writing various kinds of verse apparently kept Tate busy, if not financially comfortable, both before and after his appointment in 1692 to succeed Shadwell as Poet Laureate.[12] Among his literary productions in this period are the psalms and hymns which were combined with similar pieces by Dr. Nicholas Brady and published first in London in 1695 as **A New Version of the Psalms of David.** As a result of the adoption of this as the standard text for the Church of England and numerous subsequent editions, Tate's psalms and hymns are probably his most widely used, if not his most notorious works. It was not until after the financial failure of *The Monitor,* a tri-weekly periodical that he published in association with an M. Smith, that Tate was forced to seek refuge in the Mint.[13] He died there on July 30, 1715.[14]

In the two chapters that Golden devotes to Tate's personality and reputation, he cites evidence from the author's own work and that of his contemporaries to establish that Tate was excessively modest, industrious, morally upright, and deserving of the loyalty of such intimate friends as Dryden and Brady.[15] The sneering contempt with which Pope, Swift, and Parnell referred to him apparently derived from their perception of his lack of artistry and talent, rather than any lack of integrity or personal merit.[16] Golden takes elaborate pains to explain away any inference that Tate was "given to heavy drinking"[17] as a gross misinterpretation of the word *fuddling* that had appeared in an early account.[18]

Golden devotes considerably more attention to Tate the man than most commentators do; the usual focus is on his works and/or how they fit into the context of English literature of the Restoration Period. The comments of his contemporary Gerard Langbaine appear in *An Account of the English Dramatick Poets* (Oxford, 1691), and are probably the earliest in print:

> An Author now living; who tho' he be allow'd to be a Man of Wit and Parts, yet for *Dramatic Poetry,* he is not above the common Rank: What he has extant, for the most part is borrow'd; at least we may say, That generally he follows other Mens Models, and builds upon their Foundations: for of Eight Plays that are printed under his Name, Six of them owe their Original to other Pens; as we shall shew in the following Account.[19]

This paragraph (and the two-page discussion of plays and poetry which follows it) might seem to be merely an acknowledgement of Tate's existence; in contrast to Langbaine's evaluations of other writers past and present, however, it is almost complimentary. Th. Durfey

> is accounted by some for an Admirable Poet, but it is by those who are not acquainted much with Authors, and therefore are deceiv'd by Appearances, taking that for his own Wit, which he only borrows from Others: for Mr. *Durfey* like the *Cuckow,* makes it his business to suck other Birds Eggs.[20]

Selections from his treatment of Edward Ravenscroft provide further contrast: "One who with the Vulgar passes for a Writer . . . I rather stile him in the Number of Wit-Collectors . . . 'twill be manifest, that this Ricketty-Poet (tho' of so many Years) cannot go without others Assistance."[21] Tate was at least given credit for *building,* albeit on foundations laid by other men.

How much Langbaine's opinions were influenced by his personal reactions to the men of whom he wrote is, of course, impossible to determine now, and a comparison of his treatment of Shadwell (whom he obviously likes) and Dryden (whom he equally obviously does not like very much) makes one skeptical of the objectivity and soundness of his literary judgments. His comments on Tate, however, have been echoed and reinforced by the majority of later critics. On rare occasions they have applied other terms than those connoting mediocrity to him and particular works. Samuel Johnson's implied preference for his **King Lear** over Shakespeare's is probably the most commonly cited.[22] Within the past decade, Christopher Spencer has worked out a defense of that piece as "a new play with its own purpose," not merely an adaptation, and one which "is both coherent and entertaining."[23] Another kind of non-mediocre distinction was conferred upon Tate when D. B. Wyndham Lewis and Charles Lee chose one of his occasional poems for inclusion in *The Stuffed Owl, An Anthology of Bad Verse.*[24]

Hazelton Spencer's statements about Tate are the most relevant to the current study, and although he uses a great variety of disparaging nouns and adjectives in his discussions of Tate and others, his critical appraisal is rather consistent. At the end of his discussion of Shadwell's *Timon of Athens,* he says that it "is preferable to the ineptitudes and inanities of Nahum Tate, and the vandalism of D'Avenant."[25] At one time he refers to "Tate's murderous attempts to improve Shakespeare"[26] and at another comments that "Tate was a rather facile hack without a spark of artistic genius." He continues to explain, however, that "It is in just such men that one finds clues to literary methods and motives which abler men, like Dryden, succeed in covering up."[27]

Tate is rarely discussed alone, more frequently coupled or contrasted with others who spread the "epidemic of [particularly Shakespeare] alteration"[28] in the 1670's and 1680's. Golden voices the summary dismissal of a twentieth-century biographer when he says that Tate's "dull personality removes him farther and farther from his more colourful contemporaries until he fades into the background."[29] The reaction of those "contemporaries" was probably different, however. In particular, those other playwrights who were competing for space in London theatres between 1678 and 1687 would surely have regarded him as more than background material as they watched him offer eight plays for production in those nine years.

TATE AND THE ADAPTATION OF SHAKESPEARE FOR THE RESTORATION STAGE

Tate's career as a writer for the public stage began sometime before the summer of 1678 and had virtually ended by 1687; the bulk of the work he published as a struggling young writer (eight quartos!) can be discussed under this general heading. He did make one more attempt at drama (fifteen years after he had achieved the public recognition of the laureateship) when he adapted Webster's *The White Devil* as *Injur'd Love: Or, The Cruel Husband* (London, 1707).[30] As the title page announces, this tragedy was "Design'd to be Acted at the *THEATRE ROYAL*"; the fact that it was never actually played need not suggest that it is worse (or better) than any of Tate's other dramas. It is, in fact, merely typical of the kind of adapting, i.e., "improving," of Elizabethan plays that was a popular and sometimes lucrative practice among Restoration dramatists. The prologue (presumably by Tate himself) reflects the overt reforming motive of the new century in the last three lines:

> *You Wits the Sov'reign Summons will obey,*
> *And, First, to shew you're in a mending way,*
> *You'll often visit our* Reforming Play.[31]

However, in such features as refinement of characters and diction, simplification of plot and characterization, development and introduction of sentimental situations, and often, consequently, the changing of the central focus of the story (as in this play, from Vittoria to Isabella), *Injur'd Love* is not radically different from numerous Restoration adaptations of the comedies, tragedies, histories, farces, tragi-comedies, and pastorals of the earlier generation.

The adaptation "movement" rose to peaks of popularity twice during Tate's lifetime—around 1680 and again around 1700. Although he was only a nominal contributor to the second (with the un-played *Injur'd Love*), he was a major contributor to the first. Of course, Tate and his cohorts did not limit themselves to Shakespearean tragedy; the current study is, however, based on Tate's adaptation of one such play, i.e., his contribution to the Coriolanus tradition. Therefore, although it is impossible to avoid references to his other works and those of other authors (in the process of filling in essential background for the particular study), discussion of them is governed by a strict principle of limitation.[32]

Sir William D'Avenant's *The Law Against Lovers* (London, 1673) was the first to appear in print, but Restoration adaptations of Shakespeare's tragedies had begun to appear on London stages less than a year after Charles II returned to England.[33] According to Spencer, *Hamlet* was the first (August 24, 1661?)[34] of these, and D'Avenant's was the hand responsible for the "mangled" version that was eventually printed in 1676.[35] While the plot structure and characterization are not essentially changed in this version, there are extensive cuts (lines from the original are reprinted, but their omission from the stage version is indicated by inverted quotation marks) and there are numerous changes of diction. Some of these are obviously predicated by the principles of modernization, clarification, and purification, while others seem to be made merely for the sake of changing words. Although D'Avenant's name does not appear on the 1674 edition of *Macbeth*, there seems to be little question that he was the inventor of the spectacular operatic apparatus in the 1663 or 1664 production[36] which represents a more startling kind of modification of the original. Amalgamation of the basic conflict in *Measure for Measure* and the Beatrice-Benedick situation from *Much Ado about Nothing* was the most substantial alteration that D'Avenant himself committed, and one which he exposed to the London audience at least as early as 1662.[37] John Downes provides information about the initiation of a still more drastic kind of change in one of Shakespeare's tragedies. In his account of plays produced by D'Avenant at the new theatre in Lincoln's-Inn Fields soon after its opening in the spring of 1662,[38] he includes "*Romeo and Juliet,* Wrote by Mr. Shakespear." After listing some of the members of the cast and describing an amusing incident which occurred during the production, he adds the information that:

> This Tragedy of *Romeo* and *Juliet,* was made some time after into a Tragi-comedy, by Mr. *James Howard,* he preserving *Romeo* and *Juliet* alive; so that when the Tragedy was Reviv'd again, 'twas Play'd Alternately, Tragical one Day, and Tragicomical another; for several Days together.[39]

Although this tragi-comical version of Howard's was never printed, the precedent for the happy-ending had been set long before Tate came to London in 1672.

In addition to these early adaptations by D'Avenant and Howard, other stage versions (tailored to the taste of the London audiences of the 1670's) may have been a part of Tate's background. During his early years in London he may have seen productions of Thomas Shadwell's *The History of Timon of Athens, the Man-Hater*[40] and Thomas D'Urfey's version of *Cymbeline* which he called *The Injured Princess, or the Fatal Wager*.[41] In the two theatrical seasons immediately preceding his own debut as an adapter of Shakespearean tragedy, he certainly could have seen Edward Ravenscroft's *Titus Andronicus, or the Rape of Lavinia*,[42] John Dryden's *Troilus and Cressida: or Truth Found Too Late*,[43] and Thomas Otway's *The History and Fall of Caius Marius*,[44] a variation on the *Romeo and Juliet* theme which Spencer calls "the most absurdly incongruous of all the Restoration versions."[45] At least the first of John Crowne's two plays based on the Henry VI saga also antedates (certainly in production and probably in composition) Tate's first attempt at adapting Shakespeare. *The Misery of Civil-War, A Tragedy*,[46] and *Henry the Sixth, the First Part, with the Murder of Humphrey Duke of Glocester*[47] were both played in 1680-1681 at Dorset Garden.[48] These plays are representative of another literary activity that became popular in London between 1678 and 1682—making theatrical profits out of allusions to and satire on the contemporary political turmoils.[49] Although Crowne's particular animus in *Henry VI* (and to a lesser extent in *The Misery of Civil-War*) was against "Popery and Popish Courts,"[50] either or both of these plays may have been the immediate inspiration for Tate's use of *Richard II* and *Coriolanus* for more generalized political purposes.

One more play (often discussed in connection with what the Restoration *did* to Shakespeare, but far outside the mainstream of adaptation proper) is Dryden's *All for Love: or, The World well Lost*.[51] It is a considerably more independent, creative effort than any of Tate's adaptations of Shakespeare (and in its relationship to Shakespeare's text, occupies a position analogous to that of Thomson's *Coriolanus*[52]), but it serves a purpose here as a reminder of a third movement in Restoration drama that contributed to Tate's formation as a writer for the stage. Dryden himself had been a major figure in the development of heroic tragedy and, as Spencer delights in pointing out, that genre was a "powerful" influence in *All for Love*.[53]

According to Samuel A. Golden, Tate's first play was a part of the heroic tradition.[54] However, although there are "heroic" elements in **Brutus of Alba: or, the Enchanted Lovers** (London, 1678), it is scarcely a classic example of the genre. The play is an "original," at least in the sense that it does not obviously derive from any previous dramatic version of the Dido and Aeneas story; in fact, if it were not for Langbaine's hint,[55] one might have difficulty identifying the "source." The title suggests not only the extent of geographical displacement that the story has undergone, but also the distortion of plot, theme, and emphasis. The central characters have also been so diluted (often by tears) that they resemble Dryden's Antony and Cleopatra far more than they do the legendary founder of Rome and the lady who detained him for so long in Carthage. The central conflict produces only feeble echoes of the anguished cries that issue from breasts torn by the rival claims of love and honor. The drams is in blank verse (probably as a result of Dryden's example in *All for Love*), except for two stanzas sung by a quartet of priestesses in Act II[56] and another pair of stanzas "Written by Mr. *Wright*" and inserted just before the denouement.[57] Tate has invented two characters to fill in the background—Soziman, "a designing lord," into whose clumsy plotting Summers has read an allusion to Shaftesbury,[58] and Ragusa, "a sorceress," whose efficiency both in her own and her author's interests is probably the best feature of the play. The opening lines of Act III, scene i, "A Desart. At some distance a Fountain with the Statue of Diana," are marvelously suggestive of the whole piece.

Enter Soziman *Solus.*

Soz.

This is the dreadfull Sorceresse's Cave,
Where sullen Fiends, Hell's Male-contents conspire,
Whilst at the ghastly Board the Hag presides,
Weighs their Debates and sways the dark Cabal.
Ho *Ragusa*! dread Prophetess appear:
Assist an Heart that labours with vast mischief,
And with thy Spells secure the fatal Birth.
Enter Ragusa.

Rag.

Who interrupts when I'm at work for Hell?
Whos'e're thou art, I hate the Light and Thee.
Ha! *Soziman*? thou art a hopefull Son,
A working Head, industrious for Perdition.

Soz.

Instruct this feeble Arm to shake a Throne,
And snatch a Crown.

Rag.

Let it be steept in Bloud!

(p. 19)

A few lines later, Ragusa promises:

I will by Magick pour a Tempest down,
Hail, Rain and Fire, th'ingredients of the Storm;
Scatt'ring the Company to th' Caves for Shelter.

At the same Cell the Prince and Queen shall hide,
Where she forgetfull shall resign her Honour.

(p. 20)

Although there is no record that **Brutus of Alba** ran beyond the opening night,[59] Tate was apparently not discouraged. He had another play ready for production in December of 1679.[60] **The Loyal General** (London, 1680) is, according to Golden, "heroic tragedy at its worst,"[61] but it has many more typical "heroic" devices than **Brutus** and, probably because of the complications leading up to the denouement (which involves five deaths, two by slow poison), is much more exciting reading. Theocrin is the heroic general; he is loyal to a king who Golden thinks is "probably modelled" on Lear.[62] Tate's old king in this play is "discontented," as the author indicates in a stage direction and illustrates with such lines as

Why was my Life stretcht out to this black day?
Death might have come long since, and found me ripe
With all my Honours flourishing round my Head:
But now to Winter blasts I'm left expos'd,
Script of my Leaves, and with'ring on the Bough.

(I.ii, pp. 5-6)

However, this king is never more than a shadow of Lear. The complications (which involve a faithless queen, her two villainous henchmen Escalus and Pisander, and the loyal general who is in love with the king's sole heir Arviola) are not analogous to those in Shakespeare's treatment of the legendary king of Britain. Golden's theory does, of course, gain support from the fact that *King Lear* was the first Shakespearean tragedy that Tate attacked.

The failure of his second "original" heroic tragedy and the perennial success of other men's adaptations of "old" plays may both have been factors influencing Tate's decision to begin working directly on Shakespearean texts. Although **Lear** was, according to his own account, the first adaptation he attempted,[63] it was his version of **Richard II** that was first played (at the Theatre Royal, under the title of **The Sicilian Usurper,** and with a Sicilian dramatis personae) on Saturday, December 11, 1680; this play was promptly suppressed by a government order dated December 14.[64] **King Lear** was acted at Dorset Garden the following March[65] and advertised in the Easter *Term Catalogue* in 1681.[66] **The History of King Richard the Second** was advertised in the Trinity issue of the same year and the printed text was prefaced by "a Prefatory Epistle in Vindication of the Author, occasion'd by the Prohibition of this Play on the Stage."[67] Less than a year later, Tate had finished his third and last attempt at redoing an old play for a new audience. **The Ingratitude of a Common-Wealth: or, the Fall of Caius Martius Coriolanus** was acted at Drury Lane in December[68] and advertised in the *Term*

Catalogue for Hilary in 1682.[69] Thus within thirteen months, Tate had managed to get three "improved" Shakespearean tragedies on London stages—a record unequalled even by D'Avenant or Dryden.

Although there is no clear pattern of maturation of adaptive technique in Tate's three Shakespeare adaptations, an over-all comparison and contrast of the plays is of value as background for the detailed analysis of Tate's version of the Coriolanus story. All three of the plays printed in the early 1680's reveal Tate's alteration of plot, character, theme, and diction, but it is not always possible to establish the hierarchy of these items in the mind of the adapter. While certain theoretical principles might seem obvious to one who tries to analyze the texts, it is not always possible to find lines, incidents, or scenes that will serve as concrete illustrations. For example, changes in plot development would logically presume that changes in character action or characterization had been made; changes in plot should, of course, result in changes in theme or emphasis; changes in diction should have been made to effect the changes in plot, character, or theme. And, ideally, one should be able to discern some contemporary canon of taste, usage or propriety to explain why each of the various changes was made. In the case of Tate's adaptations—or those of any other author, probably—no such completely logical analysis is possible. One must accept the "facts" of the printed texts and rigorously avoid distortion of them to illustrate historical or critical principles.

Tate seems to have reversed the direction of creative development which D'Avenant had established in his series of adaptations. D'Avenant began by cutting some non-essential scenes for an acting version of *Hamlet,* progressed through modification and development of several characters in *Macbeth,* and eventually wrought a substantial change in two plays and fused them into *The Law Against Lovers.* Tate, on the other hand, began by making radical changes in the plot of **King Lear,** made rather superficial changes in characters and chronology in **Richard II,** and eventually relied on an ill-prepared-for and rather shocking ending to effect the major part of his adaptation of **Coriolanus.** A simple mathematical comparison of the numbers of lines of Shakespeare's and Tate's that appear in the three adaptations reveals this phenomenon in a striking manner. Shakespeare's *Lear* has 3337 lines, Tate's 2424, and of these, only 1120 (or 46%) have come either whole or in part from Shakespeare's text. Shakespeare's *Richard II* has 2760 lines, Tate's only 1955, and of these, 981 (or 50%) have been taken over word for word or tampered with slightly before they were printed in the adaptation. Of Shakespeare's 3409 lines in *Coriolanus,* Tate has kept 1274; i.e., he is directly indebted to Shakespeare for 60% of the 2124 lines in his **Ingratitude of a Common-Wealth.** Another numerical comparison adds supporting evidence that Tate's creative energy was waning. For his version of **Lear,** he wrote 1304 new lines; for **Richard II,** only 974; and for **Ingratitude,** a paltry 850, almost half of which occur in two large patches in the last act.

Tate's **Lear,** however, gives evidence of careful and principled reworking throughout. The preface to the 1681 quarto contains an ominous and now oft-quoted line. In the text which follows, he fulfills his promise to make order out of the *"Heap of Jewels, unstrung and unpolisht"* which he has *"seiz'd."*[70] He does indeed re-string the exile of Cordelia, the flight of Edgar, the wanderings of Lear (and Cordelia!), and ultimate happiness for all the good people in the play on the slender but carefully woven strand of the love between Edgar and Cordelia. He begins to interweave this new strand of plot early, with a 45 line interpolation in Act I scene i, in which Edgar confesses his love for Cordelia and she suspiciously rejects him (pp. 6-7). Edgar's love for her is still hopeful enough, however, to motivate him to flee in disguise rather than "leave my Griefs on my Sword's reeking point" (II.i, p. 17). Midway in the play, Cordelia trustingly accepts his love with the lines,

> Come to my Arms, thou dearest, best of Men,
> And take the kindest Vows that e're were spoke
> By a protesting Maid.

> (III.iii, p. 36)

(Her gratitude is not unmotivated: he has just rescued her from two Ruffians employed by Edmund to abduct her during the storm scene on the heath.) Finally, their love adds both pathos and suspense to the scene in which he rescues her a second time. He enters the prison (where she and Lear are at the mercy of official stranglers) and says

> Death! Hell! Ye Vultures hold your impious Hands,
> Or take a speedier Death than you wou'd give.

> (V.vi, p. 63)

Although he changes details, Tate leaves the Gloster-Edmund and Regan-Gonerill aspects of the plot essentially intact. He does rearrange some scenes; e.g., he opens the play with Edmund's

> Thou Nature art my Goddess, to thy Law
> My Services are bound, why am I then
> Depriv'd of a Son's Right because I came not
> In the dull Road that custom has prescrib'd?
> Why Bastard, wherefore Base, when I can boast
> A Mind as gen'rous and a Shape as true
> As honest Madam's Issue? Why are we
> Held Base, who in the lusty stealth of Nature
> Take fiercer Qualities than what compound
> The scanted Births of the stale Marriage-bed?

> (I.i, p. 1)

Shakespeare had opened the second scene of his first act with what is clearly the source of the Tate lines quoted above.

> Thou, Nature, art my goddess; to thy law
> My services are bound. Wherefore should I
> Stand in the plague of custom, and permit
> The curiosity of nations to deprive me,
> For that I am some twelve or fourteen moonshines
> Lag of a brother? Why bastard? Wherefore base?
> When my dimensions are as well compact,
> My mind as generous, and my shape as true,
> As honest madam's issue? Why brand they us
> With base? with baseness? bastardy? base, base?
> Who, in the lusty stealth of nature, take
> More composition and fierce quality
> Than doth, within a dull, stale, tired bed,
> Go to the creating a whole tribe of fops,
> Got 'tween asleep and wake?

> (I.11.1-15)[71]

Comparison of the Tate and Shakespeare versions of this passage illustrates the kind and extent of "tampering" with diction which was far from uncommon among the Restoration adapters of Shakespeare and other earlier dramatists. Here in Edmund's speech, Tate not only condenses the fifteen lines of his source into ten, but in the process of smoothing them and "clarifying" their meaning, he also distills out much of their natural passion. The most significant alteration occurs when he ameliorates Shakespeare's "Why brand they us / With base? with baseness? bastardy? base, base?" (11.9-10) to "Why are we held / Base" (11. 7-8). When Tate also simplifies Shakespeare's 11. 3-6 into his own 11. 2-3, he sustains the softened tone he has introduced by substituting "why am I then" (1.2) for Shakespeare's "Wherefore should I" (1.2). Finally, by compressing Shakespeare's 11. 12-15 into his own 11. 9-10, Tate purges the Bastard's tirade of its fierce quality and leaves him to ruminate on "The scanted Births of the stale Marriage-bed" (1. 10).

As Tate condenses the action in the middle sections of Shakespeare's version of the play and relocates a few more lines, he indulges in one digression that explicates the illicit passion between Regan and Edmund. He begins Act IV (pp. 40-41) with a scene in a grotto where they are *"amorously Seated, Listning to Musick."* In the main, however, he follows Shakespeare's sequence of events. Gloster's eyes are put out by Cornwall (III.iv, pp. 38-39), Edmund falls (V.v, p. 60) and Edgar penultimately reports that

> *Gonerill* and haughty *Regan,* both are Dead,
> Each by the other poison'd at a Banquet;
> This, Dying, they confest.

> (V.vi, p. 66)

This is Cordelia's cue to enunciate the rather un-Shakespearean

> O fatal Period of ill-govern'd Life!

> (V.vi, p. 66)

There are still 28 more lines (in which the good people exchange felicitations) but Edgar finally speaks the pure Tate tag:

> Thy bright Example shall convince the World
> (Whatever Storms of Fortune are decreed)
> That Truth and Vertue shall at last succeed.

> (p. 67)

In the course of reworking *Lear*, Tate has eliminated three characters, none of which is essential to the plot of either version, but one of which is essential to the tragedy of Shakespeare's *Lear*. With Edgar's involvement in the Lear-Cordelia plot, France is obviously redundant; Curan's few retained lines can easily be read by any anonymous servant; but by cutting out the Fool, Tate decreases the stature of the king by many inches and robs Lear of one whole tragic dimension. Without this foil to taunt him on the heath, Lear is merely a disheveled and deprived old man who fares somewhat better than he deserves when kingdom, life, and daughter are restored to him in the fifth act. The adapter does not explain his deletion of the Fool's lines. Whether it was to save time in the theatrical presentation, to avoid a mixture of comic and serious business, or to accomplish some as yet unsuspected purpose, it was a mistake that reveals to the modern reader Tate's failure to appreciate the complexity of the matter he was dealing with. Invention of Arante to act as Cordelia's companion and confidante while she is making her ill-timed and unmotivated trek across the heath is another example of Tate's short-sighted extemporizing. Of course, Cordelia needs someone to talk to in Act III, scenes ii and iii, but by providing her with an opportunity to confide her concern for her own and her father's safety, Tate robs both Lear and Cordelia of another tragic dimension that Shakespeare had given them. His resolute and almost mute Cordelia is her father's daughter and she shares responsibility with Lear for their mutual tragedy. Tate's Cordelia is really a very good girl whose father joyfully announces in the fifth act:

> *Cordelia* shall be Queen; Winds catch the Sound
> And bear it on your rosie Wings to Heav'n.
> *Cordelia* is a Queen.

> (V.vi, p. 65)

And as a queen she reigned in the theatre for many years. The popularity of this version is, however, less a testimonial to Tate's gifts as a dramatic artist than testimony of the state of theatrical taste between 1681 and the eventual revival of Shakespeare's fifth act in 1823.[72]

Richard II reigned no longer in Tate's play than he did in Shakespeare's, and his reign on the stage was considerably shorter and less glorious. Probably Tate did rush this adaptation into production (before the more thoroughly revised *Lear*) in order to take advantage of the current interest in political tensions, and shortness of time may therefore account for the fact that he depended so heavily on his source. For example, in his abridged version (only 70% as long as the 2760-line original) he made use of 400 of Shakespeare's lines—word-for-word; thus, more than 20% of his text was actually ready for the compositor before he ever penned or emended a line. However, Tate did rearrange and rewrite plot incidents, develop character relationships, delete some characters, and change the personalities of others to such an extent that *The Sicilian Usurper* (as he masked it for its first night at Drury Lane[73]) would soon have died "a natural death"[74] even if government censors had not executed it after two performances.

It was in protest against the "Prohibition from Court" that Tate wrote the six-page vindication as a preface for the text which was printed a few months later. Here he explains his most fundamental change in the play: instead of painting Richard "in the worst Colours of History" as Shakespeare had done, Tate has "every where given him the Language of an Active, Prudent Prince. Preferring the Good of his Subjects to his own private Pleasure . . . [because Tate's] Design was to engage the pitty of the Audience for him in his Distresses."[75] On this principle Tate deletes such lines as those of York (not Gaunt, to whom Tate erroneously attributes them) which criticize Richard for his absorption with foreign frivolities and refusal to listen to sage advice (II.i.17-30). This is also the principle on which Tate develops the character of the queen into a sentimentalist who bids her husband pause on his way to prison and

> Lean on my Brest whilst I dissolve to Dew,
> And wash thee fair agen with Tears of Love.

> (V.ii, p. 48)

Nine of these words are Shakespeare's, but the context and sentiment are Tate's. In the original, the Queen does meet her husband on his way to the tower, but she is speaking *of* him *to* her attendant ladies when she says:

> But soft, but see, or rather do not see,
> My fair rose wither; yet look up, behold,
> That you in pity may dissolve to dew
> And wash him fresh again with true-love tears.

> (V.i.7-10)

A few lines later, when she speaks to Richard himself, her words are not the sort that Tate would want to borrow—and he does not.

> What, is my Richard both in shape and mind
> Transform'd and weak'ned? Hath Bolingbroke depos'd
> Thine intellect? Hath he been in thy heart?
> The lion dying thrusteth forth his paw,
> And wounds the earth, if nothing else, with rage
> To be o'erpower'd; and wilt thou, pupil-like,

Take the correction, mildly kiss the rod,
And fawn on rage with base humility,
Which art a lion and the king of beasts?

(V.i.26-33)

In contrast to such substantial character changes, the omission of Bushy, Bagot, and Green (their execution is only discussed by the Gardiner and his servant in III.ii, p. 26) is obviously an accidental result of abbreviation of the original text. When Tate allows York to degenerate at times into an anemic Falstaff, however, he creates an inconsistency not only in the tone of the tragedy, but also within the character of York himself. It is difficult to take seriously the York who admonishes his liege

Think not that falsly I gave up your Pow'r,
If any Villain of 'em dares to say it,
I'le call that Villain Lyar to his teeth,
He is a Rogue, tho' it be *Bullingbrook*!

(III.iv, pp. 32-33)

after his response to the Queen's request for aid in II.ii has been

I shall dissolve to a Gelly.

(p. 17)

Unfortunately, one cannot even fall in with the author's design and "pitty . . . [Richard] in his Distresses." Poor Richard has been shorn of too much of his majesty and too many of his most poetic lines. If Tate had had the opportunity to realize that this play was a failure (in terms of audience reaction or absence) instead of being able to attribute its short run to the intervention of sensitive politicians, he might not have tried his hand at *Coriolanus*. But he did have encouragement in the success of *Lear,* and so the ink was apparently not yet dry on the order prohibiting *Richard II* before he had begun work on his second failure at adapting Shakespearean tragedy for the Restoration stage. There is no evidence that *The Ingratitude of a Common-Wealth* ran beyond the opening night in December of 1681.[76] Tate waited three years, however, before offering another adaptation to the London audience. This one, based on a farce by Aston Cokain and called *A Duke and No Duke* was considerably more successful.[77] He tried farce again the next year, but this hodge-podge of Marston, Chapman, and Jonson's *Eastward Hoe* and Jonson's *The Devil Is an Ass* which Tate called *Cuckolds-Haven: or, An Alderman no Conjurer,* failed miserably.[78] His last attempt at drama in the seventeenth century was in yet another genre—tragi-comedy. Again he adapted—Fletcher's *The Island Princess*[79]—and again he failed.

With such a box-office record before him, it is not surprising that Spencer felt an obligation to justify the separate chapter on Tate (in his 1927 book on Restoration adaptations) by repeatedly calling attention to the "extraordinary success" of *Lear.*[80] And it is comforting to know that Spencer could justify further study of Tate (published seven years later) because his work reveals "clues to literary methods and motives which abler men, like Dryden, succeed in covering up."[81]

Notes

1. Samuel A. Golden, "Nahum Tate," unpublished doctoral dissertation (Trinity College, Dublin, 1954), p. 65. In this (the most recent of the three unpublished doctoral dissertations on Tate) Golden not only refers to the other dissertations, standard reference works, and the few critical studies on Tate, but also cites local official documents and contemporary records as his sources for "new" information. Therefore, it is logical to cite Golden (whose study was available in microfilm) in this biographical section. Arthur Hawley Scouten's "Aston Cokain and his Adapter Nahum Tate" (Louisiana State University, 1942), was also available on microfilm; it has been a valuable source for Tate's method as an adapter of comedy, but did not contain biographical information not obtainable from other sources. Herbert Francis Scott-Thomas's "The Life and Works of Nahum Tate," (Johns Hopkins, 1932) was not consulted, but an article (which is probably taken from the original study) "Nahum Tate and the Seventeenth Century," *ELH,* I (1934), 250-275, did provide interesting general background on Tate's intellectual milieu.

2. Golden, pp. 17, 10, and 25.

3. Golden, p. 21.

4. Golden, p. 24.

5. Golden, p. 24.

6. See pp. lxii-lxiii, notes 7 and 8.

7. Golden, pp. 314-328, provides a more complete list of Tate's works than either *CBEL* or *BMCPB.*

8. See pp. xvii-xxxvii.

9. Heliodorus, sig. A2ᵛ. This work was originally written in Greek and Tate gives no indication that his translation was not from the original language. If further evidence of his ability to use Greek be required, however, he contributed a 50 page section, "Dialogues of the Gods: To ridicule the Fables about them," to the fourth volume of *The Works of Lucian,* translated by several eminent hands, 4 vols. (London, 1711).

10. This point is of some significance because it establishes that Tate *could* have used Alexandre Hardy's *Coriolan* (Paris, 1625) as a source for his own version of the Coriolanus story (see pp. xlv-xlvii.

11. Busbequius, sig. A2.

12. Golden, pp. 71-76, provides a thoroughly documented account of Tate's financial negotiations with the government and prospective patrons during this period.

13. Golden, pp. 58-76, discusses the history (from March 2, 1712/13 to April 20/24, 1713) and content of the 21 numbers of this periodical which was "Intended for the promoting of religion and virtue, and suppressing of vice and immorality," as the title page states.

14. Golden, p. 65, cites H. F. Scott-Thomas, "The Date of Nahum Tate's Death," *Modern Language Notes,* XLIX (March, 1934), 169-171, as his source of this fact.

15. Golden, pp. 77-85.

16. Golden, pp. 86-90.

17. *British Authors Before 1800*. ed. Stanley J. Kunitz and Howard Haycraft (New York, 1952), p. 509.

18. Golden, pp. 84-85, cites R. Southey, ed., *Specimens of the Later English Poets* (London, 1807), I, 173. Quotation of Southey's comment in its entirety will not only clarify this point but also constitute an interesting example of what Tate's reputation was in the early nineteenth century. It reads:

   The worthy successor of Shadwell as Court Poet, the worthy accomplice of Nicholas Brady in berhyming the Psalms, and the unworthy assistant of Dryden in Absalom and Achithophel. He was indeed a pitiful poet; but, says Oldys, he was a free, good-natured, fuddling companion. His latter days were spent in the Mint, as a place of refuge from his creditors.

19. Langbaine, p. 500. Although this statement appears under the heading "Nathaniel Tate," the list of works that follows leaves no doubt that Langbaine is talking about the same N. Tate.

20. Langbaine, p. 179.

21. Langbaine, pp. 417-418.

22. Samuel Johnson, *The Plays of William Shakespeare* (London, 1765), VI, 159.

23. Christopher Spencer, "A Word for Tate's *King Lear,*" *Studies in English Literature 1500-1900,* III (Spring, 1963), 251.

24. (New York, 1962). "Ode upon the New Year (1693)," which appears on pp. 38-39, is bad indeed, but Tate's name appears in the chronological "Table of Contents" with such names as Dryden, Goldsmith, Byron, Wordsworth, Poe, and Tennyson.

25. *Shakespeare Improved* (Cambridge, Mass., 1927), p. 287.

26. H. Spencer, p. 101.

27. H. Spencer, "Tate and *The White Devil,*" *ELH,* I (1934), 240.

28. H. Spencer, *Shakespeare Improved,* p. 97.

29. Golden, p. 85.

30. H. Spencer has done a thorough study of plot and character changes in this adaptation and provided numerous examples of changes in diction in his article "Tate and *The White Devil.*"

31. Sig. A2.

32. H. Spencer, *Shakespeare Improved,* treats all of the Shakespeare adaptations in considerable detail, from both historical and literary standpoints. George C. D. Odell, *Shakespeare—from Betterton to Irving* (New York, 1963), 2 vols., covers a much longer period of time and is dealing primarily with theatrical history. Both Spencer and Odell regularly cite John Downes, *Roscius Anglicanus* and John Genest, *Some Account of the English Stage from the Restoration in 1660 to 1830* as their sources. Although Downes, Genest, and at least first editions of the plays have been consulted in the course of the current study, sources cited in this chapter will frequently be Spencer or Odell since the point in question is often a conclusion drawn from the evidence in the primary source, rather than the evidence itself. Allardyce Nicoll's treatment of the adaptations of Shakespeare in *A History of English Drama 1660-1900,* Vol. I, *Restoration Drama 1660-1700* (Cambridge, 1961) is brief (pp. 171-180) and therefore much less specific. Since the fourth edition (1952) is the most recent study, however, Nicoll is occasionally cited when there is a disagreement or lack in the other sources.

33. H. Spencer, p. 68.

34. H. Spencer, p. 68; Odell, I, 25.

35. H. Spencer, pp. 178-187. D'Avenant's name does not appear on the title page, and he had died four years before this edition of *Hamlet* was printed, but the numerous similarities between the *kinds* of changes made in the texts of *Macbeth* and *Measure for Measure* and those made in the text of *Hamlet* constitute impressive evidence for his "authorship." Although Nicoll (p. 401) parenthetically refers to this edition as "or Betterton's," he lists it among D'Avenant's contributions.

36. H. Spencer, pp. 78-80 and 93. The intrusion of operatic elements occurred in tragedy before it did in comedy. The Dryden-D'Avenant adaptation of

The Tempest (with the addition of complementary characters for Miranda, Ferdinand, Caliban and Ariel) had appeared as early as November 7, 1667 (Spencer, pp. 85-86), but the Shadwell operatic treatment of this adaptation did not premier at the Theatre Royal until April 30, 1674 (Spencer, p. 94).

37. H. Spencer, pp. 72-73; Nicoll (p. 401) gives Feb. 1661/2.

38. John Downes, *Roscius Anglicanus,* ed. Montague Summers (London, [1928]), p. (20).

39. Downes, p. (22). Nicoll (p. 414) dates the first performance as "before 1665," but adds that Downes is the only source of information on this play.

40. (London, 1678). H. Spencer (p. 282) implies that it may have been played at Dorset Garden as early as 1671.

41. (London, 1682). Although Odell (I, 67) says this play was not produced until November, 1682, H. Spencer (pp. 103-104) summarizes an impressive array of facts to support the theory that it could have been on the stage as early as 1673. The most crucial fact is the statement in the epilogue that *"this Play was writ nine years ago"* (p. [56]).

42. (London, 1687). H. Spencer (pp. 97 and 109, n. 86) affirms that it was played at least as early as 1678. His most significant piece of evidence for this is Ravenscroft's own statement in the address "To the Reader" that his *Titus "first appear'd upon the Stage, at the beginning of the pretended Popish Plot"* (sig. A2).

43. (London, 1679). H. Spencer (p. 98) says it was staged at Dorset Garden in the same year it was printed.

44. (London, 1680). H. Spencer (p. 100) says this "grotesque" was acted at Dorset Garden (probably in the fall) of the 1679-1680 season. Nicoll (p. 422) dates the first performance "c. Sept. 1679."

45. H. Spencer, p. 292.

46. (London, 1680). Nicoll, p. 399, gives "c. March 1679/80" as the first performance date.

47. (London, 1681). Nicoll, p. 399, gives "c. Sept. 1681" as the first performance date.

48. H. Spencer, p. 102.

49. For a discussion of political satire on the stage in this period, see pp. lxviii-lxxiv.

50. Crowne, *The English Frier: or, The Town Sparks* (London, 1690), sig. A3ᵛ.

51. (London, 1678).

52. See pp. lxxxi-lxxxix.

53. H. Spencer, p. 221.

54. Golden, p. 186.

55. Langbaine, p. 500: "This Play is founded on *Virgil's AEneids,* Book the 4th; and *was finished under the Names of* Dido *and* AEneas, *but by the Advice of some Friends, was tranformed* [sic] *to the Dress it now wears."*

56. *Brutus,* p. 15.

57. *Brutus,* p. 55.

58. *Shakespeare Adaptations,* ed. Montague Summers (London, 1922), p. lxxv.

59. [John Genest], *Some Account of the English Stage from the Restoration in 1660 to 1830* (Bath, 1832), I, 245-246.

60. Nicoll, p. 434.

61. Golden, p. 200.

62. Golden, p. 198.

63. *The History of King Richard the Second* (London, 1681), sig. A1.

64. Nicoll, p. 434.

65. Nicoll, p. 434.

66. *Term Catalogues,* ed. Arber, I, 440.

67. *Term Catalogues,* I, 451. The advertisement also quotes from the title page.

68. Nicoll, p. 434.

69. *Term Catalogues,* I, 473.

70. Tate, *The History of King Lear* (London, 1681), sig. A2ᵛ.

71. William Shakespeare, *The Tragedy of King Lear,* in *The Complete Plays and Poems of William Shakespeare,* ed. William Allan Neilson and Charles Jarvis Hill (Cambridge, Mass., 1942). All references to lines from *Lear* and other plays will be to this edition.

72. Genest, IX, 186, remarks on the difficulty that Kean (as Lear) encountered when he had to carry the apparently lifeless body of Cordelia (a Mrs. W. West) across the stage. Despite such physical difficulties, however, Shakespeare's fifth act prevailed, and (according to Odell, I, 54) even the Fool had reappeared by 1838.

73. December, 1680. Nicoll, p. 434.

74. H. Spencer, p. 264.

75. Tate, *Richard II,* sigs. A1ᵛ-A2.

76. Genest, I, 326.

77. (London, 1685). Nicoll, p. 434, gives Mon., Nov. 3, 1684 as the date of the first production at Drury Lane. Arthur Hawley Scouten's unpublished doctoral dissertation "Aston Cokain and his Adapter Nahum Tate" (Louisiana State University, 1942) provides the texts of both the original and the adaptation as well as a critical study of the adaptation.

78. Genest, I, 440-441. Sometime during this period, Tate also wrote the libretto for an opera based on the *Dido and Aeneas* story, for which Henry Purcell had written music. Golden (pp. 263-273) discusses the opera and, after reviewing conflicting pieces of evidence, dates the first performance "after the revolution in 1688" (p. 265). Critical opinion on the work (which was not printed until 1841) is varied; Golden thinks that without Purcell's "excellent music" it "could never have survived" (p. 267).

79. Genest, I, 456-457.

80. H. Spencer, p. 274.

81. H. Spencer, "Tate and *The White Devil*," p. 240.

Timothy J. Viator (essay date 1988)

SOURCE: Viator, Timothy J. "Nahum Tate's *Richard II*." *Theatre Notebook* 42, no. 3 (1988): 109-17.

[*In the following essay, Viator presents a stage history of Tate's* Richard II, *which he says reveals important facts about the monarchy's attitude toward the stage and censorship practices during the Restoration.*]

The stage history of Nahum Tate's **The History of King Richard the Second** has long been improperly understood. According to *The London Stage,* the King's Company produced Tate's adaptation as **The Sicilian Usurper** in December 1680 and, after the censors banned it, as **The Tyrant of Sicily** in January 1681. Robert D. Hume suggests, however, that the December dates "are a misconstruction from confusing evidence".[1] After Charles Killigrew, the Master of the Revels, refused to license the play as **Richard II,** Hume argues, the King's Company staged it twice in January 1681 as **The Sicilian Usurper,** for which performances, the Earl of Arlington (Sir Henry Bennet), the Lord Chamberlain, silenced the King's Company for ten days. Thus, Tate's **Richard II** raises three questions: 1) Why did the original revised scripts trouble the Court's censors? 2) Why did the King's Company decide to stage **The Sicilian Usurper**? 3) And why did the Lord Chamberlain close Drury Lane? The answers to these questions reveal important evidence for understanding the King's Company's financial desperation in 1681 and Restoration censorship practices.

I. Background

The first problem concerns the initial denial of a licence for **Richard II.** Critics have long known the reasons why in 1680 Charles II's Court perceived **Richard II** as dangerous and antimonarchical. Particularly sensitive to attacks, whether real or imagined, upon the monarchy, the Court could not overlook a play which depicted usurpation and regicide. As Lacey Baldwin Smith summarizes the political climate in the late 1670s and early 1680s, three factors divided Restoration England: "(1) The growing resentment against the heir apparent, James, Duke of York, and his Catholic faith; (2) the wave of religious hysteria which led even Englishmen of reason and moderation to believe that papists were hidden behind every bush, plotting to murder the king and overthrow the Protestant church; and (3) the formation of a country party under the leadership of . . . Anthony Cooper, Earl of Shaftesbury".[2] This political turmoil found its way into the literature as writers aligned themselves with the "Whigs", as the country party became known, and the Tories, Royalists who supported the Court. John Dryden's "Absalom and Achitophel" illustrates well how Restoration writers turned their attentions to politics. In the poem Dryden describes the Popish Plot (1678), which more than any other development caused the religious hysteria, and its effects on London:

> This Plot, which failed for want of common sense,
> Had yet a deep and dangerous consequence:
> For, as when raging fevers boil the blood,
> The standing lake soon floats into a flood,
> And every hostile humor, which before
> Slept quiet in its channels, bubbles o'er;
> So several factions from this first ferment
> Work up to foam, and threat the government[3]

By playing upon the religious passions that the Popish Plot provoked and upon the fears that Charles's illness in August, 1680 would lead to his death, Shaftesbury and the Whigs managed to sway public opinion and to gain more power. The Whigs had one goal: to ensure that a protestant ascended to Charles's throne. By autumn 1680, they felt powerful enough to attempt to exclude the Duke of York from the line of royal ascent. The exclusion strategy infuriated Charles II; he interpreted the Whig action not only as a plan to block James but also an infringement upon the monarchical prerogative. Antonia Fraser writes that Charles thought "the campaign smacked of insult to the monarchy".[4] But more to the point, the Exclusion Bill's actual impact upon Restoration London was considerable. The Whigs had made the royal line of ascent a political issue: could and should the legislative body select the next king?

The Whigs thought so; on November 12, 1680 they forced through Commons the Exclusion Bill which excluded the Duke of York from the throne. Although the House of Lords defeated the bill, the Whig campaign greatly affected Charles's Court. For the first time, the Court must have been suspicious and anxious, ready to identify and thwart attacks upon the monarchy.

By year's end, Charles started to oppose those attacks. David Ogg writes, "Such was the state of parties in January 1681 when the danger threatening the monarchy and the succession by the dissolution of parliament may have roused Charles from the lethargy into which he had fallen a few months before".[5] Not surprisingly, then, Charles's Court was prone to react harshly to suggestive productions by London's theatre companies, and Fraser hypothesizes that Tate's *Richard II* was the victim selected to exemplify Charles's propaganda campaign.[6] Between December 1680 and July 1682, Arlington and Charles Killigrew banned or prohibited six plays and censored or held up three others.[7] For the first time in the Restoration period, the Court, recognizing drama's potential to fuel political controversy, attempted to squelch plays which might fire antimonarchism and to advocate openly plays which evidenced royalist sentiment. Thus, the Court felt compelled to ban plays like Nathaniel Lee's *Lucius Junius Brutus* (December 11, 1680), a conspicuously Whig play, Crowne's *The City Politiques* (June 26, 1682), John Dryden and Lee's *The Duke of Guise* (July 18, 1682), and Tate's *Richard II,* seemingly an antimonarchical play,[8] and to support plays like Otway's *Venice Preserv'd,* a Tory play.[9] The fact of six banned plays in 19 months does much to support Ogg's and Fraser's arguments that Charles attempted to initiate his own campaign. So Charles's Court—which had protected, supported, encouraged, and enjoyed the theatre—suddenly implemented control over any theatrical attempts to exploit political issues.

One way to understand the government's eagerness to ban Tate's *Richard II* is to consider how the seventeenth-century audience perceived literature and theatre. As John M. Wallace explains (paraphrasing Plutarch), "Instead of sitting at a lecture (or reading a poem) like a person warming himself at another man's fire, the attender to a discourse should 'think it necessary to kindle from it some illumination for himself and some thinking of his own'".[10] As a result, the seventeenth-century reader or playgoer routinely saw parallels between the text and his country's situation. If a poem or play involved a king, he probably considered how the fictive king's crisis or dilemma mirrored the actual king's reign. Hume maintains that the audience arrived at the theatre "ready and able to draw its own inferences freely, often from the midst of disguise and contradiction".[11]

Because he knew that playgoers would look for parallels, the censor objected to *Richard II*'s plot. Usurpation and regicide troubled the Court's censors throughout the Restoration, but particularly so during the Exclusion Bill Crisis. Beaumont and Fletcher's *The Maid's Tragedy* illustrates how the Crisis affected the censors. As Hume writes, Charles had seen the play acted on 23 November 1667 and apparently took no offence. By 1680, however, because of the political tensions and Charles's campaign to attack the Whigs, the Court considered *The Maid's Tragedy* a dangerous play, as Hume argues, "in that in a particular context it could take on a 'meaning' which Beaumont and Fletcher could not have envisioned and which seems not to have concerned Charles II or his officials at any time between 1660 and 1677" and the play was "quietly prohibited".[12]

II. BANNING AND RESTAGING

Killigrew refused to license *Richard II* because of its plot. Subsequently, critics have focused on two questions: Was the play politically relevant during the political turmoil and did Tate intend to draw political parallels? For example, Frank Fowell and Frank Palmer consider the play harmless since it has "nothing that might reasonably be regarded as objectionable in the piece".[13] Arthur F. White maintains that "except for the general theme of civil war, there seems little or nothing [in *Richard II*] which might give offence" to the Court.[14] On the other hand, Robert Muller concludes that because of the political situation at that time *Richard II* "must be seen as an attempt to include politics" and that it reflects the political beliefs of that time.[15] For the most part, Christopher Spencer summarizes the play well:

> The alterations of Tate, are, then, intelligently made in view of the purpose he wished to achieve: to dress up a politically relevant play with anti-Whig satire and other topical comment and to make it entertaining theatre fare . . . The principal flaw in this plan was that the play itself was unalterably anti-Tory in its essentials, and an anti-Whig veneer was insufficient to cover them. Tate's unpolitical mind failed to grasp the danger in the story of Richard II, no matter how it was told—the danger of a successful deposition.[16]

In passing over the unique stage history of Tate's adaptation, however, critics have failed to consider why Tate tried to disguise *Richard II* as *The Sicilian Usurper* and why the King's Company staged a play that the Master of the Revels had refused to license.

To try to disguise the play Tate merely changed the title from *The History of King Richard the Second* to *The Sicilian Usurper,* the setting from England to Sicily, and the characters' names. For example, King Richard became Oswald; Gaunt, Alcidore; York, Cleon. The results on the stage must have seemed strange if not incomprehensible. As Tate writes in the **"Epistle Dedicatory"**:

From the two days in which it was Acted, the changes of the Scene, Names of Persons, & c. was a great Disadvantage: many things were by this means render'd obscure and incoherent that in their native Dress had appear'd not only proper but gracefull. I call'd my Persons *Sicilians* but might as well have made 'em Inhabitants of the *Isle of Pines,* or, World in the Moon, for whom an Audience are like to have small Concern. Yet I took care from the Beginning to adorn my Prince with Such heroick Vertues, as afterwards made his distress Scenes of force to draw Tears from the Spectators; which, how much more touching they would have been had the Scene been laid at home . . .[17]

Changing the title, the characters' names, and the setting are the most superficial changes one can make, and we must wonder why Tate believed that **The Sicilian Usurper** would appear to be a different play and, thus, could pass unnoticed by the Court and its censors. Nevertheless, Tate tried to defend his play in the **"Epistle Dedicatory."** His remarks are worth quoting at length:

> They that have not seen it Acted, by its being silenc't must suspect me to have Compil'd a Disloyal or Reflecting Play. But how far distant this was from my Design and Conduct in the Story will appear to him that reads with half an Eye. To form any Resemblance between the Times here written of, and the Present, had been unpardonable Presumption in Me. If the Prohibiters conceive any such Notion I am not accountable for That. I fell upon the new-modelling of the Tragedy . . . charm'd with the many Beauties I discover'd in it, which wou'd become the Stage; with as little design of Satyr upon present Transactions, as Shakespeare himself that wrote this Story before this Age began. I am not ignorant of the posture of Affairs in King Richard the Second's Reign, how dissolute then the Age, and how corrupt the Court; a Season that beheld Ignorance and Infamy preferr'd to Office and Pow'r, exercised in Oppressing, Learning, and Merit; but why a History of those Times shou'd be supprest as a Libel upon Ours, is past my understanding.[18]

Tate asserts that his "design was to engage the pitty of the Audience for" Richard and that his Richard is not like Shakespeare's, who was "Dissolute, Careless, and Unadvisable".[19] Regardless of Tate's intentions, in December 1680 the Master of the Revels could not license a play which highlights a usurper murdering a king, Sicilian or English. Hume writes that "to suppose that this subject could be made to pass in the midst of the Exclusion Crisis must require either disingenuousness or plain stupidity".[20]

Likewise, the King's Company had to have known that **The Sicilian Usurper** was in essence the same play, yet it still staged the play. Why did the company decide to stage Tate's "new" play? The answer may well concern the financial problems the company faced in January 1681. *The London Stage* reports that by the second half of the 1680-1681 season "the receipts of Drury Lane had fallen off so drastically that the players ceased act-

ing, resumed, faltered again".[21] The company's difficulties had begun a decade earlier in 1671 when a fire destroyed the Theatre Royal. To pay for a new theatre, which ultimately cost some £2,000 to £4,000, the company incorporated, selling shares to its actors. Through mismanagement, dissension (several leading actors quit), and unexpected low attendance, however, the company's profits dwindled.[22] Thus, financial pressures perhaps compelled the King's Company to attempt desperate measures in order to compete with its rival, the more successful Duke's Company, which in January 1681 staged Aphra Behn's sequel to her popular *The Rover.*[23] Tate may have intended the play to elevate Richard II's character and to engender pity, but the King's Company management must have recognized the play's topical and parallel possibilities. In other words, while the Court wanted to keep "parallel" plays from audiences, the theatre companies must have recognized that such plays were potentially profitable. As Behn's Prologue to *The Rover, Part II* (January 1681) exemplifies, the political controversies influenced the theatrical community:

> In vain we labour to reform the Stage,
> Poets have caught too the Disease o'th'Age,
> That Pest, of not being quiet when they're well,
> That restless Fever, in the Brethen, Zeal;
> In publick Spirits call'd Good o'th'Commonwealth.
> Some for this Faction cry, others for that,
> The pious Mobile for they know not what:
> So tho by different ways the Fever seize,
> In all 'tis one and the same mad Disease.[24]

"The same mad Disease" aroused some playwrights, notably Nathaniel Lee, to write *political* plays like *Lucius Junius Brutus* for political and artistic reasons. But playwrights and managers alike must have recognized the *commercial* potential that political or parallel plays offered. For instance, Elkanah Settle's *The Female Prelate* (May 1680) must have encouraged the Drury Lane managers to consider more parallel plays. In this tragedy, which Hume describes as an "extreme anti-Catholic play",[25] Settle exploits the religious hysteria that the Popish Plot created, and although it was not a hit, it ran for three nights, becoming one of the few moneymaking productions the King's Company produced in the 1679-1680 season. So the possible political parallels in Tate's **Richard II** must have excited the managers to hope that the play might also enjoy a worthwhile run and to take a chance on a play in the repertory since 1669.

Thus, the King's Company wanted to stage Tate's play to try to capture an audience sensitive to and interested in contemporary political events. For that very reason Killigrew refused to license the script. Yet a month later the King's Company staged Tate's revised script, and one can only conclude that either Killigrew failed to recognize **The Sicilian Usurper** as **Richard II** and licensed the script, or he never saw the second script. Although the evidence is inconclusive, the latter seems probable. Killigrew surely would have known that **The Sicilian Usurper** was the same play that he had refused to license only a month before.[26] As Emmet L. Avery and Arthur H. Scouten note, "the principal companies neither fully nor promptly acquiesced" to the Master of the Revels' review of all plays.[27] Therefore, after Killigrew refused to license **The History of King Richard the Second,** the King's Company decided to perform **The Sicilian Usurper** without licence, expecting that the Court and its censors would either overlook the revised script or, at worst, simply halt the performance as was done in December when the Duke's Company staged Lee's *Lucius Junius Brutus.*

In light of the political difficulties and Charles II's programme to stop antimonarchical propaganda, Arlington wanted to demonstrate to the theatres that the Court planned to prohibit controversial plays. To this end, the Lord Chamberlain closed Drury Lane for ten days, an unprecedented decision. With only one exception, in the previous twenty years the Court had closed the theatres only for the Plague in June 1665 and for mourning royal deaths, such as the Queen Mother's death on September 3 1669.[28] Accordingly, by his decision Arlington sent two consequential messages to the theatre companies: that the Court intended to halt controversial plays, and that the Lord Chamberlain intended to use forceful measures to control the companies.

No scholars have considered the effects that Arlington's punitive orders had on the King's Company. Directly, the banning of Tate's play caused the company, which was already financially troubled, to bear the production costs of a play which might have proved profitable but was suddenly no longer capable of returning any revenue. The Duke's Company suffered a similar setback when Arlington stopped *Lucius Junius Brutus* in December, but at least it kept its doors open. Drury Lane, on the other hand, remained empty for ten nights, and that loss of revenue weakened the faltering company. Indirectly, therefore, the banning accelerated the King's Company's declining fortunes, resulting in the final closure of Drury Lane in April 1682 and the union with the Duke's Company the following November. Moreover, Charles's campaign to control the theatres proved effective. Fearing further sanctions, the King's Company must have avoided plays which appeared to attack or satirize Charles, his Court, its Roman faction, and in general the monarchy. And although one cannot conclude with any certainty, because *The London Stage* performance records are incomplete, both companies seemed to have avoided (with few exceptions) "Whig" plays and began to stage after early 1681 only "Tory" plays like Behn's *The Roundheads* (December 1681 at Dorset Garden), Tate's **The Ingratitude of the Commonwealth** (December 1681 at Drury Lane) which

Hume maintains stresses loyalty to one's king,[29] and Thomas Southerne's *The Loyal Brothers* (February 4 1682 at Drury Lane). By closing Drury Lane for ten days, Arlington hurt the King's Company more than theatre historians have acknowledged.

III. Censorial Duties after 1680

The effects of Arlington's actions do not end with the impact on the King's Company. His decision to close Drury Lane defined for decades the censorial duties of both the Lord Chamberlain and the Master of the Revels. Throughout the Restoration, as John Loftis writes, "the nature and extent of government supervision [of the theatre companies] was ambiguous and variable [because] there was neither a well-defined theory of supervision nor a well-defined delegation of authority".[30] As the King's servant, as were all managers and actors his servants, the Master of the Revels was under the Lord Chamberlain's jurisdiction, establishing the Chamberlain as the primary officer. Vincent J. Liesenfeld writes that the Lord Chamberlain's

> authority was founded on traditions, many of them imprecisely defined. It extended directly to the management of the theatres, particularly their relationships with actors and actresses. The drama itself appears to have come under his control through another court official, the Master of the Revels, who by 1660 had become his subordinate and thereby brought the drama under his jurisdiction.[31]

Yet the available sources suggest that although the Lord Chamberlain was the ranking officer, Chamberlains before Arlington either delegated or lost censorial powers to the Master of the Revels, most notably Sir Henry Herbert (in office from 1660 to 1673), who reviewed, censored, and licensed plays before production. White argues that during the Exclusion Crisis "the Lord Chamberlain [probably] asserted his greater authority at the request of the Master of the Revels".[32] Arlington, however, did not assume the censorial duties traditionally held by the Master of the Revels, the power to license plays. While White understands that "under the precedent of Arlington the Lord Chamberlain took . . . an increasingly large interest in the affairs of the theatre and their authority was frequently appealed to in matters which concerned the theatre",[33] he fails to recognize the effects of Arlington's actions.

The fate of Tate's play along with the other plays censored or banned during the Exclusion Crisis suggests a new relationship between the Master of the Revels and the Lord Chamberlain, and the way Killigrew and Arlington shared censorial duties influenced the roles of later Chamberlains. Extant sources reveal that before 1680 only the Master of the Revels and the King censored plays. For example, Herbert struck out several passages from John Wilson's *The Cheats* (1663), then approved the script, yet Charles II suppressed the play two weeks after its first performance. In the case of Edward Howard's *The Change of Crowns* (1667) the King not only banned the play after it reached the stage, he also ordered that Howard not have it published.[34] After the Exclusion Crisis, however, as the Master of the Revels continued to assess plays before they were acted, Arlington asserted the right to ban them after production should they be controversial and to close a theatre for controversial plays. Two plays from 1681 exemplify how Arlington and Killigrew performed their duties: John Crowne's *Henry the Sixth: the First Part* (April 1681) and Thomas Shadwell's *The Lancashire Witches* (September 1681). According to White, Arlington suppressed Crowne's *Henry the Sixth* "after production as a result of the influence of the Church of Rome party at Court".[35] But for the most part, Arlington let Killigrew review and license plays before production. For example, in the epistle to the reader of *The Lancashire Witches,* Shadwell writes that a "great opposition was design'd against the Play (a month before it was acted) by a Party, who . . . pretended that I had written a Satyr upon the Church of England".[36] The Master of the Revels then expunged significant passages which he had found acceptable when he had first read and licensed the play. Therefore, the histories of these two plays indicate that the two censors shared the duties to control the theatre. Killigrew censored by striking out offensive passages before production as he had done with Shadwell's play or by refusing to license a play as he had done with Tate's ***Richard II***. Arlington censored by banning plays already on stage (as only King Charles had done before) and by closing theatres for failing to comply to his or the Master of Revels' orders as he had done against Lee's *Lucius Junius Brutus* and Tate's ***The Sicilian Usurper***. Subsequent Chamberlains followed Arlington's lead and allowed the Master of the Revels to license plays. For example, Dorset, the Chamberlain in 1696, ordered that the theatre companies have all plays

> Licensed by ye Master of the Revells according to ye Antient Custome of His place and upon the Examination of the said Master I find that he Complaines that of Late severall new & Revived plays have been Acted at ye Theatres of Drury Lane and Dorsett Gardens without any License. . . . I do therefore Order and Command that for ye future noe plays shall be Acted but such as shall first be sent . . . to Charles Killegrew Esqr Master of the Revells by him to be perused and diligently Corrected & Licensed And I Order all Persons Concerned in the Management of both Companyes to take notice hereof on ye Penalty of being Silenced according to ye Antient Custom of His place for such defaults.[37]

The Chamberlains Sunderland (1697), Bertie (1699), Jersey (1703) and Kent (1704) all wrote similar instructions to the theatre managers ordering that the Master of the Revels should license all plays and threatening that they would silence the theatres if the managers failed to comply.

In conclusion, Nahum Tate's ***Richard II*** is an example of a Restoration play that most modern critics usually dismiss as merely a poor Shakespearean adaptation. But in many ways ***Richard II*** remains important. The play's unusual stage history illuminates Charles II's attitudes towards the stage, the King's Company's financial problems, and the Master of the Revels' and the Lord Chamberlain's duties. But most importantly, Tate's play demonstrates the Court's relationship to the theatres in the early 1680s: Charles and his censors tended to allow the companies to enjoy artistic freedom; but when the plays seemed to attack Charles, his family, his Court, and the monarchy itself, Charles reacted swiftly and decisively.

Notes

1. *The Development of English Drama in the Late Seventeenth Century,* Robert D. Hume, 1976, 345.

2. *This Realm of England 1399 to 1688,* Lacy Baldwin Smith, 1976, 283-284.

3. *The Works of John Dryden,* ed. H. T. Swedenberg, Jr., 1972, 9.

4. *Royal Charles,* Antonia Fraser, 1979, 372.

5. *England in the Reign of Charles II,* David Ogg, 1955, 613-614.

6. See her footnote on page 400. Tate's play is the only example she gives.

7. See Hume's "*The Maid's Tragedy* and Censorship in the Restoration Theatre", *The Philological Quarterly,* 61 (1982), 486. Tate's *Richard the Second,* Lee's *Lucius Junius Brutus,* Crowne's *Henry the Sixth* were silenced; Lee's *The Massacre of Paris* and Bank's *The Island Queens* and *The Innocent Usurper* were prohibited; Dryden and Lee's *The Duke of Guise* and Crowne's *City Politiques* were held up; and Shadwell's *The Lancashire Witches* was cut.

8. See Allardyce Nicoll's *A History of Restoration Drama 1600-1700,* 1940, 10, n4 and n5. Nicoll's source is the Lord Chamberlain's papers of the Public Record Office: LC 5/144, pp. 28, 29, 260 and 278.

9. For an analysis of Otway's play see David Bywaters' "Venice, Its Senate, and Its Plot in Otway's *Venice Preserv'd*" MP 80: 256-263.

10. "'Examples Are Best Precepts': Readers and Meanings in Seventeenth-Century Poetry", *Critical Inquiry,* 1:2 (1982), 281-282.

11. *The Development of English Drama in The Late Seventeenth Century,* Robert D. Hume, 1976, 222.

12. *"The Maid's Tragedy"*, see note 7, 486-488.

13. *Censorship in England,* F. Fowell and F. Palmer, 1913, rpt 1969, 123.

14. "The Office of Revels and Dramatic Censorship During the Restoration Period", *Western Reserve University Bulletin,* NS 34 (1931), 32.

15. "Nahum Tate's *Richard II* and Censorship during the Exclusion Bill Crisis in England", *Poetic Drama and Poetic Theory,* 26 (1975), 51.

16. *Nahum Tate,* 1972, 84.

17. *The History of King Richard II,* 1681, rpt 1969, A2v-A3r.

18. *Ibid,* A1r.

19. See Spencer for an objective analysis of Tate's alterations, 80-84.

20. *The Development of English Drama in the Late Seventeenth Century,* Robert D. Hume, 1976, 222.

21. *The London Stage,* Part 1, 1965, 289.

22. See Leslie Hotson's *A Commonwealth and Restoration Stage,* 242-277, for an extensive history of the King's Company.

23. According to *The London Stage,* Part 1 293, the date of Behn's play's first performance is not known; however, strong evidence suggests that it was acted before January 18, 1681.

24. *The Works of Aphra Behn,* ed. Montague Summers, 1915, rpt 1967, 115.

25. *The Development of English Drama in The Late Seventeenth Century,* Robert D. Hume, 1976, 346.

26. In "Exclusion Bill Crisis" (p 50), Muller speculates that Arlington, the Lord Chamberlain "was more sensitive to . . . political implications" than Killigrew. Following the *London Stage* stage history that the play appeared as *Richard II,* Muller does not realize that Killigrew probably refused to license the script. Hence, since Killigrew very likely did disapprove the script, Muller's argument must be invalid.

27. "A Critical Introduction", *The London Stage,* 1965, cxlvii.

28. On 9 September 1661 the Lord Chamberlain also ordered acting suspended, but no reason is given in the sources.

29. *The Development of English Drama in the Late Seventeenth Century,* Robert D. Hume, 1976, 344-5.

30. *The Politics of Drama in Augustan England,* 1965, 20.

31. *The Licensing Act of 1737,* 1984, 9.

32. "Office of the Revels", 16.

33. *Ibid,* 15.

34. See "Office of the Revels", 26-28, for stage histories of Wilson's and Howard's plays.

35. "Office of the Revels", 35. In addition, Arlington held up two plays before production: Crowne's *City Politiques* (June 1682) and Dryden and Lee's *The Duke of Guise* (July 1682). The sources suggest, however, that Arlington was complying with the King's orders. He was not, therefore, appropriating the Master of the Revels' duties. See pp 35-39.

36. Quoted by White, p 33.

37. L.C. 7/1, p. 43. Quoted by White, 18.

Thomas G. Olsen (essay date summer 1998)

SOURCE: Olsen, Thomas G. "Apolitical Shakespeare; or, The Restoration *Coriolanus.*" *Studies in English Literature, 1500-1900* 38, no. 3 (summer 1998): 411-25.

[*In the following essay, Olsen argues that Tate's* Coriolanus *is particularly important because it is representative of political and aesthetic tendencies on the Restoration stage.*]

Several recent critical studies of Shakespeare's historical evolution into the figure Michael Dobson calls "the national poet" have considerably enriched our understanding of how Shakespearean adaptations functioned politically and culturally on the Restoration stage. Previously, and in the shadow of early-twentieth-century critics such as George C. D. Odell and Hazelton Spencer, abstract aesthetic considerations had dominated scholarly discussion of late-seventeenth-century productions of Shakespeare, an analytical tradition in which Restoration standards were almost invariably disparaged in comparison with those of the Renaissance.[1]

Given such a critical climate, it is not surprising that Nahum Tate's adaptation of *Coriolanus* has long been overlooked, even though Tate as much as John Dryden (both poets laureate, incidentally) has come to stand for the aesthetic principles upon which the Restoration Shakespeare has usually been judged and found wanting. What is more surprising, however, is that even recent scholarship has consistently relegated Tate's ***The Ingratitude of a Common-Wealth; Or, The Fall of Caius Martius Coriolanus*** (1681) to the status of supporting evidence. In fact, the play represents a critical moment in the development of several important Restoration aesthetic and political tendencies, as important to their cultural moment as either of Tate's better-known adaptations:[2] his notorious ***King Lear,*** with its added sexual intrigues and happy ending, and ***The Sicilian Tyrant,*** his suppressed revision of ***Richard II.*** In contrast to these better-known adaptations, Tate's comparatively restrained rewriting of ***Coriolanus*** offers an opportunity to examine his aesthetic and political motives for the adaptation, as well as their relation to the cultural status of the late-seventeenth-century *Shakespear.*

Tate's most apparent changes occur primarily in the fifth act, but both the prologue and dedication to the printed version of 1682 also reveal an overt, but ultimately conflicted, ideological purpose. Tate cannot deliver on his expressed desire in the prefatory matter, to show the nefarious effects of "the ingratitude of a commonwealth," because he cannot completely efface the political indeterminacy of Shakespeare's play.[3] In attempting to enlist a partisan Shakespeare, he instead reifies an "apolitical Shakespear" that resists rather than advances tendentious political appropriation.

The printed dedication to Charles, Lord Herbert expresses an ambivalent debt to Shakespeare as both artistic source and artistic adversary, an example of a widespread Restoration tradition of borrowing from, while improving upon, Shakespeare's canon. Tate claims artistic authority from that process, his imagery figuring Shakespeare as two different kinds of foundation upon which he bases his artistic strength: "I impose not on your Lordship's Protection a work meerly of my own *Compling; having in this Aventure Launcht out in* Shakespear's *Bottom. Much of what is offered here, is Fruit that grew in the Richness of his Soil; and what ever the Superstructure prove, it was my good fortune to build upon a Rock.*"[4] Not only does Tate express mixed attitudes toward Shakespeare as an artistic source, but like other adapters of his age, he also exploits *Coriolanus* for what he considered its latent political value. His dedication continues: "*Upon a close view of this Story, there appear'd in some Passages, no small Resemblance with the busie* Faction *of our own time. And I confess, I chose rather to set the Parallel nearer to Sight, than to throw it off to further Distance*" (p. 2).

Two central, interrelated questions emerge from the prefatory matter: first, what exactly are the qualities and the status of the "Rock" that Tate imagines he builds upon—who and what was Shakespeare to Tate and his contemporaries? Second, to what extent does his appropriation of Shakespeare for the Tory cause politicize or depoliticize both *Coriolanus* and Shakespeare?[5] As I hope to show, the Restoration *Coriolanus* bodies forth a range of aesthetic and political anxieties that are as significant for what they express as for how they cannot be reconciled. The ambivalence Tate cannot avoid revealing toward his own appropriation of Shakespeare

has a darker parallel in his advocacy of the Tory cause: his political position, like his aesthetic one, is more viable as polemic than drama. Specifically, the overtly loyalist claims of his dedication and of the prologue are at variance with the dramatic impact of his ***Coriolanus.*** Although Tate successfully blackens the Whig cause by introducing one character and several actions not in Shakespeare's text, and although he exalts Charles II, he finally cannot force the play to conform to an idealized standard of royal grandeur.

The gradual movement from the staid "heroic tragedy" of the 1660s and 1670s to the infinitely more conflicted and politically volatile affective tragedy of the 1680s is the precise aesthetic milieu of Tate's three adaptations of Shakespeare. As Laura Brown has argued, the years surrounding and including the Exclusion Crisis saw a general shift in taste from drama depicting the twin ideals of royalism and aristocracy, to a tragic vision concerned with the middling sorts and sentimentalism.[6] Tate's ***Ingratitude*** draws from both traditions, fully engaging with the affective tendencies of the period but also drawing upon a slightly older set of aesthetics that stressed nobility, aristocracy, and—more to his purpose with ***Coriolanus***—royalism as themes worthy of dramatic representation.

The Shakespeare of the late 1670s and early 1680s was principally a dramatic poet of the theater and not the printed page. *Pace* Gary Taylor, who rightly sees in the 1685 Fourth Folio "an elegant and readable" tome "comparable" to the best of Continental publishing,[7] in the Restoration period there is little printed evidence of the enshrining of Shakespeare as a writer of incomparably great literature. Unlike Nicholas Rowe's 1709 *The Works of Mr. William Shakespeare,* the two Restoration folios make no claims for the transcendent quality of Shakespeare's genius that are not made in the First and Second Folios, nor any for the fixity of his canon. Quite the contrary: to the 1664 edition are added seven new plays, of which only *Pericles* has survived the trials (or the predispositions) of modern editorial scholarship. Indeed, except for a few printer's touches in the 1685 edition, both Restoration folios follow the pre-Commonwealth editions and make the same limited claims for the status of Shakespeare and his as yet unstable *oeuvre.*

Restoration adapters developed an elaborate vocabulary for justifying their uses of this malleable "anticanon" of scripts. Central to their lexicon was the notion that Shakespeare's plays were too rough, undisciplined, or obscure to be produced as written, and though the adapters are careful to avoid direct denigration of Shakespeare's genius, their imagery gives away the fact that their anxieties entail more than just aesthetics. They are often subtly subversive, despite their protestations that they act as redactors and not inventors. Thomas

Shadwell claims his *Timon of Athens* is a "*Scion* grafted upon *Shakespeare*'s stock," while to Edward Ravenscroft and John Dryden, his works constitute rubble in need of reconstruction. In the dedication to *King Lear,* Tate himself imagines his literary predecessor "a Heap of Jewels, unstrung and unpolisht; yet so dazling in their disorder." In his *Ingratitude,* he figures Shakespeare as the rock upon which he builds. Most significant, however, in his preface to *Richard II* he imagines Shakespeare as a "first-Father" to his adaptation[8]—a point to which I will return.

In the immediate period of Tate's *Ingratitude,* the years 1678-82, nine plays by Shakespeare were adapted by seven different playwrights, Tate alone authoring three of them. In sharp contrast to the adaptations of the previous generation, of which Dryden and Sir William Davenant's romantic and radically adapted *The Tempest* holds a kind of aesthetic preeminence, all of the Exclusion Crisis revisions were tragedies or Roman plays.[9] They draw upon originals deeply engaged with questions of political organization, particularly those concerning the merits of monarchical and constitutional claims to power. Likewise, other plays of the period also articulate such political concerns openly: Charles Saunders's *Tamerlane the Great*; Nathaniel Lee's *Caesar Borgia* and *Lucius Junius Brutus*; a revival of Davenant's 1673 *Macbeth;* Aphra Behn's *The Young King* and *The Roundheads*; John Banks's *The Unhappy Favourite; or, The Earl of Essex*; and, perhaps most of all, Thomas Otway's brooding, violent *Venice Preserv'd.* In addition, Dryden and Lee's *Oedipus* was reprinted in this period, possibly in conjunction with a revival. And even when the subjects of the plays to which they were appended were not overtly political, many prologues and dedications often waxed polemical.[10]

The intersection of affective tragedy and political advocacy was a *donnée* throughout the Exclusion Crisis. Far from unique to adaptations of Shakespeare, partisan politics and sentimental appeal—or in the case of works such as Behn's *The Roundheads,* partisan politics and social satire—mix easily in nearly every production of the period. But as Susan Owen argues, the political polemics of prologues and dedications during the period often do not accurately represent the usually affective tendencies of the plays themselves. They "may not simply be taken at face value,"[11] she contends, because polemical engagement was a *sine qua non* of the period's dramatic publishing conventions.

Indeed, Restoration theater was in its very inception overtly political. Henry Killigrew and Davenant were not granted their monopolies in a political vacuum, but rather as licensed, regulated servants of Charles and his new government. The relation between London theaters and topical politics was thus from the beginning of the Restoration period a matter of political control. The

years leading up to the production of Tate's adaptation saw the most extensive disruptions within the restored monarchy, including the raising of a royal army that stood ready for three years; Charles II's dissolution of the "Cavalier" Parliament; the debacle of the "Popish Plot"; the coerced exile of James, duke of York; two bills for James's exclusion from the succession; and several politically motivated murders and executions—a combination of *ad hominem* attacks upon and constitutional resistance to the Stuart claim that had no precedent except in the 1640s.[12] These events together constituted the most serious threat to date against the very constitutional basis of the restored monarchy, and it is into this political maelstrom that Tate launches out in "*Shakespear's* Bottom."

Specifically, this intervention occurred in December of 1681, a year of intense political upheavals that included the executions of two Popish Plotters; the arrest and subsequent exoneration of Anthony Ashley Cooper, earl of Shaftesbury, the prime mover of the Exclusionist cause; the publication of Dryden's *Absalom and Achitophel*; and the guarantee of James's right to succession only after bitter strife and violent disorder at all levels of society. It is also the year that the tide turned against the rising Whig party, as the Tories solidified their position with Charles's dissolution of the Oxford Parliament and numerous political gains at the local level in London and the provinces.[13] Within about a year, but certainly by late 1683, the polemic in which the dedication to *The Ingratitude of a Common-Wealth* was embroiled had been rendered moot, the Tory cause having taken the day.[14]

Amid this welter of political contention, Tate's adapted *Coriolanus* tendentiously promotes an antidemocratic orthodoxy that Shakespeare's original avoids. Though his first four acts are essentially those of Shakespeare, subtle differences in Tate's treatment of his material indicate that his title was indeed chosen for a reason. For example, in act IV, scene ii, Aufidius plots openly with Nigridius, an invented character who bears a distinct resemblance to Shaftesbury and seems intended as a stock figure of Whig wickedness. Nigridius asks a series of leading questions that make Aufidius's intentions more clearly manifest than in Shakespeare's version. In keeping with the conventions of Restoration adaptation, Tate tightens and regularizes his source, but he also seizes the opportunity to make ever starker lines of demarcation between solitary Coriolanus, Shakespeare's lonely dragon, and the many groups of conspirators against his power.

In the next scene, Brutus and Sicinius plot together, as in *Coriolanus,* and later Tate's citizens turn upon them when they learn of Coriolanus's threat to Rome, as occurs in Shakespeare's V.iv. As one of their number encourages Menenius to intercede, a subtle change in reported action suggests a political dynamic different from that implied in Shakespeare's text. Tate offers, "The *Gods* preserve you Sir, Commend my hearty Affections to him; and if it stand with his good liking, we'll hang up our *Tribunes,* and send them him for a Token" (IV.iii.110-2), but the corresponding passage in Shakespeare has none of Tate's sentiment:

MESS.

> Sir, if you'd save your life, fly to your house.
> The plebeians have got your fellow-tribune,
> And hale him up and down, all swearing, if
> The Roman ladies bring not comfort home,
> They'll give him death by inches.[15]

Here the image of a specifically public vengeance, death as a *token* of changed political allegiances, underscores the opposition between royalism and populist republicanism that drives *The Ingratitude*. Tate's rabble, it seems, have learned the lesson to which he refers in his dedication: "*Where is the harm of letting the People see what Miseries* Common-Wealths *have been involv'd in, by a blind Compliance with their popular Misleaders? Nor may it be altogether amiss, to give these Projectors themselves, examples how wretched their dependence is on the uncertain Crowd . . . The moral therefore of these Scenes being to Recommend Submission and Adherence to Establisht Lawful Power, which in a word, is* Loyalty" (p. 2).

A number of minor lexical changes throughout the first four acts also emphasize the play's topical relevance to exactly this moral. None is so significant, however, as Tate's implied elevation of Coriolanus from deposed consul to wronged, vengeful king. His Cominius tells the First Citizen that all appeals will prove meaningless to enraged Coriolanus, who "sits Thron'd in Gold, his Eye / All Red, as 'twould burn *Rome*" (IV.iii.114-5). Then, in a streamlining and extension of Shakespeare's version, Menenius confronts the hero, who is enthroned, "*seated in State, in a rich* Pavilion," and scornfully throwing aside written petitions from Roman citizens (IV.iv.*sd*). The setting for the final encounter between Coriolanus and his family, traditionally staged as a military encampment, is in *The Ingratitude of a Common-Wealth* explicitly a palace.[16]

Though the topical relevance is clear enough, Tate's revision also strains under two broad aesthetic tendencies of Exclusion Crisis drama. First, in act IV, scene iv, he conflates Menenius's supplication with that of Virgilia, Volumnia, and young Martius. The implication is that begging for Rome's salvation is not so much a political mission but a family affair; the "last old man," who in Shakespeare's text seems almost a surrogate for the father that Coriolanus lacks, is in Tate's *Ingratitude* figured even more directly as a father. These "family" members present a unified front, a sentimental appeal to

Coriolanus's emotional side, but they are also indications of a broader tendency among Restoration writers to mingle familial and political matters. It is significant evidence of Tate's failure to remake Coriolanus fully that he excises most of the speech on kinship spoken by Shakespeare's Coriolanus, in which he declares his indifference to "[f]resh embassies and suits" from statesmen, friends, and family (V.iii.8-37). This conflation of family and political life, royal and republican governance—the suggestion that Charles II is a man of the people while Coriolanus is an anointed king—completely elides the very distinction for which the Exclusion Crisis developed.

In acts I-IV, then, Tate only subtly adapts Shakespeare's text, in several places streamlining it and sharpening contrasts, but also moving the entire dramatic direction of the play toward a domestic, familial tragedy. The fifth act, as critics from Odell and Spencer onward have noted, is the locus of Tate's most significant departures, almost all of them outright additions. Beyond even the changes that make the play into an affective tragedy, however, Tate's appropriation of Shakespeare reveals a great deal about English theatrical politics in the heady years of the Exclusion Crisis and about his own conception of the "rock" upon which he claims to build. Coriolanus and Aufidius face off in act V, scene iii, wounding each other in the scuffle (mortally, it turns out). Meanwhile, Nigridius has plotted the murder of Menenius and the maiming of young Martius, and has attempted to serve as panderer to Aufidius, whose final triumph is to be the rape of Virgilia before Coriolanus's moribund eyes:

> but heark, she comes:
> I charge thee Dye not yet, till thou hast seen
> Our Scene of Pleasures; to thy Face I'll Force her;
> Glut my last Minuits with a double Ryot;
> And in Revenges Sweets and Loves, Expire.
>
> (V.iii.92-6)

Then, in rapid succession, Virgilia enters, dying from the self-inflicted wound that allows her to preserve her "chast Treasure" rather than give it up as "th' unhallowed *Pyrates* Prize" (V.iii.120-1). Aufidius expires, clearing the emotional space of the stage for the family drama that closes the play. Virgilia dies a heroine's death just before Volumnia returns, distracted and bearing the mangled body of young Martius, still "living / In quickest Sense of Pain" (V.iii.156-7).

Volumnia delivers an extended rebuke to the conspirators against Coriolanus and his family, her dying grandson innocently calls attention to his own impending death and to his dead mother, and then she snatches a partisan and delivers a death blow to Nigridius. She runs off, still distracted, young Martius asks his father why his mangled arms will not move, then strikes a stoic pose before he too dies, and leaves his father to breathe his last, his arms clutching his dead wife and child:

> Thus, as th' Inhabitant of some sack't Town,
> The Flames grown near, and Foe hard pressing on,
> In haste lays hold on his most precious Store:
> Then to some peaceful Country takes his Flight:
> So, grasping in each Arm my Treasure, I
> > Pleas'd with the Prize, to Death's calm region
> fly.

> (V.iii.230-5)

In contrast to the closing scene of Shakespeare's play, Tate's revision seems intended to unify and mobilize an audience around a cluster of sentimental family issues, but not only that. In the final analysis, Shakespeare's ambivalent dramatic presentation of Caius Martius proves insurmountable: Tate's revision cannot quite get around the fact that Coriolanus has feet of clay, that he is neither a viable political leader nor an object easily given reverence or deep pity.[17] Like that of Shakespeare's Coriolanus, the fall of Tate's Caius Martius is, in part, just deserts. His Coriolanus cannot inspire the loyalty that the playwright advocates in his dedication to Lord Herbert because Tate is caught between his ideological allegiance to the monarch and his creative allegiance to the Bard.

The larger cultural implications of this creative impasse are significant. Tate's fusion of party polemics and affective appeal is infinitely complicated by his use of *Shakespear* as a source. His dedication to Lord Herbert, the grandson of one of Charles I's most steadfast supporters and himself a model royalist, is itself a political gesture of no uncertain meaning. Relevant, too, is the prologue by Sir George Raynsford, which represents the adaptation of Shakespeare in the language of parliamentary politics:

> Our Author do's with modesty submit,
> To all the Loyal Criticks of the Pit;
> Not to the Wit-dissenters of the Age,
> Who in a Civil War do still engage,
> The antient fundamental Laws o' th' stage:
> Such who have common Places got, by stealth,
> From the Sedition of Wits Common-Wealth.
> . . . . .
> Yet he presumes we may be safe to Day,
> Since *Shakespear* gave foundation to the Play:
> 'Tis Altered—and his sacred Ghost appeas'd;
> I wish you All as easily were Pleas'd:
> He only ventures to make Gold from Oar,
> And turn to Money, what lay dead before.

> (lines 2-15)

Both the dedication and prologue to *The Ingratitude of a Common-Wealth* enlist Shakespeare as a Tory partisan. His "sacred Ghost" is "appeas'd," we are led to be-

lieve, by his being appropriated for the (apparently parallel) objectives of financial gain, dramatic improvement, and service to the royalist cause. In fact, the two objectives are less disconnected than might be assumed. Shakespeare functions in Restoration prologues and dedications, especially for Tate, as a literary forefather, an aesthetic analog to Charles II, the political patriarch. The recurring image of fatherhood, a favorite trope of the Tories woven into many plays and their extratextual apparatuses, "is a politically charged notion in the Exclusion Crisis,"[18] and Tate attempts—unsuccessfully—to reconcile an idealized patriarchal image of Charles II with the authority of Shakespeare, his literary father.

The ambivalence toward the forefather shown by Tate and nearly all other adapters of Shakespeare during the Exclusion Crisis implies political instability as much as it suggests a conflicted understanding of literary inheritance. Just as writers created an idealized image of a gifted but barbarous national poet (a rock on which to build, a stock on which to graft a scion, a ruin to be restored, a heap of jewels to be restrung, and so on), so too did they accommodate Charles's unsuitability as an ideal paterfamilias and overlook his notorious and widely publicized promiscuity.[19] One way that several political tragedies, such as Otway's *Venice Preserv'd* and *The History and Fall of Caius Marius,* suppressed or moderated the full truth of Charles's public image was to subsume the question of monarchical succession into Venetian or Roman republican settings—to blur the otherwise firm lines separating monarchs from elected or appointed rulers. In Tate's case, this blurring occurs in order to advance a hopelessly idealized political vision, one in which England's greatest dramatic artist could be made to praise its greatest political leader.

Tate's filial respect for his literary forefather runs deeper than first appears, however. Despite his revisions of the fifth act, and despite his typically Restoration attempt to create both an affective *and* political tragedy, Tate ultimately follows the trajectory set forth by Shakespeare. He does launch out in Shakespeare's bottom and does build a superstructure upon his rock. His presentation of the hero, hardly altered from the source except for what is done *to* him, proves incompatible with his avowed political objective to advance the royalist cause. Coriolanus, like Charles II, was neither a sympathetic character nor an apt representative of benign, enlightened governing, but instead a headstrong and at times scheming leader who alternately countenanced and disdained the principle of constitutional republicanism. In finally capitulating to Shakespeare's skepticism concerning Caius Martius's ability to inspire loyalty or to govern well, Tate compromises his own Tory principles. The best he can do is to blacken the sins of Aufidius, Nigridius, and the tribunes: he can make the encoded Whig conspiracy more menacing, and he can allow his rabble to see the right reason of loyalty. But out of a sense of duty and deference toward his literary forefather, he balks at the opportunity to improve Coriolanus in any of the ways he made Richard II a better ruler and a more worthy object of loyalty.[20]

In fact, Coriolanus's final embrace of young Martius seems to suggest a parodic relation to Charles's refusal to acknowledge his bastard son Monmouth, the object of the Exclusionist faction's support.[21] Subject to intensified supplication by his "family" in Tate's adaptation, Coriolanus nevertheless does not even speak Shakespeare's lines on the dilemma between blood and honor (V.iii.18-36). These words might give meaning to his death at the hands of political schemers and populist rabble; instead, the hero's great moment is a sentimental and politically irrelevant slow death that present a tableau of idealized but impotent fantasies of the family's role in state politics. Caius Martius remains essentially and fundamentally the Caius Martius of Shakespeare's profoundly skeptical play.

My title, "Apolitical Shakespear; Or, The Restoration *Coriolanus*," suggests two further considerations I hope to have addressed in offering this reading of Tate's *Ingratitude.*[22] The use of *Shakespear*, a common enough Restoration spelling, is meant to signal the indeterminate aesthetic and political status of Shakespeare and his canon among Restoration adapters. The Shakespeare plays Tate (and many others) adapted were a fluid group of scripts not yet subjected to the scrutiny of editors and scholars from Rowe onward. To the extent that the Restoration Shakespeare constitutes a canon at all, it is the mutable domain of the public theater, not the fixed one of the gentleperson's library—a repertory and not a great books list.

Shakespear's ambiguously numinous and boorish status in the period of the Exclusion Crisis made his plays appear to adapters as a kind of political *tabula rasa* for all persuasions, factions, and parties, and Tate's use of that blank slate in *The Ingratitude of a Common-Wealth* is both typical of the period and remarkably restrained. And because restrained, it constitutes not a less but actually a more radical act of appropriation. More than in Davenant and Dryden's radically altered *The Enchanted Isle* or his own **King Lear** and **Richard II,** here Tate claims both Shakespeare's words and what he imagines to be his *politics* for his own. Without the mediation of deep or radical revision, Tate is truly appropriating Shakespeare through a strategy of multiple but comparatively minor additions and deletions, not wholesale adaptation. In so doing, he attempts to make Shakespeare ventriloquize for the royalist cause and claims, as does Sir George Raynsford in his prologue, that the august "sacred Ghost" of Shakespeare has been appeased and not antagonized.

Therein lies the rub. To the extent that he does so at all, Tate accomplishes this appeasement at the direct expense of his own political purpose: complete glorification of a noble monarch that merits complete loyalty. A truly noble Coriolanus would have had to be different in kind, not in details, from the flawed and sentimentalized figure Tate retains—a great deal, in fact, less like Charles himself.

Only half whimsically, I hope also to have gestured in my title toward the Restoration convention of separating dramatic titles and subtitles by the nearly ubiquitous *or*. This textual strategy of balancing opposing notions—and often fusing them as if they were one—deserves an extended analysis someday. For my own more restricted purposes here, however, I am convinced that two largely unresolved motives are at work in Tate's **The Ingratitude of a Common-Wealth; Or, The Fall of Caius Martius Coriolanus.** His *Or* ultimately signals alternative and not synonymous or conjunctive concepts: ingratitude, politics, and civic and constitutional matters are fundamentally at odds with the second part of the title, which suggests a sentimentalized tragic fall in an apolitical world. Even Tate's additions and deletions cannot fully elide these basic differences. The title and subtitle will not square.

Tate's **Coriolanus** is political in more than its party allegiances and its engagement in the micropolemics of the Exclusion Crisis. By domesticating Restoration political polemic and giving it an affective, familial bias, he makes broader claims for the inherently orderly and hierarchical stability of royal authority—a family, in effect, with Charles as the ultimate paterfamilias.[23] But, as I have also argued, that family has a darker side. To adapt Menenius's parable of the belly, its head, like that of the English body politic during the Exclusion Crisis, is no paragon to its members.

Tate's retreat into the sentimentality of prevailing dramatic conventions announces the problems inherent in grafting scions onto Shakespeare's stock and rearranging the jewels (or rubble) of his plays to suit prevailing political needs. Tate's largely ignored play merits attention because, more than offering only an instance of Restoration polemical adaptation, it also exemplifies the political capital that is still imagined to accrue by appropriating "the national poet"'s works. By suggesting that Shakespeare's politics can be not reinscribed, but simply *conscripted* for one's self, one's party, or even one's political system, Tate marks a crucial early stage in the long and varied history of Shakespeare's appropriation for political gain. That habit and its attendant risks, of course, did not die with Tate.

Notes

1. See Michael Dobson, *The Making of the National Poet: Shakespeare, Adaptation, and Authorship, 1660-1769* (Oxford: Clarendon Press, 1992); Jean

I. Marsden, *The Re-Imagined Text: Shakespeare, Adaptation, and Eighteenth-Century Literary Theory* (Lexington: Univ. Press of Kentucky, 1995) and her introduction to *The Appropriation of Shakespeare: Post-Renaissance Reconstructions of the Works and the Myth* (New York: St. Martin's Press, 1991), pp. 1-10; and Gary Taylor, "Restoration," in *Reinventing Shakespeare: A Cultural History, From the Restoration to the Present* (New York: Weidenfeld and Nicholson, 1989), pp. 7-51. Also noteworthy is a survey article by Matthew H. Wikander, "The Spitted Infant: Scenic Emblem and Exclusionist Politics in Restoration Adaptations of Shakespeare," *SQ* 37, 3 (Autumn 1986): 340-58. Previous to these, Hazelton Spencer's *Shakespeare Improved: The Restoration Versions in Quarto and on the Stage* (Cambridge MA: Harvard Univ. Press, 1927) and George C. D. Odell's *Shakespeare: From Betterton to Irving,* 2 vols. (1920; rprt. New York: Dover Publications, 1966) had dominated in this largely neglected field. One notable exception is Gunnar Sorelius, *"The Giant Race before the Flood": Pre-Restoration Drama on the Stage and in the Criticism of the Restoration* (Upsala and Stockholm: Almqvist and Wiksells, 1966). Even studies as influential as Robert D. Hume's *The Development of English Drama in the Late Seventeenth Century* (Oxford: Clarendon Press, 1976) have little to say about the conjunction of Shakespeare, aesthetic theory, and politics.

2. Steven N. Zwicker concisely characterizes the milieu to which I refer: "the traffic between politics and art in this age allows us to see that all the work of the literary and imagination is embedded in polemic and contest. In these years ephemera and eternity have important relations, and texts that display the gestures of canonical self-celebration often allow the most complex and illuminating conversations with the local, the partisan, and the political" (introduction to *Lines of Authority: Politics and English Literary Culture, 1649-89* [Ithaca: Cornell Univ. Press, 1993], pp. 1-8, 2).

3. On the political representations of Charles II, see Paul Hammond, "The King's Two Bodies: Representations of Charles II," in *Culture, Politics, and Society in Britain, 1660-1800,* ed. Jeremy Black and Jeremy Gregory (Manchester: Manchester Univ. Press, 1991), pp. 13-48. Hammond argues that the execution of Charles I made representations of Charles II "assertive rather than simply declarative"; such representations allowed for "alternatives" that a writer such as Nahum Tate had to negotiate (p. 13).

4. Tate, *The Ingratitude of a Common-Wealth; Or, The Fall of Caius Martius Coriolanus,* in *Nahum Tate and the "Coriolanus" Tradition in English Drama with a Critical Edition of Tate's "The Ingratitude of a Common-Wealth,"* ed. Ruth McGugan (New York: Garland, 1987), pp. 2-5. All further references to *The Ingratitude of a Common-Wealth* are to this edition, the only modern one available, and appear parenthetically in the text. All references to the bodies of plays are by act, scene, and line numbers. See also Dobson, p. 5, and Pierre Danchin, ed., introduction to *1660-76,* pt. 1, vol. 1 of *The Prologues and Epilogues of the Restoration, 1660-1700* (Nancy: Publications Université Nancy II, 1981), pp. xxiii-xliii, on the importance of the dedications, prefaces, prologues, and epilogues of the period.

5. My use of the term *Tory* is intended as a convenient shorthand, not a way of reopening a basic historiographical question about the formation of political parties in Britain. Terms like *conservative* and even *royalist* have a problematic relation to the drama of the period before the Exclusion Crisis because even in the early years of the crisis, both factions claimed a conservative purpose.

6. Laura Brown, *English Dramatic Form, 1660-1760: An Essay in Generic History* (New Haven: Yale Univ. Press, 1981), especially pp. 21-5, 69, 86, and 99. In a study of the 1678-79 theatrical season, Susan Owen offers a persuasive rationale for adopting a more tightly historical view of events during the Exclusion Crisis, as well as a taxonomy for making precise sense of what other critics often amalgamate as "Restoration stage politics" ("Interpreting the Politics of Restoration Drama," *SCen* 8, 1 [Spring 1993]: 67-97).

7. Taylor, p. 31.

8. Thomas Shadwell (epilogue to his *Timon of Athens*), Edward Ravenscroft (preface to his *Titus Andronicus*), John Dryden (preface to his *Troilus and Cressida*), and Tate (dedication to his *King Lear,* preface to his *Richard II*), rprt. in *1623-92,* vol. 1 of *Shakespeare: The Critical Heritage,* ed. Brian Vickers (London: Routledge and Kegan Paul, 1974), pp. 237, 239, 250, 344, and 321, respectively. See also John Dryden's preface to *The Enchanted Isle,* where he states (almost prophetically, in the case of Tate) that "Shakespear's *pow'r* is sacred as a King's" (in *Plays: "The Tempest," "Tyrannick Love," "An Evening's Love,"* in *Works,* ed. Maximillian E. Novak and George Robert Guffey, vol. 10 [Berkeley: Univ. of California Press, 1970], pp. 6-7, line 24).

9. The nine are Shadwell's *Timon of Athens* and Ravenscroft's *Titus Andronicus* (1678); Dryden's *Troilus and Cressida* and Thomas Otway's *The*

History and Fall of Caius Marius (1679); in the following year, John Crowne's *Henry VI* and Tate's *Richard II*; and in the remaining two years, Tate's *King Lear* and his *Coriolanus,* and Thomas D'Urfey's *The Injured Princess,* based upon *Cymbeline* (William Van Lennep, ed., *1660-1700,* pt. 1 of *The London Stage, 1660-1800* [Carbondale: Southern Illinois Univ. Press, 1965], pp. 265-76).

10. Van Lennep, pp. 276-7, 281, 292, 295-6, 300, and 303. See also Wikander.

11. Owen, p. 82. In addition, Wikander describes a persistent "double drive towards both inflammatory applicability and regular romantic intrigue" among adapters of Shakespeare in the 1680s (*The Play of Truth and State: Historical Drama from Shakespeare to Brecht* [Baltimore: Johns Hopkins Univ. Press, 1986], p. 113).

12. For surveys of the Exclusion Crisis and the period leading up to it, see especially Geoffrey Holmes, *The Making of a Great Power: Late Stuart and Early Georgian Britain, 1660-1722* (London: Longman, 1993), pp. 106-42; John Miller, *Popery and Politics in England, 1660-88* (Cambridge: Cambridge Univ. Press, 1973), pp. 154-95; and J. P. Kenyon, "Charles II, 1649-85," in *The Stuarts: A Study in English Kingship* (1958; rprt. London: Fontana Collins, Fontana Library, 1966), pp. 100-43. Kenyon's *The Popish Plot* (London: Heinemann, 1972) is the most thorough treatment, though with a bias toward the religious rather than the constitutional aspects of the Exclusion Crisis.

13. Miller, pp. 189-90.

14. Holmes, p. 162.

15. William Shakespeare, *Coriolanus,* ed. Philip Brockbank (London: Methuen, 1976), V.iv.36-40. All quotations from Shakespeare's play are from this edition. Subsequent references will appear parenthetically in the text.

16. Tate anticipates editors and critics from the eighteenth century onward in this matter. See the useful note at V.iii.0.1-2 in R. B. Parker, ed., *The Tragedy of Coriolanus,* by Shakespeare (Oxford: Oxford Univ. Press, 1994).

17. On the difficulties involved in pitying Coriolanus, see Kenneth Burke, "*Coriolanus*—and the Delights of Faction," in *Language as Symbolic Action: Essays on Life, Literature, and Method* (Berkeley: Univ. of California Press, 1966), pp. 81-97, 82-94.

18. Owen, p. 89.

19. Dryden's image from *Absalom and Achitophel,* that Charles "Scatter'd his Maker's image through the Land" (2:453-93, line 10), and Rochester's

line "His sceptre and his p[ric]k are of a length" from "The Earl of Rochester's Verses for Which he was Banished" (1:423-4, line 11) are perhaps the most widely known squibs on Charles II's promiscuity. The satirical tradition, however, is much more extensive, as demonstrated throughout the anthology here quoted, *Poems on Affairs of State: Augustan Satirical Verse, 1660-1714* (ed. George deF. Lord, 7 vols. [New Haven: Yale Univ. Press, 1963-75]). To offer only a few examples, Charles was likened (unfavorably) to Henry VIII, because he had illegitimate "sons and daughters more / Than e'er has Harry by three-score" ("The History of Insipids," 1:243-51, lines 17-8), implicated in charges of incest and compared to drunken Lot ("Hodge," 2:146-53, lines 43-4), and consistently referred to by the name of "Old Rowley," that of his stud horse ("Satyre on Old Rowley," 2:184-8). By the Exclusion Crisis, his promiscuity was thoroughly conventionalized in the satiric literature, and he was among the most frequently satirized figures of the period. See also Hammond, pp. 13-7.

20. See Dobson, p. 81 and n., for a brief but useful review of Tate's adaptation of *Richard II.*

21. James, duke of Monmouth's military and civil duties were taken from him by Charles in November 1679, from which time he became a popular hero, especially for the anticourt party. Charles's rejection of him became the subject of several satires against the king; see, for example, "'Letter of the Duke of Monmouth to the King' and 'The King's Answer'" for an especially apt Tory satire (Lord, 2:253-6).

An interesting verbal parallel exists between Coriolanus's dying speech and a satire Tate wrote in approximately May 1682. The final words of his Coriolanus (see above) echo in these lines addressed to Monmouth:

> Both parties boast a star to lead their train,
> One but of late dropp'd out of Charles his wain.
> Unhappy prince! . . .
> To feed on husks, before thy father's bread!
> Fly to his arms, he like th' Almighty stands,
> Inviting penitents with both his hands.
>   ([Tate], "Old England," in Lord, 3:183-206, lines
>   227-32)

As the editor of *Poems on Affairs of State* indicates, Tate's position in the shifting political field of these years was unstable; he tried to navigate a middle position between Yorkist and Catholic zealots, to maintain "a perilous balance" between extremes that could have proved dangerous as the political landscape changed (Lord, 3:184).

22. I am also, of course, alluding to Jonathan Dollimore and Alan Sinfield, eds., *Political Shakespeare: Essays in Cultural Materialism,* 2d edn.

(Ithaca: Cornell Univ. Press, 1994), and to the larger critical problem of ascertaining (or appropriating) Shakespeare's own politics.

23. See the useful discussions by Michael Walzer, *The Revolution of the Saints: A Study in the Origins of Radical Politics* (Cambridge MA: Harvard Univ. Press, 1965), pp. 183-6, and Hammond.

Sonia Massai (essay date summer 2000)

SOURCE: Massai, Sonia. "Nahum Tate's Revision of Shakespeare's *King Lear*s." *Studies in English Literature, 1500-1900* 40, no. 3 (summer 2000): 435-50.

[*In the following essay, Massai examines Tate's use of different versions of Shakespeare's* King Lear *in his revision of the play.*]

In his 1975 edition of *The History of King Lear* (1681), James Black could still claim that Nahum Tate's notorious adaptation was "one of the most famous unread plays in English."[1] Since then, mainly as a result of an unprecedented interest in the afterlife of the Shakespearean text,[2] *The History of King Lear* has been studied both in relation to the changed stage and dramatic conventions of Restoration theaters and for its historical and political significance.[3] Despite this revival of critical interest in Shakespearean adaptations and Christopher Spencer's advocacy of Tate,[4] the stigma of mediocrity which was first associated with Tate in the nineteenth century still discourages critics and editors alike from investigating Tate's competence as a professional reader of Shakespeare.

Tate had the privilege of reading and adapting Shakespeare's *King Lear* in a preconflationist age, when no theory about the origin of the copy texts behind the Quarto or the Folio had been advanced. His adaptation is the only surviving instance of a critical assessment of the *dramatic* qualities of Quarto and Folio *King Lear* before Lewis Theobald's editorial policy of conflation and the theory of the lost original denied both texts a direct link with the author's holograph. Tate felt free to rely on his Quarto and Folio source texts independently of their *formal* qualities, thus highlighting *dramatic* differences between them which supporters of the theory of revision in *King Lear* now regard as intentional and possibly authorial. Unlike Black, who argues that Tate must have relied on his Folio source(s) more and more consistently after act I, because he had by then realized that the Quarto is *formally* inferior to the Folio,[5] I believe that Tate must have regarded his Quarto and Folio source texts as *dramatically* independent versions of the same play and that he used them according to which text provided an alternative better suited to his own strategy of revision of the Lear story.[6] This article therefore provides new indirect evidence in favor of the theory of internal revision in *King Lear*,[7] by establishing a connection between Tate's dramatic and ideological agenda as an adapter of Shakespeare and his selective and discriminating reliance on his Quarto and his Folio sources in *The History of King Lear*.

I. QUARTO VARIANTS IN ACTS I AND II OF *THE HISTORY OF KING LEAR* AND TATE'S REVISION OF THE KING

Tate's political affiliations played an important part in his decision to replace Shakespeare's tragic ending with "the King's blest Restauration" (K1v, line 10).[8] The new ending bears a close resemblance to the comic resolution in Shakespeare's main dramatic source, the anonymous *The Chronicle History of King Leir* (1605).[9] More importantly, Tate's revision is symptomatic of the progressive decline of tragedy and the increasing popularity of tragicomedy in postrevolutionary drama.[10] Similarly, Tate's expansion of the female roles and his introduction of the love affair between Edgar and Cordelia are clearly a tribute to the new practice of having women actors on the Restoration stage.[11] Further evidence of the influence of current dramatic conventions on Tate's revision is a strong concern with decorum, which, as Tate himself suggests, led him to tone down "Lear's real, and Edgar's pretended Madness" (**"Epistle Dedicatory,"** A2r, line 14; A2v, line 1). The omission of the Fool, however, seems prompted by matters of ideological rather than dramatic concern, the Fool being the main source of the vexing criticism the king is exposed to in the Shakespearean originals.

Tate's adaptation of Shakespearean tragedy into Restoration tragicomedy entailed a radical departure from both his Quarto and his Folio originals. Particularly interesting is Tate's recasting of his tragic hero in acts I and II.

In order to suit Tate's tragicomic revision of the Lear story, the king is transformed into a character with an obvious but minor flaw, easily blamed at the beginning for initiating his own fall, but also easily forgiven in the end, because of the obvious imbalance between his share of responsibility and the potential magnitude of the avoided catastrophe. Tate helps his audience detect a flaw in the king's character by introducing a new exchange between Gloucester and Kent in the opening scene:

KENT.

> I grieve to see him
> With such wild starts of passion hourly seiz'd,
> As renders Majesty beneath it self.

GLOST.

> Alas! 'tis the Infirmity of his Age,
> Yet has his Temper ever been unfixt,
> Chol'rick and suddain.

> (B1v, lines 35-8; B2r, lines 1-2)

Although Tate's Lear is a flawed character, he is guilty of a lesser crime than his predecessors in Quarto and Folio *King Lear*, his disappointment for the outcome of the love trial being partly justified by Cordelia's ulterior motives. A brief exchange between Cordelia and Edgar immediately before Lear's first entrance discloses their secret engagement. Cordelia's original integrity is therefore compromised by her divided allegiances to Lear and Edgar:

CORD.

> Now comes my Trial, how am I distrest,
> That must with cold speech tempt the chol'rick King
> Rather to leave me Dowerless, than condemn me
> To loath'd Embraces!

> (B2v, lines 6-9)

Lear's rage stems not so much from his blindness and his misjudgment of Cordelia's motives as from his perspicacity. When she retorts "So young my Lord and True" (B3r, line 2), the king, along with the audience, knows that Cordelia is lying. The king's initial surprise at his daughter's open disobedience, "And goes thy Heart with this?" (B2v, line 32), which Tate borrows from the original, is followed by an indictment of her true motives:

LEAR.

> 'Tis said that I am Chol'rick, judge me Gods,
> Is there not cause? now Minion I perceive
> The Truth of what has been suggested to Us,
> Thy Fondness for the Rebel Son of Gloster,
> False to his Father, as Thou art to my Hopes.

> (B2v, lines 33-7)

The king's reference to Edgar as "the Rebel Son of Gloster" is directly related to Tate's decision to open his adaptation with Edmund's soliloquy, "Thou Nature art my Goddess" (B1r, line 6). Toward the end of this soliloquy, Edmund informs the audience that Edgar is now unanimously regarded as a traitor as a result of his machinations:

BAST.

> Here comes the old Man [Gloucester] chaf't with
>   th'Information
> Which last I forg'd against my Brother Edgar,
> A Tale so plausible, so boldly utter'd
> And heightned by such lucky Accidents,
> That now the slightest circumstance confirms him,
> And Base-born Edmund spight of Law inherits.

> (B1r, lines 21-2; B1v, lines 1-4)

Tate's Lear is therefore misled about Edgar, but not about Cordelia. Tate, in other words, makes his audience aware that Lear is acting to the best of his knowledge as a wise and responsible monarch in opposing Edgar and Cordelia's engagement. Besides, Lear's disclaimer, "'Tis said that I am Chol'rick" (B2v, line 33), makes his flaw more easily forgivable.

According to Peter L. Sharkey, "King Lear possessed no 'tragic flaw' until Tate endowed him with one."[12] Black expands on Sharkey: "Attempting to make the king more understandable or at least more recognizable, [Tate] prepares for Lear's irrational behavior by introducing 'choler' as a tragic flaw."[13] My objection to this argument is that Tate did not have to invent a new tragic flaw for his king. He simply accentuated the tragic flaw he found in the Quarto.

Tate follows the Quarto in omitting seven extra Folio lines from Lear's first speech. As a result, Tate's Lear fails to justify his decision to divide the kingdom, and, as in the Quarto, he sounds more willful and reckless. Tate's Lear also fails to explain (or to realize) that the division of the kingdom serves a noble and selfless purpose. By omitting the Folio lines,

> We have this houre a constant will to publish
> Our daughters severall Dowers, that future strife
> May be prevented now.

> (F, lines 48-50)

Tate follows the Quarto in depicting the king as strong-willed to the point of obstinacy.[14]

The Folio additions to Lear's first speech combine to make the king look older, weaker, and consequently unable to retain his title and power. In the Folio, the king's "darker purpose" (F, line 41) coincides with his decision to abdicate not only "all cares and business" of state (Q, line 40; F, line 44), as in the Quarto, but also the "Rule, and Interest of Territory" (F, lines 54-5). His decision to abdicate is fully justified by the fact that he is too old to rule. In the Folio, the king thinks he is soon to die:

> 'tis our fast intent,
> To shake all Cares and Businesse *from our Age,*
> *Conferring* them on yonger *strengths, while we*
> *Unburthen'd crawle toward death.*

> (F, lines 43-6; Folio variants in italics)

Lear in the Quarto is still as strong as the majority of his predecessors in the sources. In John Higgins and in Raphael Holinshed, for example, Lear never resigns. The division of the kingdom and abdication are two independent issues. The king divides his kingdom into marriage portions, but succession is postponed until after his death. In Higgins, the king punishes his youngest daughter by disowning her and by dividing the kingdom between his elder daughters, retaining his title and position until his death. Cordell happily marries the king of France and only her sisters' greed brings her back to England to defend her father's right to the throne. Similarly in Holinshed, the king proclaims his eldest daughters and their husbands his successors but does not abdicate. The Lear episode in *The Faerie Queene* is the only notable exception: here the king is old and tired and, as in the Folio, he voluntarily "eases" himself of the crown. In *The True Chronicle History of King Leir,* the king expresses a wish to abdicate before the love trial, but abdication is forced upon him only by its unforeseen outcome.[15] In Shakespeare, Kent and Gloucester's opening exchange,

KENT.

> I Thought the King had more affected the Duke of Albany, then Cornwall.

GLOUC.

> It did alwayes seeme so to us: But now in the division of the Kingdome*s*, it appeares not which of the Dukes hee valewes most, for *equalities are so weigh'd, that curiosity in neither*, can make choice of eithers moity.

> (Q, lines 1-6; F, lines 1-7; Quarto variants in italics)

informs the audience that the king's decision regarding the settlement of his daughters' dowries has already taken place, and not, as it is generally assumed when this passage is read retrospectively, within the context of a conflated King Lear, that the king has decided to abdicate.

In his first speech in the Quarto, the king announces his "darker purposes": arranging Cordelia's marriage, dividing the kingdom in three parts to bestow on his daughters as their marriage portions, and testing them to decide who deserves the richest share of the kingdom. In the Quarto, chronologically closer to the sources, the succession motif is not as yet linked to the abdication motif, as it will be in the later Folio version. Lear's plan in the Quarto betrays a wish to retain, rather than resign, his power by settling the succession in his own terms and perhaps postponing it till after his death, as in the sources.

The so-called abdication speech, "Cornwall, and Albanie, / With my two Daughters Dowres, digest the third," is identical in the two versions of *King Lear.* Only in the Folio, however, does the king's abdication happen de facto. The last line of Lear's abdication speech, "This Coronet part betweene you," is not meant to prompt the king to take off his crown and hand it over to his sons-in-law, because "Coronet," as Wilfried Perrett first observed in 1904, is not a synonym for crown.[16] The first meaning of "coronet" listed in the OED is "a small or inferior crown; spec. a crown denoting a dignity inferior to that of the sovereign, worn by the nobility, and varying in form, according to rank." In his 1992 New Cambridge edition of *The Tragedy of King Lear,* Jay L. Halio specifies that "Shakespeare

uses 'coronet' for the diadem of a nobleman in *Henry VI Part I* and *Julius Caesar* and in *The Tempest,* he explicitly contrasts 'crowns and coronets.'" He therefore concludes that "it is unlikely that Lear gives his sons-in-law his own crown to divide between them," and that "probably Lear refers to the coronet he meant for Cordelia."[17] It is however worth noting that the Folio omits "one bearing a coronet" from the stage direction which marks the first entrance of the king and his retinue in the opening scene. Although the absence of this stage direction does not necessarily mean that the coronet was not brought on stage, the Folio implies a degree of ambiguity, thus reinforcing the idea that abdication and division of the kingdom are taking place simultaneously. In the Quarto, however, the king is perfectly fit to rule, expresses no wish to abdicate, and is merely forced to divide his kingdom by letting Cornwall and Albany "digest" Cordelia's dower, signified by the presence of the coronet on stage. As Sir Walter W. Greg argues, "if Shakespeare was responsible for [the Quarto's] direction, 'there is subtlety in the provision he makes. When Lear says to his "Beloued Sonnes" Cornwall and Albany "This *Coronet* part betweene you," he is bidding them share the executive office only; he retains on his own head the *crown* as symbol of "The name, and all th'addition to a King."'"[18] In the Quarto, the abdication speech is not, technically speaking, an abdication speech after all.

Other Quarto variants in act II confirm Tate's tactful avoidance of the abdication motif. The first variant occurs at the end of Kent's confrontation with Goneril's messenger outside Gloucester's castle. As in the Quarto, Tate's Gloucester begs Cornwall and Regan to reconsider their decision to punish the king's messenger. Gloucester reminds them that although "His fault is much, and the good King his Master / Will check him for't" (D1r, lines 2-3). Both in the Quarto and in Tate, Gloucester warns Cornwall that his decision will lead to a clash of authorities. Tate's king, as his Quarto counterpart, has divided his kingdom and devolved his former responsibilities but has never abdicated his power. Gloucester's warning, omitted from the Folio, reminds Lear's opponents that the latter is still a king de facto. Once again Tate retains a Quarto line which is more in keeping with his recasting of the character of the king in act I than the alternative provided by the Folio.

The second relevant Quarto variant in *The History of King Lear* occurs after Lear has found Kent-as-Caius in the stocks. Although Tate follows the Folio in assigning to Lear Goneril's lines, "Who stockt my Servant? Regan, I have hope / Thou didst not know it" (D3r, lines 23-4), he continues to refer to his Quarto source for the characterization of the king in this scene. Lear's original reaction to Oswald is expanded to read:

LEAR.

> This is a Slave whose easie borrow'd pride
> Dwells in the fickle Grace of her he follows;
> *A Fashion-fop that spends the day in Dressing,*
> *And all to bear his Ladie's flatt'ring Message,*
> *That can deliver with a Grace her Lie,*
> *And with as bold a face bring back a greater.*
> Out Varlet from my sight.

(D3r, lines 15-21)

The lines in italics represent Tate's addition to the original passage, as it appears in both the Quarto and the Folio. There is a telling similarity between Lear's new lines and Kent's billingsgate against Oswald in the original:

STEW.

> What dost thou know me for?

KENT.

> A knave, a rascall, an eater of broken meates, a base, proud, shallow, beggerly, three snyted hundred pound, filthy wosted stocken knave, a lilly lyver'd action tak-ing *knave, a* whorson glassegazing *supersinicall* rogue, one truncke inheriting slave, one that would'st bee a baud in way of good service, and art nothing but the composition of a knave, begger, coward.

(Q, lines 908-15; F, lines 1087-94; Quarto variants in italics)

Lear in Tate is not overwhelmed by "the Mother," Hysterica Passio. He borrows instead Kent's forceful idiom to express his disgust at seeing a rogue preferred to his messenger. This first alteration shows the audi-ence that the king is still as strong and capable of indig-nation as he was at the beginning of the play.

Straight after Lear's arraignment of Goneril's messen-ger, Cornwall asks the king, "What means your Grace?" (D3r, line 22), and Lear speaks the lines quoted above, "Who stockt my Servant?" Only at this point does Goneril enter. Though Tate follows the Folio in having Lear repeat his question, he moves the stage direction "Enter Gonerill." from its original position, after Cornwall's "What means your Grace?", to the end of Lear's "Who stockt my Servant?" As a consequence, Lear, who in the Folio fails to realize that Goneril has already entered, appears as alert and in control as in the Quarto, where Goneril's line "Who struck my servant" attracts everybody's attention, Lear's included. The king in *The History of King Lear* does not seem to have lost touch with reality. Tate's Lear is not mad with sorrow and overwhelmed by self-pity and hysteria be-cause of his daughters' betrayal, as is his counterpart in the Folio. Like Lear in the Quarto, Tate's king is mad with rage at seeing his power taken away from him and he struggles to resist.

The Quarto variants Tate retains in the first two acts of *The History of King Lear* contribute to presenting the audience with a strong, if unflattering, image of the king, who is as willful and reckless as in the Quarto, al-though, on the whole, guilty of a lesser crime. When Tate follows the Folio at the end of act I, he modifies Albany's mild disagreement with Goneril about the king's riotous knights from "Well, you may feare too farre" (F, line 849) to "Well, you may bear too far" (C2v, line 33). Although "bear" could be a misprint for "fear," it is intriguing that up to the end of act I, even Tate's Albany, who will act as a champion of royalty in act V and restore Lear to the throne, should appear to feel no sympathy for the willful king.

The end of act II, however, marks an inversion of strat-egy on Tate's part, and the willful king is gradually re-deemed through repentance and forbearance. The shift from the tragic to the pathetic mode becomes fully manifest only in acts III and IV. As early as the middle of act II, however, Tate retains the Folio line "Are they inform'd of this? my Breath and Blood!" (D2r, line 21), where the king draws attention to his despondency for the first time. This line represents what Black refers to as a "sentimental ingredient," a recurrent element in the second half of *The History of King Lear,* where Tate's characters "invariably turn the pathos back upon them-selves."[19] From the end of act II, Tate starts to rely on the Folio more and more consistently as a source of similar sentimental lines. As the textual evidence in section II suggests, Tate switches from his Quarto to his Folio source, because, contrary to the Folio, the Quarto provides no such lines, and, more importantly, denies its audience the opportunity to identify and sympathize with its tragic hero.

II. FOLIO VARIANTS IN ACTS III AND IV OF
THE HISTORY OF KING LEAR AND THE POLITICS
OF SENTIMENTALISM

Acts III and IV form the dramatic heart of Tate's adap-tation: here suffering is elaborately expressed and exter-nalized by the king and the good characters and, at the same time, contained and transformed into pity. Pain in Tate is never associated with a tragic sense of loss, waste, and disorientation; neither is it the source of a redemptive, but nonetheless tragic, resolution. Pain be-comes the object of a public display, thus inviting both the on-stage and the real audience to share the charac-ters' experience and values. In Tate, the feelings of sympathy, pity, and compassion imply a communion of values and beliefs between the characters and their fic-tional and real audiences, and make the happy ending not only emotionally but also ideologically desirable. Lear's delusive certainty that the Gods will take pity on Cordelia and himself, "Upon such Sacrifices / The Gods themselves throw Incense" (I1v, lines 32-3), is trans-ferred to Tate's Cordelia, who, unlike her father, is not hallucinating, but foreseeing the inevitable.

Although neither the Quarto nor the Folio version of Shakespeare's *King Lear* provides an ideal model for the dramatic technique which Tate uses in the second half of his adaptation, the Folio is followed more consistently, because, unlike the Quarto, it does not prevent identification. Tate, for example, omits all the moralizing passages which appear only in the Quarto, such as the servants' exchange after Gloucester's blinding at the end of act III, or the gentleman's description of Cordelia in act IV. His decision to ignore the Quarto might seem odd, because these passages attract the audience's attention to the characters' emotions and could have been exploited for their pathetic potential. One however only needs to look a little closer to realize that the Quarto's moralizing passages elicit a peculiar response from the audience, one which is quite irreconcilable with the sympathetic identification encouraged by Tate's adaptation.

In the Folio, the omission of the servants' exchange after Gloucester's blinding serves both dramatic and practical purposes. According to Gary Taylor, the Quarto was designed for uninterrupted performance, and this passage was meant to give Gloucester enough time to exit, change clothes and reenter after Edgar's soliloquy at the beginning of the next scene. The introduction of act intervals in the Folio made this passage theatrically redundant.[20] Its omission, however, also has interesting dramatic effects because it protects the audience from the brunt of the violence, and also from the immediacy of emotional identification.

In Tate, the servants' exchange is replaced by a long monologue in which Gloucester laments the sudden change of his fortune and exposes his inner being to the full view of the audience. Gloucester's original, heartrending "All Dark and Comfortless" is followed by twenty-six new lines. This passage is crucial to Tate's strategy of revision of the original, in that it shows how the externalization of grief can turn black despair into restoring pathos. Suicide is soon dismissed in favor of revenge. Gloucester's share of responsibility for precipitating Lear's and his own downfall does not seem to prevent him from thinking that revenge can right the play's topsy-turvy universe. Whereas Shakespeare's Gloucester is crushed by his own despair, Tate's Gloucester uses his suffering to help the king:

GLOUC.

> with these bleeding Rings
> I will present me to the pittying Crowd,
> And with the Rhetorick of these dropping Veins
> Enflame 'em to Revenge their King and me.

> (F4r, lines 24-7)

Gloucester's world is unshaken by his misfortunes and its values are never questioned. Grief does not prevent him from seeking redress; on the contrary, grief be-

comes the means whereby he will overcome his enemy. His certainty of ultimate success rests on the fact that Gloucester, like Tate, knows that an audience can be stirred to sympathy through the pathetic display of undeserved suffering. This kind of sympathy implies a shared belief in the political and aesthetic necessity of poetic justice.

Immediately after IV.ii, the Quarto provides an extra scene which Tate chooses to ignore. This scene contains an exquisite portrait of Cordelia, which exemplifies the process whereby sympathy is transformed into a visible theatrical phenomenon:

KENT.

> Did your letters pierce the queene to any demonstration of griefe.

GENT.

> I say she tooke them, read them in my presence,
> And now and then an ample teare trild downe
> Her delicate cheeke, it seemed she was a queene
> over her passion,
> Who most rebell-like, sought to be King ore her.

KENT.

> O then it moved her.

GENT.

> Not to a rage, patience and sorow streme,
> Who should expresse her goodliest you have seen,
> Sun shine and raine at once, her smiles and teares,
> Were like a better way those happie smilets,
> That playd on her ripe lip seeme not to know,
> What guests were in her eyes which parted thence,
> As pearles from diamonds dropt in briefe,
> Sorow would be a raritie most beloved,
> If all could so become it.

> (Q, lines 2104-18)

Cordelia's composure and stillness are suggestive of the emblematic quality of a precious icon: her tears are "pearls," her eyes "diamonds." The gentleman's description of Cordelia's state of mind is also highly emblematic. Cordelia's private feelings become the actors of an allegorical psychomachia. Sorrow is personified and described as striving to be "king" over Cordelia's emotions. Unlike Lear, who succumbed to the "Mother," Histerica Passio, Cordelia faces her kingly sorrow and triumphs over it. As the gentleman explains, "Sorow would be a raritie most beloved, / If all could so become it." The Quarto provides the audience with a compelling example of how grief can be turned into art. Grief becomes something "rich and strange" for the audience to admire, but not to identify with.

As with the servants' exchange at the end of act III, Tate follows the Folio and omits this Quarto passage, replacing it with a living portrait of Cordelia weeping.

Tate's Cordelia rejoins the action as early as the second half of act III, thus creating several opportunities for a pathetic anticipation of the long awaited reunion at the end of act IV:

CORD.

> As 'tis too probable this furious Night
> Has pierc'd his tender Body, the bleak Winds
> And cold Rain chill'd, or Lightening struck him
>   Dead;
> If it be so your Promise is discharg'd,
> And I have only one poor Boon to beg,
> That you'd Convey me to his breathless Trunk,
> With my torn Robes to wrap his hoary Head,
> With my torn Hair to bind his Hands and Feet,
> Then with a show'r of Tears
> To wash his Clay-smear'd Cheeks, and Die beside
>   him.
>
>   (E2r, lines 28-37)

A quick glance at the effects this spectacle of pity has on the on-stage audience is probably the best way to establish the kind of response Tate meant to elicit from his real audience. Gloucester, who has questioned Cordelia's motives for wanting to rescue her father, is finally persuaded of her good intentions: "Rise, fair Cordelia, thou hast Piety / Enough t'attone for both thy Sisters Crimes" (E2r, line 38; E2v, line 1). Far more interesting, however, is the reaction Cordelia's tears elicit from the other character on stage. Unseen by Gloucester and Cordelia, Edmund is spying on them, and like Milton's Satan in Eden, he is entranced by his vision:

BAST.

> O charming Sorrow! how her Tears adorn her
> Like Dew on Flow'rs, but she is Virtuous,
> And I must quench this hopeless Fire i'th'Kindling.
>   . . . . .
> I'll gaze no more—and yet my Eyes are Charm'd.
>   (E2r, lines 17-26)

Unlike the serpent in Milton's book 9 of *Paradise Lost,* however, Tate's Edmund is mesmerized not only by Cordelia's beauty and unspotted innocence, but also by her distress. He claims that Cordelia's tears adorn her like dew on flowers. This episode reveals a more general mechanism underlying Tate's strategy of revision. In Tate, the exposure of the good characters' inner being encourages identification not only through sympathy but also through the voyeuristic pleasure of the on-looker.

The Folio's naturalistic use of sympathy as a response to tragic experience, although substantially different from Tate's technique of exposing his characters' inner being to the full view of his audience, is not incompatible with his strategy of revision. The Quarto's moralizing passages, on the other hand, are irreconcilable with

Tate's efforts to bridge the distance between the character and the onlooker through sympathy and pathos. Tate follows the Folio because the Quarto creates a gap between the characters and the audience which ensures understanding rather than identification. The Captain's two-line speech in act V, where he seeks a motive for obeying Edmund and killing the old king and his daughter, "I cannot draw a cart, nor eate dride oats, / If it bee mans worke ile do't" (Q, lines 2697-8), is probably the best, if not the most consequential, example of another "Brechtian" passage in the Quarto which Tate chooses to ignore.

III. TATE'S "CRITICAL EDITING" OF QUARTO AND FOLIO *KING LEAR* AND THE REVISIONIST HYPOTHESIS

The theory of authorial revision in *King Lear* was first advanced when textual scholars stopped wrestling with the problem of the possible origin of a specific variant and concentrated on its function, both in relation to its immediate context and to other variants. By looking at Quarto and Folio *King Lear* as scripts, the revisionists started to notice patterns of interrelated variants which suggest a "substantial and consistent recasting of certain aspects of the play."[21] The selection of Quarto and Folio variants in *The History of King Lear* shows that Tate, who never worried about the origin of his source texts, also spotted patterns of interrelated variants. The similarity in some of the patterns of variants spotted by Tate and by the revisionists strikes me as more than a suggestive coincidence.

Tate's reliance on his Quarto source for the recasting of the old king into a stronger and more willful character, for example, is suggestively in keeping with the revisionists' view that, whereas "the behaviour of Q[uarto]'s Lear partakes of the brisk arbitrariness of myth and fairy-tale," "the Folio version lays a strong foundation for the development of sympathy," and the old king grows into a "larger and more intensely tragic" figure.[22] David Richman, who directed a performance of *King Lear* based exclusively on the Quarto, similarly realized that the shorter version of Lear's first speech conveys a stronger image of the king as ruler: "[The Quarto] presents a clear, strong image of the king which is borne out and developed during the first two acts . . . Quarto's Lear allows nothing to distract him from his division of the kingdom, his disposal of Cordelia in marriage, and the love-test of his daughters."[23]

Despite the attention paid to individual variants in relation to the character of the king, none of the revisionists has identified the abdication motif as a potential pattern of revision in *King Lear.* MacD. P. Jackson and Taylor, for example, claim that Shakespeare revised Lear's first speech in order to stress the "full political import of his abdication," by making it more "explicable" and "noble," whereas Thomas Clayton refers to Lear's plans in I.i as "division and *partial* abdication" (emphasis added).[24] The revisionists' diverging views on this issue reflect the textual ambiguity inherited from the standard conflated text. Tate's preference for the Quarto variants, on the other hand, suggests a connection between the Quarto's characterization of the king as a strong and willful ruler and his unwillingness to relinquish power. As in the Quarto and the majority of its sources, Tate's Lear never abdicates, thus departing from the revised and weaker king of the Folio, whose age and noble attempt to avoid a civil war fully justify his willingness to relinquish power.

Tate's omission of the moralizing passages analyzed above sheds light on another pattern of revision in *King Lear.* Michael Warren agrees with Steven Urkowitz that "Such cameos, in which the progress of plot is briefly arrested and an image of moral life is *presented,* are a *distinctive feature* of the *dramatic technique* of the Quarto, a readiness to allow the action to pause so that the moral impact of events can be *demonstrated verbally* and *visually.* In the Folio, by contrast, the plot just takes its mighty course" (emphasis added).[25] Warren's remarks are supported by Urkowitz's view that the Quarto passages provide "more 'meaning'" but "less 'experience'" and "fewer sensations of 'drama'" than the Folio.[26] The Quarto presents and demonstrates, thus encouraging critical detachment, whilst the Folio stresses emotional intensity, a precondition of sympathetic identification.

Tate's omission of the Quarto moralizing passages confirms Warren and Urkowitz's analysis of their function, and, more generally, the hypothesis of internal revision in *King Lear.* Tate's adaptation, in other words, provides indirect evidence to argue that these Quarto passages are a cluster of interrelated variants and that Quarto and Folio *King Lear* must have been conceived as two different tragedies, not only in terms of plot and characterization, but also in terms of their dramatic effect. In Henry Norman Hudson's view, Tate's adaptation was a distorting mirror, which marred the greatness of its original;[27] in my view **The History of King Lear** is rather a magnifying glass, through which Shakespeare's "unstrung jewels" shine even more clearly than through the thick coat of editorial dust which three centuries of conflation have laid upon them.

Notes

1. Nahum Tate, *The History of King Lear,* ed. James Black (London: Arnold, 1975), p. xv.

2. Recent reconstructions of the establishment of the Shakespeare myth and the appropriation of Shakespeare's works include Jonathan Bate, *Shakespearean Constitutions: Politics, Theatre, Criticism, 1730-1830* (Oxford: Clarendon Press, 1989) and *The Genius of Shakespeare* (London and Basingstoke: Picador, 1997); Margreta De Grazia, *Shakespeare Verbatim: The Reproduction of Authenticity and the 1790 Apparatus* (Oxford: Clarendon Press, 1991); Gary Taylor, *Reinventing Shakespeare: A Cultural History from the Restoration to the Present* (London: Vintage, 1991); Michael Dobson, *The Making of the National Poet: Shakespeare, Adaptation, and Authorship, 1660-1769* (Oxford: Clarendon Press, 1992); Paulina Kewes, *Authorship and Appropriation: Writing for the Stage in England, 1660-1710* (Oxford: Clarendon Press, 1998).

3. On the Lear narrative's relation to dramatic convention, see Harry William Pedicord, "Shakespeare, Tate, and Garrick: New Light on Alterations of *King Lear,*" *TN* 36, 1 (1982): 14-21; James Black, "An Augustan Stage History: Nahum Tate's *King Lear,*" *RECTR* 6 (1967): 36-54. Among the main historical-political interpretations of the *History,* J. Douglas Canfield, "Royalism's Last Dramatic Stand: English Political Tragedy, 1679-89," *SP* 82, 2 (Spring 1985): 234-63; Nancy K. Maguire, "Nahum Tate's *King Lear*: 'the king's blest restoration,'" in *The Appropriation of Shakespeare: Post-Renaissance Reconstructions of the Works and the Myth,* ed. Jean I. Marsden (Hemel Hempstead: Harvester, 1991), pp. 29-42; and Matthew H. Wikander, "The Spitted Infant: Scenic Emblem and Exclusionist Politics in Restoration Adaptations of Shakespeare," *SQ* 37, 3 (Autumn 1986): 340-58.

4. Christopher Spencer, "A Word for Tate's *King Lear,*" *SEL* 3, 2 (Spring 1969): 241-51; see also his *Nahum Tate* (New York: Twayne, 1972). For more details on this stigma, see *Five Restoration Adaptations of Shakespeare,* ed. Spencer (Urbana: Univ. of Illinois Press, 1965), p. 8.

5. Black, p. 99.

6. See Sonia Massai, "Tate's Critical 'Editing' of His Source-Text(s) in *The History of King Lear,*" in *AEB* n.s. 9, 4 (1995): 168-96, where it is established that, contrary to Black's conclusion, Tate uses a copy of the First Quarto and both a copy of the First and the Third Folio throughout acts I to IV. A shorter version of this article appears in *Textus: English Studies in Italy,* ed. Keir Elam and Ann Thompson (Geneva: Tilgher, 1996), pp. 501-22. For specific examples of Tate's critical "editing" of his source-texts, see Bate and Massai, "Adaptation as Edition," in *The Margins of the Text,* ed. David C. Greetham (Ann Arbor: Univ. of Michigan Press, 1997), pp. 129-51.

7. For the main studies exploring the two-text theory in *King Lear,* see Michael J. Warren, "Quarto and Folio *King Lear* and the Interpretation of Albany

and Edgar," in David Bevington and Jay L. Halio, *Shakespeare, Pattern of Excelling Nature* (Newark: Univ. of Delaware Press, 1976), pp. 95-107; Taylor, "The War in *King Lear*," *ShS* 33 (1980): 27-34; Steven Urkowitz, *Shakespeare's Revision of "King Lear"* (Princeton: Princeton Univ. Press, 1980); Peter W. M. Blayney, *The Texts of "King Lear" and Their Origins: Nicholas Okes and the First Quarto,* vol. 1 (Cambridge: Cambridge Univ. Press, 1982); and *The Division of the Kingdoms: Shakespeare's Two Versions of "King Lear,"* ed. Taylor and Warren (Oxford: Oxford Univ. Press, 1983). P. W. K. Stone, in *The Textual History of "King Lear"* (London: Scolar Press, 1980) also supports the theory of revision in *King Lear,* although, as opposed to the bitextual scholars mentioned above, he rejects the hypothesis of authorial revision. For the latest developments of the "two-text controversy," see *"Lear" from Study to Stage: Essays in Criticism,* ed. James Ogden and Arthur H. Scouten (Madison: Fairleigh Dickinson Univ. Press, 1997), and recent editions, such as Rene Weis's parallel-text edition (London: Longman, 1993) and the single-text Quarto editions prepared by Halio (Cambridge: Cambridge Univ. Press, 1994) and Graham Holderness (Hemel Hempstead: Prentice Hall, 1995).

8. All quotations from *The History of King Lear* are followed by line-reference to Nahum Tate, *The History of King Lear* (London: Cornmarket Press, 1969). All quotations represent the source exactly except in one respect: the long "s" and italic type are not preserved.

9. It is worth stressing that Black's view that this parallel is fortuitous remains virtually unchallenged. For more details, see Black, pp. 97-8.

10. Maguire suggests that the popularity of tragicomedy reflects an attempt to exorcise the specter of regicide, which was still haunting the collective memory of Tate's contemporaries. For more details, see Maguire, *Regicide and Restoration English Tragicomedy, 1660-71* (Cambridge: Cambridge Univ. Press, 1992).

11. Tate's own account of his introduction of the love affair between Edgar and Cordelia seems solely aimed at advertising his "improvements" on the Shakespearean original: "'Twas my good Fortune to light on one Expedient to rectifie what was wanting in the Regularity and Probability of the Tale, which was to run through the whole A Love betwixt Edgar and Cordelia, that never chang'd word with each other in the Original" (*The Epistle Dedicatory,* A2v, lines 12-7).

12. Peter L. Sharkey, "Performing Nahum Tate's *King Lear*: Coming Hither by Going Hence," *QJS* 54, 4 (December 1968): 398-403, 400.

13. Black, p. xx.

14. Quotations from the 1608 Quarto (hereinafter Q) and the 1623 Folio *King Lear* (hereinafter F) are followed by line reference to Warren, *The Complete King Lear: 1608-1623* (Los Angeles, Berkeley, and London: Univ. of California Press, 1989). The long "s," italic type, and the old spelling of "u" and "v" are not preserved.

15. The main sources of *King Lear* referred to in this paper are available in Geoffrey Bullough, *Narrative and Dramatic Sources of Shakespeare,* 7 vols. (London: Routledge, 1957-75). For more details on the abdication motif in the sources, see Wilfried Perrett, *The Story of King Lear: From Geoffrey of Monmouth to Shakespeare* (Berlin: Mayer and Müller, 1904), pp. 181-3.

16. Perrett, pp. 151-2.

17. Shakespeare, *The Tragedy of King Lear,* ed. Halio (Cambridge: Cambridge Univ. Press, 1992), I.i.32n.

18. Sir Walter W. Greg, quoted in MacD. P. Jackson, "Fluctuating Variation: Author, Annotator, or Actor?" in *The Division of the Kingdoms,* pp. 313-49, 338.

19. Black, p. xxxi.

20. Taylor, "The Structure of Performance: Act-Intervals in the London Theatres, 1576-1642," in Taylor and John Jowett, *Shakespeare Reshaped, 1606-1623* (Oxford: Clarendon Press, 1993), pp. 3-50, 48-9.

21. Warren, "Quarto and Folio," p. 99.

22. Jackson, p. 338; Thomas Clayton, "'Is this the promis'd end?': Revision in the Role of the King," in *The Division of the Kingdoms,* pp. 121-41, 125; Grace Ioppolo, "The Idea of Shakespeare and the Two *Lears,*" in *"Lear" from Study to Stage,* pp. 45-56, 50.

23. David Richman, "The *King Lear* Quarto in Rehearsal and Performance," *SQ* 37, 3 (Autumn 1986): 374-401, 376-7.

24. Jackson, p. 336; Taylor, "*King Lear*: The Date and Authorship of the Folio Version," in *The Division of the Kingdoms,* pp. 351-468, 382; Clayton, p. 125.

25. Warren, "The Diminution of Kent," in *The Division of the Kingdoms,* pp. 59-73, 65.

26. Urkowitz, p. 52.

27. Henry Norman Hudson, in *Five Restoration Adaptations,* p. 8.

C. B. Hardman (essay date October 2000)

SOURCE: Hardman, C. B. "'Our Drooping Country Now Erects Her Head': Nahum Tate's *History of King*

Lear." Modern Language Review 95, no. 4 (October 2000): 913-23.

[*In the following essay, Hardman examines the changes made by Tate to Edmund, Edgar, and Albany in* King Lear, *considering how Tate's audience might have responded to the characters in light of contemporary political events.*]

It was once thought that 'political considerations' had 'a minimum of direct effect' on Tate's rewriting of *King Lear.*[1] However, for some time now critics have attended to the play's contemporary political significance, placing it squarely in the political context of its period, and particularly of the exclusion crisis in the 1680s.[2] This article seeks to extend the discussion of Tate's rewriting of Edmund, Edgar, and Albany and to consider how a contemporary audience might have read them in the light of the politics of the day; for however Shakespeare's audience would have reacted to them, even names could sometimes suggest something different by the 1680s.

Tate seems to have consulted both quarto and folio versions of Shakespeare's play.[3] Beginning with the quarto, he then turned to the folio, where the conclusion is precipitated not by invasion but by civil war, which was more to his purpose, and developed that somewhat (IV.2.100). In his *King Lear* a political crisis involving banishment, exclusion, and the overturning of legitimacy (especially in the Gloster plot, which now stands more prominently at the beginning of the play) leads to the abuse of freedom and eventually to internecine conflict. Despite its justification, an uprising to restore rather than depose monarchy and traditional order fails. It is a potent warning of the consequences of the wilful disturbance of proper succession that initiated the action in the first place.

The political situation in 1680 was so tense that there was a real fear, according to Bishop Burnet, that there would be another civil war over exclusion:

> This was like either to end in a rebellion, or in an abject submission of the Nation to the humours of the Court. I confess, that which I apprehended most was rebellion, tho' it turned afterwards quite the other way. But men of more experience, and who had better advantages to make a true judgement of the temper of the Nation, were mistaken as well as myself.[4]

William Lloyd, preaching before the House of Lords on 5 November 1680, gave the same warning.[5] To supporters of the legitimate succession, the banishment of Kent, Cordelia, and Edgar would have suggested the potential predicament of the Duke of York, should the exclusionists triumph. The alternative to the legitimate Duke of York was the illegitimate Duke of Monmouth. It has already been recognized that a number of similarities between Monmouth and Edmund are suggested as the play continues. The Duke was attractive, if not particularly intelligent, and was certainly considered by many contemporaries to live a libertine life. The development of that aspect of Shakespeare's Edmund by Tate would have offered obvious parallels. By his own admission Edmund disregards conscience: 'Awe thou thy dull legitimate slaves', he says, for 'I I Was born a libertine, and so keep me' (v.5.19-20). In Shakespeare, Edmund's calculated self-interest had always had a sexual aspect in his adulterous alliances with Goneril and Regan; now this is extended and more blatant. First of all he is very quick to wish to become a part of the revelling, self-indulgent life of feasting and masking at the court of Gonerill and Regan, the noise of their entertainment drowning the storm while they callously disregard those on the heath. In Tate's play Edmund receives messages from both Gonerill and Regan before the blinding of his father and is 'sick of expectation, I [panting] for the possession' (III.2.26-27). In his opening speech in Act III, Scene 2, social aspiration combines with sexual desire:

> Oh for a taste of such majestic beauty,
> Which none but my hot veins are fit t'engage!
> Nor are my wishes desperate, for even now
> During the banquet I observed their glances
> Shot thick at me; and as they left the room
> Each cast by stealth a kind inviting smile,
> The happy earnest—
>
> (III.2.9)

Only a hundred lines later, he plans to rape Cordelia.[6] At the opening of the fourth Act he is revealed in a grotto with Regan 'amorously seated, listening to music' and protesting his affection (IV.1.3-6), though within twenty lines he leaves to meet Gonerill and offer her the same pledges. Before the battle he confesses that he has already 'enjoyed' Regan and looks forward to the 'dear variety' to be afforded by Gonerill's 'untasted beauty' (v.3.7-9).[7]

To a contemporary audience the word 'libertine' would not have suggested simply promiscuity but that Edmund was a follower of the currently popular idea of what constituted Epicurean philosophy and, motivated by self-interest, saw himself as free from the restraints of conventional morality: an incarnate opponent of legitimacy, irreligious, independent, and free thinking.[8] It is a philosophy that quickly leads to ambitious self-assertion and he very soon has his eyes on a throne: 'Thus would I reign could I but mount a throne' (III.2.2). Edmund and the Duke of Monmouth both seek to displace a legitimate brother and are libertine in their attitude to the laws of inheritance and sexual morality. One of Tate's additions to the play in the last act reinforces the argument for a connection between Edmund and Monmouth. Shakespeare's Edmund had never cast any doubt upon his paternity; Tate's Edmund does so in a way that would have reminded his contemporaries of the question of Monmouth's paternity. When Edgar says: 'The dark and vicious place where thee he got | Cost him his eyes', Shakespeare's Edmund replies: 'Th'hast spoken right.' Tate's Edgar adds to his moralizing the remark: 'From thy licentious mother | Thou draw'st thy villainy', and this provokes the response:

> Thou bear'st on thy mother's piety,
> Which I despise. Thy mother being chaste
> Thou art assured thou art but Gloster's son.
> But mine, disdaining constancy, leaves me
> To hope that I am sprung from nobler blood,
> And possibly a king might be my sire.
> But be my birth's uncertain chance as 'twill,
> Who 'twas that had the hit to father me
> I know not.
>
> (v.5.46)

At times in the course of the exclusion crisis Monmouth's paternity was questioned, along with the morals of his mother, suggesting of course that the King may not have been his father, exactly the opposite of Edmund's suggestion that a king might be his. In both cases, real and fictional, sexual immorality and dubious legitimacy are highlighted. Dying, Edmund admits that in the play, as was to be the case in contemporary Britain, 'Legitimacy | At last has got it' (v.5.77-78). In the rewriting of Edmund, Tate presents an apprehensive look into the kind of future one might expect to attend upon a policy of exclusionism before falling back with some relief into legitimacy.

The play concludes with the emergence from national and domestic disorder, the return of sanity, the endorsement of legitimacy in Edgar, and the celebration of the piety of Edgar and Cordelia inaugurating the re-establishment of empire and of peace and plenty:

> Our drooping country now erects her head,
> Peace spreads her balmy wings, and Plenty blooms.
>
> (v.6.154)

All references to piety, to empire, and to peace and plenty are Tate's, not Shakespeare's. Gloster speaks pointedly of a 'second birth of empire' and of 'the king's blest restoration' (v.6.117-18). The survival of Lear and Cordelia in Tate's version of the play necessitated the removal of the striking entrance, *'Re-enter Lear, with Cordelia dead in his arms'*, which Tate replaced with 'a reminiscence of Aeneas bringing Anchises out of Troy':[9]

> Look, sir, where pious Edgar comes
> Leading his eyeless father.
>
> (v.6.111)

It is clearly not, however, simply the replacement of one moving passage with another, for Tate's recollection of the *Aeneid* at this point in the play signals his

major change to Shakespeare's dramatic structure, the substitution of a happy ending: Shakespeare's *pietà*-like tragic tableau is replaced by a reminder of the refugees from Troy, the culmination of whose narrative was the establishment of empire. Further, this archetypal example of filial piety has a potent political significance in the 1980s, by recalling the political discourse of the 1660s. At the Restoration the idealized representation of the re-established kingdom often explicitly referred to the golden age and imperium of Augustus. Now the King is under pressure to upset the order established then. When Charles II returned to London in 1660 he had been welcomed to the city, as had his grandfather James I, as another Augustus leading back a golden age. Once again, the lines from Virgil's *Fourth Eclogue* that had first celebrated Octavius's messianic assumption of power, 'Redeunt saturnia regna', appeared on a triumphal arch, together with the explicit acknowledgement of the Augustan parallel, 'Adventus Augusti' and quotations from the epic endorsement of Roman imperial power, the *Aeneid*.[10] The association of Charles and Aeneas as the wandering exile who founds a new empire featured in contemporary national poetry of praise (Knowles, p. 25).

One further strain developed by Tate in his rewriting of the play also had its roots in the history of the Restoration. On the first arch there had been 'a trophy of "decollated heads"' under the inscription *'Sequitur Rebelles | Ultor a tergo Deus* ("Gods Vengeance Rebels at the Heels pursues")', explained by Ogilby as 'representing in a Trophy the late Example of God's justice apon the Rebels, who committed that most horrid murther upon His Majesties Royal Father of Blessed Memory' (p. 18). Ogilby linked this to the theme of the returning Augustus by recalling that Augustus likewise avenged the murder of his father when the wars had ended. Tate's Gloster and his Cordelia both express a clear wish for just vengeance for the treatment of the king which has no source in Shakespeare. Gloster asks:

> Must I then tamely die, and unrevenged?
> So Lear may fall: no, with these bleeding rings
> I will present me to the pitying crowd,
> And with the rhetoric of these dropping veins
> Enflame 'em to revenge their king and me.
>
> (III.5.83)

Cordelia regrets her inability to 'shift my sex, and dye me deep | In his opposer's blood' (IV.5.64-65), but calls on the gods to enact the revenge she cannot accomplish herself. Her conviction that an act of rebellion against the king constitutes an affront to the gods themselves emphasizes the divine ordination of kingship:

> You never-erring gods
> Fight on his side, and thunder on his foes
> Such tempest as his poor aged head sustained:
> Your image suffers when a monarch bleeds.

'Tis your own cause, for that your succors bring,
Revenge yourselves, and right an injured king.

(IV.5.64)

In the 1680s audiences would have recalled the fate of regicides after the Restoration and would no doubt have seen this as a warning against disturbing legitimacy again.

It has been suggested that by the mid-1670s the royalist vision of restoration was already anachronistic and that in Dryden's *Aureng-Zebe,* for example, one sees a retreat from the 'lost heir' trope and a shift of narrative focus 'from restoration to succession by presenting the story of a royal family whose internal divisions nearly destroy an empire. The situation calls for a successor capable of creating a consensus out of the deep divisions within the royal-family-as-state'.[11] *King Lear,* of course, both incorporates the lost-heir theme and provides a succession apparently capable of resolving the crisis within the royal family. In 1681, the motif of the return from exile was not, however, an anachronism, not just a question of remembering the past. The exile and recall of James, Duke of York, was an important issue in the current exclusion crisis. James and his Duchess had been exiled to Brussels in March 1679, only days before the Parliament that was to discuss the first Exclusion Bill met. Early in 1680 the King resisted petitions to meet Parliament: instead, it was prorogued and James was welcomed back to Court. In October 1680 he was sent to Scotland, despite his reluctance, and did not return until April 1682, though no doubt his return was looked for during 1681 by those who opposed exclusion and hoped for the triumph of the Court, with Shaftesbury in the Tower on a capital charge. It was at this time that *Absalom and Achitophel,* the most accomplished of the contemporary effusions of the propagandists, appeared. If, then, Tate's play looks back to the return of a legitimate sovereign in 1660 and in doing so reinforces the importance of stability, the preservation of time-honoured values of descent, inheritance, tradition, and legitimacy, the cry 'Legitimacy | At last has got it' (v.5.77-78) at the end of the play also looks forward optimistically to the continuance of these values in the future, to the return from exile of another pious ruler, to the resolution of family and state conflict, and to the defeat of the exclusionists and of the illegitimate libertine championed by some of them. The representations would have been by no means precise to a contemporary audience, but as Edmund would have reminded them of Monmouth, perhaps Edgar would have stood for the hopes that were placed in James.

Tate's recollection of the politically charged Virgilian narrative at the time of the exclusion crisis can be seen as one of several allusions to the re-establishment of order at the Restoration and to the disorder it resolved. The rebellion and confusion that had been then set aside was now in danger of breaking out again. The madness so prominent in *King Lear* and reflected in the nakedness of Poor Tom and the casting-off of clothes by the king recalls the depiction of Confusion on the first arch erected in the City for Charles's entry in 1660. She was 'a deformed shape [wearing] a Garment of several ill-matched Colours, and put on the wrong way', alluding to the familiar topic of a disordered and upside-down world and to madness.[12] Clarendon, when writing about the recent hostilities, observed with profound regret that they had been characterized by a loss of reverence and respect. It is no surprise to find him detailing the usual disruption of hierarchies, breakdown of order, and dissolution of family ties:

> Parents had no Manner of Authority over their Children, nor Children any Obedience or Submission to their Parents; but every one did that which was good in his own Eyes. This unnatural Antipathy had its first Rise from the Beginning of the Rebellion; when the Fathers and Sons engaged themselves in the contrary Parties. [. . .] The Relation between Masters and Servants had been long since dissolved by the Parliament, that their Army might be increased by the Prentices against their masters' Consent. [. . .] In the Place of Generosity, a vile and sordid Love of Money was entertained as the truest Wisdom, and any Thing lawful that would contribute to being rich.[13]

All this would have been familiar in Tate's source and the audience would have been well aware of the fear that the circumstances of the interregnum might easily repeat themselves.

Considerable changes were needed to Shakespeare's play for the resolution to reflect the triumph of legitimacy it was hoped would come with a decision for James as Charles's heir and assure the country once again of the harmony of the Restoration. In Shakespeare's play, Lear does not survive to enjoy a restoration, the reuniting of families is merely a prelude to the separation of death, and Lear's grasp on his sanity does not seem entirely secure. For Tate it is very different: sanity is regained, Lear and Gloster are reunited with their virtuous children, their families joined in marriage, the monarchy is restored and legitimate inheritance assured when Lear hands on his power to Cordelia and then to Cordelia and Edgar, 'this celestial pair' (v.6.151). Nancy Maguire has, however, questioned the assumption that Tate was offering a straightforward Tory resolution here and suggests that he was rather 'hedging his bets':

> The happy (and Whiggish) arrangement to have Cordelia and Edgar rule is, in a sense, elective monarchy rather than divine right, and their joint rule, of course, foreshadows the succession of William and Mary in 1688.[14]

After their accession William and Mary may indeed have thought their joint rule was reflected in that of Cordelia and Edgar. However, it is hard to see what happens as elective and 'Whiggish'. At the beginning of the play Lear chose his successors; now the more sensible choice of Cordelia, his only surviving legitimate heir, is inevitable, but the choice is still his. It is hardly consonant with Shaftesbury's rejection of the theory of divine right in 1675 as a Stuart fiction and his conviction that not God but English law determined who should rule.[15] Instead it seems to take the view expressed by Hobbes that with kings 'the disposing of the Successor is alwaies left to the Jugement and Will of the present Possessor' (Chapter 19, p. 100), for 'they that are subjects to a Monarch, cannot without his leave cast of Monarchy' (Chapter 18, p. 88).[16]

The prosperous reign of an Edgar to which the conclusion of the play looks forward would have reminded audiences of another Edgar, the British king who had often been invoked in the Stuart discourse of sovereignty, in the iconography of the Restoration, in the reconstruction of the navy, and in two contemporary plays. In the long-running claim of Britain to have dominion over the British seas in opposition to the Dutch support for *mare liberum,* it was King Edgar (959-75) who was cited as a precedent and said to have claimed maritime sovereignty and possibly actually exercised it.[17] It was part of the argument in John Selden's *Mare clausum,* written first for James I and then augmented for Charles I in 1635. Charles I had placed Edgar's effigy on the beak of his ship *The Sovereign of the Sea* and had the inscription *Carolus Edgari sceptrum stabilivit aquarum* on each of the 102 brass guns. The ship was represented on the arches welcoming Charles II, who was portrayed as the British Neptune (Knowles, pp. 32-34), emphasizing that Charles, like his royal predecessor, sought to be master of the sea. In the course of the bitter war with Holland that broke out in 1664 this ambition became hopeless.[18] However, reconstruction of the fleet followed eventually and to this end Charles provided money from his privy purse in 1677 to finance a thirty-ship programme directed by Pepys and the naval architect Anthony Deane.

The two contemporary plays that took Edgar as their subject were Edward Ravenscroft's *King Edgar and Alfreda* (London, 1677) and Thomas Rymer's *Edgar or the English Monarch* (London, 1678). Audiences for Tate's play may have known these, though there is no record of a performance of Rymer's play. Both plays speak of the importance of naval power during Edgar's reign. Ravenscroft's play has a brief life of the king as found 'in our English Chronicles' in place of a preface. It describes a king who 'had no War all his Reyn, yet [who was] always well prepar'd for warr; he govern'd the kingdome in great Peace, Honour and Prosperity, gaining thence the Sirname of Peacemaker', and particularly stresses his naval preparedness:

His Care and Wisdom was great in guarding the Coast around with Ships, to the number of Three thousand six hundred, which he divided into Four Squadrons to sayl to and fro about the Four Quarters of the Land, meeting each other. Thus he kept out wisely the Force of Strangers, prevent'd Foreign Warr and secur'd the Coasts from Pyrots.

(*King Edgar and Alfreda,* A2ᵛ)

Ravenscroft claimed in the prologue that his play had been written 'at least Ten Years ago'. If that was the case, any comparison with Charles's own reign at that time of crisis, when plague and fire had been followed by the Dutch War, would have been to its disadvantage and Edgar's care of the realm would have been an exemplary model. On the other hand, those contemporaries who frequently recorded the vice of the Court and in particular the profligacy of the King would have recognized a similarity at the end of the following passage: 'His Acts were some Virtous, some Politick, some Just, and some Pious, and some with a mixture of Vice; but those related to women.' By the time the play was published, however, it would have been easier to see the description of the reign of Edgar as offering a complimentary comparison than a contrast, although the king's vices remained the same. The advertisement to Rymer's play described it as 'an Heroick Tragedy' in which he 'chiefly sought occasion to extoll the English Monarchy'. The preliminary verses 'To the King' refer to Edgar as his 'great Fore-runner', though by comparison his ships were 'mere infants of the Main', while each of Charles's would then have seemed a 'God o' th' Sea'. 'Empire without End' is promised as other nations do homage while 'Peace [the] larger Empire happy made' and the King 'alone, great Edgar's Person bear[s]'. In the play Edgar's barge is rowed by subject kings who compare their narrow dominions with his 'Empire's vast extent' (1.9, p. 10). In Act IV there is a masque in which Neptune lays his trident at Edgar's feet and Proteus and Nereus do obeisance to him. It is his valour rather than his fleet of ships that establishes English power, and from Edgar 'England's glory grows' and 'More than one *Edgar* Fate to *England* owes' (p. 38). Yet the masque is interrupted, Edgar starts up, and this 'Dream of Majesty' is 'dethroned by Love' (p. 40). Masques had traditionally offered both praise and counsel to their patrons, and the audience in 1678 would no doubt have seen this as a delicately critical reflection on the conflict between private passion and duty. The play concludes with Edgar's denial of the power of Rome to forbid his marriage to his goddaughter. This episode asserts, if nothing more, the independence of the monarchy from the dictates of a foreign religious power at a time when Catholic plots and the threat of Popery were at the centre of British political discussion.

In these plays it seems that Edgar's empire is a type of Charles's, a promised 'Empire without End'. In Tate's play the plenty and peace of this 'second birth of empire' seem to reflect the idea of a legitimate Stuart imperium existing from the Restoration and stretching into the future as a legitimate James, like Edgar, is preferred before an illegitimate Monmouth, like Edmund.

When Charles died suddenly in 1685 Dryden was writing an opera later to be called *Albion and Albanius,* including Charles (Albion) and also his successor James (Albanius) in the title. There can be little doubt that James's part was already prominent before his brother's death, though that event may have brought about a change of title. In the work Dryden implies that both men were supporters of the naval power, which as he well knew was necessary to defend the trade on which the country's imperial future depended. In other words, it was using a different fiction to present a picture of an ideal empire essentially similar to that presented above. Albion was the name given in the chronicles to the Britain ruled over by Brute after his flight from fallen Troy and more pertinently here was, as Spenser recorded, (*Faerie Queene,* IV) the name of a mythical son of Neptune. The events of the opera clearly reflect recent history: for example, the arrival of Charles at Dover, the exile of the Duke of York, and the Popish Plot. Ronald Knowles has pointed out that Dryden certainly explicitly recalled Charles II's triumphal entry in 1660 when he took as an epigraph for his opera the Virgilian line which appeared on the first arch 'Discite justitiam moniti et non temnere divos' and when 'at the end of the first act (an allegory of the Restoration) Ogilby's triumphal arches appear as part of the stage machinery' (Knowles, pp. 24, 46 (note 102)). The choice of the name Albanius for James is interesting. It is taken from one of his titles, Duke of Albany, a title held by the Stuart family since the fourteenth century. Modern editors have suggested that Dryden may have been influenced in his choice by an association with 'the noble Duke of Albany in Shakespeare's *King Lear*',[19] but contemporary perception of Albany's character was more likely derived from Tate.

The folio version of Shakespeare's play, most recently accessible in the third folio (1663-64), had removed much of Albany's moral indignation evident in the quartos and as a result, some critics find him an ambiguous figure in this version.[20] He has been seen as morally wavering, ineffectual, and a cuckold. Albany's presence is even less apparent in Tate than in the Folio, but criticism of him is muted, he is less overtly ineffectual, and his cuckolding is less obvious. Goneril's reference in Shakespeare to 'his milky gentleness' (1.4.320-23) is entirely omitted. Her scornful, detailed criticism:

> It is the cowish terror of his spirit
> That dares not undertake. He'll not feel wrongs
> Which tie him to an answer.

(IV.2.13)

is reduced by Tate to: 'It is his coward spirit' (IV.3.13); she does not contrast him unfavourably to Edmund as in Shakespeare:

> My most dear Gloucester
> O, the difference of man and man!
> To thee a woman's services are due;
> My fool usurps my body.

(IV.2.26)

and Tate omits Goneril's outbursts, 'Milk-livered man' and 'O vain fool', in response to Albany's criticism (IV.2.32,37). In Tate, the poisoning of Regan at a banquet is planned in detail by Gonerill, and Edmund, who has already 'enjoyed' Regan (v.2,7), additionally plans to usurp Albany's bed and kingdom after the battle. The effect of all this is to blacken Gonerill's character more, to divert some of the thoughts of Albany's cuckolding by paying attention to Regan's relations with Edmund too, and to see Edmund's sexual and political ambitions as signs of his depravity rather than of Albany's weakness. In Shakespeare, Edmund speaks of Albany's indecisiveness before the battle: 'He's full of abdication | And self-reproving' (v.1.4): this is not in Tate.

The abiding impression of Albany in the last act of the Folio is of a 'worthy prince' at last trying to take control but who is not quite capable of the decisive direction needed nor able to cope with the circumstances in which he finds himself; Shakespeare's play ends with Albany's attempt to hand over power to Kent and Edgar: the first definitely declines and the second does not clearly accept. Tate's Albany gives a very different impression in the last act. It is Albany and not Edmund who enters with the prisoners after the battle. His authority is clear and his behaviour humane:

> It is enough to have conquered; cruelty
> Should ne'er survive the fight. Captain o'th' guards,
> Treat well your royal prisoners till you have
> Our further orders, as you hold our pleasure.

(v.6.1)

This is established before Gonerill (not Edmund as in Shakespeare: a further blackening of Gonerill's character) sends the captain to murder them. Albany intervenes in person to save Lear and Cordelia, releases them, directs the return of Kent and Gloster, and, in revealing the infamy of Gonerill, identifies himself with Lear's suffering:

> Ere they fought
> Lord Edgar gave into my hands this paper,
> A blacker scrowl of treason and of lust,
> Than can be found in the records of hell.
> There, sacred sir, behold the character
> Of Gonerill, the worst of daughters, but
> More vicious wife. [. . .]
> Since then my injuries Lear, fall in with thine,
> I have resolved the same redress for both.

(v.6.77, 85)

To Cordelia his voice seems 'The charming voice of a descending god' (v.6.88) and Tate's version of the speech that is so ineffectual in the Folio here offers a satisfactory resolution:

> The troops by Edmund raised I have disbanded.
> Those that remain are under my command.
> What comfort may be brought to cheer your age
> And heal your savage wrongs, shall be applied;
> For to your majesty we do resign
> Your kingdom, save what part yourself conferred
> On us in marriage.
>
> (v.6.89)

Tate's Albany may then be seen as 'the noble Duke', a man who is certainly 'more sinned against than sinning', a virtuous victim of unnatural wickedness, for 'What will not they that wrong a father do?' (v.6.84), rather than a cowed cuckold. Furthermore, by the conclusion of the play he has become a powerful directing force for good. The contemporary Duke of York and Albany would certainly have been able to see a satisfactory reflection in him.

When Tate's play was first performed, perhaps early in 1681, the conclusion seems, through the presentation of Edgar and Albany, to have been reinforcing tradition and legitimacy, looking back to the classical and native iconography used to support the restored Stuart dynasty, and promising the certainty of a future as prosperous as that enjoyed in the past in Albion, under the rule of King Edgar, or in Imperial Rome. When the play was subsequently performed before James II at Whitchall, on 9 May 1687 and 29 February 1688, things were very different. Presumably, since he saw it twice, the King found the treatment of the subject congenial. By then the promised future of 1681 had become reality, though James did not enjoy it for long. Exclusionism had failed, James had succeeded his brother, Monmouth's rebellion had been put down, the Duke executed and his supporters systematically destroyed, while the King pressed on with his religious and political agenda. The play was not seen again until it was staged at Drury Lane in 1699 and then it became very popular after 1700. Perhaps the gap after 1688 is explained partly by the association of the play with the ousted régime. By the turn of the century, on the other hand, the political readings that would have been so obvious and topical in the late 1680s would no longer have been evident.

Notes

1. Christopher Spencer, *Nahum Tate* (New York: Twayne, 1972), p. 68.

2. See James Black's introduction to his edition of Nahum Tate, *The History of King Lear* (London: Arnold, 1975); all references to Tate's Lear are from this edition. Also see Nancy Klein Maguire, 'Nahum Tate's *King Lear*: "The King's Blest Restoration"', in *The Appropriation of Shakespeare: Post-Renaissance Reconstructions of the Works and the Myth,* ed. by Jean I. Marsden (London: Harvester Wheatsheaf, 1991), pp. 29-39.

3. See Black, Appendix A. All references to Shakespeare's *King Lear* are to *The Tragedy of King Lear,* in *The Complete Works,* ed. by Stanley Wells and Gary Taylor (Oxford: Clarendon Press, 1986).

4. *History of His Own Time* (London, 1724), pp. 459-60.

5. Lloyd explicitly warned of the 'danger of another civil war' in *A Sermon Preached before the House of Lords on November 5 1680* (London, 1680), p. 37.

6. The imagery he uses identifies him with Jove, a mythological example both of sexual vigour and active aspiration and of a destructive force, for Jove too displaced his father and Semele was killed by the thunderbolts of her divine lover: 'Like the vig'rous Jove I will enjoy | This Semele in a storm' (III.2.119-20).

7. In Shakespeare, by comparison, Edmund is still undecided at this stage: 'To both of these sisters have I sworn my love, | [. . .] Which of them shall I take?—| Both?—one?—or neither? Neither can be enjoyed | If both remain alive' (v.1.46-50). Once again, Tate's Edmund is sexually more precocious than Shakespeare's.

8. Dale Underwood has written of the 'at least implied recognition by most seventeenth-century libertines that the stress upon freedom led in actuality to a state of "war" much like that which characterised the natural man for Machiavelli and Hobbes' (*Etherege and the Seventeenth-Century Comedy of Manners* (New Haven, CT: Yale University Press; London: Oxford University Press, 1957), p. 27). On Hobbes and Tate, see James Black, 'The Influence of Hobbes on Nahum Tate's *King Lear*', *Studies in English Literature,* 7 (1967), 377-85.

9. Black suggests that 'to compensate for its excision [Tate] offers one of the best things he knows' (*The History of King Lear,* p. xxii).

10. See John Ogilby, *The Entertainment of His Most Excellent Majestie Charles II in His Passage through the City of London to His Coronation* (London, 1662): A facsimile with introduction by Ronald Knowles, Medieval & Renaissance Texts & Studies, 43 (New York: Medieval & Renaissance Texts, 1988), p. 21. Knowles writes: 'As Charles approaches the first arch his symbolic position is that of Aeneas accompanied by the sibyl

viewing the torments of the Titans in Erebus; the English Titans are the rebels of the interregnum. Passing through the arch Charles becomes the imperial embodiment of the Augustus "promised oft, and long foretold", prophesied by Anchises to Aeneas in the sixth book of the *Aeneid.*' See below for Dryden's explicit recollection of the celebrations of 1660 in *Albion and Albianus* (1685), and see Knowles p. 43, note 30, for Logan's engravings of the arches, reprinted in 1685 for a version of *The Relation of His Majesties Entertainment,* which had been Ogilby's first attempt to provide a record in 1661.

11. See Richard Braverman, *Plots and Counterplots: Sexual Politics and the Body Politic in English Literature, 1660-1730* (Cambridge: Cambridge University Press, 1993), p. 117.

12. Christine Stevenson suggested that Confusion's appearance was typical of the Bedlamite, in an unpublished paper, 'Anti-masque, Pageant: Restoration and Bedlam at Moorfields', given in the series of Reading Seminars in Medieval and Renaissance Buildings, 28 May 1998. She has drawn my attention to Natsu Hattori, '"The Pleasure of your Bedlam": The Theatre of Madness in the Renaissance', *History of Psychiatry,* 6 (1995), 283 308, on dress and madness in the Renaissance. The quarto stage directions in Shakespeare's *The History of King Lear* describe Edgar as disguised as a Bedlamite. Tate simply describes the disguise as that of a madman. See also Jonathan Sawday, '"Mysteriously Divided": Civil War, Madness and the Divided Self', in *Literature and the English Civil War,* ed. by Thomas Healy and Jonathan Sawday (Cambridge: Cambridge University Press, 1990), pp. 127-43.

13. *The Continuation of the Life of Edward, Earl of Clarendon,* 2 vols (London, 1759), II, 39-41.

14. 'Nahum Tate's *King Lear*', p. 39, and see Michael Dobson, *The Making of the National Poet* (Oxford: Clarendon Press, 1992), p. 85.

15. See Paul Hammond, 'The King's Two Bodies: Representations of Charles II', in *Culture, Politics and Society in Britain, 1660 1800,* ed. by Jeremy Black and Jeremy Gregory (Manchester: Manchester University Press, 1991), p. 33.

16. *Leviathan* (London, 1651).

17. T. W. Fulton, *The Sovereignty of the Sea* (Edinburgh and London: Blackwood, 1911), pp. 27-28, 326. See F. T. Flahiff, 'Edgar: Once and Future King', in *Some Facets of King Lear: Essays in Prismatic Criticism,* ed. by Rosalie L. Colie and F. T. Flahiff (London: Heinemann, 1974), pp. 221-37. Some of what Flahiff has to

say refers to Edgar's reputation in the seventeenth century after *King Lear*: for example, Thomas Heywood's *A True Description of His Majesties Royall Ship, Built this Yeare 1637 at Wooll-witch in Kent. To the great glory of our English Nation, and not paralleled in the whole Christian World* (London, 1637) refers to Edgar as 'the first that could truely write himselfe an Absolute Monarch of this Island' (p. 30) and describes the figure of the King mounted on horseback trampling seven kings carved on the beak head of the ship.

18. At first the war was popular and was prosecuted with enthusiasm by naval men; the fleet matched the Dutch and despite some mistakes and severe losses held its own. However, in June 1667 there was a great disaster: a Dutch squadron bombarded Sheerness, penetrated as far as Chatham, destroyed half the fleet with fire ships, and took the flagship the *Royal Charles* as a prize. An ignominious peace followed and in 1672 a further unsuccessful war.

19. See *Albion and Albanius,* in *Works of John Dryden,* XV, ed. by Earl Miner, George R. Guffey, and Franklin B. Zimmerman (Berkeley: University of California Press, 1976), 329.

20. See Gary Taylor, '*King Lear*: The Date and Authorship of the Folio Version', in *The Division of the Kingdoms,* ed. by Gary Taylor and Michael Warren (Oxford: Clarendon Press, 1986), p. 425; Steven Urkowitz, *Shakespeare's Revision of 'King Lear'* (Princeton, NJ: Princeton University Press, 1980).

Deborah Payne Fisk and Jessica Munns (essay date spring 2002)

SOURCE: Fisk, Deborah Payne, and Jessica Munns. "'Clamorous with War and Teeming with Empire': Purcell and Tate's *Dido and Aeneas*." *Eighteenth-Century Life* 26, no. 2 (spring 2002): 23-44.

[*In the following essay, Fisk and Munns explore issues of gender and imperialism, the costs of conquest, and the emotional experience of loss in* Dido and Aeneas.]

Two notorious problems have beset ***Dido and Aeneas***: assessing its possible political allusions and possible political meanings, and assigning a date for its premiere performance. Early in the last century, W. Barclay Squire argued that the epilogue pointed to the revolution of 1688.[1] Other critics have since maintained that the prologue's stage directions for Phoebus' rising "*Over the Sea,*" his remarks to Venus that her "lustre . . . half Eclipses mine" (I.14-15), and the Act I song "When

Monarchs unite how happy their State / They Triumph at once on [or'e] their Foes and their Fate" (I.20-21) refer to the arrival of William III and to his joint monarchy with Mary.[2] Other political interpretations not only link the work's first performance date to the coronation of William and Mary in April 1689, but also argue that the Sorceress' machinations allude to new Catholic plots, while Aeneas' abandonment of Dido warns William III against neglecting England—although it should be noted that that would have deeply offended the new monarchs.[3] Many critics agree upon a première of 1689;[4] but others object that the opera's musical style predates 1689 and that Purcell would have been too busy with coronation music and birthday odes to have composed an opera in 1689. Instead, it is conjectured that, like Blow's *Venus and Adonis,* which was presented at court some time in 1681 or 1682 (*London Stage,* p. 301) and revived for performance at Josias Priest's girls boarding school at Chelsey, *Dido and Aeneas* may similarly have had its premiere at court, perhaps shortly after the performance of Blow's opera. However, until some firm evidence is unearthed, all of these conjectures about political meanings and dates remain tentative. A precise dating would be desirable, especially for those scholars who interpret the piece (largely the text) as politically allusive and commenting on, variously, Charles II, James II, or William and Mary. Such readings are fascinating; however, our approach differs: and we shall explore the issues the opera raises about gender and imperialism, the costs of conquest, and the emotional experience of loss. There is all but complete consensus that the opera premiered between 1684 and 1689; and we assume that it was written for a performance at Priest's school in 1689, possibly during the coronation month.

The earliest known libretto of *Dido and Aeneas* announces it was performed at Priest's school "By Young Gentlewomen. The Words Made by Mr. Nat. Tate. The Musick Compos'd by Mr. Purcell"; and that, alas undated libretto, is the earliest concrete evidence of a performance.[5] Josias Priest, a dancing master and choreographer frequently employed by the playhouses, had taken over the aristocratic girl's school in Gorges House, Cheyne Walk, in 1680, nine years before the first known performance of *Dido and Aeneas.*[6] The school had a tradition of performing musical dramas prior to Priest and under his management moved from half-spoken, half-sung dramas such as Thomas Duffett's and John Bannister's *Beauties Triumph* in 1676 (a rendering of the story of the Judgment of Paris) to fully-sung dramas—or operas—such as, on 17 April 1684, John Blow's *Venus and Adonis,* a miniature opera of the sort popularized by Marc-Antoine Charpentier in France. *Dido and Aeneas,* an opera, was part of the vogue for what Judith Milhous has aptly called "multimedia spectaculars" that flourished in the 1670s and then again in the 1690s.[7] Priest's school was obviously unable to compete with the scenic glories available to the Dorset Garden Theatre, where those spectaculars were staged; but the stage directions in the libretto indicate that the school had the machinery to stage descents, as with the arrival of Phoebus and Venus in the prologue and the cupids "*in the clouds*" at the conclusion of *Dido and Aeneas.*

On the face of it, the erotic Dido and Aeneas episode from Book IV of Virgil's *Aeneid* hardly seems appropriate for a schoolgirl performance. Nevertheless, one can imagine that Purcell, Tate, and Priest thought the putative morals embedded in the story of Dido and Aeneas—that women should not build empires or succumb to passion—might have had a certain relevance for a girls' school that sought to inculcate proper feminine virtues.[8] However, various socio-political forces rend holes in the ideological fabric of this moral. Put another way, the disjunction between social and aesthetic realms, the putative moral's not squaring with the opera's representation of Dido, resulted from 1680s ambivalence about empire-building. In order to persuade its intended audience of the legitimacy of a symbolic action—in this instance, the tragedy of Dido's death—and secure its status as a tragedy, the opera must demonstrate the inevitability of Dido's plight, a plight that arises because both characters fulfill their respective "destinies": Dido follows the dictates of passion, Aeneas, the call of duty. In its bid for tragic stature, *Dido and Aeneas* opens itself to several contradictions. On a social level, the story as received from Virgil apparently censures Dido's overreaching ambitions. After all, when Aeneas abandons her, Dido chooses suicide over leadership, thereby suggesting that female rulers, unlike their male counterparts, toss aside duty when emotions run high. On an aesthetic level, Purcell's music, by making prominent the female voice, and Tate's libretto, by presenting a diminished male warrior, throw into relief the very "moral" the story presumably upholds. While giving voice (literally) to Dido, the foreigner, the exotic, the other, *Dido and Aeneas* questions the heroism of Aeneas. Indecisive and weak, he skulks, rather than strides, to his imperial destiny.[9]

TATE'S REDACTION OF VIRGIL

The emphasis on Dido—and in particular, her musically magnificent last lament—shifts the focus of the story from duty to abandonment; and Tate's libretto, which minimizes the role of Aeneas, further undercuts the imperial theme implicit in the original story. Virgil's *Aeneid* had long been understood to be about empire; indeed, as such it formed a basic text for Roman schoolboys learning the myth of Roman origins and destiny. It is a patrilineal myth: Pater Aeneas flees devastated Troy with his son, Ascanius, and carries his own father, Anchises, on his shoulders. Aeneas' wife, Creusa, disappears. Lost, dead, or destroyed by the gods, she is excluded from the founding of Rome. Aeneas and his men are given refuge by Queen Dido, herself a refugee, who has founded the city of Carthage in North Africa. The gods Venus and Juno organize a thunderstorm during a hunt; Dido and Aeneas take refuge in a cave, make love, and, at least from Dido's perspective, are now married. Aeneas throws himself into building Carthage until the gods, petitioned by a neighboring king, Iarbas, jealous of Aeneas' presence in the city, remind Aeneas of his destiny to found a new home for his Trojans and a new realm for Ascanius. As secretly as possible, Aeneas prepares his ships and men for departure, and when confronted by Dido denies that any legal or binding marriage has taken place. Mercury again reminds Aeneas of his destiny; and, as he sails off for his ultimately successful destination in Italy, Dido organizes her suicide, killing herself with Aeneas' sword on a high funeral pyre of his deserted possessions.

In the *Aeneid* the brief moment in which a man might collaborate with woman in building and defending *her* realm, and the brief moment in which a city is founded and run by a woman, are imagined—and rejected. As Hélène Cixous and Catherine Clément put it in *The Newly Born Woman,* "The good love for a man is his country, the fatherland. A masculine land to hand down from father to son."[10] The female-founded Carthage, now destroyed, will pass into the hands of the rival African king. Aeneas, respectful of his father, careful for his son's patrimony, eager for the battles that awaits him, will found Rome. And, of course, as Virgil constantly intimates, Aeneas' Rome will eventually conquer the reborn Carthage. Empire-building, the proper business of men, has been saved from female contamination. Ironically, it is Dido's passionate nature—a "female" nature—that renders her unfit to govern. Impulsive, generous, more devoted to desire than duty (upon glimpsing Aeneas she quickly forgets her vow never to marry again), Dido represents the qualities that a man must "lose" (like his mother) on the way to founding an Empire.

Yet this brief "feminine" episode has over the centuries threatened to overwhelm the "main" narrative of masculine imperial foundation. (Only Aeneas' descent into the underworld has been as frequently invoked as the narrative of Dido's love and betrayal.) Versions of Book IV,[11] as well as pictorial images of the suicidal Dido, had made this episode widely known and much cited, and one in which the heroic founder of Rome plays second lead. From Cristine de Pisan to Hélène Cixous, Dido has been reconfigured from a casebook study in female susceptibility and love-sickness to a figure whose nobility and generosity far outweighs Aeneas' masculine piety. In the process Aeneas is also reconfigured, from empire builder to the very type of trickster male lover, as in Isabella Whitney's sixteenth-century meditation on male inconstancy: "Lord Aeneas . . . / Re-

quiting all thy steadfast love, / From Carthage took his flight, / And foully broke his oath" (ll. 10-13).[12] As Marilynn Desmond points out in her fascinating study of the medieval Dido,

> By displacing the epic hero Aeneas, the tradition of reading Dido disrupts the patrilineal focus of the *Aeneid* as an imperial foundation narrative . . . and thereby calls into question Aeneas, his destiny, the empire he founds, as well as the reiteration of imperial ideologies in the repetition of empires in the West.[13]

In the opera, as in these other versions of Book IV, Dido's tragedy threatens to overwhelm the central narrative; and Tate's changes to the script further undercut Aeneas' role as a builder of empire. No longer do the gods oversee his fate, as in Virgil's text; instead, the operatic Aeneas receives his injunction to leave Carthage from a coven of chuckling enchanters, calling into question the stature and inevitability of his mission. In part, the diminution of Aeneas resulted from Tate's immediate source for the opera: his earlier *Brutus of Alba,* a work with music and dance, which premiered in Dorset Garden in June 1678. *Brutus of Alba* began life as a Dido and Aeneas play, but as Tate explains in his preface, "They told me it wou'd appear Arrogant to attempt any Characters that had been written by the Incomparable Virgil: and therefore (though sensible enough of what I should lose by the Change) I chose to suffer any Inconvenience rather than be guilty of a breach of Modesty." Reworking the text for the libretto, Tate cast modesty aside and cut radically, removing all subplots and concentrating on a short narrative that falls into three parts. In the first, Dido describes her unrest and is reassured by her sister, renamed Belinda, that Aeneas loves her. Aeneas arrives and briefly affirms this reassurance. The second part introduces Tate's major departure from Virgil, the added plot against Dido and Carthage by the Sorceress and her band of enchanters and furies. After a storm conjured by the Sorceress sends Dido and her court hurrying back to town, a false Mercury, the Sorceress' "Trusty Elf," appears to Aeneas, commanding him to leave. This false Mercury contrasts strongly not only with Virgil's authentic messenger of the gods, but with the Mercury in *Albion and Albanius,* where he is the serious herald of the Restoration.

In constructing the Sorceress' plot, Tate drew on his *Brutus of Alba,* in which the sorceress Ragusa plots variously against the ruling family. She does not scheme directly against Brutus, who leaves for Britain and destiny after his friend Asaracus has, like Enobarbus in Dryden's *All for Love* (1677), committed suicide to bring the leader to his senses. In *Dido and Aeneas,* however, it is the Ragusa figure, now simply called "the Sorceress," who hatches the plot of separation. The third and final part opens with a none-too-subtle foreshadowing of things to come as Aeneas' sailors sing merrily about abandoning their lovers. Aeneas, after trying to justify his departure as "the Gods decree" (III.31), offers to stay. Dido, insulted, spurns him, declaring, "To your promised Empire fly" (III.39). After Aeneas leaves, Dido bids farewell to Belinda, singing "Remember me" (III.62) and preparing to die.

Neither the storm during the hunt, nor the command to leave, come from the gods but are arranged by demonic enchantment. The Sorceress' motives, insofar as she has any, are purely malicious: she simply announces that she "hates" the Queen of Carthage, as she does all "in prosperous State" (II.910).[14] She and her enchanters triumph: they send Aeneas off to found his empire and achieve the downfall of Dido. Their entrance at the start of Act II is signaled by the thrilling prelude in F minor that modulates into the Sorceress' song of hate. Both passages create a sense of power and menace. The enchanters then, however, embark on a light-hearted three-stave song of gleeful laughter. Although this laughter is appropriate to their malicious pleasure, it must also to some degree trivialize their menace and minimize imperial glory. They alone embody destiny for Aeneas in the opera; and it is not, in fact, Aeneas' destiny that concerns them. In yet another displacement of interest from Aeneas to Dido, he is not the object of their hatred, which is directed against Dido and Carthage, but is merely the instrument of their plot against the queen and her city.

Tate and Purcell's opera deviates from Virgil and also from *Brutus of Alba* to produce a tale in which female malice rules male destiny; indeed, as far as the Sorceress' plot is concerned, Aeneas is present almost by accident. The conflict in the opera occurs between two women—even though they never meet—and, in that sense, male heroic destiny turns out to be less than male, to be, in fact, female-directed. Indeed, Roger Savage has suggested that Aeneas and the sailors apart, "all the characters in the opera are really personified aspects of Dido": Belinda and the second woman voice her desire, and the Sorceress and enchanters voice her fears. In such a reading Aeneas is simply the object of female desire.[15] Aeneas, whether abandoning empire for love of Dido, or embracing empire at the command of the false Mercury, is always female-dominated; and his belief that he acts to fulfill a higher and nobler destiny—"the gods decree" (III.31)—is a delusion. The Tate/Purcell Dido is always noble, whether struggling with love, disdaining a perjured lover, or lamenting her fate; but Aeneas cannot but emerge as callow and untrustworthy, a point the libretto underscores in the jaunty sailors' song prefacing Aeneas' departure:

> Take a bouze short leave of your Nymphs on the Shore,
>   And silence their Morning,
>   With Vows of returning
> But never intend to visit them more.

As this episode indicates, the woman briefly diverts (in all senses of the word) the man from his imperial destiny; but Mercury appears or trumpets blare, reminding the man of his life elsewhere—of rule and order. Exotic love, framed by the prohibitions of gods, nation, and destiny, is always forbidden—at best, a digression, at worst, a disaster. Exotic/erotic love always derails the hero who should be elsewhere, who should be listening to the dictates of duty, not the siren song of the native woman. The foreign woman's love, sometimes fatal to the hero, always destroys the woman in complex movements of mutual betrayal and contamination. *Dido and Aeneas,* although following that basic trajectory, offers a variant on it. Aeneas' arrival introduces an element of betrayal that Dido resists initially, as she is still in mourning for her husband, Sychaeus: "Ah! Belinda I am press'd, / With torment not to be confess'd" (I.10-11). Aeneas momentarily betrays his destiny to found the Roman Empire. An alternative empire, in fact, is on offer, one that will be jointly ruled and which offers a seductive combination of sexual fulfillment and imperial rule with "Empire growing, / Pleasures flowing" (I.3-4). Whereas both Tate's *Brutus of Alba* and Dryden's *Albion and Albanius* treat the legendary hero's departure for his ordained land or his celestially heralded arrival as triumphant, in this work the departure of their analogue Aeneas is shabby.

Tate perhaps sought to temper the departure of Aeneas by excluding the rather churlish lines in the *Aeneid* where the hero denies that he ever considered himself married to Dido; instead, Tate's Aeneas offers to remain: "Let Jove say what he will, I'll stay" (III.49). This weaker, more vacillating Aeneas typifies the unheroic protagonists who form part of the period's ongoing reevaluation of psychic and social costs of male bravura. At a time when England was moving into position to challenge the Dutch and Spanish colonial empires and, if one accepts the 1689 date, equipped with a king eager to undertake military action in the European mainland, this elegiac opera functioned as a countertext to imperial expansion.

DIDO AND RESTORATION COLONIALISM

To a culture that commonly equated women with conquered lands, the abandonment of Dido would have been especially resonant, especially given the recent loss of Tangiers and other colonies. Purcell's and Tate's own vexed attitudes toward kings and conquest further destabilized what should, on the face of it, have been a straightforward version of a well-known episode from Virgil. The notion that women symbolized land would have been well known to the opera's auditors and, as Laura Brown notes, "women are the emblems and proxies of the whole male enterprise of colonialism."[16] To audiences in the middle and late 1680s, Dido would have figured as an especially apt "emblem" of troublesome colonies. Her tale is one of excess. She is "too" female in her passion for Aeneas and "too" masculine in her ambition for Carthage. Both object and subject, she embodies the colonial dilemma at the close of the Restoration: like the colonized, her passionate, "irrational" nature justifies external domination; like the colonizer, her ambition invites endless trouble and expense.

The decision by Purcell and Tate to tell the story of a Libyan queen at this historical moment is suggestive given the recent abandonment of Tangiers. The Portuguese princess, Catherine of Braganza, brought as part of her dowry the port of Tangiers and the Island of Bombay to her marriage to Charles II in 1661.[17] While this development pleased merchants who saw in the free port of Tangiers a door to the Mediterranean, maintaining a military presence in the colony displeased a financially beleaguered crown. Bombay, the other part of Catherine of Braganza's dowry, presented even more troubles. As Edwin Chappell notes, the island had to be defended against the Dutch, French, Portuguese, and Indians.[18] Merchant ships making the long voyage to and from Bombay, a voyage that took them round the Cape of Good Hope, required defense from pirates and enemy fleets—yet more expense for the crown. Pressure from the East India Company, which had received a new charter from Cromwell in 1657, increased throughout the Restoration; and trading posts in India were either revived or expanded to include Madras, Masulipatam, Balsore, and Hughli. As the Mogul Empire declined, yet more forces were needed to protect these settlements. The American colonies also demanded attention and money. In 1682 a French expedition attacked Fort Nelson in James Bay, setting off a series of French and English skirmishes along what would eventually become the Canadian border.

If the expense of maintaining these colonies gave the crown pause, the thought of maintaining standing armies in these outposts—armies that could be called home to subjugate unruly citizens—frightened the anti-militarists in Parliament from voting additional funding. Irish troops had been deployed in Tangiers; and some feared they could be recalled to force Roman Catholicism and the succession of the Duke of York on the country. Suspicions were further inflamed by the presence of Portuguese friars in Tangiers and the appointment of two successive Roman Catholic governors. Without the funds to support troops, the crown simply retreated. Charles II's 1662 *Proclamation Declaring His Majesties pleasure to Settle and Establish a Free Port at His City of Tanger in Africa* acknowledged its importance to "the welfare and prosperity of Our good Subjects" and pledged to make

> it a great part of Our Princely Care and Study to find out ways and means for the advancement and security of their general Traffique and Commerce; So We can-

not but hope that these Our just ends and purposes (which We had chiefly in Our prospect) will be very much promoted by gaining the City of Tanger in Africa as an accession unto Our Dominions.

Much to the dismay of merchants, that pledge did not last; by the late 1670s rumors circulated that the crown would relinquish Tangiers to the Moors. An anonymous letter addressed to a "Person of Quality" indicates the concern felt by merchants over the possible loss of this free port. In it the author extols the mercantile and military advantages of Tangiers and also reminds the crown that colonies such as these maintain the "vast Engin" of commerce: "What is it has rendred England so formidable, so rich, and so renown'd a Kingdom: but the strength of our Navies, and Universality of our Commerce?"[19] Nonetheless, for months in 1683 and 1684 engineers in Tangiers, under the supervision of John Luke, Samuel Pepys, and the Baron of Dartmouth, hacked and blasted its walls, its fifteen forts, and that spectacular feat of engineering, the Mole, into rubble before returning home.[20] North Africa, where Dido had long ago built her empire, was deserted. Tate's libretto registers the personal and political complexities of abandonment. In one sense, the cost to England of maintaining these colonies—like the cost to Aeneas of loving Dido—was "too high."[21] In another sense, though, "cutting one's losses" invariably entails regret for unfulfilled possibilities. Merchants and captains alike cast a longing eye on Tangiers, the one imagining the circulatory flow of luxuriant commodities through the body of England, the other envisioning the unfettered passage of boats through otherwise hazardous straits: riches and ease, the very siren call of exotic climes. These too Aeneas enjoyed, but "Fate" dictates a higher calling to leave and establish a Western empire:

> No sooner she resigns her Heart,
> But from her Armes I'm forc't to part.
> How can so hard a Fate be took,
> One night enjoy'd, the next forsook.[22]

Similarly, in 1689 all good moneyed and landed citizens were being reminded of "so hard a Fate" as they prepared for increased taxes to fund William's war against France. As early as late 1688 Jacobite pamphlets warned that English commerce would suffer from higher taxes and excises under William, as well as from Dutch domination of the New Exchange. One author, writing soon after William's conquest, warned of "reproach, violence, taxes, blood and poverty"; he also estimated the cost of William's war at £3 million per annum.[23] By spring of 1689 anxieties about the cost of warfare had heightened. The demographer Gregory King gives some indication of the wealth that might be tapped in 1688 to fund William's war. While temporal lords enjoyed an average yearly family income of £6,060, they numbered no more than 200 families, producing a total income for that social group of

£1,121,000. While "greater merchants" and "lesser merchants" enjoyed, respectively, annual incomes of £400 and £200, their joint numbers tallied 20,000, producing a total income of nearly £5,000,000.[24] If Aeneas' call to duty intimated the self-sacrifice awaiting English citizens, the abandonment of Dido recalled forfeited wealth and squandered possibilities. By the 1680s, as W. A. Speck notes, "colonial produce began to make up an increasingly large proportion of English overseas trade . . . there was also domestic demand for these products created by the fall in the price of foodstuffs and the corresponding availability of cash to spend on other commodities."[25] Increasingly, though, foreign firms were taking over the Near Europe trade, "blocking off an important avenue of diversification" (Jones, p. 249). William's war would create more pressure on commerce, closing off important trade routes and eliminating potential profit. In addition to these associations, the very aesthetic form Purcell and Tate had selected could not help but remind audiences of more expenditures, largely because of the high cost of staging these sung-through spectacles. In May of the following year, Dryden, in the prologue to *The Prophetess*, the Fletcher play adapted by Thomas Betterton ("*With Alterations and Additions, After the Manner of an Opera*"), compared the cost of staging operas to the cost of funding William's war:

> A Play which like a Prospective set right,
> Presents our vast Expences close to sight;
> But turn the Tube, and there we sadly view
> Our distant gains; and those uncertain too:
> A sweeping Tax, which on our selves we raise;
> And all like you, in hopes of better days.
> When will our Losses warn us to be wise!
> Our Wealth decreases, and our Charges rise:
> Money the sweet Allurer of our hopes,
> Ebbs out in Oceans, and comes in by Drops.[26]

So inflammatory was the alleged criticism of William's Irish campaign, that the prologue was suppressed.[27]

BAROQUE OPERA AND THE ABJECT FEMALE

The Purcell/Tate version of the abandoned Dido—and, by extension, of abandoned colonies such as Tangiers—presented the audience with "vast Expences close to sight." The cost of abandonment, a cost that would be realized in higher taxes and higher prices for imported goods, might very well prove too dear. That Purcell and Tate chose opera for their aesthetic vehicle undercut the usual exhortations to duty and self-sacrifice, virtues traditionally espoused by male leaders. Opera, an art form that specializes in emotional excess—think of its reliance on superfluity of voice, feeling, and spectacle—can tell powerfully extravagant tales of doomed encounters between cultures. Moreover, baroque opera, because of the very nature of the form, cannot help but accentuate the lure, the danger, and the tragedy of the female exotic.

Dido and Aeneas, as Purcell and Tate treat the material, stands at the head of a series of operatic narratives, beginning with Monteverdi's *Ariadne* (1608), of which only her lament remains, depicting the plight of "foreign" women abandoned as their lovers depart for "higher" male destinies and duties. From the seventeenth to the nineteenth century, operas depict distant lands amazingly ruled by a woman, or offering up fragile beauties to a conqueror, or trying vainly to protect their women from conquest. Often the settings evoke a distant time, when Romans ruled, or conjure up images of exotic locales, such as an enslaved Africa or dominated China; and in them stories take place in which the conquered territory is invariably feminized. Opera, in following this narrative logic and in showcasing the female voice, must literally give splendid utterance to the foreign women—Dido, Sélika, Norma, Lakmé, Butterfly, Aïda—who stand for, sing for, the desired, dangerous, magical, luxurious, sensual colonized land. To restate Gayatri Spivak's question, "can the subaltern speak?," one might ask, "can the subaltern sing?"[28] The answer is yes—loudly. The feminine and sexually ambiguous qualities of opera allied to its imperial themes of invasion and conquest made it a perfect form for imagining natives and foreigners. As such, opera was capable of imagining and giving voice (quite literally) to counter-forces, benign and dangerous, that either way thwart and/or temporarily derail the imperial project.[29]

Opera's narratives were based, like heroic drama, on a romantic and classical world in which the actions of noble heroes counted. Much more than in heroic drama, however, the masculine ethos of the hero are balanced against, or indeed, subsumed by the leading role given to the soprano, the castrati, or counter-tenor—any of whom might, of course, be singing the hero's role. Thus, alternative and ambiguous sexualities counter masculine privilege. In retelling the stories of male martial endeavour and imperial ambition, baroque opera privileges oppositional voices. The ensemble singing that Mozart specialized in, which literally enacted a simultaneous heteroglossia, was not yet available; instead, solos, duets, choral responses, refrains and, in the case of Purcell, tonal modulations take one through sequential experiences of assertion and denial, confidence and doubt, promise and betrayal, triumph and despair. In *Dido and Aeneas* that movement culminates in Dido's lament to her sister, not her lover, and her repeated cry of "Remember me."

The neo-classical convention requiring just rewards for heroes dictated the change to the Virgilian text made in an earlier Dido opera, *La Didone* (1641)—libretto by Busenello, music by Francesco Cavalli—in which Iarbas, the rival king, plays a role and is rewarded at the end by Dido's hand. The effect is also to lessen Aeneas' guilt and retain his heroic status. Whether Purcell and/or Tate knew of Cavelli's opera is open to debate; but certainly rather than seeking to ameliorate Dido's grief at abandonment, that grief forms one of Purcell's finest passages. There is no stress at all on the glory that awaits Aeneas, but rather on the impending death of the woman who has provided the brief interlude for the visiting male who hurries off to other places. Derek Hughes has drawn attention to the ways in which women are usually erased from the processes of memorializing in the dramas of the period.[30] In *Dido and Aeneas* the tables are turned: it is Aeneas who silently departs while Dido dictates her legacy. "Remember me, but ah! Forget my fate" (III.62), she sings, while the scene shifts to cupids hovering over her tomb, effectively indicating that both queen and her fate will be remembered.

Unlike many prose dramas from the period, baroque opera, with its emphasis on sequential singing, promotes the female voice throughout the spectacle and capitalizes on the emotion and pathos of which divas are capable. This is true of *Dido and Aeneas.* Aeneas sings "Behold, upon my bending spear," his last aria (which is short, about thirty seconds in most modern recordings), two-thirds of the way through the opera; and he sings only briefly in the final third act, responding mainly to Dido's accusations and pleas. By contrast, the audience hears Dido sing two significant arias in the final act, "Your counsel all is urg'd in vain" and "Thy hand Belinda—When I am laid in earth." Both of these arias, two of the longest except for Dido's entry piece, "Ah! Belinda, I am prest with torment," ensure the tragic queen's melodious words will haunt the audience long after the final curtain.

THE DIVIDED SOCIAL DISPOSITION OF PURCELL AND TATE

Dido and Aeneas, far from celebrating imperial expansion—indeed, an anachronistic concept for the late seventeenth century—expresses a suspicion of empire-building that may very well have proceeded from the divided social dispositions of Purcell and Tate. Neither man evinced unwavering support for Jacobite or Whig politics, nor for the foreign policies arising from those respective positions. Although appointed in 1679 to the positions of composer for the violins and organist for the Chapel Royal, Purcell, like every musician employed by Charles II, went for months, sometimes years, without payment.[31] He survived by composing for the theatre, teaching students, and selling musical scores to printers such as John Playford. He also suffered financially under William III. Traditionally, at a coronation the organist for the Chapel Royal was allowed to sell tickets for places in a specially constructed organ loft, a perquisite Purcell had enjoyed under the Stuarts. At William III's coronation, Purcell was ordered to redis-

tribute the money from ticket sales, a sizeable £492, to the other musicians—not the sort of command that promotes fealty to royal patrons—and his stipend, normally paid at Lady Day, was to "be detained in the hands of the Treasurer until further order" (Keates, p. 168). Although James II was more generous, his zealous promotion of Catholicism may have given Purcell pause. Indeed, Purcell's anthems and devotional works show a strong connection to an Anglican spirituality. At the same time, Purcell married a Roman Catholic woman and was in contact with Catholic musicians such as Giovanni Draghi, John Abell, and the convert Matthew Locke (Keates, p. 103). In short, there is little to suggest strong political or religious identification with either the Stuarts or with William III and much to suggest that Purcell was wary of such identification.

Nahum Tate, perhaps because he worked in words, not music, has left behind more sharply etched tracks. Anglo-Irish in origin but Puritan in religion, Tate's family shuttled uncomfortably between Ireland and England for three decades, suffering under both cultures.[32] Tate left Ireland for England sometime between 1672 and 1676 and initially embraced Stuart culture with alacrity. Befriended by John Dryden—who asked him to write the *Second Part of Absalom and Achitophel*—Tate was quickly assimilated into high Tory circles and became an apologist for the Stuarts. For the remainder of the 1670s and the early '80s, Tate was to explore in various adaptations of Shakespeare the theme of loyalty to the crown. *Richard II* (1681) proved especially resonant against the backdrop of the Exclusion Crisis, but after two performances the very regime Tate wrote the play to support ended up banning the production.[33] Despite lack of support from the crown, the next year Tate once again attempted to display his fealty in adapting *Coriolanus*. As one might expect from the title, *The Ingratitude of a Commonwealth* (1682) expanded on the theme of loyalty to the monarch: "The Moral therefore of these Scenes being to Recommend Submission and Adherence to Establisht Lawful Power, which in a word, is LOYALTY" (A2ᵛ). Despite such blatant fealty, the play was not actively supported by the crown. Nevertheless, Tate continued to champion the Stuarts through the accession of James II: he praised the new monarch highly in his *Second Part of Absalom and Achitophel,* as well as in the first selection in his *Poems* of 1684.

However, as revealed by Christopher Spencer, Tate stopped writing for the commercial stage after James II came to the throne. Perhaps he tired of Stuart neglect; perhaps he feared the aggressive Catholicism of James II, all too evident in post-coronation policies. Tate's Puritan upbringing no doubt made attractive the stalwart Protestantism of William III, a Protestantism, as Tony Claydon has argued recently, couched in the language of reformation.[34] After all, Tate would in the next decade lend public support to Jeremy Collier's attacks on the theatre and translate the *Psalms* for the Church of England. Nonetheless, in the dedication to the 1690 *Life of Alexander the Great,* Tate, who assisted with the translation, likens William III to Alexander (and the very comparison to a great but solipsistic military leader is itself revealing) in language at once complimentary yet qualified:

> But in all his Enterprizes, he was supported by a Constancy that was peculiar to himself, and the Result of his own extraordinary Genius. But his Sagacity, as well as Fortitude, was of a Reach beyond the most Experienced of his Council, from whose Opinion he would often dissent, but was never in the Wrong. His Resolves, (as Plutarch well observes) which in their Sentiments seemed Rash, will appear on deep and thorough Consideration to be the Result of true and well-grounded Policy. . . . All which Circumstances render him a Candidate to Your Majesties Favour, being so far Parallel to the *Alexander of the Present Age.*[35]

In a verse panegyric published in 1691, Tate further expands on William's military exploits, calling him "Our Caesar," "Jove," "Albion's Joy," and "Alcides."[36] But the poem betrays, in a series of grotesque images—some of them unfortunately deserving of inclusion in *The Dunciad*—doubts about William's pugilism: his very name "makes the unborn Years to spring / In Fate's dark Womb, and clap their unfledg'd wing" (p. 11), or to William "distant Nations call with out-stretch'd Hands, / Like longing Ghosts on black Cocytus Strands" (p. 11). Note, too, that the strained syntax suggests that, far from proving a savior, William is a slaughterer who has reduced the inhabitants of "distant nations" to unhappy "Ghosts." Tate's Anglo-Irish origins and Puritan background destined him to a position of cultural alienation not unlike that of Dido. Little wonder that Tate returned throughout his writings to Dido-like females or, for that matter, to abandoned males, such as Richard II, Coriolanus, and Lear. Betrayal and ingratitude, themes that loom large in Tate's plays and poems, suggest something of his compassion for the all too human casualties of political ambition.

GILDON AND BEYOND

Subsequent changes to Tate's libretto, as well as later operatic treatments of the Dido and Aeneas story, reveal the extent to which the skepticism of the baroque version had to be tempered. Charles Gildon included ***Dido and Aeneas*** as an entr'acte entertainment in his adaptation of *Measure for Measure* (1700).[37] His expanded prologue includes a debate between Mars and Peace. Mars insists that "Conquest is the hero's due / Glorious triumph will ensue" (ll. 3-4), while Peace urges that the

time has come to "reap the happy fruits of Peace" (l. 9). The choric reply, "Fame and Honour answer—No" (l. 11), and a "Yes, Yes" and "No, No" sequence concludes with Peace appearing to win out as the chorus sing "Let's all agree to welcome Peace" (l. 30). However, this is merely the phrase that introduces the love story between Dido and Aeneas, now framed as a debate on the conflicting merits of Fame and Honor versus Love and Peace. Necessarily, the other passage that Gildon expanded was the Grove scene, in which Aeneas gets his marching orders. The Purcell/Tate Aeneas has merely a one-word response to the news he must leave tonight ("Tonight?"), followed by lines regretting what he must tell Dido; but in Gildon's version soldier friends debate the news with him in the spirit of the expanded prologue. One friend speaks for love, another for fame and glory and "Resistless Jove's commands" (l. 6); and Aeneas is clearly drawn to Fame (l. 8). Gildon's insertion ends inconclusively: "Love with Empire trifling is but vain, / And Empire without Love a pompous pain." Yet the overall effect elevates Aeneas; and his place, rather than Dido's, is asserted in the narrative: "His valour and glory, / Shall flourish in story" (ll. 23-24). Gildon's more conventional version presents a conflict between personal pleasure and Empire in which fame, honor and "Resistless Jove's commands" must always triumph.

By the end of the eighteenth century, Dido's story had become a straightforward justification for the expansion of the British Empire.[38] Prince Hoare's opera, *Dido, Queen of Carthage* (1792), which featured new music by Storace, along with selections from Sacchini, Salieri, Andreozzi, Giordaniello, and Cimarosa, is a virtual paean to Empire. From the very opening, that opera celebrates the spoils of conquest: Iarbas, a neighboring king, attempts to woo Dido away from Aeneas with a "train of Moors . . . bringing presents," which include "An ostrich led by a young slave, two soldiers, gold vases carried by slaves . . . a camel led by a slave . . . Two cymbals, a slave, An elephant conducted by a cornac riding on his neck." (pp. 5-6). Dido refuses the gifts and the giver, invoking Enlightenment principles of freedom ("In quest of freedom, and in scorn of chains, / Hither from Tyre I came"). Subsequently, the opera depicts Iarbas as the wily Moor, deceitful, cunning, and backhanded, while Aeneas embodies nobility, honesty, and valor, all figured as European traits. In rejecting the hand of Iarbas, who is referred to as an "Afric," a "haughty Moor," and a "barbarian," Dido effectively rejects Oriental culture in favor of the Europeanized Aeneas. Even unto death, Dido prefers Europe to the Orient; and after a final rejection by Dido, Iarbas sets fire to Carthage, while Dido "ascends the steps of her palace, and, stabbing herself, falls into the flames"

(p. 37). The opera is followed by *The Masque of Neptune's Prophecy,* a short piece underscoring—as if anyone could miss the heavy-handed treatment in the opera proper—the importance of founding not Rome but "Albion." First Neptune appears, exhorting the chorus to help Aeneas on his journey. Then, "as Aeneas advances Venus descends from a Cloud with Graces, Cupids, etc. leading in her hand Ascanius, followed by a Troop of Trojan youths" (p. 39). Neptune reappears and tells Aeneas and Ascanius they are

> Ordain'd to empire yet unknown,
> On Albion's coast shall fix his throne,
> And, crown'd with laurels, spoils, and fame,
> Shall change to Britain Albion's name.

(p. 41)

Hoare's opera, unlike ***Dido and Aeneas,*** concludes with Aeneas and his son facing their imperial destiny. Whereas the baroque Dido sang plaintively to "Remember me," more than a hundred years later she not only disappears conveniently, but also expunges any taint of the native from herself. A European at heart, she recoils from the embraces of the "Afric" barbarian, Iarbas; and her speeches uphold as necessary Enlightenment principles of freedom, choice, and the purchase (or conquest) of native lands. By 1792 such statements were a foregone conclusion. During the Restoration, when England teetered on the brink of colonial expansion, attitudes were far more ambiguous. Dido's plea for remembrance confronted the audience with the doubts, anxieties, and fears they hoped, for one afternoon at least, to set aside while listening to a bit of pretty music. What they saw and heard was a tale "Teeming with Empire" that on a powerful emotional plane enacted "vast Expences close to sight."

Notes

1. Cited in Ellen T. Harris, *Henry Purcell's "Dido and Aeneas"* (Oxford: Clarendon, 1987), p. 5. There is circumstantial evidence for Squire's assumption. The epilogue, written by Thomas Durfey, was included in his miscellany *New Poems* (London, 1689). Since prologues and epilogues usually appeared in print shortly after production, it stands to reason that Durfey would want to make use of a recent effort. Furthermore, the speaker of the epilogue was one Lady Dorothy Burke, daughter of the Earl of Claricarde. Lady Dorothy had been studying at a Benedictine convent school in Dublin, but in 1689 she was transferred to Priest's school, her fees paid in part by a pension from Queen Mary. See Jonathan Keates, *Purcell: A Biography* (Boston: Northeastern Univ., 1995), pp. 184-85.

2. See, e. g., Margaret Laurie, ed., *Dido and Aeneas* (London: New Purcell Soc., 1979), p. ix. There is no music for the prologue, which may suggest it was added later.

3. Curtis Price maintains that the witches refer to Roman Catholic supporters of James II and that the opera cautions against the consequences of "a new popish plot, as mindless as the original one of 1678 but still with potentially fatal consequences" (*Purcell's "Dido and Aeneas," An Opera* [N.Y.: W. W. Norton, 1986], p. 11). See also Price's *Henry Purcell and the London Stage* (Cambridge: Cambridge Univ., 1984). John Buttery sees the opera as a warning of what might happen to England if William neglects it ("Dating Purcell's *Dido and Aeneas,*" *Proceedings of the Royal Musical Assoc.* 94 [1967-68]: 51-62). Andrew R. Walking argues that "Aeneas can be read as James, while Dido can be seen to represent England" and sees the entire opera as "an allegorical commentary on James's policies in England" ("Politics and the Restoration Masque: The Case of *Dido and Aeneas,*" in *Culture and Society in the Stuart Restoration: Literature, Drama, History,* ed. Gerald Maclean [Cambridge: Cambridge Univ. Press, 1995], p. 58). Robert D. Hume argues persuasively that political readings of *Dido* are "improvable . . . and contrary to historical logic" ("The Politics of Opera in Late Seventeenth-Century London" in *Cambridge Opera Jour.* 10 [1998]: 15-43); and it is because of the diverse and contradictory nature of attempts to impose a political allegory on *Dido* that we have avoided engaging in that controversial approach and have taken a new tack.

4. In *The London Stage, Part 1: 1660-1700* (Carbondale: Southern Illinois Univ., 1965), p. 378, Emmett L. Avery & Arthur H. Scouten give Dec. 1689 as the probable date, based on R. H. Moore's *Henry Purcell and the Restoration Theatre* (Cambridge: Harvard Univ., 1961). John Buttery, Ellen T. Harris, and Margaret Laurie posit a premiere in Apr. 1689, making the performance coterminous with the coronation. For a summary of the early dating arguments, see Keates, pp. 184-85.

The problem of dating the opera resurfaced in the 1990s in two different issues of *Early Music.* Bruce Wood & Andrew Pinnock, arguing by analogy, maintain that since Blow's *Venus and Adonis* saw a court performance, then the same must have been true of *Dido and Aeneas.* They support a performance date of 1684 with internal evidence derived from topical allusions, musical style, literary sources, even the weather ("'Unscarr'd by turning times'? The Dating of Purcell's *Dido and Aeneas*," *Early Music* 20 [1992]: 373-90). Mark Goldie, responding in the same issue ("The Earliest Notice of Purcell's *Dido and Aeneas*" p. 393), uses a letter from Mrs. Buck, the wife of a Whig MP, to one Mary Clark to date the opera 1689. Two years later, in the same journal, Andrew R. Walking rejected Wood's & Pinnock's evidence, suggesting instead that the opera may have been written in 1687 or early 1688 to celebrate James II's Declaration of Indulgence ("'The Dating of Purcell's *Dido and Aeneas*?' A Reply to Bruce Wood and Andrew Pinnock," *Early Music* 22 [1994]: 469-81). Since this exchange, two other scholars have come to support the 1684 date: Hume in "Politics" and James A. Winn in "Theatrical culture 2: theatre and music," in *The Cambridge Companion to English Literature 1650-1740,* ed. Steven N. Zwicker (Cambridge: Cambridge Univ., 1998), p. 111.

5. Henry Purcell, *Dido and* Aeneas. Libretto. (Facsimile edition?) [London]: Boosey & Hawkes, n.d., p. 1. The only known copy of the libretto is in the Royal College of Music.

6. Recently Jennifer Thorpe has cautioned scholars with regard to the identity of Josias Priest, arguing that Josias Priest the schoolmaster and dancing master may not be the same as *Joseph* Priest the choreographer. As Thorpe observes, they may be different members of the same family. See "Dance in Late 17th-Century London: Priestly Muddles," *Early Music* 26 (1998): 198-210.

7. "The Multimedia Spectacular on the Restoration Stage," in *British Theatre and the Other Arts, 1660-1800,* ed. Shirley Strum Kenny (Washington: Folger, 1984), pp. 41-66.

8. Kenneth Charlton notes the emphasis on religious education and modest conduct in the boarding schools that peppered the villages of Chelsea, Hackney, and Putney just outside of London (*Women, Religion and Education in Early Modern England* [London: Routledge, 1999], chap. 5).

9. Michael Burden has recently argued for a manly Aeneas, a hero beleaguered by a hysterical, even mad, queen who forgets herself and her duty: "Dido behaves with foolishness, verging on idiocy, her rejection of Aeneas seeming almost churlish" and "Dido brings about her own destruction by allowing the effects of suspicion to corrode her sanity" ("'Great Minds Against Themselves Conspire': Purcell's Dido as Conspiracy Theorist," in *A Woman Scorn'd: Responses to the Dido*

Myth, ed. Michael Burden [London: Faber and Faber, 1998], pp. 236-37). Our reading squares with the more traditional interpretation of the opera's Aeneas as an inadequate hero, however.

10. Trans. Betsy Wong (Minneapolis: Univ. of Minnesota, 1986), p. 45.

11. Book IV was of particular interest to the courtiers and poets who supported the Stuart dynasty. Sir Robert Stapylton, a courtier associated with Charles I and II, did a translation in 1634. Edmund Waller, cavalier poet, finished and then published (in 1658 and again in 1679) the translation originally done by Sidney Godolphin, who died fighting for the king during the Civil War. Sir Robert Howard, who became Secretary of the Exchequer under Charles II, included a version of Book IV in his *Poems* of 1660. John Ogilby, who received royal commissions from Charles II for folios of geography, published a translation in 1649 that became sufficiently popular to realize three more printings in 1654, 1665, and 1684 (Hollar did the plates for the royal folio edn. of 1654). Dryden, long an apologist for the Stuarts, included the story in his ambitious translation of Virgil's works in 1697, as well as in his edn. of Ovid's epistles in 1680.

12. "A Careful Complaint by the Unfortunate Author," in *The Longman Anthology of British Literature,* ed. David Damrosch (N. Y.: Wesley Addison Longman, 1998), p. 1001.

13. *Reading Dido: Gender, Textuality, and the Medieval Aeneid* (Minneapolis: Univ. of Minnesota, 1994), p. 2.

14. Witches and sorceresses function integrally in baroque opera, both as an occasion for scenic wonder and as blocking figures opposing heroic ends. Female, malicious, and magical, they are also the emblems of a working misogyny, by nature contrary to the law of the father and opposed to the rule of order. See Cixous & Clément, p. 105.

15. "Producing *Dido and Aeneas*," in Price, *Purcell's "Dido and Aeneas,"* pp. 255-77 & 261.

16. *Ends of Empire: Women and Ideology in Early Eighteenth-Century English Literature* (Ithaca: Cornell Univ., 1993), p. 47.

17. Christopher Lloyd, *English Corsairs on the Barbary Coast* (London: Collins, 1981), p. 5.

18. Ed., *The Tangier Papers of Samuel Pepys* (London: Navy Records Soc., 1935), p. xx.

19. *A Discourse Touching Tanger: In a Letter to a Person of Quality* (London, 1680), p. 1.

20. *Tangier at High Tide: The Journal of John Luke 1670-73,* ed. Helen Andrews Kaufman (Genève: E. Droz, 1958), p. 1.

21. John Ogilby, in his sumptuous folio, *Africa: Being An Accurate Description of the Regions of Egypt, Barbary, Lybia, and Billedulgerid* (London, 1670), argues that Portugal gave Tangiers to England because of the cost of maintaining the colony: "During this time they got also Tangier, which with great expence and trouble having kept divers years, at length finding the charge of defence to exceed the profit, they absolutely assigned over their interest to our gracious Soveraign CHARLES the Second, King of England, Scotland, France and Ireland, in part of the Marriage-Portion with Donna Catharina," p. 197.

22. Purcell, *Dido and Aeneas.* Libretto, p. 7.

23. Tony Claydon, *William III and the Godly Revolution* (Cambridge: Cambridge Univ., 1996), p. 123.

24. See Table 3.3 in D. W. Jones, *War and Economy in the Age of William III and Marlborough* (Oxford: Basil Blackwell, 1988).

25. *Reluctant Revolutionaries: Englishmen and the Revolution of 1688* (Oxford: Oxford Univ., 1988), pp. 202-03.

26. John Dryden, Prologue to *The Prophetess,* in *The Works of John Dryden,* vol. 3 (Berkeley: Univ. of California, 1969), p. 255.

27. R. P. McCutcheon, "Dryden's Prologue to *The Prophetess,*" *Modern Language Notes* 39 (1924): 123-24.

28. *In Other Worlds: Essays in Cultural Politics* (N.Y.: Methuen, 1987).

29. For a sophisticated discussion of "Female Orientalism" on stage, see Mita Choduhury's *Interculturalism and Resistance in the London Theater, 1660-1800: Identity, Performance, Empire* (Lewisburg: Bucknell Univ., 2000).

30. *English Drama 1660-1700* (Oxford: Clarendon, 1996), pp. 255-89.

31. John Hingeston told Samuel Pepys in 1666 that "many of the Musique are ready to starve, they being five years behindhand for their wages"; he further claimed that the court harper, Lewis Evans, starved to death "for mere want." As cited in Peter Holman, *Henry Purcell* (Oxford: Oxford Univ., 1994), p. 16.

32. His English Puritan grandfather, Faithful Teate, lost three children and £4000 in possessions and land in the 1641 rebellion of Irish Catholics against English settlers. After this loss, he went to England, only to return to Ireland in 1658 at the request of Henry Cromwell. Nahum's father attended Trinity College Dublin but received his B.A. and M.A. from Cambridge before returning to Ireland in 1659 to take up preaching in Limerick. A year later, having violated the Act of Uniformity, he was banned from preaching. He died five years later.

33. In the dedication to his "esteemed friend" George Raynsford, Tate protested against the suppression of *Richard II* ("I confess, I expected it wou'd have found Protection from whence it receiv'd Prohibition"); and he further complained about the "Arbitrary Courtiers of the Reign" (A2ᵛ).

34. Claydon documents how Bishop Burnet and others manipulated for propaganda purposes the language of the Protestant reformation on behalf of William, even well before his forces landed at Torbay in Devon on 5 Nov. 1688 (chap. 1).

35. *The Life of Alexander the Great. Written in Latin by Quintus Curtius Rufus, and Translated into English by several Gentlemen in the University of Cambridge* (London, 1690), A4ᵛ-A6ᵛ.

36. *A Poem, Occasioned by His Majesty's Voyage to Holland, the Congress at the Hague, and Present Siege of Mons* (London, 1691), pp. 6, 8, & 11.

37. *Measure for Measure, or Beauty the Best Advocate. Written Originally by Mr. Shakespeare: And now very much Alter'd; With Additions and Several Entertainments of Music* (London, 1700).

38. By the 19th c., as Herbert Lindenberger observes, many operas actively promoted colonial rule. In Meyerbeer's *L'Africaine* (1865) the death of the East Indian Sélika gave the audience a chance to "experience at once the plight of the abandoned colonial other and the necessity that the imperialist project (at its height among the British and French at this time) must roll on whatever the human cost"; and Berlioz's *Les Troyens* (1858) "spells out its imperial theme even more explicitly than Meyerbeer's opera: at the end we are made to witness a vision of the future Rome above the pyre of Dido" (*Opera in History: From Monteverdi to Cage* [Stanford: Stanford Univ., 1998], p. 184).

FURTHER READING

Criticism

Adler, Doris. "The Half-Life of Tate in *King Lear.*" *Kenyon Review* 7, no. 3 (summer 1985): 52-6.

Argues that many of the conventions in Tate's *King Lear* remain in modern stage productions of Shakespeare's version.

Black, James. "An Augustan Stage History: Nahum Tate's *King Lear*." *Restoration and Eighteenth Century Theatre Research* 6, no. 1 (May 1967): 36-54.
   Comments on the eighteenth-century stage versions of Tate's *King Lear*.

Canfield, J. Douglas. "Royalism's Last Dramatic Stand: English Political Tragedy, 1679-89." *Studies in Philology* 82, no. 2 (spring 1985): 234-63.
   Argues that many of the works by major and minor dramatists from 1679 to 1689 were feudal and patriarchal; uses Tate's *Loyal General* and *King Lear* as examples.

Craven, Robert R. "Nahum Tate's Third *Dido and Aeneas*: The Sources of the Libretto to Purcell's Opera." *The World of Opera* 1, no. 3 (1979): 65-78.
   Discusses Nahum's use of *Brutus of Alba*, the *Aeneid*, and other works as sources for *Dido and Aeneas*.

Hicks, Penelope. "Filling in the Gaps: Further Comments on Two Performances of Nahum Tate's *King Lear* in 1701, Their Dates and Cast." *Theatre Notebook* 49, no. 1 (1995): 3-10.
   Examines in detail the performances of Tate's *King Lear* by Thomas Betterton's company at the Lincoln's Inn Fields theatre.

Hodson, Geoffrey. "The Nahum Tate *Lear* at Richmond." *Drama*, no. 81 (summer 1966): 36-9.
   Describes a drama course in which educators learned about Tate's *King Lear* by studying the play and then staging a live performance.

Holst, Imogen. "Purcell's Librettist, Nahum Tate." In *Henry Purcell 1659-1695: Essays on His Music*, edited by Imogen Holst, pp. 35-41. London: Oxford University Press, 1959.
   Argues that part of the greatness and success of Henry Purcell's opera *Dido and Aeneas* must be attributed to Tate's libretto, which often brings the music to life.

Hook, Lucyle. "Shakespeare Improv'd, or A Case for the Affirmative." *Shakespeare Quarterly* 4, no. 2 (summer 1953): 289-99.
   Examines adaptations of Shakespeare Plays, including Tate's *King Lear*, noting the dominance of Cordelia in Tate's version.

Johnson, Odai. "Empty Houses: The Suppression of Tate's *Richard II*." *Theatre Journal* 47, no. 4 (December 1995): 503-16.

Discusses the banning of Tate's revision of *Richard II* and other works that were deemed offensive to the king.

Leaver, Robin A. "The Failure that Succeeded: The *New Version* of Tate and Brady." *Hymn* 48, no. 4 (October 1977): 22-31.
   Offers a textual history of Tate and Nicholas Brady's *The New Version of the Psalms of David*.

Maguire, Nancy Klein. "Nahum Tate's *King Lear*: 'The King's Blest Restoration.'" In *Appropriation of Shakespeare: Post-Renaissance Reconstructions of the Works and the Myth,* edited by Jean I. Marsden, pp. 29-43. New York: Harvester Wheatsheaf, 1991.
   Argues that Tate wrote his version of *King Lear* to comment on the 1678-83 Exclusion Crisis and that this contributed to the play's success and popularity among contemporary audiences.

Nameri, Dorothy E. *Three Versions of the Story of King Lear (Anonymous ca. 1594/1605; William Shakespeare 1607/1608; Nahum Tate 1681) Studied in Relation to One Another.* Vol. 1. Salzburg: Institut für Englische Sprache und Literatur, Universität Salzburg, 1976, 271 p.
   Attempts to establish a relationship between three versions of *King Lear*; considers whether Tate was aware of the anonymous 1594/1605 work *The True Chronicle History of the King Leir and his three daughters, Gonorill, Raga, and Cordelia.*

Ogden, James. "Lear's Blasted Heath." *Durham University Journal* 80, no. 1 (December 1987): 19-26.
   Claims that the use of the heath in productions of Shakespeare's *King Lear* was derived from Tate's version of the play.

Rosenthal, Laura J. "Reading Masks: The Actress and the Spectatrix in Restoration Shakespeare." In *Broken Boundaries: Women and Feminism in Restoration Drama,* edited by Katherine M. Quinsey, pp. 201-18. Lexington: University Press of Kentucky, 1996.
   Includes a discussion of male-female relations in Tate's adaptations of *King Lear* and *Coriolanus*.

Shershow, Scott Cutler. "'Higlety, Piglety, Right or Wrong': Providence and Poetic Justice in Rymer, Dryden and Tate." *Restoration: Studies in English Literary Culture, 1660-1700* 15, no. 1 (spring 1991): 17-26.
   Discusses the use of poetic justice in the works of three seventeenth-century dramatists; includes comments on Tate's *King Lear* as the most infamous example of poetic justice as it rectifies Shakespeare's original, both morally and poetically.

Spencer, Christopher. *Nahum Tate,* New York: Twayne Publishers, 1972, 184 p.

First book-length study of Tate's life and works, with individual chapters on the poems, adaptations, psalms, and his poem on tea.

Walkling, Andrew R. "Political Allegory in Purcell's *Dido and Aeneas.*" *Music & Letters* 76, no. 4 (November 1995): 540-71.

Reexamines *Dido and Aeneas,* arguing that it conceals a political commentary about the event it was written to celebrate—James II's Declaration.

Wikander, Matthew H. "The Spitted Infant: Scenic Emblem and Exclusionist Politics in Restoration Adaptations of Shakespeare." *Shakespeare Quarterly* 37, no. 3 (autumn 1986): 340-58.

Claims that the adaptation of Shakespeare to the Restoration stage in the 1680s was primarily a political activity; includes discussions of Tate's versions of *Richard II, King Lear,* and *Coriolanus.*

Additional coverage of Tate's life and career is contained in the following sources published by Thomson Gale: *Dictionary of Literary Biography,* **Vol. 80;** *Literature Resource Center***; and** *Reference Guide to English Literature,* **Ed. 2.**

How to Use This Index

The main references

Calvino, Italo
   1923-1985 .... **CLC 5, 8, 11, 22, 33, 39,
                           73; SSC 3, 48**

list all author entries in the following Gale Literary Criticism series:

AAL = Asian American Literature
BG = The Beat Generation: A Gale Critical Companion
BLC = Black Literature Criticism
BLCS = Black Literature Criticism Supplement
CLC = Contemporary Literary Criticism
CLR = Children's Literature Review
CMLC = Classical and Medieval Literature Criticism
DC = Drama Criticism
HLC = Hispanic Literature Criticism
HLCS = Hispanic Literature Criticism Supplement
HR = Harlem Renaissance: A Gale Critical Companion
LC = Literature Criticism from 1400 to 1800
NCLC = Nineteenth-Century Literature Criticism
NNAL = Native North American Literature
PC = Poetry Criticism
SSC = Short Story Criticism
TCLC = Twentieth-Century Literary Criticism
WLC = World Literature Criticism, 1500 to the Present
WLCS = World Literature Criticism Supplement

The cross-references

See also CA 85-88, 116; CANR 23, 61;
DAM NOV; DLB 196; EW 13; MTCW 1, 2;
RGSF 2; RGWL 2; SFW 4; SSFS 12

list all author entries in the following Gale biographical and literary sources:

AAYA = Authors & Artists for Young Adults
AFAW = African American Writers
AFW = African Writers
AITN = Authors in the News
AMW = American Writers
AMWR = American Writers Retrospective Supplement
AMWS = American Writers Supplement
ANW = American Nature Writers
AW = Ancient Writers
BEST = Bestsellers
BPFB = Beacham's Encyclopedia of Popular Fiction: Biography and Resources
BRW = British Writers
BRWS = British Writers Supplement
BW = Black Writers
BYA = Beacham's Guide to Literature for Young Adults
CA = Contemporary Authors
CAAS = Contemporary Authors Autobiography Series
CABS = Contemporary Authors Bibliographical Series
CAD = Contemporary American Dramatists
CANR = Contemporary Authors New Revision Series
CAP = Contemporary Authors Permanent Series
CBD = Contemporary British Dramatists
CCA = Contemporary Canadian Authors
CD = Contemporary Dramatists
CDALB = Concise Dictionary of American Literary Biography
CDALBS = Concise Dictionary of American Literary Biography Supplement
CDBLB = Concise Dictionary of British Literary Biography

CMW = *St. James Guide to Crime & Mystery Writers*
CN = *Contemporary Novelists*
CP = *Contemporary Poets*
CPW = *Contemporary Popular Writers*
CSW = *Contemporary Southern Writers*
CWD = *Contemporary Women Dramatists*
CWP = *Contemporary Women Poets*
CWRI = *St. James Guide to Children's Writers*
CWW = *Contemporary World Writers*
DA = *DISCovering Authors*
DA3 = *DISCovering Authors 3.0*
DAB = *DISCovering Authors: British Edition*
DAC = *DISCovering Authors: Canadian Edition*
DAM = *DISCovering Authors: Modules*
   DRAM: *Dramatists Module;* **MST:** *Most-studied Authors Module;*
   MULT: *Multicultural Authors Module;* **NOV:** *Novelists Module;*
   POET: *Poets Module;* **POP:** *Popular Fiction and Genre Authors Module*
DFS = *Drama for Students*
DLB = *Dictionary of Literary Biography*
DLBD = *Dictionary of Literary Biography Documentary Series*
DLBY = *Dictionary of Literary Biography Yearbook*
DNFS = *Literature of Developing Nations for Students*
EFS = *Epics for Students*
EXPN = *Exploring Novels*
EXPP = *Exploring Poetry*
EXPS = *Exploring Short Stories*
EW = *European Writers*
FANT = *St. James Guide to Fantasy Writers*
FW = *Feminist Writers*
GFL = *Guide to French Literature,* Beginnings to 1789, 1798 to the Present
GLL = *Gay and Lesbian Literature*
HGG = *St. James Guide to Horror, Ghost & Gothic Writers*
HW = *Hispanic Writers*
IDFW = *International Dictionary of Films and Filmmakers: Writers and Production Artists*
IDTP = *International Dictionary of Theatre: Playwrights*
LAIT = *Literature and Its Times*
LAW = *Latin American Writers*
JRDA = *Junior DISCovering Authors*
MAICYA = *Major Authors and Illustrators for Children and Young Adults*
MAICYAS = *Major Authors and Illustrators for Children and Young Adults Supplement*
MAWW = *Modern American Women Writers*
MJW = *Modern Japanese Writers*
MTCW = *Major 20th-Century Writers*
NCFS = *Nonfiction Classics for Students*
NFS = *Novels for Students*
PAB = *Poets: American and British*
PFS = *Poetry for Students*
RGAL = *Reference Guide to American Literature*
RGEL = *Reference Guide to English Literature*
RGSF = *Reference Guide to Short Fiction*
RGWL = *Reference Guide to World Literature*
RHW = *Twentieth-Century Romance and Historical Writers*
SAAS = *Something about the Author Autobiography Series*
SATA = *Something about the Author*
SFW = *St. James Guide to Science Fiction Writers*
SSFS = *Short Stories for Students*
TCWW = *Twentieth-Century Western Writers*
WLIT = *World Literature and Its Times*
WP = *World Poets*
YABC = *Yesterday's Authors of Books for Children*
YAW = *St. James Guide to Young Adult Writers*

Literary Criticism Series
Cumulative Author Index

al-Hariri, al-Qasim ibn 'Ali Abu Muhammad al-Basri
1054-1122 .... **CMLC 63**
See also RGWL 3

Ali, Ahmed 1908-1998 .... **CLC 69**
See also CA 25-28R; CANR 15, 34; EWL 3

Ali, Tariq 1943- .... **CLC 173**
See also CA 25-28R; CANR 10, 99

Alighieri, Dante
See Dante

Allan, John B.
See Westlake, Donald E(dwin)

Allan, Sidney
See Hartmann, Sadakichi

Allan, Sydney
See Hartmann, Sadakichi

Allard, Janet .... **CLC 59**

Allen, Edward 1948- .... **CLC 59**

Allen, Fred 1894-1956 .... **TCLC 87**

Allen, Paula Gunn 1939- ..... **CLC 84; NNAL**
See also AMWS 4; CA 112; 143; CANR 63, 130; CWP; DA3; DAM MULT; DLB 175; FW; MTCW 1; RGAL 4

Allen, Roland
See Ayckbourn, Alan

Allen, Sarah A.
See Hopkins, Pauline Elizabeth

Allen, Sidney H.
See Hartmann, Sadakichi

Allen, Woody 1935- .... **CLC 16, 52, 195**
See also AAYA 10, 51; CA 33-36R; CANR 27, 38, 63, 128; DAM POP; DLB 44; MTCW 1

Allende, Isabel 1942- ... **CLC 39, 57, 97, 170; HLC 1; SSC 65; WLCS**
See also AAYA 18; CA 125; 130; CANR 51, 74, 129; CDWLB 3; CLR 99; CWW 2; DA3; DAM MULT, NOV; DLB 145; DNFS 1; EWL 3; FW; HW 1, 2; INT CA-130; LAIT 5; LAWS 1; LMFS 2; MTCW 1, 2; NCFS 1; NFS 6, 18; RGSF 2; RGWL 3; SSFS 11, 16; WLIT 1

Alleyn, Ellen
See Rossetti, Christina (Georgina)

Alleyne, Carla D. .... **CLC 65**

Allingham, Margery (Louise)
1904-1966 .... **CLC 19**
See also CA 5-8R; 25-28R; CANR 4, 58; CMW 4; DLB 77; MSW; MTCW 1, 2

Allingham, William 1824-1889 ...... **NCLC 25**
See also DLB 35; RGEL 2

Allison, Dorothy E. 1949- .... **CLC 78, 153**
See also AAYA 53; CA 140; CANR 66, 107; CSW; DA3; FW; MTCW 1; NFS 11; RGAL 4

Alloula, Malek .... **CLC 65**

Allston, Washington 1779-1843 .... **NCLC 2**
See also DLB 1, 235

Almedingen, E. M. .... **CLC 12**
See Almedingen, Martha Edith von
See also SATA 3

Almedingen, Martha Edith von 1898-1971
See Almedingen, E. M.
See also CA 1-4R; CANR 1

Almodovar, Pedro 1949(?)- .... **CLC 114; HLCS 1**
See also CA 133; CANR 72; HW 2

Almqvist, Carl Jonas Love
1793-1866 .... **NCLC 42**

al-Mutanabbi, Ahmad ibn al-Husayn Abu al-Tayyib al-Jufi al-Kindi
915-965 .... **CMLC 66**
See also RGWL 3

Alonso, Damaso 1898-1990 .... **CLC 14**
See also CA 110; 131; 130; CANR 72; DLB 108; EWL 3; HW 1, 2

Alov
See Gogol, Nikolai (Vasilyevich)

al'Sadaawi, Nawal
See El Saadawi, Nawal
See also FW

Al Siddik
See Rolfe, Frederick (William Serafino Austin Lewis Mary)
See also GLL 1; RGEL 2

Alta 1942- .... **CLC 19**
See also CA 57-60

Alter, Robert B(ernard) 1935- .... **CLC 34**
See also CA 49-52; CANR 1, 47, 100

Alther, Lisa 1944- .... **CLC 7, 41**
See also BPFB 1; CA 65-68; CAAS 30; CANR 12, 30, 51; CN 7; CSW; GLL 2; MTCW 1

Althusser, L.
See Althusser, Louis

Althusser, Louis 1918-1990 .... **CLC 106**
See also CA 131; 132; CANR 102; DLB 242

Altman, Robert 1925- .... **CLC 16, 116**
See also CA 73-76; CANR 43

Alurista .... **HLCS 1**
See Urista (Heredia), Alberto (Baltazar)
See also DLB 82; LLW 1

Alvarez, A(lfred) 1929- .... **CLC 5, 13**
See also CA 1-4R; CANR 3, 33, 63, 101; CN 7; CP 7; DLB 14, 40

Alvarez, Alejandro Rodriguez 1903-1965
See Casona, Alejandro
See also CA 131; 93-96; HW 1

Alvarez, Julia 1950- .... **CLC 93; HLCS 1**
See also AAYA 25; AMWS 7; CA 147; CANR 69, 101, 133; DA3; DLB 282; LATS 1:2; LLW 1; MTCW 1; NFS 5, 9; SATA 129; WLIT 1

Alvaro, Corrado 1896-1956 .... **TCLC 60**
See also CA 163; DLB 264; EWL 3

Amado, Jorge 1912-2001 ... **CLC 13, 40, 106; HLC 1**
See also CA 77-80; 201; CANR 35, 74; CWW 2; DAM MULT, NOV; DLB 113, 307; EWL 3; HW 2; LAW; LAWS 1; MTCW 1, 2; RGWL 2, 3; TWA; WLIT 1

Ambler, Eric 1909-1998 .... **CLC 4, 6, 9**
See also BRWS 4; CA 9-12R; 171; CANR 7, 38, 74; CMW 4; CN 7; DLB 77; MSW; MTCW 1, 2; TEA

Ambrose, Stephen E(dward)
1936-2002 .... **CLC 145**
See also AAYA 44; CA 1-4R; 209; CANR 3, 43, 57, 83, 105; NCFS 2; SATA 40, 138

Amichai, Yehuda 1924-2000 .. **CLC 9, 22, 57, 116; PC 38**
See also CA 85-88; 189; CANR 46, 60, 99, 132; CWW 2; EWL 3; MTCW 1

Amichai, Yehudah
See Amichai, Yehuda

Amiel, Henri Frederic 1821-1881 .... **NCLC 4**
See also DLB 217

Amis, Kingsley (William)
1922-1995 ...... **CLC 1, 2, 3, 5, 8, 13, 40, 44, 129**
See also AITN 2; BPFB 1; BRWS 2; CA 9-12R; 150; CANR 8, 28, 54; CDBLB 1945-1960; CN 7; CP 7; DA; DA3; DAB; DAC; DAM MST, NOV; DLB 15, 27, 100, 139; DLBY 1996; EWL 3; HGG; INT CANR-8; MTCW 1, 2; RGEL 2; RGSF 2; SFW 4

Amis, Martin (Louis) 1949- .... **CLC 4, 9, 38, 62, 101**
See also BEST 90:3; BRWS 4; CA 65-68; CANR 8, 27, 54, 73, 95, 132; CN 7; DA3; DLB 14, 194; EWL 3; INT CANR-27; MTCW 1

Ammianus Marcellinus c. 330-c. 395 .... **CMLC 60**
See also AW 2; DLB 211

Ammons, A(rchie) R(andolph)
1926-2001 ...... **CLC 2, 3, 5, 8, 9, 25, 57, 108; PC 16**
See also AITN 1; AMWS 7; CA 9-12R; 193; CANR 6, 36, 51, 73, 107; CP 7; CSW; DAM POET; DLB 5, 165; EWL 3; MTCW 1, 2; PFS 19; RGAL 4

Amo, Tauraatua i
See Adams, Henry (Brooks)

Amory, Thomas 1691(?)-1788 .... **LC 48**
See also DLB 39

Anand, Mulk Raj 1905-2004 ...... **CLC 23, 93**
See also CA 65-68; CANR 32, 64; CN 7; DAM NOV; EWL 3; MTCW 1, 2; RGSF 2

Anatol
See Schnitzler, Arthur

Anaximander c. 611B.C.-c. 546B.C. .... **CMLC 22**

Anaya, Rudolfo A(lfonso) 1937- ...... **CLC 23, 148; HLC 1**
See also AAYA 20; BYA 13; CA 45-48; CAAS 4; CANR 1, 32, 51, 124; CN 7; DAM MULT, NOV; DLB 82, 206, 278; HW 1; LAIT 4; LLW 1; MTCW 1, 2; NFS 12; RGAL 4; RGSF 2; WLIT 1

Andersen, Hans Christian
1805-1875 .... **NCLC 7, 79; SSC 6, 56; WLC**
See also AAYA 57; CLR 6; DA; DA3; DAB; DAC; DAM MST, POP; EW 6; MAICYA 1, 2; RGSF 2; RGWL 2, 3; SATA 100; TWA; WCH; YABC 1

Andersen, C. Farley
See Mencken, H(enry) L(ouis); Nathan, George Jean

Anderson, Jessica (Margaret) Queale
1916- .... **CLC 37**
See also CA 9-12R; CANR 4, 62; CN 7

Anderson, Jon (Victor) 1940- .... **CLC 9**
See also CA 25-28R; CANR 20; DAM POET

Anderson, Lindsay (Gordon)
1923-1994 .... **CLC 20**
See also CA 125; 128; 146; CANR 77

Anderson, Maxwell 1888-1959 .... **TCLC 2, 144**
See also CA 105; 152; DAM DRAM; DFS 16, 20; DLB 7, 228; MTCW 2; RGAL 4

Anderson, Poul (William)
1926-2001 .... **CLC 15**
See also AAYA 5, 34; BPFB 1; BYA 6, 8, 9; CA 1-4R; 181; 199; CAAE 181; CAAS 2; CANR 2, 15, 34, 64, 110; CLR 58; DLB 8; FANT; INT CANR-15; MTCW 1, 2; SATA 90; SATA-Brief 39; SATA-Essay 106; SCFW 2; SFW 4; SUFW 1, 2

Anderson, Robert (Woodruff)
1917- .... **CLC 23**
See also AITN 1; CA 21-24R; CANR 32; DAM DRAM; DLB 7; LAIT 5

Anderson, Roberta Joan
See Mitchell, Joni

Anderson, Sherwood 1876-1941 .. **SSC 1, 46; TCLC 1, 10, 24, 123; WLC**
See also AAYA 30; AMW; AMWC 2; BPFB 1; CA 104; 121; CANR 61; CDALB 1917-1929; DA; DA3; DAB; DAC; DAM MST, NOV; DLB 4, 9, 86; DLBD 1; EWL 3; EXPS; GLL 2; MTCW 1, 2; NFS 4; RGAL 4; RGSF 2; SSFS 4, 10, 11; TUS

Andier, Pierre
See Desnos, Robert

Andouard
See Giraudoux, Jean(-Hippolyte)

Armah, Ayi Kwei 1939- . **BLC 1; CLC 5, 33, 136**
See also AFW; BRWS 10; BW 1; CA 61-64; CANR 21, 64; CDWLB 3; CN 7; DAM MULT, POET; DLB 117; EWL 3; MTCW 1; WLIT 2

Armatrading, Joan 1950- .... **CLC 17**
See also CA 114; 186

Armitage, Frank
See Carpenter, John (Howard)

Armstrong, Jeannette (C.) 1948- .... **NNAL**
See also CA 149; CCA 1; CN 7; DAC; SATA 102

Arnette, Robert
See Silverberg, Robert

Arnim, Achim von (Ludwig Joachim von Arnim) 1781-1831 ..... **NCLC 5; SSC 29**
See also DLB 90

Arnim, Bettina von 1785-1859 ...... **NCLC 38, 123**
See also DLB 90; RGWL 2, 3

Arnold, Matthew 1822-1888 ..... **NCLC 6, 29, 89, 126; PC 5; WLC**
See also BRW 5; CDBLB 1832-1890; DA; DAB; DAC; DAM MST, POET; DLB 32, 57; EXPP; PAB; PFS 2; TEA; WP

Arnold, Thomas 1795-1842 .... **NCLC 18**
See also DLB 55

Arnow, Harriette (Louisa) Simpson 1908-1986 .... **CLC 2, 7, 18**
See also BPFB 1; CA 9-12R; 118; CANR 14; DLB 6; FW; MTCW 1, 2; RHW; SATA 42; SATA-Obit 47

Arouet, Francois-Marie
See Voltaire

Arp, Hans
See Arp, Jean

Arp, Jean 1887-1966 .... **CLC 5; TCLC 115**
See also CA 81-84; 25-28R; CANR 42, 77; EW 10

Arrabal
See Arrabal, Fernando

Arrabal, Fernando 1932- ... **CLC 2, 9, 18, 58**
See Arrabal (Teran), Fernando
See also CA 9-12R; CANR 15; EWL 3; LMFS 2

Arrabal (Teran), Fernando 1932-
See Arrabal, Fernando
See also CWW 2

Arreola, Juan Jose 1918-2001 .... **CLC 147; HLC 1; SSC 38**
See also CA 113; 131; 200; CANR 81; CWW 2; DAM MULT; DLB 113; DNFS 2; EWL 3; HW 1, 2; LAW; RGSF 2

Arrian c. 89(?)-c. 155(?) .... **CMLC 43**
See also DLB 176

Arrick, Fran .... **CLC 30**
See Gaberman, Judie Angell
See also BYA 6

Arrley, Richmond
See Delany, Samuel R(ay), Jr.

Artaud, Antonin (Marie Joseph) 1896-1948 .... **DC 14; TCLC 3, 36**
See also CA 104; 149; DA3; DAM DRAM; DLB 258; EW 11; EWL 3; GFL 1789 to the Present; MTCW 1; RGWL 2, 3

Arthur, Ruth M(abel) 1905-1979 ..... **CLC 12**
See also CA 9-12R; 85-88; CANR 4; CWRI 5; SATA 7, 26

Artsybashev, Mikhail (Petrovich) 1878-1927 .... **TCLC 31**
See also CA 170; DLB 295

Arundel, Honor (Morfydd) 1919-1973 .... **CLC 17**
See also CA 21-22; 41-44R; CAP 2; CLR 35; CWRI 5; SATA 4; SATA-Obit 24

Arzner, Dorothy 1900-1979 .... **CLC 98**

Asch, Sholem 1880-1957 .... **TCLC 3**
See also CA 105; EWL 3; GLL 2

Ascham, Roger 1516(?)-1568 .... **LC 101**
See also DLB 236

Ash, Shalom
See Asch, Sholem

Ashbery, John (Lawrence) 1927- .. **CLC 2, 3, 4, 6, 9, 13, 15, 25, 41, 77, 125; PC 26**
See Berry, Jonas
See also AMWS 3; CA 5-8R; CANR 9, 37, 66, 102, 132; CP 7; DA3; DAM POET; DLB 5, 165; DLBY 1981; EWL 3; INT CANR-9; MTCW 1, 2; PAB; PFS 11; RGAL 4; WP

Ashdown, Clifford
See Freeman, R(ichard) Austin

Ashe, Gordon
See Creasey, John

Ashton-Warner, Sylvia (Constance) 1908-1984 .... **CLC 19**
See also CA 69-72; 112; CANR 29; MTCW 1, 2

Asimov, Isaac 1920-1992 ..... **CLC 1, 3, 9, 19, 26, 76, 92**
See also AAYA 13; BEST 90:2; BPFB 1; BYA 4, 6, 7, 9; CA 1-4R; 137; CANR 2, 19, 36, 60, 125; CLR 12, 79; CMW 4; CPW; DA3; DAM POP; DLB 8; DLBY 1992; INT CANR-19; JRDA; LAIT 5; LMFS 2; MAICYA 1, 2; MTCW 1, 2; RGAL 4; SATA 1, 26, 74; SCFW 2; SFW 4; SSFS 17; TUS; YAW

Askew, Anne 1521(?)-1546 .... **LC 81**
See also DLB 136

Assis, Joaquim Maria Machado de
See Machado de Assis, Joaquim Maria

Astell, Mary 1666-1731 .... **LC 68**
See also DLB 252; FW

Astley, Thea (Beatrice May) 1925- .. **CLC 41**
See also CA 65-68; CANR 11, 43, 78; CN 7; DLB 289; EWL 3

Astley, William 1855-1911
See Warung, Price

Aston, James
See White, T(erence) H(anbury)

Asturias, Miguel Angel 1899-1974 .... **CLC 3, 8, 13; HLC 1**
See also CA 25-28; 49-52; CANR 32; CAP 2; CDWLB 3; DA3; DAM MULT, NOV; DLB 113, 290; EWL 3; HW 1; LAW; LMFS 2; MTCW 1, 2; RGWL 2, 3; WLIT 1

Atares, Carlos Saura
See Saura (Atares), Carlos

Athanasius c. 295-c. 373 .... **CMLC 48**

Atheling, William
See Pound, Ezra (Weston Loomis)

Atheling, William, Jr.
See Blish, James (Benjamin)

Atherton, Gertrude (Franklin Horn) 1857-1948 .... **TCLC 2**
See also CA 104; 155; DLB 9, 78, 186; HGG; RGAL 4; SUFW 1; TCWW 2

Atherton, Lucius
See Masters, Edgar Lee

Atkins, Jack
See Harris, Mark

Atkinson, Kate 1951- .... **CLC 99**
See also CA 166; CANR 101; DLB 267

Attaway, William (Alexander) 1911-1986 .... **BLC 1; CLC 92**
See also BW 2, 3; CA 143; CANR 82; DAM MULT; DLB 76

Atticus
See Fleming, Ian (Lancaster); Wilson, (Thomas) Woodrow

Atwood, Margaret (Eleanor) 1939- ... **CLC 2, 3, 4, 8, 13, 15, 25, 44, 84, 135; PC 8; SSC 2, 46; WLC**
See also AAYA 12, 47; AMWS 13; BEST 89:2; BPFB 1; CA 49-52; CANR 3, 24, 33, 59, 95, 133; CN 7; CP 7; CPW; DA; DA3; DAB; DAC; DAM MST, NOV, POET; DLB 53, 251; EWL 3; EXPN; FW; INT CANR-24; LAIT 5; MTCW 1, 2; NFS 4, 12, 13, 14, 19; PFS 7; RGSF 2; SATA 50; SSFS 3, 13; TWA; WWE 1; YAW

Aubigny, Pierre d'
See Mencken, H(enry) L(ouis)

Aubin, Penelope 1685-1731(?) .... **LC 9**
See also DLB 39

Auchincloss, Louis (Stanton) 1917- .. **CLC 4, 6, 9, 18, 45; SSC 22**
See also AMWS 4; CA 1-4R; CANR 6, 29, 55, 87, 130; CN 7; DAM NOV; DLB 2, 244; DLBY 1980; EWL 3; INT CANR-29; MTCW 1; RGAL 4

Auden, W(ystan) H(ugh) 1907-1973 . **CLC 1, 2, 3, 4, 6, 9, 11, 14, 43, 123; PC 1; WLC**
See also AAYA 18; AMWS 2; BRW 7; BRWR 1; CA 9-12R; 45-48; CANR 5, 61, 105; CDBLB 1914-1945; DA; DA3; DAB; DAC; DAM DRAM, MST, POET; DLB 10, 20; EWL 3; EXPP; MTCW 1, 2; PAB; PFS 1, 3, 4, 10; TUS; WP

Audiberti, Jacques 1899-1965 .... **CLC 38**
See also CA 25-28R; DAM DRAM; EWL 3

Audubon, John James 1785-1851 . **NCLC 47**
See also ANW; DLB 248

Auel, Jean M(arie) 1936- .... **CLC 31, 107**
See also AAYA 7, 51; BEST 90:4; BPFB 1; CA 103; CANR 21, 64, 115; CPW; DA3; DAM POP; INT CANR-21; NFS 11; RHW; SATA 91

Auerbach, Erich 1892-1957 .... **TCLC 43**
See also CA 118; 155; EWL 3

Augier, Emile 1820-1889 .... **NCLC 31**
See also DLB 192; GFL 1789 to the Present

August, John
See De Voto, Bernard (Augustine)

Augustine, St. 354-430 .... **CMLC 6; WLCS**
See also DA; DA3; DAB; DAC; DAM MST; DLB 115; EW 1; RGWL 2, 3

Aunt Belinda
See Braddon, Mary Elizabeth

Aunt Weedy
See Alcott, Louisa May

Aurelius
See Bourne, Randolph S(illiman)

Aurelius, Marcus 121-180 .... **CMLC 45**
See Marcus Aurelius
See also RGWL 2, 3

Aurobindo, Sri
See Ghose, Aurabinda

Aurobindo Ghose
See Ghose, Aurabinda

Austen, Jane 1775-1817 ...... **NCLC 1, 13, 19, 33, 51, 81, 95, 119; WLC**
See also AAYA 19; BRW 4; BRWC 1; BRWR 2; BYA 3; CDBLB 1789-1832; DA; DA3; DAB; DAC; DAM MST, NOV; DLB 116; EXPN; LAIT 2; LATS 1:1; LMFS 1; NFS 1, 14, 18, 20; TEA; WLIT 3; WYAS 1

Auster, Paul 1947- .... **CLC 47, 131**
See also AMWS 12; CA 69-72; CANR 23, 52, 75, 129; CMW 4; CN 7; DA3; DLB 227; MTCW 1; SUFW 2

Austin, Frank
See Faust, Frederick (Schiller)
See also TCWW 2

MULT, POET, POP; DFS 3, 11, 16; DLB
5, 7, 16, 38; DLBD 8; EWL 3; MTCW 1,
2; PFS 9; RGAL 4; TUS; WP

Baratynsky, Evgenii Abramovich
1800-1844 .... **NCLC 103**
See also DLB 205

Barbauld, Anna Laetitia
1743-1825 .... **NCLC 50**
See also DLB 107, 109, 142, 158; RGEL 2

Barbellion, W. N. P. .... **TCLC 24**
See Cummings, Bruce F(rederick)

Barber, Benjamin R. 1939- .... **CLC 141**
See also CA 29-32R; CANR 12, 32, 64, 119

Barbera, Jack (Vincent) 1945- .... **CLC 44**
See also CA 110; CANR 45

Barbey d'Aurevilly, Jules-Amedee
1808-1889 .... **NCLC 1; SSC 17**
See also DLB 119; GFL 1789 to the Present

Barbour, John c. 1316-1395 .... **CMLC 33**
See also DLB 146

Barbusse, Henri 1873-1935 .... **TCLC 5**
See also CA 105; 154; DLB 65; EWL 3;
RGWL 2, 3

Barclay, Alexander c. 1475-1552 .... **LC 109**
See also DLB 132

Barclay, Bill
See Moorcock, Michael (John)

Barclay, William Ewert
See Moorcock, Michael (John)

Barea, Arturo 1897-1957 .... **TCLC 14**
See also CA 111; 201

Barfoot, Joan 1946- .... **CLC 18**
See also CA 105

Barham, Richard Harris
1788-1845 .... **NCLC 77**
See also DLB 159

Baring, Maurice 1874-1945 .... **TCLC 8**
See also CA 105; 168; DLB 34; HGG

Baring-Gould, Sabine 1834-1924 ... **TCLC 88**
See also DLB 156, 190

Barker, Clive 1952- .... **CLC 52; SSC 53**
See also AAYA 10, 54; BEST 90:3; BPFB
1; CA 121; 129; CANR 71, 111, 133;
CPW; DA3; DAM POP; DLB 261; HGG;
INT CA-129; MTCW 1, 2; SUFW 2

Barker, George Granville
1913-1991 .... **CLC 8, 48**
See also CA 9-12R; 135; CANR 7, 38;
DAM POET; DLB 20; EWL 3; MTCW 1

Barker, Harley Granville
See Granville-Barker, Harley
See also DLB 10

Barker, Howard 1946- .... **CLC 37**
See also CA 102; CBD; CD 5; DLB 13,
233

Barker, Jane 1652-1732 .... **LC 42, 82**
See also DLB 39, 131

Barker, Pat(ricia) 1943- ...... **CLC 32, 94, 146**
See also BRWS 4; CA 117; 122; CANR 50,
101; CN 7; DLB 271; INT CA-122

Barlach, Ernst (Heinrich)
1870-1938 .... **TCLC 84**
See also CA 178; DLB 56, 118; EWL 3

Barlow, Joel 1754-1812 .... **NCLC 23**
See also AMWS 2; DLB 37; RGAL 4

Barnard, Mary (Ethel) 1909- .... **CLC 48**
See also CA 21-22; CAP 2

Barnes, Djuna 1892-1982 .... **CLC 3, 4, 8, 11,
29, 127; SSC 3**
See Steptoe, Lydia
See also AMWS 3; CA 9-12R; 107; CAD;
CANR 16, 55; CWD; DLB 4, 9, 45; EWL
3; GLL 1; MTCW 1, 2; RGAL 4; TUS

Barnes, Jim 1933- .... **NNAL**
See also CA 108, 175; CAAE 175; CAAS
28; DLB 175

Barnes, Julian (Patrick) 1946- . **CLC 42, 141**
See also BRWS 4; CA 102; CANR 19, 54,
115; CN 7; DAB; DLB 194; DLBY 1993;
EWL 3; MTCW 1

Barnes, Peter 1931-2004 .... **CLC 5, 56**
See also CA 65-68; CAAS 12; CANR 33,
34, 64, 113; CBD; CD 5; DFS 6; DLB
13, 233; MTCW 1

Barnes, William 1801-1886 .... **NCLC 75**
See also DLB 32

Baroja (y Nessi), Pio 1872-1956 .... **HLC 1;
TCLC 8**
See also CA 104; EW 9

Baron, David
See Pinter, Harold

Baron Corvo
See Rolfe, Frederick (William Serafino
Austin Lewis Mary)

Barondess, Sue K(aufman)
1926-1977 .... **CLC 8**
See Kaufman, Sue
See also CA 1-4R; 69-72; CANR 1

Baron de Teive
See Pessoa, Fernando (Antonio Nogueira)

Baroness Von S.
See Zangwill, Israel

Barres, (Auguste-)Maurice
1862-1923 .... **TCLC 47**
See also CA 164; DLB 123; GFL 1789 to
the Present

Barreto, Afonso Henrique de Lima
See Lima Barreto, Afonso Henrique de

Barrett, Andrea 1954- .... **CLC 150**
See also CA 156; CANR 92

Barrett, Michele .... **CLC 65**

Barrett, (Roger) Syd 1946- .... **CLC 35**

Barrett, William (Christopher)
1913-1992 .... **CLC 27**
See also CA 13-16R; 139; CANR 11, 67;
INT CANR-11

Barrie, J(ames) M(atthew)
1860-1937 .... **TCLC 2**
See also BRWS 3; BYA 4, 5; CA 104; 136;
CANR 77; CDBLB 1890-1914; CLR 16;
CWRI 5; DA3; DAB; DAM DRAM; DFS
7; DLB 10, 141, 156; EWL 3; FANT;
MAICYA 1, 2; MTCW 1; SATA 100;
SUFW; WCH; WLIT 4; YABC 1

Barrington, Michael
See Moorcock, Michael (John)

Barrol, Grady
See Bograd, Larry

Barry, Mike
See Malzberg, Barry N(athaniel)

Barry, Philip 1896-1949 .... **TCLC 11**
See also CA 109; 199; DFS 9; DLB 7, 228;
RGAL 4

Bart, Andre Schwarz
See Schwarz-Bart, Andre

Barth, John (Simmons) 1930- ... **CLC 1, 2, 3,
5, 7, 9, 10, 14, 27, 51, 89; SSC 10**
See also AITN 1, 2; AMW; BPFB 1; CA
1-4R; CABS 1; CANR 5, 23, 49, 64, 113;
CN 7; DAM NOV; DLB 2, 227; EWL 3;
FANT; MTCW 1; RGAL 4; RGSF 2;
RHW; SSFS 6; TUS

Barthelme, Donald 1931-1989 ... **CLC 1, 2, 3,
5, 6, 8, 13, 23, 46, 59, 115; SSC 2, 55**
See also AMWS 4; BPFB 1; CA 21-24R;
129; CANR 20, 58; DA3; DAM NOV;
DLB 2, 234; DLBY 1980, 1989; EWL 3;
FANT; LMFS 2; MTCW 1, 2; RGAL 4;
RGSF 2; SATA 7; SATA-Obit 62; SSFS
17

Barthelme, Frederick 1943- ...... **CLC 36, 117**
See also AMWS 11; CA 114; 122; CANR
77; CN 7; CSW; DLB 244; DLBY 1985;
EWL 3; INT CA-122

Barthes, Roland (Gerard)
1915-1980 .... **CLC 24, 83; TCLC 135**
See also CA 130; 97-100; CANR 66; DLB
296; EW 13; EWL 3; GFL 1789 to the
Present; MTCW 1, 2; TWA

Bartram, William 1739-1823 .... **NCLC 145**
See also ANW; DLB 37

Barzun, Jacques (Martin) 1907- ..... **CLC 51,
145**
See also CA 61-64; CANR 22, 95

Bashevis, Isaac
See Singer, Isaac Bashevis

Bashkirtseff, Marie 1859-1884 .... **NCLC 27**

Basho, Matsuo
See Matsuo Basho
See also PFS 18; RGWL 2, 3; WP

Basil of Caesaria c. 330-379 .... **CMLC 35**

Basket, Raney
See Edgerton, Clyde (Carlyle)

Bass, Kingsley B., Jr.
See Bullins, Ed

Bass, Rick 1958- .... **CLC 79, 143; SSC 60**
See also ANW; CA 126; CANR 53, 93;
CSW; DLB 212, 275

Bassani, Giorgio 1916-2000 .... **CLC 9**
See also CA 65-68; 190; CANR 33; CWW
2; DLB 128, 177, 299; EWL 3; MTCW 1;
RGWL 2, 3

Bastian, Ann .... **CLC 70**

Bastos, Augusto (Antonio) Roa
See Roa Bastos, Augusto (Antonio)

Bataille, Georges 1897-1962 .... **CLC 29;
TCLC 155**
See also CA 101; 89-92; EWL 3

Bates, H(erbert) E(rnest)
1905-1974 .... **CLC 46; SSC 10**
See also CA 93-96; 45-48; CANR 34; DA3;
DAB; DAM POP; DLB 162, 191; EWL
3; EXPS; MTCW 1, 2; RGSF 2; SSFS 7

Bauchart
See Camus, Albert

Baudelaire, Charles 1821-1867 . **NCLC 6, 29,
55; PC 1; SSC 18; WLC**
See also DA; DA3; DAB; DAC; DAM
MST, POET; DLB 217; EW 7; GFL 1789
to the Present; LMFS 2; PFS 21; RGWL
2, 3; TWA

Baudouin, Marcel
See Peguy, Charles (Pierre)

Baudouin, Pierre
See Peguy, Charles (Pierre)

Baudrillard, Jean 1929- .... **CLC 60**
See also DLB 296

Baum, L(yman) Frank 1856-1919 .. **TCLC 7,
132**
See also AAYA 46; BYA 16; CA 108; 133;
CLR 15; CWRI 5; DLB 22; FANT; JRDA;
MAICYA 1, 2; MTCW 1, 2; NFS 13;
RGAL 4; SATA 18, 100; WCH

Baum, Louis F.
See Baum, L(yman) Frank

Baumbach, Jonathan 1933- .... **CLC 6, 23**
See also CA 13-16R; CAAS 5; CANR 12,
66; CN 7; DLBY 1980; INT CANR-12;
MTCW 1

Bausch, Richard (Carl) 1945- .... **CLC 51**
See also AMWS 7; CA 101; CAAS 14;
CANR 43, 61, 87; CSW; DLB 130

Baxter, Charles (Morley) 1947- . **CLC 45, 78**
See also CA 57-60; CANR 40, 64, 104, 133;
CPW; DAM POP; DLB 130; MTCW 2

Baxter, George Owen
See Faust, Frederick (Schiller)

Baxter, James K(eir) 1926-1972 .... **CLC 14**
See also CA 77-80; EWL 3

Baxter, John
See Hunt, E(verette) Howard, (Jr.)

Bayer, Sylvia
See Glassco, John

Benedikt, Michael 1935- .... **CLC 4, 14**
    See also CA 13-16R; CANR 7; CP 7; DLB 5

Benet, Juan 1927-1993 .... **CLC 28**
    See also CA 143; EWL 3

Benet, Stephen Vincent 1898-1943 ... **SSC 10; TCLC 7**
    See also AMWS 11; CA 104; 152; DA3; DAM POET; DLB 4, 48, 102, 249, 284; DLBY 1997; EWL 3; HGG; MTCW 1; RGAL 4; RGSF 2; SUFW; WP; YABC 1

Benet, William Rose 1886-1950 ..... **TCLC 28**
    See also CA 118; 152; DAM POET; DLB 45; RGAL 4

Benford, Gregory (Albert) 1941- ..... **CLC 52**
    See also BPFB 1; CA 69-72, 175; CAAE 175; CAAS 27; CANR 12, 24, 49, 95; CSW; DLBY 1982; SCFW 2; SFW 4

Bengtsson, Frans (Gunnar) 1894-1954 .... **TCLC 48**
    See also CA 170; EWL 3

Benjamin, David
    See Slavitt, David R(ytman)

Benjamin, Lois
    See Gould, Lois

Benjamin, Walter 1892-1940 .... **TCLC 39**
    See also CA 164; DLB 242; EW 11; EWL 3

Ben Jelloun, Tahar 1944-
    See Jelloun, Tahar ben
    See also CA 135; CWW 2; EWL 3; RGWL 3; WLIT 2

Benn, Gottfried 1886-1956 .. **PC 35; TCLC 3**
    See also CA 106; 153; DLB 56; EWL 3; RGWL 2, 3

Bennett, Alan 1934- .... **CLC 45, 77**
    See also BRWS 8; CA 103; CANR 35, 55, 106; CBD; CD 5; DAB; DAM MST; MTCW 1, 2

Bennett, (Enoch) Arnold 1867-1931 .... **TCLC 5, 20**
    See also BRW 6; CA 106; 155; CDBLB 1890-1914; DLB 10, 34, 98, 135; EWL 3; MTCW 2

Bennett, Elizabeth
    See Mitchell, Margaret (Munnerlyn)

Bennett, George Harold 1930-
    See Bennett, Hal
    See also BW 1; CA 97-100; CANR 87

Bennett, Gwendolyn B. 1902-1981 .... **HR 2**
    See also BW 1; CA 125; DLB 51; WP

Bennett, Hal .... **CLC 5**
    See Bennett, George Harold
    See also DLB 33

Bennett, Jay 1912- .... **CLC 35**
    See also AAYA 10; CA 69-72; CANR 11, 42, 79; JRDA; SAAS 4; SATA 41, 87; SATA-Brief 27; WYA; YAW

Bennett, Louise (Simone) 1919- .... **BLC 1; CLC 28**
    See also BW 2, 3; CA 151; CDWLB 3; CP 7; DAM MULT; DLB 117; EWL 3

Benson, A. C. 1862-1925 .... **TCLC 123**
    See also DLB 98

Benson, E(dward) F(rederic) 1867-1940 .... **TCLC 27**
    See also CA 114; 157; DLB 135, 153; HGG; SUFW 1

Benson, Jackson J. 1930- .... **CLC 34**
    See also CA 25-28R; DLB 111

Benson, Sally 1900-1972 .... **CLC 17**
    See also CA 19-20; 37-40R; CAP 1; SATA 1, 35; SATA-Obit 27

Benson, Stella 1892-1933 .... **TCLC 17**
    See also CA 117; 154, 155; DLB 36, 162; FANT; TEA

Bentham, Jeremy 1748-1832 .... **NCLC 38**
    See also DLB 107, 158, 252

Bentley, E(dmund) C(lerihew) 1875-1956 .... **TCLC 12**
    See also CA 108; DLB 70; MSW

Bentley, Eric (Russell) 1916- .... **CLC 24**
    See also CA 5-8R; CAD; CANR 6, 67; CBD; CD 5; INT CANR-6

ben Uzair, Salem
    See Horne, Richard Henry Hengist

Beranger, Pierre Jean de 1780-1857 .... **NCLC 34**

Berdyaev, Nicolas
    See Berdyaev, Nikolai (Aleksandrovich)

Berdyaev, Nikolai (Aleksandrovich) 1874-1948 .... **TCLC 67**
    See also CA 120; 157

Berdyayev, Nikolai (Aleksandrovich)
    See Berdyaev, Nikolai (Aleksandrovich)

Berendt, John (Lawrence) 1939- ...... **CLC 86**
    See also CA 146; CANR 75, 93; DA3; MTCW 1

Beresford, J(ohn) D(avys) 1873-1947 .... **TCLC 81**
    See also CA 112; 155; DLB 162, 178, 197; SFW 4; SUFW 1

Bergelson, David (Rafailovich) 1884-1952 .... **TCLC 81**
    See Bergelson, Dovid
    See also CA 220

Bergelson, Dovid
    See Bergelson, David (Rafailovich)
    See also EWL 3

Berger, Colonel
    See Malraux, (Georges-)Andre

Berger, John (Peter) 1926- .... **CLC 2, 19**
    See also BRWS 4; CA 81-84; CANR 51, 78, 117; CN 7; DLB 14, 207

Berger, Melvin H. 1927- .... **CLC 12**
    See also CA 5-8R; CANR 4; CLR 32; SAAS 2; SATA 5, 88; SATA-Essay 124

Berger, Thomas (Louis) 1924- .. **CLC 3, 5, 8, 11, 18, 38**
    See also BPFB 1; CA 1-4R; CANR 5, 28, 51, 128; CN 7; DAM NOV; DLB 2; DLBY 1980; EWL 3; FANT; INT CANR-28; MTCW 1, 2; RHW; TCWW 2

Bergman, (Ernst) Ingmar 1918- ...... **CLC 16, 72**
    See also CA 81-84; CANR 33, 70; CWW 2; DLB 257; MTCW 2

Bergson, Henri(-Louis) 1859-1941 . **TCLC 32**
    See also CA 164; EW 8; EWL 3; GFL 1789 to the Present

Bergstein, Eleanor 1938- .... **CLC 4**
    See also CA 53-56; CANR 5

Berkeley, George 1685-1753 .... **LC 65**
    See also DLB 31, 101, 252

Berkoff, Steven 1937- .... **CLC 56**
    See also CA 104; CANR 72; CBD; CD 5

Berlin, Isaiah 1909-1997 .... **TCLC 105**
    See also CA 85-88; 162

Bermant, Chaim (Icyk) 1929-1998 ... **CLC 40**
    See also CA 57-60; CANR 6, 31, 57, 105; CN 7

Bern, Victoria
    See Fisher, M(ary) F(rances) K(ennedy)

Bernanos, (Paul Louis) Georges 1888-1948 .... **TCLC 3**
    See also CA 104; 130; CANR 94; DLB 72; EWL 3; GFL 1789 to the Present; RGWL 2, 3

Bernard, April 1956- .... **CLC 59**
    See also CA 131

Bernard of Clairvaux 1090-1153 .. **CMLC 71**
    See also DLB 208

Berne, Victoria
    See Fisher, M(ary) F(rances) K(ennedy)

Bernhard, Thomas 1931-1989 ..... **CLC 3, 32, 61; DC 14**
    See also CA 85-88; 127; CANR 32, 57; CD-WLB 2; DLB 85, 124; EWL 3; MTCW 1; RGWL 2, 3

Bernhardt, Sarah (Henriette Rosine) 1844-1923 .... **TCLC 75**
    See also CA 157

Bernstein, Charles 1950- .... **CLC 142**
    See also CA 129; CAAS 24; CANR 90; CP 7; DLB 169

Bernstein, Ingrid
    See Kirsch, Sarah

Berriault, Gina 1926-1999 .... **CLC 54, 109; SSC 30**
    See also CA 116; 129; 185; CANR 66; DLB 130; SSFS 7,11

Berrigan, Daniel 1921- .... **CLC 4**
    See also CA 33-36R, 187; CAAE 187; CAAS 1; CANR 11, 43, 78; CP 7; DLB 5

Berrigan, Edmund Joseph Michael, Jr. 1934-1983
    See Berrigan, Ted
    See also CA 61-64; 110; CANR 14, 102

Berrigan, Ted .... **CLC 37**
    See Berrigan, Edmund Joseph Michael, Jr.
    See also DLB 5, 169; WP

Berry, Charles Edward Anderson 1931-
    See Berry, Chuck
    See also CA 115

Berry, Chuck .... **CLC 17**
    See Berry, Charles Edward Anderson

Berry, Jonas
    See Ashbery, John (Lawrence)
    See also GLL 1

Berry, Wendell (Erdman) 1934- ... **CLC 4, 6, 8, 27, 46; PC 28**
    See also AITN 1; AMWS 10; ANW; CA 73-76; CANR 50, 73, 101, 132; CP 7; CSW; DAM POET; DLB 5, 6, 234, 275; MTCW 1

Berryman, John 1914-1972 ... **CLC 1, 2, 3, 4, 6, 8, 10, 13, 25, 62**
    See also AMW; CA 13-16; 33-36R; CABS 2; CANR 35; CAP 1; CDALB 1941-1968; DAM POET; DLB 48; EWL 3; MTCW 1, 2; PAB; RGAL 4; WP

Bertolucci, Bernardo 1940- ...... **CLC 16, 157**
    See also CA 106; CANR 125

Berton, Pierre (Francis Demarigny) 1920- .... **CLC 104**
    See also CA 1-4R; CANR 2, 56; CPW; DLB 68; SATA 99

Bertrand, Aloysius 1807-1841 .... **NCLC 31**
    See Bertrand, Louis oAloysiusc

Bertrand, Louis oAloysiusc
    See Bertrand, Aloysius
    See also DLB 217

Bertran de Born c. 1140-1215 .... **CMLC 5**

Besant, Annie (Wood) 1847-1933 ..... **TCLC 9**
    See also CA 105; 185

Bessie, Alvah 1904-1985 .... **CLC 23**
    See also CA 5-8R; 116; CANR 2, 80; DLB 26

Bestuzhev, Aleksandr Aleksandrovich 1797-1837 .... **NCLC 131**
    See also DLB 198

Bethlen, T. D.
    See Silverberg, Robert

Beti, Mongo .... **BLC 1; CLC 27**
    See Biyidi, Alexandre
    See also AFW; CANR 79; DAM MULT; EWL 3; WLIT 2

Betjeman, John 1906-1984 ...... **CLC 2, 6, 10, 34, 43**
    See also BRW 7; CA 9-12R; 112; CANR 33, 56; CDBLB 1945-1960; DA3; DAB; DAM MST, POET; DLB 20; DLBY 1984; EWL 3; MTCW 1, 2

Blume, Judy (Sussman) 1938- .... **CLC 12, 30**
See also AAYA 3, 26; BYA 1, 8, 12; CA 29-
32R; CANR 13, 37, 66, 124; CLR 2, 15,
69; CPW; DA3; DAM NOV, POP; DLB
52; JRDA; MAICYA 1, 2; MAICYAS 1;
MTCW 1, 2; SATA 2, 31, 79, 142; WYA;
YAW

Blunden, Edmund (Charles)
1896-1974 .... **CLC 2, 56**
See also BRW 6; CA 17-18; 45-48; CANR
54; CAP 2; DLB 20, 100, 155; MTCW 1;
PAB

Bly, Robert (Elwood) 1926- .... **CLC 1, 2, 5,
10, 15, 38, 128; PC 39**
See also AMWS 4; CA 5-8R; CANR 41,
73, 125; CP 7; DA3; DAM POET; DLB
5; EWL 3; MTCW 1, 2; PFS 6, 17; RGAL
4

Boas, Franz 1858-1942 .... **TCLC 56**
See also CA 115; 181

Bobette
See Simenon, Georges (Jacques Christian)

Boccaccio, Giovanni 1313-1375 ... **CMLC 13,
57; SSC 10**
See also EW 2; RGSF 2; RGWL 2, 3; TWA

Bochco, Steven 1943- .... **CLC 35**
See also AAYA 11; CA 124; 138

Bode, Sigmund
See O'Doherty, Brian

Bodel, Jean 1167(?)-1210 .... **CMLC 28**

Bodenheim, Maxwell 1892-1954 .... **TCLC 44**
See also CA 110; 187; DLB 9, 45; RGAL 4

Bodenheimer, Maxwell
See Bodenheim, Maxwell

Bodker, Cecil 1927-
See Bodker, Cecil

Bodker, Cecil 1927- .... **CLC 21**
See also CA 73-76; CANR 13, 44, 111;
CLR 23; MAICYA 1, 2; SATA 14, 133

Boell, Heinrich (Theodor)
1917-1985 ..... **CLC 2, 3, 6, 9, 11, 15, 27,
32, 72; SSC 23; WLC**
See Boll, Heinrich
See also CA 21-24R; 116; CANR 24; DA;
DA3; DAB; DAC; DAM MST, NOV;
DLB 69; DLBY 1985; MTCW 1, 2; SSFS
20; TWA

Boerne, Alfred
See Doeblin, Alfred

Boethius c. 480-c. 524 .... **CMLC 15**
See also DLB 115; RGWL 2, 3

Boff, Leonardo (Genezio Darci)
1938- .... **CLC 70; HLC 1**
See also CA 150; DAM MULT; HW 2

Bogan, Louise 1897-1970 .... **CLC 4, 39, 46,
93; PC 12**
See also AMWS 3; CA 73-76; 25-28R;
CANR 33, 82; DAM POET; DLB 45, 169;
EWL 3; MAWW; MTCW 1, 2; PFS 21;
RGAL 4

Bogarde, Dirk
See Van Den Bogarde, Derek Jules Gaspard
Ulric Niven
See also DLB 14

Bogosian, Eric 1953- .... **CLC 45, 141**
See also CA 138; CAD; CANR 102; CD 5

Bograd, Larry 1953- .... **CLC 35**
See also CA 93-96; CANR 57; SAAS 21;
SATA 33, 89; WYA

Boiardo, Matteo Maria 1441-1494 .... **LC 6**

Boileau-Despreaux, Nicolas 1636-1711 . **LC 3**
See also DLB 268; EW 3; GFL Beginnings
to 1789; RGWL 2, 3

Boissard, Maurice
See Leautaud, Paul

Bojer, Johan 1872-1959 .... **TCLC 64**
See also CA 189; EWL 3

Bok, Edward W(illiam)
1863-1930 .... **TCLC 101**
See also CA 217; DLB 91; DLBD 16

Boker, George Henry 1823-1890 . **NCLC 125**
See also RGAL 4

Boland, Eavan (Aisling) 1944- .. **CLC 40, 67,
113; PC 58**
See also BRWS 5; CA 143, 207; CAAE
207; CANR 61; CP 7; CWP; DAM POET;
DLB 40; FW; MTCW 2; PFS 12

Boll, Heinrich
See Boell, Heinrich (Theodor)
See also BPFB 1; CDWLB 2; EW 13; EWL
3; RGSF 2; RGWL 2, 3

Bolt, Lee
See Faust, Frederick (Schiller)

Bolt, Robert (Oxton) 1924-1995 .... **CLC 14**
See also CA 17-20R; 147; CANR 35, 67;
CBD; DAM DRAM; DFS 2; DLB 13,
233; EWL 3; LAIT 1; MTCW 1

Bombal, Maria Luisa 1910-1980 .... **HLCS 1;
SSC 37**
See also CA 127; CANR 72; EWL 3; HW
1; LAW; RGSF 2

Bombet, Louis-Alexandre-Cesar
See Stendhal

Bomkauf
See Kaufman, Bob (Garnell)

Bonaventura .... **NCLC 35**
See also DLB 90

Bond, Edward 1934- .... **CLC 4, 6, 13, 23**
See also AAYA 50; BRWS 1; CA 25-28R;
CANR 38, 67, 106; CBD; CD 5; DAM
DRAM; DFS 3, 8; DLB 13; EWL 3;
MTCW 1

Bonham, Frank 1914-1989 .... **CLC 12**
See also AAYA 1; BYA 1, 3; CA 9-12R;
CANR 4, 36; JRDA; MAICYA 1, 2;
SAAS 3; SATA 1, 49; SATA-Obit 62;
TCWW 2; YAW

Bonnefoy, Yves 1923- . **CLC 9, 15, 58; PC 58**
See also CA 85-88; CANR 33, 75, 97;
CWW 2; DAM MST, POET; DLB 258;
EWL 3; GFL 1789 to the Present; MTCW
1, 2

Bonner, Marita .... **HR 2**
See Occomy, Marita (Odette) Bonner

Bonnin, Gertrude 1876-1938 .... **NNAL**
See Zitkala-Sa
See also CA 150; DAM MULT

Bontemps, Arna(ud Wendell)
1902-1973 ..... **BLC 1; CLC 1, 18; HR 2**
See also BW 1; CA 1-4R; 41-44R; CANR
4, 35; CLR 6; CWRI 5; DA3; DAM
MULT, NOV, POET; DLB 48, 51; JRDA;
MAICYA 1, 2; MTCW 1, 2; SATA 2, 44;
SATA-Obit 24; WCH; WP

Boot, William
See Stoppard, Tom

Booth, Martin 1944-2004 .... **CLC 13**
See also CA 93-96, 188; 223; CAAE 188;
CAAS 2; CANR 92

Booth, Philip 1925- .... **CLC 23**
See also CA 5-8R; CANR 5, 88; CP 7;
DLBY 1982

Booth, Wayne C(layson) 1921- .... **CLC 24**
See also CA 1-4R; CAAS 5; CANR 3, 43,
117; DLB 67

Borchert, Wolfgang 1921-1947 .... **TCLC 5**
See also CA 104; 188; DLB 69, 124; EWL
3

Borel, Petrus 1809-1859 .... **NCLC 41**
See also DLB 119; GFL 1789 to the Present

Borges, Jorge Luis 1899-1986 ... **CLC 1, 2, 3,
4, 6, 8, 9, 10, 13, 19, 44, 48, 83; HLC 1;
PC 22, 32; SSC 4, 41; TCLC 109;
WLC**
See also AAYA 26; BPFB 1; CA 21-24R;
CANR 19, 33, 75, 105, 133; CDWLB 3;
DA; DA3; DAB; DAC; DAM MST,

MULT; DLB 113, 283; DLBY 1986;
DNFS 1, 2; EWL 3; HW 1, 2; LAW;
LMFS 2; MSW; MTCW 1, 2; RGSF 2;
RGWL 2, 3; SFW 4; SSFS 17; TWA;
WLIT 1

Borowski, Tadeusz 1922-1951 .... **SSC 48;
TCLC 9**
See also CA 106; 154; CDWLB 4; DLB
215; EWL 3; RGSF 2; RGWL 3; SSFS
13

Borrow, George (Henry)
1803-1881 .... **NCLC 9**
See also DLB 21, 55, 166

Bosch (Gavino), Juan 1909-2001 ..... **HLCS 1**
See also CA 151; 204; DAM MST, MULT;
DLB 145; HW 1, 2

Bosman, Herman Charles
1905-1951 .... **TCLC 49**
See Malan, Herman
See also CA 160; DLB 225; RGSF 2

Bosschere, Jean de 1878(?)-1953 ... **TCLC 19**
See also CA 115; 186

Boswell, James 1740-1795 ... **LC 4, 50; WLC**
See also BRW 3; CDBLB 1660-1789; DA;
DAB; DAC; DAM MST; DLB 104, 142;
TEA; WLIT 3

Bottomley, Gordon 1874-1948 ..... **TCLC 107**
See also CA 120; 192; DLB 10

Bottoms, David 1949- .... **CLC 53**
See also CA 105; CANR 22; CSW; DLB
120; DLBY 1983

Boucicault, Dion 1820-1890 .... **NCLC 41**

Boucolon, Maryse
See Conde, Maryse

Bourdieu, Pierre 1930-2002 .... **CLC 198**
See also CA 130; 204

Bourget, Paul (Charles Joseph)
1852-1935 .... **TCLC 12**
See also CA 107; 196; DLB 123; GFL 1789
to the Present

Bourjaily, Vance (Nye) 1922- .... **CLC 8, 62**
See also CA 1-4R; CAAS 1; CANR 2, 72;
CN 7; DLB 2, 143

Bourne, Randolph S(illiman)
1886-1918 .... **TCLC 16**
See also AMW; CA 117; 155; DLB 63

Bova, Ben(jamin William) 1932- ...... **CLC 45**
See also AAYA 16; CA 5-8R; CAAS 18;
CANR 11, 56, 94, 111; CLR 3, 96; DLBY
1981; INT CANR-11; MAICYA 1, 2;
MTCW 1; SATA 6, 68, 133; SFW 4

Bowen, Elizabeth (Dorothea Cole)
1899-1973 . **CLC 1, 3, 6, 11, 15, 22, 118;
SSC 3, 28, 66; TCLC 148**
See also BRWS 2; CA 17-18; 41-44R;
CANR 35, 105; CAP 2; CDBLB 1945-
1960; DA3; DAM NOV; DLB 15, 162;
EWL 3; EXPS; FW; HGG; MTCW 1, 2;
NFS 13; RGSF 2; SSFS 5; SUFW 1;
TEA; WLIT 4

Bowering, George 1935- .... **CLC 15, 47**
See also CA 21-24R; CAAS 16; CANR 10;
CP 7; DLB 53

Bowering, Marilyn R(uthe) 1949- .... **CLC 32**
See also CA 101; CANR 49; CP 7; CWP

Bowers, Edgar 1924-2000 .... **CLC 9**
See also CA 5-8R; 188; CANR 24; CP 7;
CSW; DLB 5

Bowers, Mrs. J. Milton 1842-1914
See Bierce, Ambrose (Gwinett)

Bowie, David .... **CLC 17**
See Jones, David Robert

Bowles, Jane (Sydney) 1917-1973 ..... **CLC 3,
68**
See Bowles, Jane Auer
See also CA 19-20; 41-44R; CAP 2

Bowles, Jane Auer
See Bowles, Jane (Sydney)
See also EWL 3

Bowles, Paul (Frederick) 1910-1999 . **CLC 1, 2, 19, 53; SSC 3**
See also AMWS 4; CA 1-4R; 186; CAAS 1; CANR 1, 19, 50, 75; CN 7; DA3; DLB 5, 6, 218; EWL 3; MTCW 1, 2; RGAL 4; SSFS 17

Bowles, William Lisle 1762-1850 . **NCLC 103**
See also DLB 93

Box, Edgar
See Vidal, (Eugene Luther) Gore
See also GLL 1

Boyd, James 1888-1944 .... **TCLC 115**
See also CA 186; DLB 9; DLBD 16; RGAL 4; RHW

Boyd, Nancy
See Millay, Edna St. Vincent
See also GLL 1

Boyd, Thomas (Alexander)
1898-1935 .... **TCLC 111**
See also CA 111; 183; DLB 9; DLBD 16

Boyd, William 1952- .... **CLC 28, 53, 70**
See also CA 114; 120; CANR 51, 71, 131; CN 7; DLB 231

Boyesen, Hjalmar Hjorth
1848-1895 .... **NCLC 135**
See also DLB 12, 71; DLBD 13; RGAL 4

Boyle, Kay 1902-1992 .... **CLC 1, 5, 19, 58, 121; SSC 5**
See also CA 13-16R; 140; CAAS 1; CANR 29, 61, 110; DLB 4, 9, 48, 86; DLBY 1993; EWL 3; MTCW 1, 2; RGAL 4; RGSF 2; SSFS 10, 13, 14

Boyle, Mark
See Kienzle, William X(avier)

Boyle, Patrick 1905-1982 .... **CLC 19**
See also CA 127

Boyle, T. C.
See Boyle, T(homas) Coraghessan
See also AMWS 8

Boyle, T(homas) Coraghessan
1948- .... **CLC 36, 55, 90; SSC 16**
See Boyle, T. C.
See also AAYA 47; BEST 90:4; BPFB 1; CA 120; CANR 44, 76, 89, 132; CN 7; CPW; DA3; DAM POP; DLB 218, 278; DLBY 1986; EWL 3; MTCW 2; SSFS 13, 19

Boz
See Dickens, Charles (John Huffam)

Brackenridge, Hugh Henry
1748-1816 .... **NCLC 7**
See also DLB 11, 37; RGAL 4

Bradbury, Edward P.
See Moorcock, Michael (John)
See also MTCW 2

Bradbury, Malcolm (Stanley)
1932-2000 .... **CLC 32, 61**
See also CA 1-4R; CANR 1, 33, 91, 98; CN 7; DA3; DAM NOV; DLB 14, 207; EWL 3; MTCW 1, 2

Bradbury, Ray (Douglas) 1920- .... **CLC 1, 3, 10, 15, 42, 98; SSC 29, 53; WLC**
See also AAYA 15; AITN 1, 2; AMWS 4; BPFB 1; BYA 4, 5, 11; CA 1-4R; CANR 2, 30, 75, 125; CDALB 1968-1988; CN 7; CPW; DA; DA3; DAB; DAC; DAM MST, NOV, POP; DLB 2, 8; EXPN; EXPS; HGG; LAIT 3, 5; LATS 1:2; LMFS 2; MTCW 1, 2; NFS 1; RGAL 4; RGSF 2; SATA 11, 64, 123; SCFW 2; SFW 4; SSFS 1, 20; SUFW 1, 2; TUS; YAW

Braddon, Mary Elizabeth
1837-1915 .... **TCLC 111**
See also BRWS 8; CA 108; 179; CMW 4; DLB 18, 70, 156; HGG

Bradfield, Scott (Michael) 1955- .... **SSC 65**
See also CA 147; CANR 90; HGG; SUFW 2

Bradford, Gamaliel 1863-1932 .... **TCLC 36**
See also CA 160; DLB 17

Bradford, William 1590-1657 .... **LC 64**
See also DLB 24, 30; RGAL 4

Bradley, David (Henry), Jr. 1950- .... **BLC 1; CLC 23, 118**
See also BW 1, 3; CA 104; CANR 26, 81; CN 7; DAM MULT; DLB 33

Bradley, John Ed(mund, Jr.) 1958- . **CLC 55**
See also CA 139; CANR 99; CN 7; CSW

Bradley, Marion Zimmer
1930-1999 .... **CLC 30**
See Chapman, Lee; Dexter, John; Gardner, Miriam; Ives, Morgan; Rivers, Elfrida
See also AAYA 40; BPFB 1; CA 57-60; 185; CAAS 10; CANR 7, 31, 51, 75, 107; CPW; DA3; DAM POP; DLB 8; FANT; FW; MTCW 1, 2; SATA 90, 139; SATA-Obit 116; SFW 4; SUFW 2; YAW

Bradshaw, John 1933- .... **CLC 70**
See also CA 138; CANR 61

Bradstreet, Anne 1612(?)-1672 ...... **LC 4, 30; PC 10**
See also AMWS 1; CDALB 1640-1865; DA; DA3; DAC; DAM MST, POET; DLB 24; EXPP; FW; PFS 6; RGAL 4; TUS; WP

Brady, Joan 1939- .... **CLC 86**
See also CA 141

Bragg, Melvyn 1939- .... **CLC 10**
See also BEST 89:3; CA 57-60; CANR 10, 48, 89; CN 7; DLB 14, 271; RHW

Brahe, Tycho 1546-1601 .... **LC 45**
See also DLB 300

Braine, John (Gerard) 1922-1986 . **CLC 1, 3, 41**
See also CA 1-4R; 120; CANR 1, 33; CD-BLB 1945-1960; DLB 15; DLBY 1986; EWL 3; MTCW 1

Braithwaite, William Stanley (Beaumont)
1878-1962 .... **BLC 1; HR 2; PC 52**
See also BW 1; CA 125; DAM MULT; DLB 50, 54

Bramah, Ernest 1868-1942 .... **TCLC 72**
See also CA 156; CMW 4; DLB 70; FANT

Brammer, William 1930(?)-1978 ...... **CLC 31**
See also CA 77-80

Brancati, Vitaliano 1907-1954 .... **TCLC 12**
See also CA 109; DLB 264; EWL 3

Brancato, Robin F(idler) 1936- ...... **CLC 35**
See also AAYA 9; BYA 6; CA 69-72; CANR 11, 45; CLR 32; JRDA; MAICYA 2; MAICYAS 1; SAAS 9; SATA 97; WYA; YAW

Brand, Dionne 1953- .... **CLC 192**
See also BW 2; CA 143; CWP

Brand, Max
See Faust, Frederick (Schiller)
See also BPFB 1; TCWW 2

Brand, Millen 1906-1980 .... **CLC 7**
See also CA 21-24R; 97-100; CANR 72

Branden, Barbara .... **CLC 44**
See also CA 148

Brandes, Georg (Morris Cohen)
1842-1927 .... **TCLC 10**
See also CA 105; 189; DLB 300

Brandys, Kazimierz 1916-2000 .... **CLC 62**
See also EWL 3

Branley, Franklyn M(ansfield)
1915-2002 .... **CLC 21**
See also CA 33-36R; 207; CANR 14, 39; CLR 13; MAICYA 1, 2; SAAS 16; SATA 4, 68, 136

Brant, Beth (E.) 1941- .... **NNAL**
See also CA 144; FW

Brathwaite, Edward Kamau
1930- .... **BLCS; CLC 11; PC 56**
See also BW 2, 3; CA 25-28R; CANR 11, 26, 47, 107; CDWLB 3; CP 7; DAM POET; DLB 125; EWL 3

Brathwaite, Kamau
See Brathwaite, Edward Kamau

Brautigan, Richard (Gary)
1935-1984 .... **CLC 1, 3, 5, 9, 12, 34, 42; TCLC 133**
See also BPFB 1; CA 53-56; 113; CANR 34; DA3; DAM NOV; DLB 2, 5, 206; DLBY 1980, 1984; FANT; MTCW 1; RGAL 4; SATA 56

Brave Bird, Mary .... **NNAL**
See Crow Dog, Mary (Ellen)

Braverman, Kate 1950- .... **CLC 67**
See also CA 89-92

Brecht, (Eugen) Bertolt (Friedrich)
1898-1956 ..... **DC 3; TCLC 1, 6, 13, 35; WLC**
See also CA 104; 133; CANR 62; CDWLB 2; DA; DA3; DAB; DAC; DAM DRAM, MST; DFS 4, 5, 9; DLB 56, 124; EW 11; EWL 3; IDTP; MTCW 1, 2; RGWL 2, 3; TWA

Brecht, Eugen Berthold Friedrich
See Brecht, (Eugen) Bertolt (Friedrich)

Bremer, Fredrika 1801-1865 .... **NCLC 11**
See also DLB 254

Brennan, Christopher John
1870-1932 .... **TCLC 17**
See also CA 117; 188; DLB 230; EWL 3

Brennan, Maeve 1917-1993 ... **CLC 5; TCLC 124**
See also CA 81-84; CANR 72, 100

Brent, Linda
See Jacobs, Harriet A(nn)

Brentano, Clemens (Maria)
1778-1842 .... **NCLC 1**
See also DLB 90; RGWL 2, 3

Brent of Bin Bin
See Franklin, (Stella Maria Sarah) Miles (Lampe)

Brenton, Howard 1942- .... **CLC 31**
See also CA 69-72; CANR 33, 67; CBD; CD 5; DLB 13; MTCW 1

Breslin, James 1930-
See Breslin, Jimmy
See also CA 73-76; CANR 31, 75; DAM NOV; MTCW 1, 2

Breslin, Jimmy .... **CLC 4, 43**
See Breslin, James
See also AITN 1; DLB 185; MTCW 2

Bresson, Robert 1901(?)-1999 .... **CLC 16**
See also CA 110; 187; CANR 49

Breton, Andre 1896-1966 .. **CLC 2, 9, 15, 54; PC 15**
See also CA 19-20; 25-28R; CANR 40, 60; CAP 2; DLB 65, 258; EW 11; EWL 3; GFL 1789 to the Present; LMFS 2; MTCW 1, 2; RGWL 2, 3; TWA; WP

Breytenbach, Breyten 1939(?)- .. **CLC 23, 37, 126**
See also CA 113; 129; CANR 61, 122; CWW 2; DAM POET; DLB 225; EWL 3

Bridgers, Sue Ellen 1942- .... **CLC 26**
See also AAYA 8, 49; BYA 7, 8; CA 65-68; CANR 11, 36; CLR 18; DLB 52; JRDA; MAICYA 1, 2; SAAS 1; SATA 22, 90; SATA-Essay 109; WYA; YAW

Bridges, Robert (Seymour)
1844-1930 .... **PC 28; TCLC 1**
See also BRW 6; CA 104; 152; CDBLB 1890-1914; DAM POET; DLB 19, 98

Bridie, James .... **TCLC 3**
See Mavor, Osborne Henry
See also DLB 10; EWL 3

Bush, Ronald 1946- .... **CLC 34**
　　See also CA 136
Bustos, F(rancisco)
　　See Borges, Jorge Luis
Bustos Domecq, H(onorio)
　　See Bioy Casares, Adolfo; Borges, Jorge
　　Luis
Butler, Octavia E(stelle) 1947- .. **BLCS; CLC
　　38, 121**
　　See also AAYA 18, 48; AFAW 2; AMWS
　　13; BPFB 1; BW 2, 3; CA 73-76; CANR
　　12, 24, 38, 73; CLR 65; CPW; DA3;
　　DAM MULT, POP; DLB 33; LATS 1:2;
　　MTCW 1, 2; NFS 8; SATA 84; SCFW 2;
　　SFW 4; SSFS 6; YAW
Butler, Robert Olen, (Jr.) 1945- ...... **CLC 81,
　　162**
　　See also AMWS 12; BPFB 1; CA 112;
　　CANR 66; CSW; DAM POP; DLB 173;
　　INT CA-112; SSFS 11
Butler, Samuel 1612-1680 .... **LC 16, 43**
　　See also DLB 101, 126; RGEL 2
Butler, Samuel 1835-1902 .... **TCLC 1, 33;
　　WLC**
　　See also BRWS 2; CA 143; CDBLB 1890-
　　1914; DA; DA3; DAB; DAC; DAM MST,
　　NOV; DLB 18, 57, 174; RGEL 2; SFW 4;
　　TEA
Butler, Walter C.
　　See Faust, Frederick (Schiller)
Butor, Michel (Marie Francois)
　　1926- .... **CLC 1, 3, 8, 11, 15, 161**
　　See also CA 9-12R; CANR 33, 66; CWW
　　2; DLB 83; EW 13; EWL 3; GFL 1789 to
　　the Present; MTCW 1, 2
Butts, Mary 1890(?)-1937 .... **TCLC 77**
　　See also CA 148; DLB 240
Buxton, Ralph
　　See Silverstein, Alvin; Silverstein, Virginia
　　B(arbara Opshelor)
Buzo, Alex
　　See Buzo, Alexander (John)
　　See also DLB 289
Buzo, Alexander (John) 1944- .... **CLC 61**
　　See also CA 97-100; CANR 17, 39, 69; CD
　　5
Buzzati, Dino 1906-1972 .... **CLC 36**
　　See also CA 160; 33-36R; DLB 177; RGWL
　　2, 3; SFW 4
Byars, Betsy (Cromer) 1928- .... **CLC 35**
　　See also AAYA 19; BYA 3; CA 33-36R,
　　183; CAAE 183; CANR 18, 36, 57, 102;
　　CLR 1, 16, 72; DLB 52; INT CANR-18;
　　JRDA; MAICYA 1, 2; MAICYAS 1;
　　MTCW 1; SAAS 1; SATA 4, 46, 80;
　　SATA-Essay 108; WYA; YAW
Byatt, A(ntonia) S(usan Drabble)
　　1936- .... **CLC 19, 65, 136**
　　See also BPFB 1; BRWC 2; BRWS 4; CA
　　13-16R; CANR 13, 33, 50, 75, 96, 133;
　　DA3; DAM NOV, POP; DLB 14, 194;
　　EWL 3; MTCW 1, 2; RGSF 2; RHW;
　　TEA
Byrne, David 1952- .... **CLC 26**
　　See also CA 127
Byrne, John Keyes 1926-
　　See Leonard, Hugh
　　See also CA 102; CANR 78; INT CA-102
Byron, George Gordon (Noel)
　　1788-1824 ..... **DC 24; NCLC 2, 12, 109;
　　PC 16; WLC**
　　See also BRW 4; BRWC 2; CDBLB 1789-
　　1832; DA; DA3; DAB; DAC; DAM MST,
　　POET; DLB 96, 110; EXPP; LMFS 1;
　　PAB; PFS 1, 14; RGEL 2; TEA; WLIT 3;
　　WP
Byron, Robert 1905-1941 .... **TCLC 67**
　　See also CA 160; DLB 195
C. 3. 3.
　　See Wilde, Oscar (Fingal O'Flahertie Wills)

Caballero, Fernan 1796-1877 .... **NCLC 10**
Cabell, Branch
　　See Cabell, James Branch
Cabell, James Branch 1879-1958 .... **TCLC 6**
　　See also CA 105; 152; DLB 9, 78; FANT;
　　MTCW 1; RGAL 4; SUFW 1
Cabeza de Vaca, Alvar Nunez
　　1490-1557(?) .... **LC 61**
Cable, George Washington
　　1844-1925 .... **SSC 4; TCLC 4**
　　See also CA 104; 155; DLB 12, 74; DLBD
　　13; RGAL 4; TUS
Cabral de Melo Neto, Joao
　　1920-1999 .... **CLC 76**
　　See Melo Neto, Joao Cabral de
　　See also CA 151; DAM MULT; DLB 307;
　　LAW; LAWS 1
Cabrera Infante, G(uillermo) 1929- . **CLC 5,
　　25, 45, 120; HLC 1; SSC 39**
　　See also CA 85-88; CANR 29, 65, 110; CD-
　　WLB 3; CWW 2; DA3; DAM MULT;
　　DLB 113; EWL 3; HW 1, 2; LAW; LAWS
　　1; MTCW 1, 2; RGSF 2; WLIT 1
Cade, Toni
　　See Bambara, Toni Cade
Cadmus and Harmonia
　　See Buchan, John
Caedmon fl. 658-680 .... **CMLC 7**
　　See also DLB 146
Caeiro, Alberto
　　See Pessoa, Fernando (Antonio Nogueira)
Caesar, Julius .... **CMLC 47**
　　See Julius Caesar
　　See also AW 1; RGWL 2, 3
Cage, John (Milton, Jr.)
　　1912-1992 .... **CLC 41; PC 58**
　　See also CA 13-16R; 169; CANR 9, 78;
　　DLB 193; INT CANR-9
Cahan, Abraham 1860-1951 .... **TCLC 71**
　　See also CA 108; 154; DLB 9, 25, 28;
　　RGAL 4
Cain, G.
　　See Cabrera Infante, G(uillermo)
Cain, Guillermo
　　See Cabrera Infante, G(uillermo)
Cain, James M(allahan) 1892-1977 .. **CLC 3,
　　11, 28**
　　See also AITN 1; BPFB 1; CA 17-20R; 73-
　　76; CANR 8, 34, 61; CMW 4; DLB 226;
　　EWL 3; MSW; MTCW 1; RGAL 4
Caine, Hall 1853-1931 .... **TCLC 97**
　　See also RHW
Caine, Mark
　　See Raphael, Frederic (Michael)
Calasso, Roberto 1941- .... **CLC 81**
　　See also CA 143; CANR 89
Calderon de la Barca, Pedro
　　1600-1681 .... **DC 3; HLCS 1; LC 23**
　　See also EW 2; RGWL 2, 3; TWA
Caldwell, Erskine (Preston)
　　1903-1987 .... **CLC 1, 8, 14, 50, 60; SSC
　　19; TCLC 117**
　　See also AITN 1; AMW; BPFB 1; CA 1-4R;
　　121; CAAS 1; CANR 2, 33; DA3; DAM
　　NOV; DLB 9, 86; EWL 3; MTCW 1, 2;
　　RGAL 4; RGSF 2; TUS
Caldwell, (Janet Miriam) Taylor (Holland)
　　1900-1985 .... **CLC 2, 28, 39**
　　See also BPFB 1; CA 5-8R; 116; CANR 5;
　　DA3; DAM NOV, POP; DLBD 17; RHW
Calhoun, John Caldwell
　　1782-1850 .... **NCLC 15**
　　See also DLB 3, 248
Calisher, Hortense 1911- ..... **CLC 2, 4, 8, 38,
　　134; SSC 15**
　　See also CA 1-4R; CANR 1, 22, 117; CN
　　7; DA3; DAM NOV; DLB 2, 218; INT
　　CANR-22; MTCW 1, 2; RGAL 4; RGSF
　　2

Callaghan, Morley Edward
　　1903-1990 ..... **CLC 3, 14, 41, 65; TCLC
　　145**
　　See also CA 9-12R; 132; CANR 33, 73;
　　DAC; DAM MST; DLB 68; EWL 3;
　　MTCW 1, 2; RGEL 2; RGSF 2; SSFS 19
Callimachus c. 305B.C.-c.
　　240B.C. .... **CMLC 18**
　　See also AW 1; DLB 176; RGWL 2, 3
Calvin, Jean
　　See Calvin, John
　　See also GFL Beginnings to 1789
Calvin, John 1509-1564 .... **LC 37**
　　See Calvin, Jean
Calvino, Italo 1923-1985 .... **CLC 5, 8, 11, 22,
　　33, 39, 73; SSC 3, 48**
　　See also AAYA 58; CA 85-88; 116; CANR
　　23, 61, 132; DAM NOV; DLB 196; EW
　　13; EWL 3; MTCW 1, 2; RGSF 2; RGWL
　　2, 3; SFW 4; SSFS 12
Camara Laye
　　See Laye, Camara
　　See also EWL 3
Camden, William 1551-1623 .... **LC 77**
　　See also DLB 172
Cameron, Carey 1952- .... **CLC 59**
　　See also CA 135
Cameron, Peter 1959- .... **CLC 44**
　　See also AMWS 12; CA 125; CANR 50,
　　117; DLB 234; GLL 2
Camoens, Luis Vaz de 1524(?)-1580
　　See Camoes, Luis de
　　See also EW 2
Camoes, Luis de 1524(?)-1580 . **HLCS 1; LC
　　62; PC 31**
　　See Camoens, Luis Vaz de
　　See also DLB 287; RGWL 2, 3
Campana, Dino 1885-1932 .... **TCLC 20**
　　See also CA 117; DLB 114; EWL 3
Campanella, Tommaso 1568-1639 .... **LC 32**
　　See also RGWL 2, 3
Campbell, John W(ood, Jr.)
　　1910-1971 .... **CLC 32**
　　See also CA 21-22; 29-32R; CANR 34;
　　CAP 2; DLB 8; MTCW 1; SCFW; SFW 4
Campbell, Joseph 1904-1987 .... **CLC 69;
　　TCLC 140**
　　See also AAYA 3; BEST 89:2; CA 1-4R;
　　124; CANR 3, 28, 61, 107; DA3; MTCW
　　1, 2
Campbell, Maria 1940- .... **CLC 85; NNAL**
　　See also CA 102; CANR 54; CCA 1; DAC
Campbell, (John) Ramsey 1946- ..... **CLC 42;
　　SSC 19**
　　See also AAYA 51; CA 57-60; CANR 7,
　　102; DLB 261; HGG; INT CANR-7;
　　SUFW 1, 2
Campbell, (Ignatius) Roy (Dunnachie)
　　1901-1957 .... **TCLC 5**
　　See also AFW; CA 104; 155; DLB 20, 225;
　　EWL 3; MTCW 2; RGEL 2
Campbell, Thomas 1777-1844 .... **NCLC 19**
　　See also DLB 93, 144; RGEL 2
Campbell, Wilfred .... **TCLC 9**
　　See Campbell, William
Campbell, William 1858(?)-1918
　　See Campbell, Wilfred
　　See also CA 106; DLB 92
Campion, Jane 1954- .... **CLC 95**
　　See also AAYA 33; CA 138; CANR 87
Campion, Thomas 1567-1620 .... **LC 78**
　　See also CDBLB Before 1660; DAM POET;
　　DLB 58, 172; RGEL 2
Camus, Albert 1913-1960 ...... **CLC 1, 2, 4, 9,
　　11, 14, 32, 63, 69, 124; DC 2; SSC 9,
　　76; WLC**
　　See also AAYA 36; AFW; BPFB 1; CA 89-
　　92; CANR 131; DA; DA3; DAB; DAC;
　　DAM DRAM, MST, NOV; DLB 72; EW

Cassity, (Allen) Turner 1929- .... **CLC 6, 42**
    See also CA 17-20R; 223; CAAE 223;
    CAAS 8; CANR 11; CSW; DLB 105

Castaneda, Carlos (Cesar Aranha)
    1931(?)-1998 .... **CLC 12, 119**
    See also CA 25-28R; CANR 32, 66, 105;
    DNFS 1; HW 1; MTCW 1

Castedo, Elena 1937- .... **CLC 65**
    See also CA 132

Castedo-Ellerman, Elena
    See Castedo, Elena

Castellanos, Rosario 1925-1974 .... **CLC 66;**
    HLC 1; SSC 39, 68
    See also CA 131; 53-56; CANR 58; CD-
    WLB 3; DAM MULT; DLB 113, 290;
    EWL 3; FW; HW 1; LAW; MTCW 1;
    RGSF 2; RGWL 2, 3

Castelvetro, Lodovico 1505-1571 .... **LC 12**

Castiglione, Baldassare 1478-1529 ...... **LC 12**
    See Castiglione, Baldesar
    See also LMFS 1; RGWL 2, 3

Castiglione, Baldesar
    See Castiglione, Baldassare
    See also EW 2

Castillo, Ana (Hernandez Del)
    1953- .... **CLC 151**
    See also AAYA 42; CA 131; CANR 51, 86,
    128; CWP; DLB 122, 227; DNFS 2; FW;
    HW 1; LLW 1; PFS 21

Castle, Robert
    See Hamilton, Edmond

Castro (Ruz), Fidel 1926(?)- .... **HLC 1**
    See also CA 110; 129; CANR 81; DAM
    MULT; HW 2

Castro, Guillen de 1569-1631 .... **LC 19**

Castro, Rosalia de 1837-1885 ... **NCLC 3, 78;**
    PC 41
    See also DAM MULT

Cather, Willa (Sibert) 1873-1947 . **SSC 2, 50;**
    TCLC 1, 11, 31, 99, 132, 152; WLC
    See also AAYA 24; AMW; AMWC 1;
    AMWR 1; BPFB 1; CA 104; 128; CDALB
    1865-1917; CLR 98; DA; DA3; DAB;
    DAC; DAM MST, NOV; DLB 9, 54, 78,
    256; DLBD 1; EWL 3; EXPN; EXPS;
    LAIT 3; LATS 1:1; MAWW; MTCW 1,
    2; NFS 2, 19; RGAL 4; RGSF 2; RHW;
    SATA 30; SSFS 2, 7, 16; TCWW 2; TUS

Catherine II
    See Catherine the Great
    See also DLB 150

Catherine the Great 1729-1796 .... **LC 69**
    See Catherine II

Cato, Marcus Porcius
    234B.C.-149B.C. .... **CMLC 21**
    See Cato the Elder

Cato, Marcus Porcius, the Elder
    See Cato, Marcus Porcius

Cato the Elder
    See Cato, Marcus Porcius
    See also DLB 211

Catton, (Charles) Bruce 1899-1978 . **CLC 35**
    See also AITN 1; CA 5-8R; 81-84; CANR
    7, 74; DLB 17; SATA 2; SATA-Obit 24

Catullus c. 84B.C.-54B.C. .... **CMLC 18**
    See also AW 2; CDWLB 1; DLB 211;
    RGWL 2, 3

Cauldwell, Frank
    See King, Francis (Henry)

Caunitz, William J. 1933-1996 .... **CLC 34**
    See also BEST 89:3; CA 125; 130; 152;
    CANR 73; INT CA-130

Causley, Charles (Stanley)
    1917-2003 .... **CLC 7**
    See also CA 9-12R; 223; CANR 5, 35, 94;
    CLR 30; CWRI 5; DLB 27; MTCW 1;
    SATA 3, 66; SATA-Obit 149

Caute, (John) David 1936- .... **CLC 29**
    See also CA 1-4R; CAAS 4; CANR 1, 33,
    64, 120; CBD; CD 5; CN 7; DAM NOV;
    DLB 14, 231

Cavafy, C(onstantine) P(eter) .... **PC 36;**
    TCLC 2, 7
    See Kavafis, Konstantinos Petrou
    See also CA 148; DA3; DAM POET; EW
    8; EWL 3; MTCW 1; PFS 19; RGWL 2,
    3; WP

Cavalcanti, Guido c. 1250-c.
    1300 .... **CMLC 54**
    See also RGWL 2, 3

Cavallo, Evelyn
    See Spark, Muriel (Sarah)

Cavanna, Betty .... **CLC 12**
    See Harrison, Elizabeth (Allen) Cavanna
    See also JRDA; MAICYA 1; SAAS 4;
    SATA 1, 30

Cavendish, Margaret Lucas
    1623-1673 .... **LC 30**
    See also DLB 131, 252, 281; RGEL 2

Caxton, William 1421(?)-1491(?) .... **LC 17**
    See also DLB 170

Cayer, D. M.
    See Duffy, Maureen

Cayrol, Jean 1911- .... **CLC 11**
    See also CA 89-92; DLB 83; EWL 3

Cela (y Trulock), Camilo Jose
    See Cela, Camilo Jose
    See also CWW 2

Cela, Camilo Jose 1916-2002 .... **CLC 4, 13,**
    59, 122; HLC 1; SSC 71
    See Cela (y Trulock), Camilo Jose
    See also BEST 90:2; CA 21-24R; 206;
    CAAS 10; CANR 21, 32, 76; DAM
    MULT; DLBY 1989; EW 13; EWL 3; HW
    1; MTCW 1, 2; RGSF 2; RGWL 2, 3

Celan, Paul .... **CLC 10, 19, 53, 82; PC 10**
    See Antschel, Paul
    See also CDWLB 2; DLB 69; EWL 3;
    RGWL 2, 3

Celine, Louis-Ferdinand .. **CLC 1, 3, 4, 7, 9,**
    15, 47, 124
    See Destouches, Louis-Ferdinand
    See also DLB 72; EW 11; EWL 3; GFL
    1789 to the Present; RGWL 2, 3

Cellini, Benvenuto 1500-1571 .... **LC 7**

Cendrars, Blaise .... **CLC 18, 106**
    See Sauser-Hall, Frederic
    See also DLB 258; EWL 3; GFL 1789 to
    the Present; RGWL 2, 3; WP

Centlivre, Susanna 1669(?)-1723 .... **LC 65**
    See also DLB 84; RGEL 2

Cernuda (y Bidon), Luis 1902-1963 . **CLC 54**
    See also CA 131; 89-92; DAM POET; DLB
    134; EWL 3; GLL 1; HW 1; RGWL 2, 3

Cervantes, Lorna Dee 1954- ..... **HLCS 1; PC
    35**
    See also CA 131; CANR 80; CWP; DLB
    82; EXPP; HW 1; LLW 1

Cervantes (Saavedra), Miguel de
    1547-1616 .... **HLCS; LC 6, 23, 93; SSC
    12; WLC**
    See also AAYA 56; BYA 1, 14; DA; DAB;
    DAC; DAM MST, NOV; EW 2; LAIT 1;
    LATS 1:1; LMFS 1; NFS 8; RGSF 2;
    RGWL 2, 3; TWA

Cesaire, Aime (Fernand) 1913- .... **BLC 1;**
    CLC 19, 32, 112; DC 22; PC 25
    See also BW 2, 3; CA 65-68; CANR 24,
    43, 81; CWW 2; DA3; DAM MULT,
    POET; EWL 3; GFL 1789 to the Present;
    MTCW 1, 2; WP

Chabon, Michael 1963- ... **CLC 55, 149; SSC
    59**
    See also AAYA 45; AMWS 11; CA 139;
    CANR 57, 96, 127; DLB 278; SATA 145

Chabrol, Claude 1930- .... **CLC 16**
    See also CA 110

Chairil Anwar
    See Anwar, Chairil
    See also EWL 3

Challans, Mary 1905-1983
    See Renault, Mary
    See also CA 81-84; 111; CANR 74; DA3;
    MTCW 2; SATA 23; SATA-Obit 36; TEA

Challis, George
    See Faust, Frederick (Schiller)
    See also TCWW 2

Chambers, Aidan 1934- .... **CLC 35**
    See also AAYA 27; CA 25-28R; CANR 12,
    31, 58, 116; JRDA; MAICYA 1, 2; SAAS
    12; SATA 1, 69, 108; WYA; YAW

Chambers, James 1948-
    See Cliff, Jimmy
    See also CA 124

Chambers, Jessie
    See Lawrence, D(avid) H(erbert Richards)
    See also GLL 1

Chambers, Robert W(illiam)
    1865-1933 .... **TCLC 41**
    See also CA 165; DLB 202; HGG; SATA
    107; SUFW 1

Chambers, (David) Whittaker
    1901-1961 .... **TCLC 129**
    See also CA 89-92; DLB 303

Chamisso, Adelbert von
    1781-1838 .... **NCLC 82**
    See also DLB 90; RGWL 2, 3; SUFW 1

Chance, James T.
    See Carpenter, John (Howard)

Chance, John T.
    See Carpenter, John (Howard)

Chandler, Raymond (Thornton)
    1888-1959 .... **SSC 23; TCLC 1, 7**
    See also AAYA 25; AMWC 2; AMWS 4;
    BPFB 1; CA 104; 129; CANR 60, 107;
    CDALB 1929-1941; CMW 4; DA3; DLB
    226, 253; DLBD 6; EWL 3; MSW;
    MTCW 1, 2; NFS 17; RGAL 4; TUS

Chang, Diana 1934- .... **AAL**
    See also CWP; EXPP

Chang, Eileen 1921-1995 .... **AAL; SSC 28**
    See Chang Ai-Ling; Zhang Ailing
    See also CA 166

Chang, Jung 1952- .... **CLC 71**
    See also CA 142

Chang Ai-Ling
    See Chang, Eileen
    See also EWL 3

Channing, William Ellery
    1780-1842 .... **NCLC 17**
    See also DLB 1, 59, 235; RGAL 4

Chao, Patricia 1955- .... **CLC 119**
    See also CA 163

Chaplin, Charles Spencer
    1889-1977 .... **CLC 16**
    See Chaplin, Charlie
    See also CA 81-84; 73-76

Chaplin, Charlie
    See Chaplin, Charles Spencer
    See also DLB 44

Chapman, George 1559(?)-1634 . **DC 19; LC
    22**
    See also BRW 1; DAM DRAM; DLB 62,
    121; LMFS 1; RGEL 2

Chapman, Graham 1941-1989 .... **CLC 21**
    See Monty Python
    See also CA 116; 129; CANR 35, 95

Chapman, John Jay 1862-1933 .... **TCLC 7**
    See also AMWS 14; CA 104; 191

Chapman, Lee
    See Bradley, Marion Zimmer
    See also GLL 1

Chapman, Walker
    See Silverberg, Robert

Chulkov, Mikhail Dmitrievich
1743-1792 .... **LC 2**
See also DLB 150
Churchill, Caryl 1938- .... **CLC 31, 55, 157;
DC 5**
See Churchill, Chick
See also BRWS 4; CA 102; CANR 22, 46,
108; CBD; CWD; DFS 12, 16; DLB 13;
EWL 3; FW; MTCW 1; RGEL 2
Churchill, Charles 1731-1764 .... **LC 3**
See also DLB 109; RGEL 2
Churchill, Chick
See Churchill, Caryl
See also CD 5
Churchill, Sir Winston (Leonard Spencer)
1874-1965 .... **TCLC 113**
See also BRW 6; CA 97-100; CDBLB
1890-1914; DA3; DLB 100; DLBD 16;
LAIT 4; MTCW 1, 2
Chute, Carolyn 1947- .... **CLC 39**
See also CA 123
Ciardi, John (Anthony) 1916-1986 . **CLC 10,
40, 44, 129**
See also CA 5-8R; 118; CAAS 2; CANR 5,
33; CLR 19; CWRI 5; DAM POET; DLB
5; DLBY 1986; INT CANR-5; MAICYA
1, 2; MTCW 1, 2; RGAL 4; SAAS 26;
SATA 1, 65; SATA-Obit 46
Cibber, Colley 1671-1757 .... **LC 66**
See also DLB 84; RGEL 2
Cicero, Marcus Tullius
106B.C.-43B.C. .... **CMLC 3**
See also AW 1; CDWLB 1; DLB 211;
RGWL 2, 3
Cimino, Michael 1943- .... **CLC 16**
See also CA 105
Cioran, E(mil) M. 1911-1995 .... **CLC 64**
See also CA 25-28R; 149; CANR 91; DLB
220; EWL 3
Cisneros, Sandra 1954- .... **CLC 69, 118, 193;
HLC 1; SSC 32, 72**
See also AAYA 9, 53; AMWS 7; CA 131;
CANR 64, 118; CWP; DA3; DAM MULT;
DLB 122, 152; EWL 3; EXPN; FW; HW
1, 2; LAIT 5; LATS 1:2; LLW 1; MAI-
CYA 2; MTCW 2; NFS 2; PFS 19; RGAL
4; RGSF 2; SSFS 3, 13; WLIT 1; YAW
Cixous, Helene 1937- .... **CLC 92**
See also CA 126; CANR 55, 123; CWW 2;
DLB 83, 242; EWL 3; FW; GLL 2;
MTCW 1, 2; TWA
Clair, Rene .... **CLC 20**
See Chomette, Rene Lucien
Clampitt, Amy 1920-1994 .... **CLC 32; PC 19**
See also AMWS 9; CA 110; 146; CANR
29, 79; DLB 105
Clancy, Thomas L., Jr. 1947-
See Clancy, Tom
See also CA 125; 131; CANR 62, 105;
DA3; INT CA-131; MTCW 1, 2
Clancy, Tom .... **CLC 45, 112**
See Clancy, Thomas L., Jr.
See also AAYA 9, 51; BEST 89:1, 90:1;
BPFB 1; BYA 10, 11; CANR 132; CMW
4; CPW; DAM NOV, POP; DLB 227
Clare, John 1793-1864 .. **NCLC 9, 86; PC 23**
See also DAB; DAM POET; DLB 55, 96;
RGEL 2
Clarin
See Alas (y Urena), Leopoldo (Enrique
Garcia)
Clark, Al C.
See Goines, Donald
Clark, (Robert) Brian 1932- .... **CLC 29**
See also CA 41-44R; CANR 67; CBD; CD
5
Clark, Curt
See Westlake, Donald E(dwin)

Clark, Eleanor 1913-1996 .... **CLC 5, 19**
See also CA 9-12R; 151; CANR 41; CN 7;
DLB 6
Clark, J. P.
See Clark Bekederemo, J(ohnson) P(epper)
See also CDWLB 3; DLB 117
Clark, John Pepper
See Clark Bekederemo, J(ohnson) P(epper)
See also AFW; CD 5; CP 7; RGEL 2
Clark, Kenneth (Mackenzie)
1903-1983 .... **TCLC 147**
See also CA 93-96; 109; CANR 36; MTCW
1, 2
Clark, M. R.
See Clark, Mavis Thorpe
Clark, Mavis Thorpe 1909-1999 ...... **CLC 12**
See also CA 57-60; CANR 8, 37, 107; CLR
30; CWRI 5; MAICYA 1, 2; SAAS 5;
SATA 8, 74
Clark, Walter Van Tilburg
1909-1971 .... **CLC 28**
See also CA 9-12R; 33-36R; CANR 63,
113; DLB 9, 206; LAIT 2; RGAL 4;
SATA 8
Clark Bekederemo, J(ohnson) P(epper)
1935- .... **BLC 1; CLC 38; DC 5**
See Clark, J. P.; Clark, John Pepper
See also BW 1; CA 65-68; CANR 16, 72;
DAM DRAM, MULT; DFS 13; EWL 3;
MTCW 1
Clarke, Arthur C(harles) 1917- .... **CLC 1, 4,
13, 18, 35, 136; SSC 3**
See also AAYA 4, 33; BPFB 1; BYA 13;
CA 1-4R; CANR 2, 28, 55, 74, 130; CN
7; CPW; DA3; DAM POP; DLB 261;
JRDA; LAIT 5; MAICYA 1, 2; MTCW 1,
2; SATA 13, 70, 115; SCFW; SFW 4;
SSFS 4, 18; YAW
Clarke, Austin 1896-1974 .... **CLC 6, 9**
See also CA 29-32; 49-52; CAP 2; DAM
POET; DLB 10, 20; EWL 3; RGEL 2
Clarke, Austin C(hesterfield) 1934- .. **BLC 1;
CLC 8, 53; SSC 45**
See also BW 1; CA 25-28R; CAAS 16;
CANR 14, 32, 68; CN 7; DAC; DAM
MULT; DLB 53, 125; DNFS 2; RGSF 2
Clarke, Gillian 1937- .... **CLC 61**
See also CA 106; CP 7; CWP; DLB 40
Clarke, Marcus (Andrew Hislop)
1846-1881 .... **NCLC 19**
See also DLB 230; RGEL 2; RGSF 2
Clarke, Shirley 1925-1997 .... **CLC 16**
See also CA 189
Clash, The
See Headon, (Nicky) Topper; Jones, Mick;
Simonon, Paul; Strummer, Joe
Claudel, Paul (Louis Charles Marie)
1868-1955 .... **TCLC 2, 10**
See also CA 104; 165; DLB 192, 258; EW
8; EWL 3; GFL 1789 to the Present;
RGWL 2, 3; TWA
Claudian 370(?)-404(?) .... **CMLC 46**
See also RGWL 2, 3
Claudius, Matthias 1740-1815 .... **NCLC 75**
See also DLB 97
Clavell, James (duMaresq)
1925-1994 .... **CLC 6, 25, 87**
See also BPFB 1; CA 25-28R; 146; CANR
26, 48; CPW; DA3; DAM NOV, POP;
MTCW 1, 2; NFS 10; RHW
Clayman, Gregory .... **CLC 65**
Cleaver, (Leroy) Eldridge
1935-1998 .... **BLC 1; CLC 30, 119**
See also BW 1, 3; CA 21-24R; 167; CANR
16, 75; DA3; DAM MULT; MTCW 2;
YAW
Cleese, John (Marwood) 1939- .... **CLC 21**
See Monty Python
See also CA 112; 116; CANR 35; MTCW 1

Cleishbotham, Jebediah
See Scott, Sir Walter
Cleland, John 1710-1789 .... **LC 2, 48**
See also DLB 39; RGEL 2
Clemens, Samuel Langhorne 1835-1910
See Twain, Mark
See also CA 104; 135; CDALB 1865-1917;
DA; DA3; DAB; DAC; DAM MST, NOV;
DLB 12, 23, 64, 74, 186, 189; JRDA;
LMFS 1; MAICYA 1, 2; NCFS 4; NFS
20; SATA 100; SSFS 16; YABC 2
Clement of Alexandria
150(?)-215(?) .... **CMLC 41**
Cleophil
See Congreve, William
Clerihew, E.
See Bentley, E(dmund) C(lerihew)
Clerk, N. W.
See Lewis, C(live) S(taples)
Cleveland, John 1613-1658 .... **LC 106**
See also DLB 126; RGEL 2
Cliff, Jimmy .... **CLC 21**
See Chambers, James
See also CA 193
Cliff, Michelle 1946- .... **BLCS; CLC 120**
See also BW 2; CA 116; CANR 39, 72; CD-
WLB 3; DLB 157; FW; GLL 2
Clifford, Lady Anne 1590-1676 .... **LC 76**
See also DLB 151
Clifton, (Thelma) Lucille 1936- .... **BLC 1;
CLC 19, 66, 162; PC 17**
See also AFAW 2; BW 2, 3; CA 49-52;
CANR 2, 24, 42, 76, 97; CLR 5; CP 7;
CSW; CWP; CWRI 5; DA3; DAM MULT,
POET; DLB 5, 41; EXPP; MAICYA 1, 2;
MTCW 1, 2; PFS 1, 14; SATA 20, 69,
128; WP
Clinton, Dirk
See Silverberg, Robert
Clough, Arthur Hugh 1819-1861 ... **NCLC 27**
See also BRW 5; DLB 32; RGEL 2
Clutha, Janet Paterson Frame 1924-2004
See Frame, Janet
See also CA 1-4R; 224; CANR 2, 36, 76;
MTCW 1, 2; SATA 119
Clyne, Terence
See Blatty, William Peter
Cobalt, Martin
See Mayne, William (James Carter)
Cobb, Irvin S(hrewsbury)
1876-1944 .... **TCLC 77**
See also CA 175; DLB 11, 25, 86
Cobbett, William 1763-1835 .... **NCLC 49**
See also DLB 43, 107, 158; RGEL 2
Coburn, D(onald) L(ee) 1938- .... **CLC 10**
See also CA 89-92
Cocteau, Jean (Maurice Eugene Clement)
1889-1963 ...... **CLC 1, 8, 15, 16, 43; DC
17; TCLC 119; WLC**
See also CA 25-28; CANR 40; CAP 2; DA;
DA3; DAB; DAC; DAM DRAM, MST,
NOV; DLB 65, 258; EW 10; EWL 3; GFL
1789 to the Present; MTCW 1, 2; RGWL
2, 3; TWA
Codrescu, Andrei 1946- .... **CLC 46, 121**
See also CA 33-36R; CAAS 19; CANR 13,
34, 53, 76, 125; DA3; DAM POET;
MTCW 2
Coe, Max
See Bourne, Randolph S(illiman)
Coe, Tucker
See Westlake, Donald E(dwin)
Coen, Ethan 1958- .... **CLC 108**
See also AAYA 54; CA 126; CANR 85
Coen, Joel 1955- .... **CLC 108**
See also AAYA 54; CA 126; CANR 119
The Coen Brothers
See Coen, Ethan; Coen, Joel

Cooper, Anthony Ashley 1671-1713 .. **LC 107**
See also DLB 101

Cooper, Douglas 1960- .... **CLC 86**

Cooper, Henry St. John
See Creasey, John

Cooper, J(oan) California (?)- .... **CLC 56**
See also AAYA 12; BW 1; CA 125; CANR
55; DAM MULT; DLB 212

Cooper, James Fenimore
1789-1851 .... **NCLC 1, 27, 54**
See also AAYA 22; AMW; BPFB 1;
CDALB 1640-1865; DA3; DLB 3, 183,
250, 254; LAIT 1; NFS 9; RGAL 4; SATA
19; TUS; WCH

Cooper, Susan Fenimore
1813-1894 .... **NCLC 129**
See also ANW; DLB 239, 254

Coover, Robert (Lowell) 1932- ...... **CLC 3, 7,
15, 32, 46, 87, 161; SSC 15**
See also AMWS 5; BPFB 1; CA 45-48;
CANR 3, 37, 58, 115; CN 7; DAM NOV;
DLB 2, 227; DLBY 1981; EWL 3;
MTCW 1, 2; RGAL 4; RGSF 2

Copeland, Stewart (Armstrong)
1952- .... **CLC 26**

Copernicus, Nicolaus 1473-1543 .... **LC 45**

Coppard, A(lfred) E(dgar)
1878-1957 .... **SSC 21; TCLC 5**
See also BRWS 8; CA 114; 167; DLB 162;
EWL 3; HGG; RGEL 2; RGSF 2; SUFW
1; YABC 1

Coppee, Francois 1842-1908 .... **TCLC 25**
See also CA 170; DLB 217

Coppola, Francis Ford 1939- ... **CLC 16, 126**
See also AAYA 39; CA 77-80; CANR 40,
78; DLB 44

Copway, George 1818-1869 .... **NNAL**
See also DAM MULT; DLB 175, 183

Corbiere, Tristan 1845-1875 .... **NCLC 43**
See also DLB 217; GFL 1789 to the Present

Corcoran, Barbara (Asenath)
1911- .... **CLC 17**
See also AAYA 14; CA 21-24R, 191; CAAE
191; CAAS 2; CANR 11, 28, 48; CLR
50; DLB 52; JRDA; MAICYA 2; MAIC-
YAS 1; RHW; SAAS 20; SATA 3, 77;
SATA-Essay 125

Cordelier, Maurice
See Giraudoux, Jean(-Hippolyte)

Corelli, Marie .... **TCLC 51**
See Mackay, Mary
See also DLB 34, 156; RGEL 2; SUFW 1

Corinna c. 225B.C.-c. 305B.C. ...... **CMLC 72**

Corman, Cid .... **CLC 9**
See Corman, Sidney
See also CAAS 2; DLB 5, 193

Corman, Sidney 1924-2004
See Corman, Cid
See also CA 85-88; 225; CANR 44; CP 7;
DAM POET

Cormier, Robert (Edmund)
1925-2000 .... **CLC 12, 30**
See also AAYA 3, 19; BYA 1, 2, 6, 8, 9;
CA 1-4R; CANR 5, 23, 76, 93; CDALB
1968-1988; CLR 12, 55; DA; DAB; DAC;
DAM MST, NOV; DLB 52; EXPN; INT
CANR-23; JRDA; LAIT 5; MAICYA 1,
2; MTCW 1, 2; NFS 2, 18; SATA 10, 45,
83; SATA-Obit 122; WYA; YAW

Corn, Alfred (DeWitt III) 1943- .... **CLC 33**
See also CA 179; CAAE 179; CAAS 25;
CANR 44; CP 7; CSW; DLB 120, 282;
DLBY 1980

Corneille, Pierre 1606-1684 ... **DC 21; LC 28**
See also DAB; DAM MST; DLB 268; EW
3; GFL Beginnings to 1789; RGWL 2, 3;
TWA

Cornwell, David (John Moore)
1931- .... **CLC 9, 15**
See le Carre, John
See also CA 5-8R; CANR 13, 33, 59, 107,
132; DA3; DAM POP; MTCW 1, 2

Cornwell, Patricia (Daniels) 1956- . **CLC 155**
See also AAYA 16, 56; BPFB 1; CA 134;
CANR 53, 131; CMW 4; CPW; CSW;
DAM POP; DLB 306; MSW; MTCW 1

Corso, (Nunzio) Gregory 1930-2001 . **CLC 1,
11; PC 33**
See also AMWS 12; BG 2; CA 5-8R; 193;
CANR 41, 76, 132; CP 7; DA3; DLB 5,
16, 237; LMFS 2; MTCW 1, 2; WP

Cortazar, Julio 1914-1984 ... **CLC 2, 3, 5, 10,
13, 15, 33, 34, 92; HLC 1; SSC 7, 76**
See also BPFB 1; CA 21-24R; CANR 12,
32, 81; CDWLB 3; DA3; DAM MULT,
NOV; DLB 113; EWL 3; EXPS; HW 1,
2; LAW; MTCW 1, 2; RGSF 2; RGWL 2,
3; SSFS 3, 20; TWA; WLIT 1

Cortes, Hernan 1485-1547 .... **LC 31**

Corvinus, Jakob
See Raabe, Wilhelm (Karl)

Corwin, Cecil
See Kornbluth, C(yril) M.

Cosic, Dobrica 1921- .... **CLC 14**
See also CA 122; 138; CDWLB 4; CWW
2; DLB 181; EWL 3

Costain, Thomas B(ertram)
1885-1965 .... **CLC 30**
See also BYA 3; CA 5-8R; 25-28R; DLB 9;
RHW

Costantini, Humberto 1924(?)-1987 . **CLC 49**
See also CA 131; 122; EWL 3; HW 1

Costello, Elvis 1954- .... **CLC 21**
See also CA 204

Costenoble, Philostene
See Ghelderode, Michel de

Cotes, Cecil V.
See Duncan, Sara Jeannette

Cotter, Joseph Seamon Sr.
1861-1949 .... **BLC 1; TCLC 28**
See also BW 1; CA 124; DAM MULT; DLB
50

Couch, Arthur Thomas Quiller
See Quiller-Couch, Sir Arthur (Thomas)

Coulton, James
See Hansen, Joseph

Couperus, Louis (Marie Anne)
1863-1923 .... **TCLC 15**
See also CA 115; EWL 3; RGWL 2, 3

Coupland, Douglas 1961- .... **CLC 85, 133**
See also AAYA 34; CA 142; CANR 57, 90,
130; CCA 1; CPW; DAC; DAM POP

Court, Wesli
See Turco, Lewis (Putnam)

Courtenay, Bryce 1933- .... **CLC 59**
See also CA 138; CPW

Courtney, Robert
See Ellison, Harlan (Jay)

Cousteau, Jacques-Yves 1910-1997 .. **CLC 30**
See also CA 65-68; 159; CANR 15, 67;
MTCW 1; SATA 38, 98

Coventry, Francis 1725-1754 .... **LC 46**

Coverdale, Miles c. 1487-1569 .... **LC 77**
See also DLB 167

Cowan, Peter (Walkinshaw)
1914-2002 .... **SSC 28**
See also CA 21-24R; CANR 9, 25, 50, 83;
CN 7; DLB 260; RGSF 2

Coward, Noel (Peirce) 1899-1973 . **CLC 1, 9,
29, 51**
See also AITN 1; BRWS 2; CA 17-18; 41-
44R; CANR 35, 132; CAP 2; CDBLB
1914-1945; DA3; DAM DRAM; DFS 3,
6; DLB 10, 245; EWL 3; IDFW 3, 4;
MTCW 1, 2; RGEL 2; TEA

Cowley, Abraham 1618-1667 .... **LC 43**
See also BRW 2; DLB 131, 151; PAB;
RGEL 2

Cowley, Malcolm 1898-1989 .... **CLC 39**
See also AMWS 2; CA 5-8R; 128; CANR
3, 55; DLB 4, 48; DLBY 1981, 1989;
EWL 3; MTCW 1, 2

Cowper, William 1731-1800 ..... **NCLC 8, 94;
PC 40**
See also BRW 3; DA3; DAM POET; DLB
104, 109; RGEL 2

Cox, William Trevor 1928-
See Trevor, William
See also CA 9-12R; CANR 4, 37, 55, 76,
102; DAM NOV; INT CANR-37; MTCW
1, 2; TEA

Coyne, P. J.
See Masters, Hilary

Cozzens, James Gould 1903-1978 . **CLC 1, 4,
11, 92**
See also AMW; BPFB 1; CA 9-12R; 81-84;
CANR 19; CDALB 1941-1968; DLB 9,
294; DLBD 2; DLBY 1984, 1997; EWL
3; MTCW 1, 2; RGAL 4

Crabbe, George 1754-1832 .... **NCLC 26, 121**
See also BRW 3; DLB 93; RGEL 2

Crace, Jim 1946- .... **CLC 157; SSC 61**
See also CA 128; 135; CANR 55, 70, 123;
CN 7; DLB 231; INT CA-135

Craddock, Charles Egbert
See Murfree, Mary Noailles

Craig, A. A.
See Anderson, Poul (William)

Craik, Mrs.
See Craik, Dinah Maria (Mulock)
See also RGEL 2

Craik, Dinah Maria (Mulock)
1826-1887 .... **NCLC 38**
See Craik, Mrs.; Mulock, Dinah Maria
See also DLB 35, 163; MAICYA 1, 2;
SATA 34

Cram, Ralph Adams 1863-1942 ..... **TCLC 45**
See also CA 160

Cranch, Christopher Pearse
1813-1892 .... **NCLC 115**
See also DLB 1, 42, 243

Crane, (Harold) Hart 1899-1932 .... **PC 3;
TCLC 2, 5, 80; WLC**
See also AMW; AMWR 2; CA 104; 127;
CDALB 1917-1929; DA; DA3; DAB;
DAC; DAM MST, POET; DLB 4, 48;
EWL 3; MTCW 1, 2; RGAL 4; TUS

Crane, R(onald) S(almon)
1886-1967 .... **CLC 27**
See also CA 85-88; DLB 63

Crane, Stephen (Townley)
1871-1900 ...... **SSC 7, 56, 70; TCLC 11,
17, 32; WLC**
See also AAYA 21; AMW; AMWC 1; BPFB
1; BYA 3; CA 109; 140; CANR 84;
CDALB 1865-1917; DA; DA3; DAB;
DAC; DAM MST, NOV, POET; DLB 12,
54, 78; EXPN; EXPS; LAIT 2; LMFS 2;
NFS 4, 20; PFS 9; RGAL 4; RGSF 2;
SSFS 4; TUS; WYA; YABC 2

Cranmer, Thomas 1489-1556 .... **LC 95**
See also DLB 132, 213

Cranshaw, Stanley
See Fisher, Dorothy (Frances) Canfield

Crase, Douglas 1944- .... **CLC 58**
See also CA 106

Crashaw, Richard 1612(?)-1649 .... **LC 24**
See also BRW 2; DLB 126; PAB; RGEL 2

Cratinus c. 519B.C.-c. 422B.C. ..... **CMLC 54**
See also LMFS 1

Craven, Margaret 1901-1980 .... **CLC 17**
See also BYA 2; CA 103; CCA 1; DAC;
LAIT 5

Dahlberg, Edward 1900-1977 .. **CLC 1, 7, 14**
See also CA 9-12R; 69-72; CANR 31, 62;
DLB 48; MTCW 1; RGAL 4

Daitch, Susan 1954- .... **CLC 103**
See also CA 161

Dale, Colin .... **TCLC 18**
See Lawrence, T(homas) E(dward)

Dale, George E.
See Asimov, Isaac

Dalton, Roque 1935-1975(?) ..... **HLCS 1; PC
36**
See also CA 176; DLB 283; HW 2

Daly, Elizabeth 1878-1967 .... **CLC 52**
See also CA 23-24; 25-28R; CANR 60;
CAP 2; CMW 4

Daly, Mary 1928- .... **CLC 173**
See also CA 25-28R; CANR 30, 62; FW;
GLL 1; MTCW 1

Daly, Maureen 1921- .... **CLC 17**
See also AAYA 5, 58; BYA 6; CANR 37,
83, 108; CLR 96; JRDA; MAICYA 1, 2;
SAAS 1; SATA 2, 129; WYA; YAW

Damas, Leon-Gontran 1912-1978 .... **CLC 84**
See also BW 1; CA 125; 73-76; EWL 3

Dana, Richard Henry Sr.
1787-1879 .... **NCLC 53**

Daniel, Samuel 1562(?)-1619 .... **LC 24**
See also DLB 62; RGEL 2

Daniels, Brett
See Adler, Renata

Dannay, Frederic 1905-1982 .... **CLC 11**
See Queen, Ellery
See also CA 1-4R; 107; CANR 1, 39; CMW
4; DAM POP; DLB 137; MTCW 1

D'Annunzio, Gabriele 1863-1938 ... **TCLC 6,
40**
See also CA 104; 155; EW 8; EWL 3;
RGWL 2, 3; TWA

Danois, N. le
See Gourmont, Remy(-Marie-Charles) de

Dante 1265-1321 .... **CMLC 3, 18, 39, 70; PC
21; WLCS**
See also DA; DA3; DAB; DAC; DAM
MST, POET; EFS 1; EW 1; LAIT 1;
RGWL 2, 3; TWA; WP

d'Antibes, Germain
See Simenon, Georges (Jacques Christian)

Danticat, Edwidge 1969- .... **CLC 94, 139**
See also AAYA 29; CA 152, 192; CAAE
192; CANR 73, 129; DNFS 1; EXPS;
LATS 1:2; MTCW 1; SSFS 1; YAW

Danvers, Dennis 1947- .... **CLC 70**

Danziger, Paula 1944-2004 .... **CLC 21**
See also AAYA 4, 36; BYA 6, 7, 14; CA
112; 115; CANR 37, 132; CLR 20; JRDA;
MAICYA 1, 2; SATA 36, 63, 102, 149;
SATA-Brief 30; WYA; YAW

Da Ponte, Lorenzo 1749-1838 .... **NCLC 50**

Dario, Ruben 1867-1916 .... **HLC 1; PC 15;
TCLC 4**
See also CA 131; CANR 81; DAM MULT;
DLB 290; EWL 3; HW 1, 2; LAW;
MTCW 1, 2; RGWL 2, 3

Darley, George 1795-1846 .... **NCLC 2**
See also DLB 96; RGEL 2

Darrow, Clarence (Seward)
1857-1938 .... **TCLC 81**
See also CA 164; DLB 303

Darwin, Charles 1809-1882 .... **NCLC 57**
See also BRWS 7; DLB 57, 166; LATS 1:1;
RGEL 2; TEA; WLIT 4

Darwin, Erasmus 1731-1802 .... **NCLC 106**
See also DLB 93; RGEL 2

Daryush, Elizabeth 1887-1977 ...... **CLC 6, 19**
See also CA 49-52; CANR 3, 81; DLB 20

Das, Kamala 1934- .... **CLC 191; PC 43**
See also CA 101; CANR 27, 59; CP 7;
CWP; FW

Dasgupta, Surendranath
1887-1952 .... **TCLC 81**
See also CA 157

**Dashwood, Edmee Elizabeth Monica de la
Pasture** 1890-1943
See Delafield, E. M.
See also CA 119; 154

da Silva, Antonio Jose
1705-1739 .... **NCLC 114**

Daudet, (Louis Marie) Alphonse
1840-1897 .... **NCLC 1**
See also DLB 123; GFL 1789 to the Present;
RGSF 2

d'Aulnoy, Marie-Catherine c.
1650-1705 .... **LC 100**

Daumal, Rene 1908-1944 .... **TCLC 14**
See also CA 114; EWL 3

Davenant, William 1606-1668 .... **LC 13**
See also DLB 58, 126; RGEL 2

Davenport, Guy (Mattison, Jr.)
1927- .... **CLC 6, 14, 38; SSC 16**
See also CA 33-36R; CANR 23, 73; CN 7;
CSW; DLB 130

David, Robert
See Nezval, Vitezslav

Davidson, Avram (James) 1923-1993
See Queen, Ellery
See also CA 101; 171; CANR 26; DLB 8;
FANT; SFW 4; SUFW 1, 2

Davidson, Donald (Grady)
1893-1968 .... **CLC 2, 13, 19**
See also CA 5-8R; 25-28R; CANR 4, 84;
DLB 45

Davidson, Hugh
See Hamilton, Edmond

Davidson, John 1857-1909 .... **TCLC 24**
See also CA 118; 217; DLB 19; RGEL 2

Davidson, Sara 1943- .... **CLC 9**
See also CA 81-84; CANR 44, 68; DLB
185

Davie, Donald (Alfred) 1922-1995 .... **CLC 5,
8, 10, 31; PC 29**
See also BRWS 6; CA 1-4R; 149; CAAS 3;
CANR 1, 44; CP 7; DLB 27; MTCW 1;
RGEL 2

Davie, Elspeth 1919-1995 .... **SSC 52**
See also CA 120; 126; 150; DLB 139

Davies, Ray(mond Douglas) 1944- ... **CLC 21**
See also CA 116; 146; CANR 92

Davies, Rhys 1901-1978 .... **CLC 23**
See also CA 9-12R; 81-84; CANR 4; DLB
139, 191

Davies, (William) Robertson
1913-1995 .... **CLC 2, 7, 13, 25, 42, 75,
91; WLC**
See Marchbanks, Samuel
See also BEST 89:2; BPFB 1; CA 33-36R;
150; CANR 17, 42, 103; CN 7; CPW;
DA; DA3; DAB; DAC; DAM MST, NOV,
POP; DLB 68; EWL 3; HGG; INT CANR-
17; MTCW 1, 2; RGEL 2; TWA

Davies, Sir John 1569-1626 .... **LC 85**
See also DLB 172

Davies, Walter C.
See Kornbluth, C(yril) M.

Davies, William Henry 1871-1940 ... **TCLC 5**
See also CA 104; 179; DLB 19, 174; EWL
3; RGEL 2

Da Vinci, Leonardo 1452-1519 ..... **LC 12, 57,
60**
See also AAYA 40

Davis, Angela (Yvonne) 1944- .... **CLC 77**
See also BW 2, 3; CA 57-60; CANR 10,
81; CSW; DA3; DAM MULT; FW

Davis, B. Lynch
See Bioy Casares, Adolfo; Borges, Jorge
Luis

Davis, Frank Marshall 1905-1987 ...... **BLC 1**
See also BW 2, 3; CA 125; 123; CANR 42,
80; DAM MULT; DLB 51

Davis, Gordon
See Hunt, E(verette) Howard, (Jr.)

Davis, H(arold) L(enoir) 1896-1960 . **CLC 49**
See also ANW; CA 178; 89-92; DLB 9,
206; SATA 114

Davis, Rebecca (Blaine) Harding
1831-1910 .... **SSC 38; TCLC 6**
See also CA 104; 179; DLB 74, 239; FW;
NFS 14; RGAL 4; TUS

Davis, Richard Harding
1864-1916 .... **TCLC 24**
See also CA 114; 179; DLB 12, 23, 78, 79,
189; DLBD 13; RGAL 4

Davison, Frank Dalby 1893-1970 ..... **CLC 15**
See also CA 217; 116; DLB 260

Davison, Lawrence H.
See Lawrence, D(avid) H(erbert Richards)

Davison, Peter (Hubert) 1928- .... **CLC 28**
See also CA 9-12R; CAAS 4; CANR 3, 43,
84; CP 7; DLB 5

Davys, Mary 1674-1732 .... **LC 1, 46**
See also DLB 39

Dawson, (Guy) Fielding (Lewis)
1930-2002 .... **CLC 6**
See also CA 85-88; 202; CANR 108; DLB
130; DLBY 2002

Dawson, Peter
See Faust, Frederick (Schiller)
See also TCWW 2, 2

Day, Clarence (Shepard, Jr.)
1874-1935 .... **TCLC 25**
See also CA 108; 199; DLB 11

Day, John 1574(?)-1640(?) .... **LC 70**
See also DLB 62, 170; RGEL 2

Day, Thomas 1748-1789 .... **LC 1**
See also DLB 39; YABC 1

Day Lewis, C(ecil) 1904-1972 . **CLC 1, 6, 10;
PC 11**
See Blake, Nicholas
See also BRWS 3; CA 13-16; 33-36R;
CANR 34; CAP 1; CWRI 5; DAM POET;
DLB 15, 20; EWL 3; MTCW 1, 2; RGEL
2

Dazai Osamu .... **SSC 41; TCLC 11**
See Tsushima, Shuji
See also CA 164; DLB 182; EWL 3; MJW;
RGSF 2; RGWL 2, 3; TWA

de Andrade, Carlos Drummond
See Drummond de Andrade, Carlos

de Andrade, Mario 1892(?)-1945
See Andrade, Mario de
See also CA 178; HW 2

Deane, Norman
See Creasey, John

Deane, Seamus (Francis) 1940- ...... **CLC 122**
See also CA 118; CANR 42

**de Beauvoir, Simone (Lucie Ernestine Marie
Bertrand)**
See Beauvoir, Simone (Lucie Ernestine
Marie Bertrand) de

de Beer, P.
See Bosman, Herman Charles

de Brissac, Malcolm
See Dickinson, Peter (Malcolm)

de Campos, Alvaro
See Pessoa, Fernando (Antonio Nogueira)

de Chardin, Pierre Teilhard
See Teilhard de Chardin, (Marie Joseph)
Pierre

Dee, John 1527-1608 .... **LC 20**
See also DLB 136, 213

Deer, Sandra 1940- .... **CLC 45**
See also CA 186

De Ferrari, Gabriella 1941- .... **CLC 65**
See also CA 146

de Saint Roman, Arnaud
See Aragon, Louis

Desbordes-Valmore, Marceline
1786-1859 .... **NCLC 97**
See also DLB 217

Descartes, Rene 1596-1650 .... **LC 20, 35**
See also DLB 268; EW 3; GFL Beginnings
to 1789

Deschamps, Eustache 1340(?)-1404 .. **LC 103**
See also DLB 208

De Sica, Vittorio 1901(?)-1974 .... **CLC 20**
See also CA 117

Desnos, Robert 1900-1945 .... **TCLC 22**
See also CA 121; 151; CANR 107; DLB
258; EWL 3; LMFS 2

Destouches, Louis-Ferdinand
1894-1961 .... **CLC 9, 15**
See Celine, Louis-Ferdinand
See also CA 85-88; CANR 28; MTCW 1

de Tolignac, Gaston
See Griffith, D(avid Lewelyn) W(ark)

Deutsch, Babette 1895-1982 .... **CLC 18**
See also BYA 3; CA 1-4R; 108; CANR 4,
79; DLB 45; SATA 1; SATA-Obit 33

Devenant, William 1606-1649 .... **LC 13**

Devkota, Laxmiprasad 1909-1959 . **TCLC 23**
See also CA 123

De Voto, Bernard (Augustine)
1897-1955 .... **TCLC 29**
See also CA 113; 160; DLB 9, 256

De Vries, Peter 1910-1993 ..... **CLC 1, 2, 3, 7,
10, 28, 46**
See also CA 17-20R; 142; CANR 41; DAM
NOV; DLB 6; DLBY 1982; MTCW 1, 2

Dewey, John 1859-1952 .... **TCLC 95**
See also CA 114; 170; DLB 246, 270;
RGAL 4

Dexter, John
See Bradley, Marion Zimmer
See also GLL 1

Dexter, Martin
See Faust, Frederick (Schiller)
See also TCWW 2

Dexter, Pete 1943- .... **CLC 34, 55**
See also BEST 89:2; CA 127; 131; CANR
129; CPW; DAM POP; INT CA-131;
MTCW 1

Diamano, Silmang
See Senghor, Leopold Sedar

Diamond, Neil 1941- .... **CLC 30**
See also CA 108

Diaz del Castillo, Bernal
1496-1584 .... **HLCS 1; LC 31**
See also LAW

di Bassetto, Corno
See Shaw, George Bernard

Dick, Philip K(indred) 1928-1982 ... **CLC 10,
30, 72; SSC 57**
See also AAYA 24; BPFB 1; BYA 11; CA
49-52; 106; CANR 2, 16, 132; CPW;
DA3; DAM NOV, POP; DLB 8; MTCW
1, 2; NFS 5; SCFW; SFW 4

Dickens, Charles (John Huffam)
1812-1870 .... **NCLC 3, 8, 18, 26, 37, 50,
86, 105, 113; SSC 17, 49; WLC**
See also AAYA 23; BRW 5; BRWC 1, 2;
BYA 1, 2, 3, 13, 14; CDBLB 1832-1890;
CLR 95; CMW 4; DA; DA3; DAB; DAC;
DAM MST, NOV; DLB 21, 55, 70, 159,
166; EXPN; HGG; JRDA; LAIT 1, 2;
LATS 1:1; LMFS 1; MAICYA 1, 2; NFS
4, 5, 10, 14, 20; RGEL 2; RGSF 2; SATA
15; SUFW 1; TEA; WCH; WLIT 4; WYA

Dickey, James (Lafayette)
1923-1997 .... **CLC 1, 2, 4, 7, 10, 15, 47,
109; PC 40; TCLC 151**
See also AAYA 50; AITN 1, 2; AMWS 4;
BPFB 1; CA 9-12R; 156; CABS 2; CANR
10, 48, 61, 105; CDALB 1968-1988; CP
7; CPW; CSW; DA3; DAM NOV, POET,
POP; DLB 5, 193; DLBD 7; DLBY 1982,
1993, 1996, 1997, 1998; EWL 3; INT
CANR-10; MTCW 1, 2; NFS 9; PFS 6,
11; RGAL 4; TUS

Dickey, William 1928-1994 .... **CLC 3, 28**
See also CA 9-12R; 145; CANR 24, 79;
DLB 5

Dickinson, Charles 1951- .... **CLC 49**
See also CA 128

Dickinson, Emily (Elizabeth)
1830-1886 ... **NCLC 21, 77; PC 1; WLC**
See also AAYA 22; AMW; AMWR 1;
CDALB 1865-1917; DA; DA3; DAB;
DAC; DAM MST, POET; DLB 1, 243;
EXPP; MAWW; PAB; PFS 1, 2, 3, 4, 5,
6, 8, 10, 11, 13, 16; RGAL 4; SATA 29;
TUS; WP; WYA

Dickinson, Mrs. Herbert Ward
See Phelps, Elizabeth Stuart

Dickinson, Peter (Malcolm) 1927- .. **CLC 12,
35**
See also AAYA 9, 49; BYA 5; CA 41-44R;
CANR 31, 58, 88; CLR 29; CMW 4; DLB
87, 161, 276; JRDA; MAICYA 1, 2;
SATA 5, 62, 95, 150; SFW 4; WYA; YAW

Dickson, Carr
See Carr, John Dickson

Dickson, Carter
See Carr, John Dickson

Diderot, Denis 1713-1784 .... **LC 26**
See also EW 4; GFL Beginnings to 1789;
LMFS 1; RGWL 2, 3

Didion, Joan 1934- . **CLC 1, 3, 8, 14, 32, 129**
See also AITN 1; AMWS 4; CA 5-8R;
CANR 14, 52, 76, 125; CDALB 1968-
1988; CN 7; DA3; DAM NOV; DLB 2,
173, 185; DLBY 1981, 1986; EWL 3;
MAWW; MTCW 1, 2; NFS 3; RGAL 4;
TCWW 2; TUS

Dietrich, Robert
See Hunt, E(verette) Howard, (Jr.)

Difusa, Pati
See Almodovar, Pedro

Dillard, Annie 1945- .... **CLC 9, 60, 115**
See also AAYA 6, 43; AMWS 6; ANW; CA
49-52; CANR 3, 43, 62, 90, 125; DA3;
DAM NOV; DLB 275, 278; DLBY 1980;
LAIT 4, 5; MTCW 1, 2; NCFS 1; RGAL
4; SATA 10, 140; TUS

Dillard, R(ichard) H(enry) W(ilde)
1937- .... **CLC 5**
See also CA 21-24R; CAAS 7; CANR 10;
CP 7; CSW; DLB 5, 244

Dillon, Eilis 1920-1994 .... **CLC 17**
See also CA 9-12R, 182; 147; CAAE 182;
CAAS 3; CANR 4, 38, 78; CLR 26; MAI-
CYA 1, 2; MAICYAS 1; SATA 2, 74;
SATA-Essay 105; SATA-Obit 83; YAW

Dimont, Penelope
See Mortimer, Penelope (Ruth)

Dinesen, Isak ..... **CLC 10, 29, 95; SSC 7, 75**
See Blixen, Karen (Christentze Dinesen)
See also EW 10; EWL 3; EXPS; FW; HGG;
LAIT 3; MTCW 1; NCFS 2; NFS 9;
RGSF 2; RGWL 2, 3; SSFS 3, 6, 13;
WLIT 2

Ding Ling .... **CLC 68**
See Chiang, Pin-chin
See also RGWL 3

Diphusa, Patty
See Almodovar, Pedro

Disch, Thomas M(ichael) 1940- ... **CLC 7, 36**
See Disch, Tom
See also AAYA 17; BPFB 1; CA 21-24R;
CAAS 4; CANR 17, 36, 54, 89; CLR 18;
CP 7; DA3; DLB 8; HGG; MAICYA 1, 2;
MTCW 1, 2; SAAS 15; SATA 92; SCFW;
SFW 4; SUFW 2

Disch, Tom
See Disch, Thomas M(ichael)
See also DLB 282

d'Isly, Georges
See Simenon, Georges (Jacques Christian)

Disraeli, Benjamin 1804-1881 ... **NCLC 2, 39,
79**
See also BRW 4; DLB 21, 55; RGEL 2

Ditcum, Steve
See Crumb, R(obert)

Dixon, Paige
See Corcoran, Barbara (Asenath)

Dixon, Stephen 1936- .... **CLC 52; SSC 16**
See also AMWS 12; CA 89-92; CANR 17,
40, 54, 91; CN 7; DLB 130

Djebar, Assia 1936- .... **CLC 182**
See also CA 188; EWL 3; RGWL 3; WLIT
2

Doak, Annie
See Dillard, Annie

Dobell, Sydney Thompson
1824-1874 .... **NCLC 43**
See also DLB 32; RGEL 2

Doblin, Alfred .... **TCLC 13**
See Doeblin, Alfred
See also CDWLB 2; EWL 3; RGWL 2, 3

Dobroliubov, Nikolai Aleksandrovich
See Dobrolyubov, Nikolai Alexandrovich
See also DLB 277

Dobrolyubov, Nikolai Alexandrovich
1836-1861 .... **NCLC 5**
See Dobroliubov, Nikolai Aleksandrovich

Dobson, Austin 1840-1921 .... **TCLC 79**
See also DLB 35, 144

Dobyns, Stephen 1941- .... **CLC 37**
See also AMWS 13; CA 45-48; CANR 2,
18, 99; CMW 4; CP 7

Doctorow, E(dgar) L(aurence)
1931- .... **CLC 6, 11, 15, 18, 37, 44, 65,
113**
See also AAYA 22; AITN 2; AMWS 4;
BEST 89:3; BPFB 1; CA 45-48; CANR
2, 33, 51, 76, 97, 133; CDALB 1968-
1988; CN 7; CPW; DA3; DAM NOV,
POP; DLB 2, 28, 173; DLBY 1980; EWL
3; LAIT 3; MTCW 1, 2; NFS 6; RGAL 4;
RHW; TUS

Dodgson, Charles L(utwidge) 1832-1898
See Carroll, Lewis
See also CLR 2; DA; DA3; DAB; DAC;
DAM MST, NOV, POET; MAICYA 1, 2;
SATA 100; YABC 2

Dodsley, Robert 1703-1764 .... **LC 97**
See also DLB 95; RGEL 2

Dodson, Owen (Vincent) 1914-1983 .. **BLC 1;
CLC 79**
See also BW 1; CA 65-68; 110; CANR 24;
DAM MULT; DLB 76

Doeblin, Alfred 1878-1957 .... **TCLC 13**
See Doblin, Alfred
See also CA 110; 141; DLB 66

Doerr, Harriet 1910-2002 .... **CLC 34**
See also CA 117; 122; 213; CANR 47; INT
CA-122; LATS 1:2

Domecq, H(onorio Bustos)
See Bioy Casares, Adolfo

Domecq, H(onorio) Bustos
See Bioy Casares, Adolfo; Borges, Jorge
Luis

Domini, Rey
See Lorde, Audre (Geraldine)
See also GLL 1

Dominique
See Proust, (Valentin-Louis-George-Eugene)
Marcel

Don, A
See Stephen, Sir Leslie

Drummond of Hawthornden, William
1585-1649 .... **LC 83**
See also DLB 121, 213; RGEL 2

Drury, Allen (Stuart) 1918-1998 .... **CLC 37**
See also CA 57-60; 170; CANR 18, 52; CN
7; INT CANR-18

Dryden, John 1631-1700 ..... **DC 3; LC 3, 21;
PC 25; WLC**
See also BRW 2; CDBLB 1660-1789; DA;
DAB; DAC; DAM DRAM, MST, POET;
DLB 80, 101, 131; EXPP; IDTP; LMFS
1; RGEL 2; TEA; WLIT 3

du Bellay, Joachim 1524-1560 .... **LC 92**
See also GFL Beginnings to 1789; RGWL
2, 3

Duberman, Martin (Bauml) 1930- ..... **CLC 8**
See also CA 1-4R; CAD; CANR 2, 63; CD
5

Dubie, Norman (Evans) 1945- .... **CLC 36**
See also CA 69-72; CANR 12, 115; CP 7;
DLB 120; PFS 12

Du Bois, W(illiam) E(dward) B(urghardt)
1868-1963 ..... **BLC 1; CLC 1, 2, 13, 64,
96; HR 2; WLC**
See also AAYA 40; AFAW 1, 2; AMWC 1;
AMWS 2; BW 1, 3; CA 85-88; CANR
34, 82, 132; CDALB 1865-1917; DA;
DA3; DAC; DAM MST, MULT, NOV;
DLB 47, 50, 91, 246, 284; EWL 3; EXPP;
LAIT 2; MTCW 1, 2; NCFS 1;
PFS 13; RGAL 4; SATA 42

Dubus, Andre 1936-1999 ..... **CLC 13, 36, 97;
SSC 15**
See also AMWS 7; CA 21-24R; 177; CANR
17; CN 7; CSW; DLB 130; INT CANR-
17; RGAL 4; SSFS 10

Duca Minimo
See D'Annunzio, Gabriele

Ducharme, Rejean 1941- .... **CLC 74**
See also CA 165; DLB 60

du Chatelet, Emilie 1706-1749 .... **LC 96**

Duchen, Claire .... **CLC 65**

Duclos, Charles Pinot- 1704-1772 .... **LC 1**
See also GFL Beginnings to 1789

Dudek, Louis 1918-2001 .... **CLC 11, 19**
See also CA 45-48; 215; CAAS 14; CANR
1; CP 7; DLB 88

Duerrenmatt, Friedrich 1921-1990 ... **CLC 1,
4, 8, 11, 15, 43, 102**
See Durrenmatt, Friedrich
See also CA 17-20R; CANR 33; CMW 4;
DAM DRAM; DLB 69, 124; MTCW 1, 2

Duffy, Bruce 1953(?)- .... **CLC 50**
See also CA 172

Duffy, Maureen 1933- .... **CLC 37**
See also CA 25-28R; CANR 33, 68; CBD;
CN 7; CP 7; CWD; CWP; DFS 15; DLB
14; FW; MTCW 1

Du Fu
See Tu Fu
See also RGWL 2, 3

Dugan, Alan 1923-2003 .... **CLC 2, 6**
See also CA 81-84; 220; CANR 119; CP 7;
DLB 5; PFS 10

du Gard, Roger Martin
See Martin du Gard, Roger

Duhamel, Georges 1884-1966 .... **CLC 8**
See also CA 81-84; 25-28R; CANR 35;
DLB 65; EWL 3; GFL 1789 to the
Present; MTCW 1

Dujardin, Edouard (Emile Louis)
1861-1949 .... **TCLC 13**
See also CA 109; DLB 123

Duke, Raoul
See Thompson, Hunter S(tockton)

Dulles, John Foster 1888-1959 .... **TCLC 72**
See also CA 115; 149

Dumas, Alexandre (pere)
1802-1870 .... **NCLC 11, 71; WLC**
See also AAYA 22; BYA 3; DA; DA3;
DAB; DAC; DAM MST, NOV; DLB 119,
192; EW 6; GFL 1789 to the Present;
LAIT 1, 2; NFS 14, 19; RGWL 2, 3;
SATA 18; TWA; WCH

Dumas, Alexandre (fils) 1824-1895 ...... **DC 1;
NCLC 9**
See also DLB 192; GFL 1789 to the Present;
RGWL 2, 3

Dumas, Claudine
See Malzberg, Barry N(athaniel)

Dumas, Henry L. 1934-1968 .... **CLC 6, 62**
See also BW 1; CA 85-88; DLB 41; RGAL
4

du Maurier, Daphne 1907-1989 .. **CLC 6, 11,
59; SSC 18**
See also AAYA 37; BPFB 1; BRWS 3; CA
5-8R; 128; CANR 6, 55; CMW 4; CPW;
DA3; DAB; DAC; DAM MST, POP;
DLB 191; HGG; LAIT 3; MSW; MTCW
1, 2; NFS 12; RGEL 2; RGSF 2; RHW;
SATA 27; SATA-Obit 60; SSFS 14, 16;
TEA

Du Maurier, George 1834-1896 ..... **NCLC 86**
See also DLB 153, 178; RGEL 2

Dunbar, Paul Laurence 1872-1906 ... **BLC 1;
PC 5; SSC 8; TCLC 2, 12; WLC**
See also AFAW 1, 2; AMWS 2; BW 1, 3;
CA 104; 124; CANR 79; CDALB 1865-
1917; DA; DA3; DAC; DAM MST,
MULT, POET; DLB 50, 54, 78; EXPP;
RGAL 4; SATA 34

Dunbar, William 1460(?)-1520(?) .... **LC 20**
See also BRWS 8; DLB 132, 146; RGEL 2

Dunbar-Nelson, Alice .... **HR 2**
See Nelson, Alice Ruth Moore Dunbar

Duncan, Dora Angela
See Duncan, Isadora

Duncan, Isadora 1877(?)-1927 .... **TCLC 68**
See also CA 118; 149

Duncan, Lois 1934- .... **CLC 26**
See also AAYA 4, 34; BYA 6, 8; CA 1-4R;
CANR 2, 23, 36, 111; CLR 29; JRDA;
MAICYA 1, 2; MAICYAS 1; SAAS 2;
SATA 1, 36, 75, 133, 141; SATA-Essay
141; WYA; YAW

Duncan, Robert (Edward)
1919-1988 .... **CLC 1, 2, 4, 7, 15, 41, 55;
PC 2**
See also BG 2; CA 9-12R; 124; CANR 28,
62; DAM POET; DLB 5, 16, 193; EWL
3; MTCW 1, 2; PFS 13; RGAL 4; WP

Duncan, Sara Jeannette
1861-1922 .... **TCLC 60**
See also CA 157; DLB 92

Dunlap, William 1766-1839 .... **NCLC 2**
See also DLB 30, 37, 59; RGAL 4

Dunn, Douglas (Eaglesham) 1942- .... **CLC 6,
40**
See also BRWS 10; CA 45-48; CANR 2,
33, 126; CP 7; DLB 40; MTCW 1

Dunn, Katherine (Karen) 1945- .... **CLC 71**
See also CA 33-36R; CANR 72; HGG;
MTCW 1

Dunn, Stephen (Elliott) 1939- .... **CLC 36**
See also AMWS 11; CA 33-36R; CANR
12, 48, 53, 105; CP 7; DLB 105; PFS 21

Dunne, Finley Peter 1867-1936 ...... **TCLC 28**
See also CA 108; 178; DLB 11, 23; RGAL
4

Dunne, John Gregory 1932-2003 ..... **CLC 28**
See also CA 25-28R; 222; CANR 14, 50;
CN 7; DLBY 1980

Dunsany, Lord .... **TCLC 2, 59**
See Dunsany, Edward John Moreton Drax
Plunkett
See also DLB 77, 153, 156, 255; FANT;
IDTP; RGEL 2; SFW 4; SUFW 1

**Dunsany, Edward John Moreton Drax
Plunkett** 1878-1957
See Dunsany, Lord
See also CA 104; 148; DLB 10; MTCW 1

Duns Scotus, John 1266(?)-1308 ... **CMLC 59**
See also DLB 115

du Perry, Jean
See Simenon, Georges (Jacques Christian)

Durang, Christopher (Ferdinand)
1949- .... **CLC 27, 38**
See also CA 105; CAD; CANR 50, 76, 130;
CD 5; MTCW 1

Duras, Marguerite 1914-1996 . **CLC 3, 6, 11,
20, 34, 40, 68, 100; SSC 40**
See also BPFB 1; CA 25-28R; 151; CANR
50; CWW 2; DLB 83; EWL 3; GFL 1789
to the Present; IDFW 4; MTCW 1, 2;
RGWL 2, 3; TWA

Durban, (Rosa) Pam 1947- .... **CLC 39**
See also CA 123; CANR 98; CSW

Durcan, Paul 1944- .... **CLC 43, 70**
See also CA 134; CANR 123; CP 7; DAM
POET; EWL 3

Durfey, Thomas 1653-1723 .... **LC 94**
See also DLB 80; RGEL 2

Durkheim, Emile 1858-1917 .... **TCLC 55**

Durrell, Lawrence (George)
1912-1990 ..... **CLC 1, 4, 6, 8, 13, 27, 41**
See also BPFB 1; BRWS 1; CA 9-12R; 132;
CANR 40, 77; CDBLB 1945-1960; DAM
NOV; DLB 15, 27, 204; DLBY 1990;
EWL 3; MTCW 1, 2; RGEL 2; SFW 4;
TEA

Durrenmatt, Friedrich
See Duerrenmatt, Friedrich
See also CDWLB 2; EW 13; EWL 3;
RGWL 2, 3

Dutt, Michael Madhusudan
1824-1873 .... **NCLC 118**

Dutt, Toru 1856-1877 .... **NCLC 29**
See also DLB 240

Dwight, Timothy 1752-1817 .... **NCLC 13**
See also DLB 37; RGAL 4

Dworkin, Andrea 1946- .... **CLC 43, 123**
See also CA 77-80; CAAS 21; CANR 16,
39, 76, 96; FW; GLL 1; INT CANR-16;
MTCW 1, 2

Dwyer, Deanna
See Koontz, Dean R(ay)

Dwyer, K. R.
See Koontz, Dean R(ay)

Dybek, Stuart 1942- .... **CLC 114; SSC 55**
See also CA 97-100; CANR 39; DLB 130

Dye, Richard
See De Voto, Bernard (Augustine)

Dyer, Geoff 1958- .... **CLC 149**
See also CA 125; CANR 88

Dyer, George 1755-1841 .... **NCLC 129**
See also DLB 93

Dylan, Bob 1941- .... **CLC 3, 4, 6, 12, 77; PC
37**
See also CA 41-44R; CANR 108; CP 7;
DLB 16

Dyson, John 1943- .... **CLC 70**
See also CA 144

Dzyubin, Eduard Georgievich 1895-1934
See Bagritsky, Eduard
See also CA 170

E. V. L.
See Lucas, E(dward) V(errall)

Eagleton, Terence (Francis) 1943- .. **CLC 63,
132**
See also CA 57-60; CANR 7, 23, 68, 115;
DLB 242; LMFS 2; MTCW 1, 2

Eagleton, Terry
See Eagleton, Terence (Francis)

Early, Jack
See Scoppettone, Sandra
See also GLL 1

Ferguson, Niall 1964- .... **CLC 134**
See also CA 190

Ferguson, Samuel 1810-1886 .... **NCLC 33**
See also DLB 32; RGEL 2

Fergusson, Robert 1750-1774 .... **LC 29**
See also DLB 109; RGEL 2

Ferling, Lawrence
See Ferlinghetti, Lawrence (Monsanto)

Ferlinghetti, Lawrence (Monsanto)
1919(?)- .... **CLC 2, 6, 10, 27, 111; PC 1**
See also CA 5-8R; CANR 3, 41, 73, 125;
CDALB 1941-1968; CP 7; DA3; DAM
POET; DLB 5, 16; MTCW 1, 2; RGAL 4;
WP

Fern, Fanny
See Parton, Sara Payson Willis

Fernandez, Vicente Garcia Huidobro
See Huidobro Fernandez, Vicente Garcia

Fernandez-Armesto, Felipe .... **CLC 70**

Fernandez de Lizardi, Jose Joaquin
See Lizardi, Jose Joaquin Fernandez de

Ferre, Rosario 1938- ...... **CLC 139; HLCS 1;
SSC 36**
See also CA 131; CANR 55, 81; CWW 2;
DLB 145; EWL 3; HW 1, 2; LAWS 1;
MTCW 1; WLIT 1

Ferrer, Gabriel (Francisco Victor) Miro
See Miro (Ferrer), Gabriel (Francisco
Victor)

Ferrier, Susan (Edmonstone)
1782-1854 .... **NCLC 8**
See also DLB 116; RGEL 2

Ferrigno, Robert 1948(?)- .... **CLC 65**
See also CA 140; CANR 125

Ferron, Jacques 1921-1985 .... **CLC 94**
See also CA 117; 129; CCA 1; DAC; DLB
60; EWL 3

Feuchtwanger, Lion 1884-1958 .... **TCLC 3**
See also CA 104; 187; DLB 66; EWL 3

Feuerbach, Ludwig 1804-1872 ..... **NCLC 139**
See also DLB 133

Feuillet, Octave 1821-1890 .... **NCLC 45**
See also DLB 192

Feydeau, Georges (Leon Jules Marie)
1862-1921 .... **TCLC 22**
See also CA 113; 152; CANR 84; DAM
DRAM; DLB 192; EWL 3; GFL 1789 to
the Present; RGWL 2, 3

Fichte, Johann Gottlieb
1762-1814 .... **NCLC 62**
See also DLB 90

Ficino, Marsilio 1433-1499 .... **LC 12**
See also LMFS 1

Fiedeler, Hans
See Doeblin, Alfred

Fiedler, Leslie A(aron) 1917-2003 ..... **CLC 4,
13, 24**
See also AMWS 13; CA 9-12R; 212; CANR
7, 63; CN 7; DLB 28, 67; EWL 3; MTCW
1, 2; RGAL 4; TUS

Field, Andrew 1938- .... **CLC 44**
See also CA 97-100; CANR 25

Field, Eugene 1850-1895 .... **NCLC 3**
See also DLB 23, 42, 140; DLBD 13; MAI-
CYA 1, 2; RGAL 4; SATA 16

Field, Gans T.
See Wellman, Manly Wade

Field, Michael 1915-1971 .... **TCLC 43**
See also CA 29-32R

Field, Peter
See Hobson, Laura Z(ametkin)
See also TCWW 2

Fielding, Helen 1958- .... **CLC 146**
See also CA 172; CANR 127; DLB 231

Fielding, Henry 1707-1754 .... **LC 1, 46, 85;
WLC**
See also BRW 3; BRWR 1; CDBLB 1660-
1789; DA; DA3; DAB; DAC; DAM
DRAM, MST, NOV; DLB 39, 84, 101;
NFS 18; RGEL 2; TEA; WLIT 3

Fielding, Sarah 1710-1768 .... **LC 1, 44**
See also DLB 39; RGEL 2; TEA

Fields, W. C. 1880-1946 .... **TCLC 80**
See also DLB 44

Fierstein, Harvey (Forbes) 1954- ..... **CLC 33**
See also CA 123; 129; CAD; CD 5; CPW;
DA3; DAM DRAM, POP; DFS 6; DLB
266; GLL

Figes, Eva 1932- .... **CLC 31**
See also CA 53-56; CANR 4, 44, 83; CN 7;
DLB 14, 271; FW

Filippo, Eduardo de
See de Filippo, Eduardo

Finch, Anne 1661-1720 .... **LC 3; PC 21**
See also BRWS 9; DLB 95

Finch, Robert (Duer Claydon)
1900-1995 .... **CLC 18**
See also CA 57-60; CANR 9, 24, 49; CP 7;
DLB 88

Findley, Timothy (Irving Frederick)
1930-2002 .... **CLC 27, 102**
See also CA 25-28R; 206; CANR 12, 42,
69, 109; CCA 1; CN 7; DAC; DAM MST;
DLB 53; FANT; RHW

Fink, William
See Mencken, H(enry) L(ouis)

Firbank, Louis 1942-
See Reed, Lou
See also CA 117

Firbank, (Arthur Annesley) Ronald
1886-1926 .... **TCLC 1**
See also BRWS 2; CA 104; 177; DLB 36;
EWL 3; RGEL 2

Fish, Stanley
See Fish, Stanley Eugene

Fish, Stanley E.
See Fish, Stanley Eugene

Fish, Stanley Eugene 1938- .... **CLC 142**
See also CA 112; 132; CANR 90; DLB 67

Fisher, Dorothy (Frances) Canfield
1879-1958 .... **TCLC 87**
See also CA 114; 136; CANR 80; CLR 71,;
CWRI 5; DLB 9, 102, 284; MAICYA 1,
2; YABC 1

Fisher, M(ary) F(rances) K(ennedy)
1908-1992 .... **CLC 76, 87**
See also CA 77-80; 138; CANR 44; MTCW
1

Fisher, Roy 1930- .... **CLC 25**
See also CA 81-84; CAAS 10; CANR 16;
CP 7; DLB 40

Fisher, Rudolph 1897-1934 .... **BLC 2; HR 2;
SSC 25; TCLC 11**
See also BW 1, 3; CA 107; 124; CANR 80;
DAM MULT; DLB 51, 102

Fisher, Vardis (Alvero) 1895-1968 .... **CLC 7;
TCLC 140**
See also CA 5-8R; 25-28R; CANR 68; DLB
9, 206; RGAL 4; TCWW 2

Fiske, Tarleton
See Bloch, Robert (Albert)

Fitch, Clarke
See Sinclair, Upton (Beall)

Fitch, John IV
See Cormier, Robert (Edmund)

Fitzgerald, Captain Hugh
See Baum, L(yman) Frank

FitzGerald, Edward 1809-1883 .... **NCLC 9**
See also BRW 4; DLB 32; RGEL 2

Fitzgerald, F(rancis) Scott (Key)
1896-1940 ... **SSC 6, 31, 75; TCLC 1, 6,
14, 28, 55, 157; WLC**
See also AAYA 24; AITN 1; AMW; AMWC
2; AMWR 1; BPFB 1; CA 110; 123;
CDALB 1917-1929; DA; DA3; DAB;
DAC; DAM MST, NOV; DLB 4, 9, 86,
219, 273; DLBD 1, 15, 16; DLBY 1981,
1996; EWL 3; EXPN; EXPS; LAIT 3;
MTCW 1, 2; NFS 2, 19, 20; RGAL 4;
RGSF 2; SSFS 4, 15; TUS

Fitzgerald, Penelope 1916-2000 . **CLC 19, 51,
61, 143**
See also BRWS 5; CA 85-88; 190; CAAS
10; CANR 56, 86, 131; CN 7; DLB 14,
194; EWL 3; MTCW 2

Fitzgerald, Robert (Stuart)
1910-1985 .... **CLC 39**
See also CA 1-4R; 114; CANR 1; DLBY
1980

FitzGerald, Robert D(avid)
1902-1987 .... **CLC 19**
See also CA 17-20R; DLB 260; RGEL 2

Fitzgerald, Zelda (Sayre)
1900-1948 .... **TCLC 52**
See also AMWS 9; CA 117; 126; DLBY
1984

Flanagan, Thomas (James Bonner)
1923-2002 .... **CLC 25, 52**
See also CA 108; 206; CANR 55; CN 7;
DLBY 1980; INT CA-108; MTCW 1;
RHW

Flaubert, Gustave 1821-1880 .... **NCLC 2, 10,
19, 62, 66, 135; SSC 11, 60; WLC**
See also DA; DA3; DAB; DAC; DAM
MST, NOV; DLB 119, 301; EW 7; EXPS;
GFL 1789 to the Present; LAIT 2; LMFS
1; NFS 14; RGSF 2; RGWL 2, 3; SSFS
6; TWA

Flavius Josephus
See Josephus, Flavius

Flecker, Herman Elroy
See Flecker, (Herman) James Elroy

Flecker, (Herman) James Elroy
1884-1915 .... **TCLC 43**
See also CA 109; 150; DLB 10, 19; RGEL
2

Fleming, Ian (Lancaster) 1908-1964 . **CLC 3,
30**
See also AAYA 26; BPFB 1; CA 5-8R;
CANR 59; CDBLB 1945-1960; CMW 4;
CPW; DA3; DAM POP; DLB 87, 201;
MSW; MTCW 1, 2; RGEL 2; SATA 9;
TEA; YAW

Fleming, Thomas (James) 1927- ...... **CLC 37**
See also CA 5-8R; CANR 10, 102; INT
CANR-10; SATA 8

Fletcher, John 1579-1625 .... **DC 6; LC 33**
See also BRW 2; CDBLB Before 1660;
DLB 58; RGEL 2; TEA

Fletcher, John Gould 1886-1950 .... **TCLC 35**
See also CA 107; 167; DLB 4, 45; LMFS
2; RGAL 4

Fleur, Paul
See Pohl, Frederik

Flieg, Helmut
See Heym, Stefan

Flooglebuckle, Al
See Spiegelman, Art

Flora, Fletcher 1914-1969
See Queen, Ellery
See also CA 1-4R; CANR 3, 85

Flying Officer X
See Bates, H(erbert) E(rnest)

Fo, Dario 1926- .... **CLC 32, 109; DC 10**
See also CA 116; 128; CANR 68, 114;
CWW 2; DA3; DAM DRAM; DLBY
1997; EWL 3; MTCW 1, 2

Fogarty, Jonathan Titulescu Esq.
See Farrell, James T(homas)

Frazer, Robert Caine
  See Creasey, John
Frazer, Sir James George
  See Frazer, J(ames) G(eorge)
Frazier, Charles 1950- .... **CLC 109**
  See also AAYA 34; CA 161; CANR 126;
  CSW; DLB 292
Frazier, Ian 1951- .... **CLC 46**
  See also CA 130; CANR 54, 93
Frederic, Harold 1856-1898 .... **NCLC 10**
  See also AMW; DLB 12, 23; DLBD 13;
  RGAL 4
Frederick, John
  See Faust, Frederick (Schiller)
  See also TCWW 2
Frederick the Great 1712-1786 .... **LC 14**
Fredro, Aleksander 1793-1876 .... **NCLC 8**
Freeling, Nicolas 1927-2003 .... **CLC 38**
  See also CA 49-52; 218; CAAS 12; CANR
  1, 17, 50, 84; CMW 4; CN 7; DLB 87
Freeman, Douglas Southall
  1886-1953 .... **TCLC 11**
  See also CA 109; 195; DLB 17; DLBD 17
Freeman, Judith 1946- .... **CLC 55**
  See also CA 148; CANR 120; DLB 256
Freeman, Mary E(leanor) Wilkins
  1852-1930 .... **SSC 1, 47; TCLC 9**
  See also CA 106; 177; DLB 12, 78, 221;
  EXPS; FW; HGG; MAWW; RGAL 4;
  RGSF 2; SSFS 4, 8; SUFW 1; TUS
Freeman, R(ichard) Austin
  1862-1943 .... **TCLC 21**
  See also CA 113; CANR 84; CMW 4; DLB
  70
French, Albert 1943- .... **CLC 86**
  See also BW 3; CA 167
French, Antonia
  See Kureishi, Hanif
French, Marilyn 1929- .. **CLC 10, 18, 60, 177**
  See also BPFB 1; CA 69-72; CANR 3, 31;
  CN 7; CPW; DAM DRAM, NOV, POP;
  FW; INT CANR-31; MTCW 1, 2
French, Paul
  See Asimov, Isaac
Freneau, Philip Morin 1752-1832 .. **NCLC 1, 111**
  See also AMWS 2; DLB 37, 43; RGAL 4
Freud, Sigmund 1856-1939 .... **TCLC 52**
  See also CA 115; 133; CANR 69; DLB 296;
  EW 8; EWL 3; LATS 1:1; MTCW 1, 2;
  NCFS 3; TWA
Freytag, Gustav 1816-1895 .... **NCLC 109**
  See also DLB 129
Friedan, Betty (Naomi) 1921- .... **CLC 74**
  See also CA 65-68; CANR 18, 45, 74; DLB
  246; FW; MTCW 1, 2; NCFS 5
Friedlander, Saul 1932- .... **CLC 90**
  See also CA 117; 130; CANR 72
Friedman, B(ernard) H(arper)
  1926- .... **CLC 7**
  See also CA 1-4R; CANR 3, 48
Friedman, Bruce Jay 1930- ...... **CLC 3, 5, 56**
  See also CA 9-12R; CAD; CANR 25, 52,
  101; CD 5; CN 7; DLB 2, 28, 244; INT
  CANR-25; SSFS 18
Friel, Brian 1929- .... **CLC 5, 42, 59, 115; DC 8; SSC 76**
  See also BRWS 5; CA 21-24R; CANR 33,
  69, 131; CBD; CD 5; DFS 11; DLB 13;
  EWL 3; MTCW 1; RGEL 2; TEA
Friis-Baastad, Babbis Ellinor
  1921-1970 .... **CLC 12**
  See also CA 17-20R; 134; SATA 7
Frisch, Max (Rudolf) 1911-1991 ... **CLC 3, 9, 14, 18, 32, 44; TCLC 121**
  See also CA 85-88; 134; CANR 32, 74; CD-
  WLB 2; DAM DRAM, NOV; DLB 69,
  124; EW 13; EWL 3; MTCW 1, 2; RGWL
  2, 3

Fromentin, Eugene (Samuel Auguste)
  1820-1876 .... **NCLC 10, 125**
  See also DLB 123; GFL 1789 to the Present
Frost, Frederick
  See Faust, Frederick (Schiller)
  See also TCWW 2
Frost, Robert (Lee) 1874-1963 .. **CLC 1, 3, 4, 9, 10, 13, 15, 26, 34, 44; PC 1, 39; WLC**
  See also AAYA 21; AMW; AMWR 1; CA
  89-92; CANR 33; CDALB 1917-1929;
  CLR 67; DA; DA3; DAB; DAC; DAM
  MST, POET; DLB 54, 284; DLBD 7;
  EWL 3; EXPP; MTCW 1, 2; PAB; PFS 1,
  2, 3, 4, 5, 6, 7, 10, 13; RGAL 4; SATA
  14; TUS; WP; WYA
Froude, James Anthony
  1818-1894 .... **NCLC 43**
  See also DLB 18, 57, 144
Froy, Herald
  See Waterhouse, Keith (Spencer)
Fry, Christopher 1907- .... **CLC 2, 10, 14**
  See also BRWS 3; CA 17-20R; CAAS 23;
  CANR 9, 30, 74, 132; CBD; CD 5; CP 7;
  DAM DRAM; DLB 13; EWL 3; MTCW
  1, 2; RGEL 2; SATA 66; TEA
Frye, (Herman) Northrop
  1912-1991 .... **CLC 24, 70**
  See also CA 5-8R; 133; CANR 8, 37; DLB
  67, 68, 246; EWL 3; MTCW 1, 2; RGAL
  4; TWA
Fuchs, Daniel 1909-1993 .... **CLC 8, 22**
  See also CA 81-84; 142; CAAS 5; CANR
  40; DLB 9, 26, 28; DLBY 1993
Fuchs, Daniel 1934- .... **CLC 34**
  See also CA 37-40R; CANR 14, 48
Fuentes, Carlos 1928- .. **CLC 3, 8, 10, 13, 22, 41, 60, 113; HLC 1; SSC 24; WLC**
  See also AAYA 4, 45; AITN 2; BPFB 1;
  CA 69-72; CANR 10, 32, 68, 104; CD-
  WLB 3; CWW 2; DA; DA3; DAB; DAC;
  DAM MST, MULT, NOV; DLB 113;
  DNFS 2; EWL 3; HW 1, 2; LAIT 3; LATS
  1:2; LAW; LAWS 1; LMFS 2; MTCW 1,
  2; NFS 8; RGSF 2; RGWL 2, 3; TWA;
  WLIT 1
Fuentes, Gregorio Lopez y
  See Lopez y Fuentes, Gregorio
Fuertes, Gloria 1918-1998 .... **PC 27**
  See also CA 178; 180; DLB 108; HW 2;
  SATA 115
Fugard, (Harold) Athol 1932- . **CLC 5, 9, 14, 25, 40, 80; DC 3**
  See also AAYA 17; AFW; CA 85-88; CANR
  32, 54, 118; CD 5; DAM DRAM; DFS 3,
  6, 10; DLB 225; DNFS 1, 2; EWL 3;
  LATS 1:2; MTCW 1; RGEL 2; WLIT 2
Fugard, Sheila 1932- .... **CLC 48**
  See also CA 125
Fukuyama, Francis 1952- .... **CLC 131**
  See also CA 140; CANR 72, 125
Fuller, Charles (H.), (Jr.) 1939- .... **BLC 2; CLC 25; DC 1**
  See also BW 2; CA 108; 112; CAD; CANR
  87; CD 5; DAM DRAM, MULT; DFS 8;
  DLB 38, 266; EWL 3; INT CA-112;
  MTCW 1
Fuller, Henry Blake 1857-1929 .... **TCLC 103**
  See also CA 108; 177; DLB 12; RGAL 4
Fuller, John (Leopold) 1937- .... **CLC 62**
  See also CA 21-24R; CANR 9, 44; CP 7;
  DLB 40
Fuller, Margaret
  See Ossoli, Sarah Margaret (Fuller)
  See also AMWS 2; DLB 183, 223, 239
Fuller, Roy (Broadbent) 1912-1991 ... **CLC 4, 28**
  See also BRWS 7; CA 5-8R; 135; CAAS
  10; CANR 53, 83; CWRI 5; DLB 15, 20;
  EWL 3; RGEL 2; SATA 87

Fuller, Sarah Margaret
  See Ossoli, Sarah Margaret (Fuller)
Fuller, Sarah Margaret
  See Ossoli, Sarah Margaret (Fuller)
  See also DLB 1, 59, 73
Fulton, Alice 1952- .... **CLC 52**
  See also CA 116; CANR 57, 88; CP 7;
  CWP; DLB 193
Furphy, Joseph 1843-1912 .... **TCLC 25**
  See Collins, Tom
  See also CA 163; DLB 230; EWL 3; RGEL
  2
Fuson, Robert H(enderson) 1927- .... **CLC 70**
  See also CA 89-92; CANR 103
Fussell, Paul 1924- .... **CLC 74**
  See also BEST 90:1; CA 17-20R; CANR 8,
  21, 35, 69; INT CANR-21; MTCW 1, 2
Futabatei, Shimei 1864-1909 .... **TCLC 44**
  See Futabatei Shimei
  See also CA 162; MJW
Futabatei Shimei
  See Futabatei, Shimei
  See also DLB 180; EWL 3
Futrelle, Jacques 1875-1912 .... **TCLC 19**
  See also CA 113; 155; CMW 4
Gaboriau, Emile 1835-1873 .... **NCLC 14**
  See also CMW 4; MSW
Gadda, Carlo Emilio 1893-1973 ...... **CLC 11; TCLC 144**
  See also CA 89-92; DLB 177; EWL 3
Gaddis, William 1922-1998 ... **CLC 1, 3, 6, 8, 10, 19, 43, 86**
  See also AMWS 4; BPFB 1; CA 17-20R;
  172; CANR 21, 48; CN 7; DLB 2, 278;
  EWL 3; MTCW 1, 2; RGAL 4
Gaelique, Moruen le
  See Jacob, (Cyprien-)Max
Gage, Walter
  See Inge, William (Motter)
Gaiman, Neil (Richard) 1960- .... **CLC 195**
  See also AAYA 19, 42; CA 133; CANR 81,
  129; DLB 261; HGG; SATA 85, 146;
  SFW 4; SUFW 2
Gaines, Ernest J(ames) 1933- .. **BLC 2; CLC 3, 11, 18, 86, 181; SSC 68**
  See also AAYA 18; AFAW 1, 2; AITN 1;
  BPFB 2; BW 2, 3; BYA 6; CA 9-12R;
  CANR 6, 24, 42, 75, 126; CDALB 1968-
  1988; CLR 62; CN 7; CSW; DA3; DAM
  MULT; DLB 2, 33, 152; DLBY 1980;
  EWL 3; EXPN; LAIT 5; LATS 1:2;
  MTCW 1, 2; NFS 5, 7, 16; RGAL 4;
  RGSF 2; RHW; SATA 86; SSFS 5; YAW
Gaitskill, Mary (Lawrence) 1954- .... **CLC 69**
  See also CA 128; CANR 61; DLB 244
Gaius Suetonius Tranquillus
  See Suetonius
Galdos, Benito Perez
  See Perez Galdos, Benito
  See also EW 7
Gale, Zona 1874-1938 .... **TCLC 7**
  See also CA 105; 153; CANR 84; DAM
  DRAM; DFS 17; DLB 9, 78, 228; RGAL
  4
Galeano, Eduardo (Hughes) 1940- . **CLC 72; HLCS 1**
  See also CA 29-32R; CANR 13, 32, 100;
  HW 1
Galiano, Juan Valera y Alcala
  See Valera y Alcala-Galiano, Juan
Galilei, Galileo 1564-1642 .... **LC 45**
Gallagher, Tess 1943- .... **CLC 18, 63; PC 9**
  See also CA 106; CP 7; CWP; DAM POET;
  DLB 120, 212, 244; PFS 16

Genet, Jean 1910-1986 .. **CLC 1, 2, 5, 10, 14, 44, 46; TCLC 128**
See also CA 13-16R; CANR 18; DA3; DAM DRAM; DFS 10; DLB 72; DLBY 1986; EW 13; EWL 3; GFL 1789 to the Present; GLL 1; LMFS 2; MTCW 1, 2; RGWL 2, 3; TWA

Gent, Peter 1942- .... **CLC 29**
See also AITN 1; CA 89-92; DLBY 1982

Gentile, Giovanni 1875-1944 .... **TCLC 96**
See also CA 119

Gentlewoman in New England, A
See Bradstreet, Anne

Gentlewoman in Those Parts, A
See Bradstreet, Anne

Geoffrey of Monmouth c. 1100-1155 .... **CMLC 44**
See also DLB 146; TEA

George, Jean
See George, Jean Craighead

George, Jean Craighead 1919- .... **CLC 35**
See also AAYA 8; BYA 2, 4; CA 5-8R; CANR 25; CLR 1; 80; DLB 52; JRDA; MAICYA 1, 2; SATA 2, 68, 124; WYA; YAW

George, Stefan (Anton) 1868-1933 . **TCLC 2, 14**
See also CA 104; 193; EW 8; EWL 3

Georges, Georges Martin
See Simenon, Georges (Jacques Christian)

Gerald of Wales c. 1146-c. 1223 ... **CMLC 60**

Gerhardi, William Alexander
See Gerhardie, William Alexander

Gerhardie, William Alexander 1895-1977 .... **CLC 5**
See also CA 25-28R; 73-76; CANR 18; DLB 36; RGEL 2

Gerson, Jean 1363-1429 .... **LC 77**
See also DLB 208

Gersonides 1288-1344 .... **CMLC 49**
See also DLB 115

Gerstler, Amy 1956- .... **CLC 70**
See also CA 146; CANR 99

Gertler, T. .... **CLC 34**
See also CA 116; 121

Gertsen, Aleksandr Ivanovich
See Herzen, Aleksandr Ivanovich

Ghalib .... **NCLC 39, 78**
See Ghalib, Asadullah Khan

Ghalib, Asadullah Khan 1797-1869
See Ghalib
See also DAM POET; RGWL 2, 3

Ghelderode, Michel de 1898-1962 ..... **CLC 6, 11; DC 15**
See also CA 85-88; CANR 40, 77; DAM DRAM; EW 11; EWL 3; TWA

Ghiselin, Brewster 1903-2001 .... **CLC 23**
See also CA 13-16R; CAAS 10; CANR 13; CP 7

Ghose, Aurabinda 1872-1950 .... **TCLC 63**
See Ghose, Aurobindo
See also CA 163

Ghose, Aurobindo
See Ghose, Aurabinda
See also EWL 3

Ghose, Zulfikar 1935- .... **CLC 42**
See also CA 65-68; CANR 67; CN 7; CP 7; EWL 3

Ghosh, Amitav 1956- .... **CLC 44, 153**
See also CA 147; CANR 80; CN 7; WWE 1

Giacosa, Giuseppe 1847-1906 .... **TCLC 7**
See also CA 104

Gibb, Lee
See Waterhouse, Keith (Spencer)

Gibbon, Edward 1737-1794 .... **LC 97**
See also BRW 3; DLB 104; RGEL 2

Gibbon, Lewis Grassic .... **TCLC 4**
See Mitchell, James Leslie
See also RGEL 2

Gibbons, Kaye 1960- .... **CLC 50, 88, 145**
See also AAYA 34; AMWS 10; CA 151; CANR 75, 127; CSW; DA3; DAM POP; DLB 292; MTCW 1; NFS 3; RGAL 4; SATA 117

Gibran, Kahlil 1883-1931 . **PC 9; TCLC 1, 9**
See also CA 104; 150; DA3; DAM POET, POP; EWL 3; MTCW 2

Gibran, Khalil
See Gibran, Kahlil

Gibson, William 1914- .... **CLC 23**
See also CA 9-12R; CAD 2; CANR 9, 42, 75, 125; CD 5; DA; DAB; DAC; DAM DRAM, MST; DFS 2; DLB 7; LAIT 2; MTCW 2; SATA 66; YAW

Gibson, William (Ford) 1948- ... **CLC 39, 63, 186, 192; SSC 52**
See also AAYA 12, 59; BPFB 2; CA 126; 133; CANR 52, 90, 106; CN 7; CPW; DA3; DAM POP; DLB 251; MTCW 2; SCFW 2; SFW 4

Gide, Andre (Paul Guillaume) 1869-1951 ..... **SSC 13; TCLC 5, 12, 36; WLC**
See also CA 104; 124; DA; DA3; DAB; DAC; DAM MST, NOV; DLB 65; EW 8; EWL 3; GFL 1789 to the Present; MTCW 1, 2; RGSF 2; RGWL 2, 3; TWA

Gifford, Barry (Colby) 1946- .... **CLC 34**
See also CA 65-68; CANR 9, 30, 40, 90

Gilbert, Frank
See De Voto, Bernard (Augustine)

Gilbert, W(illiam) S(chwenck) 1836-1911 .... **TCLC 3**
See also CA 104; 173; DAM DRAM, POET; RGEL 2; SATA 36

Gilbreth, Frank B(unker), Jr. 1911-2001 .... **CLC 17**
See also CA 9-12R; SATA 2

Gilchrist, Ellen (Louise) 1935- .. **CLC 34, 48, 143; SSC 14, 63**
See also BPFB 2; CA 113; 116; CANR 41, 61, 104; CN 7; CPW; CSW; DAM POP; DLB 130; EWL 3; EXPS; MTCW 1, 2; RGAL 4; RGSF 2; SSFS 9

Giles, Molly 1942- .... **CLC 39**
See also CA 126; CANR 98

Gill, Eric 1882-1940 .... **TCLC 85**
See Gill, (Arthur) Eric (Rowton Peter Joseph)

Gill, (Arthur) Eric (Rowton Peter Joseph) 1882-1940
See Gill, Eric
See also CA 120; DLB 98

Gill, Patrick
See Creasey, John

Gillette, Douglas .... **CLC 70**

Gilliam, Terry (Vance) 1940- .... **CLC 21, 141**
See Monty Python
See also AAYA 19, 59; CA 108; 113; CANR 35; INT CA-113

Gillian, Jerry
See Gilliam, Terry (Vance)

Gilliatt, Penelope (Ann Douglass) 1932-1993 .... **CLC 2, 10, 13, 53**
See also AITN 2; CA 13-16R; 141; CANR 49; DLB 14

Gilman, Charlotte (Anna) Perkins (Stetson) 1860-1935 ...... **SSC 13, 62; TCLC 9, 37, 117**
See also AMWS 11; BYA 11; CA 106; 150; DLB 221; EXPS; FW; HGG; LAIT 2; MAWW; MTCW 1; RGAL 4; RGSF 2; SFW 4; SSFS 1, 18

Gilmour, David 1946- .... **CLC 35**

Gilpin, William 1724-1804 .... **NCLC 30**

Gilray, J. D.
See Mencken, H(enry) L(ouis)

Gilroy, Frank D(aniel) 1925- .... **CLC 2**
See also CA 81-84; CAD; CANR 32, 64, 86; CD 5; DFS 17; DLB 7

Gilstrap, John 1957(?)- .... **CLC 99**
See also CA 160; CANR 101

Ginsberg, Allen 1926-1997 .... **CLC 1, 2, 3, 4, 6, 13, 36, 69, 109; PC 4, 47; TCLC 120; WLC**
See also AAYA 33; AITN 1; AMWC 1; AMWS 2; BG 2; CA 1-4R; 157; CANR 2, 41, 63, 95; CDALB 1941-1968; CP 7; DA; DA3; DAB; DAC; DAM MST, POET; DLB 5, 16, 169, 237; EWL 3; GLL 1; LMFS 2; MTCW 1, 2; PAB; PFS 5; RGAL 4; TUS; WP

Ginzburg, Eugenia .... **CLC 59**
See Ginzburg, Evgeniia

Ginzburg, Evgeniia 1904-1977
See Ginzburg, Eugenia
See also DLB 302

Ginzburg, Natalia 1916-1991 .... **CLC 5, 11, 54, 70; SSC 65; TCLC 156**
See also CA 85-88; 135; CANR 33; DFS 14; DLB 177; EW 13; EWL 3; MTCW 1, 2; RGWL 2, 3

Giono, Jean 1895-1970 .... **CLC 4, 11; TCLC 124**
See also CA 45-48; 29-32R; CANR 2, 35; DLB 72; EWL 3; GFL 1789 to the Present; MTCW 1; RGWL 2, 3

Giovanni, Nikki 1943- ...... **BLC 2; CLC 2, 4, 19, 64, 117; PC 19; WLCS**
See also AAYA 22; AITN 1; BW 2, 3; CA 29-32R; CAAS 6; CANR 18, 41, 60, 91, 130; CDALBS; CLR 6, 73; CP 7; CSW; CWP; CWRI 5; DA; DA3; DAB; DAC; DAM MST, MULT, POET; DLB 5, 41; EWL 3; EXPP; INT CANR-18; MAICYA 1, 2; MTCW 1, 2; PFS 17; RGAL 4; SATA 24, 107; TUS; YAW

Giovene, Andrea 1904-1998 .... **CLC 7**
See also CA 85-88

Gippius, Zinaida (Nikolaevna) 1869-1945
See Hippius, Zinaida (Nikolaevna)
See also CA 106; 212

Giraudoux, Jean(-Hippolyte) 1882-1944 .... **TCLC 2, 7**
See also CA 104; 196; DAM DRAM; DLB 65; EW 9; EWL 3; GFL 1789 to the Present; RGWL 2, 3; TWA

Gironella, Jose Maria (Pous) 1917-2003 .... **CLC 11**
See also CA 101; 212; EWL 3; RGWL 2, 3

Gissing, George (Robert) 1857-1903 .... **SSC 37; TCLC 3, 24, 47**
See also BRW 5; CA 105; 167; DLB 18, 135, 184; RGEL 2; TEA

Giurlani, Aldo
See Palazzeschi, Aldo

Gladkov, Fedor Vasil'evich
See Gladkov, Fyodor (Vasilyevich)
See also DLB 272

Gladkov, Fyodor (Vasilyevich) 1883-1958 .... **TCLC 27**
See Gladkov, Fedor Vasil'evich
See also CA 170; EWL 3

Glancy, Diane 1941- .... **NNAL**
See also CA 136; 225; CAAE 225; CAAS 24; CANR 87; DLB 175

Glanville, Brian (Lester) 1931- .... **CLC 6**
See also CA 5-8R; CAAS 9; CANR 3, 70; CN 7; DLB 15, 139; SATA 42

Goryan, Sirak
    See Saroyan, William
Gosse, Edmund (William)
    1849-1928 .... **TCLC 28**
    See also CA 117; DLB 57, 144, 184; RGEL
    2
Gotlieb, Phyllis (Fay Bloom) 1926- .. **CLC 18**
    See also CA 13-16R; CANR 7; DLB 88,
    251; SFW 4
Gottesman, S. D.
    See Kornbluth, C(yril) M.; Pohl, Frederik
Gottfried von Strassburg fl. c.
    1170-1215 .... **CMLC 10**
    See also CDWLB 2; DLB 138; EW 1;
    RGWL 2, 3
Gotthelf, Jeremias 1797-1854 .... **NCLC 117**
    See also DLB 133; RGWL 2, 3
Gottschalk, Laura Riding
    See Jackson, Laura (Riding)
Gould, Lois 1932(?)-2002 .... **CLC 4, 10**
    See also CA 77-80; 208; CANR 29; MTCW
    1
Gould, Stephen Jay 1941-2002 .... **CLC 163**
    See also AAYA 26; BEST 90:2; CA 77-80;
    205; CANR 10, 27, 56, 75, 125; CPW;
    INT CANR-27; MTCW 1, 2
Gourmont, Remy(-Marie-Charles) de
    1858-1915 .... **TCLC 17**
    See also CA 109; 150; GFL 1789 to the
    Present; MTCW 2
Gournay, Marie le Jars de
    See de Gournay, Marie le Jars
Govier, Katherine 1948- .... **CLC 51**
    See also CA 101; CANR 18, 40, 128; CCA
    1
Gower, John c. 1330-1408 .... **LC 76; PC 59**
    See also BRW 1; DLB 146; RGEL 2
Goyen, (Charles) William
    1915-1983 .... **CLC 5, 8, 14, 40**
    See also AITN 2; CA 5-8R; 110; CANR 6,
    71; DLB 2, 218; DLBY 1983; EWL 3;
    INT CANR-6
Goytisolo, Juan 1931- .... **CLC 5, 10, 23, 133;**
    HLC 1
    See also CA 85-88; CANR 32, 61, 131;
    CWW 2; DAM MULT; EWL 3; GLL 2;
    HW 1, 2; MTCW 1, 2
Gozzano, Guido 1883-1916 .... **PC 10**
    See also CA 154; DLB 114; EWL 3
Gozzi, (Conte) Carlo 1720-1806 .... **NCLC 23**
Grabbe, Christian Dietrich
    1801-1836 .... **NCLC 2**
    See also DLB 133; RGWL 2, 3
Grace, Patricia Frances 1937- .... **CLC 56**
    See also CA 176; CANR 118; CN 7; EWL
    3; RGSF 2
Gracian y Morales, Baltasar
    1601-1658 .... **LC 15**
Gracq, Julien .... **CLC 11, 48**
    See Poirier, Louis
    See also CWW 2; DLB 83; GFL 1789 to
    the Present
Grade, Chaim 1910-1982 .... **CLC 10**
    See also CA 93-96; 107; EWL 3
Graduate of Oxford, A
    See Ruskin, John
Grafton, Garth
    See Duncan, Sara Jeannette
Grafton, Sue 1940- .... **CLC 163**
    See also AAYA 11, 49; BEST 90:3; CA 108;
    CANR 31, 55, 111; CMW 4; CPW; CSW;
    DA3; DAM POP; DLB 226; FW; MSW
Graham, John
    See Phillips, David Graham
Graham, Jorie 1951- .... **CLC 48, 118; PC 59**
    See also CA 111; CANR 63, 118; CP 7;
    CWP; DLB 120; EWL 3; PFS 10, 17

Graham, R(obert) B(ontine) Cunninghame
    See Cunninghame Graham, Robert
    (Gallnigad) Bontine
    See also DLB 98, 135, 174; RGEL 2; RGSF
    2
Graham, Robert
    See Haldeman, Joe (William)
Graham, Tom
    See Lewis, (Harry) Sinclair
Graham, W(illiam) S(idney)
    1918-1986 .... **CLC 29**
    See also BRWS 7; CA 73-76; 118; DLB 20;
    RGEL 2
Graham, Winston (Mawdsley)
    1910-2003 .... **CLC 23**
    See also CA 49-52; 218; CANR 2, 22, 45,
    66; CMW 4; CN 7; DLB 77; RHW
Grahame, Kenneth 1859-1932 ...... **TCLC 64,**
    136
    See also BYA 5; CA 108; 136; CANR 80;
    CLR 5; CWRI 5; DA3; DAB; DLB 34,
    141, 178; FANT; MAICYA 1, 2; MTCW
    2; NFS 20; RGEL 2; SATA 100; TEA;
    WCH; YABC 1
Granger, Darius John
    See Marlowe, Stephen
Granin, Daniil 1918- .... **CLC 59**
    See also DLB 302
Granovsky, Timofei Nikolaevich
    1813-1855 .... **NCLC 75**
    See also DLB 198
Grant, Skeeter
    See Spiegelman, Art
Granville-Barker, Harley
    1877-1946 .... **TCLC 2**
    See Barker, Harley Granville
    See also CA 104; 204; DAM DRAM;
    RGEL 2
Granzotto, Gianni
    See Granzotto, Giovanni Battista
Granzotto, Giovanni Battista
    1914-1985 .... **CLC 70**
    See also CA 166
Grass, Guenter (Wilhelm) 1927- ... **CLC 1, 2,**
    4, 6, 11, 15, 22, 32, 49, 88; WLC
    See Grass, Gunter (Wilhelm)
    See also BPFB 2; CA 13-16R; CANR 20,
    75, 93, 133; CDWLB 2; DA; DA3; DAB;
    DAC; DAM MST, NOV; DLB 75, 124;
    EW 13; EWL 3; MTCW 1, 2; RGWL 2,
    3; TWA
Grass, Gunter (Wilhelm)
    See Grass, Guenter (Wilhelm)
    See also CWW 2
Gratton, Thomas
    See Hulme, T(homas) E(rnest)
Grau, Shirley Ann 1929- .... **CLC 4, 9, 146;**
    SSC 15
    See also CA 89-92; CANR 22, 69; CN 7;
    CSW; DLB 2, 218; INT CA-89-92,
    CANR-22; MTCW 1
Gravel, Fern
    See Hall, James Norman
Graver, Elizabeth 1964- .... **CLC 70**
    See also CA 135; CANR 71, 129
Graves, Richard Perceval
    1895-1985 .... **CLC 44**
    See also CA 65-68; CANR 9, 26, 51
Graves, Robert (von Ranke)
    1895-1985 .. **CLC 1, 2, 6, 11, 39, 44, 45;**
    PC 6
    See also BPFB 2; BRW 7; BYA 4; CA 5-8R;
    117; CANR 5, 36; CDBLB 1914-1945;
    DA3; DAB; DAC; DAM MST, POET;
    DLB 20, 100, 191; DLBD 18; DLBY
    1985; EWL 3; LATS 1:1; MTCW 1, 2;
    NCFS 2; RGEL 2; RHW; SATA 45; TEA
Graves, Valerie
    See Bradley, Marion Zimmer

Gray, Alasdair (James) 1934- .... **CLC 41**
    See also BRWS 9; CA 126; CANR 47, 69,
    106; CN 7; DLB 194, 261; HGG; INT
    CA-126; MTCW 1, 2; RGSF 2; SUFW 2
Gray, Amlin 1946- .... **CLC 29**
    See also CA 138
Gray, Francine du Plessix 1930- ..... **CLC 22,**
    153
    See also BEST 90:3; CA 61-64; CAAS 2;
    CANR 11, 33, 75, 81; DAM NOV; INT
    CANR-11; MTCW 1, 2
Gray, John (Henry) 1866-1934 ...... **TCLC 19**
    See also CA 119; 162; RGEL 2
Gray, Simon (James Holliday)
    1936- .... **CLC 9, 14, 36**
    See also AITN 1; CA 21-24R; CAAS 3;
    CANR 32, 69; CD 5; DLB 13; EWL 3;
    MTCW 1; RGEL 2
Gray, Spalding 1941-2004 .... **CLC 49, 112;**
    DC 7
    See also CA 128; 225; CAD; CANR 74;
    CD 5; CPW; DAM POP; MTCW 2
Gray, Thomas 1716-1771 .... **LC 4, 40; PC 2;**
    WLC
    See also BRW 3; CDBLB 1660-1789; DA;
    DA3; DAB; DAC; DAM MST; DLB 109;
    EXPP; PAB; PFS 9; RGEL 2; TEA; WP
Grayson, David
    See Baker, Ray Stannard
Grayson, Richard (A.) 1951- .... **CLC 38**
    See also CA 85-88; 210; CAAE 210; CANR
    14, 31, 57; DLB 234
Greeley, Andrew M(oran) 1928- ...... **CLC 28**
    See also BPFB 2; CA 5-8R; CAAS 7;
    CANR 7, 43, 69, 104; CMW 4; CPW;
    DA3; DAM POP; MTCW 1, 2
Green, Anna Katharine
    1846-1935 .... **TCLC 63**
    See also CA 112; 159; CMW 4; DLB 202,
    221; MSW
Green, Brian
    See Card, Orson Scott
Green, Hannah
    See Greenberg, Joanne (Goldenberg)
Green, Hannah 1927(?)-1996 .... **CLC 3**
    See also CA 73-76; CANR 59, 93; NFS 10
Green, Henry .... **CLC 2, 13, 97**
    See Yorke, Henry Vincent
    See also BRWS 2; CA 175; DLB 15; EWL
    3; RGEL 2
Green, Julian (Hartridge) 1900-1998
    See Green, Julien
    See also CA 21-24R; 169; CANR 33, 87;
    CWW 2; DLB 4, 72; MTCW 1
Green, Julien .... **CLC 3, 11, 77**
    See Green, Julian (Hartridge)
    See also EWL 3; GFL 1789 to the Present;
    MTCW 2
Green, Paul (Eliot) 1894-1981 .... **CLC 25**
    See also AITN 1; CA 5-8R; 103; CANR 3;
    DAM DRAM; DLB 7, 9, 249; DLBY
    1981; RGAL 4
Greenaway, Peter 1942- .... **CLC 159**
    See also CA 127
Greenberg, Ivan 1908-1973
    See Rahv, Philip
    See also CA 85-88
Greenberg, Joanne (Goldenberg)
    1932- .... **CLC 7, 30**
    See also AAYA 12; CA 5-8R; CANR 14,
    32, 69; CN 7; SATA 25; YAW
Greenberg, Richard 1959(?)- .... **CLC 57**
    See also CA 138; CAD; CD 5
Greenblatt, Stephen J(ay) 1943- ...... **CLC 70**
    See also CA 49-52; CANR 115

Harvey, Caroline
See Trollope, Joanna
Harvey, Gabriel 1550(?)-1631 .... **LC 88**
See also DLB 167, 213, 281
Harwood, Ronald 1934- .... **CLC 32**
See also CA 1-4R; CANR 4, 55; CBD; CD
5; DAM DRAM, MST; DLB 13
Hasegawa Tatsunosuke
See Futabatei, Shimei
Hasek, Jaroslav (Matej Frantisek)
1883-1923 .... **SSC 69; TCLC 4**
See also CA 104; 129; CDWLB 4; DLB
215; EW 9; EWL 3; MTCW 1, 2; RGSF
2; RGWL 2, 3
Hass, Robert 1941- ... **CLC 18, 39, 99; PC 16**
See also AMWS 6; CA 111; CANR 30, 50,
71; CP 7; DLB 105, 206; EWL 3; RGAL
4; SATA 94
Hastings, Hudson
See Kuttner, Henry
Hastings, Selina .... **CLC 44**
Hathorne, John 1641-1717 .... **LC 38**
Hatteras, Amelia
See Mencken, H(enry) L(ouis)
Hatteras, Owen .... **TCLC 18**
See Mencken, H(enry) L(ouis); Nathan,
George Jean
Hauptmann, Gerhart (Johann Robert)
1862-1946 .... **SSC 37; TCLC 4**
See also CA 104; 153; CDWLB 2; DAM
DRAM; DLB 66, 118; EW 8; EWL 3;
RGSF 2; RGWL 2, 3; TWA
Havel, Vaclav 1936- ..... **CLC 25, 58, 65, 123;**
DC 6
See also CA 104; CANR 36, 63, 124; CD-
WLB 4; CWW 2; DA3; DAM DRAM;
DFS 10; DLB 232; EWL 3; LMFS 2;
MTCW 1, 2; RGWL 3
Haviaras, Stratis .... **CLC 33**
See Chaviaras, Strates
Hawes, Stephen 1475(?)-1529(?) .... **LC 17**
See also DLB 132; RGEL 2
Hawkes, John (Clendennin Burne, Jr.)
1925-1998 .. **CLC 1, 2, 3, 4, 7, 9, 14, 15,**
27, 49
See also BPFB 2; CA 1-4R; 167; CANR 2,
47, 64; CN 7; DLB 2, 7, 227; DLBY
1980, 1998; EWL 3; MTCW 1, 2; RGAL
4
Hawking, S. W.
See Hawking, Stephen W(illiam)
Hawking, Stephen W(illiam) 1942- . **CLC 63,**
105
See also AAYA 13; BEST 89:1; CA 126;
129; CANR 48, 115; CPW; DA3; MTCW
2
Hawkins, Anthony Hope
See Hope, Anthony
Hawthorne, Julian 1846-1934 .... **TCLC 25**
See also CA 165; HGG
Hawthorne, Nathaniel 1804-1864 ... **NCLC 2,**
10, 17, 23, 39, 79, 95; SSC 3, 29, 39;
WLC
See also AAYA 18; AMW; AMWC 1;
AMWR 1; BPFB 2; BYA 3; CDALB
1640-1865; DA; DA3; DAB; DAC; DAM
MST, NOV; DLB 1, 74, 183, 223, 269;
EXPN; EXPS; HGG; LAIT 1; NFS 1, 20;
RGAL 4; RGSF 2; SSFS 1, 7, 11, 15;
SUFW 1; TUS; WCH; YABC 2
Haxton, Josephine Ayres 1921-
See Douglas, Ellen
See also CA 115; CANR 41, 83
Hayaseca y Eizaguirre, Jorge
See Echegaray (y Eizaguirre), Jose (Maria
Waldo)
Hayashi, Fumiko 1904-1951 .... **TCLC 27**
See Hayashi Fumiko
See also CA 161

Hayashi Fumiko
See Hayashi, Fumiko
See also DLB 180; EWL 3
Haycraft, Anna (Margaret) 1932-
See Ellis, Alice Thomas
See also CA 122; CANR 85, 90; MTCW 2
Hayden, Robert E(arl) 1913-1980 ..... **BLC 2;**
CLC 5, 9, 14, 37; PC 6
See also AFAW 1, 2; AMWS 2; BW 1, 3;
CA 69-72; 97-100; CABS 2; CANR 24,
75, 82; CDALB 1941-1968; DA; DAC;
DAM MST, MULT, POET; DLB 5, 76;
EWL 3; EXPP; MTCW 1, 2; PFS 1;
RGAL 4; SATA 19; SATA-Obit 26; WP
Haydon, Benjamin Robert
1786-1846 .... **NCLC 146**
See also DLB 110
Hayek, F(riedrich) A(ugust von)
1899-1992 .... **TCLC 109**
See also CA 93-96; 137; CANR 20; MTCW
1, 2
Hayford, J(oseph) E(phraim) Casely
See Casely-Hayford, J(oseph) E(phraim)
Hayman, Ronald 1932- .... **CLC 44**
See also CA 25-28R; CANR 18, 50, 88; CD
5; DLB 155
Hayne, Paul Hamilton 1830-1886 . **NCLC 94**
See also DLB 3, 64, 79, 248; RGAL 4
Hays, Mary 1760-1843 .... **NCLC 114**
See also DLB 142, 158; RGEL 2
Haywood, Eliza (Fowler)
1693(?)-1756 .... **LC 1, 44**
See also DLB 39; RGEL 2
Hazlitt, William 1778-1830 ...... **NCLC 29, 82**
See also BRW 4; DLB 110, 158; RGEL 2;
TEA
Hazzard, Shirley 1931- .... **CLC 18**
See also CA 9-12R; CANR 4, 70, 127; CN
7; DLB 289; DLBY 1982; MTCW 1
Head, Bessie 1937-1986 ...... **BLC 2; CLC 25,**
67; SSC 52
See also AFW; BW 2, 3; CA 29-32R; 119;
CANR 25, 82; CDWLB 3; DA3; DAM
MULT; DLB 117, 225; EWL 3; EXPS;
FW; MTCW 1, 2; RGSF 2; SSFS 5, 13;
WLIT 2; WWE 1
Headon, (Nicky) Topper 1956(?)- ..... **CLC 30**
Heaney, Seamus (Justin) 1939- ..... **CLC 5, 7,**
14, 25, 37, 74, 91, 171; PC 18; WLCS
See also BRWR 1; BRWS 2; CA 85-88;
CANR 25, 48, 75, 91, 128; CDBLB 1960
to Present; CP 7; DA3; DAB; DAM
POET; DLB 40; DLBY 1995; EWL 3;
EXPP; MTCW 1, 2; PAB; PFS 2, 5, 8,
17; RGEL 2; TEA; WLIT 4
Hearn, (Patricio) Lafcadio (Tessima Carlos)
1850-1904 .... **TCLC 9**
See also CA 105; 166; DLB 12, 78, 189;
HGG; RGAL 4
Hearne, Samuel 1745-1792 .... **LC 95**
See also DLB 99
Hearne, Vicki 1946-2001 .... **CLC 56**
See also CA 139; 201
Hearon, Shelby 1931- .... **CLC 63**
See also AITN 2; AMWS 8; CA 25-28R;
CANR 18, 48, 103; CSW
Heat-Moon, William Least .... **CLC 29**
See Trogdon, William (Lewis)
See also AAYA 9
Hebbel, Friedrich 1813-1863 . **DC 21; NCLC**
43
See also CDWLB 2; DAM DRAM; DLB
129; EW 6; RGWL 2, 3
Hebert, Anne 1916-2000 .... **CLC 4, 13, 29**
See also CA 85-88; 187; CANR 69, 126;
CCA 1; CWP; CWW 2; DA3; DAC;
DAM MST, POET; DLB 68; EWL 3; GFL
1789 to the Present; MTCW 1, 2; PFS 20

Hecht, Anthony (Evan) 1923-2004 .... **CLC 8,**
13, 19
See also AMWS 10; CA 9-12R; CANR 6,
108; CP 7; DAM POET; DLB 5, 169;
EWL 3; PFS 6; WP
Hecht, Ben 1894-1964 ..... **CLC 8; TCLC 101**
See also CA 85-88; DFS 9; DLB 7, 9, 25,
26, 28, 86; FANT; IDFW 3, 4; RGAL 4
Hedayat, Sadeq 1903-1951 .... **TCLC 21**
See also CA 120; EWL 3; RGSF 2
Hegel, Georg Wilhelm Friedrich
1770-1831 .... **NCLC 46**
See also DLB 90; TWA
Heidegger, Martin 1889-1976 .... **CLC 24**
See also CA 81-84; 65-68; CANR 34; DLB
296; MTCW 1, 2
Heidenstam, (Carl Gustaf) Verner von
1859-1940 .... **TCLC 5**
See also CA 104
Heidi Louise
See Erdrich, Louise
Heifner, Jack 1946- .... **CLC 11**
See also CA 105; CANR 47
Heijermans, Herman 1864-1924 .... **TCLC 24**
See also CA 123; EWL 3
Heilbrun, Carolyn G(old)
1926-2003 .... **CLC 25, 173**
See Cross, Amanda
See also CA 45-48; 220; CANR 1, 28, 58,
94; FW
Hein, Christoph 1944- .... **CLC 154**
See also CA 158; CANR 108; CDWLB 2;
CWW 2; DLB 124
Heine, Heinrich 1797-1856 .... **NCLC 4, 54,**
147; PC 25
See also CDWLB 2; DLB 90; EW 5; RGWL
2, 3; TWA
Heinemann, Larry (Curtiss) 1944- .. **CLC 50**
See also CA 110; CAAS 21; CANR 31, 81;
DLBD 9; INT CANR-31
Heiney, Donald (William) 1921-1993
See Harris, MacDonald
See also CA 1-4R; 142; CANR 3, 58; FANT
Heinlein, Robert A(nson) 1907-1988 . **CLC 1,**
3, 8, 14, 26, 55; SSC 55
See also AAYA 17; BPFB 2; BYA 4, 13;
CA 1-4R; 125; CANR 1, 20, 53; CLR 75;
CPW; DA3; DAM POP; DLB 8; EXPS;
JRDA; LAIT 5; LMFS 2; MAICYA 1, 2;
MTCW 1, 2; RGAL 4; SATA 9, 69;
SATA-Obit 56; SCFW; SFW 4; SSFS 7;
YAW
Helforth, John
See Doolittle, Hilda
Heliodorus fl. 3rd cent. - .... **CMLC 52**
Hellenhofferu, Vojtech Kapristian z
See Hasek, Jaroslav (Matej Frantisek)
Heller, Joseph 1923-1999 . **CLC 1, 3, 5, 8, 11,**
36, 63; TCLC 131, 151; WLC
See also AAYA 24; AITN 1; AMWS 4;
BPFB 2; BYA 1; CA 5-8R; 187; CABS 1;
CANR 8, 42, 66, 126; CN 7; CPW; DA;
DA3; DAB; DAC; DAM MST, NOV,
POP; DLB 2, 28, 227; DLBY 1980, 2002;
EWL 3; EXPN; INT CANR-8; LAIT 4;
MTCW 1, 2; NFS 1; RGAL 4; TUS; YAW
Hellman, Lillian (Florence)
1906-1984 .. **CLC 2, 4, 8, 14, 18, 34, 44,**
52; DC 1; TCLC 119
See also AAYA 47; AITN 1, 2; AMWS 1;
CA 13-16R; 112; CAD; CANR 33; CWD;
DA3; DAM DRAM; DFS 1, 3, 14; DLB
7, 228; DLBY 1984; EWL 3; FW; LAIT
3; MAWW; MTCW 1, 2; RGAL 4; TUS
Helprin, Mark 1947- .... **CLC 7, 10, 22, 32**
See also CA 81-84; CANR 47, 64, 124;
CDALBS; CPW; DA3; DAM NOV, POP;
DLBY 1985; FANT; MTCW 1, 2; SUFW
2

Hill, George Roy 1921-2002 .... **CLC 26**
    See also CA 110; 122; 213
Hill, John
    See Koontz, Dean R(ay)
Hill, Susan (Elizabeth) 1942- ...... **CLC 4, 113**
    See also CA 33-36R; CANR 29, 69, 129;
    CN 7; DAB; DAM MST, NOV; DLB 14,
    139; HGG; MTCW 1; RHW
Hillard, Asa G. III .... **CLC 70**
Hillerman, Tony 1925- .... **CLC 62, 170**
    See also AAYA 40; BEST 89:1; BPFB 2;
    CA 29-32R; CANR 21, 42, 65, 97; CMW
    4; CPW; DA3; DAM POP; DLB 206, 306;
    MSW; RGAL 4; SATA 6; TCWW 2; YAW
Hillesum, Etty 1914-1943 .... **TCLC 49**
    See also CA 137
Hilliard, Noel (Harvey) 1929-1996 ... **CLC 15**
    See also CA 9-12R; CANR 7, 69; CN 7
Hillis, Rick 1956- .... **CLC 66**
    See also CA 134
Hilton, James 1900-1954 .... **TCLC 21**
    See also CA 108; 169; DLB 34, 77; FANT;
    SATA 34
Hilton, Walter (?)-1396 .... **CMLC 58**
    See also DLB 146; RGEL 2
Himes, Chester (Bomar) 1909-1984 .. **BLC 2;**
    CLC 2, 4, 7, 18, 58, 108; TCLC 139
    See also AFAW 2; BPFB 2; BW 2; CA 25-
    28R; 114; CANR 22, 89; CMW 4; DAM
    MULT; DLB 2, 76, 143, 226; EWL 3;
    MSW; MTCW 1, 2; RGAL 4
Hinde, Thomas .... **CLC 6, 11**
    See Chitty, Thomas Willes
    See also EWL 3
Hine, (William) Daryl 1936- .... **CLC 15**
    See also CA 1-4R; CAAS 15; CANR 1, 20;
    CP 7; DLB 60
Hinkson, Katharine Tynan
    See Tynan, Katharine
Hinojosa(-Smith), Rolando (R.)
    1929- .... **HLC 1**
    See Hinojosa-Smith, Rolando
    See also CA 131; CAAS 16; CANR 62;
    DAM MULT; DLB 82; HW 1, 2; LLW 1;
    MTCW 2; RGAL 4
Hinton, S(usan) E(loise) 1950- .. **CLC 30, 111**
    See also AAYA 2, 33; BPFB 2; BYA 2, 3;
    CA 81-84; CANR 32, 62, 92, 133;
    CDALBS; CLR 3, 23; CPW; DA; DA3;
    DAB; DAC; DAM MST, NOV; JRDA;
    LAIT 5; MAICYA 1, 2; MTCW 1, 2; NFS
    5, 9, 15, 16; SATA 19, 58, 115; WYA;
    YAW
Hippius, Zinaida (Nikolaevna) .... **TCLC 9**
    See Gippius, Zinaida (Nikolaevna)
    See also DLB 295; EWL 3
Hiraoka, Kimitake 1925-1970
    See Mishima, Yukio
    See also CA 97-100; 29-32R; DA3; DAM
    DRAM; GLL 1; MTCW 1, 2
Hirsch, E(ric) D(onald), Jr. 1928- .... **CLC 79**
    See also CA 25-28R; CANR 27, 51; DLB
    67; INT CANR-27; MTCW 1
Hirsch, Edward 1950- .... **CLC 31, 50**
    See also CA 104; CANR 20, 42, 102; CP 7;
    DLB 120
Hitchcock, Alfred (Joseph)
    1899-1980 .... **CLC 16**
    See also AAYA 22; CA 159; 97-100; SATA
    27; SATA-Obit 24
Hitchens, Christopher (Eric)
    1949- .... **CLC 157**
    See also CA 152; CANR 89
Hitler, Adolf 1889-1945 .... **TCLC 53**
    See also CA 117; 147
Hoagland, Edward 1932- .... **CLC 28**
    See also ANW; CA 1-4R; CANR 2, 31, 57,
    107; CN 7; DLB 6; SATA 51; TCWW 2

Hoban, Russell (Conwell) 1925- ... **CLC 7, 25**
    See also BPFB 2; CA 5-8R; CANR 23, 37,
    66, 114; CLR 3, 69; CN 7; CWRI 5; DAM
    NOV; DLB 52; FANT; MAICYA 1, 2;
    MTCW 1, 2; SATA 1, 40, 78, 136; SFW
    4; SUFW 2
Hobbes, Thomas 1588-1679 .... **LC 36**
    See also DLB 151, 252, 281; RGEL 2
Hobbs, Perry
    See Blackmur, R(ichard) P(almer)
Hobson, Laura Z(ametkin)
    1900-1986 .... **CLC 7, 25**
    See Field, Peter
    See also BPFB 2; CA 17-20R; 118; CANR
    55; DLB 28; SATA 52
Hoccleve, Thomas c. 1368-c. 1437 ...... **LC 75**
    See also DLB 146; RGEL 2
Hoch, Edward D(entinger) 1930-
    See Queen, Ellery
    See also CA 29-32R; CANR 11, 27, 51, 97;
    CMW 4; DLB 306; SFW 4
Hochhuth, Rolf 1931- .... **CLC 4, 11, 18**
    See also CA 5-8R; CANR 33, 75; CWW 2;
    DAM DRAM; DLB 124; EWL 3; MTCW
    1, 2
Hochman, Sandra 1936- .... **CLC 3, 8**
    See also CA 5-8R; DLB 5
Hochwaelder, Fritz 1911-1986 .... **CLC 36**
    See Hochwalder, Fritz
    See also CA 29-32R; 120; CANR 42; DAM
    DRAM; MTCW 1; RGWL 3
Hochwalder, Fritz
    See Hochwaelder, Fritz
    See also EWL 3; RGWL 2
Hocking, Mary (Eunice) 1921- .... **CLC 13**
    See also CA 101; CANR 18, 40
Hodgins, Jack 1938- .... **CLC 23**
    See also CA 93-96; CN 7; DLB 60
Hodgson, William Hope
    1877(?)-1918 .... **TCLC 13**
    See also CA 111; 164; CMW 4; DLB 70,
    153, 156, 178; HGG; MTCW 2; SFW 4;
    SUFW 1
Hoeg, Peter 1957- .... **CLC 95, 156**
    See also CA 151; CANR 75; CMW 4; DA3;
    DLB 214; EWL 3; MTCW 2; NFS 17;
    RGWL 3; SSFS 18
Hoffman, Alice 1952- .... **CLC 51**
    See also AAYA 37; AMWS 10; CA 77-80;
    CANR 34, 66, 100; CN 7; CPW; DAM
    NOV; DLB 292; MTCW 1, 2
Hoffman, Daniel (Gerard) 1923- . **CLC 6, 13,**
    23
    See also CA 1-4R; CANR 4; CP 7; DLB 5
Hoffman, Eva 1945- .... **CLC 182**
    See also CA 132
Hoffman, Stanley 1944- .... **CLC 5**
    See also CA 77-80
Hoffman, William 1925- .... **CLC 141**
    See also CA 21-24R; CANR 9, 103; CSW;
    DLB 234
Hoffman, William M(oses) 1939- ..... **CLC 40**
    See Hoffman, William M.
    See also CA 57-60; CANR 11, 71
Hoffmann, E(rnst) T(heodor) A(madeus)
    1776-1822 .... **NCLC 2; SSC 13**
    See also CDWLB 2; DLB 90; EW 5; RGSF
    2; RGWL 2, 3; SATA 27; SUFW 1; WCH
Hofmann, Gert 1931- .... **CLC 54**
    See also CA 128; EWL 3
Hofmannsthal, Hugo von 1874-1929 ... **DC 4;**
    TCLC 11
    See also CA 106; 153; CDWLB 2; DAM
    DRAM; DFS 17; DLB 81, 118; EW 9;
    EWL 3; RGWL 2, 3

Hogan, Linda 1947- ..... **CLC 73; NNAL; PC**
    35
    See also AMWS 4; ANW; BYA 12; CA 120,
    226; CAAE 226; CANR 45, 73, 129;
    CWP; DAM MULT; DLB 175; SATA
    132; TCWW 2
Hogarth, Charles
    See Creasey, John
Hogarth, Emmett
    See Polonsky, Abraham (Lincoln)
Hogg, James 1770-1835 .... **NCLC 4, 109**
    See also BRWS 10; DLB 93, 116, 159;
    HGG; RGEL 2; SUFW 1
Holbach, Paul Henri Thiry Baron
    1723-1789 .... **LC 14**
Holberg, Ludvig 1684-1754 .... **LC 6**
    See also DLB 300; RGWL 2, 3
Holcroft, Thomas 1745-1809 .... **NCLC 85**
    See also DLB 39, 89, 158; RGEL 2
Holden, Ursula 1921- .... **CLC 18**
    See also CA 101; CAAS 8; CANR 22
Holderlin, (Johann Christian) Friedrich
    1770-1843 .... **NCLC 16; PC 4**
    See also CDWLB 2; DLB 90; EW 5; RGWL
    2, 3
Holdstock, Robert
    See Holdstock, Robert P.
Holdstock, Robert P. 1948- .... **CLC 39**
    See also CA 131; CANR 81; DLB 261;
    FANT; HGG; SFW 4; SUFW 2
Holinshed, Raphael fl. 1580- .... **LC 69**
    See also DLB 167; RGEL 2
Holland, Isabelle (Christian)
    1920-2002 .... **CLC 21**
    See also AAYA 11; CA 21-24R; 205; CAAE
    181; CANR 10, 25, 47; CLR 5; CWRI
    5; JRDA; LAIT 4; MAICYA 1, 2; SATA
    8, 70; SATA-Essay 103; SATA-Obit 132;
    WYA
Holland, Marcus
    See Caldwell, (Janet Miriam) Taylor
    (Holland)
Hollander, John 1929- .... **CLC 2, 5, 8, 14**
    See also CA 1-4R; CANR 1, 52; CP 7; DLB
    5; SATA 13
Hollander, Paul
    See Silverberg, Robert
Holleran, Andrew 1943(?)- .... **CLC 38**
    See Garber, Eric
    See also CA 144; GLL 1
Holley, Marietta 1836(?)-1926 .... **TCLC 99**
    See also CA 118; DLB 11
Hollinghurst, Alan 1954- .... **CLC 55, 91**
    See also BRWS 10; CA 114; CN 7; DLB
    207; GLL 1
Hollis, Jim
    See Summers, Hollis (Spurgeon, Jr.)
Holly, Buddy 1936-1959 .... **TCLC 65**
    See also CA 213
Holmes, Gordon
    See Shiel, M(atthew) P(hipps)
Holmes, John
    See Souster, (Holmes) Raymond
Holmes, John Clellon 1926-1988 ...... **CLC 56**
    See also BG 2; CA 9-12R; 125; CANR 4;
    DLB 16, 237
Holmes, Oliver Wendell, Jr.
    1841-1935 .... **TCLC 77**
    See also CA 114; 186
Holmes, Oliver Wendell
    1809-1894 .... **NCLC 14, 81**
    See also AMWS 1; CDALB 1640-1865;
    DLB 1, 189, 235; EXPP; RGAL 4; SATA
    34
Holmes, Raymond
    See Souster, (Holmes) Raymond
Holt, Victoria
    See Hibbert, Eleanor Alice Burford
    See also BPFB 2

Inge, William (Motter) 1913-1973 ..... **CLC 1, 8, 19**
See also CA 9-12R; CDALB 1941-1968; DA3; DAM DRAM; DFS 1, 3, 5, 8; DLB 7, 249; EWL 3; MTCW 1, 2; RGAL 4; TUS

Ingelow, Jean 1820-1897 .... **NCLC 39, 107**
See also DLB 35, 163; FANT; SATA 33

Ingram, Willis J.
See Harris, Mark

Innaurato, Albert (F.) 1948(?)- ... **CLC 21, 60**
See also CA 115; 122; CAD; CANR 78; CD 5; INT CA-122

Innes, Michael
See Stewart, J(ohn) I(nnes) M(ackintosh)
See also DLB 276; MSW

Innis, Harold Adams 1894-1952 .... **TCLC 77**
See also CA 181; DLB 88

Insluis, Alanus de
See Alain de Lille

Iola
See Wells-Barnett, Ida B(ell)

Ionesco, Eugene 1912-1994 ... **CLC 1, 4, 6, 9, 11, 15, 41, 86; DC 12; WLC**
See also CA 9-12R; 144; CANR 55, 132; CWW 2; DA; DA3; DAB; DAC; DAM DRAM, MST; DFS 4, 9; EW 13; EWL 3; GFL 1789 to the Present; LMFS 2; MTCW 1, 2; RGWL 2, 3; SATA 7; SATA-Obit 79; TWA

Iqbal, Muhammad 1877-1938 .... **TCLC 28**
See also CA 215; EWL 3

Ireland, Patrick
See O'Doherty, Brian

Irenaeus St. 130- .... **CMLC 42**

Irigaray, Luce 1930- .... **CLC 164**
See also CA 154; CANR 121; FW

Iron, Ralph
See Schreiner, Olive (Emilie Albertina)

Irving, John (Winslow) 1942- ... **CLC 13, 23, 38, 112, 175**
See also AAYA 8; AMWS 6; BEST 89:3; BPFB 2; CA 25-28R; CANR 28, 73, 112, 133; CN 7; CPW; DA3; DAM NOV, POP; DLB 6, 278; DLBY 1982; EWL 3; MTCW 1, 2; NFS 12, 14; RGAL 4; TUS

Irving, Washington 1783-1859 . **NCLC 2, 19, 95; SSC 2, 37; WLC**
See also AAYA 56; AMW; CDALB 1640-1865; CLR 97; DA; DA3; DAB; DAC; DAM MST; DLB 3, 11, 30, 59, 73, 74, 183, 186, 250, 254; EXPS; LAIT 1; RGAL 4; RGSF 2; SSFS 1, 8, 16; SUFW 1; TUS; WCH; YABC 2

Irwin, P. K.
See Page, P(atricia) K(athleen)

Isaacs, Jorge Ricardo 1837-1895 ... **NCLC 70**
See also LAW

Isaacs, Susan 1943- .... **CLC 32**
See also BEST 89:1; BPFB 2; CA 89-92; CANR 20, 41, 65, 112; CPW; DA3; DAM POP; INT CANR-20; MTCW 1, 2

Isherwood, Christopher (William Bradshaw) 1904-1986 .... **CLC 1, 9, 11, 14, 44; SSC 56**
See also AMWS 14; BRW 7; CA 13-16R; 117; CANR 35, 97, 133; DA3; DAM DRAM, NOV; DLB 15, 195; DLBY 1986; EWL 3; IDTP; MTCW 1, 2; RGAL 4; RGEL 2; TUS; WLIT 4

Ishiguro, Kazuo 1954- .. **CLC 27, 56, 59, 110**
See also AAYA 58; BEST 90:2; BPFB 2; BRWS 4; CA 120; CANR 49, 95, 133; CN 7; DA3; DAM NOV; DLB 194; EWL 3; MTCW 1, 2; NFS 13; WLIT 4; WWE 1

Ishikawa, Hakuhin
See Ishikawa, Takuboku

Ishikawa, Takuboku 1886(?)-1912 ..... **PC 10; TCLC 15**
See Ishikawa Takuboku
See also CA 113; 153; DAM POET

Iskander, Fazil (Abdulovich) 1929- .. **CLC 47**
See Iskander, Fazil' Abdulevich
See also CA 102; EWL 3

Iskander, Fazil' Abdulevich
See Iskander, Fazil (Abdulovich)
See also DLB 302

Isler, Alan (David) 1934- .... **CLC 91**
See also CA 156; CANR 105

Ivan IV 1530-1584 .... **LC 17**

Ivanov, Vyacheslav Ivanovich 1866-1949 .... **TCLC 33**
See also CA 122; EWL 3

Ivask, Ivar Vidrik 1927-1992 .... **CLC 14**
See also CA 37-40R; 139; CANR 24

Ives, Morgan
See Bradley, Marion Zimmer
See also GLL 1

Izumi Shikibu c. 973-c. 1034 .... **CMLC 33**

J. R. S.
See Gogarty, Oliver St. John

Jabran, Kahlil
See Gibran, Kahlil

Jabran, Khalil
See Gibran, Kahlil

Jackson, Daniel
See Wingrove, David (John)

Jackson, Helen Hunt 1830-1885 .... **NCLC 90**
See also DLB 42, 47, 186, 189; RGAL 4

Jackson, Jesse 1908-1983 .... **CLC 12**
See also BW 1; CA 25-28R; 109; CANR 27; CLR 28; CWRI 5; MAICYA 1, 2; SATA 2, 29; SATA-Obit 48

Jackson, Laura (Riding) 1901-1991 .... **PC 44**
See Riding, Laura
See also CA 65-68; 135; CANR 28, 89; DLB 48

Jackson, Sam
See Trumbo, Dalton

Jackson, Sara
See Wingrove, David (John)

Jackson, Shirley 1919-1965 . **CLC 11, 60, 87; SSC 9, 39; WLC**
See also AAYA 9; AMWS 9; BPFB 2; CA 1-4R; 25-28R; CANR 4, 52; CDALB 1941-1968; DA; DA3; DAC; DAM MST; DLB 6, 234; EXPS; HGG; LAIT 4; MTCW 2; RGAL 4; RGSF 2; SATA 2; SSFS 1; SUFW 1, 2

Jacob, (Cyprien-)Max 1876-1944 .... **TCLC 6**
See also CA 104; 193; DLB 258; EWL 3; GFL 1789 to the Present; GLL 2; RGWL 2, 3

Jacobs, Harriet A(nn) 1813(?)-1897 .... **NCLC 67**
See also AFAW 1, 2; DLB 239; FW; LAIT 2; RGAL 4

Jacobs, Jim 1942- .... **CLC 12**
See also CA 97-100; INT CA-97-100

Jacobs, W(illiam) W(ymark) 1863-1943 .... **SSC 73; TCLC 22**
See also CA 121; 167; DLB 135; EXPS; HGG; RGEL 2; RGSF 2; SSFS 2; SUFW 1

Jacobsen, Jens Peter 1847-1885 .... **NCLC 34**

Jacobsen, Josephine (Winder) 1908-2003 .... **CLC 48, 102**
See also CA 33-36R; 218; CAAS 18; CANR 23, 48; CCA 1; CP 7; DLB 244

Jacobson, Dan 1929- .... **CLC 4, 14**
See also AFW; CA 1-4R; CANR 2, 25, 66; CN 7; DLB 14, 207, 225; EWL 3; MTCW 1; RGSF 2

Jacqueline
See Carpentier (y Valmont), Alejo

Jacques de Vitry c. 1160-1240 ...... **CMLC 63**
See also DLB 208

Jagger, Mick 1944- .... **CLC 17**

Jahiz, al- c. 780-c. 869 .... **CMLC 25**

Jakes, John (William) 1932- .... **CLC 29**
See also AAYA 32; BEST 89:4; BPFB 2; CA 57-60, 214; CAAE 214; CANR 10, 43, 66, 111; CPW; CSW; DA3; DAM NOV, POP; DLB 278; DLBY 1983; FANT; INT CANR-10; MTCW 1, 2; RHW; SATA 62; SFW 4; TCWW 2

James I 1394-1437 .... **LC 20**
See also RGEL 2

James, Andrew
See Kirkup, James

James, C(yril) L(ionel) R(obert) 1901-1989 .... **BLCS; CLC 33**
See also BW 2; CA 117; 125; 128; CANR 62; DLB 125; MTCW 1

James, Daniel (Lewis) 1911-1988
See Santiago, Danny
See also CA 174; 125

James, Dynely
See Mayne, William (James Carter)

James, Henry Sr. 1811-1882 .... **NCLC 53**

James, Henry 1843-1916 .... **SSC 8, 32, 47; TCLC 2, 11, 24, 40, 47, 64; WLC**
See also AMW; AMWC 1; AMWR 1; BPFB 2; BRW 6; CA 104; 132; CDALB 1865-1917; DA; DA3; DAB; DAC; DAM MST, NOV; DLB 12, 71, 74, 189; DLBD 13; EWL 3; EXPS; HGG; LAIT 2; MTCW 1, 2; NFS 12, 16, 19; RGAL 4; RGEL 2; RGSF 2; SSFS 9; SUFW 1; TUS

James, M. R.
See James, Montague (Rhodes)
See also DLB 156, 201

James, Montague (Rhodes) 1862-1936 .... **SSC 16; TCLC 6**
See James, M. R.
See also CA 104; 203; HGG; RGEL 2; RGSF 2; SUFW 1

James, P. D. .... **CLC 18, 46, 122**
See White, Phyllis Dorothy James
See also BEST 90:2; BPFB 2; BRWS 4; CDBLB 1960 to Present; DLB 87, 276; DLBD 17; MSW

James, Philip
See Moorcock, Michael (John)

James, Samuel
See Stephens, James

James, Seumas
See Stephens, James

James, Stephen
See Stephens, James

James, William 1842-1910 .... **TCLC 15, 32**
See also AMW; CA 109; 193; DLB 270, 284; NCFS 5; RGAL 4

Jameson, Anna 1794-1860 .... **NCLC 43**
See also DLB 99, 166

Jameson, Fredric (R.) 1934- .... **CLC 142**
See also CA 196; DLB 67; LMFS 2

James VI of Scotland 1566-1625 .... **LC 109**
See also DLB 151, 172

Jami, Nur al-Din 'Abd al-Rahman 1414-1492 .... **LC 9**

Jammes, Francis 1868-1938 .... **TCLC 75**
See also CA 198; EWL 3; GFL 1789 to the Present

Jandl, Ernst 1925-2000 .... **CLC 34**
See also CA 200; EWL 3

Janowitz, Tama 1957- .... **CLC 43, 145**
See also CA 106; CANR 52, 89, 129; CN 7; CPW; DAM POP; DLB 292

Japrisot, Sebastien 1931- .... **CLC 90**
See Rossi, Jean-Baptiste
See also CMW 4; NFS 18

Jarrell, Randall 1914-1965 .... **CLC 1, 2, 6, 9, 13, 49; PC 41**
See also AMW; BYA 5; CA 5-8R; 25-28R; CABS 2; CANR 6, 34; CDALB 1941-1968; CLR 6; CWRI 5; DAM POET; DLB 48, 52; EWL 3; EXPP; MAICYA 1, 2; MTCW 1, 2; PAB; PFS 2; RGAL 4; SATA 7

Jarry, Alfred 1873-1907 .... **SSC 20; TCLC 2, 14, 147**
See also CA 104; 153; DA3; DAM DRAM; DFS 8; DLB 192, 258; EW 9; EWL 3; GFL 1789 to the Present; RGWL 2, 3; TWA

Jarvis, E. K.
See Ellison, Harlan (Jay)

Jawien, Andrzej
See John Paul II, Pope

Jaynes, Roderick
See Coen, Ethan

Jeake, Samuel, Jr.
See Aiken, Conrad (Potter)

Jean Paul 1763-1825 .... **NCLC 7**

Jefferies, (John) Richard
1848-1887 .... **NCLC 47**
See also DLB 98, 141; RGEL 2; SATA 16; SFW 4

Jeffers, (John) Robinson 1887-1962 .. **CLC 2, 3, 11, 15, 54; PC 17; WLC**
See also AMWS 2; CA 85-88; CANR 35; CDALB 1917-1929; DA; DAC; DAM MST, POET; DLB 45, 212; EWL 3; MTCW 1, 2; PAB; PFS 3, 4; RGAL 4

Jefferson, Janet
See Mencken, H(enry) L(ouis)

Jefferson, Thomas 1743-1826 . **NCLC 11, 103**
See also AAYA 54; ANW; CDALB 1640-1865; DA3; DLB 31, 183; LAIT 1; RGAL 4

Jeffrey, Francis 1773-1850 .... **NCLC 33**
See Francis, Lord Jeffrey

Jelakowitch, Ivan
See Heijermans, Herman

Jelinek, Elfriede 1946- .... **CLC 169**
See also CA 154; DLB 85; FW

Jellicoe, (Patricia) Ann 1927- .... **CLC 27**
See also CA 85-88; CBD; CD 5; CWD; CWRI 5; DLB 13, 233; FW

Jelloun, Tahar ben 1944- .... **CLC 180**
See Ben Jelloun, Tahar
See also CA 162; CANR 100

Jemyma
See Holley, Marietta

Jen, Gish .... **AAL; CLC 70, 198**
See Jen, Lillian
See also AMWC 2

Jen, Lillian 1956(?)-
See Jen, Gish
See also CA 135; CANR 89, 130

Jenkins, (John) Robin 1912- .... **CLC 52**
See also CA 1-4R; CANR 1; CN 7; DLB 14, 271

Jennings, Elizabeth (Joan)
1926-2001 .... **CLC 5, 14, 131**
See also BRWS 5; CA 61-64; 200; CAAS 5; CANR 8, 39, 66, 127; CP 7; CWP; DLB 27; EWL 3; MTCW 1; SATA 66

Jennings, Waylon 1937- .... **CLC 21**

Jensen, Johannes V(ilhelm)
1873-1950 .... **TCLC 41**
See also CA 170; DLB 214; EWL 3; RGWL 3

Jensen, Laura (Linnea) 1948- .... **CLC 37**
See also CA 103

Jerome, Saint 345-420 .... **CMLC 30**
See also RGWL 3

Jerome, Jerome K(lapka)
1859-1927 .... **TCLC 23**
See also CA 119; 177; DLB 10, 34, 135; RGEL 2

Jerrold, Douglas William
1803-1857 .... **NCLC 2**
See also DLB 158, 159; RGEL 2

Jewett, (Theodora) Sarah Orne
1849-1909 .... **SSC 6, 44; TCLC 1, 22**
See also AMW; AMWC 2; AMWR 2; CA 108; 127; CANR 71; DLB 12, 74, 221; EXPS; FW; MAWW; NFS 15; RGAL 4; RGSF 2; SATA 15; SSFS 4

Jewsbury, Geraldine (Endsor)
1812-1880 .... **NCLC 22**
See also DLB 21

Jhabvala, Ruth Prawer 1927- . **CLC 4, 8, 29, 94, 138**
See also BRWS 5; CA 1-4R; CANR 2, 29, 51, 74, 91, 128; CN 7; DAB; DAM NOV; DLB 139, 194; EWL 3; IDFW 3, 4; INT CANR-29; MTCW 1, 2; RGSF 2; RGWL 2; RHW; TEA

Jibran, Kahlil
See Gibran, Kahlil

Jibran, Khalil
See Gibran, Kahlil

Jiles, Paulette 1943- .... **CLC 13, 58**
See also CA 101; CANR 70, 124; CWP

Jimenez (Mantecon), Juan Ramon
1881-1958 .... **HLC 1; PC 7; TCLC 4**
See also CA 104; 131; CANR 74; DAM MULT, POET; DLB 134; EW 9; EWL 3; HW 1; MTCW 1, 2; RGWL 2, 3

Jimenez, Ramon
See Jimenez (Mantecon), Juan Ramon

Jimenez Mantecon, Juan
See Jimenez (Mantecon), Juan Ramon

Jin, Ha .... **CLC 109**
See Jin, Xuefei
See also CA 152; DLB 244, 292; SSFS 17

Jin, Xuefei 1956-
See Jin, Ha
See also CANR 91, 130; SSFS 17

Joel, Billy .... **CLC 26**
See Joel, William Martin

Joel, William Martin 1949-
See Joel, Billy
See also CA 108

John, Saint 10(?)-100 .... **CMLC 27, 63**

John of Salisbury c. 1115-1180 ..... **CMLC 63**

John of the Cross, St. 1542-1591 .... **LC 18**
See also RGWL 2, 3

John Paul II, Pope 1920- .... **CLC 128**
See also CA 106; 133

Johnson, B(ryan) S(tanley William)
1933-1973 .... **CLC 6, 9**
See also CA 9-12R; 53-56; CANR 9; DLB 14, 40; EWL 3; RGEL 2

Johnson, Benjamin F., of Boone
See Riley, James Whitcomb

Johnson, Charles (Richard) 1948- .... **BLC 2; CLC 7, 51, 65, 163**
See also AFAW 2; AMWS 6; BW 2, 3; CA 116; CAAS 18; CANR 42, 66, 82, 129; CN 7; DAM MULT; DLB 33, 278; MTCW 2; RGAL 4; SSFS 16

Johnson, Charles S(purgeon)
1893-1956 .... **HR 3**
See also BW 1, 3; CA 125; CANR 82; DLB 51, 91

Johnson, Denis 1949- . **CLC 52, 160; SSC 56**
See also CA 117; 121; CANR 71, 99; CN 7; DLB 120

Johnson, Diane 1934- .... **CLC 5, 13, 48**
See also BPFB 2; CA 41-44R; CANR 17, 40, 62, 95; CN 7; DLBY 1980; INT CANR-17; MTCW 1

Johnson, E. Pauline 1861-1913 .... **NNAL**
See also CA 150; DAC; DAM MULT; DLB 92, 175

Johnson, Eyvind (Olof Verner)
1900-1976 .... **CLC 14**
See also CA 73-76; 69-72; CANR 34, 101; DLB 259; EW 12; EWL 3

Johnson, Fenton 1888-1958 .... **BLC 2**
See also BW 1; CA 118; 124; DAM MULT; DLB 45, 50

Johnson, Georgia Douglas (Camp)
1880-1966 .... **HR 3**
See also BW 1; CA 125; DLB 51, 249; WP

Johnson, Helene 1907-1995 .... **HR 3**
See also CA 181; DLB 51; WP

Johnson, J. R.
See James, C(yril) L(ionel) R(obert)

Johnson, James Weldon 1871-1938 .. **BLC 2; HR 3; PC 24; TCLC 3, 19**
See also AFAW 1, 2; BW 1, 3; CA 104; 125; CANR 82; CDALB 1917-1929; CLR 32; DA3; DAM MULT, POET; DLB 51; EWL 3; EXPP; LMFS 2; MTCW 1, 2; PFS 1; RGAL 4; SATA 31; TUS

Johnson, Joyce 1935- .... **CLC 58**
See also BG 3; CA 125; 129; CANR 102

Johnson, Judith (Emlyn) 1936- .... **CLC 7, 15**
See Sherwin, Judith Johnson
See also CA 25-28R; 153; CANR 34

Johnson, Lionel (Pigot)
1867-1902 .... **TCLC 19**
See also CA 117; 209; DLB 19; RGEL 2

Johnson, Marguerite Annie
See Angelou, Maya

Johnson, Mel
See Malzberg, Barry N(athaniel)

Johnson, Pamela Hansford
1912-1981 .... **CLC 1, 7, 27**
See also CA 1-4R; 104; CANR 2, 28; DLB 15; MTCW 1, 2; RGEL 2

Johnson, Paul (Bede) 1928- .... **CLC 147**
See also BEST 89:4; CA 17-20R; CANR 34, 62, 100

Johnson, Robert .... **CLC 70**

Johnson, Robert 1911(?)-1938 .... **TCLC 69**
See also BW 3; CA 174

Johnson, Samuel 1709-1784 .... **LC 15, 52; WLC**
See also BRW 3; BRWR 1; CDBLB 1660-1789; DA; DAB; DAC; DAM MST; DLB 39, 95, 104, 142, 213; LMFS 1; RGEL 2; TEA

Johnson, Uwe 1934-1984 .. **CLC 5, 10, 15, 40**
See also CA 1-4R; 112; CANR 1, 39; CD-WLB 2; DLB 75; EWL 3; MTCW 1; RGWL 2, 3

Johnston, Basil H. 1929- .... **NNAL**
See also CA 69-72; CANR 11, 28, 66; DAC; DAM MULT; DLB 60

Johnston, George (Benson) 1913- .... **CLC 51**
See also CA 1-4R; CANR 5, 20; CP 7; DLB 88

Johnston, Jennifer (Prudence)
1930- .... **CLC 7, 150**
See also CA 85-88; CANR 92; CN 7; DLB 14

Joinville, Jean de 1224(?)-1317 ..... **CMLC 38**

Jolley, (Monica) Elizabeth 1923- ..... **CLC 46; SSC 19**
See also CA 127; CAAS 13; CANR 59; CN 7; EWL 3; RGSF 2

Jones, Arthur Llewellyn 1863-1947
See Machen, Arthur
See also CA 104; 179; HGG

Jones, D(ouglas) G(ordon) 1929- ..... **CLC 10**
See also CA 29-32R; CANR 13, 90; CP 7; DLB 53

Klein, Joseph 1946- .... **CLC 154**
   See also CA 85-88; CANR 55
Klein, Norma 1938-1989 .... **CLC 30**
   See also AAYA 2, 35; BPFB 2; BYA 6, 7,
   8; CA 41-44R; 128; CANR 15, 37; CLR
   2, 19; INT CANR-15; JRDA; MAICYA
   1, 2; SAAS 1; SATA 7, 57; WYA; YAW
Klein, T(heodore) E(ibon) D(onald)
   1947- .... **CLC 34**
   See also CA 119; CANR 44, 75; HGG
Kleist, Heinrich von 1777-1811 ...... **NCLC 2,
37; SSC 22**
   See also CDWLB 2; DAM DRAM; DLB
   90; EW 5; RGSF 2; RGWL 2, 3
Klima, Ivan 1931- .... **CLC 56, 172**
   See also CA 25-28R; CANR 17, 50, 91;
   CDWLB 4; CWW 2; DAM NOV; DLB
   232; EWL 3; RGWL 3
Klimentev, Andrei Platonovich
   See Klimentov, Andrei Platonovich
Klimentov, Andrei Platonovich
   1899-1951 .... **SSC 42; TCLC 14**
   See Platonov, Andrei Platonovich; Platonov,
   Andrey Platonovich
   See also CA 108
Klinger, Friedrich Maximilian von
   1752-1831 .... **NCLC 1**
   See also DLB 94
Klingsor the Magician
   See Hartmann, Sadakichi
Klopstock, Friedrich Gottlieb
   1724-1803 .... **NCLC 11**
   See also DLB 97; EW 4; RGWL 2, 3
Kluge, Alexander 1932- .... **SSC 61**
   See also CA 81-84; DLB 75
Knapp, Caroline 1959-2002 .... **CLC 99**
   See also CA 154; 207
Knebel, Fletcher 1911-1993 .... **CLC 14**
   See also AITN 1; CA 1-4R; 140; CAAS 3;
   CANR 1, 36; SATA 36; SATA-Obit 75
Knickerbocker, Diedrich
   See Irving, Washington
Knight, Etheridge 1931-1991 ... **BLC 2; CLC
40; PC 14**
   See also BW 1, 3; CA 21-24R; 133; CANR
   23, 82; DAM POET; DLB 41; MTCW 2;
   RGAL 4
Knight, Sarah Kemble 1666-1727 .... **LC 7**
   See also DLB 24, 200
Knister, Raymond 1899-1932 .... **TCLC 56**
   See also CA 186; DLB 68; RGEL 2
Knowles, John 1926-2001 ... **CLC 1, 4, 10, 26**
   See also AAYA 10; AMWS 12; BPFB 2;
   BYA 3; CA 17-20R; 203; CANR 40, 74,
   76, 132; CDALB 1968-1988; CLR 98; CN
   7; DA; DAC; DAM MST, NOV; DLB 6;
   EXPN; MTCW 1, 2; NFS 2; RGAL 4;
   SATA 8, 89; SATA-Obit 134; YAW
Knox, Calvin M.
   See Silverberg, Robert
Knox, John c. 1505-1572 .... **LC 37**
   See also DLB 132
Knye, Cassandra
   See Disch, Thomas M(ichael)
Koch, C(hristopher) J(ohn) 1932- .... **CLC 42**
   See also CA 127; CANR 84; CN 7; DLB
   289
Koch, Christopher
   See Koch, C(hristopher) J(ohn)
Koch, Kenneth (Jay) 1925-2002 .... **CLC 5, 8,
44**
   See also CA 1-4R; 207; CAD; CANR 6,
   36, 57, 97, 131; CD 5; CP 7; DAM POET;
   DLB 5; INT CANR-36; MTCW 2; PFS
   20; SATA 65; WP
Kochanowski, Jan 1530-1584 .... **LC 10**
   See also RGWL 2, 3

Kock, Charles Paul de 1794-1871 . **NCLC 16**
Koda Rohan
   See Koda Shigeyuki
Koda Rohan
   See Koda Shigeyuki
   See also DLB 180
Koda Shigeyuki 1867-1947 .... **TCLC 22**
   See Koda Rohan
   See also CA 121; 183
Koestler, Arthur 1905-1983 ... **CLC 1, 3, 6, 8,
15, 33**
   See also BRWS 1; CA 1-4R; 109; CANR 1,
   33; CDBLB 1945-1960; DLBY 1983;
   EWL 3; MTCW 1, 2; NFS 19; RGEL 2
Kogawa, Joy Nozomi 1935- ...... **CLC 78, 129**
   See also AAYA 47; CA 101; CANR 19, 62,
   126; CN 7; CWP; DAC; DAM MST,
   MULT; FW; MTCW 2; NFS 3; SATA 99
Kohout, Pavel 1928- .... **CLC 13**
   See also CA 45-48; CANR 3
Koizumi, Yakumo
   See Hearn, (Patricio) Lafcadio (Tessima
   Carlos)
Kolmar, Gertrud 1894-1943 .... **TCLC 40**
   See also CA 167; EWL 3
Komunyakaa, Yusef 1947- .. **BLCS; CLC 86,
94; PC 51**
   See also AFAW 2; AMWS 13; CA 147;
   CANR 83; CP 7; CSW; DLB 120; EWL
   3; PFS 5, 20; RGAL 4
Konrad, George
   See Konrad, Gyorgy
Konrad, Gyorgy 1933- .... **CLC 4, 10, 73**
   See also CA 85-88; CANR 97; CDWLB 4;
   CWW 2; DLB 232; EWL 3
Konwicki, Tadeusz 1926- .... **CLC 8, 28, 54,
117**
   See also CA 101; CAAS 9; CANR 39, 59;
   CWW 2; DLB 232; EWL 3; IDFW 3;
   MTCW 1
Koontz, Dean R(ay) 1945- .... **CLC 78**
   See also AAYA 9, 31; BEST 89:3, 90:2; CA
   108; CANR 19, 36, 52, 95; CMW 4;
   CPW; DA3; DAM NOV, POP; DLB 292;
   HGG; MTCW 1; SATA 92; SFW 4;
   SUFW 2; YAW
Kopernik, Mikolaj
   See Copernicus, Nicolaus
Kopit, Arthur (Lee) 1937- ...... **CLC 1, 18, 33**
   See also AITN 1; CA 81-84; CABS 3; CD
   5; DAM DRAM; DFS 7, 14; DLB 7;
   MTCW 1; RGAL 4
Kopitar, Jernej (Bartholomaus)
   1780-1844 .... **NCLC 117**
Kops, Bernard 1926- .... **CLC 4**
   See also CA 5-8R; CANR 84; CBD; CN 7;
   CP 7; DLB 13
Kornbluth, C(yril) M. 1923-1958 .... **TCLC 8**
   See also CA 105; 160; DLB 8; SFW 4
Korolenko, V. G.
   See Korolenko, Vladimir Galaktionovich
Korolenko, Vladimir
   See Korolenko, Vladimir Galaktionovich
Korolenko, Vladimir G.
   See Korolenko, Vladimir Galaktionovich
Korolenko, Vladimir Galaktionovich
   1853-1921 .... **TCLC 22**
   See also CA 121; DLB 277
Korzybski, Alfred (Habdank Skarbek)
   1879-1950 .... **TCLC 61**
   See also CA 123; 160
Kosinski, Jerzy (Nikodem)
   1933-1991 .... **CLC 1, 2, 3, 6, 10, 15, 53,
70**
   See also AMWS 7; BPFB 2; CA 17-20R;
   134; CANR 9, 46; DA3; DAM NOV;
   DLB 2, 299; DLBY 1982; EWL 3; HGG;
   MTCW 1, 2; NFS 12; RGAL 4; TUS

Kostelanetz, Richard (Cory) 1940- .. **CLC 28**
   See also CA 13-16R; CAAS 8; CANR 38,
   77; CN 7; CP 7
Kostrowitzki, Wilhelm Apollinaris de
   1880-1918
   See Apollinaire, Guillaume
   See also CA 104
Kotlowitz, Robert 1924- .... **CLC 4**
   See also CA 33-36R; CANR 36
Kotzebue, August (Friedrich Ferdinand) von
   1761-1819 .... **NCLC 25**
   See also DLB 94
Kotzwinkle, William 1938- ..... **CLC 5, 14, 35**
   See also BPFB 2; CA 45-48; CANR 3, 44,
   84, 129; CLR 6; DLB 173; FANT; MAI-
   CYA 1, 2; SATA 24, 70, 146; SFW 4;
   SUFW 2; YAW
Kowna, Stancy
   See Szymborska, Wislawa
Kozol, Jonathan 1936- .... **CLC 17**
   See also AAYA 46; CA 61-64; CANR 16,
   45, 96
Kozoll, Michael 1940(?)- .... **CLC 35**
Kramer, Kathryn 19(?)- .... **CLC 34**
Kramer, Larry 1935- .... **CLC 42; DC 8**
   See also CA 124; 126; CANR 60, 132;
   DAM POP; DLB 249; GLL 1
Krasicki, Ignacy 1735-1801 .... **NCLC 8**
Krasinski, Zygmunt 1812-1859 .... **NCLC 4**
   See also RGWL 2, 3
Kraus, Karl 1874-1936 .... **TCLC 5**
   See also CA 104; 216; DLB 118; EWL 3
Kreve (Mickevicius), Vincas
   1882-1954 .... **TCLC 27**
   See also CA 170; DLB 220; EWL 3
Kristeva, Julia 1941- .... **CLC 77, 140**
   See also CA 154; CANR 99; DLB 242;
   EWL 3; FW; LMFS 2
Kristofferson, Kris 1936- .... **CLC 26**
   See also CA 104
Krizanc, John 1956- .... **CLC 57**
   See also CA 187
Krleza, Miroslav 1893-1981 .... **CLC 8, 114**
   See also CA 97-100; 105; CANR 50; CD-
   WLB 4; DLB 147; EW 11; RGWL 2, 3
Kroetsch, Robert 1927- .. **CLC 5, 23, 57, 132**
   See also CA 17-20R; CANR 8, 38; CCA 1;
   CN 7; CP 7; DAC; DAM POET; DLB 53;
   MTCW 1
Kroetz, Franz
   See Kroetz, Franz Xaver
Kroetz, Franz Xaver 1946- .... **CLC 41**
   See also CA 130; CWW 2; EWL 3
Kroker, Arthur (W.) 1945- .... **CLC 77**
   See also CA 161
Kropotkin, Peter (Aleksieevich)
   1842-1921 .... **TCLC 36**
   See Kropotkin, Petr Alekseevich
   See also CA 119; 219
Kropotkin, Petr Alekseevich
   See Kropotkin, Peter (Aleksieevich)
   See also DLB 277
Krotkov, Yuri 1917-1981 .... **CLC 19**
   See also CA 102
Krumb
   See Crumb, R(obert)
Krumgold, Joseph (Quincy)
   1908-1980 .... **CLC 12**
   See also BYA 1, 2; CA 9-12R; 101; CANR
   7; MAICYA 1, 2; SATA 1, 48; SATA-Obit
   23; YAW
Krumwitz
   See Crumb, R(obert)
Krutch, Joseph Wood 1893-1970 ..... **CLC 24**
   See also ANW; CA 1-4R; 25-28R; CANR
   4; DLB 63, 206, 275
Krutzch, Gus
   See Eliot, T(homas) S(tearns)

Krylov, Ivan Andreevich
    1768(?)-1844 .... **NCLC 1**
    See also DLB 150
Kubin, Alfred (Leopold Isidor)
    1877-1959 .... **TCLC 23**
    See also CA 112; CANR 104; DLB 81
Kubrick, Stanley 1928-1999 .... **CLC 16;**
    TCLC 112
    See also AAYA 30; CA 81-84; 177; CANR
    33; DLB 26
Kumin, Maxine (Winokur) 1925- ..... **CLC 5,**
    13, 28, 164; PC 15
    See also AITN 2; AMWS 4; ANW; CA
    1-4R; CAAS 8; CANR 1, 21, 69, 115; CP
    7; CWP; DA3; DAM POET; DLB 5;
    EWL 3; EXPP; MTCW 1, 2; PAB; PFS
    18; SATA 12
Kundera, Milan 1929- . **CLC 4, 9, 19, 32, 68,**
    115, 135; SSC 24
    See also AAYA 2; BPFB 2; CA 85-88;
    CANR 19, 52, 74; CDWLB 4; CWW 2;
    DA3; DAM NOV; DLB 232; EW 13;
    EWL 3; MTCW 1, 2; NFS 18; RGSF 2;
    RGWL 3; SSFS 10
Kunene, Mazisi (Raymond) 1930- ... **CLC 85**
    See also BW 1, 3; CA 125; CANR 81; CP
    7; DLB 117
Kung, Hans .... **CLC 130**
    See Kung, Hans
Kung, Hans 1928-
    See Kung, Hans
    See also CA 53-56; CANR 66; MTCW 1, 2
Kunikida Doppo 1869(?)-1908
    See Doppo, Kunikida
    See also DLB 180; EWL 3
Kunitz, Stanley (Jasspon) 1905- .. **CLC 6, 11,**
    14, 148; PC 19
    See also AMWS 3; CA 41-44R; CANR 26,
    57, 98; CP 7; DA3; DLB 48; INT CANR-
    26; MTCW 1, 2; PFS 11; RGAL 4
Kunze, Reiner 1933- .... **CLC 10**
    See also CA 93-96; CWW 2; DLB 75; EWL
    3
Kuprin, Aleksander Ivanovich
    1870-1938 .... **TCLC 5**
    See Kuprin, Aleksandr Ivanovich; Kuprin,
    Alexandr Ivanovich
    See also CA 104; 182
Kuprin, Aleksandr Ivanovich
    See Kuprin, Aleksander Ivanovich
    See also DLB 295
Kuprin, Alexandr Ivanovich
    See Kuprin, Aleksander Ivanovich
    See also EWL 3
Kureishi, Hanif 1954(?)- .... **CLC 64, 135**
    See also CA 139; CANR 113; CBD; CD 5;
    CN 7; DLB 194, 245; GLL 2; IDFW 4;
    WLIT 4; WWE 1
Kurosawa, Akira 1910-1998 ..... **CLC 16, 119**
    See also AAYA 11; CA 101; 170; CANR
    46; DAM MULT
Kushner, Tony 1956(?)- .... **CLC 81; DC 10**
    See also AMWS 9; CA 144; CAD; CANR
    74, 130; CD 5; DA3; DAM DRAM; DFS
    5; DLB 228; EWL 3; GLL 1; LAIT 5;
    MTCW 2; RGAL 4
Kuttner, Henry 1915-1958 .... **TCLC 10**
    See also CA 107; 157; DLB 8; FANT;
    SCFW 2; SFW 4
Kutty, Madhavi
    See Das, Kamala
Kuzma, Greg 1944- .... **CLC 7**
    See also CA 33-36R; CANR 70
Kuzmin, Mikhail (Alekseevich)
    1872(?)-1936 .... **TCLC 40**
    See also CA 170; DLB 295; EWL 3
Kyd, Thomas 1558-1594 .... **DC 3; LC 22**
    See also BRW 1; DAM DRAM; DLB 62;
    IDTP; LMFS 1; RGEL 2; TEA; WLIT 3

Kyprianos, Iossif
    See Samarakis, Antonis
L. S.
    See Stephen, Sir Leslie
Laȝamon
    See Layamon
    See also DLB 146
Labrunie, Gerard
    See Nerval, Gerard de
La Bruyere, Jean de 1645-1696 .... **LC 17**
    See also DLB 268; EW 3; GFL Beginnings
    to 1789
Lacan, Jacques (Marie Emile)
    1901-1981 .... **CLC 75**
    See also CA 121; 104; DLB 296; EWL 3;
    TWA
Laclos, Pierre Ambroise Francois
    1741-1803 .... **NCLC 4, 87**
    See also EW 4; GFL Beginnings to 1789;
    RGWL 2, 3
Lacolere, Francois
    See Aragon, Louis
La Colere, Francois
    See Aragon, Louis
La Deshabilleuse
    See Simenon, Georges (Jacques Christian)
Lady Gregory
    See Gregory, Lady Isabella Augusta (Persse)
Lady of Quality, A
    See Bagnold, Enid
**La Fayette, Marie-(Madelaine Pioche de la
    Vergne)** 1634-1693 .... **LC 2**
    See Lafayette, Marie-Madeleine
    See also GFL Beginnings to 1789; RGWL
    2, 3
Lafayette, Marie-Madeleine
    See La Fayette, Marie-(Madelaine Pioche
    de la Vergne)
    See also DLB 268
Lafayette, Rene
    See Hubbard, L(afayette) Ron(ald)
La Flesche, Francis 1857(?)-1932 ...... **NNAL**
    See also CA 144; CANR 83; DLB 175
La Fontaine, Jean de 1621-1695 .... **LC 50**
    See also DLB 268; EW 3; GFL Beginnings
    to 1789; MAICYA 1, 2; RGWL 2, 3;
    SATA 18
Laforgue, Jules 1860-1887 . **NCLC 5, 53; PC
    14; SSC 20**
    See also DLB 217; EW 7; GFL 1789 to the
    Present; RGWL 2, 3
Lagerkvist, Paer (Fabian)
    1891-1974 ..... **CLC 7, 10, 13, 54; TCLC
    144**
    See Lagerkvist, Par
    See also CA 85-88; 49-52; DA3; DAM
    DRAM, NOV; MTCW 1, 2; TWA
Lagerkvist, Par .... **SSC 12**
    See Lagerkvist, Paer (Fabian)
    See also DLB 259; EW 10; EWL 3; MTCW
    2; RGSF 2; RGWL 2, 3
Lagerloef, Selma (Ottiliana Lovisa)
    1858-1940 .... **TCLC 4, 36**
    See Lagerlof, Selma (Ottiliana Lovisa)
    See also CA 108; MTCW 2; SATA 15
Lagerlof, Selma (Ottiliana Lovisa)
    See Lagerloef, Selma (Ottiliana Lovisa)
    See also CLR 7; SATA 15
La Guma, (Justin) Alex(ander)
    1925-1985 . **BLCS; CLC 19; TCLC 140**
    See also AFW; BW 1, 3; CA 49-52; 118;
    CANR 25, 81; CDWLB 3; DAM NOV;
    DLB 117, 225; EWL 3; MTCW 1, 2;
    WLIT 2; WWE 1
Laidlaw, A. K.
    See Grieve, C(hristopher) M(urray)
Lainez, Manuel Mujica
    See Mujica Lainez, Manuel
    See also HW 1

Laing, R(onald) D(avid) 1927-1989 . **CLC 95**
    See also CA 107; 129; CANR 34; MTCW 1
Laishley, Alex
    See Booth, Martin
Lamartine, Alphonse (Marie Louis Prat) de
    1790-1869 .... **NCLC 11; PC 16**
    See also DAM POET; DLB 217; GFL 1789
    to the Present; RGWL 2, 3
Lamb, Charles 1775-1834 ..... **NCLC 10, 113;**
    WLC
    See also BRW 4; CDBLB 1789-1832; DA;
    DAB; DAC; DAM MST; DLB 93, 107,
    163; RGEL 2; SATA 17; TEA
Lamb, Lady Caroline 1785-1828 ... **NCLC 38**
    See also DLB 116
Lamb, Mary Ann 1764-1847 .... **NCLC 125**
    See also DLB 163; SATA 17
Lame Deer 1903(?)-1976 .... **NNAL**
    See also CA 69-72
Lamming, George (William) 1927- ... **BLC 2;**
    CLC 2, 4, 66, 144
    See also BW 2, 3; CA 85-88; CANR 26,
    76; CDWLB 3; CN 7; DAM MULT; DLB
    125; EWL 3; MTCW 1, 2; NFS 15; RGEL
    2
L'Amour, Louis (Dearborn)
    1908-1988 .... **CLC 25, 55**
    See Burns, Tex; Mayo, Jim
    See also AAYA 16; AITN 2; BEST 89:2;
    BPFB 2; CA 1-4R; 125; CANR 3, 25, 40;
    CPW; DA3; DAM NOV, POP; DLB 206;
    DLBY 1980; MTCW 1, 2; RGAL 4
Lampedusa, Giuseppe (Tomasi) di
    .... **TCLC 13**
    See Tomasi di Lampedusa, Giuseppe
    See also CA 164; EW 11; MTCW 2; RGWL
    2, 3
Lampman, Archibald 1861-1899 ... **NCLC 25**
    See also DLB 92; RGEL 2; TWA
Lancaster, Bruce 1896-1963 .... **CLC 36**
    See also CA 9-10; CANR 70; CAP 1; SATA
    9
Lanchester, John 1962- .... **CLC 99**
    See also CA 194; DLB 267
Landau, Mark Alexandrovich
    See Aldanov, Mark (Alexandrovich)
Landau-Aldanov, Mark Alexandrovich
    See Aldanov, Mark (Alexandrovich)
Landis, Jerry
    See Simon, Paul (Frederick)
Landis, John 1950- .... **CLC 26**
    See also CA 112; 122; CANR 128
Landolfi, Tommaso 1908-1979 ... **CLC 11, 49**
    See also CA 127; 117; DLB 177; EWL 3
Landon, Letitia Elizabeth
    1802-1838 .... **NCLC 15**
    See also DLB 96
Landor, Walter Savage
    1775-1864 .... **NCLC 14**
    See also BRW 4; DLB 93, 107; RGEL 2
Landwirth, Heinz 1927-
    See Lind, Jakov
    See also CA 9-12R; CANR 7
Lane, Patrick 1939- .... **CLC 25**
    See also CA 97-100; CANR 54; CP 7; DAM
    POET; DLB 53; INT CA-97-100
Lang, Andrew 1844-1912 .... **TCLC 16**
    See also CA 114; 137; CANR 85; CLR 101;
    DLB 98, 141, 184; FANT; MAICYA 1, 2;
    RGEL 2; SATA 16; WCH
Lang, Fritz 1890-1976 .... **CLC 20, 103**
    See also CA 77-80; 69-72; CANR 30
Lange, John
    See Crichton, (John) Michael
Langer, Elinor 1939- .... **CLC 34**
    See also CA 121

Langland, William 1332(?)-1400(?) ..... **LC 19**
    See also BRW 1; DA; DAB; DAC; DAM
    MST, POET; DLB 146; RGEL 2; TEA;
    WLIT 3

Langstaff, Launcelot
    See Irving, Washington

Lanier, Sidney 1842-1881 . **NCLC 6, 118; PC
50**
    See also AMWS 1; DAM POET; DLB 64;
    DLBD 13; EXPP; MAICYA 1; PFS 14;
    RGAL 4; SATA 18

Lanyer, Aemilia 1569-1645 .... **LC 10, 30, 83;
PC 60**
    See also DLB 121

Lao-Tzu
    See Lao Tzu

Lao Tzu c. 6th cent. B.C.-3rd cent.
    B.C. .... **CMLC 7**

Lapine, James (Elliot) 1949- .... **CLC 39**
    See also CA 123; 130; CANR 54, 128; INT
    CA-130

Larbaud, Valery (Nicolas)
    1881-1957 .... **TCLC 9**
    See also CA 106; 152; EWL 3; GFL 1789
    to the Present

Lardner, Ring
    See Lardner, Ring(gold) W(ilmer)
    See also BPFB 2; CDALB 1917-1929; DLB
    11, 25, 86, 171; DLBD 16; RGAL 4;
    RGSF 2

Lardner, Ring W., Jr.
    See Lardner, Ring(gold) W(ilmer)

Lardner, Ring(gold) W(ilmer)
    1885-1933 .... **SSC 32; TCLC 2, 14**
    See Lardner, Ring
    See also AMW; CA 104; 131; MTCW 1, 2;
    TUS

Laredo, Betty
    See Codrescu, Andrei

Larkin, Maia
    See Wojciechowska, Maia (Teresa)

Larkin, Philip (Arthur) 1922-1985 ... **CLC 3,
5, 8, 9, 13, 18, 33, 39, 64; PC 21**
    See also BRWS 1; CA 5-8R; 117; CANR
    24, 62; CDBLB 1960 to Present; DA3;
    DAB; DAM MST, POET; DLB 27; EWL
    3; MTCW 1, 2; PFS 3, 4, 12; RGEL 2

La Roche, Sophie von
    1730-1807 .... **NCLC 121**
    See also DLB 94

La Rochefoucauld, Francois
    1613-1680 .... **LC 108**

**Larra (y Sanchez de Castro), Mariano Jose
de** 1809-1837 .... **NCLC 17, 130**

Larsen, Eric 1941- .... **CLC 55**
    See also CA 132

Larsen, Nella 1893(?)-1963 .... **BLC 2; CLC
37; HR 3**
    See also AFAW 1, 2; BW 1; CA 125; CANR
    83; DAM MULT; DLB 51; FW; LATS
    1:1; LMFS 2

Larson, Charles R(aymond) 1938- ... **CLC 31**
    See also CA 53-56; CANR 4, 121

Larson, Jonathan 1961-1996 .... **CLC 99**
    See also AAYA 28; CA 156

La Sale, Antoine de c. 1386-1460(?) . **LC 104**
    See also DLB 208

Las Casas, Bartolome de
    1474-1566 .... **HLCS; LC 31**
    See Casas, Bartolome de las
    See also LAW

Lasch, Christopher 1932-1994 .... **CLC 102**
    See also CA 73-76; 144; CANR 25, 118;
    DLB 246; MTCW 1, 2

Lasker-Schueler, Else 1869-1945 ... **TCLC 57**
    See Lasker-Schuler, Else
    See also CA 183; DLB 66, 124

Lasker-Schuler, Else
    See Lasker-Schueler, Else
    See also EWL 3

Laski, Harold J(oseph) 1893-1950 . **TCLC 79**
    See also CA 188

Latham, Jean Lee 1902-1995 .... **CLC 12**
    See also AITN 1; BYA 1; CA 5-8R; CANR
    7, 84; CLR 50; MAICYA 1, 2; SATA 2,
    68; YAW

Latham, Mavis
    See Clark, Mavis Thorpe

Lathen, Emma .... **CLC 2**
    See Hennissart, Martha; Latsis, Mary J(ane)
    See also BPFB 2; CMW 4; DLB 306

Lathrop, Francis
    See Leiber, Fritz (Reuter, Jr.)

Latsis, Mary J(ane) 1927-1997
    See Lathen, Emma
    See also CA 85-88; 162; CMW 4

Lattany, Kristin
    See Lattany, Kristin (Elaine Eggleston)
    Hunter

Lattany, Kristin (Elaine Eggleston) Hunter
    1931- .... **CLC 35**
    See also AITN 1; BW 1; BYA 3; CA 13-
    16R; CANR 13, 108; CLR 3; CN 7; DLB
    33; INT CANR-13; MAICYA 1, 2; SAAS
    10; SATA 12, 132; YAW

Lattimore, Richmond (Alexander)
    1906-1984 .... **CLC 3**
    See also CA 1-4R; 112; CANR 1

Laughlin, James 1914-1997 .... **CLC 49**
    See also CA 21-24R; 162; CAAS 22; CANR
    9, 47; CP 7; DLB 48; DLBY 1996, 1997

Laurence, (Jean) Margaret (Wemyss)
    1926-1987 . **CLC 3, 6, 13, 50, 62; SSC 7**
    See also BYA 13; CA 5-8R; 121; CANR
    33; DAC; DAM MST; DLB 53; EWL 3;
    FW; MTCW 1, 2; NFS 11; RGEL 2;
    RGSF 2; SATA-Obit 50; TCWW 2

Laurent, Antoine 1952- .... **CLC 50**

Lauscher, Hermann
    See Hesse, Hermann

Lautreamont 1846-1870 .. **NCLC 12; SSC 14**
    See Lautreamont, Isidore Lucien Ducasse
    See also GFL 1789 to the Present; RGWL
    2, 3

Lautreamont, Isidore Lucien Ducasse
    See Lautreamont
    See also DLB 217

Lavater, Johann Kaspar
    1741-1801 .... **NCLC 142**
    See also DLB 97

Laverty, Donald
    See Blish, James (Benjamin)

Lavin, Mary 1912-1996 . **CLC 4, 18, 99; SSC
4, 67**
    See also CA 9-12R; 151; CANR 33; CN 7;
    DLB 15; FW; MTCW 1; RGEL 2; RGSF
    2

Lavond, Paul Dennis
    See Kornbluth, C(yril) M.; Pohl, Frederik

Lawler, Ray
    See Lawler, Raymond Evenor
    See also DLB 289

Lawler, Raymond Evenor 1922- .... **CLC 58**
    See Lawler, Ray
    See also CA 103; CD 5; RGEL 2

Lawrence, D(avid) H(erbert Richards)
    1885-1930 .... **PC 54; SSC 4, 19, 73;
TCLC 2, 9, 16, 33, 48, 61, 93; WLC**
    See Chambers, Jessie
    See also BPFB 2; BRW 7; BRWR 2; CA
    104; 121; CANR 131; CDBLB 1914-
    1945; DA; DA3; DAB; DAC; DAM MST,
    NOV, POET; DLB 10, 19, 36, 98, 162,
    195; EWL 3; EXPP; EXPS; LAIT 2, 3;
    MTCW 1, 2; NFS 18; PFS 6; RGEL 2;
    RGSF 2; SSFS 2, 6; TEA; WLIT 4; WP

Lawrence, T(homas) E(dward)
    1888-1935 .... **TCLC 18**
    See Dale, Colin
    See also BRWS 2; CA 115; 167; DLB 195

Lawrence of Arabia
    See Lawrence, T(homas) E(dward)

Lawson, Henry (Archibald Hertzberg)
    1867-1922 .... **SSC 18; TCLC 27**
    See also CA 120; 181; DLB 230; RGEL 2;
    RGSF 2

Lawton, Dennis
    See Faust, Frederick (Schiller)

Layamon fl. c. 1200- .... **CMLC 10**
    See Laȝamon
    See also DLB 146; RGEL 2

Laye, Camara 1928-1980 ..... **BLC 2; CLC 4,
38**
    See Camara Laye
    See also AFW; BW 1; CA 85-88; 97-100;
    CANR 25; DAM MULT; MTCW 1, 2;
    WLIT 2

Layton, Irving (Peter) 1912- .... **CLC 2, 15,
164**
    See also CA 1-4R; CANR 2, 33, 43, 66,
    129; CP 7; DAC; DAM MST, POET;
    DLB 88; EWL 3; MTCW 1, 2; PFS 12;
    RGEL 2

Lazarus, Emma 1849-1887 ...... **NCLC 8, 109**

Lazarus, Felix
    See Cable, George Washington

Lazarus, Henry
    See Slavitt, David R(ytman)

Lea, Joan
    See Neufeld, John (Arthur)

Leacock, Stephen (Butler)
    1869-1944 .... **SSC 39; TCLC 2**
    See also CA 104; 141; CANR 80; DAC;
    DAM MST; DLB 92; EWL 3; MTCW 2;
    RGEL 2; RGSF 2

Lead, Jane Ward 1623-1704 .... **LC 72**
    See also DLB 131

Leapor, Mary 1722-1746 .... **LC 80**
    See also DLB 109

Lear, Edward 1812-1888 .... **NCLC 3**
    See also AAYA 48; BRW 5; CLR 1, 75;
    DLB 32, 163, 166; MAICYA 1, 2; RGEL
    2; SATA 18, 100; WCH; WP

Lear, Norman (Milton) 1922- .... **CLC 12**
    See also CA 73-76

Leautaud, Paul 1872-1956 .... **TCLC 83**
    See also CA 203; DLB 65; GFL 1789 to the
    Present

Leavis, F(rank) R(aymond)
    1895-1978 .... **CLC 24**
    See also BRW 7; CA 21-24R; 77-80; CANR
    44; DLB 242; EWL 3; MTCW 1, 2;
    RGEL 2

Leavitt, David 1961- .... **CLC 34**
    See also CA 116; 122; CANR 50, 62, 101;
    CPW; DA3; DAM POP; DLB 130; GLL
    1; INT CA-122; MTCW 2

Leblanc, Maurice (Marie Emile)
    1864-1941 .... **TCLC 49**
    See also CA 110; CMW 4

Lebowitz, Fran(ces Ann) 1951(?)- ... **CLC 11,
36**
    See also CA 81-84; CANR 14, 60, 70; INT
    CANR-14; MTCW 1

Lebrecht, Peter
    See Tieck, (Johann) Ludwig

le Carre, John .... **CLC 3, 5, 9, 15, 28**
    See Cornwell, David (John Moore)
    See also AAYA 42; BEST 89:4; BPFB 2;
    BRWS 2; CDBLB 1960 to Present; CMW
    4; CN 7; CPW; DLB 87; EWL 3; MSW;
    MTCW 2; RGEL 2; TEA

Leroux, Gaston 1868-1927 .... **TCLC 25**
　　See also CA 108; 136; CANR 69; CMW 4;
　　NFS 20; SATA 65

Lesage, Alain-Rene 1668-1747 .... **LC 2, 28**
　　See also EW 3; GFL Beginnings to 1789;
　　RGWL 2, 3

Leskov, N(ikolai) S(emenovich) 1831-1895
　　See Leskov, Nikolai (Semyonovich)

Leskov, Nikolai (Semyonovich)
　　1831-1895 .... **NCLC 25; SSC 34**
　　See also Leskov, Nikolai Semenovich

Leskov, Nikolai Semenovich
　　See Leskov, Nikolai (Semyonovich)
　　See also DLB 238

Lesser, Milton
　　See Marlowe, Stephen

Lessing, Doris (May) 1919- ... **CLC 1, 2, 3, 6,**
　　10, 15, 22, 40, 94, 170; SSC 6, 61;
　　WLCS
　　See also AAYA 57; AFW; BRWS 1; CA
　　9-12R; CAAS 14; CANR 33, 54, 76, 122;
　　CD 5; CDBLB 1960 to Present; CN 7;
　　DA; DA3; DAB; DAC; DAM MST, NOV;
　　DFS 20; DLB 15, 139; DLBY 1985; EWL
　　3; EXPS; FW; LAIT 4; MTCW 1, 2;
　　RGEL 2; RGSF 2; SFW 4; SSFS 1, 12,
　　20; TEA; WLIT 2, 4

Lessing, Gotthold Ephraim 1729-1781 . **LC 8**
　　See also CDWLB 2; DLB 97; EW 4; RGWL
　　2, 3

Lester, Richard 1932- .... **CLC 20**

Levenson, Jay .... **CLC 70**

Lever, Charles (James)
　　1806-1872 .... **NCLC 23**
　　See also DLB 21; RGEL 2

Leverson, Ada Esther
　　1862(?)-1933(?) .... **TCLC 18**
　　See Elaine
　　See also CA 117; 202; DLB 153; RGEL 2

Levertov, Denise 1923-1997 .. **CLC 1, 2, 3, 5,**
　　8, 15, 28, 66; PC 11
　　See also AMWS 3; CA 1-4R, 178; 163;
　　CAAE 178; CAAS 19; CANR 3, 29, 50,
　　108; CDALBS; CP 7; CWP; DAM POET;
　　DLB 5, 165; EWL 3; EXPP; FW; INT
　　CANR-29; MTCW 1, 2; PAB; PFS 7, 17;
　　RGAL 4; TUS; WP

Levi, Carlo 1902-1975 .... **TCLC 125**
　　See also CA 65-68; 53-56; CANR 10; EWL
　　3; RGWL 2, 3

Levi, Jonathan .... **CLC 76**
　　See also CA 197

Levi, Peter (Chad Tigar)
　　1931-2000 .... **CLC 41**
　　See also CA 5-8R; 187; CANR 34, 80; CP
　　7; DLB 40

Levi, Primo 1919-1987 ...... **CLC 37, 50; SSC**
　　12; TCLC 109
　　See also CA 13-16R; 122; CANR 12, 33,
　　61, 70, 132; DLB 177, 299; EWL 3;
　　MTCW 1, 2; RGWL 2, 3

Levin, Ira 1929- .... **CLC 3, 6**
　　See also CA 21-24R; CANR 17, 44, 74;
　　CMW 4; CN 7; CPW; DA3; DAM POP;
　　HGG; MTCW 1, 2; SATA 66; SFW 4

Levin, Meyer 1905-1981 .... **CLC 7**
　　See also AITN 1; CA 9-12R; 104; CANR
　　15; DAM POP; DLB 9, 28; DLBY 1981;
　　SATA 21; SATA-Obit 27

Levine, Norman 1924- .... **CLC 54**
　　See also CA 73-76; CAAS 23; CANR 14,
　　70; DLB 88

Levine, Philip 1928- .. **CLC 2, 4, 5, 9, 14, 33,**
　　118; PC 22
　　See also AMWS 5; CA 9-12R; CANR 9,
　　37, 52, 116; CP 7; DAM POET; DLB 5;
　　EWL 3; PFS 8

Levinson, Deirdre 1931- .... **CLC 49**
　　See also CA 73-76; CANR 70

Levi-Strauss, Claude 1908- .... **CLC 38**
　　See also CA 1-4R; CANR 6, 32, 57; DLB
　　242; EWL 3; GFL 1789 to the Present;
　　MTCW 1, 2; TWA

Levitin, Sonia (Wolff) 1934- .... **CLC 17**
　　See also AAYA 13, 48; CA 29-32R; CANR
　　14, 32, 79; CLR 53; JRDA; MAICYA 1,
　　2; SAAS 2; SATA 4, 68, 119, 131; SATA-
　　Essay 131; YAW

Levon, O. U.
　　See Kesey, Ken (Elton)

Levy, Amy 1861-1889 .... **NCLC 59**
　　See also DLB 156, 240

Lewes, George Henry 1817-1878 ... **NCLC 25**
　　See also DLB 55, 144

Lewis, Alun 1915-1944 .... **SSC 40; TCLC 3**
　　See also BRW 7; CA 104; 188; DLB 20,
　　162; PAB; RGEL 2

Lewis, C. Day
　　See Day Lewis, C(ecil)

Lewis, C(live) S(taples) 1898-1963 .... **CLC 1,**
　　3, 6, 14, 27, 124; WLC
　　See also AAYA 3, 39; BPFB 2; BRWS 3;
　　BYA 15, 16; CA 81-84; CANR 33, 71,
　　132; CDBLB 1945-1960; CLR 3, 27;
　　CWRI 5; DA; DA3; DAB; DAC; DAM
　　MST, NOV, POP; DLB 15, 100, 160, 255;
　　EWL 3; FANT; JRDA; LMFS 2; MAI-
　　CYA 1, 2; MTCW 1, 2; RGEL 2; SATA
　　13, 100; SCFW; SFW 4; SUFW 1; TEA;
　　WCH; WYA; YAW

Lewis, Cecil Day
　　See Day Lewis, C(ecil)

Lewis, Janet 1899-1998 .... **CLC 41**
　　See Winters, Janet Lewis
　　See also CA 9-12R; 172; CANR 29, 63;
　　CAP 1; CN 7; DLBY 1987; RHW;
　　TCWW 2

Lewis, Matthew Gregory
　　1775-1818 .... **NCLC 11, 62**
　　See also DLB 39, 158, 178; HGG; LMFS
　　1; RGEL 2; SUFW

Lewis, (Harry) Sinclair 1885-1951 . **TCLC 4,**
　　13, 23, 39; WLC
　　See also AMW; AMWC 1; BPFB 2; CA
　　104; 133; CANR 132; CDALB 1917-
　　1929; DA; DA3; DAB; DAC; DAM MST,
　　NOV; DLB 9, 102, 284; DLBD 1; EWL
　　3; LAIT 3; MTCW 1, 2; NFS 15, 19;
　　RGAL 4; TUS

Lewis, (Percy) Wyndham
　　1884(?)-1957 .. **SSC 34; TCLC 2, 9, 104**
　　See also BRW 7; CA 104; 157; DLB 15;
　　EWL 3; FANT; MTCW 2; RGEL 2

Lewisohn, Ludwig 1883-1955 .... **TCLC 19**
　　See also CA 107; 203; DLB 4, 9, 28, 102

Lewton, Val 1904-1951 .... **TCLC 76**
　　See also CA 199; IDFW 3, 4

Leyner, Mark 1956- .... **CLC 92**
　　See also CA 110; CANR 28, 53; DA3; DLB
　　292; MTCW 2

Lezama Lima, Jose 1910-1976 .... **CLC 4, 10,**
　　101; HLCS 2
　　See also CA 77-80; CANR 71; DAM
　　MULT; DLB 113, 283; EWL 3; HW 1, 2;
　　LAW; RGWL 2, 3

L'Heureux, John (Clarke) 1934- ...... **CLC 52**
　　See also CA 13-16R; CANR 23, 45, 88;
　　DLB 244

Li Ch'ing-chao 1081(?)-1141(?) .... **CMLC 71**

Liddell, C. H.
　　See Kuttner, Henry

Lie, Jonas (Lauritz Idemil)
　　1833-1908(?) .... **TCLC 5**
　　See also CA 115

Lieber, Joel 1937-1971 .... **CLC 6**
　　See also CA 73-76; 29-32R

Lieber, Stanley Martin
　　See Lee, Stan

Lieberman, Laurence (James)
　　1935- .... **CLC 4, 36**
　　See also CA 17-20R; CANR 8, 36, 89; CP
　　7

Lieh Tzu fl. 7th cent. B.C.-5th cent.
　　B.C. .... **CMLC 27**

Lieksman, Anders
　　See Haavikko, Paavo Juhani

Li Fei-kan 1904-
　　See Pa Chin
　　See also CA 105; TWA

Lifton, Robert Jay 1926- .... **CLC 67**
　　See also CA 17-20R; CANR 27, 78; INT
　　CANR-27; SATA 66

Lightfoot, Gordon 1938- .... **CLC 26**
　　See also CA 109

Lightman, Alan P(aige) 1948- .... **CLC 81**
　　See also CA 141; CANR 63, 105

Ligotti, Thomas (Robert) 1953- ...... **CLC 44;**
　　SSC 16
　　See also CA 123; CANR 49; HGG; SUFW
　　2

Li Ho 791-817 .... **PC 13**

Li Ju-chen c. 1763-c. 1830 .... **NCLC 137**

Lilar, Francoise
　　See Mallet-Joris, Francoise

Liliencron, (Friedrich Adolf Axel) Detlev
　　von 1844-1909 .... **TCLC 18**
　　See also CA 117

Lille, Alain de
　　See Alain de Lille

Lilly, William 1602-1681 .... **LC 27**

Lima, Jose Lezama
　　See Lezama Lima, Jose

Lima Barreto, Afonso Henrique de
　　1881-1922 .... **TCLC 23**
　　See Lima Barreto, Afonso Henriques de
　　See also CA 117; 181; LAW

Lima Barreto, Afonso Henriques de
　　See Lima Barreto, Afonso Henrique de
　　See also DLB 307

Limonov, Edward 1944- .... **CLC 67**
　　See also CA 137

Lin, Frank
　　See Atherton, Gertrude (Franklin Horn)

Lin, Yutang 1895-1976 .... **TCLC 149**
　　See also CA 45-48; 65-68; CANR 2; RGAL
　　4

Lincoln, Abraham 1809-1865 .... **NCLC 18**
　　See also LAIT 2

Lind, Jakov .... **CLC 1, 2, 4, 27, 82**
　　See Landwirth, Heinz
　　See also CAAS 4; DLB 299; EWL 3

Lindbergh, Anne (Spencer) Morrow
　　1906-2001 .... **CLC 82**
　　See also BPFB 2; CA 17-20R; 193; CANR
　　16, 73; DAM NOV; MTCW 1, 2; SATA
　　33; SATA-Obit 125; TUS

Lindsay, David 1878(?)-1945 .... **TCLC 15**
　　See also CA 113; 187; DLB 255; FANT;
　　SFW 4; SUFW 1

Lindsay, (Nicholas) Vachel
　　1879-1931 .... **PC 23; TCLC 17; WLC**
　　See also AMWS 1; CA 114; 135; CANR
　　79; CDALB 1865-1917; DA; DA3; DAC;
　　DAM MST, POET; DLB 54; EWL 3;
　　EXPP; RGAL 4; SATA 40; WP

Linke-Poot
　　See Doeblin, Alfred

Linney, Romulus 1930- .... **CLC 51**
　　See also CA 1-4R; CAD; CANR 40, 44,
　　79; CD 5; CSW; RGAL 4

Linton, Eliza Lynn 1822-1898 .... **NCLC 41**
　　See also DLB 18

Li Po 701-763 .... **CMLC 2; PC 29**
　　See also PFS 20; WP

Lowell, Robert (Traill Spence, Jr.)
1917-1977 .... **CLC 1, 2, 3, 4, 5, 8, 9, 11, 15, 37, 124; PC 3; WLC**
See also AMW; AMWC 2; AMWR 2; CA 9-12R; 73-76; CABS 2; CANR 26, 60; CDALBS; DA; DA3; DAB; DAC; DAM MST, NOV; DLB 5, 169; EWL 3; MTCW 1, 2; PAB; PFS 6, 7; RGAL 4; WP

Lowenthal, Michael (Francis)
1969- .... **CLC 119**
See also CA 150; CANR 115

Lowndes, Marie Adelaide (Belloc)
1868-1947 .... **TCLC 12**
See also CA 107; CMW 4; DLB 70; RHW

Lowry, (Clarence) Malcolm
1909-1957 .... **SSC 31; TCLC 6, 40**
See also BPFB 2; BRWS 3; CA 105; 131; CANR 62, 105; CDBLB 1945-1960; DLB 15; EWL 3; MTCW 1, 2; RGEL 2

Lowry, Mina Gertrude 1882-1966
See Loy, Mina
See also CA 113

Loxsmith, John
See Brunner, John (Kilian Houston)

Loy, Mina .... **CLC 28; PC 16**
See Lowry, Mina Gertrude
See also DAM POET; DLB 4, 54; PFS 20

Loyson-Bridet
See Schwob, Marcel (Mayer Andre)

Lucan 39-65 .... **CMLC 33**
See also AW 2; DLB 211; EFS 2; RGWL 2, 3

Lucas, Craig 1951- .... **CLC 64**
See also CA 137; CAD; CANR 71, 109; CD 5; GLL 2

Lucas, E(dward) V(errall)
1868-1938 .... **TCLC 73**
See also CA 176; DLB 98, 149, 153; SATA 20

Lucas, George 1944- .... **CLC 16**
See also AAYA 1, 23; CA 77-80; CANR 30; SATA 56

Lucas, Hans
See Godard, Jean-Luc

Lucas, Victoria
See Plath, Sylvia

Lucian c. 125-c. 180 .... **CMLC 32**
See also AW 2; DLB 176; RGWL 2, 3

Lucretius c. 94B.C.-c. 49B.C. .... **CMLC 48**
See also AW 2; CDWLB 1; DLB 211; EFS 2; RGWL 2, 3

Ludlam, Charles 1943-1987 .... **CLC 46, 50**
See also CA 85-88; 122; CAD; CANR 72, 86; DLB 266

Ludlum, Robert 1927-2001 .... **CLC 22, 43**
See also AAYA 10, 59; BEST 89:1, 90:3; BPFB 2; CA 33-36R; 195; CANR 25, 41, 68, 105, 131; CMW 4; CPW; DA3; DAM NOV, POP; DLBY 1982; MSW; MTCW 1, 2

Ludwig, Ken .... **CLC 60**
See also CA 195; CAD

Ludwig, Otto 1813-1865 .... **NCLC 4**
See also DLB 129

Lugones, Leopoldo 1874-1938 .... **HLCS 2; TCLC 15**
See also CA 116; 131; CANR 104; DLB 283; EWL 3; HW 1; LAW

Lu Hsun .... **SSC 20; TCLC 3**
See Shu-Jen, Chou
See also EWL 3

Lukacs, George .... **CLC 24**
See Lukacs, Gyorgy (Szegeny von)

Lukacs, Gyorgy (Szegeny von) 1885-1971
See Lukacs, George
See also CA 101; 29-32R; CANR 62; CDWLB 4; DLB 215, 242; EW 10; EWL 3; MTCW 2

Luke, Peter (Ambrose Cyprian)
1919-1995 .... **CLC 38**
See also CA 81-84; 147; CANR 72; CBD; CD 5; DLB 13

Lunar, Dennis
See Mungo, Raymond

Lurie, Alison 1926- ..... **CLC 4, 5, 18, 39, 175**
See also BPFB 2; CA 1-4R; CANR 2, 17, 50, 88; CN 7; DLB 2; MTCW 1; SATA 46, 112

Lustig, Arnost 1926- .... **CLC 56**
See also AAYA 3; CA 69-72; CANR 47, 102; CWW 2; DLB 232, 299; EWL 3; SATA 56

Luther, Martin 1483-1546 .... **LC 9, 37**
See also CDWLB 2; DLB 179; EW 2; RGWL 2, 3

Luxemburg, Rosa 1870(?)-1919 ..... **TCLC 63**
See also CA 118

Luzi, Mario 1914- .... **CLC 13**
See also CA 61-64; CANR 9, 70; CWW 2; DLB 128; EWL 3

L'vov, Arkady .... **CLC 59**

Lydgate, John c. 1370-1450(?) .... **LC 81**
See also BRW 1; DLB 146; RGEL 2

Lyly, John 1554(?)-1606 .... **DC 7; LC 41**
See also BRW 1; DAM DRAM; DLB 62, 167; RGEL 2

L'Ymagier
See Gourmont, Remy(-Marie-Charles) de

Lynch, B. Suarez
See Borges, Jorge Luis

Lynch, David (Keith) 1946- ..... **CLC 66, 162**
See also AAYA 55; CA 124; 129; CANR 111

Lynch, James
See Andreyev, Leonid (Nikolaevich)

Lyndsay, Sir David 1485-1555 .... **LC 20**
See also RGEL 2

Lynn, Kenneth S(chuyler)
1923-2001 .... **CLC 50**
See also CA 1-4R; 196; CANR 3, 27, 65

Lynx
See West, Rebecca

Lyons, Marcus
See Blish, James (Benjamin)

Lyotard, Jean-Francois
1924-1998 .... **TCLC 103**
See also DLB 242; EWL 3

Lyre, Pinchbeck
See Sassoon, Siegfried (Lorraine)

Lytle, Andrew (Nelson) 1902-1995 ... **CLC 22**
See also CA 9-12R; 150; CANR 70; CN 7; CSW; DLB 6; DLBY 1995; RGAL 4; RHW

Lyttelton, George 1709-1773 .... **LC 10**
See also RGEL 2

Lytton of Knebworth, Baron
See Bulwer-Lytton, Edward (George Earle Lytton)

Maas, Peter 1929-2001 .... **CLC 29**
See also CA 93-96; 201; INT CA-93-96; MTCW 2

Macaulay, Catherine 1731-1791 .... **LC 64**
See also DLB 104

Macaulay, (Emilie) Rose
1881(?)-1958 .... **TCLC 7, 44**
See also CA 104; DLB 36; EWL 3; RGEL 2; RHW

Macaulay, Thomas Babington
1800-1859 .... **NCLC 42**
See also BRW 4; CDBLB 1832-1890; DLB 32, 55; RGEL 2

MacBeth, George (Mann)
1932-1992 .... **CLC 2, 5, 9**
See also CA 25-28R; 136; CANR 61, 66; DLB 40; MTCW 1; PFS 8; SATA 4; SATA-Obit 70

MacCaig, Norman (Alexander)
1910-1996 .... **CLC 36**
See also BRWS 6; CA 9-12R; CANR 3, 34; CP 7; DAB; DAM POET; DLB 27; EWL 3; RGEL 2

MacCarthy, Sir (Charles Otto) Desmond
1877-1952 .... **TCLC 36**
See also CA 167

MacDiarmid, Hugh .... **CLC 2, 4, 11, 19, 63; PC 9**
See Grieve, C(hristopher) M(urray)
See also CDBLB 1945-1960; DLB 20; EWL 3; RGEL 2

MacDonald, Anson
See Heinlein, Robert A(nson)

Macdonald, Cynthia 1928- .... **CLC 13, 19**
See also CA 49-52; CANR 4, 44; DLB 105

MacDonald, George 1824-1905 .... **TCLC 9, 113**
See also AAYA 57; BYA 5; CA 106; 137; CANR 80; CLR 67; DLB 18, 163, 178; FANT; MAICYA 1, 2; RGEL 2; SATA 33, 100; SFW 4; SUFW; WCH

Macdonald, John
See Millar, Kenneth

MacDonald, John D(ann)
1916-1986 .... **CLC 3, 27, 44**
See also BPFB 2; CA 1-4R; 121; CANR 1, 19, 60; CMW 4; CPW; DAM NOV, POP; DLB 8, 306; DLBY 1986; MSW; MTCW 1, 2; SFW 4

Macdonald, John Ross
See Millar, Kenneth

Macdonald, Ross ..... **CLC 1, 2, 3, 14, 34, 41**
See Millar, Kenneth
See also AMWS 4; BPFB 2; DLBD 6; MSW; RGAL 4

MacDougal, John
See Blish, James (Benjamin)

MacDougal, John
See Blish, James (Benjamin)

MacDowell, John
See Parks, Tim(othy Harold)

MacEwen, Gwendolyn (Margaret)
1941-1987 .... **CLC 13, 55**
See also CA 9-12R; 124; CANR 7, 22; DLB 53, 251; SATA 50; SATA-Obit 55

Macha, Karel Hynek 1810-1846 .... **NCLC 46**

Machado (y Ruiz), Antonio
1875-1939 .... **TCLC 3**
See also CA 104; 174; DLB 108; EW 9; EWL 3; HW 2; RGWL 2, 3

Machado de Assis, Joaquim Maria
1839-1908 .... **BLC 2; HLCS 2; SSC 24; TCLC 10**
See also CA 107; 153; CANR 91; DLB 307; LAW; RGSF 2; RGWL 2, 3; TWA; WLIT 1

Machaut, Guillaume de c.
1300-1377 .... **CMLC 64**
See also DLB 208

Machen, Arthur .... **SSC 20; TCLC 4**
See Jones, Arthur Llewellyn
See also CA 179; DLB 156, 178; RGEL 2; SUFW 1

Machiavelli, Niccolo 1469-1527 ... **DC 16; LC 8, 36; WLCS**
See also AAYA 58; DA; DAB; DAC; DAM MST; EW 2; LAIT 1; LMFS 1; NFS 9; RGWL 2, 3; TWA

MacInnes, Colin 1914-1976 .... **CLC 4, 23**
See also CA 69-72; 65-68; CANR 21; DLB 14; MTCW 1, 2; RGEL 2; RHW

MacInnes, Helen (Clark)
1907-1985 .... **CLC 27, 39**
See also BPFB 2; CA 1-4R; 117; CANR 1, 28, 58; CMW 4; CPW; DAM POP; DLB 87; MSW; MTCW 1, 2; SATA 22; SATA-Obit 44

Mamoulian, Rouben (Zachary)
1897-1987 .... **CLC 16**
See also CA 25-28R; 124; CANR 85

Mandelshtam, Osip
See Mandelstam, Osip (Emilievich)
See also EW 10; EWL 3; RGWL 2, 3

Mandelstam, Osip (Emilievich)
1891(?)-1943(?) .... **PC 14; TCLC 2, 6**
See Mandelshtam, Osip
See also CA 104; 150; MTCW 2; TWA

Mander, (Mary) Jane 1877-1949 ... **TCLC 31**
See also CA 162; RGEL 2

Mandeville, Bernard 1670-1733 .... **LC 82**
See also DLB 101

Mandeville, Sir John fl. 1350- ...... **CMLC 19**
See also DLB 146

Mandiargues, Andre Pieyre de .... **CLC 41**
See Pieyre de Mandiargues, Andre
See also DLB 83

Mandrake, Ethel Belle
See Thurman, Wallace (Henry)

Mangan, James Clarence
1803-1849 .... **NCLC 27**
See also RGEL 2

Maniere, J.-E.
See Giraudoux, Jean(-Hippolyte)

Mankiewicz, Herman (Jacob)
1897-1953 .... **TCLC 85**
See also CA 120; 169; DLB 26; IDFW 3, 4

Manley, (Mary) Delariviere
1672(?)-1724 .... **LC 1, 42**
See also DLB 39, 80; RGEL 2

Mann, Abel
See Creasey, John

Mann, Emily 1952- .... **DC 7**
See also CA 130; CAD; CANR 55; CD 5;
CWD; DLB 266

Mann, (Luiz) Heinrich 1871-1950 ... **TCLC 9**
See also CA 106; 164, 181; DLB 66, 118;
EW 8; EWL 3; RGWL 2, 3

Mann, (Paul) Thomas 1875-1955 .... **SSC 5,
70; TCLC 2, 8, 14, 21, 35, 44, 60;
WLC**
See also BPFB 2; CA 104; 128; CANR 133;
CDWLB 2; DA; DA3; DAB; DAC; DAM
MST, NOV; DLB 66; EW 9; EWL 3; GLL
1; LATS 1:1; LMFS 1; MTCW 1, 2; NFS
17; RGSF 2; RGWL 2, 3; SSFS 4, 9;
TWA

Mannheim, Karl 1893-1947 .... **TCLC 65**
See also CA 204

Manning, David
See Faust, Frederick (Schiller)
See also TCWW 2

Manning, Frederic 1882-1935 .... **TCLC 25**
See also CA 124; 216; DLB 260

Manning, Olivia 1915-1980 .... **CLC 5, 19**
See also CA 5-8R; 101; CANR 29; EWL 3;
FW; MTCW 1; RGEL 2

Mano, D. Keith 1942- .... **CLC 2, 10**
See also CA 25-28R; CAAS 6; CANR 26,
57; DLB 6

Mansfield, Katherine . **SSC 9, 23, 38; TCLC
2, 8, 39; WLC**
See Beauchamp, Kathleen Mansfield
See also BPFB 2; BRW 7; DAB; DLB 162;
EWL 3; EXPS; FW; GLL 1; RGEL 2;
RGSF 2; SSFS 2, 8, 10, 11; WWE 1

Manso, Peter 1940- .... **CLC 39**
See also CA 29-32R; CANR 44

Mantecon, Juan Jimenez
See Jimenez (Mantecon), Juan Ramon

Mantel, Hilary (Mary) 1952- .... **CLC 144**
See also CA 125; CANR 54, 101; CN 7;
DLB 271; RHW

Manton, Peter
See Creasey, John

Man Without a Spleen, A
See Chekhov, Anton (Pavlovich)

Manzoni, Alessandro 1785-1873 ... **NCLC 29,
98**
See also EW 5; RGWL 2, 3; TWA

Map, Walter 1140-1209 .... **CMLC 32**

Mapu, Abraham (ben Jekutiel)
1808-1867 .... **NCLC 18**

Mara, Sally
See Queneau, Raymond

Maracle, Lee 1950- .... **NNAL**
See also CA 149

Marat, Jean Paul 1743-1793 .... **LC 10**

Marcel, Gabriel Honore 1889-1973 . **CLC 15**
See also CA 102; 45-48; EWL 3; MTCW 1,
2

March, William 1893-1954 .... **TCLC 96**
See also CA 216

Marchbanks, Samuel
See Davies, (William) Robertson
See also CCA 1

Marchi, Giacomo
See Bassani, Giorgio

Marcus Aurelius
See Aurelius, Marcus
See also AW 2

Marguerite
See de Navarre, Marguerite

Marguerite d'Angouleme
See de Navarre, Marguerite
See also GFL Beginnings to 1789

Marguerite de Navarre
See de Navarre, Marguerite
See also RGWL 2, 3

Margulies, Donald 1954- .... **CLC 76**
See also AAYA 57; CA 200; DFS 13; DLB
228

Marie de France c. 12th cent. - ..... **CMLC 8;
PC 22**
See also DLB 208; FW; RGWL 2, 3

Marie de l'Incarnation 1599-1672 ...... **LC 10**

Marier, Captain Victor
See Griffith, D(avid Lewelyn) W(ark)

Mariner, Scott
See Pohl, Frederik

Marinetti, Filippo Tommaso
1876-1944 .... **TCLC 10**
See also CA 107; DLB 114, 264; EW 9;
EWL 3

Marivaux, Pierre Carlet de Chamblain de
1688-1763 .... **DC 7; LC 4**
See also GFL Beginnings to 1789; RGWL
2, 3; TWA

Markandaya, Kamala .... **CLC 8, 38**
See Taylor, Kamala (Purnaiya)
See also BYA 13; CN 7; EWL 3

Markfield, Wallace 1926-2002 .... **CLC 8**
See also CA 69-72; 208; CAAS 3; CN 7;
DLB 2, 28; DLBY 2002

Markham, Edwin 1852-1940 .... **TCLC 47**
See also CA 160; DLB 54, 186; RGAL 4

Markham, Robert
See Amis, Kingsley (William)

Markoosie .... **NNAL**
See Patsauq, Markoosie
See also CLR 23; DAM MULT

Marks, J.
See Highwater, Jamake (Mamake)

Marks, J
See Highwater, Jamake (Mamake)

Marks-Highwater, J
See Highwater, Jamake (Mamake)

Marks-Highwater, J.
See Highwater, Jamake (Mamake)

Markson, David M(errill) 1927- .... **CLC 67**
See also CA 49-52; CANR 1, 91; CN 7

Marlatt, Daphne (Buckle) 1942- .... **CLC 168**
See also CA 25-28R; CANR 17, 39; CN 7;
CP 7; CWP; DLB 60; FW

Marley, Bob .... **CLC 17**
See Marley, Robert Nesta

Marley, Robert Nesta 1945-1981
See Marley, Bob
See also CA 107; 103

Marlowe, Christopher 1564-1593 . **DC 1; LC
22, 47; PC 57; WLC**
See also BRW 1; BRWR 1; CDBLB Before
1660; DA; DA3; DAB; DAC; DAM
DRAM, MST; DFS 1, 5, 13; DLB 62;
EXPP; LMFS 1; RGEL 2; TEA; WLIT 3

Marlowe, Stephen 1928- .... **CLC 70**
See Queen, Ellery
See also CA 13-16R; CANR 6, 55; CMW
4; SFW 4

Marmion, Shakerley 1603-1639 .... **LC 89**
See also DLB 58; RGEL 2

Marmontel, Jean-Francois 1723-1799 .. **LC 2**

Maron, Monika 1941- .... **CLC 165**
See also CA 201

Marquand, John P(hillips)
1893-1960 .... **CLC 2, 10**
See also AMW; BPFB 2; CA 85-88; CANR
73; CMW 4; DLB 9, 102; EWL 3; MTCW
2; RGAL 4

Marques, Rene 1919-1979 .. **CLC 96; HLC 2**
See also CA 97-100; 85-88; CANR 78;
DAM MULT; DLB 305; EWL 3; HW 1,
2; LAW; RGSF 2

Marquez, Gabriel (Jose) Garcia
See Garcia Marquez, Gabriel (Jose)

Marquis, Don(ald Robert Perry)
1878-1937 .... **TCLC 7**
See also CA 104; 166; DLB 11, 25; RGAL
4

Marquis de Sade
See Sade, Donatien Alphonse Francois

Marric, J. J.
See Creasey, John
See also MSW

Marryat, Frederick 1792-1848 .... **NCLC 3**
See also DLB 21, 163; RGEL 2; WCH

Marsden, James
See Creasey, John

Marsh, Edward 1872-1953 .... **TCLC 99**

Marsh, (Edith) Ngaio 1895-1982 .. **CLC 7, 53**
See also CA 9-12R; CANR 6, 58; CMW 4;
CPW; DAM POP; DLB 77; MSW;
MTCW 1, 2; RGEL 2; TEA

Marshall, Garry 1934- .... **CLC 17**
See also AAYA 3; CA 111; SATA 60

Marshall, Paule 1929- .. **BLC 3; CLC 27, 72;
SSC 3**
See also AFAW 1, 2; AMWS 11; BPFB 2;
BW 2, 3; CA 77-80; CANR 25, 73, 129;
CN 7; DA3; DAM MULT; DLB 33, 157,
227; EWL 3; LATS 1:2; MTCW 1, 2;
RGAL 4; SSFS 15

Marshallik
See Zangwill, Israel

Marsten, Richard
See Hunter, Evan

Marston, John 1576-1634 .... **LC 33**
See also BRW 2; DAM DRAM; DLB 58,
172; RGEL 2

Martel, Yann 1963- .... **CLC 192**
See also CA 146; CANR 114

Martha, Henry
See Harris, Mark

Marti, Jose
See Marti (y Perez), Jose (Julian)
See also DLB 290

Marti (y Perez), Jose (Julian)
1853-1895 .... **HLC 2; NCLC 63**
See Marti, Jose
See also DAM MULT; HW 2; LAW; RGWL
2, 3; WLIT 1

Mayne, William (James Carter)
1928- .... **CLC 12**
See also AAYA 20; CA 9-12R; CANR 37,
80, 100; CLR 25; FANT; JRDA; MAI-
CYA 1, 2; MAICYAS 1; SAAS 11; SATA
6, 68, 122; SUFW 2; YAW

Mayo, Jim
See L'Amour, Louis (Dearborn)
See also TCWW 2

Maysles, Albert 1926- .... **CLC 16**
See also CA 29-32R

Maysles, David 1932-1987 .... **CLC 16**
See also CA 191

Mazer, Norma Fox 1931- .... **CLC 26**
See also AAYA 5, 36; BYA 1, 8; CA 69-72;
CANR 12, 32, 66, 129; CLR 23; JRDA;
MAICYA 1, 2; SAAS 1; SATA 24, 67,
105; WYA; YAW

Mazzini, Guiseppe 1805-1872 .... **NCLC 34**

McAlmon, Robert (Menzies)
1895-1956 .... **TCLC 97**
See also CA 107; 168; DLB 4, 45; DLBD
15; GLL 1

McAuley, James Phillip 1917-1976 .. **CLC 45**
See also CA 97-100; DLB 260; RGEL 2

McBain, Ed
See Hunter, Evan
See also MSW

McBrien, William (Augustine)
1930- .... **CLC 44**
See also CA 107; CANR 90

McCabe, Patrick 1955- .... **CLC 133**
See also BRWS 9; CA 130; CANR 50, 90;
CN 7; DLB 194

McCaffrey, Anne (Inez) 1926- .... **CLC 17**
See also AAYA 6, 34; AITN 2; BEST 89:2;
BPFB 2; BYA 5; CA 25-28R, 227; CAAE
227; CANR 15, 35, 55, 96; CLR 49;
CPW; DA3; DAM NOV, POP; DLB 8;
JRDA; MAICYA 1, 2; MTCW 1, 2; SAAS
11; SATA 8, 70, 116, 152; SATA-Essay
152; SFW 4; SUFW 2; WYA; YAW

McCall, Nathan 1955(?)- .... **CLC 86**
See also AAYA 59; BW 3; CA 146; CANR
88

McCann, Arthur
See Campbell, John W(ood, Jr.)

McCann, Edson
See Pohl, Frederik

McCarthy, Charles, Jr. 1933-
See McCarthy, Cormac
See also CANR 42, 69, 101; CN 7; CPW;
CSW; DA3; DAM POP; MTCW 2

McCarthy, Cormac .... **CLC 4, 57, 101**
See McCarthy, Charles, Jr.
See also AAYA 41; AMWS 8; BPFB 2; CA
13-16R; CANR 10; DLB 6, 143, 256;
EWL 3; LATS 1:2; TCWW 2

McCarthy, Mary (Therese)
1912-1989 .. **CLC 1, 3, 5, 14, 24, 39, 59;
SSC 24**
See also AMW; BPFB 2; CA 5-8R; 129;
CANR 16, 50, 64; DA3; DLB 2; DLBY
1981; EWL 3; FW; INT CANR-16;
MAWW; MTCW 1, 2; RGAL 4; TUS

McCartney, (James) Paul 1942- . **CLC 12, 35**
See also CA 146; CANR 111

McCauley, Stephen (D.) 1955- .... **CLC 50**
See also CA 141

McClaren, Peter .... **CLC 70**

McClure, Michael (Thomas) 1932- ... **CLC 6,
10**
See also BG 3; CA 21-24R; CAD; CANR
17, 46, 77, 131; CD 5; CP 7; DLB 16;
WP

McCorkle, Jill (Collins) 1958- .... **CLC 51**
See also CA 121; CANR 113; CSW; DLB
234; DLBY 1987

McCourt, Frank 1930- .... **CLC 109**
See also AMWS 12; CA 157; CANR 97;
NCFS 1

McCourt, James 1941- .... **CLC 5**
See also CA 57-60; CANR 98

McCourt, Malachy 1931- .... **CLC 119**
See also SATA 126

McCoy, Horace (Stanley)
1897-1955 .... **TCLC 28**
See also AMWS 13; CA 108; 155; CMW 4;
DLB 9

McCrae, John 1872-1918 .... **TCLC 12**
See also CA 109; DLB 92; PFS 5

McCreigh, James
See Pohl, Frederik

McCullers, (Lula) Carson (Smith)
1917-1967 .... **CLC 1, 4, 10, 12, 48, 100;
SSC 9, 24; TCLC 155; WLC**
See also AAYA 21; AMW; AMWC 2; BPFB
2; CA 5-8R; 25-28R; CABS 1, 3; CANR
18, 132; CDALB 1941-1968; DA; DA3;
DAB; DAC; DAM MST, NOV; DFS 5,
18; DLB 2, 7, 173, 228; EWL 3; EXPS;
FW; GLL 1; LAIT 3, 4; MAWW; MTCW
1, 2; NFS 6, 13; RGAL 4; RGSF 2; SATA
27; SSFS 5; TUS; YAW

McCulloch, John Tyler
See Burroughs, Edgar Rice

McCullough, Colleen 1938(?)- .. **CLC 27, 107**
See also AAYA 36; BPFB 2; CA 81-84;
CANR 17, 46, 67, 98; CPW; DA3; DAM
NOV, POP; MTCW 1, 2; RHW

McCunn, Ruthanne Lum 1946- .... **AAL**
See also CA 119; CANR 43, 96; LAIT 2;
SATA 63

McDermott, Alice 1953- .... **CLC 90**
See also CA 109; CANR 40, 90, 126; DLB
292

McElroy, Joseph 1930- .... **CLC 5, 47**
See also CA 17-20R; CN 7

McEwan, Ian (Russell) 1948- .... **CLC 13, 66,
169**
See also BEST 90:4; BRWS 4; CA 61-64;
CANR 14, 41, 69, 87, 132; CN 7; DAM
NOV; DLB 14, 194; HGG; MTCW 1, 2;
RGSF 2; SUFW 2; TEA

McFadden, David 1940- .... **CLC 48**
See also CA 104; CP 7; DLB 60; INT CA-
104

McFarland, Dennis 1950- .... **CLC 65**
See also CA 165; CANR 110

McGahern, John 1934- ... **CLC 5, 9, 48, 156;
SSC 17**
See also CA 17-20R; CANR 29, 68, 113;
CN 7; DLB 14, 231; MTCW 1

McGinley, Patrick (Anthony) 1937- . **CLC 41**
See also CA 120; 127; CANR 56; INT CA-
127

McGinley, Phyllis 1905-1978 .... **CLC 14**
See also CA 9-12R; 77-80; CANR 19;
CWRI 5; DLB 11, 48; PFS 9, 13; SATA
2, 44; SATA-Obit 24

McGinniss, Joe 1942- .... **CLC 32**
See also AITN 2; BEST 89:2; CA 25-28R;
CANR 26, 70; CPW; DLB 185; INT
CANR-26

McGivern, Maureen Daly
See Daly, Maureen

McGrath, Patrick 1950- .... **CLC 55**
See also CA 136; CANR 65; CN 7; DLB
231; HGG; SUFW 2

McGrath, Thomas (Matthew)
1916-1990 .... **CLC 28, 59**
See also AMWS 10; CA 9-12R; 132; CANR
6, 33, 95; DAM POET; MTCW 1; SATA
41; SATA-Obit 66

McGuane, Thomas (Francis III)
1939- .... **CLC 3, 7, 18, 45, 127**
See also AITN 2; BPFB 2; CA 49-52;
CANR 5, 24, 49, 94; CN 7; DLB 2, 212;
DLBY 1980; EWL 3; INT CANR-24;
MTCW 1; TCWW 2

McGuckian, Medbh 1950- .... **CLC 48, 174;
PC 27**
See also BRWS 5; CA 143; CP 7; CWP;
DAM POET; DLB 40

McHale, Tom 1942(?)-1982 .... **CLC 3, 5**
See also AITN 1; CA 77-80; 106

McHugh, Heather 1948- .... **PC 61**
See also CA 69-72; CANR 11, 28, 55, 92;
CP 7; CWP

McIlvanney, William 1936- .... **CLC 42**
See also CA 25-28R; CANR 61; CMW 4;
DLB 14, 207

McIlwraith, Maureen Mollie Hunter
See Hunter, Mollie
See also SATA 2

McInerney, Jay 1955- .... **CLC 34, 112**
See also AAYA 18; BPFB 2; CA 116; 123;
CANR 45, 68, 116; CN 7; CPW; DA3;
DAM POP; DLB 292; INT CA-123;
MTCW 2

McIntyre, Vonda N(eel) 1948- .... **CLC 18**
See also CA 81-84; CANR 17, 34, 69;
MTCW 1; SFW 4; YAW

McKay, Claude .... **BLC 3; HR 3; PC 2;
TCLC 7, 41; WLC**
See McKay, Festus Claudius
See also AFAW 1, 2; AMWS 10; DAB;
DLB 4, 45, 51, 117; EWL 3; EXPP; GLL
2; LAIT 3; LMFS 2; PAB; PFS 4; RGAL
4; WP

McKay, Festus Claudius 1889-1948
See McKay, Claude
See also BW 1, 3; CA 104; 124; CANR 73;
DA; DAC; DAM MST, MULT, NOV,
POET; MTCW 1, 2; TUS

McKuen, Rod 1933- .... **CLC 1, 3**
See also AITN 1; CA 41-44R; CANR 40

McLoughlin, R. B.
See Mencken, H(enry) L(ouis)

McLuhan, (Herbert) Marshall
1911-1980 .... **CLC 37, 83**
See also CA 9-12R; 102; CANR 12, 34, 61;
DLB 88; INT CANR-12; MTCW 1, 2

McManus, Declan Patrick Aloysius
See Costello, Elvis

McMillan, Terry (L.) 1951- . **BLCS; CLC 50,
61, 112**
See also AAYA 21; AMWS 13; BPFB 2;
BW 2, 3; CA 140; CANR 60, 104, 131;
CPW; DA3; DAM MULT, NOV, POP;
MTCW 2; RGAL 4; YAW

McMurtry, Larry (Jeff) 1936- .. **CLC 2, 3, 7,
11, 27, 44, 127**
See also AAYA 15; AITN 2; AMWS 5;
BEST 89:2; BPFB 2; CA 5-8R; CANR
19, 43, 64, 103; CDALB 1968-1988; CN
7; CPW; CSW; DA3; DAM NOV, POP;
DLB 2, 143, 256; DLBY 1980, 1987;
EWL 3; MTCW 1, 2; RGAL 4; TCWW 2

McNally, T. M. 1961- .... **CLC 82**

McNally, Terrence 1939- .... **CLC 4, 7, 41, 91**
See also AMWS 13; CA 45-48; CAD;
CANR 2, 56, 116; CD 5; DA3; DAM
DRAM; DFS 16, 19; DLB 7, 249; EWL
3; GLL 1; MTCW 2

McNamer, Deirdre 1950- .... **CLC 70**

McNeal, Tom .... **CLC 119**

McNeile, Herman Cyril 1888-1937
See Sapper
See also CA 184; CMW 4; DLB 77

McNickle, (William) D'Arcy
1904-1977 .... **CLC 89; NNAL**
See also CA 9-12R; 85-88; CANR 5, 45;
DAM MULT; DLB 175, 212; RGAL 4;
SATA-Obit 22

McPhee, John (Angus) 1931- .... **CLC 36**
See also AMWS 3; ANW; BEST 90:1; CA
65-68; CANR 20, 46, 64, 69, 121; CPW;
DLB 185, 275; MTCW 1, 2; TUS

McPherson, James Alan 1943- . **BLCS; CLC
19, 77**
See also BW 1, 3; CA 25-28R; CAAS 17;
CANR 24, 74; CN 7; CSW; DLB 38, 244;
EWL 3; MTCW 1, 2; RGAL 4; RGSF 2

McPherson, William (Alexander)
1933- .... **CLC 34**
See also CA 69-72; CANR 28; INT
CANR-28

McTaggart, J. McT. Ellis
See McTaggart, John McTaggart Ellis

McTaggart, John McTaggart Ellis
1866-1925 .... **TCLC 105**
See also CA 120; DLB 262

Mead, George Herbert 1863-1931 . **TCLC 89**
See also CA 212; DLB 270

Mead, Margaret 1901-1978 .... **CLC 37**
See also AITN 1; CA 1-4R; 81-84; CANR
4; DA3; FW; MTCW 1, 2; SATA-Obit 20

Meaker, Marijane (Agnes) 1927-
See Kerr, M. E.
See also CA 107; CANR 37, 63; INT CA-
107; JRDA; MAICYA 1, 2; MAICYAS 1;
MTCW 1; SATA 20, 61, 99; SATA-Essay
111; YAW

Medoff, Mark (Howard) 1940- .... **CLC 6, 23**
See also AITN 1; CA 53-56; CAD; CANR
5; CD 5; DAM DRAM; DFS 4; DLB 7;
INT CANR-5

Medvedev, P. N.
See Bakhtin, Mikhail Mikhailovich

Meged, Aharon
See Megged, Aharon

Meged, Aron
See Megged, Aharon

Megged, Aharon 1920- .... **CLC 9**
See also CA 49-52; CAAS 13; CANR 1;
EWL 3

Mehta, Gita 1943- .... **CLC 179**
See also CA 225; DNFS 2

Mehta, Ved (Parkash) 1934- .... **CLC 37**
See also CA 1-4R, 212; CAAE 212; CANR
2, 23, 69; MTCW 1

Melanchthon, Philipp 1497-1560 .... **LC 90**
See also DLB 179

Melanter
See Blackmore, R(ichard) D(oddridge)

Meleager c. 140B.C.-c. 70B.C. ...... **CMLC 53**

Melies, Georges 1861-1938 .... **TCLC 81**

Melikow, Loris
See Hofmannsthal, Hugo von

Melmoth, Sebastian
See Wilde, Oscar (Fingal O'Flahertie Wills)

Melo Neto, Joao Cabral de
See Cabral de Melo Neto, Joao
See also CWW 2; EWL 3

Meltzer, Milton 1915- .... **CLC 26**
See also AAYA 8, 45; BYA 2, 6; CA 13-
16R; CANR 38, 92, 107; CLR 13; DLB
61; JRDA; MAICYA 1; SAAS 1; SATA
1, 50, 80, 128; SATA-Essay 124; WYA;
YAW

Melville, Herman 1819-1891 ..... **NCLC 3, 12,
29, 45, 49, 91, 93, 123; SSC 1, 17, 46;
WLC**
See also AAYA 25; AMW; AMWR 1;
CDALB 1640-1865; DA; DA3; DAB;
DAC; DAM MST, NOV; DLB 3, 74, 250,
254; EXPN; EXPS; LAIT 1, 2; NFS 7, 9;
RGAL 4; RGSF 2; SATA 59; SSFS 3;
TUS

Members, Mark
See Powell, Anthony (Dymoke)

Membreno, Alejandro .... **CLC 59**

Menander c. 342B.C.-c. 293B.C. .... **CMLC 9,
51; DC 3**
See also AW 1; CDWLB 1; DAM DRAM;
DLB 176; LMFS 1; RGWL 2, 3

Menchu, Rigoberta 1959- .. **CLC 160; HLCS
2**
See also CA 175; DNFS 1; WLIT 1

Mencken, H(enry) L(ouis)
1880-1956 .... **TCLC 13**
See also AMW; CA 105; 125; CDALB
1917-1929; DLB 11, 29, 63, 137, 222;
EWL 3; MTCW 1, 2; NCFS 4; RGAL 4;
TUS

Mendelsohn, Jane 1965- .... **CLC 99**
See also CA 154; CANR 94

Menton, Francisco de
See Chin, Frank (Chew, Jr.)

Mercer, David 1928-1980 .... **CLC 5**
See also CA 9-12R; 102; CANR 23; CBD;
DAM DRAM; DLB 13; MTCW 1; RGEL
2

Merchant, Paul
See Ellison, Harlan (Jay)

Meredith, George 1828-1909 .. **PC 60; TCLC
17, 43**
See also CA 117; 153; CANR 80; CDBLB
1832-1890; DAM POET; DLB 18, 35, 57,
159; RGEL 2; TEA

Meredith, William (Morris) 1919- .... **CLC 4,
13, 22, 55; PC 28**
See also CA 9-12R; CAAS 14; CANR 6,
40, 129; CP 7; DAM POET; DLB 5

Merezhkovsky, Dmitrii Sergeevich
See Merezhkovsky, Dmitry Sergeyevich
See also DLB 295

Merezhkovsky, Dmitry Sergeevich
See Merezhkovsky, Dmitry Sergeyevich
See also EWL 3

Merezhkovsky, Dmitry Sergeyevich
1865-1941 .... **TCLC 29**
See Merezhkovsky, Dmitrii Sergeevich;
Merezhkovsky, Dmitry Sergeevich
See also CA 169

Merimee, Prosper 1803-1870 ... **NCLC 6, 65;
SSC 7, 77**
See also DLB 119, 192; EW 6; EXPS; GFL
1789 to the Present; RGSF 2; RGWL 2,
3; SSFS 8; SUFW

Merkin, Daphne 1954- .... **CLC 44**
See also CA 123

Merleau-Ponty, Maurice
1908-1961 .... **TCLC 156**
See also CA 114; 89-92; DLB 296; GFL
1789 to the Present

Merlin, Arthur
See Blish, James (Benjamin)

Mernissi, Fatima 1940- .... **CLC 171**
See also CA 152; FW

Merrill, James (Ingram) 1926-1995 .. **CLC 2,
3, 6, 8, 13, 18, 34, 91; PC 28**
See also AMWS 3; CA 13-16R; 147; CANR
10, 49, 63, 108; DA3; DAM POET; DLB
5, 165; DLBY 1985; EWL 3; INT CANR-
10; MTCW 1, 2; PAB; RGAL 4

Merriman, Alex
See Silverberg, Robert

Merriman, Brian 1747-1805 .... **NCLC 70**

Merritt, E. B.
See Waddington, Miriam

Merton, Thomas (James)
1915-1968 . **CLC 1, 3, 11, 34, 83; PC 10**
See also AMWS 8; CA 5-8R; 25-28R;
CANR 22, 53, 111, 131; DA3; DLB 48;
DLBY 1981; MTCW 1, 2

Merwin, W(illiam) S(tanley) 1927- ... **CLC 1,
2, 3, 5, 8, 13, 18, 45, 88; PC 45**
See also AMWS 3; CA 13-16R; CANR 15,
51, 112; CP 7; DA3; DAM POET; DLB
5, 169; EWL 3; INT CANR-15; MTCW
1, 2; PAB; PFS 5, 15; RGAL 4

Metcalf, John 1938- .... **CLC 37; SSC 43**
See also CA 113; CN 7; DLB 60; RGSF 2;
TWA

Metcalf, Suzanne
See Baum, L(yman) Frank

Mew, Charlotte (Mary) 1870-1928 .. **TCLC 8**
See also CA 105; 189; DLB 19, 135; RGEL
2

Mewshaw, Michael 1943- .... **CLC 9**
See also CA 53-56; CANR 7, 47; DLBY
1980

Meyer, Conrad Ferdinand
1825-1898 .... **NCLC 81; SSC 30**
See also DLB 129; EW; RGWL 2, 3

Meyer, Gustav 1868-1932
See Meyrink, Gustav
See also CA 117; 190

Meyer, June
See Jordan, June (Meyer)

Meyer, Lynn
See Slavitt, David R(ytman)

Meyers, Jeffrey 1939- .... **CLC 39**
See also CA 73-76, 186; CAAE 186; CANR
54, 102; DLB 111

**Meynell, Alice (Christina Gertrude
Thompson)** 1847-1922 .... **TCLC 6**
See also CA 104; 177; DLB 19, 98; RGEL
2

Meyrink, Gustav .... **TCLC 21**
See Meyer, Gustav
See also DLB 81; EWL 3

Michaels, Leonard 1933-2003 ..... **CLC 6, 25;
SSC 16**
See also CA 61-64; 216; CANR 21, 62, 119;
CN 7; DLB 130; MTCW 1

Michaux, Henri 1899-1984 .... **CLC 8, 19**
See also CA 85-88; 114; DLB 258; EWL 3;
GFL 1789 to the Present; RGWL 2, 3

Micheaux, Oscar (Devereaux)
1884-1951 .... **TCLC 76**
See also BW 3; CA 174; DLB 50; TCWW
2

Michelangelo 1475-1564 .... **LC 12**
See also AAYA 43

Michelet, Jules 1798-1874 .... **NCLC 31**
See also EW 5; GFL 1789 to the Present

Michels, Robert 1876-1936 .... **TCLC 88**
See also CA 212

Michener, James A(lbert)
1907(?)-1997 .. **CLC 1, 5, 11, 29, 60, 109**
See also AAYA 27; AITN 1; BEST 90:1;
BPFB 2; CA 5-8R; 161; CANR 21, 45,
68; CN 7; CPW; DA3; DAM NOV, POP;
DLB 6; MTCW 1, 2; RHW

Mickiewicz, Adam 1798-1855 . **NCLC 3, 101;
PC 38**
See also EW 5; RGWL 2, 3

Middleton, (John) Christopher
1926- .... **CLC 13**
See also CA 13-16R; CANR 29, 54, 117;
CP 7; DLB 40

Middleton, Richard (Barham)
1882-1911 .... **TCLC 56**
See also CA 187; DLB 156; HGG

Middleton, Stanley 1919- .... **CLC 7, 38**
See also CA 25-28R; CAAS 23; CANR 21,
46, 81; CN 7; DLB 14

Middleton, Thomas 1580-1627 ...... **DC 5; LC
33**
See also BRW 2; DAM DRAM, MST; DFS
18; DLB 58; RGEL 2

Migueis, Jose Rodrigues 1901-1980 . **CLC 10**
See also DLB 287

Nichols, Peter (Richard) 1927- .... **CLC 5, 36, 65**
See also CA 104; CANR 33, 86; CBD; CD 5; DLB 13, 245; MTCW 1

Nicholson, Linda ed. .... **CLC 65**

Ni Chuilleanain, Eilean 1942- .... **PC 34**
See also CA 126; CANR 53, 83; CP 7; CWP; DLB 40

Nicolas, F. R. E.
See Freeling, Nicolas

Niedecker, Lorine 1903-1970 ..... **CLC 10, 42; PC 42**
See also CA 25-28; CAP 2; DAM POET; DLB 48

Nietzsche, Friedrich (Wilhelm)
1844-1900 .... **TCLC 10, 18, 55**
See also CA 107; 121; CDWLB 2; DLB 129; EW 7; RGWL 2, 3; TWA

Nievo, Ippolito 1831-1861 .... **NCLC 22**

Nightingale, Anne Redmon 1943-
See Redmon, Anne
See also CA 103

Nightingale, Florence 1820-1910 ... **TCLC 85**
See also CA 188; DLB 166

Nijo Yoshimoto 1320-1388 .... **CMLC 49**
See also DLB 203

Nik. T. O.
See Annensky, Innokenty (Fyodorovich)

Nin, Anais 1903-1977 ..... **CLC 1, 4, 8, 11, 14, 60, 127; SSC 10**
See also AITN 2; AMWS 10; BPFB 2; CA 13-16R; 69-72; CANR 22, 53; DAM NOV, POP; DLB 2, 4, 152; EWL 3; GLL 2; MAWW; MTCW 1, 2; RGAL 4; RGSF 2

Nisbet, Robert A(lexander)
1913-1996 .... **TCLC 117**
See also CA 25-28R; 153; CANR 17; INT CANR-17

Nishida, Kitaro 1870-1945 .... **TCLC 83**

Nishiwaki, Junzaburo
See Nishiwaki, Junzaburo
See also CA 194

Nishiwaki, Junzaburo 1894-1982 .... **PC 15**
See Nishiwaki, Junzaburo; Nishiwaki Junzaburo
See also CA 194; 107; MJW; RGWL 3

Nishiwaki Junzaburo
See Nishiwaki, Junzaburo
See also EWL 3

Nissenson, Hugh 1933- .... **CLC 4, 9**
See also CA 17-20R; CANR 27, 108; CN 7; DLB 28

Nister, Der
See Der Nister
See also EWL 3

Niven, Larry .... **CLC 8**
See Niven, Laurence Van Cott
See also AAYA 27; BPFB 2; BYA 10; DLB 8; SCFW 2

Niven, Laurence Van Cott 1938-
See Niven, Larry
See also CA 21-24R; 207; CAAE 207; CAAS 12; CANR 14, 44, 66, 113; CPW; DAM POP; MTCW 1, 2; SATA 95; SFW 4

Nixon, Agnes Eckhardt 1927- .... **CLC 21**
See also CA 110

Nizan, Paul 1905-1940 .... **TCLC 40**
See also CA 161; DLB 72; EWL 3; GFL 1789 to the Present

Nkosi, Lewis 1936- .... **BLC 3; CLC 45**
See also BW 1, 3; CA 65-68; CANR 27, 81; CBD; CD 5; DAM MULT; DLB 157, 225; WWE 1

Nodier, (Jean) Charles (Emmanuel)
1780-1844 .... **NCLC 19**
See also DLB 119; GFL 1789 to the Present

Noguchi, Yone 1875-1947 .... **TCLC 80**

Nolan, Christopher 1965- .... **CLC 58**
See also CA 111; CANR 88

Noon, Jeff 1957- .... **CLC 91**
See also CA 148; CANR 83; DLB 267; SFW 4

Norden, Charles
See Durrell, Lawrence (George)

Nordhoff, Charles Bernard
1887-1947 .... **TCLC 23**
See also CA 108; 211; DLB 9; LAIT 1; RHW 1; SATA 23

Norfolk, Lawrence 1963- .... **CLC 76**
See also CA 144; CANR 85; CN 7; DLB 267

Norman, Marsha 1947- . **CLC 28, 186; DC 8**
See also CA 105; CABS 3; CAD; CANR 41, 131; CD 5; CSW; CWD; DAM DRAM; DFS 2; DLB 266; DLBY 1984; FW

Normyx
See Douglas, (George) Norman

Norris, (Benjamin) Frank(lin, Jr.)
1870-1902 .... **SSC 28; TCLC 24, 155**
See also AAYA 57; AMW; AMWC 2; BPFB 2; CA 110; 160; CDALB 1865-1917; DLB 12, 71, 186; LMFS 2; NFS 12; RGAL 4; TCWW 2; TUS

Norris, Leslie 1921- .... **CLC 14**
See also CA 11-12; CANR 14, 117; CAP 1; CP 7; DLB 27, 256

North, Andrew
See Norton, Andre

North, Anthony
See Koontz, Dean R(ay)

North, Captain George
See Stevenson, Robert Louis (Balfour)

North, Captain George
See Stevenson, Robert Louis (Balfour)

North, Milou
See Erdrich, Louise

Northrup, B. A.
See Hubbard, L(afayette) Ron(ald)

North Staffs
See Hulme, T(homas) E(rnest)

Northup, Solomon 1808-1863 ...... **NCLC 105**

Norton, Alice Mary
See Norton, Andre
See also MAICYA 1; SATA 1, 43

Norton, Andre 1912- .... **CLC 12**
See Norton, Alice Mary
See also AAYA 14; BPFB 2; BYA 4, 10, 12; CA 1-4R; CANR 68; CLR 50; DLB 8, 52; JRDA; MAICYA 2; MTCW 1; SATA 91; SUFW 1, 2; YAW

Norton, Caroline 1808-1877 .... **NCLC 47**
See also DLB 21, 159, 199

Norway, Nevil Shute 1899-1960
See Shute, Nevil
See also CA 102; 93-96; CANR 85; MTCW 2

Norwid, Cyprian Kamil
1821-1883 .... **NCLC 17**
See also RGWL 3

Nosille, Nabrah
See Ellison, Harlan (Jay)

Nossack, Hans Erich 1901-1978 .... **CLC 6**
See also CA 93-96; 85-88; DLB 69; EWL 3

Nostradamus 1503-1566 .... **LC 27**

Nosu, Chuji
See Ozu, Yasujiro

Notenburg, Eleanora (Genrikhovna) von
See Guro, Elena (Genrikhovna)

Nova, Craig 1945- .... **CLC 7, 31**
See also CA 45-48; CANR 2, 53, 127

Novak, Joseph
See Kosinski, Jerzy (Nikodem)

Novalis 1772-1801 .... **NCLC 13**
See also CDWLB 2; DLB 90; EW 5; RGWL 2, 3

Novick, Peter 1934- .... **CLC 164**
See also CA 188

Novis, Emile
See Weil, Simone (Adolphine)

Nowlan, Alden (Albert) 1933-1983 ... **CLC 15**
See also CA 9-12R; CANR 5; DAC; DAM MST; DLB 53; PFS 12

Noyes, Alfred 1880-1958 ...... **PC 27; TCLC 7**
See also CA 104; 188; DLB 20; EXPP; FANT; PFS 4; RGEL 2

Nugent, Richard Bruce 1906(?)-1987 ... **HR 3**
See also BW 1; CA 125; DLB 51; GLL 2

Nunn, Kem .... **CLC 34**
See also CA 159

Nwapa, Flora (Nwanzuruaha)
1931-1993 .... **BLCS; CLC 133**
See also BW 2; CA 143; CANR 83; CD-WLB 3; CWRI 5; DLB 125; EWL 3; WLIT 2

Nye, Robert 1939- .... **CLC 13, 42**
See also BRWS 10; CA 33-36R; CANR 29, 67, 107; CN 7; CP 7; CWRI 5; DAM NOV; DLB 14, 271; FANT; HGG; MTCW 1; RHW; SATA 6

Nyro, Laura 1947-1997 .... **CLC 17**
See also CA 194

Oates, Joyce Carol 1938- .. **CLC 1, 2, 3, 6, 9, 11, 15, 19, 33, 52, 108, 134; SSC 6, 70; WLC**
See also AAYA 15, 52; AITN 1; AMWS 2; BEST 89:2; BPFB 2; BYA 11; CA 5-8R; CANR 25, 45, 74, 113, 129; CDALB 1968-1988; CN 7; CP 7; CPW; CWP; DA; DA3; DAB; DAC; DAM MST, NOV, POP; DLB 2, 5, 130; DLBY 1981; EWL 3; EXPS; FW; HGG; INT CANR-25; LAIT 4; MAWW; MTCW 1, 2; NFS 8; RGAL 4; RGSF 2; SSFS 17; SUFW 2; TUS

O'Brian, E. G.
See Clarke, Arthur C(harles)

O'Brian, Patrick 1914-2000 .... **CLC 152**
See also AAYA 55; CA 144; 187; CANR 74; CPW; MTCW 2; RHW

O'Brien, Darcy 1939-1998 .... **CLC 11**
See also CA 21-24R; 167; CANR 8, 59

O'Brien, Edna 1936- ..... **CLC 3, 5, 8, 13, 36, 65, 116; SSC 10, 77**
See also BRWS 5; CA 1-4R; CANR 6, 41, 65, 102; CDBLB 1960 to Present; CN 7; DA3; DAM NOV; DLB 14, 231; EWL 3; FW; MTCW 1, 2; RGSF 2; WLIT 4

O'Brien, Fitz-James 1828-1862 ..... **NCLC 21**
See also DLB 74; RGAL 4; SUFW

O'Brien, Flann .... **CLC 1, 4, 5, 7, 10, 47**
See O Nuallain, Brian
See also BRWS 2; DLB 231; EWL 3; RGEL 2

O'Brien, Richard 1942- .... **CLC 17**
See also CA 124

O'Brien, (William) Tim(othy) 1946- . **CLC 7, 19, 40, 103; SSC 74**
See also AAYA 16; AMWS 5; CA 85-88; CANR 40, 58, 133; CDALBS; CN 7; CPW; DA3; DAM POP; DLB 152; DLBD 9; DLBY 1980; LATS 1:2; MTCW 2; RGAL 4; SSFS 5, 15

Obstfelder, Sigbjoern 1866-1900 .... **TCLC 23**
See also CA 123

O'Casey, Sean 1880-1964 .... **CLC 1, 5, 9, 11, 15, 88; DC 12; WLCS**
See also BRW 7; CA 89-92; CANR 62; CBD; CDBLB 1914-1945; DA3; DAB; DAC; DAM DRAM, MST; DFS 19; DLB 10; EWL 3; MTCW 1, 2; RGEL 2; TEA; WLIT 4

Orton, John Kingsley 1933-1967
See Orton, Joe
See also CA 85-88; CANR 35, 66; DAM
DRAM; MTCW 1, 2

Orwell, George ...... **SSC 68; TCLC 2, 6, 15,
31, 51, 128, 129; WLC**
See Blair, Eric (Arthur)
See also BPFB 3; BRW 7; BYA 5; CDBLB
1945-1960; CLR 68; DAB; DLB 15, 98,
195, 255; EWL 3; EXPN; LAIT 4, 5;
LATS 1:1; NFS 3, 7; RGEL 2; SCFW 2;
SFW 4; SSFS 4; TEA; WLIT 4; YAW

Osborne, David
See Silverberg, Robert

Osborne, George
See Silverberg, Robert

Osborne, John (James) 1929-1994 .... **CLC 1,
2, 5, 11, 45; TCLC 153; WLC**
See also BRWS 1; CA 13-16R; 147; CANR
21, 56; CDBLB 1945-1960; DA; DAB;
DAC; DAM DRAM, MST; DFS 4, 19;
DLB 13; EWL 3; MTCW 1, 2; RGEL 2

Osborne, Lawrence 1958- .... **CLC 50**
See also CA 189

Osbourne, Lloyd 1868-1947 .... **TCLC 93**

Osgood, Frances Sargent
1811-1850 .... **NCLC 141**
See also DLB 250

Oshima, Nagisa 1932- .... **CLC 20**
See also CA 116; 121; CANR 78

Oskison, John Milton
1874-1947 .... **NNAL; TCLC 35**
See also CA 144; CANR 84; DAM MULT;
DLB 175

Ossian c. 3rd cent. - .... **CMLC 28**
See Macpherson, James

Ossoli, Sarah Margaret (Fuller)
1810-1850 .... **NCLC 5, 50**
See Fuller, Margaret; Fuller, Sarah Margaret
See also CDALB 1640-1865; FW; LMFS 1;
SATA 25

Ostriker, Alicia (Suskin) 1937- .... **CLC 132**
See also CA 25-28R; CAAS 24; CANR 10,
30, 62, 99; CWP; DLB 120; EXPP; PFS
19

Ostrovsky, Aleksandr Nikolaevich
See Ostrovsky, Alexander
See also DLB 277

Ostrovsky, Alexander 1823-1886 .. **NCLC 30,
57**
See Ostrovsky, Aleksandr Nikolaevich

Otero, Blas de 1916-1979 .... **CLC 11**
See also CA 89-92; DLB 134; EWL 3

O'Trigger, Sir Lucius
See Horne, Richard Henry Hengist

Otto, Rudolf 1869-1937 .... **TCLC 85**

Otto, Whitney 1955- .... **CLC 70**
See also CA 140; CANR 120

Otway, Thomas 1652-1685 ... **DC 24; LC 106**
See also DAM DRAM; DLB 80; RGEL 2

Ouida .... **TCLC 43**
See De la Ramee, Marie Louise (Ouida)
See also DLB 18, 156; RGEL 2

Ouologuem, Yambo 1940- .... **CLC 146**
See also CA 111; 176

Ousmane, Sembene 1923- ... **BLC 3; CLC 66**
See Sembene, Ousmane
See also BW 1, 3; CA 117; 125; CANR 81;
CWW 2; MTCW 1

Ovid 43B.C.-17 .... **CMLC 7; PC 2**
See also AW 2; CDWLB 1; DA3; DAM
POET; DLB 211; RGWL 2, 3; WP

Owen, Hugh
See Faust, Frederick (Schiller)

Owen, Wilfred (Edward Salter)
1893-1918 ... **PC 19; TCLC 5, 27; WLC**
See also BRW 6; CA 104; 141; CDBLB
1914-1945; DA; DAB; DAC; DAM MST,
POET; DLB 20; EWL 3; EXPP; MTCW
2; PFS 10; RGEL 2; WLIT 4

Owens, Louis (Dean) 1948-2002 .... **NNAL**
See also CA 137, 179; 207; CAAE 179;
CAAS 24; CANR 71

Owens, Rochelle 1936- .... **CLC 8**
See also CA 17-20R; CAAS 2; CAD;
CANR 39; CD 5; CP 7; CWD; CWP

Oz, Amos 1939- ...... **CLC 5, 8, 11, 27, 33, 54;
SSC 66**
See also CA 53-56; CANR 27, 47, 65, 113;
CWW 2; DAM NOV; EWL 3; MTCW 1,
2; RGSF 2; RGWL 3

Ozick, Cynthia 1928- .... **CLC 3, 7, 28, 62,
155; SSC 15, 60**
See also AMWS 5; BEST 90:1; CA 17-20R;
CANR 23, 58, 116; CN 7; CPW; DA3;
DAM NOV, POP; DLB 28, 152, 299;
DLBY 1982; EWL 3; EXPS; INT CANR-
23; MTCW 1, 2; RGAL 4; RGSF 2; SSFS
3, 12

Ozu, Yasujiro 1903-1963 .... **CLC 16**
See also CA 112

Pabst, G. W. 1885-1967 .... **TCLC 127**

Pacheco, C.
See Pessoa, Fernando (Antonio Nogueira)

Pacheco, Jose Emilio 1939- .... **HLC 2**
See also CA 111; 131; CANR 65; CWW 2;
DAM MULT; DLB 290; EWL 3; HW 1,
2; RGSF 2

Pa Chin .... **CLC 18**
See Li Fei-kan
See also EWL 3

Pack, Robert 1929- .... **CLC 13**
See also CA 1-4R; CANR 3, 44, 82; CP 7;
DLB 5; SATA 118

Padgett, Lewis
See Kuttner, Henry

Padilla (Lorenzo), Heberto
1932-2000 .... **CLC 38**
See also AITN 1; CA 123; 131; 189; CWW
2; EWL 3; HW 1

Page, James Patrick 1944-
See Page, Jimmy
See also CA 204

Page, Jimmy 1944- .... **CLC 12**
See Page, James Patrick

Page, Louise 1955- .... **CLC 40**
See also CA 140; CANR 76; CBD; CD 5;
CWD; DLB 233

Page, P(atricia) K(athleen) 1916- ...... **CLC 7,
18; PC 12**
See Cape, Judith
See also CA 53-56; CANR 4, 22, 65; CP 7;
DAC; DAM MST; DLB 68; MTCW 1;
RGEL 2

Page, Stanton
See Fuller, Henry Blake

Page, Stanton
See Fuller, Henry Blake

Page, Thomas Nelson 1853-1922 .... **SSC 23**
See also CA 118; 177; DLB 12, 78; DLBD
13; RGAL 4

Pagels, Elaine Hiesey 1943- .... **CLC 104**
See also CA 45-48; CANR 2, 24, 51; FW;
NCFS 4

Paget, Violet 1856-1935
See Lee, Vernon
See also CA 104; 166; GLL 1; HGG

Paget-Lowe, Henry
See Lovecraft, H(oward) P(hillips)

Paglia, Camille (Anna) 1947- .... **CLC 68**
See also CA 140; CANR 72; CPW; FW;
GLL 2; MTCW 2

Paige, Richard
See Koontz, Dean R(ay)

Paine, Thomas 1737-1809 .... **NCLC 62**
See also AMWS 1; CDALB 1640-1865;
DLB 31, 43, 73, 158; LAIT 1; RGAL 4;
RGEL 2; TUS

Pakenham, Antonia
See Fraser, Antonia (Pakenham)

Palamas, Costis
See Palamas, Kostes

Palamas, Kostes 1859-1943 .... **TCLC 5**
See Palamas, Kostis
See also CA 105; 190; RGWL 2, 3

Palamas, Kostis
See Palamas, Kostes
See also EWL 3

Palazzeschi, Aldo 1885-1974 .... **CLC 11**
See also CA 89-92; 53-56; DLB 114, 264;
EWL 3

Pales Matos, Luis 1898-1959 .... **HLCS 2**
See Pales Matos, Luis
See also DLB 290; HW 1; LAW

Paley, Grace 1922- .. **CLC 4, 6, 37, 140; SSC
8**
See also AMWS 6; CA 25-28R; CANR 13,
46, 74, 118; CN 7; CPW; DA3; DAM
POP; DLB 28, 218; EWL 3; EXPS; FW;
INT CANR-13; MAWW; MTCW 1, 2;
RGAL 4; RGSF 2; SSFS 3, 20

Palin, Michael (Edward) 1943- .... **CLC 21**
See Monty Python
See also CA 107; CANR 35, 109; SATA 67

Palliser, Charles 1947- .... **CLC 65**
See also CA 136; CANR 76; CN 7

Palma, Ricardo 1833-1919 .... **TCLC 29**
See also CA 168; LAW

Pamuk, Orhan 1952- .... **CLC 185**
See also CA 142; CANR 75, 127; CWW 2

Pancake, Breece Dexter 1952-1979
See Pancake, Breece D'J
See also CA 123; 109

Pancake, Breece D'J .... **CLC 29; SSC 61**
See Pancake, Breece Dexter
See also DLB 130

Panchenko, Nikolai .... **CLC 59**

Pankhurst, Emmeline (Goulden)
1858-1928 .... **TCLC 100**
See also CA 116; FW

Panko, Rudy
See Gogol, Nikolai (Vasilyevich)

Papadiamantis, Alexandros
1851-1911 .... **TCLC 29**
See also CA 168; EWL 3

Papadiamantopoulos, Johannes 1856-1910
See Moreas, Jean
See also CA 117

Papini, Giovanni 1881-1956 .... **TCLC 22**
See also CA 121; 180; DLB 264

Paracelsus 1493-1541 .... **LC 14**
See also DLB 179

Parasol, Peter
See Stevens, Wallace

Pardo Bazan, Emilia 1851-1921 .... **SSC 30**
See also EWL 3; FW; RGSF 2; RGWL 2, 3

Pareto, Vilfredo 1848-1923 .... **TCLC 69**
See also CA 175

Paretsky, Sara 1947- .... **CLC 135**
See also AAYA 30; BEST 90:3; CA 125;
129; CANR 59, 95; CMW 4; CPW; DA3;
DAM POP; DLB 306; INT CA-129;
MSW; RGAL 4

Parfenie, Maria
See Codrescu, Andrei

Parini, Jay (Lee) 1948- .... **CLC 54, 133**
See also CA 97-100; CAAS 16; CANR 32,
87

Park, Jordan
See Kornbluth, C(yril) M.; Pohl, Frederik

Robinson, Marilynne 1944- ...... **CLC 25, 180**
See also CA 116; CANR 80; CN 7; DLB 206

Robinson, Mary 1758-1800 .... **NCLC 142**
See also DLB 158; FW

Robinson, Smokey .... **CLC 21**
See Robinson, William, Jr.

Robinson, William, Jr. 1940-
See Robinson, Smokey
See also CA 116

Robison, Mary 1949- .... **CLC 42, 98**
See also CA 113; 116; CANR 87; CN 7;
DLB 130; INT CA-116; RGSF 2

Rochester
See Wilmot, John
See also RGEL 2

Rod, Edouard 1857-1910 .... **TCLC 52**

Roddenberry, Eugene Wesley 1921-1991
See Roddenberry, Gene
See also CA 110; 135; CANR 37; SATA 45;
SATA-Obit 69

Roddenberry, Gene .... **CLC 17**
See Roddenberry, Eugene Wesley
See also AAYA 5; SATA-Obit 69

Rodgers, Mary 1931- .... **CLC 12**
See also BYA 5; CA 49-52; CANR 8, 55,
90; CLR 20; CWRI 5; INT CANR-8;
JRDA; MAICYA 1, 2; SATA 8, 130

Rodgers, W(illiam) R(obert)
1909-1969 .... **CLC 7**
See also CA 85-88; DLB 20; RGEL 2

Rodman, Eric
See Silverberg, Robert

Rodman, Howard 1920(?)-1985 .... **CLC 65**
See also CA 118

Rodman, Maia
See Wojciechowska, Maia (Teresa)

Rodo, Jose Enrique 1871(?)-1917 .... **HLCS 2**
See also CA 178; EWL 3; HW 2; LAW

Rodolph, Utto
See Ouologuem, Yambo

Rodriguez, Claudio 1934-1999 .... **CLC 10**
See also CA 188; DLB 134

Rodriguez, Richard 1944- .... **CLC 155; HLC 2**
See also AMWS 14; CA 110; CANR 66,
116; DAM MULT; DLB 82, 256; HW 1,
2; LAIT 5; LLW 1; NCFS 3; WLIT 1

Roelvaag, O(le) E(dvart) 1876-1931
See Rolvaag, O(le) E(dvart)
See also CA 117; 171

Roethke, Theodore (Huebner)
1908-1963 .... **CLC 1, 3, 8, 11, 19, 46,
101; PC 15**
See also AMW; CA 81-84; CABS 2;
CDALB 1941-1968; DA3; DAM POET;
DLB 5, 206; EWL 3; EXPP; MTCW 1, 2;
PAB; PFS 3; RGAL 4; WP

Rogers, Carl R(ansom)
1902-1987 .... **TCLC 125**
See also CA 1-4R; 121; CANR 1, 18;
MTCW 1

Rogers, Samuel 1763-1855 .... **NCLC 69**
See also DLB 93; RGEL 2

Rogers, Thomas Hunton 1927- .... **CLC 57**
See also CA 89-92; INT CA-89-92

Rogers, Will(iam Penn Adair)
1879-1935 .... **NNAL; TCLC 8, 71**
See also CA 105; 144; DA3; DAM MULT;
DLB 11; MTCW 2

Rogin, Gilbert 1929- .... **CLC 18**
See also CA 65-68; CANR 15

Rohan, Koda
See Koda Shigeyuki

Rohlfs, Anna Katharine Green
See Green, Anna Katharine

Rohmer, Eric .... **CLC 16**
See Scherer, Jean-Marie Maurice

Rohmer, Sax .... **TCLC 28**
See Ward, Arthur Henry Sarsfield
See also DLB 70; MSW; SUFW

Roiphe, Anne (Richardson) 1935- .. **CLC 3, 9**
See also CA 89-92; CANR 45, 73; DLBY
1980; INT CA-89-92

Rojas, Fernando de 1475-1541 ... **HLCS 1, 2;
LC 23**
See also DLB 286; RGWL 2, 3

Rojas, Gonzalo 1917- .... **HLCS 2**
See also CA 178; HW 2; LAWS 1

Roland, Marie-Jeanne 1754-1793 .... **LC 98**

Rolfe, Frederick (William Serafino Austin
Lewis Mary) 1860-1913 .... **TCLC 12**
See Al Siddik
See also CA 107; 210; DLB 34, 156; RGEL 2

Rolland, Romain 1866-1944 .... **TCLC 23**
See also CA 118; 197; DLB 65, 284; EWL
3; GFL 1789 to the Present; RGWL 2, 3

Rolle, Richard c. 1300-c. 1349 ...... **CMLC 21**
See also DLB 146; LMFS 1; RGEL 2

Rolvaag, O(le) E(dvart) .... **TCLC 17**
See Roelvaag, O(le) E(dvart)
See also DLB 9, 212; NFS 5; RGAL 4

Romain Arnaud, Saint
See Aragon, Louis

Romains, Jules 1885-1972 .... **CLC 7**
See also CA 85-88; CANR 34; DLB 65;
EWL 3; GFL 1789 to the Present; MTCW 1

Romero, Jose Ruben 1890-1952 .... **TCLC 14**
See also CA 114; 131; EWL 3; HW 1; LAW

Ronsard, Pierre de 1524-1585 . **LC 6, 54; PC
11**
See also EW 2; GFL Beginnings to 1789;
RGWL 2, 3; TWA

Rooke, Leon 1934- .... **CLC 25, 34**
See also CA 25-28R; CANR 23, 53; CCA
1; CPW; DAM POP

Roosevelt, Franklin Delano
1882-1945 .... **TCLC 93**
See also CA 116; 173; LAIT 3

Roosevelt, Theodore 1858-1919 ..... **TCLC 69**
See also CA 115; 170; DLB 47, 186, 275

Roper, William 1498-1578 .... **LC 10**

Roquelaure, A. N.
See Rice, Anne

Rosa, Joao Guimaraes 1908-1967 ... **CLC 23;
HLCS 1**
See Guimaraes Rosa, Joao
See also CA 89-92; DLB 113, 307; EWL 3;
WLIT 1

Rose, Wendy 1948- . **CLC 85; NNAL; PC 13**
See also CA 53-56; CANR 5, 51; CWP;
DAM MULT; DLB 175; PFS 13; RGAL
4; SATA 12

Rosen, R. D.
See Rosen, Richard (Dean)

Rosen, Richard (Dean) 1949- .... **CLC 39**
See also CA 77-80; CANR 62, 120; CMW
4; INT CANR-30

Rosenberg, Isaac 1890-1918 .... **TCLC 12**
See also BRW 6; CA 107; 188; DLB 20,
216; EWL 3; PAB; RGEL 2

Rosenblatt, Joe .... **CLC 15**
See Rosenblatt, Joseph

Rosenblatt, Joseph 1933-
See Rosenblatt, Joe
See also CA 89-92; CP 7; INT CA-89-92

Rosenfeld, Samuel
See Tzara, Tristan

Rosenstock, Sami
See Tzara, Tristan

Rosenstock, Samuel
See Tzara, Tristan

Rosenthal, M(acha) L(ouis)
1917-1996 .... **CLC 28**
See also CA 1-4R; 152; CAAS 6; CANR 4,
51; CP 7; DLB 5; SATA 59

Ross, Barnaby
See Dannay, Frederic

Ross, Bernard L.
See Follett, Ken(neth Martin)

Ross, J. H.
See Lawrence, T(homas) E(dward)

Ross, John Hume
See Lawrence, T(homas) E(dward)

Ross, Martin 1862-1915
See Martin, Violet Florence
See also DLB 135; GLL 2; RGEL 2; RGSF 2

Ross, (James) Sinclair 1908-1996 ... **CLC 13;
SSC 24**
See also CA 73-76; CANR 81; CN 7; DAC;
DAM MST; DLB 88; RGEL 2; RGSF 2;
TCWW 2

Rossetti, Christina (Georgina)
1830-1894 .... **NCLC 2, 50, 66; PC 7;
WLC**
See also AAYA 51; BRW 5; BYA 4; DA;
DA3; DAB; DAC; DAM MST, POET;
DLB 35, 163, 240; EXPP; LATS 1:1;
MAICYA 1, 2; PFS 10, 14; RGEL 2;
SATA 20; TEA; WCH

Rossetti, Dante Gabriel 1828-1882 . **NCLC 4,
77; PC 44; WLC**
See also AAYA 51; BRW 5; CDBLB 1832-
1890; DA; DAB; DAC; DAM MST,
POET; DLB 35; EXPP; RGEL 2; TEA

Rossi, Cristina Peri
See Peri Rossi, Cristina

Rossi, Jean-Baptiste 1931-2003
See Japrisot, Sebastien
See also CA 201; 215

Rossner, Judith (Perelman) 1935- . **CLC 6, 9,
29**
See also AITN 2; BEST 90:3; BPFB 3; CA
17-20R; CANR 18, 51, 73; CN 7; DLB 6;
INT CANR-18; MTCW 1, 2

Rostand, Edmond (Eugene Alexis)
1868-1918 .... **DC 10; TCLC 6, 37**
See also CA 104; 126; DA; DA3; DAB;
DAC; DAM DRAM, MST; DFS 1; DLB
192; LAIT 1; MTCW 1; RGWL 2, 3;
TWA

Roth, Henry 1906-1995 ..... **CLC 2, 6, 11, 104**
See also AMWS 9; CA 11-12; 149; CANR
38, 63; CAP 1; CN 7; DA3; DLB 28;
EWL 3; MTCW 1, 2; RGAL 4

Roth, (Moses) Joseph 1894-1939 ... **TCLC 33**
See also CA 160; DLB 85; EWL 3; RGWL
2, 3

Roth, Philip (Milton) 1933- ... **CLC 1, 2, 3, 4,
6, 9, 15, 22, 31, 47, 66, 86, 119; SSC
26; WLC**
See also AMWR 2; AMWS 3; BEST 90:3;
BPFB 3; CA 1-4R; CANR 1, 22, 36, 55,
89, 132; CDALB 1968-1988; CN 7; CPW
1; DA; DA3; DAB; DAC; DAM MST,
NOV, POP; DLB 2, 28, 173; DLBY 1982;
EWL 3; MTCW 1, 2; RGAL 4; RGSF 2;
SSFS 12, 18; TUS

Rothenberg, Jerome 1931- .... **CLC 6, 57**
See also CA 45-48; CANR 1, 106; CP 7;
DLB 5, 193

Rotter, Pat ed. .... **CLC 65**

Roumain, Jacques (Jean Baptiste)
1907-1944 .... **BLC 3; TCLC 19**
See also BW 1; CA 117; 125; DAM MULT;
EWL 3

Rourke, Constance Mayfield
1885-1941 .... **TCLC 12**
See also CA 107; 200; YABC 1

3; GFL 1789 to the Present; LMFS 2; MTCW 1, 2; RGSF 2; RGWL 2, 3; SSFS 9; TWA

Sassoon, Siegfried (Lorraine)
1886-1967 .... **CLC 36, 130; PC 12**
See also BRW 6; CA 104; 25-28R; CANR 36; DAB; DAM MST, NOV, POET; DLB 20, 191; DLBD 18; EWL 3; MTCW 1, 2; PAB; RGEL 2; TEA

Satterfield, Charles
See Pohl, Frederik

Satyremont
See Peret, Benjamin

Saul, John (W. III) 1942- .... **CLC 46**
See also AAYA 10; BEST 90:4; CA 81-84; CANR 16, 40, 81; CPW; DAM NOV, POP; HGG; SATA 98

Saunders, Caleb
See Heinlein, Robert A(nson)

Saura (Atares), Carlos 1932-1998 .... **CLC 20**
See also CA 114; 131; CANR 79; HW 1

Sauser, Frederic Louis
See Sauser-Hall, Frederic

Sauser-Hall, Frederic 1887-1961 ...... **CLC 18**
See Cendrars, Blaise
See also CA 102; 93-96; CANR 36, 62; MTCW 1

Saussure, Ferdinand de
1857-1913 .... **TCLC 49**
See also DLB 242

Savage, Catharine
See Brosman, Catharine Savage

Savage, Richard 1697(?)-1743 .... **LC 96**
See also DLB 95; RGEL 2

Savage, Thomas 1915-2003 .... **CLC 40**
See also CA 126; 132; 218; CAAS 15; CN 7; INT CA-132; SATA-Obit 147; TCWW 2

Savan, Glenn 1953-2003 .... **CLC 50**
See also CA 225

Sax, Robert
See Johnson, Robert

Saxo Grammaticus c. 1150-c.
1222 .... **CMLC 58**

Saxton, Robert
See Johnson, Robert

Sayers, Dorothy L(eigh) 1893-1957 . **SSC 71; TCLC 2, 15**
See also BPFB 3; BRWS 3; CA 104; 119; CANR 60; CDBLB 1914-1945; CMW 4; DAM POP; DLB 10, 36, 77, 100; MSW; MTCW 1, 2; RGEL 2; SSFS 12; TEA

Sayers, Valerie 1952- .... **CLC 50, 122**
See also CA 134; CANR 61; CSW

Sayles, John (Thomas) 1950- .... **CLC 7, 10, 14, 198**
See also CA 57-60; CANR 41, 84; DLB 44

Scammell, Michael 1935- .... **CLC 34**
See also CA 156

Scannell, Vernon 1922- .... **CLC 49**
See also CA 5-8R; CANR 8, 24, 57; CP 7; CWRI 5; DLB 27; SATA 59

Scarlett, Susan
See Streatfeild, (Mary) Noel

Scarron 1847-1910
See Mikszath, Kalman

Schaeffer, Susan Fromberg 1941- ..... **CLC 6, 11, 22**
See also CA 49-52; CANR 18, 65; CN 7; DLB 28, 299; MTCW 1, 2; SATA 22

Schama, Simon (Michael) 1945- ..... **CLC 150**
See also BEST 89:4; CA 105; CANR 39, 91

Schary, Jill
See Robinson, Jill

Schell, Jonathan 1943- .... **CLC 35**
See also CA 73-76; CANR 12, 117

Schelling, Friedrich Wilhelm Joseph von
1775-1854 .... **NCLC 30**
See also DLB 90

Scherer, Jean-Marie Maurice 1920-
See Rohmer, Eric
See also CA 110

Schevill, James (Erwin) 1920- .... **CLC 7**
See also CA 5-8R; CAAS 12; CAD; CD 5

Schiller, Friedrich von 1759-1805 ...... **DC 12; NCLC 39, 69**
See also CDWLB 2; DAM DRAM; DLB 94; EW 5; RGWL 2, 3; TWA

Schisgal, Murray (Joseph) 1926- .... **CLC 6**
See also CA 21-24R; CAD; CANR 48, 86; CD 5

Schlee, Ann 1934- .... **CLC 35**
See also CA 101; CANR 29, 88; SATA 44; SATA-Brief 36

Schlegel, August Wilhelm von
1767-1845 .... **NCLC 15, 142**
See also DLB 94; RGWL 2, 3

Schlegel, Friedrich 1772-1829 .... **NCLC 45**
See also DLB 90; EW 5; RGWL 2, 3; TWA

Schlegel, Johann Elias (von)
1719(?)-1749 .... **LC 5**

Schleiermacher, Friedrich
1768-1834 .... **NCLC 107**
See also DLB 90

Schlesinger, Arthur M(eier), Jr.
1917- .... **CLC 84**
See also AITN 1; CA 1-4R; CANR 1, 28, 58, 105; DLB 17; INT CANR-28; MTCW 1, 2; SATA 61

Schlink, Bernhard 1944- .... **CLC 174**
See also CA 163; CANR 116

Schmidt, Arno (Otto) 1914-1979 ...... **CLC 56**
See also CA 128; 109; DLB 69; EWL 3

Schmitz, Aron Hector 1861-1928
See Svevo, Italo
See also CA 104; 122; MTCW 1

Schnackenberg, Gjertrud (Cecelia)
1953- .... **CLC 40; PC 45**
See also CA 116; CANR 100; CP 7; CWP; DLB 120, 282; PFS 13

Schneider, Leonard Alfred 1925-1966
See Bruce, Lenny
See also CA 89-92

Schnitzler, Arthur 1862-1931 ..... **DC 17; SSC 15, 61; TCLC 4**
See also CA 104; CDWLB 2; DLB 81, 118; EW 8; EWL 3; RGSF 2; RGWL 2, 3

Schoenberg, Arnold Franz Walter
1874-1951 .... **TCLC 75**
See also CA 109; 188

Schonberg, Arnold
See Schoenberg, Arnold Franz Walter

Schopenhauer, Arthur 1788-1860 .. **NCLC 51**
See also DLB 90; EW 5

Schor, Sandra (M.) 1932(?)-1990 ..... **CLC 65**
See also CA 132

Schorer, Mark 1908-1977 .... **CLC 9**
See also CA 5-8R; 73-76; CANR 7; DLB 103

Schrader, Paul (Joseph) 1946- .... **CLC 26**
See also CA 37-40R; CANR 41; DLB 44

Schreber, Daniel 1842-1911 .... **TCLC 123**

Schreiner, Olive (Emilie Albertina)
1855-1920 .... **TCLC 9**
See also AFW; BRWS 2; CA 105; 154; DLB 18, 156, 190, 225; EWL 3; FW; RGEL 2; TWA; WLIT 2; WWE 1

Schulberg, Budd (Wilson) 1914- .. **CLC 7, 48**
See also BPFB 3; CA 25-28R; CANR 19, 87; CN 7; DLB 6, 26, 28; DLBY 1981, 2001

Schulman, Arnold
See Trumbo, Dalton

Schulz, Bruno 1892-1942 .. **SSC 13; TCLC 5, 51**
See also CA 115; 123; CANR 86; CDWLB 4; DLB 215; EWL 3; MTCW 2; RGSF 2; RGWL 2, 3

Schulz, Charles M(onroe)
1922-2000 .... **CLC 12**
See also AAYA 39; CA 9-12R; 187; CANR 6, 132; INT CANR-6; SATA 10; SATA-Obit 118

Schumacher, E(rnst) F(riedrich)
1911-1977 .... **CLC 80**
See also CA 81-84; 73-76; CANR 34, 85

Schumann, Robert 1810-1856 ...... **NCLC 143**

Schuyler, George Samuel 1895-1977 .... **HR 3**
See also BW 2; CA 81-84; 73-76; CANR 42; DLB 29, 51

Schuyler, James Marcus 1923-1991 .. **CLC 5, 23**
See also CA 101; 134; DAM POET; DLB 5, 169; EWL 3; INT CA-101; WP

Schwartz, Delmore (David)
1913-1966 ... **CLC 2, 4, 10, 45, 87; PC 8**
See also AMWS 2; CA 17-18; 25-28R; CANR 35; CAP 2; DLB 28, 48; EWL 3; MTCW 1, 2; PAB; RGAL 4; TUS

Schwartz, Ernst
See Ozu, Yasujiro

Schwartz, John Burnham 1965- .... **CLC 59**
See also CA 132; CANR 116

Schwartz, Lynne Sharon 1939- .... **CLC 31**
See also CA 103; CANR 44, 89; DLB 218; MTCW 2

Schwartz, Muriel A.
See Eliot, T(homas) S(tearns)

Schwarz-Bart, Andre 1928- .... **CLC 2, 4**
See also CA 89-92; CANR 109; DLB 299

Schwarz-Bart, Simone 1938- . **BLCS; CLC 7**
See also BW 2; CA 97-100; CANR 117; EWL 3

Schwerner, Armand 1927-1999 .... **PC 42**
See also CA 9-12R; 179; CANR 50, 85; CP 7; DLB 165

Schwitters, Kurt (Hermann Edward Karl Julius) 1887-1948 .... **TCLC 95**
See also CA 158

Schwob, Marcel (Mayer Andre)
1867-1905 .... **TCLC 20**
See also CA 117; 168; DLB 123; GFL 1789 to the Present

Sciascia, Leonardo 1921-1989 .. **CLC 8, 9, 41**
See also CA 85-88; 130; CANR 35; DLB 177; EWL 3; MTCW 1; RGWL 2, 3

Scoppettone, Sandra 1936- .... **CLC 26**
See Early, Jack
See also AAYA 11; BYA 8; CA 5-8R; CANR 41, 73; GLL 1; MAICYA 2; MAICYAS 1; SATA 9, 92; WYA; YAW

Scorsese, Martin 1942- .... **CLC 20, 89**
See also AAYA 38; CA 110; 114; CANR 46, 85

Scotland, Jay
See Jakes, John (William)

Scott, Duncan Campbell
1862-1947 .... **TCLC 6**
See also CA 104; 153; DAC; DLB 92; RGEL 2

Scott, Evelyn 1893-1963 .... **CLC 43**
See also CA 104; 112; CANR 64; DLB 9, 48; RHW

Scott, F(rancis) R(eginald)
1899-1985 .... **CLC 22**
See also CA 101; 114; CANR 87; DLB 88; INT CA-101; RGEL 2

Scott, Frank
See Scott, F(rancis) R(eginald)

Scott, Joan .... **CLC 65**

Scott, Joanna 1960- .... **CLC 50**
See also CA 126; CANR 53, 92

Siguenza y Gongora, Carlos de
1645-1700 .... **HLCS 2; LC 8**
See also LAW

Sigurjonsson, Johann
See Sigurjonsson, Johann

Sigurjonsson, Johann 1880-1919 ... **TCLC 27**
See also CA 170; DLB 293; EWL 3

Sikelianos, Angelos 1884-1951 .... **PC 29;**
TCLC 39
See also EWL 3; RGWL 2, 3

Silkin, Jon 1930-1997 .... **CLC 2, 6, 43**
See also CA 5-8R; CAAS 5; CANR 89; CP
7; DLB 27

Silko, Leslie (Marmon) 1948- .... **CLC 23, 74,**
114; NNAL; SSC 37, 66; WLCS
See also AAYA 14; AMWS 4; ANW; BYA
12; CA 115; 122; CANR 45, 65, 118; CN
7; CP 7; CPW 1; CWP; DA; DA3; DAC;
DAM MST, MULT, POP; DLB 143, 175,
256, 275; EWL 3; EXPP; EXPS; LAIT 4;
MTCW 2; NFS 4; PFS 9, 16; RGAL 4;
RGSF 2; SSFS 4, 8, 10, 11

Sillanpaa, Frans Eemil 1888-1964 ... **CLC 19**
See also CA 129; 93-96; EWL 3; MTCW 1

Sillitoe, Alan 1928- .. **CLC 1, 3, 6, 10, 19, 57,**
148
See also AITN 1; BRWS 5; CA 9-12R, 191;
CAAE 191; CAAS 2; CANR 8, 26, 55;
CDBLB 1960 to Present; CN 7; DLB 14,
139; EWL 3; MTCW 1, 2; RGEL 2;
RGSF 2; SATA 61

Silone, Ignazio 1900-1978 .... **CLC 4**
See also CA 25-28; 81-84; CANR 34; CAP
2; DLB 264; EW 12; EWL 3; MTCW 1;
RGSF 2; RGWL 2, 3

Silone, Ignazione
See Silone, Ignazio

Silver, Joan Micklin 1935- .... **CLC 20**
See also CA 114; 121; INT CA-121

Silver, Nicholas
See Faust, Frederick (Schiller)
See also TCWW 2

Silverberg, Robert 1935- .... **CLC 7, 140**
See also AAYA 24; BPFB 3; BYA 7, 9; CA
1-4R, 186; CAAE 186; CAAS 3; CANR
1, 20, 36, 85; CLR 59; CN 7; CPW; DAM
POP; DLB 8; INT CANR-20; MAICYA
1, 2; MTCW 1, 2; SATA 13, 91; SATA-
Essay 104; SCFW 2; SFW 4; SUFW 2

Silverstein, Alvin 1933- .... **CLC 17**
See also CA 49-52; CANR 2; CLR 25;
JRDA; MAICYA 1, 2; SATA 8, 69, 124

Silverstein, Shel(don Allan)
1932-1999 .... **PC 49**
See also AAYA 40; BW 3; CA 107; 179;
CANR 47, 74, 81; CLR 5; CWRI 5;
JRDA; MAICYA 1, 2; MTCW 2; SATA
33, 92; SATA-Brief 27; SATA-Obit 116

Silverstein, Virginia B(arbara Opshelor)
1937- .... **CLC 17**
See also CA 49-52; CANR 2; CLR 25;
JRDA; MAICYA 1, 2; SATA 8, 69, 124

Sim, Georges
See Simenon, Georges (Jacques Christian)

Simak, Clifford D(onald) 1904-1988 . **CLC 1,**
55
See also CA 1-4R; 125; CANR 1, 35; DLB
8; MTCW 1; SATA-Obit 56; SFW 4

Simenon, Georges (Jacques Christian)
1903-1989 .... **CLC 1, 2, 3, 8, 18, 47**
See also BPFB 3; CA 85-88; 129; CANR
35; CMW 4; DA3; DAM POP; DLB 72;
DLBY 1989; EW 12; EWL 3; GFL 1789
to the Present; MSW; MTCW 1, 2; RGWL
2, 3

Simic, Charles 1938- .... **CLC 6, 9, 22, 49, 68,**
130
See also AMWS 8; CA 29-32R; CAAS 4;
CANR 12, 33, 52, 61, 96; CP 7; DA3;
DAM POET; DLB 105; MTCW 2; PFS 7;
RGAL 4; WP

Simmel, Georg 1858-1918 .... **TCLC 64**
See also CA 157; DLB 296

Simmons, Charles (Paul) 1924- .... **CLC 57**
See also CA 89-92; INT CA-89-92

Simmons, Dan 1948- .... **CLC 44**
See also AAYA 16, 54; CA 138; CANR 53,
81, 126; CPW; DAM POP; HGG; SUFW
2

Simmons, James (Stewart Alexander)
1933- .... **CLC 43**
See also CA 105; CAAS 21; CP 7; DLB 40

Simms, William Gilmore
1806-1870 .... **NCLC 3**
See also DLB 3, 30, 59, 73, 248, 254;
RGAL 4

Simon, Carly 1945- .... **CLC 26**
See also CA 105

Simon, Claude (Eugene Henri)
1913-1984 .... **CLC 4, 9, 15, 39**
See also CA 89-92; CANR 33, 117; CWW
2; DAM NOV; DLB 83; EW 13; EWL 3;
GFL 1789 to the Present; MTCW 1

Simon, Myles
See Follett, Ken(neth Martin)

Simon, (Marvin) Neil 1927- ... **CLC 6, 11, 31,**
39, 70; DC 14
See also AAYA 32; AITN 1; AMWS 4; CA
21-24R; CANR 26, 54, 87, 126; CD 5;
DA3; DAM DRAM; DFS 2, 6, 12, 18;
DLB 7, 266; LAIT 4; MTCW 1, 2; RGAL
4; TUS

Simon, Paul (Frederick) 1941(?)- ..... **CLC 17**
See also CA 116; 153

Simonon, Paul 1956(?)- .... **CLC 30**

Simonson, Rick ed. .... **CLC 70**

Simpson, Harriette
See Arnow, Harriette (Louisa) Simpson

Simpson, Louis (Aston Marantz)
1923- .... **CLC 4, 7, 9, 32, 149**
See also AMWS 9; CA 1-4R; CAAS 4;
CANR 1, 61; CP 7; DAM POET; DLB 5;
MTCW 1, 2; PFS 7, 11, 14; RGAL 4

Simpson, Mona (Elizabeth) 1957- ... **CLC 44,**
146
See also CA 122; 135; CANR 68, 103; CN
7; EWL 3

Simpson, N(orman) F(rederick)
1919- .... **CLC 29**
See also CA 13-16R; CBD; DLB 13; RGEL
2

Sinclair, Andrew (Annandale) 1935- . **CLC 2,**
14
See also CA 9-12R; CAAS 5; CANR 14,
38, 91; CN 7; DLB 14; FANT; MTCW 1

Sinclair, Emil
See Hesse, Hermann

Sinclair, Iain 1943- .... **CLC 76**
See also CA 132; CANR 81; CP 7; HGG

Sinclair, Iain MacGregor
See Sinclair, Iain

Sinclair, Irene
See Griffith, D(avid Lewelyn) W(ark)

Sinclair, Mary Amelia St. Clair 1865(?)-1946
See Sinclair, May
See also CA 104; HGG; RHW

Sinclair, May .... **TCLC 3, 11**
See Sinclair, Mary Amelia St. Clair
See also CA 166; DLB 36, 135; EWL 3;
RGEL 2; SUFW

Sinclair, Roy
See Griffith, D(avid Lewelyn) W(ark)

Sinclair, Upton (Beall) 1878-1968 ..... **CLC 1,**
11, 15, 63; WLC
See also AMWS 5; BPFB 3; BYA 2; CA
5-8R; 25-28R; CANR 7; CDALB 1929-
1941; DA; DA3; DAB; DAC; DAM MST,
NOV; DLB 9; EWL 3; INT CANR-7;
LAIT 3; MTCW 1, 2; NFS 6; RGAL 4;
SATA 9; TUS; YAW

Singe, (Edmund) J(ohn) M(illington)
1871-1909 .... **WLC**

Singer, Isaac
See Singer, Isaac Bashevis

Singer, Isaac Bashevis 1904-1991 .. **CLC 1, 3,**
6, 9, 11, 15, 23, 38, 69, 111; SSC 3, 53;
WLC
See also AAYA 32; AITN 1, 2; AMW;
AMWR 2; BPFB 3; BYA 1, 4; CA 1-4R;
134; CANR 1, 39, 106; CDALB 1941-
1968; CLR 1; CWRI 5; DA; DA3; DAB;
DAC; DAM MST, NOV; DLB 6, 28, 52,
278; DLBY 1991; EWL 3; EXPS; HGG;
JRDA; LAIT 3; MAICYA 1, 2; MTCW 1,
2; RGAL 4; RGSF 2; SATA 3, 27; SATA-
Obit 68; SSFS 2, 12, 16; TUS; TWA

Singer, Israel Joshua 1893-1944 .... **TCLC 33**
See also CA 169; EWL 3

Singh, Khushwant 1915- .... **CLC 11**
See also CA 9-12R; CAAS 9; CANR 6, 84;
CN 7; EWL 3; RGEL 2

Singleton, Ann
See Benedict, Ruth (Fulton)

Singleton, John 1968(?)- .... **CLC 156**
See also AAYA 50; BW 2, 3; CA 138;
CANR 67, 82; DAM MULT

Siniavskii, Andrei
See Sinyavsky, Andrei (Donatevich)
See also CWW 2

Sinjohn, John
See Galsworthy, John

Sinyavsky, Andrei (Donatevich)
1925-1997 .... **CLC 8**
See Siniavskii, Andrei; Sinyavsky, Andrey
Donatovich; Tertz, Abram
See also CA 85-88; 159

Sinyavsky, Andrey Donatovich
See Sinyavsky, Andrei (Donatevich)
See also EWL 3

Sirin, V.
See Nabokov, Vladimir (Vladimirovich)

Sissman, L(ouis) E(dward)
1928-1976 .... **CLC 9, 18**
See also CA 21-24R; 65-68; CANR 13;
DLB 5

Sisson, C(harles) H(ubert)
1914-2003 .... **CLC 8**
See also CA 1-4R; 220; CAAS 3; CANR 3,
48, 84; CP 7; DLB 27

Sitting Bull 1831(?)-1890 .... **NNAL**
See also DA3; DAM MULT

Sitwell, Dame Edith 1887-1964 ..... **CLC 2, 9,**
67; PC 3
See also BRW 7; CA 9-12R; CANR 35;
CDBLB 1945-1960; DAM POET; DLB
20; EWL 3; MTCW 1, 2; RGEL 2; TEA

Siwaarmill, H. P.
See Sharp, William

Sjoewall, Maj 1935- .... **CLC 7**
See Sjowall, Maj
See also CA 65-68; CANR 73

Sjowall, Maj
See Sjoewall, Maj
See also BPFB 3; CMW 4; MSW

Skelton, John 1460(?)-1529 ..... **LC 71; PC 25**
See also BRW 1; DLB 136; RGEL 2

Skelton, Robin 1925-1997 .... **CLC 13**
See Zuk, Georges
See also AITN 2; CA 5-8R; 160; CAAS 5;
CANR 28, 89; CCA 1; CP 7; DLB 27, 53

Skolimowski, Jerzy 1938- .... **CLC 20**
See also CA 128

Skram, Amalie (Bertha)
1847-1905 .... **TCLC 25**
See also CA 165

Steffens, (Joseph) Lincoln
1866-1936 .... **TCLC 20**
See also CA 117; 198; DLB 303

Stegner, Wallace (Earle) 1909-1993 .. **CLC 9, 49, 81; SSC 27**
See also AITN 1; AMWS 4; ANW; BEST 90:3; BPFB 3; CA 1-4R; 141; CAAS 9; CANR 1, 21, 46; DAM NOV; DLB 9, 206, 275; DLBY 1993; EWL 3; MTCW 1, 2; RGAL 4; TCWW 2; TUS

Stein, Gertrude 1874-1946 .... **DC 19; PC 18; SSC 42; TCLC 1, 6, 28, 48; WLC**
See also AMW; AMWC 2; CA 104; 132; CANR 108; CDALB 1917-1929; DA; DA3; DAB; DAC; DAM MST, NOV, POET; DLB 4, 54, 86, 228; DLBD 15; EWL 3; EXPS; GLL 1; MAWW; MTCW 1, 2; NCFS 4; RGAL 4; RGSF 2; SSFS 5; TUS; WP

Steinbeck, John (Ernst) 1902-1968 ... **CLC 1, 5, 9, 13, 21, 34, 45, 75, 124; SSC 11, 37, 77; TCLC 135; WLC**
See also AAYA 12; AMW; BPFB 3; BYA 2, 3, 13; CA 1-4R; 25-28R; CANR 1, 35; CDALB 1929-1941; DA; DA3; DAB; DAC; DAM DRAM, MST, NOV; DLB 7, 9, 212, 275; DLBD 2; EWL 3; EXPS; LAIT 3; MTCW 1, 2; NFS 1, 5, 7, 17, 19; RGAL 4; RGSF 2; RHW; SATA 9; SSFS 3, 6; TCWW 2; TUS; WYA; YAW

Steinem, Gloria 1934- .... **CLC 63**
See also CA 53-56; CANR 28, 51; DLB 246; FW; MTCW 1, 2

Steiner, George 1929- .... **CLC 24**
See also CA 73-76; CANR 31, 67, 108; DAM NOV; DLB 67, 299; EWL 3; MTCW 1, 2; SATA 62

Steiner, K. Leslie
See Delany, Samuel R(ay), Jr.

Steiner, Rudolf 1861-1925 .... **TCLC 13**
See also CA 107

Stendhal 1783-1842 .. **NCLC 23, 46; SSC 27; WLC**
See also DA; DA3; DAB; DAC; DAM MST, NOV; DLB 119; EW 5; GFL 1789 to the Present; RGWL 2, 3; TWA

Stephen, Adeline Virginia
See Woolf, (Adeline) Virginia

Stephen, Sir Leslie 1832-1904 .... **TCLC 23**
See also BRW 5; CA 123; DLB 57, 144, 190

Stephen, Sir Leslie
See Stephen, Sir Leslie

Stephen, Virginia
See Woolf, (Adeline) Virginia

Stephens, James 1882(?)-1950 .... **SSC 50; TCLC 4**
See also CA 104; 192; DLB 19, 153, 162; EWL 3; FANT; RGEL 2; SUFW

Stephens, Reed
See Donaldson, Stephen R(eeder)

Steptoe, Lydia
See Barnes, Djuna
See also GLL 1

Sterchi, Beat 1949- .... **CLC 65**
See also CA 203

Sterling, Brett
See Bradbury, Ray (Douglas); Hamilton, Edmond

Sterling, Bruce 1954- .... **CLC 72**
See also CA 119; CANR 44; SCFW 2; SFW 4

Sterling, George 1869-1926 .... **TCLC 20**
See also CA 117; 165; DLB 54

Stern, Gerald 1925- .... **CLC 40, 100**
See also AMWS 9; CA 81-84; CANR 28, 94; CP 7; DLB 105; RGAL 4

Stern, Richard (Gustave) 1928- ... **CLC 4, 39**
See also CA 1-4R; CANR 1, 25, 52, 120; CN 7; DLB 218; DLBY 1987; INT CANR-25

Sternberg, Josef von 1894-1969 .... **CLC 20**
See also CA 81-84

Sterne, Laurence 1713-1768 .... **LC 2, 48; WLC**
See also BRW 3; BRWC 1; CDBLB 1660-1789; DA; DAB; DAC; DAM MST, NOV; DLB 39; RGEL 2; TEA

Sternheim, (William Adolf) Carl
1878-1942 .... **TCLC 8**
See also CA 105; 193; DLB 56, 118; EWL 3; RGWL 2, 3

Stevens, Mark 1951- .... **CLC 34**
See also CA 122

Stevens, Wallace 1879-1955 . **PC 6; TCLC 3, 12, 45; WLC**
See also AMW; AMWR 1; CA 104; 124; CDALB 1929-1941; DA; DA3; DAB; DAC; DAM MST, POET; DLB 54; EWL 3; EXPP; MTCW 1, 2; PAB; PFS 13, 16; RGAL 4; TUS; WP

Stevenson, Anne (Katharine) 1933- .. **CLC 7, 33**
See also BRWS 6; CA 17-20R; CAAS 9; CANR 9, 33, 123; CP 7; CWP; DLB 40; MTCW 1; RHW

Stevenson, Robert Louis (Balfour)
1850-1894 ...... **NCLC 5, 14, 63; SSC 11, 51; WLC**
See also AAYA 24; BPFB 3; BRW 5; BRWC 1; BRWR 1; BYA 1, 2, 4, 13; CDBLB 1890-1914; CLR 10, 11; DA; DA3; DAB; DAC; DAM MST, NOV; DLB 18, 57, 141, 156, 174; DLBD 13; HGG; JRDA; LAIT 1, 3; MAICYA 1, 2; NFS 11, 20; RGEL 2; RGSF 2; SATA 100; SUFW; TEA; WCH; WLIT 4; WYA; YABC 2; YAW

Stewart, J(ohn) I(nnes) M(ackintosh)
1906-1994 .... **CLC 7, 14, 32**
See Innes, Michael
See also CA 85-88; 147; CAAS 3; CANR 47; CMW 4; MTCW 1, 2

Stewart, Mary (Florence Elinor)
1916- .... **CLC 7, 35, 117**
See also AAYA 29; BPFB 3; CA 1-4R; CANR 1, 59, 130; CMW 4; CPW; DAB; FANT; RHW; SATA 12; YAW

Stewart, Mary Rainbow
See Stewart, Mary (Florence Elinor)

Stifle, June
See Campbell, Maria

Stifter, Adalbert 1805-1868 .. **NCLC 41; SSC 28**
See also CDWLB 2; DLB 133; RGSF 2; RGWL 2, 3

Still, James 1906-2001 .... **CLC 49**
See also CA 65-68; 195; CAAS 17; CANR 10, 26; CSW; DLB 9; DLBY 01; SATA 29; SATA-Obit 127

Sting 1951-
See Sumner, Gordon Matthew
See also CA 167

Stirling, Arthur
See Sinclair, Upton (Beall)

Stitt, Milan 1941- .... **CLC 29**
See also CA 69-72

Stockton, Francis Richard 1834-1902
See Stockton, Frank R.
See also CA 108; 137; MAICYA 1, 2; SATA 44; SFW 4

Stockton, Frank R. .... **TCLC 47**
See Stockton, Francis Richard
See also BYA 4, 13; DLB 42, 74; DLBD 13; EXPS; SATA-Brief 32; SSFS 3; SUFW; WCH

Stoddard, Charles
See Kuttner, Henry

Stoker, Abraham 1847-1912
See Stoker, Bram
See also CA 105; 150; DA; DA3; DAC; DAM MST, NOV; HGG; SATA 29

Stoker, Bram . **SSC 62; TCLC 8, 144; WLC**
See Stoker, Abraham
See also AAYA 23; BPFB 3; BRWS 3; BYA 5; CDBLB 1890-1914; DAB; DLB 304; LATS 1:1; NFS 18; RGEL 2; SUFW; TEA; WLIT 4

Stolz, Mary (Slattery) 1920- .... **CLC 12**
See also AAYA 8; AITN 1; CA 5-8R; CANR 13, 41, 112; JRDA; MAICYA 1, 2; SAAS 3; SATA 10, 71, 133; YAW

Stone, Irving 1903-1989 .... **CLC 7**
See also AITN 1; BPFB 3; CA 1-4R; 129; CAAS 3; CANR 1, 23; CPW; DA3; DAM POP; INT CANR-23; MTCW 1, 2; RHW; SATA 3; SATA-Obit 64

Stone, Oliver (William) 1946- .... **CLC 73**
See also AAYA 15; CA 110; CANR 55, 125

Stone, Robert (Anthony) 1937- ... **CLC 5, 23, 42, 175**
See also AMWS 5; BPFB 3; CA 85-88; CANR 23, 66, 95; CN 7; DLB 152; EWL 3; INT CANR-23; MTCW 1

Stone, Ruth 1915- .... **PC 53**
See also CA 45-48; CANR 2, 91; CP 7; CSW; DLB 105; PFS 19

Stone, Zachary
See Follett, Ken(neth Martin)

Stoppard, Tom 1937- ... **CLC 1, 3, 4, 5, 8, 15, 29, 34, 63, 91; DC 6; WLC**
See also BRWC 1; BRWR 2; BRWS 1; CA 81-84; CANR 39, 67, 125; CBD; CD 5; CDBLB 1960 to Present; DA; DA3; DAB; DAC; DAM DRAM, MST; DFS 2, 5, 8, 11, 13, 16; DLB 13, 233; DLBY 1985; EWL 3; LATS 1:2; MTCW 1, 2; RGEL 2; TEA; WLIT 4

Storey, David (Malcolm) 1933- . **CLC 2, 4, 5, 8**
See also BRWS 1; CA 81-84; CANR 36; CBD; CD 5; CN 7; DAM DRAM; DLB 13, 14, 207, 245; EWL 3; MTCW 1; RGEL 2

Storm, Hyemeyohsts 1935- ... **CLC 3; NNAL**
See also CA 81-84; CANR 45; DAM MULT

Storm, (Hans) Theodor (Woldsen)
1817-1888 .... **NCLC 1; SSC 27**
See also CDWLB 2; DLB 129; EW; RGSF 2; RGWL 2, 3

Storni, Alfonsina 1892-1938 . **HLC 2; PC 33; TCLC 5**
See also CA 104; 131; DAM MULT; DLB 283; HW 1; LAW

Stoughton, William 1631-1701 .... **LC 38**
See also DLB 24

Stout, Rex (Todhunter) 1886-1975 ..... **CLC 3**
See also AITN 2; BPFB 3; CA 61-64; CANR 71; CMW 4; DLB 306; MSW; RGAL 4

Stow, (Julian) Randolph 1935- ... **CLC 23, 48**
See also CA 13-16R; CANR 33; CN 7; DLB 260; MTCW 1; RGEL 2

Stowe, Harriet (Elizabeth) Beecher
1811-1896 .... **NCLC 3, 50, 133; WLC**
See also AAYA 53; AMWS 1; CDALB 1865-1917; DA; DA3; DAB; DAC; DAM MST, NOV; DLB 1, 12, 42, 74, 189, 239, 243; EXPN; JRDA; LAIT 2; MAICYA 1, 2; NFS 6; RGAL 4; TUS; YABC 1

Strabo c. 64B.C.-c. 25 .... **CMLC 37**
See also DLB 176

Strachey, (Giles) Lytton
1880-1932 .... **TCLC 12**
See also BRWS 2; CA 110; 178; DLB 149; DLBD 10; EWL 3; MTCW 2; NCFS 4

Sylvia
See Ashton-Warner, Sylvia (Constance)
Symmes, Robert Edward
See Duncan, Robert (Edward)
Symonds, John Addington
1840-1893 .... NCLC 34
See also DLB 57, 144
Symons, Arthur 1865-1945 .... TCLC 11
See also CA 107; 189; DLB 19, 57, 149;
RGEL 2
Symons, Julian (Gustave)
1912-1994 .... CLC 2, 14, 32
See also CA 49-52; 147; CAAS 3; CANR
3, 33, 59; CMW 4; DLB 87, 155; DLBY
1992; MSW; MTCW 1
Synge, (Edmund) J(ohn) M(illington)
1871-1909 .... DC 2; TCLC 6, 37
See also BRW 6; BRWR 1; CA 104; 141;
CDBLB 1890-1914; DAM DRAM; DFS
18; DLB 10, 19; EWL 3; RGEL 2; TEA;
WLIT 4
Syruc, J.
See Milosz, Czeslaw
Szirtes, George 1948- .... CLC 46; PC 51
See also CA 109; CANR 27, 61, 117; CP 7
Szymborska, Wislawa 1923- ... CLC 99, 190;
PC 44
See also CA 154; CANR 91, 133; CDWLB
4; CWP; CWW 2; DA3; DLB 232; DLBY
1996; EWL 3; MTCW 2; PFS 15; RGWL
3
T. O., Nik
See Annensky, Innokenty (Fyodorovich)
Tabori, George 1914- .... CLC 19
See also CA 49-52; CANR 4, 69; CBD; CD
5; DLB 245
Tacitus c. 55-c. 117 .... CMLC 56
See also AW 2; CDWLB 1; DLB 211;
RGWL 2, 3
Tagore, Rabindranath 1861-1941 .... PC 8;
SSC 48; TCLC 3, 53
See also CA 104; 120; DA3; DAM DRAM,
POET; EWL 3; MTCW 1, 2; PFS 18;
RGEL 2; RGSF 2; RGWL 2, 3; TWA
Taine, Hippolyte Adolphe
1828-1893 .... NCLC 15
See also EW 7; GFL 1789 to the Present
Talayesva, Don C. 1890-(?) .... NNAL
Talese, Gay 1932- .... CLC 37
See also AITN 1; CA 1-4R; CANR 9, 58;
DLB 185; INT CANR-9; MTCW 1, 2
Tallent, Elizabeth (Ann) 1954- .... CLC 45
See also CA 117; CANR 72; DLB 130
Tallmountain, Mary 1918-1997 .... NNAL
See also CA 146; 161; DLB 193
Tally, Ted 1952- .... CLC 42
See also CA 120; 124; CAD; CANR 125;
CD 5; INT CA-124
Talvik, Heiti 1904-1947 .... TCLC 87
See also EWL 3
Tamayo y Baus, Manuel
1829-1898 .... NCLC 1
Tammsaare, A(nton) H(ansen)
1878-1940 .... TCLC 27
See also CA 164; CDWLB 4; DLB 220;
EWL 3
Tam'si, Tchicaya U
See Tchicaya, Gerald Felix
Tan, Amy (Ruth) 1952- . AAL; CLC 59, 120,
151
See also AAYA 9, 48; AMWS 10; BEST
89:3; BPFB 3; CA 136; CANR 54, 105,
132; CDALBS; CN 7; CPW 1; DA3;
DAM MULT, NOV, POP; DLB 173;
EXPN; FW; LAIT 3, 5; MTCW 2; NFS
1, 13, 16; RGAL 4; SATA 75; SSFS 9;
YAW
Tandem, Felix
See Spitteler, Carl (Friedrich Georg)

Tanizaki, Jun'ichiro 1886-1965 ... CLC 8, 14,
28; SSC 21
See Tanizaki Jun'ichiro
See also CA 93-96; 25-28R; MJW; MTCW
2; RGSF 2; RGWL 2
Tanizaki Jun'ichiro
See Tanizaki, Jun'ichiro
See also DLB 180; EWL 3
Tanner, William
See Amis, Kingsley (William)
Tao Lao
See Storni, Alfonsina
Tapahonso, Luci 1953- .... NNAL
See also CA 145; CANR 72, 127; DLB 175
Tarantino, Quentin (Jerome)
1963- .... CLC 125
See also AAYA 58; CA 171; CANR 125
Tarassoff, Lev
See Troyat, Henri
Tarbell, Ida M(inerva) 1857-1944 . TCLC 40
See also CA 122; 181; DLB 47
Tarkington, (Newton) Booth
1869-1946 .... TCLC 9
See also BPFB 3; BYA 3; CA 110; 143;
CWRI 5; DLB 9, 102; MTCW 2; RGAL
4; SATA 17
Tarkovskii, Andrei Arsen'evich
See Tarkovsky, Andrei (Arsenyevich)
Tarkovsky, Andrei (Arsenyevich)
1932-1986 .... CLC 75
See also CA 127
Tartt, Donna 1963- .... CLC 76
See also AAYA 56; CA 142
Tasso, Torquato 1544-1595 .... LC 5, 94
See also EFS 2; EW 2; RGWL 2, 3
Tate, (John Orley) Allen 1899-1979 .. CLC 2,
4, 6, 9, 11, 14, 24; PC 50
See also AMW; CA 5-8R; 85-88; CANR
32, 108; DLB 4, 45, 63; DLBD 17; EWL
3; MTCW 1, 2; RGAL 4; RHW
Tate, Ellalice
See Hibbert, Eleanor Alice Burford
Tate, James (Vincent) 1943- ..... CLC 2, 6, 25
See also CA 21-24R; CANR 29, 57, 114;
CP 7; DLB 5, 169; EWL 3; PFS 10, 15;
RGAL 4; WP
Tate, Nahum 1652(?)-1715 .... LC 109
See also DLB 80; RGEL 2
Tauler, Johannes c. 1300-1361 ...... CMLC 37
See also DLB 179; LMFS 1
Tavel, Ronald 1940- .... CLC 6
See also CA 21-24R; CAD; CANR 33; CD
5
Taviani, Paolo 1931- .... CLC 70
See also CA 153
Taylor, Bayard 1825-1878 .... NCLC 89
See also DLB 3, 189, 250, 254; RGAL 4
Taylor, C(ecil) P(hilip) 1929-1981 .... CLC 27
See also CA 25-28R; 105; CANR 47; CBD
Taylor, Edward 1642(?)-1729 .... LC 11
See also AMW; DA; DAB; DAC; DAM
MST, POET; DLB 24; EXPP; RGAL 4;
TUS
Taylor, Eleanor Ross 1920- .... CLC 5
See also CA 81-84; CANR 70
Taylor, Elizabeth 1932-1975 ..... CLC 2, 4, 29
See also CA 13-16R; CANR 9, 70; DLB
139; MTCW 1; RGEL 2; SATA 13
Taylor, Frederick Winslow
1856-1915 .... TCLC 76
See also CA 188
Taylor, Henry (Splawn) 1942- .... CLC 44
See also CA 33-36R; CAAS 7; CANR 31;
CP 7; DLB 5; PFS 10
Taylor, Kamala (Purnaiya) 1924-2004
See Markandaya, Kamala
See also CA 77-80; 227; NFS 13

Taylor, Mildred D(elois) 1943- .... CLC 21
See also AAYA 10, 47; BW 1; BYA 3, 8;
CA 85-88; CANR 25, 115; CLR 9, 59,
90; CSW; DLB 52; JRDA; LAIT 3; MAI-
CYA 1, 2; SAAS 5; SATA 135; WYA;
YAW
Taylor, Peter (Hillsman) 1917-1994 .. CLC 1,
4, 18, 37, 44, 50, 71; SSC 10
See also AMWS 5; BPFB 3; CA 13-16R;
147; CANR 9, 50; CSW; DLB 218, 278;
DLBY 1981, 1994; EWL 3; EXPS; INT
CANR-9; MTCW 1, 2; RGSF 2; SSFS 9;
TUS
Taylor, Robert Lewis 1912-1998 .... CLC 14
See also CA 1-4R; 170; CANR 3, 64; SATA
10
Tchekhov, Anton
See Chekhov, Anton (Pavlovich)
Tchicaya, Gerald Felix 1931-1988 .. CLC 101
See Tchicaya U Tam'si
See also CA 129; 125; CANR 81
Tchicaya U Tam'si
See Tchicaya, Gerald Felix
See also EWL 3
Teasdale, Sara 1884-1933 .... PC 31; TCLC 4
See also CA 104; 163; DLB 45; GLL 1;
PFS 14; RGAL 4; SATA 32; TUS
Tecumseh 1768-1813 .... NNAL
See also DAM MULT
Tegner, Esaias 1782-1846 .... NCLC 2
Teilhard de Chardin, (Marie Joseph) Pierre
1881-1955 .... TCLC 9
See also CA 105; 210; GFL 1789 to the
Present
Temple, Ann
See Mortimer, Penelope (Ruth)
Tennant, Emma (Christina) 1937- .. CLC 13,
52
See also BRWS 9; CA 65-68; CAAS 9;
CANR 10, 38, 59, 88; CN 7; DLB 14;
EWL 3; SFW 4
Tenneshaw, S. M.
See Silverberg, Robert
Tenney, Tabitha Gilman
1762-1837 .... NCLC 122
See also DLB 37, 200
Tennyson, Alfred 1809-1892 ... NCLC 30, 65,
115; PC 6; WLC
See also AAYA 50; BRW 4; CDBLB 1832-
1890; DA; DA3; DAB; DAC; DAM MST,
POET; DLB 32; EXPP; PAB; PFS 1, 2, 4,
11, 15, 19; RGEL 2; TEA; WLIT 4; WP
Teran, Lisa St. Aubin de .... CLC 36
See St. Aubin de Teran, Lisa
Terence c. 184B.C.-c. 159B.C. ...... CMLC 14;
DC 7
See also AW 1; CDWLB 1; DLB 211;
RGWL 2, 3; TWA
Teresa de Jesus, St. 1515-1582 .... LC 18
Terkel, Louis 1912-
See Terkel, Studs
See also CA 57-60; CANR 18, 45, 67, 132;
DA3; MTCW 1, 2
Terkel, Studs .... CLC 38
See Terkel, Louis
See also AAYA 32; AITN 1; MTCW 2; TUS
Terry, C. V.
See Slaughter, Frank G(ill)
Terry, Megan 1932- .... CLC 19; DC 13
See also CA 77-80; CABS 3; CAD; CANR
43; CD 5; CWD; DFS 18; DLB 7, 249;
GLL 2
Tertullian c. 155-c. 245 .... CMLC 29
Tertz, Abram
See Sinyavsky, Andrei (Donatevich)
See also RGSF 2
Tesich, Steve 1943(?)-1996 .... CLC 40, 69
See also CA 105; 152; CAD; DLBY 1983

Trollope, Frances 1779-1863 .... **NCLC 30**
See also DLB 21, 166

Trollope, Joanna 1943- .... **CLC 186**
See also CA 101; CANR 58, 95; CPW;
DLB 207; RHW

Trotsky, Leon 1879-1940 .... **TCLC 22**
See also CA 118; 167

Trotter (Cockburn), Catharine
1679-1749 .... **LC 8**
See also DLB 84, 252

Trotter, Wilfred 1872-1939 .... **TCLC 97**

Trout, Kilgore
See Farmer, Philip Jose

Trow, George W. S. 1943- .... **CLC 52**
See also CA 126; CANR 91

Troyat, Henri 1911- .... **CLC 23**
See also CA 45-48; CANR 2, 33, 67, 117;
GFL 1789 to the Present; MTCW 1

Trudeau, G(arretson) B(eekman) 1948-
See Trudeau, Garry B.
See also AAYA 60; CA 81-84; CANR 31;
SATA 35

Trudeau, Garry B. .... **CLC 12**
See Trudeau, G(arretson) B(eekman)
See also AAYA 10; AITN 2

Truffaut, Francois 1932-1984 ... **CLC 20, 101**
See also CA 81-84; 113; CANR 34

Trumbo, Dalton 1905-1976 .... **CLC 19**
See also CA 21-24R; 69-72; CANR 10;
DLB 26; IDFW 3, 4; YAW

Trumbull, John 1750-1831 .... **NCLC 30**
See also DLB 31; RGAL 4

Trundlett, Helen B.
See Eliot, T(homas) S(tearns)

Truth, Sojourner 1797(?)-1883 ...... **NCLC 94**
See also DLB 239; FW; LAIT 2

Tryon, Thomas 1926-1991 .... **CLC 3, 11**
See also AITN 1; BPFB 3; CA 29-32R; 135;
CANR 32, 77; CPW; DA3; DAM POP;
HGG; MTCW 1

Tryon, Tom
See Tryon, Thomas

Ts'ao Hsueh-ch'in 1715(?)-1763 .... **LC 1**

Tsushima, Shuji 1909-1948
See Dazai Osamu
See also CA 107

Tsvetaeva (Efron), Marina (Ivanovna)
1892-1941 .... **PC 14; TCLC 7, 35**
See also CA 104; 128; CANR 73; DLB 295;
EW 11; MTCW 1, 2; RGWL 2, 3

Tuck, Lily 1938- .... **CLC 70**
See also CA 139; CANR 90

Tu Fu 712-770 .... **PC 9**
See Du Fu
See also DAM MULT; TWA; WP

Tunis, John R(oberts) 1889-1975 ..... **CLC 12**
See also BYA 1; CA 61-64; CANR 62; DLB
22, 171; JRDA; MAICYA 1, 2; SATA 37;
SATA-Brief 30; YAW

Tuohy, Frank .... **CLC 37**
See Tuohy, John Francis
See also DLB 14, 139

Tuohy, John Francis 1925-
See Tuohy, Frank
See also CA 5-8R; 178; CANR 3, 47; CN 7

Turco, Lewis (Putnam) 1934- ..... **CLC 11, 63**
See also CA 13-16R; CAAS 22; CANR 24,
51; CP 7; DLBY 1984

Turgenev, Ivan (Sergeevich)
1818-1883 ..... **DC 7; NCLC 21, 37, 122;
SSC 7, 57; WLC**
See also AAYA 58; DA; DAB; DAC; DAM
MST, NOV; DFS 6; DLB 238, 284; EW
6; LATS 1:1; NFS 16; RGSF 2; RGWL 2,
3; TWA

Turgot, Anne-Robert-Jacques
1727-1781 .... **LC 26**

Turner, Frederick 1943- .... **CLC 48**
See also CA 73-76, 227; CAAE 227; CAAS
10; CANR 12, 30, 56; DLB 40, 282

Turton, James
See Crace, Jim

Tutu, Desmond M(pilo) 1931- .. **BLC 3; CLC
80**
See also BW 1, 3; CA 125; CANR 67, 81;
DAM MULT

Tutuola, Amos 1920-1997 ..... **BLC 3; CLC 5,
14, 29**
See also AFW; BW 2, 3; CA 9-12R; 159;
CANR 27, 66; CDWLB 3; CN 7; DA3;
DAM MULT; DLB 125; DNFS 2; EWL
3; MTCW 1, 2; RGEL 2; WLIT 2

Twain, Mark .... **SSC 6, 26, 34; TCLC 6, 12,
19, 36, 48, 59; WLC**
See Clemens, Samuel Langhorne
See also AAYA 20; AMW; AMWC 1; BPFB
3; BYA 2, 3, 11, 14; CLR 58, 60, 66; DLB
11; EXPN; EXPS; FANT; LAIT 2; NCFS
4; NFS 1, 6; RGAL 4; RGSF 2; SFW 4;
SSFS 1, 7; SUFW; TUS; WCH; WYA;
YAW

Tyler, Anne 1941- . **CLC 7, 11, 18, 28, 44, 59,
103**
See also AAYA 18, 60; AMWS 4; BEST
89:1; BPFB 3; BYA 12; CA 9-12R; CANR
11, 33, 53, 109, 132; CDALBS; CN 7;
CPW; CSW; DAM NOV, POP; DLB 6,
143; DLBY 1982; EWL 3; EXPN; LATS
1:2; MAWW; MTCW 1, 2; NFS 2, 7, 10;
RGAL 4; SATA 7, 90; SSFS 17; TUS;
YAW

Tyler, Royall 1757-1826 .... **NCLC 3**
See also DLB 37; RGAL 4

Tynan, Katharine 1861-1931 .... **TCLC 3**
See also CA 104; 167; DLB 153, 240; FW

Tyndale, William c. 1484-1536 .... **LC 103**
See also DLB 132

Tyutchev, Fyodor 1803-1873 .... **NCLC 34**

Tzara, Tristan 1896-1963 ..... **CLC 47; PC 27**
See also CA 153; 89-92; DAM POET; EWL
3; MTCW 2

Uchida, Yoshiko 1921-1992 .... **AAL**
See also AAYA 16; BYA 2, 3; CA 13-16R;
139; CANR 6, 22, 47, 61; CDALBS; CLR
6, 56; CWRI 5; JRDA; MAICYA 1, 2;
MTCW 1, 2; SAAS 1; SATA 1, 53; SATA-
Obit 72

Udall, Nicholas 1504-1556 .... **LC 84**
See also DLB 62; RGEL 2

Ueda Akinari 1734-1809 .... **NCLC 131**

Uhry, Alfred 1936- .... **CLC 55**
See also CA 127; 133; CAD; CANR 112;
CD 5; CSW; DA3; DAM DRAM, POP;
DFS 11, 15; INT CA-133

Ulf, Haerved
See Strindberg, (Johan) August

Ulf, Harved
See Strindberg, (Johan) August

Ulibarri, Sabine R(eyes)
1919-2003 .... **CLC 83; HLCS 2**
See also CA 131; 214; CANR 81; DAM
MULT; DLB 82; HW 1, 2; RGSF 2

Unamuno (y Jugo), Miguel de
1864-1936 .. **HLC 2; SSC 11, 69; TCLC
2, 9, 148**
See also CA 104; 131; CANR 81; DAM
MULT, NOV; DLB 108; EW 8; EWL 3;
HW 1, 2; MTCW 1, 2; RGSF 2; RGWL
2, 3; SSFS 20; TWA

Uncle Shelby
See Silverstein, Shel(don Allan)

Undercliffe, Errol
See Campbell, (John) Ramsey

Underwood, Miles
See Glassco, John

Undset, Sigrid 1882-1949 ..... **TCLC 3; WLC**
See also CA 104; 129; DA; DA3; DAB;
DAC; DAM MST, NOV; DLB 293; EW
9; EWL 3; FW; MTCW 1, 2; RGWL 2, 3

Ungaretti, Giuseppe 1888-1970 ... **CLC 7, 11,
15; PC 57**
See also CA 19-20; 25-28R; CAP 2; DLB
114; EW 10; EWL 3; PFS 20; RGWL 2,
3

Unger, Douglas 1952- .... **CLC 34**
See also CA 130; CANR 94

Unsworth, Barry (Forster) 1930- .... **CLC 76,
127**
See also BRWS 7; CA 25-28R; CANR 30,
54, 125; CN 7; DLB 194

Updike, John (Hoyer) 1932- . **CLC 1, 2, 3, 5,
7, 9, 13, 15, 23, 34, 43, 70, 139; SSC 13,
27; WLC**
See also AAYA 36; AMW; AMWC 1;
AMWR 1; BPFB 3; BYA 12; CA 1-4R;
CABS 1; CANR 4, 33, 51, 94, 133;
CDALB 1968-1988; CN 7; CP 7; CPW 1;
DA; DA3; DAB; DAC; DAM MST, NOV,
POET, POP; DLB 2, 5, 143, 218, 227;
DLBD 3; DLBY 1980, 1982, 1997; EWL
3; EXPP; HGG; MTCW 1, 2; NFS 12;
RGAL 4; RGSF 2; SSFS 3, 19; TUS

Upshaw, Margaret Mitchell
See Mitchell, Margaret (Munnerlyn)

Upton, Mark
See Sanders, Lawrence

Upward, Allen 1863-1926 .... **TCLC 85**
See also CA 117; 187; DLB 36

Urdang, Constance (Henriette)
1922-1996 .... **CLC 47**
See also CA 21-24R; CANR 9, 24; CP 7;
CWP

Uriel, Henry
See Faust, Frederick (Schiller)

Uris, Leon (Marcus) 1924-2003 ... **CLC 7, 32**
See also AITN 1, 2; BEST 89:2; BPFB 3;
CA 1-4R; 217; CANR 1, 40, 65, 123; CN
7; CPW 1; DA3; DAM NOV, POP;
MTCW 1, 2; SATA 49; SATA-Obit 146

Urista (Heredia), Alberto (Baltazar)
1947- .... **HLCS 1; PC 34**
See Alurista
See also CA 45-48, 182; CANR 2, 32; HW
1

Urmuz
See Codrescu, Andrei

Urquhart, Guy
See McAlmon, Robert (Menzies)

Urquhart, Jane 1949- .... **CLC 90**
See also CA 113; CANR 32, 68, 116; CCA
1; DAC

Usigli, Rodolfo 1905-1979 .... **HLCS 1**
See also CA 131; DLB 305; EWL 3; HW 1;
LAW

Ustinov, Peter (Alexander)
1921-2004 .... **CLC 1**
See also AITN 1; CA 13-16R; 225; CANR
25, 51; CBD; CD 5; DLB 13; MTCW 2

U Tam'si, Gerald Felix Tchicaya
See Tchicaya, Gerald Felix

U Tam'si, Tchicaya
See Tchicaya, Gerald Felix

Vachss, Andrew (Henry) 1942- .... **CLC 106**
See also CA 118, 214; CAAE 214; CANR
44, 95; CMW 4

Vachss, Andrew H.
See Vachss, Andrew (Henry)

Vaculik, Ludvik 1926- .... **CLC 7**
See also CA 53-56; CANR 72; CWW 2;
DLB 232; EWL 3

Vaihinger, Hans 1852-1933 .... **TCLC 71**
See also CA 116; 166

Villa, Jose Garcia 1914-1997 .... **AAL; PC 22**
See also CA 25-28R; CANR 12, 118; EWL
3; EXPP
Villa, Jose Garcia 1914-1997
See Villa, Jose Garcia
Villarreal, Jose Antonio 1924- .... **HLC 2**
See also CA 133; CANR 93; DAM MULT;
DLB 82; HW 1; LAIT 4; RGAL 4
Villaurrutia, Xavier 1903-1950 .... **TCLC 80**
See also CA 192; EWL 3; HW 1; LAW
Villaverde, Cirilo 1812-1894 .... **NCLC 121**
See also LAW
Villehardouin, Geoffroi de
1150(?)-1218(?) .... **CMLC 38**
Villiers, George 1628-1687 .... **LC 107**
See also DLB 80; RGEL 2
Villiers de l'Isle Adam, Jean Marie Mathias
Philippe Auguste 1838-1889 ... **NCLC 3;**
SSC 14
See also DLB 123, 192; GFL 1789 to the
Present; RGSF 2
Villon, Francois 1431-1463(?) . **LC 62; PC 13**
See also DLB 208; EW 2; RGWL 2, 3;
TWA
Vine, Barbara .... **CLC 50**
See Rendell, Ruth (Barbara)
See also BEST 90:4
Vinge, Joan (Carol) D(ennison)
1948- .... **CLC 30; SSC 24**
See also AAYA 32; BPFB 3; CA 93-96;
CANR 72; SATA 36, 113; SFW 4; YAW
Viola, Herman J(oseph) 1938- .... **CLC 70**
See also CA 61-64; CANR 8, 23, 48, 91;
SATA 126
Violis, G.
See Simenon, Georges (Jacques Christian)
Viramontes, Helena Maria 1954- .... **HLCS 2**
See also CA 159; DLB 122; HW 2; LLW 1
Virgil
See Vergil
See also CDWLB 1; DLB 211; LAIT 1;
RGWL 2, 3; WP
Visconti, Luchino 1906-1976 .... **CLC 16**
See also CA 81-84; 65-68; CANR 39
Vitry, Jacques de
See Jacques de Vitry
Vittorini, Elio 1908-1966 .... **CLC 6, 9, 14**
See also CA 133; 25-28R; DLB 264; EW
12; EWL 3; RGWL 2, 3
Vivekananda, Swami 1863-1902 .... **TCLC 88**
Vizenor, Gerald Robert 1934- .... **CLC 103;**
NNAL
See also CA 13-16R, 205; CAAE 205;
CAAS 22; CANR 5, 21, 44, 67; DAM
MULT; DLB 175, 227; MTCW 2; TCWW
2
Vizinczey, Stephen 1933- .... **CLC 40**
See also CA 128; CCA 1; INT CA-128
Vliet, R(ussell) G(ordon)
1929-1984 .... **CLC 22**
See also CA 37-40R; 112; CANR 18
Vogau, Boris Andreyevich 1894-1938
See Pilnyak, Boris
See also CA 123; 218
Vogel, Paula A(nne) 1951- ... **CLC 76; DC 19**
See also CA 108; CAD; CANR 119; CD 5;
CWD; DFS 14; RGAL 4
Voigt, Cynthia 1942- .... **CLC 30**
See also AAYA 3, 30; BYA 1, 3, 6, 7, 8;
CA 106; CANR 18, 37, 40, 94; CLR 13,
48; INT CANR-18; JRDA; LAIT 5; MAI-
CYA 1, 2; MAICYAS 1; SATA 48, 79,
116; SATA-Brief 33; WYA; YAW
Voigt, Ellen Bryant 1943- .... **CLC 54**
See also CA 69-72; CANR 11, 29, 55, 115;
CP 7; CSW; CWP; DLB 120

Voinovich, Vladimir (Nikolaevich)
1932- .... **CLC 10, 49, 147**
See also CA 81-84; CAAS 12; CANR 33,
67; CWW 2; DLB 302; MTCW 1
Vollmann, William T. 1959- .... **CLC 89**
See also CA 134; CANR 67, 116; CPW;
DA3; DAM NOV, POP; MTCW 2
Voloshinov, V. N.
See Bakhtin, Mikhail Mikhailovich
Voltaire 1694-1778 .... **LC 14, 79; SSC 12;**
WLC
See also BYA 13; DA; DA3; DAB; DAC;
DAM DRAM, MST; EW 4; GFL Begin-
nings to 1789; LATS 1:1; LMFS 1; NFS
7; RGWL 2, 3; TWA
von Aschendrof, Baron Ignatz
See Ford, Ford Madox
von Chamisso, Adelbert
See Chamisso, Adelbert von
von Daeniken, Erich 1935- .... **CLC 30**
See also AITN 1; CA 37-40R; CANR 17,
44
von Daniken, Erich
See von Daeniken, Erich
von Hartmann, Eduard
1842-1906 .... **TCLC 96**
von Hayek, Friedrich August
See Hayek, F(riedrich) A(ugust von)
von Heidenstam, (Carl Gustaf) Verner
See Heidenstam, (Carl Gustaf) Verner von
von Heyse, Paul (Johann Ludwig)
See Heyse, Paul (Johann Ludwig von)
von Hofmannsthal, Hugo
See Hofmannsthal, Hugo von
von Horvath, Odon
See von Horvath, Odon
von Horvath, Odon
See von Horvath, Odon
von Horvath, Odon 1901-1938 .... **TCLC 45**
See von Horvath, Oedon
See also CA 118; 194; DLB 85, 124; RGWL
2, 3
von Horvath, Oedoen
See von Horvath, Odon
See also CA 184
von Kleist, Heinrich
See Kleist, Heinrich von
von Liliencron, (Friedrich Adolf Axel)
Detlev
See Liliencron, (Friedrich Adolf Axel) De-
tlev von
Vonnegut, Kurt, Jr. 1922- . **CLC 1, 2, 3, 4, 5,**
8, 12, 22, 40, 60, 111; SSC 8; WLC
See also AAYA 6, 44; AITN 1; AMWS 2;
BEST 90:4; BPFB 3; BYA 3, 14; CA
1-4R; CANR 1, 25, 49, 75, 92; CDALB
1968-1988; CN 7; CPW 1; DA; DA3;
DAB; DAC; DAM MST, NOV, POP;
DLB 2, 8, 152; DLBD 3; DLBY 1980;
EWL 3; EXPN; EXPS; LAIT 4; LMFS 2;
MTCW 1, 2; NFS 3; RGAL 4; SCFW 4;
SFW 4; SSFS 5; TUS; YAW
Von Rachen, Kurt
See Hubbard, L(afayette) Ron(ald)
von Rezzori (d'Arezzo), Gregor
See Rezzori (d'Arezzo), Gregor von
von Sternberg, Josef
See Sternberg, Josef von
Vorster, Gordon 1924- .... **CLC 34**
See also CA 133
Vosce, Trudie
See Ozick, Cynthia
Voznesensky, Andrei (Andreievich)
1933- .... **CLC 1, 15, 57**
See Voznesensky, Andrey
See also CA 89-92; CANR 37; CWW 2;
DAM POET; MTCW 1

Voznesensky, Andrey
See Voznesensky, Andrei (Andreievich)
See also EWL 3
Wace, Robert c. 1100-c. 1175 .... **CMLC 55**
See also DLB 146
Waddington, Miriam 1917-2004 .... **CLC 28**
See also CA 21-24R; 225; CANR 12, 30;
CCA 1; CP 7; DLB 68
Wagman, Fredrica 1937- .... **CLC 7**
See also CA 97-100; INT CA-97-100
Wagner, Linda W.
See Wagner-Martin, Linda (C.)
Wagner, Linda Welshimer
See Wagner-Martin, Linda (C.)
Wagner, Richard 1813-1883 ..... **NCLC 9, 119**
See also DLB 129; EW 6
Wagner-Martin, Linda (C.) 1936- .... **CLC 50**
See also CA 159
Wagoner, David (Russell) 1926- .... **CLC 3, 5,**
15; PC 33
See also AMWS 9; CA 1-4R; CAAS 3;
CANR 2, 71; CN 7; CP 7; DLB 5, 256;
SATA 14; TCWW 2
Wah, Fred(erick James) 1939- .... **CLC 44**
See also CA 107; 141; CP 7; DLB 60
Wahloo, Per 1926-1975 .... **CLC 7**
See also BPFB 3; CA 61-64; CANR 73;
CMW 4; MSW
Wahloo, Peter
See Wahloo, Per
Wain, John (Barrington) 1925-1994 . **CLC 2,**
11, 15, 46
See also CA 5-8R; 145; CAAS 4; CANR
23, 54; CDBLB 1960 to Present; DLB 15,
27, 139, 155; EWL 3; MTCW 1, 2
Wajda, Andrzej 1926- .... **CLC 16**
See also CA 102
Wakefield, Dan 1932- .... **CLC 7**
See also CA 21-24R, 211; CAAE 211;
CAAS 7; CN 7
Wakefield, Herbert Russell
1888-1965 .... **TCLC 120**
See also CA 5-8R; CANR 77; HGG; SUFW
Wakoski, Diane 1937- ...... **CLC 2, 4, 7, 9, 11,**
40; PC 15
See also CA 13-16R, 216; CAAE 216;
CAAS 1; CANR 9, 60, 106; CP 7; CWP;
DAM POET; DLB 5; INT CANR-9;
MTCW 2
Wakoski-Sherbell, Diane
See Wakoski, Diane
Walcott, Derek (Alton) 1930- ... **BLC 3; CLC**
2, 4, 9, 14, 25, 42, 67, 76, 160; DC 7;
PC 46
See also BW 2; CA 89-92; CANR 26, 47,
75, 80, 130; CBD; CD 5; CDWLB 3; CP
7; DA3; DAB; DAC; DAM MST, MULT,
POET; DLB 117; DLBY 1981; DNFS 1;
EFS 1; EWL 3; LMFS 2; MTCW 1, 2;
PFS 6; RGEL 2; TWA; WWE 1
Waldman, Anne (Lesley) 1945- .... **CLC 7**
See also BG 3; CA 37-40R; CAAS 17;
CANR 34, 69, 116; CP 7; CWP; DLB 16
Waldo, E. Hunter
See Sturgeon, Theodore (Hamilton)
Waldo, Edward Hamilton
See Sturgeon, Theodore (Hamilton)
Walker, Alice (Malsenior) 1944- .... **BLC 3;**
CLC 5, 6, 9, 19, 27, 46, 58, 103, 167;
PC 30; SSC 5; WLCS
See also AAYA 3, 33; AFAW 1, 2; AMWS
3; BEST 89:4; BPFB 3; BW 2, 3; CA 37-
40R; CANR 9, 27, 49, 66, 82, 131;
CDALB 1968-1988; CN 7; CPW; CSW;
DA; DA3; DAB; DAC; DAM MST,
MULT, NOV, POET, POP; DLB 6, 33,
143; EWL 3; EXPN; EXPS; FW; INT

Author Index

Williams, Charles
See Collier, James Lincoln
Williams, Charles (Walter Stansby)
1886-1945 .... **TCLC 1, 11**
See also BRWS 9; CA 104; 163; DLB 100, 153, 255; FANT; RGEL 2; SUFW 1
Williams, Ella Gwendolen Rees
See Rhys, Jean
Williams, (George) Emlyn
1905-1987 .... **CLC 15**
See also CA 104; 123; CANR 36; DAM DRAM; DLB 10, 77; IDTP; MTCW 1
Williams, Hank 1923-1953 .... **TCLC 81**
See Williams, Hiram King
Williams, Helen Maria
1761-1827 .... **NCLC 135**
See also DLB 158
Williams, Hiram Hank
See Williams, Hank
Williams, Hiram King
See Williams, Hank
See also CA 188
Williams, Hugo (Mordaunt) 1942- ... **CLC 42**
See also CA 17-20R; CANR 45, 119; CP 7; DLB 40
Williams, J. Walker
See Wodehouse, P(elham) G(renville)
Williams, John A(lfred) 1925- . **BLC 3; CLC 5, 13**
See also AFAW 2; BW 2, 3; CA 53-56, 195; CAAE 195; CAAS 3; CANR 6, 26, 51, 118; CN 7; CSW; DAM MULT; DLB 2, 33; EWL 3; INT CANR-6; RGAL 4; SFW 4
Williams, Jonathan (Chamberlain)
1929- .... **CLC 13**
See also CA 9-12R; CAAS 12; CANR 8, 108; CP 7; DLB 5
Williams, Joy 1944- .... **CLC 31**
See also CA 41-44R; CANR 22, 48, 97
Williams, Norman 1952- .... **CLC 39**
See also CA 118
Williams, Sherley Anne 1944-1999 ... **BLC 3; CLC 89**
See also AFAW 2; BW 2, 3; CA 73-76; 185; CANR 25, 82; DAM MULT, POET; DLB 41; INT CANR-25; SATA 78; SATA-Obit 116
Williams, Shirley
See Williams, Sherley Anne
Williams, Tennessee 1911-1983 . **CLC 1, 2, 5, 7, 8, 11, 15, 19, 30, 39, 45, 71, 111; DC 4; WLC**
See also AAYA 31; AITN 1, 2; AMW; AMWC 1; CA 5-8R; 108; CABS 3; CAD; CANR 31, 132; CDALB 1941-1968; DA; DA3; DAB; DAC; DAM DRAM, MST; DFS 17; DLB 7; DLBD 4; DLBY 1983; EWL 3; GLL 1; LAIT 4; LATS 1:2; MTCW 1, 2; RGAL 4; TUS
Williams, Thomas (Alonzo)
1926-1990 .... **CLC 14**
See also CA 1-4R; 132; CANR 2
Williams, William C.
See Williams, William Carlos
Williams, William Carlos
1883-1963 .... **CLC 1, 2, 5, 9, 13, 22, 42, 67; PC 7; SSC 31**
See also AAYA 46; AMW; AMWR 1; CA 89-92; CANR 34; CDALB 1917-1929; DA; DA3; DAB; DAC; DAM MST, POET; DLB 4, 16, 54, 86; EWL 3; EXPP; MTCW 1, 2; NCFS 4; PAB; PFS 1, 6, 11; RGAL 4; RGSF 2; TUS; WP
Williamson, David (Keith) 1942- ..... **CLC 56**
See also CA 103; CANR 41; CD 5; DLB 289

Williamson, Ellen Douglas 1905-1984
See Douglas, Ellen
See also CA 17-20R; 114; CANR 39
Williamson, Jack .... **CLC 29**
See Williamson, John Stewart
See also CAAS 8; DLB 8; SCFW 2
Williamson, John Stewart 1908-
See Williamson, Jack
See also CA 17-20R; CANR 23, 70; SFW 4
Willie, Frederick
See Lovecraft, H(oward) P(hillips)
Willingham, Calder (Baynard, Jr.)
1922-1995 .... **CLC 5, 51**
See also CA 5-8R; 147; CANR 3; CSW; DLB 2, 44; IDFW 3, 4; MTCW 1
Willis, Charles
See Clarke, Arthur C(harles)
Willy
See Colette, (Sidonie-Gabrielle)
Willy, Colette
See Colette, (Sidonie-Gabrielle)
See also GLL 1
Wilmot, John 1647-1680 .... **LC 75**
See Rochester
See also BRW 2; DLB 131; PAB
Wilson, A(ndrew) N(orman) 1950- .. **CLC 33**
See also BRWS 6; CA 112; 122; CN 7; DLB 14, 155, 194; MTCW 2
Wilson, Angus (Frank Johnstone)
1913-1991 . **CLC 2, 3, 5, 25, 34; SSC 21**
See also BRWS 1; CA 5-8R; 134; CANR 21; DLB 15, 139, 155; EWL 3; MTCW 1, 2; RGEL 2; RGSF 2
Wilson, August 1945- ... **BLC 3; CLC 39, 50, 63, 118; DC 2; WLCS**
See also AAYA 16; AFAW 2; AMWS 8; BW 2, 3; CA 115; 122; CAD; CANR 42, 54, 76, 128; CD 5; DA; DA3; DAB; DAC; DAM DRAM, MST, MULT; DFS 3, 7, 15, 17; DLB 228; EWL 3; LAIT 4; LATS 1:2; MTCW 1, 2; RGAL 4
Wilson, Brian 1942- .... **CLC 12**
Wilson, Colin 1931- .... **CLC 3, 14**
See also CA 1-4R; CAAS 5; CANR 1, 22, 33, 77; CMW 4; CN 7; DLB 14, 194; HGG; MTCW 1; SFW 4
Wilson, Dirk
See Pohl, Frederik
Wilson, Edmund 1895-1972 .. **CLC 1, 2, 3, 8, 24**
See also AMW; CA 1-4R; 37-40R; CANR 1, 46, 110; DLB 63; EWL 3; MTCW 1, 2; RGAL 4; TUS
Wilson, Ethel Davis (Bryant)
1888(?)-1980 .... **CLC 13**
See also CA 102; DAC; DAM POET; DLB 68; MTCW 1; RGEL 2
Wilson, Harriet
See Wilson, Harriet E. Adams
See also DLB 239
Wilson, Harriet E.
See Wilson, Harriet E. Adams
See also DLB 243
Wilson, Harriet E. Adams
1827(?)-1863(?) .... **BLC 3; NCLC 78**
See Wilson, Harriet; Wilson, Harriet E.
See also DAM MULT; DLB 50
Wilson, John 1785-1854 .... **NCLC 5**
Wilson, John (Anthony) Burgess 1917-1993
See Burgess, Anthony
See also CA 1-4R; 143; CANR 2, 46; DA3; DAC; DAM NOV; MTCW 1, 2; NFS 15; TEA
Wilson, Lanford 1937- .. **CLC 7, 14, 36, 197; DC 19**
See also CA 17-20R; CABS 3; CAD; CANR 45, 96; CD 5; DAM DRAM; DFS 4, 9, 12, 16, 20; DLB 7; EWL 3; TUS

Wilson, Robert M. 1941- .... **CLC 7, 9**
See also CA 49-52; CAD; CANR 2, 41; CD 5; MTCW 1
Wilson, Robert McLiam 1964- .... **CLC 59**
See also CA 132; DLB 267
Wilson, Sloan 1920-2003 .... **CLC 32**
See also CA 1-4R; 216; CANR 1, 44; CN 7
Wilson, Snoo 1948- .... **CLC 33**
See also CA 69-72; CBD; CD 5
Wilson, William S(mith) 1932- .... **CLC 49**
See also CA 81-84
Wilson, (Thomas) Woodrow
1856-1924 .... **TCLC 79**
See also CA 166; DLB 47
Wilson and Warnke eds. .... **CLC 65**
Winchilsea, Anne (Kingsmill) Finch
1661-1720
See Finch, Anne
See also RGEL 2
Windham, Basil
See Wodehouse, P(elham) G(renville)
Wingrove, David (John) 1954- .... **CLC 68**
See also CA 133; SFW 4
Winnemucca, Sarah 1844-1891 .... **NCLC 79; NNAL**
See also DAM MULT; DLB 175; RGAL 4
Winstanley, Gerrard 1609-1676 .... **LC 52**
Wintergreen, Jane
See Duncan, Sara Jeannette
Winters, Janet Lewis .... **CLC 41**
See Lewis, Janet
See also DLBY 1987
Winters, (Arthur) Yvor 1900-1968 .... **CLC 4, 8, 32**
See also AMWS 2; CA 11-12; 25-28R; CAP 1; DLB 48; EWL 3; MTCW 1; RGAL 4
Winterson, Jeanette 1959- .... **CLC 64, 158**
See also BRWS 4; CA 136; CANR 58, 116; CN 7; CPW; DA3; DAM POP; DLB 207, 261; FANT; FW; GLL 1; MTCW 2; RHW
Winthrop, John 1588-1649 .... **LC 31, 107**
See also DLB 24, 30
Wirth, Louis 1897-1952 .... **TCLC 92**
See also CA 210
Wiseman, Frederick 1930- .... **CLC 20**
See also CA 159
Wister, Owen 1860-1938 .... **TCLC 21**
See also BPFB 3; CA 108; 162; DLB 9, 78, 186; RGAL 4; SATA 62; TCWW 2
Wither, George 1588-1667 .... **LC 96**
See also DLB 121; RGEL 2
Witkacy
See Witkiewicz, Stanislaw Ignacy
Witkiewicz, Stanislaw Ignacy
1885-1939 .... **TCLC 8**
See also CA 105; 162; CDWLB 4; DLB 215; EW 10; EWL 3; RGWL 2, 3; SFW 4
Wittgenstein, Ludwig (Josef Johann)
1889-1951 .... **TCLC 59**
See also CA 113; 164; DLB 262; MTCW 2
Wittig, Monique 1935(?)-2003 .... **CLC 22**
See also CA 116; 135; 212; CWW 2; DLB 83; EWL 3; FW; GLL 1
Wittlin, Jozef 1896-1976 .... **CLC 25**
See also CA 49-52; 65-68; CANR 3; EWL 3
Wodehouse, P(elham) G(renville)
1881-1975 . **CLC 1, 2, 5, 10, 22; SSC 2; TCLC 108**
See also AITN 2; BRWS 3; CA 45-48; 57-60; CANR 3, 33; CDBLB 1914-1945; CPW 1; DA3; DAB; DAC; DAM NOV; DLB 34, 162; EWL 3; MTCW 1, 2; RGEL 2; RGSF 2; SATA 22; SSFS 10
Woiwode, L.
See Woiwode, Larry (Alfred)
Woiwode, Larry (Alfred) 1941- ... **CLC 6, 10**
See also CA 73-76; CANR 16, 94; CN 7; DLB 6; INT CANR-16

Yeats, William Butler 1865-1939 . **PC 20, 51; TCLC 1, 11, 18, 31, 93, 116; WLC**
See also AAYA 48; BRW 6; BRWR 1; CA 104; 127; CANR 45; CDBLB 1890-1914; DA; DA3; DAB; DAC; DAM DRAM, MST, POET; DLB 10, 19, 98, 156; EWL 3; EXPP; MTCW 1, 2; NCFS 3; PAB; PFS 1, 2, 5, 7, 13, 15; RGEL 2; TEA; WLIT 4; WP

Yehoshua, A(braham) B. 1936- .. **CLC 13, 31**
See also CA 33-36R; CANR 43, 90; CWW 2; EWL 3; RGSF 2; RGWL 3

Yellow Bird
See Ridge, John Rollin

Yep, Laurence Michael 1948- .... **CLC 35**
See also AAYA 5, 31; BYA 7; CA 49-52; CANR 1, 46, 92; CLR 3, 17, 54; DLB 52; FANT; JRDA; MAICYA 1, 2; MAICYAS 1; SATA 7, 69, 123; WYA; YAW

Yerby, Frank G(arvin) 1916-1991 ..... **BLC 3; CLC 1, 7, 22**
See also BPFB 3; BW 1, 3; CA 9-12R; 136; CANR 16, 52; DAM MULT; DLB 76; INT CANR-16; MTCW 1; RGAL 4; RHW

Yesenin, Sergei Alexandrovich
See Esenin, Sergei (Alexandrovich)

Yesenin, Sergey
See Esenin, Sergei (Alexandrovich)
See also EWL 3

Yevtushenko, Yevgeny (Alexandrovich) 1933- ...... **CLC 1, 3, 13, 26, 51, 126; PC 40**
See Evtushenko, Evgenii Aleksandrovich
See also CA 81-84; CANR 33, 54; DAM POET; EWL 3; MTCW 1

Yezierska, Anzia 1885(?)-1970 .... **CLC 46**
See also CA 126; 89-92; DLB 28, 221; FW; MTCW 1; RGAL 4; SSFS 15

Yglesias, Helen 1915- .... **CLC 7, 22**
See also CA 37-40R; CAAS 20; CANR 15, 65, 95; CN 7; INT CANR-15; MTCW 1

Yokomitsu, Riichi 1898-1947 .... **TCLC 47**
See also CA 170; EWL 3

Yonge, Charlotte (Mary) 1823-1901 .... **TCLC 48**
See also CA 109; 163; DLB 18, 163; RGEL 2; SATA 17; WCH

York, Jeremy
See Creasey, John

York, Simon
See Heinlein, Robert A(nson)

Yorke, Henry Vincent 1905-1974 ..... **CLC 13**
See Green, Henry
See also CA 85-88; 49-52

Yosano Akiko 1878-1942 .... **PC 11; TCLC 59**
See also CA 161; EWL 3; RGWL 3

Yoshimoto, Banana .... **CLC 84**
See Yoshimoto, Mahoko
See also AAYA 50; NFS 7

Yoshimoto, Mahoko 1964-
See Yoshimoto, Banana
See also CA 144; CANR 98; SSFS 16

Young, Al(bert James) 1939- ... **BLC 3; CLC 19**
See also BW 2, 3; CA 29-32R; CANR 26, 65, 109; CN 7; CP 7; DAM MULT; DLB 33

Young, Andrew (John) 1885-1971 ...... **CLC 5**
See also CA 5-8R; CANR 7, 29; RGEL 2

Young, Collier
See Bloch, Robert (Albert)

Young, Edward 1683-1765 .... **LC 3, 40**
See also DLB 95; RGEL 2

Young, Marguerite (Vivian) 1909-1995 .... **CLC 82**
See also CA 13-16; 150; CAP 1; CN 7

Young, Neil 1945- .... **CLC 17**
See also CA 110; CCA 1

Young Bear, Ray A. 1950- ... **CLC 94; NNAL**
See also CA 146; DAM MULT; DLB 175

Yourcenar, Marguerite 1903-1987 ... **CLC 19, 38, 50, 87**
See also BPFB 3; CA 69-72; CANR 23, 60, 93; DAM NOV; DLB 72; DLBY 1988; EW 12; EWL 3; GFL 1789 to the Present; GLL 1; MTCW 1, 2; RGWL 2, 3

Yuan, Chu 340(?)B.C.-278(?)B.C. . **CMLC 36**

Yurick, Sol 1925- .... **CLC 6**
See also CA 13-16R; CANR 25; CN 7

Zabolotsky, Nikolai Alekseevich 1903-1958 .... **TCLC 52**
See Zabolotsky, Nikolay Alekseevich
See also CA 116; 164

Zabolotsky, Nikolay Alekseevich
See Zabolotsky, Nikolai Alekseevich
See also EWL 3

Zagajewski, Adam 1945- .... **PC 27**
See also CA 186; DLB 232; EWL 3

Zalygin, Sergei -2000 .... **CLC 59**

Zalygin, Sergei (Pavlovich) 1913-2000 .... **CLC 59**
See also DLB 302

Zamiatin, Evgenii
See Zamyatin, Evgeny Ivanovich
See also RGSF 2; RGWL 2, 3

Zamiatin, Evgenii Ivanovich
See Zamyatin, Evgeny Ivanovich
See also DLB 272

Zamiatin, Yevgenii
See Zamyatin, Evgeny Ivanovich

Zamora, Bernice (B. Ortiz) 1938- .. **CLC 89; HLC 2**
See also CA 151; CANR 80; DAM MULT; DLB 82; HW 1, 2

Zamyatin, Evgeny Ivanovich 1884-1937 .... **TCLC 8, 37**
See Zamiatin, Evgenii; Zamiatin, Evgenii Ivanovich; Zamyatin, Yevgeny Ivanovich
See also CA 105; 166; EW 10; SFW 4

Zamyatin, Yevgeny Ivanovich
See Zamyatin, Evgeny Ivanovich
See also EWL 3

Zangwill, Israel 1864-1926 ... **SSC 44; TCLC 16**
See also CA 109; 167; CMW 4; DLB 10, 135, 197; RGEL 2

Zappa, Francis Vincent, Jr. 1940-1993
See Zappa, Frank
See also CA 108; 143; CANR 57

Zappa, Frank .... **CLC 17**
See Zappa, Francis Vincent, Jr.

Zaturenska, Marya 1902-1982 ..... **CLC 6, 11**
See also CA 13-16R; 105; CANR 22

Zayas y Sotomayor, Maria de 1590-c. 1661 .... **LC 102**
See also RGSF 2

Zeami 1363-1443 .... **DC 7; LC 86**
See also DLB 203; RGWL 2, 3

Zelazny, Roger (Joseph) 1937-1995 . **CLC 21**
See also AAYA 7; BPFB 3; CA 21-24R; 148; CANR 26, 60; CN 7; DLB 8; FANT; MTCW 1, 2; SATA 57; SATA-Brief 39; SCFW; SFW 4; SUFW 1, 2

Zhang Ailing
See Chang, Eileen
See also CWW 2; RGSF 2

Zhdanov, Andrei Alexandrovich 1896-1948 .... **TCLC 18**
See also CA 117; 167

Zhukovsky, Vasilii Andreevich
See Zhukovsky, Vasily (Andreevich)
See also DLB 205

Zhukovsky, Vasily (Andreevich) 1783-1852 .... **NCLC 35**
See Zhukovsky, Vasilii Andreevich

Ziegenhagen, Eric .... **CLC 55**

Zimmer, Jill Schary
See Robinson, Jill

Zimmerman, Robert
See Dylan, Bob

Zindel, Paul 1936-2003 ...... **CLC 6, 26; DC 5**
See also AAYA 2, 37; BYA 2, 3, 8, 11, 14; CA 73-76; 213; CAD; CANR 31, 65, 108; CD 5; CDALBS; CLR 3, 45, 85; DA; DA3; DAB; DAC; DAM DRAM, MST, NOV; DFS 12; DLB 7, 52; JRDA; LAIT 5; MAICYA 1, 2; MTCW 1, 2; NFS 14; SATA 16, 58, 102; SATA-Obit 142; WYA; YAW

Zinov'Ev, A. A.
See Zinoviev, Alexander (Aleksandrovich)

Zinov'ev, Aleksandr (Aleksandrovich)
See Zinoviev, Alexander (Aleksandrovich)
See also DLB 302

Zinoviev, Alexander (Aleksandrovich) 1922- .... **CLC 19**
See Zinov'ev, Aleksandr (Aleksandrovich)
See also CA 116; 133; CAAS 10

Zizek, Slavoj 1949- .... **CLC 188**
See also CA 201

Zoilus
See Lovecraft, H(oward) P(hillips)

Zola, Emile (Edouard Charles Antoine) 1840-1902 ...... **TCLC 1, 6, 21, 41; WLC**
See also CA 104; 138; DA; DA3; DAB; DAC; DAM MST, NOV; DLB 123; EW 7; GFL 1789 to the Present; IDTP; LMFS 1, 2; RGWL 2; TWA

Zoline, Pamela 1941- .... **CLC 62**
See also CA 161; SFW 4

Zoroaster 628(?)B.C.-551(?)B.C. ... **CMLC 40**

Zorrilla y Moral, Jose 1817-1893 .... **NCLC 6**

Zoshchenko, Mikhail (Mikhailovich) 1895-1958 .... **SSC 15; TCLC 15**
See also CA 115; 160; EWL 3; RGSF 2; RGWL 3

Zuckmayer, Carl 1896-1977 .... **CLC 18**
See also CA 69-72; DLB 56, 124; EWL 3; RGWL 2, 3

Zuk, Georges
See Skelton, Robin
See also CCA 1

Zukofsky, Louis 1904-1978 ... **CLC 1, 2, 4, 7, 11, 18; PC 11**
See also AMWS 3; CA 9-12R; 77-80; CANR 39; DAM POET; DLB 5, 165; EWL 3; MTCW 1; RGAL 4

Zweig, Paul 1935-1984 .... **CLC 34, 42**
See also CA 85-88; 113

Zweig, Stefan 1881-1942 .... **TCLC 17**
See also CA 112; 170; DLB 81, 118; EWL 3

Zwingli, Huldreich 1484-1531 .... **LC 37**
See also DLB 179

Literary Criticism Series
Cumulative Topic Index

This index lists all topic entries in Gale's *Children's Literature Review* (CLR), *Classical and Medieval Literature Criticism* (CMLC), *Contemporary Literary Criticism* (CLC), *Drama Criticism* (DC), *Literature Criticism from 1400 to 1800* (LC), *Nineteenth-Century Literature Criticism* (NCLC), *Short Story Criticism* (SSC), and *Twentieth-Century Literary Criticism* (TCLC). The index also lists topic entries in the Gale Critical Companion Collection, which includes the following publications: *The Beat Generation* (BG), and *Harlem Renaissance* (HR).

Topic Index

Topic Index

LC Cumulative Nationality Index

Nationality Index